The African Union (AU)

The African Union (AU)

Third Edition

Konstantinos D. Magliveras

Gino J. Naldi

This book was originally published as a monograph in the International Encyclopaedia of Laws/Intergovernmental Organizations.

Founding Editor: Roger Blanpain
General Editor: Frank Hendrickx
Volume Editor: Jan Wouters

Wolters Kluwer

Published by:
Kluwer Law International B.V.
PO Box 316
2400 AH Alphen aan den Rijn
The Netherlands
E-mail: lrs-sales@wolterskluwer.com
Website: www.wolterskluwer.com/en/solutions/kluwerlawinternational

Sold and distributed by:
Wolters Kluwer Legal & Regulatory U.S.
920 Links Avenue
Landisville, PA 17538
United States of America
E-mail: customer.service@wolterskluwer.com

ISBN 978-94-035-4987-3

e-Book: ISBN 978-94-035-0008-9
web-PDF: ISBN 978-94-035-0018-8

This title is available on www.kluwerlawonline.com

The Authors

Konstantinos D. Magliveras is Professor of the Law of International Organisations, Department of Mediterranean Studies, University of the Aegean. He is the author of Parts I and II.

Gino J. Naldi graduated from the Faculty of Law, University of Birmingham in 1978. He was awarded an LLM in 1979 and a PhD in 1984, both from the University of Birmingham. He is a retired university lecturer and is currently an independent scholar in international law and human rights.

Gino Naldi is the author of Parts III to V.

The Authors

Table of Contents

List of Abbreviations

AAC	African Accounting Council
ACERWC	African Committee of Experts on the Rights and Welfare of the Child
ACHR	American Convention on Human Rights
ACIRC	African Capacity for Immediate Response to Crises
ACJHR	African Court of Justice and Human Rights
ACRWC	African Charter on the Rights and Welfare of the Child
ACPF	African Child Policy Forum
ACSRT	African Centre for Study and Research on Terrorism
AEC	African Economic Community
AFCAC	African Civil Aviation Commission
AFISMA	African International Support Mission in Mali
AFREC	African Energy Commission
AHRLR	African Human Rights Law Reports
AIB	African Investment Bank
AIDA	Action Plan for Accelerated Industrial Development of Africa
AJIL	American Journal of International Law
ALSF	African Legal Support Facility
AMF	African Monetary Fund
AMIS	African Union Mission in Sudan
AMISEC	African Union Mission in the Comoros
AMISOM	African Union Mission in Somalia
APA	African Peace Academy
APSA	African Peace and Security Architecture
ATMIS	African Union Transition Mission in Somalia
ATU	African Telecommunications Union
AU	African Union

List of Abbreviations

AUBP	African Union Border Programme
AUC	African Union Commission
AUCIL	African Union Commission on International Law
AUCISS	African Union Commission of Inquiry on South Sudan
AYBIL	African Yearbook of International Law
BASE	African Bureau for Educational Sciences
BCLR	Butterworths Constitutional Law Reports
BIAT	Action Plan for Boosting Intra-Africa Trade
BLR	Botswana Law Reports
BYBIL	British Yearbook of International Law
CAADP	Comprehensive Africa Agriculture Development Program
CAR	Central African Republic
CARMMA	Campaign on Accelerated Reduction of Maternal Mortality in Africa
CEDAW	UN Convention on the Elimination of Discrimination Against Women
CEMAC	Economic and Monetary Community of Central Africa
CENSAD	Community of Sahelo-Saharan States
CETS	Council of Europe Treaty Series
CFTA	Continental Free Trade Area
CILSA	Comparative and International Law Journal of Southern Africa
CJEU	Court of Justice of the European Union
CM	Organization of African Unity Council of Ministers
COMESA	Common Market for Eastern and Southern Africa
COPAX	Council for Peace and Security in Central Africa
CRC	UN Convention on the Rights of the Child
CSOs	Civil Society Organizations
CSSDCA	Conference on Security, Stability, Development and Cooperation in Africa
Doc.	Document
DRC	Democratic Republic of Congo
EAC	Extraordinary African Chambers
EC	European Community
ECA	United Nations Economic Commission of Africa
ECCAS	Economic Community of Central African States
ECCJ	ECOWAS Community Court of Justice

ECHR	European Convention for the Protection of Human Rights and Fundamental Freedoms
ECJ	European Court of Justice
ECOMIG	Economic Community of West African States' Mission in The Gambia
ECOMOG	Economic Community of West African States Monitoring Group
ECOSOC	United Nations Economic and Social Council
ECOSOCC	Economic, Social and Cultural Council
ECOWAS	Economic Community of West African States
ECR	European Court Reports
EPA	Economic Partnership Agreement
ERM	Early Response Mechanism
ETS	European Treaty Series
EU	European Union
EX	Executive Council
FY	Financial Year
FGM	Female Genital Mutilation
GDPR	General Data Protection Regulation
HCSS	African Union Hybrid Court for South Sudan
HRC	Human Rights Committee
IACtHR	Inter-American Court of Human Rights
ICC	International Criminal Court
ICESCR	International Covenant on Economic, Social and Cultural Rights
ICCPR	International Covenant on Civil and Political Rights
ICJ	International Court of Justice
ICLQ	International and Comparative Law Quarterly
IDPs	Internally Displaced Persons
IGAD	Intergovernmental Authority on Development
IGO	Intergovernmental Organization
IHRR	International Human Rights Reports
ILC	UN International Law Commission
ILM	International Legal Materials
ILO	International Labour Organization
ILR	International Law Reports
JAL	Journal of African Law
LRC	Law Reports of the Commonwealth
LSAC	Labour and Social Affairs Commission

List of Abbreviations

MAES	African Union Electoral and Security Assistance Mission to the Comoros
MINURCAT	UN Mission in the Central African Republic
MINURSO	UN Mission for the Referendum in Western Sahara
MINUSMA	UN Multidimensional Integrated Stabilization Mission in Mali
MISCA	International Support Mission in the Central African Republic
MONUC	UN Observer Mission in the Democratic Republic of Congo
MONUSCO	UN Organization Stabilization Mission in the DRC
MPLA	Popular Movement for the Liberation of Angola
MR	Mauritius Reports
NADAF	United Nations New Agenda for the Development of Africa in the 1990s
NEPAD	New African Partnership for Africa's Development
NGO	Non-governmental Organization
NILR	Netherlands International Law Review
NQHR	Netherlands Quarterly on Human Rights
OAU	Organization of African Unity
OECD	Organization for Economic Cooperation and Development
PAAERD	United Nations Programme of Action for African Economic Recovery and Development 1986–1990
PAIDA	New United Nations and African Union Partnership on Africa's Integration and Development Agenda
PAIPO	Pan-African Intellectual Property Organization
PANWISE	Pan-African Network of the Wise
PAP	Pan-African Parliament
PAPU	Pan-African Postal Union
PATU	Pan-African Telecommunications Union
PIDA	Programme for Infrastructure Development in Africa
PRC	Permanent Representatives Committee
PSC	Peace and Security Council
PSO	Peace Support Operations
RADIC	African Journal of International and Comparative Law
REC	Regional Economic Community
SADC	Southern African Development Community
SADR	Sahrawi Arab Democratic Republic
SCSA	Supreme Council of Sports in Africa
UDHR	Universal Declaration of Human Rights

UN	United Nations
UNAMID	United Nation-African Union Mission in Darfur
UNAOU	United Nations Office to the African Union
UNCAC	UN Convention Against Corruption
UNGA	United Nations General Assembly
UNHCR	United Nations High Commission for Refugees
UNMIS	United Nations Mission in Sudan
UNMISS	UN Mission in the Republic of South Sudan
UNSC	United Nations Security Council
UNTS	United Nations Treaty Series
ZaöRV	Zeitschrift für ausländisches öffentliches Recht und Völkerrecht
ZR	Zambia Law Reports

List of Abbreviations

Preface

When our monograph 'The African Union and the predecessor Organization of African Unity' was published in 2004, it was the only reference work that not only examined and analysed the African Union (AU) in detail but also put it into the necessary context by offering a detailed account of the predecessor institution, the Organization of African Unity (OAU). Twenty years later, it continues to be the only monograph in the international literature to address the AU from an academic perspective and in an exhaustive fashion. Since the last edition of *The African Union* (2017), much has changed in the continent. Among the most significant developments has been the establishment of the African Continental Free Trade Area and, more generally, the rejuvenation of the economic integration agenda. Unfortunately, the old scourges with a very heavy toll on human life have continued, as evidenced by the seemingly never-ending cases of unconstitutional changes of government and civil strife and wars. It is not an easy task to determine if the AU is in a better state compared to when the previous edition was published. Certainly, several continental treaties and conventions of note have been concluded (including two new Protocols to the African Charter on Human and Peoples' Rights, the Protocol to the Treaty Establishing the African Economic Community Relating to Free Movement of Persons, Right of Residence and Right of Establishment, etc.), and new organs and entities have been created (including the African Space Agency, the African Medicines Agency, the African Audio Visual and Cinema Commission, etc.). Moreover, there has been an urgent drive to revise the workings of the AU principally on the basis of the so-called Kagame Report ('The Imperative to Strengthen Our Union: Report on the Proposed Recommendations for the Institutional Reform of the African Union') that was issued in 2017. On the other hand, the overreliance of AU's funding on the international partners has continued unabated. Without such funding, it is doubtful if the AU would be able to operate and carry out its activities and programmes. It is probably the single most important challenge that the AU, as a regional international organization, faces and will continue to face.

The law is stated as we understood it to be in April 2023, although some subsequent events have been recorded.

Konstantinos D. Magliveras and Gino J. Naldi

Part I. History and Evolution: From the Organization of African Unity to the African Union to the United States of Africa

1. It is a well-known fact that the countries of the African continent, with only a very few exceptions, have until recent times been occupied by foreign colonial powers. The course of African history has been and continues to be influenced to a large degree by the centuries' long foreign domination. Before World War II, Africa's participation on the international plane was rather negligible. Only four states were members of the League of Nations: Egypt (it gained its independence from Great Britain in 1922); Abyssinia-Ethiopia (an ancient kingdom whose sovereignty was recognized when the Treaty of Wuchale was concluded with Italy in May 1889);[1] Liberia (founded in 1822, became a republic in 1847); and the Union of South Africa (created in 1910). In the aftermath of World War II, these four countries remained the only independent states in Africa and three of them participated as original United Nations (UN) Member States.[2] When regional organizations were being formed in other continents in the late 1940s (in Europe, the Western European Union (WEU) in 1948 and the Council of Europe in 1949; in the Americas, the Organization of American States in 1948; in the Arab world, the League of Arab States in 1945), Africa consisted mostly of colonies. Consequently, there was no scope for political, economic or other forms of regional cooperation, not to mention integration.

2. However, the situation changed dramatically when, from the late 1950s onwards, the process of decolonization and the parallel move towards political, economic, and cultural self-determination gained momentum and swept most of Africa. The process was not completed swiftly. It took thirty-three years, from 1957, when Ghana declared its independence from Great Britain and was the first African colony to become a sovereign state, to 1990, when Namibia gained its independence from South African occupation. In the period 1957–1963, no less than thirty former colonies became sovereign states. The creation of so many new states, even

1. Also known as Treaty of Wichale or Trattato di Uccialli, text at: https://hornaffairs.com/2011/08/17/text-of-wuchale-treaty-1989-ethio-italian-treaty/.
2. Compare Council of Ministers, *Resolution on Africa's Representation at the United Nations*, OAU Doc. CM/Res. 1 (I) (11 Aug. 1963).

though they did not share many common features other than their colonial past, did offer the necessary impetus to consider the establishment of a pan-African organization, on the one hand, as a means for consolidating achievements and, on the other hand, as an institutional vehicle for bringing about the much-cherished African unity. Although these discussions, which mainly took the form of ministerial conferences,[3] showed that there was agreement to promote cooperation on the continent, it also became apparent that there was no consensus on the form that it should take. Two opposing groupings surfaced: the Brazzaville Group (from which later the Monrovia Group emerged) represented by Emperor Haile Selassie of Ethiopia, and the Casablanca Group represented by President Kwame Nkrumah of Ghana. The former group, which was constituted of Cameroon, the Central African Republic (CAR), Chad, Congo, Côte d'Ivoire, Benin, Gabon, Mauritania, Madagascar, Niger, Senegal, and Upper Volta (later Burkina Faso), advocated cooperation among African states in various fields and rejected political integration. The latter group, which was composed of Ghana, Guinea, Mali, Morocco, Egypt, and the Provisional Government of Algeria, proposed the creation of a United States of Africa. This proposal was based on the idea of Pan-Africanism, which had dated from the late nineteenth and early twentieth centuries.[4] But, this was not the only area of contention among the newly independent African states. They were further divided along the lines of the former colonial power, principally in the Anglophone countries and the Francophone countries, a division that stands until today.[5] Moreover, there were serious disagreements on the issue of their borders, which the European colonial powers had drawn artificially to accommodate their own interests and in clear disregard not only of the prevailing ethnic and tribal divisions but also of obvious geographical considerations.[6]

3. Despite the divergence of opinions, there were a considerable number of issues of common interest (the principal ones being colonialism and apartheid) allowing, on 15 May 1963, the calling of a Preparatory Conference of Foreign Ministers to discuss the creation of a pan-African political organization and to draft its constitutive instrument. A week later, a Conference of the Heads of State and Government of the then thirty-two independent African states took place in Addis

---

3. Starting in 1958, two entities had met periodically to discuss, *inter alia*, the possible association between African countries: the Conference of Independent African States and the Inter-African and Malagasy Organization. Both ceased functioning after the establishment of the OAU, since they were no longer needed; *see* H.F. Strauch, *Panafrica, kontinentale Weltmacht im Werden? Anfaenge, Wachstum und Zukunft der afrikanischen Einigungsbestrebungen* (Zürich: Atlantis, 1964), 144 et seq. The first-ever Pan-African gathering took place in Manchester, Great Britain, in 1960.
4. Generally, *see* A. Ayrton (2022), 'Des congrès panafricains à l'Organisation de l'unité africaine: les circulations transimpériales dans la formation des diplomates africains postcoloniaux' 3 *Revue d'Histoire Contemporaine de l'Afrique* (2022) 157–168.
5. *See* C. Clapham, 'Boundaries and States in the New African Order' in *Regionalism in Africa – Integration and Disintegration*, ed. D. Bach (Oxford: James Currey Publishers, 1999), 53; P. Nugent & A.I. Asiwaju (eds), *African Boundaries: Barriers, Conduits and Opportunities* (London: Pinter, 1996).
6. Generally, *see* H. Cohen, *Intervening in Africa: Superpower Peacemaking in a Troubled Continent* (New York: St. Martin's Press, 2000); V. LeVine, *Politics in Francophone Africa* (Boulder, Colorado: Rienner, 2004); A. Andereggen, *France's Relationship with Sub-saharan Africa* (Westport: Praeger, 1994).

Ababa, Ethiopia. On 25 May 1963, the Organization of African Unity (OAU) was born, and its Charter was signed by thirty states (Morocco and Togo signed it at a later stage).[7] The Charter entered into force on 13 September 1963. In the Preamble, the quest for Pan-Africanism was considerably played down although the following references were made to it:

> [c]o-operation among our States in response to the aspirations of our peoples for brotherhood and solidarity, in a larger unity transcending ethnic and national differences ... all African States should henceforth unite so that the welfare and well-being of their peoples can be assured.

At its inception, the OAU stood on two broad premises. The first was the safeguarding and consolidation of the process for liberation, territorial integrity, and sovereignty of the participating countries and the war against neocolonialism in all its forms. The second was the promotion of links between African states through the establishment of common organs, the two main ones being the Assembly of Heads of State and Government (the supreme organ) and the Council of Ministers (the executive organ).

4. In the 1960s, emerging Africa rested on very fragile foundations with the fight for decolonization continuing and with the newly born independent states fighting for survival while rejecting involvement in all its forms by the former colonial powers.[8] Given this reality, the structure and the aims of the OAU were rather basic and simplistic, at least compared to other, more sophisticated, regional organizations which had already made their mark in the international society, such as the European Economic Community. Despite these limitations, the importance in creating the OAU laid in that for the first time in African history rivalries and mutual distrust were set aside and a formal institutional entity was established, without outside interference, to address and solve problems, to enhance the much-needed joint cooperation and to allow Africa to speak with one voice on the international plane.

5. Article II(1) of the OAU Charter laid down that it was guided by the following five purposes: promotion of unity and solidarity of the African states; coordination and intensification of the efforts to achieve a better life for the African peoples; defence of Member States' sovereignty, territorial integrity and independence; eradication of all forms of colonialism from the continent; and promotion of cooperation with other parts of the world having due regard to the principles enshrined in the UN Charter. To achieve these goals, Member States agreed in Article II(2) to harmonize their policies in a wide range of fields: political and diplomatic; economic (including transport and communications); educational and cultural; health and sanitation; scientific and technical; as well as defence and security.

---

7. 479 U.N.T.S. 39; reproduced in 2 I.L.M. (1963) 766 and in G.J. Naldi (ed.), *Documents of the Organization of African Unity* (London: Mansell, 1992), 3.
8. Compare Council of Ministers, *Resolution on Africa's Non-Alignment*, OAU Doc. CM/Res. 12 (II) (29 Feb. 1964), and Assembly, *Resolution on the Interference of the Internal Affairs of African States*, OAU Doc. AHG/Res. 85 (XIV) (5 Jul. 1977).

6. These purposes were given effect through the observance of seven principles, which were enumerated in Article III and reflected the values and doctrines enshrined in Article 2 of the UN Charter: (a) sovereign equality of the entire membership; (b) non-interference in the internal affairs of other states, irrespective of whether they were Member States or not;[9] (c) respect for the sovereignty and territorial integrity of all states and for their inalienable right to independent existence; (d) settlement of disputes through the traditional peaceful means of negotiation, mediation, conciliation, and arbitration; (e) complete condemnation of political assassination and subversive activities against third countries as instruments of state policy; (f) unqualified dedication to the total emancipation of those African territories under foreign rule; and (g) affirmation of the policy of non-alignment to any political, ideological or other groups.

7. Although, pursuant to Article VI of the Charter, Members pledged to observe these principles scrupulously, the sad truth is that they were breached repeatedly. Through the adoption of declarations and resolutions, the Assembly of Heads of State and Government attempted to give additional credence to the above principles and to make Member States apply them regardless of the circumstances at hand. For example, in September 1967, on account of the serious disruption of Kenyan-Somali relations and Israel's partial occupation of Egypt, which at the time was part of the United Arab Republic, it reaffirmed adhesion to the principle of respect of sovereignty and Member States' territorial integrity.[10] The principle of detachment from any group was partly implemented through the participation of some OAU Member States in the Non-Alignment Movement (NAM), which had surfaced in the mid-1950s and in which Egypt was a leading participant.[11] However, following their independence, most of the states that had been under the domination of Great Britain and France participated in the associations which these countries had set up, namely the British Commonwealth (now the Commonwealth of Nations) and the French Community (Communauté française).[12] The relations with France, which had been particularly strong in the military assistance field, continued throughout

9. A.B. Akinyemi, 'The Organization of African Unity and the Concept of Non-Interference in Internal Affairs of Member States', *BYBIL* 46 (1972/1973): 393.
10. Respectively, *see* Assembly, *Declaration on Kenya-Somali Relations*, OAU Doc. AHG/ST. 1 (IV) and Assembly, *Declaration*, OAU Doc. AHG/ST. 2 (IV) (14 Sep. 1967). It is interesting that the latter Declaration did not name Israel as the occupying force; however later resolutions expressly referred to Israel as the aggressor state, *see*, *inter alia*, Assembly, *Resolution on the Continued Occupation by Israel of Part of the Territory of the Arab Republic of Egypt*, OAU Doc. AHG/Res. 70 (X) (28 May 1973).
11. *See* Council of Ministers, *Resolution of the Council of Foreign Ministers of Non-Aligned Countries*, OAU Doc. CM/Res. 434 (XXV) (25 Jul. 1975) proclaiming non-alignment as one of the fundamental principles of the OAU Charter. Compare Council of Ministers, *Resolution on the Forthcoming Summit Conference of the Non-Aligned Countries*, OAU Doc. CM/Res. 290 (XX) (9 Feb. 1973).
12. *See* W.H. Morris-Jones & G. Fischer (eds), *Decolonisation and After: the British and French Experience* (London: Frank Cass, 1980). Note that, as an association of nations, the French Community was officially terminated in August 1995 when, by virtue of Constitutional Act no. 95-880, the relevant provisions of the French Constitution were abrogated. Muck later, a Community of Portuguese Speaking Countries (Comunidade dos Países de Língua Portuguesa) was created. Its Statutes were signed on 17 July 1996, entered into force on 17 April 2000, 2233 U.N.T.S. 224, while its membership from Africa include Angola, Mozambique and Capo Verde.

the OAU days and have been maintained in the AU era.[13] On occasions, these relations have been to the detriment of the newly independent states. For example, the provisions of the Defence Agreement between, on the one hand, France and, on the other hand, the CAR, Congo (Brazzaville) and the Republic of Chad, which was concluded on 15 August 1960 and entered into force on 13 March 1961, allow France to intervene militarily in these countries and send armed forces to them.[14] An example of French military involvement taking the form of intervention was *Operation Serval*, which was lodged in the northern parts of Mali on 11 January 2013.[15]

8. During the Cold War, several African states favoured the Soviet bloc and signed what amounted to security agreements with the USSR; they were rather euphemistically called 'treaties of friendship and cooperation'. Among those concluded, suffice to mention the following six: the Agreement with Egypt, which was signed on 27 May 1971; the Agreement with Somalia on 11 July 1974; the Agreement with Angola on 8 October 1976; the Agreement with Mozambique in April 1977; the Agreement with Ethiopia on 20 November 1978; and the Agreement with the People's Republic of the Congo on 13 May 1981.[16] As the balance in the international community gradually changed and new alliances were struck, some African states abrogated these Agreements, for example, Egypt on 14 March 1976 and Somalia on 13 November 1977.

9. Regarding the borders of the newly independent African states, the OAU had to make a difficult choice between maintaining those inherited from the colonial era (the principle of *uti possidetis*),[17] which did not always mirror ethnic realities, and those that could have been drawn based on equity and pragmatic needs. In the event, the OAU opted for the former solution as the last disruptive option. Thus, the principle of respect for the borders existing at independence was enshrined in the OAU

---

13. *See* A. Huliaras, 'Continuity and Change in French Foreign Policy Towards Africa' in D. Frost, A. Thomson & T. Zack-Williams (eds), *Africa in Crisis* (London: Pluto Press, 2002), 161; P. Manning, *Francophone Sub-Saharan Africa 1880–1995*, 2nd edn (Cambridge: Cambridge University Press, 1999); J. Chipman, *French Power in Africa* (Oxford: Blackwell, 1989).
14. Reproduced in 821 U.N.T.S. 301; *see* R. Luckham, 'French Militarism in Africa', *Review of African Political Economy* 9 (1982): 55; P. Lellouche & D. Moisi, 'French Policy in Africa: A Lonely Battle Against Destabilization', *International Security* 3 (1979): 108; and N. Bagayoko, *Security Systems in Francophone Africa*, Institute of Development Studies, University of Sussex, Research Report 64 (Brighton, May 2010) at: http://www.ids.ac.uk/files/dmfile/RR64.pdf.
15. *See* P. Melly & V. Darrace, *A New Way to Engage? French Policy in Africa from Sarkozy to Hollande* (London: Chatham House, May 2013); S. Recchia & T. Tardy (eds), *French Interventions in Africa: Reluctant Multilateralism* (London: Routledge, 2020).
16. *See* T.B. Millar (ed.), *Current International Treaties* (London: Croom Helm, 1984), 474 et seq.; K. Somerville, 'The U.S.S.R. and Southern Africa since 1976', *The J. of Modern African Studies* 22 (1984): 73; R.E. Bissell, 'Soviet Military Aid to Africa', *Journal of Contemporary African Studies* 1 (1981): 1; and C. Coker, 'Adventurism and Pragmatism: The Soviet Union, Comecon, and Relations with African States', *Intl Affairs* 57 (1981): 618. For the Agreement with Egypt, *see* 798 U.N.T.S. 184.
17. *See* S.R. Ratner, 'Drawing a Better Line: Uti Possidetis and the Borders of New States', *AJIL* 90 (1996): 590; and S. Lalonde, *Determining Boundaries in a Conflicted World: The Role of Uti Possidetis* (Montreal: McGill-Queen's University Press, 2002), 103 et seq.

legal order.[18] Although the insistence on colonial borders has led to a considerable number of interstate conflicts, African leaders have maintained that borders' inviolability is one of the 'objectives and principles of the OAU Charter'[19] and that it has 'contributed decisively' to preserving peace and stability.[20] The principle of *uti possidetis* has found express recognition in the *Frontier Dispute Case (Burkina Faso/Mali)*, where the International Court of Justice (ICJ) held that '[i]ts obvious purpose is to prevent the independence and stability of new States being endangered by fratricidal struggles provoked by the challenging of frontiers following the withdrawal of the administering power'.[21] Finally, respect for borders as they existed at independence was laid down as one of the basic principles of the AU (Article 4(b) of the Constitutive Act).

10. Many complex conflicts and disputes between African states plagued the OAU and until today have continued posing challenges for the AU. At a Ministerial Conference on Africa held on 25 September 1997, the UN Security Council noted this fact and expressed its grave concern at the number and intensity of conflicts.[22] The following intra-state and interstate discords, frictions and armed hostilities exemplify this state of affairs.[23] Already in the first years of the OAU's existence, border disputes erupted, on the one hand, between Algeria and Morocco and, on the other hand, between Somalia, Ethiopia and Kenya. The latter lasted until 1967[24] but re-emerged in the 1970s. In 1973, a serious controversy between Rwanda and Burundi broke out, a typical result of the way colonial borders had been drawn. In 1977–1978, insurgents from Angola invaded part of Zaïre, Libya occupied Northern Chad[25] and there was an outbreak of hostilities not only between Ethiopia and

18. *See* Assembly, *Borders Disputes among African States*, OAU Doc. AHG/Res. 16 (I) adopted by the First Ordinary Session in July 1964; reproduced in Naldi, *Documents*, 49. Generally, *see* S. Touval, 'The Organization of African Unity and African Borders', *International Organization* 21 (1967): 102; R.H. Payne, 'Divided Tribes: A Discussion of African Boundary Problems', *New York University Journal of International Law & Policy* 2 (1968): 243; and D.M. Ahmed, *Boundaries and Secession in Africa and International Law: Challenging Uti Possidetis* (Cambridge: Cambridge University Press, 2015).
19. *See* Assembly, *Cairo Declaration on the OAU Mechanism for Conflict Prevention, Management and Resolution*, OAU Doc. AHG/Decl. 3 (XXIX) at para. 14 (30 Jun. 1993).
20. *See* Assembly, *Algiers Declaration*, OAU Doc. AHG/Decl. 1 (XXXV) (14 Jul. 1999).
21. I.C.J. Reports 1986, 554, para. 20 at p. 565.
22. UN Press Release SC/6465 (25 Sep. 1997). The complexity of some of these conflicts is best evidenced by the fact that, pursuant to UNGA Res. 46/37 B of 6 December 1991, the UN Secretary-General set up the UN Standing Advisory Committee on Security Questions in Central Africa (UNSAC) in May 1992. One of UNSDAC achievements is the adoption of the Central African Convention for the Control of Small Arms and Light Weapons, their Ammunition, and All Parts and Components for their Manufacture, Repair and Assembly on 30 April 2010, entered into force on 8 March 2017, 3176 UNTS I-54327. UNSAC meets twice a year.
23. Generally, *see* B. Boutros Ghali, *Les conflits de frontières en Afrique (études et documents)* (Paris: Editions techniques et économiques, 1973).
24. *See* Assembly, *Declaration on Kenya-Somali Relations*, OAU Doc. AHG/ST. 1 (IV) (14 Sep. 1967) recording the undertaking of these states to resolve their differences.
25. Assembly, *Resolution on the Libya/Chad Dispute*, OAU Doc. AHG/Res. 94 (XV) (22 Jul. 1978).

Somalia[26] but also between Ethiopia and Sudan; in the latter case, an Ad Hoc Mediation Committee was set up.[27] Moreover, serious disputes erupted between Guinea and Côte d'Ivoire and between Guinea and Senegal.[28] In 1978, the overthrow of Idi Amin of Uganda was partly achieved through the invasion of Uganda by Tanzania (October 1978–April 1979), which led to armed hostilities that lasted until 1981. This incident marked the first time in the OAU's history that a Member State had invaded another in clear disrespect of at least three of the Charter principles: non-interference in the internal affairs of third states, respect of sovereignty and territorial integrity, and unreserved condemnation of subversive activities on the part of neighbouring countries. In 1994–1995, conflict situations exploded in Burundi, Somalia, Liberia, Sierra Leone. The genocide in Rwanda also took place. Between 1996 and 1998, there were clashes between Eritrea, Ethiopia and Sudan, while between 1997 and 2000, significant armed hostilities erupted between Ethiopia and Eritrea over border disputes.[29] The latter were terminated by the Agreement of 12 December 2000, which, faithful to the principle of employing peaceful means for the settlement of disputes, established a Boundary Commission and a Claims Commission to adjudicate bilateral claims. The Claims Commission rendered its final award on damages on 17 August 2009. The Boundary Commission issued its decision on delimitation on 13 April 2002, which however does not seem to have been implemented by the two states.[30] Since 2004, the conflict in the Niger Delta has resulted in considerable human losses, while armed clashes at the Djiboutian–Eritrean border in June 2008[31] exemplified that not all matters concerning African borders have been dealt with, especially when, like in this case, the applicable boundary agreement dates from 1900. It is instructive to note that in the twenty-first century, the ICJ has given judgments on and/or has heard a considerable number of cases concerning African border disputes, including the following (in chronological order). First, a case concerning the land and maritime boundaries between Cameroon and Nigeria.[32] Second, a disagreement between Benin and Niger concerning the River Niger.[33] Third, a dispute concerning the frontier between Burkina Faso

26. Assembly, *Resolution on the Somalia/Ethiopia Conflict*, OAU Doc. AHG/Res. 90 (XV) (22 Jul. 1978). Generally, *see* G. Tareke, 'The Ethiopia-Somalia War 1977 Revisited', *International Journal of African Historical Studies* 33 (2000): 635.
27. Assembly, *Resolution on the Somalia/Sudan Dispute*, OAU Doc. AHG/Res. 97 (XVI) Rev. 1 (20 Jul. 1979). Generally, *see* S. Peterson, *Me Against My Brother: At War in Somalia, Sudan and Rwanda* (London: Routledge, 2001).
28. Assembly, *Resolution on Reconciliation between Guinea, Ivory Coast and Senegal*, OAU Doc. AHG/Res. 88 (XV) (22 Jul. 1978).
29. Assembly, *Dispute between Ethiopia and Eritrea*, OAU Doc. AHG/Dec. 130 (XXXIV) (10 June 1998); and Assembly, *Decision on the Conflict between Ethiopia and Eritrea*, OAU Doc. AHG/Dec. 144 (XXXVI) (12 Jul. 2000). Generally, *see* N. Tekeste & K. Tronvall, *Brothers at War: Making Sense of the Eritrean-Ethiopian War* (Oxford: Currey, 2000).
30. UNSC, *Report of the Secretary-General on Ethiopia and Eritrea*, UN Doc. S/2008/40 (23 Jan. 2008) para. 26 and Annex II.
31. Note that UNSC Presidential Statement 2008/20 condemned Eritrea's military action, *see* UN Doc. S/PV.5908, 12 Jun. 2008, p. 2.
32. *See Land and Maritime Boundary between Cameroon and Nigeria* (*Cameroon v. Nigeria*; Equatorial Guinea intervening), Judgment of 10 Oct. 2002, [2002] I.C.J. Reports 303.
33. *See Frontier Dispute* (*Benin v. Niger*), Judgment of 12 Jul. 2005, I.C.J. Reports 2005, 90.

and Niger.[34] Fourth, a maritime delimitation dispute in the Indian Ocean between Somalia and Kenya.[35] Finally, in March 2021, proceedings were instituted by way of a Special Agreement (Compromis) between the Gabonese Republic and the Republic of Equatorial Guinea.[36]

11. The OAU was rather ineffective in preventing and solving interstate conflicts and domestic unrest. Arguably, from its inception, the Organization was ill-equipped to undertake such missions and to fulfil such roles. Even though under Article XIX of the Charter, Member States had pledged to settle all their disputes by peaceful means and primarily through the Commission of Mediation, Conciliation and Arbitration, this organ never became functional. Fresh impetus was given in June 1993 by means of the Cairo Declaration on the Establishment of a Mechanism for Conflict Prevention, Management and Resolution, which carried out its functions with relative success.[37] It was replaced in early 2004 when the AU Peace and Security Council (PSC) became operative. Even though the Preamble of the OAU Charter referred to the aspiration of African peoples for brotherhood and solidarity (it was repeated in the Preamble of the AU Constitutive Act as the 'noble ideals which guided the founding fathers' of the OAU), the sad truth is that African leaders have chosen to disregard these principles when it has so suited them.

12. Moreover, the OAU had been confronted with a seemingly never-ending series of coups d'état. Even in these instances, the Organization showed that it did not have the capacity or the willingness to intervene. Its usual justification for inactivity was that the unconstitutional overthrow of governments amounted to domestic matters, and the OAU could not intervene even if the life of the population was at stake (and invariably it was). This justification emerged from the following two facts: Member States (a) adhered slavishly to the Charter principle of non-interference in the internal affairs of other states; and (b) usually chose to ignore the serious repercussions of coups d'état not only for the countries involved but also for the neighbouring countries and the African continent at large. For it is a fact that coups d'état are (with only limited exemptions) accompanied by human rights abuses, maladministration, and breakdowns in civil society. The OAU attitude was officially reversed during the Thirty-Fifth Ordinary Assembly Session (Algiers, July 1999), which rejected them as unacceptable and anachronistic acts. The following year, the Assembly adopted the Declaration on the Framework for an OAU Response to Unconstitutional Change of Government, which was a framework for collective response against any regime that had come into power by force instead of being elected through the applicable constitutional procedure. The irony was of

34. *See Frontier Dispute* (*Burkina Faso v. Niger*), Judgment of 16 Apr. 2013, I.C.J. Reports 2013, 44.
35. *See Maritime Delimitation in the Indian Ocean* (*Somalia v. Kenya*), Judgment of 12 October 2021, I.C.J. Reports 2021, 206.
36. *See Land and Maritime Delimitation and Sovereignty over Islands* (*Gabon v. Equatorial Guinea*), ICJ, Press Release, No. 2021/10, 5 March 2021. For the Compromis, *see* https://www.icj-cij.org/public/files/case-related/179/179-20210305-SPE-01-00-EN.pdf.
37. *See* M. Muyangwa & M.A. Vogt, 'An Assessment of the OAU Mechanism for Conflict Prevention, Management and Resolution, 1993–2000', International Peace Academy (New York, November 2000), at: https://www.ipinst.org/wp-content/uploads/publications/oau_conflict_1993_2000.pdf.

course that some of the African leaders who were so eager to condemn them had seized power in coups d'état themselves!

13. Despite the rather ineffective role that the OAU played in conflict resolution, it had considerable success in several other areas, principally, in decolonization and in eradicating racial discrimination and apartheid. For the OAU, decolonization and apartheid were not separate concerns but two interrelated issues, which, as was stated in the Declaration adopted in 1973 on the OAU's tenth anniversary, could be solved by either peaceful means or by military confrontation:

> The liberation of those areas under colonial and racist domination can be achieved either by peaceful means or by armed struggle ... we would prefer to achieve our objectives by peaceful means if that were possible. But whether the solution takes the form of intensified military confrontation or negotiations would entirely depend on the response of the racist and colonialist regimes.[38]

Ten years later, in 1984, the OAU repeated the talk of an armed confrontation against the racist African states, but this time, the issue was downplayed:

> In the light of the intransigence, ruthlessness, and consistent brutality of the Apartheid regime, both within South Africa and Namibia, we uphold the right of the Liberation Movements and the people they lead to take up arms in pursuance of the struggle for freedom. We continue to express our preference for a peaceful resolution of the Namibian and South African questions as stated in the Lusaka Manifesto. But we are convinced that the peaceful negotiations can only succeed when the Pretoria regime had convincingly demonstrated its acceptance of both the principle and the inevitability of majority rule. One such demonstration would be the unconditional release of imprisoned Liberation Movement leaders, and the subsequent negotiation with the genuine representatives of the South African and Namibian peoples.[39]

It should be noted that the compatibility of the military solution contained in the above references with the UN Charter has been a matter of some contention.[40] In its first year of operation, the OAU established the Coordinating Committee for the Liberation of Africa as a subsidiary organ.[41] Its purpose was to organize diplomatic support for the various liberation movements, which were active in colonized territories, and to channel financial, military, and logistical aid to them. The Assembly dissolved the Liberation Committee in June 1994, even though the continent had

---

38. *See* Assembly, *Solemn Declaration on General Policy*, OAU Doc. CM/ST. 9 (XXI) (25 May 1973).
39. Assembly, *Declaration on Southern Africa made by the Assembly of Heads of State and Government of the Organization of African Unity*, OAU Doc. AHG/DECL. 1 (XX) (15 Nov. 1984).
40. Generally, *see* C. Dugard, 'The Organization of African Unity and Colonialism: An Inquiry into the Plea of Self-Defence as a Justification for the Use of Force in the Eradication of Colonialism', *ICLQ* 16 (1967): 157.
41. OAU Doc. CIAS/Plen.2/Rev.2 (25 Jun. 1963).

been largely decolonized much earlier.[42] Financial assistance to the liberation movements was provided through a Special Fund, which was also set up in 1963 and was maintained by Member States' voluntary contributions. The Fund targeted, *inter alia*, the liberation struggle in Guinea-Bissau, in Angola, and in Mozambique. The OAU internationalized the fight for decolonization, especially in the context of the UN. Thus, in the case of the occupation of Namibia by the Republic of South Africa, OAU Member States were successful in having judicial action initiated before the ICJ.[43] In the struggle against apartheid, the contribution of the OAU was of pivotal significance. One of its major accomplishments was the sponsoring of the World Conference for Action against Apartheid in 1977, which adopted the Lagos Declaration for Action against Apartheid.[44] The Conference not only condemned racial discrimination and segregation but also recognized the legitimate aspirations of the South African population and committed governments to provide support for the liberation movements, which were officially accepted by the OAU. Two years later, the OAU created an ad hoc committee on Southern Africa to mobilize international diplomatic action against the pariah states, namely the Republic of South Africa and the Republic of Rhodesia (Southern Rhodesia), and to exert pressure on them to abolish apartheid policies. This entity aligned with the UN Special Committee against Apartheid, which had been set up in 1962 by virtue of General Assembly Resolution 1761(XVII).[45]

14. Although the activities of the OAU were by no means exhausted with decolonization and apartheid, they constituted fundamental aspects of its operations and, even more importantly, they served as themes unifying the whole membership. Suffice to mention the declaration of independence by Zimbabwe in 1980, the achievement of independence by Namibia in March 1990 and the transition to a multiracial and democratic society in the Republic of South Africa in 1994. Undoubtedly, the OAU had not reached the end of its life, for too much work was

---

42. Assembly, *Resolution on Dissolution of the OAU Liberation Committee*, OAU Doc. AHG/Res. 228 (XXX) (15 Jun. 1994). Note that the AU position is that the United Kingdom continues the unlawful occupation of the Chagos Archipelago denying Mauritius the exercise of its sovereignty over it, Assembly, *Resolution on Chagos Archipelago*, AU Doc. Assembly/AU/Res. 1 (XXV) (15 Jun. 2015) and, more recently, Assembly, *Decision on Decolonization of Mauritius*, AU Doc. Assembly/AU/ Dec. 836 (XXXV) (2 Feb. 2022), which took into consideration the ICJ Advisory Opinion of 25 February 2019 titled 'Legal Consequences of the Separation of the Chagos Archipelago from Mauritius in 1965', I.C.J. Reports 2019, 95; for commentary, *see* B.T. Rrecaj, 'Legal Consequences of the Separation of the Chagos Archipelago from Mauritius in 1965 (ICJ Advisory Opinion, 25 February 2019, General List No. 169)', *Utrecht Journal of International and European Law* 35 (2020): 50–55 A similar AU position exists as regards the island of Réunion in the Indian Ocean and France.
43. *See Legal Consequences for States of the Continued Presence of South Africa in Namibia (South West Africa) Notwithstanding Security Council Resolution 276 (1970)*, Advisory Opinion of 21 Jun. 1971, I.C.J. Reports 1971, 16. The Advisory Opinion had been requested by the UNSC, whose Res. 276 (1970) of 29 July 1970 had declared that the continued presence of South Africa in the territory of Namibia was illegal and, consequently, all acts taken by its government on behalf of Namibia were invalid.
44. *See Report of the World Conference for Action Against Apartheid*, Lagos, 22–26 Aug. 1977 (New York: United Nations, 1977).
45. UNGA Res. 1761(XVII) 'Politics of apartheid of the Government of the Republic of South Africa', para. 5 (6 Nov. 1962).

still required to bring about what the Preamble of its Charter referred to as 'the total advancement of our peoples in all spheres of human endeavour'. In the closing years of the 1990s, African leaders were confronted with many pressing questions, which on account of developments on the international arena (the end of Cold War, the promotion by Western countries of a 'democracy – rule of law – human rights' agenda, the emergence of what was termed 'globalization', etc.) had made them more imperative than ever: Had the OAU outlived its usefulness? Could the OAU address effectively the challenges posed by the end of the Cold War and the advent of globalization? Could the OAU enhance Africa's role in an extremely competitive international community? Could the OAU advance much-needed social and economic development in the continent? Could the OAU promote and protect human rights as well as play a positive role in democratic reforms? These and similar questions were put on the table during the Thirty-Fifth Ordinary Assembly Session, which took place in Algiers in July 1999. It was decided to hold a session specifically dealing with the revitalization of the OAU.[46] The implementation of this proposal came from perhaps a rather expected quarter: Colonel Muammar Gaddafi, who breaking away from self-imposed alienation in the OAU that had lasted for some twenty years, re-emerged dynamically in the affairs of the continent and invited all African leaders to Libya for deliberations.[47] Gaddafi's plan was grand: the creation of a United States of Africa with a single army, a single currency, and a powerful leadership, which in the initial phase would be entrusted to him. On 8–9 September 1999, the Fourth Extraordinary Assembly Session took place in Sirte, Libya under the theme 'Strengthening OAU Capacity to Enable it to Meet the Challenges of the New Millennium.' Gaddafi's plan did not find favour with Thabo Mbeki, then President of the Republic of South Africa, who persuaded most of the other leaders to restrict the Session's agenda to revising the OAU Charter to increase efficiency and effectiveness.

15. This was not the first time that the OAU's streamlining had been seriously debated. Attempts had also taken place in 1975[48] and in 1979. In the latter case, the Sixteenth Ordinary Assembly Session (Monrovia, 17–20 July 1979) established a fourteen-member Committee on the Review of the Charter as a subsidiary organ operating within the Secretariat.[49] Its terms of reference were the overhaul of the Organization to meet the challenges brought about by the changing international arena and developments in the continent, for example, the collapse of dictatorial regimes, the first universal-franchise election in Zimbabwe, the UN plan for self-determination in Namibia, etc. The Committee failed to formulate substantive amendments to the OAU Charter, even though its membership had almost doubled

---

46. *See* Assembly, *Decision on the Convening of an Extraordinary Session of the OAU Assembly of Heads of State and Government in accordance with Article 33(5) of its Rules of Procedure*, OAU Doc. AHG/Dec. 140 (XXXV) (14 Jul. 1999).
47. For Libya's comeback, *see* A. Huliaras, 'Qadhafi's Comeback: Libya and Sub-Saharan Africa in the 1990s' *African Affairs* 100 (2001): 5; and Y. Romen, 'Libya's Diplomatic Success in Africa: The Reemergence of Quadhafi on the International Stage' *Diplomacy and Statecraft* 13 (2002): 235.
48. *See* Council of Ministers, *Resolution on the Establishment of an* Ad Hoc *Committee for the Structured Reform of the OAU*, OAU Doc. CM/Res. 386 (XXIV) (21 Feb. 1975).
49. OAU Doc. AHG/Dec. 111 (XVI) Rev. 1 (20 Jul. 1979).

since its establishment.[50] However, several proposals were successfully carried forward, which, in their turn, led to concrete initiatives. The most notable is the Cairo Declaration Establishing the Mechanism for Conflict Prevention, Management and Resolution, reference to which is made later in the present monograph.

16. At the aforementioned Sirte Extraordinary Session, African leaders sponsored the namesake Declaration, which set out the following aims, most of which centred on the welfare of African peoples:

- address in an effective manner the new social, political and economic realities as they were emerging both in Africa and in the world;
- fulfil the African peoples' aspirations for greater unity, as envisaged in the OAU Charter but also in the Treaty establishing the African Economic Community (AEC), also known as 'Abuja Treaty';
- revitalize the OAU and enhance its role to meet the needs of African peoples;
- eliminate the scourge of conflicts; and
- harness the human and natural resources of the continent to improve living conditions.[51]

17. The importance of the Sirte Declaration lies in the fact that these aims were not to be realized within the context of the OAU. On the contrary, it was decided to establish a new entity to be called the 'African Union.' The title was probably coined after the European Union (EU) hoping that the new pan-African Organization would have the EU's success. It was further resolved that the AU's guiding principles would be in conformity with the ultimate objectives enshrined in the OAU Charter and in the AEC Treaty. Thus, in Sirte, Member States declared that the OAU, as originally conceived in the early 1960s, could no longer have served the continent's needs and aspirations and decided to replace it with another, more dynamic, organization capable of safeguarding its achievements and promoting Africa's role in the perplexing and demanding twenty-first century. Yet the AEC was not to be replaced, and the Sirte Declaration stipulated that measures had to be taken to accelerate its implementation, including the shortening of the transitory periods envisaged in the Abuja Treaty; the prompt establishment of all organs envisaged therein and especially the Pan-African Parliament (PAP); and the strengthening and consolidation of the African Regional Economic Communities (RECs).

18. It follows that the new organization was not conceived as an 'umbrella' institution with an expanded mandate under which the OAU and the AEC would merge and be given a renewed mandate. Thus, it was not a case akin to the creation of the EU in the early 1990s, where the European (Economic) Community comprised one of its three constituent pillars (the other two being the common foreign and security

---

50. Assembly, *Resolution on the Composition of the Charter Review Committee*, OAU Doc. AHG/ Res. 152 (XXII) (30 Jul. 1986), as proposed by the Council of Ministers, *Resolution on the Composition of the Charter Review Committee*, OAU Doc. CM/Res. 1041 (XLIV) (26 Jul. 1986).
51. Assembly, *Sirte Declaration*, OAU Doc. EAHG/Draft/Decl. (IV) Rev.1, at paras 5, 6 and 8 (9 Sep. 1999), reproduced in RADIC 11 (1999): 803.

policy (CFSP) and cooperation in the field of justice and home affairs (JHI)). African leaders could be criticized for not exploring this avenue at Sirte, especially considering the lagging performance of the AEC. Although, as is made apparent in Part III of this monograph, the AU commenced its operations with a significant degree of dynamism, the AEC continued its rather aimless course. African states abandoned their economic integration efforts through the AEC and only in the late 2010s explored other avenues to create an African Continental Free Trade Area (ACFTA).

19. The task of drafting the AU Constitutive Act was undertaken by a working group comprising lawyers, political scientists, and economists. Its task did not only include offering solutions to such issues as the smooth transition from the OAU to the AU and the functional relationship between the AU organs and those existing in the OAU structure but also the incorporation into the AU of policies, which had been agreed by OAU Summits but had never been implemented. The Republic of South Africa played a significant role in the drafting of the Constitutive Act, which was done in record time by international standards. The insertion of provisions on human rights, the rule of law and democratic principles should be attributed to South Africa. This was a rather risky endeavour since regimes in several Member States (including Libya) were in power by negating these very rights and principles to their populations. Nevertheless, the Constitutive Act was promptly placed before the Thirty-Sixth Ordinary Assembly Session, which met in Lomé, Togo between 10 and 12 July 2000. Despite some apparent inadequacies in its text, it was approved without many changes.[52] If nothing else, this showed the determination of African leaders to break away from the discredited OAU and start a new page in their cooperation.

20. The haste to create the AU was also revealed during the Fifth Extraordinary Assembly Session (Sirte, 2 March 2001), which proclaimed its establishment even though at the time the Constitutive Act had not yet entered into force.[53] To declare the advent of a new international organization when its Charter has not come into effect and when there are no provisions on its interim operation during the ratification period is rather unknown in international law. In particular, Article 28 of the Constitutive Act stipulated that it would enter into force thirty days following the deposit of instruments of ratification by at least two-thirds of OAU Members (i.e., by thirty-six states). On 26 April 2001, Nigeria became the thirty-sixth Member State to do so, and, consequently, the Act came into force on 26 May 2001. The actual date of the AU's establishment requires some clarification, as there would appear to be two relevant dates: 2 March 2001 (the day the declaration of establishment was adopted) and 26 May 2001 (the day the Constitutive Act entered into force). It is submitted that the latter date should be accepted, not least because the said declaration was a political act of an undisputed important symbolic character

52. 2158 U.N.T.S. 3, reproduced in Appendix I of this monograph, in RADIC 12 (2000): 629, and in RADIC 13 (2005): 25. For analysis, *see* K. Magliveras & G. Naldi, 'The African Union – A New Dawn for Africa?', *ICLQ* 51 (2002): 415.
53. Assembly, *Decision on the African Union*, OAU Doc. EAHG/Dec. 1 (V) (2 Mar. 2001).

but had no legal consequences from an institutional point of view. AU was officially lodged in July 2002 when the Inaugural Session of the Assembly took place in Durban, South Africa.

21. There can be no doubt that, by deciding to establish the AU, African states did not aim at setting up a new institution that was going to be a mere continuation of the OAU by another name. In the words of the OAU Secretary-General: '[African leaders] certainly had in mind an organization that would provide a framework for enhanced cohesion, cooperation, integration and strengthened capacity to deal with the crises that face the African continent today.'[54] At the Inaugural Assembly Session in July 2002, African statesmen 'rededicated' themselves more determinedly to the OAU principles and objectives, 'pledged' to strive more resolutely in pursuing its ultimate goals, and 'reiterated' their commitment to achieving the AU objectives.[55]

22. After many turbulent years, arguably the AU has made its distinctive mark. On the whole, the fears that it would be a repetition of the OAU have not materialized. The AU has managed to transform the way African affairs are conducted, although more seems to have been achieved in areas such as peace and security and less in other areas such as free trade and economic integration, even though the work undertaken in the context of NEPAD (now AUDA-NEPAD), Agenda 2063, and the African Continental Free Trade Area, which are examined later in the monograph, should not be underestimated. Several favourite conditions have contributed to these achievements, including economic growth at accelerated rates, high global prices for the raw materials and commodities produced in Africa, increased Foreign Direct Investments (FDI) from Europe, the United States,[56] and the so-called BRIC countries (Brazil, Russia, India, and China), etc.[57] At the same time, relations with the former colonial powers and with the EU at large entered a new phase. However, for a combination of reasons, including persisting ethnic conflicts and interstate problems, the inability to accept and maintain democratic ideals and the rule of law leading to endless coups d'état, large-scale human rights violations, endemic corruption, etc., the much-cherished African renaissance has still not been materialized. Mentioned for the first time by Nelson Mandela during the Thirtieth Ordinary OAU Assembly Session (Tunis, 13–15 June 1994),[58] the concept of African renaissance has been popularized by former President Thabo Mbeki of South Africa as

54. *See* Secretary-General, *Report of the Secretary-General on the Implementation of the Sirte Decision on the African Union*, OAU Doc. CM/2210 (LXXIV), para. 26 at p. 10 (2001).
55. Assembly, *Durban Declaration in Tribute to the Organization of African Unity and on the Occasion of the Launching of the African Union*, AU Doc. ASS/AU/Decl. 2 (I) (12 Jul. 2002), paras 14 and 15, reproduced in I.L.M. 41 (2002): 1029.
56. The US relationship to Africa has always been a complex one with periods of abandonment followed by periods of engagement and vice versa, *see* P. Baker & D. Walsh, 'Biden Aims to Inject New Energy Into U.S. Relations With African Nations', *The New York Times*, 14 December 2022, at: https://www.nytimes.com/2022/12/14/us/politics/biden-us-africa-summit.html.
57. J.C. Anyanwu, 'Why Does Foreign Direct Investment Go Where It Goes?: New Evidence From African Countries', *Annals of Economics and Finance* 13 (2012): 425.
58. *See* M. Meredith, *The State of Africa: A History of Fifty Years of Independence* (London: Free Press, 2005), 676 et seq.

being the third stage in the evolution of post-colonial Africa, the first two being decolonization, and the promotion of democratization.[59] However, the term is used here in a rather different context: with many an African leader of the old generation ousted, the new generation of leaders should pursue collective efforts to create the necessary conditions for breaking away from the ankyloses of the past. This will allow the continent to catch up with the rest of the world and free itself from all kinds of outside direct and indirect interferences and interventions.

23. What follows is a synopsis, in chronological order, of some of the most important events in the history of the OAU and of the AU.[60] It records milestones in the development and evolution of the two institutions, moments of triumph but also of defeat, the various multilateral agreements and other instruments negotiated and adopted under their auspices (their current status is also given) as well as other events that, directly or indirectly, have had consequences for their evolution. This record of affairs is based primarily on the work of the Assembly of Heads of State and Government, the highest-ranking organ and policymaking organ and, where pertinent, on the work of other organs as well. Many of the developments and documents mentioned in the following paragraphs are examined and analysed elsewhere in the present monograph. This part of the monograph serves as a legal history of the African continent by looking primarily at the multifaceted work and activities of the OAU and the AU, the problems and challenges encountered, and the solutions given.

24. Immediately after the establishment of the OAU in 1963, the Coordinating Committee for the Liberation of Africa, the entity responsible for streamlining the efforts for the independence of the territories still under foreign domination, was set up. Moreover, citing Portugal's and South Africa's non-compliance with the United Nations Security Council (UNSC) and United Nations General Assembly (UNGA) resolutions on the issue of apartheid and racial discrimination, African leaders resolved to boycott their goods and products and cease the supply of minerals to them.[61] In the First Ordinary Session of the OAU Assembly (Cairo, 17–21 July 1964), African leaders reaffirmed their pledge to the principle of strict observance for the colonial boundaries that were inherited at independence,[62] chose Addis Ababa, Ethiopia and not Accra, Ghana as the Organization's headquarters,[63] and

59. Thabo Mbeki, *Statement on African Renaissance*, 13 August 1998, https://www.sahistory.org.za/archive/african-renaissance-statement-deputy-president-thabo-mbeki-sabc-gallagher-estate-13-august. Generally, *see* UN Economic and Social Council, *The African Renaissance and the Challenge of Globalization*, UN Doc. E/C.12/2001/WP.1 (2 Mar. 2001).

60. For a more detailed chronology of OAU events until the early 1990s, *see* G. Harris, *The Organization of African Unity*, World Bibliographical Series/International Organizations Series, Vol. 7 (Oxford: Clio Press, 1994).

61. Council of Ministers, *Portuguese Colonialism and Apartheid in South Africa*, OAU Doc. CM/Res. 6 (1) (11 Aug. 1963).

62. Assembly, *Border Disputes Among African States*, OAU Doc. AHG/Res. 16 (I) (21 Jul. 1964).

63. Assembly, *Recommendations of the First and Second Ordinary Sessions of the Council of Ministers*, OAU Doc. AHG/Res. 2 (I) (21 Jul. 1964).

established a sub-committee within the Secretariat to promote the campaign for economic sanctions against South Africa.[64] Moreover, the person in charge of Angola's National Liberation Front (FNLA) was recognized as the country's legitimate leader,[65] a decision that later caused considerable problems to the smooth functioning of the OAU. Finally, the Protocol establishing the Commission of Mediation, Conciliation and Arbitration, which had been envisaged in Article XIX of the OAU Charter, was adopted and became an integral part of the Charter. Eight French-speaking Member States abstained from the Second Ordinary Assembly Session (Accra, 21–26 October 1965) in protest at the policy of the host state's leader to lend support to rebellious elements in their territories. At the same Session, the Declaration on the Problem of Subversion was adopted, which, *inter alia*, condemned every form of subversion conceived, organized or financed by foreign powers against the OAU and its Member States.[66] On 11 November 1965, the white supremacy regime in Rhodesia (today's Zimbabwe) unilaterally proclaimed its independence as a sovereign state. Even before this declaration of independence, the Assembly had called upon all states and international organizations to withhold recognition of the 'European minority government'.[67] The United Kingdom, the Commonwealth, and the UN regarded the declaration as illegal, while the UN imposed the first-ever economic sanctions in its history on the former British colony.[68]

25. The Third Ordinary Assembly Session (Addis Ababa, 5–9 November 1966) took no decisions of note. However, the Council of Ministers, the OAU's executive arm, during its Seventh Ordinary Session (Addis Ababa, 31 October–4 November 1966) condemned Rhodesia's unilateral proclamation of independence, called upon all Member States and third states to withhold recognition, and strongly condemned 'Britain for her refusal to crush the Southern Rhodesian rebel regime.'[69] On the question of South West Africa (Namibia), the Council considered that the continued domination by South Africa constituted 'an illegal military occupation of an African sister country'.[70] The following year, the OAU was confronted with the Biafran secessionist war in Nigeria. Owing to the serious split between its Member States on whether or not to recognize the self-declared independent state of Biafra (Eastern Nigeria) and their concern to avoid balkanization at a time when the political map of Africa was still being shaped, the Fourth Ordinary Assembly Session (Kinshasa, 11–14 September 1967) considered that the situation was an internal affair

---

64. Assembly, *Apartheid and Racial Discrimination*, OAU Doc. AHG/Res. 6 (I) (21 Jul. 1964).
65. Assembly, *The Revolutionary Government of Angola in Exile and the Popular Liberation Movement of Angola (MPLA)*, OAU Doc. AHG/Res. 18 (I) (21 Jul. 1964).
66. Assembly, *Declaration on the Problem of Subversion*, OAU Doc. AHG/Res. 27 (II) (25 Oct. 1965).
67. Assembly, *Southern Rhodesia*, OAU Doc. AHG/Res. 25 (II) (25 Oct. 1965).
68. *See* UNSC Resolutions 217(1965), 232(1966) and 253(1968). Generally, *see* C. Robinowitz, 'U.N. Application of Selective, Mandatory Sanctions against Rhodesia: A Brief Legal and Political Analysis', *Virginia Journal of International Law* 7 (1966–1967): 147; J.L. Cefkin, 'The Rhodesian Question at the United Nations', *International Organization* 22 (1968):649; and A.S. Mlambo, 'Honoured More in the Breach than in the Observance': Economic Sanctions on Rhodesia and International Response, 1965 to 1979', *South African Historical Journal* 71 (2019): 371.
69. Council of Ministers, *Resolution on Southern Rhodesia*, OAU Doc. CM/Res. 78 (VII) (4 Nov. 1966).
70. Council of Ministers, *Resolution on South West Africa*, OAU Doc. CM/Res. 87 (VII) (4 Nov. 1966).

and aligned itself with Nigeria's territorial integrity and unity.[71] The same Session adopted the Phyto-Sanitary Convention for Africa to prevent the introduction of diseases, insect pests and other threats to plants in Africa. The Convention is quite unique in the sense that it does not require it to be signed and does not feature a clause on its entry into force. It has received ten ratifications (lastly by Burundi in October 1992).

26. Already in 1967, several unresolved incidents, including the border disputes between Somalia, Kenya, and Ethiopia, which had by now lasted almost four years,[72] and the continuing presence of foreign mercenaries in Zaïre (Democratic Republic of Congo (DRC)), had resulted in what was described as the 'crumbling image' of the OAU. In 1967, the Secretariat established the Board of Refugees, which together with the Commission for Refugees, dealt with massive human dislocations in Africa.[73] In 1968, Nigeria was reconciled with those Members supporting secessionist Biafra, and the first constitutional crisis in the OAU's history ended. On 15 September 1968, the African Convention on Conservation of Nature and Natural Resources was adopted. It came into effect on 16 June 1969. So far, thirty-three Member States have ratified it (latterly by Angola in February 2014). The Convention is still being signed, e.g., by Equatorial Guinea in January 2011, by Guinea-Bissau in January 2012 and by South Sudan in January 2013. In January 1969, the Constitution of the African Civil Aviation Commission (AFCAC) was opened for signature. It entered into force on 15 March 1972. By the time a Revised Constitution was adopted on 16 December 2009, forty-four Member States had ratified and/or acceded to it. When the Revised Constitution entered into force provisionally on 11 May 2010, the old Constitution was abrogated and superseded. Therefore, the fact that the 1969 Constitution was signed by Equatorial Guinea on 31 January 2011, by Guinea-Bissau on 27 January 2012 and by South Sudan on 24 January 2013 was probably a procedural mistake, especially since the latter two states signed on the same day the Revised Constitution as well. The Revised Constitution shall enter into force definitely when ratified by fifteen Member States; so far, it has secured thirteen ratifications (lastly by San Tome and Principe in February 2018). In January 2017, the AU Assembly adopted an amendment to Article 10(4) of the (Revised) Constitution of AFCAC.[74] It should be noted that a Single African Air Transport Market (SAATM) was launched in January 2018.[75] Currently, thirty-five Member States participate in SAATM. They have all adhered to

71. African leaders reiterated their condemnation of secession in Member States and pointed out that the solution to the problem was the responsibility of Nigerians themselves, Assembly, OAU Doc. AHG/Res. 51 (IV) (14 Sep. 1967); note that the Resolution did not have a title. *See also* Assembly, *Resolution on Nigeria*, OAU Doc. AHG/Res. 54 (V) (16 Sep. 1968). For the OAU mediation in the Nigerian civil war (1967–1970), *see* T. Princen, *Intermediaries in International Conflict* (Princeton: Princeton University Press, 1992), 186.
72. Assembly, *Declaration on Kenya-Somali Relations*, OAU Doc. AHG/ST. 1 (14 Sep. 1967).
73. Generally, *see* M. Sharpe, 'Organization of African Unity and African Union Engagement with Refugee Protection: 1963–2011', *RADIC* 21 (2013): 50.
74. Assembly, *Decision on the Draft Legal Instruments*, AU Doc. Assembly/AU/Dec. 636 (XXVIII), para. 2 (31 Jan. 2017).
75. *See* Assembly, *Decision on the Establishment of a Single African Air Transport Market*, AU Doc. Assembly/AU/Dec. 665 (XXX) (29 Jan. 2018).

the Solemn Commitment to fully implement the Decision Relating to the Implementation of the Yamoussoukro Declaration Concerning the Liberalisation of Access to Air Transport Markets in Africa, which was signed in November 1999[76] and was endorsed during its Thirty-Sixth OAU Assembly Ordinary Session (July 2000, it was simultaneously held as the Fourth Ordinary AEC Assembly Session as well).[77] Despite its title, the Yamoussoukro Decision is actually a multilateral agreement and allows contracting parties to withdraw. Its principal aim is the full liberalization of air transport in Africa, and it was drafted with the AEC project in mind considering that it promotes the relaxation of non-physical barriers to the movement of persons, goods and services in the continent.

In April 1969, fifteen East and Central African countries issued the Lusaka Manifesto on the Future of southern Africa.[78] The Manifesto was subsequently adopted by the OAU and guided its stance towards the Republic of South Africa.[79] Moreover, UNGA Resolution 2505(XXIV) of 20 November 1969 brought the Manifesto 'to the attention of all States and of all peoples'. In the meantime, the OAU Council of Ministers, by suggesting that all liberation movements should be required to form a common fighting front and that no assistance be extended to those movements not recognized by the OAU, had indicated that the African struggle against decolonization and racial discrimination had to come under OAU auspices.[80] Finally, on 10 September 1969, the Convention Governing the Specific Aspects of Refugee Problems in Africa was adopted as an effective regional complement to the UN Convention Relating to the Status of Refugees (1951)[81] and its Protocol (1967).[82] All except nine Member States have currently ratified the Convention (South Sudan submitted its ratification instrument in May 2016), which entered into force on 20 June 1974.[83]

27. The 1970s were marked by gross human rights violations orchestrated by dictatorial regimes in Uganda, the CAR, and Equatorial Guinea. In 1971, several Member States (including Gabon, Lesotho, Malawi, and Madagascar) were in

---

76. The text appeared as OAU Doc. CM/2178 (LXXII) and as UN Economic and Social Council, Economic Community for Africa, UN Doc. ECA/RCID/CM.CIVAC/99/RPT, Annex I (14 Nov. 1999), at: https://repository.uneca.org/handle/10855/24568.
77. OAU Doc. AHG/OUA/AEC/Dec. 1 (IV), para. 5 (12 Jul. 2000).
78. For the text with commentary, *see The African Review* (1971): 66; *see further African Affairs* 69 (1970): 180.
79. Council of Ministers, *Declaration on the Question of Dialogue*, OAU Doc. CM/St. 5 (XVII) (19 Jun. 1971). The *Lusaka Manifesto* should be read together with the *Resolution on Decolonization* and the *Mogadiscio Declaration*, both of which were adopted by the Twenty-Third Ordinary Council of Ministers Session, OAU Doc. CM/Res.350 (XXIII) and CM/ST. 13 (XXIII) (15 Jun. 1974), respectively.
80. Council of Ministers, *Resolution on Decolonization and Apartheid*, OAU Doc. CM/Res. 206 (XIII) (6 Sep. 1969). *See further*, The USESCO Press, *The Decolonization of Africa: Southern Africa and the Horn of Africa* (Paris: The General History of Africa: Studies and Documents 5, 1981), at: https://unesdoc.unesco.org/ark:/48223/pf0000045919.
81. Entered into force on 22 Apr. 1954, 189 U.N.T.S. 150.
82. Entered into force on 4 Oct. 1967, 606 U.N.T.S. 267.
83. 1001 U.N.T.S. 45.

favour of dialogue and rapprochement with the Republic of South Africa, a suggestion that was met with distrust by other Members. In 1972–1973, a series of developments, such as the termination of the civil war in southern Sudan, the rapprochement between, on the one hand, Morocco and Algeria, and, on the other hand, Senegal and Guinea, as well the OAU's tenth anniversary gave a fresh impetus.[84] However, the mass slaughter of Hutus in Burundi in 1972 went largely unnoticed, and the OAU failed to exercise its authority.[85] Twenty-two years later, when the genocide of Tutsis by Hutu extremists in Rwanda took place, the OAU, alongside the UN and the international community at large, would once more prove unable to actively intervene and save human lives, even though the 1994 genocide was rather a continuation of the killings between these two ethnic groups that had taken place in Burundi when President Melchior Ndadaye was assassinated in October 2003.[86] By 1974, the struggle against apartheid had intensified on the international plane.[87] It was organized and directed by the OAU and was also fought at the UN through the African Group of Members in the UNGA. The African Group, established in 1964, was very often succoured by the Arab Group of Members in the UNGA to have the Republic of South Africa expelled from membership.[88] Indeed, it was instrumental in South Africa's ostracism from the UNGA Twenty-Ninth Session (November 1974) and subsequent sessions.[89] On 18 January 1974, the Constitution of the Association of African Trade Promotion Organizations was adopted. Although it came provisionally into force on the day it was opened for signature, it formally entered into force only on 28 March 2012 having secured the required twelve ratifications. Currently, it has been ratified by fifteen Member States

84. Compare Heads of State and Government, *Solemn Declaration on General Policy*, OAU Doc. CM/ST. 9 (XXI) (25 May 1973). But *see*, Council of Ministers, *Statement on Current Political Issues*, OAU Doc. CM/ST.8/Rev. 2 (XX) (9 Feb. 1973).
85. *See* J.P. Chretien & J.F. Dupaquier, *Burundi 1972: Au bord des genocides* (Paris: L'Harmattan, 2007); R. Lemarchand, 'The Burundi Genocide' in S. Totten, W. Parsons & I. Charny (eds), *Century of Genocide: Critical Essays and Eyewitness Accounts* (New York & London: Routledge, 2004) 321. In December 2021, the Truth and Reconciliation Commission established three years earlier described the 1972 crisis as 'genocide' in a report submitted to the Parliament of Burundi, *see* https://senat.bi/en/?p=8419.
86. Generally, *see* the Report of the International Commission of Inquiry in Burundi set up under UNSC Res. 1012 (1995) of 28 Aug. 1995, contained in UN Doc. S/1996/682 (22 Aug. 1996), at: https://digitallibrary.un.org/record/220451.
87. Council of Ministers, *Resolution on the Activities of the African Group at the United Nations*, OAU Doc. CM/Res. 351 (XXIII) (11 Jun. 1974), and Council of Ministers, *Resolution on South Africa*, OAU Doc. CM/Res. 428 (XXV) (25 Jul. 1977).
88. The First Afro-Arab Summit was held in Cairo on 7–9 Mar. 1977. Cooperation was implemented through the following four entities: the Coordinating Commission, the Standing Commission, the Joint Afro-Arab Ministerial Conference, and the Afro-Arab Summit Conference. Generally, *see* Council of Ministers, *Resolution on Afro-Arab Cooperation*, OAU Doc. CM/Res. 770 (XXXIV) (15 Feb. 1980); *Resolution on Afro-Arab Cooperation*, OAU Doc. CM/Res. 781 (XXXV) (28 Jun. 1980); and *Resolution on Afro-Arab Cooperation*, OAU Doc. CM/Res. 1106 (XLVI) (25 Jul. 1987).
89. Council of Ministers, *Resolution on the Expulsion of South Africa from the Twenty-Ninth Session of the United Nations General Assembly*, OAU Doc. CM/Res. 392 (XXIV) (21 Feb. 1975). Generally, *see* K. Magliveras, *Exclusion from Participation in International Organisations – The Law and Practice behind Member States' Expulsion and Suspension of Membership* (The Hague: Kluwer Law International, 1999), 209–222.

(lastly by Burkina Faso in June 2016). In April 1975, the Ninth Extraordinary Council of Ministers Session adopted the Dar-as-Salaam Declaration stipulating that the OAU strategy towards Rhodesia, Namibia, and South Africa should be primarily based on peaceful means and, if these were to fail, resort to armed struggle would be a legitimate course of action.[90] The Extraordinary Session had been convened because the collapse of Portugal's dictatorial regime had immediate effects on its African territories (Angola, Mozambique, Cape Verde (now, officially called Cabo Verde)) and had radically altered the balance of forces in southern Africa forcing the OAU to formulate a new common position. Several African leaders boycotted the Twelfth Ordinary Assembly Session (Kampala, Uganda, 28 July–1 August 1975) because they believed that, by meeting there, they were giving respectability to President Idi Amin of Uganda, whose regime had been universally condemned for atrocities and widespread human rights violations. During the Kampala Session, forty-two Member States adopted the Inter-African Convention Establishing an African Technical Cooperation Programme, as the most appropriate method of promoting the employment of African specialists by African states, an early example of the 'African solutions to African problems' line of thinking. It is noteworthy that the Convention, presently signed by twenty-nine states, was signed by only two states until 2000 and that all eight Member States that ratified it did so in the twenty-first century. That the Convention is two ratifications short of the required number to enter into force raises two crucial questions, which happen to concern other OAU/AU treaties as well. The first question is the commitment of Members to ensure that the instruments negotiated and signed under OAU/AU auspices enter into force and become operative promptly. The second question is whether there are valid grounds to continue keeping open multilateral instruments, which were concluded so many years ago and whose content no longer corresponds to contemporary realities and needs, in short, instruments that ought to have been either abrogated or revised.

28. Disagreement over the legitimate government of Angola brought to a stalemate the First Extraordinary Assembly Session, which met in Addis Ababa on 10–13 January 1976 solely for determining this very issue.[91] The forty-four voting Members were equally split between the Soviet and Cuba-backed Popular Movement for the Liberation of Angola (MPLA) and the US-backed National Union for the Total Independence of Angola (UNITA), a prime example of the Cold War's so-called proxy wars.[92] The Extraordinary Session collapsed. This complicated the question of Angola's admittance to membership.[93] However, by 2 February 1976, most Members had recognized MPLA, leading to its express recognition by the

90. *See Dar-as-Salaam Declaration on Southern Africa*, 10 Apr. 1975, which was partly endorsed by UNGA Res. 3396 (XXX), 'Question of Southern Rhodesia' (21 Nov. 1975).
91. Note that the previous year an OAU Fact-Finding Commission of Enquiry and Conciliation had been set up, *see* Assembly, *Resolution on the Situation in Angola*, OAU Doc. AHG/Res. 72 (XII) (1 Aug. 1975).
92. *See* J.I. De Maio, 'Plausible Deniability: Proxy Wars in Africa' *Fletcher Security Review* I:II (2014): 35.
93. For the disagreement over Angola's legitimate government, *see* the document titled 'OAU-Angola' released on 12 Jan. 1976 by the Central Intelligence Agency (CIA), at: http://www.faqs.org/cia/

OAU and admission on 10 February 1976. Later in the same month, Morocco and Mauritania took over the administration of the Western Sahara territory from Spain (another colonial power that had recently embraced democracy) in negation of the local population's right to self-determination. The Western Saharan issue had always been a crucial test of the OAU's effectiveness and its ability to abide by its lofty principles; until today, it remains unresolved even though the de facto presence of Morocco for so many decades has shaped a reality which is hard to ignore. On 29 June 1976, Seychelles acceded to the OAU. The Twenty-Seventh Ordinary Council of Ministers Session (Port Louis, Mauritius, 24 June–3 July 1976) adopted a decision preventing Member States from recognizing the South African Bantustans,[94] while the Thirteenth Ordinary Assembly Session (Port Louis, Mauritius, 2–6 July 1976) denounced as an act of aggression the freeing by Israeli armed forces of their countrymen who were held hostages by Palestinians hijackers in Uganda's Entebbe Airport.[95] Mauritius, as the country which at the time held the OAU Chairmanship, complained before the UNSC for Israel's 'unprecedented aggression' against Uganda. The UNSC deliberated the complaint in early July 1976, but no action was taken.[96] The Thirteenth Assembly also adopted the Cultural Charter for Africa.[97] It came into force with considerable delay on 19 September 1990 and has currently received thirty-five ratifications (lastly by Gabon on 26 September 2007). In the following year, the Fourteenth Ordinary Assembly Session (Libréville, Gabon, 2–5 July 1977) approved the Convention for the Elimination of Mercenarism in Africa. It entered into force on 22 April 1985.[98] Currently, only thirty-two Member States have deposited instruments of ratification (the last four being Algeria on 11 January 2008, Gambia on 9 July 2009, Chad on 27 October 2012, and Guinea-Bissau on 22 January 2015). In February 2022, the Assembly welcomed the initiative taken by the AUC to revise the Mercenarism Convention and to prepare a comprehensive and integrated continental stabilization strategy for addressing the security threat posed by non-State armed groups.[99]

29. In July 1978, the discussion at Assembly level on the interference of states from outside the continent in the internal affairs of African states revealed the ideological divide among Member States, when criticism of French and US intervention was counteracted by criticism of Soviet and Cuban involvement leading to cases of

index_48.html. *See further*, F. Castro, J. Risquet & G. Garcia Marquez, *Changing the History of Africa: Angola and Namibia* (Melbourne: Ocean Press, 1989).

94. Council of Ministers, *Resolution on Non-recognition of South African Bantustans*, OAU Doc. CM/Res. 492 (XXVII) (3 Jul. 1976).
95. Assembly, *Resolution on Israel Aggression against Uganda*, OAU Doc. AHG/Res. 83 (XIII) (6 Jul. 1976).
96. *See* UNSC Official Records, UN Doc. S/PV. 1939, 9 Jul. 1976, at: https://digitallibrary.un.org/record/86947.
97. Assembly, *Resolution relating to the Cultural Charter for Africa,* OAU Doc. AHG/Res. 82 (XIII) (6 Jul. 1976).
98. 1490 U.N.T.S. 95.
99. *See* Assembly, *Decision on the Report on the Activities of the Peace and Security Council (PSC) and the State of Peace and Security in Africa*, AU Doc. Assembly/AU/Dec. 815(XXXV), para. 25 (6 Feb. 2022).

instability such as in Angola.[100] It is interesting to note that the Fourteenth Ordinary Assembly Session had adopted an uncontested Decision on the question of outside interference in African affairs which promoted an African policy of non-alignment.[101] During 1978, various long-standing interstate conflicts appeared to be coming to a conclusion, including the disputes between Guinea and Ivory Coast and between Guinea and Senegal.[102] However, in other ongoing disputes (e.g., between Somalia and Ethiopia,[103] between Ethiopia and Sudan,[104] and between Libya and Chad),[105] the OAU was not a successful mediator. The OAU recognized Mugabe's Patriotic Front as the legitimate government in Zimbabwe (Rhodesia) but appealed to all political parties to participate in the general elections in the hope of avoiding a crisis like that of Angola a few years earlier. In 1978/1979, Tanzania invaded Uganda and caused the downfall of the infamous dictator Idi Amin. This led to considerable controversy among Member States which had various consequences. First, it showed the OAU's inability to deal with dictatorial regimes violating the OAU Charter principles and obligations. Second, it revealed its inability to prevent Members from resorting to extreme measures in their interstate relations, which were prohibited under the rules of international law as they invariably involved the use of force. Third, the invasion of another Member State (even one with a totalitarian regime in power) questioned the doctrine of absolute state sovereignty, which was enshrined in the OAU Charter. On 2 November 1979, Angola acceded to the OAU.

30. The Second Extraordinary Assembly Session (Lagos, Nigeria, 28–29 April 1980) was convened to discuss Africa's economic revival. It adopted the namesake Plan of Action for the Economic Development of Africa 1980–2000, which was based on the Monrovia Declaration of Commitment.[106] This was a strategy, partly devised by the UN Economic Commission for Africa (ECA),[107] for the development

100. Discussion on the issue started at the Thirty-First Ordinary Council of Ministers Session (Khartoum, Sudan, 7–18 Jul. 1978) which however rejected a decision tabled as *Draft Resolution on Measures to be Taken against Neo-Colonialist Maneuvers and Foreign Military Intervention in Africa*, *see* OAU Doc. CM/Res. 638 (XXXI), 18 Jul. 1978. The matter was then referred to the Fifteenth Ordinary Assembly Session (Khartoum, Sudan, 18–22 Jul. 1978) which failed to reach a decision as well. At the Thirty-First Council of Ministers Session, another decision tabled as *Draft Resolution on the Territorial Integrity of Africa and the Surrounding Islands* (OAU Doc. CM/Res. 676 (XXXI)) was not adopted as fifteen Member States filed reservations and another did not participate in the proceedings.
101. Assembly, *Resolution on the Interference of the Internal Affairs of African States*, OAU Doc. AHG/Res. 85 (XIV) (5 Jul. 1977).
102. Assembly, *Resolution on Reconciliation between Guinea, Ivory Coast and Senegal*, OAU Doc. AHG/Res. 88 (XV) (22 Jul. 1978).
103. Assembly, *Resolution on the Somalia/Ethiopia Conflict*, OAU Doc. AHG/Res. 90 (XV) (22 Jul. 1978).
104. Assembly, *Resolution on the Ethiopia/Sudan Dispute*, OAU Doc. AHG/Res. 93 (XV) (22 Jul. 1978).
105. Assembly, *Resolution on the Libya/Chad Dispute*, OAU Doc. AHG/Res. 94 (XV) (22 Jul. 1978).
106. Assembly, OAU Doc. EAHG/Res. 1 (II) (29 Apr. 1980).
107. It was established by the UN Economic and Social Council (ECOSOC) in 1958 as one of the UN's five regional economic commissions. The mandate of ECA, which comprises 54 African UN members (i.e. the entire AU membership bar the Sahrawi Arab Democratic Republic), is to promote economic and social development, to foster intra-regional integration, and to promote international cooperation leading to Africa's development. Note that, when created, six colonial powers were

and the creation of the necessary conditions to encourage economic growth in the agricultural, industry and energy sectors and to protect the environment in the continent. The same Session also decided to promote the more active participation of African states in international negotiations, a theme which, many years later, became an objective in the AU Constitutive Act. In June 1980, Zimbabwe acceded to the OAU, an event of immense political importance since it was a turning point in the phasing out of white regimes in southern Africa. The Polisario Front, the political entity representing the indigenous population of Western Sahara, was recognized as the legitimate government by twenty-six out of the then fifty Member States, opening the way for another constitutional crisis in the OAU. In February 1981, after many resolutions issued by the Council of Ministers, the Convention for the Establishment of the African Centre for Fertilizer Development was concluded in the hope of contributing to the stabilization and improvement of Africa's agricultural sector. The Convention contains a rather strange entry-into-force clause: it stipulates that it shall enter into force if it has been ratified by the host Government, namely Zimbabwe, as well as by the Governments of at least five other Member States. Thus, even though it has been ratified by eight Member States, it has still not entered into force (Zimbabwe signed it on 30 December 1986 but never ratified it). The Eighteenth Ordinary Assembly Session (Nairobi, 24–27 June 1981) adopted the African Charter on Human and Peoples' Rights (also known as the African Charter or Banjul Charter). It entered into force on 21 October 1986. It has been ratified by all Member States, except Morocco, which, as is later explained, acceded to the AU in January 2017. The African Charter, which is examined in detail later in the monograph, constitutes, chronologically speaking, the third regional system for the protection of human rights and has distinctive features separating it from the European and Inter-American counterparts, for example, the notion that people do not only enjoy rights but also owe obligations to fellow people as well as to their countries. Subsequent Protocols have augmented both its scope of protection (adding the rights of women, the rights of older people and the rights of persons with disabilities) and its institutional mechanism (adding a Court of Human Rights). At the same Session, the Assembly's decision to establish an OAU peacekeeping force for Chad marked the first opportunity to involve itself in peacekeeping operations, which, however, ended in an embarrassing failure.[108]

It was also during 1981 that Morocco agreed in principle on holding a referendum in Western Sahara so that the local population could exercise its alienable right to self-determination; the choice offered to the population was either independence or integration with Morocco. Until today, and despite the creation and operation of

---

ECA members, including Portugal which was expelled in 1963. The Union of South Africa (it became the Republic of South Africa in 1961) was an original ECA member but its membership was suspended in 1963. *See further*, UN ECOSOC, *Terms of Reference and Rules of Procedure of the Economic Commission for Africa*, UN Doc. E/CN.14/III/Rev.8/Corr.2 (1994).

108. Assembly, *Resolution on Chad*, OAU Doc. AHG/Res. 102 (XVIII) Rev. 1 (27 Jun. 1981), and Council of Ministers, *Resolution on Chad*, OAU Doc. CM/Res. 769 (XXXIV) (15 Feb. 1980). Generally, *see* G. Naldi, 'Peace-Keeping Attempts by the Organisation of African Unity', *ICLQ* 34 (1985): 593; T.M. Mays, *Africa's First Peacekeeping Operation: The OAU in Chad, 1981–1982* (London: Praeger Publishers, 2002).

the UN Mission for the Referendum in Western Sahara (MINURSO),[109] it has not taken place. In 2009, the UNSC described the situation as follows:

> [t]he Parties [should] continue to negotiate, without preconditions and in good faith, with a view to achieving a just, lasting and mutually acceptable political solution which will provide for the self-determination of the people of Western Sahara in the context of arrangements consistent with the principles and purposes of the Charter of the United Nations.[110]

Presumably, in this statement, the UNSC ought to have added the principles and purposes to be found in the AU Constitutive Act. And this is because the Western Sahara saga is characteristic of the issues associated with Africa's emancipation following the withdrawal of colonial powers. It is as much a problem for Africa as it is for the UN and, by extension, for the international community. However, it is an issue to be resolved primarily under AU auspices. On the other hand, it is also an issue of direct concern for the countries of the Arab Maghreb region (especially Morocco and Algeria) and, therefore, in principle, it falls within the ambit of the League of Arab States (LAS) as well. However, LAS has never addressed the Western Sahara affair earnestly,[111] while the OAU/AU and LAS, to the best of one's knowledge, have not discussed a joint effort to resolve it. It is rather an issue to be dealt with. More recently, the successful holding of the referendum in South Sudan in the summer of 2011 shows that, despite inherent difficulties, African populations can exercise their right to self-determination without fear of the outcome. And if the referendum takes place in Western Sahara and the population votes for independence, taking the case of South Sudan's referendum as precedence, effectively a vote for creating a separate state, the way should be open for eventual accession to the UN.

In 1982 and 1983, the Ordinary Sessions of the Assembly were paralysed for two reasons. The first reason was the Secretary-General's decision to admit to membership the Sahrawi Arab Democratic Republic (SADR), the political entity representing the territory of Western Sahara. The second reason was a dispute concerning the legitimate government of Chad. In April 1984, the Constitution of the Association of African Trade Promotion Organizations (AATPO), which had been adopted on 18 January 1974, came into force.[112] The Constitution has currently been ratified by fifteen Member States (lastly by Congo in March 2013 and by Burkina Faso in June 2016). AATPO became operational in 1977 and the Headquarters Agreement with

109. It was established pursuant to UNSC Res. 690(1991) of 29 Apr. 1991. As an annual ritual, MINURCO's mandate is extended for twelve-month periods, *see* UNSC Res. 2285 (2016) of 29 Apr. 2016, Res. 2351 (2017) of 27 Apr. 2017, Res. 2602 (2021) of 29 Oct. 2021, and Res. 2654 (2022) of 29 Oct. 2022 extending it until 31 October 2023. MINURCO's operation is recorded in the reports which are regularly submitted by the UN Secretary-General to the UNSC, *see, e.g.*, UNSC, *Situation concerning Western Sahara – Report of the Secretary-General*, UN Doc. S/2022/733 (3 Oct. 2022).

110. *See* UNSC Res. 1871 (2009) of 30 Apr. 2009, para. 4.

111. *See* B. Iratni, 'The Arab League and the Western Sahara Conflict: The Politics of a Sheer Neglect', *Africana Studia* 29 (2018): 103.

112. Note that, according to the official status list at: https://au.int/sites/default/files/treaties/36409-sl-CONSTITUTION-1.pdf, the Convention came into force on 28 Mar. 2012, this being the date that

Morocco was signed on 27 January 1978. In November 1984, the SADR was officially accepted as the fifty-first Member State, a move that led to Morocco's immediate withdrawal from the OAU. Morocco stayed away when the OAU was transformed into the AU. However, in the summer of 2016, it strongly indicated its wish to apply for membership, which it did later in the same year and was successful. The AU Assembly welcomed Morocco as its fifty-fifth Member State in January 2017. The Twenty-First Assembly Ordinary Session (Addis Ababa, 18–20 November 1985) strongly urged the USA to reconsider its position and not withdraw from UNESCO.[113] It also approved Africa's Priority Programme for Economic Recovery 1986–1990, where Member States reaffirmed the primary responsibility for their own economic and social development, identified areas for urgent action and promised to mobilize and utilize domestic resources for achieving the same. The Programme had been preceded by the Declaration on the Critical Economic Situation in Africa, which was approved by the Twentieth Assembly Ordinary Session (Addis Ababa, 12–15 November 1984).[114] The UNGA promptly engaged itself in deliberating Africa's economic plight[115] and, in December 1985, it resolved to convene a 'special session to focus, in a comprehensive and integrated manner, on the rehabilitation and medium-term and long-term development problems and challenges facing African countries'.[116] Six months later, the special session took place and culminated in the UN Programme of Action for African Economic Recovery and Development 1986–1990 (PAAERD).[117]

31. On 17 July 1985, the Convention for the Establishment of the African Rehabilitation Institute was adopted with the aim of harmonizing the principles and the strategy for disability prevention and the rehabilitation of the disabled. It entered into force on 2 December 1991 and has currently been signed by thirty-one and ratified by twenty-eight Member States (the last two being Rwanda on 14 July 2010 and Benin on 29 March 2016). As is later explained, on 29 January 2018, Member States adopted the Protocol to the African Charter on Human and Peoples' Rights on the Rights of Persons with Disabilities in Africa, which so far has received ten ratifications and has not entered into force. With economic and financial issues now firmly on the OAU agenda, in July 1985, on the fifth anniversary of the Lagos Plan of Action, the Addis Ababa Declaration on the Economic Situation in Africa was adopted. African leaders resolved to accelerate the implementation of the Lagos Plan and started to debate seriously the problem of the excessive foreign debt incurred by Member States. The Third Extraordinary Assembly Session was convened in November–December 1987 to deliberate the question of the continent's external debt, which at the time had reached USD 200 billion. The ensuing document, the African Common Position on Africa's External Debt Crisis, called for a

---

Benin ratified it and became the thirteenth contracting party. However, as its entry into force required twelve ratifications, arguably this was achieved when Zambia deposited its instrument of ratification in April 1984.

113. Assembly, *Resolution on UNESCO*, OAU Doc. AHG/Res. 127 (XX) (15 Nov. 1984).
114. Assembly, OAU Doc. AHG/Decl. 2 (XX) (15 Nov. 1984).
115. UNGA Res. 39/29, *Declaration on the Critical Economic Situation in Africa*, 3 Dec. 1984, Annex.
116. UNGA Res. 40/40, *Critical economic situation in Africa*, 2 Dec. 1985.
117. UNGA Res. S-13/2, 1 Jun. 1986, Annex.

ten-year moratorium. The excessive debt of African countries has remained an issue of considerable concern. Many an African state qualify as Highly Indebted Poor Countries (HIPCs). The appearance of the so-called vulture funds, namely aggressive private creditors who buy sovereign debt at very low prices and, upon maturity, demand to be paid the face value of the debt they hold, has made it a very acute problem. The practice of vulture funds to institute court proceedings against states asking to be awarded the sovereign debt's full-face value attracted the attention of the G-8 group in 2005 (at the time, more than USD 1 billion had been awarded by courts to plaintiff vulture funds). The G-8 considered this practice as a major obstacle to its attempts to arrange a debt relief programme for poor countries. Because of these and similar concerns, a few years later, the African Legal Support Facility (ALSF) was created and placed under the auspices of the African Development Bank (ADB) in April 2008. It started operating in 2010, while in May 2021, the Governing Council of the ALSF extended its term for a further fourteen years from 2023 to 2036.[118] The UNGA has also addressed the question of sovereign debt restructuring.[119]

A Ministerial Regional Conference on Security, Disarmament and Development in Africa was convened in Lomé in August 1985. It adopted the namesake Declaration and Programme of Action, which connected regional security with state commitments to socioeconomic development, justice, equity, and human dignity. The Forty-Eighth Ordinary Council of Ministers Session (Addis Ababa, 19–23 May 1988) adopted the Resolution on Dumping of Nuclear and Industrial Waste in Africa, which, *inter alia*, declared the discarding of nuclear and industrial wastes a crime against African peoples and called upon those Member States that had entered into agreements with third countries for their disposal in their territories to terminate them.[120] The last two years of the 1980s were also dominated by the external debt issue[121] to which the question of arrears in the payment of Member States' contributions to the OAU budget was added. The latter, a perennial issue of concern, endangered the financial stability of the OAU and prevented it from carrying out its programmes and projects. Finally, the Fiftieth Ordinary Council of Ministers Session (Addis Ababa, 17–22 July 1989) hailed the creation of another entity fighting racial discrimination, the African Anti-Apartheid Committee, which was described

118. *See* https://www.afdb.org/en/topics-and-sectors/initiatives-partnerships/african-legal-support-facility/. Presently, ALSF has 60 members, 53 states (five of which are not African (France, Great Britain, The Netherlands, Belgium, and Brazil)) and seven international organizations.

119. UNGA Res. 68/304, *Towards the establishment of a multilateral legal framework for sovereign debt restructuring processes*, 9 Sep. 2014. *See further*, UNGA Res. 69/247, *Modalities for the implementation of resolution 68/304, entitled 'Towards the establishment of a multilateral legal framework for sovereign debt restructuring processes'*, 24 Dec. 2014, and Res. 69/319, *Basic Principles on Sovereign Debt Restructuring Processes*, 10 Sep. 2015.

120. Council of Ministers, *Resolution on Dumping of Nuclear and Industrial Wastes in Africa*, OAU Doc. CM/Res. 1153 (XLVIII) (23 May 1988).

121. Council of Ministers, *Resolution on the Convening of the International Seminar on Africa's Common Position on External Debt Crisis*, OAU Doc. CM/Res. 1195 (XLIX) (25 Feb. 1989), and Assembly, *Resolution on Holding an Extraordinary Session of the Assembly of Heads of State and Government on Economic Problems of Africa*, OAU Doc. AHG/Res. 96 (XVI) Rev. 1 (20 Jul. 1989).

as a Non-Governmental Organization (NGO), and asked the Secretary-General to work out modalities for cooperation with it.[122] The work of this Committee has apparently never been recorded.

32. The Twenty-Sixth Ordinary Assembly Session (Addis Ababa, 9–11 July 1990) adopted two important documents. The first was the Declaration on the Political and Socio-Economic Situation in Africa and the Fundamental Changes Taking Place in Africa, in which African leaders painted a rather gloomy picture of affairs in the continent, in particular, as regards its position in the international community. However, they committed themselves to work towards the peaceful and speedy resolution of conflicts. The second instrument was the African Charter on the Rights and Welfare of the Child, which was concluded a year after a similar treaty was finalized by the UN, the Convention on the Rights of the Child. The Charter entered into force with considerable delay on 29 November 1999. Presently, five Member States (Morocco, SADR, Somalia, South Sudan, and Tunisia) have not ratified it).[123] In June 1990, Namibia acceded to the OAU, thus ending one of the last chapters of colonialism in Africa. In January 1991, the OAU Conference of Environmental Ministers meeting in Bamako, Mali, adopted the Convention on the Ban of the Import into Africa and the Control of Transboundary Movement and Management of Hazardous Wastes within Africa. The Convention, which entered into force on 22 April 1998, has currently received only twenty-nine ratifications (CAR was the last one in March 2020, preceded by Burkina Faso in August 2009 and Chad in July 2012) despite the fact that the illegal dumping of hazardous waste in the continent continues unabated.[124] In May 1991, the Kampala Document towards a Conference on Security, Stability, Development and Cooperation in Africa (CSSDCA) was proposed as the first pan-African attempt to bring together the following four pillars: security, stability, development, and cooperation. While it was forwarded to the OAU Assembly for adoption, Member States received it rather unenthusiastically. It was finally approved by the Thirty-Sixth Ordinary OAU Assembly Session in July 2000.[125]

33. The Twenty-Seventh Ordinary Assembly Session (Abuja, 3–5 June 1991) adopted the Treaty Establishing the AEC, which entered into force on 12 May 1994. Presently, it has been ratified by all Members, except Djibuti, Eritrea, Madagascar, Somalia and South Sudan. The OAU had once before played with the idea of creating a Pan-African economic integration institution to complement its political agenda.

---

122. Council of Ministers, *Resolution on the African Anti-Apartheid Committee*, OAU Doc. CM/Res. 1208 (L) (22 Jul. 1989).
123. 28 I.L.M. (1989) 1456. Generally, *see* T. Kaime, *African Charter on the Rights and Welfare of the Child – A Socio-Legal Perspective* (Pretoria: Pretoria University Law Press, 2009); J. Sloth-Nielsen (ed.), *Children's Rights in Africa: A Legal Perspective* (Aldershot: Ashgate, 2008).
124. 2101 U.N.T.S. 177; 30 I.L.M. (1991) 657.
125. *See* OAU Assembly, 'CSSDCA Solemn Declaration', OAU Doc. AHG/Decl.4 (XXXVI) (12 Jul. 2000). *See further*, OAU Assembly, *Decision on the Conference on Security, Stability, Development and Cooperation (CSSDCA)*, OAU Doc. AHG/Dec. 175 (XXXVIII) (8 Jul. 2002). Generally, *see* F.M Deng & I.W. Zartman, *A Strategic Vision for Africa. The Kampala Movement* (Washington, DC: The Brookings Institution, 2002); J. Ng, *Contesting Sovereignty: Power and Practice in Africa and Southeast Asia* (Cambridge: Cambridge University Press, 2021), 103–132.

Thus, in September 1968, the Council of Ministers declared that the continent's economic integration was a prerequisite for the realization of the OAU's objectives,[126] and in July 1977, African leaders endorsed the Kinshasa Declaration, which had been adopted by the Eleventh Extraordinary Council of Ministers Session on Economic Development and Cooperation (Kinshasa, DRC, December 1976). The Kinshasa Declaration had called for the establishment of an African Common Market within fifteen to twenty-five years, the required first step towards the creation of the AEC. It was followed by the Monrovia Strategy[127] and the Monrovia Declaration[128] in July 1979, which did not culminate in any concrete results. Even though in the early 1990s the prevailing situation appeared to be much more favourable for pursuing economic integration through a new legal entity, which was to become an integral part of the OAU, the AEC project was rather abandoned in the final years of the 1990s. It was only in the 2010s that it was again taken up principally through the adoption of Agenda 2063,[129] the creation of the African Continental Free Trade Area (AfCFTA),[130] and the conclusion of the Protocol to the AEC Treaty Relating to Free Movement of Persons, Right of Residence and Right of Establishment;[131] references to these initiatives are made later in the monograph. In addition to economic integration, a second issue that received considerable attention in the early 1990s was the need to devise and implement an effective mechanism for the settlement of disputes by peaceful means. Thus, the Twenty-Ninth Ordinary Assembly Session (Cairo, 28–30 June 1993) adopted the Cairo Declaration on the Establishment, within the OAU, of a Mechanism for Conflict Prevention, Management and Resolution to revamp the non-operational Commission of Mediation, Conciliation, and Arbitration. The Mechanism carried out its mandate relatively successfully, and, following the establishment of the AU, the PSC absorbed it. On 24 May 1993, Eritrea acceded to the OAU. However, due to unsurpassable internal problems and strife as well as hostile relations with other Member States, Eritrea's participation has been kept to a minimum and, therefore, there is some merit in the argument that it should not be considered as a fully pledged Member State.

In the course of 1994, the OAU was not only unable to prevent the genocide of Tutsis in Rwanda but also failed to intervene in a forceful manner to bring it to an end. This necessitated the intervention, albeit tardy, by the international community.

---

126. Council of Ministers, *Regional Groupings and Market Integration*, OAU Doc. CM/Res. 159 (XI) (12 Sep. 1968).
127. Council of Ministers, *Monrovia Strategy for the Economic Development of Africa*, OAU Doc. CM/Res. 722 (XXXIII) Rev. 1 (2 Jul. 1979).
128. Assembly, *Monrovia Declaration of Commitment of the Heads of State and Government of the Organization of African Unity on Guidelines and Measures for National and Collective Self-Reliance in Social and Economic Development for the Establishment of a New International Economic Order*, OAU Doc. AHG/ST. 3 (XVI) Rev. 1 (20 Jul. 1979).
129. *See* African Union Commission, *Agenda 2063: The Africa we Want*, Popular Edition, September 2015, paras 23 and 73, explaining that Africa's political unity will be the culmination of the integration process, which includes the free movement of people and the establishment of continental institutions, leading to economic integration. It should be noted that the latter is meant at a continental level because at a sub-regional level it has been pursued by various RECs acting either individually or in unison (notably, the EAC – COMESA – SADC Free Trade Area).
130. Agreement Establishing the African Continental Free Trade Area, signed on 21 Mar. 2018, entered into force on 30 May 2019.
131. Adopted on 29 Jan. 2018, not yet in force.

Four years later, the OAU created an International Panel of Eminent Personalities to investigate the genocide.[132] Too little, too late for a tragedy where the question of state responsibility appears to be still open. Thus, in 2021, a US law firm, acting on instructions from the Government of Rwanda, published its report on France's role in the genocide.[133] The AU's annual commemoration of the 1994 genocide is known as *Kwibuka*, which means 'to remember'. At the Thirtieth Ordinary Session (Tunis, 13–15 June 1994), the Assembly adopted the following two instruments. First, the Declaration on a Code of Conduct for Inter-African Relations, where fanatism and extremism were rejected as unacceptable means and as detrimental to the promotion of peace and security in the continent.[134] Second, the African Maritime Transport Charter, which entered into force provisionally.[135] Currently, it has been signed by forty and ratified by thirteen Member States (the last being Rwanda on 14 July 2010). Because of rigorous AU action in the field of maritime transport, in 2007 the Executive Council endorsed the Abuja Declaration and Plan of Action on Maritime Transport in Africa,[136] which paved the way for the negotiation of a Revised African Maritime Transport Charter. The Second African Union Conference of Ministers Responsible for Maritime Transport, held on 12–16 October 2009 in Durban, South Africa, concluded its text,[137] which was adopted by the Assembly in July 2010.[138] Finally, on 6 June 1994, the Republic of South Africa acceded to the OAU thus ending three decades of hostile relations principally due to the apartheid regime that had been in power in the country and because of its (unlawful) occupation of the territory of Namibia.

While interstate wars and the struggle for liberation from foreign dominance were the OAU's principal concerns in the 1970s and in the 1980s, the 1990s have been dominated by intra-state violence. However, it was only after 1995 that the importance of the OAU possessing its own permanent force to deal with intra-state and interstate disputes and conflicts (at the time, there were clashes in Rwanda, Burundi, Somalia, Liberia, and Sierra Leone) was seriously discussed. But several factors, including the severe shortage of funds, prevented the creation of such a force. On the contrary, peacekeeping operations continued to be launched by RECs with a considerable record of success. In particular, the Economic Community of West African States (ECOWAS) has played a pivotal role in these operations, most of

---

132. Generally, *see* AJIL 94 (2000): 692–695; M. Budeli & B. Vambe, 'The Rwandan genocide: a legal analysis', *African Identities* 8 (2010): 409–424.
133. Levy Firestone Muse LLP, *A Foreseeable Genocide: The Role of the French Government in Connection with the Genocide Against the Tutsi in Rwanda* (Washington, D.C., 19 April 2021), at: https://www.gov.rw/fileadmin/user_upload/gov_user_upload/2021.04.19_MUSE_REPORT.pdf.
134. Assembly, *Declaration on a Code of Conduct for Inter-African Relations*, OAU Doc. AHG/Decl. 2 (XXX) (15 Jun. 1994).
135. *See* L. Savadogo, 'La Charte africaine des transports maritime: Principes, règles et techniques' in T.M. Ndiaye & R. Wolfrum (eds), *Law of the Sea, Environmental Law and Settlement of Disputes: Liber Amicorum Judge Thomas A. Mensah* (The Hague: Martinus Nijhoff, 2007) 545.
136. *See* Executive Council, *Decision on the First African Union Conference of Ministers Responsible for Maritime Transport*, AU Doc. EX.CL/Dec. 358 (XI), 29 Jun. 2007.
137. The Conference also adopted the Durban Resolution on Maritime Safety, Maritime Security and Protection of the Marine Environment in Africa, AU Doc. AU/MT/MIN/DRAFT/Res. (II).
138. Assembly, *Decision on the Adoption of the African Maritime Transport Charter*, Assembly/AU/Dec. 293 (XV), 27 Jul. 2010. Presently, it has been ratified by 12 Member States and has not entered into force.

which have been endorsed by the OAU/AU and approved by the UN Security Council.[139] ECOWAS action in this area continues to this day. Apart from the ongoing deployment of the Mission in The Gambia and the Stabilization Support Mission in Guinea Bissau (SSMGB), in December 2022, the ECOWAS Authority agreed to establish a regional force to address coups d'état attempts in Member States and also to assist in the restoration of the democratic order.[140] In June 1995, the Treaty of Pelindaba, which creates a nuclear-weapon-free zone in Africa, was successfully negotiated under the OAU auspices. The Treaty opened for signature in April 1996 and entered into force with considerable delay in July 2009. Currently, it has been signed by fifty-two and ratified by forty-four Member States (the last being SADR in January 2014, Seychelles in April 2014, Angola in May 2014, Niger in June 2016, as well as the DRC and Morocco in February 2022).[141] The Treaty has three Protocols annexed, which have been signed and/or ratified by Great Britain, France, China and the Soviet Union (presently, the Russian Federation as the successor state). It could be viewed as the culmination of two previous instruments: the Declaration on the Denuclearization of Africa, which was adopted by the First Assembly Session (Cairo, July 1964)[142] and UN General Assembly Resolution 3472B (XXX) of 11 December 1975 titled 'Comprehensive study of the question of nuclear-weapon-free zones in all its aspects'. The latter instrument considered that regional nuclear weapons-free zones (NWFZ) are the most effective means for preventing their proliferation. Apart from Africa, NWFZ have been established in Latin America (1967), the South Pacific (1985), Southeast Asia (1995) and Central Asia (2006).[143]

34. In May 1997, the First Continental Conference of African Experts on Anti-Personnel Mines adopted the Kempton Park Plan of Action on a Landmine Free Africa. Endorsed by the Sixty-Sixth Ordinary Council of Ministers Session (Harare, 28–31 May 1997),[144] it committed the continent to the total ban of anti-personnel mines. Given the ongoing armed conflicts in many parts of Africa, anti-personnel land mines are an issue of considerable importance for the population of war-torn areas because they continue to kill and injure even after the cessation of hostilities. The AU has not adopted its own legal instrument, but most African states are contracting parties to the Convention on the Prohibition of the Use, Stockpiling, Production and Transfer of Anti-personnel Mines and on their Destruction, which was

139. Suffice to mention that, until the advent of the AU, ECOWAS had deployed a Ceasefire Monitoring Group (ECOMOG) in Liberia (1990–1998), in Sierra Leone (1997–2000) and in Guinea-Bissau (1999), and, after the AU was operationalized, in Liberia (2003–2006) as well as in Côte d'Ivoire (2003).
140. ECOWAS Commission, *Final Communique – Sixty-Second Ordinary Session of the Authority of Heads of State and Government*, Abuja, Nigeria, 4 December 2022, at: https://ecowas.int/wp-content/uploads/2022/12/Eng_Final-Communique_62nd-ECOWAS-Summit_Rev.pdf.
141. African Nuclear-Weapon-Free Zone Treaty, reproduced in I.L.M. 35 (1996): 702.
142. Assembly, *Denuclearization of Africa*, OAU Doc. AHG/Res. 11 (I) (21 Jul. 1964).
143. Generally, *see* https://www.un.org/disarmament/wmd/nuclear/nwfz/.
144. Council of Ministers, *Report of the Secretary-General on the Issue of Anti-Personnel Mines and International Efforts to Reach a Total Ban*, OAU Doc. CM/Dec. 363 (LXVI) (31 May 1997). Generally, *see* African Union Commission, Peace and Security Department, Defence and Security Division, *The African Union Mine Action and Explosive Remnants of War Strategic Framework: April 2014 – December 2017*, no date, at: http://www.peaceau.org/uploads/au-mine-action-project-document.pdf.

negotiated under UN auspices (the Ottawa Convention).[145] The First Meeting of the States Parties (MSP) was held in Maputo, Mozambique, in May 1999. The following month, the Thirty-Third Ordinary Assembly Session (Harare, 2–4 June 1997) issued a Common Position on the Reform of the Security Council, advocating that, in any future enlargement of the Security Council, Africa ought to be given two permanent seats.[146] This continues to be the AU common position to the present day. It is part of the so-called Ezulwini Consensus, which since 2005 has embodied the AU common positions on international relations. In September 2022, Macky Sall, the President of Senegal and at the time AU Chairperson, speaking at the podium of the UNGA Seventy-Seventh Ordinary Session, reiterated the request, adding that 'it is time to do justice to Africa's just and legitimate demand for Security Council reform, as reflected in the Ezulwini Consensus'.[147]

35. The Thirty-Fourth Ordinary Assembly Session (Ouagadougou, 8–10 June 1998) adopted the Protocol to the African Charter on Human and Peoples' Rights on the Establishment of an African Court on Human and Peoples' Rights to complement the supervisory mechanism of the Banjul Charter, which was until then carried out by the African Commission on Human and Peoples' Rights. The existence of a Court and a Commission to supervise and rule on the protection of human rights was first introduced in the European human rights system (as originally set up by the Council of Europe) and, thereafter, in the Inter-American system (set up by the Organization of American States). Finally, it has been introduced in the Arab human rights system, but the Arab Court of Human Rights is presently not yet in operation. However, when it does, Arab African states will come under the jurisdiction of both the African and Arab Courts of Human Rights, provided of course that they will have ratified their constitutive instruments. The parallel operation of two regional human rights courts with jurisdiction over the same contracting parties will probably raise legal questions. In a way, it will be somewhat similar to the parallel competencies of the European, Inter-American and African Human Rights Courts and the so-called treaty bodies established under the UN human rights treaties (the so-called core human rights treaties), e.g., the Human Rights Committee (it was created by the International Covenant on Civil and Political Right), the Committee Against Torture (CAT) (by the Convention against Torture and Other Cruel, Inhuman or Degrading Treatment or Punishment), etc. The Protocol on the African Court on Human and Peoples' Rights entered into force with considerable delay on 25 January 2004. Currently, it has been signed by all Member States except Cape Verde, Eritrea and Morocco but has received only thirty-four ratifications (the last ones being by Cameroon in December 2014, Chad in January 2016, DRC in January 2017, Guinea-Bissau and Madagascar in October 2021, and Zambia in December 2022). Despite the appalling human rights situation in parts of Africa, the Court was not promptly operationalized, the cost of its operation being apparently one of

145. It was signed on 18 September 1997, entered into force on 1 March 1999, 2056 U.N.T.S. 211.

146. Assembly, *Harare Declaration of the Assembly of Heads of State and Government of the OAU on the Reform of the UN Security Council*, OAU Doc. AHG/Decl. 3 (XXXIII) (4 Jun. 1997).

147. *See* https://qz.com/senegal-s-macky-sall-delivered-a-list-of-striking-afric-1849562146.

the reasons. The first application before the Court was lodged in 2008.[148] While no applications were lodged during 2009 and 2010, during the last decade it has received an ever-increasing number of applications.[149] The Assembly decision in 2008 to merge it with the AU Court of Justice to create the African Court of Justice and Human Rights (ACJHR), a project that has still not been completed, has arguably deprived the continent of the opportunity to have in place robust judicial organs able to tackle its persisting problems, including impunity for gross violations of fundamental freedoms.

In a move that arguably contradicted fundamental rules of international law, the Thirty-Fourth Assembly Session resolved that Member States should disregard the sanctions imposed by the UN Security Council against Libya under Resolution 748 (1992) of 31 March 1992 and Resolution 883 (1993) of 11 November 1993 for its involvement in the Lockerbie bombing.[150] Resolutions criticizing the UNSC sanctions against Libya were adopted by subsequent Assembly Sessions as well, but they did not repeat the express call to disregard them.[151] In April 1999, another noteworthy event in relation to the promotion of human rights in the continent took place: the First OAU Ministerial Conference on Human and Peoples' Rights, which adopted the Grand Bay (Mauritius) Declaration and Plan of Action, reference to which is made *infra*. The Declaration, a legally non-binding instrument, did not view the protection of human rights as an abstract matter but put it into the context of the other problems plaguing domestic and intra-African affairs, such as the lack of a democratic ethos, inadequate governance, corruption, coups d'état resulting in loss of life, internal displacement, etc.[152] The Thirty-Fifth Ordinary Assembly Session (Algiers, 12–14 July 1999) approved the Convention on the Prevention and Combating of Terrorism (also known as 'Algiers Convention'), at the time one of the few regional instruments to address the multifaceted issues of terrorism. The Convention, which entered into force on 26 December 2002 and has currently been signed by fifty Member States (including by South Sudan in January 2013) and ratified by forty-three Members,[153] excludes terrorist acts perpetrated during the struggle for liberation or the fight for self-determination. An additional Protocol to the Convention was signed on 2 July 2004 and entered into force on 26 February 2014; it has currently been ratified by twenty-one Member States. Following a Decision adopted by the Seventy-Second Ordinary Council of Ministers Session (Lomé,

148. African Court on Human and Peoples' Rights, Application No. 001/2008, *Michelot Yogogombaye v. the Republic of Senegal*, Judgment of 15 Dec. 2009.
149. For information, *see* https://www.african-court.org/cpmt/statistic. For pending cases, *see* https://www.african-court.org/wpafc/category/cases/pending-cases/.
150. Assembly, *The Crisis between the Great Socialist People's Libyan Arab Jamahiriya and the United States of America and the United Kingdom*, OAU Doc. AHG/Dec. 127 (XXXIV) (10 Jun. 1998).
151. Assembly, *Decision on the Crisis between the Libyan Arab Jamahiriya and the United States and the United Kingdom*, OAU Doc. AHG/Dec. 134 (XXXV) (14 Jul. 1999); Assembly, *Decision on the Lockerbie Issue*, OAU Doc. EAHG/Dec. 3 (V) (5 Mar. 2001); Assembly, *Decision on the Lockerbie Issue*, OAU Doc. AHG/Dec. 9 (XXXVII) (11 Jul. 2001) & UN Doc. S/2001/1152 (6 Dec. 2001); and Assembly, *Decision on the Lockerbie Issue*, OAU Doc. AHG/Dec. 174 (XXXVIII) (8 Jul. 2002).
152. CONF/HRA/DEC 1, 16 April 1999, at: https://archives.au.int/handle/123456789/2058.
153. 2219 U.N.T.S. 179.

6–8 July 2000),[154] the OAU convened a Meeting of Experts to consider a Draft Convention on Extradition and a Draft Convention on Mutual Legal Assistance in Criminal Matters. Even though similar instruments have been adopted by several RECs,[155] it appears that the plans for regulation at AU level have been abandoned.

36. The year 1999 saw the beginning of the OAU's demise. In June 1999, the now-deceased Libyan leader Muammar Gaddafi attended an Assembly Session for the first time in twenty-two years, during which period he had voluntarily abstained because the OAU had criticized the occupation of northern Chad by his troops. Arguably, Gaddafi returned because he wanted to implement his grand plan: create a new multilateral institution, to be called the United States of Africa and which would have a single currency.[156] The quite original proposals, which Gaddafi was prepared to finance handsomely, were discussed at the Fourth Extraordinary Assembly Session, which took place in Sirte, Libya, on 8 and 9 September 1999 at his invitation. Bringing back memories of the divisions between the Brazzaville Group and the Casablanca Group in the early 1960s on how to proceed with the political integration of the continent, the Extraordinary Session rejected Gaddafi's proposal for the creation of a United States of Africa. Instead, the idea of creating a new institution, the AU, to replace the OAU was pushed forward. Moreover, the same Session resolved to accelerate the emergence of the AEC and set the foundations for the creation of a constructive partnership for Africa's regeneration.

37. By the following summer, the drafting of the AU Constitutive Act had been completed, and African leaders signed it during the Thirty-Sixth Ordinary Assembly Session (Lomé, 10–12 July 2000). It entered into force on 26 May 2001. The same Session adopted two important Declarations. The first was the Declaration on the Framework for an OAU Response to Unconstitutional Change of Government. Based on this Declaration, several Member States, including the Comoros, were excluded from participating in OAU meetings. The second was the Solemn Declaration on the CSSDCA,[157] whose precise purpose was not immediately clear. However, two years later, the Memorandum of Understanding (MoU) on Security, Stability, Development, and Cooperation in Africa was adopted to give effect to the Solemn Declaration. The MoU offers clear guidelines on how Member States should pursue its objectives and envisages performance indicators and time frames.[158] On 1 December 2000, a Ministerial Conference in Bamako adopted the

154. Council of Ministers, *Decision on the Draft Conventions on Extradition and on Mutual Legal Assistance*, OAU Doc. CM/Dec. 540 (LXXII) (8 Jul. 2000).
155. *See*, *inter alia*, ECOWAS Convention on Mutual Assistance in Criminal Matters of 29 Jul. 1992; Cooperation Agreement between ECOWAS Member States' Police Forces on Investigation in Criminal Matters of December 2002; ECOWAS Convention on Extradition of 1994; IGAD Convention on Mutual Legal Assistance of 2009; SADC Protocol on Mutual Legal Assistance in Criminal Matters of 2002; and Mutual Assistance Pact between the Member States of ECCAS of 2002. The first relevant sub-regional legal instrument was the Cooperation Agreement on Police Matters between Benin, Ghana, Nigeria and Togo, signed in Lagos, Nigeria, in 1984.
156. *See* BBC, 'Gaddafi calls for United States of Africa', 20 Aug. 1999, at: http://news.bbc.co.uk/2/hi/africa/425929.stm.
157. *See* Assembly, *CSSDCA Solemn Declaration*, OAU Doc. AHG/Decl. 4 (XXXVI) (12 Jul. 2000).
158. OAU Doc. OAU/CIVILSOCIETY.3 (II) (19 Jul. 2002).

Declaration on an African Common African Position on the Illicit Proliferation, Circulation, and Trafficking of Small Arms and Light Weapons.[159] The Declaration, which was endorsed by the Council of Ministers in July 2001,[160] stipulated measures to be taken at national, regional and continental levels against these weapons that threaten peace and security and undermine efforts to improve the living conditions of Africans. Much later, the Arms Trade Treaty was concluded under the auspices of the UN in April 2013 (it was opened for signature on 1 June 2013 and entered into force on 24 December 2014).[161] The Fifth Extraordinary Assembly Session (Sirte, Libya, 1–2 March 2001) was convened to give momentum to the AU's establishment. It finally approved the Protocol to the Treaty Establishing the AEC Relating to the PAP, which entered into force on 14 December 2003 and has currently been ratified by all Member States except DRC, Eritrea, Guinea and Somalia. In June 2014, the Protocol to the Constitutive Act of the African Union (AU) relating to the PAP was concluded; it aims at making PAP a proper AU organ (under the 2001 Protocol, it was created as an AEC organ) and, at some future stage, becoming a *quasi* norms-setting body. The Protocol has not entered into force, and it is doubtful if it will in the foreseeable given that it must be ratified by twenty-seven Member States, and presently it has been signed by twenty-three and ratified by only fourteen states. In April 2001, the serious problems that the continent encountered by the spread of infectious diseases such as HIV/AIDS and tuberculosis were addressed during an Extraordinary Meeting of the Assembly, which was held in Abuja, Nigeria.[162]

Parallel to these institutional developments, the project for the continent's regeneration was being prepared. During the Thirty-Seventh Ordinary Assembly Session (Lusaka, Zambia, 9–11 July 2001), the New African Partnership for Africa's Development (NEPAD) was unanimously adopted as a comprehensive framework for socioeconomic development to be realized within the context of the AU. Human rights, conflict resolution and good economic and political governance have been at the heart of NEPAD, which moved with slow steps towards being institutionally integrated into the AU.[163] In 2005/2006, the AU/NEPAD African Action Plan (AAP) was conceived and developed. Having been reviewed by the African Development Bank, on behalf of the NEPAD Agency, it led to the AAP 2010–2015,[164] which was

---

159. At: https://au.int/en/documents/20200903/bamako-declaration-african-common-position-illicit-proliferation-circulation-and.
160. *See* Council of Ministers, OAU Doc. CM/Dec. 599 (LXXIV) (11 Jul. 2001). *See further*, SADC Protocol on the Control of Firearms, Ammunition and other Related Materials, which entered into force on 8 Nov. 2004.
161. 3013 U.N.T.S 269. For details, *see* https://thearmstradetreaty.org/.
162. *See* OAU Doc. OAU/SPS/ABUJA/3, 27 Apr. 2001, noted in UNGA Res. 56/48, *Cooperation between the United Nations and the Organization of African Unity*, 7 Dec. 2001.
163. Compare Assembly, *Decision on the Integration of NEPAD into African Union Structures and Processes,* AU Doc. Assembly/AU/Dec. 153 (VIII) (30 Jan. 2007).
164. *See* NEPAD Planning and Coordinating Agency, *Revision of the AU/NEPAD AFRICAN ACTION PLAN 2010–2015: Advancing Regional and Continental Integration Together through Shared Values*, Abridged Report 2010–2012, at: https://www.oecd.org/investment/investmentfordevelopment/47693615.pdf.

formally launched in January 2011 during the Sixteenth Ordinary Assembly Session.[165] The Convention of the African Energy Commission (AFREC) was also adopted in July 2001;[166] it entered into force on 13 December 2006. Currently, it has been signed by forty-six and ratified by thirty-five Member States (lastly by Lesotho in November 2018, Liberia in February 2014 and Swaziland (Eswatini) on 6 November 2012). AFREC is a specialized agency, supervised by the AUC's Infrastructure and Energy Department. Its mandate includes coordinating, harmonizing, protecting, developing, and integrating energy resources in the continent.

38. After a fourteen-month transition period, the OAU was replaced by the AU and the last Ordinary Sessions of the Assembly (Thirty-Eighth) and of the Council of Ministers (Seventy-Sixth) took place in Durban in late June and early July 2002, respectively. The First Ordinary AU Assembly Session was held in Durban on 9–11 July 2002 marking the official inauguration of the AU. A new chapter in the history of Africa's (primarily) political and (secondarily) economic integration had begun. The Protocol to the Constitutive Act Relating to the Establishment of the PSC was adopted. It came into operation on 26 December 2003. Currently, it has been signed by all Member States and ratified by all Members, except Cape Verde and South Sudan. That the Protocol has not been ratified by the entire membership has never been considered an obstacle for the PSC taking action against non-contracting parties.

39. The First Extraordinary Assembly Session met in Addis Ababa on 3 February 2003. It approved a Protocol of Amendments to the Constitutive Act without debate. The Protocol, which was adopted during the Second Ordinary Assembly Session (July 2003), has still not entered into force, having been ratified by only thirty Member States (a two-thirds majority is required). In May 2003, the First AU Ministerial Conference on Human Rights in Africa adopted the Kigali Declaration, which formed the basis of the continent's revised agenda on human rights.[167] This event was a follow-up to the aforementioned OAU Ministerial Conference on Human and Peoples' Rights that had adopted the Grand Bay Declaration. The Second Ordinary Assembly Session (Maputo, Mozambique, 10–12 July 2003) continued with the setting up of the remaining AU organs and adopted the Protocol of the African Court of Justice, which entered into force on 11 February 2009 and currently has nineteen contracting parties.[168] Moreover, it concluded three important treaties on themes of particular interest to Africa. First, the Convention on Preventing and Combating Corruption (it entered into force on 5 August 2006 and currently has forty-eight contracting parties);[169] the Advisory Board on Corruption

165. *See* Assembly, *Decision on the Report of Heads of State and Government Orientation Committee (HSGOC) on New Partnership for Africa's Development (NEPAD)*, AU Doc. Assembly/AU/Dec. 348 (XVI) (31 Jan. 2011).
166. OAU Assembly, *Decision on the Creation of the African Energy Commission*, OAU Doc. AHG/Dec. 167 (XXXVII) (11 July 2001).
167. At: https://achpr.au.int/en/node/880.
168. Reproduced in RADIC 13 (2005): 37.
169. Reproduced in I.L.M. 43 (2004): 5.

(AUABC) was set up on 26 May 2009 under Article 22(1) of the Convention.[170] Second, the revised version of the Convention on Conservation of Nature and Natural Resources, which entered into force in June 2016, having secured the required fifteen ratifications. Third, the Protocol to the African Charter on Human and Peoples' Rights on the Rights of Women in Africa, which came into force promptly on 25 November 2005. It has currently been signed by forty-nine Member States and has received forty-four ratifications (lastly by Cameroon in December 2012, Sierra Leone in July 2015, Algeria in November 2016, Mauritius in June 2017, Ethiopia in July 2018, Tunisia in August 2018, San Tome and Principe in April 2019, SADR in March 2022 and South Sudan in February 2023). Finally, the number of Member States that signed the MoU on the African Peer Review Mechanism (APRM) operating in the context of NEPAD increased to fifteen.[171] In December 2003, with the entry into force of the PCS Protocol, the OAU Central Organ of the Mechanism for Conflict Prevention ceased its operations, which were transferred to the PSC.

Initially, the AU addressed the internal conflict in the Sudanese region of Darfur from 2003 onwards by setting up, through the PSC, the severely understaffed AU Mission in Sudan (AMIS I). On 20 October 2004, it was replaced by a considerably larger but still inadequate force (AMIS II) with the mandate to monitor the deteriorating security conditions in the region. Although considerable criticism has been waged against AMIS, it should be regarded as a major improvement compared to the peacekeeping missions of the OAU era. Logistical support was received by the North Atlantic Treaty Organization (NATO) and the EU. As regards NATO, its involvement with AMIS broke new ground in the implementation of the so-called out of area operations. In January 2008, a hybrid UN-AU peace operation succeeded AMIS, the United Nations-African Union Mission in Darfur (UNAMID).[172] Its mandate was completed on 31 December 2020, but part of its agenda has been continued by the United Nations Integrated Transition Assistance Mission in Sudan (UNITAMS), which was established under UNSC Resolution 2524 (2020) of 3 June 2020 as a 'special political mission'. Pursuant to UNSC Resolution 2685 (2023) adopted on 2 June 2023, its mandate was extended until 3 December 2023 (previously extended to June 2023 under UNSC Resolution 2636 (2022)). UNITAMS, together with the AU and the Intergovernmental Authority on Development (IGAD), constitutes a so-called Trilateral Mechanism assisting Sudan to achieve the goals of the Constitutional Declaration of 17 August 2019, which was signed four months after President Omar

170. *See also* the AUABC Strategic Plans 2011–2015 and 2018–2022. Note that in January 2017, the AU Assembly decided to declare 2018 as 'African Year of Anti-Corruption' and the 11th of July as the 'African Anti-Corruption Day'.
171. Generally, *see* C. Manga Fombad, Z. Kebonang & H. Melber, *AU, NEPAD and the APRM Democratisation Efforts Explored*, Current African Issues No. 32 (Uppsala: Nordiska Afrikainstitutet, 2006).
172. Established under UNSC Res. 1769(2007) of 31 Jul. 2007. Generally, *see* V. Pergantis, 'UN–AU Partnerships in International Peace and Security and Issues of Responsibility Allocation in Cases of UN Support to Regional Missions', 13 *International Organizations Law Review* (2016): 74.

Al Bashir was ousted from power.[173] However, as explained later in the examination of the Peace and Security Council, a deadly fighting broke out in April 2023 in Sudan between its military and the main paramilitary force derailing any attempt towards constitutional normalcy.

40. As mentioned, in January 2004, the Protocol to the African Charter establishing the African Human Rights Court entered into force, and hopes were once more raised that, together with the African Human Rights Commission, it will lead to an effective institutional mechanism for the protection of fundamental freedoms in the continent. However, presently a large number of Member States have ratified it. Equally problematic is the fact that, at the time of writing, only six contracting parties (Burkina Faso, The Gambia, Malawi, Mali and Tunisia) have deposited declarations under Article 34 of the Protocol accepting the Court's competence to receive cases under Article 5(3) thereof, namely cases lodged by NGOs with observer status before the African Human Rights Commission as well as by individuals. In the past, four other parties (Benin, Burkina Faso, Rwanda and Tanzania) had deposited such declarations, but they subsequently withdrew them. Therefore, one could and should question the determination of the AU membership to have in place a regional human rights mechanism able to ensure that the violations of fundamental freedoms and the ethos of impunity are addressed. The Second Extraordinary Assembly (Sirte, Libya, 27–28 February 2004) adopted the Declaration on the Challenges of Implementing Integrated and Sustainable Development of Agriculture and Water in Africa,[174] which should be read in conjunction with the Maputo Declaration on Agriculture and Food Security in Africa adopted in July 2003.[175] Ten years later, when the Assembly met for its Twenty-Third Session on the theme 'African Year of Agriculture and Food Security', the Malabo Declaration on Accelerated Agricultural Growth and Transformation for Shared Prosperity and Improved Livelihoods was adopted.[176] Moreover, the Second Extraordinary Assembly examined the progress towards the adoption of a Non-Aggression and Common Defence Pact. However, as three separate and largely different drafts were proposed (one by the African Union Commission (AUC), the second by the DRC and the third by Libya, the country hosting the Session), it was decided to convene a meeting of government experts to elaborate a single document.[177] Despite this development, the Assembly adopted a lengthy document dealing with similar issues, the Solemn Declaration on a Common African Defence and Security Policy.[178] The Declaration was based on a common perception among African leaders of what is required to be done collectively to ensure that the

173. Generally, *see* B. Davies, *Sudan's 2019 Constitutional Declaration – Its Impact on the Transition* (Stockholm: International Institute for Democracy and Electoral Assistance, 2022) at: https://www.idea.int/publications/catalogue/sudans-2019-constitutional-declaration-its-impact-transition.
174. AU Doc. Ex/Assembly/AU/Decl. 1 (II).
175. AU Doc. Assembly/AU/Decl. 7 (II) (2003). At the level of SADC, these two Declarations were given effect through the Dar-Es-Salaam Declaration on Agriculture and Food Security in the SADC Region, adopted on 15 May 2004.
176. At: https://www.nepad.org/caadp/publication/malabo-declaration-accelerated-agricultural-growth.
177. *See* Assembly, *Decision on a Non-Aggression and Common Defence Pact*, AU Doc. Ext/Assembly/AU/Dec. 2 (II) (28 Feb. 2004).
178. At: https://www.peaceau.org/uploads/declaration-cadsp-en.pdf.

AU's defence and security interests and goals, as set out in Articles 3 and 4 of the Constitutive Act, are safeguarded in the face of common threats. The Pact was successfully concluded in 2005. Finally, the Inaugural and First PAP Session took place in Addis Ababa on 16–18 March 2004.[179] However, as only thirty-eight states had ratified its Protocol at the time, it did not include parliamentarians from all Member States. Even today, there are four Member States which have not ratified it.

The Third Ordinary Assembly Session (Addis Ababa, 6–8 July 2004) adopted a Protocol to the Convention on the Prevention and Combating of Terrorism (1999), which categorically states that 'acts of terrorism cannot be justified under any circumstances'.[180] Following ratification by the SADR in January 2014, the Protocol, which was based on the Dakar Declaration against Terrorism adopted in October 2001,[181] secured the required fifteen ratifications and entered into force on 26 February 2014.[182] Currently, twenty-one Member States are contracting parties. The Fourth Ordinary Assembly Session (Abuja, Nigeria, 30–31 January 2005) deliberated and adopted the AU Non-Aggression and Common Defence Pact as a framework for dealing with threats to peace, security and stability but also for providing for mutual assistance vis-à-vis use of force, aggression or threats of aggression.[183] The Pact entered into force on 18 December 2009 and has currently been signed by forty-four and ratified by the clearly inadequate number of twenty-two Member States (lastly by Comoros in July 2012, Ethiopia in April 2014 and Benin in September 2017). During the same Session, the Assembly recognized the East African Community (EAC) as a REC and, in effect, as one of the building blocks in the continental integration process.[184]

---

179. *See* Assembly, *Decision on the Launching and the Establishment of the Pan-African Parliament*, AU Doc. Assembly/AU/Dec. 39 (III) (8 Jul. 2004) determining that its seat shall be in South Africa. *See further* the decision that AU organs should be located in different regions of the continent on the basis of the principle of geographical distribution, Assembly/AU/Dec. 45 (III) (8 Jul. 2004). *See further*, Assembly, *Decision on the Location of the Headquarters of AU Institutions in various AU Regions*, Assembly/AU/Dec. 64 (IV), para. 2 (31 Jan. 2005).
180. *See* Assembly, *Decision on the Draft Protocol to the OAU Convention on the Prevention and Combating of Terrorism*, AU Doc. Assembly/AU/Dec. 36 (III) (8 Jul. 2004).
181. It was transmitted to the UN on 29 October 2001 as UN Doc. A/56/513 – S/2001/1021. For the text of the Declaration, *see* https://www.refworld.org/docid/3deb22b14.html.
182. *See also AU Plan of Action on the Prevention and Combating of Terrorism*, which was adopted in September 2002 in Algiers by the AU High-Level Intergovernmental Meeting on the Prevention and Combating of Terrorism in Africa. The Plan of Action promotes practical measures on counter-terrorism and addresses continental security challenges. As part of its implementation, the African Centre for the Study, and Research on Terrorism (ACSRT) was established in 2004 in Algiers, while in July 2011 the Seventeenth Ordinary Assembly Session endorsed the African Model Law on Counter Terrorism, which had been developed by the AU Commission, AU Doc. Assembly/AU/Dec. 369 (XVII). *See further* at: http://www.peaceau.org/en/page/64-counter-terrorism-ct.
183. *See* Assembly, *Decision on the Draft African Union Non-Aggression and Common Defence Pact*, AU Doc. Assembly/AU/Dec. 71 (IV) (31 Jan. 2005). Art. 1 of the Pact defines the term 'aggression' and lays down eleven types, including blockage of ports and aerospace, espionage and violent transnational organized crimes.
184. *See* Assembly, *Decision on Granting Accreditation to the East African Community (EAC) as one of the Regional Economic Community of the African Union*, AU Doc. Assembly/AU/Dec. 58 (IV) (31 Jan. 2005).

Finally, the Assembly deliberated the situation in the Darfur region of Sudan, where the fighting between militia groups and armed groups supported by the government in Khartoum since 2003 has led to an estimated number of 300,000 people killed and has left more than 2.7 million displaced people, with around 300,000 Darfuri refugees living in neighbouring Chad. According to the then US Secretary of State Colin Powell, the killings amounted to genocide,[185] a finding that shortly later was repeated in US domestic legislation, the Darfur Peace and Accountability Act of 2006, signed into law by President George W. Bush on 13 October 2006.[186] Although the Assembly avoided taking sides over the Darfur conflict,[187] it expressly stated that, despite the seriousness of the humanitarian situation in the region, it could not be defined as genocide. At the same time, the Assembly took no measures of substance to address the deteriorating humanitarian situation in Darfur, leaving the civilian population's protection and the armed groups' disarming to the government of Sudan, the very institution that has been accused of being responsible for serious crimes in Darfur. Arguably, the unsatisfactory way the AU has treated the Darfur crisis constitutes a very low point and has shown its limitations in addressing, as an emancipated international organization, intricate matters which are not unique to Africa but have been repeated time and time again in the continent. As regards the question of impunity for the crimes committed in Darfur, it has not been addressed at continental level. As has been argued, this could be seen as denialism on behalf of the AU, which clearly has not only a role to play but also a duty to fulfil.[188] The situation in Darfur was the first to be referred to the International Criminal Court (ICC) by the UNSC pursuant to Resolution 1593 (2005) of 31 March 2005. It was also the first ICC investigation in the territory of a state non-party to the Rome Statute establishing the ICC (1998). Finally, it was the first ICC investigation regarding allegations of genocide.[189] The ICC has issued two warrants of arrest against the former President of Sudan Omar Al Bashir (as mentioned above, he was deposed on 11 April 2019). The arrest warrants, which were issued when he was a sitting President, have still not been enforced because, *inter alia*, not only several AU Member States but also non-African states have refused to arrest him while being in their territory.[190] Since 2020, Sudanese government officials

185. *See* BBC News, 'Powell declares genocide in Sudan', 9 Sep. 2004, at: http://news.bbc.co.uk/2/hi/3641820.stm.
186. H.R. 3127, S. 1462, Public Law 109-344, at: https://www.govtrack.us/congress/bills/109/hr3127. On the basis of this and similar legislation, successive US administrations imposed sanctions on Sudan, which were considerably eased in January 2017, when President B. Obama signed Executive Order 13761 'Recognizing Positive Actions by the Government of Sudan and Providing for the Revocation of Certain Sudan-Related Sanctions', *Federal Register* Vol. 82 No. 11, p. 5331 (19 Jan. 2017). For the current US sanctions, *see* https://ofac.treasury.gov/sanctions-programs-and-country-information/sudan-and-darfur-sanctions.
187. *See* Assembly, *Decision on Darfur*, AU Doc. Assembly/AU/Dec. 54 (III) (8 Jul. 2004).
188. *See* K. Magliveras, 'International Organisations and Denialism: The Case of the African Union' in *Denialism and Human Rights*, R. Moerland, H. Nelen & J.C.M. Willems (eds.) (Cambridge: Intersentia 2016), 267.
189. The ICC investigation, which opened in June 2005, concerns alleged acts of genocide, war crimes and crimes against humanity committed in Darfur, since 1 July 2002. For details, *see* https://www.icc-cpi.int/darfur.
190. Generally, *see* K. Magliveras & G. Naldi, 'The ICC Addresses Non-Cooperation by State Parties in Arresting President Al-Bashir: The *Malawi* Decision' 6 *African Journal of Legal Studies* (2013) 1.

have reiterated that Al Bashir together with all other individuals indicted by the ICC for war crimes and genocide will be handed over to the ICC. Until now, it has not happened, a fact castigated by the ICC Prosecutor when presenting to the UNSC the Thirty-Sixth Report pursuant to Resolution 1593 (2005).[191] Presently, Al Bashir is tried by a criminal court in Khartoum for his role during the 1989 coup d'etat that brought him to power.[192] Finally, in September 2004, an Extraordinary Assembly Summit on Employment and Poverty Alleviation in Africa was held in Ouagadougou, Burkina Faso. It adopted a Declaration, drafted a Plan of Action and established a Follow-up Mechanism committing Member States to place employment at the centre of their socioeconomic policies.[193] The Fifth Ordinary Assembly Session (Sirte, Libya, 4–5 July 2005) reaffirmed its previous decision[194] to integrate the AU judicial organ and the African Human Rights Court into a single legal entity, the African Court of Justice and Human Rights. If it ever becomes operative, the ACJHR will be the first hybrid judicial organ of an international organization mandated to resolve disputes among Member States, disputes between the membership and the Organization as well as to act as a regional human rights court of justice.[195]

The Fifth Ordinary Session was dominated by the question of the reform of the UN system, and in particular the Security Council. The stance taken by the Assembly is a very good example of an AU common position and a very important one for the AU to have a voice in multilateral negotiations and transactions. In that respect, the Assembly adopted three documents, including the Sirte Declaration on the Reform of the UN, which, *inter alia*, acknowledged the need for a 'fairer world based on universalism, equity and regional balance', referred to the UNGA as a 'world parliament', and called for the establishment of two new entities: a so-called Peace-Building Commission and a new human rights body as a subsidiary UNGA organ to replace the United Nations Human Rights Commission (UNCHR).[196] The latter calls were fruitful: the Peacebuilding Commission was established in December 2005 as an intergovernmental advisory body for post-conflict reconstruction and recovery, while the following year, the Human Rights Council (HRC) was set up as an intergovernmental body within the UN system mandated to strengthen

---

191. *See* 'Sudan Not Meeting Cooperation Requirements with International Criminal Court, Prosecutor Tells Security Council, Urging Khartoum to Act Now', UNSC Meetings Coverage, UN Doc. SC/15183 (25 Jan. 2023), at https://press.un.org/en/2023/sc15183.doc.htm. For the Report, *see* https://www.icc-cpi.int/sites/default/files/2023-01/20230125-report-darfur-eng.pdf.
192. *See* 'Sudan's Bashir admits role in 1989 coup during trial', *Reuters*, 21 December 2022.
193. *See* https://www.tralac.org/news/article/5987-extraordinary-summit-of-the-african-union-on-employment-poverty-eradication-and-inclusive-development-ouagadougou-burkina-faso.html.
194. *See* Assembly, *Decision on the Seats of the African Union*, AU Doc. Assembly/AU/Dec. 45 (III) (8 Jul. 2004).
195. *See* Assembly, *Decision on the Merger of the African Court on Human and Peoples' Rights and the Court of Justice of the African Union*, AU Doc. Assembly/AU/Dec. 83 (V) (5 Jul. 2005).
196. *See* Assembly, *Decision on the Expansion of the Follow-Up Mechanism on the Reform of the United Nations*, AU Doc. Assembly/AU/Dec. 87 (V); *Sirte Declaration on the Reform of the United Nations*, AU Doc. Assembly/AU/Decl. 2 (V); and *Resolution on the United Nations Reform: Security Council*, AU Doc. Assembly/AU/Res. 1 (V) (all adopted 5 Jul. 2005). UNCHR, a so-called functional commission, was established in 1946 as a subsidiary body of the UN Economic and Social Council (ECOSOC).

the promotion and protection of human rights around the world and to address situations of human rights abuses and make recommendations on them.[197] The election of Sudan to HRC membership in 2002 and the assumption of the HRC chairmanship by Libya in 2003, states traditionally accused of widespread human rights abuses, could be criticized as being incompatible with a UN organ dedicated to safeguarding human rights.

At its Sixth Ordinary Session (Khartoum, Sudan, 23–24 January 2006), the Assembly considered the report prepared by a Committee of Seven titled 'An African Union Government: Towards a United States of Africa' and restated that the AU's ultimate goal is the full political and economic integration of the continent leading to the United States of Africa.[198] Prior to this Session, Libya had lodged with the Eighth Ordinary Executive Council Session (Khartoum, Sudan, 16–21 January 2006) six proposals on, *inter alia*, new AU symbols, the establishment of a Pan-African Stock Exchange and the setting up of a fund to alleviate the effects of oil price increases on poor Member States. The proposals were referred to the Assembly for deliberation and were later forwarded to groups of experts for consideration.[199] Some of them, for example, the revision of AU insignia and the fund to assist poorer Members with rising oil prices, materialized. Finally, the Assembly noted the proposal for the establishment of an African educational, scientific, and cultural organization and requested the Commission to consider it further.[200] Apparently, the proposal was abandoned. On 12 January 2006, the AU brokered a Peace Agreement between the fighting sides in the Darfur conflict. The Agreement, apart from the obvious military goals, dealt with the complex issue of human security in the region of Darfur. In order to supervise the implementation of the Agreement, UNSC Resolution 1769(2007) of 31 July 2007 authorized the creation of a hybrid UN-AU peace operation (UNAMID) with a predominant African character. It succeeded the AU's own Mission to Sudan (AMIS) on 1 January 2008. As mentioned above, the mandate of UNAMID was completed on 31 December 2020. It was one of the largest UN peacekeeping missions ever established with around 16,000 military personnel.[201]

---

197. For the Peace-building Commission, *see* UNGA Res. 60/180 of 20 Dec. 2005 and UNSC 1645(2005) of 30 Dec. 2005; for the Human Rights Council, *see* UNGA Res. 60/251 of 15 Mar. 2006.
198. *See* Assembly, *Decision on the Report of the Committee of Seven Heads of State and Government Chaired by the President of the Federal Republic of Nigeria*, AU Doc. Assembly/AU/Dec. 99 (VI) (24 Jan. 2006). The idea of a 'Union Government' goes back to the very first year of the OAU, *see* OAU Assembly, *Union Government For Africa*, OAU Doc. AHG/Res. 10 (I) (21 Jul. 1964).
199. *See* Assembly, *Decision on the Review of Symbols – Flag of the Union, on the Holding of Bilateral Summits Between Africa and other States and on the Non-Assimilation of North Africa into the Middle East with Regard to Nomenclature, Content and Concept*, AU Doc. Assembly/AU/Dec. 107 (VI) (24 Jan. 2006).
200. *See* Assembly, *Decision on the Establishment of an African Educational, Scientific and Cultural Organization (AFESCO)*, AU Doc. Assembly/AU/Dec. 110 (VI) (24 Jan. 2006).
201. For details, *see*, *inter alia*, UNSC Res. 2063(2012) of 31 Jul. 2012, Res. 2113(2013) of 30 Jul. 2013, and Res. 2296(2016) of 29 June 2016. For FY 2012–2013, its budget reached USD 1.51 billion, while in FY 2016–2017 USD 1.039 billion, *see* UN Doc. A/C.5/70/24, 22 Jun. 2016.

The draft Protocol to the Constitutive Act to create the ACJHR was considered by the Ninth Ordinary Executive Council Session (Banjul, 25–29 June 2006).[202] It decided to refer it to a meeting for Ministers of Justice and Attorney-Generals from Member States and to consider it again at its next Ordinary Session in January 2007.[203] Moreover, it resolved that forthwith there shall be one integrated AU budget: Staff costs, operating expenses, statutory meetings costs and top priority programmes/projects shall be assessed on Member States, while the remaining programmes' costs shall be financed through contributions to be secured from AU partners and donors.[204] The Executive Council also deliberated the draft African Charter on Democracy, Elections, and Governance, whose aim was to consolidate the collective commitments of Member States towards promoting the democratic ideals, the rule of law and good governance across the continent.[205] Finally, during this very fruitful Session, the Executive Council endorsed the AU Framework for Post-Conflict Reconstruction and Development (PCRD) as a policy towards the consolidation of peace and regeneration in areas emerging from conflict.[206] The Policy on PCRD was adopted in Banjul, the Gambia, in July 2006,[207] while in May 2016, the Inter-Departmental Task Force on Post-Conflict Reconstruction and Development was inaugurated to facilitate an effective, timely, and coordinated AUC-wide approach in implementing the PCRD Policy with the participation of the RECs Liaison Offices to the AU. The Executive Council also approved the establishment of a Democracy and Electoral Assistance Unit (DEAU) within the Political Affairs Department of the AUC with a special fund attached to it.[208] The latter constituted yet another attempt to secure the continent's stability by tackling the issue of rigged national elections. Presently, DEAU administers and maintains the African Union Electoral Roster, a database for the selection of AUC Election Observers.

The Seventh Ordinary Assembly Session (Banjul, 1–2 July 2006) adopted the African Youth Charter.[209] It came into force on 8 August 2009, and currently it has been signed by forty-three Member States and has received thirty-nine ratifications. The Charter seeks to empower the African youth by building their capacity and leadership while letting them bear responsibilities. Finally, the Assembly dealt with the question of the trial of the former President of Chad, Hissène Habré, who was accused of perpetrating crimes against humanity, war crimes and widespread acts of

202. AU Doc. EX.CL/253 (IX) (2006).
203. *See* Executive Council, *Decision on the Draft Single Legal Instrument on the Merger of the African Court on Human and Peoples' Rights and the Court of Justice of the African Union*, AU Doc. EX.CL/Dec. 283 (IX) (29 Jun. 2006).
204. *See* Executive Council, *Decision on Structure of Budget and Modality of Funding*, AU Doc. EX.CL/Dec. 278 (IX) Rev.2 (29 Jun. 2006).
205. *See* Executive Council, *Decision on the Report of the Ministerial Conference on the African Charter on Democracy, Elections and Governance*, AU Doc. EX.CL/Dec. 288 (IX) (29 Jun. 2006).
206. *See* Executive Council, *Decision on the AU Policy on Post-Conflict Reconstruction and Development,* AU Doc. EX.CL/Dec. 302 (IX) (29 Jun. 2006).
207. For the text, *see* https://au.int/node/39185. A PCDR Needs Assessment exercise was conducted in CAR in August 2016.
208. *See* Executive Council, *Decision on the Establishment and Organization of a Democracy and Electoral Assistance Unit and Fund*, AU Doc. EX.CL/Dec. 300 (IX) (29 Jun. 2006). For information on the Unit, *see* http://democracy-essentials.eu/web/au/.
209. *See* Assembly, *Decision on the Report of the Ministerial Conference on the African Youth Charter*, AU Doc. Assembly/AU/ Dec. 121(VII) (2 Jul. 2006).

torture while in power between 1982 and 1990. In 2006, the Assembly considered his trial as falling with the AU's competence and mandated Senegal, the country to which Habré had fled after being overthrown, to prosecute and try him 'on behalf of Africa'.[210] In the same year, the UN Committee Against Torture (CAT) castigated Senegal for failing to prosecute Habré.[211] His trial, a major test case of African states' ability to fight impunity promptly and efficiently, became the subject matter of litigation before international courts. The first was before the Court of Justice of ECOWAS, which in 2010 concluded that Senegal, in the context of the AU mandate, must put Habré on trial within the framework of ad hoc special procedure, as practised in international law by all civilized nations.[212] The second was before the ICJ, where Belgium had brought an application against Senegal claiming that it must either proceed with his prosecution or extradite him to Belgium. In July 2012, the ICJ upheld the claims advanced by Belgium.[213] After too many twists and turns, Senegal, in agreement with the AU, finally set up within its domestic court system the Extraordinary African Chambers (EAC) to try the international crimes committed in the territory of Chad between June 1982 and December 1990. The Chambers, whose Statute was approved by the Parliament of Senegal on 30 January 2013,[214] commenced operating on 8 February 2013.[215] They are reminiscent of the Extraordinary Chambers in the Courts of Cambodia (ECCC), the prototype of the so-called hybrid criminal courts.[216] In 2013, Habré tried unsuccessfully to halt the EAC proceedings before the Community Court of Justice of ECOWAS on the ground that they were illegitimate.[217] The trial of Habré before the EAC started on 20 July 2015 and ended on 11 February 2016. Judgment was delivered in May 2016: he was sentenced to life imprisonment, having been found guilty of crimes against humanity, war crimes and torture.[218] In June 2016, the judgment was appealed against by

210. *See* Assembly, *Decision on the Hissène Habré Case and the African Union*, AU Doc. Assembly/AU/Dec. 127 (VII) (2 Jul. 2006), para. 5.
211. CAT, *Guengueng v. Senegal*, Communication No. 181/2001, 19 May 2006.
212. ECOWAS Court of Justice, *Hissène Habré v. Senegal*, No. ECW/CCJ/JUD/06/10, Decision of 18 Nov. 2010, English translation at: https://www.asser.nl/upload/documents/20120419T034816-Habre%20Ecowa%202010.pdf.
213. ICJ, *Questions Relating to the Obligation to Prosecute or Extradite* (*Belgium v. Senegal*), Merits, Judgment of 20 Jul. 2012, I.C.J. Reports 2012, 422. For commentary, *see* S. Shah in *Human Rights L. R.* (2013) 13: 1.
214. *See Statut des Chambres africaines extraordinaires au sein des juridictions sénégalaises pour la poursuite des crimes internationaux commis au Tchad durant la période du 7 juin 1982 au 1er décembre 1990*, September 2012, unofficial English translation at: http://www.hrw.org/news/2013/09/02/statute-extraordinary-african-chambers. *See further*, S. Williams, 'The Extraordinary African Chambers in the Senegalese Courts. An African Solution to an African Problem?', *Journal of International Criminal Justice* 11 (2013) 1139.
215. For further information, *see* http://www.chambresafricaines.org/. *See further*, R.O. Savadogo, 'Les Chambres africaines extraordinaires au sein des tribunaux sénégalais: quoi de siextraordinaire?', *Études internationales* 45:1 (2014) 105.
216. Generally, *see* K. Magliveras, 'Fighting Impunity Unsuccessfully in Africa: A Critique of the African Union's Handling of the Hissène Habré Affair', *RADIC* 22:3 (2014) 420.
217. ECOWAS Court of Justice, *Hissène Habré v. Republic of Senegal*, Decision No. ECW/CCJ/RUL/05/13, 5 Nov. 2013, at: http://www.courtecowas.org (in French).
218. Chambre Africaine Extraordinaire d'Assises, *Le Procuteur Général contre Hissein Habré*, Judgment, 30 May 2016, at: http://www.chambresafricaines.org/pdf/Jugement_complet.pdf; *see* S.A.E.

lawyers representing Habré. In April 2017, the Appeals Chamber acquitted him of a rape charge but confirmed all other charges and did not alter the sentence of life imprisonment.[219]

41. In the closing months of 2006, relations between the AU and, respectively, the EU and the UN family were given considerable impetus. Thus, on 2 October 2006, the AUC and the EU Commission signed an MoU on the establishment of a partnership to foster twinning and exchange.[220] In November 2006, the UN Secretary-General and the AUC Chairperson concluded the framework for a ten-year AU capacity-building programme highlighting the key areas for cooperation, including institution-building and financial management; peace and security; human development; and food security and environmental protection.[221] A month later, the AU and the UNSC decided to set up a coordination and consultation mechanism, the United Nations-African Union Joint Task Force on Peace and Security, which is ongoing.[222] In December 2014, the UNSC requested the UN Secretary-General to present a report on UN-AU partnership in the area of peace and security in Africa, which has since been presented annually.[223] Finally, in December 2006 the Summit on Food Security in Africa was organized by the UN Food and Agricultural Organization (FAO), the AU, and NEPAD in Nigeria under the theme 'Food Security: an Engine for Growth and Poverty Alleviation in Africa.'[224]

On another front, in December 2006, Ethiopia's military assisted the Transitional Federal Government in Somalia to expel a rebel group known as the 'Union of Islamic Courts.'[225] However, not much later, Ethiopia took advantage of the turmoil

---

Høgestøl, 'The Habré Judgment at the Extraordinary African Chambers: A Singular Victory in the Fight Against Impunity', *Nordic Journal of Human Rights* 34 (2016):147.

219. Chambre Africaine Extraordinaire d'Assises d'Appel, *Le Procuteur Général contre Hissein Habré*, Judgment, 27 Apr. 2017, at: http://www.chambresafricaines.org. *See further* The Guardian, 'Ex-Chad dictator's conviction for crimes against humanity upheld by Dakar court', 27 Apr. 2017, at: https://www.theguardian.com/world/2017/apr/27/conviction-chad-hissene-habre-crimes-against-humanity-upheld.

220. Generally, *see* N. Pirozzi (ed.), *Strengthening the Africa-EU Partnership on Peace and Security: How to Engage African Regional Organizations and Civil Society* (Rome: Istituto Affairi Internazionali, 2012).

221. *See* Joint Declaration on 'Enhancing UN-AU Cooperation: Framework for the Ten-Year Capacity Building Programme for the African Union', 16 Nov. 2016. Note that on 30 May 2007, during its Forty-First Ordinary Session, the African Human Rights Commission stressed that the Framework's operationalization should also address needs in capacity-building and ensure adequate resources.

222. *See further*, UNSC Res. 1809(2008) of 16 Apr. 2008 on effective partnerships between the United Nations and regional organizations, particularly the AU, and UN Press Release SC/9301, 16 Apr. 2008, at: http://www.un.org/press/en/2008/sc9301.doc.htm.

223. UNSC, *Statement by the President of the Security Council*, UN Doc. S/PRST/2014/27 (16 Dec. 2014). For the latest Reports, *see* UNSC, *Strengthening the partnership between the United Nations and the African Union on issues of peace and security in Africa, including the work of the United Nations Office to the African Union – Report of the Secretary-General*, UN Doc. S/2023/629 (28 Aug. 2023), UN Doc. S/2022/643 (25 Aug. 2022) and UN Doc. S/2021/763 (30 Aug. 2021).

224. *See* FAO, *State of Food Insecurity in the World 2006* (Rome, 2006).

225. *See* B. Roggio, 'The Rise & Fall of Somalia's Islamic Courts: An Online History', *The Long War Journal*, 4 Jan. 2007, at: http://www.longwarjournal.org/archives/2007/01/the_rise_fall_of_som.php.

in Somalia and the lack of an effective government and invaded its territory. It is submitted that, pursuant to the principles enshrined in the AU Constitutive Act, this act amounted to unilateral intervention in another Member State's internal affairs. It was therefore prohibited, and the AU ought to have intervened. However, African leaders had only praise for Ethiopia regarding its intervention in Somalia on the invitation of the (legitimate) Transitional Federal Government: they treated it as a positive development that created an unprecedented opportunity for lasting peace in the country.[226] In January 2007, with the Ethiopian troops withdrawing, the African Union Mission in Somalia (AMISOM) was formed pursuant to a PSC decision to assist in resolving this long-standing crisis.[227] On the basis of six-month extensions of its mandate,[228] AMISOM operated until March 2022, when PSC reconfigured it to the African Union Transition Mission in Somalia (ATMIS),[229] a move endorsed by the UNSC in Resolution 2628 (2022) on 31 March 2022.[230]

Moreover, in May 2013, UNSC Resolution 2102(2013) established the UN Assistance Mission in Somalia (UNSOM) acting on the recommendations of the UN Secretary-General.[231] UNSOM replaced the UN Political Office for Somalia (UNPOS), which had completed its mandate in June 2013. Presently, its mandate has been extended to 31 October 2023 under UNSC Resolution 2657 (2022) adopted on 31 October 2022. The role of UNSOM is to offer policy advice to the Federal Government of Somalia and to AMISOM (now ATMIS) on peace-building and state-building. Both AMISOM (now ATMIS) and UNSOM have been provided logistic and life support by the UN Support Office in Somalia (UNSOS) set up under UNSC Resolution 2245(2015) of 9 November 2015.[232] Until today, the UNSC has not established is own peacekeeping mission for Somalia because, as stated in Resolution 2297(2016) of 7 July 2016, it agreed with the UN Secretary-General that conditions in Somalia were not appropriate for the deployment of such mission. It is possible that the ill-fated UN Operation in Somalia (UNOSOM I), created under UNSC Resolution 751(1992) of 24 April 1992,[233] might have played a role in this decision. It should be noted that the EU has also had a sizeable input in the Somalia situation principally by making available considerable funding. Thus, an AU-EU

226. *See* Assembly, *Decision on Somalia*, AU Doc. Assembly/AU/Dec. 142 (VIII) (30 Jan. 2007).
227. *See* PSC, *Communiqué of the 69th Meeting of the Peace and Security Council*, AU Doc. PSC/PR/Comm (LXIX) (19 Jan. 2007).
228. *See*, *inter alia*, UNSC Res. 1772 (2007) of 20 August 2007 and Res. 1801 (2008) of 20 February 2008. For further details, *see* http://unsom.unmissions.org/.
229. PSC, *Communique of the 1068th meeting of the AU Peace and Security Council on ATMIS Mandate*, AU Doc. PSC/PR/COMM.1068(2022) (8 Mar. 2022).
230. *See* para. 22 of Res. 2628 (2022): the UNSC authorized AU Member States 'to take all necessary measures, in full compliance with [their] obligations under international law, to … support peace and reconciliation efforts in Somalia [for] the development of a stable, federal, sovereign and united Somalia'.
231. *See* United Nations, *Letter of the Secretary-General addressed to the President of the Security Council on the findings and observations of the Somalia technical assessment mission*, UN Doc. S/2013/239 (19 Apr. 2013).
232. UNSOS replaced the United Nations Support Office for the African Union Mission in Somalia (UNSOA), which had been established under UNSC Res. 1863(2009) in January 2009, *see* http://unsoa.unmissions.org/.
233. Generally, *see* C.E. Philipp, 'Somalia – A Very Special Case', *Max Planck Yearbook of United Nations Law* (2005) 9: 517.

agreement signed on 20 September 2013 allocated further financial support to AMISOM to the tune of EUR 124 million from June 2013 to December 2013, bringing its contribution to AMISOM since March 2007 to EUR 411 million. Also, in September 2013, the EU and the Federal Government of Somalia organized a High-Level Conference in Brussels on 'A New Deal for Somalia' where the EU pledged EUR 650 million towards the reconstruction of the country. In subsequent years, the EU's provision of funding for state and peace-building initiatives was based on the National Indicative Programme for the Federal Republic of Somalia 2014 to 2020 (concluded on 19 June 2014).[234] But the ever-generous EU did not keep up funding AMISOM. In 2016, the EU explained that cutting its funding should not be misconstrued as a sign of bad relations but the result of competing priorities in Africa and elsewhere in the world.[235] However, the EU continued to be the principal non-African contributor to AMISOM and, therefore, when in 2017 it reduced its financial contribution, the operation of AMISOM faced a significant funding gap. Currently, the EU addresses Somalia's security challenges through the following missions: (a) the Military Training Mission (EUTM) supporting Somali security forces; (b) the EU Naval Force (EU NAVFOR) fighting piracy; and (c) the European Union Capacity Building Mission in Somalia (EUCAP Somalia), a civilian crisis management mission developing regional maritime security.

42. The Eighth Ordinary Assembly Session (Addis Ababa, 29–30 January 2007) appointed the members of the Panel of the Wise, which together with the PSC, the African Standby Force, the Military Staff Committee, and the Continental Early Warning System (CEWS), comprise the so-called African Peace and Security Architecture (APSA).[236] Moreover, it adopted the African Charter on Democracy, Elections and Governance, which entered into force on 15 February 2012 and has currently been signed by forty-six Member States but has received a rather low number of thirty-eight ratifications (indicative ratifications Benin in July 2012, Malawi in October 2012, Djibouti in January 2013, Mali in September 2013, Sudan in September 2013, Cote d'Ivoire in November 2013, SADR in January 2014, South Sudan in April 2015, Gambia in June 2018, and Angola in June 2021).[237] Building on previous instruments and similar initiatives, the Charter aims to become the main reference point for political reform in the continent based on the triptych 'democracy, human rights and the rule of law). It is often cited in PSC resolutions which are adopted for the purpose of not recognizing regimes which have come into power in an undemocratic/unconstitutional manner.

The internal structure of the African Court on Human and Peoples' Rights was approved during the Eleventh Ordinary Executive Council Session (Accra, Ghana,

234. At: https://www.eeas.europa.eu/sites/default/files/nip-somalia-20140619_en.pdf.

235. *See* 'EU Reiterates Its Continued Support For AMISOM', 27 Apr. 2016, at: http://amisom-au.org/2016/04/eu-reiterates-its-continued-support-for-amisom/.

236. *See* Assembly, *Decision on the Appointment of the Members of the Panel of the Wise*, AU Doc. Assembly/AU/Dec. 152 (VIII) (30 Jan. 2007).

237. *See* Assembly, *Decision on the African Charter on Democracy, Elections and Governance*, AU Doc. Assembly/AU/Dec. 147 (VIII) (30 Jan. 2007).

25–29 June 2007).[238] The Court's first eleven judges had been appointed by the Assembly in January 2006. Moreover, the Executive Council deliberated the modalities of the Africa-EU Summit, which was scheduled to take place in December 2007.[239] It also endorsed the Protocol regulating relations between the AU and RECs,[240] which the Assembly adopted during its Ninth Ordinary Session (Accra, Ghana, 1–3 July 2007).[241] It was signed on 27 January 2008,[242] replacing the previous Protocol concluded on 25 February 1998. The Protocol, which came into force rather belatedly on 10 November 2021, has so far been accepted by only four RECs, the last one being COMESA on 4 February 2022. This instrument should not be confused with the MoU on Cooperation in the Area of Peace and Security between the AU, RECs and the Coordinating Mechanisms of the Regional Standby Brigades of Eastern Africa and Northern Africa, which was also signed in 2008 and is mentioned *infra*.[243] Moreover, in February 2020, the Assembly approved the Protocol on Relations between the AU and RECs and authorized the AUC Chairperson to sign it on behalf of the Organization.[244] It is not clear how this instrument relates to the 2008 MOU, whether it is meant to replace it and which is its present status. The 2020 Protocol appears to have stemmed from the Assembly's mandate given to AUC in November 2018 to develop a proposal for the effective division of labour among the AU, RECs, Member States, and other continental institutions, in line with the principle of subsidiarity.[245] Finally, during its Eleventh Session, the Executive Council adopted the Declaration on the African Union Border Programme (AUBP).[246] The AUBP, which comes under the Peace and Security Department (PSD) of the AUC, centres around two principal axes: to delimit and to demark borders where it has not yet been achieved and to develop cross-border cooperation. It is associated with the AU Convention on Cross Border Cooperation, which the

---

238. *See* Executive Council, *Decision on the Structure of the African Court on Human and Peoples' Rights*, AU Doc. EX.CL/Dec. 351 (XI) (29 Jun. 2007).
239. *See* Executive Council, *Decision on Africa-European Union Dialogue*, AU Doc. EX.CL/Dec. 355 (XI) (29 Jun. 2007).
240. *See* Executive Council, *Decision on the Protocol on Relations Between the African Union and the Regional Economic Communities (RECs)*, AU Doc. EX.CL/Dec. 357 (XI) (29 Jun. 2007).
241. *See* Assembly, *Decision on the Protocol on Relations between the African Union and the Regional Economic Communities (RECs)*, AU Doc. Assembly/AU/Dec. 166 (IX) (3 Jul. 2007); it authorized the AUC Chairperson to sign it on behalf of the AU. For the outcomes of the Ninth Ordinary Assembly Session, *see* the briefing by the South African Deputy Minister of Foreign Affairs, 16 Jul. 2007, at: http://www.gov.za/s-van-der-merwe-briefing-heads-mission-african-union-summit-outcomes.
242. Text at: https://knowledge-uclga.org/IMG/pdf/protocol-on-relations-between-the-african-union-and-the-regional-economic-communities-recs.pdf.
243. Generally, *see* N.C. Ani, 'Clarifying the roles of the African Union and sub-regional organizations in peace and security', *Journal of African Union Studies* 7 (2018): 43.
244. Assembly, *Decision on the Follow Up to the First Mid-Year Coordination Meeting Between the African Union and the Regional Economic Communities*, Assembly/AU/Dec. 767 (XXXIII), para. 5 (10 Feb. 2020).
245. Assembly, *Decision on the Institutional Reform*, AU Doc. Ext/Assembly/AU/Dec. 1 (XI), para. 54 (18 Nov. 2018).
246. *See* Executive Council, *Decision on the Conference of African Ministers in Charge of Border Issues held in Addis Ababa, on 7 June 2007*, AU Doc. EX.CL/Dec. 370 (XI) (29 Jun. 2007).

Assembly approved in June 2014 and aims at ensuring peaceful resolution of border disputes.[247] The Niamey Convention, as it is also known, is another AU treaty which has not received the required number of ratification to come into force (presently, it has secured only eight ratifications, the last from Guinea in July 2021, Ghana in April 2023 and Cote d'Ivoire in June 2023). It is also of some interest to note that the Executive Council has proclaimed the 7th of June of each year as the 'African Border Day' to popularize the AUBP's importance in promoting peace and integration in the continent.[248] The first African Border Day was celebrated in 2011. So far, AUBP has held four Meetings of Ministers on African Border Issues (in June 2007, in March 2010, in May 2012 and in October 2016) to review the Programme's implementation, while the PSC has occasionally discussed its progress.[249] The Ninth Ordinary Assembly Session also discussed the consolidation of the project for a politically united Africa, as a follow-up to the deliberations held during the Tenth Extraordinary Executive Council Session (Durban, South Africa, 8–10 May 2007). The discussion was based on the document titled 'Study on an African Union Government: Towards the United States of Africa', which had appeared the previous year.[250] On 3 July 2007, the Assembly held the 'Grand Debate on the Union Government' and adopted the Accra Declaration on the Union Government of Africa and resolved to accelerate the continent's economic and political integration and to create an African Common Market with a time frame shorter than the Treaty establishing the AEC.[251] It should be noted that the political integration, a project which was pushed very hard by Colonel Gaddafi, was finally downplayed in the Accra Declaration. African leaders opted to promote economic integration, a project which got off the ground in the late 2010s.

After many years of delay, the Second Africa-EU Summit took place in Lisbon in December 2007. From the outset, the Summit was surrounded by controversy because Great Britain and other EU Member States had objected (unsuccessfully as it turned out) to the participation of President Mugabe of Zimbabwe on account of his totalitarian regime. The Summit resulted in the adoption of a Joint AU-EU Strategy and an Action Plan, which centred on an Africa-EU Strategic Partnership for the period 2008–2010. It concentrated on eight themes covering such diverse topics as human rights, climate change, migration, and space exploration. The first follow-up meeting took place on 4 February 2008 at AU Headquarters. The second meeting was organized in Brussels on 1 April 2008 under the theme 'The Africa-EU Strategic Partnership: Challenges and Prospects.' At the Third Africa-EU Summit,

---

247. Assembly, *Decision on the Draft Legal Instruments*, AU Doc. Assembly/AU/Dec. 529 (XXIII) (27 Jun. 2014).
248. Executive Council, *Decision on the Report of the Commission on the Second Conference of African Ministers in Charge of Border Issues*, AU Doc. EX.CL/Dec. 563 (XVII) (23 Jul. 2010).
249. *See, e.g.*, PSC, *Communique of the 930th meeting of the PSC held on 11 June 2020, in Commemoration of the African Border Day within the framework of the AU Master Roadmap of Practical Steps to Silence the Guns in Africa by the Year 2020*, AU Doc. PSC/PR/COMM.(CMXXX) (11 Jun. 2020).
250. Text at: https://archives.au.int/handle/123456789/2656.
251. AU Doc. Assembly/AU/Decl. 2 (IX). Generally, *see* T. Murithi (ed.), *Towards a Union Government for Africa – Challenges and Opportunities*, Institute of Security Studies Monograph Series, No. 140 (Pretoria, January 2008); B. Yao Gebe, 'The Quest for a Union Government of Africa: Reflections on the Vision and the Realities of Political Integration', *South African J. of International Affairs* 15 (2008): 41.

which took place in Libya in November 2010 and centred on investment, economic growth, and job creation, the two sides agreed to continue working on the same eight themes and, therefore, the Second Action Plan covering the period 2011–2013 retained them. However, the Second Action Plan has additionally sought to increase policy dialogue and coordination, cooperation on administrative issues, and strengthening the capacity of AU bodies mainly in the areas of human resources, financial resources and statistics.[252] The vigour with which the EU surrounded Africa at the time, arguably, had a lot to do with the inroads of several emerging economies (principally the BRIC countries)[253] into Africa and fears that it might lose its primacy in African affairs. In retrospect, the renewed interest that the EU showed towards Africa has benefited the continent because the USA has come to consider it as a foreign policy priority, arguably for the first time since the end of the Cold War. It might not have been a coincidence that the first United States–Africa Leaders Summit was held in Washington, D.C. on 4–6 August 2014,[254] exactly four months after the Fourth EU-Africa Summit (Brussels, 2–3 April 2014). There was also a striking similarity between the themes of the two meetings: that of the EU Summit was 'Investing in People, Prosperity and Peace', and that of the US Summit was 'Investing in the Next Generation'.

Much had changed since the Third Africa-EU Summit in 2010. Many an African country had rapid economic growth, and there were positive developments on the political front, while the EU had to confront a damaging fiscal and banking crisis, which revealed deep rifts among its membership. In June 2013, a four-day meeting at the AUC had prepared the AU's negotiation position during the Fourth EU-Africa Summit.[255] At the end of the Summit, a Declaration[256] as well as a Roadmap for the period 2014–2017 to complement the Joint Africa-EU Strategy (JAES) were adopted.[257] These documents reveal the EU's willingness to follow a differentiated relationship towards Africa treating it as a more equal partner while deepening its relationship with the continent.[258]

The Fifth AU-EU Summit took place on 29–30 November 2017 in Abidjan, Côte d'Ivoire. The theme centred again on human resources: 'Investing in Youth for

252. Text at: https://www.europarl.europa.eu/cmsdata/122472/Africa%20EU%20Strategy%20Action%20Plan%202011-2013.pdf.
253. Compare Assembly, *Decision on the Africa-South America Summit*, AU Doc. Assembly/AU/Dec. 159 (VIII) (30 Jan. 2007); and *Decision on the Africa-China Forum on Cooperation (FOCAC)*, AU Doc. Assembly/AU/Dec. 160 (VIII) (30 Jan. 2007). Generally, *see* A. Huliaras & K. Magliveras, 'In Search of a Policy: European Union and U.S. Reactions to the Growing Chinese Presence in Africa', *European Foreign Affairs Review* 13 (2008): 399; F. Kell & A. Vines, 'The Evolution of the Joint Africa-EU Strategy (2007–2020)' in T. Haastrup, L. Mah & N. Duggan (eds), *The Routledge Handbook of EU-Africa Relations* (Abingdon: Routledge, 2020) 105.
254. For details, *see* https://obamawhitehouse.archives.gov/us-africa-leaders-summit.
255. *See* African Union Commission, 'African Brainstorming on the future of the Africa – EU Dialogue, Zanzibar, Tanzania', Media Advisory, 13 June 2013, at: https://au.int/fr/node/26672.
256. At: http://www.ist-africa.org/home/files/FourthEU-AfricaSummitDeclaration.pdf.
257. At: https://www.consilium.europa.eu/media/21520/142094.pdf. For evaluation of JAES, *see* A. Sherriff & J. Kotsopoulos, 'Africa and the European Union: An Assessment of the Joint Africa-EU Strategy (JAES)' in T. Murithi (ed.), *Handbook of Africa's International Relations* (Abingdon: Routledge, 2013) 305.
258. *See* European Commission, *The EU-Africa Partnership*, MEMO/15/4808, 22 Apr. 2015, at: http://europa.eu/rapid/press-release_MEMO-15-4808_en.htm.

Accelerated Inclusive Growth and Sustainable Development'. The adopted Joint Declaration (Egypt attached a reservation) set out the common priorities for partnership in the following four strategic areas: (i) economic opportunities for youth; (ii) peace and security; (iii) mobility and migration; and (iv) cooperation on governance.[259] Over and above there priority areas, it was also agreed to promote their cooperation on the global scene, *inter alia*, by strengthening 'the high level policy dialogue to adopt a more coordinated approach and converging positions in international negotiations'.[260] According to the Joint Declaration, the two sides undertook to promote 'effective multilateralism', while the AU-EU-UN trilateral cooperation would be cognizant of the multilateral institutions' role in the field of peace and security. The Fifth Summit also adopted a Joint Statement on the Migrant Situation in Libya concentrating on the inhuman treatment of African migrants and refugees by criminal groups operating in the territory of lawless Libya,[261] an issue that persists to the present day.[262] However, this Statement made no reference to the decision reached in the margins of the Summit to create a joint AU-EU-UN Task Force to save and protect the lives of migrants and refugees by dismantling criminal networks, by offering opportunities of development and stability to the countries of origin and transit, and by tackling the root causes of migration in Africa.[263]

43. The Sixth EU-AU Summit was held in Brussels on 17–18 February 2022. Initially scheduled for Autumn 2020, it was postponed due to the coronavirus pandemic. In preparation for the Summit, the European Commission produced a document explaining why a new comprehensive EU strategy with Africa was required and suggested that it be built on the following five partnerships, most of which were already 'priority areas': (a) green transition and energy access; (b) digital transformation; (c) sustainable growth and jobs; (d) peace and governance; and (e) migration and mobility. It also recommended that EU-Africa engagements should continue at bilateral, regional and continental levels.[264] At the end of the Sixth Summit, the traditional joint EU-AU declaration was adopted. Titled 'A joint Vision for

259. Text at: https://www.consilium.europa.eu/media/31991/33454-pr-final_declaration_au_eu_summit.pdf.
260. *Ibid*, paras 76 et seq.
261. At: https://www.consilium.europa.eu/media/31871/33437-pr-libya20statement20283020nov2010.pdf.
262. Generally, *see* Office of the United Nations High Commissioner for Human Rights, *Unsafe and Undignified: The forced expulsion of migrants from Libya*, May 2021, at: https://www.ohchr.org/sites/default/files/2021-12/Unsafe_and_Undignified.pdf; O. Karasapan, 'Libya's migrants and crimes against humanity', *Brookings*, 2 Nov. 2021, at: https://www.brookings.edu/blog/future-development/2021/11/02/libyas-migrants-and-crimes-against-humanity/.
263. *See* European Commission, *Joint press release of the United Nations, the African Union and the European Union*, Abidjan, 29 Nov. 2017, at: https://ec.europa.eu/commission/presscorner/detail/en/STATEMENT_17_5029.
264. European Commission, *Joint Communication to the European Parliament and the Council – Towards a Comprehensive Strategy with Africa*, JOIN(2020) 4 final, 9 Mar. 2020. *See also*, Council of the European Union, *Council conclusions on Africa*, 9265/20 Annex (30 Jun. 2020). *See further*, Joint Communiqué of the Second AU-EU Foreign Affairs Ministerial Meeting, Kigali, Rwanda, 25–26 Oct. 2021, discussed by T. Yaw Voets, 'What the Second AU-EU Ministerial Meeting on Foreign Affairs means for the future relations', *Institute for a Greater Europe*, 30 November 2021, at: https://institutegreatereurope.com/what-the-second-au-eu-ministerial-meeting-on-foreign-affairs-means-for-the-future-relations/.

2030', it talked about a 'renewed EU-AU Partnership' to address immediate challenges (e.g., the pandemic, the African debt problem, combatting illicit financial flows, etc.) but also long-term possibilities. It also recorded the EU pledge of EUR 150 billion to Africa for the period 2021–2027 to be delivered through the so-called Global Gateway scheme.[265] The latter is a new EU strategy. It is implemented by the so-called Team Europe, which comprises the EU institutions, the EU Member States as well as the European Investment Bank (EIB) and the European Bank for Reconstruction and Development (EBRD). It is expected that in the period 2021–2027, it will mobilize up to EUR 300 billion in investments to boost smart, clean and secure links in the digital, energy and transport sectors as well as to strengthen health, education and research systems worldwide.[266] Finally, it is interesting to compare the EU's funding pledge to Africa with those made during other AU summits with third stakeholders in the period 2021–2022. Suffice to mention that USD 40 billion was pledged at the 2021 Forum on China-Africa Cooperation, USD 30 billion at the 2022 Tokyo International Conference on African Development, and USD 55 billion at the 2022 US-Africa Leaders Summit.[267] The Tenth Ordinary Assembly Session (Addis Ababa, 31 January–2 February 2008) dealt with two major issues. The first issue concerned the Report and Declaration of the Second Conference of African Ministers of Integration (Kigali, 26–27 July 2007). The Assembly endorsed the recommendations and requested Member States to implement them in cooperation with the UN Economic Commission of Africa (ECA), the African Development Bank, and other (undisclosed) 'development partners'.[268] Second, it deliberated the Report on the Audit of the AU, which it had requested in July 2007. The Report, which was submitted in mid-December 2007 by an independent group of experts, was the first attempt to examine the effectiveness and the impact of AU programmes. It was also associated with the project of political integration in the continent and the creation of a Union Government.[269] As the Assembly had not been adequately prepared to appraise the 197-page Report and its 172 recommendations, it authorized the convening within three months of an Executive Council session to analyse and evaluate it.[270] As was perhaps to be expected, the

265. *See 6th European Union – African Union Summit: A Joint Vision for 2030*, at: https://www.consilium.europa.eu/media/54412/final_declaration-en.pdf.
266. *See* European Commission/High Representative of the Union for Foreign Affairs and Security Policy, *Joint Communication to the European Parliament, the Council, the European Economic and Social Committee, the Committee of the Regions and the European Investment Bank – The Global Gateway*, JOIN(2021) 30 final, 1 Dec. 2021, at: https://commission.europa.eu/system/files/2021-12/joint_communication_global_gateway.pdf.
267. This was the second US-Africa Summit, which was held in December 2022, *see* Z. Usman, J. Ovadia & A. Abayo, 'The U.S.-Africa Leaders Summit Marks a Seismic Shift in Relations with the Continent', *Carnegie Endowment For International Peace*, 22 December 2022, at: https://carnegieendowment.org/2022/12/22/u.s.-africa-leaders-summit-marks-seismic-shift-in-relations-with-continent-pub-88692.
268. *See* Assembly, *Decision on Economic Integration*, AU Doc. Assembly/AU/Dec. 178 (X) (2 Feb. 2008).
269. *See* African Union, *Audit of the African Union: Towards A People-Centred Political and Socio-economic Integration and Transformation of Africa*, Addis Ababa, December 2007.
270. *See* Assembly, *Decision on the Report of the Executive Council on the Audit of the Union and the Report of the Ministerial Committee on the Union Government*, AU Doc. Assembly/AU/Dec. 185 (X) (2 Feb. 2008).

Extraordinary Session, which was held in Arusha on 7 May 2008, did not result in any breakthroughs but repeated the usual rhetoric on how to accelerate the process for setting up the remaining AU organs and to operationalize the AEC. In the years that followed, only few of the recommendations were implemented.[271] With at least one-fifth of the AU membership embroiled at the time in domestic strife and transnational conflicts (suffice to mention the DRC, Côte d'Ivoire, Burundi, Sudan, the Comoros, Chad, the CAR, Kenya, Somalia, Ethiopia, and Eritrea), six years after its inauguration, the AU (just as the OAU before it) was unable to muster the necessary strength and demand its proper place on the international arena, being one of the largest multilateral institutions. Even today, the AU struggles to find its rightful place in an ever-complex global community.

The theme of the Eleventh Ordinary Assembly Session (Sharm El Sheikh, Egypt, 24 June–1 July 2008) was 'Meeting the Millennium Development Goals on Water and Sanitation.' The Assembly carried on from the previous Session the deliberations on creating a Union Government leading to the United States of Africa (to be abbreviated U.S.A. as well?). The project concentrated, on the one hand, on addressing effectively the principal African problems through long-term solutions and, on the other hand, on mapping out an institutional framework for the AU that even for the EU would have probably been considered revolutionary. The former was an urgent task that could no longer be neglected. The latter was rather of secondary importance. And with the demise of Colonel Gaddafi three years later, the principal underwriter of political integration projects in Africa, the 'Union Government' project came to nothing. The continent had more important problems to deal with. A UN document released in 2008 listed all the conflicts around the globe with which the UNSC had been involved. The document made grim reading as most conflicts were in or about Africa.[272] This situation has continued to this day: from January 2011 until December 2013, the UNSC considered at formal meetings the situation in fifteen African states,[273] from January 2013 until December 2015 in twelve African states,[274] from January 2015 to June 2018 in sixteen so-called items that concerned situations in Africa,[275] while the same number of 'items' was considered at formal meetings between 1 January 2019 and 31 December 2021.[276]

44. The theme of the Twelfth Ordinary Assembly Session (Addis Ababa, 1–3 February 2009) was 'Infrastructure Development in Africa.' The Assembly was

271. *See* Y. Bedzigui, '28th AU summit: AU reform can't be fast-tracked', *ISS Today*, 27 Jan. 2017, at: https://issafrica.org/iss-today/28th-au-summit-au-reform-cant-be-fast-tracked.

272. *See* UNSC, *Summary statement by the Secretary-General on matters of which the Security Council is seized and on the stage reached in their consideration*, UN Doc. S/2008/10 (13 May 2008).

273. *See* UNSC, *Summary statement by the Secretary-General on matters of which the Security Council is seized and on the stage reached in their consideration*, UN Doc. S/2013/10 (2 Jan. 2013) and *Summary statement by the Secretary-General on matters of which the Security Council is seized and on the stage reached in their consideration*, UN Doc. S/2014/10 (2 Jan. 2014).

274. *See* UNSC, *Summary statement by the Secretary-General on matters of which the Security Council is seized and on the stage reached in their consideration*, UN Doc. S/2016/10 (4 Jan. 2016).

275. *See* UNSC, *Summary statement by the Secretary-General of matters of which the Security Council is seized and of the stage reached in their consideration*, UN Doc. S/2018/10/Add.22 (4 Jun. 2018).

276. *See* UNSC, *Summary statement by the Secretary-General of matters of which the Security Council is seized and of the stage reached in their consideration*, UN Doc. S/2022/10 (4 Jan. 2022).

arguably pre-occupied with the international law principle of universal jurisdiction and the fundamentally different way that African states and European states understood and apply it. Universal jurisdiction embodies the principle of international law allowing a state to prosecute and bring to trial the citizens of a third state, who have allegedly committed an array of international crimes, even though the former state might have no link with the crime committed, the perpetrator/s and/or the victim/s. According to the principle of universal jurisdiction, such prosecutions do not breach the sovereignty of other states (e.g., the state of the perpetrator's nationality). The differing opinions on this principle's applicability had resulted in considerable friction between the AU and European states. Moreover, that certain European states, including Belgium and France, had issued arrest warrants against Africans based on this very principle had led to problems in bilateral relations. European states justified the arrest warrants and the legal proceedings against Africans by, *inter alia*, invoking the ethos of impunity prevailing in Africa. According to the European view, their commission amounted to mass violations of human rights which were neither investigated nor prosecuted by African states. Apparently reacting to these accusations, the Assembly suggested that the African Court on Human and Peoples' Rights be empowered to try individuals for egregious criminal offences, namely genocide, crimes against humanity and war crimes.[277] It is not clear whether the Assembly considered the repercussions that such a move would have to the jurisdiction of other international courts of justice. Regarding the International Criminal Court (ICC) specifically, the consequences would concern those African states which are also contracting parties to its Statute as well as those situations already referred to the ICC by the UNSC (namely, the situation in Darfur – the situation in Libya was referred in 2011). Given that African states constitute the largest single group of ICC parties and that the ICC deals predominantly with situations in Africa, the implications of this suggestion were significant. In June 2014, the International Law Section of the African Court of Justice and Human Rights was created with the competence to prosecute and try several international crimes and not only the egregious criminal offences mentioned above. But as is later explained, Member States have shown no willingness to become parties to the Protocol establishing the International Law Section.

The Twelfth Ordinary Assembly Session also adopted the following three legal instruments. First, the African Charter on Statistics, which was signed on 4 February 2009 and entered into force on 8 February 2015. The Charter, which is promoted by the AU Institute for Statistics (STATAFRIC) has currently been signed by thirty-three Member States and has received twenty-four ratifications (the last two by The Gambia in July 2018 and by Botswana in February 2020).[278] Second, the Statute of the African Union Commission on International Law (AUCIL), which

277. *See* Assembly, *Decision on the Implementation of the Assembly Decision on the Abuse of the Principle of Universal Jurisdiction*, AU Doc. Assembly/AU/Dec. 213 (XII) (3 Feb. 2009).

278. *See* Assembly, *Decision on the Draft African Charter on Statistics*, AU Doc. Assembly/AU/Dec. 210 (XII) (3 Feb. 2009). *See further*, the Addis Ababa Plan of Action for Statistical Development in Africa adopted in May 1990 by the OAU Conference of Ministers in charge of Social and Economic Development. Note that the Charter on Statistics refers to the 'subsidiarity principle', which is very well developed in EU law, *see* Art. 5(3) of the Treaty on European Union as well as Protocols No. 1 and No. 2 annexed to the Treaty of Lisbon. However, in the Charter on Statistics, subsidiarity has a

came into force upon approval by the Assembly.[279] The Statute does not require signature or ratification by Member States. Third, the Protocol for the Establishment of the African Investment Bank (AIB), one of the three financial institutions envisaged in Article 19 of the Constitutive Act.[280] Currently, it has been signed by twenty-two Member States and ratified by only six (the last one was Chad in August 2018). Nine more ratifications are required to enter into force.

During its Thirteenth Ordinary Session (Sirte, Libya, 1–3 July 2009), the Assembly was again seized of the saga concerning the 'blatant abuse' by European states of the principle of universal jurisdiction. The Assembly made the novel suggestion that 'an international regulatory body' be set up with the competence to review complaints arising from the abusive exploitation of the universal jurisdiction principle by individual states.[281] The question of the application of universal jurisdiction by European courts targeting Africans has persisted and was one of the issues discussed during the aforementioned Fourth EU-Africa Summit in April 2014.[282] The Assembly also addressed the consequences of the arrest warrant issued by the ICC Prosecutor against the then President of Sudan Omar Al Bashir for allegedly committing crimes against humanity in the region of Darfur.[283] During the 2010s, the ICC arrest warrant against Al Bashir and other African dignitaries developed into a direct antiparathesis between the AU and the ICC. It is submitted that, on the whole, the Assembly's approach was not the proper one. First, because it effectively ordered Member States (including those that have chosen to become contracting parties to the Rome Statute) not to cooperate with the ICC in arresting and surrendering Al Bashir and other African dignitaries to The Hague, threatening with the imposition of sanction if they did. Second, because it regarded the arrest warrants as an affront to the dignity, sovereignty and integrity of Member States, neglecting that several African countries have been proponents of international criminal justice. Third, because it turned this affair to another point of contention with the Western world. Undoubtedly, the Assembly, as the highest-ranking organ of an intergovernmental organization, may legitimately show its opposition towards another international institution, namely the ICC, which has not been faultless in his handling of certain prosecutions against African dignitaries, e.g. the *Ruto and Sang*

---

rather different connotation. It is defined in Art. 8(10) thereof as 'taking the measures needed for the systems to function to such levels as would enable it achieve maximum effectiveness'.

279. *See* Assembly, *Decision on the Draft Statute of the African Union Commission on International Law*, AU Doc. Assembly/AU/Dec. 209 (XII) (3 Feb. 2009).

280. *See* Assembly, *Decision on the Protocol on the Establishment of the African Investment Bank*, AU Doc. Assembly/AU/Dec. 212 (XII) (3 Feb. 2009).

281. *See* Assembly, *Decision on the Abuse of the Principle of Universal Jurisdiction*, AU Doc. Assembly/AU/Dec. 243 (XIII) (3 Jul. 2009).

282. *See* Fourth EU-Africa Summit, 2–3 Apr. 2014, *Brussels Declaration*, para. 10 confirming that both sides reject impunity and commit themselves to fighting it at national and international level, at: http://www.ist-africa.org/home/files/FourthEU-AfricaSummitDeclaration.pdf; and *Roadmap 2014–2017*, para. 9, at: https://www.consilium.europa.eu/media/21520/142094.pdf.

283. ICC Pre-Trial Chamber I, *Decision on the Prosecution's Application for a Warrant of Arrest against Omar Hassan Ahmad Al Bashir*, ICC-02/05-01/09-3, 4 Mar. 2009, 48 I.L.M. (2009) 463. The following year a second arrest warrant was issued, ICC Pre-Trial Chamber I, *Second Warrant of Arrest for Omar Hassan Ahmed Al Bashir*, ICC-02/05-01/09-95, 12 Jul. 2010.

Case that was opened in September 2013.[284] However, it was at least problematic to request that Member States do not discharge their duties owed to the ICC considering that they emanate from a multilateral treaty (the ICC (Rome) Statute) to which they have freely and willingly decided to participate, when, at the same time, they have failed to address the prevailing ethos of impunity (especially as regards the crimes perpetrated in Darfur).

The Thirteenth Assembly Session also authorized the AU's accession to the UN Framework Convention on Climate Change, which was adopted in 1992,[285] and to the Kyoto Protocol, adopted in 1997,[286] in accordance with Article 22 of the Framework Convention and Article 24 of the Kyoto Protocol allowing accession by Regional Economic Integration Organizations (REIOs).[287] The EU had already acceded to both treaties, respectively, in December 1993 and in May 2002. Until today, the AU has not actually acceded to either instrument; the AU is among the over one hundred intergovernmental organizations (IGOs) which have been designated as 'Non-Party Stakeholders' to the Framework Convention on Climate Change.[288] The same Assembly Session also authorized[289] the AU to accede to the UN Convention to Combat Desertification in those Countries Experiencing Serious Drought and/or Desertification, Particularly in Africa.[290] The EU accepted the Convention in 1998 but the AU has not yet acceded to it. Finally, the Assembly adopted a decision dealing with the scourge of coups d'état and the AU's effectiveness in handling them.[291] On the whole, it repeated the content of Article 25 of the African Charter on Democracy, Elections and Governance (2007), which at the time had not entered into force. More specifically, the Assembly considered that the AU was well endowed with an array of instruments to tackle coups d'état and, therefore, the aim was not to elaborate new ones but to promote their effective implementation and, where necessary, to refine, to enrich and to update them. Arguably,

---

284. Ruto and Sang were accused of crimes against humanity (murder, deportation of population and persecution) allegedly committed during post-election violence in Kenya in 2007–2008. But ICC Trial Chamber V(A) decided, by majority, that the case against them be terminated, *see* ICC, *The Prosecutor v. William Samoei Ruto and Joshua Arap Sang*, Public redacted version of Decision on Defence Applications for Judgments of Acquittal, ICC-01/09-01/11-2027-Red-Corr, 5 Apr. 2016, at: https://www.icc-cpi.int/court-record/icc-01/09-01/11-2027-red-corr.
285. 1771 U.N.T.S. 107.
286. 2303 U.N.T.S. 148.
287. *See* Assembly, *Decision on the Accession of the African Union to the United Nations Framework Convention on Climate Change (UNFCCC) and the Kyoto Protocol Rev.1*, AU Doc. Assembly/AU/Dec. 248 (XIII) (3 Jul. 2009).
288. *See* https://unfccc.int/process/parties-non-party-stakeholders/non-party-stakeholders/admitted-igos/list-of-admitted-igos.
289. *See* Assembly, *Decision on the African Union Accession to the United Nations Convention to Combat Desertification (UNCCD) Rev. 1*, AU Doc. Assembly/AU/Dec. 255 (XIII) (3 Jul. 2009).
290. Signed in Paris on 14 October 1994, entered into force on 26 December 1996, 1954 U.N.T.S. 3. *See also* the various UNGA Resolutions titled 'Implementation of the United Nations Convention to Combat Desertification in Those Countries Experiencing Serious Drought and/or Desertification, Particularly in Africa', e.g. Res. 64/202 of 21 Dec. 2009, Res. 74/220 of 19 Dec. 2019 and Res. 75/218 of 21 Dec. 2020, as well as the UN Secretary-General Reports on its implementation, e.g. UN Doc. A/75/256 (25 Jul. 2020).
291. *See* Assembly, *Decision on the Prevention of Unconstitutional Changes of Government and Strengthening the Capacity of the African Union to Manage Such Situations*, AU Doc. Assembly/AU/Dec. 253 (XIII) (3 Jul. 2009).

the situation was slightly more complicated because the AU did not only have to address the question of the Member States' failure to discharge the obligations flowing from these instruments but also the large number of (mostly violent) coups d'état, which negated peace, security and stability in the continent. Thus, the report submitted by the AUC Chairperson to the Special Assembly Session on the Consideration and Resolution of Conflicts in Africa, held in Tripoli, Libya, on 30–31 August 2009, cited seventeen instances of interstate and intra-state conflicts, coups d'état, etc.[292]

45. Before the commencement of the Fourteenth Ordinary Assembly Session (Addis Ababa, 31 January–2 February 2010), Gaddafi attempted to secure a second term as AU Chairperson but, despite the leverage he exerted on many a Member State, he failed.[293] The Assembly took further measures to enhance the AU's effectiveness in responding to coups d'état.[294] Thus, over and above suspending from participation the Member State where the coup took place, it agreed on the following measures. First, barring the perpetrators from participating in the elections to be held to restore constitutional order in the country in question. Second, ordering sanctions, whose precise content was not given, against any Member State that was proven to have instigated or supported the coup. Third, adopting additional punitive measures, including economic sanctions. It is submitted that, as a whole, these measures, whose legal basis was lacking in the decision, constituted a de facto amendment of the Constitutive Act. And this is because Article 30 thereof stipulates a framework for the AU's response specifically to coups d'état. Moreover, these measures lacked the legal precision which is required when punitive measures are imposed against Member States. Indeed, sanctions violate, in principle, state sovereignty, but they are allowed because they have already been agreed to and accepted by the whole membership as a means to 'punish' and bring back to normalcy those Member States that had breached their duties and obligations. The Assembly decision had several weak elements. For example, it was not stipulated which organ would determine authoritatively that a Member State had instigated a coup d'état against another Member State. This was an important omission because it could only be an impartial and independent organ, not one succumbed to political manipulation, so rife in African affairs. Given that, as explained elsewhere, there is no functioning AU Court of Justice, one cannot speculate as to which organ would have fulfilled this role. Moreover, to prevent the coup perpetrators from participating in future democratic elections, correct as it might be, is arguably problematic because it could be construed as unacceptable interference in the domestic affairs of the Member State concerned. Arguably, an emancipated population should be in the position to ostracize those responsible for disrupting the country's political life.

---

292. *See* Report of the Chairperson of the Commission, *Enhancing Africa's Resolve and Effectiveness in Ending Conflict and Sustaining Peace*, AU Doc. SP/ASSEMBLY/PS/RPT(I) (2009), pp. 12 et seq.

293. *See* A. Huliaras & K. Magliveras, 'The End of an Affair? Libya and Sub-Saharan Africa', *Journal of North African Studies* 16 (2011): 167.

294. *See* Assembly, *Decision on the Prevention of Unconstitutional Changes of Government and Strengthening the Capacities of the African Union to Manage such Situations*, AU Doc. Assembly/AU/Dec. 269 (XIV) Rev. 1 (2 Feb. 2010).

The Assembly also proclaimed 2010 to be the 'Year of Peace and Security in Africa'.[295] This was largely a symbolic act. Future events showed that such initiatives are devoid of purpose if they are not accompanied by vigorous action and the assumption of specific commitments. The coup d'état in Madagascar in March 2009, which is examined in detail later, is a good illustration of how the AU's peace and security agenda could be derailed. Even though the Assembly considered the Madagascar situation as a separate issue[296] and also as one of the situations posing threats and challenges to peace and security in the continent,[297] the AU did not manage to remove Andry Rajoelina, the strongman who had assumed power in the 2009 coup, from office until presidential elections were held in December 2013. The question of whether, pursuant to the aforementioned Assembly Decision 269(XIV), Rajoelina should not have been allowed to stand as presidential candidate in the 2013 elections did not come up because, under pressure from Southern African Development Community (SADC), both Rajoelina and his arch-rival Ravalomanana consented to opt out from the race, together with seven other candidates. A so-called Special Electoral Court was formed to assist in the organization of the post-coup elections in Madagascar.[298] However, the Court did not disqualify Rajoelina as the instigator of the 2009 coup but because he had failed to file the required documentation within the prescribed deadline.[299]

Given the rather vague and unclear institutional position of NEPAD within the AU, the Fourteenth Assembly Session resolved to integrate it into the AU structures and processes. In particular, it established the NEPAD Planning and Coordinating Agency (NPCA) as a technical AU body to replace the NEPAD Secretariat and made the NEPAD Heads of State and Government Orientation Committee (HSGOC) an Assembly sub-committee to provide political leadership and strategic guidance.[300] In the course of 2018, there was another major overhaul of NEPAD as the Assembly, acting on a previous Decision, consented to the proposal[301] to transform it into the African Union Development Agency (AUDA).[302] The mandate of

295. *See* Assembly, *Decision on the Year of Peace and Security in Africa*, AU Doc. Assembly/AU/Dec. 275 (XIV) (2 Feb. 2010).
296. *See* Assembly, *Decision on Madagascar*, AU Doc. Assembly/AU/Dec. 279 (XIV) (2 Feb. 2010).
297. *See* Assembly, *Decision on the Report of the Peace and Security Council on its Activities and the Situation of Peace and Security in Africa*, AU Doc. Assembly/AU/Dec. 268 (XIV) (2 Feb. 2010).
298. SADC leaders congratulated the Special Electoral Court for its 'bold decision' to disqualify them, *see Communiqué of the 33rd Summit of SADC Heads of State and Government*, Lilongwe, Malawi, 17–18 Aug. 2013, para. 19, at: https://reliefweb.int/report/zimbabwe/communiqu%C3%A9-33rd-summit-sadc-heads-state-and-government.
299. *See* SADC, *Statement on the Publication of the Final List of Candidates for the Madagascar Presidential Elections*, 23 August 2013, at: https://www.sadc.int/; and The Carter Center, *Legislative and Second Round of Presidential Elections in Madagascar*, Final Report (Atlanta, Georgia, December 2013) 19, at: https://www.cartercenter.org/resources/pdfs/news/peace_publications/election_reports/madagascar-2013-final.pdf.
300. *See* Assembly, *Decision on the Integration of the New Partnership for Africa's Development (NEPAD) into the Structures and Processes of the African Union including the Establishment of the NEPAD Planning and Coordinating Agency (NPCA)*, AU Doc. Assembly/AU/Dec. 283 (XIV) (2 Feb. 2010).
301. Assembly, *Decision on the Outcome of the Retreat of the Assembly of the African Union on the Institutional Reform of the African Union*, AU Doc. Assembly/AU/Dec. 635 (XXVIII) (31 Jan.

what is now called *AUDA-NEPAD* is to coordinate and execute priority regional and continental integration projects in the context of Agenda 2063, to strengthen the capacity of Member States and RECs, and to serve as the continent's technical interface with all of Africa's development stakeholders and international partners.[303] Under the present structure, HSGOC, comprising thirty-three Member States, operates as an Assembly sub-committee providing the highest political leadership and strategic guidance on the priority issues of Agenda 2063. Its recommendations are sent to the full Assembly for endorsement.[304] Finally, the Fourteenth Assembly Session adopted the Annexes to the Statutes of the AIB,[305] which had been recommended by the Executive Council a few days earlier.[306] It was decided that the Special Drawing Rights (SDRs) of the International Monetary Fund will be the AIB unit of account until the introduction of an African single currency. Arguably, this was a premature move because, as mentioned above, the Protocol on the AIB had not entered into force (and still has not).

In June 2010, the Panel of the Wise, one of the components of APSA, published its report on how the AU should strengthen its preventive and management role vis-à-vis election-related disputes and conflicts. The report, while acknowledging that elections had become a core ingredient of popular participation in the governance process, cited several principles to be applied, which arguably should be considered as novelty for Africa, e.g., 'rules of orderly political competition' and 'building institutions of competition that are widely accepted by winners and losers'.[307] During the Fifteenth Ordinary Assembly Session (Kampala, Uganda, 25–27 July 2010), the first steps were taken to establish the Pan-African University (PAU), a project that had been proposed by the first African Ministerial Conference on Science and Technology in Johannesburg in 2003.[308] The University has presence in four Member States: Nigeria, where the concentration is on life and earth sciences; Kenya, on basic sciences, technology, and innovation; Cameroon, on governance,

---

2017). *See further*, Assembly, *Decision on the New Partnership for Africa's Development (NEPAD)*, AU Doc. Assembly/AU/Dec. 685 (XXX) (29 Jan. 2018).

302. Assembly, *Decision on the Transformation of the NEPAD Planning and Coordinating Agency (NPCA) Into the African Union Development Agency (AUDA)*, AU Doc. Assembly/AU/Dec. 691 (XXXI) (2 Jul. 2018).

303. As agreed in Assembly, *Decision on the Institutional Reform*, AU Doc. Ext/Assembly/AU/Dec. 1 (XI), para. 38 (18 Nov. 2018). The same Decision asked for a permanent Host Country Agreement for AUDA/NEPAD to be concluded with the Republic of South Africa, *ibid*, para. 39.

304. *See* Assembly, *Decision on the Report of the NEPAD Heads of State and Government Orientation Committee (HSGOC)*, AU Doc. Assembly/AU/Dec. 763 (XXXIII) (10 Feb. 2020), para. 2.

305. *See* Assembly, *Decision on the Annexes to the Statutes of the African Investment Bank*, AU Doc. Assembly/AU/Dec. 286 (XIV) (2 Feb. 2010).

306. *See* Executive Council, *Decision on the Annexes to the Statutes of the African Investment Bank*, AU Doc. EX.CL/Dec. 550 (XVI) (29 Jan. 2010).

307. African Union Panel of the Wise, 'Election-Related Disputes and Political Violence: Strengthening the Role of the African Union in Preventing, Managing, and Resolving Conflict', *The African Union Series* (New York: International Peace Institute, July 2010) at: http://www.peaceau.org/uploads/au-electionviolence-epub.pdf.

308. *See* Assembly, *Decision on the Establishment of the Pan-African University*, AU Doc. Assembly/AU/Dec. 290 (XV) (25 Jul. 2010). *See further*, Assembly, *Decision on the Establishment of the Pan-African University*, AU Doc. Assembly/AU/Dec. 391(XVIII) (30 Jan. 2012); Assembly, *Decision on the Establishment of the Pan-African University*, AU Doc. Assembly/AU/Dec. 418 (XIX) (16 Jul. 2012).

humanities, and social sciences; and Algeria, on water and energy sciences as well as on climate change. PAU Statutes were adopted at the Twentieth Ordinary Assembly Session (January 2013),[309] were amended in May 2013[310] and revised in January 2016 to ensure that the Council, the highest governing PAU organ, becomes more inclusive and representative of a wider spectrum of stakeholders.[311] The Fifteenth Assembly Session also adopted the Revised African Maritime Transport Charter, which at the time of writing had attracted twelve out of the fifteen ratifications required to enter into force.[312] Even though the Revised Charter aims at updating the aforementioned Charter adopted in 1994, Member States have continued to become signatory parties to the latter. Thus, Angola signed it in January 2012, Liberia in May 2011 and Equatorial Guinea in January 2011, posing the question if there is an explanation why Member States sign outdated OAU treaties. For example, Angola signed on the same day (27 January 2012) both the 1994 Charter and the 2010 Revised Charter but has ratified only the latter (August 2020). One explanation might have to do with the AU's consistent attempts to persuade Member States to sign and ratify as many OAU/AU treaties as possible, so that they come into force as early as possible, while they continue to become contracting parties to those already in force. And perhaps, in their haste, Member States sign and/or ratify the older treaties that are meant to be replaced by newer ones. Notwithstanding this rather strange situation, it will be argued that these treaties, taken as a whole, have created a body of continental legal rules which are meant to be followed universally in the continent, a process akin to the EU notion of *acquis communautaire*.[313] As has been argued, these treaties contain rules, norms and procedures with Africa-wide application. All in all, they form part of what could be called 'AU law', in other words, a distinct international legal system that has been created, developed and applied by the OAU/AU, acting through their organs, by Member States, and, to a certain extent, by RECs and other regional entities.[314] This is a legal development with obvious policy implications in most areas of AU activities, including trade and economic cooperation, peace and security, good governance, etc. But the AU itself and the Member States should acknowledge it and be willing to undertake the necessary changes in the way it operates and is structured. It is also a factor that the external partners (international organizations and individual states) should take

---

309. *See* Assembly, *Decision on the Pan-Africa University Statutes*, AU Doc. Assembly/AU/Dec. 451(XX) (28 Jan. 2013).
310. *See* Assembly, *Decision on the Amendment of Article 8.2 of the Statutes of the Pan-African University*, AU Doc. Assembly/AU/Dec. 481 (XXI) (27 May 2013).
311. *See* Assembly, *Decision on the Specialized Technical Committees*, AU Doc. Assembly/AU/Dec. 589 (XXVI), para. 2(xx) (31 Jan. 2016). Text at: https://au.int/en/treaties/revised-statute-pan-african-university-pau.
312. *See* Assembly, *Decision on the Adoption of the African Maritime Transport Charter*, AU Doc. Assembly/AU/Dec. 293 (XV) (25 Jul. 2010).
313. It is a body of common rights and obligations binding upon all the EU Member States, constantly evolving and comprising principally the founding Treaties, the EU secondary legislation (directives and regulations); the judgments of the Court of Justice of the EU; and the agreements and treaties entered into by the EU with third states and other international organizations.
314. *See* K. Magliveras, 'The Implications of African Union Law: Conceptual Analysis with Emphasis on the Institutional Consequences' in F. Amao, M. Olivier & K. Magliveras (eds), *The Emergent African Union Law: Conceptualization, Delimitation, and Application* (Oxford: Oxford University Press, 2021) 30.

into account when transacting with the AU. It is submitted that the existence of an AU (separate) legal system should be acknowledged by revising the Constitutive Act. Indeed, a new constitutive instrument might be required to regulate the AU and take cognizance of its considerable evolution. To out it otherwise, the AU is no longer just the successor to the OAU/AEC but is a continental organization with clear and unambiguous purposes and principles that aims at making Africa an economically integrated area with a collective security system, an area of human rights, democratic ideals, rule of law, and good governance, an area of education, science and technology, and so on. Moreover, the name should probably be changed from 'African Union' to 'Pan African Community' because for a transnational legal entity to be a 'union of states' (as arguably the European Union is), it must first accomplish the stage of becoming a 'community of states' (as arguably the European Economic Community was before it was transformed to the EU). Presently, the AU has not achieved the stage of 'Community', this being the goal of Agenda 2063. But on the road to becoming a 'community of states', the role and impact of the AU legal order will be instrumental, while Member States will have to strictly adhere to the commitments, duties and obligations laid down in AU law.

Moreover, the Fifteenth Assembly Session examined the commitment to gradually transform the AUC into a new organ, the Authority, in an attempt to strengthen the Organization's institutional architecture and to accelerate the integration process. However, no concrete action was taken other than to request the AUC to prepare and submit the necessary legal instruments.[315] Although the matter was to be discussed at the Nineteenth Assembly Session in July 2012, it was presumably not deemed ripe enough for deliberation. Finally, it was discussed during the Twentieth Ordinary Assembly Session in January 2013, which asked the AUC 'to first make appropriate recommendations' on its own strengthening.[316] As later explained, in July 2016, the Assembly entrusted Paul Kagame, the President of Rwanda, to conduct, in collaboration with the Commission, a study on the AU's institutional reform and on a 'system of governance' capable of addressing the challenges facing it.[317] Kagame, who presented his Report 'The Imperative to Strengthen Our Union' in January 2017, continues until now to lead the efforts for the AU's institutional reform.

During the Fifteenth Ordinary Session, the Assembly also resolved to establish and operationalize the African Petroleum Fund.[318] The idea behind it can be traced to the Seventh Ordinary Assembly Session, which had recognized the need to alleviate the impact of the oil prices' increase on poor Member States and had asked

---

315. *See* Assembly, *Decision on the Transformation of the African Union Commission into the African Union Authority*, AU Doc. Assembly/AU/Dec. 298 (XV) (25 Jul. 2010).
316. Assembly, *Decision on the Transformation of the African Union Commission into the African Union Authority*, AU Doc. Assembly/AU/Dec. 454 (XX) (28 Jan. 2013), para. 6.
317. Assembly, *Decision on the Institutional Reform of the African Union*, AU Doc. Assembly/AU/Dec. 606 (XXVII) (18 Jul. 2016).
318. *See* Assembly, *Decision on the Establishment and Operationalisation of the African Petroleum Fund*, AU Doc. Assembly/AU/Dec. 307 (XV) (25 Jul. 2010). *See also* Executive Council, *Decision on the Report of the Second African Union Conference of Ministers Responsible for Hydrocarbons (Oil & Gas)*, AU Doc. EX.CL/Dec. 546 (XVI) (29 Jan. 2010).

for the development of a strategy for cooperation and solidarity between oil-producing and non-oil producing African countries.[319] Moreover, the Cairo Declaration on African Cooperation and Solidarity in the Field of Hydrocarbons, which was adopted on 14 December 2006, promoted the idea further.[320] The Fund was set up by the African Development Bank, which has also hosted and operated it. Apparently, it has been unable to support non-oil-exporting African countries because of a lack of contributions (contributions were voluntary).[321] Presently, it does not appear to be operative. A proposal to levy a tax on hydrocarbons exported by Member States to secure resources for the Fund had been proposed but summarily rejected. Reference should also be made to the African Petroleum Producers Association (APPA), which was established in January 1987 by African oil-producing countries.[322] In March 2017, it was renamed the African Petroleum Producers' Organization (APPO). Even though at present APPO has fifteen Member States (almost one-fourth of the AU membership) and has created a financing arm to secure the necessary capital for investments in the continent's oil and gas sector (the Africa Energy Investment Corporation (AEICorp)), there has been no known collaboration with the African Petroleum Fund.[323]

Finally, the Fifteenth Ordinary Assembly Session discussed the status of implementation of decisions and resolutions which were adopted by it and by the Executive Council in previous sessions. Although decisions constitute a legal foundation for the integration process in the continent and constitute a component of the aforementioned AU legal system, in other words, they are part of AU law, arguably there has never been an effective mechanism to supervise prompt and diligent execution. As will be explained later on, pursuant to Article 23(2) of the Constitutive Act, decisions are binding and sanctions may be ordered by the Assembly against recalcitrant Member States. For several years, the AUC had prepared 'Reports on the Implementation of Previous Decisions of the Executive Council and the Assembly', which were submitted to the Assembly for deliberation. In that Session, it was requested that the format of the Reports be improved.[324] The new Report that the AUC submitted to the Executive Council in January 2011 confirmed that decisions are inadequately implemented and that there is a tendency to consistently

---

319. *See* Assembly, *Decision on the Proposal to Establish a Fund within the African Union to Alleviate the Increase in Oil Price on the Poor African Countries and the Coordination of African Oil Policies*, AU Doc. Assembly/AU/Dec. 132 (VII) (14 Dec. 2006). Generally, *see* African Development Bank & African Union, *Oil and Gas in Africa* (Oxford: Oxford University Press, 2009).
320. AU Doc. AU/MIN/OG/Decl. (I) (2006).
321. *See* 'Oil fund for Africa has no money', *Ghana Business News*, 26 Mar. 2012, at: https://www.ghanabusinessnews.com/2012/03/26/oil-fund-for-africa-has-no-money.
322. For the text of the Agreement establishing APPA, *see* 26 I.L.M. 1493 (1987).
323. Note that in 2022 the African Export-Import Bank (Afreximbank) and APPO signed an agreement for the joint establishment of an African Energy Bank, which will serve as an African-led solution to the problems encountered by the withdrawal of international banks from financing oil and gas projects in the continent, *see* 'APPO commences African Energy Bank in Angola', *Oil Review Africa*, 19 May 2022, at: https://www.oilreviewafrica.com/exploration/industry/appo-commences-african-energy-bank-in-angola.
324. *See* Assembly, *Decision on the Implementation of the Previous Decisions of the Executive Council and the Assembly*, AU Doc. Assembly/AU/Dec. 318 (XV) (25 Jul. 2010). For the text of the Report, *see* https://archives.au.int/handle/123456789/3875.

defer their execution.[325] These Reports continue to be prepared. Thus, in October 2021, the AUC submitted the Report on the process of implementation of the fifty-eight decisions approved in February and October 2020 by the AU's principal policy organs, of which twenty-three were adopted by the Executive Council and thirty-five by the Assembly.[326] Finally, in February 2022, the AUC submitted a Report on the execution of decisions which had been taken during the previous ten-year period (2011–2021).[327]

46. During its Sixteenth Ordinary Session (Addis Ababa, 30–31 January 2011), the Assembly adopted the African Charter on the Values and Principles of Public Service and Administration, a multilateral instrument promoting the AU agenda on good governance.[328] The Charter, which entered into force on 23 July 2016 (currently signed by thirty-eight and ratified by twenty Member States), aims at improving the way Member States deliver public services and at combating corruption, the latter being one of the scourges plaguing Africa.[329] The operationalization of the African Security and Peace Architecture (ASPA) was also discussed during the same Session. ASPA was established by the AU in collaboration with RECs with terms of reference to the prevention, management, and resolution of conflicts in the continent. The EU has contributed significantly to its funding through the Capacity Building Component of the African Peace Facility (APF). The latter was established in December 2003, when the EU responded to an African request for support to its peace and security agenda. The request was justified on the premise that peace is a necessary precondition for sustainable development in the continent.[330] Until July 2021, when APF was replaced by the European Peace Facility (EPF),[331] the EU had contributed more than EUR 3.6 billion towards financing sixteen African-led peace support missions in nineteen states.[332] However, as a funding tool, EPF is not directed solely towards Africa but allows the financing of all EU Common Foreign

325. AU Doc. EX.CL/623 (XVIII) (28 Jan. 2011), at: https://www.peaceau.org/uploads/ex-cl-623-xviii-e.pdf.
326. *See Report on the Implementation of the African Union Previous Decisions of the Executive Council and the Assembly – February and October 2020 Decisions*, AU Doc. EX.CL/1284 (XXXIX) Rev.1 (1 Oct. 2021), at: https://archives.au.int/handle/123456789/10330.
327. *See Progress Report on the Status of Implementation of Previous Decisions of the Executive Council and Assembly (2011–2021)*, AU Doc. EX.CL/1321 (XL) Rev.1 (3 Feb. 2022), at: https://archives.au.int/handle/123456789/10401.
328. *See* Assembly, *Decision on the African Charter on the Values and Principles of Public Service and Administration*, AU Doc. Assembly/AU/Dec. 337 (XVI) (31 Jan. 2011).
329. *See* P. Mudau, 'The role of the African Charter on Values and Principles of Public Service and Administration in promoting good governance', 26 *Law, Democracy & Development* (2022): 148.
330. For details, *see* European Commission, *African Peace Facility, Annual Report 2015* (Luxembourg: Publications Office of the European Union, 2016), 18–21, at: https://reliefweb.int/report/somalia/african-peace-facility-annual-report-2015. *See further*, Memorandum of Understanding between the African Union and the European Union on Peace, Security and Governance signed in May 2018.
331. European Union, Council Decision (CFSP) 2021/509 of 22 March 2021 establishing a European Peace Facility, and repealing Decision (CFSP) 2015/528, ST/5212/2021/INIT, O.J. L 102, 24.3.2021, 14. The Decision came into force on the same day. Note that EU Member States are entitled not to contribute to the financing of military operations or assistance measures under EPF.
332. *See*, *inter alia*, European Commission, *African Peace Facility, Annual Report 2019* (Luxembourg: Publications Office of the European Union, 2020).

and Security Policy (CFSP) external action that has military and defence implications (e.g., action in support of Ukraine following the Russian Federation's 'special military operation' against it in 2022).[333] The AU has been criticized for not presenting a common position on this matter during the aforementioned Sixth EU-AU Summit (Brussels, February 2022).[334] However, the lack of an AU common position might also reveal how differently EU assistance towards Africa is viewed by individual AU Member States. The Sixteenth Assembly also noted the successful conduct of the Amani Africa Exercise in November 2010, whose purpose was to assess the procedures relating to the deployment of the African Standby Force (ASF) and the AUC's capacity to undertake complex peace support operations.[335]

The continued reliance on external partners (whether multilateral or bilateral) does raise the legitimate question of whether ASPA could ever be financed solely by African resources and what are the consequences of its over-dependence on their goodwill. Complex AU projects, like ASPA, face multiple challenges. Thus, they must address ongoing conflicts effectively, invariably necessitating the use of force; they must also deal with security and peace threats as they develop, while reconciliation, stabilization, and reconstruction processes need to be undertaken. Given that, on the whole, the UN (principally the UNSC) is not willing to contribute to these efforts and with the scarcity of AU and RECs financial resources, the dependence on funding from outside the continent has continued unabated. Moreover, relevant initiatives taken by individual AU Member States may often lead to unnecessary complications. For example, during its Sixteenth Ordinary Session, the Assembly welcomed Egypt's proposal to establish the AU Centre for Post-Conflict Reconstruction and Development (PCRD),[336] which related to the aforementioned AU Framework for Post-Conflict Reconstruction and Development adopted in 2006. However, subsequently, Uganda also offered to host the Centre, and the two countries were not able to find an amicable solution.[337] Finally, the PCRD Centre was officially launched in Cairo on 21 December 2021. The Centre serves as the AU specialized technical agency for the implementation, monitoring and evaluation of post-conflict reconstruction and development programmes and projects in countries emerging from political and other struggles. In late 2021 and in early 2022, respectively, the PSC[338] and the Assembly[339] asked for the 'retooling' of the 2006 Framework.

333. Generally, *see* B. Immenkamp, *European Peace Facility: Investing in international stability and security*, European Parliamentary Research Service, Members' Research Service, PE 690.641, October 2021.

334. *See* S. Woldemichael, 'Africa should be better prepared for Europe's security funding shift', *ISS Today*, 12 April 2022, at: https://issafrica.org/iss-today/africa-should-be-better-prepared-for-europes-security-funding-shift.

335. *See* Assembly, *Decision on the Report of the Peace and Security Council on its activities and the state of Peace and Security in Africa*, AU Doc. Assembly/AU/Doc. 338 (XVI), para. 3 (31 Jan. 2011).

336. *See* Assembly, *Decision on the Establishment of an African Union Centre for Post-Conflict Reconstruction and Development (AUCPCRD)*, AU Doc. Assembly/AU/Dec. 351 (XVI) (31 Jan. 2011).

337. *See* PSC, *First Progress Report of the Chairperson of the Commission on AU's Efforts on Post-Conflict Reconstruction and Development*, AU Doc. PSC/PR/2/CCCLII, paras 17 et seq. (16 Jan. 2003), at: http://www.peaceau.org.

338. PSC, *Communique of the 1047th meeting of the AU Peace and Security Council held on 12 November 2021, on Post Conflict Reconstruction and Development (PCRD) in Africa*, AU Doc. PSC/COMM/1047 (12 Nov. 2021).

According to Article 3(i) of the Constitutive Act, one of the AU's principal objectives is to establish the necessary conditions enabling Africa to play its rightful role in the global economy and in international negotiations. To fulfil this objective, the AU has not only promoted bilateral relations with other international organizations but has also attempted to advance the idea of a 'united African voice' during conferences organized at a transnational level. Thus, during its Sixteenth Session, the Assembly endorsed the outcome of the Second Africa-Arab Summit, which was held on 10 October 2010.[340] It also welcomed the Declaration and Second Action Plan 2011–2013 agreed during the Third Africa-EU Summit (Libya, November 2010).[341] It is no coincidence that both these important events took place in Libya. Indeed, it was Colonel Gaddafi who had played an instrumental role in promoting the AU's foreign agenda. However, with his demise in the summer of 2011 and the country descending into chaos, Libya has been unable to play the pivotal role it used to. Until today, there has not been an African leader who can demonstrate that he is capable of continuing and promoting the AU's foreign affairs agenda, especially when the world stage continues to be very volatile. Finally, the Assembly endorsed the African Common Position on Climate Change and the African Green Development Fund, which were tabled during the Seventh Conference of Parties to the Kyoto Protocol that met in Durban, South Africa, in December 2011.[342]

The standoff between the AU and the ICC, which, as has been explained, concerned principally the arrest warrant issued against President Al Bashir, continued with the arrest warrants issued in June 2011 against the then leader of Libya Colonel Gadaffi, his son Saif Al-Islam, and his brother in law Abdullah Al-Senussi.[343] They were the culmination of the investigation carried out by the ICC Prosecutor pursuant to UNSC Resolution 1970(2011) of February 2011, which had referred, under Article 13(b) of the Rome Statute, the alleged crimes committed during the popular uprising against the Gadaffi regime to the ICC.[344] As in the case of Al Bashir, the Assembly during its Seventeenth Ordinary Session (Malabo, Equatorial Guinea, 30 June–1 July 2011) considered that these Warrants of Arrest complicated seriously the efforts to find a negotiated political solution to the Libyan crisis and, therefore, decided that Member States shall not cooperate in their execution. Moreover, it requested that the UNSC invoke Article 16 of the Rome Statute and defer

339. Assembly, *Decision on the Report on the Activities of the Peace and Security Council (PSC) and the State of Peace and Security in Africa*, AU Doc. Assembly/AU/Dec. 815 (XXXV), para. 36 (6 Feb. 2022).
340. *See* Assembly, *Decision on Africa-Arab Cooperation*, OAU Doc. Assembly/AU/Dec. 343 (XVI) (31 Jan. 2011).
341. *See* Assembly, *Decision on the Africa-European Union Dialogue*, OAU Doc. Assembly/AU/Dec. 344 (XVI) (31 Jan. 2011).
342. *See* Assembly, *Decision on the Sixteenth Conference of Parties to the United Nations Framework Convention on Climate Change and the Sixth Conference of Parties to the Kyoto Protocol*, OAU Doc. Assembly/AU/Dec. 342 (XVI) (31 Jan. 2011).
343. *See* ICC, *Prosecutor v. Muammar Mohammed Abu Minyar Gaddafi, Saif Al-Islam Gaddafi and Abdullah Al-Senussi*, Warrants of Arrest, ICC-01/11-01/11, P.-T. Ch. I, 27 June 2011, at: https://www.icc-cpi.int/court-record/icc-01/11-01/11-2.
344. Reproduced in I.L.M. 50 (2011): 287.

the ICC proceedings 'in the interest of Justice as well as peace in the Country'.[345] In another resolution, the Assembly, without offering compelling legal reasoning, repeated its request that the UNSC defer its involvement to the African initiative, which was 'the best way of achieving ... peace, democracy, the rule of law and national reconciliation in Libya'.[346] Moreover, it considered that the AU's role in the Libyan situation had been recognized under UNSC Resolution 1970(2011) and was fully consistent with Chapter VIII of the UN Charter concerning regional arrangements for the maintenance of peace and security.

The Assembly's position was prima facie in line with Chapter VIII, Article 53(1), of the UN Charter. However, the structure of Chapter VIII denotes that, once seized of a situation, UNSC retains full authority over the measures to be taken to resolve it. Arguably, these measures are not only those envisaged in the UN Charter but also those to be found in other relevant multilateral instruments (in casu, the Rome Statute) and expressly granting powers to the UNSC. Thus, if any relevant action (including enforcement action) were to be pursued by a regional arrangement (in casu, the AU), this presumably can only be undertaken in the context of (express) UNSC authorization. In these circumstances, the regional arrangement (the AU) should be understood as acting as a UNSC agent (the theory of delegated powers might find application here). It was rather clear that in the Libyan situation, the UNSC was not prepared to grant any such powers to the AU: it retained all powers and devolved none. On its part, the AU could have perhaps invoked Article 4(h) of the Constitutive Act to justify its intervention in Libya. As explained *infra*, Article 4(h) gives the AU the right to intervene in a Member State pursuant to an Assembly decision when there are grave circumstances (including war crimes) in a Member State's territory. This would have tested not only the unchartered waters of applying Article 4(g) but also its consistency with the UN Charter's provisions on non-interference in the domestic affairs of states and with the so-called Responsibility to Protect (R2P) while creating precedence for handling future situations.[347] However, the ferocity with which the 'Arab Spring' spread to North Africa showed that the AU was rather incapable of formulating a prompt and coherent response, while the Assembly has probably not used its authority and powers in accordance with the Constitutive Act.

During its Seventeenth Session, the Assembly deliberated the regular Report that is submitted by the PSC on its activities.[348] It reiterated the need for greater and better coordinated efforts to promote sustainable peace, security, and stability on the

345. *See* Assembly, *Decision on the Implementation of the Assembly Decisions on the International Criminal Court*, AU Doc. Assembly/AU/Dec. 366 (XVII) (1 Jul. 2011). In subsequent Sessions, the Assembly reiterated its call on the UNSC to defer ICC proceedings as regards Al Bashir but also as regards proceedings in the Kenyan situation, *see*, *inter alia*, Assembly, *Decision on the Implementation of the Decisions on the International Criminal Court (ICC)*, AU Doc. Assembly/AU/Dec. 419 (XIX) (16 Jul. 2012).

346. *See* Assembly, *Decision on the Situation in Libya*, AU Doc. Assembly/AU/Dec. 385 (XVII) (1 Jul. 2011).

347. Compare L. Boisson de Chazournes, *Interactions Between Regional and Universal Organizations: A Legal Perspective* (Leiden/Boston: Brill Nijhoff, 2017), 188 et seq.

348. AU Doc. Assembly/AU/4 (XVII) (2011).

continent 'based on Africa's ownership and leadership'.[349] The reference to 'Africa's ownership' is closely connected to the principle of 'African solutions to African problems,' namely, that the AU, as the pan-African political institution, ought to resolve those issues that are of central importance to the continent through its own actions and means. However, noble as this aim might be, it is clear that the AU has proven time and time again unwilling and unable to tackle the scourges plaguing it and has had to resort to the assistance of its international 'partners', including the UN and the EU.

Furthermore, the Seventeenth Session dealt with a pressing social problem which, although not restricted to Africa, is widely practised in several African countries: female genital mutilation (FGM). FGM has been condemned and prohibited in all its forms in Article 5 of the Protocol on the Rights of Women in Africa attached to the African Charter on Human and Peoples' Rights (2003). It obliges contracting parties (currently ratified by forty-four Member States) to adopt pertinent legislative measures to be enforced by criminal sanctions. The Assembly supported the proposal tabled by Burkina Faso before the UNGA Sixty-Sixth Ordinary Session to ban FGM worldwide by harmonizing Member States' actions and by strengthening regional and international legal instruments.[350] On 20 December 2012, the UNGA adopted, without a vote, Resolution 67/146 on 'Intensifying global efforts for the elimination of female genital mutilations.' Recognizing that FGM is an irreparable and irreversible abuse of the human rights of women and girls as well as a threat to their health, it urged UN Member States to condemn all harmful practices, to take all required measures protecting women and girls from this form of violence, to end impunity and to continue observing the 6th of February as the International Day of Zero Tolerance to Female Genital Mutilation. Decisions on eliminating FGM are constantly taken by the Assembly[351] and by the UNGA,[352] while the UN Secretary-General regularly submits reports on the progress made by Member States.[353]

During the Seventeenth Session, the Assembly also adopted a resolution concerning a long-standing feud between two non-African states. In particular, it called

349. *See* Assembly, *Decision on the Report of the Peace and Security Council on its Activities and the State of Peace and Security in Africa*, AU Doc. Assembly/AU/Dec. 369 (XVII), para. 3 (1 Jul. 2011).

350. *See* Assembly, *Decision on the Support of a Draft Resolution at the Sixty-Sixth Ordinary Session of the General Assembly of the United Nations to Ban Female Genital Mutilation in the World*, AU Doc. Assembly/AU/Dec. 383 (XVII) (1 Jul. 2011). Generally, *see* R. Skaine, *Female Genital Mutilation: Legal, Cultural and Medical Issues* (McFarland & Company, 2005); and A. Rahman & N. Toubia (eds), *Female Genital Mutilation: A Guide to Laws and Policies Worldwide* (London and New York: Zed Books, 2000).

351. *See*, Assembly, *Decision on Galvanizing Political Commitment Towards the Elimination of Female Genital Mutilation in Africa*, AU Doc. Assembly/AU/Dec. 737 (XXXII) (21 Feb. 2019); Assembly, *Decision on Ending Female Genital Mutilation*, AU Doc. Assembly/AU/Dec. 773 (XXXIII) (10 Feb. 2020).

352. *See* UNGA Res. 75/160 (16 Dec. 2020) with references to previous Resolutions.

353. *See*, *inter alia*, UNGA, *Intensifying global efforts for the elimination of female genital mutilation – Report of the Secretary-General*, UN Doc. A/77/312 (25 Jul. 2022). For a recent UN document addressing FGM in Mauritania, *see* UN Working Group on discrimination against women and girls, *Gender equality in Mauritania: commendable steps forward and major deadlocks*, 6 Oct. 2023, at: https://www.ohchr.org/sites/default/files/documents/issues/women/wg/EoM-visit-Mauritania-2023 1006-EN.pdf.

upon the USA to lift its 'unjustifiable' economic and trade sanctions against Cuba which had been imposed in the 1960s.[354] Similar resolutions were adopted, *inter alia*, during the Twenty-First Ordinary Session in May 2013[355] and the Twenty-Sixth Ordinary Session in January 2016.[356] As is later explained, the Assembly has continued adopting them to the present day.[357] Even though resolutions to that effect have also been issued by the UNGA on a yearly basis since 1992 (they are invariably titled 'Necessity of ending the economic, commercial and financial embargo imposed by the United States of America against Cuba'),[358] there is a fundamental difference between the action taken at AU level and the action taken at UN level because the USA and Cuba participate in the UN and, therefore, its Member States may legitimately take sides in a situation concerning fellow Members. On the contrary, the Assembly takes sides in a matter that does not concern its own Members. Finally, Namibia, supported by other Member States, proposed to the Seventeenth Session a 'Decision on AU Decision-Making Process, Lack of Implementation of Decisions, and the Need to Uphold and Respect the Integrity of Summit Decisions by All Member States of the Union'. In rather blunt language, it warned that '... no Member State that harbours good will for the future of the African Union can afford to remain indifferent in the face of blatant attempts to destabilize the normal functioning of our organization'.[359] The Assembly took note of it and resolved to defer consideration to the January 2012 session,[360] but it was not placed on the agenda, presumably because Member States wanted to avoid discussing the critical matters that Namibia and others had raised. On 27 July 2011, South Sudan acceded to the AU and became the fifty-fourth Member State; on 14 July 2011, it acceded to the UN as its 193rd Member State.

47. In the process of transforming OAU into AU, the future of the AEC was arguably not properly addressed, while the various deadlines mentioned in the AEC

---

354. *See* Assembly, *Resolution on the Lifting of the Economic and Trade Embargo Imposed on the Republic of Cuba by the United States of America*, AU Doc. Assembly/AU/Res. 1 (XVII) (1 Jul. 2011).

355. *See*, respectively, Assembly, *Resolution on the Lifting of the Economic and Trade Embargo imposed on the Republic of Cuba by the United States of America*, AU Doc. Assembly/AU/Res. 1 (XV) (27 Jul. 2010); and Assembly, *Resolution on the Lifting of the Economic and Trade Embargo imposed on the Republic of Cuba by the United States of America*, AU Doc. Assembly/AU/Res. 1 (XXI) (27 May 2013).

356. *See* Assembly, *Resolution on Recent Developments in the Cuba-United States of America Relations*, AU Doc. Assembly/AU/Res. 1 (XXVI) (31 Jan. 2016). A Declaration asking the USA to terminate its unilateral sanctions against Sudan was also adopted, *see* Assembly/AU/Decl. 2 (XXVI) (31 Jan. 2016). As mentioned above, on 13 January 2017 President Obama had signed an Executive Order easing sanctions imposed on Sudan.

357. *See* Assembly, *Resolution on the Lifting of the Economic, Commercial and Financial Blockade Imposed on the Republic of Cuba by the United States of America*, AU Doc. Assembly/AU/Res. 2 (XXXV) (6 Feb. 2022), which considered that the blockade was the main obstacle for Cuba to implement the UN 2030 Agenda for Sustainable Development.

358. *See*, *inter alia*, UNGA Res. 77/73, 3 Nov. 2022; Res. 75/289, 23 Jun. 2021; Res. 71/5, 26 Oct. 2016; Res. 70/5, 27 Oct. 2015; Res. 69/5, 18 Oct. 2014; Res. 68/8, 29 Oct. 2013; Res. 67/4, 13 Nov. 2012; and Res. 66/6, 25 Oct. 2011, all at: https://research.un.org/en/docs/ga/resolutions.

359. AU Doc. Assembly/AU/12 (XVII) Add.1 (2011), at: https://archives.au.int/handle/123456789/5475.

360. *See* Assembly/AU/Dec. 379 (XVII) (1 Jul. 2011).

Treaty to materialize the continent's economic integration project were never met. The overall negative socioeconomic situation in Africa, the fragile state institutions and the constant instability in the peace and security sector have been inhibiting factors for close economic cooperation. The Fifth AU Conference of Ministers in Charge of Integration (COMAI V), held in Nairobi in September 2011 gave the Eighteenth Ordinary Assembly Session (Addis Ababa, 29 January–30 January 2012) the opportunity to discuss developments. The Assembly adopted the first Plan of Action of the Minimum Integration Programme[361] and asked Member States to speed up the integration process and to initiate actions to promote, *inter alia*, the free movement of persons, of goods, of services, and of capital, the four cornerstones of any economic integration project. Given that all African RECs have the goal of advancing close economic cooperation among their respective Member States, the Assembly recommended that, to accelerate the establishment of the AEC, they be grouped together around two poles of integration. The first pole would comprise Common Market for Eastern and Southern Africa (COMESA), SADC, and the EAC, while the second pole, ECOWAS, the Economic Community of Central African States (ECCAS), CFN-SAD, and the AMU.[362] The plan was apparently never implemented. Moreover, the Assembly deliberated the report submitted by the AUC on the Seventh Ordinary Session of the Conference of Ministers of Trade, held in Accra, Ghana, on 29 November–3 December 2011[363] and endorsed the Framework, Road Map and Architecture for Fast Tracking the establishment of the CFTA and the Action Plan for Boosting Intra-African Trade.[364] The Assembly set the target date for achieving CFTA in 2017 but did not connect it to the revitalization of the AEC,[365] a fact indicating that integration in the context of the AEC was effectively abandoned. In July 2016, the Assembly resolved to establish a High-Level Panel of five eminent persons (one from each African region) 'to champion the fast tracking of the CFTA' and asked the AUC to present feasible options to eliminate non-trade barriers among African countries to foster their trade.[366] A Report was submitted for evaluation by the Twenty-Eighth Ordinary Assembly Session in January 2017,[367] which mandated Mahamadou Issoufou, President of Niger, to 'champion the process of the CFTA to ensure that the deadline of the end of 2017 is reached'.[368] In

361. AU Doc. EX/CL/693 (XX) (2012).
362. *See* Assembly, *Decision on African Integration*, AU Doc. Assembly/AU/Dec. 392 (XVIII) (30 Jan. 2012).
363. AU Doc. AU/MIN/TD//Rpt(VII) (2011).
364. AU Doc. EX.CL/700 (XX) (2012).
365. *See* Assembly, *Decision on Boosting Intra-African Trade and Fast Tracking the Continental Free Trade Area*, AU Doc. Assembly/AU/Dec. 394 (XVIII) (30 Jan. 2012). *See further*, Assembly, *Decision on Boosting Intra-African Trade and fast tracking the Continental Free Trade Area*, AU Doc. Assembly/AU/Dec. 426 (XIX) (16 Jul. 2012).
366. *See* Assembly, *Decision on the Continental Free Trade Area*, AU Doc. Assembly/AU/Dec. 608 (XXVII) (18 Jul. 2016).
367. *See Report on implementation of Assembly/AU/Dec.608(XXVII) on the Continental Free Trade Area and Update on the proposed mechanism for the elimination of non-tariff barriers (NTBs) in the Continental Free Trade Area (CFTA)*, AU Doc. Assembly/AU/4(XXVIII) (2017).
368. *See* Assembly, *Decision on the Continental Free Trade Area*, AU Doc. Assembly/AU/Dec. 623 (XXVIII), para. 4 (31 Jan. 2017).

the meantime, the pan-continental economic integration had become one of the stepping stones of Agenda 2063, which was approved in 2015.[369] As is later explained, in March 2018, the Agreement Establishing the African Continental Free Trade Area was adopted. Having entered into force in May 2019, presently, it has not been ratified primarily by Member States facing domestic strife and conflicts (e.g. Libya, Somalia, Sudan, South Sudan, and Eritrea). Notwithstanding this reality, it should be emphasized that the free trade area cannot be implemented at a continental level until and unless all African states have ratified and executed not only the 2018 Agreement but also all the other legal instruments that are necessary for its functioning.

African states have always been very supportive of the Palestinian claim to statehood, and during the OAU era, the African Committee on the Question of Palestine was set up. This should be attributed to the fact that, since Palestine had been waging a struggle to end Israeli occupation, African states associated themselves with a political entity fighting for its liberation from alien domination and also to the alliance between Israel and the regimes in power at the time in South Africa and in Rhodesia. The wording of a resolution adopted in 1977 by the OAU Assembly is characteristic: '...liberating Palestine … from Zionist racist colonialism … considering that the cause of Palestine is an African cause'.[370] During its Eighteenth Ordinary Session, the Assembly, noting that Palestine had on 31 October 2011 been accepted as a full Member State in UNESCO, reaffirmed its support for its efforts to obtain full membership in the UN family of organizations.[371] Moreover, in 2012, the African group in the UNGA was instrumental in securing that the status of Palestine was upgraded to that of non-Member observer state,[372] the same status that has been accorded to the Holy See. In 2016, the AU common position on the Palestinian issue was articulated. It supported the two-state solution, demanded the return of Palestinian refugees to their home and properties, and was in favour of the then-French initiative to hold an international peace conference for relaunching the negotiations to resolve the Palestine-Israeli conflict.[373] Until today, the question of Palestine has always been included in the Assembly agenda. At its Thirty-Fifth Ordinary Session (2022), the Assembly adopted a six-page Declaration, where, among others, it called upon Member States 'to end all forms of direct and indirect interaction and business with the Israeli colonial settlement regime and illegal apartheid in the territory of the State

---

369. Generally, *see* United Nations Conference on Trade and Development, *African Continental Free Trade Area: Advancing Pan-African Integration – Some Considerations*, UNCTAD/WEB/DITC/2016/5 (New York and Geneva: United Nations, November 2016), at: http://unctad.org/en/PublicationsLibrary/webditc2016d5_en.pdf.

370. *See* OAU Assembly, *Resolution on the Question of Palestine*, OAU Doc. AHG/Res. 77 (XII) (1 Aug. 1975).

371. *See* Assembly, *Decision on the Situation in Palestine and the Middle East*, AU Doc. Assembly/AU/Dec. 396 (XVIII) (30 Jan. 2012). *See further*, Assembly, *Decision on the Situation in Palestine and the Middle East*, AU Doc. Assembly/AU/Dec. 421 (XIX) (16 Jul. 2012).

372. UNGA Res. 67/19, *Status of Palestine in the United Nations*, 26 Nov. 2012. Presently, 138 states have accorded recognition to the State of Palestine, which on 23 Sep. 2011 applied for admission to full UN membership, *see* UN Doc. A/66/371 – S/2011/592 Annex I (2011). The application is pending.

373. *See* Assembly, *Declaration on the Situation in Palestine and the Middle East*, AU Doc. Assembly/AU/Decl. 2 (XXVII) (18 Jul. 2016).

of Palestine occupied in 1967 [and to give effect to AU decisions] based on the rich experience...that led to the boycott and dismantling of the apartheid regime in South Africa'.[374]

Furthermore, the Eighteenth Assembly Session deliberated again the AU-ICC antiparathesis. One of the problems that surfaced was that certain Member States and at the same time ICC parties (Malawi, Djibouti, Chad, and Kenya) had received Sudanese President Al Bashir in their territories in violation of the aforementioned Arrest Warrants. In December 2011, the ICC reacted by issuing two decisions, which, on the one hand, castigated, respectively, Malawi[375] and Chad[376] for not arresting Al Bashir even though they had the opportunity to do so and, on the other hand, held that their behaviour was in clear violation of their obligations under the Rome Statute.[377] The Assembly offered political cover to these Member States: it argued that receiving Al Bashir was justified because they were implementing its previous resolutions calling on the entire AU membership not to cooperate with the ICC as regards his arrest and surrender to The Hague. In effect, the Assembly argued that Member States' obligations flowing from its own resolutions somehow take precedence over obligations that they have freely assumed by becoming contracting parties to the Rome Statute.[378]

During the Nineteenth Ordinary Session (Addis Ababa, 15–16 July 2012), the Assembly proposed amendments to the structure of the ACJHR and the PAP. As far as the former organ is concerned, it proposed adding an International Criminal Law Section, a rather complex proposal because the ACJHR was not at the time operative due to the lack of the required fifteen ratifications for its founding instrument to enter into force.[379] The Assembly asked the AUC to prepare a study on the financial and structural implications resulting from the expansion of the ACJHR jurisdiction to cover the commission of international crimes as well.[380] As regards PAP, the Executive Council had approved during its Twenty-First Ordinary Session (Addis

---

374. *See* Assembly, *Declaration on the Situation in Palestine and the Middle East*, AU Doc. Assembly/AU/Decl. 1 (XXXV) (6 Feb. 2022), para. 7.
375. ICC, *Prosecutor v. Omar Hassan Ahmad Al Bashir*, *Decision Pursuant to Article 87(7) of the Rome Statute on the Failure of the Republic of Malawi to Comply with the Cooperation Requests Issued by the Court with respect to the Arrest and Surrender of Omar Hassan Ahmad Al Bashir*, Corrigendum, P.-T. Ch. I, ICC-02/05-01/09, 12 Dec. 2011, reproduced in I.L.M. 51 (2012): 393.
376. ICC, *Prosecutor v. Omar Hassan Ahmad Al Bashir*, *Decision Pursuant to Article 87(7) of the Rome Statute on the Failure of the Republic of Chad to Comply with the Cooperation Requests Issued by the Court with respect to the Arrest and Surrender of Omar Hassan Ahmad Al Bashir*, P.-T. Ch. I, ICC-02/05-01/09, 13 Dec. 2011.
377. For analysis of the ICC Decision on Malawi, *see* K. Magliveras & G. Naldi, 'The ICC Addresses Non-Cooperation by States Parties: The *Malawi* Decision', *African J of Legal Studies* 6 (2013): 137.
378. *See* Assembly, *Decision on the Progress Report of the Commission on the Implementation of the Assembly Decisions on the International Criminal Court (ICC)*, AU Doc. Assembly/AU/Dec. 397 (XVIII) (30 Jan. 2012).
379. *See* G. Naldi & K. Magliveras, 'African Union Debates Adding an International Criminal Law Section to Its Court', *International Enforcement Law Reporter* 28 (2012): 335.
380. *See* Assembly, *Decision on the Protocol on Amendments to the Protocol on the Statute of the African Court of Justice and Human Rights*, AU Doc. Assembly/AU/Dec. 427 (XIX) (16 Jul. 2012).

Ababa, 9–13 July 2012) the draft Protocol to the Constitutive Act of the AU relating to the PAP (it had been prepared by the Ministers of Justice),[381] with the exception of Article 8.1(a) and Article 8.2 thereof, which dealt with PAP's crucial powers to legislate and to supervise AU activities.[382] Endowing it with these powers would have turned the AU parliamentary organ into an institution somewhat resembling the European Parliament. However, the Assembly was not prepared to consent to such a significant augmentation of PAP's role. By resolving that more detailed consultations were required and that the discussion ought to be linked with the progress towards continental integration process, the Assembly deferred examination of the Draft Protocol.[383] As is later explained in the chapter on PAP, in June 2014, the Assembly finally approved its new Protocol, which, however, is nowhere near to entering into force.

During the same Session, the Assembly pressed for an intensification of efforts to promote its common position on UNSC reform and asked Member States to include it as a foreign policy priority.[384] As will be recalled, the African Common Position demands no less than two permanent seats with all the prerogatives and privileges of permanent membership (including the right of veto) and, additionally, five non-permanent seats. As explained by the representative of Mauritius, speaking on behalf of the African Group during the UNGA Sixty-Third Ordinary Session, the African common position sought to ensure that the continent was fully represented in all UN decision-making organs and especially in the UNSC. According to Mauritius, if and when the UNSC is enlarged, the AU should be solely responsible for selecting Africa's representatives and determining the criteria for selection.[385] The AU's overreliance on international partners became once more apparent in the budget for the financial year 2013. Based on the Executive Council proposals agreed at its Twenty-First Ordinary Session,[386] the Assembly adopted a budget totalling USD 278,226,622, of which less than half (USD 122,866,637) was to be assessed to Member States, while the remaining USD 155,359,986 was earmarked for various AU programmes to be funded solely by the international partners.[387]

Finally, the Nineteenth Assembly Session took the unusual step of adopting a Declaration concerning the internal situation of a specific Member State, namely Mali, where, in March 2012, army rebel groups had deposed the democratically

---

381. *See Report on the Meeting of Ministers of Justice/Attorneys General on the Review of the Protocol to the Constitutive Act of the African Union Relating to the Pan-African Parliament*, held in Addis Ababa on 14 and 15 May 2012, AU Doc. EX.CL/731 (XXI)b (2012).

382. *See* Executive Council, *Decision on the Protocol to the Constitutive Act of the African Union relating to the Pan-African Parliament*, AU Doc. EX.CL/Dec. 707 (XXI) (13 Jul. 2012).

383. *See* Assembly, *Decision on the Protocol to the Constitutive Act of the African Union relating to the Pan-African Parliament*, AU Doc. Assembly/AU/Dec. 428 (XIX) (16 Jul. 2012).

384. *See* Assembly, *Decision on the Report of the Committee of Ten on UN Reform*, AU Doc. Assembly/AU/Dec. 430 (XIX) (16 Jul. 2012).

385. *See* UNGA, Press Release GA/10786, 18 Nov. 2008.

386. *See* Executive Council, *Decision on the Budget of the African Union for the 2013 Financial Year*, AU Doc. EX.CL/Dec. 696 (XXI) (13 Jul. 2012).

387. *See* Assembly, *Decision on the Budget of the African Union for the 2013 Financial Year*, AU Doc. Assembly/AU/Dec. 438 (XIX) (16 Jul. 2012). On the overall role of 'international partners', *see* S.M. Makinda, F. Wafula Okumu & D. Mickler, *The African Union: Addressing the Challenges of Peace, Security and Governance* (2nd edn., London: Routledge, 2016), 136 et seq.

elected government of President Amadou Toumani Toure in a coup d'état causing considerable loss of life. The Assembly considered, *inter alia*, that the occupation of Mali's northern part by various armed, terrorist, and criminal groups posed a serious threat to the peace, security, and stability of the region and beyond.[388] The Assembly Declaration repeated verbatim the Communiqué that the PSC had issued on 14 July 2012 with regard to the situation in Mali.[389] The Assembly also condemned the unconstitutional regime change in Mali when it examined the regular PSC Activities Report.[390] What is noteworthy is that the PSC Communiqué had urged the UNSC and the UN Secretary-General to assist AU efforts in neutralizing the situation in Mali and that, in paragraph 12 thereof, it had expressed its determination to impose sanctions against those groups perpetuating the crisis in the country. It would appear that the envisaged sanctions were never imposed.[391] The question could be asked whether this had to do with the fact that on the previous day, 13 July 2012, the government of Mali had referred the situation in the country since January 2012 to the ICC Prosecutor, and had asked him to investigate, pursuant to Article 14 of the Rome Statute, any alleged crimes committed by armed groups. The ICC investigation, which was officially opened in January 2013, has so far led to one conviction and a Reparation Order.[392] Peaceful elections were held in Mali in July and August 2013[393] but, as of late, the situation in the country has again become chaotic due to the unconstitutional changes of government in August 2020 and in May 2021, despite the presence of a peacekeeping mission, the UN Multi-dimensional Integrated Stabilization Mission in Mali (MINUSMA). The Mission, which was set up on 25 April 2013 under UNSC Resolution 2100(2013) to stabilize the country after the 2012 coup d'etat, had its mandate augmented pursuant to Resolution 2164(2014) of 25 June 2014. Its operation had been extended to 30 June 2023

---

388. *See* Assembly, *Solemn Declaration on Mali*, AU Doc. Assembly/AU/Decl. 1 (XIX) (16 Jul. 2012).
389. *See* PSC, 327th Meeting at the Level of the Heads of State and Government, *Communiqué*, AU Doc. PSC/AHG/COMM/1 (CCCXXVII) (14 Jul. 2012). *See further*, PSC, *Report of the Chairperson of the Commission on the Evolution of the Situation in Mali*, AU Doc. PSC/AHG/3 (CCCXXVII) (2012).
390. *See* Assembly, *Decision on the Report of the Peace and Security Council on its Activities and the State of Peace and Security in Africa*, AU Doc. Assembly/AU/Dec. 432 (XIX), paras 4–6 (16 Jul. 2002). For the PSC Report, *see* AU Doc. Assembly/AU/6 (XIX) (2012).
391. Note that in April 2012 the PSC did order sanctions (taking the form of 'individual measures'), including a travel ban and assets freeze, against the Mali junta and against those natural persons and entities contributing to the maintenance of the unconstitutional *status quo* but only after sanctions had been ordered by ECOWAS, *see* AU Doc. PSC/PR/COMM(CCCXVI), paras 7–8 (3 Apr. 2012), at: http://www.peaceau.org/uploads/psc-comm-mali-03-04-2012.pdf. On 2 April 2012, ECOWAS had imposed a total embargo on Mali, closing all its borders, *see* 'Mali sanctions lifted as junta agrees to step aside', *France24*, 8 April 2012, at: https://www.france24.com.
392. *See* ICC, *The Prosecutor v. Ahmad Al Faqi Al Mahdi*, ICC-01/12-01/15-171, Decision of 27 Sep. 2016, at: https://www.icc-cpi.int/court-record/icc-01/12-01/15-171; on 8 March 2018, the Appeals Chamber delivered its judgment confirming mostly the Reparations Order, at: https://www.icc-cpi.int/court-record/icc-01/12-01/15-259-red2.
393. *See*, 'Mali election won by Ibrahim Boubacar Keïta', *The Guardian*, 13 Aug. 2013, at: http://www.theguardian.com/world/2013/aug/13/mali-election-ibrahim-boubacar-keita.

under UNSC Resolution 2640(2022) of 29 June 2022, but it was terminated under Resolution 2690 (2023) adopted on 30 June 2023.[394]

48. The theme of the Twentieth Ordinary Assembly Session (Addis Ababa, 27–28 January 2013) was 'Pan-Africanism and African Renaissance', reflecting that 2013 marked the fiftieth anniversary of the OAU establishment. Hailemariam Dessalegn, Prime Minister of Ethiopia, was elected as AU Chairperson for a one-year term. The Assembly decided to create the Pan-African Intellectual Property Organization (PAIPO).[395] Its Statute was approved in January 2016.[396] However, the fact that until now only seven Member States have signed it and only one (Tunisia) has ratified it raises the question of why African leaders adopted the PAIPO Statute even though they were evidently not prepared to sign and ratify it. The Assembly also requested that the AUCIL, which is examined later on, consider the establishment of an International Constitutional Court as proposed by Tunisia[397] and submit its observations and recommendations to the Twenty-Second Ordinary Session (January 2014).[398] The item, however, was not placed on that Session's agenda. The Twentieth Assembly also addressed several health issues affecting large parts of the continent as well as the implementation of the so-called Campaign on Accelerated Reduction of Maternal and Child Mortality in Africa (CARMMA), which has been described as an example of a successful continental initiative with national ownership. The campaign was officially launched during a Special Session of the AU Conference of Ministers of Health (CAMH4), held on the eve of Sixty-Third World Health Assembly in Geneva on 15 May 2010.[399] It would appear that CARMMA was terminated in 2020. The Assembly also endorsed Nigeria's offer to host in 2013 a follow-up summit meeting on the Abuja Summit on HIV/AIDS, held in 2001. The Summit, which took place on 12–16 July 2013, called for strong commitment of the

---

394. *See* K. Magliveras, 'The Situation in Mali: Recent Developments in the UNSC and their Consequences', *International Law Blog*, 11 Sep. 2023, at: https://internationallaw.blog/2023/09/11/the-situation-in-mali-recent-developments-in-the-unsc-and-their-consequences/.

395. *See* Assembly, *Decision on the Creation of the Pan-African Intellectual Property Organization (PAIPO)*, AU Doc. Assembly/AU/Dec. 453 (XX) (28 Jan. 2013). For the need to establish PAIPO, *see* Assembly, *Decision on the Establishment of the Pan-African Intellectual Property Organization*, AU Doc. Assembly/AU/Dec. 138 (VII)) (30 Jan. 2007). *See further*, Economic Commission for Africa, *African Union and African Development Bank Group, Assessing Regional Integration in Africa (ARIA VII): Innovation, Competitiveness and Regional Integration*, Addis Ababa, 2016.

396. *See* Assembly, *Decision on the Specialized Technical Committees*, AU Doc. Assembly/AU/Dec. 589 (XVI) (31 Jan. 2016). For analysis, *see* Y. Mupangavanhu 'African Union Rising to the Need for Continental IP Protection? The Establishment of the Pan-African Intellectual Property Organization' 59 *J.A.L.* (2015): 1; E.K. Oke, 'The Statute of the Pan-African Intellectual Property Organisation: A Human Rights Perspective' in O. Amao, M. Olivier & K.D. Magliveras (eds), *The Emergent African Union Law* (Oxford: OUP, 2021) 154.

397. *See* Assembly, *Establishment of an International Constitutional Court (Item proposed by the Republic of Tunisia)*, AU Doc. Assembly/AU/12 (XX) Add. 1 (2013), at: https://archives.au.int/handle/123456789/5491.

398. *See* Assembly, *Decision on the Establishment of an 'International Constitutional Court'*, AU Doc. Assembly/AU/Dec. 458 (XX) (28 Jan. 2013).

399. *See* Assembly, *Decision on the Reduction of Maternal, Newborn and Child Mortality and Morbidity in Africa*, AU Doc. Assembly/AU/Dec. 461 (XX) (28 Jan. 2013) and Assembly, *Actions on Maternal, Newborn and Child Health and Development in Africa By 2015*, AU Doc. Assembly/AU/Decl. 1 (XV) (25 Jul. 2010).

'Abuja Actions toward the elimination of HIV and AIDS, tuberculosis and malaria in Africa by 2030' and noted that access to medical services depended largely on the political will and commitment by Africa's top leadership.[400]

The Twentieth Ordinary Assembly Session also adopted a declaration of solidarity with Algeria regarding the terrorist attack in In Amenas, the country's third largest gas field operated by British Petroleum (BP), Norway's Statoil, and the national oil company Sonatrach, which took place on 16–20 January 2013. The events surrounding the incident were rather unclear, but the time proximity with the French military intervention in northern Mali on 11 January 2016 (*Opération Serval*) was suggestive of the attackers' identity.[401] What is noteworthy about the declaration is that the Assembly dealt with a rather isolated incident in which more non-Africans than Africans were killed, even though previous instances of considerable loss of life (e.g. post-electoral violence) had not attracted its attention. In July 2013, US prosecutors charged Mokhtar Belmokhtar, an alleged commander of Al-Qaeda's operations in North Africa, with, *inter alia*, kidnapping internationally protected persons during the In Amenas incident.[402] On another front, in mid-June 2013, the African Court on Human and Peoples' Rights issued its first judgment on merits ruling that Tanzania had breached the provisions of the Banjul Charter by not allowing its citizens to participate without impediments in government positions either directly or through representatives and regardless of party affiliation. The Court also ordered Tanzania to take any necessary constitutional, legislative, and administrative measures to remedy the violations.[403]

49. The second (Twenty-First) Ordinary Assembly Session for the year 2013 was held in Addis Ababa but not in the months of June or July as customary. It took place on 26 and 27 May 2013, exactly fifty years after the signing of the OAU

400. *See* Assembly, *Decision on the Hosting of A Special Follow-up Summit on the Abuja 2001 African Union Summit on HIV/AIDS, Tuberculosis and Other Related Infectious Diseases in the Third Quarter (July/August) of 2013*, AU Doc. Assembly/AU/Dec. 464 (XX) (28 Jan. 2013). *See further*, *African Health Strategy 2016 – 2030*, produced by the AUC Department of Social Affairs, at: https://au.int/sites/default/files/documents/24098-au_ahs_strategy_clean.pdf.

401. *See* Assembly, *Declaration of Solidarity with Algeria following the terrorist attack on Gazier site in Amenas*, AU Doc. Assembly/AU/Decl. 1 (XX) (28 Jan. 2013). Generally, *see* 'Le rescapes d'In Amenas', *Le nouvel Observateur*, 10 Apr. 2013, p. 12; *The In Amenas Attack. Report of the Investigation into the Terrorist Attack on In Amenas. Prepared for Statoil ASA's Board of Directors*, no date, at: https://www.equinor.com/news/archive/2013/09/12/12SepInAmenasreport; and N. Græger & W.Y. Lindgren, 'The Duty of Care for Citizens Abroad: Security and Responsibility in the In Amenas and Fukushima Crises', *The Hague Journal of Diplomacy* 13 (2018): 188–210.

402. *See* Federal Bureau of Investigation, *Charges Filed in Manhattan Federal Court Against Mokhtar Belmokhtar for His Role in Terror Attack in Algeria and Other Crimes*, 19 Jul. 2013, at: https://archives.fbi.gov/archives/newyork/press-releases/2013/charges-filed-in-manhattan-federal-court-against-mokhtar-belmokhtar-for-his-role-in-terror-attack-in-algeria-and-other-crimes. Belmokhtar was reportedly killed in a US airstrike in Libya in mid-June 2015, *see* http://edition.cnn.com/2015/06/14/world/mokhtar-belmokhtar/.

403. *See* African Court on Human and Peoples' Rights, *Tanganyika Law Society et al. v. The United Republic of Tanzania*, Application Nos 09/2011 and 11/2011, Judgment of 14 Jun. 2013, at: http://en.african-court.org/.

Treaty. The standoff between the AU and the ICC continued with the Assembly reaffirming that those Member States (e.g., Chad) which had welcomed Sudanese President Al Bashir did so in conformity with its decisions and, therefore, should not be penalized.[404] The Assembly also stressed the need for international justice to be conducted in a transparent and fair manner to avoid any perception of double standards and requested that the AUC, in collaboration with AUCIL, seek ways to strengthen African mechanisms to deal with African challenges and problems. The AU's very difficult financial situation was also discussed, and the Assembly accepted (with the reservation of Cape Verde) the Report on Alternative Sources of Financing the African Union prepared by a high-level panel chaired by former Nigerian President Olusegun Obasanjo.[405] The Assembly implemented one of the recommendations contained in the Report and established the African Union Foundation (it accepts voluntary contributions for financing the Organization) and called upon Member States, the private sector, donors, philanthropists, and individuals to ensure its operationalization.[406] It was launched in January 2015. Jamaica was the first non-Africa country that pledged USD 100,000 to 'underscore the commitment of the Diaspora towards African development'. The Foundation is connected to the African Economic Platform (AEP), which was formally launched at the Twenty-Seventh Ordinary Assembly Session. AEP comprises African heads of state, captains of industry and academics who discuss the continent's economic future and how to implement the Agenda 2063 priorities.

Finally, the Assembly adopted the Solemn Declaration on the fiftieth Anniversary of the OAU/AU (it appears as Appendix 3 to the present monograph). It concentrated on the following eight broad areas: (a) African Identity and Renaissance; (b) the struggle against colonialism and the right to self-determination of people still under colonial rule (the 'unlawful occupation' of the Chagos Archipelago and the Comorian Island of Mayotte as well as the right to self-determination of the people of Western Sahara were specifically mentioned); (c) political, social and economic integration; (d) social and economic development; (e) peace and security (a specific milestone was set to end all wars in Africa by 2020); (f) democratic governance; (g) Africa's destiny by taking ownership of continental issues and providing African solutions to African problems; and (h) promoting Africa's place in the world. Member States pledged to make the above ideals and goals more coherent in domestic development plans and to devise the so-called Continental Agenda 2063 by means of a people-driven process leading to an integrated, people-centred, prosperous

---

404. *See* Assembly, *Decision on International Jurisdiction, Justice and the International Criminal Court (ICC)*, AU Doc. Assembly/AU/Dec. 482 (XXI) (27 May 2013), adopted with the reservation of Botswana.

405. *See* Assembly, *Decision on Alternative Sources of Financing the African Union*, AU Doc. Assembly/AU/Dec. 486 (XXI) (27 May 2013). For the Report, *see* AU Doc. Assembly/AU/6(XXI) (2013), at: https://archives.au.int/handle/123456789/885.

406. *See* Assembly, *Decision on the Establishment of an African Union Foundation for Voluntary Contributions Towards Financing the African Union*, AU Doc. Assembly/AU/Dec. 488 (XXI) (27 May 2013). The Foundation is located in Midrand, South Africa, *see* http://www.africaunionfoundation.org/.

Africa at peace with itself.[407] For some ten years now, 'Agenda 2063', which is examined in more detail *infra*, has become a buzzword for the AU and most programmes and actions are directly or indirectly connected to it. It was officially adopted by the Twenty-Fourth Ordinary Assembly Session in January 2015[408] and was reaffirmed by the Twenty-Sixth Ordinary Session a year later, where it was described as 'a common continental framework for socio-economic development'.[409] The First Ten-Year Implementation Plan 2014–2023, adopted in 2017, envisaged seven aspirations, based on the ideals of Pan-Africanism and the vision of Africa's Renaissance.[410] During the Twenty-Eighth Ordinary Assembly Session, Agenda 2063 was cited in relation to four separate Resolutions, which concerned, respectively, achieving a universal health coverage;[411] supporting, encouraging and protecting Africa-Africa investments;[412] promoting a conflict-free Africa;[413] and repositioning the African Peer Review Mechanism.[414] The first Continental Report on the Implementation of Agenda 2063 was published in February 2020[415] and the second two years later.[416] Presently, the Second Ten Year Implementation Plan (STYIP) 2024-2033 is underway. In early October 2023, the Executive Council Retreat on Agenda 2063 took place in Rwanda.

The holding of a brainstorming session on AU's relations with the ICC, which had been agreed in May 2013, took place in October 2013 and took the form of an extraordinary Assembly session. There was a lot of speculation as to its outcome and it was even suggested that it might lead to an *en masse* withdrawal of African states from the ICC. The Declaration adopted at the end of the Extraordinary Summit did not call for withdrawal. However, the Assembly did reach several conclusions, which may have imposed upon Member States (specifically those that have

407. *See* Assembly, *Solemn Declaration on the 50th Anniversary of the OAU/AU*, AU Doc. Assembly/AU/Decl. 3 (XXI) (26 May 2013), reproduced in Annex III to this monograph.
408. Assembly, *Decision on the Report of the Commission on Development of the African Union Agenda 2063 and the Report of the Ministerial Follow-Up Committee on The Bahr Dar Retreat*, AU Doc. Assembly/AU/Dec. 565 (XXIV) (31 Jan. 2015).
409. Assembly, *Decision on the Domestication of the First Ten-Year Implementation Plan of Agenda 2063*, AU Doc. Assembly/AU/Dec. 588 (XXVI) (31 Jan. 2016). *See further*, Economic Commission for Africa and African Union, Ninth Joint Annual Meetings of the African Union Specialized Technical Committee on Finance, Monetary Affairs, Economic Planning and Integration and the Economic Commission for Africa Conference of African Ministers of Finance, Planning and Economic Development, Meeting of the Committee of Experts, Addis Ababa, 31 Mar.–2 Apr. 2016, *Draft concept note*, UN Doc. E/ECA/COE/35/Inf/1; AU Doc. AU/STC/FMEPI/EXP/Info.1(II) (27 Jan. 2016).
410. See https://au.int/en/agenda2063/ftyip.
411. *See* Assembly, *Decision on Universal Access to Immunization as a Cornerstone for Health and Development in Africa*, AU Doc. Assembly/AU/Dec. 624 (XXVIII) (31 Jan. 2017).
412. *See* Assembly, *Decision on Promotion and Protection of African Investments to Sustain Investment in the Yo*uth, AU Doc. Assembly/AU/Dec. 625 (XXVIII) (31 Jan. 2017).
413. *See* Assembly, *Decision on the African Union Master Roadmap of Practical Steps for Silencing the Guns in Africa by the Year 2020*, AU Doc. Assembly/AU/Dec. 630 (XXVIII) (31 Jan. 2017).
414. *See* Assembly, *Decision on the Revitalisation of the African Peer Review Mechanism*, AU Doc. Assembly/AU/Dec. 631 (XXVIII) (31 Jan. 2017).
415. At: https://au.int/en/documents/20200208/first-continental-report-implementation-agenda-2063.
416. African Union Development Agency – NEPAD, *Second Continental Report on the Implementation of Agenda 2063*, February 2022, at: https://www.nepad.org/microsite/2nd-continental-report-implementation-of-agenda-2063.

ratified the ICC Statute) duties of a political nature, which possibly exceed its powers and functions. In particular, the Assembly resolved that, in order to safeguard the constitutional order, stability, and integrity of Member States, no charges shall be commenced or continued before any international court or tribunal against any serving African head of state or government or anybody acting or entitled to act in such capacity during their term of office. Moreover, it decided that the ICC trials of Kenyan President Uhuru Kenyatta and Deputy President William Samoei Ruto should be suspended until they have completed their terms of office and that the former should not appear before the ICC until such time as the AU concerns had been adequately addressed by the UNSC and the ICC. Finally, it resolved that any AU Member State wishing to refer a case to the ICC (e.g., as mentioned above, the government of Mali did so in July 2012) should first inform and seek the advice of the AU.

It is rather problematic that the Assembly believed that it had the right to tell international courts and tribunals (including presumably the Courts of Justice of the various RECs) not to hear cases brought against serving African heads of state or government. Arguably, this could be construed as giving them a carte blanche to impunity for as long as they remain in power, and that would give them the incentive to stay in power beyond what is constitutionally accepted. At the same time, the Assembly's stance is most likely incompatible with 'the AU's unflinching commitment to fight impunity, promote human rights and democracy, and the rule of law and good governance', as stipulated in Articles 3 and 4 of the Constitutive Act and reiterated in the Preamble of the Declaration.[417]

On 30 December 2013, the PSC met for its 411th meeting held at the level of Heads of State and Government. It requested that an African Union Commission of Inquiry on South Sudan (AUCISS) be created. In particular, it asked the AUC, in consultation with the African Human Rights Commission and 'other relevant AU structures', to urgently establish a Commission to investigate the human rights violations and international humanitarian law abuses committed during South Sudan's armed conflict and to make recommendations on ensuring accountability, reconciliation and healing among all local communities.[418] The five-member AUCISS was appointed in March 2014,[419] apparently the first-ever such commission of enquiry in OAU/AU history. Its Final Report, which was submitted to PSC on 15 October 2014 (but was published exactly one year later[420]), makes interesting reading despite the Commission's inability to have direct access to primary sources. In particular, AUCISS complained that it could not reach key witnesses, even though they

417. *See* Assembly, *Decision on Africa's Relationship with the International Criminal Court (ICC)*, AU Doc. Ext/Assembly/AU/Dec. 1 (12 Oct. 2013).

418. *See* PSC, Communiqué, AU. Doc. PSC/AHG/COMM.1 (CDXI), 31 Dec. 2013.

419. African Union, Directorate of Information and Communication, Press Release N° 039/2014, 7 March 2014, at: http://www.peaceau.org/en/article/south-sudan-commission-of-inquiry-established-and-members-appointed.

420. The PSC had decided not to make public the Report in order not to complicate the peace process in South Sudan, but many NGOs reprimanded it for this decision, *see* Amnesty International, *South Sudan: Joint open letter to Members of the AU Peace and Security Council on the publication of the AU Commission of Inquiry Report*, Index Number: AFR 65/2149/2015, 23 Jul. 2015, at: https://www.amnesty.org/en/documents/afr65/2149/2015/en/.

had previously provided information to other international organizations that had already investigated the conflict.[421] Arguably, the reference was to the Human Rights Division of the UN Mission in the Republic of South Sudan (UNMISS), which had explored and documented events in the country since 15 December 2013 and whose Report had been submitted earlier in 2014.[422] Indeed, there appears to have been considerable friction between the two entities: AUCISS protested that it had no access to data in UNMISS' possession. And this despite UNSC Resolution 2155 (2014) of 27 May 2014, which had welcomed AUCISS 'inaugural meeting and the initiation of work … as critical steps in independent and public human rights monitoring, investigation and reporting' and had determined that the mandate of UNMISS included coordinating with and offering technical support to AUCISS. Finally, the findings of the AUCISS Final Report were of considerable importance because in June 2015, IGAD had proposed the creation of a hybrid court of criminal jurisdiction to prosecute and try alleged crimes committed in the territory of South Sudan. The creation of the hybrid court, reference to which is made later, was by means of an MOU concluded by the AU, the UN and the country's transitional government.

50. The Twenty-Second Ordinary Assembly Session (Addis Ababa, 30–31 January 2014) decided to declare the period 2014–2024 as 'The Madiba Nelson Mandela Decade of Reconciliation in Africa'. On the basis of 'the lessons learnt from his indelible legacy in the areas of truth, reconciliation and peace building', the aim has been to promote reconciliation as a means of securing peace, stability and development in the continent.[423] The Assembly also took steps in implementing further existing pan-African policies while adopting new ones, e.g., the Maternal New Born and Child Health policy,[424] the 2050 Africa's Integrated Maritime Strategy,[425] the African Capacity for Immediate Response to Crises (ACIRC),[426] the Sharm El

---

421. *See* para. 25 of the Final Report, at: http://www.peaceau.org/en/article/final-report-of-the-african-union-commission-of-inquiry-on-south-sudan.
422. *See* United Nations Mission in the Republic of South Sudan, *Conflict in South Sudan: A Human Rights Report*, 8 May 2014, at: http://www.refworld.org/docid/5371c1924.html.
423. *See* Assembly, *Decision on the Report of the Peace and Security Council on its Activities and the State of Peace and Security in Africa*, AU Doc. Assembly/AU/Dec. 501 (XXII) (31 Jan. 2014), para. 17.
424. *See* Assembly, *Decision on Progress on Maternal New Born and Child Health (MNCH)*, AU Doc. Assembly/AU/Dec. 494 (XXII) (31 Jan. 2014). Generally, *see* African Union, Second Session of the Specialised Technical Committee on Health, Population and Drug Control (STC-HPDC-2), 20–24 March 2017, *2017 Status Report on Maternal Newborn Child and Adolescent Health: Focusing on Unfinished Business in Africa*.
425. *See* Assembly, *Decision on the Adoption and Implementation of the 2050 Africa's Integrated Maritime Strategy (2050 AIM Strategy)*, AU Doc. Assembly/AU/Dec. 496 (XXII) (31 Jan. 2014).
426. *See* Assembly, *Decision on the Operationalisation of the African Capacity for Immediate Response to Crises*, AU Doc. Assembly/AU/Dec. 515 (XXII) (31 Jan. 2014). ACIRC had been established under Assembly/AU/Dec. 489 (XXI) (2013) as the interim mechanism until the African Standby Force became operationalized.

Sheikh Commitments on Accelerating Water and Sanitation Goals,[427] etc. Previously, the Twenty-Fourth Ordinary Executive Council Session (Addis Ababa, 21–28 January 2014) had adopted the new Financial Rules and Regulations of the Organization (except of Article 22).[428] As has been mentioned, the AU relies on partnerships and financial assistance received by non-African parties. Indeed, had it not been for such funding it would have probably been incapable of operating. The AUC Report on Multilateral Cooperation with respect to Africa's Strategic Partnerships,[429] which was endorsed by the Executive Council,[430] reveals how extensive these links were. They have continued to be extensive. Presently, the AU recognizes the following nine partnerships: with the League of Arab States (at the time the Third Africa-Arab Summit had taken place in Kuwait in November 2013); with the EU (examined in other parts of the monograph); with South America (principally through the Africa-South America (ASA) Partnership, which includes a Financing Mechanism and a Fund for the implementation of agreed specific projects); with India (through the Africa-India Partnership, which at the time was implementing the Plan of Action of the Enhanced Framework for Cooperation of the Second Africa-India Forum Summit 2011–2014[431]); with South Korea (through the Africa-Korea Forum); with Turkey (at the time the Second Africa-Turkey Summit had taken place in Malabo, Equatorial Guinea, in November 2014); with China (through the Forum for China–Africa Cooperation (FOCAC)); with the United States of America; and with Japan (through the Tokyo International Conference on African Development (TICAD), at the time the Fifth Summit had taken place in Yokohama in June 2013).[432] Finally, as regards refugees and Internally Displaced Persons (IDPs), another perennial African problem, the Executive Council asked for the implementation of a previous Decision,[433] which had called for doubling (from 2% to 4%) the amount in the AU operational budget destined for emergency humanitarian interventions.[434]

---

427. *See* Assembly, *Decision on the Report on the Implementation of Sharm El Sheikh Commitments on Accelerating Water and Sanitation Goals in Africa*, AU Doc. Assembly/AU/Dec. 516 (XXII) (31 Jan. 2014).
428. *See* Executive Council, *Decision on the Revised Financial Rules and Regulations of the African Union*, AU Doc. EX.CL/Dec. 784 (XXIV) (28 Jan. 2014).
429. AU Doc. EX.CL/802(XXIV)iv (Jan. 2014).
430. *See* Executive Council, *Decision on the Report of the PRC Sub-Committee on Multilateral Cooperation with respect to Africa's Strategic Partnerships*, AU Doc. EX.CL/Dec. 786 (XXIV) (28 Jan. 2014).
431. *See* Second Africa-India Forum Summit 2011, *Addis Ababa Declaration*, adopted on 25 May 2011, at: https://au.int/sites/default/files/documents/30662-doc-addis_declar-1_0.pdf. Generally, *see* R. Modi, 'India-Africa Forum Summits and Capacity Building' 16 *African and Asian Studies* (2017): 139.
432. Note that TICAD I had been held in 1993, TICAD II in 1998, and TICAD III in 2003. For the corresponding Declarations, *see* M. Juma (ed.), *Compendium of Key Documents Relating to Peace and Security in Africa* (Pretoria: Pretoria University Law Press, 2006), 491 et seq.
433. *See* Executive Council, *Decision on the Implementation of the Plan of Action for the Outcomes of the Special Summit on Refugees, Returnees and Internally Displaced Persons in Africa*, Decision EX.CL/Dec. 567 (XVII) (23 July 2010).
434. *See* Executive Council, *Decision on the report of the Sub-Committee on Refugees, Returnees and Internally Displaced Persons in Africa,* AU Doc. EX.CL/Dec. 787 (XXIV) (28 Jan. 2014).

51. The Twenty-Third Ordinary Assembly Session (Malabo, Equatorial Guinea, 26–27 June 2014) approved six multilateral instruments. Three of them concerned the AU's institutional architecture: the Protocol on Amendments to the Protocol on the Statute of the ACJHR; the Protocol on the Establishment of the African Monetary Fund (AMF); and the Protocol to the Constitutive Act of the AU relating to PAP. The other three broadened the scope of AU's activities, namely the Convention on Cyber Security and Personal Data Protection; the African Charter on the Values and Principles of Decentralisation, Local Governance and Local Development; and the AU Convention on Cross-Border Cooperation (Niamey Convention).[435] Most of these treaties are explored elsewhere in the present monograph. Suffice to mention that nine years later, Member States are still hesitant to sign/ratify them. Indeed, of these six treaties, none has come into force. This situation poses the question of whether Member States are under a duty to sign and ratify treaties approved by the Assembly. To put it otherwise, when the Assembly gives its consent to a treaty's adoption, in effect, it is the whole membership that signifies its agreement to the treaty in question. Therefore, there is the legitimate expectation not only that treaties will enter into force but will do so within a reasonable period of time. After all, the purpose of these treaties is to benefit the population of Member States without undue delay. The question of treaties that linger unsigned/unratified over long periods of time is of particular concern to the AU. It is submitted that if the Constitutive Act were to be revised in the future, this matter ought to be addressed, for example, by stipulating that if a certain number of years has lapsed and a treaty has not entered into force, it shall be considered as revoked. Alternatively, this matter ought to be regulated separately in the treaties to be approved by the Assembly in the future.

Regarding the creation of PAIPO, which the Assembly had already envisaged in a previous resolution,[436] at the Twenty-Third Session, it asked the AUC to submit the Draft Statute to the Specialized Technical Committee on Justice and Legal Affairs for consideration.[437] Given that the continent already has two relevant institutions, namely the African Organisation for Intellectual Property (OAPI, created by the Bangui Protocol in 1977) and the African Regional Intellectual Property Organization (ARIPO, created by the Lusaka Agreement in 1976), the obvious question is why did the Assembly consider it worthwhile to create another legal entity in the same field. As was mentioned above, the PAIPO Statute was approved in January 2016. However, on 9 February 2017, OAPI and ARIPO signed a Cooperation Agreement establishing a comprehensive framework for collaboration as well as a Working Programme for the period 2017–2018, which does not mention the AU

435. Assembly, *Decision on the Protocol and the Statute for the Establishment of the African Monetary Fund*, AU Doc. Assembly/AU/Dec. 517 (XXIII); and *Decision on the Draft Legal Instruments*, AU Doc. Assembly/AU/Dec. 529 (XXIII) (27 Jun. 2014).

436. Assembly, *Decision on the Creation of the Pan-African Intellectual Property Organization*, AU Doc. Assembly/AU/Dec. 453 (XX) (28 Jan. 2013).

437. Assembly, *Decision on Pan-African Intellectual Property Organization (PAIPO)*, AU Doc. Assembly/AU/Dec. 522 (XXIII) (27 Jun. 2014).

dimension on intellectual property matters.[438] PAIPO was established on the day that the Assembly adopted its Statute and, according to Article 2 thereof, it is an AU Specialized Agency. Arguably, the entire AU membership should be considered *ipso facto* PAIPO Member States, and therefore AU members should not be free not to participate. On the other hand, it is true that the term 'Specialized Agency' does not appear in the Constitutive Act, even though they have seemingly become part of the AU's institutional architecture. An AU document described them as follows: 'independent bod[ies] established by [AU] Member States outside the managerial and budgetary rules and regulations as well as control of the [AU] or the Commission to carry out a specific or specialized but related function of the mandate of the [AU]. A specialized agency ... may not be necessarily created by the [AU] but it has to be incorporated or affiliated or linked by way of Assembly decision into the [AU] system'.[439] There are some quite interesting provisions in the PAIPO Statute, including the disputes settlement clause (Article 19, whereby States Parties may consent to refer disputes to the African Court of Justice and Human Rights), the clause on its dissolution (Article 20, whereby the relevant decision shall be taken by the Conference of States Parties) and the withdrawal clause (Article 28, whereby no state may withdraw from PAIPO within the first three years of the Statute's coming into force). For the first time since July 2009,[440] the Assembly's agenda contained an item dealing specifically with maritime piracy. Even though not a matter of concern to the continent as a whole, it has been a point of contention between Western states and certain African states. The decision reached did not actually discuss any of the ramifications of maritime piracy,[441] which, however, continues to be an issue of concern to this day as revealed by several PSC decisions,[442] the Code of Conduct concerning the Repression of Piracy, Armed Robbery against Ships and Illicit Maritime Activity in West and Central Africa (Yaoundé Code of Conduct), adopted in June 2013 but also by UNSC action.[443]

Not long after the creation of the state of South Sudan, a deadly conflict among the supporters of the main political parties erupted. As mentioned above, in 2015, it was resolved to set up an 'independent hybrid judicial body' to prosecute those most

---

438. For details and the relevant documents, *see* H. Muheebwa, 'ARIPO, OAPI To Harmonise Practices On Intellectual Property In Africa', *Intellectual Property Watch*, 21 Feb. 2017, at: https://www.ip-watch.org/2017/02/21/aripo-oapi-harmonise-practices-issues-intellectual-property-africa/.

439. *See* 'Concept Note on Specialized Institutions and Agencies of the African Union', no date, at: https://au.int/sites/default/files/newsevents/conceptnotes/14601-cn-olc_conecpt_note_specialized_agencies_and_institutions.pdf.

440. *See* Assembly, *Decision on the Report of the Peace and Security Council on its Activities and on the Peace and Security Situation in Africa*, AU Doc. Assembly/AU/Dec. 252 (XIII), para. 18 (3 Jul. 2009); and Assembly, *Decision to Combat the Payment of Ransom to Terrorist Groups*, AU Doc. Assembly/AU/Dec. 256 (XIII), para. 1 (3 Jul. 2009).

441. Assembly, *Decision on Maritime Piracy*, AU Doc. Assembly/AU/Dec. 534 (XXIII) (27 Jun. 2014).

442. *See*, *inter alia*, Communique PSC/PR/COMM. (DCCCLVIII), 16 July 2019; Communique PSC/PR/COMM.1012(2021), 23 July 2021; and Communique PSC/PR/COMM. 1090(2022), 28 June 2022 concerning piracy and armed robbery at sea at the Gulf of Guinea and reiterating that the responsibility for combating these illegal activities rests with the concerned littoral states.

443. UNSC Res. 2634 (2022) adopted on 31 May 2021; UNSC Presidential Statement 2022/6, 31 August 2022; and UN Secretary-General, *Report on the situation of piracy and armed robbery at sea in the Gulf of Guinea*, UN Doc. S/2022/818 (1 Nov. 2022).

responsible for violating international humanitarian law. It culminated in the African Union Hybrid Court for South Sudan (HCSS). More specifically, its creation was envisaged in Chapter V(3) of the Agreement on the Resolution of the Conflict in South Sudan, signed on 17 August 2015 by the South Sudanese government and various domestic stakeholders under the auspices of IGAD. The HCSS, which was described 'as an African-led and Africa-owned legal mechanism',[444] was the second ad hoc criminal court to be created during 2015 to try crimes committed during internal conflicts in Africa, the other being the Special Criminal Court (SCC) competent to investigate and prosecute serious violations of international humanitarian law (including crimes against humanity, war crimes and genocide) in the CAR since January 1, 2003. SCC was established in February 2015, while the relevant legislation was promulgated on 3 June 2015.[445] After being in limbo for several years and despite forming part of the Revitalized Agreement on the Resolution of the Conflict in the Republic of South Sudan (R-ARCSS, 2018),[446] the government of South Sudan approved the establishment of HCSS on 30 January 2021. It has still not been operationalized. Theoretically speaking, the Assembly could do so pursuant to the power of intervention in Member States when grave circumstances are present (Article 4(h) of the Constitutive Act). However, as is later explained, the Assembly has so far desisted from applying it despite the apparent attempts to promote the 'African solutions to African problems' policy. Finally, the UNSC could refer the situation in South Sudan to the ICC Prosecutor (Article 13(b) of the Rome Statute) but, again, this is unlikely to happen. These internationalized criminal courts appear to be the only answer to ensure that justice is served in those African states plagued by conflict and considerable loss of life (in the South Sudan civil war, some 400,000 people are estimated to have died), especially considering that the Protocol of the ACJHR International Criminal Law Section lingers unratified, that the ICC is often unable to exercise its role promptly and effectively and that not all AU members are contracting parties to the Rome Statute, and that domestic criminal judicial systems in Africa are often incapable to function and perform their duties.

During the Twenty-Fourth Ordinary Session (Addis Ababa, 30–31 January 2015), the Assembly dealt with the consequences of the Ebola virus in affected Member

---

444. *See* PSC, *Communiqué of 547th meeting of the PSC, at the level of Heads of State and Government, on the situation in South Sudan*, AU Doc. PSC/AHG/COMM.3(DXLVII), 26 Sep. 2015, para. 22.

445. *See* Loi Organique N° 15.003 portant creation, organisation et fonctionnement de la Cour Penale Speciale, at: https://www.fidh.org/IMG/pdf/loi_organique_portant_cre_ation_organisation_et_fonctionnement_de_la_cps.pdf. *See also* K. Magliveras, 'The Special Criminal Court of the Central African Republic', *International Enforcement Law Reporter* 32 (2016): 69. Note that SCC was first envisaged in the Memorandum of Understanding on Urgent Temporary Measures, signed on 7 Aug. 2014 between the UN Multidimensional Integrated Stabilization Mission in the Central African Republic (MINUSCA) and CAR's transitional government. On MINUSCA role, *see* A. Gilder, 'UN Peace Operations and the Role of the Local in (Re)Building the Rule of Law', *Utrecht Law Review* 17 (2021): 70, 73 et seq.

446. Note that R-ARCSS also envisages the establishment of a Commission for Truth, Reconciliation and Healing and a Compensation and Reparation Authority. *See* K. Magliveras, 'The (Unfinished Story of the) Hybrid Court for South Sudan', *International Enforcement Law Reporter* 36 (2015): 410.

States (Guinea, Liberia, and Sierra Leone). It asked Member States to lift all restrictions imposed upon these states, as had already been requested by the Executive Council meeting in Extraordinary Session on 8 September 2014. In particular, the Executive Council had called for the non-closure of their borders and for the non-stigmatization of their nationals on account of Ebola.[447] Additionally, the Assembly requested that the international financial institutions and the so-called partner countries cancel the debt of affected states to alleviate the virus' impact on their economies and to assist in their economic recovery and development, and, presumably as a token measure of solidarity, it asked the AUC to pay directly to each of these Members the amount of USD 500,000.[448] To further its decision, it urged the setting up of a High-Level Contact Group composed of Member States, the AUC, the African Development Bank and the UN Economic Commission for Africa to negotiate the terms of debt cancellation in the affected states.[449] Despite similar calls made by the UN Economic Commission for Africa[450] and 'partner countries',[451] apparently, only partial debt cancellation was made, but, thereafter, affected states had to borrow more funds to overcome the economic and financial consequences of Ebola.[452] As a result of the significant financial problems to which the outbreak of Ebola led, the International Monetary Fund set up the Catastrophe Containment and Relief Trust (CCR), which is also intended to assist other 'low income countries' affected by public health disasters.[453] In 2019, the Assembly discussed debt cancellation in relation to Somalia. It asked Member States to fully cancel its debt obligations 'in the spirit of African solidarity' but also external creditors to relieve Somalia from the debt-servicing burden 'that may hinder its transition from conflict to peace and sustainable'.[454] During the Twenty-Fourth Session, the Assembly also congratulated Tunisia for the successful democratic transition, having held free and fair legislative and presidential elections in October and November 2014. The Assembly

447. Executive Council, *Decision on the Ebola Virus Disease (EVD) Outbreak*, AU Doc. Ext/EX.CL/Dec. 1 (XVI) (8 Sep. 2014).

448. Assembly, *Decision on Ebola Virus Disease (EVD) Outbreak*, AU Doc. Assembly/AU/Dec. 553 (XXIV) (31 Jan. 2015). *See also* Assembly, *Special Declaration Acknowledging the Role of African Volunteers in the Fight Against Ebola*, AU Doc. Assembly/AU/Decl. 4 (XXIII) (31 Jan. 2015).

449. Assembly, *Resolution on Debt Cancellation of Countries Affected by Ebola Virus Disease*, AU Doc. Assembly/AU/Res. 1 (XXIV), para. 4 (31 Jan. 2015).

450. UN Economic Commission for Africa, *A case for external debt cancellation for Ebola affected countries*, Addis Ababa, January 2015, at: https://repository.uneca.org/handle/10855/22828.

451. *See, e.g.*, A.Yukhananov, 'U.S. urges IMF to cancel debt of Ebola-stricken countries', *Reuters*, 12 November 2014, at: https://www.reuters.com/article/us-health-ebola-usa-debt-idUSKCN0IV28L20141111.

452. *See* T. Jones, 'Sierra Leone: Ebola debt to IMF contributes to big cuts in public spending', *Debt Justice*, 19 December 2018, at: https://debtjustice.org.uk/blog/sierra-leone-debt-payments-from-imf-ebola-loans-contribute-to-big-cuts-in-public-spending.

453. *See* M. Cangul, C. Sdralevich & I. Sian, 'Beating Back Ebola', 54:2 *Finance & Development* (2017): 54. On the CCR, *see* https://www.imf.org/external/np/fin/ccr/.

454. Assembly, *Decision on the Debt Cancellation as a Means Towards Enhancing Peace, Security, Development and Durable Solutions for Displaced Somalis*, AU Doc. Assembly/AU/Dec. 731 (XXXII) (21 Feb. 2019).

considered 'the successful of the Tunisian experience as possible model for democratization process in Africa'.[455] But Tunisia's political success (including the promulgation of a democratic Constitution in 2014)[456] proved short-lived and has relapsed to authoritarianism.[457]

52. The Twenty-Fifth Ordinary Assembly Session (Johannesburg, South Africa, 14–15 June 2015) was held under the theme 'Year of Women Empowerment and Development towards Africa's Agenda 2063.' The Assembly discussed, as it has been doing in every session for arguably far too many years, the question of UNSC reform. It reserved the right to determine the criteria for the selection of the two AU Member States that at the time believed that they must represent the continent as permanent UNSC members.[458] More recently, the Assembly articulated the continent's demands as follows: (a) not less than two permanent UNSC seats with all the prerogatives and privileges of permanent membership, including the right of veto;[459] (b) five non-permanent seats; and (c) that the AU reserves the right to select its representatives for election to the UNSC acting in the name of Africa and on its behalf.[460] There is no doubt that the AU has invested a lot in its common position on UNSC reform. However, it will be submitted that these demands are not realistic. Moreover, even though at the UN level the UNSC reform agenda has been in stalemate for several years now, the AU continues to consider it a priority while the resources put into it might have been used more productively elsewhere. During the same Session, the Assembly took an important decision concerning the streamlining of its meetings and the Organization's working methods.[461] Taking onboard the Executive Council's recommendations,[462] the Assembly resolved, *inter alia*, to: (a)

455. Assembly, *Decision on Democratic Transition in Tunisia*, AU Doc. Assembly/AU/Dec. 568 (XXIV), para. 1 (31 Jan. 2015).
456. English translation at: https://www.constituteproject.org/constitution/Tunisia_2014.pdf. Amendments to the Constitution, which were approved in July 2022 with 94.6% of votes in favour but with a turnout that was lower than 31%, gave the President powers that are evidently not in line with a democratic state, *see* F. Eardley, *Tunisian constitutional referendum and reform*, House of Lords Library, 29 July 2022, at: https://lordslibrary.parliament.uk/tunisian-constitutional-referendum-and-reform/.
457. Generally, *see* T. Hill & S. Yerkes, *Tunisian Foreign Policy Under Kais Saied*, Carnegie Endowment for International Peace, 11 January 2023, at: https://carnegieendowment.org/2023/01/11/tunisian-foreign-policy-under-kais-saied-pub-88770.
458. Assembly, *Decision on the Sixteenth Report of the Committee of Ten Heads of State and Government on the Reform of the United Nations Security Council*, AU Doc. Assembly/AU/Dec. 574 (XXV), para. 8 (15 Jun. 2015).
459. Note that, in principle, the AU is opposed to the veto power but its position is that, as long as it exists, it is 'a matter of common justice' to be made available to all permanent members, *see* Assembly, *Decision on the Reform of the United Nations Security Council*, AU Doc. Assembly/AU/Dec. 766 (XXXIII), para. 9 (10 Feb. 2020).
460. Assembly, *Decision on Annual Report of the Union and Its Organs Including the Specific Thematic Issues by the Heads of States, Champions*, AU Doc. Assembly/AU/Dec. 819 (XXXV), para. 77 (6 Feb. 2022).
461. Assembly, *Decision on Streamlining of the AU Summits and the Working Methods of the African Union*, AU Doc. Assembly/AU/Dec. 582 (XXV) (15 Jun. 2015).
462. Presumably this topic was discussed in the context of Executive Council, *Decision on the Report of the Commission on the Review of the Rules of Procedure of the Policy Organs*, AU Doc. EX.CL/Dec. 884 (XXVII) (12 Jun. 2015).

delineate the decision-making process by it and by the Executive Council and to delegate to the latter the power and mandate to take decisions, except those on key strategic issues (it did not define which these issues are but arguably they comprise continental integration, peace and security, governance, and financial matters); (b) empower the Specialized Technical Committees (STCs) (they are composed of Member States' Ministers) to reach decisions on issues falling under their competence, except for decisions having financial and structural implications and with the provisio that, if a Member State objects to decision-making by an STC, it will be the Executive Council that will consider the matter ; (c) not repeat the adoption of those decisions already taken at the level of the Executive Council; (d) hold 'closed sessions' meetings to discuss strategic issues, which will be convened 'in a Retreat format'; (e) continue the mode of two (sessions) Summits per year, where one will focus on policy issues with the participation of 'partners' in accordance with the Assembly Rules of Procedure and the other on the implementation of decisions; and (f) conduct the opening of its sessions in a business-like manner and in accordance with the Rules of Procedure, i.e., only the AU Secretary-General and the President of the State of Palestine (on account of the 'historical African solidarity' with the Palestinian struggle) would be allowed to address the Assembly in person, while the other invited guests would have to use 'alternative platforms'. Finally, the Assembly adopted six declarations, of which two were quite important. The first dealt with the need for self-reliance, a recurring issue closely connected to the need to implement the Agenda 2063 programmes and initiatives.[463] The second had to do with intra-continental migration. African leaders committed themselves to offer all Africans the same opportunities accorded to the citizens of countries within the respective RECs by the year 2018 and requested the AUC to 'urgently organize a retreat of the Executive Council to consider [the] development of a Protocol on Free Movement of Persons.[464] As explained elsewhere, the latter was adopted in January 2018 as the Protocol to the Treaty Establishing the African Economic Community Relating to Free Movement of Persons, Right of Residence and Right of Establishment; it has not entered into force.

53. During the Twenty-Sixth Ordinary Session (Addis Ababa, 30–31 January 2016), the Assembly adopted the impressive number of twenty legal texts, which were a mixture of new multilateral legal instruments (e.g., the Road Safety Charter and the Model Law on Medicine Regulation); additions to existing instruments (e.g., the Protocol to the African Charter on Human and Peoples' Rights on the Rights of Older Persons); changes to existing legal instruments (e.g., the Amended Statute of the Pan-African University); Statutes of new subsidiary organs and other entities/bodies (e.g., the Africa Sports Council; the Legal Aid Fund for the AU Human Rights Organs[465] (it has still not been operationalized[466]); the African Minerals Development Centre (AMDC);[467] the Africa Centres for Disease Control and

463. Assembly, *Declaration on Self-Reliance*, Assembly/AU/Decl. 5 (XXV) (15 Jun. 2015).
464. Assembly, *Declaration on Migration*, AU Doc. Assembly/AU/Decl. 6 (XXV) (15 Jun. 2015).
465. The Statute of the Legal Aid Fund is not subject to ratification but entered into force upon adoption by the Assembly. The African Human Rights Court's Legal Aid Scheme was established in 2012 to support unrepresented applicants to have access to free legal assistance before the Court in the

Prevention (Africa CDC); the African Science Research and Innovation Council (ASRIC)); as well as changes to the Rules of Procedure of Specialized Technical Committees (e.g., the Committee on Social Development, Labour and Employment; the Committee on Health Population and Drug Control; and the Committee on Public Service, Local Government, Urban Development and Decentralisation)).[468] Presently, none of these multilateral instruments establishing new organs and bodies has entered into force. Indeed, relatively few Member states have signed and/or ratified them, confirming the question put earlier, namely why were they concluded in the first place. For example, the Protocol to the African Charter on the Rights of Older Persons has so far received only twelve ratifications.

On another front, during the Twenty-Sixth Session, the Assembly attempted to link up the various decisions adopted by the PSC with the resolutions adopted on similar issues and situations by the UNSC. In particular, by invoking Article 7(3) of the PSC Protocol stipulating that Member States have agreed to accept and implement PSC decisions, the Assembly not only concluded that the three African members sitting on the UNSC 'have special responsibility to ensure that the decisions of the PSC are well reflected in the decision-making process of the UNSC on peace and security issues of concern to Africa' but also requested that they present reports to it on their efforts at the UNSC level as well as on their promotion of common African positions as these have been articulated by the PSC.[469] This demand may actually be against the principle of sincere cooperation which, even though more developed in the law of the EU, should be considered to be part of the law of international organizations. In the UN Charter, this principle is manifested in Article 2(2), which obliges all Member States to fulfil in good faith all their obligations. And if there happens to be a conflict between the UN Charter's obligations and their obligations under another international agreement (in case, under the AU Constitutive Act), Article 103 of the UN Charter expressly states that their obligations under it shall prevail. This provision should be interpreted that if AU organs and the UNSC happen to follow completely different policies in a specific matter, AU Member States have the duty to align with the latter's policy because in the present case

---

interest of justice. The Scheme was authorized by the Executive Council, *Decision on the 2014 Activity Report of the African Court on Human and Peoples' Rights*, AU Doc. EX.CL/Dec. 865 (XXVI) (27 Jan. 2015). The Fund has been accorded full juridical personality and capacity to contract, acquire and dispose of immovable and moveable property and institute legal proceedings.

466. Despite the Executive Council repeatedly urging the AUC Chairperson to do so, *see*, Executive Council, *Decision on the Activity Report of the African Court on Human and Peoples' Rights* (AfCHPR), AU Doc. EX.CL/Dec. 1153 (XL), para. 10 (3 Feb. 2022); *Decision on the Activity Report of the African Court on Human and Peoples' Rights (AfCHPR) Including Outcome of the PRC-AFCHPR Retreat Held in Arusha, Tanzania, March 2022*, AU Doc. EX.CL/Dec. 1197, para. 15 (16 Feb. 2023).

467. Even though the AMDC Statute had not entered into force, in 2018 the Assembly decided that it will be hosted by Guinea, Assembly, *Decision on the Report on the Hosting of the African Minerals Development Centre (AMDC)*, AU Doc. Assembly/AUDec. 697 (XXXI) (2 Jul. 2018).

468. Assembly, *Decision on the Specialized Technical Committees*, AU Doc. Assembly/AU/Dec. 589 (XXVI) (31 Jan. 2016), para. 2. The recommendation to adopt them was made by the Executive Council on the basis of the Report of the First Extraordinary Session of the Specialized Technical Committee on Justice and Legal Affairs, AU Doc. EX.CL/935(XXVIII) (2014).

469. *See* Assembly, *Decision on the Activities of the Peace and Security Council and the State of Peace and Security in Africa*, AU Doc. Assembly/AU/Dec. 598 (XXVI) (31 Jan. 2016), para. 24.

they act as UN Member States and, therefore, they are required to follow and give effect to the view taken by the majority of members in the UNSC. Should they not do so, they must produce reasons which concern the UN policy itself and not the policy which another international organization (namely, the AU) happens to have adopted. To put it otherwise, UNSC members are under the obligation to act only in their capacity as members of this organ irrespective of the continent or region in which they are geographically located and the commitments they may have already made in the context of any regional political organization. Presumably, if they fail to do so, they could be considered as recalcitrant UN Member States.

54. At the Twenty-Seventh Ordinary Session (Kigali, Rwanda, 17–18 July 2016), the Assembly discussed the continental free movement of people, aspects of which, as a protected right, are laid down in the African Charter on Human and Peoples' Rights and in the Treaty establishing the AEC. Article 12 of the former, which concerns domestic and transborder migration, guarantees to every individual the right to freedom of movement and residence within the borders of a contracting party as long as he/she abides by its law, the right to leave any country including his/her own, and the right to return to the country of origin. It also guarantees that non-nationals legally admitted to a contracting party may only be expelled by virtue of a decision taken in accordance with domestic law, while the mass expulsion of non-nationals forming national, racial, ethnic or religious groups is prohibited. Building on this *acqui*, the Assembly confirmed the decision which had been taken by the Executive Council in January 2016 mandating the AUC to develop the Protocol on Free Movement of Persons in Africa.[470] Moreover, the Assembly launched the African Passport to be issued by the AUC and Member States. It asked third states to recognize it as a valid travel document.[471] The Assembly also pressed for the implementation of the CFTA project. It asked the AUC to draft and circulate to Member States negotiating texts on trade in goods and on trade in services while presenting feasible options on the elimination of non-trade barriers among African states to foster continental trade. Finally, it called on Member States to speak with one voice on all issues related to trade negotiations with third parties.[472] All three projects, which are 'Aspirations' of Agenda 2063, materialized rather promptly. As already mentioned, the Protocol to the AEC Treaty Relating to Free Movement of Persons, Right of Residence and Right of Establishment was adopted in January 2018, while the Agreement Establishing the African Continental Free Trade Area in March 2018.

As has been noted above, in May 2016, the African Extraordinary Chambers in Senegal found Hissène Habré, the former dictator of Chad, guilty of most of the charges brought against him. However, regarding the question of victims' reparations, while the Statute of the Chambers provided for the establishment of a reparation fund, the necessary measures to implement it had not been taken. In

470. *See* Executive Council, *Decision on the Mekele Retreat of the Executive Council*, AU Doc. EX.CL/Dec. 908 (XXVIII) (31 Jan. 2017).
471. *See* Assembly, *Decision on the Free Movement of Persons and the African Passport*, AU Doc. Assembly/AU/Dec. 607 (XXVII) (18 Jul. 2016).
472. Assembly, *Decision on the Continental Free Trade Area (CFTA)*, AU Doc. Assembly/AU/Dec. 608 (XXVII) (18 Jul. 2016).

particular, in July 2016, Habré was ordered to pay 20 million CFA francs (circa USD 34,000) for each surviving victim of rape and sexual slavery, 15 million CFA francs (circa USD 25,400) for each surviving victim of torture and arbitrary detention, and 10 million CFA francs (circa USD 17,000) for the surviving family members of victims. Thus, the Assembly resolved that the Trust Fund be created under AU auspices and that the AUC together with Chad organize a pledging conference with the participation of as many African and international stakeholders as possible.[473] In April 2017, the judgment on the appeal lodged by Habré was handed down. It ordered, *inter alia*, that he pay compensation to 7,396 victims (the applications of 3,489 other alleged victims were rejected), confirmed the reparations as decided by the Trial Chamber (a total of 82,290 billion CFA francs (circa USD 130 million)) but denied the claim advanced by civil parties that Habré must also be ordered to pay collective reparations. The Thirty-First Ordinary Executive Council Session (2017) had before it the Statute of the Trust Fund for Victims of Hissène Habré Crimes.[474] It requested that the AUC submit it to the Specialized Technical Committee on Justice and Legal Affairs for consideration.[475] During the Thirtieth Ordinary Assembly Session, the Statute was approved.[476] The amounts that the Trust Fund has managed to collect are quite insignificant compared to the total damages that Habré was ordered to pay. On 24 August 2021, Habré died while serving a life sentence in Senegal for crimes against humanity. Soon thereafter, an AU delegation visited the capital N'Djamena to discuss indemnifications from the Trust Fund.[477] Since then, Chad voluntarily contributed the amount of ten billion CFA francs (circa USD 16.3 million).[478] It should be noted that the right to compensation for gross human rights violations is stated in several global and regional legal instruments.[479]

Given the developments in 2017 as regards the Trust Fund for Victims, it is interesting that the theme of the Twenty-Seventh Assembly Session was 'The African Year of Human Rights with Particular Focus on the Rights of Women'. The Assembly expressed its determination to protect and promote human rights as embodied in the Protocol on the African Charter on Human and People's Rights on the Rights of

---

473. Assembly, *Decision on the Hissene Habre Case*, AU Doc. Assembly/AU/Dec. 615 (XXVII) (18 Jul. 2016). Generally, *see* C. Sperfeldt, 'The Trial Against Hissène Habré: Networked Justice and Reparations at the Extraordinary African Chambers', *The International Journal of Human Rights* 21 (2017): 1243.
474. *See* AU Doc. EX.CL/1040(XXXI), Annex (June 2017), text at: https://www.hrw.org/sites/default/files/supporting_resources/statute_trust_fund_victims_english.pdf.
475. Executive Council, *Decision on the Report of the Commission on the Hissene Habre Case*, AU Doc. EX.CL/Dec. 972 (XXXI) para. 6 (1 Jul. 2017).
476. Assembly, *Decision on the Legal Instruments*, AU Doc. Assembly/AU/Dec. 676 (XXX) para. 2a (29 Jan. 2018).
477. *See* M. Soumaré, 'Mission de l'UA au Tchad: les victimes d'Hissène Habré bientôt indemnisées?', *Jeune Afrique*, 21 September 2021, at: https://www.jeuneafrique.com/.
478. *See* Executive Council, *Decision on the Operationalization of the Secretariat of the Hissene Habre Victims Compensation Fund*, AU Doc. EX.CL/Dec. 1193 (XLII), para. 5 (16 Feb. 2023).
479. *See*, *inter alia*, UNGA, Res. 60/147, *Basic Principles and Guidelines on the Right to a Remedy and Reparation for Victims of Gross Violations of International Human Rights Law and Serious Violations of International Humanitarian Law* (21 Mar. 2006); and African Commission on Human and Peoples' Rights, *Resolution 111 on the Right to a Remedy and Reparation for Women and Girls Victims of Sexual Violence*, November 2007.

Women in Africa (the Maputo Protocol) and in the Solemn Declaration on Gender Quality in Africa, adopted during its Third Ordinary Session (Addis Ababa, 6–8 July 2004). Member States 're-committed' themselves to expedite the ratification, domestication and implementation of the Maputo Protocol, and called upon the AUC to introduce measures and modalities to support the establishment of capacities and processes to monitor domestication efforts.[480] Arguably, the proper organ to do so would have been the African Commission on Human and Peoples' Rights and not the AUC. Finally, the Assembly took the decision to ensure that the AU is adequately financed, including the introduction of a 0.2% levy 'on all eligible imported goods' into Africa (i.e. from non-AU Member States).[481] It was expected that the levy would create sufficient income to finance the AU Operational Budget, the Programme Budget, and the Peace Support Operations Budget. As regards the practical aspects, the amounts collected by the levy would be automatically paid by national administrations into an account that the AU would open with the Central National or Reserve Bank of each Member State for the purpose of transmitting each Member's assessed budgetary contribution to the AU. Finally, the AUC was asked to study the management of African mineral resources, in particular how revenue may be optimized through harmonization of royalties and fiscal regimes.[482] The idea behind a levy on imports to be collected by a regional international organization is not novel: it is customary in those regional institutions engaged in economic integration (in Africa, ECOWAS, ECCAS and CEMAC had already introduced it). Interestingly enough, the Assembly had adopted the levy on imports before the African Continental Free Trade Area project was initiated.[483] In early 2019, sixteen Member States had introduced domestic legislation allowing them to collect the 0.2% levy in favour of the AU.[484] The current number is not known but it should not have increased dramatically.

55. The Twenty-Eighth Ordinary Assembly Session (Addis Ababa, 30–31 January 2017) had the theme 'Harnessing the demographic dividend through investments in the youth'. Before it, the Thirtieth Executive Council Ordinary Session had taken place (25–27 January 2017) and, before it, the Thirty-Third Permanent Representatives Committee Ordinary Session (22–24 January 2017). The question of

480. Assembly, *Declaration of the Assembly on the Theme of the Year*, AU Doc. Assembly/AU/Decl. 1 (XXVII) Rev. 1 (18 Jul. 2016).

481. *See* African Union, *Draft – Guidelines for the Implementation of the Assembly Directive on the Financing of the Union*, August 2016, at: https://au.int/sites/default/files/pages/31902-file-guidelines20english2028129.pdf.

482. Assembly, *Decision on the Outcome of the Retreat of the Heads of States and Government, Ministers of Foreign Affairs and Ministers of Finance on the Financing of the African Union*, AU Doc. Assembly/AU/Dec. 605 (XXVII) (18 Jul. 2016). It is also known as 'Kigali Decision on Financing the Union' (Mauritius entered a reservation). *See also* Assembly, *Decision on the Implementation of the Financing of the Union*, AU Doc. Assembly/AU/Dec. 641 (XXVIII) (31 Jan. 2017).

483. Generally, *see* U. Engel, 'State of the Union', *Yearbook on the African Union* 1 (2020): 23.

484. *See* 'Africa is financing its development agenda through domestic resource mobilization', *AU Monthly Bulletin*, March 2019, at: https://au.int/es/node/36397. For implementation in Ghana, *see* African Union Import Levy Act, 2017 (Act 952) and Parliament of Ghana, *Report of the Finance Committee on the 2021 Annual Report on the Collection and Utilization of the African Union Import Levy*, 2 November 2022, at: http://ir.parliament.gh/.

the AU's relationship towards the ICC was again the dominant issue. Despite formal reservations entered by Cabo Verde, Nigeria, Senegal and Liberia, the Assembly adopted the so-called ICC Withdrawal Strategy[485] and asked Member States to consider implementing its recommendations. The Assembly also expressed its deep concern at the slow pace of ratification of the 2014 Protocol on Amendments to the Protocol on the Statute of the African Court of Justice and Human Rights (Malabo Protocol),[486] which still stands unratified. The Assembly regarded those states that had already submitted to the ICC notices of withdrawal (Burundi, the Republic of South Africa, and The Gambia) as 'pioneer implementers of the Withdrawal Strategy'.[487] However, subsequent events proved that this jubilation was rather premature. The Gambia changed course when the new President, Adama Barrow, advocated that the withdrawal process will be terminated and the country will follow a rapprochement with international institutions (including the Commonwealth). And, in February 2017, the High Court in South Africa decreed that the notice to withdraw from the ICC was unconstitutional and, therefore, invalid because the government had failed to consult Parliament;[488] in April 2017, the South African government officially withdrew its notice of withdrawal. Only Burundi withdrew with effect from 27 October 2017.[489] However, two days earlier, the ICC Prosecutor had been authorized to investigate alleged crimes against humanity committed in Burundi or in other countries by nationals of Burundi during the period April 2015–October 2017.[490] The investigation is ongoing and so far has not led to any alleged perpetrators being named.

The Twenty-Eighth Assembly also considered a topic introduced by Ethiopia titled 'Universal Access to Immunization as a Cornerstone for Health and Development in Africa,' which is closely linked to the Pharmaceutical Manufacturing Plan for Africa (PMPA), whose implementation calls for investing in the continent's capacity to develop and produce vaccines.[491] Moreover, it asked Member States in partnership with all relevant stakeholders to negotiate with manufacturers

485. *See* African Union, *Withdrawal Strategy Document*, Draft 2, Version 12.1.2017, at: https://www.hrw.org/sites/default/files/supporting_resources/icc_withdrawal_strategy_jan._2017.pdf.
486. Assembly, *Decision on the International Criminal Court*, AU Doc. Assembly/AU/Dec. 622 (XXVIII) (31 Jan. 2017).
487. *Ibid*, paras 6 and 8. *See further*, M. Ssenyonjo, 'State Withdrawal Notifications from the Rome Statute of the International Criminal Court: South Africa, Burundi and the Gambia', *Criminal Law Forum* 29 (2018): 63.
488. North Gauteng High Court, Pretoria, *Democratic Alliance v. Minister of International Relations and Cooperation and Others (Council for the Advancement of the South African Constitution Intervening)*, Case no. 83145/2016, Order, 22 Feb. 2017, [2017] ZAGPPHC 53, at: http://saflii.org/za/cases/ZAGPPHC/2017/53.html.
489. Generally, *see* K. Magliveras, 'The Withdrawal of African States from the ICC: Good, Bad or Irrelevant?', *Netherlands International Law Review* 66 (2019): 419.
490. ICC, Pre-Trial Chamber III, *Public Redacted Version of 'Decision Pursuant to Article 15 of the Rome Statute on the Authorization of an Investigation into the Situation in the Republic of Burundi'*, ICC-01/17-X-9-US-Exp, 25 Oct. 2017.
491. *See* AU Commission and United Nations Industrial Development Organization, *Pharmaceutical Manufacturing Plan for Africa (PMPA): Business Plan*, Addis Ababa, November 2012, at:https://www.unido.org/sites/default/files/2013-02/PMPA_Business_Plan_Nov2012_ebook_0.PDF.

the provision of vaccines at affordable prices.[492] Arguably, PMPA has not been a success. This was unfortunately revealed during the COVID-19 pandemic when it became apparent that the continent was not in the position to produce the necessary medicaments to curb the disease but also to manufacture the so-called personal protective equipment to prevent its spread. However, the entry into force on 5 November 2021 of the Treaty for the Establishment of the African Medicines Agency (AMA), which was adopted at the Thirty-Second Ordinary Assembly Session on 11 February 2019, may address some of the challenges.[493] During its previous Session (July 2016), the Assembly had resolved to establish the AU Special Fund on the Prevention and Combating Terrorism and Violent Extremism in Africa and had entrusted AUC to draft its Statute,[494] which was thereafter submitted to the Specialized Technical Committee on Justice and Legal Affairs for consideration.[495] However, this Fund does not appear to have been operationalized.[496] In a similar development, the Twenty-Eighth Assembly adopted the Statute of the African Union Mechanism for Police Cooperation (AFRIPOL),[497] which had been established following the recommendations of the African Conference of Police Directors and Inspector-Generals (Algiers, 10–11 February 2014)[498] and the endorsement of the Executive Council.[499] AFRIPOL is located in Algiers and operates as an independent mechanism for police cooperation for AU Member States. It has its own institutional structure comprising of a General Assembly, a Steering Committee and a Permanent Secretariat.[500]

Other items on the agenda of the Twenty-Eighth Assembly included the tenth anniversary of the functioning of the African Court on Human and Peoples' Rights, where the question of whether the Court and the African Commission on Human and Peoples' Rights will finally become part of the AU's institutional structure, was

---

492. Assembly, *Decision on Universal Access to Immunization as a Cornerstone for Health and Development in Africa*, AU Doc. Assembly/Dec. 624 (XXVIII) (31 Jan. 2017).
493. Generally, *see* B.M. Ncube, A. Dube & K. Ward, 'Establishment of the African Medicines Agency: progress, challenges and regulatory readiness', *Journal of Pharmaceutical Policy and Practice* 14 (2021): 29.
494. Assembly, *Decision on the Establishment of an African Union Special Fund on Prevention and Combating Terrorism and Violent Extremism in Africa*, AU Doc. Assembly/AU/Dec. 614 (XXVII) (18 Jul. 2016).
495. Assembly, *Decision on the African Union Special Fund on the Prevention and Combating of Terrorism and Violent Extremism in Africa*, AU Doc. Assembly/AU/Dec. 627 (XXVIII) (31 Jan. 2017).
496. In 2021, PSC asked AUC to take the necessary measures for its implementation, PSC, 1040th Meeting, Communiqué, AU Doc. PSC/MIN/COMM.1040(2021), para. 14 (22 Oct. 2021) and *see further*, Assembly, AU Doc. Assembly/AU/Dec. 819 (XXXV), *infra*.
497. Assembly, *Decision on the Draft Legal Instruments*, AU Doc. Assembly/AU/Dec. 636 (XXVIII), para. 2 (31 Jan. 2017). The Statute was not subject to signature and ratification and came into effect upon adoption by the Assembly.
498. For the text of the Algiers Declaration, *see* https://afripol.africa-union.org/old/index.php/declarations/algiers-declaration.
499. Executive Council, *Decision on the Establishment of the African Union Mechanism for Police Cooperation – AFRIPOL*, AU Doc. EX.CL/Dec. 820 (XXV) (24 Jun. 2014).
500. For further information, *see* https://afripol.africa-union.org/.

not discussed,[501] and Morocco's official application to accede to the AU. In July 2016, King Mohammed VI made known Morocco's intention to return,[502] while the official request was submitted on 22 September 2016.[503] The Assembly decision accepting the application does not reveal how many Member States voted in favour and how many against (reportedly, thirty-nine Members expressed their agreement in writing and nine voted against) and only praised the outcome:

> [Morocco's accession] provides the opportunity to reunite the African community of states around the Pan-African core values of the Founders of solidarity, unity, freedom and equality, in accordance with the Principles and Objectives of the Constitutive Act. This will strengthen the ability of the African Union to find African solutions to African problems.[504]

Morocco became the fifty-fifth Member State when it deposited its instrument of accession to the Constitutive Act on 31 January 2017. Since then, there have been no changes in AU membership. At a time when there is a leadership crisis in the AU and those Members which in the past had played a pivotal role (including Libya, Egypt, and South Africa) are no longer able or willing to do so, other very important states (e.g. Nigeria) are more inclined to pursue sub-regional integration, Morocco could fulfil this role. However, the conflict in Western Sahara would no doubt prove to be a major issue of contention. Its description as 'a non-self-governing territory', an anathema to Morocco, and the insistence that a self-determination referendum for the people must be held,[505] a development that Morocco has managed to prevent until now, could lead to a clash between it and a large group of Member States. Lest it be forgotten, many an African state still regard Morocco as a colonial power suppressing fellow Africans. To that extent, there is a credible possibility that those which disagreed with Morocco's accession will oppose its assuming a larger role, especially if it immediately pursues a policy to

---

501. Assembly, *Declaration on the Commemoration of the Tenth Anniversary of the Operationalization of the African Court on Human and Peoples' Rights*, AU Doc. Assembly/Decl. 2 (XXVIII) (31 Jan. 2017).
502. It took the form of a Royal Message handed over to the Chadian President and then to AU Chairperson Idriss Deby. Note that in February 2017 Morocco told ECOWAS that it will be seeking full membership, a move arguably signifying its determination of pursuing deeper relations with other African states. In June 2017, ECOWAS leaders gave the go ahead but decided that the implications of Morocco's membership still needed to be considered before it could formally join, *see* Fifty-First Ordinary Session of the ECOWAS Authority of Heads of State and Government, *Final Communique*, 4 June 2017, para. 61, at: https://ecowas.int/wp-content/uploads/2022/08/2017-51st-Session-June.pdf; and Policy and Legal Advocacy Centre, 'Morocco's Bid to Join ECOWAS', 31 December 2017, at: https://placng.org/Legist/moroccos-bid-to-join-ecowas/. At the time of writing, there was no prospect of Morocco joining ECOWAS, especially on account of Nigeria's economic concerns about its accession.
503. *See*, AU, Directorate of Information and Communication, 'Morocco officially requests to join the African Union', Press Release No. 324/2016, at: https://au.int/en/pressreleases/20160923.
504. Assembly, *Decision on the Admission of the Kingdom of Morocco to the African Union*, AU Doc. Assembly/AU/Dec. 639 (XXVIII), para. 3 (31 Jan. 2017).
505. *See* Assembly, *Decision on the Report of the Peace and Security Council on its Activities and the State of Peace and Security in Africa*, AU Doc. Assembly/AU/Dec. 629 (XXVIII), para. 11 (31 Jan. 2017). para. 10.

disrupt the participation of the SADR in AU affairs or even have it excluded completely from the Organization. There are already signs that this is Morocco's intention. In March 2017, Morocco failed to attend a PSC meeting on the situation in Western Sahara even though it had been invited.[506] The PSC asked it 'to extend the necessary cooperation in conformity with the ... Constitutive Act' and, presumably to accommodate a hostile Morocco, it resolved to reactivate the Ad hoc Committee of Heads of State and Government on the conflict in Western Sahara, which had been established by the OAU Assembly in July 1978.[507] Moreover, some days later, a meeting between the AU and the UN Economic Commission for Africa (ECA) was postponed because Morocco demanded the exclusion of SADR as it does not participate in ECA. Given that SADR does not participate in any international organization and institution bar the AU (there are no formal relations between SADR and the League of Arab States) and has not become a contracting party to any multilateral treaty bar the OAU/AU ones, no doubt Morocco has been pursuing a policy of disruption that has arguably led to SADR's isolation.

The Assembly met for the Twenty-Ninth Ordinary Session in Addis Ababa on 3–4 July 2017 and decided that the theme of the year 2017 would be 'Harnessing the Demographic Dividend through Investments in Youth'.[508] The first item on the agenda was the approval of the budget for the Financial Year (FY) 2018. The Assembly, *inter alia*, discussed the European Union's reduction by 20% of its annual contribution to the AU Mission in Somalia (AMISOM), which had led to a funding gap of USD 81.8 million. To give a measure of the problem, suffice to note that the total AU budget for FY 2018 was USD 769 million. The Assembly asked the AUC to refer the matter to the PSC for consideration. As was explained above, in 2022, AMISOM was reconfigured to the African Union Transition Mission in Somalia (ATMIS), which has also been facing funding shortfalls. To that effect, the PSC has appealed to the UNSC for its financing through UN-assessed contributions.[509] Indeed, it is a standing request of African states to the UNSC that AU-led peace support missions should be assisted through UN-assessed contributions.[510] Whether it will ever happen is open to question. Thus, for the USA, no such discussion can start until and unless the AU has implemented compliance frameworks

---

506. PSC, Communiqué, 668th Meeting, PSC/PR/COMM(DCLVIII), 20 Mar. 2017, at: http://www.peaceau.org/en/article/communique-of-the-668th-meeting-of-the-peace-and-security-council-of-the-african-union-au-on-the-situation-in-western-sahara.
507. *See* OAU Doc. AHG/Res. 92 (XV) (22 Jul. 1978).
508. Assembly, *Decision on the Implementation of the Theme of the Year*, AU Doc. Assembly/AU/Dec. 660 (XXIX) (4 Jul. 2017). *See further*, Assembly, *Declaration on the 2017 AU Theme 'Harnessing the Demographic Dividend through Investments in Youth'*, AU Doc. Assembly/AU/Decl. 1 (XXIX) (4 Jul. 2017).
509. PSC, *Consideration of the Report of the Chairperson of the Commission on the Situation in Somalia and the Mandate of the AU Transition Mission in Somalia (ATMIS)*, Communique, 1112th Meeting, AU Doc. PSC/PR/COMM.1112, 10 October 2022, para. 9.
510. For example Kenya, *see* United Nations Meetings Coverage and Press Releases, 'Stronger United Nations-African Union Partnership Vital to Tackle Increasing Terrorism, Governance Gaps, Humanitarian Plight in Africa, Speakers Tell Security Council', UN Doc. SC/15058, 11 October 2022, at: https://press.un.org/en/2022/sc15058.doc.htm.

in international humanitarian law and human rights and has strengthened monitoring and accountability.[511] Returning to the approval of the AU budget and given that Member States are notoriously unreliable in their payment of budgetary contributions, the Assembly asked the AUC to employ a new format when preparing AU budgets to be supported by projections on future contributions.[512] Moreover, the Assembly deliberated the regular PSC Report on conflicts and tensions in the continent and how it had dealt with them. The following passage taken from an Assembly decision requires some explication:

> [Assembly] … welcomed the commitment of the A3 Group, namely Egypt, Ethiopia and Senegal, to continue to promote and defend African common interests and positions on peace and security issues within the UN Security Council, in line with the conclusions of the High Level Seminars on Peace and Security held in Oran, Algeria.[513]

In particular, the 'A3 Group' refers to the three non-permanent UNSC members to which African states are entitled,[514] while the High-Level Seminars were inaugurated in December 2013 to strengthen coherence, cooperation and coordination between the PSC and the A3 countries.[515] In particular, the Seminars aim at ensuring that A3 Group members promote and defend the AU common positions in an effective way, as well as AU interests and concerns when the UNSC deliberates peace and security issues pertaining to the continent and to its people. The Seminars, which have been held in Oran, the second largest city in Algeria (for this reason, they are also known as the 'Oran process'), have been supported by the United Nations Institute for Training and Research (UNITAR).[516] They take place once a year during the month of December. The most recent (Ninth) Seminar was held on 7–9 December 2022,[517] which, *inter alia*, deliberated the 'imposition and application of sanctions by international organizations and partners on AU Member States'. Arguably, the discussion revealed that African states may have difficulties reconciling their AU membership with that of other international organizations, an issue that was also touched upon above. More specifically, Seminar participants 'expressed

---

511. *Ibid*, statement by the US representative to the UNSC. Note the existence of a tripartite project (African Union, EU and UN) on the 'Human Rights Compliance Framework' for peacekeeping operations. The question of the accountability of AU peace missions' members is discussed *infra*.
512. Assembly, *Decision on the Budget of the African Union for the 2018 Financial Year*, AU Doc. Assembly/AU/Dec. 642 (XXIX) (4 Jul. 2017).
513. Assembly, *Decision on the Report of Peace and Security Council on its Activities and the State of Peace and Security in Africa*, AU Doc. Assembly/AU/Dec. 644 (XXIX) (4 Jul. 2017).
514. *See* UNGA Res. 1991 A (XVIII), *Question of Equitable Representation in the Security Council and in the Economic and Social Council*, 17 Dec. 1963.
515. Pursuant to PSC, *Communique of the 397th Meeting at the Level of Heads of State and Government*, AU Doc. PSC/AHG/COMM/1. (CCCXCVII) (23 Sep. 2013).
516. *See* https://unitar.org/about/news-stories/news/unitar-participates-second-high-level-seminar-peace-and-security-africa.
517. *See* Conclusions of the 9th High-Level Seminar on Peace and Security in Africa, Oran Process 'Enhancing Cooperation Between the AU PSC and the A3', AU Doc. PSC/HLS/09 (2022), at: https://www.peaceau.org/uploads/9th-hls-concl-en.pdf.

deep concern over the imposition of sanctions by the United Nations and some international organizations against [AU] Member States struggling to protect their sovereignty, national unity and territorial integrity'. To that effect, they recommended that '[AU] Member States support the call for the lifting of unilateral sanctions imposed by some international organizations against some AU Member States'. Even though (presumably for diplomatic reasons) no specific cases were mentioned, to criticize punitive measures ordered, presumably, by the UNSC is at least problematic considering that the UNSC acts on behalf of the entire UN membership.[518] Thus, it is submitted that when states (including African members) cast their votes in UN organs, they should not be guided (certainly not dictated) by the regional institution/s to which they happen to belong, in casu the AU. On the contrary, what they must uphold are the membership duties and obligations to which they agreed when they joined the UN, even if these might conflict with the AU's common positions. During the Twenty-Ninth Session, the Assembly also discussed the implementation of the Common Position concerning the social problem of child marriage.[519] The Common Position is an outcome of the AU Campaign to End Child Marriage in Africa, which was launched on 29 May 2014 during the Fourth AU Conference of Ministers of Social Development. A Special Rapporteur on Child Marriage was appointed in 2014 from among the members of the African Committee of Experts on the Rights and Welfare of the Child.[520] The Campaign lasted until 2018, when a new strategy was agreed for the period 2019–2023.[521] The Assembly urged Member States to specify the minimum age of marriage in line with the African Charter on the Rights of the Child and with the Maputo Protocol on the Rights of Women and to legally recognize marriages only if recorded in writing and registered in accordance with national laws.[522] Finally, the Assembly adopted its customary declaration on the situation in Palestine and the maintenance of peace and security in the Middle East,[523] as well as a resolution on the crisis that had erupted in the Gulf region between the Kingdom of Saudi Arabia and the United Arab Emirates on the one hand and the State of Qatar on the other hand.[524]

518. *See* Articles 24(1) and 25 of the UN Charter.

519. *See Common African Position on Ending Child Marriage in Africa*, at: https://au.int/sites/default/files/documents/31010-doc-cap_on_ending_child_marriage_-english_0.pdf. Generally, *see* United Nations Entity for Gender Equality and the Empowerment of Women, *Prospects for Ending Child Marriage in Africa: Implications on Legislation, Policy, Culture & Interventions*, Executive Brief, no date, at: https://africa.unwomen.org/.

520. Executive Committee, *Decision on the Report of the African Committee of experts on the Rights and Welfare of the Child (ACERWC)*, AU Doc. EX.CL/Dec. 843 (XXV) (24 Jun. 2014).

521. The Campaign, which maintains its own webpage at: https://www.aucecma.org/en/, is closely pursued with the AU action against female genital mutilation, reference to which has been made above. *See, e.g.*, the Cairo Call to Action on Ending Child Marriage and Female Genital Mutilation (2019), and the Niamey Call to Action and Commitment on Eliminating Harmful Practices, adopted at the Third African Girls Summit on 18 November 2021. For the previous two African Girls Summits, *see* Assembly, *Decision on the African Union Campaign on Ending Child Marriage in Africa*, AU Doc. Assembly/AU/Dec. 727 (XXXII) (11 Feb. 2019).

522. Assembly, *Decision on Ending Child Marriage in Africa*, AU Doc. Assembly/AU/Dec. 659 (XXIX) (4 Jul. 2017).

523. Assembly, *Declaration on the Situation in Palestine and the Middle East*, AU Doc. Assembly/AU/Decl. 2 (XXIX) (4 Jul. 2017).

524. Assembly, *Resolution on the Gulf Crisis*, AU Doc. Assembly/AU/ Res. 1 (XXIX) (4 Jul. 2017).

At the Thirtieth Ordinary Session (28–29 January 2018, Addis Ababa), the Assembly continued its antiparathesis with the ICC. The Assembly condemned the ICC for opening an investigation into the situation of Burundi (as explained above, it had withdrawn from the ICC in October 2017[525]). It mentioned three grounds: it was prejudicial to the peace process pursued in the country under the East African Community's auspices, it constituted a violation of the sovereignty of Burundi and it aimed at destabilizing Burundi.[526] Clearly, the ICC investigation was in line with the stipulations of the Rome Statute pertaining to the situation following contracting parties' withdrawal. It is rather difficult to see how it violated Burundi's sovereignty. Moreover, the Assembly adopted a score of legal instruments in different areas of endeavour.[527] Suffice to mention the following: (a) the Statute of the Trust Fund for the victims of the crimes committed by the former Chadian president Hissène Habré, reference to which has been made above; (b) amendments to Articles 10 and 14 of ECOSOCC Statutes;[528] and (c) the Statute of the African Institute for Remittances (AIR), which entered into force upon adoption. Even though AIR was established as a Specialized Technical Office of the AUC, it was given full international legal personality and, therefore, it may conclude agreements with non-Member States, enter into contracts, institute legal proceeding, be sued, etc. Before the AIR Statute was adopted, the Executive Council had already selected Kenya to host it; (d) the Protocol to the AEC Treaty relating to Free Movement of Persons, Rights of Residence and Right of Establishment as well as the Implementation Roadmap, reference to which is made elsewhere in this monograph; (e) the African Union Model Law for the implementation of the Convention for the Protection of and Assistance to Internally Displaced Persons in Africa;[529] (f) the Protocol to the African Charter on Human and Peoples' Rights on the Rights of Persons with Disability in Africa. The Protocol has not yet entered into force as it has been ratified by eight out of the required fifteen states (the last one was the Republic of South Africa in February 2023); (g) the Statute of the African Space Agency (AfSA), which entered into force upon adoption by the Assembly. It was established as an 'Organ of the African Union' in accordance with Article 5(2) of the Constitutive Act;[530] and (h) the Model Law on the implementation of the Kampala Convention on IDPs to assist Member States' Parliaments.[531]

525. *See* M. SSENYONJO, 'State Withdrawal Notifications from the Rome Statute of the International Criminal Court: South Africa, Burundi and The Gambia', *Criminal Law Forum* 29 (2018):63.
526. Assembly, *Decision on the International Criminal Court*, AU Doc. Assembly/AU/Dec. 672 (XXX) (29 Jan. 2018).
527. Assembly, *Decision on the Legal Instruments*, AU Doc. Assembly/AU/Dec. 676 (XXX) (29 Jan. 2018).
528. These changes were envisaged in ECOSOCC's Strategic Plan 2017–2018 adopted in December 2016.
529. Text at: https://www.refworld.org/docid/5afc3a494.html.
530. *See* K. Magliveras, 'The African Union's Outer Space Agenda and the African Space Agency: An Assessment, Zeitschrift *für Luft- und Weltraumrecht* 70 (2021): 52. For the staffing of AfSA (with an estimated annual cost of USD 13.1 million), *see* Assembly, *Decision on Sub-Committee on Structural Reforms*, AU Doc. Assembly/AU/Dec. 814 (XXXV), p. 22 (6 Feb. 2022). The seat of AfSA is in Cairo.
531. *See* AU Commission on International Law, *African Union Model Law for the Implementation of the African Union Convention for the Protection of and Assistance to Internally Displaced Persons in Africa*, April 2018, at: https://www.refworld.org/docid/5afc3a494.html.

Regarding the ongoing project of the AU's institutional reform, the Thirtieth Ordinary Assembly Session resolved, *inter alia*, that: (a) the AUC must ensure by 2025 the equal representation of women and men in AU organs and institutions; (b) from 2019 onwards, there will be only one (instead of two) ordinary Assembly session per year; (c) pursuant to the provisions of Article 9.2 of the Constitutive Act, the Assembly's budget adoption powers and relevant functions be delegated to the Executive Council. The later was instructed to adopt the AU budget during the months of June/July at a dedicated budget session to be attended by the Ministers of Foreign Affairs and the Ministers of Finance; (d) the decision-making roles of the Assembly and of the Executive Council be properly delineated to ensure the disaggregation of the types of decisions that are adopted by these two organs, respectively under Article 9 and Article 13 of the Constitutive Act; and (e) the implementation of resolutions and policies be monitored by the AUC and by the PRC (meeting monthly), by the Executive Council (mid-year meeting reviews) and by the Assembly, which will also take the decisions on compliance.[532] The Assembly also adopted a declaration on Internet governance and on the development of an African digital economy.[533] Finally, the Assembly adopted a declaration commemorating the fifteenth anniversary of the African Peer Review Mechanism (APRM), where it was noted that the APRM Statute (it was approved in August 2016)[534] 'marked a historic step to put the Mechanism on solid legal basis and secure its future as an institution central to our enduring pursuit of transformative governance on the continent'.[535] It should be noted that the transformation of APRM into an autonomous entity operating within the AU system and acting as a voluntary organization of Member States with financial and budgetary autonomy had taken place in 2014.[536] In 2017, the Assembly stated that the APRM should be strengthened to track implementation and oversee monitoring and evaluation in key governance areas on the continent,[537] including Agenda 2063 and the UN Sustainable Development Goals Agenda 2030.[538] The following year, the Assembly resolved to integrate the APRM budget into the 'statutory [AU] budget funded by Member States' (it was implemented for the first time in the budget for FY 2020), and urged those Member States that were not part of APRM to accelerate their accession 'to achieve universality by 2023'.[539] Presently, forty-two Member States participate in APRM,

---

532. Assembly, *Decision on the Progress Report on the Status of Implementation of Assembly Decision Assembly/AU/Dec.635(XXVIII) on the Institutional Reform of the African Union*, AU Doc. Assembly/AU/Dec. 687 (XXX) (29 Jan. 2018).
533. Assembly, *Declaration on Internet Governance and Development of Africa's Digital Economy*, AU Doc. Assembly/AU/Decl. 3 (XXX) (29 Jan. 2018).
534. Text at: https://www.aprm-au.org/wp-content/uploads/2014/11/Statute-of-the-APRM.pdf.
535. Assembly, *Declaration on the Commemoration of the Fifteenth Anniversary of the African Peer Review Mechanism*, AU Doc. Assembly/AU/Decl. 4 (XXX) (29 Jan. 2018).
536. Assembly, *Decision on the Integration of the APRM into the African Union*, AU Doc. Assembly/AU/Dec. 527 (XXIII) (27 Jun. 2014).
537. *See* AU Doc. Assembly/AU/Dec. 635 (XXVIII), *supra*, and Assembly, *Decision on the Revitalisation of the APRM*, AU Doc. Assembly/AU/Dec. 631 (XXVIII) (31 Jan. 2017).
538. Adopted under UNGA Resolution 70/1, *Transforming our world: the 2030 Agenda for Sustainable Development*, 25 Sep. 2015.
539. Assembly, *Decision on the Institutional Reform*, AU Doc. Ext/Assembly/AU/Dec. 1 (XI) (18 Nov. 2018).

which is in the process of realizing its Five Year Strategic Plan (2020–2024) endorsed by the Assembly in February 2020.[540]

The Tenth Extraordinary Assembly Session (Kigali, Rwanda, 21 March 2018) had a single item on the agenda: the launch of the African Continental Free Trade Area (AfCFTA) and the adoption of the namesake Agreement as well as the Protocols on Trade in Goods, on Trade in Services and on Rules and Procedures on the Settlement of Disputes.[541] The AfCFTA Agreement, which entered into force on 30 May 2019, has presently been ratified by forty-seven Member States (Eritrea is the only one that has not signed it) and is being implemented satisfactorily considering the multifaceted challenges that the continent faces. The Thirty-First Ordinary Assembly Session (Nouakchott, Mauritania, 1–2 July 2018) decided that in the services sector, there will be five AfCFTA priority areas, namely transport, communication, tourism, financial services, and business services. It also resolved that external AfCFTA partners will be engaged as one block and that the AU will 'speak with one voice'.[542]

At its Thirty-First Ordinary Session (1–2 July 2018, Nouakchott, Mauritania), the Assembly expressed deep concern at the continued stalemate over the Western Sahara situation and its impact on the AU's functioning. To address it, it resolved to establish an African mechanism comprising the AU Troika (namely the outgoing, the current and the incoming Assembly Chairpersons)[543] as well as the AUC Chairperson to support the UN-led efforts to find a compromise.[544] This Decision has been regarded as the AU limiting its own peace efforts in Western Sahara to assist the UN process and as 'a big win for Morocco, which believes the AU-led efforts are biased'.[545] However, at its Twenty-Ninth Ordinary Session, the Assembly had considered that the conflict in Western Sahara should be tackled in the context of the Joint UN-AU Framework for Enhancing Partnership on Peace and Security.[546] The Framework had been signed on 19 April 2017 following the first Joint UN-AU Annual Conference, which had focused on the complementarity between the aforementioned UN Agenda for Sustainable Development 2030 and Agenda 2063, on the fight against terrorism and on the financing of AU operations.[547] More specifically

---

540. Assembly, *Decision on the Report of the African Peer Review Mechanism (APRM)*, AU Doc. Assembly/AU/Dec. 765 (XXXIII), para. 26 (10 Feb. 2020).
541. Assembly, *Decision on the Draft Agreement Establishing the African Continental Free Trade Area (AfCFTA)*, AU Doc. Ext/Assembly/AU/Dec. 1 (X) (21 Mar. 2018). The Assembly has adopted Annexes to the Protocol on Trade in Goods and to the Protocol on Rules and Procedures on the Settlement of Disputes, *see* Assembly, *Decision on the Draft Legal Instruments*, AU Doc. Assembly/AU /Dec. 698 (XXXI) (2 Jul. 2018).
542. Assembly, *Decision on the African Continental Free Trade Area (AfCFTA)*, AU Doc. Assembly/AU/Dec. 692 (XXXI) (2 Jul. 2018).
543. On the establishment of the Troika, which aims at ensuring continuity and effective implementation of Assembly decisions, *see* AU Doc. Assembly/AU/Dec. 635 (XXVIII), *supra*.
544. Assembly, *Decision on the Report of the Chairperson of the Commission of the African Union on the Issue of Western Sahara*, Assembly/AU /Dec. 693 (XXXI) (2 Jul. 2018).
545. *See* 'How the latest AU decision on Western Sahara could affect other crises', *ISS PSC Report*, 22 Aug. 2018, at: https://issafrica.org/pscreport/psc-insights/how-the-latest-au-decision-on-western-sahara-could-affect-other-crises.
546. Assembly, *Decision on the Issue of Western Sahara*, AU Doc. Assembly/AU/Dec. 653 (XXIX)Rev.1, para. 5 (4 Jul. 2017).
547. Text at: https://unoau.unmissions.org/sites/default/files/signed_joint_framework.pdf.

in Assembly/AU/Dec. 653 (XXIX)Rev.1, the Assembly requested the AU and the AUC Chairpersons to take appropriate measures and support the UN efforts to resolve the Western Sahara conflict and to 'encourage the parties, both of whom are now members of the African Union, to cooperate in good faith'.[548] Interestingly enough, the text of the Decision did not name them: they were of course Morocco (as mentioned above, it rejoined the AU in January 2017 and was elected to PSC membership in January 2018) and the Saharawi Arab Democratic Republic (SADR). Arguably, this was a concession to Morocco considering that it does not recognize the existence of SADR. Finally, the Thirty-First Ordinary Assembly Session resolved that the theme for 2019 will be 'The Year of Refugees, Returnees and Internally Displaced Persons: Towards Durable Solutions to Forced Displacement in Africa'.[549] The Assembly also issued a declaration on the theme that had been chosen for the year 2018, namely 'Winning the Fight Against Corruption: A Sustainable Path to Africa's Transformation'. Corruption is one of the continent's scourges.[550] Even though the Constitutive Act does not expressly refer to corruption, it does mention good governance as an AU objective and principle. The two concepts, corruption and good governance, are very closely associated: as has been explained by the UN Office on Drugs and Crime: '[they] have a two-way causal relationship with each other and feed off each other in a vicious circle'.[551] It was explained above that the Convention on Preventing and Combating Corruption (it entered into force on 5 August 2006 and currently has forty-eight contracting parties) envisages the operation of the Advisory Board on Corruption (AUABC), which was set up on 26 May 2009. At its Thirty-First Session, the Assembly requested AUABC to make appropriate recommendations on amending the Convention to strengthen its mandate. Moreover, it resolved to combat illicit financial flows and suggested that Member States, *inter alia*, establish effective ownership registers, engage in country-by-country reporting of financial information, participate in the automatic exchange of information under tax information agreements,[552] and adopt measures to ensure that public personalities declare their assets and that such assets are verified. Finally, the Assembly called upon the AU's international partners and allies to promote the recovery and return of stolen assets to Africa with due respect

548. Assembly, *Decision on the Issue of Western Sahara*, AU Doc. Assembly/AU/Dec. 653 (XXIX)Rev.1, para. 5 (4 Jul. 2017).
549. Assembly, *Decision on the 2019 Theme of the Year*, AU Doc. Assembly/AU/Dec. 707 (XXXI) (2 Jul. 2018).
550. *See, e.g.*, Transparency International, Global Corruption Barometer (GCB) – Africa, 10th ed., 2019, at: https://www.transparency.org/en/gcb/africa/africa-2019.
551. *See* https://www.unodc.org/e4j/en/anti-corruption/module-2/key-issues/corruption-and-bad-governance.html. All AU Member States, except SADR, as contracting parties to the UN Convention against Corruption, adopted on 31 October 2003, entered into force on 14 December 2005, 2349 U.N.T.S. 41. *See further*, Thirteenth United Nations Congress on Crime Prevention and Criminal Justice, Doha, 12–19 April 2015, *Doha Declaration on Integrating Crime Prevention and Criminal Justice into the Wider United Nations Agenda to Address Social and Economic Challenges and to Promote the Rule of Law at the National and International Levels, and Public Participation* (United Nations Office at Vienna, July 2015).
552. Note that one African country (Liberia) has concluded several agreements based on the Model Agreement on Exchange of Information in Tax Matters, which was prepared by the OECD in April 2002, *see* https://web-archive.oecd.org/2012-07-16/71427-taxinformationexchangeagreementstieas.htm.

for state sovereignty.[553] These efforts culminated in the adoption of a Common African Position on Asset Recovery (CAPAR) in February 2020.[554] CAPAR is based on the following pillars: detection; identification recovery and return of illicitly removed assets; management of recovered assets; and cooperation in promoting harmonized processes of identification and recovery.[555] The first workshop on the implementation of CAPAR was held in September 2022.[556]

In November 2018, another Extraordinary Assembly Session was held to discuss, among others, developments in the AU's institutional reform; the new sanctions regime for the non-payment of contributions to the AU budget (it is examined later in the monograph);[557] and the ongoing discussions on cooperation with the EU in the post-Cotonou Agreement era (also discussed later).[558] As regards the first item, it was resolved that the AUC be restructured and be composed of a Chairperson, a Deputy Chairperson and six Commissioners. These persons constitute the 'senior leadership of the Commission', whose election process was also changed, for example, a five-member Panel of Eminent Africans is now to oversee the preselection of candidatures.[559] The overhaul of the AUC's structure continued during the Thirty-Third Ordinary Assembly Session.[560] It was also in November 2018 that the High-Level Committee (HLC), which had been instituted in May 2018 by the AUC Chairperson to investigate allegations of harassment against women, submitted its final Report. The HLC broadened the ambit of the investigation and reviewed forty-four cases that involved claims of abuse of authority, bribery, bullying, corruption, fraud, intimidation, impunity, whistleblowing, etc. The Report makes distressing reading: 'It is the finding of the Committee that incidents of sexual harassment exists in the Commission … Senior departmental staff, who position themselves as 'gate-keepers' and 'king-makers, are well-positioned to make believable promises to young women that they will be offered contracts … .' The HLC made several key recommendations, and the AUC Chairperson announced the intention to appoint an internal committee to look into all of them.[561]

During its Thirty-Second Ordinary Session (Addis Ababa, 10 – 11 February 2019), the Assembly discussed the regular PSC Report on crises, conflicts, disputes

553. Assembly, *Declaration on the African Anti-Corruption Year*, AU Doc. Assembly/AU/Decl. 1 (XXXI) (2 Jul. 2018).
554. Assembly, *Decision on the Common African Position on Asset Recovery*, AU Doc. Assembly/AU/Dec. 774 (XXXIII) (10 Feb. 2020).
555. AU Doc. EX.CL/1213(XXXVI) Add.1 Rev.1, at: https://au.int/sites/default/files/documents/42297-doc-COMMON-AFRICAN-POSITION-ON-ASSEST-RECOVERY-ENGLISH-NEWLY-PROOFREAD-1.pdf.
556. AU, Information & Communication Directorate, Press Release No: 000003456/2022, 19 September 2022.
557. Assembly, *Decision on the New African Union Sanctions Regime for the Non-Payment of Contributions*, AU Doc. Ext/Assembly/AU/Dec. 3 (XI) (18 Nov. 2018).
558. Assembly, *Decision on Post-Cotonou Negotiations*, AU Doc. Ext/Assembly/AU/Dec. 4 (XI) (18 Nov. 2018).
559. *See* AU Doc. Ext/Assembly/AU/Dec. 1 (XI), *supra*.
560. Assembly, *Decision on the Structures of the African Union Commission, Organs and Specialized Agencies*, AU Doc. Assembly/AU/Dec. 750 (XXXIII) (10 Feb. 2020).
561. *See* AU, *Outcome of the Investigation of allegations of harassment against women and other institutional malpractices in the African Union Commission*, Press Release, 22 November 2018, at:

and tensions in the continent.[562] It noted developments in the following Member States: Libya;[563] Madagascar; the Comoros; Somalia; Sudan (it concerned peace in the Darfur region); Sudan and South Sudan (the issue of the Two Areas of South Kordofan and the Blue Nile), again Sudan and South Sudan (the final status of Abye); South Sudan (the signing of the Revitalized Agreement on the Resolution of the Conflict in the Republic of South Sudan (R-ARCSS) on 12 September 2018[564]); Ethiopia and Eritrea; Eritrea and Djibouti; DRC; CAR; Burundi; Guinea-Bissau; and Mali.[565] According to the PSC Report, almost one-fourth of the AU membership was embroiled in some kind of conflict or had just come out of it. Moreover, a close reading of the Assembly decision reveals that several stakeholders not only from inside Africa (principally RECs and the Lake Chad Basin Commission) but also from outside Africa were engaged in the resolution of the disputes. This raises the rather obvious question of to which extent does the AU actually own the solutions to these situations and whether its role has not been restricted to that of an overall supervision. Considering that some of these conflicts had been going on for many years and persist to this day, arguably the continent requires a different peace and security architecture, where delineating the differing roles of the AU, of RECs and other (sub)regional peace and security mechanisms, of the UN, of the EU, and so on is of paramount importance. The Thirty-Second Ordinary Session also dealt with the ever-complex issue of migration and took further action in establishing technical bodies to deal with legal and illegal migration, with trafficking in human beings and with migrant smuggling. Thus, it endorsed the Executive Council's proposal to set up as a specialized AU technical office the Continental Operational Centre in Sudan for Combating Irregular Migration (known as 'Khartoum Centre'),[566] and, in 2020, it approved its Statute.[567] The Assembly also resolved to create an African Migration Observatory (AMO) in Morocco as the body to implement the

---

https://au.int/en/pressreleases/20181122/outcome-investigation-allegations-harassment-against-women-and-other, where the HLC Terms of Reference are also available. *See also*, 'African Union hit by sexual harassment claims', *BBC News*, 23 Nov. 2018, at: https://www.bbc.com/news/world-africa-46319227.

562. Assembly, *Decision on the Report of the Peace and Security Council on its Activities and the State of Peace and Security in Africa*, AU Doc. Assembly/AU/Dec. 718 (XXXII) (11 Feb. 2019).

563. Note that developments in Libya were also discussed in the context of Assembly, *Decision on the Report of the High-Level Committee on Libya*, AU Doc. Assembly/AU/Dec. 722 (XXXII) (11 Feb. 2019). The separate discussion of the same topic is explained because this Decision deliberated the action undertaken not by the PSC but by another AU body set up solely for resolving the crisis, the African Union High-Level Committee on Libya.

564. Text at: https://www.peaceagreements.org/viewmasterdocument/2112.

565. Note that the Assembly reiterated its request to the European Union to immediately lift the targeted sanctions imposed against certain DRC political actors as well as the unilateral sanctions imposed on Burundi, on which *see also infra*.

566. Assembly, *Decision on the Establishment of Continental Operational Centre in Khartoum for Combating Irregular Migration*, AU Doc. Assembly/AU/Dec. 728 (XXXII) (11 Feb. 2019).

567. AU Doc. Assembly/AU/26(XXXIII)vii; *see* Assembly, *Decision on the Structures of the African Union Commission, Organs and Specialized Agencies*, AU Doc. Assembly/AU/Dec. 750 (XXXIII) (20 Feb. 2020).

Global Compact on Safe, Orderly and Regular Migration in the continent.[568] The Host Agreement between Morocco and AUC to operationalize AMO was signed on 10 December 2018, even though its Statute had not been completed at the time.[569] Finally, in 2020, the Assembly consented to the establishment of the African Centre for the Study and Research on Migration (CARIM) in Bamako, Mali.[570] CARIM was officially launched in March 2021. It serves as a specialized technical office to advance the knowledge base of the continent on migration and mobility, and to contribute to evidence-based interventions on migration in Africa.[571] As regards the ongoing topic of restructuring the AU's working methods, in January 2016, the Assembly had dissolved the (Ministerial) Drafting Committee (it was involved in elaborating the draft decisions proposed by the AUC, which were then considered by the PRC, before being submitted to the Assembly through the Executive Council for adoption).[572] However, at the Thirty-Second Session and without giving any reason, other than that it was recommended by the Executive Council, the Assembly resolved to re-establish the Drafting Committee composed of fifteen members at the ambassadorial level (the five members of the AU Bureau and two Member States from each of the five regions).[573] The Assembly also adopted a revised scale of assessment for Member States' contributions to the AU budget (*see* the section on Finances).[574] Reference should also be made to the adoption of a declaration on the 400th anniversary of the transatlantic slave trade, which, however, did not mention the issue of reparations for slavery and other crimes committed during the colonization of the continent.[575] Indeed, the AU has been criticized for not taking a more resolute stance on this matter.[576] But, acting individually, some African states have negotiated settlement agreements with the former colonial states. Thus, in 2021, the governments of Germany and Namibia announced the conclusion of a joint declaration concerning the atrocities perpetrated between 1904 and 1908 during German colonial rule in the territory of today's Namibia. According to the draft declaration, the German government agreed to disburse, in the form of a grant, EUR 1.1 billion over a period of 30 years principally for a reconstruction and development support

568. The Compact was approved during the Intergovernmental Conference that took place in Marrakech, Morocco, on 10 and 11 December 2018. It was endorsed under UNGA Resolution 73/195 of 19 December 2018.
569. Assembly, *Decision on the Follow-Up on the Establishment of the African Migration Observatory in Morocco*, AU Doc. Assembly/AU/Dec. 730 (XXXII) (11 Feb. 2019).
570. AU Doc. Assembly/AU/Dec. 750 (XXXIII), *supra*.
571. *See* https://au.int/en/pressreleases/20210313/official-inauguration-african-centre-study-and-research-migration.
572. *See* Assembly/AU/Dec. 597(XXVI), *supra*, para. 2 (iv).
573. Assembly, *Decision on the Report of the Commission on Re-Establishing the Drafting Committee*, AU Doc. Assembly/AU/Dec. 745 (XXXII) (11 Feb. 2019).
574. *See* Assembly, *Decision on the Scale of Assessment for the Regular Budget and the Peace Fund*, AU Doc. Assembly/AU/Dec. 734 (XXXII) (11 Feb. 2019).
575. Assembly, *Declaration on the AU Recognition of the 400th Anniversary of the Transatlantic Slave Trade*, AU Doc. Assembly/AU/Decl. 2 (XXXII) (11 Feb. 2019).
576. *See* I. Kaledzi, 'Africa revives push for colonial-era reparations', *DW*, 8 April 2022, at: https://www.dw.com/en/africa-revives-push-for-colonial-era-reparations/a-62710366.

programme 'for the benefit of the descendants of the particularly affected communities'.[577] The declaration has apparently not yet been signed as the Namibian side has asked for a renegotiation of the settlement amount, and the German side has rejected the request. Moreover, there appear to be outstanding legal issues, e.g. whether the document is an agreement under international law and, therefore, requires ratification by the respective Parliaments (the German Parliament has said that no ratification is required[578]). This is a crucial issue because if it were not regarded as a bilateral (legal) agreement, the German grant would not be a legally binding promise and, therefore, failure to execute it would not be actionable. This incident shows the importance that should be attached to the AU negotiating reparation agreements on behalf of its Member States. Finally, the Thirty-Second Ordinary Session adopted two documents on the conduct of members of Peace Support Operations (PSO), the 'African Union Policy on Conduct and Discipline for Peace Support Operations' and the 'African Union Policy on Prevention and Response to Sexual Exploitation and Abuse for Peace Support Operations'.[579] Improper conduct by peacekeeping operations is a matter of particular concern for the UN as well.[580] Especially in cases of sexual and other crimes, the accountability and the responsibility of the alleged perpetrators and/or of their superiors has to be addressed. The AU Policy on Prevention and Response to Sexual Exploitation and Abuse defines accountability as the 'measures taken to acknowledge, assume responsibility for, and remedy violations of international humanitarian and human rights law'. These measures include AU policies, AU rules and regulations as well as mission-specific regulations. More specifically, for accountability to exist, systems must have been set up to ensure that the AU personnel serving in PSO 'act in accordance with their international and internal obligations and duties'. Thus, section 8 of said Policy stipulates that acts of sexual exploitation and abuse (SEA) committed by PSO members constitute acts of serious misconduct and, therefore, grounds for disciplinary action, including termination of employment contracts with the AU as well as criminal prosecution. Moreover, since SEA also constitutes a violation of international humanitarian law and of international and regional human rights law, the question of safeguarding the rights of victims and the question of their compensation invariably arises. Pursuant to section 10 of said Policy, victims of SEA have the right to

---

577. Joint Declaration by the Federal Republic of Germany and the Republic of Namibia: United in Remembrance of Our Colonial Past, United in Our Will to Reconcile, United in Our Vision of the Future, May 2021, para. 18, at: https://www.dngev.de/images/stories/Startseite/joint-declaration_2021-05.pdf. *See* H. Melber, 'Germany and reparations: the reconciliation agreement with Namibia', *The Round Table*, 2022 (111): 475.

578. *See* D. Pelz, 'Germany rejects new negotiations over Namibia genocide', *GW*, 9 February 2022, at: https://www.dw.com/en/germany-rejects-new-negotiations-over-namibia-genocide/a-63002889.

579. The documents appear as Annexes to Assembly, *Declaration on the 11th Ordinary Meeting of the Specialized Technical Committee on Defence, Safety and Security (STCDSS) Addis Ababa, 12 October 2018*, AU Doc. Assembly/AU/Decl. 5 (XXXII) (11 Feb. 2019). Texts, respectively, at: https://www.peaceau.org/uploads/english-final-au-policy-for-conduct-discipline-in-pso.pdf and at: https://www.peaceau.org/uploads/english-final-sea-policy-for-au-psos.pdf.

580. *See*, *inter alia*, UNGA, Resolution 57/306, *Investigation into sexual exploitation of refugees by aid workers in West Africa*, 15 April 2003, which prompted the UN Secretary-General to issue the Bulletin on special measures for protection from sexual exploitation and sexual abuse, UN Doc. ST/SGB/2003/13, 9 October 2003. *See further*, UNGA, *Special measures for protection from sexual exploitation and abuse: Report of the Secretary-General*, UN Doc. A/76/702, 16 Feb. 2022.

remedies for harm suffered, including access to justice and reparations. However, it is also laid down that assistance and support offered by the PSO cannot be construed as acknowledgement on the validity of claims of SEA. The effect of this clause is arguably to exclude a priori the AU's responsibility, given that PSO operate under its authority. Therefore, it is not clear with its responsibility in such instances, including the question of whether (alleged) victims and their families are entitled to demand compensation from the AU. These are no doubt intricate legal questions, which should be clarified considering the many cases of SEA during PSO. According to said Policy, the AUC must ensure that resources for delivery of assistance and redress to victims are specifically designated in the budget of the relevant PSO. Moreover, victims, with the assistance of the AUC, should additionally be entitled to obtain redress from the perpetrators, for the country of origin of the perpetrators, and from other sources that the PSO may deem appropriate. Redress includes monetary or material compensation, public apologies, and acceptance of responsibility for the harm suffered. Finally, it is submitted that, notwithstanding the significance of this framework on the conduct of PSOs, the question of how to avoid the impunity of those accused of sexual crimes and other human rights violations is not adequately addressed.

The Twelfth Extraordinary Assembly Session was held in Niamey, Niger, on 7 July 2019. As will be recalled, the Assembly had decided that, from 2019 onwards, there will only be one ordinary session per year. Thus, even though, under the previous arrangement, another ordinary session would have taken place during the months of June/July, it did not. Therefore, important, urgent affairs have to be deliberated during extraordinary sessions. There was only one item on the agenda of the Twelfth Extraordinary Session: the launch of AfCFTA's operational phase, following the entry into force of the AfCFTA Agreement, which as mentioned above took place on 30 May 2019.[581] At the time, only half of the Member States had deposited their instruments of ratification. Africa's largest economy, Nigeria, as well as other heavy-weight economies (e.g. Algeria, Morocco, Kenya) were not among them but became contracting parties at a later stage. On the contrary, countries with small or feeble economies (e.g. The Gambia, São Tomé and Príncipe, Djibouti) had already ratified the Agreement. Presently, there are more than forty-three parties.[582] The Assembly decided that Ghana will host the AfCFTA Secretariat,[583] pursuant to the rules on hosting AU organs.[584] Finally, the Assembly adopted a declaration on AfCFTA's launch, where, among others, it reaffirmed the 'commitment to continue

581. Assembly, *Decision on the Launch of the Operational Phase of the African Continental Free Trade Area (AfCFTA)*, AU Doc. Ext/Assembly/AU/ Dec. 1(XII) (7 Jul. 2019).
582. For updated information, *see* https://au-afcfta.org/state-parties/.
583. Assembly, *Decision on Hosting of the Secretariat of the African Continental Free Trade Area (AfCFTA)*, AU Doc. Ext/Assembly/AU/ Dec. 2 (XII) (7 Jul. 2019).
584. *See* AU Doc. EX.CL/195 (VII) Rev.1 on AU hosting criteria (July 2005). In 2021, the Executive Council reviewed this document 'by developing relevant, quantifiable and evaluable criteria, including a rating for each criterion', Executive Council, *Decision on the Reports of the Sub-Committees of the Permanent Representatives' Committee (PRC)*, AU Doc. EX.CL/Dec. 1126 (XXXIX), para. 46 (15 Oct. 2021).

the journey of establishing the AEC as outlined in the Abuja Treaty of 1991'.[585] However, while the Abuja Treaty is still in operation, to the extent that it has not been repealed or otherwise terminated, as an international organization, the AEC should be considered to be in disuse and not functionable. Moreover, one could raise some caution as to whether the AfCFTA Agreement is aligned with the Abuja Treaty (e.g. as concerns the question of dispute settlement). One can understand why African leaders did not want to engage with the subtle legal and institutional issues arising from the arguably defunct AEC. However, at some stage, they will have to be addressed because economic integration is a complicated project full of rules, norms, and legal procedures. At the Thirty-Third Ordinary Assembly Session (Addis Ababa, 9–10 February 2020), the Assembly adopted a declaration on the theme for the previous year (2019), namely 'Refugees, Returnees and Internally Displaced Persons: Towards Durable Solution to Forced Displacement in Africa'.[586] This was an attempt to further the declaration on that theme adopted during the Thirty-Second Ordinary Session,[587] and to connect it with the theme for the year 2020 ('Silencing the Guns: Creating Conducive Conditions for Africa's Development'). The 'Silencing the Guns' project is part of the Agenda 2063's aim for a conflict-free Africa.[588] It was meant to have been achieved by 2020. Furthermore, the Assembly talked about bolstering 'the collaborative mechanisms [with RECs] on geometrically implementing the regional and continental initiatives to strengthen Member States' capacities in addressing the phenomena of illicit proliferation, circulation and trafficking of Small Arms and Light Weapons'.[589] Moreover, the Assembly took up again the issue of the imposition of unilateral sanctions by third states against African and non-African countries (namely, Cuba). It considered that unilateral coercive measures and domestic legislation are contrary to international law, to international humanitarian law, to the UN Charter as well as to the norms and principles on peaceful interstate relations, while they have a negative impact on the right to development, on trade and investment, and on peace and stability.[590] In support of its assertion, the Assembly invoked two relevant UN documents: (a) a UNGA resolution urging the international community to adopt urgent and effective measures to eliminate the use of unilateral economic, financial or trade measures that

585. Assembly, *Niamey Declaration on the Launch of the Operational Phase of the African Continental Free Trade Area (AfCFTA)*, AU Doc. Ext/Assembly/AU/ Decl. 1 (XII) (7 Jul. 2019).

586. Assembly, *Declaration on the 2019 Theme of the Year*, AU Doc. Assembly/AU/Decl. 1 (XXXII) (9 Feb. 2020).

587. Assembly, *Declaration on the African Union Theme of the Year 2019: 'The Year of Refugees, Returnees and Internally Displaced Persons: Towards Durable Solutions to Forced Displacement in Africa'*, AU Doc. Assembly/AU/Decl. 8 (XXXII) (11 Feb. 2019).

588. *See* AU Doc. Assembly/AU/Dec. 630 (XXVIII), *supra*.

589. Assembly, *Decision on Strengthening National Capacities for Effective Management of Weapon Stockpiles*, AU Doc. Assembly/AU/Dec. 775 (XXXIII) (10 Feb. 2020).

590. Assembly, *Resolution on the Impact of Sanction and Unilateral Coercive Measures*, AU Doc. Assembly/AU/Res. 1 (XXXII) (10 Feb. 2020). *See further*, Assembly, *Resolution on the Impact of Sanctions and Unilateral Coercive Measures on African Union Member States*, AU Doc. Assembly/AU/Res. 1 (XXXV) (6 Feb. 2022); as regards Cuba, *see* Assembly, *Resolution on the Lifting of the Economic, Commercial and Financial Blockade Imposed on the Republic of Cuba by the United States of America*, AU Doc. Assembly/AU/Res. 2 (XXXV) (6 Feb. 2022).

are not authorized by the UN, that are inconsistent with the principles of international law or contravene the basic principles of the multilateral trading system and affect developing countries;[591] and (b) a UN Human Rights Council resolution castigating unilateral coercive measures due to their negative impact on the right to life, the right to health, the right to freedom from hunger and the right to an adequate standard of living, food,[592] education, work and housing.[593] In particular, the Assembly urged the USA to lift the sanctions imposed 'on the Government and People' of Zimbabwe, of South Sudan and of Sudan;[594] asked the UN to consider lifting the arms embargo against South Sudan;[595] and requested that the EU lift all unilateral sanctions against Burundi.[596] Finally, it decided that the coercive measures imposed on Somalia should be lifted but did not clarify which were the states and/or international organizations that had ordered them. Judging from the aforementioned Oran process Seminars, and in particular the one held in December 2022, it is obvious that the question of unilateral sanctions continues to be of considerable importance to the AU. A quite different matter that was discussed again during the Thirty-Third Session was adding Spanish as an AU working language.[597] According to the Constitutive Act, the AU does not have official languages but only working languages. Pursuant to Article 25 thereof, these are (unspecified) African languages,[598] Arabic, English, French and Portuguese. The Assembly urged Member States and the AUC to operationalize the use of Spanish as a working language

591. Although the Assembly did not cite specifically the document, it was probably UNGA Res. 74/200, *Unilateral economic measures as a means of political and economic coercion against developing countries*, adopted on 19 Dec. 2019.
592. *See* in this regard, PAP, *Résolution du Bureau du Parlement Panafricain sur l'impact des sanctions sur la sécurité alimentaire de l'Afrique*, 27 Jan. 2023, at: https://pap.au.int/en/documents/2023-01-27/resolution-du-bureau-du-parlement-panafricain.
593. Human Rights Council, Resolution 27/21, *Human rights and unilateral coercive measures*, 26 September 2014. Note that during the UNGA 74th Session another relevant document was adopted (Res. 74/154, *Human rights and unilateral coercive measures*, 18 Dec. 2019) but the AU Assembly did not take it into consideration.
594. For updated information, *see* U.S. Department of the Treasury, Office of Foreign Assets Control, *Sanctions Programs and Country Information*, at: https://ofac.treasury.gov/sanctions-programs-and-country-information.
595. Note that in May 2023 when the UNSC extended, under Res. 2683(2023), the sanctions regime against South Sudan for one year (it includes freezing of assets, travel bans and an arms embargo), several of its members stressed that, instead of sanctions, what South Sudan needed was a carefully managed support system 'to facilitate its transitional journey' and to overcome its security issues, *see* UNSC Press Release, UN Doc. SC/15297, 30 May 2023.
596. Note that, in October 2022, the EU reviewed its restrictive measures (as sanctions are called in the EU) against Burundi in view of the developing situation in the country and decided to renew the sanctions regime that had originally been established for one year under Council Decision (CFSP) 2015/1763 of 1 October 2015 concerning restrictive measures in view of the situation in Burundi, O.J. L 257, 2.10.2015, p. 37, *see* Council Decision (CFSP) 2022/2051 of 24 October 2022 amending Decision (CFSP) 2015/1763 concerning restrictive measures in view of the situation in Burundi, O.J. L 275, 25.10.2022, p. 72.
597. *See* OAU Council of Ministers, *Decision Relating to the Introduction of Spanish as a Working Language of the OAU/AU*, OAU Doc. CM/Dec. 45 (LXXIV) (8 Jul. 2001) and, further, Assembly, *Decision on the Use of Spanish within the African Union*, AU Doc. Assembly/AU/Dec. 388 (XVII) (1 Jul. 2011).
598. Kiswahili has been recognized in the UN as the first African language, while in November 2021 UNESCO designated the seventh of July as 'Kiswahili Language Day' (Resolution 41 C/61). In

by July 2020.[599] Arguably, this was another instance of a de facto amendment of the Constitutive Act. Furthermore, the Assembly deliberated the precarious situation in Libya and in the Sahel. It is made obvious from the adopted decision that, especially in the Sahel, the AU must work together with the relevant RECs, other regional institutions but also with the UNSC, which maintains the overall global responsibility for the restoration of peace and security.[600] Thus, as regards the Sahel and the challenges it faces from the operation of terrorist groups, the Assembly requested that the AUC develop a framework on a possible deployment of an operation to be composed of the Joint Multinational Task Force (JMTF)[601] and 3,000 troops for a period of six months to address terrorism in the region and asked ECOWAS to urgently disburse the funds that it had pledged in support of Mali, Niger and Burkina Faso (USD 100 million) so as to assist its deployment. The Assembly also welcomed the ECOWAS 2020–2024 Priority Plan of Action to eradicate terrorism, which had been agreed at the end of 2019 at an estimated cost of USD 2.3 billion.[602] However, as has been argued, the parallel involvement and engagement of different actors in the region has led to competing agendas.[603] Indeed, the AU acting through its African Peace and Security Architecture (ASPA) does appear to be in the position to act as coordinator, to set clear priorities and to respond when and as required.[604] Arguably, the simultaneous actions by different stakeholders could be a liability. During the Thirty-Third Session, the Assembly also discussed climate

---

Assembly, *Decision on the Use of Kiswahili as an AU Working Language of the African Union*, AU Doc. Assembly/AU/Dec. 832 (XXXV) (6 Feb. 2022), it was decided to make Kiswahili a working AU language and to promote it as a language of wider communication in the continent. The Thirty-Ninth SADC Summit in August 2019 approved Kiswahili as the fourth SADC official working language in recognition of its contribution in peace-building and liberation struggles of Southern Africa and Africa in general.

599. Assembly, *Project Decision on the Use of Spanish as an AU Working Language*, AU Doc. Assembly/AU/Dec. 794 (XXXIII) (10 Feb. 2020). Note that the first Assembly and Executive Council decisions to appear in Spanish were in February 2022 when, respectively, their Thirty-Fifth and Fortieth Ordinary Sessions took place. The official AU website shows that it is also available in Spanish and in Kiswahili but, at the time of writing, the relevant webpages were not working. However, the website of the AfCFTA Secretariat (https://au-afcfta.org/) has a version in both these languages.
600. Assembly, *Decision on Libya and the Sahel*, AU Doc. Assembly/AU/Dec. 792 (XXXIII) (10 Feb. 2020).
601. The deployment of JMTF, an initiative of the Member States of the Lake Chad Basin Commission and Benin, was authorized by the 484th PSC Meeting, which met at the level of Heads of States and Governments on 29 January 2015. It is mandated to create a safe and secure environment in the areas affected by the activities of Boko Haram and other terrorist groups. Presently, JMTF activities cover affected areas in the countries of Lake Chad Basin, in Cameroon, in Chad, in Niger, and in Nigeria.
602. Text at: https://remo-psd-soudir.org/english_version.pdf. The EU has expressed its readiness to lend support to the Action Plan, *see* Twenty-Third EU-ECOWAS Ministerial Dialogue, Joint Communique, 6 Feb. 2023, at: https://www.eeas.europa.eu/eeas/23rd-eu-ecowas-ministerial-dialogue_en.
603. Apart of ECOWAS, the involvement of the Group of Five for the Sahel (G5 Sahel), which was formed in 2014 by Burkina Faso, Chad, Mali, Mauritania and Niger, should be mentioned. *See* S. Kwarkye, ‘Slow progress for West Africa’s latest counter-terrorism plan’, *ISS Today*, 17 September 2021, at: https://issafrica.org/iss-today/slow-progress-for-west-africas-latest-counter-terrorism-plan.
604. Generally, *see* C. de Coning, A.E. Yaw Tchie & A.O. Grand, ‘Ad-hoc Security Initiatives, an African Response to Insecurity’, *African Security Review* 2022 (31): 383.

change, the consequences of which affect the whole continent. One of the interesting aspects of the adopted decision concerned the nature and outcome of the measures taken to combat climate change in relation to the goals of AfCFTA. According to the Assembly, such measures (whether joint or unilateral) should not constitute discrimination or restrict exports from Member States.[605] Moreover, climate change has been, *inter alia*, linked to political instability and security challenges (especially in the Sahel region).[606] However, it is debatable whether it should be addressed at a continental (AU) level or at a sub-regional (REC) level. Often, the answer is given by the developments themselves. Thus, RECs were the first to address climate change. Suffice to mention that COMESA adopted the Comprehensive Framework for Climate Change Initiative 2009–2013; presently, it implements the Strategy on Climate Change 2020–2030.[607] The AU acted at a much later stage: in February 2022, it adopted the African Union Climate Change and Resilient Development Strategy and Action Plan (2022–2032).[608] In AU parlance, the Strategy is built on the foundations of Agenda 2063, is African-led and African-owned, and follows a common but differentiated approach with intersectionality at its centre. Regarding the ever-crucial question of who is going to finance the actions envisaged in it, the Strategy says that 'the continent must … innovate new, predictable and sustainable sources of funding'. The Assembly approved the establishment of another subsidiary organ, the African Inclusive Market Excellence Centre (AIMEC), which is hosted by Tunisia.[609] AIMEC was developed in association with the UN Economic Commission for Africa to 'promote regional economic integration through transformative regional value chains starting with the Food Industry'. It will provide products and services to the AUC, to RECs and to their Member States to support them in their economic development policies to involve the poor and the vulnerable as producers, employees and consumers.[610]

605. Assembly, *Decision on the Report of the Committee of African Heads of State and Government on Climate Change (CAHOSCC)*, AU Doc. Assembly/AU/Dec. 764 (XXXIII) (10 Feb. 2020).
606. Note that on 25 September 2022 the UN, together with the AUC, ECOWAS and the G5 Sahel, launched the Independent High-Level Panel on Security and Development in the Sahel to assess the situation in the area and to make recommendations on ways to foster international engagement. According to the UN Secretary-General, the crisis in the Sahel has been compounded by climate change, *see* 'High-level independent panel on security and development in crisis-torn Sahel region launched at UN', *UN News*, 25 September 2022, at: https://news.un.org/en/story/2022/09/1127931.
607. *See COMESA Strategy on Climate Change 2020–2030*, no date, at: https://fanrpan.org/wp-content/uploads/2021/05/COMESA-CIMATE-CHANGE-STRATEGY.pdf, with references to actions undertaken by other RECs.
608. Assembly, *Decision on Annual Report of the Union and its Organs Including the Specific Thematic Issues by the Heads of States, Champions*, AU Doc. Assembly/AU/Dec. 819 (XXXV), para. 125 (6 Feb. 2022). Text of the Strategy at: https://repository.uneca.org/handle/10855/47738.
609. Assembly, *Decision on the Hosting of the African Inclusive Market Excellence Centre (AIMEC)*, Assembly/AU/Dec. 780 (XXXIII) (10 Feb. 2020).
610. *See* Economic Commission for Africa/African Union, *African Inclusive Markets Center of Excellence (AIMEC) Concept Note – Working Document*, Draft 11, 27 November 2014, E/ECA/COE/35/19 – AU/STC/FMEPI/EXP/19(II) (26 Mar. 2016), p. 2, at: https://repository.uneca.org/handle/10855/23011. *See further*, Economic Commission for Africa/African Union, *Business plan for African Inclusive Markets Center of Excellence (AIMEC)*, December 2016, E/ECA/CM/50/1 – AU/STC/FMEPI/MIN/1(III) (8 Feb. 2017).

Finally, the Assembly decided to hold on 30 May 2020 in South Africa and back-to-back its Thirteenth and Fourteenth Extraordinary Sessions, respectively on AfCFTA and on 'Silencing the Guns'.[611] When this did not materialize, the Assembly provisionally resolved to have them organized in December 2020,[612] which it later confirmed.[613] Both were held by means of virtual platforms. As regards the Thirteenth Extraordinary Session, the Assembly essentially confirmed a previous Decision[614] postponing the commencement of preferential trade under AfCFTA to 1 January 2021.[615] It also adopted a Declaration, where, *inter alia*, it (a) acknowledged the existence of negotiation issues regarding the full implementation of the Protocols to the AfCFTA Agreement on Trade in Goods and Services (Phase I negotiations); (b) repeated that the Phase II and III negotiations on competition policy, investments, intellectual property and e-commerce had to be completed as a prerequisite for the continent's sustainable economic growth and for its integration into the global economy; (c) requested that the Council of Ministers responsible for trade prepare to launch trade under AfCFTA on 1 January 2021 and to oversee the full implementation of the tariff reduction commitments on trade in goods; and (d) urged the remaining Member States to ratify the AfCFTA Agreement in order to increase the volume of transcontinental trading. It is interesting that the Assembly regarded the start of trading as 'a novel undertaking which requires collective responsibility to generate results that will improve the welfare of each and every African in the spirit of inclusiveness'.[616] Given that several RECs either individually or in unison have already experience in barrier-free trade in goods, it could hardly be regarded as a 'novel experiment'. As regards the Fourteenth Extraordinary Session, the Assembly, *inter alia*, asked the PSC, with the support of the AUC and the Panel of the Wise, to strictly adhere to the Constitutive Act, the PSC Protocol and the relevant policy frameworks, to promptly respond to looming crises and to avoid violent conflict from escalating; mandated PSC to name and shame those denying emerging crises, as stipulated in the AU Master Roadmap on Silencing the Guns,[617] and to complete the process of building a platform for the Roadmap. Importantly, the Assembly resolved to declare the African Standby Force (ASF) fully operational, directed the PSC to utilize its framework in mandating and authorizing AU peace support operations – presumably, this constituted a delegation of powers from the Assembly to PSC – and decided to dissolve the African Capacity for Immediate

611. *See*, respectively, AU Doc. Assembly/AU/Dec. 751 (XXXIII) and Assembly/AU/Dec. 755 (XXXIII) (10 Feb. 2020).
612. *See* AU Doc. Assembly/AU/OSP/Dec. 1 (06-20)II (17 Jun. 2020), adopted online through a silent procedure.
613. *See* AU Doc. Assembly/AU/OSP/Dec. 1 (11-20) (12 Nov. 2020), adopted online through a silent procedure.
614. AU Doc. Assembly/AU/OSP/Dec. 1 (06.20)II, *supra*, para. 9.
615. Assembly, *Decision on the Start of Trading under the African Continental Free Trade Area* (AfCFTA), AU Doc. Ext/Assembly/AU/Dec. 1 (XIII) (5 Dec. 2020).
616. Assembly, *Johannesburg Declaration on the Start of Trading Under the Agreement Establishing the African Continental Free Trade Area*, AU Doc. Ext/Assembly/AU/Decl. 1 (XIII) (5 Dec. 2020).
617. The Assembly resolved to prolong the Master Roadmap for a ten-year period, *i.e.* until 2030.

Response to Crisis (ACIRC) and wind it down before February 2021.[618] In the Declaration adopted at the same Session,[619] the Assembly set out the 'multiple and complex challenges' that Africa faces and which continue to prevent its accelerated integration and socioeconomic development: gaps in governance; terrorism; violent extremism; the surge of foreign terrorist fighters from outside the continent; illicit circulation of arms and weapons; corruption; illicit financial flows; transnational organized crime (drug trafficking, human trafficking, siphoning of benefits from natural resources away from the population); foreign political and military interference; outbreaks of epidemics and pandemic; the impact of climate change; and the slow process of ratification of AU instruments. Even though many of these issues are not connected to the illicit circulation and use of arms and weapons, it is significant to understand how African states view them to be somehow connected and interrelated. On the other hand, the Declaration does not appear to move matters significantly further; for example, the so-called Africa Amnesty Month, which takes place in the month of September of each year and aims at collecting and disposing of arms and weapons, is no doubt a commendable effort, but one cannot expect that its results will overturn the present situation.

At its Thirty-Fourth Ordinary Session (Addis Ababa, 6–7 February 2021), the Assembly adopted the customary decision on the theme of the year, which for 2021 was 'Arts, Culture and Heritage: Levers for Building the Africa We Want'.[620] The Assembly, *inter alia*, urged Member States to ratify the Charter for African Cultural Renaissance (2006)[621] as well as the Statute of the African Audio-Visual and Cinema Commission[622] and to ensure their earliest possible entry into force. The Assembly also approved the proposal presented by Togo to declare the period 2021–2031 as the 'Decade of African Roots and Diasporas',[623] arguably a follow-up to the Declaration of the Global African Diaspora Summit that had taken place

618. Assembly, *Decision of the 14th Extraordinary Session of the Assembly of the Union on Silencing the Guns in Africa*, AU Doc. Ext/Assembly/AU/Dec. 1 (XIV) (6 Dec. 2020).
619. Assembly, *Johannesburg Declaration on Silencing the Guns in Africa 'Silencing the Guns: Creating Conducive Conditions for Africa's Development'*, AU Doc. Ext/Assembly/AU/Decl. 1 (XIV) (6 Dec. 2020).
620. Assembly, *Decision on the Launch of the Theme of the Year for 2021*, AU Doc. Assembly/AU/Dec. 796 (XXXIV) (7 Feb. 2021).
621. Assembly, *Decision on the Revised Charter for the Cultural Renaissance of Africa*, AU Doc. Assembly/AU/Dec. 94 (VI) (24 Jan. 2006). Although originally Art. 35 of the Charter stipulated that it will 'come into force immediately upon receipt by the [AUC] of the instruments of ratification and adhesion from two-thirds of the total [AU] membership', the Assembly amended this provision in 2019 to read that it will enter into force after the deposit of the fifteenth instrument of ratification, *see* Assembly, *Decision on the Draft Legal Instruments*, AU Doc. Assembly/AU/Dec. 735 (XXXII), para. 2(v) (8 Feb. 2019). According to the ratification table on the AU's website, it entered into force on 14 October 2020, *see* https://au.int/sites/default/files/treaties/37305-sl-CHARTER_FOR_AFRICAN_CULTURAL_RENAISSANCE_0.pdf. Note that on 5 July 1976 the OAU had adopted the Cultural Charter for Africa, entered into force on 19 September 1990, presently ratified by 35 Member States.
622. The Commission was established as an AU Specialized Agency and its Statute was approved during the Thirty-Second Assembly Session, *see* Assembly/AU/Dec. 735 (XXXII), ibid, para. 2(ii). For the text of the Statute, AU Doc. EX.CL/1142(XXXIV), *see* https://archives.au.int/handle/123456789/6513.
623. Assembly, *Decision on the Proposal to Decree 2021–2031 as 'Decade of African Roots and Diasporas'*, Assembly/AU/Dec. 807 (XXXIV) (7 Feb. 2021).

in Johannesburg on 25 May 2012.[624] Finally, the Assembly approved the Aligned Rules of Procedures of the Assembly and the Aligned Statute of the AUC, in line with the project on the AU's institutional reform of November 2018.[625] Before that, the Executive Council had adopted its own aligned Rules of Procedures as well as those of the Permanent Representatives' Committee in October 2020.[626]

At its Thirty-Fifth Ordinary Session (Addis Ababa, 5–6 February 2022), the Assembly endorsed the proposal that the year 2022 be dedicated to nutrition and adopted the following theme of the year: 'Strengthening Resilience in Nutrition and Food Security on the African Continent: Strengthening Agro-Food Systems, Health and Social Protection Systems for the Acceleration of Human, Social and Economic Capital Development'.[627] Presently, the AU is implementing the revised Africa Regional Nutrition Strategy (ARNS) 2016–2025.[628] The Assembly had also before it the Report prepared by the President of Algeria, Abdelmadjid Tebboune, in his capacity as Coordinator on the Fight against Terrorism and Violent Extremism. The Assembly requested the AUC to operationalize the Special Fund for the Prevention and Combating of Terrorism and Violent Extremism in Africa (reference to which has already been made) as well as to activate the PSC's Sub-Committee on Counter-Terrorism, reiterated the need to urgently establish an African list of persons, groups and entities involved in terrorist acts, including foreign terrorist fighters, and that the project on a (continental) arrest warrant be implemented.[629] In relation to the latter, it should be noted that in 2014, the African Commission on Human and Peoples' Rights adopted the Guidelines on the Conditions of Arrest, Police Custody and Pre-Trial Detention in Africa (Luanda Guidelines).[630] Moreover, the Assembly noted the entry into force of the Treaty establishing the African Medicines Agency (AMA) on 5 November 2021, which it had adopted in February 2019.[631] As thirteen Member States had offered to host the AMA Headquarters, the Assembly authorized the Forty-First Executive Council Ordinary Session to reach, on its behalf, the decision on hosting AMA on the basis of the recommendation to be reached by the AMA Conference of State Parties.[632] The Executive Council decided that the headquarters will be in Rwanda.[633] AMA was established as an AU Specialized Agency with the mandate to improve Africans' access to quality, safe and efficacious medical products. Even though the AMA Treaty came into force relatively soon, presently,

624. AU Doc. Diaspora/Assembly/AU/Decl (I), at: https://au.int/en/documents/20120525/global-diaspora-summit-declaration.
625. Assembly, *Decision on the Draft Rules of Procedures of the Assembly, and Statute of the Commission*, AU Doc. Assembly/AU/Dec. 806 (XXXIV) (7 Feb. 2021).
626. AU Doc. EX.CL/Dec. 1099 (XXXVII) (14 Oct. 2020).
627. AU Doc. Assembly/AU/Dec. 813 (XXXV) (6 Feb. 2022).
628. Text at: https://au.int/sites/default/files/pages/32895-file-arns_english.pdf.
629. AU Doc. Assembly/AU/Dec. 819 (XXXV), *supra*, paras 40 *et seq*.
630. Text at: https://www.achpr.org/public/Document/file/Any/guidelines_on_arrest_police_custody_detention.pdf.
631. *See* Assembly/AU/Dec. 735 (XXXII), *supra*, para. 2(i).
632. Assembly, *Decision on the Progress Report on Ratification of the Treaty to Establish the African Medicines Agency (AMA Treaty)*, AU Doc. Assembly/AU/Dec. 830 (XXXV) (6 Feb. 2022).
633. Executive Council, *Decision on the Report of the Conference of State Parties of the African Medicines Agency (AMA) on the Hosting of the AMA Headquarters*, AU Doc. EX.CL/Dec. 1179 (XLI) (15 Jul. 2022).

less than half of the Member States have ratified it, while 'heavyweight' countries (South Africa, Nigeria, Kenya, etc.) have not signed it. As regards the human rights protection system in the continent, the Assembly reinforced it by approving the Protocol to the African Charter on Human and Peoples' Rights on the Rights of Citizens to Social Protection and Social Security, which is examined later in the monograph.[634] Presently, the Protocol had been signed by only two states (Niger and Sao Tome & Principe). It could be argued that with the addition of this Protocol the African human rights system has become the most complete of all the regional systems as regards the coverage of protected human rights and fundamental freedoms. Given that it is debatable if the previous two Protocols to the African Charter (respectively, the Protocol on the Rights of Persons with Disabilities (2019) and the Protocol on the Rights of Older Persons (2016)) will enter into force anytime soon, the policy of adopting further Protocols without having secured that a large part of the membership is willing to ratify the previous ones is rather questionable. The AU should perhaps reconsider the number of ratifications that are required for the various treaties to enter into force. This number has usually been set at fifteen ratifications, and even with a membership of fifty-five states, as explained elsewhere in this monograph, it is proven very difficult and occasionally impossible to secure them. Perhaps lowering the required number to ten ratifications might provide a solution.

The Sixteenth Extraordinary Assembly Session took place in Malabo, Equatorial Guinea, on 28 May 2022. It dealt specifically with the continental scourges of terrorism and unconstitutional changes of government. There were no decisions adopted, only a Declaration.[635] As with the aforementioned Assembly Declaration adopted at its Fourteenth Extraordinary Session (December 2020), the Assembly again connected many issues and challenges, repeating several mentioned in the 2020 Declaration. In particular, it mentioned the resurgence of coups d'état; the expanding threat of terrorism and violent extremism and the presence of foreign terrorist fighters, private military companies and mercenaries in the continent; the proliferation of armed groups; and transnational organized crime.[636] According to the Assembly, these factors have a negative impact on the peace, security, stability, sovereignty, and territorial integrity of some Member States (they were not named), but the AU and RECs have made gradual progress to consolidate democracy and constitutionalism and to counter terrorism and violent extremism.[637] Moreover, the

---

634. Assembly, *Decisions on Draft Legal Instruments*, AU Doc. Assembly/AU/Dec. 821 (XXXV) (6 Feb. 2022).
635. Assembly, *Declaration on Terrorism and Unconstitutional Changes of Government in Africa 'Robust Response, Deepening Democracy and Collective Security'*, AU Doc. Ext/Assembly/AU/Decl. (XVI) (28 May 2022).
636. Note that on 30 July 2018 ECOWAS and ECCAS Heads of State and Government held a joint Summit in Lomé, Togo, on peace, security, radicalization and violent extremism, which identified the following security-related risks: terrorism, arms trafficking, money laundering, and cybercrime. For the text of the Summit Declaration, *see* https://www.eip.org/wp-content/uploads/2020/07/Lom%C3%A9-Declaration-on-Peace-Security-Stability-and-the-Fight-Against-Terrorism-and-Violent-Extremism.pdf.
637. *See further*, African Journal on Terrorism, Special Edition on Implications of Coups d'Etat and Political Instability on Terrorism and Violent Extremism in the Sahel, October 2022, at: https://au.int/sites/default/files/documents/42553-doc-African_Journal_on_Terrorism_Special_Edition_Oct.2022.pdf.

Assembly called again for the prompt full operationalization of the ASF, (re)established a Counter-Terrorism Unit within ASF,[638] and endorsed the Accra Declaration on Unconstitutional Changes of Government. The latter was adopted in March 2022 during a 'Reflection Forum' that met in Accra, Ghana, from 15–17 March 2022 to address the resurgence of unconstitutional changes of government in Africa, following a decision reached during an open PSC Session in January 2022 under the theme 'Promoting Constitutionalism, Democracy and Inclusive Governance to Strengthen Peace, Security and Stability in Africa'.[639] The Forum was attended by AU Member States, PSC members, other AU organs, RECs and Regional Mechanisms for Conflict Prevention, Management and Resolution, representatives of African CSOs, academia, professional bodies, youth and women groups and other stakeholders.[640] Paragraph 16 of the Accra Declaration mentioned, *inter alia*, 'the need for the AU to finalise and adopt the AU guidelines on the amendment of constitutions in Africa *based on the AU's existing laws*, policies and practice relating to constitutionalism and rule of law … ' (emphasis added). Arguably, this reference to 'the AU's existing laws' confirms the argument advanced in the present monograph and elsewhere that a distinct legal system has been developed in the AU. Three months after the Sixteenth Extraordinary Assembly Session, the PSC took up again the issue of coups d'état. After reaffirming its 'condemnation of the recent upsurge in unconstitutional changes of government … as manifested by the unprecedented suspension of four (4) Member States from the activities of the AU', it directed the AUC to create a monitoring and evaluation group that will assess the implementation of sanctions imposed against Member States and, by underlining the need to refine 'existing sanctions pronouncements into consistent frameworks that are aligned with the current evolution of the challenges they are meant to address', asked the AUC, in collaboration with the UN stakeholders UN (including the UNSC permanent members) and relevant African research institutions and think tanks to develop an effective collaborative mechanism to strengthen the AU sanctions regime.[641]

The Thirty-Sixth Ordinary Assembly Session took place on 18–19 February 2023 in Addis Ababa. The first noteworthy aspect is that the Assembly extended again the

---

638. *See also*, Assembly, *Decision on the Report of the Peace and Security Council on its Activities and the State of Peace and Security in Africa*, AU Doc. Assembly/AU/Dec. 753 (XXXIII) (10 Feb. 2020), and Assembly, *Decision on the Report of the Peace and Security Council on its Activities and the State of Peace and Security in Africa*, AU Doc. Assembly/AU/Dec. 815 (XXXV) (6 Feb. 2022).

639. PSC, Communique, 1061st Meeting, AU Doc. PSC/PR/COMM.1061(2022) (27 Jan. 2022). Additionally, it was requested that the AUC reactivates the PSC's Sub-Committee on Sanctions to provide support and follow up on the implementation of PSC imposed sanctions and to coordinate with RECs as well as that it undertakes an in-depth analysis of the Lomé Declaration on Unconstitutional Change of Government (2000).

640. Text at: http://www.peaceau.org/uploads/eng-declaration-on-unconstitutional-changes-of-government-in-africa-15-17-march-2022.pdf.

641. PSC, 1100th Meeting on Sanctions and Enforcement Capacities: Deterrence Against Unconstitutional Changes of Government, Communiqué, AU Doc. PSC/PR/COMM.1100 (2022), paras 6 and 8 (15 Aug. 2022).

deadline for realizing the Organization's institutional reform to July 2023,[642] a rather inadequate extension considering the divergent opinions among Member States as to how to proceed, while the AUC faces increasing pressure to deliver. Moreover, the Assembly regarded unconstitutional changes of government and the threat posed by terrorism and violent extremism as 'twin security issues' to which the PSC should 'robustly respond'.[643] It should be noted that the PSC has increasingly intensified its engagement with most RECs and other relevant continental institutions (e.g. AU-NEPAD). Thus, in November 2022, the Second PSC – APRM Joint Retreat was held in Durban, South Africa.[644] The Assembly also adopted the Consensus Paper on Predictable, Adequate and Sustainable Financing for African Union Peace and Security Activities.[645] The Consensus Paper (the AUC Commissioner for Political Affairs, Peace and Security brought it to the attention of the UNSC in May 2023)[646] aims, *inter alia*, at the following two different goals.[647] First, the operationalization of the AU Peace Fund grounded on financial autonomy and reduced dependency; prudent management of resources and improved accountability; and the timely and predictable payment of all Member States' assessed contributions to the AU budget following the principles of the ability to pay, of solidarity, and of equitable burden-sharing. Second, to uphold compliance with human rights during Peace Support Operations (PSO), reference to which has been made *supra*.

Over the years, the organizers of the Summits of the G20 Group have invited the AU to participate. It is the prerogative of the G20 member holding the Presidency to determine which third states and international organizations will be invited, and, therefore, there is no guarantee that invitations will be made in the following years. For the first time now, the Assembly moved to a bid to have an 'African Union seat' in G20. According to the Assembly, G20 is 'the main forum for global economic, trade and financial dialogue for growth and sustainable development', and the continent needs to be more fully involved in the decision-making processes on global political, economic, financial, security, environmental and health governance, the latter being one of AU's objective as stipulated in Article 3(i) of the Constitutive Act.[648] To the best of one's knowledge, the bid has not garnished adequate support. During 9-10 September 2023, India organized the Eighteenth G20 Summit in New Delhi. India had asked the President of Nigeria in his capacity as head of state, the

642. Assembly, *Decision of the Institutional Reforms of the African Union by H.E. Paul Kagame, President of the Republic of Rwanda*, AU Doc. Assembly/AU/Dec. 839 (XXXVI) (19 Feb. 2023).
643. *See* Assembly, *Decision on the Report on the Activities of the Peace and Security Council (PSC) and the State of Peace and Security in Africa*, AU Doc. Assembly/AU/Dec. 842 (XXXVI), para. 2 (19 Feb. 2023).
644. *See Conclusions of the Second Joint Retreat of the African Peer Review Mechanism and the African Union Peace and Security Council*, AU Doc. PSC/APRM/Retreat.2 (2022) (15 Nov. 2022).
645. AU Doc. Assembly/AU/Dec. 842 (XXXVI), *supra*, para. 31.
646. UNSC, Meetings Coverage, UN Doc. SC/15294, 25 May 2023, at: https://press.un.org/en/2023/sc15294.doc.htm.
647. Text at: https://www.securitycouncilreport.org/un-documents/document/consensus-paper-on-predictable-adequate-and-sustainable-financing-for-african-union-peace-and-security-activities.php.
648. Assembly, *Decision on the Report on Granting a Seat to African Union within G20 by H.E. Macky Sall, President of the Republic of Senegal*, AU Doc. Assembly/AU/Dec. 845 (XXXVI) (19 Feb. 2023).

President of Comoros in his capacity as the AU Chairperson for 2023 and the Chair of AU-NEPAD to participate as 'invited guests'.[649] Presumably, the Assembly would have liked to see the AU Chairperson being invited as 'participating international organization guest', a status accorded in the past, for example, to the UN Secretary-General, the Secretary-General of the Organisation for Economic Co-operation and Development (OECD), the President of the International Solar Alliance, the President of the Asian Development Bank. But the G20 Meeting proved a triumph for the AU, a rare diplomatic victory: it was accepted as a permanent member of the G20. According to Declaration issued, G20 countries 'strongly believe that inclusion of the African Union … will significantly contribute to addressing the global challenges of our time. We commend the efforts of all G20 members which paved the way for [its] accession. Africa plays an important role in the global economy. We commit to strengthen our ties with and support the African Union realise the aspirations under Agenda 2063'.[650] In addition, the Thirty-Sixth Ordinary Assembly Session dealt for yet another time with the aspirations of a better African representation at the UNSC. In its previous Ordinary Session (February 2022), the Assembly had decided that 'given the wide-ranging divergences in views and positions of the respective interest groups vis-à-vis the interconnectedness of the five key clusters as set out in [UNGA] Decision 62/557,[651] engaging in a text-based negotiation, at this stage, without agreeing on the principles will not only be premature but counter-productive'.[652] This revealed that there was still considerable division on the matter among the membership. The Assembly asked all Member States 'to reflect in their respective National statements at the opening of the 78th Session of the [UNGA] in September 2023, a concise common language to advance the Common African Position, and to reiterate the call for a comprehensive reform of the [UNSC]'.[653] It is also of interest to note that, even though AU finances are very tight, the Assembly decided to increase the budget allocation to fund the activities of the Committee of Ten Heads of State and Government on the United Nations Security Council Reforms (C-10). Finally, the Assembly took up the aforementioned issue of reparations for slavery and other crimes committed by foreign powers on the continent. The Assembly had before it the Accra Declaration that had emanated as a non-binding document from a Conference on 'Advancing Justice: Reparations and Racial Healing' held in Ghana in August 2022.[654] Even though the Conference was not associated with the AU (participants came from all parts of the word), the Assembly took advantage of the Declaration's

---

649. *See* https://www.g20.org/en/g20-india-2023/new-delhi-summit/.

650. G20 New Delhi Leaders' Declaration, 10 September 2023, para. 96, at: https://www.g20.org/content/dam/gtwenty/gtwenty_new/document/G20-New-Delhi-Leaders-Declaration.pdf.

651. In accordance with UNGA Decision 62/557 of 15 September 2008, UN Member States commenced intergovernmental negotiations on UNSC reform. *See further*, UNGA Decision 69/650, *Question of equitable representation on and increase in the membership of the Security Council and related matters*, 14 Sep. 2015.

652. Assembly/AU/Dec. 819 (XXXV), *supra*, para. 81.

653. Assembly, *Decision on the Report of the AU Committee of Ten (C-10) Heads of State and Government on the Reform of the UN Security Council, by H.E. Julius Maada Bio, President of the Republic of Sierra Leone*, AU Doc. Assembly/AU/Dec. 853 (XXXVI), para. 8 (19 Feb. 2023).

654. Text at: https://ibw21.org/docs/accra-ghana-reparations-summit-2022/accra-ghana-2022-declaration_english.pdf.

call upon African countries, populations and political leaders to enforce the demands for full reparation from responsible states, institutions and governments on account of the negative impact that slavery, colonialism, apartheid and genocide has had in the continent. It also resolved to establish an African Committee of Experts on Reparations to develop a Common African Position on Reparations and an African Reparatory Programme of Action.[655] Reference should also be made to the Resolution on Africa's Reparations Agenda and the Human Rights of Africans in the Diaspora and People of African Descent Worldwide, which was adopted by the African Commission on Human and People's Rights in 2022.[656] The Declaration is of interest because it calls upon AU Member States, on the one hand, to establish a committee to 'conceptualise reparations from Africa's perspective … establish a case for reparations (or Africa's claim), and pursue justice for the trade and trafficking in enslaved Africans, colonialism and colonial crimes … ' and, on other hand, to protect the human rights of African migrant workers worldwide, including in the Middle East and in the Gulf states.

655. Assembly, *Decision on building a united front to advance the cause of justice and the payment of reparations to Africans (Item proposed by the Republic of Ghana)*, AU Doc. Assembly/AU/Dec. 847 (XXXVI) (19 Feb. 2023).

656. ACHPR/Res. 543 (LXXIII) (9 Dec. 2022), at: https://achpr.au.int/index.php/en/adopted-resolutions/543-resolution-africas-reparations-agenda-and-human-rights-africans.

Part II. The African Union

Chapter 1. The Transition from the OAU to the AU

56. The Constitutive Act, which entered into force on 26 May 2001, did not expressly stipulate that the replacement of the OAU was a case of succession between international organizations. This followed from the wording of Article 33(1) thereof, the clause dealing with the question of transition, which, on the one hand, provided that the Constitutive Act would replace the OAU Charter and, on the other hand, referred to the devolution of all OAU assets and liabilities to the AU. It was not clear from the wording of Article 33(1) whether the arrears owed to the OAU from unpaid budgetary contributions were to be regarded as Member States' debts to be paid to the AU. In the balance sheet of 31 December 2002, which showed the OAU assets and liabilities to be transferred to the AU, the sum of USD 21 million representing arrears in contributions had been written off for two reasons. First, it was highly unlikely that they would ever be recovered. Second, without such a provision, the balance sheet would not have reflected the prevailing at the time financial situation.[657] There was disagreement as to how this issue should be handled. The AUC took the view that all arrears ought to be considered as dues owed and measures be taken to claim them. On the other hand, the Permanent Representatives Committee (PRC), the organ composed of the Member States' representatives appointed to the AU, regarded that they should be written off entirely,[658] a rather expected reaction. In the event, the latter recommendation was approved by the Executive Council, and no effort was made to persuade recalcitrant Member States to even pay a part of the monies owed.[659]

57. Pursuant to Article 33(1), once the Constitutive Act had entered into force, the OAU Charter was to remain operative for a transitional period of one year or for any further period that was determined by the Assembly. Therefore, the transitional period ought to have lasted until 26 May 2002. However, the Thirty-Seventh Ordinary Assembly Session (Lusaka, July 2001) decided, 'due to the magnitude of

657. *See Report of the Fifth Ordinary Session of the Advisory Sub-Committee on Administrative, Budgetary and Financial Matters on the Report of Ernst & Young*, AU Doc. EX/CL/69 (IV) (2004).

658. *See* Permanent Representatives Committee, Seventh Ordinary Session, 12–13 Mar. 2004, AU Doc. PRC/Rpt (VII), 8.

659. *See* Executive Council, *Decision on the Balance Sheet of the African Union as at 31 December 2002*, OAU Doc. EX/CL/Dec. 75 (IV) (16 Mar. 2004).

the tasks to be performed and bearing in mind the need for consultations with Member States', to extend it to mid-July 2002.[660] As it turned out, setting the transition period to just under fourteen months (May 2001–July 2002) was a most ambitious goal and failed to take into consideration the following parameters which complicated the procedure. First, Member States had a varying degree of adaptability to the new state of affairs that the AU was bringing about. Second, as it turned out, not all OAU Member States had ratified the Constitutive Act by the time the transition period had expired. Third, there were extraneous circumstances in several Member States (e.g., ongoing armed hostilities, breakdown of state functions, etc.) preventing the smooth cooperation between the whole membership, a fundamental condition for completing promptly the transition. Fourth, the OAU lacked the necessary manpower, facilities and expertize for undertaking such a massive project, which involved reconstituting an organization that had existed for almost forty years and the setting up of fifteen organs, most of which did not previously exist.

58. The transition from the OAU to the AU was supervised by the Secretary-General and the Eminent Persons Advisory Panel, a group of experts convened for this specific purpose. On 8 May 2002, the Panel recommended that the transition period be extended, a view shared by the Secretary-General. Although it was generally expected that African leaders would agree with the recommendation, they decided to proceed as planned and inaugurate the AU in July 2002. There is no doubt that considerations of pragmatism drove this decision. A delay in launching the AU would have tarnished its image and might have dealt a severe blow to the continent's morale at a crucial moment.[661] However, with the benefit of hindsight, one cannot but criticize the decision to keep the transition period shorter than longer, not least because even today not all AU organs are in operation.

59. There were four methods used to set up the various organs. The first method concerns those organs (namely, the Assembly of Heads of State and Government, the Executive Council, the Commission, the Specialized Technical Committees, and the PRC that were envisaged in the Constitutive Act and no further action was required on behalf of Member States. The second method concerned those organs (namely, the Pan-African Parliament (PAP, originally envisaged in Article 14 of the AEC Treaty), the African Court of Justice (a Court of Justice was envisaged in Article 18 of the AEC Treaty) and the three Financial Institutions (the African Investment Bank – AIB, the African Monetary Fund – AMF and the African Central Bank – ACB)), whose setting up required the negotiation, conclusion, and adoption of corresponding protocols by Member States.[662] This is a method not generally found in international institutions and, particularly, in regional Intergovernmental Organizations (IGOs) of a politico-economic nature. The PAP Protocol was concluded in March 2001 and entered into force in December 2003, while the Protocol

660. *See* Assembly, *Decision on the Implementation of the Sirte Summit Decision on the African Union*, para. 15, OAU Doc. AHG/Dec. 160 (XXXVII) (11 Jul. 2001).
661. *See* the Acts of the Symposium on *African Union and the New Pan-Africanism: Rushing to Organize or Timely Swift?* in *Transnational Law & Contemporary Problems* 13/1 (2003): 1.
662. For PAP, *see* Art. 17(2) of the Constitutive Act, for the African Court of Justice, *see* Art. 18(2), and for the Financial Institutions, *see* Art. 19 thereof.

on the African Court of Justice was concluded in July 2003 and entered into force in February 2009, but it has not yet been operationalized. As regards the Financial Institutions, so far the Protocol on the AIB and the Protocol on the AMF have been concluded (respectively, in February 2009 and June 2014) but have not entered into force. Protocol on the ACB has not yet been concluded, and, arguably, it cannot be concluded because it requires a level of continental economic and monetary integration which has not been achieved. The Constitutive Act did not stipulate the number of ratifications necessary for these Protocols to enter into force. Even though one would assume that they would require the same number as the Constitutive Act itself (namely, two-thirds of all Member States), they contain different stipulations. Thus, the PAP Protocol requires a simple majority of the total membership (at the time of its conclusion, it meant twenty-eight ratifications), while the Protocol on the Court of Justice and the Protocol on the AIB require fifteen ratifications, this being the number of ratifications required for most OAU/AU treaties.

A few general comments on these Protocols should be made. First, these Protocols apply only to those Member States which choose to ratify them. In effect, two classes of organs have been created: (a) those established directly by the Constitutive Act and to which all Member States participate as contracting parties to the Act and (b) those which have been set up by protocols and to which only the Member States that have become contracting parties participate. This rather awkward situation was amply manifested in March 2004 during the Inaugural PAP Session, where only thirty-eight Member States took part. Currently, there are still four states which have not ratified it. Even though they are countries where basic state functions have collapsed and/or are facing serious domestic strife (Somalia, Eritrea, DRC, and Guinea), the question cannot be avoided if, twenty years after its inauguration, PAP should be regarded the 'pan-African' entity that it claims to be. Second, to the extent that they introduce new rules and principles, these protocols do not modify the Constitutive Act de jure because they were not adopted as amending protocols under Article 32 thereof. Nevertheless, they have resulted in many important de facto changes.

60. It will be argued that the Constitutive Act has given the Assembly the authority to adopt the protocols setting up the organs of the second method without necessitating their prior ratification to enter into force. Thus, since these organs were already named and envisaged in the Constitutive Act, the Assembly was authorized (and mandated for that matter) to conclude the relevant protocols, which could have come into force upon their adoption.[663] Since, however, these protocols require their prior ratification by a specific number of Member States, the latter have effectively been given the opportunity to decide whether they wish their operationalization, a desire manifested by ratifying the respective protocol. But was this the real aspiration of the Constitutive Act's drafters? To put it otherwise, it would be improper to reach the conclusion that Member States may determine anew whether these organs will be set up. However, as things have developed, this is exactly what has happened: by being asked to ratify these protocols, several Member States have still not

663. As has been mentioned above, many a Statute of AU subsidiary organs have entered into force the same day they were approved by the Assembly.

approved them, a move that presumably shows that they do not want to participate. This Member States' attitude is ill-conceived and should be criticized: the AU's institutional architecture was devised in a specific manner and should be respected by the whole membership. This is a very well-known problem and has been discussed in other parts of this monograph. Suffice to mention here that the establishment of Ministerial Committees to address the challenges of non-ratification/ accession and implementation of OAU/AU treaties[664] are rather face-saving exercises convoluting the membership's duty to sign, ratify and implement these Protocol without delay.

It follows from the above that the AU membership has effectively been divided into two categories: those states which have ratified the Protocols and are bound by the decisions adopted by the respective organs on the one hand and those which have not ratified them on the other hand. This is like having membership a la carte: with the exception of those organs, which were expressly created by the Constitutive Act (the Assembly, the Executive Council, and the Commission), participation in the other organs is subject to Member States' discretion whether or not to ratify the applicable Protocols, which arguably goes against the very logic of pursuing institutional cooperation in the context of an international organization.

61. The third category concerns only one organ, the Economic, Social and Cultural Council (ECOSOCC). Its establishment required an Assembly resolution laying down its functions, powers, composition and organization. This was done during the Third Ordinary Assembly Session (Addis Ababa, 6–8 July 2004).[665] Finally, the fourth category concerns those organs that the Assembly has decided to create pursuant to the power granted under Article 5(2) of the Constitutive Act. Until today, several such organs have been established, the most important being PSC, which was set up through the adoption of a separate Protocol attached to the Constitutive Act.[666] Another such organ is the AUCIL. It was set up through a Statute, which was adopted by the Executive Council during its Fourteenth Ordinary Session in January 2009[667] and was approved by the Assembly at its Twelfth Ordinary Session in February 2009.[668] The AUCIL Statute is not attached to the Constitutive Act. The same is true with the Statute of another Article 5(2) organ, the African Space Agency, the establishment of which has been noted above.

62. The procedure for setting up the organs is laid down in the third paragraph of Article 33 of the Constitutive Act, which reads as follows:

664. Such a Committee was created by the Executive Council within the context of the OAU's fiftieth anniversary, *see* Executive Council, *Decision on the Status of Signature and Ratification of OAU/ AU Treaties*, AU Doc. EX.CL/Dec. 705 (XXI) (13 Jul. 2012).
665. *See* Assembly, *Decision on the Economic, Social and Cultural Council (ECOSOCC)*, AU Doc. Assembly/AU/Dec. 48 (III) (8 Jul. 2004).
666. Note that the setting up of the PSC is envisaged in Art. 9 of the Protocol on Amendments to the Constitutive Act of 2003, which inserted a new Art. 20*bis* in the Constitutive Act. As is later explained, it is doubtful if the Protocol will ever enter into force.
667. AU Doc. EX.CL/478 (XIV) a (30 Jan. 2009).
668. *See* Assembly, *Decision on the Draft Statute of the African Union Commission on International Law*, AU Doc. Assembly/AU//Dec. 209 (XII) (3 Feb. 2009).

> Upon the entry into force of this Act, all necessary measures shall be undertaken to implement its provisions and to ensure the establishment of the organs provided for under the Act in accordance with any directives or decisions which may be adopted in this regard by the Parties thereto within the transitional period stipulated [in Article 33(1)].

This is arguably a rather vague and badly drafted provision raising a number of problems and questions. First, it diminished the importance of the transitional period because it referred solely to 'directives or decisions' adopted during that stage and not that the implementation and execution of such instruments would also have to be effected within the same deadline. Second, it was not explained whether it would be the Member States or the AU itself (acting through the Assembly) that would implement the Act's provisions and set up the organs in question. This is a crucial question because, as the wording of Article 33(3) contains what would appear to be a legally binding obligation, it should have been determined upon whom the burden falls and, in particular, whether the Member States are under a duty to give effect to any 'necessary measures' adopted. Third, the reference to the adoption of 'directives or decisions by the Parties [to the Constitutive Act' was legally not sound because when the Constitutive Act' entered into force the AU started existing as a distinct and separate legal entity and, therefore, the necessary 'directives or decisions' had to be taken by the Member States acting through the Assembly. By definition, the contracting parties to the Constitutive Act are the Member States and the Assembly; pursuant to Article 6(2) thereof, it is the 'supreme' AU organ where all Members are represented. Consequently, it has always had the general competence to adopt the required measures. Fourth, considering that the Constitute Act's entry into force required ratification by two-thirds of OAU Member States, it could have reasonably been expected (and indeed this is what happened) that not all states would be able to ratify it before coming into force and, consequently, be allowed to participate in the adoption of the relevant decisions.

63. The official launching of the AU was scheduled to take place in mid-July 2002 and was planned to coincide with the Assembly's inaugural session. However, there was still one state which had not ratified the Constitutive Act (Madagascar) and another which, even though it had ratified it, had not deposited the instrument of ratification (Guinea-Bissau).[669] Therefore, as these two states could not have participated in the AU, the delicate issue of permitting them to be present in the Assembly's inaugural session was raised. It was argued by certain Member States that, since they were part of the OAU whose assets and liabilities were being transferred to the AU, they should be allowed to attend as observers. Other states advanced the rather impossible argument that, since they had signed the Constitutive Act, they

669. T. Maluwa, 'International Law-Making in Post-Colonial Africa: The Role of the Organization of African Unity', *Netherlands International Law Review* 49 (2002): 81, 101–102 might be wrong in writing that the DRC had also not ratified the Act, as it had deposited its ratification on 9 Jul. 2002; *see List of States which Have Signed, Ratified/ Acceded to the Constitutive Act of the African Union as at 26 November 2002*, OAU Doc. CAB/LEG/23.15 (2002).

already had the status of AU Member State. The matter was referred to the Acting Legal Counsel for an opinion. He was categorical that, since they had not completed the ratification process or had not acceded to the Constitutive Act, its provisions were not binding upon them, and, consequently, they had neither rights nor obligations. In the event, it was decided that the Council of Ministers would invite them under the status of 'prospective Members'.[670]

This solution was nothing more than a legal machination, which could only be explained by the importance attached to the presence of all OAU Members at the launching of the AU. Moreover, it was probably driven by the expectation that by then they would have completed the ratification process. However, as Madagascar deposited its instrument of ratification on 10 June 2003 (it had ratified the Act five days earlier) and Guinea-Bissau on 7 July 2003,[671] the fact that they were treated as full Members (Guinea-Bissau was even allowed to sign the Protocol establishing the PSC on 9 July 2002, which incidentally it ratified only in December 2011) is highly questionable. To conclude, by affording these states the status of 'prospective Members', the AU, even though it secured, from a political perspective, the participation of all states, arguably committed unconstitutional acts.

670. *See Report of the Fifteenth Ordinary Session of the Committee of Ambassadors and Other Plenipotentiaries*, OAU Doc. Cttee/AMB/Rpt (XV) at paras 83–86 (30 Jun. 2002).

671. *See Report of the Interim Chairperson of the Commission on the Status of AU Treaties as at 17 June 2003*, AU Doc. EX/CL/36 (III) (2003), and the Constitutive Act's ratification table at: https://au.int/sites/default/files/treaties/7758-sl-constitutive_act_of_the_african_union_2.pdf.

Chapter 2. Objectives and Principles

64. The Constitutive Act follows the structure of the OAU Charter and contains the AU objectives (Article 3) separately from its principles (Article 4). There are fourteen objectives laid down covering an extremely broad spectrum of activities primarily in the fields of political cooperation and economic integration. They range from greater unity and solidarity between the countries and peoples of Africa, to the promotion of peace, security and stability, on the one hand, and democratic principles and good governance, on the other hand, to the protection of human rights, to coordination and harmonization between the RECs and the AU, etc. Moreover, the objectives include the creation of the necessary conditions enabling the continent to play its rightful role in the global economy and in international negotiations while advancing and defending common positions on those issues that are of shared interest. A good example is the UN reform and specifically the restructuring of UNSC, where Africa has been pressing to reverse the fact that it is the only continent without a permanent seat. Even though this matter was discussed in Part I, where reference was made to, *inter alia*, the Sirte Declaration on the Reform of the UN of July 2005,[672] suffice to mention here the role played by the Committee of Ten Heads of State and Government on the Reform of the UN Security Council (C-10),[673] as it is characteristic of the way the AU transacts its business. In particular, a Committee comprising a small number of heads of state or government is established, the Committee submits reports, the reports are deliberated by the Assembly, the Assembly either rubber stamps the recommendations and proposals contained in the reports or requests updated reports or takes no action. Over time, this process has perpetuated. Often the Assembly's concern is to ensure that Member States are not seen to have divergent opinions and that 'Africa speaks with one voice'.[674] In July 2016, the Committee of Ten's Eighteenth Report was examined by the Assembly, which repeated verbatim the demand: Africa's full representation in the Security Council cannot be with less than two permanent seats with all the prerogatives, privileges and the veto right attached as well as five additional non-permanent seats (more recently, the number has been reduced to two). According to the Assembly, it is a historical injustice that the continent has no permanent representation on the UNSC.[675] In February 2023, the Assembly adopted the Twenty-Third Report of the Committee of Ten, which arguably had nothing new to add. Indeed, it would appear

672. Assembly/AU/ Decl. 2 (V) (5 Jul. 2005). *See further* Executive Council, *The Common African Position on the Proposed Reform of the United Nations: The Ezulwini Consensus,* AU Doc. Ext/EC.CL/2 (VII) (8 Mar. 2005). Generally, *see* D. Bourantonis & K. Magliveras, 'The Enlargement of the UN Security Council: Reflections from the Current Debate', *Politics* 22 (2002): 24, 27. For the African position vis-à-vis the enlargement of the Security Council in the mid-1990s, *see* D. Bourantonis, *The History and Politics of UN Security Council Reform* (Abingdon: Routledge, 2005), 59–60.

673. *See* Assembly, *Decision on the Reform of the United Nations Security Council*, AU Doc. Assembly/AU/Dec. 184 (X) (2 Feb. 2008).

674. *See* Assembly, *Decision on the Reform of the United Nations Security Council*, AU Doc. Assembly/AU/Dec. 285 (XIV) (2 Feb. 2010), para. 2.

675. *See* Assembly, *Decision on the Reform of the United Nations Security Council*, AU Doc. Assembly/AU/Dec. 616 (XXVII) (18 Jul. 2016).

that if African demands were ever met, it would not be the outcome of the work of this Committee but the change in the stance on UNSC reform by non-African UN Member States,[676] including the USA.[677]

Regarding AU objectives, some are vague (e.g., 'to promote cooperation in all fields of human activity to raise the living standards of African peoples'); others are rather devoid of specific meaning and content (e.g., 'to promote sustainable development at the … cultural level') and others were at the time rather wishful thinking but as of late they have been pursued at an accelerated rate (e.g., 'to promote … the integration of African economies'). Finally, the Protocol on Amendments adopted in 2003 added three new objectives as subparagraphs (i), (p), and (q) to Article 3: First, the effective participation of women in decision-making in all areas. Second, the development and promotion of common policies on trade, defence, and foreign relations ensuring the defence of the continent's interests and strengthening its negotiating position. Third, the encouragement of the African Diaspora's full participation in building up the AU and its recognition as an important stakeholder.[678] The dynamics of the Diaspora were addressed during the Global African Diaspora Summit, which took place in South Africa on 25 May 2012 with the participation of African, Caribbean and South American leaders.[679] The Summit culminated in the so-called Five Legacy Projects, which were endorsed by the Assembly in July 2012. A South African proposal to establish self-funding Technical Committees of Experts for the implementation of these projects was adopted by the Assembly in May 2013.[680] The next Summit took place in November 2015, where it was argued that the Diaspora should be considered as the sixth region of Africa.[681]

65. While OAU objectives were almost exclusively concerned with political issues, the AU broke away from this tradition. The Constitutive Act has advanced all kinds of economic and developmental questions and topics promoted democratic principles and institutions as well as issues which in the 1990s had started to appear in the constitutive instruments of international organizations, namely, the

---

676. *See, e.g.*, the 2016 statements of, *inter alia*, Norway and Belgium at the podium of the UNGA, UN Press Release, *Updated Security Council Must Reflect Changing Global Reality, Member States Say, as General Assembly Debates Ways to Advance Progress on Reform*, UN Doc. GA/11854, 7 Nov. 2016, at: https://www.un.org/press/en/2016/ga11854.doc.htm.
677. *See* United States Mission to the United Nations, *Remarks by Senior Administration Official During a Background Briefing on Ambassador Linda Thomas-Greenfield's Travel to Ghana, Mozambique, and Kenya*, 23 January 2023, at: https://usun.usmission.gov/.
678. Generally, *see* T. Maluwa, 'Fast-Tracking African Unity or Making Haste Slowly? A Note on the Amendments to the Constitutive Act of the African Union', *Netherlands International Law Review* 51 (2004): 195. On the African Diaspora, *see*, *inter alia*, Executive Council, *Decision on the Definition of the African Diaspora*, AU Doc. EX.CL/ Dec. 173 (VI) (28 Jan. 2005); Executive Council, *Decision on the Definition of the African Diaspora*, AU Doc. EX.CL/Dec. 221 (VII) (2 Jul. 2005); and Executive Council, *Decision on the First African Union Diaspora Ministerial Conference*, EX.CL/Dec. 386 (XII) (29 Jan. 2008).
679. *See Declaration of the Global African Diaspora Summit*, AU Doc. Diaspora/Assembly/AU/Decl (I) (25 May 2012).
680. *See* Assembly, *Decision on the Implementation of the Global African Diaspora Legacy Projects*, AU Doc. Assembly/AU/Dec. 478 (XXI) (27 May 2013).
681. AU ECOSOCC, Global Africa Diaspora Stakeholder Convention, 19–22 Nov. 2015, Washington DC and Maryland, USA, *Official Report*, at: http://www.globalafricadiaspora.org.

democratic principle, good governance and popular participation. That the popular participation was included in the Act should not be underestimated since it marked a significant change in Member States' attitude. Whereas previously there was almost no institutionalized cooperation between the OAU and NGOs and the civil society at large (possibly because of suspiciousness towards NGO activities),[682] this policy of exclusion was partly overturned with the African Charter for Popular Participation in Development and Transformation (1990)[683] and was further consolidated with the aforementioned Sirte Declaration of September 1999, which expressly referred to involving African peoples and 'their grassroots organizations'.

This aspect of the Sirte Declaration, which, as will be recalled, also decided to establish the AU, was carried on to the Constitutive Act, whose seventh recital puts forward 'the need to build a partnership between governments and all segments of civil society … in order to strengthen solidarity and cohesion among our peoples'. Almost two years later, the First OAU/Civil Society Conference took place in June 2001 and a follow-up Second Conference in Addis Ababa on 11–14 June 2002 to establish a mechanism facilitating and deepening the interface among the continent's civil society and the AU.[684] Since then, this interface has largely been institutionalized twofold: through the setting up of the ECOSOCC, envisaged in Article 22 of the Constitutive Act as an AU advisory organ composed of different social and professional groups, and through the New Economic Partnership for Africa's Development (NEPAD), which, as explained above, has been transformed into the African Union Development Agency (AUDA). As was noted by the AUC, the decision to establish ECOSOCC signifies the will to make the AU 'a tool to build a new equilibrium between state and non-state actors on solid foundations'.[685]

66. The Article 3 objectives are to be materialized and implemented pursuant to the sixteen principles that are laid down in Article 4 of the Constitutive Act. Some of these principles are repetition of those set out in Article III of the OAU Charter and include the fundamental doctrines of sovereign equality between all Member States, the peaceful resolution of disputes and the non-intervention in the internal affairs of other states. However, many significant new objectives were added, and it is particularly worthwhile to note (again) the participation of African peoples in AU activities, the establishment of a common defence policy, the promotion of the continent's self-reliance, the advancement of gender equality and of social justice and, last but not least, the condemnation and rejection of political assassination, of acts

---

682. *See* E. Gyimah-Boadi, 'Civil Society in Africa', *Journal of Democracy* 7 (1996): 118.

683. The Charter, which was a declaration of intent, was adopted in February 1990 at the International Conference on Popular Participation in the Recovery and Development Process in Africa, held under the auspices of the UN Economic Commission for Africa in Arusha, text in UN Doc. A/45/427 (22 Aug. 1990). *See also*, S.J. Kpundeh (ed.), *Democratization in Africa: African Views, African Voices* (Washington, DC: National Research Council/National Academy Press, 1992), 34–36.

684. *See* T. Murithi, *The African Union: Pan-Africanism, Peacebuilding and Development* (London: Ashgate, 2005) 117–118.

685. *See* Commission of the African Union, *Vision of the African Union and Missions of the African Union Commission*, Final Draft, March 2004, 31.

of terrorism, of subversive activities and of unconstitutional changes of government. Finally, the Protocol on Amendments of 2003 added the principle of restraining Member States from entering into any treaty or alliance incompatible with AU principles and objectives as Article 4 subparagraph (q) and the principle of prohibiting Member States from allowing the use of their territory as a base for subversion against other Members as Article 4 subparagraph (r). The latter echoes Article III(5) of the OAU Treaty, and it was probably the drafters' omission not to include it in the Constitutive Act.

67. Several observations should be made in relation to the Article 4 principles. First, there are arguably two doctrines essential to the functioning of international organizations which were omitted: (a) that Member States shall fulfil in good faith all the obligations assumed by ratifying the Constitutive Act;[686] and (b) that Member States shall facilitate the achievement of AU tasks and shall abstain from any measure that could jeopardize the attainment of its objectives.[687] It should be noted that the latter doctrine (the so-called solidarity clause) has been partly covered by the Protocol on Amendments of 2003, which inserted Article 4(q) in the Constitutive Act. The second observation relates to the principle of condemnation and rejection of acts of terrorism. It was inserted in a strict and unqualified manner even though some quarters of the international community (including in Africa) would justify terrorist activities if they were undertaken against totalitarian regimes; if the right to self-determination has been unlawfully negated; or where regimes have come into power by forcibly overthrowing legitimate governments.[688] Indeed, in the Algiers Declaration of July 1999, African leaders accepted the connection between acts of terrorism and the legitimate struggle 'waged by peoples for freedom and self-determination'.[689] Considering that contemporary African history has been marked by a continuous struggle against colonialism, dictatorships, and human rights abuses, that Member States have directly interfered in the internal affairs of other Members (even though the OAU and the AU would not be prepared to admit that much) and that the term 'terrorism' has many political shades and has not yet received a universally acceptable legal definition, it is submitted that the AU should think again the strictness of this principle. Arguably, it should reconsider the legitimacy of terrorist activities directed against governments which have come into

---

686. Compare Art. 2(2) of the UN Charter; Art. 4(3) of the Treaty on European Union (Consolidated version 2016), Official Journal of the European Union, C 202, 7.6.2016, p. 15.
687. Compare Art. 4(3) of the Treaty on European Union, ibid.
688. *See further*, Organization of the Islamic Conference (now the Organization of Islamic Cooperation (OIC)), *Code of Conduct on Combating International Terrorism*, adopted in 1994, and *Convention on Combating International Terrorism*, adopted on 1 Jul. 1999, at: https://www.files.ethz.ch/isn/125385/268.pdf; *Kuala Lumpur Declaration on International Terrorism*, adopted by the Extraordinary Session on Terrorism of the Islamic Conference of Foreign Ministers, 1–3 Apr. 2002, UN Doc. A/56/911 – S/2002/362 (8 Apr. 2002); and Twenty-Ninth Session of the Islamic Conference of Foreign Ministers, Resolution No. 6/29-LEG on the OIC Convention on Combating International Terrorism (27 Jun. 2002). The OIC Convention is presently undergoing a process of reform aiming at dealing with new trends, including the fight against cyber space terrorism and transboundary terrorist networks. Note that thirty African countries participate in the OIC.
689. *See* Assembly, *Algiers Declaration*, OAU Doc. AHG/Decl. 1 (XXXV) (14 Jul. 1999), reproduced in RADIC 11 (1999): 788.

power by quashing the rule of law and by abolishing democratic institutions and also terrorist acts perpetrated against foreign occupation troops. Moreover, this strict principle would appear to be against the OAU Convention on the Prevention and Combating of Terrorism of July 1999 (in force since December 2002), whose Article 3(1) expressly stipulates that:

> the struggle waged by peoples in accordance with the principles of international law for their liberation or self-determination, including armed struggle against colonialism, occupation, aggression and domination by foreign forces shall not be considered as terrorist acts.

However, it could be counterargued that, in view of the Protocol to the Terrorism Convention, concluded in July 2004 and in force since February 2014, the provision of Article 3(1) no longer represents the AU position. And, this is because the fifth preambular paragraph of the Protocol reads: '[The Member States of the African Union] convinced that acts of terrorism cannot be justified under any circumstances … .'[690] Therefore, there would appear to be a prima facie conflict between the Constitutive Act, the Terrorism Convention, and the Protocol raising a point of interpretation. However, the three instruments in question stipulate separate methods for resolving disputes on interpretation. Thus, Article 26 of the Constitutive Act envisages resort to the African Court of Justice (now, the ACJHR) pending the establishment of which the Assembly shall be responsible; Article 22 of the Convention envisages amicable solution between the disagreeing parties, failing which resort to the ICJ or to arbitration; and, finally, Article 7 of the Protocol is an amalgamation of the other methods: it stipulates that should the difference not be settled amicably, either party may refer it to the ACJHR, but if either or both parties do not participate in said Court, they may refer it to the ICJ for a settlement in conformity with the latter's Statute. There have also been decisions expressing the AU's determination to fight any form of terrorism.[691] Presently, there are two relevant entities in operation, the Africa Centre for the Study and Research on Terrorism (ACSRT) and the Committee of Intelligence and Security Service of Africa (CISSA), while in 2022, it was resolved to create a Counter-Terrorism Unit within the African Standby Force (ASF).[692] Finally, it should be noted that in 28 May 2022 the Sixteenth Extraordinary Assembly Session took place in Malabo, Equatorial Guinea, to discuss 'Terrorism and Unconstitutional Changes of Government in Africa'. A Declaration was adopted, which was titled 'Robust Response, Deepening Democracy and Collective Security', which connected the 'expanding threat of terrorism' with the resurgence of unconstitutional changes of government; violent extremism across the Continent, including the influx of foreign terrorist fighters, private military companies and mercenaries; as well as the proliferation of armed groups and transnational

690. Compare Executive Council, *Decision on Terrorism*, AU Doc. Ext/EX/CL/Dec. 4 (III) (24 May 2003), which rejected the perpetration of terrorism in all its forms and recalled Africa's stand to unequivocally condemn all terrorist acts.
691. *See* Assembly, *Decision on the Prevention and Combating of Terrorism*, AU Doc. Assembly/AU/311 (XV) (27 Jul. 2010).
692. AU Doc. Assembly/AU/Dec. 815 (XXXV) (6 Feb. 2022).

organized crime. One of the measures that the Assembly approved was the establishment of an AU Ministerial Committee on Counter Terrorism as a mechanism to coordinate, monitor and evaluate the commitments made in the Declaration and their implementation by Member States.[693]

68. The third observation relates to the fact that the principle of non-intervention in the internal affairs of Member States has been qualified in the Constitutive Act by providing for a right of intervention. The Constitutive Act is the only multilateral instrument to expressly stipulate the right of intervention in Member States in the following two instances. The first is laid down in Article 4(h), as revised by the Amendment Protocol of 2003. It could be described as involuntary intervention in the sense that the targeted Member State may not object to it. Article 4(h), a provision reflecting the collective inability during the OAU era to deal effectively with numerous cases of genocide and ethnic cleansing,[694] endows the AU with the right to intervene on the basis of an Assembly decision, following a PSC recommendation, when grave circumstances (i.e., war crimes, genocide, crimes against humanity as well as a serious threat to legitimate order) are present in a Member State and it is necessary to restore peace and stability. It is submitted that what constitutes a threat to legitimate order in the context of domestic affairs should be treated as a legal and not as a political matter, and, consequently, it ought to be ultimately determined, in case of dispute, by the ACJHR (once it becomes operative).

69. The second instance is voluntary intervention in accordance with Article 4(j) of the Constitutive Act. It stipulates that Member States have the right to request AU intervention to restore peace and security. The wording of this provision raises a point of interpretation: is intervention to be demanded only by the Member State concerned or could any other Member request it? An AU Legal Adviser has argued for the latter interpretation by offering a grammatical interpretation of Article 4(j). According to him, this provision 'refers to Member States and not to a member State, and therefore does not restrict the right to request intervention of the Union to the member State concerned'.[695] Even though this interpretation moves towards expanding the ambit of Article 4(j) (undoubtedly, this could lead to protecting the population of Member States from civil strife, human rights violations, etc.), it is submitted that it could lead to unwanted consequences. Thus, it might be used as a weapon by a Member State to create internal problems in another state or to support a minority in that state. In such instances, the Member State invoking Article 4(j) should be required to show an adequate and justifiable legal interest. Moreover, there is nothing to suggest that the drafters of the Constitutive Act wanted such a significant departure from the way the OAU Mechanism for Conflict Prevention and

---

693. AU Doc. Ext/Assembly/AU/Decl. (XVI) (28 May 2022), para. 16.

694. *See* B. Kioko, 'The Right of Intervention under the African Union's Constitutive Act: From Non-Interference to Non-Intervention', *International Review of the Red Cross* 85 (2003), No. 852: 807; D. Kuwali, 'The End of Humanitarian Intervention: Evaluation of the African Union's Right of Intervention', *African Journal of Conflict Resolution* 9 (2009): 41.

695. Kioko, *ibid.*, 817.

Management operated.[696] Finally, Article 4(j) introduces several supranational elements, which the AU arguably does not possess.

70. The modalities of AU involvement pursuant to either Article 4(h) or Article 4(j) have not been laid down in the Constitutive Act. Especially, in the case of Article 4(j), it does not even specify which would be the competent organ to order it. Following the adoption of the Rules of Procedure of the Assembly, it is clear that both actions require its prior decision.[697] However, since the operationalization of the PSC in 2004 the situation has changed. In particular, as regards Article 4(h), the PSC is able to recommend to the Assembly intervention on behalf of the AU, while, as regards Article 4(j), it has been mandated to approve the modalities for intervention once the Assembly has reached the relevant decision.[698] Another issue left unresolved is whether the AU involvement could take the form of armed intervention on its own volition. Leaving aside instances where this would be absolutely necessary under the circumstances (e.g., to prevent a genocide), on the whole it would be questionable. Thus, were it undertaken to address breaches of regional peace and security, it should require the UNSC's prior authorization, as stated in Article 53(1) of the UN Charter. Indeed, the UNSC functions as the principle guardian of international peace and security, the notion of having 'primary responsibility' pursuant to Article 24 of the UN Charter. On numerous occasions, the UNSC has emphasized that it considers itself competent to deal not only with issues of international peace and security but with regional peace and security and/or internal conflicts as well.[699] Finally, it should be noted that the ASF has been established to enable the PSC perform its responsibilities vis-à-vis deploying of peace support missions and (direct) intervention pursuant to Article 4(h) and Article 4(j). Presently, the ASF is not fully operational, even though this was declared during the Fourteenth Extraordinary Assembly on Silencing the Guns which was held on 6 December 2020. However, the fact that military intervention may be ordered and undertaken by the AU cannot be ruled out.[700]

If it were to happen, the question arises whether the targeted Member State or rather its government in power is obligated to accept the intervention. The provisions of Article 4(h) of the Constitutive Act have never been applied. There was, however, an incident in 2015–2016 where the PSC came to propose its application against Burundi but the Assembly chose a different course of action. In particular, the incident concerned the crisis that had broken out in Burundi when in 2015 the then President Pierre Nkurunziza sought a third term, which was not allowed by the

---

696. For analysis *see* K. Magliveras & G. Naldi, *The African Union* (Alphen aan den Rijn: Kluwer Law International, 2009), 59 et seq.
697. *See* Art. 9(1) of the Constitutive Act in conjunction with Rule 4(1)(e) and (f) of the Rules of Procedure of the Assembly. *See also* T. Maluwa, 'Reimagining African Unity: Some Preliminary Reflections on the Constitutive Act of the African Union', *African Yearbook of International Law* 8 (2002): 29.
698. *See* Art. 7(1) of the PSC Protocol.
699. As the examples of Somalia, Rwanda, and Sudan clearly show. Generally, *see* N.M. Blokker & M. Kleiboer, 'The Internationalization of Domestic Conflict: The Role of the UN Security Council', *Leiden Journal of International Law* 9 (1996): 7.
700. *See* Art. 13 of the PSC Protocol.

Constitution. This led to mass protests, an attempted coup d'état, the intervention of the army and more than 1,100 dead Burundians. The PSC addressed the matter and recommended to the Assembly the deployment of a 5,000-strong African Prevention and Protection Mission in Burundi (MAPROBU). The following extract from the PSC is of direct relevance:

> [PSC] Expresses its determination to take all appropriate measures against any party or actor, whomsoever, who would impede the implementation of the present decision.
>
> In this regard, [PSC] decides, in the event of non–acceptance of the deployment of
>
> MAPROBU, to recommend to the Assembly ..., in accordance with the powers which are conferred to [PSC], jointly with the [AUC] Chairperson, under article 7(e) of the [PSC] Protocol, *the implementation of article 4 (h) of the Constitutive Act relating to intervention in a Member State in certain serious circumstances.*
>
> [PSC] further decides that, in such a situation, and on the basis of a communication from the [AUC] Chairperson confirming the non–acceptance of the deployment, [PSC] shall recommend to the Assembly to take additional measures in conformity with the Constitutive Act. [PSC] finally decides that all those whose action could jeopardize the inter–Burundian dialogue, including attacks by armed groups against governmental facilities and other targets ... shall be subjected to sanctions as provided for in the relevant decisions of [PSC] and other measures to be agreed upon (emphasis added).[701]

Thus, what PSC resolved was to recommend to the Assembly the implementation of Article 4(h) if Burundi were to refuse the deployment of MAPROBU. Moreover, it resolved to ask the Assembly 'to take additional measures in conformity with the Constitutive Act', arguably a reference to Article 23(2) of the Constitutive Act, which, as explained later, has never been applied. It follows that the PSC does not have the power to invoke and apply Article 4(h). This is the prerogative of the Assembly, which could possibly delegate it to the Executive Council on the basis of Article 9(1)(g) in conjunction with Article 9(2) of the Constitutive Act. In the present case, the Assembly did not deliberate the PSC's recommendation but decided to dispatch a high-level delegation to consult with the Burundian government and other domestic actors on how the AU could contribute to the resolution of the crisis.[702] Six months later, with the situation unchanged, the Assembly did not discuss the possibility of ordering forceful measures,[703] and it was only in January 2017 that it urged the government of Burundi to sign the MoU on the deployment

701. PSC, 565th Meeting, *Communiqué*, AU Doc. PSC//PR/COMM.(DLXV), para. 13(c)(4) (17 Dec. 2015).
702. Assembly, *Decision on the Activities of the Peace and Security Council and the State of Peace and Security in Africa*, AU Doc. Assembly/AU/Dec. 598 (XXVI) (31 Jan. 2016), para. 13.
703. Assembly, *Decision on the State of Peace and Security in Africa*, AU Doc. Assembly/AU/Dec. 612 (XXVII) (18 Jul. 2016), para. 1.

of the authorized 200 AU Human Rights Observers and Military Experts.[704] Finally, Nkurunziza agreed not to be a presidential candidate allowing for the successful holding of elections on 20 May 2020.[705]

71. The above considerations beg the question of whether the AU, in its present form, constitutes a regional arrangement within the meaning of Chapter VIII of the UN Charter. Articles 52–54 thereof allow the existence of arrangements dealing with the maintenance of peace and security in a manner appropriate for regional action, if they act under the primacy of the UNSC and in accordance with the relevant UN Charter provisions. Such arrangements, which have included, *inter alia*, NATO, the League of Arab States, the Warsaw Pact (dissolved in July 1991), the Bagdad Pact (renamed the Central Treaty Organization and dissolved in 1979), the Western European Union (as conceived in the late 1940s and early 1950s), ASEAN, and the Organization of American States (OAS), could be understood as agencies and/or acting as agents of the UN Security Council.[706] At the time the Constitutive Act was signed, arguably the AU did not possess the structures that are characteristic of such arrangements. However, subsequent events, including the entry into force in December 2003 of the PSC Protocol and the wide powers and functions entrusted to it in conjunction with the way the PSC has performed its mandate as well as in December 2009 of the aforementioned Non-Aggression and Common Defence Pact, clearly lead to the conclusion that it has become a Chapter VIII regional arrangement. The first major AU action in this area was the setting up of

---

704. Assembly, *Decision on the Report of the Peace and Security Council on its Activities and the State of Peace and Security in Africa*, AU Doc. Assembly/AU/Dec. 629 (XXVIII), 31 Jan. 2017, para. 9. *See also*, UNSC, *Report of the Secretary-General on Burundi*, UN Doc. S/2017/165, 23 Feb. 2017; and *Security Council Press Statement on Situation in Burundi*, UN Doc. SC/12750, 13 Mar. 2017.

705. *See* PSC, *Communique of the 993rd meeting on the African Union Human Rights Observers and Military Experts Mission in Burundi*, AU Doc. PSC/PR/COMM.3(CMXCIII) (27 Apr. 2021).

706. In order to define and make more concrete its relationship with regional arrangements, the UNSC has adopted over the years numerous instruments, including the following of particular interest to Africa: Res. 1269(1999) of 19 Oct. 1999 on the responsibility of the Security Council in the maintenance of peace and security, reproduced in 39 I.L.M. (2000) 238; Res. 1308(2000) of 17 Jul. 2000 on the responsibility of the Security Council in the maintenance of peace and security; Res. 1625(2005) of 14 Sep. 2005 on threats to international peace and security; Res. 1631(2005) of 17 Oct. 2005 on cooperation between the United Nations and regional organizations for the maintenance of international peace and security; Presidential Statement of 20 Sep. 2006 on cooperation between the United Nations and regional organizations in the maintenance of international peace and security, UN Doc. S/PRST/2006/39 (20 Sep. 2006); Presidential Statement S/PRST/2009/11 (5 May 2009) and Presidential Statement S/PRST/2021/9 (19 April 2021). *See further* the open UNSC debate 'Cooperation between the United Nations and regional and sub-regional organizations: peace operations – the United Nations-African Union partnership and its evolution', held in December 2014, UN Doc. S/2014/879 (9 Dec. 2014) and UN Doc. S/PV.7343 (16 Dec. 2014) as well as UNSC, *Strengthening the partnership between the United Nations and the African Union on issues of peace and security in Africa, including the work of the United Nations Office to the African Union – Report of the Secretary-General*, UN Doc. S/2022/643 (25 Aug. 2022). *See also* the following UNGA instruments: Res. 60/1, *2005 World Summit Outcome*, 16 Sep. 2005, para. 68(h); Res. 55/2, *United Nations Millennium Declaration*, 18 Sep. 2000, para. 28; and Res. 49/57, *Declaration on the Enhancement of Cooperation between the United Nations and Regional Arrangements or Agencies in the Maintenance of International Peace and Security*, 9 Dec. 1994.

AMIS (2004), a peacekeeping force that operated in the region of Darfur and reference to which has been made above. The following year, UNSC Resolution 1590 (2005) of 24 March 2005 requested that the United Nations Mission in Sudan (UNMIS) 'closely and continuously liaise and coordinate at all levels' with AMIS.[707]

Although there is a growing rapport between the UN and the AU in addressing collective security challenges in the continent,[708] the two institutions may understand their priorities differently. The UNSC has recognized that in some cases it may authorize the AU to deal with such challenges,[709] while the AU has time and time again called upon the UN to fund its peacekeeping operations.[710] A UN Secretary-General Report issued in 2008 might have blurred the issues when it referred to 'the potential for misunderstanding and misrepresentation concerning the meaning and scope of [UN-AU] partnerships'.[711] On 16 April 2008, the Republic of South Africa, taking advantage of holding the rotating monthly UNSC Presidency, organized a high-level meeting on the security challenges facing Africa. The PSC participated in the meeting. Even though this was an excellent opportunity to appraise the situation, address the then multifaceted problems (e.g., the deployment of the UN-AU hybrid mission in Darfur), and negotiate a working relationship between the UN and the AU, the UNSC instrument adopted later on the same day failed to offer pertinent answers. In November 2016, the UNSC said that the UN-AU partnership should further develop into a systematic and strategic partnership adapted to the

707. *See also* UNSC Res. 1564 (2004), 18 Sep. 2004. Note that, without expressly saying so, UNSC Res. 2320(2016) of 18 Nov. 2016 considers that, as a regional mechanism, the AU comes under Chapter VIII of the UN Charter.

708. Based on the *Declaration on Enhancing UN – AU Cooperation: Framework for the Ten-Year Capacity-Building Programme of the African Union*, signed in Addis Ababa between the UN Secretary-General and the AUC Chairperson on 16 Nov. 2006, UN Doc. A/61/630, 12 Dec. 2006. *See also* United Nations, *Report of the African Union-United Nations panel on modalities for support to African Union peacekeeping operations*, UN Doc. A/63/666-S/2008/813 (31 Dec. 2008).

709. For the developing dynamics of the relationship, *see* UNSC, Presidential Statement of 28 Mar. 2007 on the relationship between the United Nations and regional organizations, in particular the African Union, in the maintenance of international peace and security, UN Doc. S/PRST/2007/7 (28 Mar. 2007); UNSC Res. 2033(2012) on Cooperation between the United Nations and regional and subregional organizations in maintaining international peace and security (12 Jan. 2012); and UNSC, *Report on the activities of the Ad Hoc Working Group on Conflict Prevention and Resolution in Africa for the period January-December 2013*, UN Doc. S/2013/778 (30 Dec. 2013).

710. *See, inter alia*, Assembly, *Decision on the Activities of the Peace and Security Council of the African Union and the State of Peace and Security in Africa*, para. 6, AU Doc. Assembly/AU/Dec. 408 (XVIII) (30 Jan. 2012); Assembly, *Decision on the Activities of the Peace and Security Council of the African Union and the State of Peace and Security in Africa*, para. 17, AU Doc. Assembly/AU/Dec. 177 (X) (2 Feb. 2008); and Assembly, *Decision on the Activities of the Peace and Security Council of the African Union and the State of Peace and Security in Africa*, AU Doc. Assembly/AU/Dec. 145 (VIII) (30 Feb. 2007).

711. *See* United Nations, *Report of the Secretary-General on the relationship between the United Nations and regional organizations, in particular the African Union, in the maintenance of international peace and security*, UN Doc. S/2008/186 (7 Apr. 2008). *See further* United Nations, *Concept paper on the relationship between the United Nations and regional organizations, in particular the African Union, in the maintenance of international peace and security*, UN Doc. S/2007/148 (14 Mar. 2007).

continent's complex security challenges.[712] It culminated in the signing on 19 April 2017 of a Joint UN-AU Framework for Enhancing Partnership in Peace and Security between the Secretariats of the two Organizations at the UN Headquarters in New York.[713]

72. Before the advent of the AU in 2002, several RECs had already come into the ambit of Article 52 of the UN Charter, and, importantly, they had established a tradition of peacekeeping at a sub-regional level. The most important of the RECs, in terms of activities, was ECOWAS. Although it was established in 1975 as a regional economic integration organization,[714] it gradually acquired a collective security dimension which brought it under Chapter VIII of the UN Charter. In particular, ECOWAS adopted on 22 April 1978 a Non-Aggression Protocol prohibiting Member States from using force as a means for settling disputes; on 29 May 1981, it concluded the Protocol on Mutual Assistance in Defence, which came into force in October 1987; later it established the Defence and Security Commission (CDC); and, finally, on 10 December 1999, it concluded the Protocol relating to the Mechanism for Conflict Prevention, Management, Resolution of Conflicts, Peacekeeping and Security, which created a Mediation and Security Council.[715] Reference should also be made to the ECOWAS Vision 2020 Towards a Democratic and Prosperous Community, where peace and collective regional security is mentioned as one of its building blocks. In December 1989, ECOWAS created a peacekeeping force, the Economic Community of West African States Monitoring Group (ECOMOG), which has been deployed with considerable success in the territory of several Member States. At an international level, ECOMOG has attracted attention for its involvement in the civil wars in Liberia (1990–2005),[716] which was approved and

712. *See* UNSC Res. 2320(2016), *supra*. *See further*, UNSC, *Report of the Secretary-General on strengthening the partnership between the United Nations and the African Union on issues of peace and security in Africa, including the work of the United Nations Office to the African Union*, UN Doc. S/2016/780 (13 Sep. 2016).

713. *See* AU Commission, Directorate of Information and Communication, Press Release N° 060/2017, 18 Apr. 2017. *See further*, UNSC, *Report of the Secretary-General on options for authorization and support for African Union peace support operations*, UN Doc. S/2017/454, 26 May 2017, para. 4, and the discussion at the UNSC on 19 Jul. 2017 (8006th Meeting), UN Doc. SC/12915. For the Framework's text, *see* https://unoau.unmissions.org/sites/default/files/signed_joint_framework.pdf.

714. *See* the Treaty of Lagos establishing ECOWAS, signed on 28 May 1975, reproduced in 14 I.L.M. (1975) 1200. A Revised Treaty was signed in Cotonou, Benin, on 24 Jul. 1993, entered into force on 30 Jul. 1995, reproduced in 35 I.L.M. (1996) 660; RADIC 8 (1996): 187.

715. *See* ECOWAS Decision A/DEC. 11/10/98, which was approved by Member States in Abuja, Nigeria, on 31 Oct. 1998. The Protocol entered provisionally into force upon signature; *see* A. Abass, 'The New Collective Security Mechanism of ECOWAS: Innovations and Problems', *Journal of Conflict and Security Law* 5 (2000): 211. Generally, *see* A. Adebajo & I. Rashid (eds), *West Africa's Security Challenges – Building Peace in a Troubled Region* (London: Lynne Reiner, 2004); and M. Pitts, 'Sub-Regional Solutions for African Conflict: The ECOMOG Experiment', *Journal of Conflict Studies* 19 (1999): 49.

716. *See* K. Kufuor, 'The Legality of the Intervention in the Liberian Civil War by the Economic Community of West African States', *RADIC* 5 (1993): 525. Generally, *see* J. Boulden (ed.), *Dealing with Conflict in Africa: The United Nations and Regional Organizations* (New York: Palgrave Macmillan, 2003); and C. Borgan, 'The Theory and Practice of Regional Organization Intervention in Civil Wars', *New York University Journal of International Law & Policy* 26 (1994): 797.

endorsed by the UN Security Council,[717] in Sierra Leone (1997–2005),[718] in Guinea-Bissau (1998–1999)[719] as well as for its efforts to promote reconciliation in Côte d'Ivoire and to organize democratic presidential and legislative elections in the country (2005–2010).[720] Reference should also be made to the ECOWAS Conflict Prevention Mechanism, which has incorporated traditional African mediation notions such as the Council of Elders.[721] Moreover, it has deployed a military force, the Economic Community of West African States' Mission in The Gambia (ECOMIG), to support peace and stability in the country following the friction caused in December 2016 when the presidential election was won by the party in opposition. The UNSC endorsed it under Resolution 2337(2017) of 19 January 2017 and held that the government bears primary responsibility for protecting human rights as well as the civilian population. On 5 June 2017, ECOWAS extended ECOMIG for another year. Finally, in December 2022, ECOWAS resolved to establish a regional force to fight terrorism and restore constitutional order.[722]

Briefly, other RECs having a collective security dimension include the SADC, the ECCAS and the Economic and Monetary Community of Central Africa (CEMAC), which shares characteristics with ECCAS. SADC acquired a regional security dimension in two phases. First, though the conclusion on 14 August 2001 of the Protocol on Politics, Defence, and Security Cooperation, which established the namesake Organ. Second, through the signing on 26 August 2003 of a Mutual Defence Pact.[723] Regarding ECCAS, a Non-Aggression Pact was signed on 9 September 1994. Following its reactivation in 1999, ECCAS adopted on 24 February 2000 the Protocol Relating to the Establishment of a Council for Peace and Security in

717. *See*, *inter alia*, UNSC Res. 788(1992) of 19 Nov. 1992; Res. 856(1993) of 10 Aug. 1993; Res. 866(1993) of 22 Sep. 1993; Res. 911(1994) of 21 Apr. 1994; Res. 950(1994) of 21 Oct. 1994; Res. 1083(1996) of 27 Nov. 1996; Res. 1100(1997) of 27 Mar. 1997; Res. 1116(1997) of 27 Jun. 1997; Res. 1343(2001) of 7 Mar. 2001, reproduced in 40 I.L.M. (2001) 1024; Res. 1497(2003) of 1 Aug. 2003; and Res. 1626(2005) of 19 Sep. 2005.
718. For the relevant UNSC instruments, *see*, *inter alia*, Res. 1132(1997) of 8 Oct. 1997; Res. 1315(2000) of 14 Aug. 2000; Res. 1385(2001) of 19 Dec. 2001; Res. 1400(2002) of 28 Mar. 2002; Res. 1470(2003) of 28 Mar. 2003; Res. 1508(2003) of 19 Sep. 2003; Res. 1562(2004) of 17 Sep. 2004; and Res. 1626(2005) of 19 Sep. 2005.
719. For the relevant UNSC instruments, *see*, *inter alia*, Res. 1216(1998) of 21 Dec. 1998; and Res. 1233(1999) of 6 Apr. 1999.
720. For the relevant UNSC instruments, *see*, *inter alia*, Res. 1609(2005) of 24 Jun. 2005; Res. 1633(2005) of 21 Oct. 2005; Res. 1708(2006) of 14 Sep. 2006; Res. 1721(2006) of 1 Nov. 2006; Res. 1765(2007) of 16 Jul. 2007; Res. 1782(2007) of 29 Oct. 2007; Res. 1795(2008) of 15 Jan. 2008; Res. 1865(2009) of 27 Jan. 2009; and Res. 1880(2009) of 30 Jul. 2009. Generally, *see* A. Orahbelashvili, *Collective Security* (Oxford: Oxford University Press, 2011), 294 et seq.
721. *See* UNSC Res. 1197(1998) of 18 Sep. 1998, para. 7.
722. ECOWAS, Sixty-Second Ordinary Session of the Authority of Heads of State and Government, *Final Communique*, 4 December 2022, paras 21 and 25.
723. For criticism of SADC's record in this area, *see* M. Aeby, *Peace and Security Challenges in Southern Africa: Governance Deficits and Lacklustre Regional Conflict Management*, Nordiska Afrikainstitutet/The Nordic Africa Institute, Policy Note No 4:2018, May 2018, at: https://www.diva-portal.org/smash/get/diva2:1206571/FULLTEXT01.pdf.

Central Africa (COPAX).[724] The Protocol, which envisages that COPAX includes the Defence and Security Commission (CDC), the Multinational Force of Central Africa (FOMAC) and the Early Warning Mechanism of Central Africa (MARAC), entered into force in early 2004. In 2008, it was decided that the Multinational Force maintained by CEMAC (FOMUC) be taken over by COPAX,[725] while in October 2007, the Multinational Force deployed in the CAR had been transferred to ECCAS.

---

724. *See* A. Meyer, *Peace and Security Cooperation in Central Africa: Developments, Challenges and Prospects*, Discussion Paper 56 (Nordiska Afrikainstitutet, Uppsala, 2011); H. Besada (ed.), *Crafting an African Security Architecture: Addressing Regional Peace and Conflict in the 21st Century* (London: Routledge, 2016) 196–198.
725. *See Final Communiqué of the Council of Ministers of COPAX*, 27 Feb. 2008, at: http://www.ceeac-eccas.org.

Chapter 3. Admission to and Withdrawal from the AU: The Amendment of the Constitutive Act – The Question of Unratified OAU/AU Treaties

73. As far as admission to AU membership is concerned, there are two relevant provisions in the Constitutive Act. The first is Article 27(1) stipulating that it is open to signature and accession only by OAU Member States. The second is Article 29 stipulating that, after the Constitutive Act has entered into force, any interested African state may notify the AUC Chairperson of its intention to be admitted as a Member State. Accession to the Constitutive Act is a requirement. Once a state's intention has been received, the Chairperson communicates the notification to all Member States, which is decided by a simple majority. This provision is almost identical to the admission to membership clause in Article XXVIII of the OAU Charter. However, one notable difference is that the Constitutive Act does not expressly confer upon African countries the right to become AU Members, as was the case under Article IV of the OAU Charter.[726] The fact that the states capable of becoming original AU Members were restricted to those which were at the time OAU Members served to emphasize the continuity between them and the fact that the former institution succeeded the latter. The practical effect of Article 27(1) was that Morocco, which withdrew from the OAU in November 1985, could not have signed the Constitutive Act in July 2000. Although in the previous editions of this monograph it was argued that Morocco did not appear willing to seek membership,[727] in the summer of 2016, the situation changed dramatically and, as already mentioned, in January 2017, its application for membership was accepted by the majority of Member States and became the fifty-fifth Member State.

Before Morocco, the Republic of South Sudan had become the fifty-fourth Member State. On 27 July 2011, the AUC Chairperson announced that thirty-three Member States, including the Republic of Sudan, had submitted their written communications supporting South Sudan's application. Its accession was rather exceptional, and presumably it was induced by the need to consolidate its statehood, following its secession from Sudan. Secession was achieved when the population freely and fairly exercised its right to self-determination in a referendum held on 9–15 January 2011. Already at its Sixteenth Ordinary Session (January 2011), the Assembly had adopted a Declaration on Sudan indirectly promising AU accession.[728] When the Constitutive Act was drafted, the opportunity was there to lay down which conditions ought to be met to examine a state's request for admission. But none is mentioned. One obvious condition would have been that it is considered capable of fulfilling the obligations and the duties emanating from membership.[729] Arguably, the Republic of South Sudan, being a newly created state, could not have met this condition if the necessary state institutions and procedures were

726. For analysis, *see* K. Magliveras & G. Naldi, *The African Union* (Alphen aan den Rijn: Kluwer Law International, 2009), 41 et seq.
727. *See ibid.*, p. 45.
728. *See* AU Doc. Assembly/AU/Decl. 3 (XVI).
729. Compare Art. 4(1) of the UN Charter.

not in place. For example, it was only in late 2012 that it adopted the necessary legislative procedures for signing and ratifying treaties and conventions. South Soudan submitted the ratification instrument to the African Charter on Human and Peoples' Rights in May 2016 but has still not ratified its Protocol on the Rights of Women in Africa and the African Charter on the Rights and Welfare of the Child (it signed both instruments in January 2013), and has not signed the Protocol on the Rights of Older Persons as well as the Protocol on the Rights of Persons with Disabilities in Africa.

74. Regarding the granting of observer status in the AU and the rules of accreditation, in July 2005, the Executive Council adopted the Criteria for Granting Observer Status and a System of Accreditation,[730] while previously it had determined that states as well as IGOs outside Africa could in principle be granted accreditation and this status would confer them the right to attend public sessions and to receive documents of general circulation.[731] These criteria also apply to NGOs, and, currently, more than fifty NGOs have been granted observer status. When the NGO Lions Club International applied for observer status, the Executive Council withheld its decision and, at the same time, asked the PRC to reconsider the criteria for granting AU observer status.[732] Apparently, the matter was never resolved. Finally, it should be noted that the Assembly has allowed representatives of the African Diaspora to follow its meetings as observers.[733]

75. Article 31(1) of the Constitutive Act, almost a repetition of Article XXXI of the OAU Charter,[734] expressly stipulates that Member States have the unfettered right to renounce and, consequently, to terminate their membership by forwarding a written notification to that effect to the AUC Chairperson. According to Article 31(1), at the end of one year, commencing from the date of the written notification, 'the Act shall cease to apply with respect to the renouncing State, which shall thereby cease to belong to the Union', unless the notification has in the meantime been withdrawn. During the twelve-month period, the withdrawing Member is obliged to comply with the provisions of the Constitutive Act and to discharge all duties and obligations (Article 31(2)). It is submitted that this obligation, which was

---

730. *See* Executive Council, *Decision on the criteria for granting observer status and a system of accreditation to the AU*, AU Doc. EX.CL/Dec. 230 (VII) (2 Jul. 2005). For the draft text, *see* AU Doc. EX.CL/195 (VII) Annex IV (May 2005).

731. *See* Executive Council, *Decision on the criteria for granting observer status and a system of accreditation to the AU*, AU Doc. EX.CL/Dec. 168 (VI) (28 Jan. 2005). For the OAU criteria, *see* OAU Doc. CAB/LEG/117/82, adopted by the Fourteenth Ordinary Assembly Session (Libreville, 5 Jul. 1977).

732. *See* Executive Council, *Decision on the application by Lions Club International for accreditation with the AU*, AU Doc. EX.CL/Dec. 238 (VIII) (21 Jan. 2006). For the text of the application, *see* AU Doc. EX.CL/212 (VIII).

733. *See* AU Doc. Assembly/AU/Res. 1 (XVIII) (July 2012). For the AUC Protocol Division's list of accredited non-African states and IGOs as at 10 February 2021, *see* African Union Commission and New Zealand Ministry of Foreign Affairs and Trade, *African Union Handbook 2022*, 205, at: https://au.int/en/handbook.

734. *See* Magliveras & Naldi, *supra*, 45–46.

not included in the OAU Charter but, in varying forms, has been inserted in the constitutive instruments of international organizations for 100 years,[735] is unlikely to be legally enforceable. Thus, it will be up to the withdrawing Member State to fulfil its obligations, especially to pay in full any outstanding budgetary contributions.

In a most puzzling move, Article 12 of the Protocol on Amendments of 2003 deleted Article 31. Although it is not unusual for constitutive instruments not to include a withdrawal clause,[736] there is no previous experience with abrogating the right of Member States to withdraw. Clearly, if a Member State is determined to terminate its membership, it will do so even if the constitutive instrument does not contain a relevant clause. If one attempted to explain why it was imperative to remove Article 31, one could possibly suggest the wish to emphasize that AU membership is perpetual and that it will operate in perpetuity. Indeed, this was offered as an explanation why in 1957 the Treaty of Rome establishing the European Economic Community had no withdrawal clause. It was only in 2004 when the draft Treaty Establishing a Constitution for Europe overturned this understanding by permitting Member States to withdraw subject to concluding an agreement with the EU.[737] The draft Treaty was never ratified by the required number of states, and further negotiations led to the Treaty of Lisbon, which was signed in December 2007 and entered into force in 2009. While the Treaty of Lisbon differed in several respects from the draft Constitution for Europe, it did include a withdrawal clause,[738] which was invoked for the first time by the United Kingdom in March 2017.

76. Notwithstanding the existence of Article 31 and the apparent right of Member States to withdraw, the question could be posed if the AU itself or individual Members could block the withdrawal of a Member whose government seized power in a coup d'état or through other unconstitutional means. In particular, suppose that such a government was, by virtue of Article 30 of the Constitutive Act, suspended from participating in AU activities and, in order to antagonize the AU and show that it will not be intimidated, announced its withdrawal and, once the twelve-month period of notice had lapsed, it officially declared that it no longer has the status of a Member State. In these circumstances, could the other Member States and/or the AU treat the act of withdrawal as null and void on the ground that the unconstitutional government cannot legally bind the state in question on the international plane and, consequently, they continue to treat it as a Member State and demand that it fulfil all its membership's obligations and duties? The answer should be in

735. Starting with Art. 1(3) of the Covenant of the League of Nations of 1919; K. Magliveras, 'Withdrawal from the League of Nations Revisited' *Dickinson Journal of International Law* 10 (1991): 25.

736. The classic example is the UN Charter, whose drafters feared that the mass exodus of states from the League of Nations could have been replicated if withdrawal was expressly allowed. However, the understanding is that, while Member States may not withdraw, they will not be prevented if there are compelling reasons.

737. *See* Art. I-60 of the draft Treaty Establishing a Constitution for Europe.

738. *See* Art. 50 of the Treaty on European Union. Generally, *see* G. Naldi & K. Magliveras, 'The Right to Revoke Withdrawal Notices from International Organisations: The Case of Brexit and the European Union' [2021] 28:1 *Maastricht Journal of European and Comparative Law* 30.

the negative because withdrawal would appear to occur automatically and be tantamount to secession from membership. Moreover, the AU does not seem to be able to examine either the legality of the intention to withdraw or the legitimacy of the act of secession, even though, if and when the ACJHR commences its operation, these questions could form the subject matter of a request for an advisory opinion in accordance with Articles 53 et seq. of the Protocol establishing the Court. However, if the unconstitutional regime were to be overturned and replaced by a legitimate government within a reasonable period of time following the expiration of the twelve-month period, it could be argued that the AU, acting though the Assembly, could determine that the membership had never been terminated and, should the new regime wish to re-establish ties with the AU, it is not required to seek membership anew under Article 29 of the Constitutive Act.

77. The procedure for the amendment and revision of the Constitutive Act is laid down in Article 32 of the Constitutive Act, which resembles the corresponding clause in the OAU Charter (Article XXXIII), and in Rule 28 of the Rules of Procedure of the Assembly. Any Member State may submit proposals to the AUC Chairperson, who is instructed to transmit them to the other Members within thirty days. The Assembly will then examine the proposals within a period of one year, and the Executive Council will give its advice on them. Amendments or revisions will be adopted by the Assembly by consensus or, failing which, by a two-thirds majority and shall be submitted to all Member States for ratification under domestic constitutional procedures. Amendments shall enter into force after two-thirds of the membership have ratified them. This provision signifies that once the amendments have entered into force, they become mandatory upon any Members which had voted against them. Although this provision ensures that the amended Constitutive Act will be binding upon all Members, it could prove to be problematic if certain Members are unwilling to follow the adopted changes.

78. As already mentioned, so far there has been one attempt to modify the Constitutive Act. The fact that it was deemed necessary so soon after its entry into force could be explained by the haste with which the Constitutive Act was drafted.[739] The Protocol on Amendments was approved by the First Extraordinary Assembly Session (Addis Ababa, 3 February 2003) without any debate,[740] and was adopted by the Assembly at the Second Ordinary Session on 11 July 2003. The only difference between the two texts would appear to be that in the latter the clause on withdrawal was deleted.[741]

739. *See* E. Baimu & K. Sturman, 'Amendment to the African Union's Right to Intervene', *African Security Review* 12(2) (2003): 37, 38–39, offering a different explanation, namely that the aim was to prevent the alienation of Libya, which in July 2002 was unsuccessful in pushing through its own amendments to the Constitutive Act.

740. *See Report of the First Extraordinary Session of the Assembly of the African Union*, AU Doc. EX/Assembly/Rpt (I) (3 Feb. 2003) at para. 23.

741. *See* Assembly, *Decision on the Amendments to the Constitutive Act*, AU Doc. Assembly/AU Dec. 26 (II) (11 Jul. 2003). The text of the Protocol is reproduced in RADIC 13 (2005): 37.

79. The Protocol on Amendments contains cosmetic changes in the wording of the Constitutive Act. For example, the words 'founding fathers' in Article 2 and the words 'Chairman of the Assembly' in Article 6 are substituted, respectively, by the gender-neutral words 'founders' and 'Chairperson,' while the term 'working languages' in Article 25 is replaced by the term 'official languages'. Moreover, it endows the AU with a collective security dimension by including the PSC to the AU principal organs and by extending the AU's powers in this area. To avoid unnecessary duplication, the various changes to be brought about by the Protocol of Amendments, if it ever enters into force, are discussed in the relevant sections of the present monograph. It will enter into force when ratified by thirty-six states. Currently, the Protocol has been signed by fifty Member States and has received thirty ratifications. (the last three ratifications were by Sao Tome and Principe in February 2018, Morocco in January 2017 and Congo in December 2012. Even if the Protocol were to enter into force in the foreseeable future, arguably, it can no longer play the role for which it was adopted because its content has been surpassed by the AU's evolution and the many de facto amendments that have taken place during the twenty-one years of its operation. It is only advisable that Member States opt for abrogating the 2003 Protocol and negotiate a new Protocol of Amendments. In particular, the negotiations ought to take into account the new organs and entities that have been added to the AU's institutional architecture, update the AU principles and values, ensure that there are no inconsistencies between the Constitutive Act and the Rules of Procedure of the various organs, make the provisions on measures of a punitive nature (sanctions) more concrete, include provisions on the AU's privileges and immunities, regulate the question of the AU's responsibility and liability, address the needs of the African Continental Free Trade Area (AfCFTA) and reconfigure the relationship between the AU and the AEC, address the operation of the ACJHR, etc. Finally, stock should be taken of the fact that a certain AU legal system has already emerged, and its rules and norms should be included and explicated in the Constitutive Act. The ongoing economic cooperation at the level of AfCFTA should be included in this 'AU law', as it will prove necessary when the continent moves to proper economic integration.

80. In January 2016, the Assembly decided, on the one hand, to 'revise and review the Constitutive Act of the AU for it to be an effective legal instrument to accelerate, facilitate and deepen the efficiency and the integration process on the continent' and, on the other hand, to empower individuals to directly petition the African Court on Human and Peoples' Rights as regards the implementation of the decisions taken by the AU policy organs, subject to the following conditions: (a) such individuals come from Member States, which are contracting parties to the 1998 Protocol establishing the African Human Rights Court; and (b) such contracting parties have also accepted the Court's jurisdiction to receive communications from individuals in conformity with Article 36 of the Protocol.[742] It is not immediately clear why the African Human Rights Court should be competent to rule on such cases unless they directly concern decisions having a specific human rights

742. *See* Assembly, *Decision on Streamlining of the African Union Summits and the Working Methods of the African Union*, AU Doc. Assembly/AU/Dec. 597 (XXVI) (31 Jan. 2016), para. 2.

content. Arguably, what effectively the Assembly was saying was that the population of Member States should be able to supervise whether their governments give full effect to the decisions adopted, principally, by the Assembly, by the Executive Council, and by the PSC. The question of the AU's institutional reform was discussed on 16 July 2016 during a retreat of Heads of State and Government, of Foreign Affairs Ministers and of Finance Ministers held in Kigali, Rwanda. Although the outcome was apparently never made public, the Twenty-Seventh Ordinary Assembly Session, which took place a few days later, resolved to entrust the preparation of a study on reform to Paul Kagame, the President of Rwanda. His task was to submit a report on proposed reforms aiming at 'put[ting] in place a system of governance capable of addressing the challenges facing the Union'.[743]

81. Kagame's Report, which was titled 'The Imperative to Strengthen our Union: Report on the Proposed Recommendations for the Institutional Reform of the African Union', was presented at the Second Retreat of Heads of State and Government held at AU Headquarters in Addis Ababa on 27 January 2017.[744] According to the Report, the AU had to deal with the following challenges: (a) it was a highly fragmented international organization focusing on too many areas; (b) its complicated structure and limited managerial capacity led to inefficient working methods, poor decision-making and a lack of accountability; (c) as it was neither financially independent nor self-sustaining, it had to rely on funding provided for by its partners; and (d) there was limited coordination with RECs.[745] Addressing these challenges, the Report identified the following five focal areas as being key for the AU's transformation: (a) it had to concentrate on fewer priority areas with continental scope; (b) its structure and operations required to be reviewed to ensure 'institutional realignment for better service delivery'; (c) it should connect with the African citizenry; (d) it should become operationally effective and efficient when performing its mandate; and (e) it ought to implement sustainable financing for its programmes and, moreover, to reduce overreliance on development partners. A few days later, following deliberations among the Member States and subject to certain amendments, the Twenty-Eighth Ordinary Assembly Session adopted the Report's recommendations,[746] including the following five. First, the AUC should establish women and youth quotas as well as ensure the private sector's participation in AU activities. Second, as regards the Assembly, it will deal with no more than three strategic items at each of its sessions, delegate 'other appropriate business' to the Executive Council, hold one (instead of two) ordinary sessions per year, and extraordinary sessions as needed. Third, a troika arrangement consisting of the outgoing, the current, and the incoming AU Chairpersons will be established to ensure

743. *See* Assembly, *Decision on the Institutional Reform of the African Union*, AU Doc. Assembly/AU/Dec. 606 (XXVII) (18 Jul. 2016).

744. Text at: https://au.int/en/documents/20170129/report-proposed-recommendations-institutional-reform-african-union.

745. *See* African Union, *AU Reforms Report: Building a more relevant African Union*, January 2017, at: https://au.int/en/documents/20170115/au-reforms-report-building-more-relevant-african-union.

746. *See* Assembly, *Decision on the Outcome of the Retreat of the Assembly of the African Union on the Institutional Reform of the African Union*, AU Doc. Assembly/AU/Dec. 635 (XXVIII), Annex I (31 Jan. 2017).

continuity and the effective implementation of Assembly decisions. Fourth, the sanctions mechanism will be strengthened and enforced, and participation in AU's deliberations will be made contingent on Member States' adherence to Assembly decisions. Fifth, the scale of Member States' contributions to the AU budget will be revised based on the principles of the ability to pay, of solidarity, and of equitable burden-sharing. Arguably, the execution of these recommendations did not require the amendment of the Constitutive Act, for example, the establishment of a troika necessitated only a change in the Assembly Rules of Procedure, and as regards the mechanism for inflicting sanctions, the Constitutive Act contains authorization clauses (Article 23(2)).

82. While not directly concerned with the questions of membership, the fact that many a treaty concluded under the OAU and AU auspices have not been ratified by the required number of Member States to enter into force should be addressed. Arguably, the long period of time elapsed since these treaties were negotiated and adopted partly negates their aims and usefulness because they no longer reflect the current state of affairs. Even though updating and revising them would be the logical step to take, this has happened in only a few cases. At the same time, Member States have continued to sign and/or to ratify treaties which had been concluded many years ago and are clearly outdated, for example, the Inter-African Convention Establishing an African Technical Cooperation Programme (concluded in August 1975, lastly ratified by Gambia in July 2009 and lastly signed by Angola in January 2012) and the Convention for the Establishment of the African Centre for Fertilizer Development (concluded on 1 July 1985, lastly ratified by Burkina Faso in May 2016, and lastly signed by Mautitania in June 2018).

But, even in instances where a new and revised instrument was concluded, the fact that it only entered into force after a very long period of time having lapsed arguably defies the purpose of adopting it in the first place. Thus, the revised version of the African Convention on the Conservation of Nature and Natural Resources was adopted in July 2003 (the original was concluded in September 1968), but it only attracted the last of the required fifteen ratifications, the usual number of ratifications envisaged in OAU/AU treaties, in the summer of 2016. Despite the fact that fifteen ratifications is not such an onerous condition to meet, the ratification rate of OAU/AU treaties has always been rather low. In turn, this has hampered the AU's ability to function in areas where the close and coordinated cooperation of Member States is required, e.g., in the case of the African Nuclear-Weapon-Free Zone Treaty, which was signed in April 1996 and came into force only in July 2009; currently, eleven Member States are not contracting parties.

Over the years, the Executive Council has, on the one hand, appealed to Member States to expedite the ratification process and, on the other hand, has instructed the Commission to undertake a review of OAU/AU treaties.[747] A Conference of Ministers of Justice and of Attorneys General, which was held in Kigali, Rwanda,

747. *See* Executive Council, *Decision on the Report of the Status of OAU/AU Treaties*, AU Doc. EX.CL/Dec. 352 (XI) (29 Jun. 2007); *Decision on the Status of Signature and Ratification of OAU/AU Treaties*, AU Doc. EX.CL/Dec. 390 (XII) (29 Jan. 2008).

between 27 October and 4 November 2008 took up this specific issue. They suggested that Member States commence the process of ratification within one year from the adoption of each treaty and institutionalize the so-called AU Treaty Signing Week that has taken place during the month of December of each year.[748] In January 2012, the Executive Council authorized the establishment of a Ministerial Committee on the challenges of ratification/accession and implementation of OAU/AU treaties. The Rules of Procedure of this Committee, which was created within the context of the fiftieth anniversary of the OAU in 2013,[749] were adopted by the Executive Council in 2014.[750] The Ministerial Committee analysed the Member States' ratification pattern, which showed that, while most of them were comfortable in ratifying foundational, institutional and human rights treaties that further strengthened the AU's integration agenda of the Union, there was reluctance to ratify economic, environmental, and judicial related treaties. This was attributed 'to cost implication of ratifying these treaties and possible overlaps or tension between AU treaties and national or international commitments.'[751] In approving the Report, the Executive Council decided that the Committee will meet in ordinary session once a year.[752]

748. *See* Executive Council, *Decision on the Status of Signature and Ratification of OAU/AU Treaties and the Harmonization of Ratification procedures*, AU Doc. EX.CL/Dec. 459 (XIV) (30 Jan. 2009).

749. *See* Executive Council, *Decision on the Status of Signature and Ratification of OAU/AU Treaties*, AU Doc. EX.CL/ Dec. 705 (XXI) (13 Jul. 2012). Generally, *see* T. Maluwa, 'Ratification of African Union Treaties by Member States: Law, Policy and Practice', *Melbourne Journal of International Law* 13 (2012):1; T. Maluwa, 'Beyond Rhetoric: Commitment to and Ratification of African Human Rights and Human Rights-Related Treaties' in *Law Politics and Rights – Essays in Memory of Kader Asmal*, T. Maluwa (ed.) (Leiden/Boston: Martinus Nijhoff, 2014), 58.

750. Executive Council, *Decisions on the Rules of Procedure of the Ministerial Committee on the Challenges of Ratification/Accession and Implementation of the OAU/AU Treaties*, AU Doc. EX.CL/ Dec. 837 (XXV) (24 Jun. 2014).

751. *See Progress Report of Ministerial Committee on the Challenges of Ratification/Accession and Implementation of the OAU/AU Treaties*, AU Doc. EX.CL/950 (XXVIII) Rev.2, para. 17 (2016).

752. Executive Council, *Decision on the Progress Report of the Ministerial Committee on the Challenges of Ratification/Accession Implementation of OAU/AU Treaties*, AU Doc. EX.CL/Dec. 905 (XXVIII) (28 Jan. 2016).

Chapter 4. Imposition of Punitive Measures (Sanctions) by the AU

83. Unlike the OAU Charter, which did not stipulate at all punitive action against recalcitrant Member States, the Constitutive Act contains elaborate provisions.[753] This impressive shift in attitude was arguably brought about by reality: Member States (and some of them consistently) were (often deliberately) violating or failing to observe their various obligations. Thus, African leaders appeared to be determined to deal with them by allowing the infliction of sanctions and other penalties of a punitive nature. While there are three different provisions in the Constitutive Act dealing with recalcitrant Members, it should be noted that their stipulations have been augmented by the Rules of Procedure of the Assembly, arguably leading to a de facto amendment of the Constitutive Act.

The first provision is Article 23(1), which empowers the Assembly to determine the sanctions to be imposed upon any Member State defaulting in paying its contributions to the AU budget. The content of Article 23(1) is very strict. Unlike the relevant provisions in other constitutive instruments), where the infliction of sanctions requires that the Member in question has been in arrears for two or more years,[754] the Assembly is mandated (it does not have the discretion) to impose the following punitive measures on any Member State defaulting for any amount of contributions: denial of its right to speak at meetings; denial of right to vote; denial of right to present candidates for any AU position and professional post; and denial of the right to benefit from any AU activities or commitments. Clearly, there is a grading severity in these measures, in the sense that to refuse the right to vote is evidently far more important than not being allowed to address meetings; equally, to deny activities and commitments is more significant than the right to present candidates for professional posts. Even though it is not expressly stipulated in the Constitutive Act, there is a general rule of law pertaining to IGOs that the sanctions to be imposed must be proportional to the seriousness of the infraction. Therefore, if, for the sake of argument, the denial of AU benefits to a Member State is the toughest sanction, it should be inflicted when the state in question has repeatedly, consistently, and deliberately failed in paying its budgetary contributions.

Rule 35 of the Assembly Rules of Procedure partly answers these issues, but the question should again be put whether a secondary instrument, such as a set of Rules of Procedure, may effectively lead to the modification and the de facto amendment of the Constitutive Act. In particular, Rule 35 stipulates that, on the basis of recommendations by the Executive Council and the PRC as well as on the basis of information provided by the Commission, the Assembly shall act differently depending on whether the arrears in payment amount to two but not more than five years of assessed contributions or amount to more than five years. In the former case, the Member State in question shall suffer the following: suspension of its right to speak, of its right to vote, and to receive documentation at AU meetings; of its right to offer to host sessions of the Assembly and the Executive Council; and of its

753. *See* K. Magliveras, 'The Multiple Sanctioning Regimes in the African Union: Analysis and Synthesis' in F. Amao, M. Olivier & K. Magliveras (eds), *The Emergent African Union Law: Conceptualization, Delimitation, and Application* (Oxford: Oxford University Press, 2021) 359.

754. Compare Art. 19 of the UN Charter.

right to present candidates for Union positions and posts. In the latter case, its right to have contracts of employment of its nationals renewed and to receive AU funds for new projects in its territory shall be suspended. A temporary lifting of sanctions is envisaged when the recalcitrant Member has paid at least 50% of outstanding arrears and payment has been made thirty days before the next scheduled session of the Executive Council.

Arguably, Article 23(1) of the Constitutive Act and Rule 35 do not consider the fact that at any given time a considerable number of African countries are facing economic/financial/monetary problems and, consequently, that the non-payment of budgetary contributions could be attributed to a situation akin to force majeure and not be treated as a deliberate act of disregarding their obligations. It should be noted that the constitutive instruments of the AEC and of certain African RECs not only envisage this possibility but expressly exonerate such states from the obligation to pay financial contributions.[755] Therefore, it is suggested that the AU should lay down in any future Protocol of Amendments a specific mechanism whereby Member States facing significant problems or hardship would either be alleviated, wholly or partly, of their obligation to pay up their contributions or have the payment suspended without suffering in the enjoyment of their membership rights and privileges. It should be mentioned that in a number of instances, temporary and exceptional exemptions have been granted (e.g., to Sierra Leone in July 2003[756] or to the DRC in January 2012 but with conditions attached).[757] However, as in the case of the OAU, these were rather ad hoc arrangements.

The importance attached to engaging all Member States, rich and poor, in the political and socioeconomic integration promised by the AU cannot be underestimated, especially now that the continental free trade project is gaining momentum. Therefore, it is crucial not to prevent the full participation in AU activities of those Members, which can justify, on objective grounds, their inability to fulfil their budgetary obligations. Several of the states under sanctions were objectively unable to pay contributions. On the other hand, the AU should not treat those Member States that deliberately owe contributions solely through the imposition of punitive measures. On the contrary, it should consider how other international organizations have addressed this issue, e.g., by imposing accrued interest on the amount of contributions in arrears or by setting off the arrears against sums owed by the organization to the recalcitrant Member.

84. Article 23(1) of the Constitutive Act should be read in conjunction with its second paragraph. The latter, on the one hand, stipulates that any Member State failing to comply with AU decisions and policies may be subjected to further

755. Generally, *see* K. Magliveras, 'African International Organisations: Suspension and Expulsion of Members', *Australian International Law Journal* (1999): 158, 169–170. For example, Art. 171 of the COMESA Treaty (1994) stipulates the non-payment of budgetary contributions when public or natural calamities or exceptional circumstances have gravely affected the economy of a Member State.

756. *See* Executive Council, *Decision on the Report of the Sub-committee on Contributions*, AU Doc. EX/CL/Dec. 25 (III) (8 Jul. 2003).

757. *See* Executive Council, *Decision on the Contributions of Member States' to the Budget of the African Union*, AU Doc. EX.CL/ Dec. 673 (XX) (27 Jan. 2012).

sanctions, such as the denial of transport and communications links with fellow Member States, and, on the other hand, empowers the Assembly to determine the imposition of any other 'measures of a political and economic nature'. A first point to clarify is whether the Article 23(2) sanctions are over and above those envisaged in the first paragraph. In other words, whether a Member State defaulting in its financial obligations may face the sanctions envisaged in both paragraphs. The answer should be in the negative, as the principle of specialization and/or the principle of *non bis in idem* should apply. Thus, Article 23(1) is the only provision dealing with punitive measures to be imposed for contributions in arrears.

85. The wording of Article 23(2) is inordinately unclear. By effectively giving the Assembly a carte blanche to establish additional political or economic punitive measures, the drafters may have opened a dangerous door to political manoeuvring. In particular, the Assembly may be driven to consider incidents of non-compliance on a case-by-case basis instead of applying the same rules to similar instances. Undoubtedly, Article 23(2) lacks the legal clarity that is required of constitutive instruments of international institutions and may violate the principles of legitimate expectations and legal certainty, which run through the law of international institutions. Notwithstanding these considerations, it should be noted that the Assembly will probably be subject to checks and balances in implementing its Article 23(2) powers since any Member State which has a vested interest in disputing the legality of the sanctions imposed would be able to resort to the AU judicial organ and file an action akin to judicial review. However, since the AU judicial organ (the African Court of Justice according to the Constitutive Act) has not yet been operationalized, this is a theoretical argument.

86. A final point arising from Article 23(2) is whether the additional measures to be determined by the Assembly could ever go as far as ordering the expulsion of the recalcitrant Member State. The answer should be in the negative because the wording of this provision refers exclusively to punitive measures of a political or economic nature. Even though expulsion could be described as a measure of political character, it is submitted that the term 'political' in the context of Article 23(2) does not cover measures bearing upon the membership status. Finally, it is interesting to note that the OAU Secretariat has indicated that since the Constitutive Act does not provide for expulsion, it follows that the Assembly lacks the required legal basis for ordering it.[758]

Rule 36 of the Assembly Rules of Procedure, which corresponds to Article 23(2), does not shed any light on the above questions. The gist of Rule 36, which arguably contradicts the spirit of Article 23(2), is that, upon the Executive Council's recommendation, the Assembly shall record that a Member State has not, without good and reasonable cause, complied with AU decisions and policies and shall determine the sanctions to be imposed. However, the wording of the third paragraph of Rule 36:

---

758. *See Report of the Meeting of OAU Permanent Representatives and Experts on the African Union*, 21–25 January 2002, Addis Ababa, Ethiopia, at para. 27.

> [3] When taking any decision in this regard, the Assembly shall stipulate the time frame for compliance and indicate when the failure to comply with that decision will trigger the sanctions regime provided for under Article 23(2) of the Constitutive Act and this Rule.

would suggest that sanctions are not automatic, but the Member in question shall first be given the opportunity to observe the decision and only if he does not, will the sanctions be imposed. Finally, Rule 36, in a rather cryptic manner, stipulates that Members under sanctions are entitled to present their case to the Assembly. Presumably, the object of this move would be to ask the Assembly to lift or vary the sanctions.

87. The third instance for the imposition of punitive measures is when governments have come into power through unconstitutional means.[759] According to Article 30 of the Constitutive Act, such governments 'shall not be allowed to participate in the activities of the Union'. This provision is in line with the aforementioned principle of condemnation and rejection of unconstitutional changes of government. Moreover, it was influenced by developments since the early 1990s in several international organizations, where the realization of the democracy principle (i.e., states must be governed by regimes subscribing to the rule of law, human rights and fundamental freedoms must always be protected, and undemocratic overthrows of governments are not tolerated) has led to the inclusion of similar clauses in their constitutive instruments. Suffice to mention two examples. First, the Protocol of Washington of 14 December 1992, which amended the Charter of the Organization of American States (OAS) by adding a new Article 9 to it.[760] Second, Article 7 of the Treaty on European Union and Article 309 of the Treaty Establishing the European Community, which were inserted by the Treaty of Amsterdam of 1997; following the entry into force of the Lisbon Reform Treaty (it revised the EU Founding Treaties in 2009), the relevant provisions are laid down in Article 7 of the Consolidated Version of the Treaty on European Union.[761]

88. The gist of Article 30 of the Constitutive Act is that only those governments coming into power through unconstitutional means and not the Member States in question shall be prevented from participating in AU activities. Thus, the membership of the relevant states is neither affected nor compromised, and once they return to constitutional normalcy, they will be allowed to participate again. Considering

759. *See* J. Grauvogel, K. Newbery & C. von Soest, *Stabilität durch regionale Sanktionen in Afrika?*, German Institute of Global and Area Studies, GIGA Focus Afrika 3, 2013, at: http://www.ssoar.info/ssoar/handle/document/34799.

760. The Protocol is reproduced in 33 I.L.M. (1994) 1005; for commentary, *see* K. Magliveras, *Exclusion from Participation in International Organisations: The Law and Practice Behind Member States' Expulsion and Suspension of Membership* (The Hague: Kluwer Law International, 1999), 171–174. *See also* the Inter-American Democratic Charter, adopted by the OAS on 11 Sep. 2001, reproduced in 40 I.L.M. (2001) 1289.

761. *See* K. Magliveras & G. Naldi, 'The Question of Recalcitrant Member States in the Context of the European Union', *Evrigenis Yearbook of International and European Law* 3 (2021): 205.

that Article 30 does not stipulate which organ will be competent to order non-participation, it is submitted that the process is an automatic one, and this is signified by the words 'shall not be allowed'. To put it otherwise, contrary to the aforementioned provisions of Article 23, the sanction of non-participation does not involve political discretion. If this submission were correct, the AU would be required to establish authoritatively, as evidenced by a concurring vote of most of the Member States, that the government in question did come into power through unconstitutional means. Although the Assembly would probably assume this function, in its capacity as the highest-ranking organ encompassing the whole membership, one could also suggest two reasons why the AU judicial organ should be called upon to decide it. First, the determination would have to be based on legal grounds; there should be no place for political considerations. Second, as the determination would be a judicial pronouncement, it would have the effect of a legally binding judicial decision.

89. Article 30 does not offer any guidance on the ambit of the unconstitutional government's non-participation in AU activities. As has already been indicated, it will not bring about the suspension of the membership of the Member State in question. It is rather a measure of a punitive nature aiming at putting considerable pressure on the relevant government to restore constitutional normality and the rule of law. It is submitted that the scope of non-participation includes the sanctions referred to in Article 23(1) of the Constitutive Act but not those envisaged in the second paragraph of the same Article because the latter are measures of a general nature and not directly related to AU activities. Finally, it should be accepted that for as long as an unconstitutional government is not allowed to participate in the proceedings of the Union, all obligations of the Member in question remain intact and, consequently, they must continue paying budgetary contributions, comply with mandatory Assembly decisions, etc. Rule 37 of the Assembly Rules of Procedure, the provision corresponding to Article 30, has considerably augmented the latter's arguably insufficient content, and some of its provisions run contrary to the submissions made here. More specifically, the fourth paragraph of Rule 37 lays down a five-stage procedure for dealing with unconstitutional changes of government. It should be noted that the following actions are to be jointly taken by the Assembly Chairperson and the AUC Chairperson: (a) on behalf of the AU, condemn coups d'état promptly and demand that constitutional order be reinstated immediately; (b) convey a clear and unequivocal warning that the illegal change of government shall neither be tolerated nor recognized; (c) ensure consistency in the action to be taken against the unconstitutional regime at the bilateral, sub-regional and international levels; (d) request the PSC to convene and discuss the matter; and (e) suspend the Member in question from the AU and from participating in its organs at once, provided that such non-participation shall not affect its membership and its obligations towards the organization. As far as the sanctions against the unconstitutional regime itself are concerned, the fifth paragraph of Rule 37 endows the Assembly to inflict the following measures in a non-exclusive fashion. First, visa denials for the perpetrators of the unconstitutional change (and presumably their entourage as well). Second, restrictions in the contact between the illegal regime and the governments of the other Member States. Third, trade restrictions. Fourth, the sanctions provided for in the aforementioned Article 23(2) and in the Assembly Rules. Fifth, any additional sanctions that might be recommended by the PSC. Finally, the sixth paragraph of Rule 37 entrusts to the AUC Chairperson the role of assisting the peaceful reinstatement of the democratic order. It could be described as a mixture of mediation and good offices. In particular, the Chairperson is asked to, *inter alia*, establish appropriate contacts with the perpetrators without recognizing or legitimizing them and to enlist the contribution of African leaders and personalities as a conduit for securing cooperation between the perpetrators and the AU.

In January 2017, the Assembly resolved that the current sanctions mechanism should be strengthened and enforced and proposed to make participation in the AU deliberations 'contingent on adherence to Summit decisions'.[762] Even though the Assembly did not specifically refer to the sanctions for non-payment of assessed contributions, the two Reports submitted by the AUC Chairperson dealt specifically with strengthening this sanctions regime.[763] Building upon these two Reports and the deliberations at the Twentieth Extraordinary Executive Council Session (14–15 November 2018), a few days later the Eleventh Extraordinary Assembly Session decided, in a de facto amendment of the Constitutive Act, to introduce a new sanctions regime from July 2019,[764] whose basic parameters are as follows: (a) those Member States which fail to meet their budgetary obligations, and which have not settled at least 50% of their current assessed contributions after the second quarter of each financial year (i.e., six months from the beginning of each calendar year) in which the contribution was due, are deemed to be in arrears; (b) Member States in arrears are divided into three groups, namely short-term period (in arrears for six months), intermediate period (one year) and long-term period (two years); (c) sanctions shall be applied incrementally in three stages, starting from cautionary sanctions against Member States in the short-term period, moving to intermediate sanctions for those states in the intermediate period and ending with comprehensive sanctions for those in the long-term period. As regards the content of the sanctions, it was agreed that: (i) 'cautionary sanctions' will deprive Member States in arrears of their rights to speak at AU meetings; (ii) 'intermediate sanctions' will include, on the one hand, all sanctions that are laid down in Article 23(1) of the Constitutive Act, in Rules 5, 26, and 35(2(a) of the Assembly Rules of Procedure, in Article 78(6) of the AU Financial Rules and Regulations and in Article 18(8) of the AUC Statute (one could call them 'statutory sanctions') and, on the other hand, the suspension of the following Member States' rights: to become a member of a Bureau of any AU organ and to host an AU organ in its territory; to have their nationals participate in electoral observation missions and/or in human rights observation missions and to be invited in any AU organized meeting; and to have their nationals appointed as elected and non-elected AU staff; and (iii) 'comprehensive sanctions'

762. Assembly, *Decision on the Outcome of the Retreat of the Assembly of the African Union on the Institutional Reform of the African Union*, AU Doc. Assembly/AU/Dec. 635 (XXVIII), para. 5(c) (31 Jan. 2017).

763. *See* AU Doc. Assembly/AU/3(XXX) (January 2018) and AU Doc. Ext/Assembly/AU/2(XI)) (November 2018).

764. Assembly, *Decision on the New African Union Sanctions Regime for the Non-Payment of Contributions*, AU Doc. Ext/Assembly/AU/Dec. 3 (XI) (18 Nov. 2018).

will include all the aforementioned sanctions as well as the suspension of the Member States' right to participate in AU meetings.

Finally, the Assembly decided that it has the discretion to consider written requests from Member States that experience force majeure circumstances, making them temporarily unable to pay their assessed contributions. The wording of the relevant section in the Decision makes it clear that the Assembly is neither obligated to consider such requests nor to take a decision on them. As is made apparent in the chapter dealing with the AU finances, the Assembly has not only considered the possibility of writing off budgetary contributions owed by Member States but has also proposed it (e.g., to Libya in 2022) as a means to persuade them to pay up at least part of the contributions. While these measures are drawn no doubt from necessity, the fact that so far they have not been laid down in an Assembly decision is highly problematic. However, as argued in other parts of this monograph, the Constitutive Act is in dire need of revision. And while Member States appear not to object to these de facto amendments, an international organization's proper functioning is in jeopardy when it deviates from its constitutive instrument.

As mentioned above, the triptych 'democracy, rule of law and human rights' has been introduced in the legal orders of several regional international organizations, and the Constitutive Act subscribes to it. In 2007, the African Charter on Democracy, Elections and Governance was adopted to give fresh impetus to these principles. In particular, Article 4 thereof commits contracting parties to promote them and to 'recognize popular participation through universal suffrage as the inalienable right of the people', while Article 10 entrenches the principle of the constitution's supremacy in the political organization of contracting parties. Article 11 obliges contracting parties to establish and strengthen a culture of democracy and peace. Moreover, Article 14 stipulates that those who attempt to remove an elected government through unconstitutional means must be dealt with in accordance with the law, and contracting parties must cooperate with each other to that end. It follows that the Charter introduces a supranational element in tackling the unconstitutional removal of elected governments, a rather common phenomenon in Africa. Thus, the unconstitutional change of government is a focal point of the Charter, and it could be seen as an elaboration of the relevant provisions in the Constitutive Act. Pursuant to Article 23 of the Charter, the following five instances must be treated as 'unconstitutional change of government' and shall result in ordering appropriate sanctions: (a) any putsch or coup d'état against a democratically elected government; (b) any intervention by mercenaries to replace such a government; (c) any replacement of a democratically elected government by armed dissidents or rebels; (d) any refusal by an incumbent government to relinquish power to the winning party or candidate after free, fair and regular elections; and (e) any amendment or revision of the constitution constituting an infringement of the principle of democratic change of government. Should such a situation take place in a contracting party, the competent organ to address it is the PSC, which is mandated under Article 24 to exercise its responsibilities to maintain constitutional order.

More specifically, Article 25 of the Charter provides that when the PSC observes that there has been an unconstitutional change of government in a contracting party, and if diplomatic initiatives have not been successful, it must suspend its right to participate in AU activities with immediate effect (Article 30 of the Constitutive Act and Article 7(g) of the Protocol). However, suspension does mean termination of any engagement between the party in question and the AU: the latter must maintain diplomatic contacts and undertake any initiatives that are deemed necessary to restore democracy. As regards the perpetrators of the unconstitutional change of government, they shall be barred from participating in any future elections to restore democratic order and from holding positions of political responsibility in their country; additionally, they may be tried 'before the competent court of the Union'. As regards the former provision, the Charter dictates that contracting parties follow a specific norm: not to allow perpetrators to get involved in domestic politics. As regards the latter provision, it should be noted that no continental court with such competence existed at the time the Charter was adopted. It was much later, in June 2014, when the Assembly approved the Protocol on Amendments to the Protocol on the Statute of the African Court of Justice and Human Rights, that the crime of unconstitutional change of government came under the jurisdiction of the International Criminal Law Section of the ACJHR. Pursuant to Article 28E of the ACJHR Statute, as amended by the 2014 Protocol, the constituent elements of this crime comprise the situations laid down in Article 23 of the Charter as well as the substantial modification of domestic electoral laws at least six months before the date of elections without the prior consent of the majority of political actors.

In addition to the role that the PSC has to play, under Article 25(6)-(7) of the Charter, the Assembly must impose, in conformity with Article 23 of the Constitutive Act, sanctions on any Member State shown to have instigated or supported the unconstitutional change of government in another Member State. The Charter does not elaborate on how such instigation or support will be proven: will it be on the basis of an Assembly decision or will it require a judicial pronouncement? Moreover, the Assembly has the discretion to order other forms of sanctions against perpetrators, including punitive economic measures. Moreover, Article 25(8)-(9) of the Charter attaches obligations to all other contracting parties: they must not harbour or give sanctuary to the perpetrators and must bring them to justice or take the necessary steps to extradite them. Arguably, these provisions treat the unconstitutional change of government as a crime to which the principle of universal jurisdiction applies, in the sense that any contracting party has the duty to ensure that there will be no impunity for the perpetrators. Finally, Article 26 of the Charter provides that the PSC shall lift sanctions 'once the situation that led to the suspension is resolved'. It is not clear if the PSC will lift all sanctions, i.e., also those imposed by the Assembly against the perpetrators, or against third Member States found to have been involved in the coup d'etat, etc.

Chapter 5. Organs

90. According to Article 5(1) of the Constitutive Act, the AU comprises the following organs: The Assembly of Heads of State and Government, the Executive Council, the PAP, the Court of Justice, the Commission, the PRC, the Specialized Technical Committees, the Economic and Cultural Council, and the Financial Institutions. This array of organs would suggest that the AU has, to an extent, been modelled on the EU. More than twenty years after the AU's operationalization, it is evident that the large number of organs in conjunction with the Assembly's power to establish new ones under Article 5(2) of the Constitutive Act have posed significant hurdles, which arguably the AU has not yet addressed in a coherent and effective manner. However, it is an undisputed fact that the AU has been endowed with all the necessary organs to carry out its aims and goals.

91. As has been explained above, for several organs – and principally those that did not exist in the OAU – the Constitutive Act postponed their immediate operation until, for each of these organs, a separate Protocol had entered into force laying down its functions, powers, composition, etc. The Fifth Extraordinary OAU Assembly Session (Sirte, 1–2 March 2001) entrusted to the next Ordinary Session to, *inter alia*, prepare the necessary Protocols.[765] To that effect, the OAU Secretary-General prepared a report, which was submitted to the Seventy-Fourth Ordinary Session of the OAU Council of Ministers (Lusaka, Zambia, 5–8 July 2001).[766] At its Thirty-Seventh Ordinary Session (Lusaka, 9–11 July 2001), the OAU Assembly mandated the OAU Secretary-General to undertake the necessary consultations with Member States to elaborate the modalities for launching the AU organs and to prepare their Rules of Procedure, giving priority to the 'key Organs', namely the Assembly of Heads of State and Government, the Executive Council, the Commission and the PRC.[767] That the OAU Assembly did not consider the Court of Justice to be a 'key Organ' was undoubtedly characteristic of an international organization that was not used to have a judicial organ embedded in its operation.

§1. The Assembly of Heads of State and Government

92. Article 6(2) of the Constitutive Act proclaims the Assembly to be the supreme organ of the AU. It is composed of all Heads of States or Government or their duly accredited representatives. The OAU Assembly was meeting in ordinary session once a year. However, Article 6(3) of the Constitutive provides that the AU Assembly will meet at least once a year, and this is verbatim repeated in Rule 7 of the Assembly Rules of Procedure.[768] In 2004, the AU Assembly decided to meet

765. *See* Assembly, *Decision on the African Union*, OAU Doc. EAHG/Dec. 1 (V) (2 Mar. 2001).
766. OAU Doc. CM/2210 (LXXIV) (July 2001).
767. Assembly, *Decision on the Implementation of the Sirte Summit Decision on the African Union*, OAU Doc. AHG/Dec. 1 (XXXVII), para. 4 (11 Jul. 2001).
768. The *Rules of Procedure of the Assembly* were adopted in July 2002 pursuant to Art. 8 of the Constitutive Act, AU Doc. ASS/AU/2(I)-a, reproduced in RADIC 13 (2005): 41.

twice a year, and in practice one session was held in Winter (January/February) and the other in Summer (June/July).[769] As was explained above, in 2018, it was decided that henceforth there will be only one Assembly session per year. Until 2019, one of the two sessions would usually take place in Addis Ababa at AU Headquarters and the other in the territory of a Member State that had proposed to host a session. From a diplomatic point of view, this had the advantage of being an first-rate public relations event and offering prestige to the host Member State, which however had to cover the cost. Theoretically speaking, all Member States could be proposers, but in reality, several could not afford the cost or the security situation would be so complicated (e.g., Somalia, South Sudan, Eritrea, Mali, etc.) that it would not be realistic to host Assembly sessions. For many years, Assembly sessions have been held around a specific theme, which is topical or of particular importance to Africa. Later, the practice of the Assembly has been to adopt a theme for its calendar year. Thus, the Tenth Ordinary Assembly Session held in January/February 2008 concerned the 'Industrial Development of Africa,' the July 2008 Session concerned 'Water and Sanitation', while the theme for the year 2016 was 'The African Year of Human Rights with Particular Focus on the Rights of Women'[770] and for the year 2017 it was 'Harnessing Demographic Dividend through investments in the Youth.'[771] The themes of the other years have been noted in Part I of the monograph. The theme for the year 2023 is 'Acceleration of AfCFTA Implementation'. Moreover, occasionally, special summits have been scheduled to deal with pressing issues, but they have not always materialized. Thus, the special summit of Heads of State and Government scheduled for November 2008 to deal with refugees, returnees and IDPs and to adopt the Convention for the Protection and Assistance of IDPs in Africa[772] took place one year later in Kampala, Uganda, where the IDP Convention was approved on 23 October 2009.[773]

Any Member State may request the holding of an extraordinary Assembly session, which must be met with the approval of two-thirds of all Member States within the period specified by the AUC Chairperson. Thus, if a state does not reply to the request within the deadline set by the AUC, this is understood as a negative vote (Article 6(3) of the Constitutive Act and Rule 11 of the Assembly Rules of Procedure). Pursuant to the Protocol on Amendments of 2003, the initiative of holding

---

769. Assembly, *Decision on the Periodicity of the Ordinary Sessions of the Assembly*, AU Doc. Assembly/AU/Dec. 53 (III) (8 Jul. 2004).

770. *See* Assembly, *Declaration of the Assembly on the Theme of the Year*, AU Doc. Assembly/AU/Decl. 1 (XXVII) Rev.1 (19 Jul. 2016). It was induced by the fact that the UN Secretary-General had included water and sanitation among the topics in Africa's priority development agenda. *See further*, Executive Council, *Decision on the Proposal to Make Water and Sanitation the Theme of the July 2008 Summit*, AU Doc. EX.CL/Dec. 392 (XII) (29 Jan. 2008).

771. *See* Assembly, *Decision on the Dates and Venue of the 28th Ordinary Session of the Assembly of the African Union*, AU Doc. Assembly/AU/Dec. 620 (XXVII) (19 Jul. 2016).

772. *See* Executive Council, *Decision on the Situation of Refugees, Returnees and Internally Displaced Persons in Africa*, AU Doc. EX.CL/Dec. 381 (XII) (29 Jan. 2008).

773. *See* Executive Council, *Decision on the Situation of Refugees and Internally Displaced Persons in Africa*, AU Doc. EX/CL/Dec. 413 (XIII) (28 Jun. 2008); *Decision on the Report on the Situation of Refugees Returnees and Internally Displaced Persons in Africa*, AU Doc. EX/CL/Dec. 462 (XVI) (30 Jan. 2009); *Decision on the Report on the Situation of Refugees Returnees and Internally Displaced Persons in Africa*, AU Doc. EX.CL/Dec. 494 (XV) Rev.1 (30 Jun. 2009).

extraordinary sessions lies with the Assembly Chairperson as well. Decisions, except for procedural matters, are reached by consensus, failing which by a two-thirds majority (Article 7(1) of the Constitutive Act). Interestingly enough, the corresponding Rule 30 does not refer to consensus and subjects all decisions on substantive issues to a 'secret ballot of Member States eligible to vote'. In the past, the Assembly resolved to hold an extraordinary summit not as a separate decision but in the context of a decision dealing with other matters. Thus, when the Twenty-Fifth Ordinary Assembly Session (Johannesburg, June 2015) discussed the PSC Report, it resolved to hold in Lomé, Togo, an Extraordinary Summit on Maritime Security and Safety and Development in Africa.[774] This was a follow-up action to the 2050 Africa's Integrated Maritime Strategy (2050 AIM Strategy) adopted on 27 January 2014. It was postponed to ensure adequate preparation, and in January 2016, it was decided to take place on 15 October 2016 following preparatory sessions of the PRC and the Executive Council.[775] The Extraordinary Summit adopted the African Charter on Maritime Security and Safety and Development in Africa (the Lomé Charter), which has so far received only three ratifications (Benin, Senegal and Togo).

93. The Office of the Assembly Chairperson is established under Article 6(4) of the Constitutive Act. Although it is to be held for one-year periods by a Head of State or Government, who was elected following consultations among Member States, the OAU practice that the Head of State in whose territory the session takes place becomes Chairperson has been continued. Thus, Thabo Mbeki of South Africa became Chairperson from July 2002 to July 2003, Joaquim Chissamo of Mozambique from July 2003 to July 2004, and Olusegun Obasanjo of Nigeria from July 2004 to January 2006. However, this understanding was disrupted during the Sixth Ordinary Assembly Session (Khartoum, 23–24 January 2006). Many African leaders objected to Sudanese President Omar Hassan Al Bashir assuming the Chairmanship on account of his government's direct involvement in the civil war waged in the south of the country (the area that later became the Republic of South Sudan) and in the Darfur region. The opposition was strong enough to disrupt the meeting in reminiscence of similar events during the OAU years. In the event, the Sudanese President accepted the postponement of his term until 2007, a gesture which in the African tradition of exaggeration was demonstrated as 'a true reflection of [his] great sense of responsibility and leadership'.[776]

It was further resolved that a committee would be instructed to examine the implementation of a rotation principle in the years to come.[777] In the event, Denis

---

774. *See* Assembly, *Decision on the Report of the Peace and Security Council on its Activities and the State of Peace and Security in Africa*, AU Doc. Assembly/AU/Dec. 583 (XXV), para. 22 (15 Jun. 2015).

775. *See* Assembly, *Decision on the Extraordinary African Union Summit on Maritime Security and Safety and Development in Africa*, AU Doc. Assembly/AU/Dec. 593 (XXV) (30 Jan. 2016).

776. *See* Assembly, *Declaration of the Assembly of the African Union*, AU Doc. Assembly/AU/ Decl. 2 (VI) (24 Jan. 2006).

777. *See* Assembly, *Recommendation of the Committee on the Chairmanship of the African Union*, AU Doc. Assembly/AU/Recommendation (VI) (24 Jan. 2006).

Sassou-Nguesso of Congo became Chairperson until January 2007. In the following year, there was apparently no discussion of the Sudanese President assuming the Chairmanship, which went to John Kofi Agyekum Kufuor of Ghana. He was followed by Jakaya Kikwete, the President of Tanzania, in January 2008, and by Colonel Gaddafi in January 2009. He was followed by Bingu wa Mutharika from Malawi (he took office on 31 January 2010), by Teodoro Obiang Nguema Mbasogo from the Equatorial Guinea (31 January 2011), by Yayi Boni from Benin (29 January 2012), by Hailemariam Desalegn from Ethiopia (27 January 2013), by Mohamed Ould Abdel Aziz of Maritania (30 January 2014), by Robert Mugabe of Zimbabwe (30 January 2015), by Idriss Déby of Chad (30 January 2016), by Alpha Condé of Guinea (28 January 2017), by Paul Kagame of Rwanda (28 January 2018), by Abdel Fattah el-Sisi of Egypt (10 February 2019), by Cyril Ramaphosa of South Africa (10 February 2020), by Félix Tshisekedi of DRC (6 February 2021), by Macky Sall of Senegal (5 February 2022), and by Azali Assoumani of the Union of Comoros (18 February 2023). Although the Constitutive Act did not elaborate on the Chairperson's duties, these were laid down in Rule 16 of the Assembly Rules of Procedure. In particular, he/she is responsible for a number of procedural duties, such as convening sessions, submitting to vote matters under discussion, and, in-between sessions, acting as the AU representative 'in conformity with the fundamental objectives and principles enshrined in the Constitutive Act'. Interestingly enough, the Protocol on Amendments of 2003 envisages a new Article 7*bis* to the Constitutive Act, which will lay down the Chairperson's functions, including the convening of other organs' meetings. There is also the Bureau of the Assembly, which comprises five Member States, each representing one of the five African regions. For the year 2023, the composition of the Bureau is as follows: AU Chairperson – Azali Assoumani (Union of Comoros, representing the East African region); First AU Vice Chair – (it will be occupied by a Member State from the Northern region when consultations among them are finalized); Second AU Vice Chair (Botswana, representing the Southern region); Third AU Vice Chair (Burundi, representing the Central region); and Rapporteur (Senegal, representing the West African region). The members of the Bureau are elected by the Assembly.[778]

94. The Assembly's powers and functions are contained in Article 9(1) of the Constitutive Act and in Rule 4 of the Assembly Rules of Procedure. They are in line with the powers traditionally exercised by the supreme organs of international organizations. In particular, it determines the AU's common policies; considers and acts upon reports and recommendations issued by other organs; considers requests from African states seeking membership; monitors the implementation of and compliance with AU policies and decisions; adopts the budget; directs the Executive Council on the management of conflicts, war, and other emergency situations and the restoration of peace; appoints the Commission members and determines their functions; and appoints the judges to serve at the Court of Justice and terminates their appointment (it has never become operationalized). Finally, as already mentioned,

778. *See, e.g.*, Assembly, *Decision on the Election of the Bureau of the Assembly of the African Union for 2022*, AU Doc. Assembly/AU/Dec. 822 (XXXV) (6 Feb. 2022).

Article 5(2) of the Constitutive Act authorizes the Assembly to decide on the establishment of other organs. This provision is repeated in Article 9(1) thereof, which stipulates that '[t]he functions of the Assembly shall be to ... establish any organ of the Union'. It is submitted that this is a badly drafted clause because surely the Assembly cannot set up any of the organs envisaged in Article 5(1) but solely supplementary ones. The PSC and the African Space Agency have, among others, been established pursuant to Article 5(2).

95. It is submitted that Article 9(2) of the Constitutive Act, which stipulates that the Assembly may delegate any of its powers and functions to any other organ, is problematic because of its wide formulation. Although it might be conceivable to hand over specific powers (e.g., delegating to the ACJHR (when it becomes operative) the power to ensure that Member States comply with AU decisions (as is the case with the Court of Justice of the EU)), it is submitted that there is an array of other powers and functions which should never be delegated on the ground that they express the whole membership's will and, consequently, they should be exercised solely by the Assembly. An example of delegation of specific powers, which however might be explained by considerations of urgency, is the authorization granted by the Second Ordinary Assembly Session (Maputo, 10–12 July 2003) to the Executive Council to adopt the necessary measures for the operationalization of the PSC, including the election of its first members and the adoption of its Rules of Procedure.[779]

96. The Assembly's powers and functions contained in Article 9 are supplemented with further powers envisaged in other provisions of the Constitutive Act. The most important are: (a) the imposition of sanctions on the recalcitrant Member States (Article 23 of the Constitutive Act); (b) until the operation of the AU's judicial organ (initially this was the African Court of Justice but, following its merger with the African Court on Human and Peoples' Rights, it is the ACJHR), the interpretation of the Constitutive Act (Article 26), a power which has apparently never been exercised; and (c) the deliberation and adoption of amendments to the Constitutive Act (Article 32(3)–(4)).

97. It should be noted that the Assembly has not followed to the letter the aforementioned provisions and has adopted new practices. The following examples will illustrate this argument. First, there have been instances where the Executive Council reached decisions of importance, to be later rubber-stamped by the Assembly. Thus, the Twelfth Ordinary Executive Council Session (Addis Ababa, 25–29 January 2008) elected the new Commissioners[780] and recommended them for appointment to the Tenth Ordinary Assembly Session, which simply consented to the

779. *See* Assembly, *Decision on the Operationalization of the Protocol Relating to the Establishment of the Peace and Security Council*, AU Doc. Assembly/AU/Dec. 11 (II), para. 8 (12 Jul. 2003).

780. *See* Executive Council, *Decision on the Election of AU Commissioners*, AU Doc. EX.CL/Dec. 414 (XII) (29 Jan. 2008).

recommendation.[781] Second, as already mentioned, ordinary Assembly sessions are invariably organized under a theme of common interest to the continent, while the Member State hosting the session is often requested to hold various high-level meetings to promote it. Third, the OAU practice to set up committees with limited participation of heads of state and government (usually ranging between seven and ten members and coming from Africa's five regions) and to entrust them with the elaboration of common positions in selected topics has been carried on to the AU. These entities are not established pursuant to the aforementioned Article 5(2) but are rather ad hoc institutional arrangements giving the Assembly a measure of flexibility as regards their mandate and their terms of reference. Suffice to mention the Committee of Seven Heads of State and Government on the United States of Africa, the seven-member Committee on the Chairmanship of the AU, the Committee of Twelve Heads of State and Government on the AU Government created in 2008, and the twelve-member Committee of African Heads of State and Government on Climate Change (CAHOSCC) established in July 2009.[782] These Committees often work together with other (subsidiary) bodies and entities, for example, CAHOSCC works together with the African Ministerial Conference on Environment (AMCEN) and the African Group of Negotiators on Climate Change (AGN), which promotes the African Common Position on Climate Change at global fora and negotiations, such as the annual Conference of the Parties (COP) of the UN Convention on Climate Change.[783]

§2. The Executive Council, the Specialized Technical Committees and Other Specialized Agencies

98. According to Article 10 of the Constitutive Act and Rule 3 of its Rules of Procedure,[784] the Executive Council is composed of the Ministers of Foreign Affairs or any other Ministers duly accredited by the governments of Member States. It meets at least twice a year in ordinary session and in extraordinary session when so requested by a Member State and approved by a two-thirds majority of the total membership. Extraordinary sessions have been held, *inter alia*, in the following cities: Sun City, South Africa (21–25 May 2003), Addis Ababa (12–16 March 2004, 6 December 2004, 7–8 March 2005 and 11 October 2013), Khartoum (19 January 2006),[785] Arusha (8 May 2008), and in Tripoli (15–16 April 2009). To offer an example, the Sixteenth Extraordinary Session took place in Addis Ababa in September 2014 to discuss the outbreak of the Ebola virus.[786] There has been one case where the extraordinary session held was followed by an extraordinary Assembly

781. *See* Assembly, *Decision on Appointment of AU Commissioners*, AU Doc. Assembly/AU/Dec. 190 (X) (3 Feb. 2008).
782. Assembly Decision/AU/Dec. 257(XIII) Rev.1 (2009).
783. *See* https://unfccc.int/process/bodies/supreme-bodies/conference-of-the-parties-cop.
784. *See Rules of Procedure of the Executive Council*, adopted during the First Ordinary Assembly Session in July 2002, AU Doc. ASS/AU/2 (I)-b, reproduced in RADIC 13 (2005): 55.
785. It took place while the Eighth Ordinary Executive Council Session was ongoing (it lasted from 16–21 Jan. 2006) and dealt exclusively with budgetary matters.
786. *See* AU Doc. Ext/EX.CL/Dec. 1 (XVI) (8 Sep. 2014).

session. Thus, the Eighteenth Extraordinary Executive Council Session took place in Kigali, Rwanda, on 19 March 2018 with two items on the agenda: the establishment of AfCFTA[787] and the Draft African Common Position for the negotiation of a new Cooperation Agreement with the European Union in the context of Post-Cotonou 2020.[788] Two days later, the Tenth Extraordinary Assembly Session was held in Kigali, which, as has been explained above, launched AfCFTA.[789] Since then, the Executive Council has not met in extraordinary session. As is made clear in Article 13(2) of the Constitutive Act, the Executive Council is an organ subsidiary to the Assembly. It is mandated to consider issues referred to it by the Assembly and, moreover, to monitor the implementation of AU policies and decisions.

99. Its main task is to coordinate and take decisions on policies in areas which are of common interest to the Member States. Article 13(1) of the Constitutive Act refers to twelve such areas, whose common characteristic is that they primarily concern economic and social issues rather than political issues. To that end, the third paragraph of Article 13 stipulates that the Executive Council may decide to delegate its powers and functions to any of the Specialized Technical Committees. The areas of common interest are quite diverse and include: foreign trade; energy and industry; agriculture; water resources; protection of the environment and humanitarian action; transport and communications; education, culture, and health; science and technology; immigration matters; and social security. Decisions are reached by consensus, failing which by a two-thirds majority of Member States. It is not known whether the Executive Council has ever resorted to vote-taking, while the text of the approved decisions does not reveal any dissenting Member States. According to Article 11 of the Constitutive Act, the same majority constitutes a quorum at all its meetings.

100. Although, as already mentioned, the Assembly is empowered to direct the Executive Council regarding the management of conflicts and similar situations, Article 13 of the Constitutive Act does not envisage any corresponding competence for the Executive Council. The situation becomes more complicated because the PSC, the organ charged with the primary duty to handle such situations, was not originally envisaged in the Constitutive Act but was created through the Protocol of July 2002. The Protocol on Amendments of 2003 only partly dealt with this situation, in the sense that it added the PSC to the principal AU organs but did not delineate competences between the PSC and the Executive Council. It is submitted that the Assembly, when exercising its right to delegate powers pursuant to Article 9(2), is entitled to involve the Executive Council in the management of conflicts and the restoration of peace in the territory of Member States, while the Executive Council shall be obliged to act in accordance with the Assembly directions. Even though this has apparently never happened, were a Member State to dispute the validity of the

787. Executive Council, *Decision on the Draft Agreement Establishing the African Continental Free Trade Area (AfCFTA)*, AU Doc. Ext/EX.CL/Dec. 1 (XVIII) (19 Mar. 2018).
788. Executive Council, *Decision on the African Common Position for Negotiations for a New Cooperation Agreement with the European Union*, AU Doc. Ext/EX.CL/Dec. 2 (XVIII) (19 Mar. 2018).
789. AU Doc. Ext/Assembly/AU/Dec. 1 (X) (21 Mar. 2018), *supra*.

actions undertaken, the AU judicial organ should be competent to rule on the matter. During the AU's first years of operation, the Executive Council did address instances of civil war and interstate strife (e.g., in Somalia,[790] in Cote d'Ivoire,[791] in Burundi,[792] in Liberia,[793] and in the DRC[794]), but its relevant decisions did not contain action requiring implementation but rather reviewed the situations at hand and recorded developments. For many years now, the Executive Council has not deliberated cases relating to peace and security in the continent, presumably because they are considered to be in the sole purview of the PSC. Most of its sessions are devoted to examining the reports on activities submitted by other AU organs (both primary[795] and subsidiary), including the Specialized Technical Committees,[796] electing the members of various organs.

101. A practice that has been carried on from the OAU is for the Executive Council to meet before the scheduled ordinary sessions of the Assembly and in the same venue as the Assembly.

102. Article 5 in conjunction with 14(1) of the Constitutive Act establish the following seven Specialized Technical Committees (STCs), which cover the AU's non-political activities: (a) the Committee on Rural Economy and Agricultural Matters; (b) the Committee on Monetary and Financial Affairs; (c) the Committee on Trade, Customs and Immigration Matters; (d) the Committee on Industry, Science and Technology, Energy, Natural Resources and Environment; (e) the Committee on Transport, Communications and Tourism; (f) the Committee on Health, Labour and Social Affairs; and (g) the Committee on Education, Culture and Human Resources. STCs were originally created under Article 25 of the AEC Treaty and were carried on to the AU's institutional structure. They are subordinate to the Executive Council, which is empowered to restructure them or to establish new ones. They are composed of Ministers or senior officials from the Member States responsible for sectors falling within their respective areas of competence, while their functions are set out in Article 15 of the Constitutive Act. These include the following: preparing AU projects and programmes, ensuring that they are coordinated and harmonized, and submitting to the Executive Council, on their own initiative or at the latter's request, reports and recommendations relating to the implementation of the Constitutive Act. The process of setting up the Specialized Technical Committees has been slow. In July 2003, the Executive Council requested the PRC to submit a report on the

790. *See*, *inter alia*, AU Doc. EX.CL/Dec. 270 (XIII) (21 Jan. 2006).
791. *See*, *inter alia*, AU Doc. Ext/EX/CL/Dec. 12 (III) (25 May 2003); and EX.CL/Dec. 271 (XIII) (21 Jan. 2006).
792. *See*, *inter alia*, AU Doc. Ext/EX/CL/Dec. 13 (III) (25 May 2003).
793. *See*, *inter alia*, AU Doc. Ext/EX/CL/Dec. 11 (III) (25 May 2003).
794. *See*, *inter alia*, AU Doc. Ext/EX/CL/Dec. 8 (III) (25 May 2003).
795. *See*, *inter alia*, Executive Council, *Decision on the Reports of the Sub-Committees of the Permanent Representatives' Committee (PRC)*, AU Doc. EX.CL/Dec. 1168 (XLI) (25 Jul. 2022).
796. *See*, *inter alia*, Executive Council, *Decision on the Reports of the Specialized Technical Committees* (STCs), AU Doc. EX.CL/Dec. 1169 (XLI) (15 Jul. 2022).

issue,[797] while, during its Eleventh Extraordinary Session (Arusha, 6–7 May 2008), it requested that they be established pursuant to Article 14(3) of the Constitutive Act and that their number be finalized by the PRC and the AUC. The meeting, originally scheduled for the summer of 2008, was postponed to November 2008.

In the end, the Fourteenth Ordinary Assembly Session in February 2009 decided to 'reconfigure' STCs and increase their number to fourteen, as follows:

(1) Committee on Agriculture, Rural Development, Water and Environment.
(2) Committee on Finance, Monetary Affairs, Economic Planning and Integration.
(3) Committee on Trade and Industry and Minerals.
(4) Committee on Transport, Transcontinental, and Interregional Infrastructures, Energy and Tourism.
(5) Committee on Gender and Women Empowerment.
(6) Committee on Justice and Legal Affairs.
(7) Committee on Social Development, Labour and Employment.
(8) Committee on the Public Service, Local Government, Urban Development and Decentralization.
(9) Committee on Health, Population and Drug Control.
(10) Committee on Migration, Refugees and IDPs.
(11) Committee on Youth, Culture and Sports.
(12) Committee on Education, Science and Technology.
(13) Committee on Communication and Information Communications Technology.
(14) Committee on Defence, Safety and Security.

It also requested that the AUC avoid overlap with the STCs and ensure coherence and harmony with its own portfolios.[798] Based on an AUC Report,[799] in July 2011, the Assembly adopted, in principle, the proposed detailed activities of the Committees; resolved that each Committee should meet at the level of ministers and experts once every two years (with the exception of the Committees on Finance, Monetary Affairs, Economic Planning and Integration, on Gender and Women Empowerment, and on Defence and Security which are to meet once a year); and decided that the AUC will be responsible for convening and servicing all their meetings and ensure synergy with other AU organs.[800] Finally, in June 2015, the Assembly decided, on the one hand, to empower STCs to take decisions on issues falling within their competence with the exception of those having financial and structural

797. *See* Executive Council, *Decision on the Launching of the Specialized Technical Committees*, AU Doc. EX/CL/Dec. 72 (III) (8 Jul. 2003).
798. *See* Assembly, *Decision on the Specialised Technical Committee (STCS)*, AU Doc. Assembly/AU/Dec. 227 (XII) (3 Feb. 2009).
799. *See* AU Doc. Doc. EX.CL/666 (XIX) (2011).
800. *See* Assembly, *Decision on the Specialised Technical Committee (STCS)*, AU Doc. Assembly/AU/Dec. 365 (XVII) (1 Jul. 2011); *Decision on the Specialized Technical Committees*, AU Doc. Assembly/AU/Dec. 589 (XXVI) (31 Jan. 2016).

implications and, on the other hand, that the Executive Council should consider STC decisions at the request of Member States.[801]

103. During the OAU era, several Conferences at ministerial level had been set up to deal with specific issues. There are certain similarities between these Conferences and the STCs, as will be shown in the following five examples. First, the Labour and Social Affairs Commission (LSAC), which was organized jointly with the International Labour Organization (ILO) and has the characteristic tripartite participation structure of the ILO, namely representatives from the participating governments, from the unions of employers and from the workers' unions. Second, the Conference of Ministers of Health, which was organized in conjunction with the World Health Organization (WHO). Third, the Conference of Ministers of Industry, which was formed with the assistance of the UN Economic Commission for Africa (ECA), the United Nations Industrial Development Organization (UNIDO), and the Regional Office for Africa of the Food and Agricultural Organization (FAO). Fourth, the African Population Commission, which was set up jointly with the African Development Bank (ADB) and the ECA in 1994. Fifth, the Ministerial Conference on Drug Control, which adopted a Plan of Action for 2002–2006 in cooperation with the UN International Drug Control Programme (UNDCP).[802] In January 2008, the AU launched a Plan of Action on Drug Control and Crime Prevention (2008–2012).[803] It was followed by the Plan of Action on Drug Control (2013–2017).[804] Presently, the AU Plan of Action on Drug Control and Crime Prevention (2019–2023) (AUPA) is implemented,[805] which mirrors the African Common Position for the Thirteenth UN General Assembly Special Session held in New York in April 2016 (UNGASS 2016) on the World Drug Problem.[806]

---

801. *See* Assembly, *Decision on Streamlining of the AU Summits and the Working Methods of the African Union*, AU Doc. Assembly/AU/Dec. 582 (XXV), para. 1 (14 Jun. 2015). For the current composition of STCs, *see* African Union Commission & New Zealand Ministry of Foreign Affairs and Trade, *African Union Handbook 2022*, 45 *et seq.*
802. *See* UN Doc. AFR/410 – SOC/NAR/843 (14 May 2002). *See also* Executive Council, *Decision on the Report of the 2nd Session of the Ministerial Conference on Drug Control in Africa*, AU Doc. EX.CL/Dec. 169 (VI) (28 Jan. 2005). The functions of the UN Programme have in the meantime been assumed by the UN Office on Drugs and Crime, http://www.unodc.org.
803. *See also*, Assembly, *Decision on the Threat of Drug Trafficking in Africa*, AU Doc. Assembly/AU/Dec. 239 (XII) (3 Feb. 2009).
804. *See* AU Doc. CAMDC/EXP/2(V) (October 2012), approved by Executive Council, *Decision on the Report of the Fifth Session of the African Union Conference of Ministers in Charge of Drug Control*, AU Doc. EX.CL/Dec. 743(XXII) (25 Jan. 2013).
805. AU Doc. STC-HPDC-3/EXP/ SA24677 (2019), at: https://idpc.net/publications/2020/08/african-union-plan-of-action-on-drug-control-and-crime-prevention-2019-2023. Generally, *see* L. Raineri & F. Strazzari, 'The data that we do (not) have: studying drug trafficking and organised crime in Africa', *Trends in Organized Crime* (2023), https://doi.org/10.1007/s12117-023-09482-5.
806. *See* United Nations Office on Drugs and Crime, *Outcome Document of the 2016 United Nations General Assembly Special Session on the World Drug Problem – Our joint commitment to effectively addressing and countering the world drug problem* (Vienna, 2016); UNGA, Resolution S-30-1, Annex, 19 April 2016, at: https://www.unodc.org/documents/postungass2016/outcome/V1603301-E.pdf.

104. As there was a risk in duplication of the operation of STCs and these Ministerial Conferences and since similar organs exist in the RECs, rationalization and streamlining of activities were required. Thus, already in 2001, the Lusaka OAU Assembly Summit mandated the Secretary-General to come up with pertinent suggestions.[807] A year later, the Durban Assembly Summit, the last OAU Assembly to take place, requested the Secretary-General to determine the position of the African Population Commission[808] and of the LSAC within the AU structure.[809] However, this streamlining was apparently never achieved. Presently, a considerable number of ministerial bodies and other institutions are active in the AU.[810] Apart from LSAC,[811] the Conference of Ministers of Health,[812] and the African Population Commission (APC),[813] suffice to mention the following two entities: (a) the African Ministerial Conference on Housing and Urban Development (AMCHUD);[814] and (b) the African Energy Commission (AFREC),[815] which, as has been mentioned, was established by the namesake Convention of 2001 and has the status of an AU specialized agency.[816] It should be noted that these organs have a different status within the AU institutional architecture: some come under the aforementioned Article 5(2) of the Constitutive Act and are invariably referred to as 'Organs of the Union', others are established as specialized agencies (the terms 'specialized technical office' or 'specialized advisory body' or 'specialized institution' are also used),

---

807. Assembly, *Decision on the Implementation of the Sirte Summit Decision on the African Union*, OAU Doc. AHG/Dec. 160 (XXXVII), para. 9 (11 Jul. 2001).
808. Assembly, *Decision on the Place of the African Population Commission in the African Union*, OAU Doc. AHG/Dec. 176 (XXXVIII) (8 Jul. 2002).
809. Assembly, *Decision on the Place of the OAU Labour and Social Affairs Commission in the African Union*, OAU Doc. AHG/Dec. 177 (XXXVIII) (8 Jul. 2002).
810. Compare Executive Council, *Decision on the Specialized Technical Committees (STCs)*, AU Doc. EX.CL/Dec. 921 (XXIX) (15 Jul. 2016).
811. The First Ordinary Session of the Labour and Social Affairs Commission was held in Mauritius in April 2003 (*see* Executive Council Decision EX/CL/Dec. 49 (III) (8 Jul. 2003)), the Second Ordinary Session in Cotonou on 20 Apr. 2004, the Third Ordinary Session in 2005 (*see* Executive Council Decision EX.CL/Dec. 201 (VII) (2 Jul. 2005)), the Fourth Ordinary Session in April 2006 in Cairo, the Fifth Ordinary Session in Addis Ababa on 16–21 Apr. 2007, and the Sixth Ordinary Session in Addis Ababa on 21–25 Apr. 2008. Generally, *see* AUC, *Report of the Chairperson of AU Commission on the Activities Falling within the Competence of the Labour and Social Affairs Commission* (May 2007–April 2008), AU Doc. LSC/EXP/2 (VI) (2008). The Ninth Ordinary Session was held in Addis Ababa on 8–12 Apr. 2013. A special session took place in Namibia in April 2014 under the theme 'Employment, Poverty Eradication and Inclusive Development'.
812. Executive Council, *Decision on the Report of the First Ordinary Session of the AU Conference of African Ministers of Health*, AU Doc. EX/CL/Dec. 50 (III) (8 Jul. 2003).
813. The Fifth Ordinary Session of its General Assembly took place in 2005; *see* Executive Council Decision EX.CL/Dec. 202 (VII) (2 Jul. 2005). The Sixth Ordinary Session was held in Johannesburg on 16–17 Jul. 2007; for the Declaration adopted, *see* AU Doc. ACP/Draft/Decl. (VI) (17 Jul. 2007). *See further* the Addis Ababa Declaration on Population and Development in Africa Beyond 2014 adopted on 4 October 2013.
814. Executive Council, *Draft Decision on the Report of the First Session of the African Ministerial Conference on Housing and Urban Development (AMCHUD)*, AU Doc. EX/CL/Dec. 200 (VII) (2 Jul. 2005).
815. *See* Conference of the African Union Ministers in Charge of Energy, *Algiers Declaration on the Official Launching of the African Energy Commission*, 15–17 Feb. 2008, AU Doc. AU/EXP/EN/Decl. (III) Rev. (2008).
816. Convention of the African Energy Commission, at: http://afrec-energy.org/En/convention.html.

e.g. the African Union Institute for Statistics (STATAFRIC), which has the status of a specialized technical agency of the AUC answering to the Office of Strategic Planning and Delivery (OSPD).[817] Sometimes, there is more than one organ operating in the same field of activities. For example, in the broad area of science and research there are three (not counting the Pan-African University): (a) the African Union Scientific, Technical and Research Commission (AU-STRC), which developed from the STRC created in 1965, which was originally established as the Commission for Technical Co-operation in Africa, South of the Sahara (CCTA) by the European colonial powers in 1950;[818] (b) the African Scientific, Research and Innovation Council (ASRIC), which was established in 2013,[819] but launched in 2018 and whose Secretariat is AU-STRC; and (c) the African Observatory of Science, Technology and Innovation (AOSTI), which was established in 2009.[820] In July 2010, the AUC and the Government of Equatorial Guinea signed a hosting agreement for the Observatory to be headquartered in Malabo. AOSTI was formally created in January 2013,[821] while its Statute was adopted three years later.[822] As regards which Member States participate in these organs, a rule of thumb is the following: if the organ in question was created by an AU treaty and the treaty requires ratification to enter into force, only those Member States that have ratified it participate as contracting parties; if created by an Assembly decision, *ab initio* and *de jure* the whole membership are participants, unless the decision provides otherwise.

§3. The Pan-African Parliament (PAP)

105. The creation of PAP, the parliamentary organ envisaged in Article 17 of the Constitutive Act, had already been envisaged in Article 14 of the Treaty establishing the AEC.[823] Like the parliamentarian organs operating in the framework of

817. Its establishment was approved by the Assembly at its January 2013 Session, AU Doc. Assembly/ AU/ 462 (XX), while in January 2018 the AUC and the Government of Tunisia signed the Host Agreement. Its structure was approved the following year, *see* Executive Council, *Decision on the Reports of the Sub-Committees of the Permanent Representatives Committee (COREP)*, AU Doc. EX.CL/Dec. 1057(XXXV), para. 27 (5 Jul. 2019). The African Statistics Day is celebrated every year on the 18th of November.
818. Presently, it implements the Science Technology and Innovation Strategy for Africa 2024 (STISA 2024), adopted by the Twenty-Third Ordinary Assembly Session (June 2014), *see* https://au.int/sites/default/files/newsevents/workingdocuments/33178-wd-stisa-english_-_final.pdf.
819. Executive Council, *Decision on African Research and Innovation Council*, AU Doc. EX.CL/ Dec.747(XXII) (25 Jan. 2013).
820. Assembly, *Decision on the Proposal by the Government of the Republic of Equatorial Guinea to host the African Observatory of Science, Technology and Innovation*, AU Doc. Assembly/AU/ Dec. 235 (XII) (3 Feb. 2009).
821. Assembly, *Decision on the Creation of the African Observatory on Science, Technology and Innovation in the Republic of Equatorial Guinea*, AU Doc. Assembly/AU/Dec. 452 (XX) (28 Jan. 2013).
822. Assembly, *Decision on the Specialized Technical Committees*, AU Doc. Assembly/AU/Dec. 589 (XXVI), para. 2 (31 Jan. 2016).
823. The attempts in the context of the AEC were never pursued thoroughly; e.g., in March 1999, the Fourth Ordinary Session of the AEC Council of Ministers played with the idea of setting up a Consultative Forum of African Parliamentarians as a prelude to creating the proper PAP, *see* AEC Doc. CM/AEC/Regl.1 (IV), para. 2 (23 Mar. 1999).

RECs,[824] PAP's purpose is to ensure the full participation of African peoples in the continent's development and economic integration. The Constitutive Act did not contain any provisions on its composition, powers, functions, and organization but, as is true with other organs, left the details to be defined in a future protocol. But, more importantly, it did not deal with the relationship between the AU PAP and the namesake organ of the AEC Treaty, which was part of a larger issue: the proper incorporation of the AEC institutions and organs into the AU's structures and architecture (assuming that the AEC would eventually become the regional economic integration organization (REIO) of the African continent). However, the fact that the wording of the aforementioned two provisions is almost identical could suggest that the drafters intended that the two organs be unified and merged into a single parliamentarian entity to serve both the AEC and the AU. Notwithstanding this argument, the Protocol relating to the PAP was adopted by the Fifth Extraordinary OAU Assembly Session (Sirte, 2 March 2001) as a Protocol attached to the AEC Treaty and not to the Constitutive Act,[825] presumably because the latter had not yet come into force (it did so on 26 May 2001). Following its ratification by a simple majority of Member States, the PAP Protocol entered into force on 27 November 2003.[826] In a nutshell, PAP was originally meant to function in the AEC's context and promote what is known as parliamentary diplomacy in international organizations,[827]

---

824. The first African attempt to set up a parliamentarian organ within an IGO was the East African Legislative Assembly (EALA), envisaged as an organ of the East African Community and Common Market; *see* Art. 56 of the Treaty for East African Co-Operation, concluded on 6 Jun. 1967; reproduced in I. Brownlie, *Basic Documents on African Affairs* (Oxford: Clarendon Press, 1971), 63. Following the rejuvenation of EAC through the namesake Treaty of 30 Nov. 1999, in force on 7 Jul. 2000, EALA was formally inaugurated on 30 Nov. 2001 as an independent organ. Moreover, Arts 6 and 13 of the Revised Treaty of ECOWAS envisaged the creation of a Community Parliament as a forum for dialogue, consultation and consensus for representatives of the peoples of West Africa and as a vehicle to promote regional integration. The founding Protocol was signed on 6 Aug. 1994 and entered into force on 14 Mar. 2002. Other parliamentary entities currently in operation include the Network of Parliamentarians at the Economic Community of Central African States (ECCAS), the Interparliamentary Committee at the West African Economic and Monetary Union (UEMOA), and the Parliamentary Forum at the Southern Africa Development Community (SADC). Generally, *see* D. Jancic, 'Regional Parliaments and African Economic Integration', *The European Journal of International Law* 2019 (30): 199.

825. Wrongly some authors have written that the PAP Protocol has accompanied the Constitutive Act, *see, e.g.*, Jancic, ibid, 206.

826. *See* OAU Assembly, *Decision on the Draft Protocol to the Treaty Establishing the African Economic Community Relating to the Pan-African Parliament*, OAU Doc. EHAG/Dec. 2 (V) (2 Mar. 2001). The text of the Protocol is reproduced in RADIC 13 (2005): 86. *See* K. Magliveras & G. Naldi, 'The Pan-African Parliament of the African Union: An Overview', *African Human Rights Law Journal* 3 (2003): 222; K. Magliveras & A. Huliaras, 'Understanding Success and Failure in the Quest for Peace: The Pan-African Parliament and the Amani Forum', *The Hague Journal of Diplomacy* 11 (2016): 275; O.E. Nwebo & C.M. Fombad, 'Reflections on the Role of the Pan-African Parliament in Advancing Democratic Governance in Africa' in A. Adeola & M.W. Mutua (eds), *The Palgrave Handbook of Democracy, Governance and Justice in Africa* (Cham: Palgrave Macmillan, 2022) 85. Currently, the Protocol has been ratified by fifty-one Member States. DRC, Guinea and Somalia have not ratified it, while Eritrea is the only Member State not to have even signed it; however, given that its National Assembly has apparently not met since February 2002, the participation of parliamentarians from Eritrea would be a moot point.

827. *See* S. Stavridis & D. Jancic (eds), *Parliamentary Diplomacy in European and Global Governance* (Leiden: Brill, 2017).

but necessary changes had to be accommodated in the 2001 Protocol to be able to function as a principal AU organ. According to Article 2(2) of the Protocol, PAP is the representative of the peoples of Africa. It held its inaugural session on 18 March 2004, which is commemorated as 'the Pan-African Parliament Day'. Its Rules of Procedure were approved by the Second Ordinary PAP Session (Midrand, South Africa, 16 September–1 October 2004), and have since been amended in October 2011 and in 2022.[828]

106. Each Member State participating in the PAP is entitled to five members, at least one of whom must be a woman.[829] Pursuant to Article 5 of the Protocol, members shall either be elected or designated by national legislatures, be it parliaments or other deliberative bodies, from among their members. A former PAP President, Gertrude Mongella, cited in May 2007 the fact that the membership keeps on changing between sessions on account of national general elections taking place during the in-between periods[830] as one of the grounds preventing the PAP from establishing strong foundations. Article 6 specifies that members shall vote in their personal and independent capacity and, consequently, they should not receive directions from governments or other state bodies. Under Article 7, holders of domestic executive or judicial posts are specifically barred from participating in the PAP. No uniform electoral procedure is envisaged. It is ultimately expected that its members will be elected by universal adult suffrage,[831] no doubt a lofty aim which, has been achieved in the context of the EU with the direct elections for the European Parliament. However, developments so far do not suggest that the PAP will evolve into a fully democratically elected body.[832] This could call into question the AU's own stated commitment to democracy, popular participation and good governance, which, as explained, are enshrined in Article 3(g) and Article 3(h) of the Constitutive Act. Although in accordance with Article 4(3) of the Protocol parliamentarians must reflect the diversity of political opinions in national legislatures, there would appear to be no restraint on dictatorial regimes to manipulate the nomination process.

---

828. *See*, Parliament of the Republic of South Africa, *Media Release: Pan-African Parliament Makes History as it Unanimously Adopts its Rules of Procedure*, 3 November 2022, at: https://www.parliament.gov.za/press-releases/media-release-pan-african-parliament-makes-history-it-unanimously-adopts-its-rules-procedure.
829. Article 4(2) of the Protocol. This reflects the AU's commitment to promote gender equality pursuant to Art. 4(l) of the Constitutive Act. *See further*, AU Gender Policy of 2009; Aspiration 6 of Agenda 2063 ('An Africa, whose development is people-driven, relying on the potential of African people, especially its women and youth, and caring for children'); and AU Strategy for Gender Equality and Women's Empowerment 2018–2028 (GEWE), at: https://au.int/sites/default/files/documents/36195-doc-52569_au_strategy_eng_high.pdf.
830. This occurs because, pursuant to Art. 5(3) of the Protocol, a PAP member's term runs concurrently with his/her term of office in the national legislature.
831. According to Art. 2(3) of the Protocol, the transition to universal suffrage will not occur automatically but will necessitate an amendment to the Protocol to that effect. However, the PAP Protocol adopted in 2014 has not promoted this goal, which is rather progressive for the continent.
832. Nevertheless, the European Court of Justice's *dictum* in Case 138/79 *Roquette Frères v. Council* [1980] E.C.R. 3333 at para. 33 referring to the 'fundamental democratic principle that the peoples should take part in the exercise of power through the intermediary of a representative assembly' would appear to be met by the PAP in its present status.

107. As Africa experiences elections which cannot be described as free and fair by basic standards, it will be suggested that provision ought to have been made to exclude parliamentarians, who were elected by means of fraudulent, violent or highly undemocratic elections and/or elected or appointed following a coup d'état, which has been condemned by the AU and other international organizations. It is submitted that the Protocol or the Rules of Procedure should have included a provision akin to Rule 8 of the Rules of Procedure of the Parliamentary Assembly of the Council of Europe.[833] It stipulates that the credentials of a national delegation may be challenged *in toto* on the grounds that the basic principles guiding the Council of Europe, namely the rule of law, democratic ideals and the enjoyment by all people of human rights and fundamental freedoms, are seriously violated in the territory of the Member State in question or that the latter has persistently failed to honour obligations and commitments and has not cooperated in the Parliamentary Assembly's monitoring procedure.[834]

108. The proper place for envisaging this possibility would be Article 5 of the PAP Protocol, which, in conjunction with Rule 8 of the Rules of Procedure, lays down the instances leading to vacation of seats in the PAP. These include: death; resignation; inability to perform one's duties for reasons of physical or mental incapacity; removal on grounds of misconduct; when the parliamentarian ceases to be a member of the national legislature; or when he/she is recalled by the national legislature; and automatically when the parliamentarian's Member State has withdrawn from the AEC.[835] The manner of filling vacant seats is not addressed in the Protocol. The Rules of Procedure envisage that, depending on the circumstances, the Member State of the parliamentarian shall be notified accordingly, and it will then be up to it to arrange for the replacement. Unlike the Parliamentary Assembly of the Council of Europe, there are no substitute parliamentarians.

109. Pursuant to Articles 8(1) and 9(1) of the PAP Protocol, parliamentarians exercising their functions shall enjoy in the territory of all Member States, respectively, the immunities and privileges extended to Member States' representatives under the OAU General Convention on the Privileges and Immunities and the Vienna Convention on Diplomatic Relations. They shall also enjoy parliamentary immunity. Parliamentarians shall, therefore, not be liable to civil or criminal proceedings, arrest, imprisonment or damages for anything said or done within or outside the PAP, provided they were discharging their duties. The scope of Articles 8(1) and 9(1) has been augmented in Rule 10 of the Rules of Procedure. However, Rules 11–12 allow the PAP to waive immunity on the ground of committing a criminal offence. The request for waiver shall be heard by the Permanent Committee on Rules, Privileges, and Discipline. The PAP meets in ordinary session at least twice

833. For the Rules of Procedure, which were adopted under Parliamentary Assembly Res. 1202 (1999) in November 1999, as in force in January 2023, *see* https://assembly.coe.int/nw/xml/RoP/RoP-XML2HTML-en.asp.

834. *See* Parliamentary Assembly Res. 1115 (1997) of 29 January 1997 on the setting up of an Assembly committee on the honouring of obligations and commitments by member states of the Council of Europe (Monitoring Committee), as lastly modified by Res. 2325 (2020).

835. *See* Art. 19 of the PAP Protocol and Rule 8(1)(g).

a year[836] and in extraordinary session at the request of two-thirds of parliamentarians, of the AEC Assembly (now the AU Assembly) or of the AEC Council of Ministers (now the AU Executive Council).[837] The quorum for a meeting is a simple majority.[838] Notwithstanding the fact that each parliamentarian has one vote, the general rule is that decisions are reached by consensus.[839] Failing that, however, decisions could be taken by a two-thirds majority of all the members being present and voting.[840] This rule reflects the general AU position that a majority vote shall be employed if consensus cannot be achieved.[841] Procedural matters are decided by a simple majority of those present and voting.[842] In the event of a tie, the presiding official has the casting vote.[843]

110. PAP is meant to provide a forum for African people and their grassroots organizations to become more involved in deliberations and decision-making on African problems and challenges. Its objectives include facilitating the implementation of AU/AEC policies, promoting human rights and democracy, encouraging good governance, transparency, and accountability in Member States, promoting peace, security and stability, advancing economic recovery, assisting cooperation among RECs, and assisting cooperation and stability in Africa.[844] Accordingly, PAP has been authorized to discuss and make recommendations on issues relating to human rights, democracy, and good governance, to harmonize the laws of Member States, to make recommendations advancing the AU/AEC objectives, to promote the AU/AEC in the Member States, and to harmonize the policies and programmes of RECs.[845] PAP itself has described its objectives and functions as follows: 'The mission … is to provide a common platform for African peoples to represent, and to act as a voice of the people of Africa presenting their opinions, their concerns and aspirations, and thus effectively hold the governing institutions of the AU accountable in the implementation of policies and programmes as well as in the allocation and use of public resources for promoting just, equitable and sustainable development for all the peoples of Africa'.[846]

111. As regards the budget, the PAP can draw it up, discuss it but not adopt it as long as it has no legislative powers.[847] Moreover, the Protocol envisages that the

836. Article 14(2) of the Protocol. These sessions may last a month. It should be noted that, according to Art. 16, PAP may convene in the territory of any Member State at the latter's invitation.
837. Article 14(3) of the Protocol.
838. Article 12(11) of the Protocol.
839. Article 12(12) of the Protocol.
840. Unless stipulated to the contrary in the Rules of Procedure, *see* Art. 12(12) of the Protocol.
841. Compare Art. 7(1) of the Constitutive Act referring to the Assembly.
842. Unless stipulated to the contrary in the Rules of Procedure, *see* Art. 12(12) of the Protocol.
843. *Ibid.*
844. Article 3 of the Protocol.
845. Compare Art. 11 of the Protocol setting out its functions and powers.
846. Cited by O.C. Ruppel & L.-J. Houston, 'The Pan-African Parliament of the African Union: Composition, mandate and partnerships, and its quest for sustainable development' in O.C. Ruppel & H. Ginzky (eds), *African Soil Protection Law* (Baden-Baden: Nomos Verlag, 2021) 485, 486.
847. Article 11(2) in conjunction with Art. 15(2) of the Protocol. Until then, its budget is approved by the Assembly.

PAP has the function of discussing the AEC budget and 'make recommendations thereon prior to its approval to the Assembly'.[848] Other PAP powers include requesting AU/AEC officials to attend its sessions and to produce documents.[849] Finally, it has been authorized to perform such other functions as it deems appropriate to achieve its objectives.[850] This latter provision could potentially be of significance because, if used boldly and imaginatively, it could turn functions into real powers.[851] Given that the PAP is composed of the peoples' direct representatives, no doubt it could invoke its legitimacy vis-à-vis the Assembly, regardless if this would lead to tense relations between them. However, a power struggle as the one that has taken place in the EC between the European Parliament and the Council of Ministers during the 1980s and the 1990s, a struggle that sometimes was brought before the European Court of Justice (ECJ),[852] is not envisaged.[853] Under Article 12(13) of the Protocol, the PAP has been authorized to establish any committees that it deems necessary. Currently, the following eleven Permanent Committees operate and their functions are aligned to those of the AU Specialized Technical Committees: the Committee on Rural Economy, Agriculture, Natural Resources, and Environment; the Committee on Monetary and Financial Affairs; the Committee on Trade, Customs, and Immigration Matters; the Committee on Cooperation, International Relations, and Conflict Resolutions; the Committee on Transport, Industry, Communications, Energy, Science, and Technology; the Committee on Health, Labour, and Social Affairs; the Committee on Education, Culture, Tourism, and Human Resources; the Committee on Gender, Family, Youths, and People with Disabilities; the Committee on Justice and Human Rights;[854] the Committee on Rules, Privileges, and Discipline; and the Committee on Audit and Public Accounts (CAPA).[855] These Committees implement programmes and projects based on the

848. Article 11(2) of the Protocol. Note that the corresponding provision in the Rules of Procedure (Rule 4(g)) refers to examining and debating the AU budget, which should be regarded as being separate from the AEC budget.
849. Article 11(5) of the Protocol.
850. Article 11(9) of the Protocol.
851. Note that this possibility has been played down in Rule 4(i) and Rule 5(f), which stipulate that the PAP may exercise functions and powers that are of an incidental or auxiliary nature.
852. *See*, *inter alia*, European Court of Justice, Case 13/83 *European Parliament v. Council* [1985] E.C.R. 1513; Case C-70/88 *European Parliament v. Council* (The Chernobyl Case) [1990] E.C.R. 2041; and Case C-21/94 *Parliament v. Council* [1995] E.C.R. I–1827.
853. *See also* T. Demeke, 'The New Pan-African Parliament: Prospects and Challenges in View of the Experience of the European Parliament', *African Human Rights Law Journal* 4 (2004): 53.
854. The Committee has launched the Guidelines for Parliamentarians on eliminating harmful practices and other human rights violations. The Guidelines aim at contributing to safe communities where all persons, regardless of status, are free of all forms of harm stemming from accusations of witchcraft and ritual attacks, *see* PAP, 'PAP reaches milestone with the launch of Guidelines on eliminating harmful practices, human rights violations', Press Release, 15 March 2023, at: https://pap.au.int/en/news/press-releases/2023-03-15/pap-reaches-milestone-launch-guidelines-eliminating-harmful-pract.
855. The AU Office of Internal Audit (OIA), the internal oversight body mandated to ensure the effectiveness of AU rules and procedures, has urged CAPA to conduct periodic self-assessments to help it identify opportunities for improving its activities, *see* PAP, 'African Union Office of Internal Audit engages CAPA in its oversight function', Press Release, 14 March 2023, at: https://pap.au.int/en/news/press-releases/2023-03-14/african-union-office-internal-audit-engages-capa-its-oversight.

PAP Strategic Plan 2019–2023[856] and take into consideration the overall PAP vision, the goals of Agenda 2063, the horizontal AU programmes, and the theme of the year, which, as explained, is decided by the Assembly.

112. The following two examples serve to illustrate the kind of issues that the PAP addresses. The first example concerns the PAP Committee on Rural Economy, Agriculture, Natural Resources, and Environment. During the second half of 2007, it undertook a fact-finding mission to Côte d'Ivoire to establish the facts on an incident concerning toxic waste dumping in December 2006. The aim was to make recommendations to the Assembly so as to avoid repetition of such events. In the second example, a member from the South African Parliament tabled in May 2007 a motion calling for a fact-finding mission to Zimbabwe to investigate matters relating to human rights protection, good governance, transparency and the rule of law, arguing that the mission was pertinent to the PAP's mandate. The motion was put to the vote, and 149 parliamentarians voted in favour, twenty against and three abstained. Arguably, even though the PAP does not possess direct rights in this area, the above mandate emanates from Rule 4(b) of its Rules of Procedure, which envisages that it shall promote fundamental freedoms as well as consolidate democratic institutions and culture in all Member States. However, such a broad mandate would appear to fall also within the ambit of the African Commission on Human and Peoples' Rights,[857] begging the question of whether they should cooperate.[858] The overlap of mandates between the various AU organs and entities is a complex matter that the AU has attempted to address but not with much success.[859] Finally, reference could be made to a meeting held in Rwanda in late May 2008 on the African Charter on Democracy, Elections, and Governance, where the PAP delegation proposed that it acts as promoter for the Charter's ratification and popularization processes. On occasions, PAP has undertaken the task to urge Member States to ratify important AU treaties. For example, in March 2023, it asked them to ratify the Protocol to the African Charter on Human and People's Rights on the Rights of Persons with Disabilities, and the Protocol on the Rights of Older Persons in Africa.[860] According to a commentator, PAP resolutions and recommendations are often very brief, insufficiently substantiated, and poorly drafted but there is room for improvement.[861]

113. As mentioned, pursuant to Article 11(7) of the Protocol, the PAP has been entrusted with facilitating coordination and harmonization of policies and programmes of RECs and the other African parliamentary fora.[862] This objective is

856. At: https://pap.au.int/en/documents/2022-04-12/strategic-plan-2019-2023-pap.
857. *See* Art. 45(1)(a) of the African Charter on Human and Peoples' Rights.
858. Compare *ibid.*, Art. 45(1)(c).
859. In the present case, considering that the situation in Zimbabwe has security implications for the region, the Peace and Security Council might have a role to play; Compare Art. 18 of the PSC Protocol delineating its relationship with PAP.
860. Note that in October 2019 PAP adopted the Draft Model Law on Disability and submitted it to the Summit Session held in February 2020. So far, it has not been discussed by the Assembly.
861. *See* F. Viljoen, *International Human Right Law in Africa*, 2nd edition (Oxford: Oxford University Press, 2012), 175.
862. Compare Rule 4(e) and Rule 5(b), (d) and (e) of the Rules of Procedure.

further elaborated in Article 18, which arguably has a wider ambit, as it envisages that the cooperation shall extend to cover national parliaments or other deliberative organs operating in Member States. Apparently, the envisaged cooperation is nothing more than the possibility for the PAP to convene joint annual consultative meetings to 'discuss matters of common interest'. Arguably, representatives from the parliamentary organs of RECs could be invited to participate as observers at PAP sessions.[863] Thus, Rule 5(d) provides that the PAP could issue invitations to the representatives of RECs in order to 'furnish explanations on issues affecting or likely to affect the life of the African Union'.

114. During the initial (undefined in terms of duration) stage, it was decided that the PAP powers will only be consultative and advisory. However, it is expected that through an evolutionary process, it could acquire legislative powers as well. This derives from the combined reading of Articles 2(3) and 11 of the Protocol. However, the wording of these provisions raises issues of interpretation because the former provision says that it will necessitate an amendment to the Protocol to be decided by the Member States, while the latter says that the legislative powers will be defined by the Assembly. It was probably considerations of pragmatism that dictated the decision not to grant legislative powers to the PAP from the onset. However, this evolutionary process is imperative, as the full and effective functioning of the PAP would only be beneficial and would confer democratic legitimacy to the AU. It should be noted that the Seventh Ordinary PAP Session, which ended on 19 May 2007, recommended to the Assembly that it be transformed into a legislative organ.

115. The powers of the PAP were enhanced by the Protocol establishing the African Court of Justice, adopted by the Assembly in July 2003. These favourable for the PAP provisions were carried on to the 2008 Protocol and the appended Statute, which, as has been explained, merged the African Court of Justice with the African Court on Human and Peoples' Rights to create the ACJHR. In particular, under Article 29 of the ACJHR Statute, PAP will be entitled to submit to it cases relating, e.g., to the interpretation and application of the Constitutive Act, the interpretation, application and validity of all AU treaties, as well as to decisions issued by other AU organs. Equally, were PAP to misuse its powers, an action could be brought against it before the ACJHR by the other organs. Finally, under Article 53 of the ACJHR Statute, PAP has also been granted the right to ask the ACJHR to issue advisory opinions on any legal question. Arguably, were these provisions to be used constructively by the PAP once the ACJHR has become operative, it could strengthen its position considerably in the AU institutional architecture.

---

863. Compare Arts 4(2)(a) and 6(2) of the AEC Treaty envisaging collaboration with the RECs, which was initially formalized by the Protocol on the Relationship between the African Economic Community and the Regional Economic Communities of 25 Feb. 1998, reproduced in RADIC 10 (1998):157. *See further* Art. 6(2)(f)(v) of the AEC Treaty envisaging the harmonization and coordination process to be achieved during the AEC's fifth and final stage of creation (originally scheduled to be completed by 2034), and OAU Assembly, *Relaunching Africa's Economic and Social Development: The Cairo Agenda for Action*, OAU Doc. AHG/Res. 236 (XXXI) (26 Jun. 1995) which considered the achievement of regional economic integration a top priority.

116. As has been noted, Article 19 of the PAP Protocol deals with parliamentarians from a contracting party which has withdrawn from the AEC and stipulates that they shall automatically cease holding their office. The corresponding provision in the Rules (Rule 8(1)(g)) refers to withdrawal from the AU and not from the AEC, presumably because the Rules, without explaining why, regard that the AEC has been incorporated in the AU and does no longer exist (Eritrea signed the AEC Treaty in April 2012 and South Sudan in January 2013, while Morocco acceded to it in April 2017). As has been argued above, for as long as the AEC is not officially dissolved, this argument is very difficult to sustain because participation in the AEC is distinct from AU participation. Indeed, at the time of the AU's inauguration, there were six AU Member States which were not AEC Members.[864] Today, AEC membership is five states short of the AU membership. Moreover, Article 19 of the PAP Protocol does not specifically confer upon contracting parties the right to withdraw from it but only sets out the consequences when they have withdrawn from the AEC: 'The Pan-African Parliamentarians from a Member State which withdraws from the [AEC] shall automatically cease to be Pan-African Parliamentarians'.

117. As has been explained, even though the PAP Protocol was prepared based on the AEC Treaty's mandate, it regulates the functioning of a principal AU organ (Article 5 of the Constitutive Act). Therefore, the sensible thing had always been to disassociate it from the AEC and bring it into the AU's institutional architecture as its parliamentary organ. In 2009, the Assembly requested that the AEC initiate a review process in consultation with the PRC and the PAP.[865] Two years later, the Fifth Meeting of the Government Experts on the Legal Instruments on the Transformation of the AUC into AU Authority and on Review of the Protocols relating to the Pan-African Parliament and the African Court on Human and Peoples' Rights adopted a draft Protocol to replace the 2001 Protocol.[866] After it was reviewed by the Ministers of Justice and the Attorneys General of Member States in mid-May 2012,[867] the Executive Council approved it, except of Article 8.1(a) and 8.2, the provisions on PAP's legislative and oversight powers. It recommended that it be deferred in line with developments in the continental integration process.[868] The Assembly adopted the recommendation.[869] Presumably because national sovereignty continues to be the determining factor in how African leaders approach

864. Namely Djibouti, Equatorial Guinea, Eritrea, Gabon, Somalia and Swaziland; *see List of Countries which Have Signed, Ratified/Acceded to the Treaty Establishing the African Economic Community as at 26 September 2002*, AU Doc. CAB/LEG/28.1 (2002).

865. *See* Assembly, *Decision on the Review of the Protocol Relating to the Pan-African Parliament (PAP)*, AU Doc. Assembly/AU/Dec. 223 (XII) (3 Feb. 2009).

866. *See* Draft Protocol to the Constitutive Act of the African Union Relating to the Pan-African Parliament, AU Doc. Exp/Legal/AUC-Auth./4(V) (May 2011).

867. AU Doc. EX.CL/731(XXI)b (May 2012).

868. *See* Executive Council, *Decision on the Protocol to the Constitutive Act of the African Union Relating to the Pan-African Parliament*, EX.CL/ Dec. 707 (XXI) (13 Jul. 2012).

869. *See* Assembly, *Decision on the Protocol to the Constitutive Act of the African Union relating to the Pan-African Parliament*, AU Doc. Assembly/AU/Dec. 455 (XX) (28 Jan. 2013).

political integration,[870] the PAP's legislative and oversight powers caused considerable contention among them. The draft PAP Protocol was discussed in a previous edition of this monograph.[871] It was finally accepted by the Assembly in June 2014.[872] Until the very end, Article 8 proved to be a most contentious matter. It was the only issue that the First Ministerial Meeting of the Specialized Technical Committee on Justice and Legal Affairs, held in May 2014, was asked to deliberate,[873] leading the Executive Council to recommend to the Assembly that Article 8(1) be worded as follows:

a. The Assembly shall determine the subjects/areas on which PAP may propose draft model laws;
b. The Pan-African Parliament may on its own make proposals on the subjects/areas on which it may submit or recommend draft Model Laws to the Assembly for its consideration and approval.[874]

Presently, twenty-two Member States have signed the 2014 PAP Protocol, and fourteen have ratified it (Mali was the first to ratify it in April 2015 and Morocco the last in February 2022). According to Article 23, it shall enter into force when approved by a simple majority of Member States and pursuant to Article 27(1), it shall replace the 2001 Protocol. Some observations will be made, even though it is unknown when it will come into force. First, an obvious matter that that has not been addressed in the 2014 Protocol is whether the initial participation in PAP will be restricted to those parliamentarians coming from the contracting parties to the 2014 Protocol or from all Member States that have approved the 2001 Protocol, irrespective of whether they have ratified the 2014 Protocol as well. Presumably, the operation of PAP should not be interrupted, but its continuation should be ensured. However, under the former solution, which appears to be the correct one from a legal point of view, the PAP, as a proper AU organ, will operate with parliamentarians from the first twenty-eight contracting parties. The 2014 Protocol does not stipulate the parallel operation of both the old and new PAP. On the contrary, Article 2(1) refers to the continuation of the existing PAP (there will be no legal succession as such) pursuant to the new rules, while Article 27(2) stipulates that the term of office of PAP Members shall terminate no later than one year after the 2014 Protocol's entry into force.

Second, as regards the contentious Article 8, the 2014 Protocol limits considerably the PAP's legislative powers. In particular, the first paragraph thereof envisages that it shall be the AU legislative organ but without any lawmaking powers of

870. *See* O. Nzewi, *The Challenges of Post-1990 Regional Integration in Africa: Pan-African Parliament*, Centre for Policy Studies, Policy Brief 57, Johannesburg, April 2009, p. 11.
871. *See* K. Magliveras &G. Naldi, *The African Union* (Alphen aan den Rijn: Wolters Kluwer, 2014), para. 116.
872. Protocol to the Constitutive Act of the African Union Relating to the Pan-African Parliament, *see* Assembly, *Decision on the Draft Legal Instruments,* AU Doc. Assembly/AU/Dec. 529 (XXIII) (27 Jun. 2014).
873. *See* AU Doc. STC/Legal/Min/7(I) Rev.1 (2014).
874. *See* Executive Council, *Decision on the Draft Legal Instruments*, AU Doc. EX.CL/Dec. 835 (XXV) (24 Jun. 2014), para. 3.

its own. As mentioned above, the Assembly shall determine the subjects or the areas in which the PAP may propose draft model laws, whose adoption shall be decided by the Assembly. But, at the same time, the PAP is also entitled, on the one hand, to propose such subjects and areas and, on the other hand, to recommend draft model laws for the Assembly's consideration and approval. Clearly, the outcome of compromise, the implementation of this provision requires sincere rapport between the two organs. Third, the new PAP will acquire the consultative and oversight powers laid down in Article 8(2). They include receiving and considering reports issued by AU organs, provided they are referred to it by the Executive Council and the Assembly; debating but not adopting its own budget and making recommendations on the AU budget; discussing any matter relevant to the AU and making pertinent recommendations; promoting AU programmes and objectives in Member States; receiving, considering, and submitting opinions on draft legislative instruments and international agreements as may be referred to it by the Executive Council and the Assembly (arguably the mandate of AUCIL should have been taken into consideration); and liaising with the parliamentarian bodies of Member States and of RECs on issues concerning the AU and continental integration.

Fourth, the new PAP is also authorized to carry out any other activities which it deems appropriate to achieve the objectives of Article 3 of the 2014 Protocol. These objectives have been unchanged from the 2001 Protocol, and, *inter alia*, include the following: giving a voice to African people and the African Diaspora while encouraging the latter's full participation in African affairs;[875] facilitating the effective implementation of AU policies; promoting human rights and democracy; encouraging good governance, respect for the rule of law, transparency and accountability; promoting peace, security, and stability; encouraging collective self-reliance and economic recovery; strengthening African solidarity, cooperation, and development, and building a sense of common destiny; and encouraging national parliaments to ratify and to implement AU treaties into their legal systems. A new provision on how the PAP is to exercise these powers and functions has been inserted as Article 8(3). It is another restrictive provision because, while it may carry out fact-finding, enquiry and observer missions, it may do so if not in conflict with the mandate of other organs. The priority to be given to other organs may be acceptable in the case of fact-finding missions to establish, e.g., violations of peace and (the PSC should have priority on account of its mandate and/or the AUC if so instructed by the Assembly), but not as regards, e.g., observer missions to report on electoral processes in the territory of contracting parties. Moreover, the question of duplication of efforts and complementarity comes into play. Clearly, the AU should adopt guidelines to that effect which should not be based on an assumed superiority of one organ over another but which organ can carry out the mission more effectively, economically, and faster.

Fifth, as has been mentioned above, the clause in the 2001 Protocol on the circumstances justifying the vacation of parliamentarians' seats did not include those elected through fraudulent, violent or highly undemocratic elections or appointed by

875. *See* B.R. Dinokopila, 'The Pan-African Parliament and African Union Human Rights Actors, Civil Society and National Human Rights Institutions: The Importance of Collaboration', *African Human Rights Law Journal* 13 (2013): 302.

a regime which came to power in a coup d'état and similar situations. The 2014 Protocol covers this lacuna: Article 6(3)(h) stipulates that the seat of a parliamentarian shall become vacant if the holder represents a contracting party which has been suspended from participating in AU activities. Arguably, this provision means that parliamentarians from a Member State which participates in the PAP will not only be denied participation, but their seats will be considered to be untaken for as long as the state in question remains suspended as regards AU activities, a sanction provided for in Article 30 of the Constitutive Act. However, it is rather unclear if parliamentarians will be allowed to speak at meetings, to vote, etc., if the state they represent has been subjected to sanctions imposed by the Assembly pursuant to Article 23(1) of the Constitutive Act for having defaulted in paying budgetary contributions.

Sixth, the 2014 Protocol[876] maintains the Bureau (Article 12) and introduces the office of the Secretary-General (Article 13). The former consists of a President and four Vice Presidents representing the five regions of the continent and is responsible for developing policies to manage and administer the PAP's affairs and property. The latter will be the Head of the Secretariat, the Accounting Officer and will also be responsible for day-to-day activities. Moreover, Article 20 in the 2014 Protocol regulates PAP's relations with other organs. In particular, the Assembly Chairperson will deliver a speech on the state of the AU at the beginning of each PAP session, the AUC and the other organs will present Activity Reports to PAP, and PAP will forward its own Activity Report to them. Finally, the 2014 Protocol does not solve satisfactorily the question of the interpretation of its provisions. While Article 21 thereof provides that it will be interpreted by the ACJHR, the drafters deleted the reference in the corresponding Article 20 of the 2001 Protocol, which stipulates that, pending the establishment of the AU judicial organ, matters of interpretation will be resolved by the Assembly acting by a two-thirds majority. However, if the ACJHR Protocol comes into force before the 2014 Protocol, there will be no organ competent to deliver decisions on interpretation, a matter of considerable concern as important legal issues might be involved.

§4. The African Court of Justice and Human Rights (ACJHR)

118. The process for establishing the AU's judicial organ, the African Court of Justice (ACJ), was explained in some detail in a previous edition of the present monograph.[877] The ACJ Protocol was adopted in July 2003 and entered into force in February 2009. However, in July 2008, the Assembly decided to merge it with the African Court on Human and Peoples' Rights. To that end, it adopted the

876. Note that the aforementioned Art. 19 of the 2001 Protocol on withdrawal from the AEC and its effect on parliamentarians was deleted from the 2014 Protocol.

877. *See* K. Magliveras & G. Naldi, *The African Union* (Alphen aan den Rijn: Kluwer Law International, 2009) paras 177–187.

Protocol on the ACJHR (2008 Protocol),[878] which at the time of writing had only secured eight out of the required fifteen ratifications (in total, thirty-three Member States have signed it). Since the AU has apparently abandoned the project of operationalizing the ACJ, even for the period until the 2008 Protocol comes into force, only the ACJHR will be examined here. The present authors maintain their argument that the merger between the ACJ and the African Human Rights Court was ill-advised and that it would lead to complicated institutional problems.[879] If and when the 2008 Protocol enters into force, the ACJHR will operate on the basis of its provisions as well as of the Statute appended to it.

119. According to Article 2(1) of the Statute, the ACJHR will be 'the main judicial organ of the African Union'.[880] Article 16 thereof stipulates that it will comprise a General Affairs Section, which corresponds to the ACJ jurisdiction,[881] and a Human Rights Section, which corresponds to the jurisdiction of the African Court on Human and Peoples' Rights.[882] The former section will be competent to hear all cases except those expressly reserved for the latter. Either section may constitute chambers. A third section, the 'International Criminal Law Section,' is envisaged in the Malabo Protocol adopted in June 2014 and will be examined later.[883] Each Section will be entitled to refer any case it has received to the Full Court for consideration. Pursuant to Article 20 of the Statute, the ACJHR will hold ordinary sessions, which will be determined on an annual basis, and extraordinary sessions, to be convened at the discretion of the President or at the request of most judges.

120. The ACJHR will have both contentious jurisdiction (Article 28 of the Statute) and advisory jurisdiction (Articles 53–56 of the Statute). The former will comprise all legal disputes relating to: (a) the interpretation and application of the Constitutive Act; (b) the interpretation, application or validity of other OAU/AU Treaties and subsidiary legal instruments adopted within their framework; (c) the interpretation and the application of the African Charter on Human and Peoples' Rights (the Banjul Charter) and its Protocols on the Rights of Women in Africa, on the Rights of Older Persons, on the Rights of Older Persons, on the Rights of Persons with Disabilities in Africa and on the Rights of Citizens to Social Protection and Social Security (the latter three when they enter into force), of the Charter on

---

878. *See* G. Muigai, 'From the African Court on Human Rights and Peoples' Rights to the African Court of Justice and Human Rights' in *The African Regional Human Rights System. 30 Years After the African Charter on Human and Peoples' Rights*, M. Ssenyoujo (ed.) (Leiden: Martinus Nijhoff Publishers, 2012), 265.

879. Magliveras & Naldi, *The African Union*, *supra*, paras 188–191.

880. For further analysis, *see* G. Naldi & K. Magliveras, 'The African Court of Justice and Human Rights: A Judicial Curate's Egg', *International Organizations Law Review* 9 (2012): 383.

881. *See* G. Naldi, 'Aspects of the African Court of Justice and Human Rights' in *International Law and Dispute Settlement: New Problems and Techniques*, D. French, M. Saul, & N.D. White (eds) (Oxford: Hart Publishing, 2010), 321.

882. *See* G. Naldi, 'The Role of the Human Rights Section of the African Court of Justice and Human and Rights' in *Protecting Human Security in Africa*, A. Abass (ed.) (Oxford: Oxford University Press, 2010), 284.

883. Protocol on Amendments to the Protocol on the Statute of the African Court of Justice and Human Rights, signed on 27 Jun. 2014, not yet in force.

the Rights and Welfare of the Child, as well as of any other legal instrument pertaining to human rights, even if it is a non-OAU/AU instrument but provided it has been ratified by the contracting parties concerned; (d) any question of international law; (e) all acts, decisions, regulations and directives adopted by AU organs; (f) all matters specifically stipulated in any other agreement, which has been concluded among contracting parties or concluded with the AU; (g) the existence of any fact which, if established, would constitute a breach of an obligation owed to a contracting party or to the AU; and (h) the nature or extent of the reparation to be made for the breach of an international obligation.

According to Article 29(1) of the Statute, the persons and entities entitled to submit cases on any issue or dispute stipulated in Article 28 fall into three categories. First, the contracting parties to the 2008 Protocol. Second, the Assembly, the PAP and other AU organs (e.g., the Executive Council, the Commission, and the PSC) provided that the Assembly has so authorized them. Third, AU employees, who, in accordance with Regulation 14 of the AU Staff Regulations and Rules,[884] have appealed against a decision rendered in the context of a labour dispute with the AU. The first category could be described as privileged applicants, i.e., they may approach the ACJHR on any dispute falling within the ambit of its general jurisdiction, which could also include human rights violations. However, as far as alleged violations of human rights are specifically concerned, Article 30 of the Statute contains a very broad *locus standi* clause encompassing the following six categories of applicants. First, the contracting parties to the 2008 Protocol. Second, the African Commission on Human and Peoples' Rights.[885] Third, the African Committee of Experts on the Rights and Welfare of the Child. Fourth, the 'African Intergovernmental Organizations' which have been accredited to the AU or to its organs, a term which covers all RECs. In this respect, it should be noted that: (a) the Court of Justice of ECOWAS has stated that it has been assigned responsibility for protecting human rights, including those enshrined in the Banjul Charter,[886] (b) the East African Community (EAC) has contemplated adding jurisdiction on human rights to its Court of Justice[887] but backed down,[888] and (c) the SADC Tribunal's pronouncements on human rights issues largely led to its demise in its original form in

884. AU Doc. Assembly/AU/4(XV); they were adopted in 2010, *see* Assembly, *Decision on the Staff Regulations and Rules*, AU Doc. Assembly/AU/Dec. 305 (XV) (27 Jul. 2010).

885. *See* M. Hansungule, 'African Courts and the African Commission on Human and Peoples' Rights' in *Human Rights in Africa – Legal Perspectives on their Protection and Promotion*, A. Boesl & J. Diescho (eds) (Windhoek: Konrad Adenaueur Stiftung, 2009), 233, 253–255.

886. *See* ECOWAS Community Court of Justice, *Hadijatou Mani Koraou v. Republic of Niger*, Judgment No. ECW/CCJ/JUD/06/08, 27 Oct. 2008, paras 41–42; AHRLR (2008): 182, at: http://www.refworld.org/docid/496b41fa2.html, discussed by H. Duffy, '*Hadijatou Mani Koroua v. Niger:* Slavery Unveiled by the ECOWAS Court', *Human Rights Law Review* 9 (2009): 151–170; and more recently, *Amnesty International Togo et al v. The Togolese Republic*, Judgment No. ECW/CCJ/JUD/09/20, 25 Jun. 2020, para. 24. *See also* Supplementary Protocol A/SP.1/01/05 Amending the Preamble and Arts 1, 2, 9 and 30 of Protocol A/P.1/7/91 Relating to the Community Court of Justice and Art. 4 para. 1 of the English Version of the Said Protocol, which was signed on 19 Jan. 2005 and inserted new Arts 9(4) and 10(d) in the Protocol of the ECOWAS Court of Justice, at: http://www.courtecowas.org/wp-content/uploads/2018/11/Supplementary_Protocol_ASP.10105_ENG.pdf.

887. *See* S. Lawena, 'The Human Rights Jurisdiction of the East African Court of Justice: Challenges and Prospects', *Journal of African and International Law* 6 (2013):119; S. Kingah, *Regional Courts*

2010.[889] Fifth, African National Human Rights Institutions. Sixth, individuals or NGOs accredited to the AU or to its organs but subject to the satisfaction of the conditions envisaged in Article 8 of the 2008 Protocol. In particular, Article 8(3) states that '[a]ny Member State may … make a declaration accepting the competence of the Court to receive cases under Article 30(f) [of the Statute] involving a State which has not made such a declaration'.

It is not clear what the intention of the drafters was. Were the intention to allow the ACJHR to receive petitions from individuals and NGOs contingent upon contracting parties making a separate optional declaration, it should have stipulated that the ACJHR would not receive any petition involving a contracting party which has not made such a declaration. However, if indeed a separate declaration is required, then it might lead to a negation of justice because contracting parties with a record of serious human rights abuses are highly unlikely to accept the ACJHR's jurisdiction in this respect. Finally, it should be emphasized that, under the Statute, a complainant is not required to be the victim of the alleged human rights violation. Thus, the drafters have opted for the Inter-American human rights system, which is based on a *laissez-passer* attitude and, pursuant to Article 44 of the American Convention on Human Rights (ACHR), it allows (almost) anyone to file a petition alleging violations. The justification for such extensive standing has been based on the fact that several ACHR contracting parties face poverty, lack of education, and lack of legal assistance, while human rights defenders are often hindered from pursuing petitions for alleged violations (that much is also true for African states).[890] However, it is not clear whether, once operative, the ACJHR will allow petitions amounting to *actio popularis*, even though there is the precedence of the African Commission on Human and Peoples' Rights that has permitted it when interpreting the Banjul Charter's admissibility requirements.[891]

---

and Human Rights in the Developing World, UNU-CRIS Working Papers W-2013/11, 2013, 7–8, at: http://cris.unu.edu/regional-courts-and-human-rights-developing-world; and L. Chula, 'The East African Court of Justice and Human Rights Jurisdiction: Drawing the Line', *Strathmore Law Review* (June 2018):1.

888. *See* Communiqué of the 16th Summit of EAC Heads of State, Nairobi, Kenya, 20 Feb. 2015, para. 9.
889. Generally, *see* G. Naldi & K. Magliveras, 'The New SADC Tribunal – or the Emasculation of an International Tribunal', *Netherlands Journal of International Law* 63 (2016): 133; and K. Magliveras & G. Naldi, 'When Politics Prevail Over the Rule of Law: The Demise of the SADC Tribunal', *International Human Rights Law Review* 10 (2021): 124.
890. *See* F. Viljoen, 'Admissibility under the African Charter' in *The African Charter on Human and Peoples' Rights: The System in Practice, 1986–2000*, M.D. Evans & R. Murray (eds) (Cambridge: Cambridge University Press, 2002), 61, 75. *See also Contribution of the International Federation for Human Rights (FIDH) and the World Organisation Against Torture (OMCT) before the African Commission on Human and Peoples' Rights*, Fifty-Third Ordinary Session, Banjul, Gambia, 9–23 Apr. 2013, under agenda item 9: 'Situation of human rights defenders', 13 Apr. 2013.
891. *See*, *inter alia*, African Commission on Human and Peoples' Rights, *Article 19 v. Eritrea*, Communication No. 275/2003, *22nd Activity Report 2006–2007*, annex II, para. 65; AHRLR (2007): 73; and *The Social and Economic Rights Action Center and the Center for Economic and Social Rights v. Nigeria*, Communication No. 155/96, *15th Activity Report 2001–2002*, para. 49; AHRLR(2001): 60.

121. As far as the incidental jurisdiction is concerned, the Statute covers provisional (interim) measures, intervention, and reparations but does not cover preliminary objections and friendly settlement. Regarding provisional measures, Article 35(1) of the Statute authorizes the ACJHR to indicate, *proprio motu* or at the request of a litigant party, any measures necessary to preserve the respective rights of litigant parties. Although it breaks away from the corresponding provisions governing other international courts (it does not require the existence of extreme gravity and urgency and/or the need to avoid irreparable harm as preconditions to ordering provisional measures), its brief content leaves many questions unanswered, which presumably will be addressed in the ACJHR Rules of Procedure. Suffice to briefly mention the following four questions. First, may a request for provisional measures be submitted to the ACJHR at the same time as the main proceedings are instituted? Second, should the ACJHR satisfy itself that it has jurisdiction, *prima facie* or otherwise, before ordering provisional measures? Third, which will be the consequences when another competent organ (principally the African Commission on Human and Peoples' Rights) has already adopted interim measures in the context of the same dispute? Fourth, will the orders prescribing provisional measures be legally binding?[892] The latter is a perennial question for international courts and tribunals. It can only be hoped that the ACJHR will follow the trend of, *inter alia*, the ICJ, the Inter-American Court of Human Rights, and the European Court of Human Rights, which have established that such orders enjoy binding effect and litigant parties must obey them and act according to their stipulations.[893]

Article 49(1) of the Statute allows any Member State or any AU organ to petition the ACJHR to intervene, provided that it has a legal interest in the outcome of the case and could be affected by the judgment to be given. There is no guidance in the Statute as to the precise content of the term 'legal interest' and as to the required degree of interest. The ACJHR might be influenced by the practice of other international courts, such as the ICJ, which has applied a strict policy.[894] The fact that Article 49 refers to 'Member States,' if read in conjunction with Article 1 of the Statute, would suggest that the whole AU membership is entitled to request intervention, irrespective of whether they are contracting parties to the 2008 Protocol. Moreover, all AU organs have the opportunity to intervene and can do so without the Assembly's prior authorization. It is commendable that Article 49(2) stipulates that the interpretation to be given by the ACJHR will be binding upon the Member State/s or the AU organ/s which were allowed to intervene. This will potentially prevent speculative intervention, especially in politicized interstate litigation. Finally,

---

892. Generally, *see* G. Naldi, 'Interim Measures of Protection in the African System for the Protection of Human and Peoples' Rights', *African Human Rights Law Journal* 2 (2002): 1.

893. Generally, *see* E. Sánchez Madrigal & G. Zyberi, *The Function and Legal Status of Interim Measures Indicated by Various Human Rights Bodies and the International Court of Justice*, Norwegian Centre for Human Rights, Occasional Paper Series No. 15, 2022.

894. *See* Art. 81(2)(a) of the ICJ Rules of Procedure requiring the intervening state to indicate the interest of a legal nature that will be affected. In *Case Concerning Sovereignty over Pulau Litigan and Pulau Sipadan (Indonesia/Malaysia),* Application by Philippines to Intervene, Judgment of 23 Oct. 2001, *I.C.J. Reports 2001*, p. 575, the ICJ explained the meaning of 'interest of a legal nature'. *See further*, ICJ, *Obligations concerning Negotiations relating to Cessation of the Nuclear Arms Race and to Nuclear Disarmament* (*Marshall Islands v. United Kingdom*), Judgment of 5 Oct. 2016, *I.C.J. Reports* 2016, p. 833.

as regards intervention in cases concerning the interpretation of treaties, the Statute distinguishes between the interpretation of the Constitutive Act (Article 50) and the interpretation of 'other treaties' (Article 51). According to Article 50(3), the decisions concerning the interpretation and application of the Constitutive Act shall be binding on all Member States and AU organs, notwithstanding that not all of them might have intervened by taking advantage of the opportunity offered under Article 50(2). In contradistinction, the interpretation to be given in another treaty shall bind only those contracting parties and/or AU organs which opted to exercise their right to intervene.

122. The issue of reparations is dealt with in Article 28 (h) of the Statute. It allows the ACJHR, acting at the request of a litigant party, to determine the nature and the extent of the reparations to be made or the 'fair compensation' to be paid by the losing party for breaching its obligations. Moreover, Article 45, which deals specifically with situations where the ACJHR has established a violation of human rights by the respondent state, authorizes it to order 'any appropriate measures' to remedy the situation, including granting fair compensation. Arguably, the wording of this provision leads to the conclusion that the ACJHR has the discretion to make an award on its own motion, provided that a human rights violation has been established. Moreover, the ACJHR has a broad mandate to order suitable remedies, of which fair compensation is only one of the options. Thus, it could order consequential measures requiring parties to adopt positive measures to rectify the situation and avoid the infraction's repetition in the future. It is unclear whether the Statute envisages restitution in kind as a remedy. However, it could be covered by the concept of 'reparations' and be deemed to form part of the general structure of Article 45. Equally, what constitutes 'fair compensation' will have to be determined by the ACJHR presumably on a case-to-case basis. Suffice to mention that the African Commission on Human and Peoples' Rights has in the past accepted the principle of compensatory damages as a form of indemnity.[895] Finally, there exists the considerable practice of the Inter-American Court of Human Rights on reparations with ample examples of the nature and the forms that they may take.[896]

123. Regarding the ACJHR's incidental jurisdiction, the drafters have not covered the issues of preliminary objections and amicable or friendly settlement.

---

895. *See, inter alia*, African Commission on Human and Peoples' Rights, *Malawi African Association, Amnesty International, Ms Sarr Diop, Union Interafricaine des Droits de l'Homme and RADDHO, Collectif des Veuves et Ayant-droit, and Association Mauritanienne des Droits de l'Homme v. Mauritania*, Communication Nos 54/91, 61/91, 98/93, 164/97-196/97, and 210/98, Decision of 11 May 2000, *13th Activity Report 1999–2000*, OAU Doc. AHG/222 (XXXVI), p. 138; *AHRLR* (2000): 149. *See also* G. Naldi, 'Reparations in the Practice of the African Commission on Human and Peoples' Rights', *Leiden Journal of International Law* 14 (2001): 681; Redress, *Reaching for Justice: The Right to Reparation in the African Human Rights System*, October 2013, at: https://redress.org/publication/reaching-for-justice-the-right-to-reparation-in-the-african-human-rights-system/.

896. Generally, *see* Human Rights Clinic at the University of Texas School of Law, *Collective and Moral Reparations in the Inter-American Court of Human Rights*, November 2009, at: https://law.utexas.edu/wp-content/uploads/sites/11/2015/04/2009-HRC-Cambodia-CollectiveReparations.pdf; D.O. Contreras-Garduno, *Collective Reparations: Tensions and Dilemmas between Collective Reparations with the Individual Right to Receive Reparations* (Intersentia, 2018) 121.

Regarding the former, based on the established practice of international litigation, it cannot be ruled out that the ACJHR's jurisdiction will not be challenged. Therefore, it is rather curious that the ability to determine its own jurisdiction (the so-called principle of *Kompetenz-Kompetenz/compétence de la compétence*) has not been envisaged in the Statute. However, considering that 'the inherent power of a tribunal to interpret the text establishing its jurisdiction' has long been recognized as a principle of international law,[897] the ACJHR should be in the position to assert this implied capacity if and when necessary. Regarding the latter omission, it is rather problematic that the Statute does not envisage amicable or friendly settlements, especially as concerns the competence of the Human Rights Section and given that it is envisaged in the African Court on Human and Peoples' Rights. If, once operative, the ACJHR wanted to adopt procedures for friendly settlement, presumably it will do so by including them in the Rules of Procedure. However, it is submitted that the Rules should not be used as a vehicle for adding processes that are not already envisaged in the 2008 Protocol.

124. Article 53(1) of the Statute stipulates that the ACJHR has the competence to issue advisory opinions. This suggests that they will be given by the Full Court and not by the respective Section. Advisory opinions may be issued (i.e., the ACJHR has only a discretion) on any legal question when requested by the Assembly, PAP, the Executive Council, PSC, ECOSOCC, the Financial Institutions or any other AU organ so authorized by the Assembly (presumably this means the AUC and the Specialized (Technical) Committees). It follows that contracting parties will be barred from requesting advisory opinions. Although this is also the case with the judicial organs of other international organizations having a primarily political nature, including the ICJ, it is regrettable that the AU Member States (and not just those which are contracting parties to the 2008 Protocol) will be unable to do so. There is no compelling reason why organs such as ECOSOCC are permitted to seek advisory opinions but not Member States. Moreover, the decision of the contracting parties to the European Convention on Human Rights (ECHR) to allow their highest courts and tribunals to request the European Court of Human Rights to give advisory opinions on questions of principle relating to the interpretation or application of ECHR protected rights and freedoms is an interesting development to be considered by African states.[898] While the advisory opinions of transnational courts (e.g., the ICJ and the Inter-American Court of Human Rights) are non-binding, over time, they have been regarded as influential judicial pronouncements. Thus, if the ACJHR opinions were to be followed consistently by AU organs, they could lead to an important body of legal statements to be applied across the continent and would contribute to the further consolidation of AU law and the evolution of the AU legal system. Regarding the advisory jurisdiction's procedural aspects, it follows from

897. *See*, *inter alia*, ICJ, *Norwegian Loans Case (France v. Norway)*, Judgment of 6 Jul. 1957, Separate Opinion of Judge Lauterpacht, *I.C.J. Reports 1957*, pp. 9, 34.

898. *See* Protocol No. 16 to the Convention on the Protection of Human Rights and Fundamental Freedoms, adopted on 2 October 2013, entered into force on 1 August 2018, Council of Europe Treaty Series No. 214; and European Court of Human Rights, *Guidelines on the implementation of the advisory-opinion procedure introduced by Protocol No. 16 to the Convention*, approved on 18 September 2017 and updated on 18 October 2021.

Articles 55 and 56 of the Statute that the ACJHR will be guided by the procedure applicable in contentious cases (including delivering separate or dissenting opinions).

In exercising its various heads of jurisdiction, the law to be applied by the ACJHR is laid down (presumably in descending order) in Article 31(1) of the Statute as follows:

a. The Constitutive Act.
b. International treaties, whether of general or particular content, which have been ratified by litigant parties.
c. International custom, as evidence of a general practice accepted as law.
d. General principles of law recognized either universally or by African states.
e. Judicial decisions, academic writings and decisions issued by AU organs but only as subsidiary means for the determination of the rules of law in a specific case, and
f. Any other law relevant to the case under consideration.

Moreover, under Article 31(2), the ACJHR will have the power to decide a case *ex aequo et bono* should the litigant parties so agree.

125. Other procedural issues of note include the following. Pursuant to Article 36 of the Statute, contracting parties will be represented by agents, with the assistance of counsel, if necessary, those AU organs with *locus standi* before the ACJHR will be represented by the AUC Chairperson, while the African Commission on Human and Peoples' Rights, other African IGOs and the Member States' national human rights institutions will be represented by a person of their choice. The same applies to individuals and NGOs. Regrettably, the Statute does not provide for free legal representation in the interests of justice, a significant oversight especially in cases involving human rights violations and given that the African Court on Human and Peoples' Rights does envisage legal aid. This omission might be rectified by inserting a provision to that effect in the Rules of Procedure. All persons appearing before the ACJHR are guaranteed the protection necessary for properly discharging their functions and duties, a welcome development since arbitrary detention, ill-treatment, and disappearances for defying national authorities are all too common in parts of Africa.[899] However, this does not address how individuals (e.g., complainants and witnesses) will be protected from reprisals in the territory of litigant parties. In such situations, the ACJHR could and should use creatively its competence to indicate provisional measures under the aforementioned Article 35 of the Statute. Pursuant to Article 41 of the Statute, if a litigant party fails to appear or does not defend the case against it, the ACJHR is authorized to consider the case and give judgment. However, it will first satisfy itself that it has jurisdiction, then that the

899. Generally, *see* UNGA, Resolution 68/181, *Promotion of the Declaration on the Right and Responsibility of Individuals, Groups and Organs of Society to Promote and Protect Universally Recognized Human Rights and Fundamental Freedoms: protecting women human rights defenders*, 18 December 2013.

claim is well founded in fact and in law, and, finally, that due notice was given to the defaulting party. Presumably because the non-appearing party is likely to prejudice its case, it is offered ninety days from the date of notification of the default judgment to lodge an objection against it.

The provisions concerning judgments in contentious cases are laid down in Articles 42 et seq. of the Statute. Judgments will be taken by a majority, will be reasoned, will be read in open court (but no provision is made as regards their publication), while separate and dissenting opinions may be attached. Compared to other international courts, Article 43(1) innovates in that it requires the ACJHR to render its judgment within ninety days once deliberations have been completed. Pursuant to Article 46(2), judgments rendered by a section or by the Full Court shall be final. This should be interpreted as not allowing appeals. Although appealing against a judgment given by the Full Court might be inappropriate (taking into account the same position followed by other international courts as well), challenging a Section's judgment before the Full Court should perhaps be contemplated if and when the ACJHR becomes operative.

According to Article 47 of the Statute, litigant parties may ask the ACJHR to interpret the meaning and scope of a judgment if a dispute over it has arisen. No deadline is envisaged for this procedure. Article 48 authorizes the ACJHR to review its judgments in the light of new facts subject to a number of conditions. These include that the application shall be lodged no later than six months after the new facts' discovery, which if known at the time might have influenced the ACJHR's determination, but not later than ten years from the day the judgment was delivered, and that the party claiming revision has already complied with it. Regarding compliance, Article 46(3) stipulates that litigant parties are obliged to comply with the judgment promptly and guarantee its execution. However, whether parties will actually comply or not is a matter that cannot be influenced by the ACJHR: like other international judicial organs, it has no power to enforce its judgments. Should a party fail to comply, Article 46(4) directs the ACJHR to refer it to the Assembly for a decision.[900] But how will non-compliance be monitored? Presumably, this is another matter to be addressed in the Rules of Procedure. It will be submitted that the best means will be for the losing party/ies to notify the ACJHR and/or the AUC of the measures taken to give effect to judgments. Under Article 47(6), failure to comply with a judgment empowers (but does not compel) the Assembly to impose sanctions pursuant to the aforementioned Article 23(2) of the Constitutive Act.

126. Article 3(1) of the Statute stipulates that the ACJHR will be composed of sixteen judges, to be divided equally between the General Affairs Section and the Human Rights Section. However, this choice of number is problematic. For example, in those judicial organs of international organizations where the number of judges is not equal to the number of Member States, their number is invariably

900. Compare Art. 94(2) of the UN Charter: If a litigant party fails to perform the obligations emanating from an ICJ judgment, the other party may bring it to the attention of the UNSC, which may, if it deems necessary, make recommendations or decide upon measures to be taken to give effect to the judgment.

odd so as to avoid ties. Moreover, given that the entry into force of the 2008 Protocol necessitates fifteen ratifications, it follows that the number of judges will exceed the number of contracting parties. This situation will remain so until there is a sixteenth ratification of the 2008 Protocol. However, since Article 3(2) of the Statute prohibits two judges from being nationals of the same state, it is unclear from which contracting party the sixteenth judge will be appointed. However, when this situation arises, the AU would probably delay its operationalization until the sixteenth ratification has been secured.

Article 7(1)(2) of the Statute envisages a two-stage procedure for confirming judges: first election by the Executive Council in a secret ballot and then appointment by the Assembly. It is neither clear what this two-stage procedure serves nor which is the legal basis. Certainly, it is not to be found in the Constitutive Act, whose Article 9(1)(h) envisages the appointment of judges as a function reserved for the Assembly, while the judges of the African Court on Human and Peoples' Rights are elected by the Assembly. Furthermore, Article 13(1) of the Constitutive Act describes the Executive Council's functions as coordinating and taking decisions in areas of common interest to Member States, ranging from foreign trade to immigration to science and to technology. However, it could be counterargued that the Assembly may delegate the appointment of judges to the Executive Council pursuant to Article 9(2) of the Constitutive Act. But in that case, it would not make sense for the Executive Council to elect as well as appoint them. Finally, the Statute does not stipulate whether the Assembly is obliged to accept the election (thus making their appointment a rubber-stamp exercise) or whether it could (wholly or partly) challenge it and, in the latter case, how the procedure will proceed. Again, the ACJHR Rules of Procedure might determine the precise process for the confirmation of judges.

Finally, according to Article 7 of the Statute, the election of judges will require a two-thirds majority of all AU Member States with voting rights. Therefore, until and unless the whole membership has ratified the 2008 Protocol, non-contracting parties will vote in a matter which, arguably, is not of direct concern to them. Moreover, they could potentially use their vote to support friendly countries or in exchange of favours and benefits given to them by those contracting parties promoting their nationals to be elected to the ACJHR. Pursuant to Article 10(3), the same procedure will apply in case of vacancies resulting from the death, resignation or judges' removal from office. Finally, Article 7(4) stipulates that Africa's regions and its principal juridical traditions (presumably, the civil, the Roman-Dutch, the common law, and the Islamic legal systems) must be represented on the ACJHR.

127. In 2010, the AU started discussing adding a third Section to the ACJHR, the 'International Criminal Law Section' (ICL Section), when the Assembly requested a feasibility study to empower the African Court on Human and Peoples' Rights to try international crimes.[901] The determining factors for African states to seek a localized solution to the question of international criminal justice were, on

901. *See* Assembly, *Decision on the Abuse of the Principle of Universal Jurisdiction*, AU Doc. Assembly/AU/Dec. 292 (XV), para. 5 (27 Sep. 2010).

the one hand, Africa's disenchantment with the ICC[902] and, on the other hand, the controversy over the ICC arrest warrants issued at the time against African dignitaries, including the former President Al Bashir of Sudan and the late Colonel Gaddafi.[903] One could brush away this attempt on two grounds. First, despite Article 4(h) of the Constitutive Act, the AU lacks a clear and developed agenda on international criminal justice. Second, the existence of the ICC has made such moves rather superfluous because the largest part of the international community (including the majority of African states) has decided that the ICC should be the principal multilateral judicial entity to deal with war crimes, crimes against humanity, aggression, etc. In other words, there is a clear choice of most states to task the ICC with fighting impunity. Although any regional international organization is entitled to have its own criminal justice tribunal (provided that it has been expressly granted the necessary powers to create it), it should have very good reasons to do so, and it must meet the standards set by the ICC. And as has been argued, it could be feasible to have 'ICC regional chambers', which could potentially replace the need for regional criminal tribunals.[904]

128. In May 2012, a Draft Protocol on Amendments to the Protocol on the Statute of the ACJHR was produced for consideration by the Assembly;[905] it proposed adding the ICL Section and granting to the ACJHR 'original and appellate jurisdiction' to hear cases referred by, *inter alia*, RECs and other international organizations. The Draft Protocol did not address the following legal technicality. As the 2008 Protocol setting up the ACJHR had not yet entered into force, amendments to it and to the ACJHR Statute could not be contemplated before it became operational. And this is because Article 58(2) of the Statute stipulates that proposed amendments will be adopted by the Assembly only '*after* the Court has given its opinion on it' (emphasis added). Arguably, this is another manifestation of the rather careless approach towards the AU's judicial organ. After further elaboration,[906] the Protocol was approved by the Assembly in June 2014 (the 'Malabo Protocol').[907]

---

902. *See* discussion above and K. Magliveras & G. Naldi, 'The International Criminal Court's Involvement with Africa: Evaluation of a Fractious Relationship', *Nordic Journal of International Law* 82 (2013): 417.
903. *See* K. Magliveras & G. Naldi, 'The International Criminal Court and the African Union: A Problematical Relationship' in *The International Criminal Court and Africa*, C. Jelloh & I. Bantekas (eds) (OUP, 2017), 111.
904. *See* K. Magliveras, 'The Withdrawal of African States from the ICC: Good, Bad or Irrelevant?', *Netherlands International Law Review* 66 (2019): 419.
905. *See* Meeting of Government Experts and Ministers of Justice/Attorneys General on Legal Matters, 7–11 and 14–15 May 2012, Addis Ababa, Ethiopia, *Draft Protocol on Amendments to the Protocol on the Statute of the African Court of Justice and Human Rights*, AU Doc. Exp/Min/IV/Rev. 7 (15 May 2012).
906. *See* Assembly, *Decision on the Progress Report of the Commission on the Implementation of the Decisions on the International Criminal Court*, AU Doc. Assembly/AU/Dec. 493 (XXII), para. 13 (31 Jan. 2014).
907. *See* Assembly, *Decision on the Draft Legal Instruments*, AU Doc. Assembly/AU/Dec. 529 (XXIII) (27 Jun. 2014). According to information on the AU's website, the Protocol has been signed by fifteen Member States but has not received any ratifications. For analysis, *see* G. Naldi & K. Magliveras, 'The African Union's International Criminal Court: An Appraisal', *African Yearbook of*

129. The ICL Section is mirrored on the ICC. It will be composed of a Pre-Trial Chamber, a Trial Chamber and an Appellate, or Appeals, Chamber. A novelty is the establishment of a Defence Office to ensure the rights of suspects, the accused and any other person entitled to legal assistance.[908] The Assembly is authorized to establish, within the ACJHR's jurisdiction, a Trust Fund to provide legal aid and assistance to the victims of crimes or human rights violations and their families.[909] The Court may order any kind of property collected through fines or forfeiture to be transferred to the Trust Fund.[910] Decisions of the Pre-Trial Chamber or the Trial Chamber may be appealed to the Appellate Chamber by the Prosecutor or by the accused. Cases will be brought by the Prosecutor, who may initiate investigations *proprio motu*, following a referral by a contracting party, by the Assembly or by the PSC.[911] It is not clear whether crimes allegedly committed in the territory of non-contracting parties might be referred to the ICL Section. Regarding jurisdictional competence, contracting parties automatically accept the ICL Section's jurisdiction upon ratification of the Malabo Protocol, while non-contracting parties may do so on an *ad hoc* basis by means of a declaration. The jurisdiction *ratione materiae* of the ICL Section is far broader than that of the ICC, perhaps overly ambitious. In addition to the core international crimes of aggression,[912] genocide, crimes against humanity and war crimes, its jurisdiction also includes the crime of unconstitutional change of government, mercenarism, piracy, terrorism, corruption, money laundering, drug trafficking, trafficking in persons and the illicit exploitation of natural resources, among others.[913] Even though addressing this criminal behaviour is a reflection of African concerns and priorities, not all of them are generally categorized as international crimes. Thus, while coups d'état constitute a violation of Article 4(p) of the Constitutive Act, it is rather premature to claim that they are contrary to general international law, provided that they do not negate directly the principle of self-determination.[914] Moreover, although the aforementioned Convention on Mercenarism in Africa condemns mercenarism as an international crime, it is unclear whether it is also prohibited under customary international law, notwithstanding the existence of the International Convention against the Recruitment, Use,

---

International Law 21 (2015): 297; G. Werle & M. Vormbaum (eds), *The African Criminal Court – A Commentary on the Malabo Protocol* (The Hague: T.M.C. Asser Press, 2016).

908. *See* Arts 19*bis*, 221A, 22B and 22C of the ACJHR Statute, as amended by the Malabo Protocol.
909. Compare the Trust Fund for Victims (TFV) provided for in Art. 79 of the ICC Rome Statute. It became operative in 2007.
910. *See* Art. 46M of the ACJHR Statute, as amended by the Malabo Protocol.
911. *Ibid.*, respectively, Arts 34A(1), 46G, and 29)1)(b).
912. *Ibid.*, Art. 28M defines the crime of aggression.
913. *Ibid.*, Art. 28A.
914. In *Sir Dawda K. Jawara v. Gambia*, Communication Nos 147/95 and 149/96, 13th *Activity Report 1999–2000*, para. 73; AHRLR (2000) 107, the African Commission on Human and Peoples' Rights relied on the internal dimension of self-determination to uphold democratic values and to condemn military coups. It held that the military coup that overthrew Gambia's democratic system 'was a grave violation of the right of the Gambian people to freely choose their government as entrenched in Art. 20(1) [of the Banjul Charter]'.

Financing, and Training of Mercenaries.[915] The ever increased use of private military/security companies and contractors around the world, including Africa, complicates the situation.[916]

Finally, several OAU/AU treaties require that contracting parties pass legislation designating certain acts and practices as criminal offences, which, arguably, do not yet amount to international crimes.[917] The question could, therefore, be legitimately posed whether they amount to the 'most serious crimes of concern to the international community', as understood, for example, in Article 5(1) of the Rome Statute. As regards jurisdiction *ratione personae*, the ICL Section will be able to prosecute natural persons but also legal persons, which includes corporations but not states.[918] The inclusion of corporate legal liability is welcome, especially in light of the sometimes questionable practices pursued by multinational corporations. Notwithstanding the attempts to impose human rights standards on transnational corporations,[919] there are problems given the limited international legal personality recognized to multinational companies.[920] The principle of complementarity, which constitutes the bedrock of the ICC, also applies to the ICL Section.[921] Therefore, it will only have competence when and if the domestic courts of contracting parties are unwilling or unable to prosecute alleged perpetrators.

130. The Malabo Protocol does not contain a savings clause, and the important question of the relationship between the ACJHR and the ICC is not addressed. In effect, African contracting parties to both the Rome Statute and the ACJHR Statute, as amended by the Malabo Protocol, may be faced with the awkward question of conflicting obligations. In line with customary law over incompatibility between

915. Adopted pursuant to UNGA Resolution 44/34 of 4 December 1989, entered into force on 20 October 2001, 2163 *UNTS* 75. The fact that presently the UN Convention has received only thirty-seven ratifications is indicative of the opinion of most states on this matter.
916. *See* 'Mercenaries and private military security: Africa's thin grey line', *ISS Today*, 1 December 2021; N. El Mquirmi, 'Private Military and Security Companies: A New Form of Mercenarism?', *Policy Center for the New South*, 14 February 2022, at: https://www.policycenter.ma/.
917. For example, Art. 9(2) of the OAU Convention on the Ban of the Import of Hazardous Wastes into Africa and on the Control of their Transboundary Movements within Africa (1991), and Art. 5(1) of the AU Convention on Preventing and Combating Corruption (2003).
918. Article 46C of the ACJHR Statute, as amended by the Malabo Protocol.
919. Generally, *see* UN Sub-Commission on the Promotion and Protection of Human Rights, *Norms on the Responsibilities of Transnational Corporations and Other Business Enterprises with Regard to Human Rights*, UN Doc. E/CN.4/Sub.2/2003/12/Rev.2 (2003; *see* D. Weissbrodt & M. Kruger, 'Norms on the Responsibilities of Transnational Corporations and Other Business Enterprises with Regard to Human Rights', *American Journal International Law* 97 (2003): 901; and D. Kinley & R. Chambers, 'The UN Human Rights Norms for Corporations: The Private Implications of Public International Law', *Human Rights Law Review* 6 (2006): 452. *See further*, the Guiding Principles on Business and Human Rights, UN Doc. A/HRC/17/31. They were endorsed by Human Rights Council Resolution 17/4 of 16 June 2011, which also established the Working Group on the issue of human rights and transnational corporations and other business enterprises. Additionally, *see* the Business and Human Rights (BHR) Africa Project, which started in January 2022 as a project of the Office of the UN High Commissioner for Human Rights and is financed by the Deutsche Gesellschaft für Internationale Zusammenarbeit (GIZ) on behalf of the German government.
920. *See* P. Malanczuk, *Akehurst's Modern Introduction to International Law* 7th rev. ed. (Routledge, London, 1997), 100–103.
921. *See* Art. 46H of the ACJHR Statute, as amended by the Malabo Protocol.

successive treaties on the same subject matter, as reflected in Article 30(3) of the Vienna Convention on the Law of Treaties (1969), the ACJHR Statute, when it enters into force, would be deemed to prevail over the Rome Statute. However, if the ICC were to rule that it has jurisdiction over an African situation, as it was conferred by a UNSC resolution in accordance with Article 13(b) of the Rome Statute,[922] and a clash arose between an African state's obligations under the ACJHR Statute and a suitable ICC decision, the latter would probably prevail. This argument flows from the wording of Article 103 of the UN Charter.

131. It is a worrisome development that, even though the 2003 Protocol setting up the African Court of Justice, the judicial entity envisaged in the Constitutive Act, entered into force in February 2009 and Member States continue to ratify it (e.g., Angola in February 2020), it has never been operationalized. On account of the convoluted manner by which this affair has been handled and the Member States' unwillingness to ratify the 2008 Protocol, the AU does not presently have a functionable judicial organ. In the meantime, many complicated legal issues remain unanswered. Moreover, the provision of Article 26 of the Constitutive Act has never been applied. It stipulates that, pending the establishment of the African Court of Justice (presumably this provision should now be read 'pending the establishment of the ACJHR'), matters of interpretation arising from the Constitutive Act's application or implementation will be submitted to the Assembly, which shall decide by a two-thirds majority. The Assembly has never assumed this *quasi*-judicial role.

Finally, in 2013, the Twentieth Ordinary Assembly Session took onboard a proposal by the then Tunisian President Marzouki to establish an International Constitutional Court as 'an advisory and jurisdictional body responsible for ensuring the respect and promotion of democratic principles, human rights and the rule of law', ultimately leading to the abolition of dictatorships. The Assembly requested that AUCIL examine the proposal and submit recommendations to its Twenty-Second Ordinary Session in January 2014.[923] Judging from the proposal, which was not apparently never placed on the Assembly's agenda, one could not see any major differences from the scope and jurisdiction of the African Human Rights Commission and the African Human Rights Court working in unison with the PSC.[924]

922. *See* ICC, Pre-Trial Chamber I, *Prosecutor* v. *Omar Hassan Ahmad Al Bashir,* Decision Pursuant to Art. 87(7) of the Rome Statute on the Failure of the Republic of Malawi to Comply with the Cooperation Requests Issued by the Court with respect to the Arrest and Surrender of Omar Hassan Ahmad Al Bashir, Corrigendum, ICC-02/05-01/09, 13 Dec. 2011, para. 36, reproduced in I.L.M. 51 (2012): 393.

923. *See* Assembly, *Decision on the Establishment of an 'International Constitutional Court'*, AU Doc. Assembly/AU/Dec. 458 (XX) (28 Jan. 2013). Marzouki made the same proposal in a speech delivered in the UN General Assembly on 27 Sep. 2012.

924. *See further*, UK House of Commons, International Courts: Constitutional and Administrative Law: Written question 12816, tabled on 21 Oct. 2015, answered on 29 Oct. 2015, at: http://www.parliament.uk/business/publications/written-questions-answers-statements/written-question/Commons/2015-10-21/12816/.

§5. The Commission (AUC)

132. A Commission is set up under Article 20 of the Constitutive Act. Its structure, functions and regulations were left to be determined by the Assembly. Effectively, it is the AU's Secretariat catering for its day-to-day activities.[925] It is composed of the Chairperson, a Deputy Chairperson, and six Commissioners, assisted by the necessary staff. Although the number of Commissioners is not laid down in the Constitutive Act, until 2018 there had been the following eight: The Commissioner for Political Affairs; the Commissioner for Social Affairs; the Commissioner for Trade and Industry; the Commissioner for Economic Affairs; the Commissioner for Peace and Security; the Commissioner for Infrastructure and Energy; the Commissioner for Human Resources, Science, and Technology; and the Commissioner for Rural Economy and Agriculture. But during the Eleventh Extraordinary Assembly Session (2018), it was decided that, from 2021, their number would be reduced to six and that they would be both elected and appointed by the Executive Council (previously appointed by the Assembly), as follows: the Commissioner for Agriculture, Rural Development, Blue Economy and Sustainable Environment; the Commissioner for Economic Development, Trade, Industry and Minerals; the Commissioner for Education, Science, Technology and Innovation; the Commissioner for Infrastructure and Energy; the Commissioner for Political Affairs, Peace and Security; and the Commissioner for Health, Humanitarian Affairs and Social Development.[926] It is submitted that PAP should have a role in the selection process of Commissioners, of the AUC Chairperson and of the Deputy Chairperson, given that it is meant to be the organ representing the African people. Doing so will give more credence to the selection process and increase the AUC's legitimacy. The role of Commissioners is to offer their support to the Chairperson and are responsible for the implementation of the decisions, policies and programmes that relate to their portfolio. Commissioners are responsible for the eight portfolios of which the AUC is made up: Peace and Security; Political Affairs; Trade and Industry; Infrastructure and Energy; Social Affairs; Rural Economy and Agriculture; Human Resources, Science and Technology; and Economic Affairs. Thus, Article 3 of the AUC Statutes, which the Assembly approved in July 2002, lays down more than thirty areas of activities. Suffice to mention the following functions: the implementation and the monitoring of the decisions taken by other organs; the elaboration of common African positions on a variety of issues; and acting as the custodian of the Constitutive Act, its protocols and the treaties and legal instruments adopted under OAU/AU auspices.[927] In October 2020, the Executive Council

---

925. *See* Secretary-General, *Report of the Secretary-General on the Implementation of the Sirte Decision on the African Union*, OAU Doc. CM/2210 (LXXIV), para. 27 at p. 11 (2001).

926. Assembly, *Decision on the Institutional Reform*, AU Doc. Ext/Assembly/AU/Dec. 1 (XI), para. 3 (18 Non. 2018). For the current Commissioners and the content of their portfolios, *see* African Union Commission & New Zealand Ministry of Foreign Affairs and Trade, *African Union Handbook 2022*, 102 et seq. For the names and portfolios of previous Commissioners, *see* Magliveras & Naldi, The *African Union*, Second Edition, *supra*, 162–163. Their appointment must conform to the AU rules in respect to regional and gender balance.

927. *See Statutes of the Commission of the African Union*, AU Doc. ASS/AU/2(I)-d (2002), reproduced in RADIC 13 (2005): 74.

provisionally adopted amendments to the Statute to align it with the AU's institutional reform,[928] which were ratified by the Assembly in February 2021.[929]

133. On 16 September 2003, Alpha Oumar Konare, former President of Mali, was elected as the first AUC Chairperson. The Tenth Ordinary Assembly Session (Addis Ababa, 31 January–2 February 2008) elected, by a two-thirds majority, his successor Jean Ping, the Vice Prime Minister and Minister of Foreign Affairs of Gabon. The same Session elected Erastus Mwenda, a citizen of Kenya and Secretary-General of COMESA, as Deputy Chairperson to replace Patrick Mazimhak from Rwanda.[930] On 16 July 2012, Dr Nkosazana Dlamini-Zuma, a South African minister of state and ex-wife of the South African President Jacob Zuma, was elected as Chairperson, marking the first time that a female person was chosen to hold a post of such significance in the continent.[931] Unlike previous occasions where the decision was a rather rubber-stamp procedure, this was a most contested process: Dlamini-Zuma secured her election against the incumbent Chairperson Jean Ping after three voting rounds and following a deadlocked vote in January 2012.[932] Some commentators interpreted this event as showing that finally the AU started functioning as a proper intergovernmental organization. However, it might show that Member States cast votes according to predetermined patterns (e.g., the Anglophone states voting in favour of their 'own' candidate and against the candidate preferred by the Francophone states) and neglect which are the AU's best interests. The Twenty-Seventh Ordinary Assembly Session (Kigali, Rwanda, July 2016) ought to have elected the new Chairperson (Dlamini-Zuma did not include herself in the nomination process because she wanted to return to South African politics)[933] but proved to be another thriller as none of the three contenders for the position obtained the required two-thirds majority, after seven rounds of voting. As a result, the Assembly decided to suspend the election and extend the term of office of Commissioners until new elections were held in January 2017, and reopened the nomination process.[934] Five contenders emerged, all experienced in foreign affairs and with a fair representation of women: Pelonomi Venson-Moitoi (Foreign Minister of Botswana), Moussa Faki Mahamat (Foreign Minister of Chad), Agapito Mba Mokuy (Foreign Minister of Equatorial Guinea), Amina Mohamed (Foreign Minister of Kenya), and Bathily Abdoulaye from Senegal (at the time UN special envoy

928. Executive Council, *Decision on the Draft Rules of Procedures of the Assembly, Executive Council, Permanent Representatives' Committee and Statute of the Commission*, AU Doc. EX.CL/Dec. 1099 (XXXVII) (14 Oct. 2020).

929. Assembly, *Decision on the Draft Rules of Procedures of the Assembly, and Statute of the Commission*, AU Doc. Assembly/AU/Dec. 806 (XXXIV) (7 Feb. 2021).

930. Assembly, *Decision on Elections of Chairperson and Deputy Chairperson*, AU Doc. Assembly/AU/Dec. 189 (X), and AU Press Release No. 21/2008 (1 Feb. 2008).

931. *See* Assembly, *Decision on Election of the Chairperson of the African Union (AU) Commissio*n, AU Doc. Assembly/AU/Dec. 445 (XIX) (16 Jul. 2012). Thereafter, Erastus J.O. Mwencha was elected as Deputy Chairperson, *see* AU Doc. Assembly/AU/Dec. 446 (XIX) (16 Jul. 2012).

932. AU Doc. Assembly/AU/Dec. 414 (XVIII).

933. *See* A. Harding, 'Nkosazana Dlamini-Zuma: What Next for African Union boss?', *BBC News*, 30 Jan. 2017, at: http://www.bbc.com/news/world-africa-38795674.

934. *See* Assembly, *Decision on the Election of Members of the Commission*, Assembly/AU/Dec. 610 (XXVII) (18 Jul. 2016).

for Central Africa). A Western-style public debate with live broadcast was held on 9 December 2016 among them, while according to rumours, a group of (unnamed) Member States were seeking that the second round of the election process be also deadlocked.[935] On 30 January 2017, a secret ballot cast during the Twenty-Eighth Ordinary Assembly Session elected Moussa Faki Mahamat as the new Chairperson, ending an impasse which could have obstructed the AU's functioning.[936] In 2021, he was re-elected and appointed Chairperson for another four-year period.[937]

134. In 2014, AUC had a total of 1,444 staff; presently, it has less than 1,000. The seat has remained in Addis Ababa. A Headquarters Agreement between the AU and Ethiopia was signed on 25 April 2008. Effectively, it is a bilateral treaty regulating the legal position of the AUC in the territory of Ethiopia and the application of the latter's legislation upon the AU.[938] Considering that the General Convention on the Privileges and Immunities of the OAU (1965, discussed *infra*) is also applicable to the extent that it lays down the Organization's privileges and immunities in the territory of the Member States, the two instruments apply in parallel.[939] Thus, Article 24 of the Headquarters Agreement stipulates that its provisions as well as those of the General Convention shall be treated as complementary, both will be applicable, neither shall narrow the effect of the other, and, in case of absolute conflict, the Agreement shall prevail. The Commission operates on the basis of the following values: Respect for diversity and team work; 'Think Africa above all'; transparency and accountability; integrity and impartiality; efficiency and professionalism; and information and knowledge-sharing. Originally, the AUC comprised several 'Departments', some of which were carried on from the OAU, while others were established when the AU commenced operating.[940] Its current organizational structure could be summarized as follows: (A) Cabinet of the Chairperson, whose activities are managed by the Chief of Staff; (B) Office of the Director-General under whose purview are these entities: (a) Office of Strategic Planning and Delivery (OSPD); (b) Office of Internal Oversight (OIO); (c) Quality Assurance and Control Division; (d) Ethics, Integrity and Standards Directorate (EISD); (e) Office of the Secretary to the Commission (OSC); (f) Office of the Legal Counsel (OLC); (g)

935. *See* V.S. Makhan, 'Election of the Chairperson of the African Union Commission: The AU at a Crossroads', *Pambazuka News*, 15 Dec. 2016, at: https://www.pambazuka.org/pan-africanism/election-chairperson-african-union-commission-au-crossroads.
936. Assembly, *Decision on the Election of the Chairperson and Deputy Chairperson of the African Union (AU) Commission*, AU Dec. Assembly/AU/Dec. 637 (XXVIII) (31 Jan. 2017).
937. Assembly, *Decision on Election and Appointment of the Chairperson and Deputy Chairperson of the AU Commission*, AU Doc. Assembly/AU/Dec. 799 (XXXIV) (7 Feb. 2021). *See also*, Bureau of the Chairperson, *Taking Stock, Charting the Future: African Union Commission End of Term Report 2017–2021*, no date, at: https://au.int/sites/default/files/documents/40232-doc-au_end_of_term_report_e.pdf.
938. Text at: https://archives.au.int/handle/123456789/6617. *See* Executive Council, *Criteria for Hosting the AU Organs*, AU Doc. EX/CL. 195 (VII) Rev.1 Annex III, July 2005; the Criteria were endorsed by the Fifth Ordinary Assembly Session in July 2005.
939. *See also* Art. 19 of the AUC Statutes.
940. *See* Executive Council, *Report of the 3rd Ordinary Session of the Executive Council on the Proposed Structure, Human Resource Requirements and Conditions of Service for the Staff of the Commission of the African Union and their Financial Implications*, AU Doc. EX/CL/39 (III) (8 Jul. 2003).

Office of Protocol; (h) Partnerships Management and Resource Mobilisation Directorate (PMRM); (i) Women, Gender and Youth Directorate (WGYD); (k) Information and Communication Directorate (ICD); (l) Peace Fund Secretariat (PFS); (m) Committee of Intelligence and Security Services of Africa (CISSA) Liaison Unit; and (n) AUDA-NEPAD Coordination Unit; (o) AU Reform Implementation Unit; and (C) Cabinet of the Deputy Chairperson, whose activities are managed by the Deputy Chief of Staff and under whose purview are these entities: (a) Human Resources Management Directorate (HRMD); (b) Finance Directorate; (c) Operations Support Services Directorate (OSSD); (d) Management of Information Systems Directorate (MISD); (e) Directorate of Conference Management and Publications (DCMP); (f) Enterprises and Resource Planning (ERP) Unit; (g) Office for Safety and Security Services; (h) Citizens and Diaspora Directorate (CIDO); (i) Medical and Health Services Directorate (MHSD); (k) Financial Control Unit; (l) F15 Secretariat and Contribution Unit (F15SC); and (m) Secretariat to the Board of External Auditors (SboEA). The Commission acts as the AU's legal representative in its relations with third states and other international institutions. It maintains offices in New York (AU Permanent Observer to the United Nations), in Geneva (AU Permanent Representative to the United Nations and World Trade Organization), in Washington, D.C., in Brussels (Permanent Mission to the European Union (EU) and African, Caribbean and Pacific (ACP) states), in Cairo (Permanent Delegation to the League of Arab States), and in Beijing (African Union Permanent Mission to China).

135. In January 2013, Erastus Mwencha, the then Deputy Chairperson, outlined the AUC's strategic plan for the period 2014–2017. Its overall aims were to improve, to strengthen and to maintain accountability while ensuring operational efficiency. Moreover, to achieve sustainable financing and to promote synergies with the other AU organs, with the RECs and third multilateral institutions (or 'stakeholders' in AU jargon) such as the African Development Bank and the UN Economic Community for Africa. The strategic plan had been developed pursuant to the SMART model, which stands for Specific, Measurable, Achievable, Realistic, and Timely.[941] The Executive Council requested the Commission 'to closely and continuously engage the Permanent Representatives Committee … in the further development of the [Strategic] Plan'.[942] It also resolved to hold an Extraordinary Session to consider the Plan together with other 'urgent strategic issues', namely the draft 2063 AU Strategic Framework, the preparations for the OAU Fiftieth Anniversary, the question of the proliferation of AU structures and institutions, and the question of the implementation of adopted decisions.[943] The Fourteenth Extraordinary Executive Council Session took place on 8 April 2013.

---

941. *See* AU Commission, Directorate of Information and Communication, *AU Echo*, Issue 06, 28 Jan. 2013, p. 8.

942. *See* Executive Council, *Decision on the Development of the African Union Commission Strategic Plan 2014–2017*, AU Doc. EX.CL/Dec. 734 (XXII) (25 Jan. 2013).

943. *See* Executive Council, *Decision on Decision on the Activity Report of the Commission*, AU Doc. EX.CL/Dec. 758 (XXII) (25 Jan. 2013).

§6. The Permanent Representatives Committee (PRC)

136. According to Article 21 of the Constitutive Act, PRC is composed of the Member States' permanent representatives or other plenipotentiaries accredited to the AU. The origins of this organ could be traced to the Committee of Ambassadors and other plenipotentiaries established by the Sixty-First Ordinary Session of the OAU Council of Ministers (Addis Ababa, 23–27 January 1995) as an auxiliary organ mandated with the preparation of Council meetings.[944] Unlike the other AU organs, the Constitutive Act did not stipulate how the PRC's structure, functions and regulations were to be determined. However, in July 2002, during the First Ordinary Assembly Session, the Executive Council adopted its Rules of Procedure presumably under the authority of being the organ to which the RPC is responsible.[945] The Rules were amended by the Eighth Ordinary Assembly Session (January 2007)[946] and by the Thirty-Seventh Ordinary Executive Council Session (October 2020) to align them with the AU's institutional reform.[947] It is rather unclear if the ACJHR, when it becomes operative, will have jurisdiction over the RPC, considering that its competence extends only to acts, decisions, regulations and directives issued by AU organs and that Rule 26 of the RPC Rules of Procedure stipulates that its decisions are recommendations until adopted by the Executive Council. Thus, PRC acts do not have a legally binding effect, and, consequently, they could not be subjected to judicial review by the ACJHR.

137. Rule 4 of the PRC Rules of Procedure, which sets out its powers and functions, reveals that it is an organ very closely connected to the Executive Council, which, as will be recalled, is composed of the Ministers of Foreign Affairs of all Member States. In particular, it is mandated to prepare Executive Council meetings, agendas and draft decisions, to monitor the implementation of the policies and decisions adopted by the Executive Council, to make recommendations to the Executive Council on matters relating to administrative, budgetary and financial matters and, generally, to consider any matter assigned to it by the Executive Council. The AU Executive Council decided in June 2018 that the PRC would hold its sessions at least two weeks prior to the ordinary Executive Council sessions.[948] Furthermore, the PRC has been authorized to examine and make recommendations to the Financial Report issued by the AUC as well as to the report prepared by the Board of External Auditors. While all Member States are entitled to be represented on the

944. *See* Council of Ministers, *Resolution on the Methodology of the Sessions of the Council of Ministers*, OAU Doc. CM/Res. 1557 (LXI) (27 Jan. 1995).
945. *See* Assembly, *Rules of Procedure of the Permanent Representatives' Committee*, AU Doc. ASS/AU/2 (I)-c (10 Jul. 2002).
946. *See* Assembly, *Decision on the Proposed Amendments to the Rules of Procedure of the Assembly of the Union, The Executive Council and the Permanent Representatives' Committee, and the Statutes of the Commission*, UN Doc. Assembly/AU/Dec. 146 (VIII) (30 Jan. 2017); and Permanent Representatives' Committee, *Report on the Proposed Amendments to the Rules of Procedure of the Assembly, the Executive Council, the PRC and the Statutes of the Commission*, AU Doc. EX.CL/298 (X) Rev.I (2017) at: https://archives.au.int/handle/123456789/4433.
947. *See* AU Doc. EX.CL/Dec. 1099 (XXXVII), op. cit.
948. *See* Executive Council, *Decision on the Holding of Sessions of the Permanent Representatives' Committee (PRC) Prior to African Union Summits*, AU Doc. EX.CL/1030(XXXIII) (7 Feb. 2021).

PRC, it principally functions as a Bureau consisting of a Chairperson, three Vice-Chairpersons and a Rapporteur. These positions are occupied by the same Member States sitting on the Assembly Bureau and on the Executive Council Bureau and serve for one-year periods. The PRC meets in ordinary session at least once a month in Addis Ababa, in extraordinary sessions when required and reaches decisions by a two-thirds majority, failing which by consensus. Its meetings are closed. Pursuant to Article 21(2) of the Constitutive Act and Rule 4 of the Rules of Procedure, the PRC is authorized to set up sub-committees or working groups as necessary. Presently, the following are in operation (some are composed of all Member States and some of only fifteen Member States): Sub-Committee on General Supervision and Coordination on Budgetary, Financial and Administrative Matters; Sub-Committee on Audit Matters; Sub-Committee on Headquarters and Host Agreements; Sub-Committee of the Whole on Multilateral Cooperation; Sub-Committee on the New Partnership for Africa's Development (NEPAD); Sub-Committee on Programmes and Conferences; Sub-Committee on Refugees, Returnees and Internally Displaced Persons in Africa; Policy Sub-Committee of the Special Emergency Assistance Fund for Drought and Famine Relief in Africa; Sub-Committee on Structural Reforms; Sub-Committee on Rules, Standards and Credentials; Sub-Committee on Human Rights, Democracy and Governance; Sub-Committee on Environmental Issues; and Sub-Committee on Budget Matters. There is a Drafting Committee, reference to which has already been made.[949] Finally, reference should be made to the African Union Ethics Office, which was established in July 2016. It is an independent and autonomous body overseeing ethical matters in all AU organs and institutions. It is managed and directed by the Chief of Ethics, who reports to the PRC.

§7. The Economic, Social and Cultural Council (ECOSOCC)

138. Article 5(1) in conjunction with Article 22 of the Constitutive Act creates ECOSOCC. Even though it is one of the principal AU organs, it bears more than a simple resemblance to the Economic and Social Committee, one of the advisory organs operating in the EU, which operates as 'a bridge between Europe and organised civil society'.[950] ECOSOCC is an advisory organ composed of different social and professional groups active in Member States. It facilitates the principle stated in the third indent of Article 4 of the Constitutive Act, namely the participation of African people and the civic society at large in all AU activities. It should be noted that Articles 90 and 91 of the AEC Treaty provide for the establishment of consultative mechanisms between, on the one hand, the AEC and, on the other hand, African NGOs and socioeconomic organizations and associations. The purpose of these mechanisms is to encourage and ensure their involvement in the integration process while allowing the AEC to mobilize their technical and financial support. To that

949. *See* AU Doc. Assembly/AU/Dec. 745 (XXXII), op. cit.

950. According to Art. 13(4) of the Treaty on European Union, the European Parliament, the Council and the Commission shall, *inter alia*, be assisted by an Economic and Social Committee acting in an advisory capacity. The same provision is repeated in Art. 300 of the Treaty on the Functioning of the European Union, Art. 304 of which sets out its role and function.

extent, the OAU Secretary-General had suggested that ECOSOCC could also double as the consultative mechanism envisaged in the AEC Treaty and urged Member States to reconsider its structure, format and other procedural questions.[951] His remarks reinforce the submission made in this monograph, namely that the urgency with which the Constitutive Act was drafted and adopted did not allow for a proper and in-depth analysis of the consequences of having a complicated institutional architecture.

139. Although the Assembly was empowered to determine the functions, powers, composition, and organization of ECOSOCC, it delegated this authority to the Executive Council. In May 2003, the draft Statutes of ECOSOCC were presented.[952] At its Third Ordinary Session (Maputo, Mozambique, 4–12 July 2003), the Executive Council requested the Commission Chairperson to submit revised draft Statutes before its Fourth Ordinary Session in March 2004.[953] The Assembly adopted the Statutes four months later;[954] they were amended in 2018.[955] However, its Rules of Procedure were adopted with considerable delay in 2016;[956] they were based on the Report of the First Extraordinary Session of the Specialized Technical Committee on Justice and Legal Affairs.[957] Since the end of 2019, the ECOSOCC Secretariat has been operating in Lusaka, following Zambia's offer to host it (it relocated from the AU Headquarters in Addis Ababa).[958] According to Articles 3 and 4 thereof, ECOSOCC is composed of the following entities: social groups representing women, children, disabled persons, etc.; professional groups such as associations of artists, engineers, teachers, lawyers, chambers of commerce, etc.; NGOs; organizations of workers and employers; and religious and cultural organizations. The maximum number of participating Civil Society Organizations (CSOs) has been set at 150. Each Member State is represented by two organizations, whereas the remaining are allocated to the African Diaspora (twenty), to organizations operating at regional level (ten) and at continental level (eight), and, finally, six organizations participate in an ex officio capacity. Articles 5 and 6 of the Statutes lay down the modalities and the specific eligibility for ECOSOCC members to be elected. The term in office runs for four years, and members are entitled to re-election only once. As far as the functions of ECOSOCC are concerned, Article

---

951. *See* Secretary-General, *Report of the Secretary-General on the Implementation of the Sirte Decision on the African Union*, OAU Doc. CM/2210 (LXXIV), paras 30 and 31 at p. 12 (2001).
952. *See Draft Statutes of the Economic, Social and Cultural Council of the African Union*, AU Doc. Exp/Draft/ECOSOCC Statutes/Rev. 2 (14 May 2003).
953. *See* Executive Council, *Decision on the Report of the Interim Chairperson on the Operationalization of ECOSOCC*, EX/CL/Dec. 21 (III) (8 Jul. 2003).
954. Assembly, *Decision on the Economic, Social and Cultural Council (ECOSOCC)*, AU Doc. Assembly/AU/Dec. 48 (III) Rev. 1 (8 Jul. 2004). Text at: https://au.int/sites/default/files/documents/30971-doc-ecosocc_statutes-english_1.pdf.
955. *See* Assembly, Decision on the Legal Instruments, AU Doc. Assembly/AU/Dec. 676 (XXX) (29 Jan. 2018).
956. Assembly, *Decision on the Specialized Technical Committees*, AU Doc. Assembly/AU/Dec. 589 (XXVI), para. 1 (31 Jan. 2016).
957. AU Doc. EX.CL/935 (XXVIII) (2016).
958. *See* Assembly, *Decision on the Budget of the African Union for the 2018 Financial Year*, AU Doc. Assembly/AU/Dec. 642 (XXIX) (4 Jul. 2017).

7 of the Statutes stipulates, *inter alia*, the following: to contribute, through advise, to the effective translation of the AU objectives, principles, and policies into concrete programmes and the evaluation thereof; to undertake studies recommended by other AU organs and submit recommendations accordingly; to contribute to the promotion of popular participation, sharing of best practices and expertise, and to the realization of the AU vision and objectives; to contribute to the promotion of human rights, the rule of law, good governance, democratic principles, gender equality and child rights; to promote and support the efforts undertaken by institutions engaged in reviewing the future of Africa and forging Pan-African values; and, finally, to foster and consolidate partnership between the AU and CSOs through effective public enlightenment, mobilization and feedback on AU activities.

140. Unlike most other AU organs which are unitary, that is, they are not made up by separate entities, ECOSOCC has its own institutional architecture. It is composed of a General Assembly, a Bureau, a Standing Committee, Ten Sectoral Cluster Committees (these are so-called operational thematic mechanisms mirroring the AUC technical departments), and a Credentials Committee. The General Assembly, which has adopted its own Rules of Procedure, is the highest decision and policy-making body with a tenure of four years. All ECOSOCC members participate in it. It has been entrusted with the following tasks and duties: to elect the eighteen members of the Standing Committee for a term of two years and to oversee its work; to elect a Bureau composed of a Presiding Officer and five Deputy Presiding Officers for two years on the basis of equitable geographical distribution and rotation, including one from the Africa Diaspora; to prepare and submit advisory opinions and reports (including reports on the AU budget); and to approve the Code of Ethics and Conduct for the CSOs that are affiliated to or working with the AU.

The role of the Standing Committee is to run ECOSOCC in-between sessions of the General Assembly. It consists of the Presiding Officer and the other members of the Bureau, the Chairpersons of the ten Sectoral Cluster Committees as well as of two representatives of the AUC. Its functions are auxiliary to those of the General Assembly and include coordinating ECOSOCC work; preparing and submitting annual reports to the Assembly; and determining the criteria and the modalities for granting observer status to ECOSOCC. The Sectoral Cluster Committees (SCCs) operate as the key mechanisms of ECOSOCC in formulating opinions and offering input in AU policies, programmes, and activities. To that end, the subject matter of the ten Clusters mirrors the principal areas of AU activities and the AUC Directorates. Presently, the thematic areas of SCCs are the following: Peace and Security; Political Affairs (including human rights; rule of law, democratic and constitutional rule; and humanitarian assistance); Infrastructure and Energy; Social Affairs and Health; Human Resources, Science and Technology; Trade and Industry; Rural Economy and Agriculture; Economic Affairs; Women and Gender; and Cross-Cutting Programmes. Finally, the Credentials Committee is composed of representatives of the CSOs from each of Africa's five regions and the African Diaspora, one nominated representative for special interest groups (e.g., vulnerable groups, the aged, the physically challenged, and people living with HIV/AIDS) and two representatives of the AUC.

141. The process towards operationalizing the General Assembly and electing its first members proved lengthy. The role of the Credentials Committee was instrumental in completing the procedure for the General Assembly.[959] Although ECOSOCC was officially launched in Dar-es-Salam, Tanzania, in September 2008,[960] and the first meeting of its General Assembly was held in December 2008,[961] not all components and necessary instruments were promptly completed and adopted, revealing a degree of ineffectiveness on behalf of the AU.[962] The elections for the Second ECOSOCC General Assembly took place in December 2014.[963] The Third Permanent General Assembly was inaugurated in December 2018 in Nairobi, Kenya, and the Fourth Permanent General Assembly was inaugurated and constituted in December 2022. For the Financial Year (FY) 2013, ECOSOCC was allocated USD 1,015,372 from the AU budget. For purposes of comparison, the amount of USD 972,336 was allocated to the Advisory Board on Corruption, USD 587,275 to AUCIL, and USD 10,492,998 to PAP.[964] In FY 2014, ECOSOCC's funding was curtailed (USD 993,710), while other organs' funding was augmented significantly, including the Advisory Board on Corruption (increased to USD 1,507,857) and PAP (increased to USD 14,292,124).[965] In FY 2017, ECOSOCC's funding slightly increased to USD 1,119,557, but it paled compared to the Advisory Board on Corruption's funding (USD 2,396,246). Six years later, the situation has been reversed: for FY 2023, ECOSOCC was allocated USD 2.7 million, surpassing the Advisory Board on Corruption's funding (USD 2.05 million), while PAP's funding has been reduced to under USD 12 million.[966] And for FY 2024, ECOSOCC's funding will be proportionally larger (it will receive USD 3.6 million) compared to the Advisory Board on Corruption (USD 1.6 million) and PAP (USD 10.2 million).[967] As regards its operation, it is important to note that ECOSOCC acquired a Strategic Plan only in December 2016. It served as the framework and general guidance for the formulation of programmes and prioritization of its policies for the period 2017–2018.[968] Since then, the Strategic Plan does not appear to have been updated or renewed.

---

959. *See* Executive Council, *Decision on the Report on the Interim Standing Committee of the Economic, Social and Cultural Council (ECOSOCC)*, AU Doc. EX.CL/Dec. 384 (XII) (29 Jan. 2008).
960. *See* Executive Council, *Decision on the Economic, Social and Cultural Council (ECOSOCC)*, AU Doc. EX.CL/Dec. 477 (XIV) (30 Jan. 2009).
961. *See* Executive Council, *Decision on the Economic, Social and Cultural Council (ECOSOCC)*, AU Doc. EX.CL/Dec. 508 (XV) Rev.1 (1 Jul. 2009).
962. Compare Executive Council, *Decision on the Economic, Social and Cultural Council (ECOSOCC)*, AU Doc. EX.CL/Dec. 633 (XVIII) (28 Jan. 2011) and *Decision on the Economic, Social and Cultural Council (ECOSOCC)*, EX.CL/Dec. 656 (XIX) (28 Jun. 2011).
963. For the results, *see* https://au.int/web/sites/default/files/newsevents/workingdocuments/27443-wd-members_of_2nd_general_assembly_of_ecosocc_kenya_december_2014.pdf.
964. *See* Executive Council, *Decision on the Budget of the African Union for the 2013 Financial Year*, AU Doc. EX.CL/ Dec. 696 (XXI) (13 Jul. 2012).
965. *See* Executive Council, *Decision on the Budget of the African Union for the 2014 Financial Year*, AU Doc. EX.CL/ Dec. 767 (XXIII) (23 May 2013).
966. *See* Executive Council, *Decision on the Reports of the Sub-Committees of the Permanent Representatives' Committee (PRC)*, AU Doc. EX.CL/Dec. 1168 (XLI), p. 12 (15 Jul. 2022).
967. *See* Executive Council, *Decision on the African Union Budget for 2024*, AU Doc. EX.CL/Dec. 1217 (XLIII) (14 Jul. 2023).
968. Text at: https://ecosocc.au.int/en/strategic-plan.

Recently, the reputation of ECOSSOC was tarnished on account of improprieties committed by members of its General Assembly. More specifically, in 2021, the Executive Council requested that the Office of Internal Oversight of the AUC conduct an independent investigation 'into current and future alleged violations' of the AU Code of Ethics and Conduct by members of the General Assembly and recommend appropriate sanctions.[969] The ensuing Investigation Report concluded that seven members of the General Assembly had infringed 'AU legal norms', namely Rule 8 of the ECOSOCC Rules of Procedure and the AU Code of Ethics and Conduct, by perpetrating quite serious acts, including: abuse of authority/office and unlawful signing of MoUs with third parties on behalf of ECOSOCC; illegal convening of the General Assembly and destabilization of ECOSOCC; illegal appointments; illegal opening of a bank account in the name of ECOSOCC in Nigeria; etc. In June 2022, these seven individuals were suspended with immediate effect and indefinitely.[970] The investigation was also carried out in accordance with the broader mandate, which had been given to the AUC Chairperson by the AU Assembly in February 2020 directing him ' … to continue to take effective actions to address all acts of misconduct in the [AU], and to use his financial and administrative statutory oversight authority over all non-Policy Organs and Institutions … , including the Pan-African Parliament, the African Court of Human and Peoples' Rights, the African Commission on Human and Peoples Rights, and their elected officials'.[971] During its Fortieth Ordinary Session, the Executive Council expressed its grave concern not only because these violations were recurring but also because the ECOSOCC General Assembly had not been taking any action against those alleged to have violated the AU legal norms. It directed the AUC Chairperson to ensure that any acts of ECOSOCC members that expose the AU to 'legal, financial and reputational risks are cancelled by issuance of public notices' from his Office; to immediately and indefinitely suspend individuals found to have committed misconducts or any breach of AU legal norms including the infringement of AU intellectual property rights and acts of forgery; and to communicate officially to their respective Member States to prevent these individuals from participating in future AU activities.[972] Moreover, the Executive Council asked the AUC Chairperson to send an official communication to the Permanent Mission of Nigeria informing it of the illegal actions of the two General Assembly members having Nigerian nationality, namely

969. Executive Council, *Decision on the Activity Report of the Economic, Social and Cultural Council (ECOSOCC)*, AU Doc. EX.CL/Dec. 1115 (XXXVIII) (4 Feb. 2021).

970. For their names and infractions, *see* African Union, 'Public Notice: Immediate and Indefinite Suspension of Some Members of ECOSSOC Found to Have Committed Misconducts and Breach of AU Legal Norms', 21 June 2022, at: https://au.int/sites/default/files/pressreleases/41958-pr-Public_Notice-English.pdf.

971. Assembly, *Decision on Consequence Management and the Oversight Role of the Chairperson of the AU Commission Within the Union on the Functioning of the AUC and other AU Organs*, AU Doc. Assembly/AU/Dec. 757 (XXXIII), para. 3 (10 Feb. 2020), which also noted the sanctions, including dismissal, that had been taken against AU staff members found guilty of irregularities and violations of the Staff and Financial Regulations and Rules. The infliction of sanctions had been ordered by the Executive Council in Decision EX.CL./Dec. 1057 (XXXV), para. 40 (5 Jul. 2019).

972. Executive Council, *Decision on the Reports of the Sub-Committees of the Permanent Representatives' Committee (PRC)*, AU Doc. EX.CL/Dec. 1143 (XL), paras 26 *et seq*. (3 Feb. 2022).

that they had opened a bank account in the name of ECOSSOC, requesting its closure and the taking of legal action to hold them accountable pursuant to Nigeria's domestic legislation.[973] Arguably, the Executive Council could have also asked the AUC to institute directly (i.e., in the name of the AU) legal proceedings against the two Nigerians before the competent courts of Nigeria and seek the award of damages. However, the criminal law dimension of the acts committed by the ECOSSOC General Assembly members may be far from apparent, including whether they may be prosecuted in accordance with the laws of Zambia, the seat of ECOSSOC. Thus, when the Executive Council warned all ECOSOCC members to exercise the highest degree of confidentiality in the discharge of their mandate and duties, for otherwise they would be held accountable, it is not clear what it meant.[974]

§8. The Financial Institutions

142. Article 19 of the Constitutive Act establishes three financial institutions: the African Central Bank (it was also envisaged in the final stage of creating the AEC), the African Monetary Fund (AMF), and the African Investment Bank (AIB).[975] The Constitutive Act has not laid down its aims, purposes, structure, composition, etc., leaving everything to be defined and regulated in future protocols. Despite calls to have the financial institutions set up (e.g., during the Extraordinary Executive Council Session in May 2008), the Protocol on the AIB was adopted in February 2009 and the Protocol on the AMF in June 2014. Neither has entered into force. The Protocol on the African Central Bank has apparently not been negotiated because it presupposes that the AMF is in operation.

I. The African Investment Bank (AIB)

143. The Protocol establishing the AIB was adopted by the Twelfth Ordinary Assembly Session on 4 February 2009.[976] A Statute containing the substantive provisions for the AIB's operations has been appended to the Protocol. Both will enter

973. *Ibid*, para. 30.
974. *Ibid*, para. 33. *See further*, Executive Council, *Decision on the Report of the Commission on Implementation of Executive Decision EX.CL/Dec.1143(XL) of February 2022 on ECOSSOC*, AU Doc. EX.CL/Dec. 1172 (XLI) (15 Jul. 2022) requesting the AUC to come up with concrete proposals to address the governance and operational issues burdening ECOSOCC as well as a mechanism to ensure the accountability of its members and their accredited representatives for violation of AU rules and norms.
975. These institutions should not be confused with the African Development Bank, which is a multilateral financial institution set up in 1964. Its current membership comprises all African states as well as twenty-six states from the Americas, Europe and Asia (the so-called 'non-regional Members').
976. *See* Assembly, *Decision on the Protocol on the Establishment of the African Investment Bank*, AU Doc. Assembly AU/Dec. 212 (XII) (3 Feb. 2009).

into force on the same day.[977] According to Article 3 of the Protocol, the purpose of the AIB is to foster economic integration and development through investments in development projects in line with AU objectives. Article 4 lays down its four functions, which concern both the public and the private sectors. First, to offer financing in accordance with banking principles. Second, to advance regional economic integration among contracting parties. Third, to support the strengthening of private sector activities. Fourth, to assist the modernization of the rural sector in low-income contracting parties. Article 5 of the Protocol stipulates that its seat will be in Tripoli, Libya. This reflected the policy pursued by the late Colonel Gaddafi to use his country's wealth to house the headquarters of various AU organs and, at the same time, to augment his stature within the AU. However, given the precarious political and economic situation in Libya due to the civil war waged since 2011 and the collapse of state functions and institutions, it is questionable if it is a safe enough country to host it.

144. Article 7 of the Protocol envisages the procedure for the AIB's dissolution; it involves a recommendation by the plenary organ, the General Assembly of shareholders, and a discretionary decision by the AU Assembly, which will also determine the terms and the conditions of the dissolution. While the Protocol does not envisage withdrawal, Article 16 of the Statute provides that 'Any member may withdraw from the Bank at any time by delivering a notice in writing to the Bank at its Headquarters.' Withdrawal will become effective, and, consequently, membership will cease at least six months after the notification was lodged. Until that time, the withdrawing contracting party will remain liable for all direct and contingent obligations to the AIB. The Statute does not explain how these obligations will be honoured. As has been noted when examining withdrawal from the AU, it is a perennial issue to ensure that Member States fulfil all their duties and obligations before they withdraw. Article 18 of the Statute contains provisions on the settlement of accounts with shareholders having ceased to be Members: the remaining contracting parties will purchase the former Members' shares. It is submitted that the Statute could have envisaged that, before such purchase takes place, the AIB will set off any sums owed by the former Members with the shares they hold, a scenario offering two possibilities. First, the AIB would get ownership in a number of shares enough to cover the sums owed to it and subsequently sell them to other Members (possibly at a discount) and recover the sums owed. Second, the sale and purchase of shares would go ahead, but the Members acquiring them would not pay directly to the former Member their whole value but only what remains after subtracting the sums owed to the AIB.

The fact that the Statute, on the one hand, stipulates the dissolution of the AIB and, on the other hand, allows contracting parties to withdraw should be considered problematic. And, this is because the AIB (as well as the other two Financial Institutions), pursuant to Article 5(1) in conjunction with Article 19 of the Constitutive Act, are principal AU organs. To put it otherwise, the AIB is *not* an organ that the

977. According to Art. 9(1), the Protocol is open only to AU Member States. Fifteen ratifications are required to enter into force. At the time of writing, twenty-two Member States had signed it, of which only six have ratified it (the last two being Chad in August 2018 and Togo in June 2016).

Assembly has decided to establish in accordance with the power vested in it under Article 5(2) of the Constitutive Act. It follows that the decision to dissolve it would be tantamount to dissolving any other principal AU organ through a mere Assembly resolution. This is not in line with the law of international organizations prescribing that the dissolution of principal organs (as opposed to terminating subsidiary or auxiliary organs) must follow the procedure for amending or revising the founding instrument, in casu Article 32 of the Constitutive Act. Moreover, it dictates that Member States are not to withdraw at wish from only one organ but only from the international organization as a whole. Thus, it would be possible for a Member State to withdraw from the AU but continue participating in the AIB. The Protocol and Statute treat the AIB as a separate institution possessing full international personality (Article 23 of the Statute), but it is not very clear what the latter entails. Arguably, from a legal point of view, the AIB is not identical or equal to, e.g., the International Bank for Reconstruction and Development (IBRD) or the International Monetary Fund (IMF), which, although part of the UN family as Specialized Agencies, were established as autonomous international institutions and where UN Member States do not have an entitlement to membership.[978]

145. Article 6 of the Statute envisages two separate types of membership, even though the Protocol does not mention it. The first (Article 6(1)) comprises only states and, in particular, those AU Member States which have resolved to become contracting parties to the Protocol. As has already been argued, their participation in the Protocols to the Constitutive Act setting up AU organs ought to be obligatory and not discretionary. The second (Article 6(2)) comprises different categories of shareholders: (a) public financial institutions incorporated in the territory of contracting parties; (b) nationals or legal entities registered in contracting parties with 51% of the capital owned by nationals of the relevant contracting party, as well as the African Diaspora; and (c) financial institutions established in the context of RECs.[979] The division into two types of membership is reflected in the capital of the AIB (the authorized initial capital is set at USD 25 billion to be divided into 2.5 million shares with a par value of USD 10,000 each.) Thus, according to Article 7 section 2(3) of the Statute, contracting parties will subscribe to 'A' shares, which will represent at least 75% of total capital stock,[980] while all other Members will subscribe to 'B' shares, not to exceed 25% of the total capital stock. Strangely enough, the Statute does not stipulate how the 'other Members' will accede to the

978. According to Art. II(2) of the IBRD Articles of Agreement, 'Membership shall be open to other members of the [IMF], at such times and in accordance with such terms as may be prescribed by the Bank'; Art. II(2) of the IMF Articles of Agreement reads: 'Membership shall be open to other countries at such times and in accordance with such terms as may be prescribed by the Board of Governors.'

979. It would appear that no such institutions are currently operating in RECs. Indeed, investment is not an area where RECs have primary but only incidental competence. *See*, *inter alia*, the SADC Protocol on Finance and Investment, which was adopted in August 2006 and entered into force in April 2010, at: https://investmentpolicy.unctad.org/international-investment-agreements/treaty-files/2730/download.

980. For the individual Member States' subscriptions to the authorized capital stock and the corresponding voting power, *see*, respectively, Annex A and Annex B of the Statute.

AIB. The only relevant provisions are Article 7 section 2(4), providing that the number of 'B' shares will be determined by the AU Assembly and Article 7 section 2B(1) reading: 'Entities as referred under Article 6(2) eligible for membership shall subscribe to 'B' shares.' Finally, Article 13 section 1(2) on the powers and functions of the General Assembly, reads '… (g) Decide on the admission of new members and conditions of this admission, as provided in Article 5 of this Statute'.[981] While the reference to 'Article 5' is obviously a typing error (the relevant provision is Article 6), it does not elaborate on how the first 'other Members' envisaged in Article 6(2) will join.

146. One of the General Assembly's powers will be to elect the members of the Board of Directors, which, together with the President, completes the AIB's institutional structure. Like all other decisions, it will require a double majority of shares and shareholders, with the majority of shares prevailing in the event of a tie. The AIB President, who will be appointed by the General Assembly, is designated as the Chief Executive and Legal Representative (Article 13 section 3(1) of the Statute). There exists a considerable degree of delegation of powers between these three organs. However, the way it has been stipulated is rather problematic. In particular, according to Article 13 section (1) paragraph 3, the General Assembly is empowered to delegate all or some of its powers to the Board as necessary 'with the exception of those listed in paragraph 2 of this section'. Considering that it is exactly paragraph 2 that lays down the General Assembly's powers, it is unclear which powers may be delegated. In its turn, the Board is entitled, pursuant to Article 13 section (2) paragraph 7, to delegate its own powers to the AIB President, with the exception of the power to elect its own Chairperson. As most of the Board of Directors' powers are of a sensitive nature (e.g., deciding on the granting of loans, preparing the General Assembly sessions, approving the AIB's annual budget, etc.), arguably, they should not be delegated to the President, whose role is quite different.

147. A broad reading of Article 13 of the Statute leads to the conclusion that it might be possible for the President to carry out those General Assembly's powers delegated to the Board of Directors, in effect, a succession of handing over powers. Article 17 of the Statute, the clause on the suspension of Members failing to fulfil their obligations, offers an illustration. The General Assembly has the discretion to order suspension (the Statute does not lay down which are the precise obligations that failure to meet them could lead to suspension). One year later, the participation of the suspended Member will automatically cease unless the General Assembly decides to restore it to good standing. Taking into account that the power to suspend and to restore to good standing is not envisaged in Article 13 section (1) paragraph

981. According of Art. 13 of the Statute, the General Assembly will consist of the shareholders, namely the Members irrespective of whether they are states, individuals or companies, or their representatives.

2, the General Assembly may delegate either or both powers to the Board of Directors. But it is a basic rule of the law of international organizations that decisions on membership issues should always be adopted by the highest-ranking organ, in casu, the General Assembly.

There are further problematic aspects of Article 17. Thus, it creates a mechanism for imposing sanctions on recalcitrant Member States without linking it up with the general provision on punitive measures laid down in the aforementioned Article 23(2) of the Constitutive Act. In effect, Article 17 should be considered as *lex specialis*. This could be explained by the fact that the AIB is endowed with an international personality, which probably differentiates it from the other organs mentioned in Article 5(1) of the Constitutive Act. However, if this is the case, the Constitutive Act should have at least indicated it. Moreover, if suspension was ordered under Article 17, no further sanctions may be imposed under Article 23(2), as this would violate the double jeopardy/*ne bis in idem* rule. Furthermore, Article 17(3) allows suspended Members to withdraw from the AIB. Notwithstanding the arguments advanced above why withdrawal from the AIB is inappropriate, it is rather awkward to offer recalcitrant Members the opportunity to 'save face' and withdraw. While they will lose access to AIB services and benefits, governments could use secession for purposes of domestic consumption and conveniently blame it on AIB tactics and behaviour.

II. The African Monetary Fund (AMF)

148. A feasibility study to establish an African Monetary Fund was undertaken by the UN Economic Commission for Africa in 1985 as part of the Lagos Plan of Action for the economic development of Africa 1980-2000. But perhaps at the time the OAU was not in a position to consider and implement such a project. But the new era ushered by the AU changed the perspectives of African states. In June 2014, the Assembly adopted the Protocol and Statute on the AMF.[982] These texts had already been approved by the Specialised Technical Committee (STC) on Justice and Legal Affairs, which had met in May 2014 at the level of Experts and then at the level of Ministers of Justice and Attorneys Generals.[983] The text of the AMF Protocol is almost identical to AIB Protocol, and the issues concerning dissolution, withdrawal, and suspension of membership are treated in the same way. To avoid unnecessary repetitions, the arguments advanced above apply, *mutatis mutandis*, here as well. The Statute has drawn from the Articles of Agreement of the Arab Monetary Fund concluded in April 1976.[984] Unlike the AMF, the Arab Monetary Fund is an independent international financial institution and is only affiliated to the

982. *See* Assembly, *Decision on the Protocol and the Statute for the Establishment of the African Monetary Fund*, AU Doc. Assembly/AU/Dec. 517 (XXIII) (27 Jun. 2014), reproduced in 54 I.L.M. 507 (2015).

983. *See* Executive Council, *The Report, the Draft Legal Instruments and Recommendations of the Specialized Technical Committee on Justice and Legal Affairs*, AU Doc. EX.CL/846 (XXV) (2014), at: https://www.justsecurity.org/wp-content/uploads/2014/07/Legal-Instruments-Adopted-in-Malabo-July-2014.pdf.

984. At: http://www.amf.org.ae.

League of Arab States. The AMF is not the first African experiment in monetary issues: the West African Monetary Institute was established in Accra, Ghana, in January 2001 and became operational two months later.[985]

The AMF Headquarters will be in Yaoundé, the capital of Cameroon. According to Article 3 of the Protocol, its purpose is to foster macroeconomic stability, sustainable shared economic growth, and balanced development in the continent to facilitate the effective integration of African economies. The objectives, laid down in Article 2 of the Statute, are quite ambitious and include: correcting disequilibria in contracting parties' balances of payments; ensuring stability of exchange rates among their currencies and mutual convertibility; promoting African monetary cooperation to facilitate economic integration and economic development; assisting contracting parties to design and implement debt management policies; promoting African financial markets and the settlement of commercial debts; and establishing a clearing system for trade transactions. These objectives will be fulfilled through the following functions and activities: enabling trade; encouraging capital flows; providing short-term and medium-term credit facilities to sustain balances of payments; offering technical assistance and policy advice; cooperating with other international financial institutions; and conducting periodic consultations with contracting parties on economic policies.

Unlike the AIB, Article 4 of the AMF Statute provides only one class of membership, namely the AU Member States that have ratified the AMF Protocol. Yet, like the AIB, there is considerable reluctance among Member States to become parties to the AMF Protocol; according to the information on the AU's website, twelve have signed it, and only Chad has ratified it in September 2018. It is rather difficult to explain why Cameroon, which signed it on 4 October 2016, has not ratified it. Entry into force of the AMF Protocol requires the deposit of fifteen instruments of ratifications and the payment of at least 25% of the minimum paid up capital (Article 9 of the Protocol). As it cannot be known when these requirements will be met, any discussion to which extent the AMF could or would weaken the IMF position and role in Africa is premature. At the same time, one should entertain the thought whether the AMF's operationalization could be hastened if it were to act as the IMF's African arm.[986]

Pursuant to Article 28 of the AMF Statute, any disputes concerning its interpretation or application shall be resolved amicably within a time limit of one year, failing which they may be referred to the AU Court of Justice. But since, as explained above, this organ has never been operationalized (wrongly Article 28 thereof mentions that it has not been established), any unresolved disputes are to be submitted to the Assembly, whose determination will require a two-thirds majority. Article 28 does not explain if it governs only interstate disputes or disputes between the AMF and contracting parties as well.

According to Article 5 of the AMF Statute, the authorized (i.e., the maximum) share capital shall be USD 22.640 billion, denominated in shares of USD 100 each.

985. For further information, *see* http://www.wami-imao.org/.

986. Compare International Monetary Fund, *On the IMF's Role and Activities in Africa*, Speech by Thomas C. Dawson, Director of External Relations, 28 Apr. 2013, at: https://www.imf.org/en/News/Articles/2015/09/28/04/53/sp042803.

The capital subscription calculation for each of the contracting states is envisaged in Annex 2 of the Statute. Using a mathematical formula, it will be determined, taking into account each contracting party's GDP and population. Each Member State's subscription to the capital, given as a percentage, will also determine the number of voting rights that it will have, the total being 500,000 voting rights. South Sudan will have the smallest capital subscription (0.57%) resulting in 2,829.81 voting rights, while the Republic of South Africa will have the largest number of voting rights (40,249.06) by subscribing to 8.05% of the capital. The majority of parties will subscribe to less than 1.5% of the capital, but South Africa, Nigeria, Egypt and Algeria will hold between them more than 25% of the voting rights, which, as will be explained, effectively gives them the opportunity to run the AMF, if they so decide.

149. Institutionally, the AMF will comprise a Board of Governors, a Board of Directors, and a Managing Director. As regards the former, according to section 1 of Article 10 of the Statute, each party will be represented by a Governor or alternate Governor, who will be either the Finance Minister or the Central Bank Governor. Its mandate is to oversee the AMF. It will meet at least once every year and will have the 'highest executive powers'. These include confirming the members of the Board of Directors; appointing the Managing Director, who must have the nationality of a contracting party but may not be a member of the Board of Governors or the Board of Directors either Boards; admitting new members and determining the conditions of admission. This is a rather curious provision because the aforementioned Article 4 stipulates that, upon ratification of the Protocol, participation in the AMF is automatic. Indeed, it could not have been otherwise because the AMF is a principal AU organ, and all Member States have a right to join it.

According to section 2 of Article 10 of the Statute, the Board of Directors will be composed of the Managing Director, the Permanent Members, five Substantive Directors, one for each region of Africa, and five Alternate Directors, again one per region.[987] It will meet at least once every quarter. Under section 3 thereof, only those parties having at least 4% of the voting rights shall be allowed to hold a permanent seat. But, given the mathematical formula in Annex 2, there will be only four parties able to become Permanent Members (clearly an unacceptable small number). However, it is submitted that if the threshold was lowered to 2.3% of the voting rights, six more states would be entitled to permanent seats, a total of ten (a more acceptable number). Arguably, the following situation has not been addressed: that none of the first fifteen states to ratify the Protocol will have at least 4% of the voting rights, in which case there would be no permanent seats in the Board of Directors, a situation which could affect the taking of decisions. But as this is a matter to be addressed in the AMF Rules and Regulations, which will be adopted when it becomes operationalized, no answer can be given at this stage. The Board of Directors will be responsible for adopting the Code of Conduct; taking decisions on lending conditions and borrowing terms; approving the annual report; approving the

987. These are geographical regions defined in OAU Council of Ministers Resolution CM/Res. 464 (XXVI), adopted in March 1976.

conclusion of cooperation agreements with other similar international institutions; and approving the annual operating budget.

The Managing Director, whose role is to administer the AMF, is also its Chief Executive and legal representative. He is assisted by several Deputy Managing Directors to whom all or part of his duties may be delegated. He is entitled to attend the Board of Governors meetings, to anticipate in the deliberations but not to vote. His main duties are laid down in section 3 of Article 10 of the Statute: recruit, appoint and discipline AMF staff; implement the Statute and the Boards of Governors and Directors' decisions; prepare the annual budget; sign agreements on behalf of the AMF; and carry out those duties assigned by the Board of Governors. Article 11 of the Statute stipulates that the Code of Conduct concerns the Managing Director and the staff, who promise that while performing their duties, they shall neither accept nor receive instructions from governments or other authorities (presumably the central banks of contracting parties). Equally, parties undertake to respect the 'exclusive nature of the responsibilities' of the Managing Director and staff and refrain from influencing them. Should the Managing Director fail to comply with his duties and obligations, the Board of Governors will establish an ad hoc Committee to recommend what action should be taken. Other procedures are envisaged when a Deputy Managing Director or members of staff are found to be in breach of their obligations.

If a contracting party were to violate any of the obligations towards the AMF, the Board of Governors may suspend both its voting rights and borrowing rights. Article 13(2) of the Statute stipulates that this organ will determine the conditions for suspension, while Article 14(2) provides that the suspended party shall remain liable for any outstanding loans extended by the AMF and for any other commitments towards it. Finally, the Board of Directors is entitled under Article 15 to temporally suspend the extension or release new or existing credit facilities to any contracting party until 'outstanding issues have been resolved', while Article 16 permits the Board of Governors to terminate the operations of the AMF but its resolution must be 'duly adopted by the Assembly of the Union'.

§9. The Peace and Security Council (PSC)

150. The idea of establishing a pan-African entity to deal with security issues and breaches of the peace had been debated for many years in the OAU. However, it was never set up as most Member States were not in favour, fearing that it would encroach upon their sacred sovereignty.[988] When the Central Organ of the OAU Mechanism for Conflict Prevention, Management, and Resolution was created in 1993 under the Cairo Declaration,[989] the discussion was apparently abandoned. However, with the advent of the AU, it was decided to institutionalize the ad hoc

988. *See* OAU Secretary-General, *Report of the Secretary-General on Conflicts in Africa*, OAU Doc. CM/1710 (LVI), June 1992, reproduced in RADIC 4 (1992): 1072, 1076–1077.

989. OAU Assembly, *Declaration of the Assembly of Heads of State and Government on the Establishment Within the OAU of a Mechanism for Conflict Prevention, Management and Resolution*, OAU Doc. AHG/DECL. 3 (XXIX) (30 Jun. 1993).

operations of the Central Organ and to incorporate it into the new Organization by turning it into a proper organ pursuant to Article 5(2) of the Constitutive Act; it stipulates that the Assembly has the power to create new organs. Thus, on 9 July 2002, the First Ordinary Assembly Session adopted the Protocol establishing the PSC, whose entry into force required ratification by the majority of Member States.[990] It swiftly came into effect on 26 December 2003. Under Article 22 thereof, it replaced the 1993 Cairo Declaration and superseded those OAU instruments relating to the Conflict Prevention Mechanism and in conflict with the Protocol. To that extent, the PSC, whose First Session took place on 16 March 2004, should be considered as the successor to the Mechanism. At the time of writing, there were two Member States which have not ratified the Protocol (Cape Verde and South Sudan). Finally, pursuant to the Protocol of Amendments to the Constitutive Act (2003), which, as has been explained, never entered into force, the PSC has been included in the AU's institutional architecture as a principal organ.

151. The relationship between the PSC and the contracting parties to the 2002 Protocol is based on the notion of agency. In particular, Article 7(2) thereof stipulates: 'The Member States agree that in carrying out its duties under the present Protocol, the PSC acts on their behalf.' This provision echoes Article 24(1) of the UN Charter, which provides that the Member States agree that any action taken by the UNSC when performing its duties, pursuant to the duty to maintain international peace and security, shall be considered to have been on their behalf.

However, there are differences as regards agency in the UN and in the AU. Thus, while Article 24(1) was based on the premise that UN Member States had from the beginning conferred the primary responsibility to preserve peace and security specifically to the UNSC, the same is not true as regards the PSC. Three reasons justify this conclusion. First, the PSC was not envisaged as an AU original organ and still remains an Assembly-created body with all the restrictions that this entails in its autonomy. Second, in view of this fact, the functions relating to what is generally referred to as 'peace and security' were initially given to the Assembly. Thus, Article 9(1)(g) of the Constitutive Act allows the Assembly to give instructions to the Executive Council 'on the management of conflicts, war and other emergency situations and the restoration of peace'. The inference is that the Assembly enjoys original powers in this area, which it may delegate to the Executive Council. Although practice shows that this aspect of the mandate has been entrusted to the PSC, it is submitted that the principal responsibility as regards 'peace and security' still rests with the Assembly, which in any given case could intervene and take the necessary measures to address a situation. Third, the description of the PSC in Article 2(1) of the 2002 Protocol as 'a standing decision-making organ for the prevention, management and resolution of conflicts' does not alter the previous arguments. In conclusion, agency has different legal foundations in the AU and in the UN. Notwithstanding these considerations, the consistent practice of the AU Assembly,

990. The Protocol is reproduced in RADIC 13 (2005): 96. The PSC Rules of Procedure were adopted by the Executive Council on behalf of the Assembly in March 2004, *see* Executive Council, *Decision on the Operationalization of the Peace and Security Council*, AU Doc. EX/ CL/Dec. 79 (IV) (16 Mar. 2004).

as the highest-ranking organ representing all Member States and having a general mandate to act, is that when the PSC takes measures, including of a punitive nature, it acts on behalf of the entire membership. To the best of one's knowledge, in all the years that the PSC has been active, the Assembly has not objected or criticized its actions, even though it has not always followed its recommendations and suggestions. In short, the Assembly has given a carte blanche to the PSC allowing it to handle affairs as it sees fit.

152. Although the 2002 Protocol does not expressly lay down that the PSC should be regarded as a regional arrangement in the maintenance of international peace and security within the meaning of Chapter VIII of the UN Charter,[991] this derives both from the Preamble and several provisions of the 2002 Protocol, including Article 17(1), which stipulates that the PSC shall cooperate and work closely with the UNSC. To that end, representatives from the two entities met in Addis Ababa on 17 June 2007 in the context of implementing the ten-year capacity-building programme, which had been concluded between the UN Secretariat and the AUC. At the end of the session, an MoU was signed committing them to the development of a stronger and more structured relationship on conflict prevention, management and resolution, peacekeeping and peace-building, including post-conflict reconstruction and development, to sharing information on conflict situations and to holding a joint meeting at least once a year.[992] As mentioned above, presently, the PSC and the UNSC are in a strategic partnership that falls under the Joint UN-AU Framework for Enhanced Partnership in Peace and Security.[993] Moreover, the PSC figured prominently in the Solemn Declaration on a Common African Defence and Security Policy, which was adopted by the Second Extraordinary Assembly Session (Sirte, 27–28 February 2004),[994] as one of the main actors in implementing the AU's defence and security agenda.

Finally, reference should be made to the Ezulwini Framework for the Enhancement of the Implementation of Measures of the African Union in Situations of Unconstitutional Changes of Governments in Africa. It was adopted during a Retreat of the PSC held in Ezulwini, Swaziland, in December 2009,[995] and the last

991. Strictly legally speaking, it is not correct to term the PSC as a 'regional arrangement' in the sense that only the African Union could be regarded as an arrangement, while the PSC is simply the organ (or one of the organs) authorized to achieve the pacific settlement of regional (or sub-regional or localized) disputes.

992. Compare Assembly, *Decision on Enhancing UN-AU Cooperation: Framework for the Ten-Year Capacity-Building Programme for the African Union*, AU Doc. Assembly/AU/Dec. 140 (VIII) (30 Jan. 2007).

993. For current developments, *see* 'Stronger United Nations-African Union Partnership Vital to Tackle Increasing Terrorism, Governance Gaps, Humanitarian Plight in Africa, Speakers Tell Security Council', Press Release, UN Doc. SC/15058 (11 Oct. 2022), at: https://press.un.org/en/2022/sc15058.doc.htm.

994. At: http://www.peaceau.org/uploads/declaration-cadsp-en.pdf, reproduced in M. Juma, *Compendium of Key Documents Relating to Peace and Security in Africa* (Pretoria: Pretoria University Law Press, 2006) 100. Generally, *see* O.A. Touray, 'The Common African Defence and Security Policy', *African Affairs* 104 (2005): 635.

995. At: http://www.peaceau.org/uploads/ezulwini-framework-english.pdf.

time it was mentioned in an official AU instrument was in the Declaration on Terrorism and Unconstitutional Changes of Government in Africa adopted by the Sixteenth Extraordinary Assembly SESSION (2022).[996] The principal purpose of the Ezulwini Framework was to implement a previous PSC Decision establishing a Committee on Sanctions,[997] in conformity with Article 8(1) of the PSC Protocol. The Committee is meant to complement the AU efforts to combat and prevent unconstitutional changes of government and operates with five PSC members appointed on the principle of regional representation. Its mandate is to monitor and make recommendations on the execution of sanctions already ordered by the PSC. Sanctions are to be imposed in a graduated manner from the moment a coup d'état has taken place. The functioning of this Committee appears to be similar to the ad hoc Sanctions Committees established by the UNSC to control compliance by Member States with resolutions ordering mandatory punitive measures under Chapter VII of the UN Charter.

153. Moreover, the PSC Protocol delineates the relationship between the PSC and the African (sub) regional mechanisms for conflict prevention, management, and resolution by subjecting the latter to (what appears) its superior authority. In particular, Article 16(1) thereof provides that '[t]he Regional Mechanisms are part of the overall security architecture of the [African] Union, which has the primary responsibility for promoting peace, security and stability in Africa'. It will be argued that these are rather false premises, because on many an occasion the AU has shown that it is unable, incapable or unwilling or a combination thereof to tackle urgent issues affecting peace and stability in parts of the continent, to promote an ethos of accountability, to combat impunity; and to ensure that all Africans are treated as equals irrespective of status, wealth and origin. Indeed, as has been maintained, the attitude shown by the AU could result in denialism as regards tackling matters over which it does have 'primary responsibility'.[998] Notwithstanding these observations, Article 16 of the Protocol instructs the PSC and the AUC Chairperson to harmonize and coordinate the regional mechanisms' activities so that their actions are consistent with the AU objectives and principles. It is rather difficult to justify, from a strictly legal point of view, the subjecting of organs already in existence and belonging to different IGOs (namely the RECs) and having separate international legal personality to the jurisdiction of an organ, which has been set up in the context of another, separate, international organization (namely the AU).

The fact that the membership, respectively, in the AU and in these regional mechanisms invariably coincides is of no relevance because, unlike the AEC, there is no institutional rapport between the AU and those RECs which have established such mechanisms. Even if it were argued that the AU was conceived as the supreme

996. AU Doc. Ext/Assembly/AU/Decl. (XVI) (28 May 2022).

997. *See* PSC, *Communique of the 178th Meeting of the Peace and Security Council*, PSC/PR/COMM.3(CLXXVIII), 13 Mar. 2009.

998. *See* K. Magliveras, 'International Organisations and Denialism: The Case of the African Union' in *Denialism and Human Rights*, H. Nelen, J.C.M. Willems & R. Moerland (eds) (Cambridge: Intersentia, 2016) 267.

political and security institution in Africa, its relationship with the other mechanisms cannot be similar to that established under Articles 52 et seq. of the UN Charter, namely the relationship existing between the UNSCl and the peace and security regional arrangements. Notwithstanding these considerations, in 2008 the AU and the RECs concluded an MoU on peace and security, whose Article II describes it as a binding legal instrument.[999] This is an interesting contention because, apparently, the MOU did not require to be approved by the plenary organs of the participating organizations; under Article XXVI it came into force upon signature by five of the participating parties, including the AUC. Adherence to the principles of subsidiarity, complementarity and comparative advantage guides the MOU's operation.[1000]

154. Pursuant to Article 2(2) of the Protocol, the PSC is composed of the following five separate entities (also referred to as 'pillars'). First, the so-called Panel of the Wise, which according to Article 11 thereof is a body advising PSC on all issues relating to the promotion and maintenance of peace and stability. It is made up of five leading African personalities from various segments of society, each representing an African region. They are expected to intervene early in the outbreak of a dispute and attempt to solve it through discreet diplomacy. The first members of the Panel were appointed during the Eighth Ordinary Assembly Session (Addis Ababa, 23–30 January 2007) for three years: Salim Ahmed Salim, former OAU Secretary-General; Brigalia Bam, Chairperson of the Independent Electoral Commission (IEC) of South Africa; Ahmed Ban Bella, former President of Algeria; Elisabeth K. Pognon, President of the Constitutional Court of Benin; and Miguel Trovaoda, former President of Sao Tome and Principe.[1001] There was considerable delay in the Panel becoming operative (the modalities for its functioning were adopted in April 2008). Presently, the Fifth Panel is in operation (February 2022 to February 2025) and is composed of Domitien Ndayizeye, former President of Burundi (representing Central Africa); Effie Owuor, retired judge of the Court of Appeal of Kenya (Eastern Africa); Amr Mahmoud Abu Zaid Moussa, Egypt, former Secretary-General of the League of Arab States (Northern Africa); Phumzile Mlambo-Ngcuka, former Deputy President of the Republic of South Africa (Southern Africa); and Babacar Kanté, former Vice President of the Constitutional Court of Senegal (Western Africa).[1002] It should be noted that the representative of Southern Africa was appointed at a later date by the Executive Council pursuant to Rule 4(2) of the Assembly Rules of Procedures on delegation of authority.[1003] Second, a

999. *See Memorandum of Understanding on Cooperation in the Area of Peace and Security between the African Union, the Regional Economic Communities and the Coordinating Mechanisms of the Regional Standby Brigades of Eastern Africa and Northern Africa*, at: http://www.peaceau.org/uploads/mou-au-rec-eng.pdf.

1000. *See* father J. Akokpari & S. Ancas, 'The African Union and Regional Economic Communities: A Partnership for Peace and Security' in *Handbook of Africa's International Relations*, T. Murithi (ed.) (Abingdon: Routledge, 2014) 73.

1001. *See* Assembly, *Decision on the Appointment of the Members of the Panel of the Wise*, AU Doc. Assembly/AU/Dec. 152(VIII) (30 Jan. 2007).

1002. They were appointed by Assembly, *Decision on Appointment of Members of the Panel of the Wise*, AU Doc. Assembly/AU/Dec. 824 (XXXV) (6 Feb. 2022).

1003. Executive Council, *Decision on the Nomination and Appointment of the One (1) Representative of Southern Africa for the 5th Panel of the Wise*, AU Doc. EX.CL/Dec. 1183 (XLI) (14 Jul. 2022).

Continental Early Warning System (CEWS), which, pursuant to Article 12 of the Protocol, is the body facilitating the anticipation and prevention of conflicts.[1004] It is responsible for data collection and conflict analysis, no doubt a service of value to Member States. It is also mandated to cooperate closely not only with the observation and monitoring systems that RECs have put in place but also with the UN and its agencies, with research centres and academic institutions, and with NGOs. Based on the Framework for the Operationalization of the CEWS, adopted in 2006 and endorsed by the Tenth Ordinary Executive Council Session held in January 2007, it was meant to be fully operational by the end of 2009. However, due to a number of reasons (limited human resources, lack of training, underfunding, and lack of coordination with the Early Warning Systems (EWS) of RECs), it was finally operationalized in 2012.[1005]

Third, an African Standby Force (ASF), which, according to Article 13 of the PSC Protocol, is a body composed of multidisciplinary civilian,[1006] police and military contingents (of roughly 15,000 troops) for rapid deployment of peace support missions and intervention pursuant to Article 4(h) and 4(j) of the Constitutive Act.[1007] ASF was meant to coordinate the following five sub-regional standby forces operating in the context of RECs: the East African Standby Force (EASF); the ECOWAS Standby Force (ESF); the ECCAS Standby Force; the North African Regional Capability (NARC) Standby Force; and the SADC Standby Force (SSF). As the years was going by and the ASF was not being deployed, in 2013, following a South African initiative, the African Capacity for Immediate Response to Crises (ACIRC) was set up as an interim measure. Fourteen Member States offered assistance to ACIRC, but soon there was competition between it and ASF as to which will attract resources that were anyway in short supply; as with so many other AU projects, they both had to rely on funding from non-African stakeholders for their implementation. In 2016, the Member States participating in ACIRC declared that it was ready to respond swiftly to crises and to contribute to PSC-mandated Peace Support Operations (PSO) pursuant to Article 4 (h) and (j) of the Constitutive Act.[1008] Four years later, the Assembly, on the one hand, called for the establishment of a Special Unit within the ASF to combat terrorism[1009] and, on the other hand, promoted the

1004. *See* J. Cilliers, *Towards a Continental Early Warning System for Africa*, ISS Paper 102 (Pretoria: Institute of Security Studies, April 2005).

1005. Compare UNSC Res. 65/283 of 17 Jun. 2011 titled 'Strengthening the role of mediation in the peaceful settlement of disputes, conflict prevention and resolution', where at para. 16 the UNSC welcomed the AU efforts in developing its mediation capacities and structures, including its early warning assessment systems.

1006. *See* C. de Coning & Y. Kasumba (ed.), *The Civilian Dimension of the African Standby Force*, African Union Commission/ African Centre for the Constructive Resolution of Disputes (ACCORD), 2010, at: https://www.files.ethz.ch/isn/121430/2010_TheCivilianDimension.pdf.

1007. For an unsuccessful attempt to create a defence force during the OAU era, *see* Council of Ministers, *Resolution of the Establishment of the OAU Defence Force*, OAU Doc. CM/Res. 867 (XXXVII) (26 Jun. 1981).

1008. *See* African Capacity for Immediate Response to Crises (ACIRC), Second Extraordinary Summit, Addis Ababa, 9 November 2016, *Declaration*, at: https://www.peaceau.org/uploads/acirc-summit-declaration-09-nov-16-final-eng.pdf.

1009. Assembly, *Decision on the Report of the Peace and Security Council on its Activities and the State of Peace and Security in Africa*, AU Doc. Assembly/AU/Dec. 753 (XXXIII), para. 17 (10 Feb. 2020).

adoption of the AU Doctrine on Peace Support Operations,[1010] which was finally done at the Third Extraordinary Session of the Specialized Technical Committee on Defence, Safety and Security (STCDSS) on 30 January 2021. In the meantime, the Assembly had declared the ASF to be fully operational and directed the PSC to use its framework in mandating and authorizing AU PSOs and also dissolved ACIRC.[1011] In conclusion, ASF has become a framework and tool for implementing PSOs within the context of the aforementioned Doctrine.

Fourth, a Military Staff Committee (MSC), which hierarchically comes under the ASF. Pursuant to Article 13(8)(12) of the Protocol, it will advise and assist the PSC in all questions relating to military and security requirements for the promotion and maintenance of peace and security. In effect, it is a subsidiary organ of the PSC and operates according to the Policy Framework Document on the establishment of the African Standby Force and the Military Staff Committee adopted by the Assembly in 2004.[1012] MSC comprises senior military representatives from the fifteen Member States that are elected to the PSC and is chaired by the military or defence attaché of the Member State that has the monthly rotating chair in the PSC. Fifth, a Peace Fund, which, according to Article 21 of the PSC Protocol, is a special fund to provide the necessary financial resources for peace support missions and other operational activities. Details on the Peace Fund are given later. Over and above these entities, the PSC has also been authorized to establish subsidiary bodies and sub-committees. Finally, it should be noted that the AUC has been mandated to support the PSC logistically through its relevant Directorate, a fact which could lead to duplication of efforts and depletion of the limited recourses available.

In line with the PSC Protocol and the aforementioned MoU of 2008 between the AU and RECs, in June 2012, the Panel of the Wise agreed to establish a Pan-African Network of the Wise (PANWISE). The purpose of this entity is to bring under one umbrella (and presumably under AU leadership as well) the following organs operating in the context of separate African institutions: the AU Panel of the Wise; the ECOWAS Council of the Wise; the COMESA Committee of Elders; the SADC Mediation Reference Group and Panel of Elders; the IGAD Mediation Contact Group; as well as any other similar structure to be set up in the future in another REC. Its operation shall be based on the Framework for the Operationalization of the PANWISE, which was meant to be submitted for consideration to the AU and the respective RECs during 2013.[1013] As it becomes obvious, the necessary qualifications for individuals to gain membership in it are to have reached a certain age and have the status of elders. This insistence on the age of members derives from

1010. Assembly, Decision on the Outcome of the 12th Ordinary Meeting of the Specialized Technical Committee on Defence, Safety and Security, AU Doc. Assembly/AU/Dec. 753 (XXXIII) (10 Feb. 2020).

1011. Assembly, *Decision of the 14th Extraordinary Session of the Assembly of the Union on Silencing the Guns in Africa*, AU Doc. Ext/Assembly/AU/Dec. 1 (XIV); *Johannesburg Declaration on Silencing the Guns in Africa 'Silencing the Guns: Creating Conducive Conditions for Africa's Development'*, AU Doc. Ext/Assembly/AU/Decl. 1 (XIV) (6 Dec. 2020).

1012. Assembly, *Decision on the African Standby Force (ASF) and the Military Staff Committee (MSC)*, AU Doc. Assembly/AU/Dec. 35 (III) (8 Jul. 2004).

1013. *See* AU Commission, Directorate of Information and Communication, *AU Echo*, Issue 06, 28 Jan. 2013, p. 10.

indigenous African customs and traditions, pursuant to which elders are called upon to offer advice, to mediate between the parties to a dispute, and to undertake other conflict prevention measures. While even in contemporary Africa such methods continue to be official practice in several states (e.g., Ghana, Lesotho, and Rwanda), the question should be asked whether peace and security problems encountered in almost all parts of the continent do not require the participation, whether on an equal basis or not, of a younger generation of experienced and competent technocrats, who could very well come from the African Diaspora.

As has already been submitted, the abundance of organs is a theme characterizing the whole AU institutional architecture. However, in the case of the PSC, it should seriously be questioned whether it is viable to have different structures operating on the basis of separate rules and at a financial cost that the AU can ill-afford and, consequently, has to appeal (time after time) to the international community for assistance.[1014] It is further submitted that African conflicts and the various threats to peace and security that the continent has been experiencing require centralization and not decentralization and, in that respect, RECs have a significant role to play. Given the multitude of institutions active in the field of peace and security and the invariable lack of (human and financial) resources, it might be more appropriate to reinforce the role of RECs even if this meant the downgrading of AU's role.

155. Article 7 of the PSC Protocol lays down the multifaceted powers with which it has been endowed. The most important are the following: to undertake peacemaking and peace-building functions; to authorize the deployment of peace missions; to recommend to the Assembly intervention in a Member State in case of grave circumstances; to institute sanctions in cases of unconstitutional change of governments; to implement the AU common defence policy; to take appropriate action where a Member's independence and sovereignty is threatened by acts of aggression; and to exercise any powers that might be delegated to it by the Assembly. The power to introduce sanctions for coups d'état would appear to be problematic in view of the Assembly's primary responsibility to impose punitive measures pursuant to Article 23 of the Constitutive Act. Generally speaking, the charters of international organizations stipulate that the imposition of sanctions is the prerogative of the highest-ranking organ encompassing all Member States; in the case of the AU, this would be the Assembly. As has been noted (*supra*, paragraphs 90 et seq.), the regime for the imposition of sanctions against illegal regimes is not without problems. The adoption, variation and rescinding of punitive measures by the PSC without (at least ex post facto) approval by the Assembly should be regarded as a problematic state of affairs and arguably is not consistent with the AU's institutional architecture. If the ACJHR ever becomes operative and a Member State, which has been the object of PSC sanctions, were to challenge their legality before it, it is submitted that these considerations will surface.

156. Pursuant to Article 5(2) of the PSC Protocol, the Assembly has been empowered to elect its Members by applying the principles of equitable regional

1014. Compare Assembly, *Decision on the African Standby Force (ASF) and the Military Staff Committee (MSC)*, AU Doc. Assembly/AU/Dec. 35 (III) (8 Jul. 2004).

representation and rotation as well as by applying a number of other criteria. However, until now, Members have been elected by the Executive Council under delegation of powers and subsequently appointed by the Assembly.[1015] Thus, during the Fortieth Ordinary Executive Council Session, five Member States were elected to PSC seats for a three-year term, and ten were elected for a two-year term, all beginning on 1 April 2022.[1016] They were appointed during the Thirty-Fifth Ordinary Assembly Session.[1017] In particular, the Members serving until March 2024 are for Central Africa: Burundi and Congo Republic; for Eastern Africa: Tanzania and Uganda; for Northern Africa: Tunisia; for Southern Africa: South Africa and Zimbabwe and for Western Africa: Gambia, Ghana and Senegal, while those Members serving until 31 March 2025 are for Central Africa: Cameroon; for Eastern Africa: Djibouti; for Northern Africa: Morocco; for Southern Africa: Namibia; and for Western Africa: Nigeria.

157. The PSC functions on a continuous basis, and, therefore, all its Members are required to be represented at AU headquarters. Ordinarily it holds closed sessions (Article 8(9) of the Protocol)) but Article 8(10) envisages open meetings as well, in which case any CSO involved or interested in the matter under consideration may be invited to participate, without vote, in the discussion. This provision as well as Article 20 of the Protocol, which urges the PSC to encourage NGOs and other community-based organizations to participate in the common effort to promote peace and security in the continent, further the Constitutive Act's goal to have the civil society involved as much as possible in African affairs. In December 2008, the PSC held in Livingstone, Zambia, a retreat to discuss appropriate mechanisms for its interaction with CSO, which led to the adoption of the Livingstone Formula.[1018] Thus, on 26 March 2013, the PSC during its 364th Meeting devoted an Open Session on the theme 'Women and Children in Situations of Violent Conflict in Africa: Contribution and Role of Women,' which was held pursuant to a previous decision adopted on 30 March 2010 (223rd meeting).[1019] Moreover, on 19 August 2013 (391st meeting), the PSC held an Open Session on the occasion of the World Humanitarian Day, where it was briefed on the protection of civilians and the humanitarian situation in the CAR and the DRC by the AUC, the UN, and CSO.[1020] More recently, it held its Fourth Open Session on youth, peace and security on 3

1015. For the first such delegation of powers, *see* Assembly, *Decision on the Operationalization of the Protocol Relating to the Establishment of the Peace and Security Council*, AU Doc. ASS/AU/Dec. 16 (II) (12 Jul. 2003).

1016. Executive Council, *Decision on the Election of Fifteen (15) Members of the Peace and Security Council of the African Union*, AU Doc. EX.CL/Dec. 1167 (XL) (3 Feb. 2022).

1017. Assembly, *Decision on Appointment of Fifteen (15) Members of the PSC*, AU Doc. Assembly/AU/Dec. 823 (XXXV) (6 Feb. 2022). For all previous PSC elections and appointments as well as for the question if all appointed Members meet the standards envisaged in Art. 5(2) of the PSC Protocol, *see* Magliveras & Naldi, *The African Union*, Second Edition, *supra*, 182–183.

1018. PSC, *Conclusions on a Mechanism for Interaction Between the Peace and Security Council and Civil Society Organizations in the Promotion of Peace, Security and Stability in Africa*, AU Doc. PSC/PR/Comm (CLX), at: http://www.au.int/en/sites/default/files/documents/30974-doc-psc_conclusion_-_livingstone.pdf.

1019. *See* PSC, Press Statement, AU Doc. PSC/PR/BR.(CCCLXIV) (26 Mar. 2013).

1020. *See* PSC, Press Statement, AU Doc. PSC/PR/BR.(CCCXCI) (19 Aug. 2003).

March 2022,[1021] where it examined the progress made in the implementation of the Continental Framework for Youth, Peace and Security,[1022] a policy document that domesticates UNSC Resolution 2250(2015) of 9 December 2015 in Africa.[1023]

158. Each Member of the PSC has one vote with the exception of those Members, which happen to be parties to a conflict or to a situation under consideration. The term 'party' is not defined in the Protocol, and this could lead to questions of interpretation. Suppose that State A, which is embroiled in a belligerency situation with State B, accuses State C, a PSC Member, of aiding and abetting State B, a fact strenuously denied by State C. Would State C be considered a 'party' to the conflict and, consequently, denied participation in the deliberations and/or the right to vote? Notwithstanding that this is an issue to be resolved by the other PSC Members, it could derail discussions and prevent a prompt solution of the conflict.

159. Decisions are reached by consensus, failing which by a two-thirds majority of the Members present and voting. Considering that ten Members constitute a quorum (Article 8(13) of the PSC Protocol), decisions could be taken by seven Members, that is, by less than half of its membership and almost one-eighth of the total AU membership. Arguably, some doubts could be raised about the authority such decisions carry, especially as regards those imposing sanctions or dealing with sensitive issues pertaining to the sovereignty of Member States embroiled in armed conflict or in a civil war. Any such issues could be resolved if the decisions in question were forwarded to the Assembly for approval. However, as the PSC invariably addresses cases where urgent action is required and considering that the Assembly meets in ordinary session only once a year (and it would be impractical to meet in extraordinary session each time the PSC orders measures of a punitive nature), the problems associated with this proposal become obvious.

160. According to Article 7(3) of the Protocol, all Member States are obliged to accept and implement PSC decisions. This is a rather curious provision as it attaches a strict obligation to all Member States irrespective of whether they have ratified the Protocol or not. As has been explained, there are still Member States which have not ratified it.[1024] Moreover, considering that the PSC was not envisaged as an original AU organ but was created later under the authority of Article 5(2) of the Constitutive Act, the validity of any decisions dealing with non-contracting parties could be challenged. Indeed, it is a fundamental rule of the law of international organizations that participating states are legally bound by the decisions of organs only to the extent that they have already accepted their jurisdiction and competence, a rule that is evidently not satisfied in the present circumstances. Notwithstanding these

1021. *See* AU Information & Communication Directorate, Press Release No: 000003456/2021, 28 Feb. 2022.
1022. Text at: https://au.int/en/documents/20200821/continental-framework-youth-peace-and-security.
1023. *See further*, UNSC Res. 2419(2018) of 6 June 2018 and Res. 2535(2020) of 14 July 2020.
1024. Note that on occasions the PSC has dealt with conflicts and situations concerning Member States which were not contracting parties, e.g., with Somalia during its Seventy-Third Meeting on 19 Mar. 2007.

observations, to the best of one's knowledge, the PSC's decision-making power has never been officially challenged by Member States.

161. For the PSC to operate efficiently and effectively and to bring to fruition its goals, it is imperative that it possesses adequate financial resources. It relies primarily on the Peace Fund, the continuation of the fund which had financed the operations of the OAU Central Organ since June 1993. The Peace Fund is supported by appropriations from the regular AU budget (originally, they exceeded 6% of the regular AU budget), from voluntary contributions by Member States and other African stakeholders (the private sector, the civil society and individuals) as well as from contributions by non- African stakeholders.[1025] During the Special Assembly Summit, held in Tripoli in August 2009, Member States agreed to increase the contribution to the Peace Fund to 12% of the regular budget. However, with hindsight, doubling the contribution was considered not feasible and, therefore, during the Sixteenth Ordinary Executive Council Session (Addis Ababa, January 2010), it was agreed to maintain the target of 12% but implement it over a period of three years starting from 2011. However, considering that there are always several Member States defaulting on their compulsory budget contributions, the PSC's ability to function effectively and carry out its mandate cannot be guaranteed. Moreover, it is instructive to note that the Protocol allows the PSC to resort to the UN to secure financial and logistical support. However, as has been explained in other sections of the present monograph, the UN and more specifically the UNSC are rather unwilling to heed to AU's requests.

162. During more recent times, the Twenty-Fifth Ordinary Assembly Session (Johannesburg, 14–15 June 2015) resolved 'to enhance ownership of the budget of the Union' and that Member States should finance, *inter alia*, 25% of the peace and security budget, incrementally over a five year period.[1026] Moreover, in July 2016, the Assembly determined that the Peace Fund shall be structured around three so-called Windows: The first Window will concern 'Mediation and Preventive Diplomacy'; the second 'Institutional Capacity'; and the third 'Peace Support Operation'.[1027] The latter Window, by definition, takes up most of the resources, leaving the other two Windows underfunded. To offer an illustration, at the time, the yearly cost of AMISOM (with an approved strength of more than 22,000 uniformed personnel) was around USD 900 million and exceeded the AU budget for FY 2017

1025. Thus, on 1 Nov. 2002, it was announced that Japan contributed USD 200,000 towards the Peace Fund; *see* AU Press Release No. 45/2002. Moreover, on 31 Dec. 2003, Finland and the AU signed an agreement, according to which the former contributed EUR 750,000 to the Peace Fund until December 2005; *see* AU Press Release No. 122/2003. In mid-December 2012 Russia contributed USD 2 million.

1026. *See further*, PSC Press Statement, PSC/PR/BR.(DLXXXII), 14 Mar. 2016. The Assembly decision concerned possible alternative sources for securing the adequate funding of the AU budget, AU Doc. Assembly/AU/Dec. 561 (XXXIV).

1027. Assembly, *Decision on the Outcome of the Retreat of the Heads of States and Government, Ministers of Foreign Affairs and Ministers of Finance on the Financing of the African Union*, AU Doc. Assembly/AU/Dec. 605 (XXVII), para. 5b (18 Jul. 2016).

(it stood at USD 782 million)! According to a Report on the challenges surrounding the financing of peace activities submitted in the summer of 2016 by the AU High Representative for the Peace Fund:

> The percentage contribution from the regular budget has only reached 7%. This is mainly because of high levels of arrears and late payments of Member States' assessed contributions. While some AU Member States have made additional voluntary contributions to the Peace Fund, these payments are irregular and unpredictable. As a result, the Fund is highly dependent on external partners.[1028]

As has been noted, in July 2016, the Assembly took concrete measures to address the perennial problem of the precarious AU finances by creating a 0.2% levy on the importation of goods into Africa. Regarding specifically the Peace Fund, it was resolved to have it endowed from this levy with an initial amount of USD 325 million rising to USD 400 million in 2020. Each of the five African regions was expected to contribute an equal amount to the Peace Fund.[1029] The goal was apparently never reached.

Contributions from the EU and from individual Member States have always been instrumental in maintaining PSC activities. However, accepting EU funding should pose a moral dilemma to those African countries blaming the former European colonial powers for most of their problems. On 2 April 2003, the AU and the EU signed a EUR 12 million financial agreement, of which EUR 10 million was earmarked for supporting the peace and security agenda. Moreover, in July 2003, the Second Ordinary Assembly Session had requested that the EU examine the possibility of setting up a Peace Support Operation Facility to fund peacekeeping operations carried out under AU authority.[1030] Promptly, the EU created the Peace Facility for Africa with an initial endowment of EUR 250 million to support African-led peace support operations and enhance the institutional capacities of the AU and the RECs in peacekeeping and conflict prevention for a period of three years.[1031] In April 2006, the EU Council determined to extend it until 2010 and allocated the amount of EUR 300 million.[1032] Later, the funding of the Peace Facility was increased to EUR 440 million. In June 2004, the AU Mission in Sudan (AMIS) became the first peacekeeping operation to be supported by the Peace Facility; originally, it received EUR

1028. *See* AU Peace Fund Silencing the Guns, *Securing Predictable and Sustainable Financing for Peace in Africa*, Report, August 2016, para. 20, at: http://www.peaceau.org/uploads/auhr-progress-report-final-020916-with-annexes.pdf.
1029. *See* Assembly/AU/Dec. 605 (XXVII), *supra*.
1030. *See* Assembly, *Decision on the Establishment by the European Union of a Peace Support Operation Facility for the African Union*, AU Doc. Assembly/AU/Dec. 21 (II), para. 5 (12 Jul. 2003).
1031. *See* ACP-EC Council of Ministers, *Decision 2003/3 of 11 December 2003 on the use of resources from the long-term development envelope of the ninth EDF for the creation of a Peace Facility for Africa*, Official J. of the Eur. Communities (O.J.) L 345 of 31 Dec. 2003.
1032. *See* EU Council, *Regulation 617/2007/EC of 14 May 2007 on the implementation of the 10th European Development Fund under the ACP-EC Partnership Agreement*, O.J. L 152 of 13 Jun. 2007, and ACP-EC Council of Ministers, *Decision No 2/2007 of 25 May 2007 allowing additional bilateral contributions, to be managed by the Commission, in support of the objectives of the African Peace Facility*, O.J. L 175 of 5 Jul. 2007.

12 million; an additional EUR 40 million was pledged by the EU Council in May 2007.[1033] To offer some examples, the Peace Facility supported, *inter alia*, peacekeeping efforts in the CAR (FOMUC), in Somalia (AMISOM), as well as the African Union Mission in the Comoros (AMISEC). The African Peace Fund (APF) envelope under the Tenth European Development Fund (EDF)[1034] was EUR 600 million, broken down into two tractions of EUR 300 million each, one for the Action Programme 2008–2010 and the other for the Action Programme 2011–2013.[1035] The Eleventh EDF initially foresaw a total contribution of EUR 750 million to the African Peace Facility, but another EUR 150 million was allocated in December 2015 due to increased needs. Until December 2015, AMISOM had received a total of EUR 901.2 million from European sources,[1036] while by the end of 2016, more than EUR 2.1 billion had been allocated to the African Peace Fund since its creation.[1037] It has already been noted that in July 2021 APF was replaced by the European Peace Facility (EPF), which consists of two pillars (military operations and assistance measures). During 2021–2023, EPF has provided assistance to and/or supported projects in Niger (the financial reference amount is EUR 40 million),[1038] the deployment of Rwandan forces in Mozambique (EUR 20 million),[1039] the armed forces of Mauritania (EUR 12 million),[1040] of Nigeria (EUR 25 million),[1041] and of Mali (EUR 24 million),[1042] as well as the military units trained by the EU in Mozambique (EUR 85 million).[1043] Finally, the reference amount for the

1033. *See* European Commission, *Bulletin of the European Union 5-2007*, point 1.34.40, and *Bulletin of the European Union 6-2007*, point 1.34.72.
1034. EDF was created in 1957 by the Treaty of Rome establishing the European Economic Community and is the EU's main instrument challenging development aid to African, Caribbean and Pacific (ACP) states.
1035. Generally, *see European Commission, Annual Report 2011 – The African Peace Facility*, Publications Office of the European Union, 2012, at: https://data.europa.eu/doi/10.2841/4184.
1036. *See* European Commission, *Annual Report 2015 – The African Peace Facility*, Publications Office of the European Union, 2016, at: https://reliefweb.int/report/somalia/african-peace-facility-annual-report-2015.
1037. *See* European Commission, *Annual Report 2016 – The African Peace Facility*, Publications Office of the European Union, 2017, 7.
1038. Council Decision (CFSP) 2023/509 of 7 March 2023 on an assistance measure under the European Peace Facility to support the Nigerien Armed Forces in conjunction with the EU military partnership mission in Niger, O.J. L 70, 8.3.2023, p. 51.
1039. Council Decision (CFSP) 2022/2354 of 1 December 2022 on an assistance measure under the European Peace Facility to support the deployment of the Rwanda Defence Force in Mozambique, Council Decision (CFSP) 2022/2354 of 1 December 2022 on an assistance measure under the European Peace Facility to support the deployment of the Rwanda Defence Force in Mozambique, O.J. L 311, 2.12.2022, p. 153.
1040. Council Decision (CFSP) 2022/2355 of 1 December 2022 on an assistance measure under the European Peace Facility to strengthen the capacities of the armed forces of the Islamic Republic of Mauritania, O.J. L 311, 2.12.2022, p. 157.
1041. Council Decision (CFSP) 2022/1236 of 18 July 2022 on an assistance measure under the European Peace Facility to support the Nigerien Armed Forces, O.J. L 190, 19.7.2022, p. 121.
1042. Council Decision (CFSP) 2021/2137 of 2 December 2021 on an Assistance Measure under the European Peace Facility to support the armed forces of the Republic of Mali in conjunction with the EU Training Mission in Mali, O.J. L 432, 3.12.2021, p. 67.
1043. European Union, Council Decision (CFSP) 2021/2032 of 19 November 2021 on an assistance measure under the European Peace Facility to support military units trained by the EU Training Mission in Mozambique, O.J. L 415, 22.11.2021, p. 25.

assistance measures supporting the African Union for the period 2022–2024 is EUR 600 million. To give some illustrations of the actions approved and the amounts involved: in March 2023, EUR 25 million to support the Somali National Army and EUR 85 million to the military component of ATMIS (for the whole of 2023); in January 2023, EUR 80 million to the Multi-National Joint Task Force (MNJTF) against Boko Haram (for 2023 and 2024), in September 2022 EUR 15 million to support the SADC Mission in Mozambique (SAMIM), etc.[1044]

163. Regarding contributions from the international community (bar the EU), reference could be made to a joint project between the AUC and the Regional Bureau for Africa of the United Nations Development Programme (UNDP). On 15 May 2003, it agreed on a USD 7.2 million project titled 'Support for the Implementation of the Peace and Security Agenda of the African Union' that ran to the end of 2013.[1045] It was a follow-up to a UNDP-supported project dating from 1997 and titled 'Capacity Building for the OAU Mechanism for Conflict Prevention, Management and Resolution.' The financial input of UNDP amounted to USD 2 million, while other donors (including Germany, Norway, Sweden, Canada and the Netherlands) committed themselves to cover the remainder. This is an overarching scheme with specific objectives (e.g., to improve the management skills and the technical level of staff at the Commission's Directorate of Peace and Security), but states may finance other actions as well. Thus, on 17 March 2006, Japan and UNDP signed a USD 2 million agreement, whereby the former agreed to finance an AU plan to demobilize, disarm, rehabilitate, and reintegrate young ex-combatants in the war-torn Great Lakes region.

164. The constitutional crisis in the Comoros in the period 2007–2008, though rather dated now, does however present a good illustration of the fact that the PSC handles all matters coming under its purview. Perhaps the small size of the Comoros and the fact that its role in AU affairs was almost negligible might have been reasons not to show any real interest in it. Moreover, it was not likely that it would have become a regional security threat and, like so many African states, the Comoros had been facing unending constitutional and institutional problems. The Union of the Comoros Islands, which is made up by the Autonomous Islands of Grande-Comoros, Anjouan, and Mwali, gained its independence from France on 6 July 1975. Since then, it had been plagued by over twenty coups d'état. In December 2001, a new Constitution was adopted, which provided for a rotating presidency among the islands as well as a separate Union president and granted more autonomy to each of the islands.[1046] When the Union President called for the election of the

---

1044. European Union, Council Decision (CFSP) 2022/667 of 21 April 2022 on an assistance measure taking the form of a general programme for support to the African Union under the European Peace Facility for the period 2022–2024, O.J. L 121, 22.4.2022, p. 38.

1045. *See* UNDP, Final Report Project: Support for the Implementation of the Peace and Security Agenda of the African Union Commission July 2009 –December 2013, UNDP/RAULOE Addis Ababa, December 2013.

1046. At: http://www.wipo.int/wipolex/en/details.jsp?id=8667.

islands' presidents to take place on 10 June 2007, the PSC authorized the deployment of the African Union Electoral and Security Assistance Mission to the Comoros (MAES), which included civilian personnel but also a police and a military component with forces coming from the Republic of South Africa (which later played the role of coordinator in the regional efforts to solve the crisis), Senegal, Sudan, and Tanzania.[1047] The deployment of MAES was financially assisted by the League of Arab States, of which the Comoros has been a Member State since 1993.[1048]

A few days before the elections, the President of the Comoros decided to postpone them for a week in the island of Anjouan because the prevailing conditions were not conducive for holding free, fair and transparent elections. Even though it could be argued that this was an internal affair of a Member State, the PSC issued a Communiqué where it 'took note' of this decision, 'endorsed' the assessment that the conditions in Anjouan did not guarantee democratic voting and indicated that the results of any elections that might be held against its decision would not be recognized by the AU and the international community.[1049] In the event, the island's authorities held the vote on 10 June 2007 as scheduled. General Mohamed Bacar, who had held the office from 2002 to 2007, won 73% of the vote. Notwithstanding that the other four candidates boycotted the elections and the result was never recognized by the Union government, he was sworn-in on 14 June 2007. As the crisis with the 'de facto' authorities in Anjouan was not resolved, a so-called Ministerial Committee of the Countries of the Region on the Comoros was established and coordinated by South Africa with the participation of Tanzania, Mozambique, Mauritius, Seychelles, Kenya, and Madagascar. Although it would appear that at the time its setting up was not sanctioned by the PSC or any other AU organ, the Committee met twice on 19 June 2007 and on 8–9 July 2007.[1050] The Committee formulated a number of recommendations for which the PSC expressed its full support.[1051] The recommendations did not receive the expected positive response from the 'de facto' authorities in Anjouan, and in mid-August 2007, the PSC 'deplored the intransigence displayed' and the lack of cooperation with the regional initiative.[1052]

According to the PSC Communiqué issued in October 2007, the fact that the 'illegal authorities of Anjouan' had continued to reject the Ministerial Committee's recommendations in conjunction with the fact that 'any further delay in the resolution

1047. *See* Peace and Security Council, Seventy-Seventh Meeting, Communiqué PSC/MIN/Comm.1 (LXXVII), 9 May 2007.

1048. *See Africa Research Bulletin: Politics, Social and Cultural Series*, vol. 44, 171134–17115A (July 2007).

1049. *See* Peace and Security Council, Communiqué PSC/PR/COMM (LXXVIII), Seventy-Eighth Meeting, 9 Jun. 2007.

1050. Note that in the past the OAU Council of Ministers had recommended to the Assembly the taking of military measures against the Anjouanese separatists and had requested the countries of the region, under the Republic of South Africa's coordination, to take all appropriate steps, *see* Council of Ministers, *Decision on the Com*oros, OAU Doc. CM/Dec. 523 (LXXII) Rev. 1 (8 Jul. 2000). The Assembly approved the recommendations and authorized the countries of the region and the Central Organ to determine the modalities of the military measures to be taken, Assembly, *Decision on the Comoros*, OAU Doc. AHG/Dec. 149 (XXXVI) (12 Jul. 2000).

1051. *See* PSC, Press Statement PSC/PR/PS (LXXXII), Eighty-Second Meeting, 23 Jul. 2007.

1052. *See* PSC, Communiqué PSC/PR/COMM (LXXXVII), Eighty-Seventh Meeting, 13 Aug. 2007.

of the crisis would further destabilize' the country led the PSC to 'reiterate' its determination to ensure that the Anjouanese authorities comply fully and unconditionally with, *inter alia*, the demands of the countries of the region. It also approved the further recommendations that the Ministerial Committee had submitted on 18 September 2007 and decided that Member States shall impose against the 'illegal authorities of Anjouan' for an initial period of forty-five days, namely prevent the entry into their territories of the authorities and all other persons constituting a threat to the peace and security in the Comoros and freeze their financial assets. It also resolved to review the mandate of MAES and instructed it to support the implementation of the above sanctions, establish in Anjouan an internal security force, and facilitate the restoration of the central government's authority in the island. Finally, it created a follow-up mechanism consisting of two of its Members (Angola and Senegal) as well as representatives of the countries of the region, the Union government, and the AUC.[1053] The PSC extended twice the imposed sanctions and the mandate of MAES until 22 February 2008 'pending the envisaged ministerial meeting of the countries of the region that would review the situation and submit recommendation on the way forward'.[1054]

The role played by the Ministerial Committee in the crisis requires clarification: it did not confine itself to the role of intermediary or conciliator but moved on to formulate concrete recommendations, which were converted into PSC policy. Even though the South African Foreign Ministry has claimed that the Committee was mandated by the AU to facilitate peace and national reconciliation in the Comoros, this was not apparently corroborated by the action of PSC, which 'delegated' the handling of the situation to the Ministerial Committee and was happy to go along with its suggestions. Given the geography of the Comoros and its domestic strife since independence, the constitutional crisis could have not escalated into a regional security threat. Therefore, the PSC felt that it had to ensure that the presidential elections in the islands would be free and transparent and, to that end, it established MEAS. However, as the voting in Anjouan took place as planned and the crisis escalated, the PSC was only happy to let the Ministerial Committee take the initiative, work out the solutions and back it up by adopting the necessary decisions.

Reference should also be made to the way the Assembly dealt with the Comoros situation during its Tenth Ordinary Session (Addis Ababa, 31 January–2 February 2008), as it addressed it in two different instances. The first was when it examined the PSC Report on its activities for the year 2007. The second was as a separate matter on the agenda. In the first instance, the Assembly simply expressed its full support for the efforts 'in pursuant of the pertinent decisions of the PSC with a view to restoring State authority in Anjouan and put a definite end to the crisis from the attitude of Anjouan's illegal authorities'.[1055] But in the second instance, it referred specifically to MAES, avoided making any reference to the aforementioned Ministerial Committee and, finally, urged the UNSC Council to adopt a resolution endorsing

1053. *See* PSC, Communiqué PSC/PR/COMM (XCV), Ninety-Fifth Meeting, 10 Oct. 2007.

1054. *See* PSC, Communiqué PSC/PR/COMM (CII), Hundred-Second Meeting, 26 Nov. 2007, and Communiqué PSC/PR/COMM (XVII), Hundred-Seventh Meeting, 21 Jan. 2008.

1055. *See* Assembly, *Decision on the Activities of the Peace and Security Council of the African Union and the State of Peace and Security in Africa*, AU Doc. Assembly/AU/Dec. 177 (X) (2 Feb. 2008).

the sanctions already imposed by the PSC.[1056] As the Comoros crisis could not have posed a threat to regional peace and security, the Assembly's attempt to get the UNSC involved is questionable, unless the aim was to seek, even belatedly, its approval and legitimation. However, since the UNSC had not already addressed the situation, it was rather improbable that it would approve the PSC's punitive measures. Apparently, the Security Council had never in the past dealt with the Comoros and, when the final communique and the resolutions adopted by the Islamic Conference of Foreign Ministers in June 2004 were submitted to it,[1057] the matter was brought to its attention but was not discussed.[1058]

Based on the presumed authorization contained in Decision Assembly/Dec. 186(X), on 25 March 2008, Operation 'Democracy in the Comoros' was launched by Comorian forces backed by Tanzania, Sudan, Libya, and Senegal (France and the USA provided transportation and logistics support) and removed the 'illegal regime' of General Bacer from power.[1059] With constitutional order restored in Anjouan, new elections were planned and, to that effect, on 30 April 2008, the PSC extended for six months the MAES mandate, which was, *inter alia*, requested to provide 'assistance in the establishment of an internal security force in Anjouan'.[1060] Elections for the President of the Autonomous Island of Anjouan took place on 15 June 2008. When a few weeks later, the Eleventh Ordinary Assembly Session met in Sharm El Sheikh, Egypt (30 June–1 July 2008), it did not discuss the PSC actions.[1061] Finally, it is of some interest to note that on 30 July 2018, a referendum revised the 2001 Constitution as it had already been amended. Among other changes, referendum presidential term limits were extended, and the power-sharing system that had rotated the presidency every five years between the islands of Grand Comore, Anjouan and Moheli was abolished.[1062]

165. As has been mentioned, one of the roles of the PSC is to address promptly unconstitutional changes of government. What follows is an oversight of several of the incidents handled by the PSC, especially during the first formative years of operation.[1063] Additional relevant action undertaken as well as measures ordered by other AU organs and the competent RECs are also recorded.[1064]

1056. *See* Assembly, *Decision on the Situation on the Comoros*, AU Doc. Assembly/AU/Dec. 186 (X) (2 Feb. 2008).
1057. *See* UN Doc. S/2004/582 and Corr. 1 (15 Jul. 2004). This was the executive organ of the Organization of the Islamic Conference (now the Organization of Islamic Cooperation).
1058. *See* UNGA, *Report of the Security Council 1/8/2004 – 31/7/2005*, UN Doc. A/60/2, p. 187 (2005).
1059. PSC, Press Statement PSC/PR/BR (CXVII), 117th Meeting, 28 Mar. 2008.
1060. PSC, Communiqué PSC/PR/COMM (CXXIV), 124th Meeting, 30 Apr. 2008.
1061. *See* Assembly, *Decision on the Report of the Peace and Security Council*, AU Doc. Assembly/AU/Dec. 193 (XI) (1 Jul. 2008).
1062. For the text of the 2018 Constitution, *see* https://www.constituteproject.org/constitution/Comoros_2018.pdf?lang=en.
1063. For situations during the OAU era, *see* K.O. Kufuor, 'The OAU and the Recognition of Governments in Africa: Analyzing Its Practice and Proposals for the Future', *American University International Law Review* 17 (2002): 369.
1064. For the Member States and the regions on the PSC agenda of the PSC until the end of 2020, *see* Amani Africa Media and Research Services, *The AU Peace and Security Council Handbook 2021*, 2021, pp. 172 et seq., at: https://amaniafrica-et.org/wp-content/uploads/2021/10/Amani-Africa-Handbook-2021-English.pdf.

I. Central African Republic (March 2003–June 2005)

166. Following the coup d'état in the CAR on 15 March 2003, the Central Organ of the OAU Mechanism for Conflict Prevention, Management, and Resolution met immediately and decided at its Nineteenth session to suspend the CAR from AU activities.[1065] In June 2005, the PSC, which had in the meantime replaced the Central Organ, considered that the holding of legislative and presidential elections in the country had marked the return to constitutional rule and resolved to lift the suspension.[1066] Legally speaking, there was an irregularity in that the PSC dealt with this situation because the CAR had not ratified the 2002 Protocol establishing the PSC (it did so in June 2016). Therefore, it should not have been regarded as competent to deal with those Member States that effectively had not recognized it. On the contrary, the lifting of the sanctions should have been determined by the Assembly, it being the highest-ranking AU organ having primary responsibility in all matters, including peace and security.

II. Togo (February 2005–May 2005)

167. Following the death of President Gnassingbé Eyadéma on 5 February 2005, the armed forces assumed power, revised the Constitution and committed other acts, which the PSC regarded at its Twenty-fourth Meeting held a few days later as blatant and unacceptable violation of the Lomé Declaration on the Framework for an OAU Response to Unconstitutional Change of Government, which the OAU Assembly had adopted in July 2000,[1067] the AU principles, and the 2002 Protocol.[1068] The PSC demanded that the armed forces refrain from interfering in the political life on pain of suffering sanctions if they did not restore constitutional legality. Two weeks later, the PSC condemned the 'constitutional modifications' carried out by the armed forces, which were 'intended to legally window dress the coup d'état', 'confirmed' the suspension of the de facto authorities from participating in AU activities, and requested the AUC to ensure its scrupulous implementation.[1069] It is submitted that the PSC could not but have ordered suspension because, on 19 February 2005, the ECOWAS had imposed its own sanctions against the illegal regime, which were far stricter than merely suspending participation.[1070] On

1065. OAU Doc. Central Organ/MEC/AMB/Comm. (XC) (17 Mar. 2003).
1066. AU Doc. PSC/PR/Comm (XXXIII) – (ii) (24 Jun. 2005).
1067. OAU Doc. AHG/Decl. 5 (XXXVI) (12 Jul. 2000).
1068. AU Doc. PSC/PR/Comm(XXIV) (7 Feb. 2005).
1069. AU Doc. PSC/PR/Comm(XXV) (25 Feb. 2005).
1070. The sanctions were based on Art. 45 of the ECOWAS Protocol A/SP1/12/01 on Democracy and Good Governance Supplementary to the Protocol relating to the Mechanism of Conflict Prevention, Management, Resolution, Peacekeeping and Security, which was adopted on 21 Dec. 2001 and entered into force on 20 Feb. 2008, reproduced in S. Ebobrah & A. Tanoh (eds), *Compendium of African Sub-Regional Human Rights Documents* (Pretoria: Pretoria University Law Press, 2010), 203. Generally, *see* F. Cowell, 'The Impact of the ECOWAS Protocol on Good Governance and Democracy', *RADIC* 19 (2011): 331.

account of the country's return to constitutional legality, ECOWAS lifted all sanctions on 26 February 2005, and the PSC followed suit three months later.[1071]

III. Mauritania (August 2005–April 2007)

168. On 3 August 2005, a military coup d'état deposed President Maaouya Ould Sid'Ahmed Taya while he was abroad. Taya himself had come to power through a (bloodless) coup in December 1984. Thereafter, he introduced a democratic Constitution (July 1991)[1072] and organized the first multiparty elections (April 1992), which he won and kept winning. Therefore, the question arose whether Taya's regime ought to have been regarded a 'constitutional' regime, the overthrow of which through a military coup d'état could not be condoned, or whether it remained 'unconstitutional'. When it met the following day, the PSC did not discuss this issue but moved to suspend Mauritania from AU activities until constitutional order was restored.[1073] The elections in March 2007, which culminated in the democratic election of President Sidi Mohamed Ould Cheikh Abdallahi, in conjunction with the positive recommendation by the AUC Chairperson,[1074] led the PSC to lift 'the suspension measure' in April 2007.[1075]

IV. Mauritania (August 2008–June 2009)

169. In August 2007, Mauritanian President Abdallahi named General Abdel Aziz, the leading figure behind the August 2005 coup, as his Chief of Staff. On 6 August 2008, the Presidential Guard arrested the President, the Prime Minister, and the Minister of the Interiors. Mauritania was to be governed by an eleven-member High Council of State, headed by General Aziz, until new presidential elections were held. The PSC met the following day: it condemned the coup d'état, demanded the release of those arrested and that their dignity be respected, ordered the restoration of constitutional order but did not order the unconstitutional authorities' suspension from AU activities. On the contrary, it cited Article 30 of the Constitutive Act, the Lomé Declaration, and the PSC Protocol and held that these instruments 'provide in particular for the automatic suspension of the participation of the country concerned in the activities of the AU until the restoration of constitutional order'.[1076] Effectively, the PSC was saying that it was unnecessary to order the illegal authorities' suspension because it is a sanction imposed automatically and, consequently, does not require an express decision to that effect.

1071. AU Doc. PSC/PR/Comm(XXX) (27 May 2005).
1072. For the text of the Constitution with subsequent amendments, *see* https://www.constituteproject.org/constitution/Mauritania_2012.pdf?lang=en.
1073. AU Doc. PSC/PR/Stat.(XXXVI)-(ii) (4 Aug. 2005).
1074. *See Report of the Chairperson of the Commission on the Evolving Developments in the Islamic Republic of Mauritania*, AU Doc. PSC/PR/2(LXXVI) (10 Apr. 2007).
1075. AU Doc. PSC/PR/Comm(LXXVI) (10 Apr. 2007).
1076. AU Doc. PSC/PR/Comm(CLIV) (7 Aug. 2008).

It is submitted that the argument that there is automaticity in Article 30 of the Constitutive Act making the illegal regimes' suspension redundant cannot be sustained. On the contrary, the wording of Article 30 suggests that the AU is under an obligation to do so and has no discretion because there are no circumstances justifying the use of unconstitutional means for coming into power. But this is not tantamount to saying that suspension is automatically applied without a prior decision to that effect. Moreover, Article 7(1) of the PSC Protocol, on the one hand, authorizes the PSC to institute sanctions in cases of unconstitutional changes of government and, on the other hand, imposes upon it the duty to do so. Article 7 does not cite Article 30 of the Constitutive Act but only the Lomé Declaration, whose wording suggests that there might be discretion in ordering suspension:

> [F]ollowing the initial response of condemning the unconstitutional change by the Central Organ [now the PSC]: (a) A period of up to six months should be given to the perpetrators of the unconstitutional change to restore constitutional order. During the six month period, the government concerned should be suspended from participating in the Policy Organs of the OAU [now the AU].

In late September 2008, the PSC held its 151st Meeting at the fringe of the UNGA Annual Session in New York. After noting the lack of progress in the case of Mauritania, it linked it with the fact that Mauritania (under the overthrown regime) was the first Member State to ratify the African Charter on Democracy, Elections, and Governance in July 2008. It is not clear why the Charter was invoked: if the PSC had wanted to infer that the illegal regime was additionally bound by the Charter, this was wrong because at the time it had not entered into force and did not produce any legal effects. Finally, the PSC resolved to declare null and void all constitutional and legislative measures adopted by the military authorities and issued an ultimatum: either unconditionally restore President Abdallahi to power by 6 October 2008 or 'the authors of the coup d'état and their civilian supporters' would face 'sanctions and isolation'.[1077] A month after the deadline had expired, the PSC met to consider the situation. Surprisingly, it did not impose sanctions but requested the AUC to propose urgently concrete measures on the basis of its September 2008 Communiqué and the Lomé Declaration.[1078] The AUC recommended that, if by 5 January 2009 no progress had been made, the PSC consider imposing limited and targeted sanctions, including travel restrictions on and freezing the assets of all civilian personnel, military personnel, and economic operators, whose actions maintained the illegal regime in power.[1079] Finally, it suggested that the UNSC be encouraged to assess the impact of the concerted international measures taken to restore constitutional order pursuant to the Presidential Statement of

1077. AU Doc. PSC/MIN/Comm.2(CLI) (22 Sep. 2008).
1078. AU Doc. PSC/PR/Comm(CLVI) (11 Nov. 2008).
1079. *See Report of the Chairperson of the Commission on the Situation in Mauritania*, AU Doc. PSC/MIN/3 (CLXIII) (22 Dec. 2008).

19 August 2008 on Mauritania and to consider additional measures. In that statement,[1080] the UNSC had condemned the overthrow of the democratically elected government; had demanded the immediate release of President Abdallahi and the restoration of democratic institutions; had recognized the important role played by the AU and the support given by regional and international partners; had commented the UN Secretary-General's involvement through his Special Representative for West Africa Said Djinnit, who had been appointed in February 2008;[1081] had called on all UN Member States to assist in restoring constitutional order; and had resolved to monitor developments.

At its 163rd Meeting in December 2008, the PSC espoused the AUC's recommendations and repeated them almost verbatim with one exception: the sanctions were to be imposed if by 5 February 2009 the constitutional order had not been fully restored. Presumably, the deadline was extended by one month because, in the meantime, Abdallahi had been released, a move showing some progress towards returning to constitutional normalcy.[1082] The PSC met on the day the ultimatum expired and resolved that the aforementioned sanctions had entered into force, that all AU Member States must scrupulously implement them, and that the AUC must monitor their effective implementation. Moreover, it stressed that the sanctions were not an end by themselves but should be accompanied by diplomatic efforts to ensure prompt return to constitutional order. These efforts were to be undertaken by the AU and its partners and involved all Mauritanian parties.[1083] One of the main problems surrounding the implementation of sanctions imposed against an undefined group of individuals is to determine their identity.

In March 2009, the PSC distinguished among three groups of targeted individuals: (a) the members of the High Council of State; (b) the members of the government; and (c) all other persons, whether civilians or military, whose activities were designed to maintain the unconstitutional *status quo*. Even though the identities of those falling into the first and second categories were largely clear, this was not the case for the third category. The task was entrusted to the AUC: it had to present the three lists by 24 April 2009.[1084] On 4 June 2009, a political solution culminated in the Dakar Framework Agreement envisaging, *inter alia*, the formation of a national transitional unity government.[1085] The Agreement proved adequate for the PSC to declare that Mauritania had returned to constitutional order, to lift the suspension from participation in AU activities and to lift all sanctions.[1086] Interestingly enough, the PSC did not wait for the presidential elections, which were scheduled for July 2009, as the most appropriate sign to conclude authoritatively that democratic institutions were again fully observed. The results of the free and fair elections held on

1080. UN Doc. S/PRST/2008/30 (19 Aug. 2008).
1081. UN Doc. SG/A/1121 – BIO/3964 (28 Feb. 2008).
1082. AU Doc. PSC/MIN/Comm.3(CLXIII) (22 Dec. 2008).
1083. AU Doc. PSC/PR/(CLXVIII) (5 Feb. 2009).
1084. AU Doc. PSC/PR/COMM(CLXXXII) (24 Mar. 2009).
1085. *See* AU Doc. PSC/PR//Comm.3(CEXCII) (10 Jun. 2009), at: https://www.peaceau.org/uploads/mauritaniaen.pdf.
1086. AU Doc. PSC/MIN/COMM.(CXCVI) (29 Jun. 2009). The Dakar Agreement was principally the outcome of the work of the International Contact Group on Mauritania, which included, among others, the AU and the Organisation of Islamic Cooperation.

18 July 2009 showed that a population does not always turn its back on those violating democratic norms: 52% of the electorate voted for Aziz to become the new president, the very individual who had orchestrated the coups d'état in August 2005 and in August 2008.

V. Guinea (December 2008–December 2010)

170. On 22 December 2008, President Lansana Conté died. Elements of the armed forces took advantage and, under the command of Captain Moussa Dadis Camara, staged a bloodless coup d'état suspending the Constitution and state institutions. A few days later, the PSC condemned it. Although one would have expected that the new authorities' participation in AU activities would have been automatically suspended (as in the case of Mauritania in August 2008), it did not happen. The PSC Communiqué simply stated that the perpetrators and those committing human rights violations would be held accountable and dealt with accordingly.[1087] Less than a week later, the PSC suspended the new regime's participation in AU activities and reaffirmed its determination to take, in due course, all other measures envisaged in the Lomé Declaration to accelerate the process of return to constitutional order.[1088] Arguably, the PSC delayed the imposition of sanctions for purposes of political expediency; it would appear that ECOWAS was not convinced that the coup d'état was such a bad thing for a country suffering from misrule for so many years. President Conte had been in power for twenty-four years, having staged his own coup in 1984. The then Executive President of ECOWAS, Mohammed Ibn Chambas, had expressed to the BBC his surprise that the coup enjoyed support among political parties, civilians, and trade unions.[1089] However, on 10 January 2009, an ECOWAS Authority Extraordinary Session held in Nigeria ordered the suspension of participation of the new regime in its activities pending free and fair elections. The following month, the Twelve Ordinary Assembly Session (Addis Ababa, 1–4 February 2009) supported the decisions taken by the PSC.[1090]

In mid-September 2009, the PSC reviewed the situation in Guinea. In view of lack of any positive developments, it decided to impose 'appropriate' sanctions against Captain Camara, who had assumed the office of President of the National Council for Development and Democracy (NCDD), and against a number of other individuals, both civilian and military. However, the sanctions were not imposed with immediate effect, but targeted individuals were given one month to comply with the demands.[1091] Before the deadline had expired, the PSC asked the AUC, in collaboration with ECOWAS and other AU partners, to finalize the measures to be taken and to produce the list of the relevant individuals.[1092] In the meantime, Guinea

1087. AU Doc. PSC/PR/Comm(CLXIV) (24 Dec. 2008).
1088. AU Doc.PSC/PR/Comm(CLXV) (29 Dec. 2008).
1089. *See* BBC News, 'African Union bars Guinea on coup', 29 Dec. 2008, at: http://news.bbc.co.uk/go/pr/fr/-/2/hi/africa/7802803.stm.
1090. AU Assembly, *Decision on the Resurgence of the Scourge of Coups d'état in the Africa*, AU Doc. Assembly/AU/Dec. 220 (XII) (4 Feb. 2009).
1091. AU Doc. PSC/PR/Comm(CCIV) (17 Sep. 2009).
1092. AU Doc. PSC/PR/BR.1(CCVI) (15 Oct. 2009).

had been facing a rapidly deteriorating political, security and human rights situation. On 28 September 2009, security forces under NCDD authority massacred 150 peaceful pro-democracy demonstrators and engaged in mass rapes. It was obvious that the deadline would not be observed. In late October 2009, the PSC requested the AUC, in close collaboration with ECOWAS and the International Contact Group on Guinea (ICG–G), to take all necessary measures for the targeted sanctions' implementation (principally denial of visas, travel restrictions and freezing of assets) against the President, members of NCDD, government ministers as well as civilians and military personnel involved in maintaining the unconstitutional *status quo*. AUC was asked to circulate the list identifying these individuals within a week. Finally, as in previous occasions, the PSC moved to universalize the adopted sanctions by communicating them to the UNSC and to 'all other AU partners', namely, the EU, the Organization of the Islamic Cooperation, the International Organization of La Francophonie, and the League of Arab States.[1093]

At the time, the PSC did not have much room for manoeuvring because on 17 October 2009, an ECOWAS Authority Extraordinary Session had discussed, *inter alia*, the massacre. It resolved to work with the AU on a 'regime of targeted sanctions' against those individuals deliberately preventing the return to constitutional order as well as to impose an arms embargo on Guinea pursuant to the ECOWAS Convention on Small Arms and Light Weapons, their Ammunitions, and Related Materials, which incidentally had entered into force on the day of the massacre.[1094] Finally, it asked for the AU's support in implementing and enforcing the sanctions.[1095] In early December 2010, free and fair elections led to the election of a new civilian President and, later in the same month, all AU sanctions were lifted.

VI. Niger (August 2009–March 2011)

171. On 4 August 2009, a constitutional referendum took place asking the population whether it agreed to dissolve the state of Niger and create the so-called Sixth Republic of Niger with a presidential system of government. Even though the Constitutional Court had already ruled that the plan was illegal, the referendum returned a majority for the 'yes' vote, and President Mamadou Tandja changed the constitutional regime. The opposition regarded it as a coup d'état aiming at turning Niger into a dictatorship. The ECOWAS reacted first and during the aforementioned Extraordinary Authority Summit of October 2009 imposed two of the sanctions

1093. AU Doc. PSC/AHG/COMM.2(CCVII) (29 Oct. 2009).

1094. This Convention, signed on 14 Jun. 2006, at: https://www.sipri.org/node/2934, should not be confused with similar treaties adopted by other RECs, e.g., the Protocol on the Control of Firearms, Ammunition and Other Related Materials in the Southern African Development Community (SADC) Region (signed on 14 Aug. 2001, in force since 8 Nov. 2004), the Central African Convention for the Control of Small Arms and Light Weapons, their Ammunition, Parts and Components that can be used for their Manufacture, Repair or Assembly (the Kinshasa Convention, adopted in April 2010, in force on 8 Mar. 2017); and the Nairobi Protocol for the Prevention, Control and Reduction of Small Arms and Light Weapons in the Great Lakes Region and the Horn of Africa (adopted on 21 Apr. 2004, in force on 5 May 2005).

1095. *See* Final Communiqué, at: https://emansion.gov.lr/doc/Final_communiqu__of_ECOWAS_HS_17%20October_2009.pdf.

stipulated in Article 45(2) of the Supplementary Protocol on Democracy and Good Governance: first, to refuse supporting Niger's candidates for elective posts in international organizations and, second, to refuse to organize any future ECOWAS meetings in Niger. Moreover, it threatened that if Tandja failed to comply with its decisions, this would lead to 'the automatic and immediate imposition of [the] full sanctions [of Article 45]', and the case would be referred to the AU for similar action.[1096] The PSC considered the developing situation in Niger on 29 October 2009, where it did not pronounce on the legality of the new constitutional regime but endorsed the ECOWAS decision.[1097] Thus, the PSC, by endorsing the ECOWAS sanctions, concurred that Tandja's actions had violated the Constitution and had resulted in a very serious political crisis but failed to expressly denounce him. Although in early February 2010, the Fourteenth Ordinary Assembly Session called upon all parties in Niger to cooperate fully with the mediator, who had been appointed by the ECOWAS,[1098] it was too late. The rapidly deteriorating situation culminated, on 18 February 2010, in a coup d'état staged by the military. It resulted in the formation of a junta (the Supreme Council for the Restoration of Democracy (CSRD)), which promised to turn Niger into an example of democracy and good governance and save the population from poverty and corruption. Reportedly, the population was not against the overthrow of President Tandja and the opposition Co-ordination of Democratic Forces for the Republic (CFDR), a coalition of political parties, trade unions and human rights groups formed in 2009 to protest against the constitutional changes, welcomed this development.[1099]

The following day, the PSC (216th Meeting) condemned the government's overthrow and decided 'in accordance with the relevant legal instruments of the AU' to suspend Niger's participation in all AU activities until the restoration of constitutional order, which was defined 'as the internal situation [which] stood before the referendum of 4 August 2009'.[1100] Since the PSC regarded the August 2009 referendum as unconstitutional, it is submitted that it ought to have reacted at that time and condemned it. The formation of the junta was dissociated from the referendum. Therefore, the PSC dealt simultaneously with two different events – the military coup d'état and Tandja's attempt to remain in power through unconstitutional means – in a rather unsatisfactory way. The PSC also referred to the Decision on Prevention of Unconstitutional Changes of Government and Strengthening of the Capacity of the AU to Manage such Situations, which the Assembly had adopted a few weeks earlier during its Fourteenth Ordinary Session.[1101] Even though the Decision's stated purpose was to revamp the way the AU addressed coups d'état, in reality, it

1096. Ibid.

1097. AU Doc. PSC/AHG/Comm.3(CCVII) (29 Oct. 2009).

1098. *See* Assembly, *Decision on the Report of the Peace and Security Council on its Activities and the State of Peace and Security in Africa*, AU Doc. Assembly/AU/Dec. 268 (XIV) Rev.1, para. 21 (2 Feb. 2010).

1099. *See* BBC News, 'African Union suspends Niger after military coup', 20 Feb. 2010, at: http://news.bbc.co.uk/2/hi/africa/8525665.stm.

1100. AU Doc. PSC/PR/COMM.2(CCXVI) (19 Feb. 2010).

1101. Assembly, *Decision on the Prevention of Unconstitutional Changes of Government and Strengthening the Capacities of the African Union to Manage such Situations*, AU Doc. Assembly/AU/Dec. 269 (XIV) Rev.1 (2 Feb. 2010).

failed to enhance the AU's effectiveness, did not propose any new strategy, and merely repeated the provisions of Article 25 of the Charter on Democracy, Elections and Governance.

A close reading of the Decision reveals that the Assembly considered that, from a regulatory point of view, the AU was adequately equipped to tackle coups d'état and, therefore, the aim should be to promote efficient implementation and, where necessary, to refine it. Thus, the Decision emphasized the need for a comprehensive approach based on zero tolerance for coups d'état and violations of democratic standards. Moreover, it stipulated that, in addition to the sanction of suspending participation in AU activities, the following four measures shall be applied. First, perpetrators shall be barred from any elections held to restore constitutional order in the Member State concerned. Second, sanctions shall be ordered against any Member State proven to have instigated or supported coups d'état in another Member's territory. Third, the Assembly shall order additional punitive measures, including economic sanctions. Fourth, Members shall not recognize the de facto authorities. Finally, the Decision called on all non-African international organizations not to grant accreditation to de facto authorities and not to take any action undermining AU efforts to restore constitutional legality. This primacy that the AU reserves for itself may be difficult to be comprehended: why should other non-African regional organizations, and specifically the League of Arab States and the Organisation of Islamic Cooperation, heed to AU action?

In October 2010, with the active involvement of ECOWAS, parliamentary elections were held in Niger. They were followed by presidential elections between January and March 2011. In mid-March 2011, the PSC decided to cancel the suspension of Niger's participation in AU activities.[1102] A week later, the Thirty-Ninth ECOWAS Authority Ordinary Session also lifted sanctions.[1103] In the present case, the PSC left the initiative to ECOWAS and to Nigeria, its most important Member State.

VII. Madagascar (March 2009–January 2014)

172. The political crisis in Madagascar, one of the longest in the AU history, started with a rather minor incident: in December 2008, the government of President Marc Ravalomanana closed a TV station owned by Andry Rajoelina, the Mayor of the capital. Rajoelina accused him of authoritarianism and organized a public demonstration, which attracted tens of thousands of people but resulted in several days of rioting, burning and looting, leaving at least 100 people dead. When Rajoelina announced that he was taking over the government and forming a parallel cabinet, Ravalomanana removed him from office, and the Mayor found refuge in the French embassy. With mounting pressure and the death toll rising, on 17 March

1102. AU Doc. PSC/PR/COMM(CCLXVI) (16 Mar. 2011).

1103. *See* Final Communique, Abuja, 23–24 March 2011, https://ecowas.int/wp-content/uploads/2022/08/39tht-ECOWAS-Summit-Abuja-23-24-March-20113.pdf.

2009, Ravalomanana announced that he was handing power to the military, which almost immediately allowed Rajoelina to form a transitional government with a promise to hold elections.

The PSC met promptly to discuss the situation. It condemned the unconstitutional change of government; noted that it 'mark[ed] another serious setback in the ongoing democratization processes on the continent and reinforce[d] the concern over the resurgence of the scourge of coups d'état'; and resolved to suspend Madagascar from participation in AU activities.[1104] On 30 March 2009, the situation was also discussed during an Extraordinary Summit of the SADC Summit of Heads of State and Government. It condemned the illegal ousting of the democratically elected government and called for an immediate restoration of constitutional order; decided not to recognize the Rajoelina regime because the Malagasy Constitution, the SADC Treaty's core principles and values, the AU Constitutive Act and the UN Charter had been violated; and, without citing any legal basis, suspended Madagascar '[f]rom all Community's institutions and organs until the return of the country to constitutional normalcy with immediate effect'.[1105] At the end of April 2009, the inaugural meeting of the International Contact Group on Madagascar (ICG–M) took place. This ad hoc entity comprised of representatives from a wide array of actors: the AU, the COMESA, the EU, the Indian Ocean Commission, the International Organization of la Francophonie, the SADC, the UN, the Member States holding the Chair at the AU and the PSC, the African states elected to the Security Council as non-permanent members as well as the latter's permanent members. The ICG–M has been instrumental in maintaining open channels with the Rajoelina regime at difficult times.

During the summer of 2009, two important events occurred. First, Rajoelina formed the 'government of National Unity', excluding, however, all other political powers. Second, the Maputo Agreements were signed on 9 August 2009 among the principal Malagasy political stakeholders. Revised on 6 November 2009, they contained a roadmap for a peaceful and consensual transition to constitutionality. In September 2009, the PSC threatened the Rajoelina regime and its supporters with 'appropriate measures, including targeted sanctions', if they failed to implement the terms of the Maputo Agreements.[1106] In mid-February 2010, the PSC repeated the threat to impose sanctions. But this time, they were to be automatically applied, if by 16 March 2010 'the de facto authorities borne out of the unconstitutional change' had not implemented fully the Maputo Agreements and the Addis Ababa Additional Act.[1107] Never before had the PSC threatened such wide-ranging and comprehensive sanctions, which included:

1104. AU Doc. PSC/PR/COMM(CLXXXI) (20 Mar. 2009).

1105. The Communiqué is available at: https://reliefweb.int/report/madagascar/extraordinary-summit-sadc-heads-state-and-government-30-mar-2009. For criticism of the SADC handling, *see* International Crisis Group, *Implementing Peace and Security Architecture (II): Southern Africa*, Africa Report No. 191, 15 Oct. 2012, pp. 14–16, at: http://www.crisisgroup.org.

1106. AU Doc. PSC/PR/BR(CCII) (10 Sep. 2009).

1107. AU Doc. PSC/PR/COMM.1(CCXVI) (19 Feb. 2010).

(a) a travel ban against the de facto authorities and all other followers of the 'Rajoelina camp' whose actions impeded AU and SADC efforts to restore constitutional order. At its own initiative or upon request and on a case-by-case basis, the PSC reserved the power to grant, on humanitarian grounds, exemptions;
(b) freezing funds and other assets of all individuals and entities contributing to the maintenance of the unconstitutional *status quo* and impeding AU and SADC efforts. Again, the PSC could determine exemptions; and
(c) the diplomatic isolation of the de facto authorities. This was to be effected through concerted action by the other Member States, which were mandated to challenge the de facto authorities' participation in the activities of non-African international organizations, including the UN and its Specialized Agencies.

Unlike precious instances where the PSC had imposed sanctions against individuals and entities but had not established their identity in advance, in the present case, it requested the AUC to compile, in close collaboration with the SADC, the relevant lists before the sanctions had entered into force. When the ultimatum expired, the PSC (221st Meeting) noted that the Rajoelina regime had not complied with its obligations and decided that the sanctions had come into force as of 17 March 2010 against those individuals whose names appeared in the list attached to the Communiqué issued.[1108] In July 2010, when the PSC discussed next the situation in Madagascar, it was clear that the sanctions and the Rajoelina regime's suspension from AU activities were not having the desired effects. With no other ammunition left, the PSC stressed the need for renewed efforts to ensure that sanctions are scrupulously implemented and called on the international community to assist in strengthening their effectiveness and on international organizations to coordinate their action.[1109] The Assembly also discussed the situation during its Seventeenth Ordinary Session in June 2011. As no tangible proposals on forcing the Rajoelina regime to abide by constitutional principles were tabled, its response was reduced to calling upon the SADC and the AU to continue working together for a consensual and sustainable solution to the crisis, in full compliance with the relevant AU instruments on unconstitutional changes of government and also called for a holding of an ICG-M meeting.[1110] A week later, the PSC met to give effect to the Assembly's Decision but took no concrete action.[1111]

During 2012 and 2013, there were various attempts to organize elections in Madagascar and to return the country to constitutional normalcy. In the end, the first round of presidential elections was successfully held on 25 October 2013, and the second round, together with legislative elections, took place on 20 December 2013. The final results on the second round were announced in early January 2014. In September 2013, based on the fact that the timetable for elections appeared to be on track, the PSC resolved to immediately lift the sanctions which had been imposed

1108. AU Doc. PSC/PR/BR(CCXXI) (17 Mar. 2010).
1109. AU Doc. PSC/PR/COMM-2(CCXXXVII) (21 Jul. 2010).
1110. Assembly, *Decision on the Report of the Peace and Security Council on its Activities and the State of Peace and Security in Africa*, AU Doc. Assembly/AU/Dec. 369 (XVII) (1 Jul. 2011), para. 5.
1111. AU Doc. PSC/PR/BR.(CCLXXXIII) (6 Jul. 2011 & 12 Jul. 2011).

on 109 Malagasy 'political personalities', pursuant to the aforementioned Communiqués of 19 February and 17 March 2010.[1112] However, as regards the resumption of the country's participation in AU activities, the PSC decided to postpone it after the elected President had assumed his duties.[1113] The President's inauguration on 25 January 2014 satisfied the condition that the country should return to democratic normalcy and, two days later, the PSC invited Madagascar to immediately resume its participation in the AU.[1114] An Extraordinary SADC Summit lifted the suspension as well.[1115] It has been suggested that the Charter on Democracy, and in particular Article 25(4) prohibiting perpetrators of coups d'état to partake in elections held to restore the democratic order, had a role to play in ending the impasse.[1116] Considering that Madagascar was not a party to the Charter (and still is not despite signing it on 31 January 2014), it is open to doubt to which extent the fighting sides were swayed by its stipulations.

This protracted coup d'état in Madagascar clearly showed the limitations of the AU's machinery to address unconstitutional overthrow of governments even if acting in consort with RECs. Arguably, if the political turmoil had taken place in previous decades, it could have resulted in the de facto authorities remaining in power for much longer or even being considered as a legitimate (or legitimized) regime. However, the trend towards democratization in Africa has no doubt changed attitudes and has allowed populations to choose freely who will govern them.

VIII. Côte d'Ivoire (December 2010–April 2011)

173. Even though elections in November 2010 had ousted President Laurent Gbagbo, he refused to recognize the results, as proclaimed by the Independent Electoral Commission and certified by the Special Representative of the UN Secretary-General appointed pursuant to UNSC Resolution 1765(2007) of 16 July 2007. It was not the first time that Côte d'Ivoire had been embroiled in political turmoil following presidential elections: in 2005, the AU had appointed the then President of South Africa, Thabo Mbeki, as Mediator and, while the PSC had expressed its willingness, upon his recommendation, to impose appropriate sanctions against those blocking the constitutional process,[1117] no sanctions were ever imposed. When it became clear that the President-Elect, Alassane Ouattara, was prevented from exercising his authority, first, the ECOWAS and, then, the AU responded swiftly. On 7 December 2010, an Extraordinary ECOWAS Authority Session told Gbagbo that he

1112. AU Doc. PSC/PR/COMM.(CCCXCIV) (5 Sep. 2013).

1113. This was in line with the position adopted in a previous Communiqué, *see* AU Doc. PSC/MIN/COMM.(CCCLXVIII), para. 10 (22 Apr. 2013).

1114. AU Doc. PSC/PR/COMM.(CDXV) (27 Jan. 2014).

1115. At: https://www.sadc.int/document/communique-extraordinary-summit-sadc-heads-state-and-government-30-january-2014.

1116. S. Choudhry & S. Bisarya, 'Regional Organizations and Threats to Constitutional Democracy from Within: Self Coups and Authoritarian Backsliding' in *Rule of Law and Constitution Building: The Role of Regional Organizations*, International Institute for Democracy and Electoral Assistance (ed.) (Stockholm: 2014) 183, 195.

1117. AU Doc. PSC/Min/Comm.(XXXIV)–(ii) (3 Jul. 2005).

must go.[1118] A few days later, the PSC decided to suspend Côte d'Ivoire's participation in AU activities until Ouattara had assumed power.[1119] Despite universal condemnation, Gbagbo refused to cede power, and the country was driven to chaos and anarchy with heavy casualties among the population. The PSC met twice at the level of Heads of State or Government in January 2011 and in March 2011 but did not adopt any sanctions (a rather indirect threat was made in the latter meeting but was never materialized).[1120] However, the UNSC imposed targeted sanctions on five high-ranking officials, including Gbagbo, under Resolution 1975(2011) of 30 March 2011.[1121]

The impasse ended when in mid-April 2011 Gbagbo was placed under house arrest. Following the assumption of power by President Ouattara, the AUC issued a report where it argued that it was necessary to lift the suspension so as to 'help consolidate the positive development recorded in Côte d'Ivoire, while allowing it to make its contribution to the attainment of the objectives of our Union'.[1122] On 21 April 2011, the PSC cancelled the suspension, noting that this decision 'will help consolidate the positive development recorded in Côte d'Ivoire, while allowing it to make its contribution to the attainment of the objectives of our Union'.[1123] It should be noted that the ICC has assumed competence to investigate the crimes committed during the period of post-election violence between December 2010 and April 2011 and prosecute those allegedly responsible. Thus, in November 2011, former President Laurent Gbagbo was transferred to ICC custody, and in February 2003 the charges brought against him as indirect co-perpetrator for crimes against humanity were confirmed; in February 2012, a Warrant of Arrest was issued against his wife Simone Gbagbo for the same alleged crimes, and in December 2011, a Warrant of Arrest was issued against Charles Blé Goudé, who was described not only as being 'part of Mr Gbagbo's inner circle' but also as his mouthpiece and 'spin doctor'. He surrendered to ICC custody on 27 March 2014, and on 11 December 2014, he was committed to trial. The cases against Laurent Gbagbo and Charles Blé Goudé were

---

1118. *See also* ECOWAS Authority Extraordinary Session, *Final Communiqué*, 24 Dec. 2010, threatening to use legitimate force to oust Gbagbo, ECW/CEG/ABJ/EXT/FR./Rev.0, para. 10, at: http://www.ecowas.int. *See further*, J. Dubé Gagnon, 'ECOWAS's Right to Intervene in Côte d'Ivoire to Install Alassane Ouattara as President-Elect' *Notre Dame J. of Int'l & Comparative L.* III (2013) 51 claiming that ECOWAS had no power to interfere.

1119. AU Doc. PSC/PR/COMM.1(CCLII) (9 December 2010). For criticism of the AU's handling of the affair, *see* E. Abatan &Y. Spies, 'African Solutions to African Problems? The AU, R2P and Côte d'Ivoire', *South African Journal of International Affairs* 23 (2016): 21.

1120. AU Docs PSC/AHG/COMM(CCLIX) (28 Jan. 2011) and PSC/AHG/COMM.1(CCLXV) (10 Mar. 2011).

1121. The UNSC had expressed its readiness to impose targeted measures against those individuals threatening the peace process, obstructing the work of the United Nations Operation in Côte d'Ivoire (UNOCI) or committing serious human rights violations, *see* Press Statement on Côte d'Ivoire, UN Doc. SC/10105-AFR/2079, 8 Dec. 2010, at: https://www.un.org/press/en/2010/sc10105.doc.htm. Further, *see* UNSC Res. 1946(2010) of 15 Oct. 2010.

1122. *See Report of the Chairperson of the Commission on the Situation in Cote d'Ivoire*, AU Doc. PSC/PR/2 (CCLXXIII), 21 Apr. 2011. Note that in July 2011 Gbagbo challenged the legality of the house arrest before the ECOWAS Court of Justice, which held that it was illegal, arbitrary and violated Art. 6 of the African Human Rights Charter, *Simone & Michel Gbagbo v. Cote d'Ivoire*, Decision No. ECW/CCJ/JUD/03/13, 22 Feb. 2013, at: http://www.courtecowas.org (in French).

1123. AU Doc. PSC/PR/2 (CCLXXIII) (21 Apr. 2011), para. 18.

joined on 11 March 2015 and the trial commenced on 28 January 2016.[1124] On 15 January 2019, Laurent Gbagbo and Charles Blé Goudé were acquitted from all charges of crimes against humanity allegedly committed in 2010 and 2011. On 31 March 2021, the Appeals Chamber confirmed, by majority, the acquittal decision.[1125]

IX. Mali (April 2012–October 2012)

174. In March 2012, army rebels deposed the democratically elected government of Malian President Amadou Toumani Toure in a coup d'état causing considerable loss of life. The PSC convened promptly, and given that Mali had also been confronted with rebellion by armed groups in its northern territory, it regarded that the situation was not only posing a threat to national unity and territorial integrity but also to regional peace and security.[1126] A few days later, the PSC ordered the immediate suspension of Mali from AU activities.[1127] After the ECOWAS had adopted its own punitive measures against the insurgents on 27 March 2012,[1128] sanctions were also ordered by the PSC in early April 2012. In particular, the PSC decided to impose 'individual measures', including a travel ban and asset freeze, against the junta but also against other individuals and entities deemed to be contributing to the maintenance of the unconstitutional status quo. It also 'recalled' that, pursuant to Article 25(5) of the African Charter on Democracy, Elections, and Governance, coup d'état perpetrators are liable to prosecution.[1129] However, the implementation of the AU sanctions seems to have been delayed because the list of targeted individuals was not promptly finalized.

It should be observed that the Malian case should be distinguished from previous instances of coups d'état because, over and above the issue of the culpability of those responsible for the loss of life, there was also the responsibility for severe attacks against religious and historic monuments, many of which are protected as UNESCO World Heritage sites. In early July 2012, the UNSC emphasized the cultural dimension of the rebellion and argued that these attacks could constitute violations of international law, possibly falling under the Rome Statute establishing the

1124. *See further*, Statement *of ICC Prosecutor at the Commencement of Trial in the case against Messrs. Laurent Gbagbo and Charles Blé Goudé*, 28 Jan. 2016, at: http://www.icc-cpi.int. Note that Côte d'Ivoire signed the ICC Rome Statute on 30 Nov. 1998 but ratified it only on 15 Feb. 2013.

1125. *See The Prosecutor v. Laurent Gbagbo and Charles Blé Goudé*, ICC-02/11-01/15-1400, Judgment in the appeal of the Prosecutor against Trial Chamber I's decision on the no case to answer motions, 31 March 2021, Appeals Chamber, at: https://www.icc-cpi.int/sites/default/files/CourtRecords/CR2021_03218.PDF.

1126. AU Doc. PSC/PR/COMM(CCCXI), 20 Mar. 2012.

1127. AU Doc. PSC/PR/COMM(CCCXV), 23 Mar. 2012.

1128. ECOWAS Authority Extraordinary Summit, *Final Communiqué*, 27 Mar. 2012, at: https://reliefweb.int/report/mali/final-communique-extraordinary-summit-ecowas-heads-state-and-government. It also established the Contact Group of Mali, composed of Benin, Burkina Faso, Côte d'Ivoire, Liberia, Niger, Nigeria and Togo.

1129. AU Doc. PSC/PR/COMM(CCCXVI), 3 Mar. 2012.

ICC.[1130] Two weeks later, the government of Mali, as a contracting party to the Rome Statute since 16 August 2000, referred 'the situation in Mali since January 2012' to the ICC Prosecutor and requested its investigation because domestic courts were unable to prosecute alleged perpetrators.[1131] Thus far, Ahmad Al Faqi Al Mahdi has been found guilty of the war crime of intentionally directing attacks against religious and historic buildings in Timbuktu in September 2016, and, as has been mentioned above, he was sentenced to nine years' imprisonment, while a Reparations Order concluded that he was liable for EUR 2.7 million in expenses for individual and collective reparations for the community of Timbuktu;[1132] and on 27 March 2018 an arrest warrant was issued against Al Hassan Ag Abdoul Aziz Ag Mohamed Ag Mahmoud, who was surrendered to the ICC on 31 March 2018. His trial opened on 15 July 2020, and in May 2023, the closing statements of the Prosecutor, the Legal Representatives, of Victims, and the Defence were scheduled to take place.[1133] Moreover, in July 2012, the PSC, for the first time ever, asked the African Commission on Human and People's Rights[1134] to investigate the human rights situation in northern Mali since January 2012,[1135] and 'to submit a comprehensive report with concrete recommendations on the way forward'.[1136]

Finally, in mid-July 2012, the Nineteenth Ordinary Assembly Session discussed the situation in the northern part of Mali. Instead of a decision, the Assembly adopted a Solemn Declaration on Mali which, *inter alia*, authorized the PSC to take all appropriate measures on behalf of the AU membership.[1137] However, developments were swift: on 20 August 2012, a Government of National Unity was formed and this led the PSC to declare, a fortnight later, its readiness to review its decision, suspending Mali from participation in AU organs.[1138] Arguably, the PSC could have lifted the suspension at its September 2012 meeting. However, it probably wanted to play it safe and wait for more concrete progress. But when the UNSC adopted Resolution 2071(2012) on 12 October 2012 and, *inter alia*, called on regional and international organizations, including the AU, to provide as soon as possible coordinated assistance, expertise, training and capacity-building to the Malian armed and security forces, the PSC could not have continued maintaining the suspension and, on 24 October 2012, it was lifted.[1139]

1130. UNSC Res. 2056(2012) of 5 Jul. 2012, para. 16.
1131. ICC Press Release, ICC-OTP-20120718-PR829, 18 Jul. 2012.
1132. *See* K. Magliveras, 'The ICC Orders Wide-Ranging Reparations for Destroying Religious and Cultural Sites in the Al Mahdi Case' (2017) 33 *International Enforcement Law Reporter* 335–339.
1133. For further information, *see* https://www.icc-cpi.int/mali.
1134. For previous Resolutions of the African Human Rights Commission on Mali, *see* Res. 209 (24 Feb. 2012) and Res. 217 (3 May 2012), at: http://www.achpr.org.
1135. The question could be asked whether the UNSC ought to have referred the situation in Mali to the ICC, as it did with Darfur and Libya. Note that during UNSC deliberations in October 2012 on promoting the rule of law and maintaining peace and security with a special focus on the ICC, Togo argued that to achieve impartiality, consistency and transparency, the UNSC ought to establish clear criteria for determining which situations should be referred to the ICC and which not, *see* UN Doc. S/PV. 6849, p. 21 (17 Oct. 2012).
1136. AU Doc. PSC/AHG/COMM/1(CCCXXVII), para. 15 (14 Jul. 2013). *See further*, Res. 238 (24 Jul. 2013) and Res. 258 (5 Nov. 2013) of the African Human Rights Commission on Mali.
1137. AU Doc. Assembly/AU/Decl. 1 (XIX), para. 16(e) (16 Jul. 2012).
1138. AU Doc. PSC/PR/COMM(CCCXXXII), 4 Sep. 2012.
1139. AU Doc. PSC/MIN/COMM.2(CCCXXXIX), para. 6 (24 Oct. 2012).

X. Guinea-Bissau (April 2012–April 2014)

175. A(nother) coup d'état took place in Guinea-Bissau on 12 April 2012, two weeks before the second round of the presidential elections scheduled for that month. The first round had been deemed free and fair. A week later, the PSC suspended, with immediate effect, the country's participation in AU activities until the effective restoration of constitutional order. Moreover, invoking the frequency of coups d'état in Guinea-Bissau and using as legal basis the African Charter on Democracy Elections and Governance, it requested the AUC, in consultation with the ECOWAS and (unnamed) AU partners, to submit within two weeks proposals on additional sanctions, against the perpetrators and their civilian and military supporters, including a travel ban and an asset freeze.[1140] But a week later, the PSC met and, *inter alia*:

> Request[ed] the [AUC], in view of the refusal of the coup perpetrators to respond positively to the calls from the AU, ECOWAS, the CPLP [Community of Portuguese Speaking Countries] and the UN Security Council and other members of the international community, for the restoration of constitutional order, to compile and disseminate to all Member States, after appropriate consultations, the list of the members of the military junta and their military and civilian supporters, for application of the individual measures mentioned in paragraph 6 of communiqué PSC/PR/COMM(CCCXVIII).[1141] Council call[ed] on all Member States to fully implement these sanctions. Council further request[ed] the [AUC] to expedite, in consultation with ECOWAS, the finalization of its proposals on additional sanctions to be imposed on members of the junta and their military and civilian supporters (emphasis added)[1142]

The wording of the text raises again the aforementioned issue of the automaticity of AU sanctions. And, this is because the envisaged 'individual measures' had not actually been imposed at the previous PSC Meeting but were treated as if they had been imposed. Moreover, although the Nineteenth Ordinary Assembly Session discussed the situation in Guinea-Bissau in the context of reviewing PSC activities (as it did with the situation in Mali),[1143] it only condemned the coup d'état[1144] and did not adopt a separate instrument (as it did with Mali). The progress of the transitional organs in Guinea-Bissau towards restoring constitutional order divided ECOWAS and the AU on whether to maintain the sanctions imposed: at the end of June 2012, ECOWAS suspended them and called for lifting Guinea-Bissau's exclusion

1140. AU Doc. PSC/PR/COMM(CCCXVIII), para. 6 (17 Apr. 2012).

1141. Compare UNSC Res. 2048(2012) of 18 May 2012 imposing a travel ban on five junta members and establishing a Sanctions Committee to monitor implementation. The UNSC was influenced by the Report submitted by the UN Secretary-General on the situation in Guinea-Bissau following the coup d'état, UN Doc. S/2012/280 (30 Apr. 2012).

1142. AU Doc. PSC/MIN/COMM/1(CCCXIX), para. 8 (24 Apr. 2012).

1143. Assembly, *Decision on the Report of the Peace and Security Council on its Activities and the State of Peace and Security in Africa*, AU Doc. Assembly/AU/Dec. 432 (XIX), para. 4 (16 Jul. 2012).

1144. *Ibid.*, para. 7.

from AU activities.[1145] But in January 2013, the PSC decided to maintain them.[1146] On 17 July 2013, the ECOWAS Mediation and Security Council reiterated the call that the AU recognize the ongoing transition process and urged 'international partners' to consider lifting sanctions and resume bilateral cooperation.[1147] Later on the same day, the Forty-Third Ordinary ECOWAS Authority Session repeated the call emphatically.[1148] However, it turned out that the AU was right to continue excluding it because, at the time, the planned Presidential and legislative elections were considerably delayed, a fact also criticized by the UNSC.[1149] The elections finally took place on 13 April 2014, and three days later when the new President had assumed office, the PSC invited Guinea-Bissau to resume its participation in AU's activities.[1150]

XI. The (So-Called) Arab Spring (Tunisia, Egypt, Libya) and the Problem of Very Long Serving Heads of State (2010/2011 – Today)

176. Judging by events, the AU was rather ill-prepared to handle the uprisings in its northern Member States, even though there were good reasons to believe that the pro-democracy trend which had been developing in other parts of the continent would at some stage engulf the autocratic and dictatorial North Africa as well. Indeed, a high-level meeting organized by the PSC in April 2014 noted the weaknesses and gaps in the AU's normative framework which had impacted its response to the uprisings.[1151] While the PSC did condemn the violence which followed the popular uprisings in Tunisia, in Egypt, and in Libya and asked the incumbent regimes to honour the legitimate aspirations of their populations,[1152] the more urgent and important matter of democratic governance in Africa was not addressed. Given that the relevant AU instruments (including the Constitutive Act, the PSC Protocol, and the African Charter on Democracy Elections and Governance) talk only about democratic change of government, the question not tackled (or avoided for political reasons) was whether these uprisings (or rebellions) resulted in undemocratic regime changes. It is submitted that the answer should be in the affirmative. The international community never challenged the authority of President Zine El Abidine Ben Ali (Tunisia), of President Hosni Mubarak (Egypt) and of Colonel Gaddafi (Libya), always accepted them as the legitimate representatives of their states, always transacted with them, and always held them responsible for criminal acts committed by the regimes in power (e.g. Libya and the Lockerbie bombing). That they run their countries as autocrats, as dictators, with little or no respect for human rights and fundamental freedoms was a well-known fact, but

1145. *See* UNSC, *Report of the Secretary-General on the restoration of constitutional order in Guinea-Bissau*, UN Doc. S/2012/704, para. 14 (12 Sep. 2012).
1146. AU Doc. PSC/PR/COMM(CCCLI), para. 6 (16 Jan. 2013).
1147. ECOWAS Press Release, No. 208/2013, 17 Jul. 2013.
1148. ECOWAS Press Release, No. 210/2013, 17 Jul. 2013.
1149. *See* Statement by the President of the Security Council, UN Doc. S/PRST/2013/19 (9 Dec. 2013).
1150. AU Doc. PSC/PR/COMM.(CDXXIX), 16 Apr. 2014, para. 8.
1151. PSC, Press Statement of the 432nd Meeting, PSC/PR/BR.(CDXXXII), 29 Apr. 2014.
1152. *See, inter alia*, PSCPR/COMM.(CCLXI), 23 Feb. 2011.

other states and international organizations (including the AU as is later explained) never challenged the validity of the credentials that they issued, inadvertently accepting that democratic and undemocratic /totalitarian countries co-exist on the global plane and are treated equally.

In particular, the aforementioned AU instruments fail to stipulate if the undemocratic overthrow of dictatorial/unconstitutional regimes (especially when violence has been used) could, under certain circumstances, be treated as a legitimate act. But, while these instruments regard all coups d'état to be *a priori* illegal, a sizeable number of African states have been ruled for so many years by tyrants and despots. It follows that, when adopted, these instruments did not acknowledge what the real status of democratic governance in the continent was. On the contrary, they rather assumed that all African states had functional constitutional regimes in power and, therefore, to be unconstitutionally overturned (forcefully or not) does constitute an illegal act. At the beginning of 2014, there were at least six heads of state with extremely long periods in office: Teodoro Obiang Nguema Mbasogo of Equatorial Guinea (in office for thirty-six years), José Eduardo dos Santos of Angola (thirty-six years), Robert Mugabe of Zimbabwe (twenty-seven years), Paul Biya of Cameroon (thirty-three years), Yoweri Museveni of Uganda (twenty-eight years), and Blaise Compaoré of Burkina Faso (twenty-six years). At the beginning of 2017, five of them were still in office, allowing the argument that they have long exceeded what should be democratically accepted and tolerated. The only President who lost power in the meantime was Compaoré in October 2014, when hundreds of thousands took to the streets of Burkina Faso to complain for his attempt to prolong his office. He was forced to resign.[1153] In September 2017, dos Santos left the presidency and two months later Mugabe. At the time of writing, Biya and Museveni were still Presidents. It is no secret that several African leaders have promoted the idea of becoming 'Presidents for Life' despite strong opposition from the population. Thus, the decision by President Pierre Nkurunziza of Burundi to seek in 2015 a third term in office at all costs (the Constitution did not allow it) resulted in violence and considerable loss of life,[1154] while Presidents Dennis Sassou-Nguesso of Congo-Brazzaville and Paul Kagame of Rwanda put in motion the procedure to extend the length of their office.[1155] Presently, both are serving Presidents. Finally, President Joseph Kabila of DRC wanted to follow suit when his second term in office was to expire at the end of 2016.[1156] He was not successful and on 31 December 2016 he signed an AU-facilitated political agreement with his opponent Étienne Tshisekedi on the country's consensual management until the next elections which

1153. *See* 'Burkina Faso general takes over as Compaore resigns', *BBC News*, 1 Nov. 2014, at: http://www.bbc.com/news/world-africa-29851445.

1154. In the event, he won the July 2015 Presidential elections but domestic strife continued unabated: compare UNSC Res 2248(2015) of 12 Nov. 2015, Res. 2279(2016) of 1 Apr. 2016, and Res. 2303(2016) of 29 Jul. 2016, whose lack of implementation was lamented in a UNSC Statement in March 2017, *see* UN Doc. SC/1275 (13 Mar. 2017), at: https://www.un.org/press/en/2017/sc12750.doc.htm. Nkurunziza remained President until his death on 8 June 2020.

1155. In October 2015, the necessary constitutional amendments were overwhelmingly approved, respectively, by a referendum in Congo-Brazzaville and by the Rwandan Parliament.

1156. K. Roth & I. Sawyer, 'Joseph Kabila Forever: The Dangers of an Extended Presidency in the Democratic Republic of the Congo', *Foreign Policy*, 28 Jul. 2015, at: http://foreignpolicy.com/2015/07/28/joseph-kabila-forever-congo-president-extend-term/.

had to be organized by December 2017. Until then, Kabila remained President, and he was obliged to ensure a peaceful transfer of power to the winner of the presidential election in which he could not have been a contender.[1157] In the event, the presidential elections were held in December 2018; they were won by Felix Tshisekedi, but the result was hotly disputed.[1158]

In the discussion of what constitutes democratic governance in Africa and when the undemocratic overthrow of a legitimate government may be condoned, events in Egypt after the overthrow of the Mubarak regime by popular uprising, the formation of the Mohamed Morsi government in June 2012 through democratic elections, and its non-democratic overthrow by means of military intervention in July 2013 are of particular interest, not least because the AU reacted differently from other international organizations. In the beginning of the North African uprisings, the PSC was quick to side with those fighting the incumbent regimes and to express its solidarity. More specifically, in a Communiqué issued in February 2011, the PSC 'took note of the ardent aspirations of the Egyptian people … for change and the opening of the … political space … to democratically establish and designate institutions that are truly representative and respectful of human rights and freedoms'.[1159] Two aspects stand out. The first is that AU organs had not in the past questioned seriously the legitimacy of incumbent regimes. This begs the question of how Mubarak was permitted to participate in the AU, even though he had ruled as a dictator for almost thirty years and, according to the Communiqué, his regime did not respect fundamental freedoms and, therefore, it was not representative of Egyptians for so long. To put the question otherwise: what was the material difference between the Mubarak and the 'illegal authorities' in another African state that had assumed power by forcefully overthrowing the previous totalitarian regime? Because in the latter case, as has been seen from the coups d'état examined in the previous pages, the 'illegal authorities' were not only suspended from AU activities but often sanctions were imposed against the coup leaders and their associates.

The answer should lie in the fact that, when at the turn of this century democratic values were embedded in the AU as guiding principles, Member States ought to have put words into deeds and abandon the long-held view that undemocratic regimes are acceptable and could remain in office. In other words, the AU membership had been presented with a choice: either commence a long and arduous process towards democratization or maintain the status quo of undemocratic regimes. Evidently, they chose the latter, which has resulted in totalitarian governments being perpetuated, often with devastating effects for the populations. This situation is reminiscent of one of the major issues which the OAU founders had to address. It concerned the borders of the newly independent African states and the dilemma of whether to redraw them to accommodate the local populations' desires or keep them as determined by the colonial powers to suit their own needs. Faithful to the principle of international law that newly independent states should maintain the borders

---

1157. Compare Statement by the President of the UNSC, UN Doc. S/PRST/2017/1, 4 Jan. 2017, and Res. 2277(2016) of 30 Mar. 2016.

1158. *See* 'DR Congo presidential election: Outcry as Tshisekedi named winner', *BBC News*, 10 Jan. 2019, at: https://www.bbc.com/news/world-africa-46819303.

1159. AU Doc. PSCPR/COMM.(CCLX), 16 Feb. 2011.

existing before independence (*uti possidetis juris*), they chose the latter. And this choice has led to many anomalies and conflicts plaguing Africa until today.

The second aspect is that when the Communiqué was issued in mid-February 2011, the uprising in Egypt was still a domestic matter.[1160] It did not pose a threat to regional peace and security, and no war crimes or crimes against humanity had arguably taken place. Putting this state of affairs into the context of the Constitutive Act, Article 4(g) provides that Member States will not interfere in the internal affairs of another Member. Moreover, as explained above, Article 4(h) endows the AU with the right to intervene in a Member State but only when grave circumstances (defined as war crimes, genocide and crimes against humanity) are present. Arguably, the PSC used the apparent violation by the Mubarak regime of the commitments Egypt had assumed as a contracting party to the Constitutive Act (i.e. to promote democratization and good governance, to respect for human rights, etc.) to dispute the regime's legality. By doing so, it is submitted that at that stage the PSC intervened in Egypt's domestic affairs.

The Egyptian uprising culminated in democratic elections in July 2012, returning Mohammed Morsi of the Muslim Brotherhood as the first democratically elected President. Five months later, a free and fair referendum approved the new Constitution,[1161] but a year later, Morsi was overturned and the Constitution was suspended. While the new military-controlled regime apparently had the support of a considerable part of the population, both the EU and the UN chose to play politics: they failed to outrightly denounce the army-orchestrated coup d'état and to demand the return to constitutional normalcy but signalled their readiness to work with the new regime.[1162] However, the PSC treated it as an illegal seizure of power. On 5 July 2013, it issued a Communiqué where, after recalling that the relevant AU instruments on unconstitutional change of government 'provide[d] for the automatic implementation of specific measures whenever an unconstitutional change of Government occurs', it suspended Egypt from participating in the AU until restoration of the constitutional order. The PSC also emphasized the AU's solidarity with the Egyptian population as well as its commitment to 'support long-term efforts to address the structural problems facing Egypt'.[1163] In effect, the PSC followed the relevant instruments to the letter without taking into consideration the ideological struggle which dominated these events, namely the Islamist regime run by Morsi versus the lay regime run by the military.[1164]

1160. For an overview, *see* O. Varol, 'The Democratic Coup d'Etat', *Harvard International Law Journal* 53 (2012): 291.

1161. For unofficial translation, *see* http://constitutionaltransitions.org/wp-content/uploads/2013/05/Egypt-Constitution-26-December-2012.pdf.

1162. *See* Statement by EU High Representative Catherine Ashton on developments in Egypt, 3 Jul. 2013, at: http://eeas.europa.eu/delegations/egypt/press_corner/all_news/news/2013/20130704_en.htm, and Statement by the UN Secretary-General, who, even though he regarded that the 'military interference in the affairs of any State is of concern', was happy not to condemn it as long as an 'inclusive approach' was taking place, UN Press Release SG/SM/15151-AFR/2657, 3 Jul. 2013, at: http://www.un.org/press/en/2013/sgsm15151.doc.htm.

1163. AU Doc. PSC/PR/COMM.(CCCLXXXIV), 5 Jul. 2013, paras 6 and 9.

1164. Compare E. Hellquist, *Regional Organizations and Sanctions Against Members – Explaining the Different Trajectories of the African Union, the League of Arab States, and the Association of*

The PSC justified the suspension on the ground that the Egyptian Constitution did not condone the overthrow of a democratically elected President.[1165] Arguably, no democratic constitution would ever excuse such an act. However, more importantly, constitutions are domestic legal instruments having a legal effect within the boundaries of the respective state and, therefore, their stipulations should, in principle, not be invoked to justify imposing punitive measures by an intergovernmental organization. To put it otherwise, were the Egyptian Constitution to tolerate undemocratic acts, would this have prevented the PSC from exercising its powers as it thought fit? The answer should be in the negative because the PSC draws its mandate and its legitimacy from multilateral instruments which are founded on the collective agreement of all Member States to promote and protect democratic values. To that extent, it could be argued with some persuasion that these instruments stand higher than domestic constitutions. But even if one agreed that the PSC acted correctly as regards the events of July 2013, one cannot but accuse it of double standards. And, this is because, while it overlooked the totalitarian rule during the Mubarak era, it was quick to suspend the participation of the military-backed regime in the AU, even though it was clear that increasingly a substantial part of the population supported it. Thus, when in late May 2014 the planned presidential elections took place, Abdel Fatah el-Sisi, the former chief of the Egyptian army, overwhelmingly won them with 96% of the votes cast,[1166] a percentage that does bring to mind non-democratic electorate processes. The military regime had already drafted a new Constitution, which was approved by a referendum held on 14 and 15 January 2014 and considered to be free and fair.[1167]

On account of these political developments, it was difficult and politically inexpedient for the PSC to press for Egypt's continued exclusion from AU activities. In particular, the PSC would need to explain why these events did not amount to restoration of constitutional order in the country. Clearly, this position would have been hard to sustain, and the PSC was already criticized for the way it handled the change in government in July 2013. Thus, in June 2014, two weeks after el-Sisi was elected President, it adopted a Communiqué resolving to lift the suspension of participation and invited Egypt to immediately resume its seat.[1168] By following to the letter the provisions of the AU instruments against coups d'état, the PSC may have fulfilled its role and mandate, but, in retrospect, its action could have been questioned, especially since, as has been explained, other international organizations never took an expressly negative stance vis-à-vis the perpetrators of the July 2013 coup. This reality should explain the fact that in the June 2014 Communiqué, the PSC was so eager

---

Southeast Asian Nations, Freie Universität Berlin (KFG Working Paper Series, No. 59, January 2014) 14, at: http://userpage.fu-berlin.de/kfgeu/kfgwp/wpseries/WorkingPaperKFG_59.pdf.

1165. *See* Art. 6 of the Constitution of 2012 stipulating that the political system is based, *inter alia*, on the peaceful transfer of power.

1166. *See The Guardian*, 'Abdel Fatah al-Sisi won 96.1% of vote in Egypt presidential election, say officials', 2 Jun. 2014, at: https://www.theguardian.com/world/2014/jun/03/abdel-fatah-al-sisi-presidential-election-vote-egypt.

1167. For the official AU record of events in Egypt since January 2011, *see* PSC, *Final Report of the African Union High-Level Panel for Egypt*, AU Doc. PSC/AHG/4.(CDXVI), 17 Jun. 2014, at: http://www.peaceau.org/uploads/auhpe-report-egypt-16-06-2014.pdf.

1168. AU Doc. PSC/PR/COMM.2(CDXLII), 17 Jun. 2014, para. 8, at: http://www.peaceau.org/uploads/psc-com-442-egypt-17-06-2014.pdf.

to defend its actions by reaffirming 'the correctness of its decision characterising the events of 3 July 2013 in Egypt as falling under the definition of unconstitutional changes of Government as stipulated in the relevant AU instruments'.[1169]

At the same time, the adoption of the Communiqué had to overcome a hurdle of some importance: both Article 25(4) of the Charter on Democracy and the Assembly Decision on Prevention of Unconstitutional Changes of Government[1170] stipulate that the perpetrators of coups d'état are not to be allowed to participate in any elections held to restore constitutional order. Evidently, the problem was that, since el-Sisi had come to power in a manner conflicting with the aforementioned Article 6 of the Constitution of 2012 (effectively, it amounted to a coup d'état), he could not have been a contender in the May 2014 presidential elections.[1171] From a legal perspective, the PSC could not have bypassed these prohibitions: rules are rules and may not be varied according to prevailing circumstances. Nevertheless, there might be political considerations diluting legal normativity. Thus, a compromise solution was necessary, one which would allow Egypt to resume participation but would not compromise the PSC's authority as the Member States' constitutional watchdog. In the event, the PSC lifted Egypt's suspension but only 'on the understanding that this does not constitute a precedent in terms of adherence' to the relevant AU instruments.[1172] In other words, the PSC let it be known that this was an extraordinary case justifying extraordinary treatment. When ten days later the Assembly discussed the work of the PSC during the first semester of 2014, it did not touch upon this rather crucial and delicate issue but only noted with satisfaction Egypt's return.[1173] The question of when would an undemocratic change of government be regarded as 'popular uprising' and, consequently, the new regime would not be suspended from participating in AU activities and its perpetrators and supporters would not face punitive measures was left unanswered, even though the PSC was of view that it ought to be dealt with at the level of AU Heads of State and Government.[1174]

Regarding the general handling of the 'Arab Spring', the AU, and especially the PSC, has been criticized for not applying (particularly in the case of the Libyan uprising with its heavy toll on human life) the aforementioned Article 4(h) of the Constitutive Act.[1175] Article 4(h) has been considered to be a manifestation of the Responsibility to Protect (R2P), a concept developed by the UN[1176] but not without

1169. *Ibid.*, para. 2.
1170. Assembly/AU/Dec. 269 (XIV) Rev.1, *supra*.
1171. Under Art. 5 of the Amended Constitution of 2014 the political system is based on the peaceful rotation of power, *see* https://www.constituteproject.org/constitution/Egypt_2014.pdf.
1172. PSC/PR/COMM.2(CDXLII), *supra*.
1173. Assembly, *Decision on the Report of the Peace and Security Council on its Activities and the State of Peace and Security in Africa*, AU Doc. Assembly/AU/Dec. 536 (XXIII), 27 Jun. 2014, para. 8.
1174. PSC/PR/COMM.2(CDXLII), *supra* para. 9.
1175. *See*, *inter alia*, J.F. Mutton, 'Article 4(h) and the Citizen's Right to be Protected' in *Africa and the Responsibility to Protect – Article 4(h) of the African Union Constitutive Act,* D. Kuwali & F. Viljoen (eds) (London: Routledge, 2014), 97, 105 et seq.; A. Girmachew, *A Study of the African Union's Right of Intervention Against Genocide, Crimes Against Humanity and War Crimes* (Nijmegen: Wolf Legal Publishers, 2011). Specifically, as regards the Arab Spring, *see* K.N. Obse, 'The "African Spring" and the Question of Legitimacy of Democratic Revolution in Theory and Practice', *Human Security Perspectives* 10 (2014): 232, 265.
1176. *See* UNGA Resolution 60/1, *World Summit Outcome*, 16 Sep. 2005, paras 138–139.

ambiguities.[1177] As argued elsewhere in the present monograph, the application of Article 4(h) is surrounded by a number of issues, which for present purposes include the following. First, should the AU have devised a specific set of rules for the purpose of coups d'état? Second, irrespective of Article 4(h), could the AU, acting through the Assembly and/or the PSC, have applied the R2P concept directly?[1178] Third, does the AU have an independent right to hold the alleged perpetrators of humanitarian and human rights violations, which took place during popular revolts, personally accountable?

The situation in Libya offers a good illustration because, over and above the proceedings pursued domestically, the ICC has opened an investigation pursuant to the referral made in February 2011 by the UNSC Resolution 1970(2011).[1179] Thus, could the AU have initiated criminal proceedings against, on the one hand, dignitaries of the old regime (including Saif Al-Islam Gaddafi, the son of the late Colonel Gaddafi)[1180] and, on the other hand, those allegedly responsible for killing civilians loyal to the Gaddafi regime?[1181]

These are not theoretical questions. It is true that, following the Gaddafi regime's demise, the AU was not forthcoming to discuss what actually happened during the uprising,[1182] but has rather been content to leave the matter to be handled by others (including European countries) despite the consequences for neighbouring countries.[1183] Only in January 2016, the Assembly decided to establish the High-Level Committee of Heads of State and Government,[1184] as had been agreed by the PSC eighteen months earlier to support peace and reconstruction in Libya,[1185] and at its Twenty-Ninth Ordinary Session, it reaffirmed the intention to convene a Libyan

---

1177. *See* J. Genser & I. Cotler, *The Responsibility to Protect* (Oxford: Oxford University Press, 2012), 28 et seq.

1178. While it has been submitted that R2P is widely acknowledged within the AU, N. Zähringer, 'Norm Evolution Within and Across the African Union and the United Nations: The Responsibility to Protect (R2P) as a Contested Norm', *South African Journal of International Affairs* 20 (2013): 187, arguably this is quite separate from actually invoking it, applying it, and implementing it during a specific situation.

1179. *See* ICC, Pre-Trial Chamber I, ICC-01/11-01/11, *The Prosecutor v. Saif Al-Islam Gaddafi and Abdullah Al-Senussi*. Further *see*, K.D. Magliveras, 'Recent Developments in the 'Situation in Libya' and the Trial of Saif Al-Islam Gaddafi', *International Enforcement Law Reporter* 28 (2012): 294.

1180. In late July 2015 he was sentenced to death by a court in Tripoli, *see* C. Stephen, 'Gaddafi's son Saif al-Islam sentenced to death by court in Libya', *The Guardian*, 28 Jul. 2015, at: http://www.theguardian.com/world/2015/jul/28/saif-al-islam-sentenced-death-by-court-in-libya-gaddafi-son.

1181. *See* generally, E. O'Shea, 'Responsibility to Protect (R2P) in Libya: Ghosts of the Past Haunting the Future', *International Human Rights Law Review* 1 (2012): 173.

1182. The UN organized two investigations, *see Report of the International Commission of Inquiry to investigate all alleged violations of international human rights law in the Libyan Arab Jamahiriya*, UN Doc. A/HRC/17/44, 1 Jun. 2011, and *Report of the International Commission of Inquiry on Libya*, UN Doc. A/HRC/19/68 (8 Mar. 2012).

1183. Principally, the Ministerial Committee of Libya's Neighbours and the International Contact Group for Libya (ICG-L). *See* Assembly, *Decision on the Report of the Peace and Security Council on its Activities and the State of Peace and Security in Africa*, AU Doc. Assembly/AU/Dec. 583 (XXV), para. 17 (15 Jun. 2015).

1184. Assembly, *Decision on the Activities of the Peace and Security Council and the State of Peace and Security in Africa*, AU Doc. Assembly/AU/Dec. 598(XXVI), 31 Jan. 2016, para. 21.

1185. PSC Communique, AU Doc.PSC/MIN/COMM.(CDLIX), 23 Sep. 2014, para. 17.

national reconciliation dialogue at AU headquarters but set no date. However, if the aforementioned Malabo Protocol attaching an International Criminal Law (ICL) Section to the ACJHR and the annexed Statute had entered into force (they still have not), the ICL Section would have been competent to adjudicate criminal prosecutions brought against individuals allegedly involved in unconstitutional changes of government. To that extent, the AU would have been directly involved, alongside the ICC and any domestic criminal proceedings.[1186] Although not stated in the Malabo Protocol, the ICL Section fulfils Article 25(5) of the Charter on Democracy, stipulating that the illegal acts envisaged therein may also be tried before the AU Court. Indeed, under new Article 28(F) of the ACJHR Statute, the international crime of unconstitutional changes of government goes far beyond coups d'état and covers additionally the refusal of a government to relinquish power following free and fair elections as well as the promulgation of Constitutional amendments which are considered to be incompatible with democratic principles.

Of the three North African states where the so-called Arab Spring erupted, only Tunisia managed to become a democratic (by Western standards) regime.[1187] The PSC did not intervene in the situation in Tunisia, and although it condemned the excessive use of force against the demonstrators, resulting in deaths, it took no action.[1188] Based on this and other statements,[1189] the question has been asked whether, in reality, the AU continued to recognize the incumbent regimes or favoured the populations' democratic aspirations,[1190] which, by necessary implication, negated the legitimacy of the former. It is submitted that for the AU the parallel anti-establishment uprisings in North Africa (and in the case of the League of Arab States in the Middle East as well) could not have been coped with effectively because the relevant procedures and mechanisms are only meant to address single instances of unconstitutional change of government and not repetitive situations having similar characteristics. Regional political organizations are always wary of such incidents because, from a certain point onwards, repetitive negative events that are not addressed and coped with could lead to paralysis. In April 2023, the PSC issued a Communique where it reviewed the situation in Libya. It was mostly a recount of the various initiatives undertaken by various actors towards finding a durable solution to the crisis. However, what stands out is that the PSC recalled its decision to undertake a field mission to Libya to express solidarity with the population and to 'gather first-hand information on the situation on the ground with a

---

1186. *See* K. Magliveras, 'African Human Rights Court Castigates Libya for Violating Saif Al-Islam Kadhafi's Rights to Liberty and Security of Person', *International Enforcement Law Reporter* 32 (2016): 306.
1187. A new Constitution was adopted on 26 Jan. 2014, English translation at: https://www.constituteproject.org/constitution/Tunisia_2014.pdf. Art. 2 stipulates that Tunisia is based on the will of the people and the supremacy of law (rule of law), a provision which cannot be amended.
1188. PSC, Press Statement, PSC/PR/COMM.2(CCLVII), 15 Jan. 2011.
1189. PSC, Communique, PSC/PR/COMM.(CCLX), 16 Feb. 2011 regarding the situation in Egypt; Communique PSC/PR/COMM(CCLXI), 23 Feb. 2011 regarding the situation in Libya.
1190. *See* M. Eriksson & K. Zetterlund, *Dealing with Change: EU and AU Responses to the Uprisings in Tunisia, Egypt and Libya* (Swedish Defence Research Agency, Report No. FOI-R-3589-SE, January 2013) 38, at: https://www.foi.se/en/foi.html.

view to adopt more informed decisions on the next steps in favor of Libya'.[1191] This part of the Communique is striking for at least two reasons. First, because it was not resolved when this field mission will take place. Second, because arguably the PSC admitted that it does not actually know what is happening in Libya. It would appear that the tools that the PSC has at its disposal to deal with situations such as Libya are inadequate and that it is high time it devised new mechanisms to handle them. The latter suggestion is reinforced by the events in Sudan.

XII. Sudan (April 2023–Present)

177. Exactly four years after the overthrow of President Omar Al Bashir in April 2019, clashes broke out between the two main factions of the ruling military regime (the Sudanese Armed Forces and the Rapid Support Forces (RSF)), leaving many people dead. The PSC's reaction was to ask that 'the guns be silenced in Sudan' and to announce that it will undertake a field mission to engage with all domestic stakeholders.[1192] A month later and with the situation deteriorating, it issued a Press Release where, on the one hand, warned that all perpetrators of criminal actions will be held accountable and, on the other hand, called again for an immediate, unconditional, and comprehensive ceasefire.[1193] But it did not take any action of substance or indeed any punitive measures against the two fighting factions. The reason might be that at the time the latter were engaged, under the auspices of Saudi Arabia and the USA, in direct negotiations in Jeddah, where on 11 May 2023, they signed a Declaration of Commitment to Protect the Civilians of Sudan.[1194] The PSC Press Statement did note the talks in Jeddah but insisted that there was a 'need for inclusivity', which could be construed to show its dissatisfaction because the crisis in Sudan was handled outside an African context. On 20 May 2023, the two sides, again with the assistance of Saudi and U.S. facilitators, signed in Jeddah an Agreement on a Short-Term Ceasefire and Humanitarian Arrangements.[1195] The PSC welcomed the Agreement but emphasized 'the necessity for inclusivity, adequate representation and participation of … African regional and continental bodies in the negotiations towards a permanent and comprehensive ceasefire and the political transition in Sudan'.[1196] Moreover, it adopted the African Union Roadmap for the Resolution of the Conflict in Sudan, which comprised of six elements, the first being

1191. PSC, 1150th Meeting, PSC/MIN/COMM.1150 (2023), 18 April 2023, para. 13, at: https://papsrepository.africa-union.org/handle/123456789/1848.
1192. PSC, 1149th Meeting on the Briefing on the Situation in Sudan, *Communiqué*, AU Doc. PSC/PR/COMM.1149 (2023), para. 8 (16 Apr. 2023), at: https://papsrepository.africa-union.org/handle/123456789/1851.
1193. PSC, 1154th Meeting, *Press Statement*, AU Doc. PSC/PR/BR.1154 (2023) (16 May 2023), at: https://papsrepository.africa-union.org/handle/123456789/1865.
1194. Text at: https://reliefweb.int/report/sudan/jeddah-declaration-commitment-protect-civilians-sudan.
1195. At: https://www.state.gov/agreement-on-a-short-term-ceasefire-and-humanitarian-arrangements/.
1196. PSC, 1156th meeting at the level of Heads of State and Government on the Situation in Sudan, *Communique*, AU Doc. PSC/HoSG/COMM.1156 (2023), para. 9 (27 May 2023), at: https://www.peaceau.org/uploads/1156.comm-en.pdf.

the establishment of a coordination mechanism to ensure harmonization of all efforts by regional and global actors and ensuring that they are 'impactful towards silencing the guns in Sudan'.[1197] The implementation of the Roadmap was discussed on 31 May 2023 during the Third Meeting of the Expanded Mechanism on Sudan, which was created by the AUC Chairperson at the end of April 2023. The Meeting brought together representatives from the Trilateral Mechanism (AU, IGAD and UN), the League of Arab States (Sudan is a Member State), the EU, the permanent UNSC members, the African members of the UNSC, Sudan's neighbouring countries (Central African Republic, Chad, Egypt, Eritrea, Ethiopia, Libya and South Sudan), the countries designated by IGAD to engage the belligerents sides in Sudan (South Sudan, Kenya and Djibouti), Comoros as AU Chair, the Quad (USA, UK, Saudi Arabia, and UAE), the Troika (USA, UK and Norway), Germany, and Qatar. It is obvious that several states participated with multiple designations, e.g. the USA and the UK as permanent UNSC members, as part of the Quad and as part of the Troika; South Sudan as both a neighbouring country and as an IGAD designated country, etc. Given the wide participation of international organizations and third states, arguably, the AU, and specifically the PSC, have been sidelined and are unable to shape developments. Since then, there has been no Assembly session (as mentioned above, it now meets once a year and it had already met in February 2023) while the Executive Council met in mid July 2023 but it did not discuss any matter that had to do with peace and security. At the time of writing (November 2023), there has been no other PSC meeting to discuss the situation.

§10. The African Union Commission on International Law (AUCIL)

178. The Statute of the AUCIL was adopted by the Executive Council at its Fourteenth Ordinary Session in January 2009[1198] and came into force, upon its approval by the Assembly, the following month.[1199] The AUCIL was created as an 'independent advisory organ' of the AU pursuant to the provision on the establishment of subsidiary organs (Article 5(2) of the Constitutive Act). Its functions, objectives and structure have been defined in the Statute and elaborated in its Rules of Procedure.[1200] The setting up of the AUCIL was originally envisaged in Article 14 of the AU Non-Aggression and Common Defence Pact, adopted in January 2005, in force in December 2009. In particular, contracting parties undertook to establish the AUCIL and decided that its objectives shall be to study legal matters pertaining to the protection of peace and security in Africa, including the demarcation of borders.

1197. *Ibid*, para. 4.

1198. *See* Executive Council, *Decision on the Draft Statutes of the African Union Commission on International Law*, AU Doc. EX.CL/Dec. 474 (XIV) (30 Jan. 2009).

1199. *See* Assembly, *Decision on the Draft Statute of the African Union Commission on International Law*, AU Doc. Assembly/AU//Dec. 209 (XII) (4 Feb. 2009).

1200. *See* AU Doc. AUCIL/Legal/Doc. 4 (III). The Rules were adopted by the Executive Council and revised by the AUCIL during its Third Ordinary Session (23 Mar.–1 Apr. 2011). However, in 2016 the Assembly adopted a document titled 'Rules of Procedure of the African Union Commission on the International Law', *see* Assembly, *Decision on the Specialized Technical Committees*, AU Doc. Assembly/AU/Dec. 589 (XXVI), para. 2 (31 Jan. 2016).

Moreover, according to Article 11 of the Pact, the AUCIL together with the African Peace Academy (APA) and the African Centre for Study and Research on Terrorism (ACSRT) were asked to assist the PSC in its activities. APA has apparently never been established, while the ACSRT was established in accordance with the provisions of the AU Action Plan for the Prevention and Fight against Terrorism in Africa, which was agreed at the AU High-Level Intergovernmental Meeting on the Prevention and Combating of Terrorism in Africa in Algiers in September 2002. ACSRT was inaugurated on 13 October 2004 and its seat is in Algeria.[1201] However, the AUCIL was additionally envisaged (albeit with considerably augmented objectives) in the Report of Experts on the Review of OAU/AU Treaties, which was discussed during the Fifth Ordinary Executive Council Session in 2004.[1202] By taking note of the proposal to establish it and by requesting the AUC to come up with proposals,[1203] effectively, the Executive Council disassociated the AUCIL's further development from its role as envisaged in the Non-Aggression and Common Defence Pact. As stated in the Preamble of the AUCIL Statute, the need for establishing it was reaffirmed by the Assembly in Decision 66(IV) of January 2005. This should be a mistake because Decision 66(IV) was concerned solely with the situation in the DRC and its relations with Rwanda. The only Assembly reference appears to be in Decision 118(VII) requesting the AUC and the PRC to, *inter alia*, elaborate the document on the AUCIL establishment and submit a report to the Executive Council in January 2007.[1204]

The AUCIL consists of eleven members, who are nationals of Member States and serve in their personal capacity.[1205] They are elected for a period of five years (re-election for another term is possible) by secret ballot. Pursuant to Article 13 of the Statute, members may resign (there is no requirement to give reasons) and may be suspended or removed from office upon the recommendation of two-thirds of the other members if they are deemed to be unable to continue meeting the required conditions of office. The Statute does not stipulate which organ will be competent to decide on the recommendation and has left it to be determined in the Rules of Procedure. The latter do not contain any relevant provisions. However, this is not the only omission: according to Article 11 of the Statute, the act of the election of members is also governed by the Rules, but no such provisions have been included. In the event, the first members were elected by the Executive Council in June

1201. Note that in October 2010 the AUC Chairperson appointed the AU Special Representative for Counter-Terrorism Cooperation, who also acts as the Director of ACSRS.

1202. *See* AU Doc. EX.CL/95 (V) (2004).

1203. *See* Executive Council, *Decision on the Meeting of the Experts on the Review of OAU/AU Treaties*, AU Doc. EX.CL/Dec. 129 (V), para. 5 (3 Jul. 2004).

1204. *See* Assembly, *Decision on the Draft Single Instrument on the Merger of the African Court on Human and Peoples' Rights and the Court of Justice of the African Union*, AU Doc. Assembly/AU/Dec. 118 (VII) (2 Jul. 2006).

1205. *See also*, Assembly, *Decision on Structures*, UN Doc. Assembly/AU/Dec. 850 (XXXVI), para. 8, 19 Feb. 2023.

2009,[1206] and their appointment was effected by the Assembly during its Thirteenth Ordinary Session the following month.[1207]

The AUCIL objectives are laid down in Article 4 of the Statute. Its activities include the codification of international law, which is further elaborated in Article 6; the progressive development of international law (Article 5); the revision of existing OAU/AU treaties (Article 8); the teaching and dissemination of international law (Article 9); and the carrying out of studies on legal issues of interest to the AU and the Member States (Article 7). Regarding the codification of international law, the functions to be performed by the AUCIL are similar to those of the UN International Law Commission (ILC), which was created as a subsidiary organ of the Sixth Committee of the UN General Assembly in 1948. Indeed, under Article 25(3) of the Statute, the AUCIL is mandated to establish close cooperation with the ILC in order to promote international law in Africa. On 17 July 2012, representatives from the AUCIL visited the ILC in Geneva.[1208]

The AUCIL acts upon the requests for codification submitted by the Assembly and other (not named in the Statute) organs, prepares drafts in the form of Articles (as the ILC does) and, through the Executive Council, submits them to the Assembly together with commentaries. Following consultations with Member States, the AUCIL sends to the Assembly a final draft report and recommends that the Assembly undertake one of the following: take no action; take note of the report; adopt the report; or recommend to Member States the conclusion of a convention based on the report. However, according to Article 6(12) of the Statute, the Assembly may refer the draft report back to the AUCIL for reconsideration and further elaboration. In January 2013, and in the context of the Twentieth Ordinary Assembly Session, the AUCIL President said that its work has dealt with a broad aspect of legal issues, including the harmonization of ratification procedures in Member States (presumably this would require considerable changes in national constitutions); the immunity of states officials under the Rome Statute of the ICC (as already explained, a particularly thorny issue in Africa given the arrest warrants that the ICC has issued against African dignitaries); the revision of OAU/AU Treaties (clearly a daunting task); the juridical basis for reparations for slavery in the African continent (a long-standing theme that the AU may not have pursued actively); a Model Law assisting Member States in implementing the provisions of the Kampala Convention on IDPs; and a definition of the crime of unconstitutional change of governments.[1209]

The Eleventh Ordinary AUCIL Session was held in Cairo in October 2015, the first-ever session outside the AU Headquarters. It considered a number of ongoing studies, including the Continental Legal Framework on Migration, a review of the African Charter on the Rights and Welfare of the Child, the Continental Legal Framework on Piracy, and the African Convention on Judicial Cooperation and Mutual Legal Assistance. To the best of one's knowledge, the work of AUCIL is not

1206. *See* Executive Council, *Decision on Election of Members of the African Union Commission on International Law (AUCIL)*, AU Doc. EX.CL/Dec. 498 (XV) (30 Jun. 2009).

1207. *See* Assembly, *Decision on the Report on the Election of Members of The African Union Commission on International Law*, AU Doc. Assembly/AU/Dec. 249 (XII) (3 Sep. 2009).

1208. *See* UN Doc. A/CN.4/SR.3146 (13 Aug. 2012).

1209. *See* AU, Directorate of Information and Communication, Press Release N°18/20th AU Summit, 25 Jan. 2013.

widely disseminated, and in a rather cryptic resolution in July 2016, the Executive Council requested that it focuses its reports in line with its mandate, namely the development and codification of international law, and to align AU treaties with the vision of Agenda 2063. It is not easy to decipher whether the Executive Council was showing its displeasure with the topics the AUCIL has been considering or with the priorities it has set. However, as it further urged Member States to pay greater attention to AUCIL activities and to participate in its deliberations,[1210] the conclusion could be reached that the AUCIL operated in the AU fringes, and its role and mandate were not widely known. Since December 2012, the AUCIL has organized an annual Forum engaging in discussions on issues concerning the continent specifically as it relates to the application and development of international and African Union law. Presently, there is no proper African Union law (at least as one understands it in the context of the legal system of a regional international organization viz. European Union law),[1211] but, as is argued in the present monograph, an AU legal system is no doubt in development and will probably continue expanding as various projects (and primarily the project for continental economic integration) take shape and progress. The Ninth AUCIL Forum was held under the theme 'International Law, Business Law and Human Rights in Africa' on 15–16 May 2023. Its objectives were to identify and explore areas where Member States could contribute to creating new guiding principles on the topic of 'Business and Human Rights in Africa', to analyse the legislative framework for demanding corporate accountability, to identify challenges when corporate-related violations are perpetrated and to examine ways to develop international law in response to these issues. Finally, the present work of AUCIL, as revealed by the topics deliberated during its Twentieth Session held in March 2022, includes a draft African Convention against Slavery, the prohibition on intervention in international law, a draft African Convention on Judicial Cooperation and Mutual Assistance (a long project that had been abandoned in the past), a draft Continental Convention on the Avoidance of Double Taxation, immunities under international law, maritime piracy, as well as draft Model Laws for the domestication of the African Charter on the Rights and Welfare of the Child and for the domestication of the Protocol to the African Charter on Human and People's Rights on the Rights of Women in Africa.

1210. *See* Executive Council, *Decisions on the Activity Report of the African Union Commission on International Law (AUCIL)*, AU Doc. EX.CL/Dec. 932 (XXIX) (15 Jul. 2016).

1211. *See* K. Magliveras, 'The Implications of African Union Law: Conceptual Analysis with Emphasis on the Institutional Consequences' in F. Amao, M. Olivier & K. Magliveras (eds), *The Emergent African Union Law: Conceptualization, Delimitation, and Application*(Oxford: Oxford University Press, 2021), 30–44.

Chapter 6. Privileges and Immunities

179. The Constitutive Act is silent on the question of privileges and immunities.[1212] However, given that the AU has substituted the OAU (a case of succession between two international organizations where the latter was established to specifically succeed the former), the totality of the privileges and immunities enjoyed by the OAU were transferred *in toto* to the AU. As the OAU Charter did not contain any clauses on privileges and immunities, a General Convention on the Privileges and Immunities of the OAU was adopted on 25 October 1965.[1213] The Convention, whose provisions follow closely the Convention on the Privileges and Immunities of the UN,[1214] has a rather obscure and peculiar clause as regards its entry into force. Thus, Article X provides that it is submitted to every Member State for accession, which would be effected by the respective Head of State and Government's signature, and the very act of signing would imply its immediate entry into force. This clause, while allowing the General Convention to enter into force on the day it was adopted, has led to some strange consequences. First, it has still not come into force for the entire membership, forty-four states have ratified it, and therefore not all Member States have recognized the AU's privileges and immunities. Second, the Republic of South Africa, which has not even signed the Convention, hosts the seat of PAP. Even though Article 9 of the Protocol establishing PAP stipulates that 'The Pan-African Parliamentarians shall enjoy parliamentary immunity in each Member State', this provision does not apply to the Member States that are still not contracting parties to the PAP Protocol. The matter has also been dealt with in Article 9 of the Host Country Agreement between the AU and the Government of the Republic of South Africa on the Seat of the PAP, concluded in 2004.[1215] It stipulates that PAP, its members, the Clerk and the Deputy Clerks shall enjoy full diplomatic immunities as provided for in the 1965 Convention as well as in the Vienna Convention on Diplomatic Relations of 1961.[1216] It follows that South Africa is obliged to guarantee specific privileges and immunities not as a contracting party to the 1965 Convention but only because it has ratified the Host Country Agreement. Equally, the Member States, which are not contracting parties to the 1965 Convention but have ratified the PAP Protocol, presumably must secure parliamentary immunity as an obligation emanating only from the latter.

180. Article I of the General Convention stipulates that the OAU (references will now be to the AU) possesses international legal personality (an issue on which

1212. On the associated question of AU responsibility, *see* K. Magliveras & G. Naldi, 'Question of Responsibility and Non-Contractual Liability in African International Organizations: The African Union and the African Regional Economic Communities' in V. Pergantis (ed.), *The Responsibility of the European Union in the International Legal Order – Volume B: Comparative and Special Issues* (Athens: Sakkoulas Publications, 2023) (forthcoming).

1213. 1000 U.N.T.S. 393, reproduced in Naldi, *Documents*, 38. For further details, *see* K. Magliveras & G. Naldi, *The African Union* (Alphen aan den Rijn: Kluwer Law International, 2009) para. 99.

1214. Signed on 13 Feb. 1946, 1 U.N.T.S. 16.

1215. Reproduced in Republic of South Africa, Government Gazette, Vol. 471, 22 September 2004, No. 26816.

1216. Entered into force on 24 Apr. 1964, 500 U.N.T.S. 95.

both the OAU Charter and the AU Constitutive Act are silent) and has the capacity to enter into contracts, including the acquisition and disposal of movable property and the lodging of legal proceedings. Under Article II, the AU premises and assets enjoy immunity from every form of legal proceedings, except when the AU itself has waived immunity, are inviolable and may not be searched, confiscated or expropriated. In accordance with Article III, the AU, its income, assets, and properties are exempt from all direct taxes, from import and export duties as well as from quantitative restrictions on imports and exports in respect of goods used for official purposes and from customs duties in respect of publications. Even though the Convention does not exempt AU from sales taxes, when it acquires property on a large scale for official use, the Member States, in whose territory the acquisition has taken place, are directed to refund all taxes paid.

181. Article V of the General Convention concerns the privileges and immunities of Member States' representatives[1217] attending the meetings of the AU principal and subsidiary organs. Thus, they will enjoy the following: immunity from personal arrest or detention and from any legal process in respect of opinions expressed and acts performed in the exercise of their official functions; inviolability for their documents and the right to use diplomatic bags; exemption of their families from any immigration restrictions and alien registration; and exemption from currency and exchange restrictions, including customs duties on goods imported and sales tax. Interestingly enough, the complete freedom of speech and opinion and the immunity from legal proceedings will continue to be accorded even when representatives have ceased acting as ones. The provision of Article V(4) merits particular mention. It stipulates that these privileges and immunities are not accorded to representatives for their personal benefit but in order to protect the independent discharge of their functions in the AU. Consequently, Member States are placed under the duty to waive the immunity of their representatives when they believe that the exercise of immunity would impede the course of justice.

182. Article VI of the General Convention dealing with AU officials is not applicable to all categories of officials but only to those which are specified by the OAU Secretary-General (now the AUC Chairperson) and approved by the Assembly.[1218] Their immunities and privileges resemble those of Member States' representatives. Additionally, AU officials are exempt from taxation on their salaries and emoluments and, in times of international crisis, are accorded the same repatriation facilities as diplomatic envoys.[1219] Article VI(3) stipulates that the AUC Chairperson shall enjoy, in addition, 'the privileges and immunities, exemptions and facilities accorded to diplomatic envoys'. The immunity granted to officials may be waived

1217. The term 'representatives' has been given a rather broad interpretation and covers not only delegates but also deputy delegates, advisers, technical experts and secretaries of delegations; *see* Art. V(6) of the Convention.

1218. Experts performing missions for the OAU are not included in the term 'officials'. On the contrary, their privileges and immunities are regulated separately in Art. VII of the General Convention and are similar to those granted to representatives of foreign governments.

1219. Compare Art. 44 of the Vienna Convention on Diplomatic Relations.

by the AUC Chairperson in instances like those applying to Member States' representatives. In their turn, the Chairperson's immunities may be waived by the Council of Ministers (now the Executive Council). Finally, the AU must cooperate at all times with Member States' appropriate authorities to assist the proper administration of justice, to ensure that police regulations are observed and that its officials do not abuse the privileges and immunities accorded to them.

183. Article IX of the General Convention contains the dispute settlement clause. Four different categories of disputes are envisaged. The first concerns those arising out of contracts or other disputes of a private law nature to which the AU is a party (e.g., acquisition of land or the construction of new buildings). The second category concerns disputes involving any AU official enjoying immunity and provided that such immunity has not been waived by the AUC Chairperson. In these two categories, Article IX does not prescribe specific dispute settlement mechanisms but stipulates that the AU shall make provisions for appropriate modes of settlement. The third category deals with disputes arising out of the interpretation or application of the Convention, irrespective of the parties involved. These are to be settled by arbitration through the OAU Commission on Mediation, Conciliation, and Arbitration, unless the parties have agreed to a different settlement method. Given that this organ does no longer exist (it was established by virtue of a protocol attached to the OAU Charter in 1964),[1220] the provision should be considered as inoperative. However, a different conclusion might be reached on the basis of Article 28 of the Protocol establishing the ACJHR, which stipulates that the ACJHR's jurisdiction encompasses, *inter alia*, the interpretation, application or validity of any treaty adopted within the framework of the OAU/AU. Therefore, it could be assumed that if the conditions for *locus standi* are fulfilled, such disputes could be adjudicated by the ACJHR once it becomes operative. Finally, the fourth category also involves disputes relating to the Convention's interpretation or application but only between the AU and a Member State. These shall be settled by negotiation or any other agreed method, failing which, they shall be submitted to an arbitral tribunal for ad hoc arbitration. The tribunal shall consist of three arbitrators, one of whom shall be named by the AUC Chairperson, the other by the Member State concerned and the third by the arbitrators themselves. There are no reported cases dealing with private law litigation involving the AU or with disputes concerning the interpretation and application of the General Convention.

184. When the General Convention was adopted in 1965, there were no OAU-specialized agencies in operation. However, their subsequent establishment raised the question of whether it applied to their personnel as well. This led the OAU Assembly to adopt in June 1980 an Additional Protocol to extend privileges and immunities to such personnel. In line with the General Convention, the Additional Protocol was not opened for signature by the Member States but was submitted to each of them for accession, as stipulated in Article 10(1) of the Additional Protocol. Thus, its entry into force did not require its ratification by a certain number of signatory parties, but once a Member State had deposited the instrument of accession,

1220. Reproduced in 3 I.L.M. (1964) 1116.

it came into force between that Member and the OAU (now the AU). So far, only thirteen Member States have deposited instruments of accession (three in the course of 2022 (Zimbabwe, Namibia and Algeria)). The immunities and privileges granted to officials of the specialized agencies depend on whether the nationality of the official is that of a Member State (Article 2 of the Protocol) or of another state (Article 3). The former enjoy far more immunities compared to the latter: they are immune from any legal proceedings in respect of words spoken and written; exempt from taxation on emoluments paid; immune from arrest and detention; from national service obligations; from immigration restrictions and alien registration, etc. Finally, Article 5 stipulates that the OAU/AU may issue laissez-passer to an agency's officials, which must be recognized and accepted as valid travel documents by Member States, while Article 6 provides that it may issue travel certificates to those officials who are not nationals of a Member State. It is not clear to which extent the Additional Protocol was taken into account when drafting the constitutive instruments of specialized agencies. The example of the African Energy Commission will be given. Article 19 of the Convention establishing the Commission (adopted on 11 July 2001 and entered into force on 13 December 2006) does not mention the Additional Protocol but stipulates that the Commission, its property and assets as well as its staff shall enjoy in the territory of each contracting party (there are now thirty-five) the privileges and immunities provided for in the General Convention. But reference should also be made to the African Audio Visual and Cinema Commission (AACC), the most recent AU specialized agency. Its Statute was adopted by the Assembly in February 2019,[1221] and presently has been signed by only Kenya. According to Article 7 of the Statute, contracting parties undertake to accord to the AACC, and all its personnel, premises, property and assets, but also experts on mission providing advice or assistance to the AACC, the privileges and immunities as stipulated in the General Convention and the Additional Protocol.

It is clear that the AU has not paid the attention it should have to the issue of privileges and immunities. The fact that the General Convention and the Additional Protocol have not been accepted by all Member States is in itself problematic. Moreover, it is very doubtful if they cover the current needs of the AU. In particular, the fact that the AU's institutional architecture is very different from that of the OAU is adequate reason to advocate the drafting of new rules, which would have to take the form of a new treaty substituting the existing two instruments and cover additionally the totality of the organs (principal and subsidiary) which have been established since 2002 pursuant to the Constitutive Act.

1221. Assembly, *Decision on the Draft Legal Instruments*, AU Doc. Assembly/AU/Dec. 735 (XXXII), para. 2 (11 Feb. 2019).

Chapter 7. Finances

185. Unlike OAU, in the AU, the financial year coincides with the calendar year (January to December). As regards the size of AU budgets, they have been considerably increased compared to OAU budgets, given that the AU finances not only considerably more organs but also many more activities and programmes of action. Thus, the budget for the financial year (FY) 2004, which the Second Ordinary Assembly Session approved in July 2003, was set at USD 43 million,[1222] compared to USD 35.6 million for FY 2003.[1223] During the Fourth Ordinary Assembly Session (Addis Ababa, 4–8 July 2004), the Commission asked for a USD 570 million budget for FY 2005 but it was denied. In the event, the Assembly did not reach a decision but authorized the Executive Council to consider and adopt the budget at an extraordinary session.[1224] Five months later, the Sixth Extraordinary Executive Council Session met: the approval of the budget was the sole agenda item. It adopted a USD 158 million budget, a four-fold increase compared to the previous year, of which USD 63 million represented operational costs to be shared among Member States as assessed contributions, while the remaining amount represented the 'Programme-Budget', which Member States were asked to cover on a voluntary basis.[1225]

186. The scale of budgetary assessments had been under review since 2002. In July 2003, the Executive Council followed the conclusions of the Ad Hoc Ministerial Committee on the Review of the Scale of Assessment and recommended to the Assembly new rates with an 8.25% upper ceiling and two low floors of 0.25% and 0.75%. Moreover, it recommended that, as an exception, Algeria be granted, due to the natural disasters it had faced, a five-year grace period during which it would continue to pay its contributions based on the previous rate of 7.25%.[1226] Although the Second Ordinary Assembly Session approved the Executive Council's recommendations,[1227] some Member States indicated that their new assessment rates were too high and requested a review.[1228] This proved to be a contentious issue.[1229] However, the report prepared by the aforementioned Ad Hoc Ministerial

1222. *See* Assembly, *Decision on the Programme-Budget for the Year 2004*, AU Doc. Assembly/AU/Dec. 8 (II) (12 Jul. 2003), which was based on the recommendations of the Executive Council, AU Doc. EX/CL/26 (III) Rev. 1 (4 Jul. 2003).

1223. *See* Assembly, *Decision on the Budget for the Period January–August 2003 and the Budget for the Period September–December 2003*, AU Doc. Assembly/AU/Dec. 7 (II) (12 Jul. 2003).

1224. *See* Assembly, *Decision on the Draft Programme Budget for the 2005 Financial Year*, AU Doc. Assembly/AU/Dec. 47 (III) (8 Jul. 2004).

1225. *See* Executive Council, *Decision on the Reprioritized Priority Programme, the Solidarity Budget and the 2005 Programme-Budget*, AU Doc. EXT/EX.CL/Dec. 1 (VI) (6 Dec. 2005).

1226. *See* Executive Council, *Recommendation on the Review of the Scale of Assessment of the African Union*, AU Doc. EX/CL/Dec. 35 (III), which was based on AU Doc. EX/CL/40 (III) (4 July 2003). Note that Egypt attached a reservation.

1227. *See* Assembly, *Decision on the Review of the Scale of Assessment of the African Union*, AU Doc. Assembly/AU/Dec. 31 (II) (12 Jul. 2003).

1228. *See Report of the Sub-Committee on Contributions*, AU Doc. EX.CL/70 (IV) (2004).

1229. *See* Executive Council, *Decision on the Scale of Assessment*, AU Doc. EX.CL/Dec. 191 (VI) (28 Jan. 2005).

Committee[1230] was approved by the Seventh Ordinary Executive Council Session (Sirte, 28 June–2 July 2005)[1231] and was adopted by the Fifth Ordinary Assembly Session (Sirte, 4–5 July 2005).[1232] The revised Scale of Assessment, effective 1 January 2006, was based on the principle of the Member States' capacity to pay and featured an upper ceiling of 15% with no floor rate. Algeria, Egypt, Libya, Nigeria, and South Africa offered to contribute 15% of the regular budget each. As a result, 75% of the regular budget was to be covered by only five Member States, while the remaining forty-eight Members were asked to pay between them the remaining 25% of the budget. To offer two examples, Ethiopia's contribution was set at 0.63% and Botswana's at 0.83% of the budget.[1233]

187. Despite the new scale, disagreement among Member States persisted, prompting the Fifth Ordinary Assembly Session to authorize the convening of another extraordinary Executive Council session to resolve the matter. It took place in Khartoum on 19 January 2006 and approved the budget for FY 2006, which amounted to USD 129.6 million. As in previous years, the budget was divided into an assessed part of USD 69.4 million for operational costs to be contributed by all Member States, and a voluntary part (the 'Programme-Budget') to be financed on a voluntary basis by Member States and with the support of non-African states. South Africa appended a reservation to the resolution objecting to dividing the budget, as it was contrary to the AU Financial Rules and Regulations. In its opinion, it should have been presented as a joint, composite budget and assessed to all Member States.[1234] FY 2007 budget was set at USD 133 million, which in absolute numbers was lower than the 2006 budget because it also included the costs associated with the PAP (circa USD 6.4 million) and the African Court on Human and Peoples' Rights (circa USD 2.4 million).[1235] Finally, FY 2008 budget was approved by the Twelfth Ordinary Executive Council Session (Addis Ababa, 25–29 January 2008). It was again a separate budget totalling USD 140 million, of which USD 106.5 million were assessed to the Member States pursuant to the 2005 Scale of Assessments, USD 32.4 million were earmarked for AU programmes to be secured by the so-called international partners, and USD 1 million came from arrears in contributions.[1236]

1230. *See* AU Doc. EX.CL/192 (VII) (2005).
1231. *See* Executive Council, *Decision on the Scale of Assessment*, AU Doc. EX.CL/Dec. 223 (VII) (2 Jul. 2005).
1232. *See* Assembly, *Decision on the Scale of Assessment*, AU Doc. Assembly/AU/Dec. 88 (V) (5 Jul. 2005).
1233. *See* Executive Council, *Statement of Contributions of Member States to the African Union Budget as at 12 June 2006*, AU Doc. EX.CL/249 (IX) (25 Jun. 2006).
1234. *See* Executive Council, *Decision of the Eighth Extraordinary Session of the Executive Council on the Budget for 2006*, AU Doc. Ext/EX.CL/Dec. 1 (VIII) (19 Jan. 2006).
1235. *See* Assembly, *Decision on the Budget of the African Union for 2007*, AU Doc. Assembly/AU/Dec. 154 (VIII) (30 Jan. 2007), which was based on the recommendations of Executive Council, *see* Executive Council, *Decision of the Tenth Ordinary Session Council on the Budget for 2007*, AU Doc. EX.CL/Dec. 340 (X) (26 Jan. 2007).
1236. *See* Executive Council, *Decision on the Draft Budget for the AU Commission for 2008*, AU Doc. EX.CL/Dec. 378 (XII) (29 Jan. 2008).

188. As the Scale of Assessments is to be reviewed every three years, in July 2010, a new Scale was adopted by the Seventeenth Ordinary Executive Council Session to cover FY 2011–2013. It followed the recommendations of the Ministerial Committee on the Review of the Scale of Assessments, namely that the new scale with a ceiling of 13.271% and without a floor rate be introduced. Moreover, it asked those Member States with the capacity and the ability to pay over and above their assessed contribution to do so. Thus, Algeria, Egypt, Libya, Nigeria, and South Africa agreed to contribute 13.271% of the budget each, another five Member States agreed to pay more than 1% of the budget each, while the remaining membership was to pay less than 1% each. The latter included Burundi (0.063% of the budget), the Comoros (0.034%), Djibouti (0.075%), Gambia (0.037%), Liberia (0.037%), South Sudan (0.016%), San Tomé and Principe (0.010), and Seychelles (0.067%).[1237]

The Twenty-Second Ordinary Executive Council Session (Addis Ababa, 21–25 January 2013) adopted the Scale of Assessments for FY 2014–2016 based on a maximum rate (ceiling) of 12.898% without the imposition of a minimum (floor) rate. Moreover, it endorsed the recommendation of the Ministerial Committee on the Review of the Scale of Assessment that South Sudan be assessed at 0.599% and agreed that the assessed contribution of Sudan be fixed temporarily at 2%, both with effect from January 2012. Finally, the Executive Council asked the PRC to review the statutory contributions of small island Member States, to take into account their vulnerability, as well as to make suitable recommendations as regards the minimum amount to be paid by Member States in arrears of contributions to avoid sanctions.[1238] The Scale of Assessments for FY 2016–2018, approved by the Assembly in January 2016, envisaged three tiers. The first covered Nigeria, South Africa, Egypt and Algeria, each having to pay 12% of the budget, i.e., USD 20.391 million for FY 2016. The second concerned thirteen Member States and ranged between 8% (Angola) and 1.141% (Uganda), giving a total of 37,478% of the budget. All other Member States were in the third tier, which ranged from 1.095% (Gabon) to 0.017% (San Tome and Principe), which had to pay USD 28,888 for FY 2016. This new Scale reflected the voluntary decision of four states to increase their assessed contributions: Cote d'Ivoire to 3% (almost double the previous assessment), Ethiopia to 4%, Kenya to 4.1% and Chad to 0.942%.[1239] According to the Assembly, the scale was based 'on the principles of solidarity, equitable payment and capacity to pay', and ensured that no single Member State country bears a disproportionate share of the budget.[1240]

As has been mentioned, in February 2019, the Assembly approved a new scale of assessments for the period 2020–2022,[1241] which, for the reasons explained later, is still in force. The new scale, which maintained the three-tier system, was also based

1237. *See* Executive Council, *Decision on the Scale of Assessment*, AU Doc. EX.CL/Dec. 582 (XVII) (23 Jul. 2010).

1238. *See* Executive Council, *Decision by the Ad Hoc Ministerial Committee on the Scale of Assessment*, AU Doc. EX.CL/Dec. 756 (XXII) (25 Jan. 2013).

1239. *See* Assembly, *Decision on the Scale of Assessment and the Implementation of Alternative Sources of Financing the African Union*, AU Doc. Assembly/AU/Dec. 602 (XXVI) (31 Jan. 2016).

1240. *See* Assembly, *Decision on the Scale of Assessment and Alternative Sources of Financing the African Union*, AU Doc. Assembly/AU/Dec. 578 (XXV), paras 2 and 4 (15 Jun. 2015).

1241. AU Doc. Assembly/AU/Dec. 734 (XXXII), *supra*.

on the recommendations of the AU Ministers of Finance in 2017 that, to ensure equity and effective risk management, there should be 'caps' and 'minima', that each Member State should pay a minimum flat contribution and that no state or group of states pays more than a specified share of the budget. In particular, Tier 1 Member States were assessed at 45.151% of the budget, Tier 2 at 32.749% and Tier 3 at 22.1%, with the provisio that (a) no Member State shall pay less than USD 350,000 or more than USD 35 million as contribution for the regular budget and Peace Fund combined, and (b) so as to address the growing budgetary burden to the membership, the regular budget for FY 2020 would be reduced by USD 32 million compared to FY 2019. According to this scale, there were six states in Tier 1 (Nigeria, Egypt, South Africa, Algeria, Angola and Morocco) each contributing 7.525% of the budget and each receiving a savings of USD 2.4 million in the 2020 budget; twelve states were in Tier 2 (the largest contributor being Ethiopia with 3.999% budgetary contribution and USD 1.27 million savings, the smallest contributor being Zambia with respectively 1.599% and USD 511,618 savings); and all other states were in Tier 3 (the largest contributor being Zimbabwe contributing 1.108% of the budget and having a savings of USD 354,544.78, and the smallest Sao Tome and Principe with 0.115% of the budget and a savings of USD 36,949).[1242]

In October 2021, the Executive Council directed AUC to expedite the new scale of assessment for the period 2023–2025.[1243] But as in February 2022, the AUC had not presented it (the consequences of the COVID-19 pandemic were a major reason), the Executive Council's recommendation to the Assembly that the 2020–2022 scale was extended to 2023[1244] was accepted.[1245] Thereafter, the Executive Council asked AUC to develop a new scale for the period 2024–2026 but, at the same time, approved the request by Member States for additional time to undertake further consultations because the pandemic's enduring social and economic challenges, the effects of the Russian-Ukraine conflict, inflationary pressures, the increasing negative effects of climate change, etc. have impacted their capacity to pay contributions. For this reason, AUC and the F15 Experts were asked to develop a roadmap for regional consultations, and 'following due process, present a single option for consideration and adoption by the Executive Council in July 2023'.[1246] To do so, the Assembly had already delegated its powers of adoption to the Executive Council.[1247]

1242. *Ibid.* Interestingly enough, Seychelles appended a reservation because the scale was deemed 'inequitable and require[ing] deeper consultations at capital level'. Seychelles pays 0.204% of the budget.

1243. Executive Council, *Decision on the Report of the Joint-Sitting of the Ministerial Committee on Scale of Assessment and Contributions and the Committee of* F15, AU Doc. EX.CL/Dec. 1138 (XXXIX), para. 15 (15 Oct. 2021).

1244. Executive Council, *Decision on the Report of the Joint Sitting of the Ministerial Committee on Scale of Assessment and Contributions and Committee of Fifteen Ministers of Finance* (F15), AU Doc. EX.CL/Dec. 1162 (XL) (3 Feb. 2022).

1245. Assembly, *Decision on the Scale of Assessment and Contributions*, Assembly/AU/Dec. 838 (XXXV), (6 Feb. 2022).

1246. AU Doc. EX.CL/Dec. 1213 (XLII), *infra*, paras 17 et seq.

1247. Assembly, *Decision on the African Union Scale of Assessment*, AU Doc. Assembly/AU/Dec. 863 (XXXVI) (19 Feb. 2023).

But to return to the development of AU budgets: in May 2013, the Twenty-Third Executive Council Ordinary Session approved a total regular budget of USD 308 million for FY 2014: USD 137.8 million as AU operating costs and USD 170.1 million for AU programmes.[1248] What was extraordinary and unprecedented for international organizations was that USD 170 million were to be secured from the international partners, and only USD 126 million were to be assessed to Member States (the remaining funding came mostly from existing AU financial resources). The funding of NEPAD was very illustrative of what became a financing trend for the AU: of the total allocated budget of USD 36 million, only USD 4.4 million would be paid by Member States. The significant financial resources offered by international partners probably explain why NEPAD's funding exceeded considerably the funding of the PAP (USD 14.3 million) as well as of the African Human Rights Commission and of the African Human Rights Court (in total USD 14.2 million). In the case of these three organs, the Member States' assessments were considerably higher than the funds to be offered by international partners. However, the overall financial contribution by the international partners was not restricted to the above figure. In particular, the Executive Council also approved a (separate) budget to cover: (a) Special Projects in the tune of USD 24.2 million; (b) the so-called Pass-Through Funds (USD 90.5 million); and (c) Technical Assistance (USD 37.7 million), giving a total of USD 152.4 million, to be 'mobilized' from non-African partners. Finally, it authorized the AUC to 'mobilize' even more funds from the international partners, this time for closing until the end of 2013 the funding gap of USD 78.1 million in the 'Programmes-Budget'. In conclusion, the total amount which the AU would seek to secure from its partners exceeded USD 400 million until the end of FY 2014.

Dividing the budget into two amounts, one to be assessed on Member States and the other to be raised from international partners, has become a permanent fixture for the AU. The budget for FY 2017 was set at USD 782.108 million, broken down into USD 488.525 million as Operating Budget and USD 293.582 million as Programmes Budget, of which USD 205.149 million were assessed on Member States and USD 576.958 million were raised from international partners. In particular, AUC was allocated USD 348.8 million, PAP USD 22 million, the African Human Rights Court USD 10.3 million, the African Human Rights Commission USD 5.5 million, ECOSSOC USD 1.1 million, NEPAD USD 41.4 million, AUCIL USD 731.000, the Advisory Board on Corruption USD 2.3 million, and PSC USD 1 million. Finally, AMISOM, which was at the time active, was to receive USD 335.9 million raised solely from international partners.[1249]

1248. *See* Executive Council, *Decision on the Budget of the African Union for the 2014 Financial Year*, AU Doc. EX.CL/Dec. 767 (XXIII) (23 May 2013).

1249. *See* Executive Council, *Decision on the Budget of the African Union for the 2017 Financial Year*, AU Doc. EX.CL/Dec. 919 (XXIX) (15 Jul. 2016). For the FY 2016 budget, *see* Executive Council, *Decision on the Budget of the African Union for the 2016 Financial Year*, AU Doc. EX.CL/Dec. 873 (XXVII) (12 Jun. 2015) and for the FY 2015 budget *see* Executive Council, *Decision on the Budget of the African Union for the 2015 Financial Year*, AU Doc. EX.CL/Dec. 813 (XXV) (24 Jun. 2014).

189. Six years later, the total AU budget for FY 2023, as approved by the Executive Council in July 2022, was considerably downsized to USD 654.8 million broken down as follows: (a) a Regular Budget of USD 402.7 million, of which 163.9 million was allocated to the Operating Budget and USD 239 million to the Programme Budget; and (b) a Peace Support Operations Budget of USD 252.1 million. Overall, the 2023 budget would be financed to the tune of 66% by international partners (specifically, they will fully fund the Peace Support Operations Fund and 77% of the Programme Budget) and the rest by Member States.[1250] According to the Executive Council, due to the effects of COVID-19, the Russia-Ukraine crisis and the food insecurity on the continent, the 2023 budget continued to be 'an austerity budget'. It also reiterated the need to limit reliance on the funding by the international partners.[1251] The total amounts allocated to the various organs were agreed as follows: AUC to receive USD 2.321 million; PAP USD 11.9 million; African Human Rights Court USD 11.9 million; African Human Rights Commission USD 5.4 million; ECOSSOC USD 2.7 million; AUDA-NEPAD 29 million; AUCIL USD 0.3 million; Advisory Board on Corruption USD 2 million; and PSC USD 1.9 million. As regards the peace operations, the funding of AMISOM was set at USD 223.8 million and that of the Multinational Joint Task Force (MNJTF) at USD 11.9 million. MNJTF, which is formed of military units from Cameroon, Chad, Niger, and Nigeria (members of the Lake Chad Basin Commission) as well as Benin, has the mandate to terminate the Boko Haram insurgency.

190. As was the case with the OAU, the AU continued to be plagued by arrears in the payment of the financial obligations. In February 2003, outstanding contributions amounted to USD 42.5 million, which included outstanding assessed contributions from January to December 2002 of USD 10.2 million.[1252] By December 2004, Member States had paid only USD 26 million out of the USD 43 million budget for FY 2004. On account of the chronic problem of underfunding, the AU has attempted to seek alternative sources of funding. A report, which was prepared by the Interim Chairperson to deal with this matter,[1253] was transmitted to Member States for consideration, while the Executive Council set up a Commission to promote this idea.[1254] The latter failed to make any headway because its first two meetings in December 2003 and in February 2004 were not held due to lack of quorum.[1255] A select group of fifteen experts from Member States was then

1250. Executive Council, *Decision on the Reports of the Sub-Committees of the Permanent Representatives' Committee* (PRC), AU Doc. EX.CL/Dec. 1168 (XLI), paras 74 *et seq.* (15 Jul. 2022).

1251. *Ibid.*, paras 78–79.

1252. *See* National Assembly of the Republic of South Africa, Question No. 36 to the Minister of Foreign Affairs, 19 Mar. 2003.

1253. *See Report of the Interim Chairperson on Alternative Sources of Funding the African Union*, AU Doc. EX/CL/24 (III) (2003).

1254. *See* Executive Council, *Decision on the Synoptic Report on Alternative Sources of Funding the African Union*, EX/CL/Dec. 22 (III) (8 Jul. 2003).

1255. *See Progress Report of the Chairperson of the Commission on the Implementation of Decision EX.CL/Dec.22(III) on Alternative Sources of Funding the African Union*, AU Doc. EX.CL/71 (IV) (2004).

established to discuss the report and submit views by 31 May 2004.[1256] Apparently, these efforts did not lead to any concrete results, characteristic perhaps of the AU's inability to handle promptly and efficiently issues of major importance affecting its operation.

191. Regarding the imposition of sanctions against Members in arrears, the Third Ordinary Executive Council Session, acting on the basis of the Report of the Sub-Committee on Contributions,[1257] determined that eight Members (Guinea-Bissau, Liberia, CAR, DRC, San Tomé and Principe, Seychelles, Somalia, and the Comoros) shall remain under sanctions; determined that the sanctions imposed on Niger be lifted; and decided that a temporary and exceptional exemption be granted to Sierra Leone.[1258] This decision raised a number of issues. First, pursuant to Article 23(1) of the Constitutive Act, the competent organ for imposing sanctions on Member States in arrears is the Assembly. As there was apparently no delegation of power to the Executive Council, the legal basis for these sanctions was at least ambiguous. Second, since the sanctions against most of the above-mentioned Member States were originally imposed under OAU rules,[1259] it was rather inappropriate that the AU maintained them without reaching its own separate resolutions. Third, it was unclear which punitive measures of those envisaged in Article 23(1) were actually imposed since they differ from OAU sanctions.

192. During the 2000s, the Executive Council imposed sanctions against Member States even though several of them had been facing internal turmoil and strife of such magnitude that their involvement in AU activities has been problematic (reportedly, certain countries had even been unable to pay the expenses of their representatives to attend AU meetings). Thus, during its Eighth Extraordinary Session (Khartoum, 19 January 2006) the Executive Council affirmed that eight Members continued to be under sanctions (CAR, DRC, Eritrea, Guinea-Bissau, Sao Tomé and Principe, Somalia, Liberia, and Seychelles, i.e., almost the same states which were under OAU sanctions); imposed sanctions on Benin, Cape Verde, Côte d'Ivoire, Guinea, and Mauritania; lifted sanctions imposed on Niger, Djibouti and Gabon, which had paid their arrears in contributions; and, finally, determined that Sierra Leone would not be subjected to sanctions for as long as it honoured the agreed payment schedule.[1260] Two years later and with only twenty-nine Member States being

1256. *See* Permanent Representatives Committee, Seventh Ordinary Session, 12–13 Mar. 2004, AU Doc. PRC/Rpt (VII), 9–10, and Executive Council, *Decision on the Alternative Sources of Funding the African Union*, AU Doc. EX/CL/Dec. 77 (IV) (16 Mar. 2004).

1257. *See* AU Doc. EX/CL/27 (III) (2003).

1258. *See* Executive Council, *Decision on the Report of the Sub-Committee on Contributions*, AU Dec. EX/CL/Dec. 25 (III) (4 Jul. 2003). Sanctions were maintained by virtue of Executive Council, *Decision on the Report of the Sub-Committee on Contributions*, AU Doc. EX/CL/Dec. 76 (IV) (16 Mar. 2004).

1259. *See, inter alia*, OAU Council of Ministers, Decision CM/Dec. 2 (LXXIV), adopted at its Seventy-Fourth Ordinary Session in July 2001.

1260. *See* Executive Council, *Decision of the Eighth Extraordinary Session of the Executive Council on the Contributions by Member States*, AU Doc. Ext/EX.CL/Dec. 2 (VIII) (19 Jan. 2006).

up-to-date with the payment of contributions to the general budget, the situation had not changed considerably (Liberia and Somalia were no longer in the list of Member States under sanctions).[1261]

It is of some interest to note that there have been instances where several Member States, against whom sanctions were lifted (they had cleared their arrears from previous years), failed to keep up payments to the AU budget and, consequently, found themselves again the target of sanctions. For example, although the Eleventh Ordinary Executive Council Session (Accra, 25–29 June 2007) had cleared Guinea-Bissau and CAR (they had paid arrears up to FY 2004, had partially paid for FY 2005 and therefore were not for more than two years in arrears),[1262] they failed to continue paying outstanding contributions for FY 2006 and the Twelfth Ordinary Executive Council Session (Addis Ababa, 25–29 January 2008) reinstated the sanctions. In early 2008, the following Member States were under sanctions: Guinea-Bissau, CAR, Cape Verde (it did not present the repayment schedule that the Executive Council had requested in June 2007), DRC, Eritrea, San Tomé and Principe, and Seychelles.[1263]

Arguably, these states did not choose not to fulfil their AU budgetary obligations, but their precarious politico-economic situation led to arrears in other international organizations as well, including the UN. Thus, in January 2008, eight of the fifteen UN Member States, whose arrears had reached the stage where their voting rights in the UNGA had been suspended under the aforementioned Article 19 of the UN Charter, were African states under AU sanctions as well.[1264] Equally, during the UNGA Sixty-Seventh Session (2012), there were five African states (CAR, the Comoros, Guinea-Bissau, Sao Tome and Principe, and Somalia) falling into the scope of Article 19. However, the UNGA decided that this was due to conditions beyond their control and allowed them to participate in voting.[1265] During the UNGA Seventy-first Session (2016–2017), it was again these states (except CAR) against which Article 19 was not applied on account of conditions beyond their control.[1266] In January 2023, there were nine UN Member States (eight of which were from Africa (Comoros, Dominica, Equatorial Guinea, Gabon, Lebanon, Sao Tome and Principe, Somalia, South Sudan) and Venezuela) which, if they failed to reduce the amounts owed on their budgetary contributions, would come under Article

1261. *See* Executive Council, *Decision on the Contributions of Member States*, AU Doc. EX.CL/Dec. 379 (XII) (31 Jan. 2008).
1262. *See* Executive Council, *Decision on Contributions*, AU Doc. EX.CL/Dec. 377 (XI) (29 Jun. 2007). *See also* Permanent Representatives Committee, *Report on the Status of Contributions by Member States*, AU Doc. EX.CL/337 (XI) (2007).
1263. *See* Decision EX.CL/Dec. 379 (XII), *supra*. The Decision was based on *Report on the Contributions of Member States*, AU Doc. EX.CL/369(XII)c (2008).
1264. *See* UNGA, *Letter dated 18 January 2008 from the Secretary-General to the President of the General Assembly*, UN Doc. A/62/657 (21 Jan. 2008), and UNGA Res. 62/1 of 15 Oct. 2007. In the case of Benin and Cape Verde, the amount of USD 20,000 each would have reinstated them to good standing.
1265. *See* UNGA Res. 67/2 of 11 Oct. 2012 and Official Records, Sixty-seventh Session, *Report of the Committee on Contributions*, Supplement No. 11, UN Doc. A/67/11 (2012).
1266. *See* UNGA Res. 71/2 of 3 Oct. 2016; *See also* UNGA Res. 70/2 of 12 Oct. 2015 and Res. 69/2 of 22 Sep. 2014.

19.[1267] In the event, all except Venezuela settled their accounts, while Comoros, Sao Tome and Principe and Somalia were allowed to continue voting because their inability to pay the full minimum amount necessary to avoid the application of Article 19 was considered to be beyond their control.[1268]

193. In the AU, the situation regarding arrears gradually ameliorated. Thus, the Twenty-Second Ordinary Executive Council Session (2013) imposed sanctions only on Guinea-Bissau and Madagascar and decided that Somalia's temporary exemption from sanctions be maintained.[1269] However, whether the other Member States had been paying assessed contributions on time is questionable because, as will be recalled, the sanctions under Article 23(1) of the Constitutive Act are triggered only when they have been in arrears for more than two years. In July 2016, the Executive Council expressed its concern over Member States' non-compliance with paying assessed contributions as and when due and lamented 'the persistent pattern of arrears which is impacting adversely on the [AU's] financial situation'.[1270]

In January 2017, the Assembly resolved that the current sanctions mechanism should be strengthened and enforced and proposed to make Member States' participation in the AU deliberations 'contingent on adherence to Summit decisions'.[1271] Even though the Assembly did not specifically referred to the sanctions for non-payment of assessed contributions, the two Reports submitted by the AUC Chairperson dealt specifically with strengthening this sanctions regime.[1272] Building upon these two Reports and the deliberations at the Twentieth Extraordinary Executive Council Session (14–15 November 2018), a few days later the Eleventh Extraordinary Assembly Session decided, in a clear de facto amendment of the Constitutive Act, to introduce a new sanctions regime from July 2019,[1273] whose basic parameters are as follows: (a) those Member States which fail to meet their budgetary obligations, and which have not settled at least 50% of their current assessed contributions after the second quarter of each financial year (i.e., six months from the beginning of each calendar year) in which the contribution was due, are deemed to be in arrears; (b) Member States in arrears are divided into three groups, namely short-term period (in arrears for six months), intermediate period (one year) and long-term period (two years); (c) sanctions shall be applied incrementally in three stages, starting from cautionary sanctions against Member States in the short-term period, moving to intermediate sanctions for those states in the intermediate period and ending with comprehensive sanctions for those in the long-term period.

1267. UNGA, *Letter dated 17 January 2023 from the Secretary-General addressed to the President of the General Assembly*, UN Doc. A/77/702 (2023).
1268. UNGA, Res. 77/2, *Scale of assessments for the apportionment of the expenses of the United Nations: requests under Article 19 of the Charter*, 7 Oct. 2022.
1269. *See* Executive Council, *Decision on Contribution of the African Union Member States towards the 2012 Budget of the African Union*, AU Doc. EX.CL/Dec. 731 (XXII) (25 Jan. 2013).
1270. *See* Executive Council, *Decision on the Oversight and Accountability Mechanism(s)*, AU Doc. EX.CL/Dec. 931 (XXIX), para. 5 (15 Jul. 2016).
1271. AU Doc.Assembly/AU/Dec. 635 (XXVIII), *supra*, para. 5(c)(viii).
1272. *See* AU Doc. Assembly/AU/3(XXX) (January 2018) and AU Doc. Ext/Assembly/AU/2(XI)) (November 2018).
1273. Assembly, *Decision on the New African Union Sanctions Regime for the Non-Payment of Contributions*, AU Doc. Ext/Assembly/AU/Dec. 3 (XI) (18 Nov. 2018).

As regards the content of the sanctions, it was agreed that:

(i) 'cautionary sanctions' will deprive Member States in arrears of their rights to speak at AU meetings;
(ii) 'intermediate sanctions' will include, on the one hand, all sanctions that are laid down in Article 23(1) of the Constitutive Act, in Rules 5, 26, and 35(2(a) of the Assembly Rules of Procedure, in Article 78(6) of the AU Financial Rules and Regulations and in Article 18(8) of the AUC Statute (one could call them 'statutory sanctions') and, on the other hand, the suspension of the following Member States' rights: to become a member of a Bureau of any AU organ and to host an AU organ in its territory; to have their nationals participate in electoral observation missions and/or in human rights observation missions and to be invited in any AU organized meeting; and to have their nationals appointed as elected and non-elected AU staff; and
(iii) 'comprehensive sanctions' will include all the aforementioned sanctions as well as the suspension of the Member States' right to participate in AU meetings. Finally, the Assembly decided that it has the discretion to consider written requests from Member States that experience *force majeure* circumstances, making them temporarily unable to pay their assessed contributions. The wording of the relevant section in the Decision makes it clear that the Assembly is neither obligated to consider such requests nor to take a decision on them. But it is also true to say that the Assembly has not only considered the possibility of writing off budgetary contributions owed by Member States but has also proposed it (e.g. to Libya in 2022, see *infra*) as a means to persuade them to pay up at least part of the contributions in arrears. While these are no doubt measures of necessity, the fact that so far they have not been laid down as accepted practice in an Assembly decision is highly problematic. However, as argued in other parts of this monograph, the Constitutive Act is in dire need of revision. And while Member States appear not to object to these de facto amendments, an international organization's proper functioning is probably in jeopardy when it deviates from its constitutive instrument.

During the last few years, the situation vis-à-vis arrears in budgetary contributions and the imposition of sanctions was as follows. As regards Somalia and Libya, on account of their security and political situation, in July 2019, the Executive Council had not imposed sanctions against them and had asked the AUC to agree on a payment plan with both states aiming at clearing arrears by July 2023.[1274] Somalia's payment plan to clear arrears was endorsed by the Assembly in 2021, as was also the plan agreed with Seychelles.[1275] However, negotiations with Libya were not fruitful, and in October 2021, the Executive Council urged Libya again to agree on a payment plan.[1276] Finally, in February 2022, the Assembly decided

1274. Executive Council, *Decision on the Report of Ministerial Committee on Scale of Assessment and Contributions*, AU Doc. EX.CL/Dec. 1071 (XXXV) (5 Jul. 2019).
1275. Assembly, *Decision on the Scale of Assessment and Contributions*, AU Doc. Assembly/AU/Dec. 802 (XXXIV), para. 5 (7 Feb. 2021).
1276. Executive Council, AU Doc. EX.CL/Dec. 1138 (XXXIX), *supra*.

exceptionally that, given the complex situation in Libya, upon its full payment of 50% of its arrears, the AUC will write off 50% of Libya's contributions to the regular budget that were in arrears.[1277] As regards SADR and Burundi, in 2020, they had notified the AU that they faced challenges in meeting their annual budgetary contributions and had requested for special consideration. The Assembly instructed AUC 'to engage with Member States facing difficulties paying their contributions … and those in arrears for two or more years in order to agree on the payment plan for clearing their arrears'.[1278] The Assembly endorsed Burundi's payment plan in 2021.[1279] As regards Sudan, in 2021, it had asked the Executive Council to review its assessed contributions. The Executive Council requested that AUC agree with Sudan on a payment plan 'to clear the arrears as soon as possible', which actually meant before February 2025.[1280] However, no plan had been agreed by February 2023, and Sudan's arrears have been accumulating. The Executive Council asked AUC to press Sudan to agree to a payment plan and to report back in July 2023.[1281] As regards Mali, Guinea, and Sao Tome and Principe, in February 2023, the Executive Council imposed sanctions because they had fallen back on the payment of their assessed contributions.[1282] Finally, in July 2023, the Executive Council imposed sanctions on those Member States that had fallen back on the payment of their assessed contributions as follows: cautionary sanctions against Benin, Cape Verde, CAR, Congo, Eswatini, Guinea Bissau, Lesotho, Liberia, Madagascar, Malawi, Mali, South Sudan and Togo, and comprehensive sanctions against Guinea and Sao Tome and Principe. Thus, almost one-fourth of the membership is presently under sanctions for unpaid budgetary contributions, no doubt a cause of serious concern for the AU's financial viability. As regards Libya and Sudan, it was decided that no measures will be taken against them and that they should come to agreement with the AUC by February 2024. The Executive Council also resolved to maintain the Scale of Assessment for 2020–2023 and apply it during the period 2024–2026.[1283]

Since 2013, there have been renewed efforts in securing alternative sources for financing the AU. In the course of 2013, a panel of African dignitaries under the chairmanship of Olusegun Obasanjo, the former President of Nigeria, produced a report to that effect, which was approved by the Twenty-First Ordinary Assembly Session (Addis Ababa, 26–27 May 2013). The Assembly committed itself to 'self-reliance in the mobilization of resources in the financing of the AU programmes to

1277. AU Doc. Assembly/AU/Dec. 838 (XXXV), *supra*.
1278. Assembly, *Decision of the Joint Sitting Report of the Ministerial Committee on Scale of Assessment and Contributions and the Committee of Fifteen Ministers of Finance (F15)*, AU Doc. Assembly/AU/Dec. 752 (XXXIII) (10 Feb. 2020).
1279. AU Doc. Assembly/AU/Dec. 802 (XXXIV), *supra*, para. 5.
1280. Executive Council, *Decision on the Report of the Joint-Sitting of the Ministerial Committee on Scale of Assessment and Contributions and the Committee of Fifteen Ministers of Finance (F15)*, AU Doc. EX.CL/Dec. 1119 (XXXVIII) (4 Feb. 2021).
1281. Executive Council, *Decision on the Report of the Joint-Sitting of the Ministerial Committee on Scale of Assessment and Contributions and the Committee of F15*, AU Doc. EX.CL/Dec. 1213 (XLII), para. 14 (16 Feb. 2023).
1282. *Ibid*, para. 15.
1283. *See* Executive Council, *Decision on the Report of the Joint Sitting of the Ministerial Committee on Scale of Assessment and Contributions and the Committee of Fifteen Ministers of Finance (F15)*, AU Doc. EX.CL/Dec. 1223 (XLIII) (14 Jul. 2023).

avert undue dependency' (presumably, the reference to dependency concerned the international partners, whose contributions, as has been explained, keep the AU largely operating). However, as it is characteristic of the Assembly when facing difficult issues requiring complex decisions, no concrete measures were taken, but deliberations were postponed for its Twenty-Second Ordinary Session (January 2014) by which time the ministers of finance ought to have come up with concrete proposals.[1284] The matter was not placed on that session's agenda. After many delays, the Assembly dealt with it in earnest in July 2016. Resolving that the AU must be 'financed in a predictable, sustainable, equitable and accountable manner with the full ownership by its Member States', it took the following measures. First, it created a 0.2% levy on all eligible goods imported into Africa to finance the operational, programme, and peace support operations budgets starting from 2017. The amounts collected from the levy are to be automatically paid by the national administrations into an account to be opened for the AU with the Central Banks of each Member State. Second, it instructed AUC to put in place strong oversight and accountability mechanisms to ensure that resources are effectively and prudently used. Third, it instructed AUC to complete the AU's ongoing institutional reform and to provide for the careful use of resources. Fourth, it decided that, when preparing the annual budget, a Committee of Ministers of Finance comprising ten Member States, representing Africa's five regions, will participate in the process, a move presumably giving to the membership a more direct say over the budget already at the drafting stage.[1285] These measures have not ameliorated the situation. The troubling reality of the over-reliance on third states and international organizations poses many difficult issues, which could be summarized by the following extract from the Kagame Report (2017): 'This level of dependence on external partner funds raises a fundamental question: How can member states own the African Union if they do not set its agenda?'[1286]

1284. *See* Assembly, *Decision on Alternative Sources of Financing the African Union*, AU Doc. Assembly/AU/Dec. 486 (XXI) (27 May 2013). *See further*, Executive Council, *Decision on Alternative Sources of Financing the African Union*, AU Doc. EX.CL/Dec. 760 (XXII) (25 Jan. 2013).

1285. Assembly, *Decision on the Outcome of the Retreat of the Heads of States and Government, Ministers of Foreign Affairs and Ministers of Finance on the Financing of the African Union*, AU Doc. Assembly/AU/Dec. 605 (XXVII), para. 5 (18 Jul. 2016).

1286. *See*, African Union, 'The Imperative to Strengthen our Union: Report on the Proposed Recommendations for the Institutional Reform of the African Union', Report presented at the Second Retreat of Heads of State and Government of the African Union, Addis Ababa, 27 January 2017, at: https://static.pmg.org.za/Kagame_Report.pdf.

Part III. Activities

Chapter 1. Settlement of Disputes

194. One of the guiding principles of the OAU was the peaceful settlement of disputes.[1287] In fact, it has been observed that 'the principle of the peaceful settlement of international disputes has been recognized and accepted as a binding principle of international law by African States'.[1288] To facilitate its commitment to dispute settlement, the OAU had available to it various institutional and informal arrangements. In the former category was the Commission of Mediation, Conciliation, and Arbitration,[1289] but it never became operational as African States regarded formal dispute settlement procedures with suspicion.[1290] Rather, resort to diplomatic or political procedures was for many years the preferred mode of dispute settlement.[1291] Indeed, the OAU was distinctive for its lack of a judicial organ. These modes of dispute settlement proved to be remedial and reactive and therefore failed in general to address the root causes of many disputes, ultimately proving inadequate as preventative problem solvers. All in all these efforts often yielded disappointing results.[1292]

195. In establishing a Mechanism for Conflict Prevention, Management, and Resolution in 1993, the OAU proclaimed its readiness to adopt a more resolute

1287. Charter of the Organization of African Unity Arts III(4), XIX (25 May 1963), 479 U.N.T.S. 39, 2 I.L.M. 766 (1963). The latter provision required the Member States to settle *all* their disputes by peaceful means. *See Democratic Republic of Congo v. Burundi, Rwanda and Uganda*, Communication No. 227/99, 20th Activity Report 2005–2006, paras 66, 74–75; *Association Pour la Sauvegarde de la Paix au Burundi v. Tanzania, Kenya, Uganda, Rwanda, Zaire and Zambia*, Communication No. 157/96, 17th Activity Report, 2003–2004. Cooperation between the OAU and the UN was common in this area, B. Boutros-Ghali, *Confronting New Challenges* (New York: United Nations, 1995), 340–341.

1288. T. Maluwa, 'The Peaceful Settlement of Disputes among African States, 1963–1983: Some Conceptual Issues and Practical Trends', *I.C.L.Q.* 38 (1986): 299.

1289. *See* K.D. Magliveras & G.J. Naldi, *The African Union* (The Hague: Kluwer Law International, 2009), paras 74–79.

1290. Maluwa, 305–307.

1291. T. Maluwa, *International Law in Post-Colonial Africa* (The Hague: Kluwer Law International, 1999), 241. *See* generally J.G. Merrills, *International Dispute Settlement* (3rd edn, Cambridge: Cambridge University Press, 1998), Chs 1, 2, 4.

1292. Maluwa, International Law in Post-Colonial Africa, 241–245.

approach to dispute settlement.[1293] The Mechanism, designed to be preventative and proactive, put in place an institutional framework for the peaceful and speedy resolutions of disputes.[1294] Its primary objective was the prevention of conflicts, with emphasis on anticipatory and preventive measures; it was therefore directed to undertake confidence-building measures and peacemaking functions.[1295] It was also designed to prevent conflicts escalating. Prompt and decisive action should have acted as a deterrent to conflicts and preclude the need to resort to complex peace-keeping operations. The Mechanism's record was mixed,[1296] and with the advent of the AU, the Mechanism became an organ of the AU.[1297]

196. The AU is similarly committed to the settlement of disputes. The 'peaceful resolution of conflicts' is one of its founding principles.[1298] The AU thus inherited the Mechanism from the OAU but which was soon transformed into the PSC.[1299] This transformation was necessitated by the need to enhance the AU's conflict resolution and management capacities and to establish an operational structure for the more effective implementation of the relevant decisions. To this end, the APSA was established as the continent's overarching strategic security framework to enhance continental and regional capabilities for the prevention, management and resolution of conflict, including post-conflict reconstruction and peace-building, of which the PSC is but one element. The PSC is the main pillar of APSA.

1293. Declaration of the Assembly of Heads of State and Government on the Establishment Within the OAU of a Mechanism for Conflict Prevention, Management and Resolution (the Cairo Declaration), 6 R.A.D.I.C. 158 (1994).

1294. Cairo Declaration para. 14, reaffirmed the OAU's commitment to the principle of peaceful settlement of disputes in Africa. The Mechanism was described as 'a new and deliberate attempt to institutionalize the *political* means of dispute settlement in preference to *legal* mechanisms', Maluwa, International Law in Post-Colonial Africa, 249. *See further* Magliveras & Naldi, paras 74–79.

1295. Cairo Declaration paras 15, 19, 22.

1296. *See* Magliveras & Naldi, paras 232–233.

1297. At its Thirty-Seventh Ordinary Session in Lusaka, Zambia, in July 2001, Decision AHG/Dec. 160 (XXXVII), the OAU Assembly incorporated the Mechanism as one of the organs of the AU in accordance with the Constitutive Act of the African Union, Art. 5(2) (26 May 2001), 2158 U.N.T.S. 3.

1298. Constitutive Act, Art. 4(e). *See also* Fifteenth Anniversary Solemn Declaration para. E, Assembly, Twenty-First Ordinary Session, 26 May 2013; Agenda 2063, Assembly, *Decision on the Report of the Commission on Development of the African Union Agenda 2063*, AU Doc. Assembly/AU/Dec. 565(XXIV) (30–31 Jan. 2015).

1299. *See* Protocol Relating to the Establishment of the Peace and Security Council of the African Union (9 Jul. 2002), https://www.au.int/en/treaties, C. Heyns & M. Killander (eds), *Compendium of Key Human Rights Documents of the African Union* (7th ed., Pretoria: Pretoria University Law Press, 2022), 17. The PSC Protocol entered into force on 26 Dec. 2003 and the PSC became operational in 2004, *see supra* para. 151. By April 2022 it had been ratified by fifty-three States. Note that the Protocol on Amendments to the Constitutive Act Art. 5 (9 Jul. 2002), https://www.au.int/en/treaties, Heyns & Killander, 12, not yet in force, classifies the PSC as one of the organs of the AU. For fuller discussion of the PSC *see supra* paras 151–166; F. Viljoen, *International Human Rights Law in Africa* (Oxford: Oxford University Press, 2007), 205–211.

197. According to Article 2(1) of the PSC Protocol, the PSC is a 'standing decision-making organ for the prevention, management and resolution of conflicts'.[1300] Additionally, it is a 'collective security and early-warning arrangement to facilitate timely and efficient response to Conflict and crisis situations in Africa'. As such, the PSC is the organ that cooperates with relevant regional mechanisms and the UN.[1301] The objectives of the PSC include, according to Article 3 of the PSC Protocol, promoting peace, security and stability in Africa, anticipating and preventing conflicts, undertaking peacemaking and peace-building functions, promoting and implementing peace-building and post-conflict reconstruction activities, and promoting and encouraging democratic practices, good governance and the rule of law, and protecting human rights.[1302] According to Article 4 of the PSC Protocol, its guiding principles include the peaceful settlement of disputes and early responses to crisis situations.

198. The functions of the PSC, according to Article 6 of the Protocol, include the promotion of peace, security and stability in Africa, early warning and preventive diplomacy,[1303] peacemaking, including the use of good offices, mediation, conciliation and enquiry, peace support operations,[1304] peace-building and post-conflict reconstruction[1305] and humanitarian action and disaster management.[1306] It has the power, under Article 7, *inter alia*, to anticipate and prevent disputes and conflicts, to undertake peacemaking and peace-building functions, to authorize and mount peace support missions, to follow up the progress towards the promotion of democratic practices, good governance and the rule of law, and the protection of human rights, and to support and facilitate humanitarian action.[1307]

199. Since the PSC became operational, it has been active in a number of spheres, including Peace Support Operations (PSOs).[1308] These include peacekeeping, capacity-building, maintaining public order and mediation activities, more specifically the African Union Mission in Somalia (AMISOM), African Union–United Nations Mission in Darfur (UNAMID) and Regional Cooperation Initiative for the Elimination of the Lord's Resistance Army (RCI-LRA). Sub-regional security

1300. *See also* Protocol on Amendments to the Constitutive Act Art. 9.
1301. PSC Protocol Arts 16 and 17.
1302. Another AU organ that has a role in promoting peace, security and stability in Africa is the Pan-African Parliament, Protocol Establishing the African Economic Community relating to the Pan-African Parliament Art. 3(5) (2 Mar. 2001), https://www.au.int/en/treaties, Heyns & Killander 14. The Protocol entered into force on 14 Dec. 2003. It should be superseded by the Protocol to the Constitutive Act of the African Union Relating to the Pan-African Parliament (27 Jun. 2014), https://www.au.int/en/treaties, not yet in force.
1303. *See also* PSC Protocol Art. 12.
1304. *See also* PSC Protocol Art. 13.
1305. *See also* PSC Protocol Art. 14.
1306. *See also* PSC Protocol Art. 15.
1307. Note that under the African Charter on Democracy, Elections and Governance Art. 38(2) (30 Jan. 2007), https://www.au.int/en/treaties, Heyns & Killander, 164 (African Charter on Democracy), in force 15 Feb. 2012, State Parties undertake to support the conflict prevention and resolution initiatives of the PSC.
1308. Viljoen, 210–211. PSOs come within the definition of 'regional arrangements or agencies for enforcement action' in accordance with Art. 53(1) UN Charter. *See further* PSC Protocol Art. 13(4).

arrangements include the Multinational Joint Task Force (MNJTF) against Boko Haram and G5 Sahel Joint Force. One significant development, based on Article 12 of the PSC Protocol, is the Continental Early Warning System (CEWS) mandated to anticipate and prevent conflicts. It has an intelligence-gathering capacity to warn the PSC on threats to peace and security, and advises on courses of action. Another important body is the Panel of the Wise, established under Article 11 of the PSC Protocol, to support the PSC's mission, particularly in the area of conflict prevention, but generally in the promotion and maintenance of peace, security and stability in Africa.[1309] The Panel is composed of five members,[1310] who are appointed by the AU Assembly, on the recommendation of the Chair of the Commission, for a three-year period. The Panel may act at the request of the PSC, the Chair of the Commission, or at its own initiative. In 2010, the AU Assembly supported enhancing the Panel's role by establishing the Friends of the Panel of the Wise.[1311] The Friends, composed of five to ten eminent African personalities, supports the Panel in its activities, particularly fact-finding missions and negotiations. Another subsidiary body of the Panel of the Wise is the Network of African Women in Conflict Prevention and Mediation, or Fem Wise-Africa, which seeks to strengthen the role of women in conflict prevention and mediation efforts by providing a platform for strategic advocacy, capacity-building and networking.[1312] The UN supports the activities of Fem Wise-Africa, providing assistance in the development of policy documents, and other areas such as training, and capacity-building.[1313] Of particular importance is the African Standby Force (ASF), a multidisciplinary force composed of military, civilian and police elements, regionally located for rapid deployment in crisis situations. Its responsibilities include peace support missions,[1314] and in particular, observation and monitoring missions, intervention in a Member State in respect of grave circumstances or at the request of a Member State in order to restore peace and security, preventive deployment to stop a dispute or conflict from escalating, peace-building, including post-conflict disarmament and demobilization, and humanitarian assistance.[1315] However, while the ASF became

---

1309. J. El Abdellaoui, *The Panel of the Wise: A comprehensive introduction to a critical pillar of the African Peace and Security Architecture*, ISS Paper 193 (Pretoria: Institute of Security Studies, August 2009).

In 2016 the Panel of the Wise was involved in defusing a constitutional crisis in Madagascar, Report of the UN Secretary-General on strengthening the partnership between the United Nations and the African Union on issues of peace and security in Africa, UN Doc. S/2016/780, para. 27.

1310. '[H]ighly respected African personalities … who have made outstanding contributions to the cause of peace, security and development' in Africa, PSC Protocol Art. 11(2).

1311. Assembly, *Decision on the Appointment of the Members of the Panel of the Wise*, AU Doc. Assembly/AU/Dec. 310 (XV) (25–27 Jul. 2010).

1312. Assembly, *Decision on the Appointment of the New Members of the Panel of the Wise*, AU Doc. Assembly/AU/Dec. 663(XXIX) (3–4 Jul. 2017), para. 8.

1313. Report of the UN Secretary-General on strengthening the partnership between the United Nations and the African Union on issues of peace and security in Africa, including on the work of the United Nations Office to the African Union, UN Doc. S/2020/860, para. 37.

1314. PSC Protocol Art. 13(1). A number of such missions have been deployed over the years, often in association with the UN, including AMISOM and UNAMID.

1315. PSC Protocol Art. 13(3).

fully operational, the AU set up, as an interim mechanism, the African Capacity for Immediate Response to Crises (ACIRC).[1316] The ACIRC is a rapid deployment military force designed to respond swiftly to emergency situations. Agenda 2063 aims to ensure that all these initiatives are established and fully operational within a couple of years.[1317]

200. The African Peace Facility (APF), which is a multidisciplinary force with military, police and civilian components for deployment in crisis situations, channels political support and resources from the EU for PSOs.[1318] In 2009, the Early Response Mechanism (ERM) was established to support the APF with funding, presently until mid-2018. The ERM's areas of activities include mediation, human rights and post-conflict building. Recent initiatives include the AU High-Level Implementation Panel on Sudan and South Sudan in 2014 and the appointment of the AU High Representative for Libya in 2016.[1319]

201. It has long been an article of faith that African States have little confidence in international third-party adjudication.[1320] However, that received wisdom needs to be challenged given the fact that over the last twenty-five years, African States have 'ranked high as a source of cases' before the ICJ.[1321] Furthermore, recourse has been had to other international tribunals.[1322] In light of recent developments, it can be safely asserted that African States have come to accept judicial settlement as an accepted means of dispute resolution. Particular note should be taken of the fact that the Constitutive Act makes provision for a Court of Justice for the resolution of

1316. Assembly, *Decision on the Establishment of an African Capacity for Immediate Response to Crises,* AU Doc. Assembly/AU/Dec. 489(XXI) (26–27 May 2013).

1317. Assembly, *Decision on the Report of the Commission on Development of the African Union Agenda 2063*, AU Doc. Assembly/AU/Dec. 565(XXIV) (30–31 Jan. 2015).

1318. Assembly, *Decision on the Establishment by the European Union of a Peace Support Operation Facility for the African Union*, AU Doc. Assembly/AU/Dec. 21(II) (10–12 Jul. 2003); *The Africa-EU Partnership: 2 unions, 1 vision*, 9.

1319. Report of the UN Secretary-General on strengthening the partnership between the United Nations and the African Union on issues of peace and security in Africa, UN Doc. S/2016/780, para. 26.

1320. Maluwa, International Law in Post-Colonial Africa, 236, 305–307.

1321. Judge Stephen Schwebel, then President of the ICJ, in a speech to the UN General Assembly, ICJ Communiqué No. 98/33. For recent examples *see Immunities and Criminal Proceedings (Equatorial Guinea v. France)*, I.C.J. Reports 2020, p. 300; *Maritime Delimitation in the Indian Ocean (Somalia v. Kenya)*, I.C.J. Reports 2021, p. 206.

1322. Including the International Tribunal on the Law of the Sea, *see M.V. Saiga (No. 2) (Saint Vincent and the Grenadines v. Guinea)* 37 I.L.M. 1202 (1998), and *The M/V 'Virginia G' (Panama/Guinea-Bissau)*, Judgment, 14 Apr. 2014, ITLOS Case No. 19; and international arbitral tribunals, *see Chagos Marine Protected Area Arbitration (Mauritius v. United Kingdom)*, Award, 18 Mar. 2015) PCA Case No. 2011-03. A significant number of African States, thirty-three, have ratified the Rome Statute of the International Criminal Court (17 Jul. 1998), 2187 U.N.T.S. 91, 37 I.L.M. 999 (1998) (Rome Statute) (Burundi withdrew from the Rome Statute with effect from 27 October 2017). It is interesting to note that many of the cases on the ICC's docket or under examination relate to Africa, Report of the International Criminal Court on its activities in 2022/23, UN Doc. A/78/322.

inter-African disputes.[1323] Although the Protocol of the Court of Justice was adopted in 2003 and entered into force in February 2009, it has not been operationalized.[1324]

202. Instead, the AU's Court seems to have finally emerged in the form of the ACJHR.[1325] Since the ACJHR is discussed elsewhere,[1326] it is unnecessary to enter into detail here except to recall that the ACJHR is composed of two divisions, a General Affairs Section and a Human Rights Section. The Human Rights Section is considered below and therefore will not be discussed further.[1327] Under Article 29(1) of the Statute, the applicants entitled to submit cases to the General Affairs Section fall into three categories, only two of which have relevance here: first, the contracting parties to the 2008 Protocol; second, the Assembly, the PAP and other AU organs authorized by the Assembly (e.g., the EX or the PSC). Member States must take the conscious decision to sign up to the Protocol since the ACJHR's jurisdiction does not extend automatically over states merely by virtue of participation in the AU.[1328] Article 29(2) of the Statute makes it clear that the ACJHR does not have jurisdiction over disputes involving AU Member States that have not ratified the Protocol.[1329] Since the ACJHR is the 'main judicial organ' of the AU, it is submitted that it ought to have been conferred automatic jurisdiction over the whole membership. Nonetheless, in one circumstance, the ACJHR's decisions bind all Member States regardless of whether or not they have ratified the Protocol: according to Article 50(3) of the Statute, decisions on the Constitutive Act's interpretation and application are binding on all Members. The Statute does not extend *locus standi* to non-AU Member States even if a dispute should arise with the AU itself or a Member State. Such disputes would have to be resolved by some other body. The ACJHR's contentious jurisdiction is set out in Article 28 of the Statute, which reflects Article 36(2) of the ICJ Statute, although the former has a specifically African perspective and is considerably broader in scope. The ACJHR is competent to hear all cases and legal disputes submitted to it concerning, *inter alia*, the interpretation and application of the Constitutive Act, the interpretation, application or validity of other AU treaties and subsidiary legal instruments, any question of international law, all secondary legislation adopted by AU organs, all matters specifically provided for in other agreements that the contracting parties to the Statute may

1323. *See* Constitutive Act Arts 5(1), 18. Art. 26 thereof states that the Court of Justice shall be seized of matters of interpretation arising from the Constitutive Act's application or implementation. It should be further observed that African regional organizations, such as COMESA, ECOWAS, and EAC, have established courts or tribunals for the settlement of disputes.

1324. Protocol of the Court of Justice of the African Union (1 Jul. 2003). As of June 2020, the Protocol has been ratified by nineteen Member States. *See* K. Magliveras and G. Naldi, 'The African Court of Justice', *Zeitschrift für ausländisches öffentliches Recht und Völkerrecht* 66 (2006): 187.

1325. Protocol on the Statute of the African Court of Justice and Human Rights (1 Jul. 2008), https://www.au.int/en/treaties, 48 I.L.M. 337 (2009) (2008 Protocol). As of June 2020, the 2008 Protocol has been ratified by eight Member States.

1326. *See supra*, paras 119–132.

1327. *See infra*, Ch. 2 s. 5.

1328. While according to the UN Charter Art. 93(1), all UN Member States are *ipso facto* parties to the ICJ Statute, acceptance of its compulsory jurisdiction is dependent on a declaration to that effect pursuant to the ICJ Statute Art. 36(2).

1329. The Statute, Art. 28(f), rules out the possibility of a non-party submitting a case to the ACJHR by special agreement. Compare ICJ Statute Art. 36(1).

conclude among themselves or with the AU which confer jurisdiction on the ACJHR, the existence of any fact which, if established, would constitute a breach of an obligation owed to a State Party or to the AU, and the nature or extent of the reparation to be made for the breach of an obligation. Whether the drafters of the 2008 Protocol intended to establish an alternative, regional, forum to the ICJ for African States is unclear, but a solid argument can be made that the primary responsibility for determining general questions of international law should lie with the ICJ which, as 'the principal judicial organ of the United Nations', is uniquely placed to examine such issues.[1330] Of course, it could simply be that it was merely intended to ensure that the ACJHR has the specific authorization to consider a wide range of international law issues. In the absence of such a provision, the ACJHR, as an institutionalized judicial body, would nevertheless have had the inherent right to consider international law issues as they arose. In fact, it should be noted that the ICJ is not mentioned at all in the Statute, which does not contain a savings clause. Therefore, the important question of the relationship between these two bodies is not addressed.

203. Since its founding, the OAU put in place mechanisms for the peaceful settlement of disputes. Subsequently, various initiatives were adopted, particularly the Mechanism for Conflict Prevention, Management, and Resolution, to promote the OAU's capacity for dispute resolution. These were almost exclusively diplomatic or political rather than legal. Some modest attempts were made to deploy observers in conflict situations. However, OAU peacemaking and conflict management were hampered by a lack of adequate resources and a lack of confidence. For too long, the emphasis had been on short-term conflict prevention measures. Although the OAU had some successes, there were also too many failures. Recourse was more often had to non-African settlement mechanisms, with the onus often on the UN.[1331] The claim that a practice had evolved in Africa whereby disputes should initially be submitted for resolution to the regional organization[1332] did not seem to stand scrutiny. To its credit, the OAU/AU recognized that the root causes of conflict had to be addressed. The establishment of the PSC, which mirrors the UN's preventive diplomacy and conflict resolution initiatives, has been a significant step forward. The ACJHR may add another dimension for dispute resolution. The willingness of ECOWAS to assume a proactive and determined regional role in peace-enforcement is significant.[1333] But, it is important for the international community to continue to support the AU and ECOWAS with the necessary resources

1330. In recent years fears have been expressed that the proliferation of international judicial bodies could lead to the fragmentation of international law, *see*, *e.g.*, G. Guillaume, 'The Future of International Judicial Institutions', *I.C.L.Q.*44 (1995): 848.

1331. In recent years the UN and the AU have established a collaborative relationship in the maintenance of peace and security under the Ten-Year Capacity-Building Programme for the African Union, UN Doc. A/61/630 (2006). *See further infra*, Part IV, Ch. 2 s. 1.

1332. *Land and Maritime Boundary between Cameroon and Nigeria (Cameroon v. Nigeria)*, Preliminary Objections, I.C.J. Reports 1998, paras 48–60. Compare, *contra*, Maluwa, International Law in Post-Colonial Africa, 249.

1333. *See* generally C. Gray, *International Law and the Use of Force*(3rd edn, Oxford: Oxford University Press, 2008), 392–396, 400–407, 411–417.

and capacity to meet the difficult challenges that it is facing in Mali, Somalia, and elsewhere.[1334] Without the political willingness to provide the resources necessary to support a more resolute approach by the AU, its chances of providing successfully the means for dispute resolution will remain haphazard.

1334. *See infra*, Part IV, Ch. 2.

Chapter 2. Human Rights

§1. The African Union and Human Rights

204. The transformation of the OAU into the AU propelled human rights to the top of the agenda. Unlike the OAU Charter, express references to human rights and democratic values are made in the Constitutive Act of the AU. The AU not only reinforces the OAU's endeavours in these fields[1335] but also places respect for human rights at the forefront of its policies in the knowledge that progress in development, poverty eradication and conflict resolution are dependent on the guaranteeing of human rights. Significantly, through the PSC, the AU has armed itself with the capacity to take concrete action to promote and protect human rights. The express commitments to democracy and human rights are especially desirable developments and constitute welcome improvements on the OAU Charter, which was silent on these matters. The wording of the relevant provisions in the Constitutive Act would indicate that they create binding obligations for the Member States. The AU would thus appear to have a democratic legitimacy that the discredited OAU had always lacked. Yet human rights and democratic values can only be enhanced if the AU takes its pertinent pledges seriously. If so, the frequently abysmal human rights record in certain African States should be ameliorated.[1336]

205. The AU's commitment to these ideals is clearly established in the Constitutive Act's Preamble, where the AU undertakes to 'promote and protect human and peoples' rights, consolidate democratic institutions and culture, and to ensure good governance and the rule of law'. Significantly, these norms have not remained at a theoretical level, but effect has been given to them by enshrining them in the operative sections of the Act, and subsequently reinforced by the Protocol on the PAP and the PSC Protocol. Among the AU's objectives, as set out in Article 3 of the Constitutive Act, are the promotion of democratic principles and institutions, popular participation and good governance,[1337] and the promotion and protection of human

1335. *See* in particular the African Charter on Human and Peoples' Rights, *infra*, s. 2.

1336. The human rights record of African States varies widely. The Mo Ibrahim Foundation, a civil society organization, rated Seychelles as the leader in its Participation, Rights & Inclusion index for 2021, with Cabo Verde, Mauritius and South Africa following, *2021 Ibrahim Index of African Governance – Index Report* https://assets.iiag.online/2022/2022-Index-Report.pdf. Equatorial Guinea and South Sudan had the dubious honour of worst rated countries, with Eritrea, Somalia, and Egypt close behind. According to the website of Freedom House, https://freedomhouse.org/countries/freedom-world/scores, most African States are classified as 'Not Free' or 'Partly Free', with Botswana, Cabo Verde, Ghana, Mauritius, Namibia, Seychelles, São Tomé and Príncipe and South Africa classified as 'Free'.

1337. Constitutive Act of the African Union Art. 3(g) (26 May 2001), 2158 U.N.T.S. 3. *See further* Protocol Establishing the African Economic Community relating to the Pan-African Parliament Art. 3(3) (2 Mar. 2001), https://www.au.int/en/treaties, C. Heyns & M. Killander (eds), *Compendium of Key Human Rights Documents of the African Union*(7th edn, Pretoria: Pretoria University Law Press, 2022), 14 (PAP Protocol), and Protocol Relating to the Establishment of the Peace and Security Council of the African Union Art. 3(f) (9 Jul. 2002), https://www.au.int/en/treaties, Heyns & Killander, 17 (PSC Protocol). An important development in this regard, reinforcing the AU's commitments to these values, is the adoption of the African Charter on Democracy, Elections and

rights in accordance with the African Charter on Human and Peoples' Rights and other relevant human rights instruments.[1338] It is also interesting to observe that the statement of the AU's objectives reveals the realization by the African States that the attainment of sustainable economic development cannot be achieved without respecting and encouraging the principles of democracy, popular participation, and good governance, and the protection of human rights. By making a direct connection between sustainable economic development and human rights, the Constitutive Act acknowledges that a human rights culture is indispensable in fostering economic growth.

206. The objectives are to be attained through the strict observance of a number of fundamental principles, in accordance with which the AU shall function. Included among these principles is respect for democratic principles, human rights, the rule of law, and good governance.[1339] Particularly noteworthy is the inclusion of a 'democracy clause' whereby unconstitutional changes of government are condemned and rejected.[1340] This appears to follow rationally from the objectives of promoting democratic principles and institutions, and good governance throughout the continent. Crucially, the AU can reinforce democracy among Member States through the imposition of punitive measures. Article 30 stipulates that regimes coming to power through unconstitutional means shall be prohibited from participating in the activities of the AU.[1341] Its proper and consistent application should hopefully act as a deterrent to attempts at unconstitutional removals of legitimate governments. Of significant interest also is the fact that war crimes, genocide and crimes against humanity are viewed so seriously that the AU is authorized to intervene in a Member State where these atrocities are being perpetrated.[1342] Also worthy of note is the commitment to the promotion of gender equality.[1343] Given that the crises affecting many African countries often manifest themselves through ethnic and cultural tensions and conflicts, it seems regrettable that non-discrimination is not expressly made a key element of the Constitutive Act.

Governance (30 Jan. 2007), https://www.au.int/en/treaties, Heyns & Killander, 164, which entered into force 15 Feb. 2012. *See also* Fifteenth Anniversary Solemn Declaration para. F, Assembly, Twenty-First Ordinary Session, 26 May 2013.

1338. Constitutive Act Art. 3(h). *See further* PSC Protocol Art. 3(f), and African Charter on Democracy Art. 2(1).

1339. Constitutive Act Art. 4(g). *See further* PAP Protocol Art. 3(2), PSC Protocol Art. 4(c), and African Charter on Democracy Arts 3 and 4(1).*See Actions pour la Protection des Droit de l'Homme (APDH) v. Côte d'Ivoire*, African Court of Human and Peoples' Rights, App. No. 001/2014 (18 Nov. 2016).

1340. Constitutive Act Art. 4(p). *See further* African Charter on Democracy Arts 2(4), 3(10) and 5.

1341. *See also* African Charter on Democracy Art. 25(1). In addition, under the Constitutive Act Art. 23(2) the failure by any Member State to comply with the decisions and policies of the AU may lead to the imposition of sanctions. *See further* PSC Protocol Art. 7(g), and African Charter on Democracy Art. 23.

1342. Constitutive Act Art. 4(h). *See further* PSC Protocol Art. 7(e).

1343. Constitutive Act Art. 4(l). *See further* African Charter on Democracy Art. 3(6).

§2. The African Charter on Human and Peoples' Rights

207. The adoption of the African Charter on Human and Peoples' Rights (hereinafter 'the African Charter') in 1981 gave rise to expectations that human rights in Africa would be adequately promoted and protected.[1344] It is only in recent years, however, that these expectations, after many false starts, are beginning to be fulfilled. One of the reasons why the road to the effective protection of human rights in Africa has been laboured may lie with the African Charter itself which many commentators have considered as fatally flawed.[1345] The features of the African Charter which have given cause for concern will initially be considered.

I. Is the African Charter Fundamentally Flawed?

208. The African Charter is distinctive for providing in a sole binding legal document all three categories of human rights.[1346] Civil and political rights, essentially corresponding to those protected by the familiar human rights treaty texts, are guaranteed by Articles 3–14 and include the right to life, the prohibition of torture and other forms of ill-treatment, the prohibition of arbitrary deprivations of liberty, the right to a fair trial, the freedom of conscience, expression, association and assembly, and the right to property.[1347] Second-generation rights are set out in Articles 15–18 and include the right to work, the right to health, the right to education and to culture, and the rights of

1344. African Charter on Human and Peoples' Rights (17 Jun. 1981), 1520 U.N.T.S. 217, 21 I.L.M. 58 (1982). The African Charter entered into force on 21 Oct. 1986 and has been ratified by all of the AU's Member States with the sole exception of Morocco which joined the AU in 2017.

1345. The African Charter has been described as 'modest in its objectives and flexible in its means', *see* B. Obinna Okere, 'The Protection of Human Rights in Africa and the African Charter on Human and Peoples' Rights: A Comparative Analysis with the European and American Systems', *Human Rights Quarterly* 6 (1984): 141, 158. For other sceptical assessments, *see* R. Gittleman, 'The African Charter on Human and Peoples' Rights: A Legal Analysis', *Virginia J.I.L.* 22 (1981–1982): 667; P. Amoah, 'The African Charter on Human and Peoples' Rights – An Effective Weapon for Human Rights?', *R.A.D.I.C.* 4 (1992): 226; G. Robertson, *Crimes Against Humanity: The Struggle for Global Justice*(London: Penguin, 1999), 57–58.

1346. In *Good v. Botswana*, Communication No. 306/2005, 28th Activity Report 2009–2010, paras 227–234, the African Commission on Human and Peoples' Rights dismissed Botswana's submission that the African Charter was not a legally binding treaty. The Arab Charter on Human Rights (22 May 2004) I.H.R.R. 12 (2005): 893 is probably the closest comparable instrument in this regard.

1347. For an in-depth analysis of the specific rights, *see* A.H. Ankumah, *The African Commission on Human and Peoples' Rights* (The Hague: Martinus Nijhoff, 1996), 111–142; H.B. Jallow, *The Law of the African (Banjul) Charter on Human and Peoples' Rights* (Victoria, BC: Trafford Publishing, 2007), 178–291; C. Heyns, 'Civil and Political Rights in the African Charter', in *The African Charter on Human and Peoples' Rights: The System in Practice, 1986–2000*, M. Evans & R. Murray (eds) (Cambridge: Cambridge University Press, 2002), 137–177; B. Manby, 'Civil and Political Rights in the African Charter on Human and Peoples' Rights: Arts 1–7', in *The African Charter on Human and Peoples' Rights: The System in Practice, 1986–2006*, M. Evans & R. Murray (eds) (2nd edn, Cambridge: Cambridge University Press, 2008), 171–212; K. Olaniyan, 'Civil and Political Rights in the African Charter on Human and Peoples' Rights: Arts 8–17', in *The African Charter on Human and Peoples' Rights: The System in Practice, 1986–2006*, Evans & Murray (eds) (2nd edn, Cambridge: Cambridge University Press, 2008), 213–243; U.O. Umozurike, *The African Charter on Human and Peoples' Rights* (The Hague: Martinus Nijhoff, 1997), 29–43.

the family.[1348] Third generation or peoples' rights are listed in Articles 19–24 and include the right of self-determination, the right to peace and security, the right to environment, the right to natural resources, and the right to development.[1349] The African Commission on Human and Peoples' Rights[1350] (Commission) considers these categories of rights as indivisible and has stated that States parties are under a 'duty to respect, protect, promote, and fulfil' all the Charter obligations, entailing a combination of negative and positive duties.[1351] More so than other comparable human rights treaty texts, the substantive provisions of the African Charter are equivocally or broadly phrased.[1352] This on occasion has led the Commission to develop unenumerated rights that are not explicitly mentioned in provisions which are nevertheless considered to embody them implicitly.[1353]

209. The perceived inadequate protection of civil and political rights has attracted considerable criticism.[1354] The statist bias of the African Charter is manifest. In particular, extensive use is made of 'clawback' clauses that appear to

---

1348. For an in-depth analysis of the specific rights, *see* Ankumah, 143–159; Jallow, 293–305; C.A. Odinkalu, 'Implementing Economic, Social and Cultural Rights under the African Charter on Human and Peoples' Rights', in *The African Charter on Human and Peoples' Rights: The System in Practice, 1986–2000*, Evans & Murray (eds) (Cambridge: Cambridge University Press, 2002),178–218.
1349. The Commission has stated that the inclusion of third-generation rights in the African Charter constitutes one of its main distinctive features, *Bissangou v. Republic of Congo*, Communication No. 253/2002, 21st Activity Report 2005–2006, para. 80. For an in-depth analysis of the specific rights, *see* Ankumah, 160–170; Jallow, 305–323; C. Baldwin & C. Morel, 'Group Rights', in *The African Charter on Human and Peoples' Rights: The System in Practice, 1986–2006*, Evans & Murray (eds) (2nd edn, Cambridge: Cambridge University Press, 2008), 244–288.
1350. The Commission has the responsibility under the African Charter of promoting and protecting human and peoples' rights, *see infra*, paras 286–330. The Commission's decisions on communications can be consulted at the following sources: the Commission's website, http://www.achpr.org, the website of the University of Pretoria's Centre for Human Rights, http://www.up.ac.za/chr/ahrdb/acomm_decisions.html, and the website of the University of Minnesota's Human Rights Library, http://www1.umn.edu/humanrts/africa; International Human Rights Reports (I.H.R.R.); R. Murray & M. Evans (eds), *Documents of the African Commission on Human and Peoples' Rights* (Oxford: Hart Publishing, 2001), and Vol. II (Oxford: Hart Publishing, 2008).
1351. *The Social and Economic Rights Action Center and the Center for Economic and Social Rights v. Nigeria*, Communication No. 155/96, 15th Activity Report 2001–2002, paras 43–48. Briefly, the Commission explained that the obligation to respect 'entails that the State should refrain from interfering in the enjoyment of all fundamental rights'; the obligation to protect requires, *inter alia*, the creation and maintenance of an environment based on an effective framework of laws and regulations where individuals can realize their rights and freedoms; the obligation to promote requires States to ensure an environment of tolerance and awareness that allows that individuals can exercise their rights and freedoms; and the obligation to fulfil requires States to secure the realization of these rights. *See further Association of Victims of Post Electoral Violence & INTERIGHTS v. Cameroon*, Communication No. 272/2003, 27th Activity Report 2009, paras 87–92.
1352. Gittleman, 685; R.M. D'Sa, 'The African Charter on Human and Peoples' Rights: Problems and Prospects for Regional Action', *Australian Y.B.I.L.* 10 (1981/1983): 101, 107–108.
1353. Examples include elements of the right to a fair trial, *infra* paras 235–243, and a right to shelter or housing, *The Social and Economic Rights Action Center and the Center for Economic and Social Rights v. Nigeria*, Communication No. 155/96, 15th Activity Report 2001–2002, para. 60.
1354. *See*, *e.g.*, Gittleman.

make the rights subject to municipal law, or at the discretion of the national authorities. They seek to provide a justification for a violation.[1355] There are numerous examples. Thus, Article 8, which guarantees the freedom of conscience and religion, states that '[n]o one may, *subject to law and order*, be submitted to measures restricting the exercise of these freedoms' (emphasis added). Article 9(2) guarantees the freedom of expression 'within the law'. Article 10(1) guarantees individuals the right of association 'provided that he abides by the law'. Article 13(1) guarantees the right to participate in government 'in accordance with the provisions of the law'. Clawback clauses are therefore especially insidious because, through their vagueness, they 'do not provide the required external control over State behaviour'.[1356] It has therefore been observed that the 'legal reasons and conditions for invoking these limitations are not defined in the Charter'.[1357]

210. Commentators have been critical of the wording of these provisions. Ankumah has observed that they 'could render previously granted rights meaningless'.[1358] Gittleman has written that the African Charter is 'incapable of supplying even a scintilla of external restraint upon a government's power to create laws contrary to the spirit of the rights granted'.[1359] Kunig has expressed the view that since 'there are no provisions to ensure that a core of the human rights guarantees prevails against legislative restrictions, this represents a considerable structural defect'.[1360] And Murray has commented that '[t]he limitations are not defined exactly in the Charter, arguably leaving it purely to the discretion of states, and thus, in effect, allowing rights to be denied'.[1361] The African Commission itself has stated that 'if "law" is interpreted to mean any domestic law regardless of its effect, States Parties to the Charter would be able to negate the rights conferred upon individuals by the Charter'.[1362]

211. It is interesting to observe, however, that the practice of the Commission and the African Court of Human and Peoples' Rights (Human Rights Court) clearly demonstrate that the legality of a restraint that leaves its precise scope and nature to the whim of the State will not be upheld.[1363] Indeed, the Commission has cautioned

1355. Jallow, 163. According to Higgins, clawback clauses permit 'in normal circumstances, breach of an obligation for a specified number of published reasons', R. Higgins, 'Derogations under Human Rights Treaties', *B.Y.B.I.L.* 48 (1976–1977): 281.
1356. Gittleman, 692. *See also* D'Sa, 110.
1357. E. Bello, 'The African Charter on Human and Peoples' Rights', *Hague Recueil* 194 (1985/1986): 13, 70.
1358. Ankumah, 176.
1359. Gittleman, 694.
1360. P. Kunig, 'The Protection of Human Rights by International Law in Africa', *German Y.B. I. L.* 25 (1982): 138, 155.
1361. R. Murray, *The African Commission on Human and Peoples' Rights and International Law*(Oxford: Hart Publishing, 2000), 127.
1362. *Article 19 v. Eritrea*, Communication No. 275/2003, 22nd Activity Report 2006–2007, para. 91.
1363. *See further*, G.J. Naldi, 'Limitation of Rights under the African Charter on Human and Peoples' Rights: The Contribution of the African Commission on Human and Peoples' Rights', *S.A.J.H.R.* 17 (2001): 109.

against a 'too easy resort to the limitation clauses in the African Charter'.[1364] In *Media Rights Agenda and Constitutional Rights Project v. Nigeria*, which was mainly concerned with the proscription of various publications critical of the Nigerian military regime, the Commission gave a comprehensive, reasoned explanation of its interpretation of the nature and scope of clawback clauses in the Charter. It stated:

> Governments should avoid restricting rights, and have special care with regard to those rights protected by constitutional or international human rights law. No situation justifies the wholesale violation of human rights. In fact, general restrictions on rights diminish public confidence in the rule of law and are often counter-productive.
>
> According to Article 9(2) of the Charter, dissemination of opinions may be restricted by law. This does not mean that national law can set aside the right to disseminate one's opinions; this would make the protection of the right to express one's opinions ineffective. To allow national law to have precedent over the international law of the Charter would defeat the purpose of the rights and freedoms enshrined in the Charter. International human rights standards must always prevail over contradictory national law. Any limitation on the rights of the Charter must be in conformity with the provisions of the Charter.
>
> The only legitimate reasons for limitations to the rights and freedoms of the African Charter are found in Article 27(2), that is that the rights of the Charter 'shall be exercised with due regard to the rights of others, collective security, morality and common interest.'
>
> The reasons for possible limitations must be founded in a legitimate state interest and the evils of limitations of rights must be strictly proportionate with and absolutely necessary for the advantages which are to be obtained.
>
> Even more important, a limitation may never have as a consequence that the right itself become illusory.[1365]

212. The Commission has cautioned against reliance on clawback clauses as a means of 'giving credence' to violations of the African Charter. In the alternative, it has interpreted clawback clauses as 'constituting a reference to international law, meaning that only restrictions on rights which are consistent with the Charter and with States Parties' international obligations should be enacted by the relevant national authorities'.[1366] It has therefore made it manifest that the applicable standard is that of International Human Rights Law, which prevails over any

1364. *Amnesty International v. Zambia*, Communication No. 212/98, 12th Activity Report 1998–1999, para. 42.

1365. Communication Nos 105/93, 128/94, 130/94, 152/96, 12th Activity Report 1998–1999, paras 65–70. *See also Constitutional Rights Project, Civil Liberties Organisation and Media Rights Agenda v. Nigeria*, Communication Nos 140/94, 141/94, 145/95, 13th Activity Report 1999–2000, para. 42; *Interights, Institute for Human Rights and Development in Africa, and Association Mauritaniene des Droits de l'Homme v. Mauritania*, Communication No. 242/2001, 17th Activity Report 2003–2004, paras 76–79. And *see Tanganyika Law Society et al. v. Tanzania*, African Court of Human and Peoples' Rights, App. Nos 009/2011 and 011/2011 (14 Jun. 2013), para. 107.

1366. *Article 19 v. Eritrea*, Communication No. 275/2003, 22nd Activity Report 2006–2007, para. 92.

inconsistent municipal law.[1367] The Commission has thus held that where a State claims to be acting under legislation 'previously laid down by law', it must show that such law is consistent with its obligations under the African Charter.[1368] Moreover, a limitation can be justified only by reference to the criteria listed in Article 27(2) of the African Charter.[1369] Consequently, in relation to the protection of the freedoms of assembly and expression, the Commission stated that these 'actions and expressions are among the most important exercises of human rights and as such should be given substantial protection that do not allow the State to suspend these rights for frivolous reasons and in a manner that is thus disproportionate to the interference with the exercise of these fundamental rights'.[1370] In addition, the Commission has further extended the scope of a State's obligation by placing upon it the burden of proof, stating in *Amnesty International v. Zambia* that the 'onus is on the State to prove that it is justified to resort to the limitation clause'.[1371] Nevertheless, the Commission and the Human Rights Court, in common with other human rights systems, accept that the doctrine of margin of appreciation informs the African Charter.[1372] The Human Rights Court has held that 'the scope of the margin of appreciation enjoyed by the national authorities will depend not only on the nature of the aim of the restriction but also on the nature of the right involved. Moreover, that the margin of appreciation must be applied in good faith'.[1373]

213. While the wording of the African Charter with respect to clawback clauses leaves much to be desired, it is encouraging to observe that through its jurisprudence, the Commission has interpreted the relevant provisions to conform with international human rights standards. And it should be observed that the Commission's approach has been approved by the Human Rights Court.[1374] Given in addition the fact that the African Charter omits a derogation clause,[1375] there is every cause to be optimistic that the protection of human rights will prove effective.

1367. *Amnesty International v. Mauritania*, Communication No. 61/91, 13th Activity Report 1999–2000, para. 102.
1368. *Sir Dawda K. Jawara v. Gambia*, Communication Nos 147/95 and 149/96, 13th Activity Report 1999–2000, paras 43, 58–59.
1369. Heyns, 140–141; *Tanganyika Law Society et al. v. Tanzania*, African Court of Human and Peoples' Rights, App. Nos 009/2011 and 011/2011 (14 Jun. 2013), para. 107. In *Legal Resources Foundation v. Zambia*, Communication No. 211/98, 14th Activity Report 2000–2001, para. 70, the Commission stated that the African Charter must be interpreted holistically and all provisions must reinforce each other.
1370. *The Law Office of Ghazi Suleiman v. Sudan*, Communication No. 228/99, 16th Activity Report 2002–2003, para. 62.
1371. Communication No. 212/98, 12th Activity Report 1998–1999, para. 42.
1372. *Garreth Anver Prince v. South Africa*, Communication No. 255/2002, 18th Activity Report 2002–2003, paras 51–52. *See also Tanganyika Law Society et al. v. Tanzania*, African Court of Human and Peoples' Rights, App. Nos 009/2011 and 011/2011 (14 Jun. 2013), para. 112; *Kambole v. Tanzania*, African Court of Human and Peoples' Rights, App. No. 018/2018 (15 Jul. 2020) paras 79–81.
1373. *Tanganyika Law Society et al. v. Tanzania*, African Court of Human and Peoples' Rights, App. Nos 009/2011 and 011/2011 (14 Jun. 2013), paras 106.2–106.3.
1374. *Tanganyika Law Society et al. v. Tanzania*, African Court of Human and Peoples' Rights, App. Nos 009/2011 and 011/2011 (14 Jun. 2013), paras 107.3–110.
1375. In *Media Rights Agenda and Constitutional Rights Project v. Nigeria*, Communication Nos 105/93, 128/94, 130/94, 152/96, 12th Activity Report 1998–1999, para. 67, the Commission stated

214. A salient feature of the African Charter is the fact that it incorporates a list of duties owed by the individual.[1376] The individual's obligations towards 'his family and society, the State and other legally recognized communities and the international community' are emphasized.[1377] While this section of the African Charter has been inspired by traditional African values, it is apparent that the scope and extent of these obligations go considerably further than those imposed by other international documents.[1378] This aspect of the African Charter is difficult to reconcile with the individualistic approach of liberal democratic thought, but it should not be overlooked that even the European Convention on Human Rights (ECHR) recognizes that individuals have responsibilities, implied or otherwise, towards their social environment. The African Charter is more explicit in articulating elements of the social contract, but the danger lies in their sweeping nature which could adversely affect the enjoyment of rights protected by the African Charter.[1379] Questions arise as to whether legally binding obligations have been imposed upon the individual and to what extent these duties are enforceable. By definition, many of these duties are of a general nature which place a moral rather than a legal obligation upon the individual, but answers to these questions are particularly important; for example, can an individual be prosecuted under municipal law because s/he has not placed her/his physical and intellectual abilities at the service of the community as required by Article 29(2)? What is the relationship between such an obligation and the guarantee against forced labour or the right to (intellectual) property? How can the Commission seek to enforce these duties when individuals cannot be arraigned before the Commission? Could a complaint be brought against a State that did not seek to enforce these duties? During the drafting conference, it was stated that not all the duties were expected to be followed exactly but reference was made to principles acceptable to the community but whose immediate application is not envisaged.[1380] Nevertheless, some duties are considered enforceable, and the individual who failed in her/his duty would be answerable under municipal law.[1381] It may be that the concept of duties as a whole serves as a code of good citizenship for the people of Africa.[1382]

---

accordingly that 'limitations on the rights and freedoms enshrined in the Charter cannot be justified by emergencies or special circumstances', not even the existence of war or other turmoil, *Commission Nationale des Droits de l'Homme et des Libertés v. Chad*, Communication No. 74/92(1995); *Article 19 v. Eritrea*, Communication No. 275/2003, 22nd Activity Report 2006–2007, para. 87. In *Groupe de Travail sur les Dossiers Judiciaires Stratégiques v. Democratic Republic of Congo*, Communication No. 259/2002 (2011) para. 66, the Commission explained that this omission was based on a desire to avoid abusive restrictions of rights.

1376. African Charter Arts 27–29. *See further* Ankumah, 170–172; Umozurike, 63–65.

1377. African Charter Art. 27(1).

1378. *See, e.g.*, Universal Declaration of Human Rights Art. 29(1), UN General Assembly Res. 217A (III) (UDHR); American Convention on Human Rights Art. 32 (22 Nov. 1969), 1144 U.N.T.S. 144 (ACHR).

1379. Ankumah, 171; Umozurike, 65.

1380. International Commission of Jurists, *Human and Peoples' Rights in Africa and the African Charter* (International Commission of Jurists: Geneva, 1986), 54–55.

1381. Enforceable duties would appear to include the obligation under Art. 28 to respect other individuals without discrimination; the duty under Art. 29(1) to maintain one's parents in case of need; the

215. In addition to the general obligation to give effect to the African Charter in accordance with Article 1 thereof, and the fact that rights, by implication, impose duties on States, the African Charter curiously sets forth a number of State duties.[1383] These include the duty to promote and ensure awareness of and respect for rights guaranteed in the African Charter through teaching, education and publication, and the duty to guarantee the independence of the courts.[1384]

216. The African Charter attracted criticism for incorporating all three categories of rights. In its Preamble, the African Charter justifies its approach by indicating that civil and political rights cannot be dissociated from economic, social, and cultural rights and that to guarantee the former, the latter must be satisfied. In this, the African Charter reflects the position adopted by the Universal Declaration on Human Rights (UDHR) regarding the universality and indivisibility of all human rights.[1385] But it should not be overlooked that the African Charter is also inspired by the African philosophy of rights which emphasizes the nexus between the individual and the wider community.[1386] The OAU/AU reaffirmed its comprehensive stance on the subject in the Grand Bay Declaration 1999, proclaiming 'the principle that human rights are universal, indivisible, interdependent and inter-related' and calling for parity to be given to economic, social, and cultural rights.[1387] The Grand Bay Declaration goes on to hold third-generation rights as 'universal and inalienable rights which form an integral part of fundamental human rights'.[1388] The Commission has stressed the 'uniqueness' of the African situation and the 'special qualities' of the African Charter, which obliges international human rights to be responsive to African needs,[1389] commenting that 'collective rights, environmental rights, and economic and social rights are essential elements of human rights in Africa'.[1390]

217. A frequently voiced criticism is that the implementation of second-generation rights is programmatic, requiring State intervention. Critics therefore

---

duty under Art. 29(3) not to compromise the security of the State; the duty under Art. 29(5) to contribute to the defence of one's country, which would appear to include military service; and the duty under Art. 29(6) to pay taxes.

1382. D'Sa, 77.

1383. African Charter Arts 25–26.

1384. The Commission has found the independence of the courts to have been compromised in a number of cases concerning Nigeria, *see, e.g., International Pen, Constitutional Rights Project, Interights on behalf of Ken Saro-Wiwa Jr. and Civil Liberties Organisation v. Nigeria*, Communication Nos 137/94, 139/94, 154/96, 161/97, 12th Activity Report 1998–1999.

1385. T. Buergenthal, D. Shelton, D. Stewart & C. Vásquez, *International Human Rights* (5th edn, St. Paul: West Academic Publishing, 2017, 40–48).

1386. Umozurike, 17–18.

1387. Grand Bay (Mauritius) Declaration and Plan of Action 1999 para. 1, Heyns & Killander, 187. *See also* African Charter on Democracy Art. 6.

1388. Grand Bay Declaration para. 2.

1389. In *Constitutional Rights Project and Civil Liberties Organisation v. Nigeria*, Communication Nos 143/95, 150/96, 13th Activity Report 1999–2000, para. 26, the Commission expressed the view that the African Charter 'should be interpreted in a culturally sensitive way'.

1390. *The Social and Economic Rights Action Center and the Center for Economic and Social Rights v. Nigeria*, Communication No. 155/96, 15th Activity Report 2001–2002, para. 68.

consider them purely aspirational, social, and political desiderata to be progressively realized as resources permit but incapable of enforcement. In addition, it is argued that the State is under no legal duty to provide these societal goals. The extent to which a State provides social assistance to its citizens is viewed as a political and not a legal matter. Yet these views do not take account of the growing awareness of the importance of these 'rights' and of the work of international bodies to achieve their full realization. It is instructive to note that the Commission has stressed that once ratified States Parties are legally bound by the provisions of the African Charter.[1391] In *Commission Nationale des Droits de l'Homme et des Libertés v. Chad* the Commission stated:

> The Charter specifies in Article 1 that the States Parties shall not only recognize the rights, duties and freedoms adopted by the Charter, but they should also 'undertake … measures to give effect to them'. In other words, if a state neglects to ensure the rights in the African Charter, this can constitute a violation.[1392]

According to Odinkalu, 'the obligations that States Parties assume with respect to these rights are clearly stated as being of immediate application'.[1393] Significantly, it is no longer true that second-generation rights are non-justiciable. There is an increasing acceptance of the justiciability of positive obligations.[1394] Indeed, the Commission has taken the stance that 'there is no right in the African Charter that cannot be made effective' and that it will apply any of the diverse rights contained' therein.[1395] Crucially, as will be considered more fully below, the Commission has pronounced on these areas.[1396]

218. The importance of third-generation rights, or 'peoples' or group rights, as an element of the African concept of human rights is illustrated by its inclusion in

1391. *International Pen, Constitutional Rights Project, Interights on behalf of Ken Saro-Wiwa Jr. and Civil Liberties Organization v. Nigeria*, Communication Nos 137/94, 139/94, 154/96, 161/97, 12th Activity Report 1998–1999.
1392. Communication No. 74/92, 9th Activity Report 1995–1996. Furthermore, the Commission considers that each State is under a 'minimum core obligation' to ensure the satisfaction of, at the very least, minimum essential levels for each right under the Charter and that concerted action is sometimes required from States to ensure meaningful enjoyment of these rights, *The Social and Economic Rights Action Center and the Center for Economic and Social Rights v. Nigeria*, Communication No. 155/96, 15th Activity Report 2001–2002, para. 48.
1393. Odinkalu, 196.
1394. Thus Hatem Kotrane, independent expert on the question of a draft optional protocol to the International Covenant on Economic, Social and Cultural Rights has expressed the view that, 'In light of the experience gained in recent years from the application of international, regional and national human rights instruments and mechanisms, the independent expert notes that there is no longer any doubt about the essentially justiciable nature of the rights guaranteed by the [International Covenant on Economic, Social and Cultural Rights], UN Doc. E/CN.4/2003/53, para. 2.
1395. *International Pen, Constitutional Rights Project, Interights on behalf of Ken Saro-Wiwa Jr. and Civil Liberties Organization v. Nigeria*, Communication Nos 137/94, 139/94, 154/96, 161/97, 12th Activity Report 1998–1999, para. 68.
1396. *See infra* paras 268–284.

the African Charter, specifically in Articles 19–24.[1397] African traditional life has focused on collective, rather than individual, responsibility. It is the well-being of the community as a whole that is important; by protecting the community, the individual is thereby also protected. However, the problem with this argument is that it is difficult to reconcile with any classical theory of human rights, with its emphasis on an individualistic approach. It is therefore still unusual in legal and political theory to view peoples' rights as human rights. The criticisms made of second-generation rights apply equally here, and the Commission has spoken of 'gradual implementation' although immediate obligations may also arise.[1398] But it is interesting to note that more recently, the Commission has expressed the view that 'peoples' rights are not 'solely or exclusively collective' but can also have an individual dimension and that the two can converge.[1399] The safer conclusion is that at the present stage of development of international law, the majority of States are unwilling to accept the concept of peoples' rights.[1400] However, in practice, there has been widespread recognition of some of these rights, for example, relating to the protection of the environment.[1401] The jurisprudence of the Commission in relation to these rights will be discussed below.

II. The Application of the African Charter

219. Article 1 of the African Charter imposes a binding legal obligation on States Parties to recognize and uphold the rights, duties and freedoms therein.[1402] In

1397. Ankumah, 159–170; Umozurike, 51–61; *Bissangou v. Republic of Congo*, Communication No. 253/2002, 21th Activity Report 2005–2006, para. 80.
1398. *Open Society Justice Initiative v. Côte d'Ivoire*, Communication No. 318/06 (2015) para. 183.
1399. *Ibid.*
1400. Although the International Commission of Jurists has expressed the view that these provisions of the African Charter impose a positive obligation upon States parties to realize these rights, 29.
1401. *Legality of the Threat or Use of Nuclear Weapons*, Advisory Opinion, I.C.J. Reports 1996, 266, para. 29; *Gabcíkovo-Nagymaros Project Case (Hungary v. Slovakia)* I.C.J. Reports 1997, 7, paras 53, 111–114. In a landmark ruling, *Indigenous Communities of the Lhaka Honhat (Our Land) Association v. Argentina*, Inter-American Court of Human Rights, Ser. C No. 420 (Merits, reparations and costs) (6 Feb. 2020), the Inter-American Court of Human Rights (IACtHR) found violations of the rights to a healthy environment, food, water, and cultural identity under ACHR Art. 26. Although the ECHR does not recognize a right to a healthy environment per se, the European Court of Human Rights has determined that environmental harm and risks can breach Convention rights such as the right to life and right to respect for private and family life and home, *see* e.g. *Öneryildiz v. Turkey* [GC], European Court of Human Rights, App. No. 48939/99 (Judgment) (30 Nov. 2004); *Brincat and Others v. Malta*, European Court of Human Rights, App. Nos. 60908/11, 62110/11, 62129/11, 62312/11 and 62338/11 (Judgment) (24 Jul. 2014); *Jugheli and Others v. Georgia*, European Court of Human Rights, App. No. 38342/05 (Judgment) (13 Jul. 2017).
1402. *Sir Dawda K. Jawara v. Gambia*, Communication Nos 147/95 and 149/96, 13th Activity Report 1999–2000, para. 46; *International Pen, Constitutional Rights Project, Interights on behalf of Ken Saro-Wiwa Jr. and Civil Liberties Organisation v. Nigeria*, Communication Nos 137/94, 139/94, 154/96 and 161/97, 12th Activity Report 1998–1999, para. 116. Or as the Commission put it in *Association of Victims of Post Electoral Violence & INTERIGHTS v. Cameroon*, Communication No. 272/2003, 27th Activity Report 2009, para. 87, to respect, protect, promote and implement the rights. In *Purohit and Moore v. The Gambia*, Communication No. 241/2001, 16th Activity Report 2002–2003, para. 43, the Commission stated that if this were not true the significance of

so doing, the Commission assumes the task of being able to examine the extent to which domestic law complies with the provisions of the African Charter.[1403] States that have ratified the African Charter have a clear responsibility to incorporate the treaty in national law by adopting legislative or other measures to give effect to it.[1404] This should result in its practical implementation producing tangible results.[1405] In *Malawi African Association et al. v. Mauritania*, the Commission stated that the 'entry into force of the Charter in Mauritania created for that country an obligation of consequence, deriving from the customary principle *pacta sunt servanda*. It consequently has the duty to adjust its legislation to harmonize it with its international obligations'.[1406] In *Lawyers for Human Rights v. Swaziland*, the Commission found that by ratifying the African Charter without at the same time taking appropriate measures to bring domestic laws in conformity with it, Swaziland was defeating the object and spirit of the African Charter, violating Article 1

---

ratifying a human rights treaty would be seriously defeated. The Commission has therefore described it as an obligation of means and of result, *Mbianku v. Cameroon*, Communication No. 389/10 (2015) para. 126. *See also African Commission on Human and Peoples' Rights v. Libya*, African Court of Human and Peoples' Rights, App. No. 002/2013 (3 Jun. 2016), Separate Opinion of Judge Ouguergouz, para. 12.

1403. *Purohit and Moore v. The Gambia*, Communication No. 241/2001, 16th Activity Report 2002–2003, para. 43; *Good v. Botswana*, Communication No. 306/2005, 28th Activity Report 2009–2010, para. 240. In *Legal Resources Foundation v. Zambia*, Communication No. 211/98, 14th Activity Report 2000–2001, paras 59, 61, the Commission stated that it has no jurisdiction in interpreting and applying domestic law or adjudicating on its validity, but it can examine a State's compliance with the African Charter; 'the point of the exercise is to interpret and apply the African Charter rather than to test the validity of domestic law for its own sake'. In *Garreth Anver Prince v. South Africa*, Communication No. 255/2002, 18th Activity Report 2002–2003, paras 50–52, the Commission expressed the view that its mandate incorporated the principle of subsidiarity and the doctrine of margin of appreciation.

1404. In *Purohit and Moore v. The Gambia*, Communication No. 241/2001, 16th Activity Report 2002–2003, para. 41, the Commission stated that, 'When States ratify … the African Charter, they do so voluntarily and very much awake to their responsibilities to implement' its provisions. Whether a State adheres to the dualist or monist tradition is immaterial, *Good v. Botswana*, Communication No. 306/2005, 28th Activity Report 2009–2010, paras 236–239. In *Civil Liberties Organisation v. Nigeria*, Communication No. 129/94, 9th Activity Report 1995–1996, the Commission condemned Nigeria's purported revocation of the domestic effect of the African Charter, describing it as a 'serious irregularity'. It held that Nigeria could not negate the effects of its ratification of the African Charter through domestic action. In an Extraordinary Session the Commission proceeded to maintain that the African Charter remained legally binding on Nigeria, *Account of the Internal Legislation of Nigeria and the Disposition of the African Charter on Human and Peoples' Rights*, Communication Nos 129/94 and 101/93, in Murray & Evans, Documents Vol. I, 468. *See also Sir Dawda K. Jawara v. Gambia*, Communication Nos 147/95 and 149/96, 13th Activity Report 1999–2000, para. 49. It should be observed that the African Charter does not contain a denunciation clause but it is accepted that States do have a right to withdraw from the African Charter subject to reasonable notice in accordance with the terms of the Vienna Convention on the Law of Treaties Art. 56(2) (22 May 1969), 1155 U.N.T.S. 331, *see Civil Liberties Organisation v. Nigeria*, Communication No. 129/94, 9th Activity Report 1995–1996, para. 12. This also follows from the ruling of the Human Rights Court in *Ingabire Victoire Umuhoza v. Rwanda*, Ruling on Jurisdiction, African Court of Human and Peoples' Rights, App. No. 003/2014 (3 Jun. 2016) paras 54–59.

1405. *Association of Victims of Post Electoral Violence & INTERIGHTS v. Cameroon*, Communication No. 272/2003, 27th Activity Report 2009, para. 108.

1406. Communication Nos 54/91, 61/91, 98/93, 164/97–196/97, 210/98, 13th Activity Report 1999–2000, para. 84.

thereof.[1407] Where a domestic law is found to be incompatible with the African Charter, the State has the obligation to restore harmony.[1408] In keeping with fundamental principles of international law, the Human Rights Court has held that a State cannot seek to evade its international obligations by reference to its municipal law.[1409] However, the Commission has decided that the effect of Article 1 goes further, expressing the view that 'Any violation of the provisions of the African Charter automatically means a violation of Article 1 and that goes to the root of the African Charter since the obligations imposed by Article 1 of the African Charter are peremptory.'[1410] Consequently, any violation additionally engages automatically the responsibility of the State.[1411]

220. Failure to secure the rights in the African Charter can give rise to a violation of Article 1.[1412] In *Zimbabwe Human Rights NGO Forum v. Zimbabwe*, the Commission held that an amnesty given to the perpetrators of violent crimes committed in the run-up to elections in Zimbabwe in 2000, thus preventing victims from seeking redress and encouraging impunity, amounted to a violation of Article 1.[1413] The Commission stated further that Article 1 requires States Parties to ensure that 'effective and enforceable remedies are available'.[1414] In order to guarantee effective protection of human rights, States are under a positive obligation to ensure that rights and freedoms are additionally protected from unwarranted interference by third parties and, in accordance with the principle of due diligence, must carry out

---

1407. Communication No. 251/2002, 18th Activity Report 2004–2005, para. 51.

1408. *Legal Resources Foundation v. Zambia*, Communication No. 211/98, 14th Activity Report 2000–2001, para. 68. In *Women's Legal Aid Centre (on behalf of Sophia Moto) v. Tanzania*, Communication No. 243/2001, 18th Activity Report 2002–2003, paras 45–46, the Commission stated that the substantive rights enshrined in the African Charter rely on domestic procedural rules for their effective enjoyment but that their application may sometimes result in a negation of these rights. Domestic procedures to implement the African Charter must not frustrate the obligations Member States assumed in ratifying the treaty.

1409. *Tanganyika Law Society et al. v. Tanzania*, African Court of Human and Peoples' Rights, App. Nos 009/2011 and 011/2011 (14 Jun. 2013), paras 108–109. *See, e.g., Treatment of Polish Nationals in Danzig Case*, Advisory Opinion, P.C.I.J., Series A/B, No. 44 (1931).

1410. *Zimbabwe Human Rights NGO Forum v. Zimbabwe*, Communication No. 245/2002, 21st Activity Report 2005–2006, para. 78. *See also Sir Dawda K. Jawara v. Gambia*, Communication Nos 147/95 and 149/96, 13th Activity Report 1999–2000, *ibid.* The Commission's jurisprudence has been endorsed by the Human Rights Court, *Alex Thomas v. Tanzania*, African Court of Human and Peoples' Rights, App. No. 005/2013 (20 Nov. 2015), paras 135–136; *Rajabu and others v. Tanzania*, African Court of Human and Peoples' Rights, App. No. 007/2015, Judgment (28 Nov. 2019) para. 124.

1411. *Sudan Human Rights Organization and Sudan Centre for Housing Rights and Evictions v. Sudan* Communication Nos 279/03, 296/05, 28th Activity Report, 2010, para. 227; *Monim Elgak, Osman Hummeida and Amir Suleiman (represented by FIDH and OMCT) v. Sudan*, Communication No. 379/09 (2014) para. 140.

1412. *Commission Nationale des Droits de l'Homme et des Libertés v. Chad*, Communication No. 74/92, 9th Activity Report 1995–1996, para. 20; *Gunme et al. v. Cameroon*, Communication No. 266/2003, 26th Activity Report 2008–2009, para. 213.

1413. *Zimbabwe Human Rights NGO Forum v. Zimbabwe*, Communication No. 245/2002, 21st Activity Report 2005–2006, para. 215. *See also Mouvement Ivorien des Droits Humains (MIDH) v. Côte d'Ivoire*, Communication No. 246/2002, 25th Activity Report 2008, para. 98.

1414. *Zimbabwe Human Rights NGO Forum v. Zimbabwe*, Communication No. 245/2002, 21st Activity Report 2005–2006, para. 171.

proper investigations of alleged violations.[1415] But according to the Commission, this obligation extends additionally to one of result, giving the State the freedom of choice and action to achieve the required result.[1416]

221. Article 2 of the African Charter enshrines the 'fundamental' principle of non-discrimination;[1417] it guarantees every individual[1418] the rights and freedoms guaranteed in the Charter without distinction on a wide number of specified grounds, including race, ethnic or national origin,[1419] language,[1420] sex,[1421] political opinion,[1422] or religion.[1423] However, the term 'or any status' means this list is neither 'absolute nor comprehensive.'[1424] Discrimination has been defined as a 'differentiation of persons or situations on the basis of one or several unlawful criterion/

1415. *Amnesty International et al. v. Sudan*, Communication Nos 48/90, 50/91, 52/91, 89/93, 13th Activity Report 1999–2000, para. 50; *Zimbabwe Human Rights NGO Forum v. Zimbabwe*, Communication No. 245/2002, 21st Activity Report 2005–2006; *Association of Victims of Post Electoral Violence & INTERIGHTS v. Cameroon*, Communication No. 272/2003, 27th Activity Report 2009, para. 110; *Institute for Human Rights and Development in Africa v. Angola*, Communication No. 292/2004, 24th Activity Report 2008, para. 83; *Egyptian Initiative for Personal Rights and INTERIGHTS v. Egypt*, Communication No. 323/2006 (2011), para. 166.
1416. *Association of Victims of Post Electoral Violence & INTERIGHTS v. Cameroon*, Communication No. 272/2003, 27th Activity Report 2009, para. 111.
1417. *Good v. Botswana*, Communication No. 306/2005, 28th Activity Report 2009–2010, para. 218.
1418. According to the Commission States are obliged to secure the rights protected by the African Charter to all persons within their jurisdiction, nationals and non-nationals alike, *Rencontre Africaine pour la Defense des Droits de l'Homme v. Zambia*, Communication No. 71/92, 10th Activity Report, 1996–1997, para. 22. *See also African Institute for Human Rights and Development (on behalf of Sierra Leonean refugees in Guinea) v. Republic of Guinea*, Communication No. 249/2002, 20th Activity Report 2005–2006, para. 68; *Institute for Human Rights and Development in Africa v. Angola*, Communication No. 292/2004, 24th Activity Report 2008, para. 80.
1419. *Organisation Mondiale contre la Torture et al. v. Rwanda*, Communication Nos 27/89, 46/91, 49/91, 99/93, 10th Activity Report 1993–1994, para. 22; *Zimbabwe Lawyers for Human Rights and the Institute for Human Rights and Development (on behalf of Andrew Barclay Meldrum) v. Zimbabwe*, Communication No. 294/2004, 26th Activity Report 2008–2009, paras 93–94; *Open Society Justice Initiative v. Côte d'Ivoire*, Communication No. 318/06 (2015) para. 146; *The Nubian Community in Kenya v. Kenya*, Communication No. 317/06 (2015), paras 134–135. *See also* African Charter on Democracy Art. 8(1).
1420. *Gunme et al. v. Cameroon,* Communication No. 266/2003, 26th Activity Report 2008–2009, para. 108.
1421. *Egyptian Initiative for Personal Rights and INTERIGHTS v. Egypt*, Communication No. 323/2006 (2011), paras 121–122, 137. It should be observed that under the African Charter Art. 18(3) States Parties are under an obligation to eliminate discrimination against women. In *Egyptian Initiative for Personal Rights and INTERIGHTS v. Egypt*, Communication No. 323/2006 (2011), paras 142–153, the Commission found that acts of violence carried out on a number of women was based on their sex only and was therefore gender-specific and discriminatory. *See* Protocol to the African Charter on Human and Peoples' Rights on the Rights of Women in Africa Arts 2, 3(4), 4 (11 Jul. 2003), https://www.au.int/en/treaties, Heyns & Killander, 65 (Maputo Protocol). *See also* UN Convention on the Elimination of Discrimination against Women (18 Dec. 1979); Inter-American Convention on the Prevention, Punishment and Eradication of Violence Against Women (9 June 1994) (Convention of Belem do Para) I.L.M. 33 (1994): 1534; European Convention on preventing and combating violence against women and domestic violence Arts 3(a), 4 (11 May 2011), C.E.T.S. No. 210 (Istanbul Convention).
1422. *Zimbabwe Human Rights NGO Forum v. Zimbabwe*, Communication No. 245/2002, 21st Activity Report 2005–2006; *Good v. Botswana*, Communication No. 306/2005, 28th Activity Report 2009–2010, paras 220–221. *See also* African Charter on Democracy Art. 8(1).

criteria',[1425] and covers both direct and indirect discrimination.[1426] According to the Commission, Article 2 'guarantees that those in the same circumstances are dealt with equally in law and practice'.[1427] However, it 'does not stipulate a general banning of discrimination; it only prohibits discrimination where it affects the enjoyment of a right or freedom guaranteed by the Charter'.[1428] Its aim is 'to ensure equality of treatment for individuals irrespective' of the specified grounds.[1429] Certain differential practices will be considered permissible as long as some rational and objective basis, proportionate to the legitimate aim pursued, exists.[1430]

1423. In *Zimbabwe Human Rights NGO Forum v. Zimbabwe*, Communication No. 245/2002, 21st Activity Report 2005–2006, para. 170, the Commission defined discrimination as 'applying any distinction, exclusion, restriction or preference' based on grounds such as 'race, colour, sex, language, religion, political or other opinion, national or social origin, property, birth or other status, and which has the purpose or effect of nullifying or impairing the recognition, enjoyment or exercise by all persons, on equal footing, of all rights and freedoms'. Accordingly, a 'universal 'composite concept of discrimination' can contain the following elements, stipulates a difference in treatment, has a certain effect and is based on a certain prohibited ground.' In *Malawi African Association et al. v. Mauritania*, Communication Nos 54/91, 61/91, 98/93, 164/97–196/97, 210/98, 13th Activity Report 1999–2000, para. 131, the Commission described discrimination on the basis of colour as an 'unacceptable' attitude that violated the very spirit of the African Charter and of the letter of the provision. *See also* African Charter on Democracy Art. 8(1).

1424. *Open Society Justice Initiative v. Côte d'Ivoire*, Communication No. 318/06 (2015) para. 145. In *African Commission on Human and Peoples' Rights v. Kenya*, African Court of Human and Peoples' Rights, App. No. 006/2012 (26 May 2017) para. 138, the Human Rights Court held that Art. 2 encompasses other types of discrimination not foreseen when the African Charter was adopted. In determining whether a ground falls under this category, the Human Rights Court will take account of the general spirit of the African Charter; *see also Kambole v. Tanzania*, African Court of Human and Peoples' Rights, App. No. 018/2018 (15 Jul. 2020) para. 73.

1425. *Actions pour la Protection des Droit de l'Homme (APDH) v. Côte d'Ivoire*, African Court of Human and Peoples' Rights, App. No. 001/2014 (18 Nov. 2016) para. 147.

1426. *Kambole v. Tanzania*, African Court of Human and Peoples' Rights, App. No. 018/2018 (15 Jul. 2020) paras 68–70. In cases of indirect discrimination 'the key indicator is not necessarily different treatment based on visible or unlawful criteria but the disparate effect on groups or individuals as a result of specified measures or actions', *Legal & Human Rights Centre and Tanzania Human Rights Defenders Coalition v. Tanzania*, African Court of Human and Peoples' Rights, App. No. 039/2020 (13 Jun. 2023) para. 106.

1427. *Good v. Botswana*, Communication No. 306/2005, 28th Activity Report 2009–2010, para. 218. An intention to discriminate is not required so that an apparently neutral law or measure that results in an unjustified distinction is covered, *Open Society Justice Initiative v. Côte d'Ivoire*, Communication No. 318/06 (2015) para. 144.

1428. *Bissangou v. Republic of Congo*, Communication No. 253/2002, 21st Activity Report 2005–2006, para. 69. However, in *Malawi African Association et al. v. Mauritania*, Communication Nos 54/91, 61/91, 98/93, 164/97–196/97, 210/98, 13th Activity Report 1999–2000, para. 131, the Commission stated that, 'Article 2 of the Charter lays down a principle that is essential to the spirit of this convention, one of whose goals is the elimination of all forms of discrimination and to ensure equality among all human beings … it is apparent that international human rights law and the community of States accord a certain importance to the eradication of discrimination in all its guises.' *See also Purohit and Moore v. The Gambia*, Communication No. 241/2001, 16th Activity Report 2002–2003, para. 49.

1429. *Legal Resources Foundation v. Zambia*, Communication No. 211/98, 14th Activity Report 2000–2001, para. 63; *Zimbabwe Human Rights NGO Forum v. Zimbabwe*, Communication No. 245/2002, 21st Activity Report 2005–2006, para. 169.

1430. *Kambole v. Tanzania*, African Court of Human and Peoples' Rights, App. No. 018/2018 (15 Jul. 2020) para. 72; *Good v. Botswana*, Communication No. 306/2005, 28th Activity Report

222. Article 2 of the African Charter has been described as a 'non-derogable' provision that must be respected in all circumstances.[1431] This is because the rights guaranteed in Article 2 'are an important entitlement as the availability or lack of them affects the capacity of one to enjoy many other rights';[1432] they 'provide the foundation for the enjoyment of all human rights'.[1433] Consequently, Article 2 will often be considered in conjunction with other provisions of the African Charter.[1434] In *Sissoko v. Mali*, the Human Rights Court stated that the principle of non-discrimination is interlinked with the right to equality before the law and to equal protection before the law guaranteed by Article 3 of the African Charter.[1435] In *Legal Resources Foundation v. Zambia*, the Commission drew attention to the political instability caused in recent years by the adoption of discriminatory practices based on birth and social origin which excluded a section of the citizenry from participating in the democratic process and which therefore undermined the legitimacy of elections. The Commission held such practices to breach Article 2.[1436]

223. In *Zimbabwe Human Rights NGO Forum v. Zimbabwe*, it was alleged that the Zimbabwean Government had encouraged a deliberate policy of violence against the political opposition, consequently discriminating against persons holding an alternative political opinion. This was denied by the State which argued that it was not responsible for the actions of non-State actors and that it had in fact taken steps to try to deal with the situation. The Commission found that the legislative and other measures taken by the government to contain the violence did not suggest a discriminatory pattern against the complainants.[1437] However, by way of contrast, in *Association of Victims of Post Electoral Violence & INTERIGHTS v. Cameroon*, the failure of the State to take adequate measures to protect the victims from post-electoral violence did violate their rights under Article 2.[1438]

2009–2010, para. 219; *African Commission on Human and Peoples' Rights v. Kenya*, African Court of Human and Peoples' Rights, App. No. 006/2012 (26 May 2017) para. 139.

1431. *Purohit and Moore v. The Gambia*, Communication No. 241/2001, 16th Activity Report 2002–2003, para. 49.

1432. *Zimbabwe Human Rights NGO Forum v. Zimbabwe*, Communication No. 245/2002, 21st Activity Report 2005–2006, paras 81, 169; *Legal Resources Foundation v. Zambia*, Communication No. 211/98, 14th Activity Report 2000–2001, para. 63; *The Nubian Community in Kenya v. Kenya*, Communication No. 317/06 (2015), paras 150, 168. Accordingly described as 'imperative', *African Commission on Human and Peoples' Rights v. Kenya*, African Court of Human and Peoples' Rights, App. No. 006/2012 (26 May 2017) para. 137.

1433. *Kambole v. Tanzania*, African Court of Human and Peoples' Rights, App. No. 018/2018 (15 Jul. 2020) para. 71; *Zimbabwe Human Rights NGO Forum v. Zimbabwe*, Communication No. 245/2002, 21st Activity Report 2005–2006, para. 169.

1434. *See, e.g., Ivorien Human Rights Movement (MIDH) v. Côte d'Ivoire*, Communication No. 262/2002, 26th Activity Report 2008–2009, paras 74–78.

1435. *Sissoko and 74 others v. Mali*, African Court of Human and Peoples' Rights, App. No. 037/2017, Judgment (25 Sep. 2020), paras 95–96.

1436. Communication No. 211/98, 14th Activity Report 2000–2001, paras 63–64. *See also Mouvement Ivorien des Droits Humains (MIDH) v. Côte d'Ivoire*, Communication No. 246/2002, 26th Activity Report 2008–2009, para. 86.

1437. Communication No. 245/2002, 21st Activity Report 2005–2006, para. 172.

1438. Communication No. 272/2003, 27th Activity Report 2009, paras 122–126.

III. Civil and Political Rights

224. Article 3 of the African Charter guarantees the individual's right to equality before the law and the right to equal protection before the law, complementing the prohibition on discrimination set out in Article 2.[1439] It has been described as 'fundamental principles' of human rights law.[1440] The Commission has expressed the view that Article 3 is necessarily important 'because it guarantees fair and essential treatment of individuals within a legal system of a given country'.[1441] According to the Commission, equality before the law, under Article 3(1), 'relates to the status of individuals before the law', that everyone is subject to the same laws, whereas equal protection by the law, under Article 3(2), reflects a 'fundamental fairness'[1442] that 'relates to the implementation of the law and is applicable where the rights of the Complainant are implemented unequally'.[1443] More specifically, the Commission has described this right as guaranteeing persons the same access to the law and courts and the same treatment in procedure and substance by the law and courts.[1444] The Human Rights Court has referred to the principle of equality of

1439. *Bissangou v. Republic of Congo*, Communication No. 253/2002, 21st Activity Report 2005–2006, para. 70; *Egyptian Initiative for Personal Rights and INTERIGHTS v. Egypt*, Communication No. 323/2006 (2011), para. 175. The Human Rights Court has stated that equality in law 'presupposes that the law protects everyone without discrimination', *Actions pour la Protection des Droit de l'Homme (APDH) v. Côte d'Ivoire*, African Court of Human and Peoples' Rights, App. No. 001/2014 (18 Nov. 2016) para. 146. In *Open Society Justice Initiative v. Côte d'Ivoire*, Communication No. 318/06 (2015) para. 155, the Commission was of the view that a violation of Art. 2 would inexorably lead to a violation of Art. 3. In *Purohit and Moore v. The Gambia*, Communication No. 241/2001 16th Activity Report 2002–2003, para. 49, the Commission described Art. 3 as a 'non-derogable' provision that must be respected in all circumstances. *See also* African Charter on Democracy Art. 10 (3).

1440. *Sissoko and 74 others v. Mali*, African Court of Human and Peoples' Rights, App. No. 037/2017, Judgment (25 Sep. 2020), para. 83.

1441. *Purohit and Moore v. The Gambia*, Communication No. 241/2001, 16th Activity Report 2002–2003, para. 49.

1442. *Zimbabwe Lawyers for Human Rights and the Institute for Human Rights and Development v. Zimbabwe*, Communication No. 293/2004, 24th Activity Report 2008, para. 124. In *Zimbabwe Human Rights NGO Forum v. Zimbabwe*, Communication No. 245/2002, 21st Activity Report 2005–2006, para. 174, the Commission stated that for 'there to be equal protection of the law, the law must not only be fairly applied but must be seen to be fairly applied'.

1443. *Bissangou v. Republic of Congo*, Communication No. 253/2002, 21st Activity Report 2005–2006), para. 70. *See also Zimbabwe Lawyers for Human Rights and the Institute for Human Rights and Development (on behalf of Andrew Barclay Meldrum) v. Zimbabwe*, Communication No. 294/2004, 26th Activity Report 2008–2009, para. 96. In *Open Society Justice Initiative v. Côte d'Ivoire*, Communication No. 318/06 (2015) para. 153, the Commission considered Art. 3(1) to refer to 'equality in law or legal equality inherent to any individual subject of law as a result of his human nature and which places him on equal legal terms with other human persons', whereas Art. 3(2) refers to the 'guarantees introduced in order to give substance to the subjective law deriving from equality before the law or in law.'

1444. *Zimbabwe Lawyers for Human Rights and the Institute for Human Rights and Development v. Zimbabwe*, Communication No. 293/2004, 24th Activity Report 2008, para. 124; *Zimbabwe Lawyers for Human Rights and the Institute for Human Rights and Development (on behalf of Andrew Barclay Meldrum) v. Zimbabwe*, Communication No. 294/2004, 26th Activity Report 2008–2009, para. 99; *Egyptian Initiative for Personal Rights and INTERIGHTS v. Egypt*, Communication No. 323/2006 (2011), para. 177. In *Dino Noca v. Democratic Republic of the Congo*, Communication

arms.[1445] However, this is not to say that all cases must necessarily be treated in exactly the same manner but which is dependent on the particular circumstances of each case.[1446]

225. The Commission has stated that for Article 3 to apply, the inequality 'should follow from the "law"'.[1447] It has expressed the view that a violation of Article 3 would occur if a State exercised a power or judgment conferred by law in a discriminatory or arbitrary manner.[1448] It must be established that the State must have treated the complainants differently from others in the same position.[1449] The outbreak of politically motivated violence in Zimbabwe since 2000 gave rise to the African Commission having to consider the submission in *Zimbabwe Human Rights NGO Forum v. Zimbabwe* that in refusing to investigate complaints of attacks on members of the political opposition, the police selectively enforced the law to the detriment of the victims, amounting to unequal protection of the law in breach of Article 3(2) of the African Charter. However, the Commission was unable to make a determination on the evidence available to it.[1450]

226. Article 4 of the African Charter guarantees the right to life. It was initially believed that the right to life was not an absolute right; that it was the 'arbitrary' deprivation of life that was proscribed.[1451] In *Forum of Conscience v. Sierra Leone*, the Commission emphasized the essential importance of this right, stating that it 'is the fulcrum of all other rights. It is the fountain through which other rights flow,

---

No. 286/2004 (2012), para. 203, a violation of Art. 3 was found on the ground that only the case put by one party was taken into account by the court.

1445. *Mohamed Abubakri v. Tanzania*, African Court of Human and Peoples' Rights, App. No. 007/2013 (3 Jun. 2016), para. 193.

1446. *Kambole v. Tanzania*, African Court of Human and Peoples' Rights, App. No. 018/2018 (15 Jul. 2020) para. 87; *Sissoko and 74 others v. Mali*, African Court of Human and Peoples' Rights, App. No. 037/2017, Judgment (25 Sep. 2020), para. 70.

1447. *Bissangou v. Republic of Congo*, Communication No. 253/2002, 21st Activity Report 2005–2006, para. 71.

1448. *Ibid.*; *Zimbabwe Lawyers for Human Rights and the Institute for Human Rights and Development (on behalf of Andrew Barclay Meldrum) v. Zimbabwe*, Communication No. 294/2004, 26th Activity Report 2008–2009, para. 96.

1449. *Zimbabwe Lawyers for Human Rights and the Institute for Human Rights and Development v. Zimbabwe*, Communication No. 293/2004, 24th Activity Report 2008, para. 127.

1450. Communication No. 245/2002, 21th Activity Report 2005–2006, paras 175–176. However, in *Kazeem Aminu v. Nigeria*, Communication Nos 205/97, 13th Activity Report 1999–2000, para. 15, the Commission found that repeated arrests and detention of the victim which led him to go into hiding for fear of his life violated this provision.

1451. General Comment No. 3 on the African Charter on Human and Peoples' Rights: The Right to Life (Art. 4), paras 12–14, in Heyns & Killander, 432 (General Comment 3); *Sudan Human Rights Organization and Sudan Centre for Housing Rights and Evictions v. Sudan* Communication Nos 279/03, 296/05, 28th Activity Report, 2010, para. 147; *African Commission on Human and Peoples' Rights v. Kenya*, African Court of Human and Peoples' Rights, App. No. 006/2012 (26 May 2017) para. 152. In *Kazeem Aminu v. Nigeria*, Communication Nos 205/97, 13th Activity Report 1999–2000, the Commission was confronted with the problem whether the victim's going into hiding for fear of his life violated this provision. It stated, at para. 18, that, 'It would be a narrow interpretation to this right to think that it can only be violated when one is deprived of it. It cannot be said that the right to respect for one's life … would be protected in a state of constant fear and/or threats.'

and any violation of this right without due process amounts to arbitrary deprivation of life'.[1452] In fact, the Commission has expressed the view that the right to life is a norm of customary law.[1453] But in an important development, in *Groupe de Travail sur les Dossiers Judiciaires Stratégiques v. Democratic Republic of Congo*, the Commission went further and stressed that the right to life was inviolable and permitted no limitations.[1454] State Parties are under an obligation to provide a reasonably secure environment and to take effective measures not only to prevent and punish the loss of life[1455] but also to desist from the excessive or inappropriate use of force.[1456] Moreover, States are under a procedural obligation to investigate suspicious deaths[1457] and provide redress, including fair compensation if necessary.[1458] Extrajudicial killings have also been condemned by the Commission.[1459] In *Organisation Mondiale contre la Torture et al. v. Rwanda*, the Commission found that large numbers of Rwandan villagers had been massacred by the Rwandan military for membership of a particular ethnic group.[1460] In *Zimbabwe Human Rights NGO Forum v. Zimbabwe*, the Commission expressed the view that extrajudicial killings are 'caused by the State or through its agents or acquiescence'.[1461] The responsibility of the State can extend to killings by non-State actors where the State has

1452. Communication No. 223/98, 14th Activity Report 2000–2001, para. 19. In *Sudan Human Rights Organization and Sudan Centre for Housing Rights and Evictions v. Sudan* Communication Nos 279/03, 296/05, 28th Activity Report, 2010, para. 146, the Commission described the right to life as 'the supreme right of the human being. It is basic to all human rights and without it all other rights are without meaning'. In *Kasingachire et al. v. Zimbabwe*, Communication No. 295/04 (2012), para. 138, the Commission stated that the right to life was the 'foundational, or bedrock human right'. The Human Rights Court has described it as 'the cornerstone on which the realisation of all other rights and freedoms depend', *African Commission on Human and Peoples' Rights v. Kenya*, African Court of Human and Peoples' Rights, App. No. 006/2012 (26 May 2017) para. 152. The Court proceeded to observe that Art. 4 refers to 'the physical rather than the existential understanding of the right to life', *ibid.*, para. 154.

1453. *Kasingachire et al. v. Zimbabwe*, Communication No. 295/04 (2012), para. 137.

1454. Communication No. 259/2002 (2011) para. 68. The Commission has described it as 'non-derogable', General Comment 3, para. 1.

1455. *Sudan Human Rights Organization and Sudan Centre for Housing Rights and Evictions v. Sudan* Communication Nos 279/03, 296/05, 28th Activity Report, 2010, para. 147; *Kasingachire et al. v. Zimbabwe*, Communication No. 295/04 (2012), para. 123.

1456. Such as in *Krischna Achutan (on behalf of Aleke Banda) v. Malawi*; *Amnesty International on behalf of Orton and Vera Chirwa v. Malawi*, Communication Nos 64/92, 68/92, 78/92, 8th Activity Report 1994–1995, where the police opened fire on workers on a peaceful strike. *See also Kasingachire et al. v. Zimbabwe*, Communication Nos 295/04 (2012), paras 105–123. *See also* General Comment 3, paras 27–31.

1457. *Gunme et al. v. Cameroon,* Communication No. 266/2003, 26th Activity Report 2008–2009, para. 112; *Kasingachire et al. v. Zimbabwe*, Communication No. 295/04 (2012), para. 133; General Comment 3, paras 15–17.

1458. *Zimbabwe Human Rights NGO Forum v. Zimbabwe*, Communication No. 245/2002, 21st Activity Report 2005–2006; *Association of Victims of Post Electoral Violence & INTERIGHTS v. Cameroon*, Communication No. 272/2003, 27th Activity Report 2009, para. 136; *Kasingachire et al. v. Zimbabwe*, Communication No. 295/04 (2012), paras 127–128; General Comment 3, para. 19.

1459. *Free Legal Assistance Group v. Zaire*, Communication No. 25/89, 9th Activity Report 1995–1996; *Sudan Human Rights Organization and Sudan Centre for Housing Rights and Evictions v. Sudan* Communication Nos 279/03, 296/05, 28th Activity Report, 2010.

1460. Communication Nos 27/89, 46/91, 49/91, 99/93, 10th Activity Report 1993–1994, para. 24.

1461. Communication No. 245/2002, 21st Activity Report 2005–2006, para. 181.

failed to be diligent in taking adequate measures of protection.[1462] In this instance, the Commission found no violation of Article 4 because it accepted the State's submissions that it bore no responsibility for the terror gangs and suspicious deaths were investigated and perpetrators prosecuted for murder.[1463] Indeed, the Commission requires that extrajudicial killings must be investigated 'by entirely independent individuals, provided with the necessary resources, and their findings must be made public and prosecutions initiated in accordance with the information uncovered'.[1464] Thus, in *Sudan Human Rights Organization and Sudan Centre for Housing Rights and Evictions v. Sudan*, arising out of the violence in the Darfur region, the Commission found a violation of Article 4 because of the State's failure to conduct effective investigations.[1465]

227. The imposition of the death penalty in accordance with the law is sanctioned by Article 4,[1466] although the Commission has repeatedly called for its suspension.[1467] However, in *Groupe de Travail sur les Dossiers Judiciaires Stratégiques v. Democratic Republic of Congo*, the Commission cast doubt on this position, intimating that the death penalty was not admitted under Article 4.[1468] It

1462. *Ibid.*; General Comment 3, paras 38–39.
1463. Communication No. 245/2002, 21st Activity Report 2005–2006, *ibid.*
1464. *Amnesty International et al. v. Sudan*, Communication Nos 48/90, 50/91, 52/91, 89/93, 13th Activity Report 1999–2000, para. 51.
1465. Communication Nos 279/03, 296/05, 28th Activity Report, 2010, paras 150–153.
1466. As long as it is not arbitrary, *Rajabu and others v. Tanzania*, African Court of Human and Peoples' Rights, App. No. 007/2015, Judgment (28 Nov. 2019) para. 98. Although the death penalty cannot be imposed on a child, *see* African Charter on the Rights and Welfare of the Child Art. 5(3) (1 Jul. 1990), https://www.au.int/en/treaties, 28 I.L.M. 1456 (1989), *Groupe de Travail sur les Dossiers Judiciaires Stratégiques v. Democratic Republic of Congo*, Communication No. 259/2002 (2011), para. 71, or carried out on pregnant or nursing women, *see* Maputo Protocol Art. 4(j). As of 2021 fourteen African States were classified as retentionist countries, including Botswana, Egypt, Nigeria, Sudan, Uganda and Zimbabwe, while thirteen were abolitionist in practice, including Algeria, Kenya, Tanzania and Tunisia. Twenty-nine countries are completely abolitionist, including Angola, Benin, Cabo Verde, Ghana, Mauritius, Mozambique, Namibia, Senegal, Seychelles and South Africa. *See* Amnesty International, Abolitionist and Retentionist Countries as of December 2022, https://www.amnesty.org/en/documents/act50/6591/2023/en/. *See further* Report of the Secretary-General, Moratorium on the use of the death penalty, UN Doc. A/77/274 (8 Aug. 2022). In *S v. Makwanyane and Mchunu* 1995 (3) SA 391 (CC) the Constitutional Court of South Africa ruled that capital punishment was unconstitutional as violating, *inter alia*, the right to life. Compare, contra, *Catholic Commission for Justice and Peace in Zimbabwe v. Attorney-General, Zimbabwe* 1993 (4) SA 239 (ZS); *Mbushuu and Another v. Republic* [1995] 1 L.R.C. 216 (Tanzania Court of Appeal); *Ntesang and Others v. State* [1995] B.L.R. 151 (Botswana Court of Appeal); *Kigula and Others v. Attorney-General* (2005) A.H.R.L.R. 197 (Constitutional Court of Uganda) para. 49.
1467. The Commission's obiter dictum in *Interights (on behalf of Mariette Sonjaleen Bosch) v. Botswana*, Communication No. 240/2001, 17th Activity Report 2003–2004, para. 52, is worth noting. It drew attention to the trend towards the abolition of the death penalty in international law, including the Second Optional Protocol to the International Covenant on Civil and Political Rights Aiming at the Abolition of the Death Penalty, 15 Dec. 1989, 1642 U.N.T.S. 414, and the Commission's own Resolution Urging States to envisage a Moratorium on the Death Penalty, adopted at the Twenty-Sixth Ordinary Session of the African Commission, 1999, and therefore encouraged all States Parties to refrain from exercising the death penalty and calling for it abolition. *See also Interights & Ditshwanelo v. Botswana*, Communication No. 319/06 (2015).
1468. Communication No. 259/2002 (2011), para. 69.

based its conclusion chiefly on the fact that there is no mention of the death penalty in Article 4.[1469] But in a later case, *Interights & Ditshwanelo v. Botswana*, the Commission backed away from this radical position, indicating that given its previous rulings on the matter, it would be improper if it were suddenly to hold that the death penalty 'would in all cases' constitute a violation of Article 4.[1470] However, given the evolution of human rights law, the Commission regarded it as 'increasingly difficult to envisage a case in which the death penalty can be found to have been applied in a way that is not in some way arbitrary. As a result, it is difficult to conceive that, if called upon in future to do so, the Commission will find that the death penalty, however it is executed, is any longer compatible with the African Charter.'[1471] Indeed, the Human Rights Court has observed that the prohibition of the death sentence in international law is not absolute[1472] but has noted the trend in Africa towards its abolition and suspension.[1473] Accordingly, the death penalty 'should exceptionally be reserved only for the most heinous of offences committed in seriously aggravating circumstances.'[1474] What is beyond question is that the method of execution may be incompatible with the obligation to uphold human dignity under Article 5.[1475] The Commission has therefore proceeded to hold that hanging as a method of execution causes excessive suffering and is inhuman and degrading.[1476] This conclusion has also been reached by the Human Rights Court.[1477] However, it is imperative that due process in capital cases is scrupulously

---

1469. *Ibid.*, para. 68.
1470. Communication No. 319/06 (2015) para. 66.
1471. *Ibid.*
1472. *Rajabu and others v. Tanzania*, African Court of Human and Peoples' Rights, App. No. 007/2015, Judgment (28 Nov. 2019) para. 96.
1473. *Ghati Mwita v. Tanzania*, African Court of Human and Peoples' Rights, App. No. 012/2019, Judgment (1 Dec. 2022) para. 65.
1474. *Ibid.*, para. 66.
1475. *Spilg and Mack & Ditshwanelo (on behalf of Lehlohonolo Bernard Kobedi) v. Botswana*, Communication No. 277/2003(2011), paras 167, 169; *Interights & Ditshwanelo v. Botswana*, Communication No. 319/06 (2015) para. 84. In *Interights (on behalf of Mariette Sonjaleen Bosch) v. Botswana*, Communication No. 240/2001, 17th Activity Report, 2003–2004, para. 41, the Commission expressed the view that a criminal justice system must have 'a human face in matters of execution of death sentences'. The Commission has also expressed the view that the 'death row' phenomenon is incompatible with Art. 5, *Interights & Ditshwanelo v. Botswana*, Communication No. 319/06 (2015) para. 93. The Human Rights Court has held similarly that prolonged and indefinite detention on death row is 'inherently inhuman' and contrary to human dignity, *Ghati Mwita v. Tanzania*, African Court of Human and Peoples' Rights, App. No. 012/2019, Judgment (1 Dec. 2022) para. 87. *See also Catholic Commission for Justice and Peace in Zimbabwe v. Attorney-General, Zimbabwe* 1993 (4) SA 239 (ZS); *Kigula and Others v. Attorney-General* (2005) A.H.R.L.R. 197 (Constitutional Court of Uganda) paras 116–120.
1476. *Interights & Ditshwanelo v. Botswana*, Communication No. 319/06 (2015) para. 87. In *S v. Makwanyane and Mchunu* 1995 (3) SA 391 (CC) the Constitutional Court of South Africa ruled that the death penalty was cruel, inhuman and degrading punishment. *See also Mbushuu and Another v. Republic* [1995] 1 L.R.C. 216. Compare, contra, *Catholic Commission for Justice and Peace in Zimbabwe v. Attorney-General, Zimbabwe* 1993 (4) SA 239 (ZS) para. 4; *Kigula and Others v. Attorney-General* (2005) A.H.R.L.R. 197 (Constitutional Court of Uganda) para. 49.
1477. *Rajabu and others v. Tanzania*, African Court of Human and Peoples' Rights, App. No. 007/2015, Judgment (28 Nov. 2019) paras 118–119; *Amini Juma v. Tanzania*, African Court of Human and Peoples' Rights, App. No. 024/2016 (30 Sep. 2021) para. 136.

observed and arbitrariness avoided, including the holding of a trial, an adequate defence, a right of appeal and a right to seek pardon or commutation of sentence.[1478] This requirement is exemplified by the notorious case concerning the poet and human rights activist Ken Saro-Wiwa who was found guilty of murder in a travesty of justice by a special military tribunal which lacked the most elementary standards of a fair trial, and who was later judicially murdered by the Nigerian military regime in defiance of international public opinion. The Commission found that since the trial itself violated the right to a fair trial guaranteed by Article 7 of the African Charter, the resultant implementation of the death sentence was rendered arbitrary and in violation of Article 4.[1479] Such conclusions have been upheld by the Human Rights Court which has held the mandatory imposition of the death penalty as arbitrary and in violation of due process.[1480] The courts must have the discretionary power to impose an appropriate sentence on the basis of proportionality and individual circumstances of a convicted person.[1481]

228. Article 4 additionally declares, 'Human beings are inviolable. Every human being shall be entitled to respect for ... the integrity of his person.' The African Charter hence 'establishes the link between the right to life and the inviolable nature and integrity of the human being'.[1482] State Parties are under an obligation to provide the 'necessary conditions of a dignified life',[1483] a duty that has a very wide scope. Consequently, cavity searches performed in an unreasonable manner have been found to interfere with a person's physical integrity.[1484]

1478. *Forum of Conscience v. Sierra Leone,* Communication No. 223/98, 14th Activity Report 2000–2001, para. 19; *Interights (on behalf of Mariette Sonjaleen Bosch) v. Botswana*, Communication No. 240/2001, 17th Activity Report, 2003–2004, para. 43; *Ghati Mwita v. Tanzania*, African Court of Human and Peoples' Rights, App. No. 012/2019, Judgment (1 Dec. 2022) para. 75. Clemency procedures are not in themselves arbitrary, *Interights & Ditshwanelo v. Botswana*, Communication No. 319/06 (2015) para. 81.

1479. *International Pen, Constitutional Rights Project, Interights on behalf of Ken Saro-Wiwa Jr. and Civil Liberties Organisation v. Nigeria*, Communication Nos 137/94, 139/94, 154/96 and 161/97, 12th Activity Report 1998–1999, para. 103. *See also Malawi African Association et al. v. Mauritania*, Communication Nos 54/91, 61/91, 98/93, 164/97–196/97, 210/98, 13th Activity Report 1999–2000, para. 120; *Interights & Ditshwanelo v. Botswana*, Communication No. 319/06 (2015) paras 64–65.

1480. *Rajabu and others v. Tanzania*, African Court of Human and Peoples' Rights, App. No. 007/2015, Judgment (28 Nov. 2019) paras 109–114. *See also Amini Juma v. Tanzania*, African Court of Human and Peoples' Rights, App. No. 024/2016 (30 Sep. 2021) paras 120–131; *Ghati Mwita v. Tanzania*, African Court of Human and Peoples' Rights, App. No. 012/2019, Judgment (1 Dec. 2022) para. 79.

1481. *Gozbert Henerico v. Tanzania*, African Court of Human and Peoples' Rights, App. No. 056/2016, Judgment (10 Jan. 2022) para. 148.

1482. *African Commission on Human and Peoples' Rights v. Kenya*, African Court of Human and Peoples' Rights, App. No. 006/2012 (26 May 2017) paras 152, 154.

1483. General Comment No. 3, para. 36; *Mugesera v. Rwanda*, African Court of Human and Peoples' Rights, App. No. 012/2017, Judgment (27 Nov. 2020) para. 103.

1484. *Rashidi v. Tanzania*, African Court of Human and Peoples' Rights, App. No. 009/2015, Judgment (28 Mar. 2019) para. 97.

229. Article 5 of the African Charter protects human dignity, extending to the physical and mental integrity of the individual,[1485] although it can take many forms and needs to be assessed on an individual basis.[1486] It occupies a central place in the African Charter[1487] and is an absolute and fundamental right.[1488] In *Purohit and Moore v. The Gambia*, the Commission defined human dignity as an:

> inherent basic right to which all human beings, regardless of their mental capabilities or disabilities ... are entitled to without discrimination. It is therefore an inherent right which every human being is obliged to respect by all means possible and on the other hand it confers a duty on every human being to respect this right.[1489]

In *Open Society Justice Initiative v. Côte d'Ivoire*, the Commission described it thus:

> Dignity is consubstantial, intrinsic and inherent to the human person ... when the individual loses his dignity, it is his human nature itself which is called into question, to the extent that it is likely to interrogate the validity of continuing to belong to human society.[1490]

The Commission added that the right to enjoy a decent life, as normal and full as possible, lay at the core of the right to human dignity.[1491] It also provides for recognition of an individual's legal status. This denotes the ability to have rights and obligations.[1492] Nationality has been held to be a fundamental component of this right.[1493] The provision additionally prohibits all forms of exploitation and

1485. *Sudan Human Rights Organization and Sudan Centre for Housing Rights and Evictions v. Sudan* Communication Nos 279/03, 296/05, 28th Activity Report 2010, para. 155; *Mugesera v. Rwanda*, African Court of Human and Peoples' Rights, App. No. 012/2017, Judgment (27 Nov. 2020) para. 80. The right to dignity is designed to give the broadest possible protection against physical or psychological abuse, *Hoja Mwendesha v. Rwanda*, African Court of Human and Peoples' Rights, App. No. 032/2016, Judgment (13 Jun. 2023) para. 69.

1486. *Hoja Mwendesha v. Rwanda*, African Court of Human and Peoples' Rights, App. No. 032/2016, Judgment (13 Jun. 2023) para.69.

1487. *Open Society Justice Initiative v. Côte d'Ivoire*, Communication No. 318/06 (2015) para. 139.

1488. *Huri-Laws v. Nigeria*, Communication No. 225/98, 14th Activity Report 2000–2002, para. 41; *Rashidi v. Tanzania*, African Court of Human and Peoples' Rights, App. No. 009/2015, Judgment (28 Mar. 2019) para. 88; *Penessis v. Tanzania*, African Court of Human and Peoples' Rights, App. No. 0013/2015, Judgment (28 Nov. 2019) para. 87.

1489. Communication No. 241/2001, 16th Activity Report 2002–2003, para. 57. The Commission held that branding people with mental illness as 'lunatics' and 'idiots' dehumanized them and denied them dignity, para. 59. *See also Sudan Human Rights Organization and Sudan Centre for Housing Rights and Evictions v. Sudan* Communication Nos 279/03, 296/05, 28th Activity Report, 2010, para. 163.

1490. Communication No. 318/06 (2015) para. 139.

1491. *Purohit and Moore v. The Gambia*, Communication No. 241/2001, 16th Activity Report 2002–2003, para. 61.

1492. *Open Society Justice Initiative v. Côte d'Ivoire*, Communication No. 318/06 (2015) para. 96.

1493. *Ibid.*, para. 97; *Penessis v. Tanzania*, African Court of Human and Peoples' Rights, App. No. 0013/2015, Judgment (28 Nov. 2019) para. 87. In *The Nubian Community in Kenya v. Kenya*, Communication No. 317/06 (2015), para. 151, non-recognition of the legal status of the Nubian

degradation, including slavery, torture, cruel, inhuman or degrading punishment and treatment,[1494] for which there is no justification.[1495] This list is not exhaustive, however. In *International Pen, Constitutional Rights Project, Interights on behalf of Ken Saro-Wiwa Jr. and Civil Liberties Organisation v. Nigeria*, the Commission held that the prohibition in Article 5 included 'not only actions which cause serious physical or psychological suffering, but also actions which humiliate the individual or force him or her to act against his will or conscience'.[1496]

230. The Commission has adopted the definition of torture contained in the UN Convention Against Torture[1497] and has described its prohibition as being a norm *jus cogens.*[1498] It has taken the reasonable stance that the phrase 'cruel, inhuman or degrading punishment and treatment' must be interpreted so as to provide the widest possible protection against abuse.[1499] It has thus observed that '[p]ersonal suffering and indignity can take many forms, and will depend on the particular circumstances of each communication brought before the Commission'.[1500] An analysis of the Commission's jurisprudence can assist in determining what type of ill-treatment can amount to violations of Article 5. Included are beatings,[1501]

community, resulting in discriminatory and arbitrary measures for the acquisition of identity documents, constituted a violation of Art. 5. *See also Conaïde Togla Latondji Akouedenoudje v. Benin*, African Court of Human and Peoples' Rights, App. No. 024/2020 (13 Jun. 2023) paras 77–85.

1494. According to the Commission, the phrase 'cruel, inhuman or degrading punishment and treatment' should be interpreted 'so as to extend to the widest possible protection against abuses, whether physical or mental', *Purohit and Moore v. The Gambia*, Communication No. 241/2001, 16th Activity Report 2002–2003, para. 58. *See also Huri-Laws v. Nigeria*, Communication No. 225/98, 14th Activity Report 2000–2002, para. 40.

1495. Even combating terrorism, *Gunme et al. v. Cameroon,* Communication No. 266/2003, 26th Activity Report 2008–2009, paras 113–114.

1496. Communication Nos 137/94, 139/94, 154/96 and 161/97, 12th Activity Report 1998–1999, para. 79. *See further*, *Egyptian Initiative for Personal Rights and INTERIGHTS v. Egypt*, Communication No. 323/2006 (2011), paras 187–196. In *Huri-Laws v. Nigeria*, Communication No. 225/98, 14th Activity Report 2000–2001, para. 40, the Commission stated that not knowing the reason or duration of detention constituted mental trauma.

1497. Convention Against Torture and Other Cruel, Inhuman or Degrading Treatment or Punishment Art. 1(1) (10 Dec. 1984), 1465 U.N.T.S. 85. *See Sudan Human Rights Organization and Sudan Centre for Housing Rights and Evictions v. Sudan* Communication Nos 279/03, 296/05, 28th Activity Report, 2010, paras 155–156; *Monim Elgak, Osman Hummeida and Amir Suleiman (represented by FIDH and OMCT) v. Sudan*, Communication No. 379/09 (2014) para. 98.

1498. *Mohamed Abdullah Saleh al-Asad v. Djibouti*, Communication No. 383/10 (2014), para. 179.

1499. *Sudan Human Rights Organization and Sudan Centre for Housing Rights and Evictions v. Sudan* Communication Nos 279/03, 296/05, 28th Activity Report, 2010, para. 158.

1500. *Purohit and Moore v. The Gambia*, Communication No. 241/2001, 16th Activity Report 2002–2003, para. 58.

1501. *Krischna Achutan (on behalf of Aleke Banda) v. Malawi*; *Amnesty International on behalf of Orton and Vera Chirwa v. Malawi*, Communication Nos 64/92, 68/92, 78/92, 8th Activity Report 1994–1995; *International Pen, Constitutional Rights Project, Interights on behalf of Ken Saro-Wiwa Jr. and Civil Liberties Organisation v. Nigeria*, Communication Nos 137/94, 139/94, 154/96 and 161/97, 12th Activity Report 1998–1999; *Malawi African Association et al. v. Mauritania*, Communication Nos 54/91, 61/91, 98/93, 164/97–196/97, 210/98, 13th Activity Report 1999–2000; *Rights International v. Nigeria*, Communication No. 215/98, 13th Activity Report 1999–2000, para. 26.

applying physical violence to individuals in the form of public lashings,[1502] rape,[1503] poor conditions of detention or incarceration,[1504] including excessive solitary confinement,[1505] no or poor quality food,[1506] shackling within a cell,[1507] overcrowded or unhygienic cells,[1508] denial of access to medical care,[1509] repeated deportations,[1510] separation from one's family,[1511] forced evictions,[1512] and

---

1502. *Doebbler v. Sudan*, Communication No. 236/2000, 16th Activity Report 2002–2003, para. 42, which the Commission said would be 'tantamount to sanctioning State sponsored torture under the Charter and contrary to the very nature of this human rights treaty'.

1503. *Krischna Achutan (on behalf of Aleke Banda) v. Malawi*; *Amnesty International on behalf of Orton and Vera Chirwa v. Malawi*, Communication Nos 64/92, 68/92, 78/92, 8th Activity Report 1994–1995; *Malawi African Association et al. v. Mauritania*, Communication Nos 54/91, 61/91, 98/93, 164/97–196/97, 210/98, 13th Activity Report 1999–2000).

1504. *Institute for Human Rights and Development in Africa v. Angola*, Communication No. 292/2004, 24th Activity Report 2008, para. 51. In *Zegveld and Ephrem v. Eritrea*, Communication No. 250/2002, 17th Activity Report 2003–2004, para. 55, the Commission expressed the view that 'all detentions must be subject to basic human rights standards. There should be no secret detentions and States must disclose the fact that someone is being detained as well as the place of detention. Furthermore, every detained person must have prompt access to a lawyer and to their families and their rights with regards to physical and mental health must be protected as well as entitlement to proper conditions of detention.' *See Civil Liberties Organisation v. Nigeria*, Communication No. 151/96, 13th Activity Report 1999–2000, para. 25.

1505. *Krischna Achutan (on behalf of Aleke Banda) v. Malawi*; *Amnesty International on behalf of Orton and Vera Chirwa v. Malawi*, Communication Nos 64/92, 68/92, 78/92, 8th Activity Report 1994–1995; *Malawi African Association et al. v. Mauritania*, Communication Nos 54/91, 61/91, 98/93, 164/97–196/97, 210/98, 13th Activity Report 1999–2000; *Zegveld and Ephrem v. Eritrea*, Communication No. 250/2002, 17th Activity Report 2003–2004, para. 55.

1506. *Krischna Achutan (on behalf of Aleke Banda) v. Malawi*; *Amnesty International on behalf of Orton and Vera Chirwa v. Malawi*, Communication Nos 64/92, 68/92, 78/92, 8th Activity Report 1994–1995; *Malawi African Association et al. v. Mauritania*, Communication Nos 54/91, 61/91, 98/93, 164/97–196/97, 210/98, 13th Activity Report 1999–2000); additionally a violation of Art. 4, *Malawi African Association et al. v. Mauritania*, Communication Nos 54/91, 61/91, 98/93, 164/97–196/97, 210/98, 13th Activity Report 1999–2000, para. 120.

1507. *Ibid.*; *International Pen, Constitutional Rights Project, Interights on behalf of Ken Saro-Wiwa Jr. and Civil Liberties Organisation v. Nigeria*, Communication Nos 137/94, 139/94, 154/96 and 161/97, 12th Activity Report 1998–1999.

1508. *Ibid.*

1509. *Ibid.*; additionally, a violation of Art. 4, *International Pen, Constitutional Rights Project, Interights on behalf of Ken Saro-Wiwa Jr. and Civil Liberties Organisation v. Nigeria*, Communication Nos 137/94, 139/94, 154/96 and 161/97, 12th Activity Report 1998–1999, para. 104, where the Commission stated that the State was under a duty not to let persons in their custody deliberately die. Also a violation of the right to health under Art. 17, *Monim Elgak, Osman Hummeida and Amir Suleiman (represented by FIDH and OMCT) v. Sudan*, Communication No. 379/09 (2014) paras 136–137. The Commission has held that there must be prompt access to medical personnel, *Egyptian Initiative for Personal Rights and INTERIGHTS v. Egypt*, Communication No. 334/06 (2011), paras 172–177.

1510. *Modise v. Botswana*, Communication No. 97/93, 14th Activity Report 2000–2001, para. 91.

1511. *Modise v. Botswana*, Communication No. 97/93, 10th Activity Report 1996–1997, para. 32; *Amnesty International et al. v. Sudan*, Communication Nos 48/90, 50/91, 52/91, 89/93 13th Activity Report 1999–2000, para. 54; *The Law Office of Ghazi Suleiman v. Sudan*, Communication Nos 222/98 and 229/99, 16th Activity Report 2002–2003, para. 44.

1512. *Sudan Human Rights Organization and Sudan Centre for Housing Rights and Evictions v. Sudan* Communication Nos 279/03, 296/05, 28th Activity Report 2010, para. 164.

disappearances.[1513] Such acts have also been condemned by the Human Rights Court.[1514] By way of contrast, the prohibition on the possession and use of drugs does not violate human dignity.[1515] Acts that appear to constitute torture include the application of electric shocks and weights to particularly sensitive parts of the body,[1516] 'water boarding',[1517] and being burnt and buried in sand and left to die a slow death.[1518] In addition, a State is prohibited from deporting, expelling or extraditing a person to another State where s/he will or is likely to face torture.[1519] Certainly, the Human Rights Court, in keeping with international standards, has taken the view that cruel, inhuman and degrading punishment and treatment must meet a threshold of 'severity, intention, and severe humiliation'.[1520]

231. As with other protective rights under the African Charter above mentioned, the State is under an obligation to take timely and appropriate steps to deal with allegations of torture. The State is therefore under an obligation to prove that the allegations are unfounded.[1521] In *The Law Office of Ghazi Suleiman v. Sudan*, the Commission stated that it was important for the State 'to take preventive measures', to take legal action proportionate to the abuses against those who have committed torture, to 'search for effective solutions in a transparent legal system', and to investigate allegations of torture.[1522]

232. According to the Human Rights Court, Articles 4 and 5 of the African Charter are mutually reinforcing and protect the rights relating to the integrity of human beings, the purpose of which is to protect life, integrity and dignity.[1523]

233. The right to liberty and security of the person is guaranteed by Article 6 of the African Charter and applies to all deprivations of liberty and not solely in

1513. *Mouvement Burkinabé des Droits de l'Homme et des Peuples v. Burkina Faso*, Communication No. 204/97, 14th Activity Report 2000–2001, para. 44.
1514. *Mugesera v. Rwanda*, African Court of Human and Peoples' Rights, App. No. 012/2017 (27 Nov. 2020) para. 90. In *Rashidi v. Tanzania*, African Court of Human and Peoples' Rights, App. No. 009/2015 (28 Mar. 2019) para. 96, the Human Rights Court held that callous cavity searches constituted a violation of the right to dignity and not to be subjected to degrading treatment.
1515. *Garreth Anver Prince v. South Africa*, Communication No. 255/2002, 18th Activity Report 2002–2003, para. 49.
1516. *Malawi African Association et al. v. Mauritania*, Communication Nos 54/91, 61/91, 98/93, 164/97–196/97, 210/98, 13th Activity Report 1999–2000.
1517. *Ibid.*
1518. *Ibid.*, additionally a violation of Art. 4.
1519. *Mohamed Abdullah Saleh al-Asad v. Djibouti*, Communication No. 383/10 (2014), para. 179.
1520. *Alex Thomas v. Tanzania*, African Court of Human and Peoples' Rights, App. No. 005/2013 (20 Nov. 2015), para. 146; *Mugesera v. Rwanda*, African Court of Human and Peoples' Rights, App. No. 012/2017, Judgment (27 Nov. 2020) para. 81.
1521. *Egyptian Initiative for Personal Rights and INTERIGHTS v. Egypt*, Communication No. 334/06 (2011), paras 169–170.
1522. Communication Nos 222/98 and 229/99, 16th Activity Report 2002–2003, para. 46. *See also Amnesty International et al. v. Sudan*, Communication Nos 48/90, 50/91, 52/91, 89/93, 13th Activity Report 1999–2000, para. 56.
1523. *Ajavon v. Benin*, African Court of Human and Peoples' Rights, App. No. 062/2019 (4 Dec. 2020), para. 166.

relation to the criminal law.[1524] The Commission has defined the right to liberty as 'the right to be free ... freedom from restraint ... in accordance with established law', whereas security of the person includes national and individual security.[1525] As the Commission has indicated, 'this is not an absolute right because the African Charter allows the deprivation of this right through lawful means'.[1526] The Commission has added that deprivation of liberty 'is only acceptable if it is authorised by law and is compatible with the obligations of States Parties under the African Charter'; it does not mean that any domestic law may justify the loss of a person's freedom.[1527] The Human Rights Court has stated similarly that the grounds for deprivation of liberty must be 'clear or reasonable'.[1528] While 'an arrest or detention may be legal according to the letter of domestic law' it may nonetheless be 'arbitrary and therefore illegal by reason of its inappropriate, unjust or unpredictable nature'.[1529] Certainly, what are specifically prohibited are arbitrary arrests and detentions.[1530] In *Purohit and Moore v. The Gambia*, the Commission stated that 'Prohibition against arbitrariness requires among other things that deprivation of liberty shall be under the authority and supervision of persons procedurally and

---

1524. *Purohit and Moore v. The Gambia*, Communication No. 241/2001, 16th Activity Report 2002–2003, para. 64; *Sudan Human Rights Organization and Sudan Centre for Housing Rights and Evictions v. Sudan* Communication Nos 279/03, 296/05, 28th Activity Report, 2010, para. 179.

1525. *Sudan Human Rights Organization and Sudan Centre for Housing Rights and Evictions v. Sudan* Communication Nos 279/03, 296/05, 28th Activity Report, 2010, paras 172–175.

1526. *Zegveld and Ephrem v. Eritrea*, Communication No. 250/2002, 17th Activity Report 2003–2004, para. 52; *Alex Thomas v. Tanzania*, African Court of Human and Peoples' Rights, App. No. 005/2013 (20 November 2015), para. 150. The limitations are subject to 'the strict requirements of legitimacy and legality', *Paulo v. Tanzania*, African Court of Human and Peoples' Rights, App. No. 020/2016 (21 Sep. 2018) para. 61.

1527. *Purohit and Moore v. The Gambia*, Communication No. 241/2001, 16th Activity Report 2002–2003, para. 64. *See Amnesty International et al. v. Sudan*, Communication Nos 48/90, 50/91, 52/91, 89/93, 13th Activity Report 1999–2000, para. 59; *African Commission on Human and Peoples' Rights v. Libya*, African Court of Human and Peoples' Rights, App. No. 002/2013 (3 Jun. 2016) paras 80–83.

1528. *Onyachi and Njoka v. Tanzania*, African Court of Human and Peoples' Rights, App. No. 003/2015 (28 Sep. 2017) para. 134.

1529. *Article 19 v. Eritrea*, Communication No. 275/2003, 22nd Activity Report 2006–2007, para. 93. In *Onyachi and Njoka v. Tanzania*, African Court of Human and Peoples' Rights, App. No. 003/2015 (28 Sep. 2017) para. 130, the Human Rights Court stated that 'arbitrariness also covers deprivation of liberty contrary to the standard of reasonableness, that is, whether it is just, necessary, proportionate and equitable in opposition to unjust, absurd and arbitrary.'

1530. *Constitutional Rights Project, Civil Liberties Organisation and Media Rights Agenda v. Nigeria*, Communication Nos 140/94, 141/94, 145/95, 13th Activity Report 1999–2000, para. 51; *Zegveld and Ephrem v. Eritrea*, Communication No. 250/2002, 17th Activity Report 2003–2004, para. 52; *Institute for Human Rights and Development in Africa v. Angola*, Communication No. 292/2004, 24th Activity Report 2008, para. 54; *Monim Elgak, Osman Hummeida and Amir Suleiman (represented by FIDH and OMCT) v. Sudan*, Communication No. 379/09 (2014) paras 104–107., In *Organisation Mondiale contre la Torture et al. v. Rwanda,* Communication Nos 27/89, 46/91, 49/91, 99/93, 10th Activity Report 1993–1994, para. 28, the Commission held that the arrests and detentions of people on grounds of ethnic origin alone constituted arbitrary deprivation of liberty in clear violation of Art. 6. The Human Rights Court stated that arrest or detention that lacks any legal basis is arbitrary, *Onyachi and Njoka v. Tanzania*, African Court of Human and Peoples' Rights, App. No. 003/2015 (28 Sep. 2017) para. 132.

substantively competent to certify it.'[1531] In *Amnesty International et al. v. Sudan*, the Commission said that Article 6 had to be interpreted 'in such a way as to permit arrests only in the exercise of powers normally granted to the security forces in a democratic society'. The Commission found Article 6 to have been breached because the decree allowed individuals to be arrested 'for vague reasons, and upon suspicion, not proven acts'.[1532] The Human Rights Court has stated that an 'arrest or detention becomes arbitrary if it is not in accordance with the law, lacks clear and reasonable grounds or is conducted in the absence of procedural safeguards against arbitrariness.'[1533]

234. Article 6 fails to specify the guarantees against loss of liberty in any detail. This is regrettable because deprivation of liberty by the State constitutes one of the most serious infringements of a person's fundamental rights, and it would therefore have been appropriate to have enumerated some of these guarantees. Significantly, the Commission has found that the right of habeas corpus comes within the scope of Article 6.[1534] Nevertheless, the Commission has partially addressed this omission by adopting the Resolution on the Right to Recourse Procedure and Fair Trial which reflects accepted international human rights standards,[1535] such as the right to be informed at the time of the arrest for the reasons of the arrest,[1536] the right to be brought promptly before a judicial officer, and the right to challenge the lawfulness of the detention before a court[1537] and to be released if the lawfulness is not established. This soft law instrument has influenced the Commission's jurisprudence which has held that detention without charge or trial for a prolonged period of time constitutes an arbitrary deprivation of liberty.[1538] In *Zegveld and Ephrem v. Eritrea*, the Commission stated that the:

1531. Communication No. 241/2001, 16th Activity Report 2002–2003, para. 65.
1532. Communication Nos 48/90, 50/91, 52/91, 89/93, 13th Activity Report 1999–2000, para. 59.
1533. *Penessis v. Tanzania*, African Court of Human and Peoples' Rights, App. No. 0013/2015, Judgment (28 Nov. 2019) para. 108. They are cumulative conditions, *Onyachi and Njoka v. Tanzania*, African Court of Human and Peoples' Rights, App. No. 003/2015 (28 Sep. 2017) para. 131.
1534. *Constitutional Rights Project and Civil Liberties Organisation v. Nigeria*, Communication Nos 143/95, 150/96, 13th Activity Report 1999–2000, paras 22–27. *See also Constitutional Rights Project v. Nigeria*, Communication No. 153/96, 13th Activity Report 1999–2000, para. 18.
1535. Adopted at the Commission's Eleventh Ordinary Session, 1992, 5th Activity Report, 1991–1992.
1536. *Media Rights Agenda and Constitutional Rights Project v. Nigeria*, Communication Nos 105/93, 128/94, 130/94, 152/96, 12th Activity Report 1998–1999, para. 84; *The Law Office of Ghazi Suleiman v. Sudan*, Communication Nos 222/98 and 229/99, 16th Activity Report 2002–2003, para. 49.
1537. *Krischna Achutan (on behalf of Aleke Banda) v. Malawi*; *Amnesty International on behalf of Orton and Vera Chirwa v. Malawi*, Communication Nos 64/92, 68/92, 78/92, 8th Activity Report 1994–1995, para. 9; *International Pen, Constitutional Rights Project, Interights on behalf of Ken Saro-Wiwa Jr. and Civil Liberties Organisation v. Nigeria*, Communication Nos 137/94, 139/94, 154/96 and 161/9712th Activity Report 1998–1999, para. 83. In *Amnesty International et al. v. Sudan*, Communication Nos 48/90, 50/91, 52/91, 89/93, 13th Activity Report 1999–2000, para. 60, found a breach of Art. 6 in relation to a situation where the 'appeal in the case of arrest lies to the body whose president orders the arrests. Such a remedy provides no guarantee of good administration of justice and is more akin to an appeal for clemency than a judicial appeal'.
1538. *Free Legal Assistance Group v. Zaire*, Communication No. 25/89, 9th Activity Report 1995–1996, para. 42; *Constitutional Rights Project and Civil Liberties Organisation v. Nigeria*, Communication No. 102/93, 12th Activity Report 1998–1999, para. 55; *International Pen, Constitutional*

> lawfulness and necessity of holding someone in custody must be determined by a court or other appropriate judicial authority. The decision to keep a person in detention should be open to review periodically so that the grounds justifying the detention can be assessed. In any event, detention should not continue beyond the period for which the State can provide appropriate justification. Therefore, persons suspected of committing any crime must be promptly charged with legitimate criminal offences and the State should initiate legal proceedings that should comply with fair trial standards.[1539]

Furthermore, the Human Rights Court has had recourse to the guarantees enumerated in Article 9 of the International Covenant on Civil and Political Rights (ICCPR).[1540] It has therefore held that incommunicado detention constitutes a 'gross violation of human rights'.[1541]

235. The right to a fair trial is enshrined in Article 7 of the African Charter,[1542] described by the Commission as 'fundamental tenets of any democratic state'.[1543] The Human Rights Court has described this right as 'the prerogative of anyone who claims to be a victim of violation of their basic rights to go to court.'[1544] It has further identified it as a fundamental human right which 'implies that every individual accused of a crime or an offence shall receive all the guarantees under the procedure'.[1545] It includes the right to be present and to take part in the proceedings.[1546]

Rights Project, Interights on behalf of Ken Saro-Wiwa Jr. and Civil Liberties Organisation v. Nigeria, Communication Nos 137/94, 139/94, 154/96 and 161/97, 12th Activity Report 1998–1999, para. 83; *The Law Office of Ghazi Suleiman v. Sudan*, Communication Nos 222/98 and 229/99, 16th Activity Report 2002–2003, para. 50; *Zegveld and Ephrem v. Eritrea*, Communication No. 250/2002, 17th Activity Report 2003–2004, paras 94–95; *Article 19 v. Eritrea*, Communication No. 275/2003, 22nd Activity Report 2006–2007, para. 94; *Institute for Human Rights and Development in Africa v. Angola*, Communication No. 292/2004, 24th Activity Report 2008, para. 54; *Jean-Marie Atangana Mebara v. Cameroon*, Communication No. 416/12 (2015) para. 119.

1539. *Zegveld and Ephrem v. Eritrea*, Communication No. 250/2002, 17th Activity Report 2003–2004, para. 56.
1540. *African Commission on Human and Peoples' Rights v. Libya*, African Court of Human and Peoples' Rights, App. No. 002/2013 (3 Jun. 2016) paras 82–83.
1541. *Ibid.*, para. 684.
1542. In *Civil Liberties Organisation, Legal Defence Centre, Legal Defence and Assistance Project v. Nigeria*, Communication No. 218/98, 14th Activity Report 2000–2001, para. 27, the Commission described the provisions of Art. 7 as 'non-derogable'. *See also Good v. Botswana*, Communication No. 306/2005, 28th Activity Report 2009–2010, para. 175, where the Commission stated that the right to a fair trial is absolute and cannot be derogated from in any circumstance.
1543. *Gunme et al. v. Cameroon*, Communication No. 266/2003, 26th Activity Report 2008–2009, para. 126.
1544. *Ajavon v. Benin*, African Court of Human and Peoples' Rights, App. No. 062/2019, Judgment (4 Dec. 2020), para. 228.
1545. *African Commission on Human and Peoples' Rights v. Libya*, African Court of Human and Peoples' Rights, App. No. 002/2013 (3 Jun. 2016) para. 89; *Werema and Werema v. Tanzania*, African Court of Human and Peoples' Rights, App. No. 024/2015 (7 Dec. 2018) para. 68. Failure to consider the medical evaluation report of the accused's mental health status has been held to violate the right to a fair trial, *Gozbert Henerico v. Tanzania*, African Court of Human and Peoples' Rights, App. No. 056/2016 (10 Jan. 2022) para. 160.
1546. *Rajabu v. Tanzania*, African Court of Human and Peoples' Rights, App. No. 008/2016 (25 Jun. 2021) paras 78–79.

The right to an effective remedy, although not explicitly mentioned, has been read into Article 7(1). It is composed of three elements, namely, the remedy must be effective, that is, it must be capable of providing redress for a violation of human rights, which implies real access to a court, the scope of the provision must relate to laws, conventions and customs, and the organ competent to secure the defence of human rights must be a judicial body.[1547] Attention should be drawn to the use of the noun 'cause' which suggests a wider application to encompass not only civil actions[1548] and criminal cases but also non-judicial disputes and traditional dispute settlement by village or tribal elders. Thus, in *Purohit and Moore v. The Gambia*, a case concerning the rights of mental health patients, the Commission stated that the 'guarantees in Article 7(1) extend beyond hearings in the normal context of judicial determinations or proceedings'.[1549] According to the Commission in *Zimbabwe Human Rights NGO Forum v. Zimbabwe* Article 7:

> encompasses the right of every individual to access the relevant judicial bodies competent to have their causes heard and be granted adequate relief. If there appears to be any possibility of an alleged victim succeeding at a hearing, the applicant should be given the benefit of the doubt and allowed to have their matter heard.[1550]

Furthermore, the 'right of access to judicial protection to ensure respect for a legal right requires available and effective recourse for the violation of a right protected under the Charter or the Constitution of the country concerned'.[1551] The Commission therefore found that the amnesty law, which prohibited the prosecution of, and set free, perpetrators of politically motivated acts, prevented victims

1547. *Noudehouenou v. Benin*, African Court of Human and Peoples' Rights, App. No. 003/2020, Judgment (4 Dec. 2020), para. 88.
1548. *Kambole v. Tanzania*, African Court of Human and Peoples' Rights, App. No. 018/2018 (15 Jul. 2020) para. 98; *Zimbabwe Lawyers for Human Rights and the Institute for Human Rights and Development v. Zimbabwe*, Communication No. 293/2004, 24th Activity Report 2008, para. 130.
1549. Communication No. 241/2001, 16th Activity Report 2002–2003, para. 72.
1550. Communication No. 245/2002, 21th Activity Report 2005–2006, para. 213; *Good v. Botswana*, Communication No. 306/2005, 28th Activity Report 2009–2010, paras 162–163. The right to be heard is protected by Art. 7, *Bissangou v. Republic of Congo*, Communication No. 253/2002, 21st Activity Report 2005–2006, para. 75. In *Sudan Human Rights Organization and Sudan Centre for Housing Rights and Evictions v. Sudan* Communication Nos 279/03, 296/05, 28th Activity Report, 2010, para. 181, the Commission stated that the right to be heard gives complainants 'unfettered access to a tribunal of competent jurisdiction'. *See also Zimbabwe Lawyers for Human Rights and the Institute for Human Rights and Development (on behalf of Andrew Barclay Meldrum) v. Zimbabwe*, Communication No. 294/2004, 26th Activity Report 2008–2009, paras 106–107, where the deportation of the victim effectively prevented him from being heard. The Commission has held the nullification of court cases in progress by the Nigerian military regime breached Art. 7(1)(a), *Constitutional Rights Project, Civil Liberties Organisation and Media Rights Agenda v. Nigeria*, Communication Nos 140/94, 141/94, 145/95, 13th Activity Report 1999–2000, para. 27.
1551. Communication No. 245/2002, 21th Activity Report 2005–2006, para. 213. In *Bissangou v. Republic of Congo*, Communication No. 253/2002, 21th Activity Report 2005–2006, para. 75, the Commission stated that Art. 7 included the right to the execution of a judgment.

from seeking an effective remedy and eroded their opportunity to have their complaint heard, rendering them helpless and depriving them of justice.[1552] It held that the amnesty law breached Article 7(1) because it:

> foreclosed access to any remedy that might be available to the victims to vindicate their rights, and without putting in place alternative adequate legislative or institutional mechanisms to ensure that perpetrators ... were punished, and victims ... duly compensated or given other avenues to seek effective remedy.[1553]

The Human Rights Court has stated similarly that 'an amnesty law is compatible with human rights only if it is accompanied by restorative measures for the benefit of the victims.'[1554]

236. In a similar vein, the Commission has condemned ouster clauses. In International Pen, Constitutional Rights Project, Interights on behalf of Ken Saro-Wiwa Jr. and Civil Liberties Organisation v. Nigeria, the Commission stated that ouster clauses 'render local remedies non-existent, ineffective or illusory. They create a legal situation in which the judiciary can provide no check on the executive branch of government'.[1555] In Civil Liberties Organization v. Nigeria, the Commission was outspoken in its criticism, describing the ousting of the jurisdiction of the courts as 'an attack of incalculable proportions on Article 7 ... . An attack of this sort on the jurisdiction of the courts is especially invidious because while it is a violation of human rights itself, it permits other violations of rights to go unredressed'.[1556] The Human Rights Court has also been critical of ouster clauses. It curtails the right to be heard and 'divests the judiciary of their role as independent and impartial interpreters of the law.'[1557]

237. The right to a fair trial set out in Article 7 consists of four elements.[1558] First, the right of access or to appeal to a competent national organ.[1559] Accordingly, in *Purohit and Moore v. The Gambia*, the Commission recognized that the

---

1552. Communication No. 245/2002, 21th Activity Report 2005–2006, paras 211, 213.

1553. *Ibid.*, para. 215. *See also Mouvement Ivorien des Droits Humains (MIDH) v. Côte d'Ivoire*, Communication No. 246/2002, 25th Activity Report 2008, para. 98.

1554. *Ajavon v. Benin*, African Court of Human and Peoples' Rights, App. No. 062/2019, Judgment (4 Dec. 2020), para. 238.

1555. Communication Nos 137/94, 139/94, 154/96 and 161/97, 12th Activity Report 1998–1999, para. 76. *See also Good v. Botswana*, Communication No. 306/2005, 28th Activity Report 2009–2010, para. 179.

1556. Communication No. 129/94, 9th Activity Report, 1995–1996, para. 13. *See also Lawyers for Human Rights v. Swaziland*, Communication No. 251/2002, 18th Activity Report 2002–2003. In *Civil Liberties Organisation v. Nigeria*, Communication No. 151/96, 13th Activity Report 1999–2000, para. 17, the Commission recommended an end to the use of ouster clauses.

1557. *Legal & Human Rights Centre and Tanzania Human Rights Defenders Coalition v. Tanzania*, African Court of Human and Peoples' Rights, App. No. 039/2020 (13 Jun. 2023) para. 150.

1558. All of these provisions are mutually dependent or interlinked and infringement of the right to be heard can lead to other violations, *Amnesty International et al. v. Sudan*, Communication Nos 48/90, 50/91, 52/91, 89/93, 13th Activity Report 1999–2000, para. 62; *The Law Office of Ghazi Suleiman v. Sudan*, Communication Nos 222/98 and 229/99, 16th Activity Report 2002–2003,

provision necessitated a legal remedy[1560] and that 'in circumstances where persons are to be detained, such persons should at the very least be presented with the opportunity to challenge the matter of their detention before the competent jurisdictions that should have ruled on their detention'.[1561] Moreover, the Commission has held that the impossibility of 'any avenue of appeal to "competent national organs" in criminal cases' constitutes a clear violation of this provision.[1562] This is imperative where the accused is facing the death penalty.[1563] In fact, the Commission has expressed the view that the right to appeal is a right recognized by international

---

para. 52. The Human Rights Court has stated that the right to be heard, *Onyachi and Njoka v. Tanzania*, African Court of Human and Peoples' Rights, App. No. 003/2015 (28 Sep. 2017) para. 117.

1559. African Charter Art. 7(1)(a);*Kambole v. Tanzania*, African Court of Human and Peoples' Rights, App. No. 018/2018 (15 Jul. 2020) para. 96. In *Amnesty International et al. v. Sudan*, Communication Nos 48/90, 50/91, 52/91, 89/93, 13th Activity Report 1999–2000, para. 37, the Commission described the right of appeal as 'a general and non-derogable principle of international law'. This includes the right to be heard, *Women's Legal Aid Centre (on behalf of Sophia Moto) v. Tanzania*, Communication No. 243/2001, 18th Activity Report 2002–2003, para. 44, and the right to a second hearing, *Groupe de Travail sur les Dossiers Judiciaires Stratégiques v. Democratic Republic of Congo*, Communication No. 259/2002 (2011) para. 75. *See further Egyptian Initiative for Personal Rights and INTERIGHTS v. Egypt*, Communication No. 334/06 (2011), paras 220–222. Denial of a right of access to a national court constitutes a 'definite and inexcusable violation' of Art. 7(1)(a), *Tembani and Freeth v. Angola and Thirteen Others*, Communication No. 409/12 (2013) para. 138.

1560. *See also Ajavon v. Benin*, African Court of Human and Peoples' Rights, App. No. 062/2019, Judgment (4 Dec. 2020), para. 229. In *Zongo and Others v. Burkina Faso*, African Court of Human and Peoples' Rights, App. No. 013/2011 (28 Mar. 2014) para. 156, the Court found that the Respondent had failed to act with due diligence in dealing with the murder of the victim.

1561. Communication No. 241/2001, 16th Activity Report 2002–2003, para. 72. *See also Krischna Achutan (on behalf of Aleke Banda) v. Malawi*; *Amnesty International on behalf of Orton and Vera Chirwa v. Malawi*, Communication Nos 64/92, 68/92, 78/92(1995), para. 9; *Rencontre Africaine pour la Defense des Droits de l'Homme v. Zambia*, Communication No. 71/92, 10th Activity Report, 1996–1997, para. 29; *Union Interafricaine des Droits de l'Homme et al. v. Angola*, Communication No. 159/96, 11th Activity Report 1997–1998, para. 19; *International Pen, Constitutional Rights Project, Interights on behalf of Ken Saro-Wiwa Jr. and Civil Liberties Organisation v. Nigeria*, Communication Nos 137/94, 139/94, 154/96 and 161/97, 12th Activity Report 1998–1999, para. 93; *Amnesty International v. Zambia*, Communication No. 212/98, 12th Activity Report 1998–1999, para. 53; *Institute for Human Rights and Development in Africa v. Angola*, Communication No. 292/2004, 24th Activity Report 2008, para. 58.

1562. *Constitutional Rights Project (in respect of Waheb Akamu, G. Adega and Others) v. Nigeria*, Communication No. 60/91, 8th Activity Report, 1994–1995, para. 7; *Constitutional Rights Project (in respect of Zamani Lakwot and Others) v. Nigeria*, Communication No. 87/93, 8th Activity Report 1994–1995, para. 8; *The Law Office of Ghazi Suleiman v. Sudan*, Communication Nos 222/98 and 229/99, 16th Activity Report 2002–2003, para. 53. *See also Sudan Human Rights Organization and Sudan Centre for Housing Rights and Evictions v. Sudan* Communication Nos 279/03, 296/05, 28th Activity Report, 2010, para. 182. In *Werema and Werema v. Tanzania*, African Court of Human and Peoples' Rights, App. No. 024/2015 (7 Dec. 2018), para. 69, the Human Rights Court stated that the right to be heard does not cease with the completion of appellate proceedings; a mechanism to review findings must exist.

1563. *Civil Liberties Organisation, Legal Defence Centre, Legal Defence and Assistance Project v. Nigeria*, Communication No. 218/98, 14th Activity Report 2000–2001, para. 33; *Forum of Conscience v. Sierra Leone*, Communication No. 223/98, 14th Activity Report 2000–2001, para. 17; *Egyptian Initiative for Personal Rights and INTERIGHTS v. Egypt*, Communication No. 334/06 (2011), para. 221; *Groupe de Travail sur les Dossiers Judiciaires Stratégiques v. Democratic Republic of Congo*, Communication No. 259/2002 (2011) para. 75.

law.[1564] In addition, it is important to note that the Commission has held that the appeal process must be authentic and effective. In *Malawi African Association et al. v. Mauritania*, it found that the appeal court:

> simply confirmed the sentences without considering all the elements of fact and law. Such a practice can not be considered a genuine appeal procedure. For an appeal to be effective, the appellate jurisdiction must, objectively and impartially, consider both the elements of fact and of law that are brought before it.[1565]

In *Amnesty International et al. v. Sudan*, the Commission stated further:

> An effective appeal is one that, subsequent to the hearing by the competent tribunal of first instance, may reasonably lead to a reconsideration of the case by a superior jurisdiction, which requires that the latter should, in this regard, provide all necessary guarantees of good administration of justice.[1566]

This means, for example, that parties should be provided with court records or copies of judgments within a reasonable time in order to pursue an appeal or review of a court judgment.[1567]

238. What constitutes a 'competent organ' in such instances raises another point. The Commission has defined a competent tribunal as one having the power to hear the case by law, having 'jurisdiction over the subject matter and the person, and the trial is being conducted within any applicable time limit prescribed by law'.[1568] One other aspect refers to 'facets such as the expertise of the judges and the inherent justice of the laws under which they operate'.[1569] Although not set out in Article 7, the Human Rights Court has endorsed the finding that the right to a reasoned decision derives from the right to seize a competent organ.[1570]Another includes 'the duty of

---

1564. *Egyptian Initiative for Personal Rights and INTERIGHTS v. Egypt*, Communication No. 323/2006 (2011), para. 220.
1565. Communication Nos 54/91, 61/91, 98/93, 164/97–196/97, 210/98, 13th Activity Report 1999–2000, para. 94.
1566. Communication Nos 48/90, 50/91, 52/91, 89/93, 13th Activity Report 1999–2000, para. 37. *See also Women's Legal Aid Centre (on behalf of Sophia Moto) v. Tanzania*, Communication No. 243/2001, 18th Activity Report 2002–2003, para. 43, where the Commission stated that the principle of natural justice underlies Art. 7(1)(a).
1567. *Alex Thomas v. Tanzania*, African Court of Human and Peoples' Rights, App. No. 005/2013 (20 Nov. 2015), para. 109; *Onyachi and Njoka v. Tanzania*, African Court of Human and Peoples' Rights, App. No. 003/2015 (28 Sep. 2017) paras 118–119.
1568. *Sudan Human Rights Organization and Sudan Centre for Housing Rights and Evictions v. Sudan* Communication Nos 279/03, 296/05, 28th Activity Report, 2010, para. 181; *Good v. Botswana*, Communication No. 306/2005, 28th Activity Report 2009–2010, para. 169.
1569. *Amnesty International et al. v. Sudan*, Communication Nos 48/90, 50/91, 52/91, 89/93, 13th Activity Report 1999–2000, para. 62.
1570. *Mulindahabi v. Rwanda*, African Court of Human and Peoples' Rights, App. No. 004/2017 (26 Jun. 2020) para. 64.

everyone, including the state, to respect and follow' the judgments of the courts.[1571] The Commission has expressed its unhappiness at military courts exercising jurisdiction over civilians.[1572] In *The Law Office of Ghazi Suleiman v. Sudan*, the Commission found that 'the fact that the decisions of the military court are not subject to appeal and that civilians are brought to a military court constitutes a de jure procedural irregularity'.[1573] These elements have been upheld by the Human Rights Court.[1574]

239. Second, the presumption of innocence,[1575] which the Commission has described as 'a fundamental principle which protects everybody against being treated by public officials as if they were guilty of an offence ... No guilt should be presumed until a charge has been proved beyond reasonable doubt. It is, therefore, a duty for all public authorities to refrain from prejudging the outcome of a trial'.[1576] The Human Rights Court has stated that the presumption of innocence applies to the entire procedure, from arrest to the delivery of the final judicial decision.[1577] It is binding not only on the criminal court but also on all other judicial, quasi-judicial and administrative authorities.[1578] Additionally, the prosecution has the burden of proof beyond a reasonable doubt, and any doubt should benefit the accused.[1579] In *Malawi African Association et al. v. Mauritania*, the Commission found that this presumption had been violated when the presiding judge had

---

1571. *Media Rights Agenda and Constitutional Rights Project v. Nigeria*, Communication Nos 105/93, 128/94, 130/94, 152/96, 12th Activity Report 1998–1999, para. 62.
1572. *Gunme et al. v. Cameroon*, Communication No. 266/2003, 26th Activity Report 2008–2009, paras 127–128; *Koso and Others v. Democratic Republic of Congo*, Communication No. 281/2003, 26th Activity Report 2008–2009, paras 83–87; *Egyptian Initiative for Personal Rights and INTERIGHTS v. Egypt*, Communication No. 334/06 (2011), paras 199–200.
1573. Communication Nos 222/98 and 229/99, 16th Activity Report 2002–2003, para. 53. *See also Civil Liberties Organisation v. Nigeria*, Communication No. 151/96, 13th Activity Report 1999–2000, paras 2, 22, where the decisions of a special military tribunal could not be appealed but was only subject to confirmation by the highest decision-making body of the Nigerian military regime, the Provisional Ruling Council.
1574. *Mallya v. Tanzania*, African Court of Human and Peoples' Rights, App. No. 018/2015 (26 Sep. 2019), para. 43.
1575. African Charter Art. 7(1)(b); *Haregewoin Gabre-Selassie and IHRDA (on behalf of former Dergue officials) v. Ethiopia*, Communication No. 301/05 (2011) paras 184–194. *See Civil Liberties Organisation, Legal Defence Centre, Legal Defence and Assistance Project v. Nigeria*, Communication No. 218/98, 14th Activity Report 2000–2001, para. 40, where the Commission went on to state that this extended to the right to silence, i.e., the right not to incriminate oneself, nor to testify against oneself, nor to confess under duress.
1576. *Haregewoin Gabre-Selassie and IHRDA (on behalf of former Dergue officials) v. Ethiopia*, Communication No. 301/05 (2011) para. 190; *Tsikata v. Ghana*, Communication No. 322/2006 (2014), paras 116–119. *See also Ingabire Victoire Umuhoza v. Rwanda*, African Court of Human and Peoples' Rights, App. No. 003/2014, Judgment (24 Nov. 2017) para. 81. In *Jean-Marie Atangana Mebara v. Cameroon*, Communication No. 416/12 (2015) paras 97–103, the Commission stated that the decision of the trial or appeals courts must not be influenced by members of the executive.
1577. *Noudehouenou v. Benin*, African Court of Human and Peoples' Rights, App. No. 003/2020, Judgment (4 Dec. 2020), para. 100.
1578. *Ibid.*, para. 101.
1579. *Legal & Human Rights Centre and Tanzania Human Rights Defenders Coalition v. Tanzania*, African Court of Human and Peoples' Rights, App. No. 039/2020 (13 Jun. 2023) para. 123.

declared that the refusal of the accused to defend themselves was tantamount to an admission of guilt.[1580] The same conclusion was reached with regard to the fact that the court had based its verdict on statements coerced from the accused by the police.[1581] The Commission has further held that negative pretrial publicity by the State aimed at casting guilt on the victims before a competent court has had the opportunity of ruling on the matter violates the presumption of innocence.[1582] The same applies to the media.[1583] The Human Rights Court has stated similarly that the presumption of innocence is 'violated if, without establishing the judicial guilt of an individual, a judicial or administrative decision suggests that they are guilty. In the same vein, presumption of innocence is violated when authorities, including judicial authorities, undertake acts that lead the public to believe in the guilt of accused persons.'[1584] Detention on mere suspicion also violates this provision,[1585] as does prolonged imprisonment without conviction.[1586] The Human Rights Court has held that criminal sentences must be based on 'strong and credible evidence'.[1587]

240. Third, the right to a defence, including the right to be defended by counsel of choice.[1588] The Commission stressed the importance of this right in *Amnesty International et al. v. Sudan*, where doubts existed as to whether the accused could choose their own lawyers and whether the tribunal could bar certain lawyers from the court. The Commission stated that:

1580. Communication Nos 54/91, 61/91, 98/93, 164/97–196/97, 210/98, 13th Activity Report 1999–2000, para. 95.
1581. *Ibid.*; *Egyptian Initiative for Personal Rights and INTERIGHTS v. Egypt*, Communication No. 334/06 (2011), paras 212–219.
1582. *International Pen, Constitutional Rights Project, Interights on behalf of Ken Saro-Wiwa Jr. and Civil Liberties Organisation v. Nigeria*, Communication Nos 137/94, 139/94, 154/96 and 161/97, 12th Activity Report 1998–1999, para. 96; *Media Rights Agenda v. Nigeria*, Communication No. 224/98, 14th Activity Report 2000–2001, paras 47–48; *The Law Office of Ghazi Suleiman v. Sudan*, Communication Nos 222/98 and 229/99, 16th Activity Report 2002–2003, paras 54, 56.
1583. *Tsikata v. Ghana*, Communication No. 322/2006 (2014), para. 116.
1584. *Conaïde Togla Latondji Akouedenoudje v. Benin*, African Court of Human and Peoples' Rights, App. No. 024/2020 (13 Jun. 2023) para. 64.
1585. *Annette Pagnoulle (on behalf of Abdoulaye Mazou) v. Cameroon*, Communication No. 39/90, 10th Activity Report 1996–1997, para. 21.
1586. *Haregewoin Gabre-Selassie and IHRDA (on behalf of former Dergue officials) v. Ethiopia*, Communication No. 301/05 (2011) para. 209.
1587. *Mohamed Abubakri v. Tanzania*, African Court of Human and Peoples' Rights, App. No. 007/2013 (3 Jun. 2016), para. 174; *Werema and Werema v. Tanzania*, African Court of Human and Peoples' Rights, App. No. 024/2015 (7 Dec. 2018), paras 59–60.
1588. African Charter Art. 7(1)(c). The right to defence applies at each stage of the criminal proceedings and implies the accused's presence throughout, *Avocats Sans Frontières (on behalf of Gaëtan Bwampamye) v. Burundi*, Communication No. 231/99, 14th Activity Report 2000–2001, para. 28; *Egyptian Initiative for Personal Rights and INTERIGHTS v. Egypt*, Communication No. 334/06 (2011), para. 209; *African Commission on Human and Peoples' Rights v. Libya*, African Court of Human and Peoples' Rights, App. No. 002/2013 (3 Jun. 2016) paras 89, 93; *Alex Thomas v. Tanzania*, African Court of Human and Peoples' Rights, App. No. 005/2013 (20 Nov. 2015), para. 96. It has been held that legal representation must be effective, *Amini Juma v. Tanzania*, African Court of Human and Peoples' Rights, App. No. 024/2016 (30 Sep. 2021) para. 91; *Ghati Mwita v. Tanzania*, African Court of Human and Peoples' Rights, App. No. 012/2019, Judgment (1 Dec. 2022) para. 123.

> the right to freely choose one's counsel is essential to the assurance of a fair trial. To give the tribunal the power to veto the choice of counsel of defendants is an unacceptable infringement of this right. There should be an objective system for licensing advocates, so that qualified advocates cannot be barred from appearing in particular cases. It is essential that the national bar be an independent body which regulates legal practitioners, and that the tribunals themselves not adopt this role, which will infringe the right to defence.[1589]

Where the accused cannot afford legal counsel, the Commission has urged that they be represented by counsel at state expense.[1590] In such a circumstance, the right to counsel of choice is not absolute.[1591] The Commission has stressed that the right to legal assistance is a fundamental element of the right to a fair trial.[1592] Indeed, the Human Rights Court has emphasized that legal aid is a right designed to ensure a fair judicial process and avoid miscarriages of justice and should be available automatically in appropriate cases.[1593] The Commission found violations of this provision in *Krischna Achutan (on behalf of Aleke Banda) v. Malawi*; *Amnesty International on behalf of Orton and Vera Chirwa v. Malawi*, where the applicants had been tried without counsel,[1594] *Constitutional Rights Project (in respect of Zamani Lakwot) v. Nigeria*, where the defence counsel had been harassed and intimidated into resigning from a trial,[1595] *Media Rights Agenda and Constitutional*

1589. *Amnesty International et al. v. Sudan*, Communication Nos 48/90, 50/91, 52/91, 89/93, 13th Activity Report 1999–2000, para. 64. *See also Civil Liberties Organisation v. Nigeria*, Communication No. 151/96, 13th Activity Report 1999–2000, para. 24; *Groupe de Travail sur les Dossiers Judiciaires Stratégiques v. Democratic Republic of Congo*, Communication No. 259/2002 (2011) para. 81.
1590. *Civil Liberties Organisation, Legal Defence Centre, Legal Defence and Assistance Project v. Nigeria*, Communication No. 218/98, 14th Activity Report 2000–2001, para. 29; *Groupe de Travail sur les Dossiers Judiciaires Stratégiques v. Democratic Republic of Congo*, Communication No. 259/2002 (2011) para. 82.
1591. *Evodius Rutechura v. Tanzania*, African Court of Human and Peoples' Rights, App. No. 004/2016 (26 Feb. 2021), para. 73.
1592. *Avocats Sans Frontiéres (on behalf of Gaëtan Bwampamye) v. Burundi*, Communication No. 231/9914th Activity Report 2000–2001, para. 30. *See* Rule 126 which authorizes the to facilitate access to free legal representation and free legal aid.
1593. *Alex Thomas v. Tanzania*, African Court of Human and Peoples' Rights, App. No. 005/2013 (20 Nov. 2015), paras 114–124; *Wilfred Onyango Nganyi & 9 Others v. Tanzania*, African Court of Human and Peoples' Rights, App. No. 006/2013 (18 Mar. 2016), paras 156–184; *Mohamed Abubakri v. Tanzania*, African Court of Human and Peoples' Rights, App. No. 007/2013 (3 Jun. 2016), paras 138–139; *Mugesera v. Rwanda*, African Court of Human and Peoples' Rights, App. No. 012/2017, Judgment (27 Nov. 2020) para. 52. In 2016 the AU adopted a treaty establishing a Fund to provide legal assistance to indigent applicants before AU human rights organs, Statute on the Establishment of the Legal Aid Fund of Human Rights Organs of the African Union (30 Jan. 2016), not yet in force.
1594. Communication Nos 64/92, 68/92, 78/92, 8th Activity Report 1994–1995, para. 10.
1595. Communication No. 87/93, 8th Activity Report, 1994–1995, para. 9. *See also International Pen, Constitutional Rights Project, Interights on behalf of Ken Saro-Wiwa Jr. and Civil Liberties Organisation v. Nigeria*, Communication Nos 137/94, 139/94, 154/96 and 161/97, 12th Activity Report 1998–1999, para. 101.

Rights Project v. Nigeria, where the applicant had been denied access to a lawyer,[1596] and *Civil Liberties Organisation, Legal Defence Centre, Legal Defence and Assistance Project v. Nigeria*, where the accused had been assigned military lawyers.[1597]

241. Although not expressly spelt out in the provision, it has been established that the right to a fair trial includes other guarantees, including the right to prepare adequately one's defence.[1598] In *William A. Courson v. Equatorial Guinea*, the Commission held that the right to defence 'includes the right to be informed of the charges … as well as the evidence of the said charges; all sorts of elements required to prepare his defence', and that failure to bring those elements to the knowledge of the accused resulted in a breach of Article 7(1)(c).[1599] Access to case files and documents is also an essential factor.[1600] There is a right to call witnesses,[1601] although subject to certain limitations.[1602] In a number of cases, the evidence relied upon to secure convictions has been challenged. The Human Rights Court has stated on a number of occasions that while it is not its role to investigate the evidence used in domestic proceedings, it may ascertain in general whether consideration of the evidence by the municipal courts is in conformity with the requirements of a fair trial.[1603] Manifest errors in national proceedings have also been taken to undermine

1596. Communication Nos 105/93, 128/94, 130/94, 152/96, 12th Activity Report 1998–1999, para. 88. *See also Constitutional Rights Project and Civil Liberties Organisation v. Nigeria*, Communication Nos 143/95, 150/96, 13th Activity Report 1999–2000, para. 29.

1597. Communication No. 218/98, 14th Activity Report 2000–2001, para. 31.

1598. *See African Commission on Human and Peoples' Rights v. Libya*, African Court of Human and Peoples' Rights, App. No. 002/2013 (3 Jun. 2016) para. 94; *Mugesera v. Rwanda*, African Court of Human and Peoples' Rights, App. No. 012/2017, Judgment (27 Nov. 2020) paras 45–46. It includes the chance to examine pleadings concerning the case, *Oumar Mariko v. Mali*, African Court of Human and Peoples' Rights, App. No. 029/2018, Judgment (24 Mar. 2022) para. 53.

1599. Communication No. 144/95, 11th Activity Report, 1997–1998, para. 21. *See also International Pen, Constitutional Rights Project, Interights on behalf of Ken Saro-Wiwa Jr. and Civil Liberties Organisation v. Nigeria*, Communication Nos 137/94, 139/94, 154/96 and 161/97, 12th Activity Report 1998–1999, para. 101. In *Mohamed Abubakri v. Tanzania*, African Court of Human and Peoples' Rights, App. No. 007/2013 (3 Jun. 2016), para. 158, the Human Rights Court stated that the right to be informed of the charges was a 'key element' of the right to a fair trial. In *Tsikata v. Ghana*, Communication No. 322/2006 (2014), para. 138, the Commission explained that the State 'must clearly outline the arraigned acts and the law under which the accused … is being charged.'

1600. *Jean-Marie Atangana Mebara v. Cameroon*, Communication No. 416/12 (2015) paras 104–109; *African Commission on Human and Peoples' Rights v. Libya*, African Court of Human and Peoples' Rights, App. No. 002/2013 (3 Jun. 2016) para. 94; *Ingabire Victoire Umuhoza v. Rwanda*, African Court of Human and Peoples' Rights, App. No. 003/2014, Judgment (24 Nov. 2017) para. 98; *Mulindahabi v. Rwanda*, African Court of Human and Peoples' Rights, App. No. 004/2017 (26 Jun. 2020) para. 58.

1601. *Ingabire Victoire Umuhoza v. Rwanda*, African Court of Human and Peoples' Rights, App. No. 003/2014, Judgment (24 Nov. 2017) paras 93, 98.

1602. *Tsikata v. Ghana*, Communication No. 322/2006 (2014), paras 144–145.

1603. *See, e.g.*, *Rajabu v. Tanzania*, African Court of Human and Peoples' Rights, App. No. 008/2016 (25 Jun. 2021), paras 69–70.

the right to a fair trial.[1604] Another guarantee is the right to equal treatment. In *Avocats Sans Frontiéres (on behalf of Gaëtan Bwampamye) v. Burundi*, the Commission explained what this right meant, especially in criminal cases. It stated that first:

> both the defence and the public prosecutor shall have equal opportunity to prepare and present their pleas and indictment during the trial. Simply put, they should argue their cases before the jurisdiction on an equal footing. Secondly it entails the equal treatment of all accused persons by jurisdictions charged with trying them. This does not mean that identical treatment should be meted to all accused. The idea here is the principle that when objective facts are alike, the response of the judiciary should also be similar. There is a breach of the principle of equality if judicial or administrative decisions are applied in a discriminatory manner.[1605]

242. And fourth, the right to a trial within a reasonable time by an impartial court or tribunal,[1606] said by the Commission to be a cardinal element.[1607] Insofar as the concept of 'a reasonable time' is concerned, in the absence of a standard period[1608] three criteria have been adopted: the complexity of the case, the conduct of the applicant and other parties, and the conduct of the relevant national or judicial authorities.[1609] It has proceeded to state that in 'a criminal case, especially one in which the accused is detained until trial, the trial must be held with all possible speed to minimize the negative effects on the life of a person who, after all, may be

1604. *Alex Thomas v. Tanzania*, African Court of Human and Peoples' Rights, App. No. 005/2013 (20 Nov. 2015), paras 125–131. In *Mohamed Abubakri v. Tanzania*, African Court of Human and Peoples' Rights, App. No. 007/2013 (3 Jun. 2016), para. 194, the Court opined that alibi claims had to be properly investigated.

1605. Communication No. 231/99, 14th Activity Report 2000–2001, para. 28. The Human Rights Court has endorsed the principle of equality of arms, *Werema and Werema v. Tanzania*, African Court of Human and Peoples' Rights, App. No. 024/2015 (7 Dec. 2018), para. 77.

1606. African Charter Art. 7(1)(d). This right also applies to the appeals process, *Alex Thomas v. Tanzania*, African Court of Human and Peoples' Rights, App. No. 005/2013 (20 Nov. 2015), paras 100–110; *Mallya v. Tanzania*, African Court of Human and Peoples' Rights, App. No. 018/2015 (26 Sep. 2019), para. 49.

1607. *Haregewoin Gabre-Selassie and IHRDA (on behalf of former Dergue officials) v. Ethiopia*, Communication No. 301/05 (2011) para. 215; *Rajabu v. Tanzania*, African Court of Human and Peoples' Rights, App. No. 008/2016 (25 Jun. 2021), para. 92. In *Tsikata v. Ghana*, Communication No. 322/2006 (2014), para. 146, the Commission stated that this was an absolute right with no exceptions. In *Wilfred Onyango Nganyi & 9 Others v. Tanzania*, African Court of Human and Peoples' Rights, App. No. 006/2013 (18 Mar. 2016), para. 127, the Court stressed the importance of a 'speedy judicial process'.

1608. *Wilfred Onyango Nganyi & 9 Others v. Tanzania*, African Court of Human and Peoples' Rights, App. No. 006/2013 (18 Mar. 2016), para. 135.

1609. *Article 19 v. Eritrea*, Communication No. 275/2003 (2007), paras 97–100; *Wilfred Onyango Nganyi & 9 Others v. Tanzania*, African Court of Human and Peoples' Rights, App. No. 006/2013 (18 Mar. 2016), paras 136–155; *Rashidi v. Tanzania*, African Court of Human and Peoples' Rights, App. No. 009/2015, Judgment (28 Mar. 2019) para. 107; *Mallya v. Tanzania*, African Court of Human and Peoples' Rights, App. No. 018/2015 (26 Sep. 2019), para. 50.

innocent.'[1610] It has therefore held that indefinite detention,[1611] detention without trial,[1612] unclear indictments,[1613] or the passage of a number of years before the matter is brought to trial breach this provision.[1614] Certainly, the Human Rights Court has held that any individual arrested or detained for a criminal offence must be brought before a judge with 'minimum delay'.[1615] In relation to civil actions, a case pending for more than five years was deemed in breach of this provision.[1616]

243. The requirement of 'an impartial court or tribunal' is considered one of the 'pillars' of a fair trial.[1617] This Commission is interlinked with Article 26 of the African Charter which guarantees the independence of the judiciary.[1618] As a general principle, the Commission has stated that it covers the subjective impartiality of a

---

1610. *Constitutional Rights Project v. Nigeria*, Communication No. 153/96, 13th Activity Report 1999–2000, para. 19; *Haregewoin Gabre-Selassie and IHRDA (on behalf of former Dergue officials) v. Ethiopia*, Communication No. 301/05 (2011) para. 215. The Human Rights Court has held that where a person is in custody that State has an obligation to ensure that the proceedings are handled with due diligence and expeditiously, *Armand Guehi v. Tanzania (Côte d'Ivoire intervening)*, African Court of Human and Peoples' Rights, App. No. 001/2015, Judgment (7 Dec. 2018) para. 124.
1611. *Krischna Achutan (on behalf of Aleke Banda) v. Malawi*; *Amnesty International on behalf of Orton and Vera Chirwa v. Malawi*, Communication Nos 64/92, 68/92, 78/92, 8th Activity Report 1994–1995, para. 9. In *Sir Dawda K. Jawara v. Gambia*, Communication Nos 147/95 and 149/96, 13th Activity Report 1999–2000, para. 61, the Minister was authorized to extend the period of detention *ad infinitum*.
1612. *Constitutional Rights Project and Civil Liberties Organisation v. Nigeria*, Communication Nos 143/95, 150/96, 13th Activity Report 1999–2000, para. 28.
1613. *Haregewoin Gabre-Selassie and IHRDA (on behalf of former Dergue officials) v. Ethiopia*, Communication No. 301/05 (2011) paras 231–232.
1614. *Annette Pagnoulle (on behalf of Abdoulaye Mazou) v. Cameroon*, Communication No. 39/90, 10th Activity Report 1996–1997, para. 19 (two years); *Alhassan Abubakar v. Ghana*, Communication No. 103/93, 10th Activity Report 1996–1997, para. 12 (seven years); *Constitutional Rights Project v. Nigeria*, Communication No. 153/96, 13th Activity Report 1999–2000, para. 20 (two years); *Mouvement Burkinabé des Droits de l'Homme et des Peuples v. Burkina Faso*, Communication No. 204/97, 14th Activity Report 2000–2001, para. 40 (fifteen years); *Haregewoin Gabre-Selassie and IHRDA (on behalf of former Dergue officials) v. Ethiopia*, Communication No. 301/05 (2011) paras 233–239; *Jean-Marie Atangana Mebara v. Cameroon*, Communication No. 416/12 (2015) paras 113–115. *See also Odjouoriby Cossi Paul v. Benin*, Communication No. 199/97, 17th Activity Report, 2003–2004. Ten years has been held unreasonable, *Richard v. Tanzania*, African Court of Human and Peoples' Rights, App. No. 035/2016, Judgment (2 Dec. 2021) paras 44–50; in *Kouadio Kobena Fory v. Côte d'ivoire*, African Court of Human and Peoples' Rights, App. No. 034/2017, Judgment (2 Dec. 2021), the period in question was twenty years.
1615. *African Commission on Human and Peoples' Rights v. Libya*, African Court of Human and Peoples' Rights, App. No. 002/2013 (3 Jun. 2016) para. 91. In *Rajabu v. Tanzania*, African Court of Human and Peoples' Rights, App. No. 008/2016 (25 Jun. 2021), para. 92, the Human Rights Court stated that undue prolongation of a case at appellate level breaches Art. 7(1)(d).
1616. *Association of Victims of Post Electoral Violence & INTERIGHTS v. Cameroon*, Communication No. 272/2003, 27th Activity Report 2009, para. 130.
1617. *Mohamed Abubakri v. Tanzania*, African Court of Human and Peoples' Rights, App. No. 007/2013 (3 Jun. 2016), para. 110.
1618. *Zimbabwe Lawyers for Human Rights and the Institute for Human Rights and Development v. Zimbabwe*, Communication No. 293/2004, 24th Activity Report 2008, paras 138–41; *Koso and Others v. Democratic Republic of Congo*, Communication No. 281/2003, 26th Activity Report 2008–2009, paras 76–77; *Egyptian Initiative for Personal Rights and INTERIGHTS v. Egypt*,

judge and the objective impartiality of a court.[1619] The Human Rights Court has stated that it entails the absence of bias or prejudice in the consideration of a case.[1620] The Commission has deemed the following criteria to be essential elements: to be established by law with adjudicative functions on the basis of the rule of law; no interference with the judicial function; no review of decisions except through judicial review; independence from the executive branch which the government must respect; and decisions based on objective evidence, arguments and facts before it.[1621] The fact that judicial appointments may be made by the executive does not in itself undermine the independence of the judiciary but it depends on context. If a judicial appointment is made seemingly to deal with a specific case, the appearance of independence and impartiality is brought into question.[1622] In *Lawyers for Human Rights v. Swaziland*, the Commission held that vesting judicial power in the king, including the authority to appoint and dismiss judges, not only violated Article 7 but also compromised the independence of the judiciary guaranteed by Article 26 of the African Charter.[1623] It has taken the view that such courts or tribunals must meet judicial standards.[1624] It has therefore held that military tribunals with jurisdiction over civilians cannot be considered impartial, stating that their 'composition alone, creates the appearance, if not actual lack of impartiality'.[1625] Similarly, review panels composed of presidential appointees and representatives of the executive branch,[1626] or special tribunals.[1627]

Communication No. 323/2006 (2011), paras 216–218; *Tembani and Freeth v. Angola and Thirteen Others*, Communication No. 409/12 (2013) para. 144; *Ajavon v. Benin*, African Court of Human and Peoples' Rights, Judgment, App. No. 062/2019 (4 Dec. 2020) para. 278.

1619. *Jean-Marie Atangana Mebara v. Cameroon*, Communication No. 416/12 (2015) para. 116. Procedures should be in place to govern the recusal of judges, *Oumar Mariko v. Mali*, African Court of Human and Peoples' Rights, App. No. 029/2018, Judgment (24 Mar. 2022) paras 62–65.

1620. *Mulindahabi v. Rwanda*, African Court of Human and Peoples' Rights, App. No. 004/2017 (26 Jun. 2020) para. 70. It proceeded to state that bias cannot be presumed and must be indisputably proven by the party alleging it, *ibid.*

1621. *Egyptian Initiative for Personal Rights and INTERIGHTS v. Egypt*, Communication No. 323/2006 (2011), para. 223; *Egyptian Initiative for Personal Rights and INTERIGHTS v. Egypt*, Communication No. 334/06 (2011), para. 197.

1622. In *Tsikata v. Ghana*, Communication No. 322/2006 (2014), paras 158–159, the reconstitution of the Supreme Court panel suggested tacit interference with its independence. *See also Mugesera v. Rwanda*, African Court of Human and Peoples' Rights, App. No. 012/2017, Judgment (27 Nov. 2020) para. 71.

1623. Communication No. 251/2002, 18th Activity Report 2002–2003, para. 54; *Amnesty International et al. v. Sudan*, Communication Nos 48/90, 50/91, 52/91, 89/93, 13th Activity Report 1999–2000, para. 69.

1624. *Constitutional Rights Project v. Nigeria*, Communication No. 153/96, 13th Activity Report 1999–2000, para. 15; *Egyptian Initiative for Personal Rights and INTERIGHTS v. Egypt*, Communication No. 334/06 (2011), paras 206–207. According to the Human Rights Court, to ensure impartiality, a court must offer sufficient guarantees to exclude any legitimate doubt, *Woyome v.* Ghana, African Court of Human and Peoples' Rights, App. No. 001/2017, Judgment (28 Jun. 2017) para. 128.

1625. *Constitutional Rights Project (in respect of Waheb Akamu, G. Adega and Others) v. Nigeria*, Communication No. 60/91, 8th Activity Report, 1994–1995, para. 8; *Constitutional Rights Project (in respect of Zamani Lakwot) v. Nigeria*, Communication No. 87/93, 8th Activity Report, 1994–1995, para. 10; *Amnesty International et al. v. Sudan*, Communication Nos 48/90, 50/91,

244. Article 7(2) of the African Charter enshrines the principle of non-retroactivity of the criminal law and criminal penalties.[1628] In addition, punishment is declared to be personal and may only be imposed on the offender.[1629] In *Media Rights Agenda and Constitutional Rights Project v. Nigeria*, the Commission expressed what it believed was at the core of this principle. It stated that:

> Article 7(2) must be read to prohibit not only condemnation and infliction of punishment for acts which did not constitute crimes at the time they were committed, but retroactivity itself. It is expected that citizens must take the laws seriously. If laws change with retroactive effect, the rule of law is undermined since individuals cannot know at any moment if their actions are legal. For a law-abiding citizen, this is a terrible uncertainty, regardless of the likelihood of eventual punishment.

The Commission was underwhelmed at the State's defence that the retroactive law was not actually enforced, declaring that, 'Potential prosecution is a serious threat. An unjust but unenforced law undermines … the sanctity in which the law should be held.'[1630]

245. It should be observed that Article 7 omits a number of internationally accepted express elements of a fair trial, although some are listed in the Resolution

---

52/91, 89/93, 13th Activity Report 1999–2000, para. 68; *Centre for Free Speech v. Nigeria*, Communication No. 206/97, 13th Activity Report 1999–2000, paras 15–16; *Malawi African Association et al. v. Mauritania*, Communication Nos 54/91, 61/91, 98/93, 164/97–196/97, 210/98, 13th Activity Report 1999–2000, para. 98; *The Law Office of Ghazi Suleiman v. Sudan*, Communication Nos 222/98 and 229/99, 16th Activity Report 2002–2003, paras 61–67; *Egyptian Initiative for Personal Rights and INTERIGHTS v. Egypt*, Communication No. 334/06 (2011), paras 199–200. In *Media Rights Agenda v. Nigeria*, Communication No. 224/98, 14th Activity Report 2000–2001, para. 60, the breach was caused by the fact that the members of the tribunal were serving military officers with little or no knowledge of the law. Compare *Civil Liberties Organisation, Legal Defence Centre, Legal Defence and Assistance Project v. Nigeria*, Communication No. 218/98, 14th Activity Report 2000–2001, para. 44, where the Commission expressed the view that military tribunals per se were not contrary to the terms of the African Charter if they met the requirements of fairness, openness, justice, independence and due process.

1626. *Constitutional Rights Project v. Nigeria*, Communication No. 153/96, 13th Activity Report 1999–2000, para. 15. In *Sir Dawda K. Jawara v. Gambia*, Communication Nos 147/95 and 149/96, 13th Activity Report 1999–2000, para. 61, the Commission found that the discretion vested in the Minister to extend detention 'will render favour rather than vindicating a right'.

1627. *Civil Liberties Organisation v. Nigeria*, Communication No. 151/96, 13th Activity Report 1999–2000, para. 21.

1628. *Civil Liberties Organization in respect of Nigerian Bar Association v. Nigeria*, Communication No. 101/93, 8th Activity Report 1994–1995, para. 12; *Sir Dawda K. Jawara v. Gambia*, Communication Nos 147/95 and 149/96, 13th Activity Report 1999–2000, para. 63; *Tsikata v. Ghana*, Communication No. 322/2006 (2014), para. 128; *Ingabire Victoire Umuhoza v. Rwanda*, African Court of Human and Peoples' Rights, App. No. 003/2014, Judgment (24 Nov. 2017) paras 108–109.

1629. *See Mohamed Abubakri v. Tanzania*, African Court of Human and Peoples' Rights, App. No. 007/2013 (3 Jun. 2016), para. 105.

1630. Communication Nos 105/93, 128/94, 130/94, 152/96, 12th Activity Report 1998–1999, paras 59–60.

on the Right to Recourse Procedure and Fair Trial,[1631] but misgivings over their omission has been lessened by the fact that the Commission considers them as implicit constituents of the right. These include the requirement that cases be heard in public,[1632] the right to examine witnesses, the right to be present at one's trial, the right not to be retried according to the principle of *ne bis in idem*, the right to understand the charges,[1633] the right to be informed promptly of any charges,[1634] and the right to the free assistance of an interpreter in court.[1635]

246. Article 8 of the African Charter protects freedom of conscience, the profession and the free practice of religion. The freedom of conscience and of religion allows people to gather together to worship, to establish and maintain places of worship, and to celebrate ceremonies in connection thereto.[1636] The Commission has accepted the symbiotic relationship between practice and religious freedom.[1637] While it has stated that while the right to hold religious beliefs is absolute, the right to act on those beliefs is not since the latter right must sometimes yield to the overriding interests of society, such as protecting the health, welfare, and safety of children.[1638] However, any restriction 'must be based on exceptionally good reasons',

1631. Adopted at the Commission's Eleventh Ordinary Session, 1992, 5th Activity Report, 1991–1992. *See Lawyers for Human Rights v. Swaziland*, Communication No. 251/2002, 18th Activity Report 2002–2003, para. 53.

1632. In *Civil Liberties Organisation, Legal Defence Centre, Legal Defence and Assistance Project v. Nigeria*, Communication No. 218/98, 14th Activity Report 2000–2001, paras 35–39, the Commission held that hearings in public were an important safeguard and that holding trials in secret therefore violated the right to a fair hearing enshrined in the African Charter Art. 7. *See also Media Rights Agenda v. Nigeria*, Communication No. 224/98, 14th Activity Report 2000–2001, paras 50–53.

1633. In *Malawi African Association et al. v. Mauritania*, Communication Nos 54/91, 61/91, 98/93, 164/97–196/97, 210/98, 13th Activity Report 1999–2000, para. 97, the Commission held this right should come within the scope of the African Charter Art. 7(1)(c). *See also Gunme et al. v. Cameroon*, Communication No. 266/2003, 26th Activity Report 2008–2009, paras 129–130.

1634. In *Huri-Laws v. Nigeria*, Communication No. 225/98, 14th Activity Report 2000–2001, para. 44, the Commission found a violation of the right to a fair trial following the State's failure to give reasons for arrest and failure to bring charges. *See also Media Rights Agenda v. Nigeria*, Communication No. 224/98, 14th Activity Report 2000–2001, paras 42–44.

1635. The Human Rights Court has held that accused persons have the right to an interpreter in accordance with a combined reading of the African Charter Art. 7(1)(c) and the ICCPR Art. 14(3)(a), *Armand Guehi v. Tanzania (Côte d'Ivoire intervening)*, African Court of Human and Peoples' Rights, App. No. 001/2015, Judgment (7 Dec. 2018) para. 73. *See also Yahaya Zumo Makame v. Tanzania*, African Court of Human and Peoples' Rights, App. No. 023/2016, Judgment (25 Jun. 2021) para. 93.

1636. *Free Legal Assistance Group, Lawyers Committee for Human Rights, Union Interafricaine des Droits de l'Homme, and Les Temoins Jehoves v. Zaire*, Communication Nos 25/89, 47/90, 59/91, 100/93, 9th Activity Report 1995–1996, para. 45; *Centre for Minority Rights Development (Kenya) and Minority Rights Group International on behalf of Endorois Welfare Council v. Kenya*, Communication No. 276/2003, 27th Activity Report 2009, paras 165–168. The Human Rights Court has given Art. 8 a broad interpretation that extends to non-belief, *African Commission on Human and Peoples' Rights v. Kenya*, African Court of Human and Peoples' Rights, App. No. 006/2012 (26 May 2017) para. 163.

1637. *Amnesty International et al. v. Sudan*, Communication Nos 48/90, 50/91, 52/91, 89/93, 13th Activity Report 1999–2000, paras 71–76.

1638. *Garreth Anver Prince v. South Africa*, Communication No. 255/2002, 18th Activity Report 2002–2003, paras 41–42.

must be proportionate and reasonable, and minimal.[1639] The Commission has found violations of Article 8 where the State has harassed, oppressed and persecuted religious believers.[1640] It has also held that the forceful removal of indigenous peoples from their ancestral lands sacred to their religion constituted an unjustified interference with their religious practices.[1641] In a finding of especial significance the Commission has addressed the application of religious laws to non-adherents. It has held such situations to be 'fundamentally unjust' and that individuals should have the right to be tried by secular courts.[1642]

247. These freedoms are, however, limited. In *Garreth Anver Prince v. South Africa*, the Commission had to consider whether the State's prohibition on the possession and use of cannabis infringed the freedom of the complainant, a Rastafari, to practise his religion.[1643] The Commission held that the State had a legitimate interest in addressing the problems associated with drugs and that the law in place was both proportionate and necessary, coming therefore within the scope of the limitations in Articles 8 and 27(2) of the African Charter.[1644]

248. Article 9 of the African Charter guarantees what is one of the fundamental pillars of a free and democratic society, the right to receive information (paragraph 1), and to express and disseminate opinion (paragraph 2).[1645] The Commission has stated that these two elements are indivisible concepts that must be guaranteed simultaneously,[1646] whereas the Human Rights Court has observed that the freedom

---

1639. *Centre for Minority Rights Development (Kenya) and Minority Rights Group International on behalf of Endorois Welfare Council v. Kenya*, Communication No. 276/2003, 27th Activity Report 2009, para. 172; *African Commission on Human and Peoples' Rights v. Kenya*, African Court of Human and Peoples' Rights, App. No. 006/2012 (26 May 2017) para. 167.

1640. *Free Legal Assistance Group, Lawyers Committee for Human Rights, Union Interafricaine des Droits de l'Homme, and Les Temoins Jehoves v. Zaire*, Communication Nos 25/89, 47/90, 59/91, 100/93, 9th Activity Report 1995–1996, para. 45; *Amnesty International et al. v. Sudan*, Communication Nos 48/90, 50/91, 52/91, 89/93, 13th Activity Report 1999–2000, paras 71–76.

1641. *Centre for Minority Rights Development (Kenya) and Minority Rights Group International on behalf of Endorois Welfare Council v. Kenya*, Communication No. 276/200327th Activity Report 2009, para. 173.

1642. *Amnesty International et al. v. Sudan*, Communication Nos 48/90, 50/91, 52/91, 89/93, 13th Activity Report 1999–2000, para. 73.

1643. Communication No. 255/2002, 18th Activity Report 2002–2003.

1644. *Ibid.*, para. 43.

1645. The freedom of opinion and the freedom of expression have been described as 'the foundation of any democratic society', *Ajavon v. Benin*, African Court of Human and Peoples' Rights, App. No. 062/2019, Judgment (4 Dec. 2020), para. 119. *See also International Pen, Constitutional Rights Project, Interights on behalf of Ken Saro-Wiwa Jr. and Civil Liberties Organisation v. Nigeria*, Communication Nos 137/94, 139/94, 154/96 and 161/97, 12th Activity Report 1998–1999, para. 110; *Sir Dawda K. Jawara v. Gambia*, Communication Nos 147/95 and 149/96, 13th Activity Report 1999–2000, para. 65; *Egyptian Initiative for Personal Rights and INTERIGHTS v. Egypt*, Communication No. 323/2006 (2011), para. 250. The ECOWAS Community Court of Justice (ECCJ) has stated that African Charter Art. 9 has created derivative rights to receive, impart and access information and ideas of all kinds regardless of the means, such as writing, artwork or social media, *SERAP v. Nigeria*, ECOWAS Community Court of Justice, Judgment No. ECW/CCJ/JUD/40/22 (14 Jul. 2022) paras 66–67.

1646. *Scanlen and Holderness v. Zimbabwe*, Communication No. 297/2005, 26th Activity Report 2009, para. 108.

of opinion and the freedom of expression are intimately linked.[1647] According to the Human Rights Court, Article 9(1) means 'that every citizen in a democratic country has the right to access information held by the State. This right is ... necessary to ensure the respect for the principle of transparent government'.[1648] It is interesting to note that the Commission has established a link between the right to receive information and the right to a fair trial, so that a person has a right to be informed of the reasons for the actions taken against him/her.[1649] Although freedom of speech or other forms of expression are not explicitly mentioned per se it is clear that they come within the scope of the provision.[1650] Thus, in *Media Rights Agenda and Constitutional Rights Project v. Nigeria*, the Commission stated that Article 9 'reflects the fact that freedom of expression is a basic human right, vital to an individual's personal development, his political consciousness, and participation in the conduct of public affairs in his country'.[1651] Furthermore, in its Declaration of Principles on Freedom of Expression in Africa the Commission asserts the 'fundamental importance of freedom of expression and information as an individual human right, as a cornerstone of democracy and as a means of ensuring respect for all human rights and freedoms'.[1652] A blanket restriction on the freedom of expression breaches Article 9(2).[1653] The Human Rights Court has stated similarly that the freedom of expression is a fundamental right, respect for which 'is crucial and indispensable for the free development of the human person and to create a democratic society'.[1654]

249. The reach of the provision extends to the freedom of political expression.[1655] Hence in *The Law Office of Ghazi Suleiman v. Sudan*, the Commission stated that speech that contributed to political debate had to be protected.[1656] The

1647. *Ajavon v. Benin*, African Court of Human and Peoples' Rights, App. No. 062/2019, Judgment (4 Dec. 2020), para. 119.
1648. *XYZ v. Benin*, African Court of Human and Peoples' Rights, App. No. 010/2020 (27 Nov. 2020), para. 113.
1649. *Good v. Botswana*, Communication No. 306/2005, 28th Activity Report 2009–2010, paras 193–194.
1650. *Ibid.*, paras 186–187; *Scanlen and Holderness v. Zimbabwe* Communication No. 297/2005, 26th Activity Report 2009, para. 81; *Egyptian Initiative for Personal Rights and INTERIGHTS v. Egypt*, Communication No. 323/2006 (2011), para. 243.
1651. Communication Nos 105/93, 128/94, 130/94, 152/96, 12th Activity Report, 1998–1999, para. 54. *See also Constitutional Rights Project, Civil Liberties Organisation and Media Rights Agenda v. Nigeria*, Communication Nos 140/94, 141/94, 145/95, 13th Activity Report 1999–2000, para. 36; *Egyptian Initiative for Personal Rights and INTERIGHTS v. Egypt*, Communication No. 323/2006 (2011), para. 244. *See also* African Charter on Democracy Art. 27(8).
1652. Adopted at the Commission's Thirty-Second Ordinary Session on 23 Oct. 2002, 16th Activity Report, 2002–2003. *See Zegveld and Ephrem v. Eritrea*, Communication No. 250/2002, 17th Activity Report 2003–2004, para. 59.
1653. *Amnesty International et al. v. Sudan*, Communication Nos 48/90, 50/91, 52/91, 89/93, 13th Activity Report 1999–2000, para. 80.
1654. *Ingabire Victoire Umuhoza v. Rwanda*, African Court of Human and Peoples' Rights, App. No. 003/2014, Judgment (24 Nov. 2017) para. 131.
1655. *Good v. Botswana*, Communication No. 306/2005, 28th Activity Report 2009–2010, para. 197; *Egyptian Initiative for Personal Rights and INTERIGHTS v. Egypt*, Communication No. 323/2006 (2011), paras 246–247.
1656. Communication No. 228/99, 16th Activity Report 2002–2003, para. 53.

essential role played by the press in society has been emphasized by the Commission. In *Constitutional Rights Project, Civil Liberties Organisation and Media Rights Agenda v. Nigeria*, the Commission found that the military regime had been harassing the press by proscribing specified newspapers and sealing their premises arbitrarily which gave rise to the danger of self-censorship.[1657] In *Article 19 v. Eritrea*, the Commission found that a wholesale ban on the press and the imprisonment of those holding views contrary to those of the State violated the spirit and purpose of Article 9. Banning 'the entire press on the grounds that it constitutes a threat to the … government is a violation of the right to freedom of expression, and is the type of action that Article 9 is intended to proscribe. A free press is one of the tenets of a democratic society, and a valuable check on potential excesses by government'.[1658] Furthermore, the imprisonment of journalists 'deprives not only the journalists of their rights to freely express and disseminate their opinions, but also the public, of their right to information'.[1659] It constitutes a disproportionate interference in the exercise of the freedom of expression.[1660] Does a law that requires newspapers to register with a licensing authority and pay a registration fee interfere with the freedom of expression? The Commission addressed this question in *Media Rights Agenda and Constitutional Rights Project v. Nigeria* and held that in itself it did not. However, the fee should not be so excessive as to constitute a disincentive or restriction. In addition, the licensing authority should not be the puppet of the government giving it the power to prohibit the publication of any periodical they choose since this would invite censorship.[1661] However, in *Konaté v. Burkina Faso* the Human Rights Court was of the view that the licensing of journalists was unwarranted under Article 9 which guaranteed the freedom of expression to *all* citizens and not just journalists.[1662] Similarly, in *Scanlen and Holderness v. Zimbabwe*, the Commission held that the compulsory accreditation of journalists was incompatible with the freedom of expression.[1663]

250. Moreover, politicians, who thereby assume a public position, or other public figures must accept a wide degree of criticism.[1664] The press has a role as a

---

1657. Communication Nos 140/94, 141/94, 145/95, 13th Activity Report 1999–2000, para. 37.
1658. Communication No. 275/2003, 22nd Activity Report 2006–2007, paras 105, 107. *See also Constitutional Rights Project and Civil Liberties Organisation v. Nigeria*, Communication No. 102/93, 12th Activity Report 1998–1999, para. 59.
1659. *Article 19 v. Eritrea*, Communication No. 275/2003, 22nd Activity Report 2006–2007, para. 106; *Sir Dawda K. Jawara v. Gambia*, Communication Nos 147/95 and 149/96, 13th Activity Report 1999–2000, para. 63. *See also Constitutional Rights Project and Civil Liberties Organisation v. Nigeria*, Communication No. 102/93, 12th Activity Report 1998–1999.
1660. *Konaté v. Burkina Faso*, African Court of Human and Peoples' Rights, App. No. 004/2013 (5 Dec. 2014), para. 164. *See M.J. Duffy, Konaté v. Burkina Faso: An Analysis of a Landmark Ruling on Criminal Defamation in Africa*, 6 J. Int'l Media & Entertainment Law (2015–2016) 1.
1661. Communication Nos 105/93, 128/94, 130/94, 152/96, 12th Activity Report, 1998–1999, paras 54–57.
1662. App. No. 004/2013 (5 Dec. 2014), paras 57–58.
1663. Communication No. 297/200526th Activity Report 2009, paras 84–98.
1664. *Media Rights Agenda and Constitutional Rights Project v. Nigeria*, Communication Nos 105/93, 128/94, 130/94, 152/96, 12th Activity Report 1998–1999, para. 74; *Good v. Botswana*, Communication No. 306/2005, 28th Activity Report 2009–2010, para. 198; *Konaté v. Burkina Faso*, African Court of Human and Peoples' Rights, App. No. 004/2013 (5 Dec. 2014), paras 155–156. A

public watchdog in politics and to restrict or prevent the press from passing legitimate comment, criticizing the government or making value judgments would amount to censorship.[1665] A prohibition on the publication of 'falsehoods' has also been found to be excessive.[1666]

251. A distinction seems to be drawn between the two rights. Thus, while the right to receive information seems to be absolute,[1667] the freedom to express an opinion is not and must be exercised 'within the law'.[1668] The Human Rights Court has stated that 'laws' in this context must be 'sufficiently clear, foreseeable and compatible with the purpose of the Charter and international human rights conventions and has to be of general application.'[1669] It is generally accepted that the freedom of expression entails duties and responsibilities[1670] and therefore that some interference may be necessary, for example, to deal with libel, hate speech or national security, but such restrictions must be provided for by laws that meet international human rights standards.[1671] Consequently, restrictions must be provided by law, serve a legitimate interest and be necessary in a democratic society.[1672] If the

---

number of cases have been heard in Zimbabwe concerning 'insulting' the President, *see*, *e.g.*, *Mwonzora v. State* (Constitutional Court of Zimbabwe, Judgment No. CCZ 17/2016, 23 Nov. 2016).

1665. *Media Rights Agenda and Constitutional Rights Project v. Nigeria*, Communication Nos 105/93, 128/94, 130/94, 152/96, 12th Activity Report 1998–1999, paras 73–75.
1666. *Scanlen and Holderness v. Zimbabwe*, Communication No. 297/2005, 26th Activity Report 2009, para. 117.
1667. *Constitutional Rights Project, Civil Liberties Organisation and Media Rights Agenda v. Nigeria*, Communication Nos 140/94, 141/94, 145/95, 13th Activity Report 1999–2000, para. 38; *Good v. Botswana*, Communication No. 306/2005, 28th Activity Report 2009–2010, para. 193. Compare *Scanlen and Holderness v. Zimbabwe*, Communication No. 297/2005, 26th Activity Report 2009, para. 121.
1668. *Ajavon v. Benin*, African Court of Human and Peoples' Rights, App. No. 062/2019, Judgment (4 Dec. 2020), para. 119.
1669. In *Ingabire Victoire Umuhoza v. Rwanda*, African Court of Human and Peoples' Rights, App. No. 003/2014, Judgment (24 Nov. 2017) para. 134.
1670. *Zegveld and Ephrem v. Eritrea*, Communication No. 250/2002, 17th Activity Report 2003–2004, para. 59; *Scanlen and Holderness v. Zimbabwe*, Communication No. 297/2005, 26th Activity Report 2009, para. 108.
1671. *Ajavon v. Benin*, African Court of Human and Peoples' Rights, App. No. 062/2019, Judgment (4 Dec. 2020), paras 119, 122–123, 126; *Zegveld and Ephrem v. Eritrea*, Communication No. 250/2002, 17th Activity Report 2003–2004, paras 59–60; *Good v. Botswana*, Communication No. 306/2005, 28th Activity Report 2009–2010, paras 187–189. Note also African Charter Art. 27(2). In *Constitutional Rights Project and Civil Liberties Organisation v. Nigeria*, Communication No. 102/93, 12th Activity Report 1998–1999, para. 59, the Commission found that given that Nigerian law made provision for a law of libel 'a government proscription of a publication, by name, is of particular concern.' *See also Media Rights Agenda and Constitutional Rights Project v. Nigeria*, Communication Nos 105/93, 128/94, 130/94, 152/96, 12th Activity Report 1998–1999, para. 71.
1672. *Ajavon v. Benin*, African Court of Human and Peoples' Rights, App. No. 062/2019, Judgment (4 Dec. 2020), para. 119; *Egyptian Initiative for Personal Rights and INTERIGHTS v. Egypt*, Communication No. 323/2006 (2011), para. 248; *Monim Elgak, Osman Hummeida and Amir Suleiman (represented by FIDH and OMCT) v. Sudan*, Communication No. 379/09 (2014) para. 114. According to the Human Rights Court any criminal sanctions must be subject to the criteria of necessity and proportionality, *Konaté v. Burkina Faso*, African Court of Human and Peoples' Rights, App. No. 004/2013 (5 Dec. 2014), para. 166.

exercise of the freedom of expression appears to offend the law then 'there should be due process and all affected persons should be allowed to seek redress in a court of law'.[1673] This limitation appears to be no more sweeping than that contained in comparable international documents where the limitation constitutes the exception to the general rule and the Commission has interpreted it in such a way that governments are not allowed to enact arbitrary or punitive measures which would unnecessarily curb these freedoms or amount to prior censorship.[1674] It has therefore stated that while according to Article 9(2), dissemination of opinions may be restricted by law, this 'does not mean that national law can set aside the right to disseminate one's opinions; this would make the protection of the right to express one's opinions ineffective'.[1675] Criminal sanctions should be contemplated only for 'serious and very exceptional circumstances', such as incitement to international crimes, or incitement to hatred or violence.[1676]

252. Article 10 of the African Charter protects in broad terms the right of free association. This implies that individuals must be free to come together[1677] and to create and join political parties,[1678] trades unions, and professional bodies.[1679] It is therefore both an individual and a collective right.[1680] Thus, in *Civil Liberties Organisation in respect of Nigerian Bar Association v. Nigeria*, the African Commission held that, 'Freedom of association is enunciated as an individual right and is first and foremost a duty for the State to abstain from interfering with the free formation of associations. There must always be a general capacity for citizens to

1673. *Zegveld and Ephrem v. Eritrea*, Communication No. 250/2002, 17th Activity Report 2003–2004, para. 60. *See also Scanlen and Holderness v. Zimbabwe*, Communication No. 297/2005, 26th Activity Report 2009, para. 102.
1674. *See supra* para. 246 where the Commission has stated that limitations must be both proportionate and necessary.
1675. *Media Rights Agenda and Constitutional Rights Project v. Nigeria*, Communication Nos 105/93, 128/94, 130/94, 152/96, 12th Activity Report 1998–1999, para. 66; *Article 19 v. Eritrea*, Communication No. 275/2003, 22nd Activity Report 2006–2007, para. 105; *Scanlen and Holderness v. Zimbabwe*, Communication No. 297/2005, 26th Activity Report 2009, para. 121.
1676. *Malawi African Association et al. v. Mauritania*, Communication Nos 54/91, 61/91, 98/93, 164/97–196/97, 210/98, 13th Activity Report 1999–2000, para. 102; *Konaté v. Burkina Faso*, African Court of Human and Peoples' Rights, App. No. 004/2013 (5 Dec. 2014), para. 165. However, a number of judges were of the view that no criminalization of speech by criminal defamation laws could be justified under African Charter Art. 27(2), *ibid.* Separate Opinion of Judge Thompson, Judge Akuffo, Judge Ngoepe and Judge Tambala, para. 4.
1677. *The Law Office of Ghazi Suleiman v. Sudan*, Communication No. 228/99, 16th Activity Report 2002–2003, para. 56.
1678. *Ajavon v. Benin*, African Court of Human and Peoples' Rights, App. No. 062/2019 (4 Dec. 2020), para. 201; *Amnesty International v. Zambia*, Communication No. 212/98, 12th Activity Report 1998–1999, para. 49; *Lawyers for Human Rights v. Swaziland*, Communication No. 251/2002, 18th Activity Report 2002–2003, para. 62.
1679. In *Ouko v. Kenya*, Communication No. 232/99, 14th Activity Report 2000–2001, para. 29, the Commission upheld a violation of Art. 10 with regard to the political persecution of a student union leader. In *Huri-Laws v. Nigeria*, Communication No. 225/98, 14th Activity Report 2000–2001, paras 47–48, the persecution of employees of a NGO amounted to violations of the African Charter Arts 9 and 10.
1680. *Monim Elgak, Osman Hummeida and Amir Suleiman (represented by FIDH and OMCT) v. Sudan*, Communication No. 379/09 (2014) para. 118.

join, without State interference, in association in order to attain various ends.'[1681] Accordingly, the dissolution of a political party was deemed an excessive sanction since it had the right to hold public debates in accordance with democratic rules.[1682] Again this provision is subject to limitations. As in Article 9, Article 10 contains a general exception in that the right is conditional on the individual abiding by the law. While concern had been expressed that the freedom guaranteed could be rendered worthless the Commission has nevertheless held that limitations must be compatible with the obligations of States under the African Charter so that the right is not rendered illusory. It has expressed the view that while States may regulate the exercise of this right under domestic law such regulation must conform to the provisions of the African Charter which requires legitimate and proportionate reasons for any restrictions.[1683] Consequently, any national law on associations 'should include an objective description that makes it possible to determine the criminal nature' of an organization.[1684] The Human Rights Court has further observed that this provision must be read in light of the general limitation clause of the African Charter, Article 27(2), which it claims allows State Parties some measure of discretion [to restrict] the freedom of association in the interest of collective security and the rights and freedoms of others among others.[1685]

253. Article 10(2) contains a correlative right in that 'no one may be compelled to join an association', which implies the freedom not to associate. However, this guarantee is made subject to the obligation of solidarity contained in Article 29 of the African Charter which imposes upon the individual duties towards the family, the community and the State. While the sentiment of these obligations may be laudable in that they reflect traditional African values and attempt to imbue the individual with civic values the potential for abuse exists. For example, individuals may be compelled to join a political party not of their choice under the guise that it preserves and strengthens social and national solidarity.

1681. Communication No. 101/93, 8th Activity Report 1994–1995, para. 14. *See also International Pen, Constitutional Rights Project, Interights on behalf of Ken Saro-Wiwa Jr. and Civil Liberties Organisation v. Nigeria*, Communication Nos 137/94, 139/94, 154/96 and 161/97, 12th Activity Report 1998–1999, para. 108.

1682. *Interights, Institute for Human Rights and Development in Africa, and Association Mauritaniene des Droits de l'Homme v. Mauritania*, Communication No. 242/2001, 17th Activity Report 2003–2004, para. 80. In *Sir Dawda K. Jawara v. Gambia*, Communication Nos 147/95 and 149/96, 13th Activity Report 1999–2000, para. 68, the Commission condemned the banning of political parties. The Human Rights Court has stated that the dissolution of a political party should be the exception and be based on reasonable and objective grounds, *Ajavon v. Benin*, African Court of Human and Peoples' Rights, App. No. 062/2019 (4 Dec. 2020), para. 188.

1683. *Interights, Institute for Human Rights and Development in Africa, and Association Mauritaniene des Droits de l'Homme v. Mauritania*, Communication No. 242/2001, 17th Activity Report 2003–2004, paras 76–79; *Monim Elgak, Osman Hummeida and Amir Suleiman (represented by FIDH and OMCT) v. Sudan*, Communication No. 379/09 (2014) para. 118. *See supra* paras 208-213, for fuller discussion of this topic.

1684. *Malawi African Association et al. v. Mauritania*, Communication Nos 54/91, 61/91, 98/93, 164/97–196/97, 210/98, 13th Activity Report 1999–2000, para. 107.

1685. *Tanganyika Law Society et al. v. Tanzania*, African Court of Human and Peoples' Rights, App. Nos 009/2011 and 011/2011 (14 Jun. 2013), para. 112.

254. Article 11 of the African Charter guarantees the right of assembly, which includes demonstrations or rallies,[1686] subject to certain restrictions and limitations. The right of assembly cannot be absolute because it impacts on the rights of others and because of the threat of disorder and these reasonable restrictions can be found in all democratic societies.[1687] At the same time States must do their utmost to uphold this right.[1688] As has already been discussed in relation to other limitations, the African Commission has sought to ensure that restrictions on this right are objectively justified and are not excessive or arbitrary.[1689] A blanket ban on the formation of political parties thus violated the right of assembly.[1690]

255. The Commission has stressed the close relationship between the freedom of expression, the right of association and the right of assembly,[1691] considering expression as one of the objectives of the latter.[1692] This affinity is considered particularly important in the case of political parties, given 'their essential role for the maintenance of pluralism and the proper functioning of democracy'.[1693]

256. Article 12 of the African Charter secures various aspects of the right of free movement, described by the Commission as 'a fundamental human right to all individuals within States',[1694] including the right to enter and leave a country.[1695] First,

---

1686. *International Pen, Constitutional Rights Project, Interights on behalf of Ken Saro-Wiwa Jr. and Civil Liberties Organisation v. Nigeria*, Communication Nos 137/94, 139/94, 154/96 and 161/97, 12th Activity Report 1998–1999, para. 106; *The Law Office of Ghazi Suleiman v. Sudan*, Communication No. 228/99, 16th Activity Report 2002–2003, para. 56.

1687. *Ajavon v. Benin*, African Court of Human and Peoples' Rights, App. No. 062/2019 (4 Dec. 2020), paras 149–151.

1688. *Gunme et al. v. Cameroon*, Communication No. 266/2003, 26th Activity Report 2008–2009, para. 138.

1689. *Malawi African Association et al. v. Mauritania*, Communication Nos 54/91, 61/91, 98/93, 164/97–196/97, 210/98, 13th Activity Report 1999–2000, para. 111; *Lawyers for Human Rights v. Swaziland*, Communication No. 251/2002, 18th Activity Report 2002–2003, para. 60; *Gunme et al. v. Cameroon*, Communication No. 266/2003, 26th Activity Report 2008–2009, para. 138; Resolution on the Right to Freedom of Association, adopted at the Commission's Eleventh Ordinary Session, 1992, 5th Activity Report, 1991–1992. *See supra* paras 208-213 for fuller discussion of this topic.

1690. *Sir Dawda K. Jawara v. Gambia*, Communication Nos 147/95 and 149/96, 13th Activity Report 1999–2000, para. 69; *Lawyers for Human Rights v. Swaziland*, Communication No. 251/2002, 18th Activity Report 2002–2003, para. 60.

1691. *International Pen, Constitutional Rights Project, Interights on behalf of Ken Saro-Wiwa Jr. and Civil Liberties Organisation v. Nigeria*, Communication Nos 137/94, 139/94, 154/96 and 161/97, 12th Activity Report 1998–1999, para. 110.

1692. *Interights, Institute for Human Rights and Development in Africa, and Association Mauritaniene des Droits de l'Homme v. Mauritania*, Communication No. 242/2001, 17th Activity Report 2003–2004, para. 80.

1693. *Ibid.*

1694. *Sudan Human Rights Organization and Sudan Centre for Housing Rights and Evictions v. Sudan* Communication Nos 279/03, 296/05, 28th Activity Report, 2010, para. 187. In principle, Art. 12 can also be invoked by refugees, *Doebbler v. Sudan*, Communication No. 235/2000, 27th Activity Report 2009), para. 167.

1695. *Sudan Human Rights Organization and Sudan Centre for Housing Rights and Evictions v. Sudan* Communication Nos 279/03, 296/05, 28th Activity Report, 2010, para. 187. In *Sir Dawda K. Jawara v. Gambia*, Communication Nos 147/95 and 149/96, 13th Activity Report 1999–2000,

under paragraph 1, individuals, of whatever nationality, can move freely within the State.[1696] Second, they can elect where they wish to reside, both important considerations in view of apartheid's restrictions on these rights.[1697] Flight because of fear of persecution is incompatible with this right.[1698] Particularly important has been the Commission's condemnation of forced evictions and population displacement as a result of the violence in Darfur.[1699] The individual's right to freedom of movement or residence is guaranteed provided the person 'abides by the law'. This not only suggests that the individual must be lawfully within the territory, having complied with immigration requirements, but that their continued presence is contingent on observing domestic law, a requirement that seems to be wholly legitimate.[1700]

257. Article 12(2) grants the individual the right to leave and return to a State subject to restrictions imposed by law for the protection of national security, law and order, public health or morality.[1701] In principle, therefore, a person should not be denied a passport but inability to leave as a result of having to serve a lawful prison sentence would not violate this right. In *Amnesty International v. Zambia*, the African Commission held that the State must prove that it is justified in invoking these conditions and that the rules of natural justice must apply.[1702] With specific

para. 70, the Commission held that travel restrictions violated Art. 12. This was also the case in *Open Society Justice Initiative v. Côte d'Ivoire*, Communication No. 318/06 (2015) para. 161, where the difficulties of the Dioula community in obtaining identity and travel documents interfered with their freedom of movement. *See also Ouko v. Kenya*, Communication No. 232/99, 14th Activity Report 2000–2001, para. 31. For a national decision *see Nyirongo v. Attorney-General* (1990–1992) Z.R. 92 (SC).

1696. *The Law Office of Ghazi Suleiman v. Sudan*, Communication No. 228/99, 16th Activity Report 2002–2003, para. 60; *Penessis v. Tanzania*, African Court of Human and Peoples' Rights, App. No. 0013/2015, Judgment (28 Nov. 2019) para. 123.
1697. In *Malawi African Association et al. v. Mauritania*, Communication Nos 54/91, 61/91, 98/93, 164/97–196/97, 210/98, 13th Activity Report 1999–2000, para. 126, the Commission found that the mass eviction of people from their property violated Art. 12(1). The compulsory mass transfer of people from one State to another has been held to breach this provision, *Democratic Republic of Congo v. Burundi, Rwanda and Uganda*, Communication No. 227/99, 20th Activity Report 2005–2006, para. 81.
1698. *Sudan Human Rights Organization and Sudan Centre for Housing Rights and Evictions v. Sudan* Communication Nos 279/03, 296/05, 28th Activity Report, 2010, para. 190; *Monim Elgak, Osman Hummeida and Amir Suleiman (represented by FIDH and OMCT) v. Sudan*, Communication No. 379/09 (2014) para. 123.
1699. *Sudan Human Rights Organization and Sudan Centre for Housing Rights and Evictions v. Sudan* Communication Nos 279/03, 296/05, 28th Activity Report, 2010, paras 188–190.
1700. But *see Modise v. Botswana*, Communication No. 97/93, 14th Activity Report 2000–2001, para. 93. In *Rencontre Africaine pour la Defense des Droits de l'Homme v. Zambia*, Communication No. 71/92, 10th Activity Report 1996–1997, para. 31, the Commission stated that it would not dispute the right of the State to bring legal action against illegal migrants and to deport them if justified.
1701. *Mouvement Burkinabé des Droits de l'Homme et des Peuples v. Burkina Faso*, Communication No. 204/97, 14th Activity Report 2000–2001, para. 47; *Penessis v. Tanzania*, African Court of Human and Peoples' Rights, App. No. 0013/2015, Judgment (28 Nov. 2019) para. 124. In *Rights International v. Nigeria*, Communication No. 215/98, 13th Activity Report 1999–2000, para. 30, the Commission held that the fact that the victim had been forced to flee his country for his safety violated Art. 12(1)–(2). *See Nyirongo v. Attorney-General* (1990–1992) Z.R. 92 (SC).
1702. Communication No. 212/98, 12th Activity Report 1998–1999, para. 42.

reference to the limitation on the ground of law and order the Commission stated that the State had to prove that the individuals were indeed a danger to law and order; that they posed a 'likely' danger was too vague.[1703] The right of an individual to enter their own State is also guaranteed[1704] but the African Charter, in accordance with international law, restricts the right of entry to nationals only.[1705] However, it should be observed that the African Charter is unique in seemingly making the nationals' right to enter their own country subject to the restrictions. This provision would appear to be incompatible with international law.[1706]

258. A positive feature is Article 12(3) which grants a right to seek and obtain asylum. This provision is inspired by, and is a complement to, the OAU Convention on Refugees 1969 and is considered in more detail below.[1707] Nevertheless, it is worth observing that the Commission has stated that this provision includes 'a general protection of all those who are subject to persecution, that they may seek refuge in another state'.[1708]

259. Article 12(4) protects a non-national who is legally within another State from summary expulsion as such sanctions can only be legitimate by virtue of a decision taken in accordance with the law. While this provision is too broadly worded and fails to stipulate any procedural guarantees, such as the right to be given reasons against expulsion, the jurisprudence of the Commission requires that the provision must be interpreted to prevent arbitrary expulsions.[1709] Consequently, expulsions must be consistent with the due process of law;[1710] States must have laws

1703. *Ibid.*

1704. *Democratic Republic of Congo v. Burundi, Rwanda and Uganda*, Communication No. 227/99, 20th Activity Report, 2005–2006, para. 81. In *Huri-Laws v. Nigeria*, Communication No. 225/98, 14th Activity Report 2000–2001, paras 50–51, the Commission held that harassment and arrests at re-entry points infringed the freedom of movement. Fear of persecution upon return also constitutes a violation of Art. 12(2), *Monim Elgak, Osman Hummeida and Amir Suleiman (represented by FIDH and OMCT) v. Sudan*, Communication No. 379/09 (2014) para. 126.

1705. General comment 15, UN Doc. HRI/GEN/1/Rev.2, para. 5. However, this right may also extend to family members who are aliens, *Dow v. Attorney-General* [1992] L.R.C. (Const) 623 (Botswana Court of Appeal); *Rattigan and Others v. Chief Immigration Officer of Zimbabwe* 1995 (2) SA 182 (ZS).

1706. Compare International Covenant on Civil and Political Rights Art. 12(4) (16 Dec. 1966), 999 U.N.T.S. 171, American Convention on Human Rights Art. 22(5) (22 November 1969), O.A.S.T.S. No. 36, ECHR Fourth Protocol 4 Art. 3(2) (16 Sep. 1963), E.T.S. No. 46; *East African Asians v. United Kingdom*, 3 E.H.R.R. 76 (1981); D.J. Harris, M. O'Boyle & C. Warbrick, *Law of the European Convention on Human Rights* (2nd edn, Oxford: Oxford University Press, 2009), 743–744.

1707. *See infra* Ch. 3, para. 415.

1708. *Organisation Mondiale contre la Torture et al. v. Rwanda,* Communication Nos 27/89, 46/91, 49/91, 99/93, 10th Activity Report 1993–1994, para. 30.

1709. *Organisation Mondiale contre la Torture et al. v. Rwanda*, Communication Nos 27/89, 46/91, 49/91, 99/93, 10th Activity Report 1993–1994, para. 30.

1710. *Institute for Human Rights and Development in Africa v. Angola*, Communication No. 292/2004, 24th Activity Report 2008, paras 63–65; *Zimbabwe Lawyers for Human Rights and the Institute for Human Rights and Development (on behalf of Andrew Barclay Meldrum) v. Zimbabwe*, Communication No. 294/2004, 26th Activity Report 2008–2009, paras 114–115.

in place to regulate this area which must meet international standards.[1711] Furthermore, if the procedure for expulsion entails arrest, the safeguards relating to deprivation of liberty are applicable, as is the right to have the case reviewed.[1712]

260. Finally, Article 12(5) prohibits the mass expulsion of non-nationals aimed at national, racial, ethnic or religious groups. Expulsion based purely on nationality is therefore forbidden.[1713] A link thus exists between this provision and Article 2 of the African Charter that enshrines the principle of non-discrimination.[1714] The rationale for the proscription contained in Article 12(5) was that 'the drafters of the Charter believed that mass expulsions presented a special threat to human rights'.[1715] In *Rencontre Africaine pour la Defense des Droits de l'Homme v. Zambia*, which concerned the expulsion of over five hundred illegal residents, the Commission stated that while the African Charter did not prohibit deportations as such Zambia's right to deport people did not justify the manner in which it had done so.[1716] Again the Commission requires that due process be observed.[1717]

261. Article 13(1) of the African Charter broadly guarantees the right to participate freely in the government of one's country, either directly or through freely chosen representatives.[1718] A right to participate, and stand,[1719] in elections on the basis

1711. *Good v. Botswana*, Communication No. 306/2005, 28th Activity Report 2009–2010, paras 203–204.
1712. *Organisation Mondiale contre la Torture et al. v. Rwanda*, Communication Nos 27/89, 46/91, 49/91, 99/93, 10th Activity Report 1993–1994, para. 34; *Good v. Botswana*, Communication No. 306/2005, 28th Activity Report 2009–2010, para. 205; *Amnesty International v. Zambia*, Communication No. 212/98, 12th Activity Report 1998–1999.
1713. *Rencontre Africaine pour la Defense des Droits de l'Homme v. Zambia*, Communication No. 71/92, 10th Activity Report, 1996–1997; *Organisation Mondiale contre la Torture et al. v. Rwanda*, Communication Nos 27/89, 46/91, 49/91, 99/93, 10th Activity Report 1993–1994; *African Institute for Human Rights and Development (on behalf of Sierra Leonean refugees in Guinea v. Republic of Guinea*, Communication No. 249/2002, 20th Activity Report 2005–2006.
1714. *Rencontre Africaine pour la Defense des Droits de l'Homme v. Zambia*, Communication No. 71/92, 10th Activity Report, 1996–1997, para. 21; *Organisation Mondiale contre la Torture et al. v. Rwanda*, Communication Nos 27/89, 46/91, 49/91, 99/93, 10th Activity Report 1993–1994, para. 32; *African Institute for Human Rights and Development (on behalf of Sierra Leonean refugees in Guinea v. Republic of Guinea*, Communication No. 249/2002, 20th Activity Report 2005–2006, para. 69.
1715. *Rencontre Africaine pour la Defense des Droits de l'Homme v. Zambia*, Communication No. 71/92, 10th Activity Report 1996–1997, para. 20; *Institute for Human Rights and Development in Africa v. Angola*, Communication No. 292/2004, 24th Activity Report 2008, para. 68.
1716. *Rencontre Africaine pour la Defense des Droits de l'Homme v. Zambia*, Communication No. 71/92, 10th Activity Report 1996–1997, para. 23. *See also African Institute for Human Rights and Development (on behalf of Sierra Leonean refugees in Guinea v. Republic of Guinea*, Communication No. 249/2002, 20th Activity Report, 2005–2006.
1717. *Institute for Human Rights and Development in Africa v. Angola*, Communication No. 292/2004, 24th Activity Report 2008, para. 70.
1718. *See also* the African Charter on Democracy. Independent and impartial electoral bodies are also required, *Actions pour la Protection des Droit de l'Homme (APDH) v. Côte d'Ivoire*, African Court of Human and Peoples' Rights, App. No. 001/2014 (18 Nov. 2016) paras 135–136.
1719. *Ajavon v. Benin*, African Court of Human and Peoples' Rights, App. No. 062/2019, Judgment (4 Dec. 2020), para. 206; *Modise v. Botswana*, Communication No. 97/93, 14th Activity Report

of universal adult suffrage and a right to elected representative government[1720] seems to be secured by this provision according to the Commission. Indeed, the Commission has proceeded to describe this right as 'a fundamental civil liberty and human right, and should be enjoyed by citizens without discrimination'.[1721] Thus the right to 'participate freely in government entails, among other things, the right to vote for the representative of one's choice. An inevitable corollary of this right that the results of free expression of the will of the voters are respected; otherwise, the right to vote freely is meaningless'.[1722] The right to vote has been described as the 'bedrock of modern democratic systems'.[1723] In addition, citizens can participate in governance through political parties.[1724] Hence a ban on individuals or political parties from participating in political activity contravenes this provision.[1725] Similarly, the annulment of the results of democratic elections.[1726] These opinions are important in light of recent events which witnessed the manipulation of the electoral process in Kenya in 2007 and Zimbabwe in 2008 and the extreme reluctance of the respective Governments to accept the outcome of the people's decision. Too many ruling regimes in Africa simply pay lip service to the values of liberal democracy. They observe the trappings of democracy and expect that merely holding elections, neither free nor fair necessarily, will suffice.[1727] They therefore lack popular support or genuine democratic mandate.[1728] The Commission has affirmed that the best form of government is one elected by and accountable to the

---

2000–2001, para. 95; *Mouvement Ivorien des Droits Humains (MIDH) v. Côte d'Ivoire*, Communication No. 246/2002, 25th Activity Report 2008, para. 77. *See also Open Society Justice Initiative v. Côte d'Ivoire*, Communication No. 318/06 (2015) paras 165–169.

1720. *See also* African Charter on Democracy Art. 3(3) and Art. 4(2). Under Arts 17 and 32(7) thereof State Parties commit themselves to holding regular, transparent free and fair elections.

1721. *Mouvement Ivorien des Droits Humains (MIDH) v. Côte d'Ivoire*, Communication No. 246/2002, 25th Activity Report 2008, para. 77.

1722. *Constitutional Rights Project and Civil Liberties Organisation v. Nigeria*, Communication No. 102/93, 12th Activity Report 1998–1999, para. 50.

1723. *Open Society Justice Initiative v. Côte d'Ivoire*, Communication No. 318/06 (2015) para. 164.

1724. *Lawyers for Human Rights v. Swaziland*, Communication No. 251/2002, 18th Activity Report 2002–2003, para. 63. *See also* African Charter on Democracy Arts 3(11), 27(1) and 32(6).

1725. *Sir Dawda K. Jawara v. Gambia*, Communication Nos 147/95 and 149/96, 13th Activity Report 1999–2000, paras 66–67; *Lawyers for Human Rights v. Swaziland*, Communication No. 251/2002, 18th Activity Report 2002–2003, paras 62–63. In *Tanganyika Law Society et al. v. Tanzania*, African Court of Human and Peoples' Rights, App. Nos 009/2011 and 011/2011 (14 Jun. 2013), para. 109, the African Court on Human and Peoples' Rights held that a prohibition on individual candidatures in elections was in breach of the African Charter Art. 13(1).

1726. *Constitutional Rights Project and Civil Liberties Organisation v. Nigeria*, Communication No. 102/93, 12th Activity Report 1998–1999, para. 53.

1727. *See* the UK Foreign and Commonwealth Office's critique of the disputed 2008 election in Zimbabwe, conducted in an atmosphere of intimidation and violence, *United Kingdom Foreign & Commonwealth Office Annual Report on Human Rights 2008* http://www.gov.uk/government/publications/systems/annual-report-on-human-rights-2008. In a landmark decision, the Supreme Court of Kenya annulled the result of the presidential election held in August 2017 as a result of numerous irregularities and illegalities on the part of the Electoral Commission, *Odinga and Others v. Independent Electoral and Boundaries Commission and Others* Supreme Court of Kenya, Judgment of 20 Sep. 2017.

1728. The OAU acknowledged the relationship between poor governance and human rights abuses, *see* Grand Bay Declaration para. 8(g)–(i), (p)(r). The UN Commission on Human Rights has declared that democracy fosters the full realization of human rights, Res. 1999/57, UN Doc. E/CN.4/1999/

people.[1729] It has therefore condemned military seizures of power as a clear violation of the fundamental principle of democracy that governments should be based on the consent of the people and has called upon military governments to respect the right of free participation in government and, additionally, to hand over political power to democratically elected governments.[1730] In fact, the Commission has pronounced that one of its roles is that of promoting democracy in Africa.[1731] It may be that the Commission was emboldened to adopt this stance by the AU's explicit commitment to an agenda of democracy, human rights, and good governance.[1732] The Commission has held that the right contained in Article 13(1) can be denied only in limited circumstances, either by reason of legal incapacity or because the individual is not a citizen of the State.[1733] However, while the Commission has accepted that restrictions on the basis of nationality are understandable in the context of high offices of the nation it considers it unjustifiable and discriminatory to impose such restrictions on citizens by virtue of descent.[1734]

262. It should be noted that the right in Article 13(1) contains a limitation in that participation in government must be in accordance with the law. The Human Rights Court has stated that such limitations must serve a legitimate purpose and be based on legitimate public interests; they must be strictly proportionate to and absolutely necessary for their purpose.[1735] Consequently, States have the right to legislate to regulate elections, to determine voting age, criteria for eligibility, etc. but these must

---

167, 194. *See further* R. Murray, *Human Rights in Africa: From the OAU to the African Union* (Cambridge: Cambridge University Press, 2004), 235–266.

1729. Resolution on Electoral Process and Participatory Governance, adopted at the Commission's Nineteenth Ordinary Session, 1996, 9th Activity Report, 1995–1996. In *Mouvement Ivorien des Droits Humains (MIDH) v. Côte d'Ivoire*, Communication No. 246/2002, 25th Activity Report 2008, para. 77, the Commission expressed the view that a freely elected government 'provide the soundest guarantee that the basic human rights will be observed and protected'. In *Constitutional Rights Project and Civil Liberties Organisation v. Nigeria*, Communication No. 102/93, 12th Activity Report 1998–1999, para. 48, the Commission stated that the 'criteria for what constitutes free and fair elections are internationally agreed upon, and international observers are put in place to apply these criteria. It would be contrary to the logic of international law if a national government with a vested interest in the outcome of an election, were the final arbiter of whether the election took place in accordance with international standards'.

1730. Resolution on the Human Rights Situation in Africa, Resolution on The Gambia, and Resolution on Nigeria, adopted at the Commission's Sixteenth Ordinary Session, 1994, 8th Activity Report, 1994–1995.

1731. *The Law Office of Ghazi Suleiman v. Sudan*, Communication No. 228/99, 16th Activity Report 2002–2003, para. 53.

1732. Among the AU's objectives and principles, as set out in the Constitutive Act Arts 3(g) and 4(m), are the promotion of, and respect for, democratic principles and institutions, popular participation and good governance, human rights, and the rule of law. These aims are reinforced by the African Charter on Democracy.

1733. *Purohit and Moore v. The Gambia*, Communication No. 241/2001, 16th Activity Report 2002–2003, para. 75. The Commission proceeded to find that mentally disabled persons could be excluded from political participation only on the basis of objective and reasonable criteria established by law, *ibid.*, para. 76.

1734. *Mouvement Ivorien des Droits Humains (MIDH) v. Côte d'Ivoire*, Communication No. 246/2002, 25th Activity Report 2008, paras 80–87.

1735. *Konaté v. Burkina Faso*, African Court of Human and Peoples' Rights, App. No. 004/2013 (5 Dec. 2014) paras 132–133.

be objective, reasonable, and justifiable and must not negate the essence of the right.[1736] In *Interights, Institute for Human Rights and Development in Africa, and Association Mauritanienne des Droits de l'Homme v. Islamic Republic of Mauritania,* the Commission accepted that there were circumstances in which restrictions could be imposed upon political parties, for example, if they incited violence or threatened public order, but that any restrictions had to be proportionate, based on a legitimate public purpose and conform to international human rights standards.[1737] While some regimes may no doubt be tempted to invoke this limitation to undermine the political opposition it is nevertheless gratifying to observe that the Commission itself is committed to democratic principles and pluralism.[1738]

263. The question of the independence and impartiality of electoral commissions has given rise to controversy. The Human Rights Court has stated that such bodies occupy a 'critical space in a country's democratic architecture.'[1739] In view of the diversity of such bodies across Africa the Human Rights Court has said that it would not be appropriate to impose a uniform policy applicable throughout Africa.[1740] Nevertheless, a number of elements underpin the independence and impartiality of electoral commissions. They must have administrative and financial autonomy and offer sufficient guarantees under law of their members' independence and impartiality.[1741] The Human Rights Court has also held that returning officers must hold appropriate qualifications for their office.[1742]

264. Article 13(2) gives the citizen the right of equal access to the public service of one's country but the concept of 'public service' is not defined.[1743] It is unclear whether this refers to use of social services such as educational or health facilities,[1744] and/or employment opportunities.[1745] However, the Commission has

1736. *Mouvement Ivorien des Droits Humains (MIDH) v. Côte d'Ivoire*, Communication No. 246/2002, 25th Activity Report 2008, para. 83.
1737. Communication No. 242/2001, 17th Activity Report 2003–2004.
1738. *Ibid.*, para. 84.
1739. *Bob Chacha Wangwe and Legal and Human Rights Centre v. Tanzania*, African Court of Human and Peoples' Rights, App. No. 011/2020 (13 Jun. 2023) para. 82.
1740. *Suy Bi Gohore Emile and Others v. Côte d'Ivoire*, African Court of Human and Peoples' Rights, App. No. 044/2019 (15 Jul. 2020) paras 169–170.
1741. *Actions pour la Protection des Droits de l'Homme (APDH) v. Côte d'Ivoire*, African Court of Human and Peoples' Rights, App. No. 001/2014 (18 Nov. 2016) paras 118, 123.
1742. *Bob Chacha Wangwe and Legal and Human Rights Centre v. Tanzania*, African Court of Human and Peoples' Rights, App. No. 011/2020 (13 Jun. 2023) para. 108.
1743. Compare the European Court of Justice's interpretation of 'public service' in Treaty on the Functioning of the European Union Art. 45(4) (13 Dec. 2007), [2010] O.J. C 83/47, as referring to activities which involve participation in the exercise of powers conferred by public law or safeguard the general interests of the State, such as the armed forces, the police, or the judiciary, Case 149/79 *Commission v. Belgium* [1980] ECR 3881; Case 225/85 *Commission v. Italy* [1987] ECR 2625.
1744. Note that the African Charter on Democracy Art. 41, requires States Parties to provide and enable access to basic social services.
1745. Compare *Glasenapp v. Germany* Series A, Vol. 104 (1986) and *Kosiek v. Germany* Series A, Vol. 105 (1986) where the European Court of Human Rights held that the ECHR does not recognize a right of recruitment to the civil service.

adopted the view that it refers to political participation.[1746] Article 13(3) grants every individual, thereby including non-nationals, the right of equal access to public property and services before the law.

265. Article 14 of the African Charter guarantees the right to property, which is one enjoyed by every individual.[1747] The Commission has described the right to property as 'a fundamental right in democratic and liberal societies'.[1748] According to the Commission it includes 'the principle of ownership and peaceful enjoyment of property',[1749] the 'right to use, enjoy and dispose of something in an exclusive and absolute manner'[1750] and the effective benefit of this right 'necessarily includes a right to have access to property of one's own and the right not for one's property to be removed'.[1751] Property has been given a wider interpretation to include other assets,[1752] including land.[1753] Traditional lands belonging to indigenous communities also constitute property.[1754] As a necessary corollary, and in association with other rights, it extends to housing.[1755] A burning question that arises concerns the compatibility of African customary laws or religious law, where women are often disadvantaged in terms of family law and succession, with this provision in

1746. *Modise v. Botswana*, Communication No. 97/93, 14th Activity Report 2000–2001, para. 96.
1747. *Dino Noca v. Democratic Republic of the Congo*, Communication No. 286/2004 (2012), para. 128. However, the Human Rights Court has held that the right to property may additionally be a collective right, *African Commission on Human and Peoples' Rights v. Kenya*, African Court of Human and Peoples' Rights, App. No. 006/2012 (26 May 2017) para. 123. *See similarly Indigenous Communities of the Lhaka Honhat (Our Land) Association v. Argentina*, Inter-American Court of Human Rights, Ser. C No. 420 (Merits, reparations and costs) (6 Feb. 2020).
1748. *Interights et al. v. Mauritania*, Communication No. 373/2006, 28th Activity Report 2009–2010, para. 43.
1749. *Ibid.*, para. 44.
1750. *Mbianku v. Cameroon*, Communication No. 389/10 (2015) para. 106.
1751. *Media Rights Agenda and Constitutional Rights Project v. Nigeria*, Communication Nos 105/93, 128/94, 130/94, 152/96, 12th Activity Report 1998–1999, para. 77. *See also Constitutional Rights Project, Civil Liberties Organisation and Media Rights Agenda v. Nigeria*, Communication Nos 140/94, 141/94, 145/95, 13th Activity Report 1999–2000, para. 54. The Commission has also referred to 'the right to undisturbed possession, use and control of … property however the owner(s) deem fit', *Centre for Minority Rights Development (Kenya) and Minority Rights Group International on behalf of Endorois Welfare Council v. Kenya*, Communication No. 276/2003, 27th Activity Report 2009, para. 186.
1752. In *Bissangou v. Republic of Congo*, Communication No. 253/2002, 21st Activity Report 2005–2006, para. 76, the Commission found that monetary compensation awarded by a court judgment was to be considered an asset.
1753. *Malawi African Association et al. v. Mauritania*. Communication Nos 54/91, 61/91, 98/93/164/97–196/97, 210/98, 13th Activity Report 1999–2000, para. 128; *Centre for Minority Rights Development (Kenya) and Minority Rights Group International on behalf of Endorois Welfare Council v. Kenya*, Communication No. 276/2003, 27th Activity Report 2009, para. 186.
1754. *Centre for Minority Rights Development (Kenya) and Minority Rights Group International on behalf of Endorois Welfare Council v. Kenya*, Communication No. 276/2003, 27th Activity Report 2009, para. 187. The Commission proceeded to state that special measures may be necessary to secure such property, and that at the very least, traditional possession of land is equivalent to full title, *ibid.*, paras 187–209. *See also African Commission on Human and Peoples' Rights v. Kenya*, African Court of Human and Peoples' Rights, App. No. 006/2012 (26 May 2017) paras 126–128.
1755. *Mbianku v. Cameroon*, Communication No. 389/10 (2015) paras 121–123.

association with Article 2 of the African Charter.[1756] A curious decision is that of *Rabah v. Mauritania* where the Commission held that for a mother to deprive her children of their inheritance for the benefit of a third party with no specific reason contravened Article 14.[1757] This conclusion led to what appears to be a unique occurrence in the Commission's practice, the appending of a dissenting opinion.[1758] Commissioner El Hassan could not see how the law in Mauritania, which gave the owner of property, a rational and mature person, the freedom to dispose of property as she saw fit, could be considered incompatible with the African Charter. In fact, in his view, the Commission was in essence restraining the owner from disposing freely of her property and depriving the recipient of property he had lawfully inherited.

266. The right to property is not absolute[1759] and its enjoyment of may be limited or encroached upon 'in the interest of public need or in the general interest of the community' in accordance with the law, which means that interference with, or deprivation of, property must not be arbitrary or without good reason.[1760] The Commission has held that this test is conjunctive[1761] and must meet a higher threshold

1756. *See* the controversial judgment of the Supreme Court of Zimbabwe in *Magaya v. Magaya* [1999] 3 L.R.C. 35, noted in 43 J.A.L. 248 (1999). However, in *Bhe and Others v. The Magistrate, Khayelitsha and Others* 2005 (1) SA 580 (CC) the Constitutional Court of South Africa held that the African customary rule of male primogeniture in relation to the inheritance of property discriminated against women and illegitimate children.

1757. Communication No. 197/97, 17th Activity Report, 2003–2004.

1758. Neither the African Charter nor the Commission's Rules of Procedure make explicit provision for dissenting opinions. According to the Rules, revised in 2020, one Rapporteur is appointed for each Communication, Rule 93(1).

1759. *Institute for Human Rights and Development in Africa v. Angola*, Communication No. 292/2004, 24th Activity Report 2008, para. 73; *Dino Noca v. Democratic Republic of the Congo*, Communication No. 286/2004 (2012), para. 143.

1760. *Media Rights Agenda and Constitutional Rights Project v. Nigeria*, Communication Nos 105/93, 128/94, 130/94, 152/96, 12th Activity Report, 1998–1999, para. 77; *Constitutional Rights Project, Civil Liberties Organisation and Media Rights Agenda v. Nigeria*, Communication Nos 140/94, 141/94, 145/95, 13th Activity Report 1999–2000, para. 54; *African Institute for Human Rights and Development (on behalf of Sierra Leonean refugees in Guinea v. Republic of Guinea*, Communication No. 249/2002, 20th Activity Report, 2005–2006; *Scanlen and Holderness v. Zimbabwe*, Communication No. 297/2005, 26th Activity Report 2009, para. 179; *Interights et al. v. Mauritania*, Communication No. 373/2006, 28th Activity Report 2009–2010, para. 45; *Open Society Justice Initiative v. Côte d'Ivoire*, Communication No. 318/06 (2015) para. 174; *The Nubian Community in Kenya v. Kenya*, Communication No. 317/06 (2015), para. 165. The Commission has further stated that any limitation must be proportionate to a legitimate need, *Centre for Minority Rights Development (Kenya) and Minority Rights Group International on behalf of Endorois Welfare Council v. Kenya*, Communication No. 276/2003, 27th Activity Report 2009, paras 213–215; *Dino Noca v. Democratic Republic of the Congo*, Communication No. 286/2004 (2012), para. 145. Property can be regulated by the State to meet, for example, environmental standards, health and safety standards, building and planning regulations, and rent controls, UN Doc. E/CN.4/1993/15, pp. 75–76. The jurisprudence of the European Court of Human Rights demonstrates that the State has wide powers to take and to control the use of property, Harris, O'Boyle, Warbrick, 677–692. The policy of land redistribution pursued by the Zimbabwean Government in recent years has proven disastrous. The expropriation of farms in Zimbabwe for the purpose of social equity was held to be legitimate in the public interest, *Davies v. Minister of Land, Agriculture and Water Development* 1997 1 SA 228 (ZS). However, the Zimbabwean Government was either unable or unwilling to abide by its own laws and follow proper procedure, permitting or instigating the infamous violent farm invasions. This anarchical situation was condemned by the Supreme Court, which found that resettlement in such

with regard to encroachment on traditional lands.[1762] If evictions are contemplated then prior, bona fides consultation is required.[1763] The fact that only a limited number of people may be affected is immaterial.[1764] It should be observed that the African Charter makes no express reference as to the appropriate level of compensation for the expropriation of property.[1765] However, in *Centre for Minority Rights Development (Kenya) and Minority Rights Group International on behalf of Endorois Welfare Council v. Kenya*, the Commission held that where it is not possible to return land, the dispossessed owners should, *inter alia*, receive compensation at full replacement cost prior to their the dispossession.[1766] The Commission found a violation of this provision in *Malawi African Association et al. v. Mauritania* where the property of black Mauritanians had been confiscated and looted as part of a campaign of harassment.[1767] Another violation was found in *Union Interafricaine des Droits de l'Homme et al. v. Angola* where the mass expulsion of West Africans resulted in the loss of property.[1768]

---

circumstances was unconstitutional, being incompatible with the right to property and the protection from arbitrary search or entry, *Commercial Farmers Union v. Minister of Lands, Agriculture and Rural Resettlement and Others* 2001 2 SA 925 (ZS). The Supreme Court's defence of constitutionalism in turn led to the ousting of the firmly independent justices referred to *infra*, para. 285. The reconstituted Supreme Court subsequently upheld the constitutionality of the land resettlement programme, *Minister of Lands, Agriculture and Rural Resettlement & Others v. Commercial Farmers Union* (SC 111/01). *See also Mike Campbell (Pvt) Ltd. v. Minister of National Security Responsible for Land, Land Reform and Resettlement & Others* (SC 49/07). However, in *Mike Campbell (Pvt) Ltd. et al. v. The Republic of Zimbabwe* the SADC Tribunal, in its first judgment, held that Zimbabwe's land reform programme was in breach of the SADC Treaty, SADC (T) Case No. 2/2007 (2008), http://www.saflii.org/sa/cases/SADCT/2008/2.pdf.

1761. *Centre for Minority Rights Development (Kenya) and Minority Rights Group International on behalf of Endorois Welfare Council v. Kenya*, Communication No. 276/2003, 27th Activity Report 2009, para. 211.

1762. *Ibid.*, para. 212. *See also African Commission on Human and Peoples' Rights v. Kenya*, African Court of Human and Peoples' Rights, App. No. 006/2012 (26 May 2017) para. 130.

1763. *Ibid.*, para. 226; *The Nubian Community in Kenya v. Kenya*, Communication No. 317/06 (2015), para. 165.

1764. *Ivorien Human Rights Movement (MIDH) v. Côte d'Ivoire*, Communication No. 262/2002, 26th Activity Report 2008–2009, para. 77.

1765. At present international law requires compensation to be prompt, adequate and effective but developing States maintain that the less rigid standard of adequate compensation is appropriate, *see Texaco v. Libya* 17 I.L.M. 1 (1978) where the arbitrator observed that developed States regarded the latter formulation as *contra legem*. In *Institute for Human Rights and Development in Africa v. Angola*, Communication No. 292/2004, 24th Activity Report 2008, para. 73, and in *Dino Noca v. Democratic Republic of the Congo*, Communication No. 286/2004 (2012), para. 147, the Commission referred to 'adequate compensation'. Note that in *Lithgow v. United Kingdom* Series A, Vol. 102 (1986) the European Court of Human Rights declared that under the ECHR First Protocol Art. 1 (20 Mar. 1952), E.T.S. No. 9, the taking of property without payment of an amount reasonably related to its value would normally constitute a disproportionate interference which could not be considered justifiable.

1766. Communication No. 276/2003, 27th Activity Report 2009, paras 234–237.

1767. Communication Nos 54/91, 61/91, 98/93/164/97–196/97, 210/98, 13th Activity Report 1999–2000, para. 128.

1768. Communication No. 159/96, 11th Activity Report, 1997–1998; *African Institute for Human Rights and Development (on behalf of Sierra Leonean refugees in Guinea v. Republic of Guinea*, Communication No. 249/2002, 20th Activity Report 2005–2006; *Institute for Human Rights and Development in Africa v. Angola*, Communication No. 292/2004, 24th Activity Report 2008, para. 73.

267. It is interesting to note that the right to property does not extend to tax evasion since Article 29(6) of the African Charter, in another cultural variation, imposes an obligation upon the individual to pay taxes according to the law in the interest of society.

IV. Social and Economic Rights

268. Articles 15–18 of the African Charter provide for economic, social and cultural rights, otherwise classified as second-generation rights. Some of these rights have a plural nature, transcending both first- and second-generation rights; the right to property and the rights of the family are but two examples of rights which may be said to have a dual nature.[1769] The Commission has stated that States must respect the free use of resources owned or at the disposal of individuals for the purpose of rights-related needs.[1770] Additionally, the obligation on States to promote and fulfil these rights could amount to the provision of basic needs such as food or social security.[1771]

269. The right to work is guaranteed by Article 15 of the African Charter.[1772] While not as detailed as the ICESCR, it has been held tacitly to encompass the different aspect enumerated therein.[1773] While the right to work is deemed essential for the realization of other economic, social and cultural rights and forms an inseparable and inherent part of human dignity,[1774] it does not equate to an 'absolute and unconditional right to obtain employment', rather 'the State has the obligation to facilitate employment through the creation of an environment conducive to the full employment of individuals within society under conditions that ensure the realisation of the dignity of the individual'.[1775] It 'implies the right to enter employment, and the right not to be deprived of employment unfairly'.[1776] The Human Rights Court has stated that the rights enshrined in the provision are those of access and enjoyment.[1777] The right to remuneration also forms a critical component of this

1769. *See The Social and Economic Rights Action Center and the Center for Economic and Social Rights v. Nigeria*, Communication No. 155/96, 15th Activity Report 2001–2002.

1770. *Ibid.*, para. 45.

1771. *Ibid.*, para. 47.

1772. A corollary of the right to work is the right to strike, *Ajavon v. Benin*, African Court of Human and Peoples' Rights, App. No. 062/2019, Judgment (4 Dec. 2020), para. 132.

1773. *Mulindahabi v. Rwanda*, African Court of Human and Peoples' Rights, App. No. 004/2017 (26 Jun. 2020) para. 89. The Human Rights Court has stated that there is equivalence between the two instruments, *Karata and others v. Tanzania*, African Court of Human and Peoples' Rights, Judgment, App. No. 002/2017 (30 Sep. 2021) para. 100.

1774. *Almas Mohamed Muwinda and others v. Tanzania*, African Court of Human and Peoples' Rights, Judgment, App. No. 030/2017 (24 Mar. 2022) para. 54.

1775. *Monim Elgak, Osman Hummeida and Amir Suleiman (represented by FIDH and OMCT) v. Sudan*, Communication No. 379/09 (2014) para. 129.

1776. *Ibid.*, para. 130. It also implies a right to promotion, *Sissoko and 74 others v. Mali*, African Court of Human and Peoples' Rights, App. No. 037/2017, Judgment (25 Sep. 2020), para. 108.

1777. *Mulindahabi v. Rwanda*, African Court of Human and Peoples' Rights, App. No. 004/2017 (26 Jun. 2020) para. 89.

right.[1778] The Commission has stated that one of the purposes of this provision is 'to ensure that States respect and protect the right of everyone to have access to the labour market without discrimination. The protection should be construed to allow certain restrictions depending on the type of employment'.[1779] While the Commission has found violations of Article 15 on various occasions,[1780] in *Garreth Anver Prince v. South Africa*, the Commission found no violation because the complainant was deemed to have disqualified himself from pursuing his occupation through his use of drugs, which the State had a legitimate interest in controlling.[1781]

270. Other second-generation rights include the right to health enshrined in Article 16,[1782] and the right to education guaranteed by Article 17(1).[1783] In an important case on the right to health, *Purohit and Moore v. The Gambia*, the Commission upheld a number of complaints against the legislation governing mental health.[1784] The Commission emphasized the significance of the right to health describing it as 'vital to all aspects of a person's life and well-being, and is crucial to the realisation of all the other fundamental human rights and freedoms'.[1785] In *Egyptian Initiative for Personal Rights and INTERIGHTS v. Egypt*, the Commission underlined its significance, stating that the right to health 'is an entitlement which is derived from specific obligations claimed by individuals from States, and it is very fundamental to the exercise of other human rights enshrined in the African Charter … States have a legal obligation to protect the right to health of its citizens, including … taking concrete and targeted steps towards the full realization of the

1778. *Almas Mohamed Muwinda and others v. Tanzania*, African Court of Human and Peoples' Rights, Judgment, App. No. 030/2017 (24 Mar. 2022) para. 54.
1779. *Garreth Anver Prince v. South Africa*, Communication No. 255/2002, 18th Activity Report 2002–2003, para. 46.
1780. *Annette Pagnoulle (on behalf of Abdoulaye Mazou) v. Cameroon*, Communication No. 39/90, 10th Activity Report 1996–1997; *Institute for Human Rights and Development in Africa v. Angola*, Communication No. 292/2004, 24th Activity Report 2008, para. 76; *Scanlen and Holderness v. Zimbabwe*, Communication No. 297/2005, 26th Activity Report 2009, para. 179; *Open Society Justice Initiative v. Côte d'Ivoire*, Communication No. 318/06 (2015) paras 176–177.
1781. *Garreth Anver Prince v. South Africa*, Communication No. 255/2002, 18th Activity Report 2002–2003, para. 46.
1782. *Union Interafricaine des Droits de l'Homme v. Zaïre*, Communication 100/93 (failure by the State to provide safe drinking water, electricity and medicines); *Media Rights Agenda and Constitutional Rights Project v. Nigeria*, Communication Nos 105/93, 128/94, 130/94, 152/96 (denial of medical assistance to detainee in deteriorating health); *International Pen, Constitutional Rights Project, Interights on behalf of Ken Saro-Wiwa Jr. and Civil Liberties Organisation v. Nigeria*, Communication Nos 137/94, 139/94, 154/96, 161/97, 12th Activity Report 1998–1999 (denial of medical assistance to detainee); *Malawi African Association et al. v. Mauritania*, Communication Nos 54/91, 61/91, 98/93/164/97–196/97, 210/98, 13th Activity Report 1999–2000 (lack of medical attention for detainees); *Democratic Republic of Congo v. Burundi, Rwanda and Uganda*, Communication No. 227/99, 20th Activity Report, 2005–2006 (stopping essential services in a hospital).
1783. *Union Interafricaine des Droits de l'Homme v. Zaïre*, Communication No. 100/93 (closure of universities and secondary schools for a number of years); *Democratic Republic of Congo v. Burundi, Rwanda and Uganda*, Communication No. 227/99, 20th Activity Report, 2005–2006.
1784. Communication No. 241/2001, 16th Activity Report 2002–2003.
1785. *Ibid.*, para. 80.

right, and adopting legislation or other measures to ensure equal access to health-related services and health care'.[1786] It extends to the right to control one's health and body and to be free from intrusions.[1787] With specific reference to mental health patients, the Commission in *Purohit and Moore v. The Gambia* clarified the standard of care that they were entitled to expect; failure to meet these standards breached Articles 16 and 18.[1788] But in an important passage, the Commission spelt out its position on this issue:

> The African Commission would ... like to state that it is aware that millions of people in Africa are not enjoying the right to health maximally because African countries are generally faced with the problem of poverty which renders them incapable to provide the necessary amenities, infrastructure and resources that facilitate the full enjoyment of this right. Therefore, having due regard to this depressing but real state of affairs, the African Commission would like to read into Article 16 the obligation on part of States ... to take concrete and targeted steps, while taking full advantage of its available resources, to ensure that the right to health is fully realized in all its aspects without discrimination of any kind.[1789]

A seminal case is that of *The Social and Economic Rights Action Center and the Center for Economic and Social Rights v. Nigeria*, where the Commission considered these rights in some detail.[1790] The Ogoni people claimed that a number of their fundamental rights had been violated by the Nigerian military regime, acting through the state oil company, which had failed to take measures to protect the local population from acts harmful to the environment. The Commission found violations of, *inter alia*, the right to health, the right to protection of the family, the right to housing and the right to food. The Commission's approach to this case is particularly interesting because it found that a number of rights protected by different provisions were in fact mutually dependent and mutually reinforcing. In addition, by adopting a broad view of the combined effect of a number of provisions it was able to read into the African Charter a right that was not explicitly guaranteed, namely, a right to shelter or housing.[1791]

1786. Communication No. 323/2006 (2011), para. 264.

1787. *Monim Elgak, Osman Hummeida and Amir Suleiman (represented by FIDH and OMCT) v. Sudan*, Communication No. 379/09 (2014) para. 134.

1788. Communication No. 241/2001, 16th Activity Report 2002–2003, para. 84. *See also* African Charter on Democracy Art. 41 according to which State Parties undertake to provide and enable access to basic social services.

1789. *Ibid.*, paras 81–83.

1790. Communication No. 155/96, 15th Activity Report 2001–2002. For comment, *see* G. Bekker, 'The Social and Economic Rights Action Center and the Center for Economic and Social Rights/ Nigeria', *J.A.L.* 47(2003): 126.

1791. Communication No. 155/96, 15th Activity Report 2001–2002, para. 60. *See also Mbianku v. Cameroon*, Communication No. 389/10 (2015) paras 121–123.

271. The right to cultural life assured by Article 17(2) requires the State to tolerate cultural diversity and to protect minority groups.[1792] Given the challenges faced by indigenous peoples, the State is under a higher duty to take positive steps to promote their culture and way of life.[1793] Culture in this context has been defined by the Commission as 'that complex whole which includes a spiritual and physical association with one's ancestral land, knowledge, belief, art, law, morals, customs, and any other capabilities and habits acquired by humankind as a member of society – the sum total of the material and spiritual activities and products of a given social group that distinguish it from other similar groups'.[1794] It has a dual dimension in that it has individual and collective elements, ensuring the individual's participation in cultural life and required state protection of traditional community values.[1795] Thus, culture encompasses the total way of life of a particular group, including its languages, its rituals, its dress codes and its economic activities.[1796] In *Malawi African Association et al. v. Mauritania*, the Commission considered stating that language is an integral part of cultural expression that enables the individual to take an active part in the life of the community. Preventing individuals expressing themselves in a particular language deprives them of their identity.[1797] However, the right to cultural life is not absolute, and restrictions may legitimately be imposed on certain cultural practices, such as the use of drugs, for the overall good of society.[1798]

272. The rights of the family is guaranteed by Article 18 of the African Charter. The family is described as 'the natural unit and basis of society'.[1799] According to the Commission, Article 18 imposes both positive and negative obligations upon the State, in that the State must protect the family and assist it in meeting its needs and interests, while refraining from unwarranted interference with the family.[1800] In this latter context the State must avoid separating arbitrarily family members.[1801] As the Human Rights Court has stated, the right to family implies being able to live together or that family members can contact each other.[1802]The Commission has

1792. *Centre for Minority Rights Development (Kenya) and Minority Rights Group International on behalf of Endorois Welfare Council v. Kenya*, Communication No. 276/2003, 27th Activity Report 2009, para. 246.
1793. *Ibid.*, para. 248; *African Commission on Human and Peoples' Rights v. Kenya*, African Court of Human and Peoples' Rights, App. No. 006/2012 (26 May 2017) paras 177–179.
1794. *Centre for Minority Rights Development (Kenya) and Minority Rights Group International on behalf of Endorois Welfare Council v. Kenya*, Communication No. 276/2003, 27th Activity Report 2009, para. 241.
1795. *Ibid.*
1796. *African Commission on Human and Peoples' Rights v. Kenya*, African Court of Human and Peoples' Rights, App. No. 006/2012 (26 May 2017) para. 179.
1797. Communication Nos 54/91, 61/91, 98/93/164/97–196/97, 210/98, 13th Activity Report 1999–2000.
1798. *Garreth Anver Prince v. South Africa*, Communication No. 255/2002, 18th Activity Report 2002–2003, para. 48.
1799. African Charter Art. 18(1). *See* ACHR Art. 17(1).
1800. *Good v. Botswana*, Communication No. 306/2005, 28th Activity Report 2009–2010, para. 212.
1801. *Ibid.*; *Open Society Justice Initiative v. Côte d'Ivoire*, Communication No. 318/06 (2015) para. 179.
1802. *Mugesera v. Rwanda*, African Court of Human and Peoples' Rights, App. No. 012/2017, Judgment (27 Nov. 2020) para. 116.

found violations of Article 18 on numerous occasions[1803] but an important decision is that of *Sudan Human Rights Organization and Sudan Centre for Housing Rights and Evictions v. Sudan.*[1804] Here, the Commission found that the failure of the State to protect the victims from the Janjaweed militia who killed and forcibly evicted people from their homes, while others fled for their lives, violated Article 18.[1805] It stated that this state of affairs threatened the very foundation of the family and rendered enjoyment of the right difficult.[1806]

V. Peoples' Rights

273. The significance attributed to the concept of the rights of 'peoples', or third-generation rights, as a component of African human rights philosophy is illustrated by its inclusion in the African Charter, specifically in Articles 19–24.[1807] It requires States to respect the resources belonging to a collective group.[1808] The definition of the concept of 'peoples' is troublesome because there is little consensus and it is difficult to identify the peoples or groups entitled to these rights as well as the entities that owe them these rights.[1809] The African Charter does not provide a definition of the African notion of a 'people',[1810] but depending on context it appears capable of either referring to the national community as a whole, or the State itself,[1811] or collective, as in distinct ethnic or tribal, communities.[1812] However, in *Gunme et al. v. Cameroon*, the Commission engaged with this controversial

1803. *Union Interafricaine des Droits de l'Homme et al. v. Angola*, Communication No. 159/96, 11th Activity Report, 1997–1998; *Amnesty International v. Zambia*, Communication No. 212/98, 12th Activity Report 1998–1999; *Malawi African Association et al. v. Mauritania*, Communication Nos 54/91, 61/91, 98/93/164/97–196/97, 210/98, 13th Activity Report 1999–2000; *Constitutional Rights Project and Civil Liberties Organisation v. Nigeria*, Communication Nos 143/95, 150/96, 14th Activity Report 1999–2000; *Modise v. Botswana*, Communication No. 97/93, 14th Activity Report 2000–2001; *Democratic Republic of Congo v. Burundi, Rwanda and Uganda*, Communication No. 227/99, 20th Activity Report, 2005–2006; *Article 19 v. Eritrea*, Communication No. 275/2003, 22nd Activity Report 2006–2007; *Good v. Botswana*, Communication No. 306/2005, 28th Activity Report 2009–2010; *Egyptian Initiative for Personal Rights and INTERIGHTS v. Egypt*, Communication No. 323/2006 (2011), paras 142–153.

1804. Communication Nos 279/03, 296/05, 28th Activity Report 2010.

1805. *Ibid.*, para. 216.

1806. *Ibid.*

1807. *Bissangou v. Republic of Congo*, Communication No. 253/2002, 21st Activity Report 2005–2006, para. 80. *See* Baldwin & Morel.

1808. *The Social and Economic Rights Action Center and the Center for Economic and Social Rights v. Nigeria*, Communication No. 155/96, 15th Activity Report 2001–2002, para. 45.

1809. A. Kiss, 'The Peoples' Right to Self-Determination', *H.R.L.J.* 7 (1986): 165, 172–173; T. van Boven, 'The Relations Between Peoples' Rights and Human Rights in the African Charter', *H.R.L.J.*7 (1986): 183; J.-B. Marie, 'Relations Between Peoples' Rights and Human Rights: Semantic and Methodological Distinctions', *H.R.L.J.*7(1986): 195.

1810. A. Kiwanuka, 'The Meaning of 'People' in the African Charter of Human and Peoples' Rights', *A.J.I.L.* 82 (1988): 80.

1811. *Katangese Peoples' Congress v. Zaire,* Communication No. 75/92, 8th Activity Report 1994–1995; *African Commission on Human and Peoples' Rights v. Kenya*, African Court of Human and Peoples' Rights, App. No. 006/2012 (26 May 2017) para. 198.

question.[1813] The central argument in this case centred on the claim that the people of southern Cameroon had been denied the right of self-determination at the time of decolonization and continued to be denied that right. The respondent government argued that the people of southern Cameroon were not a 'separate and distinct' people entitled to self-determination. The Commission interpreted the concept of 'people' broadly, combining both objective and subjective elements. It took the view that the following characteristics were crucial: a common historical tradition, a racial or ethnic identity, cultural homogeneity, linguistic unity, religious and ideological affinities, territorial connections, and a common economic life. Additionally, the group may consider itself a 'people' by virtue of their consciousness that they constitute a people.[1814] Identity, said the Commission, 'is an innate characteristic within a people' and the fact that a group sees itself as having a separate and distinct identity was important, as was its recognition by others. Ethno-anthropological attributes, while important, were not determinative, except in the case of indigenous peoples.[1815] Significantly, the Commission expressed the view that the African Charter applied to all peoples in Africa, regardless of origin, including therefore, communities of Asian or European descent.[1816] In *Sudan Human Rights Organization and Sudan Centre for Housing Rights and Evictions v. Sudan*, an added feature was that of 'mixed racial composition'.[1817] In such cases the Commission stated that race became a determinant factor, just as ethnic identity could also play a part.[1818] The Commission took the opportunity to celebrate Africa's rich diversity.[1819]

274. The African Charter does not expressly recognize indigenous peoples, partly due to a fear that to have done so could have had a destabilizing effect.[1820] However, in 2000 the Commission established a Working Group on Indigenous Populations/Communities, thus recognizing the existence of indigenous peoples in Africa.[1821] But it was the case of *Centre for Minority Rights Development (Kenya) and Minority Rights Group International on behalf of Endorois Welfare Council v. Kenya* that advanced the rights of indigenous people.[1822] In this case the Endorois

1812. *Malawi African Association et al. v. Mauritania*, Communication Nos 54/91, 61/91, 98/93, 164/97–196/97, 210/98, 13th Activity Report 1999–2000; *African Commission on Human and Peoples' Rights v. Kenya*, African Court of Human and Peoples' Rights, App. No. 006/2012 (26 May 2017) *ibid.*
1813. Communication No. 266/2003, 26th Activity Report 2008–2009.
1814. *Ibid.*, para. 170. *See also Centre for Minority Rights Development (Kenya) and Minority Rights Group International on behalf of Endorois Welfare Council v. Kenya*, Communication No. 276/2003, 27th Activity Report 2009, para. 151. Self-identification as a factor is stressed by the I.L.O. Convention No. 169 on Indigenous and Tribal Peoples in Independent Countries Art. 1(2) (27 Jun. 1989) 1650 U.N.T.S. 28383.
1815. *Ibid.*, para. 178.
1816. *Ibid.*
1817. Communication Nos 279/03, 296/05, 28th Activity Report 2010, para. 220.
1818. *Ibid.*
1819. *Ibid.*, para. 221.
1820. Viljoen, 279–281.
1821. Resolution on Indigenous Populations/Communities, Twenty-Eighth Ordinary Session 2000. *See further* Baldwin & Morel, 248–249.
1822. Communication No. 276/2003, 27th Activity Report 2009.

community alleged multiple violations of the African Charter, complaining that they had been forcibly removed from their ancestral lands without proper consultation or compensation, thereby separating them from their spiritual, cultural, and economic ties to the land. The Commission identified four criteria for recognizing indigenous peoples: the occupation and use of a specific territory; the voluntary perpetuation of cultural distinctiveness; self-identification as a distinct collectivity, as well as its recognition by others; and a history of subjugation, marginalization, dispossession or discrimination.[1823] The Commission found that the Endorois culture, religion, and traditional way of life was intimately linked to their ancestral lands and that without access thereto they could not fully exercise their cultural and religious rights.[1824]

275. Article 19 of the African Charter puts in context the rights that are elaborated further in the subsequent provisions. It extends the principle of non-discrimination to the community as a whole by proclaiming the equality of all peoples. Considering the African notion of 'peoples' as a national community this provision would appear to refer to the principles of equal rights and sovereign equality contained in Articles 1(2) and 2(1) of the UN Charter. Moreover, the total prohibition on the domination of one people over another would appear to be a reference to the principles of political independence and political and economic self-determination. In addition, it can also be interpreted as Africa's rejection of the policies of racial oppression and intolerance, not only as characterized by apartheid and white-minority rule, but also the ethnic and tribal hatreds that have descended into massacres in parts of Africa.[1825]

276. Article 20 of the African Charter enshrines a principle of international law long cherished by the OAU/AU, the inalienable right to political and economic self-determination.[1826] Because this right can assume different manifestations the precise the content and scope of self-determination is still the subject of considerable debate. According to the Human Rights Court, Article 20 'offers broader and stronger protection' to self-determination that the International Covenants.[1827] It imposes both positive and negative obligations on State Parties. The former comprise the duty to protect, promote, and fulfil conditions for the right's realization. States are required to take individual and joint actions to facilitate its realization, including by

1823. *Ibid.*, para. 150. These criteria were endorsed by the Human Rights Court in *African Commission on Human and Peoples' Rights v. Kenya*, African Court of Human and Peoples' Rights, App. No. 006/2012 (26 May 2017) para. 107.

1824. *Ibid.*, para. 156. Note *Sesana and Others v. Attorney-General* (2006) A.H.R.L.R. 183, where the High Court of Botswana held that the San people (Bushmen) had been evicted illegally from their ancestral lands and that they had the right to live on such land.

1825. *See Malawi African Association et al. v. Mauritania*, Communication Nos 54/91, 61/91, 98/93, 164/97–196/97, 210/98, 13th Activity Report 1999–2000, para. 142, where discriminatory practices against the Black population of Mauritania was condemned. *See also Sudan Human Rights Organization and Sudan Centre for Housing Rights and Evictions v. Sudan*, Communication Nos. 279/03, 296/05, 28th Activity Report, 2010, para. 223.

1826. *Mornah v. Benin et al.*, African Court of Human and Peoples' Rights, App. No. 028/2018, Judgment (22 Sep. 2022) paras 290–292.

1827. *Ibid.*, para. 295.

offering assistance to people struggling for independence and freedom from domination. The latter involve the duty to respect the right, i.e., abstaining from engaging in acts or taking measures that adversely affect people from fully enjoying their right to self-determination. This includes not recognizing an illegal situation resulting from a violation of that right.[1828] One facet of self-determination is as a corollary of sovereignty, necessarily associated with the principle of non-intervention.[1829] Paragraph 1 enshrines the right of peoples to determine freely their political status. The Commission has therefore been able to rely on the internal dimension of self-determination to uphold democratic values and to condemn military coups. In *Sir Dawda K. Jawara v. Gambia*, the Commission held that the military coup that overthrew Gambia's democratic system 'was a grave violation of the right of the Gambian people to freely choose their government as entrenched in Article 20(1)'.[1830]

277. The right to self-determination extends to colonized and oppressed people.[1831] This is apparent from paragraphs 2 and 3 of the provision, and the practice and *opinio juris* of African States and the OAU/AU. In this context, self-determination, in its external manifestation, is synonymous with decolonization.[1832] Indeed, the Human Rights Court has pronounced that the right to self-determination

1828. *Ibid.*, paras 297-298. *See Legal Consequences of the Separation of the Chagos Archipelago from Mauritius in 1965*, Advisory Opinion, I.C.J. Reports 2019, *95*, para. 180.

1829. *Democratic Republic of Congo v. Burundi, Rwanda and Uganda*, Communication No. 227/99, 20th Activity Report, 2005–2006, para. 68.

1830. Communication Nos 147/95 and 149/96, 13th Activity Report 1999–2000, para. 73.

1831. The reference to 'oppressed peoples' was designed to include the majority of the inhabitants of Rhodesia, South Africa, and Namibia who were labouring under unrepresentative minority governments.

1832. It is now established that the inhabitants of non-self-governing territories have a legal right freely to determine their future political, economic and cultural status; independence must be an available choice. *See* in particular UN General Assembly Res. 1514(XV) 1960, Declaration on the Granting of Independence to Colonial Countries and Peoples, Res. 1541(XV) 1960, and Res. 2625(XXV) 1970, Declaration on Friendly Relations Among States in Accordance with the Charter of the United Nations, the relevant jurisprudence of the ICJ, in particular *Legal Consequences for States of the Continued Presence of South Africa in Namibia (South West Africa) notwithstanding Security Council Res. 276 (1970)*, Advisory Opinion, I.C.J. Reports 1971, 16, *Western Sahara Case*, Advisory Opinion, I.C.J. Reports 1975, 12, and *East Timor Case (Portugal v. Australia)* I.C.J. Reports 1995, 90. *See further* General comment 12 paras 6–7, UN Doc. HRI/GEN/1/Rev.2. Mauritius and the United Kingdom have been locked in a dispute as to whether the decolonization of Mauritius was carried out in conformity with international law in light of the separation of the Chagos Archipelago from Mauritius. In *Chagos Marine Protected Area Arbitration (Mauritius v. United Kingdom)*, Award, 18 Mar. 2015) PCA Case No. 2011-03, paras 70–72, Dissenting and Concurring Opinion of Judges Kateka and Wolfrum, the view was expressed that this fact was contrary to the principles of decolonization and self-determination. This conclusion was shared by the ICJ which stated further that *the* United Kingdom's continued administration of the Chagos Islands amounted to 'a wrongful act entailing the international responsibility of that State', *Legal Consequences of the Separation of the Chagos Archipelago from Mauritius in 1965*, **Advisory Opinion,** I.C.J. Reports 2019, *para. 177.* In January 2023, *the* United Kingdom and Mauritius commenced talks on the sovereignty of the Chagos Archipelago, Africanews, 'Mauritius and UK launch sovereignty talks over Chagos Islands', 2 Jan. 2023, https://www.africanews.com/2023/01/02/mauritius-and-uk-launch-sovereignty-talks-over-chagos-islands//.

is a norm *jus cogens* giving rise to an obligation *erga omnes*.[1833] The main case of frustrated self-determination in Africa is that of the Sahrawis of Western Sahara, a conflict that remains unresolved to this day. There is near universal agreement that the Sahrawi people have a right to self-determination,[1834] which may have been exercised through the founding of the SADR in 1976. The statehood of the SADR is contested notwithstanding the SADR's admission to the OAU in 1982; the UN still considers the situation as one of decolonization which has yet to be brought to fruition and Western Sahara continues on the UN list of non-self-governing territories. Morocco's presence in Western Sahara may be categorized as one of occupation, a view shared by the Human Rights Court which has held that the continued occupation of the SADR by Morocco is incompatible with the right to self-determination.[1835]

278. However, if self-determination is a right of all people does this mean that secession is legitimized? The international community is reluctant generally to accept such a possibility. African States are adamantly opposed to any interpretation of self-determination that involves a threat of unilateral, or contested, secession.[1836] The Commission has therefore held that it is obliged to uphold the sovereignty and territorial integrity of States and that self-determination must be exercised in a manner compatible with the sovereignty and territorial integrity of states.[1837] Accordingly, 'secession is not recognised as a variant of the right of self-determination within the context of the African Charter'.[1838] It has therefore stated

1833. *Mornah v. Benin et al.*, African Court of Human and Peoples' Rights, App. No. 028/2018, Judgment (22 Sep. 2022) para. 298. The ICJ has repeatedly reaffirmed that respect for the right to self-determination is an obligation *erga omnes*, *East Timor Case (Portugal v. Australia)* I.C.J. Reports 1995, para. 29; *Legal Consequences of the Separation of the Chagos Archipelago from Mauritius in 1965,* Advisory Opinion, I.C.J. Reports 2019, para. 180.

1834. *Western Sahara Case*, Advisory Opinion, I.C.J. Reports 1975, 12; Case C-104/16 P, *Council v. Front Polisario*, Judgment of 21 Dec. 2016, C:2016:973; Case T-279/19, *Front Polisario v. Council*, Judgment of 29 Sep. 2021, ECLI:EU:T:2021:639.

1835. *Mornah v. Benin et al.*, African Court of Human and Peoples' Rights, App. No. 028/2018, Judgment (22 Sep. 2022) para. 303. These issues are discussed in greater detail in G.J. Naldi and C. d'Orsi, 'The Sahrawi Arab Democratic Republic: A State That Never Was?', in Abidde, S.O. (ed.), *Palestine, Taiwan, and Western Sahara: Statehood, Sovereignty, and the International System* (Lanham: Lexington Books, 2023) (forthcoming).

1836. Constitutive Act Art. 3(b), PSC Protocol Art. 4(e). *See also* AHG/Res. 51(IV) (1967) whereby the OAU condemned secession in Member States, reaffirmed its support for the principle of territorial integrity and declared that the right of self-determination did not apply to cases of secession. The AU continues to refuse recognition to the Republic of Somaliland, which declared its independence in May 1991, despite meeting the criteria of statehood. *See* B.R. Farley, 'Calling a State a State: Somaliland and International Recognition', *Emory I.L.R.* 24 (2010): 777. *See* generally G.J. Naldi, 'Secession: The African Experience', in *Shielding Humanity: Essays in International Law and Policy in Honour of Abdul Koroma*, C. C. Jalloh & O. Elias (eds) (The Hague: Martinus Nijhoff Brill, 2015), 873–902.

1837. *Katangese Peoples' Congress v. Zaire*, Communication No. 75/92, 8th Activity Report 1994–1995, para. 4; *Gunme et al. v. Cameroon,* Communication No. 266/2003, 26th Activity Report 2008–2009, paras 190, 200.

1838. *Gunme et al. v. Cameroon*, Communication No. 266/2003, 26th Activity Report 2008–2009, para. 200. *See also African Commission on Human and Peoples' Rights v. Kenya*, African Court of Human and Peoples' Rights, App. No. 006/2012 (26 May 2017) para. 199.

that it 'cannot envisage, condone or encourage secession, as a form of self-determination'.[1839] In this sense, self-determination operates 'externally' and once independence is attained no further recourse to the right is permissible. Nevertheless, the internal dimension of self-determination must be complied with, by proving for autonomy or some form of self-government.[1840] It should be observed that there exists considerable support for the view, known as the 'remedial theory', that internal self-determination requires good and democratic governance and that in extreme cases of oppression and persecution of minorities, secession is justified.[1841] A link with Article 13 of the African Charter may thereby be established.[1842]

279. Paragraphs 2 and 3 of Article 20 confer on colonized and oppressed people the right to free themselves by resorting to any means recognized by the international community, and the right to the assistance of African States in their liberation struggle against foreign domination.[1843] Developing States have traditionally argued that the use of force in furtherance of wars of national liberation[1844] is valid on the grounds that these conflicts are being waged in support of a norm of international law, the principle of self-determination, and because the forcible deprivation of a people's right to self-determination constitutes a breach of international law. Material aid, including that of a military nature, is therefore justified. The generally adopted stance of Western States has been that aid to nature liberation movements is limited to humanitarian assistance and political and moral support.[1845] These rights have less contemporary relevance with the virtual elimination of colonialism from Africa.

1839. *Ibid.* The Commission thus rejected a secessionist claim to independence from Senegal by Casamance separatists, *Report on the Mission of Good Offices to Senegal of the African Commission on Human and Peoples' Rights* (1–7 Jun. 1996), 10th Activity Report 1996–1997, in Murray & Evans, Documents Vol. I, 530.
1840. *Katangese Peoples' Congress v. Zaire*, Communication No. 75/92, 8th Activity Report 1994–1995, para. 4; *Gunme et al. v. Cameroon*, Communication No. 266/2003, 26th Activity Report 2008–2009, para. 190.
1841. *Katangese Peoples' Congress v. Zaire,* Communication No. 75/92, 8th Activity Report 1994–1995, para. 6; *Gunme et al. v. Cameroon*, Communication No. 266/2003, 26th Activity Report 2008–2009, paras 197, 199; *Reference Re Secession of Quebec* 37 I.L.M. 1340 (1998); A. Cassese, *Self-Determination of Peoples: A Legal Reappraisal* (Cambridge: Cambridge University Press, 1995), 108–125.
1842. *Katangese Peoples' Congress v. Zaire,* Communication No. 75/92, 8th Activity Report 1994–1995, para. 6; *Gunme et al. v. Cameroon*, Communication No. 266/2003, 26th Activity Report 2008–2009, para. 190.
1843. *See also* UN General Assembly Res. 3103 (XXVIII) 1973 Basic Principles on the Legal Status of the Combatants Struggling Against Colonial and Alien Domination and Racist Regimes, para. 1.
1844. Wars of national liberation have been defined as 'armed conflicts in which peoples are fighting against colonial domination and alien occupation and against racist regimes in the exercise of their right to self-determination', Protocol I Additional to the Geneva Conventions relating to the Protection of Victims of International Armed Conflicts, Art. 1(4) 1977, 1125 U.N.T.S. 3. *See* generally N. Ronzitti, 'Wars of National Liberation – A Legal Definition', *Italian Y.B.I.L.* 1 (1975): 192; H. Wilson, *International Law and the Use of Force by National Liberation Movements* (Oxford: Oxford University Press, 1988).
1845. In *Military and Paramilitary Activities in and against Nicaragua (Nicaragua v. United States)* (Merits) I.C.J. Reports 1986, 14, 351, Judge Schwebel stated that 'it is lawful for a foreign State or movement to give to a people struggling for self-determination moral, political and humanitarian assistance'.

280. As has been stated Article 20 includes economic self-determination and the content of this right assumes various manifestations. Article 21 of the African Charter clearly refers to the concept of permanent sovereignty over natural resources and must be viewed in the context of the negative legacy of the colonial era[1846] and the attempts of the Developing States over the last fifty years to create a New International Economic Order.[1847] The Commission has clarified that Article 21 refers to a group right and not an individual right.[1848] The firm language in which this provision is couched reflects the strength of feeling among African States that true economic and political independence was largely dependent on exercising control over their natural resources. Thus, paragraph 1 declares that '[a]ll peoples shall freely dispose of their wealth and natural resources', a right that must be exercised in their exclusive interest and of which they cannot be deprived. In *The Social and Economic Rights Action Center and the Center for Economic and Social Rights v. Nigeria*, the Commission found that the 'destructive and selfish role' played by oil development in Ogoniland, which did not involve the local population in any decision-making and which failed to bring them any material benefits, constituted a violation of this Article.[1849] If the natural resources are in the land of indigenous peoples the Commission has held that the right also vests in them, but in this instance limited to such resources put to traditional, cultural and religious uses.[1850] Paragraph 4 extends this right to the States themselves, with the added obligation of strengthening African unity and solidarity.[1851] Moreover, in order for their people to benefit fully from the riches of their natural resources paragraph 5 obliges Member States to eliminate all forms of foreign economic exploitation, particularly that practised by international monopolies.[1852] Paragraph 2 is of special interest because it states that in cases of spoliation the dispossessed people shall have the right to the

---

1846. *The Social and Economic Rights Action Center and the Center for Economic and Social Rights v. Nigeria*, Communication No. 155/96, 15th Activity Report 2001–2002, para. 56.

1847. *See* UN General Assembly Res. 1803(XVII) 1962, Declaration on Permanent Sovereignty over Natural Resources, 3201 (S-VI) 1974, Declaration on the Establishment of a New International Economic Order, and 3281(XXIX) 1974, Charter on the Economic Rights and Duties of States.

1848. *Bissangou v. Republic of Congo*, Communication No. 253/2002, 21st Activity Report 2005–2006, para. 81.

1849. Communication No. 155/96, 15th Activity Report 2001–2002, paras 55–58.

1850. *The Social and Economic Rights Action Center and the Center for Economic and Social Rights v. Nigeria*, Communication No. 155/96, 15th Activity Report 2001–2002, paras 56–58; *Centre for Minority Rights Development (Kenya) and Minority Rights Group International on behalf of Endorois Welfare Council v. Kenya*, Communication No. 276/2003, 27th Activity Report 2009, paras 255, 263. *See also African Commission on Human and Peoples' Rights v. Kenya*, African Court of Human and Peoples' Rights, App. No. 006/2012 (26 May 2017) para. 201.

1851. In *Democratic Republic of Congo v. Burundi, Rwanda and Uganda*, Communication No. 227/99, 20th Activity Report 2005–2006, para. 94, the Commission held that the illegal exploitation and looting of the Congo's natural resources, including minerals, lumber coffee and livestock, by neighbouring States breached Art. 21.

1852. On the relationship between the enjoyment of human rights and the activities of transnational corporations, *see* the reports of the UN Secretary-General, UN Docs. E/CN.4/Sub.2/1995/11 and E/CN.4/Sub.2/1996/12. *See also The Social and Economic Rights Action Center and the Center for Economic and Social Rights v. Nigeria*, Communication No. 155/96, 15th Activity Report 2001–2002, para. 58, where the Commission found that Nigeria had facilitated the destruction of Ogoniland in league with oil companies.

lawful recovery of their property and adequate compensation.[1853] It is not altogether clear by whom the compensation will be payable, or what appropriate levels of compensation should be, but in *The Social and Economic Rights Action Center and the Center for Economic and Social Rights v. Nigeria*, the Commission asked the respondent State to pay compensation.[1854] This provision must be read in light of the moderating influence of paragraph 3 which imposes an obligation to 'promote international cooperation based on mutual respect, equitable exchange and the principles of international law'.

281. Article 22(1) of the African Charter enshrines the right to economic, social and cultural development, described as an inalienable human right.[1855] This appears to refer to factors such as opportunities for the advancement of the individual, enabling people to participate in and contribute to economic, social and cultural development, including political development,[1856] and is designed to address problems such as poverty, housing, and illiteracy. The Commission has stated that the right to development is comprised of two indivisible elements, constitutive and instrumental, or 'useful both as a means and an end'.[1857] Five principal criteria must be fulfilled: it must be equitable, non-discriminatory, participatory, accountable and transparent, with equity and choice as overarching themes.[1858] If development projects that are likely to have a major impact are undertaken, the people affected must be consulted and their prior informed consent must be obtained.[1859] Paragraph 2 thereof imposes a concomitant duty upon States individually or collectively to ensure the exercise of this right. This reflects the view that development can only take place in the context of a favourable and equitable economic order, both national and international.

282. Article 22(1) additionally declares the right of peoples to the equal enjoyment of the common heritage of humankind. The common heritage of humankind

1853. In *Bissangou v. Republic of Congo*, Communication No. 253/2002, 21st Activity Report 2005–2006, paras 80–82, the Commission made clear that this provision referred to the wealth and natural resources of a group or a population, and not to the assets of any individual.
1854. Communication No. 155/96, 15th Activity Report 2001–2002. *See also Centre for Minority Rights Development (Kenya) and Minority Rights Group International on behalf of Endorois Welfare Council v. Kenya*, Communication No. 276/2003, 27th Activity Report 2009, para. 268.
1855. *XYZ v. Benin*, African Court of Human and Peoples' Rights, App. No. 010/2020 (27 Nov. 2020), para. 125. In *Democratic Republic of Congo v. Burundi, Rwanda and Uganda*, Communication No. 227/99, 20th Activity Report, 2005–2006, para. 87, the Commission held that the indiscriminate dumping of and mass burial of victims of massacres by occupying forces violated the peoples' right to cultural development.
1856. *XYZ v. Benin*, African Court of Human and Peoples' Rights, App. No. 010/2020 (27 Nov. 2020), para. 125.
1857. *Centre for Minority Rights Development (Kenya) and Minority Rights Group International on behalf of Endorois Welfare Council v. Kenya*, Communication No. 276/2003, 27th Activity Report 2009, para. 277.
1858. *Ibid.*
1859. *Ibid.*, para. 291. *See also African Commission on Human and Peoples' Rights v. Kenya*, African Court of Human and Peoples' Rights, App. No. 006/2012 (26 May 2017) para. 210.

is a concept that has received some limited recognition by the international community right and which seeks to bring about its realization by having fair access to natural resources beyond national jurisdiction.[1860]

283. Article 23(1) of the African Charter promotes a principle fundamental to the stability of the international community, that of national and international peace and security. It may seem a trite observation that the optimum realization of human rights is dependent on the maintenance of peace and security.[1861] While the African Charter does not explicitly define what is meant by the term 'peace and security',[1862] it does refer to the principles of solidarity and friendly relations affirmed by the UN and the OAU. Additionally, it would seem that the principles contained in the UN Declaration on the Principles of International Law Concerning Friendly Relations and Cooperation Among States in Accordance with the UN Charter are directly relevant.[1863] In *Democratic Republic of Congo v. Burundi, Rwanda and Uganda*, the African Commission established a link between this provision and the principle of the peaceful settlement of disputes, Article 33 and Chapter VII of the UN Charter, and Article III of the OAU Charter.[1864] It proceeded to hold that the occupation of the DRC by the armed forces of neighbouring States was 'impermissible' and a violation of Article 23.[1865] The Human Rights Court has stated that peace 'symbolizes the absence of worry, turmoil, conflict or violence. Its symbiosis with security contributes to social well-being. Indeed, the assurance of living without danger, without the risk of being affected in its physical integrity and its heritage gives citizens the confidence of national stability.'[1866]

284. The African Charter pioneered the environment as a human right.[1867] The right to environment is not defined in Article 24, but coming within its scope is protection of the environment from, *inter alia*, pollution and polluting activities.[1868]

1860. *See* Agreement Governing the Activities of States on the Moon and other Celestial Bodies Art. 11(1) (5 Dec. 1979), 1363 U.N.T.S. 3, and UN Convention on the Law of the Sea Art. 136 (10 Dec. 1982), 1833 U.N.T.S. 3. An alternative interpretation is that the concept of common heritage of humankind refers to the protection for posterity of the cultural heritage of a nation or the wonders of nature, a species of international conservation law.

1861. This nexus is acknowledged by the African Charter on Democracy Arts 38 and 39. The Human Rights Court has stated that the right to peace encompasses the full range of rights, *XYZ v. Benin*, African Court of Human and Peoples' Rights, App. No. 010/2020, Judgment (27 Nov. 2020), para. 134.

1862. In *Malawi African Association et al. v. Mauritania*, Communication Nos 54/91, 61/91, 98/93, 164/97–196/97, 210/98, 13th Activity Report 1999–2000, para. 140, the Commission held that unprovoked attacks on villages amounted to a denial of the right to live in peace and security.

1863. *Democratic Republic of Congo v. Burundi, Rwanda and Uganda*, Communication No. 227/99, 20th Activity Report, 2005–2006, para. 73.

1864. *Ibid.*, paras 66, 74–75.

1865. *Ibid.*, para. 76.

1866. *XYZ v. Benin*, African Court of Human and Peoples' Rights, App. No. 010/2020, Judgment (27 Nov. 2020), para. 133.

1867. Ankumah, 168–70.

1868. *See also* African Charter on Democracy Art. 42, under which States commit themselves to implement policies to protect the environment to achieve sustainable development for the benefit of present and future generations.

Thus, in *The Social and Economic Rights Action Center and the Center for Economic and Social Rights v. Nigeria*, the African Commission found a violation of the right of peoples to a clean and safe environment protected by Article 24 of the African Charter when Nigerian exploitation of oilfields polluted the environment of the Ogoni people.[1869] A complementary measure is the Bamako Convention banning the import of toxic waste into Africa.[1870]

285. Article 26 of the African Charter obliges States parties to guarantee the independence of the courts[1871] and, additionally, to allow the establishment and improvement of appropriate national institutions entrusted with the promotion and protection of the rights and freedoms enshrined in the Charter. For the Human Rights Court the independence of the judiciary is 'one of the fundamental pillars of a democratic society. The notion of judicial independence essentially implies the ability of courts to discharge their functions free from external interference and without depending on any other authority'.[1872] It has stated that judicial independence is composed of two elements, institutional and individual, the former denoting the relationship of the judiciary with the other branches of government, the latter referring to the personal independence of judges and their ability to perform their functions without fear of reprisal.[1873] An independent judiciary is vital to the existence of a State governed by the rule of law and committed to human rights and many African countries have fallen short in upholding this guarantee.[1874] The campaign of threats and harassment against the robustly independent justices of the Supreme Court of Zimbabwe,[1875] and other members of the judiciary, in 2000–2001 by state-sponsored thuggery that eventually led to the resignations of the justices is common knowledge. The African Commission has stated that this provision 'speaks of the institutions which are essential to give meaning and content' to the rights protected by Article 7 of the African Charter and 'clearly envisions the protection of the courts which have traditionally been the bastion of protection of the individual's rights against the abuses of State power'.[1876] The institutional independence of the

1869. Communication No. 155/96, 15th Activity Report 2001–2002.

1870. *See infra* Ch. 5.

1871. 'Courts' in this context refers to national judicial organs and not international courts, *Tembani and Freeth v. Angola and Thirteen Others*, Communication No. 409/12 (2013) para. 144.

1872. *Action pour la protection des droits de l'homme (APDH) v. Côte d'Ivoire*, African Court of Human and Peoples' Rights, App. No. 001/2014 (18 Nov. 2016), para. 117; *Ajavon v. Benin*, African Court of Human and Peoples' Rights, App. No. 062/2019 (4 Dec. 2020), paras 277-278, 310-313.

1873. *Ajavon v. Benin*, African Court of Human and Peoples' Rights, App. No. 062/2019 (4 Dec. 2020), paras 278-280.

1874. *See Amnesty International et al. v. Sudan*, Communication Nos 48/90, 50/91, 52/91, 89/93, 13th Activity Report 1999–2000, para. 69, where over one hundred judges opposed to special and military tribunals were dismissed. In *Sir Dawda K. Jawara v. Gambia*, Communication Nos 147/95 and 149/96, 13th Activity Report 1999–2000, para. 74, the Commission found that the military regime ignored court judgments and ousted the competence of the ordinary courts to consider human rights cases. But *see* African Charter on Democracy Art. 32(3).

1875. The years 1985–2001 have been rightly described as the 'golden era of human rights litigation' in Zimbabwe, A. de Bourbon, 'Human Rights Litigation in Zimbabwe: Past, Present and Future', *A.H.R L.J.* 3 (2003): 195, 206.

1876. *Civil Liberties Organization v. Nigeria*, Communication No. 129/94, 9th Activity Report 1995–1996, para. 14. *See also* African Charter on Democracy Art. 32(3).

courts is determined by factors such as its separation from the executive and legislative branches, its administrative independence in everyday management, its ability to function without improper and unnecessary interference, and sufficient resources to enable it to perform its functions properly.[1877] The personal independence of individual judges is determined by the mode of appointment and security of tenure, especially the existence of clear criteria for selection, appointment, duration of tenure in addition to satisfactory guarantees against external pressure.[1878] The Commission considers that it has a mandate on this issue to consider complaints of 'undue interference by the executive with judicial independence'.[1879] In *Lawyers for Human Rights v. Swaziland*, the Commission found that vesting all judicial powers in the Head of State, with the capability of hiring and firing judges, directly threatened the independence of the judiciary.[1880] In addition, the Commission held this situation to undermine the doctrine of separation of powers.[1881] The Human Rights Court has held similarly that the absence of criteria for the renewal of judges' mandate in addition to the discretionary power of the appointing authority undermines the independence of the judiciary.[1882] However, in *Article 19 v. Eritrea,* the Commission dismissed the argument that the removal of the Chief Justice in a manner inconsistent with international standards rendered domestic remedies ineffective.[1883] The Commission has held that 'ouster clauses' are incompatible with Article 26,[1884] as are the creation of special courts to try civilians.[1885]

§3. THE AFRICAN COMMISSION ON HUMAN AND PEOPLES' RIGHTS

286. The African Commission on Human and Peoples' Rights (hereinafter 'the Commission') is one of the bodies entrusted with the implementation of the rights

1877. *Oumar Mariko v. Mali*, African Court of Human and Peoples' Rights, App. No. 029/2018 (24 Mar. 2022) para. 75.
1878. *Ibid.*, para. 80.
1879. *Tsikata v. Ghana*, Communication No. 322/2006, 21st Activity Report 2005–2006, para. 32. *See also* Resolution on the Respect and Strengthening on the Independence of the Judiciary, adopted at the Commission's Nineteenth Ordinary Session, 1996.
1880. Communication No. 251/2002, 18th Activity Report 2004–2005, para. 58.
1881. *Ibid.*, para. 56. On the commitment to the doctrine of separation of powers, *see* African Charter on Democracy Art. 3(5). *See further Gunme et al. v. Cameroon,* Communication No. 266/2003, 26th Activity Report 2008–2009, para. 211; *Ajavon v. Benin*, African Court of Human and Peoples' Rights, App. No. 062/2019 (4 Dec. 2020), para. 313.
1882. *Oumar Mariko v. Mali*, African Court of Human and Peoples' Rights, App. No. 029/2018 (24 Mar. 2022) paras 84-86.
1883. Communication No. 275/2003, 22nd Activity Report 2006–2007, paras 66–67.
1884. *Civil Liberties Organization v. Nigeria*, Communication No. 129/94, 9th Activity Report 1995–1996.
1885. *International Pen, Constitutional Rights Project, Interights on behalf of Ken Saro-Wiwa Jr. and Civil Liberties Organisation v. Nigeria*, Communication Nos 137/94, 139/94, 154/96 and 161/97, 12th Activity Report 1998–1999, para. 95; *Media Rights Agenda v. Nigeria*, Communication No. 224/98, 14th Activity Report 2000–2001, para. 66.

enshrined in the African Charter. By virtue of Article 30 the Commission is mandated with promoting human and peoples' rights and ensuring their protection.[1886] It is an 'autonomous treaty body'.[1887] It has described itself as 'an international quasi-judicial institution established to promote and protect the rights enshrined in the African Charter'.[1888] It is composed of eleven members, serving in their personal capacities, from among African personalities of the highest reputation with legal experience and competence in the field of human rights.[1889] The odd number of commissioners facilitates the taking of decisions in that a tie in voting may thus be avoided but in the event of a tie Article 64 provides that the Chairperson has the casting vote.[1890] Article 34 stipulates that the members of the Commission must be the nationals of one of the State parties to the African Charter. Each State party may nominate a maximum of two candidates who must not be of the same nationality. In addition, according to Article 32, the Commission may not include more than one national of the same State. The size of the Commission is supposed to correspond to an equitable geographic distribution.[1891] The members of the Commission enjoy diplomatic privileges and immunities in the performance of their duties.[1892]

287. The members of the Commission are elected by secret ballot by the, now, AU Assembly from a list of persons nominated by the States parties to the African Charter.[1893] They serve a renewable six-year term.[1894] The Commission's Chairperson and Vice-Chairperson are elected by its members for a renewable two-year term,[1895] who together constitute the bureau.[1896] It should be noted that the Chairperson has few executive powers.[1897]

1886. *See also* Rule 3 of the Commission's Rules of Procedure, hereinafter 'Rules', adopted in 2020, https://achpr.au.int/en/rules-procedure; Heyns & Killander, 206. The Commission, which became operational in 1987, is based in Banjul, The Gambia. The Commission is assisted by a secretariat, Art. 41 and Rules 20–24.
1887. Rule 3(1). In *Good v. Botswana*, Communication No. 306/2005, 28th Activity Report 2009–2010, paras 53–55, Botswana argued that the Commission had ceased to exist along with the OAU. The Commission dismissed this submission on the ground that only the termination of the African Charter could affect the Commission's existence. The continuing operation of the African Charter amounted to an acceptance of the Commission's jurisdiction. Furthermore, as a body working within the framework of the OAU, it devolved to the AU, *ibid.*, paras 75–79.
1888. *Interights, Institute for Human Rights and Development in Africa, and Association Mauritaniene des Droits de l'Homme v. Islamic Republic of Mauritania*, Communication No. 373/2009 (formerly 242/2001), 28th Activity Report 2010, para. 83.
1889. Article 31. *See also* Rule 4. Art. 38 and Rule 10 require the members of the Commission upon their election to make a solemn declaration that they will discharge their duties impartially and faithfully.
1890. *See also* Rule 54(3).
1891. According to Ankumah, 17–18, the important consideration is ensuring the representation of the different legal and language traditions from across Africa.
1892. Article 43.
1893. Article 33.
1894. Article 36 and Rule 5(1).
1895. Article 42(1) and Rule 14(1). Election is by secret ballot, Rule 14(2). *See also* Rule 59.
1896. Rule 13.
1897. Rule 17.

288. In the event of the death or resignation of a member, the seat is declared vacant by what is now the Chair of the AU Commission.[1898] The Chair of the AU Commission can additionally declare the seat vacant if, in the unanimous opinion of colleagues, a member ceases to fulfil his/her functions or is incapable of continuing to fulfil them, unless such failure is of a temporary nature.[1899] In either case, the AU Assembly shall fill that seat unless the remaining period of office is less than six months, in which event the seat will be filled in due course. A member of the Commission elected to replace another member shall complete their predecessor's mandate.[1900] In order to avoid conflicts of interest, a member of the Commission must not be present or participate in any communication where s/he is a national of the respondent State, has a personal interest in the case, has previously been involved in the case, has expressed public pronouncements that may give rise to a perception of impartiality, or is engaged in any activity that may lead his/her impartiality and independence to be questioned.[1901]

289. The Commission holds four Ordinary Sessions a year.[1902] In addition, extraordinary sessions may be convened.[1903] Sessions are both public and private.[1904] At least seven members must be present to be quorate,[1905] and decisions are taken by a majority of the voting members,[1906] with the Chairperson having the casting vote in the event of a tie.[1907] However, decisions may be taken by consensus.[1908]

290. The Commission's mandate is defined by a number of guidelines set out in Article 45. It should be noted at the outset that while the Commission was created to promote and protect human rights[1909] in Africa its competence in the field of protection is not exclusive but is shared not only with the African Court on Human and Peoples' Rights[1910] and the African Committee of Experts on the Rights and Welfare of the Child[1911] but also with the AU policy organs which have a

1898. Article 39(1) and Rule 9(1).
1899. Article 39(2) and Rule 9(1).
1900. Article 39(3) and Rule 5(3).
1901. Rule 94. In *Interights, Institute for Human Rights and Development in Africa, and Association Mauritaniene des Droits de l'Homme v. Mauritania*, Communication No. 373/2009, 28th Activity Report, 2009–2010, paras 47–62, a challenge to the impartiality of the Commission because a Commissioner who was a national of the respondent State was present during the deliberations was dismissed on the ground that he 'did not take part in the deliberations'. Under the new Rules this case would be decided differently.
1902. Rule 28(1), Art. 64(2) notwithstanding.
1903. Rule 29.
1904. Rule 28(1) and Rule 32.
1905. Article 42(3) and Rule 41.
1906. Rule 55.
1907. Article 42(4) and Rule 54(3).
1908. Rule 54(1).
1909. Article 30 and Rule 3; *Bissangou v. Republic of Congo*, Communication No. 253/2002, 21st Activity Report 2005–2006, para. 47.
1910. Rule 128. *See further infra* paras 333–374.
1911. Rule 137. *See further infra* paras 385–390.

supervisory role, including the implementation of its decisions.[1912] However, the Commission does perform a quasi-judicial function and it possesses jurisdiction to interpret the African Charter and to carry out tasks conferred upon it by the AU Assembly.[1913] It is therefore necessary to consider separately the various functions of the Commission, which may be divided into three categories: promotion; protection; and other areas of competence.

291. The first, and fundamental, function of the Commission, as provided for by the African Charter, is to promote human rights in Africa, which it is doing with the assistance of partners such as National Human Rights Institutions and NGOs.[1914] There appear to be three elements to its promotional function: a studies and information function; a quasi-legislative function; and cooperative functions.[1915]

292. Article 45(1)(a) requires the Commission to perform its study and information function in several ways.[1916] Thus, the Commission acts as a documentation centre. It therefore gathers and classifies information on human rights in Africa. In addition, it is responsible for disseminating information, either systematically or in response to enquiries, and one method of achieving this is by organizing conferences or seminars. Furthermore, the Commission can undertake studies and conduct research. The Commission is also entrusted with encouraging national and local institutions concerned with human and peoples' rights. Finally, the Commission can advise governments.

293. Article 45(1)(b) endows the Commission with a quasi-legislative function by giving it responsibility for developing principles and rules aimed at solving legal problems relating to human rights generally upon which governments may base their legislation.

294. Finally, Article 45(1)(c) requires the Commission to cooperate with other African and international institutions concerned with human rights.[1917] The Commission has thus cooperated with non-governmental agencies, such as the United Nations High Commission for Refugees (UNHCR), and NGOs such as Amnesty International and IGOs.

295. The Commission has two other areas of competence in this regard. According to Article 45(3) it can interpret the provisions of the African Charter at the request of a State party, the AU, or an African organization recognized by the

1912. Rule 138.
1913. Article 45(4).
1914. Rules 67–68, 71-72.
1915. Article 45(1). *See* Ankumah, 21–22; Murray, African Commission on Human and Peoples' Rights, 14–15. *See further* V. Dankwa, 'The Promotional Role of the African Commission on Human and Peoples' Rights', in *The African Charter on Human and Peoples' Rights: The System in Practice, 1986–2000*, Evans & Murray (eds) (Cambridge: Cambridge University Press, 2002), 335–352.
1916. *See also* Rules 75–77.
1917. *See also* Rule 70.

AU,[1918] and it has additionally adopted the practice of interpreting some Charter provisions at its own initiative.[1919] The Commission's powers in this context are important given that it is performing a quasi-judicial function, similar to the advisory jurisdiction of international judicial bodies, in defining and declaring the extent of fundamental freedoms and duties, drawing up soft law. The Commission has therefore adopted resolutions on general human rights concerns or specific problems and countries.[1920] In this context, the State reporting system should be mentioned. Under Article 62, States parties must submit every two years a report on legislative or other measures taken to give effect to the rights and freedoms guaranteed by the African Charter.[1921] The system is designed to reveal the extent of implementation through 'constructive dialogue'.[1922] The Commission can thereby identify the issues that require urgent attention by States.[1923] This system is virtually identical to the supervisory functions that exist under the UN control machinery. To date the record of compliance is unsatisfactory.[1924]

296. The Commission has an extremely important role to play in the protection of human rights,[1925] and its mandate is set out in Articles 46–58, as supplemented by the Rules of Procedure. The Commission has broad investigative powers in that it may resort to any appropriate method of investigation in accordance with international law and the African Charter.[1926] Its primary function seems to be to uncover the facts and attempt to reach an amicable settlement based on respect for human rights.[1927] It appears that the Commission has used these powers creatively by appointing thematic rapporteurs and sending missions to conduct on-site

1918. *See also* Rule 127, which additionally describes this procedure as 'Advisory Opinions'.
1919. Ankumah, 26.
1920. *See* https://achpr.au.int/en/category/soft-law.
1921. Although Art. 62 does not make it clear that the Commission has been expressly assigned this supervisory role it assumed this responsibility, Ankumah, 79. The Commission has issued guidelines to assist States parties in drafting their reports, amended in 1998, https://achpr.au.int/en/documents/1989-04-14/guidelines-national-periodic-reports. *See* generally M. Evans, T. Ige & R. Murray, 'The Reporting Mechanism of the African Charter on Human and Peoples' Rights', in *The African Charter on Human and Peoples' Rights: The System in Practice, 1986–2000*, Evans & Murray (eds), (Cambridge: Cambridge University Press, 2002), 36–60.
1922. Ankumah, 80.
1923. Rule 83(1).
1924. Evans, Ige & Murray, 41–42. By January 2013 only eight States were up-to-date with their reporting obligations, Commission's Combined Thirty-second and Thirty-third Activity Report 2013, pt. IV. There is little that the Commission can do except to remind States of their obligations, Rule 81.
1925. Article 45(2). In this context the Commission has therefore stated that 'its role consists precisely in pronouncing on allegations of violations of the human rights protected by the Charter', *Malawi African Association et al. v. Mauritania*, Communication Nos 54/91, 61/91, 98/93, 164/97–196/97, 210/98, 13th Activity Report 1999–2000, para. 83. *See also Good v. Botswana*, Communication No. 306/2005, 28th Activity Report 2009–2010, paras 80–82.
1926. Article 46.
1927. *See* Rules 112, 123. This role has become an established part of the Commission's mandate, F. Viljoen, 'Communications under the African Charter: Procedure and Admissibility', in *The African Charter on Human and Peoples' Rights: The System in Practice, 1986–2006*, Evans & Murray (eds) (Cambridge: Cambridge University Press, 2008), 80–85.

investigations.[1928] The latter, known as 'protection missions', is now specifically provided for in the Rules.[1929] Additionally, special provision is made for the Commission to refer 'matters of emergency' to the AU policy organs under Article 58(3)[1930] as well as serious or massive violations of human and peoples' rights.[1931]

297. In *Bissangou v. Republic of Congo*, the respondent State argued that Article 45 had established a non-jurisdictional mechanism and that the Commission's decisions were not binding but simply had a moral significance.[1932] It is certainly the case that there is nothing in the African Charter to indicate that the Commission's decisions have the binding force of a ruling of a court of law;[1933] at best, they may be said to have a persuasive authority akin to the Opinions of the HRC. However, an expectation of compliance does appear to have been engendered.[1934] This is evident from Rule 125 which, *inter alia*, empowers the Commission to refer a State Party's non-compliance with its decision to the competent AU policy organs.

298. An important tool in the Commission's protective mandate is the capacity to examine interstate complaints and 'other communications'.[1935] Parties to a Communication have a duty to cooperate fully with the proceedings.[1936] Articles 47–54 govern interstate complaints.[1937] Provision is made for a negotiation

---

1928. Murray, 21–24. *See* Rule 25.
1929. Rule 76.
1930. *See also* Rule 85.
1931. Rule 99.
1932. Communication No. 253/2002, 21st Activity Report 2005–2006, para. 46.
1933. *See* Art. 59 and Rule 120; Ankumah, 24, 74–75. However, in its Introduction to the first volume of law reports published by the Commission available on the website of the University of Pretoria, the Commission has stated that, 'As the only existing body with the power to examine communications, mandated by Article 45.2 to ensure the protection of human and peoples' rights under the conditions laid down by the present Charter, the Commission considers that its decisions with regard to these communications are legally binding upon the states parties concerned,' http://www.up.ac.za/chr/ahrdb/acomm_decisions.html. One commentator writes that the Commission has relied on these provisions to declare that there have been violations of the Charter, R. Murray, 'Decisions by the African Commission on Individual Communications under the African Charter on Human and Peoples' Rights,' *I.C.L.Q.* 46 (1997): 412, 428. A 'decision' may be procedurally distinct from a 'judgment', M.O. Hudson, *The Permanent Court of International Justice 1920-1942* (New York: MacMillan, 1943), 583–584. *See also Ekollo Moundi Alexandre v. Republic of Cameroon and Federal Republic of Nigeria*, African Court of Human and Peoples' Rights, App. No. 008/2011 (23 Sep. 2011) paras 3–4.
1934. This approach would appear to be required under the African Charter, Art. 1, *see Civil Liberties Organization v. Nigeria*, Communication No. 129/94, 9th Activity Report 1995–1996. *See further* C. Anyangwe, 'Obligations of States Parties to the African Charter on Human and Peoples' Rights', *R.A.D.I.C.* 10 (1998): 625. It may be that the Commission has come to regard its decisions on communications as binding, *see International Pen, Constitutional Rights Project, Interights on behalf of Ken Saro-Wiwa Jr. and Civil Liberties Organisation v. Nigeria*, Communication Nos 137/94, 139/94, 154/96 and 161/97, 12th Activity Report 1998–1999, paras 113–116; Murray, The African Commission on Human and Peoples' Rights and International Law, 53–55.
1935. Rule 88(1).
1936. Rule 92.
1937. Ankumah, 23–24. *See also* Rules 88, 108–114. In *Interights (on behalf of Pan-African Movement and Citizens for Peace in Eritrea) and Interights (on behalf of Pan-African Movement and Inter Africa Group) v. Eritrea*, Communication Nos 233/99, 234/99, 16th Activity Report 2002–2003,

procedure and a complaint procedure. Under Article 47, which is a permissive, not mandatory, procedure,[1938] the complainant State can draw the attention of the accused State to possible violations of the African Charter through a written communication. This requirement, according to the Commission, 'is to avoid a situation of springing surprises on the States involved'. It also 'enables the Respondent States to decide whether to settle the complaint amicably or not'.[1939] At the same time, this communication is also submitted to the Chair of the AU Commission and the Chairperson of the Commission, providing a detailed account of the facts denounced and the Charter provisions allegedly violated.[1940] The accused State then has three months in which to respond in writing, providing information on the relevant laws and administrative measures applied or applicable and any redress given or the course of action available.[1941] If the complainant State is not satisfied with this statement or if no reply is forthcoming and the question is not settled through bilateral negotiation or 'any other peaceful procedure' either State may submit the matter to the Commission.[1942] The phrase 'any other peaceful procedure' appears to refer to 'regional or international procedures of settlement or good offices'.[1943] According to the Commission, these provisions are aimed at conciliation.[1944]

299. Alternatively, a State can submit a complaint directly to the Commission.[1945] After due deliberation on the parties' submissions, the Commission will adopt a decision on the merits.[1946] It is interesting to note that the jurisdiction of the Commission is not dependent upon a State party's prior acceptance of its competence, that is, a State automatically accepts the compulsory jurisdiction of the Commission upon ratification or accession to the African Charter.

300. A third party with a direct interest in the case can apply to intervene in a Communication;[1947] it must prove that he or she will benefit directly or suffer a loss

---

para. 44, the Commission stated that the 'initiation of an interstate complaint is dependent on the voluntary exercise of the sovereign will of a State party to the Charter, which decision can only be made by States in accordance with the Charter'. Individual communications cannot be converted into interstate communications, *ibid.* To date only one complaint has been submitted, *Democratic Republic of Congo v. Burundi, Rwanda and Uganda*, Communication No. 227/99, 20th Activity Report 2005–2006.

1938. *Democratic Republic of Congo v. Burundi, Rwanda and Uganda*, Communication No. 227/99, 20th Activity Report 2005–2006, para. 58.

1939. *Ibid.*, para. 60.

1940. Rule 108(2).

1941. *See also* Rule 110(1).

1942. Article 48 and Rules 109–114.

1943. Rule 109(2)(b).

1944. *Democratic Republic of Congo v. Burundi, Rwanda and Uganda*, Communication No. 227/99, 20th Activity Report 2005–2006, para. 57.

1945. Article 49. *See also* Rule 109. According to the Commission, Art. 49 allows the States to avoid engagement where 'such contacts will not be diplomatically either effective or desirable', *Democratic Republic of Congo v. Burundi, Rwanda and Uganda*, Communication No. 227/99, 20th Activity Report 2005–2006, para. 61.

1946. Rule 114(1).

1947. Rule 106.

from the outcome of the case.[1948] In reaching a decision on the request, Commission must consider whether the procedure would thereby be unduly disrupted or prolonged.[1949] The language of the provision suggests that this right is conferred upon any party, including individuals and NGOs and is not limited to States.

301. The Commission is authorized to invite or grant leave to an *amicus curiae* to intervene in the case to help it in determining a factual or legal issue.[1950] Any third party may assume the role of *amicus curiae*.[1951]

302. The Commission's jurisdiction *ratione materiae* is broad since Article 47 clearly indicates that its attention may be drawn to any violation, whether by omission or commission, of the African Charter. Its jurisdiction *ratione personae* extends to acts committed by, or imputable to, a State party in accordance with the doctrine of state responsibility. In relation to its jurisdiction *ratione loci* it is clear from the wording of the African Charter that many of the rights guaranteed are available not only to the nationals of State parties but also to *any* individual under their jurisdiction.

303. Article 50 requires the exhaustion of all existing local remedies.[1952] However, States cannot profit by deliberately delaying redress since the Commission can ignore this stricture if it is apparent that exhausting those remedies would entail an inordinate length of time or do not exist.[1953]

304. The Commission's investigative powers are contained in Articles 51 and 52. Once an issue has been referred to it, the Commission can request the States concerned to provide it with all relevant information which shall be provided by both parties within ninety days.[1954] During this stage the States concerned may be represented before the Commission and may submit written or oral observations.[1955] In addition, the Commission can approach 'other sources' for any information it deems necessary[1956] and this would appear to include other States, individuals, NGOs, the AU and other international organizations. Nonetheless, during this time the Commission must attempt by all possible means to reach an amicable settlement based on respect for human and peoples' rights.[1957]

305. If no settlement is forthcoming, the Commission is required to draft a report stating the facts and its findings which it must subsequently submit to the States

1948. Rule 106(2)(a).
1949. Rule 106(1).
1950. Rule 104(1). *See also* Rule 105.
1951. Rule 104(2).
1952. *See also* Rule 109(2)(b).
1953. *Democratic Republic of Congo v. Burundi, Rwanda and Uganda*, Communication No. 227/99, 20th Activity Report 2005–2006, paras 62–63.
1954. *See also* Rule 110(3)(a).
1955. *See also* Rule 91(1).
1956. Article 52.
1957. *See also* Rule 112(1).

concerned and the AU Assembly.[1958] The Commission may make such recommendations as it considers necessary to the AU Assembly when submitting the report, so that it could recommend that the matter be closed and no further action be taken, or that the report be published.[1959] The ultimate responsibility, however, lies with the AU Assembly. However, it has to be borne in mind that this procedure applies solely to Article 48 Communications.

306. The African Charter also envisages complaints, or 'communications', 'other than those of State parties' under Article 55. Rule 115(1) refers to 'natural or legal persons', and Rule 115(2)(a) confirms that individuals and NGOs have standing to approach the Commission as complainants.[1960] It is interesting to note that the *locus standi* requirements before the Commission are comparatively broad since individuals and organizations other than the victim can submit a complaint.[1961] In fact, the Commission has stated that it has adopted an *actio popularis* approach.[1962]

1958. *See also* Rule 113.

1959. Article 53.

1960. It was clearly established in the Commission's practice that it was competent to receive complaints from individuals and NGOs, *see, e.g., Sir Dawda K. Jawara v. Gambia*, Communication Nos 147/95 and 149/96, 13th Activity Report 1999–2000, paras 41–42. In *Bissangou v. Republic of Congo*, Communication No. 253/2002, 21st Activity Report 2005–2006, para. 47, described this aspect of its promotional and protective function, that 'in seizing the Commission, the complainant does not have any other intention than to request the latter to play its role by controlling the conformity to … the Charter of an action … of a State party'. It is important to note NGOs must have observer status before the Commission. In the Final Communiqué of its 73rd ordinary session held in Banjul, The Gambia, from 20 October to 9 November 2022, the Commission rejected the applications of the three NGOs on the ground that 'sexual orientation is not an expressly recognized right or freedom under the African Charter' and is 'contrary to the virtues of African values'.

1961. Rule 115(2)(a); *Zitha & Zitha v. Mozambique*, Communication No. 361/08, 29th Activity Report 2010, para. 106; *Haregewoin Gabre-Selassie and IHRDA (on behalf of former Dergue officials) v. Ethiopia*, Communication No. 301/05 (2011) paras 61–62. This includes NGOs such as Amnesty International and International Pen; *see further* Viljoen, Communications under the African Charter, 76. Nor need the applicant be a national or registered in the Respondent State, *Spilg and Mack & Ditshwanelo (on behalf of Lehlohonolo Bernard Kobedi) v. Botswana*, Communication No. 277/2003, paras 83–84; *Haregewoin Gabre-Selassie and IHRDA (on behalf of former Dergue officials) v. Ethiopia*, Communication No. 301/05 (2011) para. 64. In *Interights (on behalf of Pan-African Movement and Citizens for Peace in Eritrea) and Interights (on behalf of Pan-African Movement and Inter Africa Group) v. Eritrea*, Communication Nos 233/99, 234/99, 16th Activity Report 2002–2003, paras 32, 34, Ethiopia questioned the neutrality, credibility and integrity of the NGO but the Commission expressed the view that such a matter did not fall within the conditions of admissibility under Art. 56. In *Malawi African Association et al. v. Mauritania*, Communication Nos 54/91, 61/91, 98/93, 164/97–196/97, 210/98, 13th Activity Report 1999–2000, para. 78, the Commission justified this situation thus, 'This characteristic of the African Charter reflects sensitivity to the practical difficulties that individuals can face in countries where human rights are violated. The national or international channels of remedy may not be accessible to the victims themselves or may be dangerous to pursue.'

1962. *Article 19 v. Eritrea*, Communication No. 275/2003, 22nd Activity Report 2006–2007, para. 65; 'wisely allowed', *see The Social and Economic Rights Action Center and the Center for Economic and Social Rights v. Nigeria*, Communication No. 155/96, 15th Activity Report 2001–2002, para. 49; *Spilg and Mack & Ditshwanelo (on behalf of Lehlohonolo Bernard Kobedi) v. Botswana*, Communication No. 277/2003, para. 81; *Haregewoin Gabre-Selassie and IHRDA (on behalf of former Dergue officials) v. Ethiopia*, Communication No. 301/05 (2011) para. 61. In *The*

A number of procedural hurdles have to be initially overcome before the Commission will consider the substance of a communication, which it will do by a simple majority of its members.[1963] Article 56 enumerates seven admissibility requirements and although similar criteria are to be found in comparable international instruments the African Charter goes further in introducing unique and, in theory, more restrictive requirements of admissibility.[1964] It is important to take cognizance of the fact that the admissibility requirements are cumulative, or 'conjunctive, meaning that if any one of them is absent, the communication will be declared inadmissible'.[1965] Consequently, all seven conditions must generally be fulfilled.[1966] The conditions are designed 'to sieve frivolous and vexatious communications before they reach the merits stage'.[1967] However, if any information is lacking, the complainant is awarded the opportunity to remedy the situation.[1968] This provision takes into account the conditions *ratione materiae, loci*, *personae* and *temporis*.[1969] It is important to note that no prescribed form of submission of a communication is required.[1970]

307. The first condition of admissibility is that the communication must indicate the author, even if the author requests anonymity, so that 'adequate information with a certain degree of specificity concerning the victim' must be provided.[1971] However, the names of the victims where they are not complainants must also be provided.[1972] The Commission has stated that the 'existence of a direct interest (like being a victim) to bring the matter before the Commission is not a requirement

Law Office of Ghazi Suleiman v. Sudan, Communication Nos 222/98 and 229/99, 16th Activity Report 2002–2003, para. 39, the Commission stated that States' obligations were of an *erga omnes* nature not dependent on individuals, an apparent reference to the special character of human rights treaties. It should be observed that the Commission may receive amicus curiae briefs on communications, Rule 99(16).

1963. Article 55(2); *Amnesty International v. Zambia*, Communication No. 212/98, 12th Activity Report 1998–1999, para. 24.
1964. Ankumah, 61–67.
1965. Rule 106; *Article 19 v. Eritrea*, Communication No. 275/2003, 22nd Activity Report 2006–2007, para. 43; *Zimbabwe Lawyers for Human Rights & Associated Newspapers of Zimbabwe v. Zimbabwe*, Communication No. 284/2003, 26th Activity Report 2008–2009, para. 81. *See also Omary and Others v. Tanzania*, African Court of Human and Peoples' Rights, App. No. 001/2012 (28 Mar. 2014), para. 86.
1966. *Zimbabwe Human Rights NGO Forum v. Zimbabwe*, Communication No. 245/2002, 21st Activity Report 2005–2006, para. 36.
1967. *Chinhamo v. Zimbabwe*, Communication No. 307/2005, 23rd Activity Report 2007, para. 45; *Majuru v. Zimbabwe*, Communication No. 308/2005, 25th Activity Report 2008, para. 70.
1968. Rule 115(4), (6).
1969. Viljoen, Communications under the African Charter, 69; Murray, Decisions by the African Commission on Individual Communications, 418–421.
1970. *Haregewoin Gabre-Selassie and IHRDA (on behalf of former Dergue officials) v. Ethiopia*, Communication No. 301/05 (2011) paras 119–120.
1971. *Centre for Independence of Judges and Lawyers v. Algeria*, Communication Nos 104/94, 109–126/94, 8th Activity Report 1994–1995, para. 5. *See also* Rule 115(2)(a), (c). Communications can be rejected on the grounds that they are vague or unclear, *Bakweri Land Claims Committee v. Cameroon,* Communication No. 260/02, 18th Activity Report 2002–2003, para. 47.
1972. Rule 115(2)(e).

under the African Charter'.[1973] This situation has been justified on the grounds that the 'African Charter reflects sensitivity to the practical difficulties that individuals can face in countries where human rights are violated. The national or international channels of remedy may not be accessible to the victims themselves or may be dangerous to pursue.'[1974] The Commission has therefore held that in the context of grave and massive violations there is no need for all the victims to be identified and named by the complainants.[1975] If there are fears of reprisals, a real fear in much of Africa, or other dangers the Commission can protect the author's identity.[1976]

308. The second condition is that the communication must be compatible with the AU Constitutive Act or the African Charter. It has been held by the Human Rights Court that these instruments should be read independently.[1977] It cannot be that mere submission of a complaint in itself gives rise to incompatibility. In a general sense 'compatibility' signifies 'in compliance with' or 'in conformity with'.[1978] As the Commission has observed, this procedure is designed to protect human rights and States are duty bound to adhere to the obligations they have assumed.[1979] However, a claim that the people of Katanga had a right to secede from Zaïre in accordance with the right to self-determination raised the question of compatibility with the basic principles of the OAU regarding territorial integrity.[1980] The Commission has summarized the requirements of this condition: that the communication be brought against a State Party to the African Charter; that it claims prima facie violations of the African Charter; that the communication be brought in respect of violations that occurred after ratification of the African Charter, or in relation to continuing violations if they commenced before ratification of the African Charter; and that the communication contain a degree of specificity.[1981] In *Omary and Others v. Tanzania*, Tanzania argued that the Court lacked jurisdiction because the application failed to cite either instrument.[1982] However, the Court ruled that an application could not be adjudged inadmissible on this ground as long as the rights alleged to have been violated were guaranteed by the African Charter or some other human rights instrument ratified by the State.[1983]

1973. *Bakweri Land Claims Committee v. Cameroon,* Communication No. 260/02, 18th Activity Report 2002–2003, para. 46.
1974. *Ibid.*, para. 78.
1975. *Ibid.*, para. 79.
1976. *Ibid.*, paras 78–79. *See also* Rule 115(2)(b).
1977. *Omary and Others v. Tanzania*, African Court of Human and Peoples' Rights, App. No. 001/2012 (28 Mar. 2014), paras 74, 93.
1978. *Mohamed Abdullah Saleh al-Asad v. Djibouti*, Communication No. 383/10 (2014), para. 128.
1979. *Sudan Human Rights Organization and Sudan Centre for Housing Rights and Evictions v. Sudan* Communication Nos 279/03, 296/05, 28th Activity Report, 2010, paras 90–91.
1980. *Katangese Peoples Congress v. Zaire*, Communication No. 75/92, 8th Activity Report 1994–1995.
1981. *Gunme et al. v. Cameroon,* Communication No. 266/2003, 26th Activity Report 2008–2009, para. 38.
1982. *Omary and Others v. Tanzania*, African Court of Human and Peoples' Rights, App. No. 001/2012 (28 Mar. 2014), para. 55. *See also Wilfred Onyango Nganyi & 9 Others v. Tanzania*, African Court of Human and Peoples' Rights, App. No. 006/2013 (18 Mar. 2016), para. 57.
1983. *Ibid.*, paras 74–76, 92–93.

309. It has been established that this particular provision should be interpreted as a reference to the conditions *ratione materiae, loci, personae,* and *temporis.*[1984] With regard to subject matter, it is not necessary to list in a communication which specific articles of the African Charter are alleged to have been violated[1985] as long as the substance of the issue at stake is raised[1986] and a prima facie case is established,[1987] in that the complaint 'should be one that compels the conclusion that a human rights violation has occurred'[1988] There is no need for evidence of systematic violations to prove a prima facie case.[1989] In *Katangese Peoples Congress v. Zaïre*, the Commission found no evidence of violations of human rights which could justify secession and was therefore without 'merit' under the African Charter.[1990] Vague complaints about the general political climate cannot suffice either.[1991]

310. Complaints can only be submitted against States parties.[1992] In fact, quite a number of communications have been declared inadmissible on the ground of being lodged against non-State parties, including States beyond Africa.[1993] The alleged violation must have occurred within the territorial jurisdiction of a State party.[1994]

311. Finally, as regards the time of the alleged violation, communications must be submitted against African States that were parties to the African Charter at the time the violations were alleged to have occurred.[1995] However, it should be observed that both the Commission and the Human Rights Court have expressed approval of the concept of 'continuing violations', that is, that they will assume

1984. *Mohamed Abdullah Saleh al-Asad v. Djibouti*, Communication No. 383/10 (2014), paras 129–137.
1985. Rule 115(2)(g); *Haregewoin Gabre-Selassie and IHRDA (on behalf of former Dergue officials) v. Ethiopia*, Communication No. 301/05 (2011) para. 106; *Wilfred Onyango Nganyi & 9 Others v. Tanzania*, African Court of Human and Peoples' Rights, App. No. 006/2013 (18 March 2016), para. 58.
1986. *Majuru v. Zimbabwe*, Communication No. 308/2005, 25th Activity Report 2008, para. 73; *Muzerengwa and 110 Others (represented by Zimbabwe Lawyers for Human Rights) v. Zimbabwe*, Communication No. 306/2005, 29th Activity Report 2010, para. 56; *Southern Africa Human Rights NGO Network and Others v. Tanzania*, Communication No. 333/200, 28th Activity Report 2009–2010, para. 51. Rule 93(2)(d) requires that an account of the act or situation complained of be provided.
1987. *Wilfred Onyango Nganyi & 9 Others v. Tanzania*, African Court of Human and Peoples' Rights, App. No. 006/2013 (18 Mar. 2016), para. 79.
1988. *Chinhamo v. Zimbabwe*, Communication No. 307/2005, 23rd Activity Report 2007, para. 48. *See also Uhuru Kenyatta and William Ruto (represented by Innocence Project Africa) v. Kenya*, Communication No. 464/14 (2014), para. 20.
1989. *Priscilla Njeri Echaria (represented by Federation of Women Lawyers, Kenya and International Center for the Protection of Human Rights) v. Kenya*, Communication No. 375/09 (2011), para. 35.
1990. Communication No. 75/92, 8th Activity Report 1994–1995.
1991. *Centre for Independence of Judges and Lawyers v. Algeria*, Communication Nos 104/94, 109–126/94, 8th Activity Report 1994–1995.
1992. *See* Rule 115(2)(g).
1993. *See* generally 7th Activity Report 1993–1994.
1994. *Muzerengwa and 110 Others (represented by Zimbabwe Lawyers for Human Rights) v. Zimbabwe*, Communication No. 306/2005, 29th Activity Report 2010, para. 58; *Mohamed Abdullah Saleh al-Asad v. Djibouti*, Communication No. 383/10 (2014), paras 151–177.
1995. *See* generally 7th Activity Report; *Malawi African Association et al. v. Mauritania*, Communication Nos 54/91, 61/91, 98/93, 164/97–196/97, 210/98, 13th Activity Report 1999–2000, paras 104, 109.

jurisdiction even though the violation had taken place before the State had become a party to the African Charter because its effects continued after that time. Thus in *Amnesty International et al. v. Sudan*, the Commission made it plain that continuing violations fall within its competence.[1996] In *Annette Pagnoulle (on behalf of Abdoulaye Mazou) v. Cameroon*, the Commission expressed the view that if 'irregularities in the original sentence have consequences that constitute a continuing violation of any of the Articles of the African Charter, the Commission must pronounce on these'.[1997] In *Zitha & Zitha v. Mozambique*, the Commission held that the phenomenon of forced disappearances constitutes a continuing violation of human rights which continued to occur after the State party had ratified the African Charter even though the initial fact had taken place before the date of ratification.[1998] In the Commission's view, this principle 'presupposes the failure by the State party to adopt measures, as required by Article 1 of the African Charter to redress the violations and their effects'.[1999]

312. The third condition is that the communication must not be disparaging or insulting towards the State concerned, its institutions or the AU.[2000] The Commission has stated that while it must strike a balance between the freedom of expression and the reputation of others vital state institutions must not be exposed to comments which bring them into disrepute or undermine their effectiveness.[2001] Hence it has the authority to dismiss patently absurd complaints that amount to an abuse of the right of petition. It is important that the adjectives 'disparaging' and 'insulting' should not be interpreted too broadly, and can be dependent on context,[2002]

1996. Communication Nos 48/90, 50/91, 52/91, 89/93, 13th Activity Report 1999–2000, para. 40; *Wilfred Onyango Nganyi & 9 Others v. Tanzania*, African Court of Human and Peoples' Rights, App. No. 006/2013 (18 Mar. 2016), para. 66; *African Commission on Human and Peoples' Rights v. Kenya*, African Court of Human and Peoples' Rights, App. No. 006/2012 (26 May 2017) para. 65.
1997. Communication No. 39/90, 10th Activity Report 1996–1997, para. 15.
1998. Communication No. 361/08, 29th Activity Report 2010, paras 85–94.
1999. *Gunme et al. v. Cameroon*, Communication No. 266/2003, 26th Activity Report 2008–2009, para. 96.
2000. *See Ligue Camerounaise des Droits de l'Homme v. Cameroon*, Communication No. 65/92, 10th Activity Report 1996–1997; *Bakweri Land Claims Committee v. Cameroon*, Communication No. 260/02, 18th Activity Report 2002–2003, para. 48; *Ahmed Ismael and 528 Others v. Egypt*, Communication No. 467/14 (2015) paras 141–145. *See further* Viljoen, Communications under the African Charter, 78–80.
2001. *Ilesanmi v. Nigeria*, Communication No. 268/2003, 18th Activity Report 2002–2003, para. 40. *See also Zimbabwe Lawyers for Human Rights and the Institute for Human Rights and Development v. Zimbabwe*, Communication No. 293/2004, 24th Activity Report 2008, paras 46–56; *Zimbabwe Lawyers for Human Rights & Associated Newspapers of Zimbabwe v. Zimbabwe*, Communication No. 284/2003, 26th Activity Report 2008–2009, paras 83–97.
2002. The applicant's subjective opinion about the regime or its leaders cannot per se be considered insulting, *Bakweri Land Claims Committee v. Cameroon*, Communication No. 260/02, 18th Activity Report 2002–2003, para. 48; *Jean-Marie Atangana Mebara v. Cameroon*, Communication No. 416/12 (2015) para. 55. In *Ivorien Human Rights Movement (MIDH) v. Côte d'Ivoire*, Communication No. 262/2002, 26th Activity Report 2008–2009, para. 47, the terms 'xenophobia' and 'discriminatory' were accepted as accurate descriptions of the state of affairs.

but abusive language is not acceptable.[2003] The Commission has accepted that this provision imposes an objective test.[2004]

313. The fourth condition is that the communication must not be based exclusively on information obtained from the mass media. The rationale for this requirement seems to be that communications should not be based on secondary and unsubstantiated allegations given the African Charter's relaxed requirements of individual standing[2005] but on primary evidence although events reported by the media have been taken into account by the Commission. Thus, in *Sir Dawda K. Jawara v. Gambia*, the Commission stated that, 'While it would be dangerous to rely *exclusively* on news disseminated from the mass media, it would be equally damaging if the Commission were to reject a communication because some aspects of it are based on news disseminated through the mass media' (emphasis added).[2006] The Commission went on to state that the test was not whether the information had been obtained from the media but whether it was correct. The crucial question was whether the applicant had tried to verify the truth and whether it was possible for him to have done so in the circumstances.[2007]

314. The fifth condition requires the exhaustion of existing domestic, or local or internal, remedies.[2008] This provision reflects a general principle of international law

2003. Statements such as 'regime of torturers' and 'government barbarisms' were considered insulting by the Commission in *Ligue Camerounaise des Droits de l'Homme v. Cameroon*, Communication No. 65/92, 10th Activity Report 1996–1997, para. 15. Other unacceptable terms include 'sickening' and 'charade', *Uhuru Kenyatta and William Ruto (represented by Innocence Project Africa) v. Kenya*, Communication No. 464/14 (2014), para. 18. *See also Ilesanmi v. Nigeria*, Communication No. 268/2003, 18th Activity Report 2002–2003, paras 22–29. The Commission has stated that the language used must 'unequivocally demonstrate the intention of the Complainant to bring the State and its institutions into disrepute', *Eyob B. Asemie v. Lesotho*, Communication No. 435/12 (2014), para. 59. *See also Zimbabwe Lawyers for Human Rights & Associated Newspapers of Zimbabwe v. Zimbabwe*, Communication No. 284/2003, 26th Activity Report 2008–2009, paras 88-91. Facts or allegations of African Charter violations are not deemed incompatible with this provision, *Tsikata v. Ghana*, Communication No. 322/2006, 21st Activity Report 2005–2006, paras 32–33.

2004. *Ahmed Ismael and 528 Others v. Egypt*, Communication No. 467/14 (2015) para. 142. Although in a previous case, *Gunme et al. v. Cameroon,* Communication No. 266/2003, 26th Activity Report 2008–2009, para. 75, the Commission had suggested the provision had a subjective character.

2005. Viljoen, Communications under the African Charter, 80.

2006. Communication Nos 147/95 and 149/96, 13th Activity Report 1999–2000, para. 24. In *Zimbabwe Human Rights NGO Forum v. Zimbabwe*, Communication No. 245/2002, 21st Activity Report 2005–2006, para. 43, the Commission stressed the 'operative term being "exclusively"'. In *Ahmed Ismael and 528 Others v. Egypt*, Communication No. 467/14 (2015), para. 151, the applicants had relied on sources derived from NGOs. In *Sudan Human Rights Organization and Sudan Centre for Housing Rights and Evictions v. Sudan* Communication Nos 279/03, 296/05, 28th Activity Report 2010, paras 92–93, the Commission accepted the fact that the conflict in Darfur had attracted the attention of the mass media.

2007. *Sir Dawda K. Jawara v. Gambia*, Communication Nos 147/95 and 149/96, 13th Activity Report 1999–2000, para. 26. Security risks and difficulties in obtaining access to documents and victims were accepted as legitimate reasons by the Commission, *Ahmed Ismael and 528 Others v. Egypt*, Communication No. 467/14 (2015) para. 150.

2008. The emphasis is on the availability of remedies in the State where the violation allegedly occurred and not in other jurisdictions, *Crawford Lindsay von Abo v. Zimbabwe*, Communication No. 477/14 (2015) para. 97.

granting the State the initial opportunity to right any wrongdoing[2009] and exists in all major human rights instruments. The Commission has pointed out that the international system plays a subsidiary and complementary role and that access to an international organ is a last, rather than initial, resort.[2010] It is of the view that this condition is one of the most important and is invariably the first requirement to be examined.[2011] Its 'essential characteristic' is its 'demonstrable effectiveness in redressing a particular violation.'[2012] The Commission has held that domestic remedies refer to 'the ordinary remedies of common law',[2013] or 'those normally available in the domestic court system and excluding those available only as a pure

---

2009. *See* generally C.F. Amerasinghe, *Local Remedies in International Law* (2nd edn, Cambridge: Cambridge University Press, 2004). The principle of exhaustion of local remedies has been described as the 'cornerstone of the Commission's adjudicatory function ... which safeguard prevents the Commission from acting as a court of first instance', *Crawford Lindsay von Abo v. Zimbabwe*, Communication No. 477/14 (2015) para. 66. In *Free Legal Assistance Group, Lawyers Committee for Human Rights, Union Interafricaine des Droits de l'Homme, and Les Temoins Jehoves v. Zaïre*, Communication Nos 25/89, 47/90, 59/91, 100/93, 9th Activity Report 1995–1996, para. 36, the Commission reaffirmed this principle, stating that, 'The requirement of exhaustion of local remedies is founded on the principle that a government should have notice of a human rights violation in order to have the opportunity to remedy such violations before being called before an international body.' In *Haregewoin Gabre-Selassie and IHRDA (on behalf of former Dergue officials) v. Ethiopia*, Communication No. 301/05 (2011) para. 113, the Commission referred to the State being given ample time and notice to redress the situation. *See also Rencontre Africaine pour la Defense des Droits de l'Homme v. Zambia*, Communication No. 71/92, 10th Activity Report 1996–1997, para. 11; *Mohammed Lamine Diakité v. Gabon*, Communication No. 73/92, 13th Activity Report 1999–2000, para. 16; *Malawi African Association et al. v. Mauritania*, Communication Nos 54/91, 61/91, 98/93, 164/97–196/97, 210/98, 13th Activity Report 1999–2000, para. 80; *Sir Dawda K. Jawara v. Gambia*, Communication Nos 147/95 and 149/96, 13th Activity Report 1999–2000, para. 31; *Anuak Justice Council v. Ethiopia*, Communication No. 299/05, 20th Activity Report 2005–2006, para. 47; *Muzerengwa and 110 Others (represented by Zimbabwe Lawyers for Human Rights) v. Zimbabwe*, Communication No. 306/2005, 29th Activity Report 2010, para. 65; *Zimbabwe Lawyers for Human Rights & Associated Newspapers of Zimbabwe v. Zimbabwe*, Communication No. 284/2003, 26th Activity Report 2008–2009, para. 100. In *Mbianku v. Cameroon*, Communication No. 389/10 (2015) para. 71, the Commission stated that Art. 56(5) was an expression of the principle of subsidiarity.

2010. *Anuak Justice Council v. Ethiopia*, Communication No. 299/05, 20th Activity Report 2005–2006, para. 48, though the Commission went on to state that this condition 'should not constitute an unjustifiable impediment to access to international remedies', para. 49. However, in *Crawford Lindsay von Abo v. Zimbabwe*, Communication No. 477/14 (2015) para. 99, the Commission explained that its role was subsidiary to that of the respondent State and it was not a 'last resort' while the applicant pursued remedies in other jurisdictions.

2011. *Amnesty International v. Zambia*, Communication No. 212/98, 12th Activity Report 1998–1999, para. 24; *Sir Dawda K. Jawara v. Gambia*, Communication Nos 147/95 and 149/96, 13th Activity Report 1999–2000, para. 30; *The Law Office of Ghazi Suleiman v. Sudan*, Communication No. 228/99, 16th Activity Report, 2002–2003, para. 29.

2012. *Human Rights Council and Others v. Ethiopia*, Communication No. 445/13 (2015) para. 59; *Groupe de Travail sur les Dossiers Judiciaires Stratégiques v. Democratic Republic of Congo*, Communication No. 259/2002 (2011) para. 46.

2013. *Interights, Institute for Human Rights and Development in Africa, and Association Mauritaniene des Droits de l'Homme v. Mauritania*, Communication No. 242/2001, 17th Activity Report, 2003–2004, para. 27; *Koso and Others v. Democratic Republic of Congo*, Communication No. 281/2003, 26th Activity Report 2008–2009, para. 51. Approved by the Human Rights Court, *Alex Thomas v. Tanzania*, African Court of Human and Peoples' Rights, App. No. 005/2013 (20 Nov. 2015), para. 64. The Court proceeded to state that constitutional remedies or applications for review constitute 'exceptional remedies' which the applicant is not expected to use, *ibid.*, paras

discretionary matter from the executive'.[2014] Moreover, it 'must operate in strict observance of the procedural guarantees of a fair hearing by a competent, independent and impartial organ … [and] must be based on enforceable law from which the relief it offers earns its mandatory or coercive force, as opposed to being merely discretionary.'[2015] The remedy should therefore be primarily a judicial one[2016] which is not 'subordinated to the discretionary power of public authorities'.[2017] In *Article 19 v. Eritrea*, the Commission expanded on the necessary criteria:

> (i) the existence of domestic procedures for dealing with the claim; (ii) the justiciability or otherwise, domestically, of the subject-matter of the complaint; (iii) the existence under the municipal legal order of provisions for redress of the type of wrong being complained of; and (iv) available effective local

---

63–64. In *Socio-Economic Rights and Accountability Project v. Nigeria*, Communication No. 300/2005, 25th Activity Report 2008, para. 69, the question was whether socioeconomic rights could be litigated in Nigerian courts.

2014. *Account of the Internal Legislation of Nigeria and the Disposition of the African Charter on Human and Peoples' Rights*, Communication Nos 129/94 and 101/93, in Murray & Evans, Documents Vol. I, 468. *See also Amnesty International et al. v. Sudan*, Communication Nos 48/90, 50/91, 52/91, 89/93, 13th Activity Report 1999–2000, para. 31; *Ilesanmi v. Nigeria*, Communication No. 268/2003, 18th Activity Report 2002–2003, para. 42; *Bissangou v. Republic of Congo*, Communication No. 253/2002, 21st Activity Report 2005–2006, paras 56, 61; *Good v. Botswana*, Communication No. 306/2005, 28th Activity Report 2009–2010, para. 89; *Muzerengwa and 110 Others (represented by Zimbabwe Lawyers for Human Rights) v. Zimbabwe*, Communication No. 306/2005, 29th Activity Report 2010, para. 74.

2015. *Human Rights Council and Others v. Ethiopia*, Communication No. 445/13 (2015) para. 59.

2016. In *Zimbabwe Lawyers for Human Rights and the Institute for Human Rights and Development (on behalf of Andrew Barclay Meldrum) v. Zimbabwe*, Communication No. 294/2004, 26th Activity Report 2008–2009, para. 51, the Commission stated that, 'Administrative or quasi judicial remedies which do not operate impartially are … inadequate and ineffective.' *See also Alfred B. Cudjoe v. Ghana*, Communication No. 221/98, 12th Activity Report 1998–1999, para. 13; *Constitutional Rights Project (in respect of Waheb Akamu, G. Adega and Others) v. Nigeria*, Communication No. 60/91, 8th Activity Report 1994–1995, para. 5. Administrative remedies have also been discounted unless they are capable and effective under domestic law, *Ilesanmi v. Nigeria*, Communication No. 268/2003, 18th Activity Report 2002–2003, para. 42; *Article 19 v. Eritrea*, Communication No. 275/2003, 22nd Activity Report 2006–2007, para. 70; *Mbianku v. Cameroon*, Communication No. 389/10 (2015) para. 66. Diplomatic protection does not constitute a judicial remedy, *Crawford Lindsay von Abo v. Zimbabwe*, Communication No. 477/14 (2015) para. 94. In *Zimbabwe Human Rights NGO Forum v. Zimbabwe*, Communication No. 245/2002, 21st Activity Report 2005–2006, para. 45, the Commission rejected the State's argument that the complainant could have pursued a remedy with the Ombudsman, who was mandated to investigate human rights violations, holding that the Ombudsman did not provide a judicial remedy. The Commission has therefore established a nexus between this remedy and Art. 7 African Charter which guarantees the right to a fair trial, *Amnesty International et al. v. Sudan*, Communication Nos 48/90, 50/91, 52/91, 89/93, 13th Activity Report 1999–2000, para. 31. In a number of cases concerning Nigeria the Commission has held that ouster clauses remove the possibility of a local remedy, *see, e.g.*, *Constitutional Rights Project and Civil Liberties Organisation v. Nigeria*, Communication Nos 143/95, 150/96, 13th Activity Report 1999–2000, paras 16–19.

2017. *Good v. Botswana*, Communication No. 306/2005, 28th Activity Report 2009–2010, para. 88. *See also Amnesty International et al. v. Sudan*, Communication Nos 48/90, 50/91, 52/91, 89/93, 13th Activity Report 1999–2000, para. 31; *Groupe de Travail sur les Dossiers Judiciaires Stratégiques v. Democratic Republic of Congo*, Communication No. 259/2002 (2011) para. 43.

remedies, that is, remedies sufficient or capable of redressing the wrong complained of.[2018]

An obvious example would be to approach the highest court of the land with the grievance and fail to obtain a remedy.[2019] The burden of proof is initially on the applicant[2020] but if met the onus shifts on to the State.[2021]

315. The Commission has declared a large number of communications inadmissible on the ground of failure to exhaust local remedies. The reasons are various and include the fact that the case was pending before the domestic courts,[2022] failure to institute legal proceedings,[2023] failure to appeal to a higher court,[2024] making general and uncorroborated allegations,[2025] and that denial of human rights violations by the government in general terms did not mean that the matter had been exhausted before the domestic courts.[2026]

2018. Communication No. 275/2003, 22nd Activity Report 2006–2007, para. 47. *See also Ivorien Human Rights Movement (MIDH) v. Côte d'Ivoire*, Communication No. 262/2002, 26th Activity Report 2008–2009, para. 55. Denial in general terms by the government of human rights violations does not mean the matter had been considered by the domestic courts, *International Pen (in respect of Kemal al-Jazouli) v. Sudan*, Communication No. 92/93, 8th Activity Report, 1994–1995. The Commission has held that the applicant need not be physically present in the country in order to access local remedies, *Chinhamo v. Zimbabwe*, Communication No. 307/2005, 23rd Activity Report 2007, para. 82.

2019. *Zimbabwe Lawyers for Human Rights & Associated Newspapers of Zimbabwe v. Zimbabwe* Communication No. 284/2003, 26th Activity Report 2008–2009, para. 113; *Lawyers for Human Rights (Swaziland) v. Swaziland*, Communication No. 414/12 (2013), para. 40.

2020. *See Rule 93(2)(i)* and further, e.g., *Nziwa Buyingo v. Uganda*, Communication No. 8/88, 8th Activity Report 1994–1995; *Sana Dumbuya v. The Gambia*, Communication No. 127/94, 8th Activity Report 1994–1995; *Mouvement des Réfugiés Mauritaniens in Senegal v. Senegal*, Communication No. 254/02, 16th Activity Report 2002–2003, para. 21; *Chinhamo v. Zimbabwe*, Communication No. 307/2005, 23rd Activity Report 2007, para. 62. In *Anuak Justice Council v. Ethiopia*, Communication No. 299/05, 20th Activity Report 2005–2006, para. 50, the Commission stated, *inter alia*, that applicants 'must provide some prima facie evidence of an attempt to exhaust local remedies'.

2021. *Rencontre Africaine pour la Defense des Droits de l'Homme v. Zambia*, Communication No. 71/92, 10th Activity Report 1996–1997, para. 13.

2022. *El Hadj Boubacare Diawara v. Benin*, Communication No. 18/88 joined with Nos 16/88 and 17/88, 8th Activity Report, 1994–1995; *Kenya Human Rights Commission v. Kenya*, Communication No. 135/94, 9th Activity Report 1995–1996; *Tsikata v. Ghana*, Communication No. 322/2006, 21st Activity Report 2005–2006, para. 35. As the Commission has observed, 'exhaustion' refers to the conclusion of an action, *Mbianku v. Cameroon*, Communication No. 389/10 (2015) para. 71.

2023. *Alfred B. Cudjoe v. Ghana*, Communication No. 221/98, 12th Activity Report 1998–1999. However, this requirement is dependent on circumstances and where the State is aware of the situation but fails to act the complainants may not be obliged to exhaust local remedies, *Monim Elgak, Osman Hummeida and Amir Suleiman (represented by FIDH and OMCT) v. Sudan*, Communication No. 379/09 (2014) paras 60–63.

2024. *Paul S. Haye v. The Gambia*, Communication No. 90/93, 8th Activity Report, 1994–1995; *Darfur Relief and Communication Centre v. Sudan*, Communication No. 310/2005, 27th Activity Report 2009, para. 73.

2025. *Chinhamo v. Zimbabwe*, Communication No. 307/2005, 23rd Activity Report 2007, para. 76; *Majuru v. Zimbabwe*, Communication No. 308/2005, 25th Activity Report 2008, para. 92; *Socio Economic Rights and Accountability Project (SERAP) v. Nigeria*, Communication No. 338/07, 29th Activity Report 2010, para. 66.

2026. *International Pen (in respect of Kemal al-Jazouli) v. Sudan*, Communication No. 92/93, 8th Activity Report 1994–1995.

316. The Commission has pointed out that this condition is not a strict requirement that must always be satisfied.[2027] It has, for instance, adopted the principle of 'constructive' exhaustion of local remedies where the complainant is prevented from accessing existing remedies.[2028] Domestic remedies must therefore exist not just in theory but in practice, otherwise it is not accessible, and their exhaustion is not required where it is apparent that such procedures would be 'unduly prolonged'.[2029] It has been held that this test applies to local remedies 'in their entirety as utilised or likely to be utilised by those concerned.'[2030] Although the wording of the African Charter may appear prima facie restrictive[2031] the practice of the Commission demonstrates a more liberal approach.[2032] In determining the rule on the exhaustion of domestic remedies the Commission has resolved on three principal elements: the remedy must be available, effective and sufficient.[2033] It has therefore held that a remedy is 'considered *available* if the petitioner can pursue it without impediment, it is deemed *effective* if it offers a prospect of success, and it

2027. *Institute for Human Rights and Development in Africa v. Angola*, Communication No. 292/2004, 24th Activity Report 2008, para. 39.

2028. *Rights International v. Nigeria*, Communication No. 215/98, 13th Activity Report 1999–2000, para. 24; *Doebbler v. Sudan*, Communication No. 236/2000, 16th Activity Report 2002–2003, para. 27. In *Zimbabwe Lawyers for Human Rights and the Institute for Human Rights and Development (on behalf of Andrew Barclay Meldrum) v. Zimbabwe*, Communication No. 294/2004, 26th Activity Report 2008–2009, paras 52–56, the victim was deported in defiance of court orders which in itself amounted to a violation of the African Charter Art. 26.

2029. There are no standard criteria to determine this particular point but is dependent on a variety of factors, *Zimbabwe Lawyers for Human Rights and the Institute for Human Rights and Development v. Zimbabwe*, Communication No. 293/2004, 24th Activity Report 2008, paras 58–61; *Jean-Marie Atangana Mebara v. Cameroon*, Communication No. 416/12 (2015) paras 60–73. The Commission has stated that if it is proven that a State has had ample time and notice to remedy the situation the State will be deemed to have been properly informed and will be expected to take the necessary steps to rectify the violation, *Article 19 v. Eritrea*, Communication No. 275/2003, 22nd Activity Report 2006–2007, para. 77. *See also Wilfred Onyango Nganyi & 9 Others v. Tanzania*, African Court of Human and Peoples' Rights, App. No. 006/2013 (18 March 2016), paras 90–95.

2030. *Zongo and Others v. Burkina Faso*, African Court of Human and Peoples' Rights, App. No. 013/2011 (28 Mar. 2014) para. 90.

2031. Ankumah, 67–69.

2032. In *Malawi African Association et al. v. Mauritania*, Communication Nos 54/91, 61/91, 98/93, 164/97–196/97, 210/98, 13th Activity Report 1999–2000, para. 85, the Commission stated that it 'interprets the provisions of Art. 56(5) in the light of its duty to protect human and peoples' rights as stipulated in the Charter'. Moreover, in *Bakweri Land Claims Committee v. Cameroon*, Communication No. 260/02, 18th Activity Report 2002–2003, para. 55, the Commission stated that this requirement 'should be interpreted liberally so as not to close the door on those who have made at least a modest attempt to exhaust local remedies. Under this Article [56(5)], all the African Commission wishes to hear from the complainant is that it has approached either local or national judicial bodies'.

2033. *Anuak Justice Council v. Ethiopia*, Communication No. 299/05, 20th Activity Report 2005–2006, para. 51; *African Commission on Human and Peoples' Rights v. Libya*, African Court of Human and Peoples' Rights, App. No. 002/2013 (3 Jun. 2016) para. 67. Additionally, the remedy must be both 'theoretical and practical', *Institute for Human Rights and Development in Africa (on behalf of Jean Simbarakiye) v. Democratic Republic of Congo*, Communication No. 247/2002, 16th Activity Report 2002–2003, para. 26.

is found *sufficient* if it is capable of redressing the complaint'.[2034] In addition, the 'existence of a remedy must be sufficiently certain, not only in theory but also in practice, failing which, it will lack the requisite accessibility and effectiveness'.[2035] Thus remedies do not need to be exhausted if they are 'unavailable, ineffective or unreasonably prolonged',[2036] are 'certain to yield no results',[2037] are 'non-existent'[2038] or 'impractical or undesirable', or impossible.[2039] However, if there is

2034. *Sir Dawda K. Jawara v. Gambia*, Communication Nos 147/95 and 149/96, 13th Activity Report 1999–2000, para. 32; *Ahmed Ismael and 528 Others v. Egypt*, Communication No. 467/14 (2015), paras 155–169. In *Zongo and Others v. Burkina Faso*, African Court of Human and Peoples' Rights, App. No. 013/2011 (28 Mar. 2014) para. 68, the Human Rights Court held that an effective remedy refers to 'that which produces the expected result … the effectiveness of a remedy is therefore measured in terms of its ability to solve a problem raise by the Applicant'. In *Kazeem Aminu v. Nigeria*, Communication No. 205/97, 13th Activity Report 1999–2000, paras 11–13, the Commission decided that it would not insist on the exhaustion of domestic remedies given the fact that the complainant's life was in danger in the chaotic situation prevailing under the military regime. *See also African Institute for Human Rights and Development (on behalf of Sierra Leonean refugees in Guinea v. Republic of Guinea*, Communication No. 249/2002, 20th Activity Report, 2005–2006, para. 33, where the victims were in constant danger.

2035. *Sir Dawda K. Jawara v. Gambia*, Communication Nos 147/95 and 149/96, 13th Activity Report 1999–2000, para. 35; *Zimbabwe Lawyers for Human Rights & Associated Newspapers of Zimbabwe v. Zimbabwe*, Communication No. 284/2003, 26th Activity Report 2008–2009, para. 119; *Justice Thomas S. Masuku v. Swaziland*, Communication No. 444/13 (2014) paras 58–59. In *Article 19 v. Eritrea*, Communication No. 275/2003, 22nd Activity Report 2006–2007, para. 73, the Commission found that merely listing remedies *in abstracto* without showing how they might provide effective redress did not prove domestic remedies existed. In *Ivorien Human Rights Movement (MIDH) v. Côte d'Ivoire*, Communication No. 262/2002, 26th Activity Report 2008–2009, paras 50–51, remedies could be pursued only by certain classes of citizen.

2036. *Alberto Capitao v. Tanzania*, Communication No. 53/91, 8th Activity Report, 1994–1995, para. 3; *Mohammed Lamine Diakité v. Gabon*, Communication No. 73/92, 13th Activity Report 1999–2000, para. 16; *Lawyers for Human Rights v. Swaziland*, Communication No. 251/2002, 18th Activity Report 2002–2003, para. 27; *Bissangou v. Republic of Congo*, Communication No. 253/2002, 21st Activity Report 2005–2006, para. 61; *Zimbabwe Lawyers for Human Rights & Associated Newspapers of Zimbabwe v. Zimbabwe*, Communication No. 284/2003, 26th Activity Report 2008–2009, para. 118. In *Haregewoin Gabre-Selassie and IHRDA (on behalf of former Dergue officials) v. Ethiopia*, Communication No. 301/05 (2011) paras 111–112, the complainants could not access the courts. Similarly, *African Commission on Human and Peoples' Rights v. Libya*, African Court of Human and Peoples' Rights, App. No. 002/2013 (3 Jun. 2016) paras 68–70, where the victim was kept in secret detention by rebels without access to lawyers. In *Monim Elgak, Osman Hummeida and Amir Suleiman (represented by FIDH and OMCT) v. Sudan*, Communication No. 379/09 (2014) paras 54–55, fear of persecution meant that domestic remedies were unavailable. In *Modise v. Botswana*, Communication No. 97/93, 10th Activity Report 1996–1997, para. 20, the Commission found that the complainant had instituted domestic legal proceedings sixteen years previously but that they had been repeatedly interrupted and wilfully obstructed. In *Bakweri Land Claims Committee v. Cameroon*, Communication No. 260/02, 18th Activity Report 2002–2003, para. 24, the Commission found that the State had had forty years in which to address the grievances of the complainants. In *Association of Victims of Post Electoral Violence & INTERIGHTS v. Cameroon*, Communication No. 272/2003, 27th Activity Report 2009, paras 63–68, the case had been before the court for five years. Moreover, the Commission found an ad hoc body set up to settle the dispute amicably 'highly inefficient' for its failure to produce a report after twelve years of existence, *ibid.*, paras 64, 69. In *Article 19 v. Eritrea*, Communication No. 275/2003, 22nd Activity Report 2006–2007, para. 48, the Commission also referred to situations where no justice is available, e.g., where the judiciary is not independent, or where the wrong is due to an executive act which is not justiciable. *See also Mouvement Ivorien des Droits Humains (MIDH) v. Côte d'Ivoire*, Communication No. 246/2002, 25th Activity Report

some prospect of success the remedies must be pursued.[2040] Neither can a remedy be deemed sufficient if it meets only part of the claim rather than the full claim.[2041] Furthermore, if the availability of the remedies is not obvious, they 'cannot be invoked by the State to the detriment of the complainant'.[2042] In *Ilesanmi v. Nigeria*, the Commission set the applicable procedure where it was argued that local remedies were unavailable as follows: first, the complainant submits that the remedy is ineffective, unavailable or insufficient this does not have to be proven; second, the Respondent State must then demonstrate that the remedy is available, effective and sufficient; if the Respondent State establishes this fact, the complainant must then either show that s/he did exhaust the remedy, or that it could not have been effective in this specific case even if effective in general.[2043] Account has also

---

2008, para. 49. However, simply maintaining that local remedies are not likely to be effective is not a persuasive argument, *Bakweri Land Claims Committee v. Cameroon,* Communication No. 260/02, 18th Activity Report 2002–2003, para. 55; *Anuak Justice Council v. Ethiopia*, Communication No. 299/05, 20th Activity Report 2005–2006, para. 58; *Chinhamo v. Zimbabwe*, Communication No. 307/2005, 23rd Activity Report 2007, para. 84.

2037. *Constitutional Rights Project and Civil Liberties Organisation v. Nigeria*, Communication Nos 143/95, 150/96, 13th Activity Report 1999–2000, para. 17. In an interesting decision, *Konaté v. Burkina Faso*, African Court of Human and Peoples' Rights, App. No. 004/2013 (5 Dec. 2014), paras 108–115, the Human Rights Court found an exception to the requirement of the exhaustion of local remedies when it held that the Applicant could not have expected a ruling in his favour from the highest court of the land which was not in a position to annul the impugned law. *See also, e.g., Actions pour la Protection des Droit de l'Homme (APDH) v. Côte d'Ivoire*, African Court of Human and Peoples' Rights, App. No. 001/2014 (18 Nov. 2016) para. 103, where the Human Rights Court held that there is 'no need to go through the same judicial process the outcome of which was known'.

2038. *Centre for Free Speech v. Nigeria*, Communication No. 206/97, 13th Activity Report 1999–2000, para. 10. In *Malawi African Association et al. v. Mauritania*, Communication Nos 54/91, 61/91, 98/93, 164/97–196/97, 210/98, 13th Activity Report 1999–2000, para. 85, the Commission held that the amnesty law adopted by the State rendered all domestic remedies obsolete.

2039. *Free Legal Assistance Group, Lawyers Committee for Human Rights, Union Interafricaine des Droits de l'Homme, and Les Temoins Jehoves v. Zaïre*, Communication Nos 25/89, 47/90, 59/91, 100/93, 9th Activity Report 1995–1996, para. 37; *Article 19 v. Eritrea,* Communication No. 275/ 2003, 22nd Activity Report 2006–2007, para. 48; *Malawi African Association et al. v. Mauritania*, Communication Nos 54/91, 61/91, 98/93, 164/97–196/97, 210/98, 13th Activity Report 1999–2000, para. 85 (large number of victims); *African Institute for Human Rights and Development (on behalf of Sierra Leonean refugees in Guinea v. Republic of Guinea*, Communication No. 249/2002, 20th Activity Report, 2005–2006, para. 34 (large number of potential complainants required to return to Guinea). In *Koso and Others v. Democratic Republic of Congo*, Communication No. 281/2003, 26th Activity Report 2008–2009, para. 53, the fact that no appeal was possible from the rulings of the Military Tribunal meant that the exhaustion of local remedies was 'impossible'. In *Purohit and Moore v. The Gambia*, Communication No. 241/2001, 16th Activity Report 2002–2003, paras 32–38, the Commission found that the remedies available, in the absence of legal aid, were not realistic for poor mental health patients.

2040. *Anuak Justice Council v. Ethiopia*, Communication No. 299/05, 20th Activity Report 2005–2006, para. 58; *Nixon Nyikadzino (represented by Zimbabwe Human Rights NGO Forum) v. Zimbabwe*, Communication No. 340/07 (2012), paras 89–91.

2041. *Crawford Lindsay von Abo v. Zimbabwe*, Communication No. 477/14 (2015) para. 86.

2042. *Sir Dawda K. Jawara v. Gambia*, Communication Nos 147/95 and 149/96, 13th Activity Report 1999–2000, para. 34.

2043. Communication No. 268/2003, 18th Activity Report 2002–2003, para. 46. *See also Zimbabwe Lawyers for Human Rights & Associated Newspapers of Zimbabwe v. Zimbabwe*, Communication No. 284/2003, 26th Activity Report 2008–2009, para. 102.

been taken of the circumstances of the complainant, for example, refugees, who because of their vulnerability, deprivation and fear may not have the means or wherewithal to pursue local remedies.[2044] But generally it is important that the complainant takes all necessary steps to exhaust, or attempt to exhaust, domestic remedies as s/he may otherwise find that the case will be dismissed.[2045] Since it is not necessary for the complainant to be physically present in the territory of the Respondent State to exhaust local remedies,[2046] the onus is on the complainant to explain why it was not possible to institute legal proceedings or have them started on his or her behalf.[2047]

317. It is important to note that the Commission has established that the requirement of exhaustion of local remedies will not apply in cases of serious or massive violations of human rights under Article 58 of the African Charter.[2048] This is because given the scale and nature of the alleged violations and the number of people involved the remedies are deemed not to be available or effective in such extreme circumstances.[2049]

318. The sixth condition is that the communication must be submitted within a reasonable period from the time local remedies were exhausted or from the date the Commission was seized of the matter.[2050] This is to ensure that the complainant is 'vigilant and to discourage tardiness'.[2051] No indication is given as to what constitutes 'reasonable' but the Commission seems to have considerable flexibility[2052] and

2044. *Doebbler v. Sudan*, Communication No. 235/2000, 27th Activity Report 2009, para. 116.

2045. *Chinhamo v. Zimbabwe*, Communication No. 307/2005, 23rd Activity Report 2007, para. 86.

2046. *Mbianku v. Cameroon*, Communication No. 389/10 (2015) para. 75.

2047. *Zitha & Zitha v. Mozambique*, Communication No. 361/08, 29th Activity Report 2010, paras 108–109; *Nixon Nyikadzino (represented by Zimbabwe Human Rights NGO Forum) v. Zimbabwe*, Communication No. 340/07 (2012), paras 81–82.

2048. *See, e.g., Free Legal Assistance Group, Lawyers Committee for Human Rights, Union Interafricaine des Droits de l'Homme, and Les Temoins Jehoves v. Zaïre*, Communication Nos 25/89, 47/90, 59/91, 100/93, 9th Activity Report 1995–1996, para. 37; *Open Society Justice Initiative v. Côte d'Ivoire*, Communication No. 318/06 (2015) paras 42–50.

2049. *Article 19 v. Eritrea*, Communication No. 275/2003, 22nd Activity Report 2006–2007, para. 71; *Doebbler v. Sudan*, Communication No. 235/2000, 27th Activity Report 2009, para. 117; *Sudan Human Rights Organization and Sudan Centre for Housing Rights and Evictions v. Sudan* Communication Nos 279/03, 296/05, 28th Activity Report 2010, paras 97–102. *See also* Viljoen, Communications under the African Charter, 86–88.

2050. *See Majuru v. Zimbabwe*, Communication No. 308/2005, 25th Activity Report 2008, paras 108-110.

2051. *Darfur Relief and Communication Centre v. Sudan*, Communication No. 310/2005, 27th Activity Report 2009, para. 78. In *Crawford Lindsay von Abo v. Zimbabwe*, Communication No. 477/14 (2015) para. 97, the Commission held that the applicant had not been diligent in pursuing alternative remedies in other jurisdictions when there was no such requirement under the African Charter.

2052. *See* Ankumah, 65–66, who writes that the Commission should take account of factors 'such as the general nature of the case, the continuity or lack thereof of the alleged violation, the seriousness of the alleged violation and the domestic remedies procedure in the country concerned.' In *Tsikata v. Ghana*, Communication No. 322/2006, 21st Activity Report 2005–2006, para. 38, the Commission stated that despite the fact that no time period is specified that early submission is advisable.

the reasonableness of time is considered in each case on its own merits.[2053] In *Tsikata v. Ghana*, the Commission held that this provision was related to the previous paragraph which meant that the 'Commission estimates the timeliness of a Communication from the date that the last available local remedy is exhausted by the Complainant. In the case of unavailability or prolongation of local remedies, it will be from the date of the Complainant's notice thereof.'[2054] This should ensure that any imputed State does not profit from delaying tactics. Nevertheless, the Commission considers the six-month rule applied by the European and American systems as a useful guide unless there is a 'good and compelling reason' or justification to the contrary or to ensure 'fairness and justice'.[2055] Periods of eleven years[2056] and thirteen years[2057] have been deemed unreasonable unsurprisingly but so have periods of two years[2058] and two years and five months.[2059]

319. The seventh and final condition is that the communication must not be concerned with cases that have previously been settled in accordance with the principles of the UN Charter, the OAU/AU Charter/Act or the African Charter.[2060] According to the Commission the rationale for this requirement 'is to desist from faulting Member States twice for the same alleged violations of human rights ... the

2053. *Darfur Relief and Communication Centre v. Sudan*, Communication No. 310/2005, 27th Activity Report 2009, para. 74; *Article 19 and Others v. Zimbabwe*, Communication No. 305/05, 29th Activity Report 2010, para. 91. This stance has been approved by the Human Rights Court, *Mohamed Abubakri v. Tanzania*, African Court of Human and Peoples' Rights, App. No. 007/2013 (3 Jun. 2016), para. 91.

2054. Communication No. 322/2006, 21st Activity Report 2005–2006, para. 37. In *Centre for Minority Rights Development (CEMIRIDE) and Truth be Told Network v. Kenya*, Communication No. 332/06 (2014) para. 103, the Commission added that the Communication must be brought within a reasonable time from the time the alleged violation occurred. The time period often applied by the Human Rights Court is the date on which the State accepted the jurisdiction of the Court to receive individual communications and the date it was seized of the case, *Mohamed Abubakri v. Tanzania*, African Court of Human and Peoples' Rights, App. No. 007/2013 (3 Jun. 2016), para. 93.

2055. *Chinhamo v. Zimbabwe*, Communication No. 307/2005, 23rd Activity Report 2007, paras 88–89; *Majuru v. Zimbabwe*, Communication No. 308/2005, 25th Activity Report 2008, paras 109–110; *Darfur Relief and Communication Centre v. Sudan*, Communication No. 310/2005, 27th Activity Report 2009, paras 75–79; *Article 19 and Others v. Zimbabwe*, Communication No. 305/05, 29th Activity Report 2010, paras 95–97. The Human Rights Court has not discounted the six-month rule, *Mohamed Abubakri v. Tanzania*, African Court of Human and Peoples' Rights, App. No. 007/2013 (3 Jun. 2016), paras 86–94.

2056. *Southern Africa Human Rights NGO Network and Others v. Tanzania*, Communication No. 333/200, 28th Activity Report 2009–2010, paras 74–76.

2057. *Zitha & Zitha v. Mozambique*, Communication No. 361/08, 29th Activity Report 2010, para. 113.

2058. *Article 19 and Others v. Zimbabwe*, Communication No. 305/05, 29th Activity Report 2010, para. 96.

2059. *Darfur Relief and Communication Centre v. Sudan*, Communication No. 310/2005, 27th Activity Report 2009, para. 77.

2060. *See Amnesty International v. Tunisia*, Communication No. 69/92, 7th Activity Report 1993–1994. In *Interights (on behalf of Pan-African Movement and Citizens for Peace in Eritrea) and Interights (on behalf of Pan-African Movement and Inter Africa Group) v. Eritrea*, Communication Nos 233/99, 234/99, 16th Activity Report 2002–2003, paras 52–56, the Commission found that the Claims Commission established under the Peace Agreement of 2000 between Ethiopia and Eritrea came within the scope of this provision.

non bis in idem rule'.[2061] To come within the ambit of this provision the communication should involve 'the same parties, the same issues ... and must have been settled by an international or regional mechanism'.[2062] The Commission can therefore reject communications which have been determined by the HRC for example, or some other international human rights adjudicatory body.[2063] The critical element is that this provision envisages mechanisms 'capable of granting declaratory or compensatory relief to victims, not mere political resolutions and declarations' by bodies such as the UN Security Council.[2064] However, the Commission has held that it is not precluded from receiving communications identical to those *submitted* to another international body so long as a decision on the merits has not been reached.[2065] The fact that the case has been discussed is not fatal.[2066] This amounts to recognition of the principle of res judicata.[2067] This provision also refers to cases where an amicable settlement has been reached. But there is another issue that the Commission has had to address, namely, whether a government is deemed responsible for the misdeeds of its predecessors. Relying on the principle of state responsibility the Commission's established practice is that successor governments do indeed inherit the responsibility for their predecessors' wrongdoings.[2068]

320. No other formal conditions of admissibility are required and it appears that these criteria are exhaustive. However, prior to the substantive examination of any communication accepted Article 57 requires that the State concerned be notified by the Commission.[2069] The complainant then has two months in which to present evidence and arguments on admissibility,[2070] while the respondent State is then given

2061. *Bakweri Land Claims Committee v. Cameroon,* Communication No. 260/02, 18th Activity Report 2002–2003, para. 52.
2062. *Gunme et al. v. Cameroon,* Communication No. 266/2003, 26th Activity Report 2008–2009, para. 86.
2063. *Sudan Human Rights Organization and Sudan Centre for Housing Rights and Evictions v. Sudan* Communication Nos 279/03, 296/05, 28th Activity Report 2010, para. 104.
2064. *Ibid.*, para. 105. Nor, it would appear, the I.C.J., *Gunme et al. v. Cameroon,* Communication No. 266/2003, 26th Activity Report 2008–2009, para. 86.
2065. *Bob Ngozi Njoku v. Egypt,* Communication No. 40/90, 11th Activity Report 1997–1998, paras 54–56; *Bakweri Land Claims Committee v. Cameroon,* Communication No. 260/02, 18th Activity Report 2002–2003, paras 49–53.
2066. *Haregewoin Gabre-Selassie and IHRDA (on behalf of former Dergue officials) v. Ethiopia,* Communication No. 301/05 (2011) para. 117.
2067. *Bakweri Land Claims Committee v. Cameroon,* Communication No. 260/02, 18th Activity Report 2002–2003, para. 52; *Sudan Human Rights Organization and Sudan Centre for Housing Rights and Evictions v. Sudan* Communication Nos 279/03, 296/05, 28th Activity Report 2010, para. 104.
2068. *See, e.g., Krischna Achutan (on behalf of Aleke Banda) v. Malawi*; *Amnesty International on behalf of Orton and Vera Chirwa v. Malawi,* Communication Nos 64/92, 68/92, 78/92, 8th Activity Report 1994–1995, para. 12; *Civil Liberties Organisation, Legal Defence Centre, Legal Defence and Assistance Project v. Nigeria,* Communication No. 218/98, 14th Activity Report 2000–2001, para. 21; *Media Rights Agenda v. Nigeria,* Communication No. 224/98, 14th Activity Report 2000–2001, paras 36–38.
2069. *See also* Rule 116(2).
2070. *Ibid. See SERAP (on behalf of Daniel Nso for and Osayindwinde Agbomien) v. Nigeria,* Communication No. 427/12 (2015).

a further two months in which to respond to the allegations.[2071] The complainant can exercise a right of reply within a month.[2072]

321. Failure of a Respondent State to appear does not prevent the Commission from proceeding with the case nor does it absolve the State from the Commission's decision.[2073] Where a State fails to respond to a Communication it forfeits its right to seek review of a decision declaring the case admissible unless there are compelling reasons.[2074]

322. The Commission has the power to reconsider communications that have been declared inadmissible in the light of new facts presented by the complainant or the respondent State'.[2075] The new fact must be a 'decisive' one, 'not known to the party seeking the review, provided that such lack of knowledge was not due to negligence',[2076] for example, if local remedies that had not been exhausted at the time of the Communication turn out subsequently not to be available.[2077] In *Interights, Institute for Human Rights and Development in Africa, and Association Mauritaniene des Droits de l'Homme v. Mauritania*, the Commission held that review was appropriate where the application introduced a 'new or compelling element, the failure to consider which would be an affront to fairness, justice and good conscience.'[2078] At greater length, it has stated:

> the application would be granted where it is proved that some facts have been discovered which intrinsically might have had a decisive influence on the judgment had it been brought to the attention of the Commission at the time the decision was made, but which at the time was unknown to both the Commission and the party making the application and also which could not, with reasonable diligence, have been discovered by the party before the judgment was made or on account of some mistake, fraud or error on the face of the record or because an injustice has been done.[2079]

2071. Rule 116(2). Note further Rule 98(2) which allows for a single extension of one month.
2072. Rule 116(2).
2073. *Organisation Mondiale contre la Torture et al. v. Rwanda*, Communication Nos 27/89, 46/91, 49/91, 99/93, 10th Activity Report 1993–1994, para. 20. The established practice of the Commission in such instances is that the burden of proof lies with the State, *see, e.g.*, *Amnesty International et al. v. Sudan*, Communication Nos 48/90, 50/91, 52/91, 89/93, 13th Activity Report 1999–2000, para. 52. There the Commission stated that, 'If the government provides no evidence to contradict an allegation of human rights allegation made against it, the Commission will take it as proven, or at the least probable or plausible.'
2074. Rule 119(4).
2075. Rule 119(1), (2). *See Modise v. Botswana*, Communication No. 97/93, 14th Activity Report 2000–2001, para. 69.
2076. Rule 119(3).
2077. *S.O.S. – Esclaves v. Mauritania*, Communication No. 198/97, 12th Activity Report 1998–1999, para. 18; *Bakweri Land Claims Committee v. Cameroon,* Communication No. 260/02 (2014), paras 1–9.
2078. Communication No. 373/2009 (2010), para. 11.
2079. *Bakweri Land Claims Committee v. Cameroon,* Communication No. 260/2002 (2014),para. 17, citing *Kevin Ngwang Gumne v. Cameroon,* Communication No. 384/09 (2012), para. 37 (unreported).

However, the Commission cannot dismiss a communication once it has been declared admissible.[2080]

323. The Commission may also review its decisions on the merits at the request of one of the parties.[2081] The request must be submitted within six months of new facts coming to light[2082] but in any case no later than three years after the decision.[2083] The request must be based on the discovery of a fact of a decisive factor which was not known at the time to the Commission and the party requesting revision, provided that such ignorance was not due to negligence.[2084] Where a State fails to make submissions on the merits it forfeits its right to seek review of the decision unless there are compelling reasons.[2085] In *Interights, Institute for Human Rights and Development in Africa, and Association Mauritaniene des Droits de l'Homme v. Mauritania*, decided before the adoption of the new Rules, the Commission revised its decision on the ground that it had been *infra petita*, that is, that it had failed to address all the allegations in the original complaint.[2086] Allegations of bias were also considered by the Commission but dismissed on the facts.[2087]

324. The Rules make provision for parties to file preliminary objections, a common feature of international litigation, both at the stage of admissibility or at the merits stage.[2088] An objection must be raised within thirty days after notification to submit on admissibility or on the merits.[2089] Any objection must be determined before any other question.[2090]

325. Provision is made under Article 58 for exceptional cases where communications reveal 'the existence of a series of serious or massive violations of human and peoples' rights'. This phrase is defined as 'grave human rights violations as distinguished by their scale and importance'[2091] but specific, isolated violations, however serious, lie beyond the scope of this provision; instead it refers to a pattern of

2080. *Zegveld and Ephrem v. Eritrea*, Communication No. 250/2002, 17th Activity Report 2003–2004, paras 43–45; *Article 19 v. Eritrea*, Communication No. 275/2003, 22nd Activity Report 2006–2007, para. 85.
2081. Rule 122(1); *Interights, Institute for Human Rights and Development in Africa, and Association Mauritaniene des Droits de l'Homme v. Mauritania*, Communication No. 373/2009, 28th Activity Report, 2009–2010, paras 8–12. The Commission's ability to review its decisions *propio motu* has been dropped from the latest Rules.
2082. Rule 122(1).
2083. *Ibid.*
2084. Rule 122(2).
2085. Rule 122(4).
2086. Communication No. 373/2009, 28th Activity Report 2009–2010, paras 16–39.
2087. *Ibid.*, paras 47–62.
2088. Rule 117. *See Interights & Ditshwanelo v. Botswana*, Communication No. 319/06 (2015) paras 37–38.
2089. *Ibid.*
2090. Rule 117(4).
2091. Rule 2.

large-scale violations.[2092] The Commission has proceeded to define 'massive' in terms of scale as 'where a significant number of people are targeted either within a specific area or across the territory of a State', whereas in terms of nature where it is 'the product of a consistent and predetermined action that impacts on a right or … rights guaranteed under the African Charter.'[2093] Widespread allegations of human rights violations lead the Commission to presume a series of serious or massive violations as established.[2094] It has adopted the stance that 'the state will be presumed to have notice of the violations within its territory and the State is expected to act accordingly to deal with whatever human rights violations'.[2095] The Commission has determined that it must act promptly in such cases[2096] and bring the matter to the attention of the Assembly and the PSC.[2097]

326. Under Article 58(2) the AU Assembly may request the Commission to undertake in-depth studies of such cases and present factual reports with findings and recommendations. In addition, under paragraph 3 thereof a case of emergency duly noted by the Commission shall be submitted to the AU Chairman who may request an in-depth study. The Commission may also take 'any appropriate action'.[2098] A case, or matter, of emergency is one of serious or massive human rights violations or presents a risk of irreparable damage or requires urgent action to avoid irreparable harm.[2099]

327. An important protective power is the Commission's ability to issue provisional, or interim, measures of protection.[2100] The purpose of interim measures is to

2092. *See Anuak Justice Council v. Ethiopia*, Communication No. 299/05, 20th Activity Report 2005–2006, para. 61. Compare *Jean Yaovi Degli (au nom du Caporal N. Bikagni), Union Interafricaine des Droits de l'Homme, Commission Internationale de Juristes v. Togo* Communication Nos 83/92, 88/93, 91/93, 8th Activity Report 1994–1995, where torture and ill-treatment, extortion and killings, electoral irregularities, and a general breakdown in law and order, amounted to grave and massive violations. *See also Malawi African Association et al. v. Mauritania*, Communication Nos 54/91, 61/91, 98/93/164/97–196/97, 210/98, 13th Activity Report 1999–2000, para. 80; *Amnesty International et al. v. Sudan*, Communication Nos 48/90, 50/91, 52/91, 89/93 13th Activity Report 1999–2000, para. 32. Rule 84(1)(b) also refers to 'the danger of irreparable harm' or 'irreparable damage'.

2093. *Ahmed Ismael and 528 Others v. Egypt*, Communication No. 467/14 (2015) para. 172; *The Kenyan Section of the International Commission of Jurists v. Kenya*, Communication No. 385/10 (2013) paras 63–64.

2094. *Free Legal Assistance Group, Lawyers Committee for Human Rights, Union Interafricaine des Droits de l'Homme, and Les Temoins Jehoves v. Zaïre*, Communication Nos 25/89, 47/90, 59/91, 100/93, 9th Activity Report 1995–1996.

2095. *Anuak Justice Council v. Ethiopia*, Communication No. 299/05, 20th Activity Report 2005–2006, para. 60.

2096. *Free Legal Assistance Group, Lawyers Committee for Human Rights, Union Interafricaine des Droits de l'Homme, and Les Temoins Jehoves v. Zaïre*, Communication Nos 25/89, 47/90, 59/91, 100/93, 9th Activity Report 1995–1996.

2097. Rules 85(1), 99.

2098. Rule 85(2).

2099. Rule 84(1).

2100. Rule 100. *See* G.J. Naldi, 'Interim Measures of Protection in the African System for the Protection of Human and Peoples' Rights', *A.H.R.L.J.* 2 (2002): 1.

'prevent irreparable damage to the victim ... as urgently as the situation demands' and/or to protect the interests of the parties or the proper conduct of the proceedings.[2101] An important safeguard is the requirement on States to report back on the implementation of the measures within fifteen days.[2102] Provisional measures do not prejudge the case on the merits.[2103] The Commission is competent to decide on its own motion, or at the request of a party, whether interim measures should be indicated in any particular case.[2104]

328. Although there is nothing in the African Charter nor the Rules to assert that interim measures are considered as binding on the parties to the case,[2105] the case of *International Pen, Constitutional Rights Project, Interights on behalf of Ken Saro-Wiwa Jr. and Civil Liberties Organisation v. Nigeria*, which concerned the detention and trial of the writer Ken Saro-Wiwa and others, would appear to suggest otherwise. Here, the Commission observed that Nigeria was bound by Article 1 of the African Charter and that one of the Commission's functions was to assist States parties to implement their obligations under the Charter.[2106] In its reasoning, the Commission found that the trial and implementation of the death sentence were in violation of the African Charter. Moreover, the:

> violation is compounded by the fact that there were pending communications before the African Commission at the time of the executions, and the Commission had requested the government to avoid causing any 'irreparable prejudice' to the subjects of the communications before the Commission had concluded its consideration. Executions had been stayed in Nigeria in the past on the invocation by the Commission of its rules on provisional measures ... and the

---

2101. Rule 100(1); *Association pour la Defence des Droits de l'Homme et des Libertés v. Djibouti*, Communication No. 133/94, 13th Activity Report 1999–2000, para. 5; *Constitutional Rights Project, Civil Liberties Organisation and Media Rights Agenda v. Nigeria*, Communication Nos 140/94, 141/94, 145/95, 13th Activity Report 1999–2000, para. 17. *See also International Pen, Constitutional Rights Project, Interights on behalf of Ken Saro-Wiwa Jr. and Civil Liberties Organisation v. Nigeria*, Communication Nos 137/94, 139/94, 154/96 and 161/97, 12th Activity Report 1998–1999, para. 114.

2102. Rule 100(5).

2103. Rule 100(6).

2104. Rule 100(1). *See further Constitutional Rights Project, Civil Liberties Organisation and Media Rights Agenda v. Nigeria*, Communication Nos 140/94, 141/94 and 145/95, 13th Activity 1999–2000, para. 17.

2105. In *Anuak Justice Council v. Ethiopia*, Communication No. 299/05, 20th Activity Report 2005–2006, para. 18, the complainant explicitly asked the Commission to declare interim measures binding but the request was not addressed by the Commission.

2106. *International Pen, Constitutional Rights Project, Interights on behalf of Ken Saro-Wiwa Jr. and Civil Liberties Organisation v. Nigeria*, Communication Nos 137/94, 139/94, 154/96 and 161/97, 12th Activity Report 1998–1999, paras 113–114. *See* similarly *Piandiong, Morallos and Bulan v. The Philippines* Communication No. 869/1999, UN Doc CCPR/C/70/D/869/1999 (19 Oct. 2000) (UN Human Rights Committee).

> Commission had hoped that a similar situation will obtain in the case of Ken Saro-Wiwa and others. It is a matter of deep regret that this did not happen.[2107]

The Commission therefore held that the Nigerian Government had, 'in ignoring its obligations to institute provisional measures', violated Article 1 of the Charter.[2108] The Commission added that:

> To have carried out the execution in the face of pleas to the contrary by the Commission and world opinion is something which we pray will never happen again. That it is a violation of the Charter is an understatement' (emphasis added).[2109]

329. Under Articles 60 and 61 of the African Charter the Commission is authorized to draw inspiration from various sources of law.[2110] The primary sources include international human rights law, such as the UDHR[2111] and the ICCPR[2112] which many African States have ratified. Other sources include other international treaties, such the ACHR and the ECHR, insofar as they reflect rules expressly recognized by the AU Member States, customs generally accepted as law, general principles of law and legal precedents and doctrines.[2113] While the Commission may look to other treaties it has stated that it is not tasked with ensuring the monitoring of their implementation nationally.[2114]

2107. *International Pen, Constitutional Rights Project, Interights on behalf of Ken Saro-Wiwa Jr. and Civil Liberties Organisation v. Nigeria*, Communication Nos 137/94, 139/94, 154/96 and 161/97, 12th Activity Report 1998–1999, para. 103.
2108. *Ibid.*, p. 285.
2109. *Ibid.*, para. 115.
2110. *Civil Liberties Organisation, Legal Defence Centre, Legal Defence and Assistance Project v. Nigeria*, Communication No. 218/98, 14th Activity Report 2000–2001, para. 24; *African Institute for Human Rights and Development (on behalf of Sierra Leonean refugees in Guinea v. Republic of Guinea*, Communication No. 249/2002, 20th Activity Report 2005–2006, paras 37–38. The Human Rights Court has also relied on these provisions, *African Commission on Human and Peoples' Rights v. Kenya*, African Court of Human and Peoples' Rights, App. No. 006/2012 (26 May 2017) para. 108.
2111. *See, e.g., Zimbabwe Human Rights NGO Forum v. Zimbabwe*, Communication No. 245/2002, 21st Activity Report 2005–2006, para. 180.
2112. International Covenant on Civil and Political Rights (16 Dec. 1966), 999 U.N.T.S. 171. *See, e.g., Civil Liberties Organisation, Legal Defence Centre, Legal Defence and Assistance Project v. Nigeria*, Communication No. 218/98, 14th Activity Report 2000–2001; *Purohit and Moore v. The Gambia*, Communication No. 241/2001, 16th Activity Report 2002–2003, para. 76; *Garreth Anver Prince v. South Africa*, Communication No. 255/2002, 18th Activity Report 2002–2003, para. 42; *African Commission on Human and Peoples' Rights v. Libya*, African Court of Human and Peoples' Rights, App. No. 002/2013 (3 Jun. 2016) paras 89, 92.
2113. *See, e.g., Democratic Republic of Congo v. Burundi, Rwanda and Uganda*, Communication No. 227/99, 20th Activity Report 2005–2006, paras 70, 78, where the Commission invoked the Geneva Conventions 1949 and the Additional Protocols 1977 as general principles of law recognized by African States. The case of *Zimbabwe Human Rights NGO Forum v. Zimbabwe*, Communication No. 245/2002, 21st Activity Report 2005–2006, is an especially interesting illustration because of the extensive references to international law, including the jurisprudence of the European Court of Human Rights, the IACtHR and the International Criminal Tribunal for the Former Yugoslavia. *See also Zitha & Zitha v. Mozambique*, Communication No. 361/08, 29th Activity Report 2010, paras 89–92, where the Commission made extensive references to the jurisprudence

330. There is an important omission in the African Charter and that is on a right to reparation, although the Human Rights Court is empowered to award remedies under Article 27(1) of the Protocol. Nevertheless, in its early jurisprudence the Commission adopted the view that the State was 'responsible for the reparation' of its abuses[2115] and accepted the principle of compensatory damages as a form of indemnity.[2116] In subsequent cases a right to reparation has become established and has been applied in different forms, spanning administrative and judicial measures, such as reform of the law and prosecution of the perpetrators, *restitution in integrum* to monetary compensation.[2117] Significant in the latter context was the case of *Egyptian Initiative for Personal Rights and INTERIGHTS v. Egypt*, where the Commission for the first time requested the payment of a specific sum of money.[2118] In *Jean-Marie Atangana Mebara v. Cameroon*, the Commission itself assessed the appropriate amount of monetary compensation.[2119] Ultimately, the Commission's stance is that the reparation has to be 'fair, adequate, effective, sufficient, appropriate, satisfactory to the victim and proportionate to the damage suffered.'[2120] Rule 121 now acknowledges the Commission's ability to make awards on reparations.

§4. The African Court on Human and Peoples' Rights

331. In a historic decision at its Thirty-Fourth Ordinary Session in Burkina Faso in June 1998 the OAU Assembly adopted the Protocol on the African Court on

---

of the Inter-American Court of Human Rights in relation to the issue of forced disappearances. In *Centre for Minority Rights Development (Kenya) and Minority Rights Group International on behalf of Endorois Welfare Council v. Kenya*, Communication No. 276/2003, 27th Activity Report 2009, the Commission made extensive references to the jurisprudence of the Inter-American Court of Human Rights on the rights of indigenous peoples. In *Purohit and Moore v. The Gambia*, Communication No. 241/2001, 16th Activity Report 2002–2003, and *Lawyers for Human Rights v. Swaziland*, Communication No. 251/2002, 18th Activity Report 2002–2003, the Commission relied on UN soft law in the form of the UN Principles for the Protection of Persons with Mental Illness and the Improvement of Mental Illnesses and the Improvement of Mental Health Care, and the UN Basic Principles on the Independence of the Judiciary respectively. Such inspiration also extends to procedural points of law, *Darfur Relief and Communication Centre v. Sudan*, Communication No. 310/2005, 27th Activity Report 2009, paras 75–76.

2114. *Groupe de Travail sur les Dossiers Judiciaires Stratégiques v. Democratic Republic of Congo*, Communication No. 259/2002 (2011) para. 59.

2115. *Krischna Achutan (on behalf of Aleke Banda) v. Malawi*; *Amnesty International on behalf of Orton and Vera Chirwa v. Malawi*, Communication Nos 64/92, 68/92, 78/92 (1995), para. 12.

2116. *See, e.g.*, African Commission on Human and Peoples' Rights, *Malawi African Association, Amnesty International, Ms Sarr Diop, Union Interafricaine des Droits de l'Homme and RADDHO, Collectif des Veuves et Ayant-droit, and Association Mauritanienne des Droits de l'Homme v. Mauritania*, Communication Nos. 54/91, 61/91, 98/93, 164/97-196/97, and 210/98 (2000). *See further* G. Naldi, 'Reparations in the Practice of the African Commission on Human and Peoples' Rights', *Leiden Journal International Law* 14 (2001) 681.

2117. *See, e.g.*, *Good v. Botswana*, Communication No. 306/2005, 28th Activity Report 2009–2010, para. 245; *Egyptian Initiative for Personal Rights and INTERIGHTS v. Egypt*, Communication No. 323/2006 (2011), para. 275; *Jean-Marie Atangana Mebara v. Cameroon*, Communication No. 416/12 (2015) para. 137.

2118. Communication No. 323/2006 (2011), para. 275.

2119. Communication No. 416/12 (2015) paras 141–142.

2120. *Jean-Marie Atangana Mebara v. Cameroon*, Communication No. 416/12 (2015) para. 135.

Human and Peoples' Rights.[2121] The adoption of the Protocol corrects the gravest omission in the African Charter, namely the failure to make provision for a court to interpret, apply and enforce the rights guaranteed thereunder. The lack of a judicial remedy attracted considerable criticism as undermining the effective application and enforcement of human rights in Africa.[2122] Consequently, continued opposition to the establishment of a court could no longer be credibly maintained as compatible with respect for human rights. But it was a few years before the Human Rights Court became operational, its first ruling on a matter of substantive law was delivered in 2013.[2123]

332. The seat of the Human Rights Court is Arusha, Tanzania,[2124] but if the Court deems it desirable it may convene in the territory of any AU Member State with its prior permission.[2125] The official and working languages of the Human Rights Court are those of the AU.[2126] The Human Rights Court meets four times a year, each session lasting a month[2127] but extraordinary sessions may also be convened.[2128]

333. The general role of the Human Rights Court is to reinforce the work of the Commission. Thus, according Article 2 of the Protocol the Human Rights Court is to complement the protective mandate of the Commission in accordance with the terms of the African Charter.[2129] However, with many questions between the two

---

2121. Protocol to the African Charter on Human and Peoples' Rights on the Establishment of an African Court on Human and Peoples' Rights (10 Jun. 1998) http://www.au.int/en/treaties, Heyns & Killander, 41 (Protocol). The Protocol entered into force on 25 Jan. 2004. As of July 2023 it had been ratified by thirty-four States. The Protocol cites the OAU but such references must now be taken to indicate the AU. For analysis *see* J. Harrington, 'The African Court on Human and Peoples' Rights,' in *The African Charter on Human and Peoples' Rights: The System in Practice, 1986–2000*, Evans & Murray (eds) (Cambridge: Cambridge University Press, 2002), 305–334; V.O. Nmehielle, *The African Human Rights System: Its Laws, Practice and Institutions* (The Hague: Martinus Nijhoff, 2001), 259–308; F. Viljoen, *International Human Rights Law in Africa* (Oxford: Oxford University Press, 2007), 418–475; G.J. Naldi & K.D. Magliveras, 'Reinforcing the African System of Human Rights: The Protocol on the Establishment of a Regional Court on Human and Peoples' Rights,' *N.Q.H.R.* 16 (1998): 431; N.J. Udombana, 'Toward the African Court on Human and Peoples' Rights: Better Late than Never', *Yale H.R. & Dev. Law Journal* 3 (2000): 45.
2122. D'Sa, African Charter on Human and Peoples' Rights; Gittleman.
2123. *Tanganyika Law Society et al. v. Tanzania*, App. Nos 009/2011 and 011/2011 (14 Jun. 2013). Its first judgment was handed down on 15 Dec. 2009 in the case of *Michelot Yogogombaye v. Senegal*, African Court of Human and Peoples' Rights, App. No. 001/2008. Its case law can be accessed at http://www.african-court.org/en/.
2124. Assembly, *Decision on the Activity Report of the African Court on Human and Peoples' Rights for 2006*, AU Doc. Assembly/AU/Dec. 144(VIII) (29-30-1-2007).
2125. Protocol Art. 25(1).
2126. Rule of Court 27(1)-(2). Compare Protocol on Amendments to the Constitutive Act Art. 11. The new Rules of Court, adopted in 2020, are available at https://www.african-court.org/en/images/Basic%20Documents/Rules_of_Court_-_25_September_2020.pdf; Heyns & Killander, 458.
2127. Rule of Court 22(1).
2128. Rule of Court 23(1).
2129. *See also* Commission Rule 128(1). This principle enables the Commission to refer any matter to the Human Rights Court, *African Commission on Human and Peoples' Rights v. Kenya*, African Court of Human and Peoples' Rights, App. No. 006/2012 (26 May 2017) para. 53.

bodies left unanswered,[2130] it was important that their working relationship be clarified through rules of procedure. Pursuant to Article 33 of the Protocol the Human Rights Court and the Commission set to work on drafting a harmonized set of rules and in 2010 the Court adopted its first Rules of Procedure, updated in September 2020.[2131] Thus the two bodies are to meet at least once a year or whenever considered necessary in order to ensure a good working relationship between them.[2132] A potential source of conflict arises in relation to the Commission's quasi-judicial function under Article 45(3) of the African Charter to interpret the provisions of the African Charter at the request of a State party, the AU, or an African organization recognized by the AU. The Commission retains this power notwithstanding the creation of the Human Rights Court. It is unclear what effect the establishment of the Court will have in practice since the potential for duplication exists, although it needs to be observed that the Commission's interpretative mandate is narrower than the Human Rights Court's.[2133] One can only speculate that it may be that this specific role of the Commission will fall into desuetude or it may be that the Human Rights Court will be asked to review the Commission's interpretations and provide definitive comment.[2134]

334. It is self-evident that the effective guarantee of human and peoples' rights will be largely dependent on the jurisdiction conferred upon, and assumed by, the Human Rights Court. The Protocol provides for both contentious and advisory jurisdiction. Under Article 3(1) and Rule of Court 29(1)(a) the jurisdiction of the Human Rights Court thus extends to all cases and disputes submitted to it concerning the interpretation and application of the African Charter, the Protocol and any other relevant human rights instrument which a State has ratified.[2135] This final clause is particularly interesting because of its innovative character. It is extremely broad in scope and has been described as conferring upon the Human Rights Court an 'almost unlimited substantive jurisdiction'.[2136] It extends the jurisdiction of the Court over not only other OAU/AU human rights treaties, for example, the African Charter on the Rights and Welfare of the Child,[2137] but also ECOWAS

2130. Harrington, 316–317; Nmehielle, 261–262; Udombana, 97.
2131. Rule of Court 92.
2132. Rule of Court 34; Commission Rule 129(1).
2133. Protocol Art. 3.
2134. Nmehielle, 262.
2135. *See Femi Falana v. African Union*, African Court of Human and Peoples' Rights, App. No. 001/2011 (26 Jun. 2012) para. 63; *Ingabire Victoire Umuhoza v. Rwanda* African Court of Human and Peoples' Rights, App. No. 003/2014 (5 Sep. 2016) para. 52. The Human Rights Court has stressed that it does not have appellate jurisdiction, *Ernest Francis Mtingwi v. Malawi*, African Court of Human and Peoples' Rights, App. No. 001/2013 (15 Mar. 2015) para. 14. In *Mohamed Abubakri v. Tanzania*, African Court of Human and Peoples' Rights, App. No. 007/2013 (3 Jun. 2016), para. 28, the Human Rights Court stated that scrutinizing the national courts for compliance with the State's human rights obligations did not amount to exercising appellate jurisdiction.
2136. Harrington, 318. *See Mkandawire v. Malawi,* African Court of Human and Peoples' Rights, App. No. 003/2011 (21 Jun. 2013) para. 34.
2137. *Request for Advisory Opinion by the African Committee of Experts on the Rights and Welfare of the Child on the Standing of the African Committee of Experts on the Rights and Welfare of the Child before the African Court of Human and Peoples' Rights*, African Court of Human and Peoples' Rights, Request No. 002/2013 (5 Dec. 2014) para. 97. In *Actions pour la Protection des*

treaties[2138] and UN treaties such as the ICCPR.[2139] The Human Rights Court also makes extensive references to the ACHR and ECHR.[2140] The Human Rights Court has interpreted the term 'instrument' broadly, enabling it to consider and apply the UDHR.[2141] This particular power of the Human Rights Court is an interesting development, seemingly justified by a desire to promote the effective protection of human rights in Africa.[2142]

335. Given the traditional reluctance among African States to submit to third-party adjudication, the power of the Human Rights Court to *apply* the law is a welcome and necessary development if human rights are to have any meaningful protection in Africa.[2143] The concern that the jurisdiction of the Human Rights Court might have been restricted to issuing declaratory judgments only, similar to that of the Commission under Article 45(3) of the African Charter described above, has been allayed. However, the composition of the Human Rights Court assumes added significance if the judges are prepared to interpret the law in a dynamic and

---

Droit de l'Homme (APDH) v. Côte d'Ivoire, African Court of Human and Peoples' Rights, App. No. 001/2014 (18 Nov. 2016) paras 49–65, the Human Rights Court held that the African Charter on Democracy was a human rights instrument. The Human Rights Court stated that in answering this question it was necessary to consider the purpose of the instrument, reflected either by an express enunciation of rights or by binding obligations on States for the enjoyment of those rights, *ibid.* para. 57. The Respondent was held in violation of the African Charter on Democracy in *Ajavon v. Benin*, African Court of Human and Peoples' Rights, App. No. 062/2019 (4 Dec. 2020), para. 257. The Human Rights Court has also held that it is competent to consider the human rights provisions of the Constitutive Act, *Mohamed Abubakri v. Tanzania*, African Court of Human and Peoples' Rights, App. No. 007/2013 (3 Jun. 2016), para. 51.

2138. For instance, *Zongo and Others v. Burkina Faso*, African Court of Human and Peoples' Rights, App. No. 013/2011 (28 Mar. 2014) para. 48; *Actions pour la Protection des Droit de l'Homme (APDH) v. Côte d'Ivoire*, African Court of Human and Peoples' Rights, App. No. 001/2014 (18 Nov. 2016) para. 65; *Ajavon v. Benin*, African Court of Human and Peoples' Rights, App. No. 062/ 2019, Judgment (4 Dec. 2020); *Suy Bi Gohore Emile & ors v. Côte d'Ivoire*, App. No. 044/2019 (15 Jul. 2020).

2139. *Actions pour la Protection des Droit de l'Homme (APDH) v. Côte d'Ivoire*, African Court of Human and Peoples' Rights, App. No. 001/2014 (18 Nov. 2016) paras 107, 145; *Wilfred Onyango Nganyi & 9 Others v. Tanzania*, African Court of Human and Peoples' Rights, App. No. 006/2013 (18 Mar. 2016), para. 165; *Rashidi v. Tanzania*, African Court of Human and Peoples' Rights, App. No. 009/2015 (28 Mar. 2019) para. 98; *Sissoko and 74 others v. Mali*, African Court of Human and Peoples' Rights, App. No. 037/2017 (25 Sep. 2020), para. 94; *Noudehouenou v. Benin*, African Court of Human and Peoples' Rights, App. No. 003/2020 (4 Dec. 2020), para. 87. In *Ajavon v. Benin*, African Court of Human and Peoples' Rights, App. No. 062/2019 (4 Dec. 2020), para. 257, the Respondent was found in violation of the International Covenant on Economic, Social and Cultural Rights (ICESCR). *See also Sissoko and 74 others v. Mali*, African Court of Human and Peoples' Rights, App. No. 037/2017 (25 Sep. 2020), paras 121, 129.

2140. *Rashidi v. Tanzania*, African Court of Human and Peoples' Rights, App. No. 009/2015 (28 Mar. 2019) para. 98.

2141. *Omary and Others v. Tanzania*, African Court of Human and Peoples' Rights, App. No. 001/2012 (28 Mar. 2014), paras 71–73; *Sissoko and 74 others v. Mali*, African Court of Human and Peoples' Rights, App. No. 037/2017, Judgment (25 Sep. 2020), paras 114, 124, 126; *Ajavon v. Benin*, African Court of Human and Peoples' Rights, App. No. 062/2019, Judgment (4 Dec. 2020), para. 124.

2142. Nmehielle, 264.

2143. *See further* Protocol Arts 7 and 27.

teleological fashion so as to make it truly effective.[2144] Nevertheless, this provision has the potential of giving the Human Rights Court ample opportunities to develop a significant and distinctive human rights jurisprudence.

336. If the jurisdiction of the Human Rights Court is disputed Article 3(2) of the Protocol and Rule of Court 29(3) declare that the matter shall be settled by the decision of the Human Rights Court.[2145] This corresponds to a fundamental principle of international law, namely, 'the inherent power of a tribunal to interpret the text establishing its jurisdiction'.[2146]

337. The Protocol itself does not make express provision for parties to file preliminary objections,[2147] rather this important procedure is governed by Rule of Court 60.[2148] A preliminary objection may be raised within the time limit set by the Court,[2149] and the other party has the right to reply.[2150] As a rule, objections will not operate so as to suspend the proceedings on the merits.[2151] Objections may be decided upon separately by the Human Rights Court in what would be a preliminary judgment or joined to the merits.[2152] The Human Rights Court's rulings on preliminary objections must be reasoned.[2153] The fact that under Rule 49(1) the Human Rights Court must at the outset satisfy itself that it has jurisdiction and that the application is admissible would suggest that the party entering an objection has to make a compelling case to convince the Court.

2144. In *Request for Advisory Opinion by the African Committee of Experts on the Rights and Welfare of the Child on the Standing of the African Committee of Experts on the Rights and Welfare of the Child before the African Court of Human and Peoples' Rights* Request No. 002/2013 (5 Dec. 2014) para. 98, the Human Rights Court rejected the use of the purposive approach to override the clear and unambiguous intention of the legislators discernible from the plain and ordinary meaning of the text. This approach would be in keeping with the Vienna Convention on the Law of Treaties Art. 31(1).

2145. *See Femi Falana v. African Union*, African Court of Human and Peoples' Rights, App. No. 001/2011 (26 Jun. 2012); *Ingabire Victoire Umuhoza v. Rwanda*, African Court of Human and Peoples' Rights, App. No. 003/2014 (5 Sep. 2016) para. 52.

2146. *Nottebohm (Liechtenstein v. Guatemala)*, Preliminary Objection, I.C.J. Reports 1953, 111; *Constitutional Court v. Peru*, Competence, Ser. A, No. 55 (1999) paras 33–34.

2147. Although Art. 3(2) would appear to envisage this procedure by envisaging challenges to the Human Rights Court's jurisdiction.

2148. *See Michelot Yogogombaye v. Senegal*, African Court of Human and Peoples' Rights, App. No. 001/2008 (15 Dec. 2009) para. 38.

2149. Rule of Court 60(1).

2150. Rule of Court 60(4).

2151. Rule of Court 60(2).

2152. *Ibid.* This was the case in *Tanganyika Law Society et al. v. Tanzania*, African Court of Human and Peoples' Rights, App. Nos 009/2011 and 011/2011 (14 Jun. 2013) paras 79–88; *Wilfred Onyango Nganyi & 9 Others v. Tanzania*, African Court of Human and Peoples' Rights, App. No. 006/2013 (18 Mar. 2016), paras 69–103. However, in *Zongo and Others v. Burkina Faso*, Preliminary Objection, African Court of Human and Peoples' Rights, App. No. 013/2011 (21 Jun. 2013), the Court for the first time considered a number of objections to its jurisdiction in a separate phase.

2153. Rule of Court 71(1)(h). *See Tanganyika Law Society et al. v. Tanzania*, African Court of Human and Peoples' Rights, App. Nos 009/2011 and 011/2011 (14 Jun. 2013) *ibid.*

338. Article 5 of the Protocol governs the contentious jurisdiction of the Human Rights Court. According to Article 5(1) the following are entitled to submit contentious cases: (a) the Commission; (b) a State Party which has lodged a complaint to the Commission; (c) a State Party against which a complaint has been lodged at the Commission; (d) a State Party whose citizen is a victim of a human rights violation; and (e) African IGOs.[2154] These, in contrast to applicants under Article 5(3), could be described as privileged applicants since access is automatic upon ratification of the Protocol and is not dependent on further declarations by State Parties. The wording of this provision suggests that only the Commission and, somewhat unusually, African IGOs have unlimited access to the Human Rights Court. It appears that States do not have direct access to the Human Rights Court but must come within one of the categories specified in subparagraphs (b)–(d). It is certainly curious that African IGOs should have unrestricted access to the Human Rights Court but not States.

339. In certain instances the Protocol envisages a two-tier system comparable to that currently operating under the ACHR with the Commission as the preliminary jurisdictional body, acting as a filter mechanism.[2155] Where the Commission submits a case to the Human Rights Court in accordance with Article 5(1)(a) of the Protocol and Rule of Court 36(1)(a) the application must be accompanied by the Commission's Report and other documents.[2156] The Human Rights Court may hear the Commissioners[2157] or the individual or NGO that initiated the communication to the Commission.[2158] Cases referred to the Human Rights Court can include those of serious or massive violations of human rights under Article 58 of the African Charter perpetrated by a State Party to the Protocol but is seems regrettable that the Commission's explicit mandate to refer such cases under its old Rules has been dropped.[2159] Rule of Court 37(1) provides that a communication before the Commission must be withdrawn if the case submitted to the Human Rights Court relates to issues in said communication. This is an expression of the *lis pendens* principle.

2154. *See also* Rule of Court 39(1)(a)-(e). In *Request for Advisory Opinion by the African Committee of Experts on the Rights and Welfare of the Child on the Standing of the African Committee of Experts on the Rights and Welfare of the Child before the African Court of Human and Peoples' Rights* Request No. 002/2013 (5 Dec. 2014) paras 60–76,94, the Human Rights Court had to consider whether the Committee on the Rights of the Child had the capacity to bring contentious cases. Since the Committee was not specifically listed in Art. 5(1) it was submitted that it qualified as an IGO under indent (e). However, the Court, with reluctance given that it felt that it would be 'highly desirable' that the Committee did have access, concluded that the Committee did not meet the definition of an IGO.
2155. Udombana, 98.
2156. Rule of Court 36(1). *See also* Commission Rule 133(1).
2157. Rule of Court 36(2). *See also* Commission Rule 132(1).
2158. Rule of Court 36(3).
2159. Commission Rule 118(3) 2010, Heyns & Killander, 168. *See In the Matter of the African Commission on Human and Peoples' Rights v. Libyan Arab People's Jamahiriya (Provisional Measures)*, African Court of Human and Peoples' Rights, App. No. 004/2011 (3 Mar. 2011); *African Commission on Human and Peoples' Rights v. Kenya*, African Court of Human and Peoples' Rights, App. No. 006/2012 (26 May 2017) para. 53.

340. The Protocol also recognizes the *locus standi* of other applicants under Article 5(3). Thus, the Human Rights Court *may* allow individuals and NGOs with observer status before the Commission to bring cases directly before it.[2160] Clearly the Human Rights Court has a discretion whether to accept an application, jurisdiction is optional in this instance.[2161] Moreover, the competence of the Human Rights Court to entertain an application against a particular State is dependent on that State's prior acceptance of the Human Rights Court's jurisdiction in accordance with Article 34(6) of the Protocol.[2162] Under this provision States must make a separate declaration accepting the competence of the Human Rights Court to receive petitions from these complainants.[2163] This position is regrettable since it is likely that some of the worst perpetrators of serious human rights abuses will not be brought to account given that it is improbable that they will accept the Human Rights Court's exceptional jurisdiction under Article 5(3).[2164] These issues came to the fore in its first case, *Michelot Yogogombaye v. Senegal*. For the Human Rights Court to exercise jurisdiction it was necessary that the respondent State Party, Senegal, must have deposited said declaration under Article 34(6) of the Protocol accepting the competence of the Human Rights Court to receive applications from individuals in accordance with Article 5(3) thereof.[2165] However, in the absence of such declaration the Human Rights Court was unable to entertain the case.[2166] In *Association Juriste d'Afrique pour la Bonne Gouvernance v. Ivory Coast* the

2160. Rule of Court 39(1)(f). *See, e.g., Zongo and Others v. Burkina Faso*, African Court of Human and Peoples' Rights, App. No. 013/2011 (28 Mar. 2014) para. 49.

2161. Udombana, 87. Thus in *Tanganyika Law Society et al. v. Tanzania*, African Court of Human and Peoples' Rights, App. Nos 009/2011 and 011/2011 (14 Jun. 2013) para. 86, the Human Rights Court used the term 'can consider'.

2162. *Mohamed Abubakri v. Tanzania*, African Court of Human and Peoples' Rights, App. No. 007/2013 (3 Jun. 2016), para. 33. The Human Rights Court has made it plain that Art. 34(6) does not apply to the Commission, *African Commission on Human and Peoples' Rights v. Kenya*, African Court of Human and Peoples' Rights, App. No. 006/2012 (26 May 2017) para. 60. Note that under Rule of Court 38(2) should the Human Rights Court receive an Application involving a State that has neither ratified the Protocol nor made the declaration under Art. 34(6) thereof, the Registry shall inform the Applicant that the Court lacks jurisdiction but that the Applicant that may file the matter before the Commission. *See, e.g., Soufiane Ababou v. Algeria*, African Court of Human and Peoples' Rights, App. No. 002/2011 (16 Jun. 2011).

2163. *Femi Falana v. African Union*, African Court of Human and Peoples' Rights, App. No. 001/2011 (26 Jun. 2012) para. 73; *Omary and Others v. Tanzania*, African Court of Human and Peoples' Rights, App. No. 001/2012 (28 Mar. 2014), para. 80. The applicants do not have to be nationals of the respondent State, *Wilfred Onyango Nganyi & 9 Others v. Tanzania*, African Court of Human and Peoples' Rights, App. No. 006/2013 (18 Mar. 2016), para. 63. And only States may be respondents, Separate Opinion by Judge Mutsinzi, *Femi Falana v. African Union*, African Court of Human and Peoples' Rights, App. No. 001/2011 (26 Jun. 2012). African Court of Human and Peoples' Rights, App. No. 003/2 paras 5–59.

2164. On the controversy surrounding the drafting history of these provisions, *see* Harrington, 320–321; Nmehielle, 266–267; Udombana, 87–88.

2165. *Michelot Yogogombaye v. Senegal*, African Court of Human and Peoples' Rights, App. No. 001/2008 (15 Dec. 2009) paras 35–37. *Tanganyika Law Society et al. v. Tanzania*, African Court of Human and Peoples' Rights, App. Nos 009/2011 and 011/2011 (14 Jun. 2013) para. 86.

2166. *Ibid.*, para. 37. *See also Soufiane Ababou v. Algeria*, African Court of Human and Peoples' Rights, App. No. 002/2011 (16 Jun. 2011) paras 5–11; *Daniel Amare and Mulugeta Amare v. Republic of Mozambique and Mozambique Airlines*, African Court of Human and Peoples' Rights, App. No. 005/2011 (16 Jun. 2011) paras 6–8; *Ekollo Moundi Alexandre v. Cameroon and Nigeria*, African

problem was that the applicant NGO did not have observer status with the Commission as required by Article 5(3) of the Protocol.[2167] Another peculiar attribution is that while the Human Rights Court decides on the admissibility of a case under Article 5(3) it may, according to Article 6(1) of the Protocol, request an opinion from the Commission. The Commission is obliged to respond promptly according to Commission Rule 131(1) and under Rule of Court 37(2) the Human Rights Court will indicate the time limit within which it wishes to receive the Commission's opinion. For its part, the Commission will consider the matter in light of the African Charter and the Rules.[2168] No indication is given as to the sort of circumstances that might prompt the Human Rights Court to invoke this provision. Nevertheless, the wisdom of introducing any delay, however brief, in such urgent circumstances appears questionable. It should also be noted that individuals and NGOs must overcome hurdles of admissibility.

Twelve States have made the declaration under Article 34(6) of the Protocol: Benin, Burkina Faso, Côte d'Ivoire, Gambia, Ghana, Guinea-Bissau, Malawi, Mali, Niger, Tanzania and Tunisia. But four, Rwanda, Tanzania, Benin and Côte d'Ivoire, have subsequently withdrawn them.[2169] In *Ingabire Victoire Umuhoza v. Rwanda* the question arose whether the Human Rights Court still had jurisdiction despite Rwanda's notice of withdrawal.[2170] The issue was complicated by the fact the Protocol does not contain a withdrawal clause. It was argued that in such an instance a unilateral denunciation is governed by Article 56(1) of the Vienna Convention on the Law of Treaties has been held to reflect customary international law,[2171] which

---

Court of Human and Peoples' Rights, App. No. 008/2011 (23 Sep. 2011) paras 5–9; *National Convention of Teachers Trade Union v. Republic of Gabon*, African Court of Human and Peoples' Rights, App. No. 012/2011 (15 Dec. 2011); *Delta International Investments SA, Mr AGL de Lange and Mrs M. de Lange v. Republic of South Africa*, African Court of Human and Peoples' Rights, App. No. 002/2012 (30 Mar. 2012); *Amir Adam Timan v. Republic of Sudan*, African Court of Human and Peoples' Rights, App. No. 005/2012 (30 Mar. 2012). Judge Ouguergouz has argued that in such circumstances applications should not be dealt with by the Human Rights Court but should be 'dismissed *de plano* by a simple letter from the Registry' on grounds of time and resources, *see, e.g.*, his Separate Opinion in *Amir Adam Timan v. Republic of Sudan*, African Court of Human and Peoples' Rights, App. No. 005/2012 (30 Mar. 2012); *Baghdadi Ali Mahmoudi v. Republic of Tunisia*, African Court of Human and Peoples' Rights, App. No. 007/2012 (30 Mar. 2012).

2167. *Association Juriste d'Afrique pour la Bonne Gouvernance v. Ivory Coast*, African Court of Human and Peoples' Rights, App. No. 006/2011 (16 Jun. 2011) paras 7–9. *See also National Convention of Teachers Trade Union v. Republic of Gabon*, African Court of Human and Peoples' Rights, App. No. 012/2011 (15 Dec. 2011). Compare contra *Tanganyika Law Society et al. v. Tanzania*, African Court of Human and Peoples' Rights, App. Nos 009/2011 and 011/2011 (14 Jun. 2013) para. 86.

2168. Commission Rule 131(2). According to Judge Ouguergouz's Dissenting Opinion in *Ekollo Moundi Alexandre v. Cameroon and Nigeria*, African Court of Human and Peoples' Rights, App. No. 008/2011 (23 Sep. 2011) para. 17, it is a condition precedent that the Human Rights Court should determine that it has jurisdiction over the case.

2169. The reasons for withdrawal are various and can be found at: https://www.african-court.org/wpafc/declarations/.

2170. *Ingabire Victoire Umuhoza v. Rwanda*, Ruling on Jurisdiction, African Court of Human and Peoples' Rights, App. No. 003/2014 (5 Sep. 2016) Corrigendum.

2171. This provision has been held to reflect customary international law, *Military and Paramilitary Activities in and Against Nicaragua (Nicaragua v. United States of America)* (Jurisdiction and Admissibility) I.C.J. Reports 1984 392, p. 420.

states the treaty is not subject to denunciation or withdrawal unless (a) it is established that the parties intended to allow the possibility of denunciation or withdrawal, or (b) a right to do so is implied from the nature of the treaty. The Human Rights Court upheld the legality of the withdrawal as a legitimate exercise of state sovereignty and paid no attention to the special character of human rights treaties.[2172] It stated that the declarations are unilateral and optional acts of States and therefore not subject to the Vienna Convention.[2173] As unilateral acts not subject to the Vienna Convention, the declarations are separable from the Protocol and can, therefore, be withdrawn separately without resulting in a denunciation of the Protocol.[2174] The optional and unilateral nature of declarations stem from the principle of state sovereignty which grants States the discretion to withdraw their treaty commitments in accordance with the relevant rules.[2175] However, Rwanda's discretion to withdraw was 'not absolute' and could not have immediate effect but, in the interests of legal certainty, was subject to a notice period of one year.[2176] This is in keeping with Article 56(2) of the Vienna Convention. Furthermore, the withdrawal does not have retroactive effect.[2177] This ruling by the Human Rights Court should ensure that States do not have to take the extreme step of denouncing the Protocol to do away with the right of individual petition.

341. The Human Rights Court must initially satisfy itself that it has jurisdiction and that the application is admissible.[2178] The issue of jurisdiction will be considered at the outset and if it is convinced that it has jurisdiction to hear it will then proceed to rule on admissibility.[2179] The Human Rights Court has declared that 'jurisdiction has four dimensions: personal, material, temporal and territorial. The

2172. *Ingabire Victoire Umuhoza v. Rwanda*, Ruling on Jurisdiction, African Court of Human and Peoples' Rights, App. No. 003/2014 (5 Sep. 2016) para. 58, Corrigendum. *See also Hossou and Adelakoun v. Benin*, African Court of Human and Peoples' Rights, App. No. 016/2020 (2 Dec. 2021) para. 33.

2173. *Ingabire Victoire Umuhoza v. Rwanda*, Ruling on Jurisdiction, African Court of Human and Peoples' Rights, App. No. 003/2014 (5 Sep. 2016) para. 54, Corrigendum; *Hossou and Adelakoun v. Benin*, African Court of Human and Peoples' Rights, App. No. 016/2020 (2 Dec. 2021) para. 29.

2174. *Ingabire Victoire Umuhoza v. Rwanda*, Ruling on Jurisdiction, African Court of Human and Peoples' Rights, App. No. 003/2014 (5 Sep. 2016) para. 58, Corrigendum; *Hossou and Adelakoun v. Benin*, African Court of Human and Peoples' Rights, App. No. 016/2020 (2 Dec. 2021) para. 32.

2175. *Ingabire Victoire Umuhoza v. Rwanda*, Ruling on Jurisdiction, African Court of Human and Peoples' Rights, App. No. 003/2014 (5 Sep. 2016) para. 58, Corrigendum; *Hossou and Adelakoun v. Benin*, African Court of Human and Peoples' Rights, App. No. 016/2020 (2 Dec. 2021) para. 33.

2176. *Ingabire Victoire Umuhoza v. Rwanda*, Ruling on Jurisdiction, African Court of Human and Peoples' Rights, App. No. 003/2014 (5 Sep. 2016) paras 60-66, Corrigendum; *Cheusi v. Tanzania*, Judgment, African Court of Human and Peoples' Rights, App. No. 004/2015 (26 Jun. 2020) para. 38.

2177. *Ingabire Victoire Umuhoza v. Rwanda*, Ruling on Jurisdiction, African Court of Human and Peoples' Rights, App. No. 003/2014 (5 Sep. 2016) para. 67, Corrigendum; *Cheusi v. Tanzania*, Judgment, African Court of Human and Peoples' Rights, App. No. 004/2015 (26 Jun. 2020) paras 38-39.

2178. Rule of Court 49(1). *See Michelot Yogogombaye v. Senegal*, African Court of Human and Peoples' Rights, App. No. 001/2008 (15 Dec. 2009) para. 40; *Wilfred Onyango Nganyi & 9 Others v. Tanzania*, African Court of Human and Peoples' Rights, App. No. 006/2013 (18 Mar. 2016), para. 51.

2179. *Mkandawire v. Malawi*, African Court of Human and Peoples' Rights, App. No. 003/2011 (21 Jun. 2013) para. 3.

Court further recalls that all applications must fulfil the four dimensions of jurisdiction before they can be considered.[2180] It therefore needs to ensure that the complaint impleads a State Party,[2181] and, as already observed, have made the declaration under Article 34(6) of the Protocol, that it possesses jurisdiction *ratione materiae,*[2182] which, as previously observed, includes other human rights instruments, or that the applicants have *locus standi*. With regard to jurisdiction *ratione temporis*, the Human Rights Court has held that the relevant dates are those of the entry into force of the African Charter, the Protocol and the deposit of the declaration accepting the Court's jurisdiction.[2183] In *Tanganyika Law Society et al. v. Tanzania* the Respondent argued that the Human Rights Court lacked jurisdiction *ratione temporis* because the violation occurred before the Protocol had entered into force. Dismissing this challenge to its jurisdiction the Human Rights Court found that the rights in question were protected by the African Charter which had been in force for Tanzania at the material time. Moreover, the alleged violation was of a continuing nature which continued when the Protocol was ratified and the optional declaration made.[2184] It must be observed that absent this latter contingency, emphasis has been placed on the crucial date being that of the State's ratification of the Protocol.[2185] In the context of continuing violations the Human Rights Court has drawn a distinction between 'instantaneous' or 'complete' violations completed at an identifiable point in time before the entry into force of the instrument which therefore fall outside the temporal jurisdiction of the Court and those that continue

2180. *Kambole v. Tanzania*, Judgment, African Court of Human and Peoples' Rights, App. No. 018/2018 (15 Jul. 2020) para. 16.

2181. In *Youseff Ababou v. Kingdom of Morocco*, African Court of Human and Peoples' Rights, App. No. 007/2011 (2 Sep. 2011) para. 12, the Human Rights Court found it lacked jurisdiction because Morocco was not then a member of the AU and thus not a party to the Protocol. *See also Femi Falana v. African Union*, African Court of Human and Peoples' Rights, App. No. 001/2011 (26 Jun. 2012) where the applicant sought to implead, unsuccessfully, the AU itself. In *Boateng & 351 ors v. Ghana*, Jurisdiction, African Court of Human and Peoples' Rights, App. No. 059/2016 (27 Nov. 2020) para. 35, the Human Rights Court dismissed an action against individuals. In *African Commission on Human and Peoples' Rights v. Libya*, African Court of Human and Peoples' Rights, App. No. 002/2013 (3 Jun. 2016) paras 49–50, the Human Rights Court held Libya responsible for the actions of rebels within its territory.

2182. *See Efoua Mbozo'o Samuel v. Pan-African Parliament*, African Court of Human and Peoples' Rights, App. No. 010/2011 (30 Sep. 2011) para. 6, where the Human Rights Court found it lacked jurisdiction on the ground that the application was based exclusively upon breach of an employment contract. But *see* Judge Ouguergouz's Dissenting Opinion, *ibid.*, para. 12. The established practice of the Human Rights Court is that the applications do not have to specify which African Charter rights were violated since it itself will look for any human rights violations, *Chacha v. Tanzania*, African Court of Human and Peoples' Rights, App. No. 003/2012 (28 Mar. 2014) paras 112-114.

2183. *Zongo and Others v. Burkina Faso*, Provisional Measures, African Court of Human and Peoples' Rights, App. No. 013/2011 (15 Mar. 2013) para. 62.

2184. App. Nos 009/2011 and 011/2011 (14 Jun. 2013) para. 84; *Mkandawire v. Malawi,* African Court of Human and Peoples' Rights, App. No. 003/2011 (21 Jun. 2013) para. 32.

2185. *See Mkandawire v. Malawi,* African Court of Human and Peoples' Rights, App. No. 003/2011 (21 Jun. 2013), Joint Dissenting Opinion of Judge Niyungeko and Judge El Hadji Guisse, paras 5–8.

over the entire period to affect the rights of a person.[2186] With regard to jurisdiction *ratione loci*, or temporal jurisdiction, the Human Rights Court has to date simply satisfied itself that the violations took place on the territory of the respondent State.[2187]

342. It is important to note that the Human Rights Court has stressed that its role is not that of a court of appeal in relation to national courts, sometimes known as the fourth instance doctrine, but that it complements the national judiciary and does not supplant it.[2188] It has stated, in the context of the exhaustion of local remedies, that the domestic system has primacy in the protection of human rights vis-à-vis the Court.[2189]

343. Article 6(2) of the Protocol states that the Human Rights Court shall rule on the admissibility of cases taking account of Article 56 of the African Charter, which governs communications submitted by individuals and NGOs to the Commission.[2190] Rule of Court 50(2)(a)-(g) makes it clear that applications must satisfy all the hurdles of admissibility, which are cumulative,[2191] and which in every material respect are identical to those listed in Article 56 of the African Charter with the exception of sub-rule (f) which makes the necessary adjustment in that the case must be filed within a reasonable period from the time local remedies were exhausted[2192] or from the date set by the Human Rights Court as being the commencement of the time limit within which it shall be seized of the matter. While there is no specific time frame[2193] the Human Rights Court has the discretion to

---

2186. *Zongo and Others v. Burkina Faso*, Provisional Measures, African Court of Human and Peoples' Rights, App. No. 013/2011 (15 Mar. 2013) paras 66-68, 73; *Boateng & 351 ors v. Ghana*, Jurisdiction, African Court of Human and Peoples' Rights, App. No. 059/2016 (27 Nov. 2020) paras 55–56.

2187. *See, e.g., XYZ v. Benin*, African Court of Human and Peoples' Rights, App. No. 010/2020 (27 Nov. 2020), para. 38iii.

2188. *Abubakari v. Tanzania*, African Court of Human and Peoples' Rights, App. No. 007/2013 (3 Jun. 2016) paras 25, 28; *Umuhoza v. Rwanda*, African Court on Human and Peoples' Rights, App. No. 003/2014 (24 Nov. 2017) para. 54.

2189. *African Commission on Human and Peoples' Rights v. Kenya*, African Court of Human and Peoples' Rights, App. No. 006/2012 (26 May 2017) para. 93.

2190. *See also* Rule 50(2). *See Mkandawire v. Malawi,* African Court of Human and Peoples' Rights, App. No. 003/2011 (21 Jun. 2013) para. 38.1; *African Commission on Human and Peoples' Rights v. Libya*, African Court of Human and Peoples' Rights, App. No. 002/2013 (3 Jun. 2016) para. 63. *See further supra* paras 306–320. The Human Rights Court has held that while the rules of admissibility of the Commission of the Court are very similar they are in fact distinct and should not be conflated, *African Commission on Human and Peoples' Rights v. Kenya*, African Court of Human and Peoples' Rights, App. No. 006/2012 (26 May 2017) para. 78.

2191. *Omary and Others v. Tanzania*, Admissibility, African Court of Human and Peoples' Rights, App. Nos 001/2012 (28 Mar. 2014) para. 86.

2192. In *Tanganyika Law Society et al. v. Tanzania*, African Court of Human and Peoples' Rights, App. Nos 009/2011 and 011/2011 (14 Jun. 2013) para. 83, the Human Rights Court found that one year was not an unreasonable period of time.

2193. *Christopher Jonas v. Tanzania*, African Court of Human and Peoples' Rights, App. No. 011/2015 (28 Sep. 2017) para. 48.

determine its reasonableness.[2194] The Human Rights Court has endorsed the Commission's jurisprudence on admissibility.[2195] The Human Rights Court will dismiss applications without merit (manifestly ill-founded) giving reasons for its decision.[2196]

344. The first condition in Rule of Court 50(2) requires that the Application indicate the authors even if they request anonymity. The Human Rights Court has often granted an Applicant's request for anonymity, such as on grounds of personal security.[2197]

345. The second requirement is that the Application must be compatible with the Constitutive Act and the African Charter. The Human Rights Court has declared that the Application must refer to rights guaranteed by the African Charter or other human rights instrument ratified by the State concerned, without necessarily requiring that the rights alleged to have been violated be specified.[2198]

346. The third factor is that the Application must not be written in abusive terms. The Human Rights Court has stated that, in general, disparaging or insulting language 'is that which is meant to soil the dignity, reputation or integrity of a person.'[2199] It has endorsed the Commission's jurisprudence on this issue that the language used must seek to undermine the integrity and status of the State and its institutions and bring them into disrepute'.[2200] The Human Rights Court has held

2194. *Onyachi and Njoka v. Tanzania*, African Court of Human and Peoples' Rights, App. No. 003/2015 (28 Sep. 2017) para. 61.
2195. *See supra* paras 306–320.
2196. Rule of Court 48(1). *See Amare v. Republic of Mozambique and Mozambique Airlines*, African Court of Human and Peoples' Rights, App. No. 005/2011 (16 Jun. 2011) para. 8. Judge Ouguergouz has argued that in such circumstances the application should not be 'considered judicially by the Court' but should be 'dismissed *de plano* by a simple letter from the Registry' on grounds of time and resources, *see, e.g.*, his Separate Opinion in *Michelot Yogogombaye v. Senegal*, African Court of Human and Peoples' Rights, App. No. 001/2008 (15 Dec. 2009), and his Dissenting Opinion in *Ekollo Moundi Alexandre v. Cameroon and Nigeria*, African Court of Human and Peoples' Rights, App. No. 008/2011 (23 Sep. 2011) para. 7. *See also XYZ v. Benin*, African Court of Human and Peoples' Rights, App. No. 010/2020 (27 Nov. 2020) para. 42.
2197. *See, e.g., XYZ v. Benin*, African Court of Human and Peoples' Rights, App. No. 010/2020 (27 Nov. 2020) paras 8–9.
2198. *Chacha v. Tanzania*, African Court of Human and Peoples' Rights, App. No. 003/2012 (28 Mar. 2014) para. 118; *Abubakari v. Tanzania*, African Court of Human and Peoples' Rights, App. No. 007/2013 (3 Jun. 2016) para. 50.
2199. *Ajavon v. Benin*, Merits, African Court of Human and Peoples' Rights, App. No. 013/2017 (29 Mar. 2019) para. 71.
2200. *Konaté v. Burkina Faso*, African Court of Human and Peoples' Rights, App. No. 004/2013 (5 Dec. 2014) para. 70, citing, e.g., *Zimbabwe Lawyers for Human Rights & Associated Newspapers of Zimbabwe v. Zimbabwe*, Communication No. 284/2003, 26th Activity Report 2008–2009, paras 88–91. In *Gihana and others v. Rwanda*, Merits and Reparations, African Court of Human and Peoples' Rights, App. No. 017/2015 (28 Nov. 2019) paras 50–52, the Applicant's claims that the Rwandan judiciary were biased and not independent was held not to be insulting or disparaging because 'mere complaints, perceptions and opinions of an applicant, on the State and its institutions in the circumstances of his case do not amount to disparaging language.'

further finds that public figures such as politicians are legitimately exposed to criticism so that for remarks to be regarded as being disparaging, they must be of 'extreme gravity and manifestly affect their reputation.'[2201]

347. The fourth criterion is that the Application must not be based exclusively on news disseminated through the mass media. In *Omary v. Tanzania*, it was noted that the use of newspaper clippings to support allegations in the Application did not render the Application inadmissible.[2202]

The fifth condition requires the exhaustion of any local remedies unless it is obvious that they are unduly prolonged. It refers 'primarily to judicial remedies'.[2203] The remedies must be ordinary domestic judicial remedies;[2204] an applicant is therefore not compelled to exhaust remedies that are non-judicial or extraordinary in nature.[2205] In *Tanganyika Law Society v. Tanzania*, the Human Rights Court rejected the notion of a parliamentary process, a political process which was discretionary and could be abandoned at any time.[2206] For domestic remedies to be exhausted they must be 'available, effective and sufficient'.[2207] Availability means that the remedies must be capable of being used by the applicant without impediment or hindrance.[2208] Effective and sufficient refer to the fact that they are capable of satisfying the complainant or of remedying the situation.[2209] Unduly prolonged means proceedings that are 'excessively or unjustifiably' delayed[2210] and should be examined

---

2201. *Ajavon v. Benin*, Merits, African Court of Human and Peoples' Rights, App. No. 013/2017 (29 Mar. 2019) para. 73.

2202. *Omary and Others v. Tanzania*, Admissibility, African Court of Human and Peoples' Rights, App. No. 001/2012 (28 Mar. 2014) paras 95–96.

2203. *Mkandawire v. Malawi,* African Court of Human and Peoples' Rights, App. No. 003/2011 (21 Jun. 2013) para. 38.1; *Tanganyika Law Society et al. v. Tanzania*, African Court of Human and Peoples' Rights, App. Nos 009/2011 and 011/2011 (14 Jun. 2013) para. 82.1.

2204. *Wilfred Onyango Nganyi & 9 Others v. Tanzania*, African Court of Human and Peoples' Rights, App. No. 006/2013 (18 Mar. 2016), para. 95.

2205. *Alex Thomas v. Tanzania*, African Court of Human and Peoples' Rights, App. No. 005/2013 (20 Nov. 2015) para. 64; *Onyachi and Njoka v. Tanzania*, African Court of Human and Peoples' Rights, App. No. 003/2015 (28 Sep. 2017) para. 56. In *Actions pour la Protection des Droit de l'Homme (APDH) v. Côte d'Ivoire*, African Court of Human and Peoples' Rights, App. No. 001/2014 (18 Nov. 2016) para. 97, the Human Rights Court held that in the circumstance administrative jurisdictions were not competent.

2206. *Tanganyika Law Society et al. v. Tanzania*, African Court of Human and Peoples' Rights, App. Nos 009/2011 and 011/2011 (14 Jun. 2013) para. 82.3.

2207. *Konaté v. Burkina Faso*, African Court of Human and Peoples' Rights, App. No. 004/2013 (5 Dec. 2014), para. 95; *African Commission on Human and Peoples' Rights v. Kenya*, African Court of Human and Peoples' Rights, App. No. 006/2012 (26 May 2017) para. 93.

2208. *Konaté v. Burkina Faso*, African Court of Human and Peoples' Rights, App. No. 004/2013 (5 Dec. 2014), para. 96; *Ajavon v. Benin*, Merits, African Court of Human and Peoples' Rights, App. No. 013/2017 (29 Mar. 2019) para. 86.

2209. *Konaté v. Burkina Faso*, African Court of Human and Peoples' Rights, App. No. 004/2013 (5 Dec. 2014), para. 108; *Ajavon v. Benin*, Merits, African Court of Human and Peoples' Rights, App. No. 013/2017 (29 Mar. 2019) para. 86.

2210. *Wilfred Onyango Nganyi & 9 Others v. Tanzania*, African Court of Human and Peoples' Rights, App. No. 006/2013 (18 Mar. 2016), para. 91.

on a case-by-case-basis.[2211] A period of almost ten years has met this test.[2212] Factors which may normalize delays include civil strife or war which may impact the functioning of the judiciary or situations where the delay is partly caused by the victim, the family or representatives.[2213]

348. There will exist other circumstances where local remedies need not be exhausted. There is therefore no need for the Applicants to go through the same domestic judicial process where the outcome is known.[2214] Or where the domestic court had failed to address allegations of violations of the accused's rights.[2215]

349. The seventh and final condition is that there must be no conflicting settlements. The Human Rights Court has stated that the concept of 'settlement' consists of three major conditions: the case should have involved the same parties, the same issues and must have been settled by an international or regional mechanism.[2216] The Human Rights Court considered these issues in some detail in the case of *Johnson v. Ghana*. It found that the UN Human Rights Committee had delivered a decision on the merits on a communication filed by the Applicant against the Respondent State which were substantively on the same issues before the Court. Moreover, if the later Application is not detachable from the earlier one examined by another body, it will be deemed to have been settled.[2217]

350. Individuals and NGOs may be further disadvantaged by the fact that under Article 6(3) the Human Rights Court is not compelled to entertain an admissible case but has the discretion of referring it to the Commission. Rule of Court 38(1)(a) makes reference to this procedure but apart from the fact that paragraph 2 therefore mentions a State that has neither ratified the Protocol nor made the Declaration under Article 34 (6) of the Protocol, no further indication is given as to what factors may motivate the Human Rights Court to take such a step. However, the Human Rights Court's case law is providing some answers to this question. In instances where it has found that it does not possess jurisdiction because a complainant under Article 5(3) of the Protocol lacks standing, either because a State Party has not made a declaration under Article 34(6) of the Protocol or an NGO does not have observer status with the Commission, in light of the claims made it has transferred them to

2211. *Zongo and Others v. Burkina Faso*, African Court of Human and Peoples' Rights, App. No. 013/2011 (28 Mar. 2014) para. 92.
2212. *Wilfred Onyango Nganyi & 9 Others v. Tanzania*, African Court of Human and Peoples' Rights, App. No. 006/2013 (18 Mar. 2016), para. 94.
2213. *Wilfred Onyango Nganyi & 9 Others v. Tanzania*, African Court of Human and Peoples' Rights, App. No. 006/2013 (18 Mar. 2016), para. 91.
2214. *Tanganyika Law Society et al. v. Tanzania*, African Court of Human and Peoples' Rights, App. Nos 009/2011 and 011/2011 (14 Jun. 2013) para. 82.3; *Konaté v. Burkina Faso*, African Court of Human and Peoples' Rights, App. No. 004/2013 (5 Dec. 2014), para. 112.
2215. *Onyachi and Njoka v. Tanzania*, African Court of Human and Peoples' Rights, App. No. 003/2015 (28 Sep. 2017) para. 54.
2216. *Johnson v. Ghana*, Jurisdiction and Admissibility, African Court of Human and Peoples' Rights, App. No. 016/2017 (28 Mar. 2019) para. 48.
2217. *Ibid.*, paras 49–53.

the Commission.[2218] The Human Rights Court appears to be guided by a desire to avoid a denial of justice. However, such emergent practice has attracted strong disapproval from Judge Ouguergouz who has argued that it 'is not founded in law' and that the Human Rights Court has 'deviated from the original purpose of that provision'.[2219] Implicit in his criticism is the opinion that the issues of jurisdiction and admissibility have not been determined correctly.[2220] In his view, this procedure 'applies primarily to the consideration of the admissibility of a case over which the jurisdiction of the Court has already been established'.[2221] Judge Ouguergouz additionally contends that the principle of legal certainty demands that clear reasoned objective criteria should guide the Human Rights Court in its practice of referrals to the Commission since the current policy was haphazard and unpredictable and was in danger of becoming 'systematic'.[2222] In his view the Human Rights Court could play 'the role of an "early warning mechanism" for the Commission' and that the procedure in question should be reserved for those cases where the former lacks jurisdiction displaying 'exceptional circumstances' such as those envisaged by Article 58 of the African Charter.[2223] He sees no reason why the Human Rights Court should not use its discretion to transfer cases over which it has jurisdiction to the Commission to rule on the merits.[2224] He advocates such a policy in order to lessen the workload on the Human Rights Court.[2225] His suggestions seem eminently sensible if the Human Rights Court is to avoid the significant delays caused by a backlog of cases.

351. Article 5(2) enshrines what appears to be a welcome development in human rights instruments in that it permits a State Party that has an interest in a case to request the Human Rights Court to be permitted to join, essentially to intervene. The decision whether to grant a request for intervention naturally rests with the Human Rights Court; the views of the applicant or the parties to the case cannot bind it. While Rule of Court 61(2) makes it clear that the interest must be one of a 'legal' nature no further guidance is provided as to the meaning of the noun 'interest' but the Human Rights Court may choose to be guided by the practice of other tribunals.[2226] Intervening States must additionally state the object of the intervention

---

2218. *Amare v. Mozambique and Mozambique Airlines*, African Court of Human and Peoples' Rights, App. No. 005/2011 (16 Jun. 2011) para. 9; *Ekollo Moundi Alexandre v. Cameroon and Nigeria* App. No. 008/2011 (23 Sep. 2011) para. 11; *Association Juriste d'Afrique pour la Bonne Gouvernance v. Ivory Coast*, African Court of Human and Peoples' Rights, App. No. 006/2011 (16 Jun. 2011) para. 10; *Ababou v. Algeria*, African Court of Human and Peoples' Rights, App. No. 002/2011 (16 Jun. 2011).
2219. *Ekollo Moundi Alexandre v. Cameroon and Nigeria*, African Court of Human and Peoples' Rights, App. No 008/2011 (23 Sep. 2011), Dissenting Opinion of Judge Ouguergouz, paras 12, 20.
2220. *Ibid.*, paras 14–19.
2221. *Ibid.*, para. 13.
2222. *Ibid.*, paras 21–26.
2223. *Ibid.*, paras 22–29.
2224. *Ibid.*, paras 31–33.
2225. *Ibid.*, para. 35.
2226. This the Human Rights Court did in *Mornah v. Benin et al., Application for Intervention by Mauritius*, Order, African Court of Human and Peoples' Rights, App. No. 028/2018 (25 Sep. 2020) para. 16, and *Mornah v. Benin et al., Application for Intervention by Sahrawi Arab Democratic Republic*, Order, African Court of Human and Peoples' Rights, App. No. 001/2020 (25 Sep. 2020)

and the Applicant's interest in the case.[2227]The Human Rights Court has decided that whether an intervenor has an interest in a case depends on the nature of issues involved, the identity of the intervenor and the potential impact of any of decision of the Court on the intervenor and third parties.[2228] In *Mornah v. Benin et al., Application for Intervention by Sahrawi Arab Democratic Republic*, where the substance of the case concerned alleged violations of the African Charter as a result of the continued occupation of territory of the SADR by Morocco and the failure of the Respondent States to protect the sovereignty, territorial integrity and independence of SADR, the Human Rights Court held that the SADR had an interest in the case and its outcome, which could have a direct bearing on the rights and of its people.[2229] In *Mornah v. Benin, Intervention by Mauritius*, Mauritius argued successfully that as an AU Member State whose process of decolonization was still incomplete and considering the *erga omnes* character of the right to self-determination, it should be granted leave to intervene in order to make submissions regarding the right to self-determination and decolonization.[2230] Any possible delays to the proceedings should be minimized by the fact that the Human Rights Court will fix a time limit within which the intervening State must submit its written observations.[2231]

352. Article 26(1) of the Protocol obliges the Human Rights Court to hear submissions by all parties and if necessary hold an enquiry. Rule of Court 55(3) provides the Human Rights Court with the discretion to conduct an enquiry at any time during the proceedings by one or more of the judges, to carry out visits to scenes or gather evidence in any other manner. Considering the often uncooperative and obstructive behaviour of impugned States in such circumstances the Human Rights Court's ability to visit scenes or conduct enquiries is of considerable importance in marshalling the facts and attempting to arrive at the truth.

353. By virtue of Article 26(2) of the Protocol and Rule of Court 55 the Human Rights Court may receive written and oral evidence including expert testimony. Evidence may be obtained by the Human Rights Court *propio motu* or at the request of a party.[2232] No new evidence may be submitted by the parties after the closure of

---

para. 16, citing the ICJ. ICJ practice under its Statute Art. 62 reveals that it has applied a very strict policy in this area, *see* C. Chinkin, 'Third Party Intervention Before the International Court of Justice,' *A.J.I.L.* 80 (1986): 495. The European Convention on Human Rights Art. 36(2) (4 Nov. 1950) (as amended), E.T.S. No. 155, which is limited under para. 1 thereof to cases where a national of a contracting party is an applicant, requires the intervention to be in the interest of the proper administration of justice. *See further* Harris, O'Boyle & Warbrick, 853–856.

2227. Rule of Court 61(3)(b), (c).
2228. *Mornah v. Benin et al., Application for Permission to Intervene by Mauritius*, Order, African Court of Human and Peoples' Rights, App. No. 028/2018 (25 Sep. 2020), para. 16.
2229. *Mornah v. Benin et al., Application for Intervention by Sahrawi Arab Democratic Republic*, Order, African Court of Human and Peoples' Rights, App. No. 001/2020 (25 Sep. 2020) para. 18.
2230. *Mornah v. Benin et al., Application for Permission to Intervene by Mauritius*, Order, African Court of Human and Peoples' Rights, App. No. 028/2018 (25 Sep. 2020) para. 17.
2231. Rule of Court 61(6).
2232. Rule of Court 55(1).

pleadings save with the leave of the Human Rights Court.[2233] That the Human Rights Court has a wide discretion as to the evidence and witnesses it will admit is confirmed by its rules. Hence Rule of Court 55(1) states that the Human Rights Court may 'obtain any evidence which in its opinion may provide clarification of the facts of a case'.[2234] To this end it can 'decide to hear as a witness or expert or in any other capacity any person whose evidence, assertions or statements it deems likely to assist it'. Moreover, the Human Rights Court 'may ask any person or institution of its choice to obtain information, express an opinion or submit a report to it on any specific point'.[2235] According to Rule of Court 71(1)(f) *amici curiae* seem to be included. It is evident, although not set out in explicit terms, that parties may object to a witness or expert given that the Human Rights Court is authorized to rule on any such challenge.[2236] Questions may be put by the Human Rights Court to witnesses, experts or other persons appearing before it.[2237] They may be examined, cross-examined and re-examined by the parties and the Commission.[2238]

354. The possibility of failure of witnesses to appear, of contempt of court or of perjury are not addressed by either the Protocol or the Rules of Court. Article 10(3) guarantees protection to any person, witness or representative of parties who appears before the Human Rights Court necessary for the proper discharging of their functions and duties before the Human Rights Court.[2239] Individuals and others should therefore be able to appear before the Human Rights Court without fear of retribution, and is a welcome development since arbitrary detention and disappearances are all too common in parts of Africa for defying the authorities. It is unclear therefore, how, if at all, individuals are to be effectively protected within the jurisdiction of a State party to the Protocol but it is submitted that this guarantee could be strengthened were the Human Rights Court to use creatively its competence to indicate provisional measures under Article 27(2). In addition, explicit provision should have been made for the imposition of sanctions on States that failed to protect effectively or persecuted such people.

355. The rules contain a reaffirmation of the principle *pacta sunt servanda* in that States Parties to a case are under an obligation to cooperate with the Human Rights Court so that all notices, communications and summonses addressed to persons in their territory or under their jurisdiction are executed.[2240] This is also true

2233. Rule of Court 46(4).
2234. Judge Ouguergouz has stressed the importance of the Court satisfying itself as to the veracity of facts by making full use of its ability to gather evidence and question witnesses, *African Commission on Human and Peoples' Rights v. Libya*, African Court of Human and Peoples' Rights, App. No. 002/2013 (3 Jun. 2016), Separate Opinion of Judge Ouguergouz, paras 16–25.
2235. Rule of Court 55(2).
2236. Rule of Court 56(5).
2237. Rule of Court 54(4).
2238. Rule of Court 54(5).
2239. *See also* Rule of Court 33(2).
2240. Rule of Court 33(1).

for any proceeding that the Human Rights Court holds in the territory of a State Party to a case.[2241] This duty extends also to other States.[2242] Given a real fear of retribution for challenging State authorities the Human Rights Court, in providing some protection for applicants, witnesses, or legal representatives, is seeking to preserve the integrity of the proceedings; a State that failed to protect such individuals could ultimately be found to be in breach of its treaty obligations.

356. Under Article 27(2) the Human Rights Court must adopt such interim, or provisional, measures as it deems necessary in cases of 'extreme gravity and urgency', and 'to avoid irreparable harm to persons'.[2243] They are also designed to preserve the *status quo ante* pending the determination of the case.[2244] Stringent requirements must therefore be met. The Human Rights Court has stated that 'urgency, which is linked to extreme gravity, means a real and imminent likelihood that irreparable harm will be caused before it renders its final decision ... Further, there is urgency whenever acts that are likely to cause irreparable harm can "occur at any time" before it renders its final decision in the matter'.[2245] It found that 'circumstances ... of great urgency' relating especially to the rights to life and physical integrity during the revolution in Libya in early 2011 compelled it to order such measures.[2246] In *African Commission on Human and Peoples' Rights v. Kenya (Provisional Measures)*, the Human Rights Court took notice of prejudice to the substantive matter before it.[2247] In cases of extreme urgency, the President of the Human Rights Court shall obtain the views of the Judges, presumably to decide on measures to be taken.[2248]

2241. Rule of Court 33(3).
2242. Rule of Court 33(4).
2243. *See also* Rule of Court 59(1). The Human Rights Court has described provisional measures as 'a consequence of the right to protection under the [African] Charter', *African Commission on Human and Peoples' Rights v. Libya (Order of Provisional Measures)*, African Court of Human and Peoples' Rights, App. No. 002/2013 (15 Mar. 2013) para. 13. They have also been described as 'of a preventive character', *XYZ v. Benin*, Provisional Measures, African Court of Human and Peoples' Rights, App. No. 010/2020 (3 Apr. 2020) para. 25. In *General Kayumba Nyamwasa and Six Others v. Rwanda (Order of Provisional Measures)*, African Court of Human and Peoples' Rights, App. No. 016/2015 (24 Mar. 2017) para. 35, the Human Rights Court declined to grant interim measures since the object of the request had been overtaken by events.
2244. Rule of Court 33(2). *African Commission on Human and Peoples' Rights v. Republic of Kenya (Order of Provisional Measures)*, African Court of Human and Peoples' Rights, App. No. 006/2012 (15 Mar. 2013) para. 23.
2245. *XYZ v. Benin*, Provisional Measures, African Court of Human and Peoples' Rights, App. No. 010/2020 (3 Apr. 2020) para. 26.
2246. *In the Matter of the African Commission on Human and Peoples' Rights v. Libyan Arab People's Jamahiriya (Provisional Measures)*, African Court of Human and Peoples' Rights, App. No. 004/2011 (25 Mar. 2011) paras 22–23. *See also Selemani v. Tanzania*, Provisional Measures, African Court of Human and Peoples' Rights, App. No. 042/2019 (20 Nov. 2020) para. 23.
2247. *African Commission on Human and Peoples' Rights v. Republic of Kenya (Order of Provisional Measures)*, African Court of Human and Peoples' Rights, App. No. 006/2012 (15 Mar. 2013) para. 22.
2248. Rule of Court 59(2).

357. Interim measures can be given at the request of a party to the case, which may include the Commission[2249] or the Human Rights Court on its own accord. In *African Commission on Human and Peoples' Rights v. Libya (Provisional Measures)*, the Human Rights Court ordered measures *proprio motu*.[2250] The fact that the Human Rights Court can order any measures 'it deems necessary' suggests that they could be 'in whole or in part other than those requested'. The Human Rights Court need not satisfy itself that it has jurisdiction on the merits but simply that prima facie jurisdiction exists.[2251] This it can do by establishing that the applicant is an entity entitled to submit a case to the Human Rights Court and that the Respondent has ratified the African Charter and the Protocol.[2252] There is certainly no need to engage in prior consideration of the substantive issues in the case.[2253] The Human Rights Court has stated that the indication of interim measures does not prejudge the question of jurisdiction, the admissibility or merits of the case.[2254]

358. A number of questions remain unaddressed however. What will the Human Rights Court's approach be towards interim measures adopted by the Commission? Furthermore, no explicit provision is made for the revocation or modification of interim measures. However, the absence in the previous Rules of the Court of any explicit guidance to the question of whether interim measures have binding effect seems to have been addressed.[2255] Rule of Court 72(2) states that the Court's decisions, not just judgments, are binding on the parties. This is supported by the use of

---

2249. *See, e.g., African Commission on Human and Peoples' Rights v. Republic of Kenya (Order of Provisional Measures)*, African Court of Human and Peoples' Rights, App. No. 006/2012 (15 Mar. 2013).

2250. *African Commission on Human and Peoples' Rights v. Libyan Arab People's Jamahiriya (Provisional Measures)*, African Court of Human and Peoples' Rights, App. No. 004/2011 (25 Mar. 2011) paras 9–12; *African Commission on Human and Peoples' Rights v. Libya (Order of Provisional Measures)*, African Court of Human and Peoples' Rights, App. No. 002/2013 (15 Mar. 2013).

2251. *African Commission on Human and Peoples' Rights v. Libya (Provisional Measures)*, African Court of Human and Peoples' Rights, App. No. 004/2011 (25 Mar. 2011) para. 15; *African Commission on Human and Peoples' Rights v. Republic of Kenya (Order of Provisional Measures)*, African Court of Human and Peoples' Rights, App. No. 006/2012 (15 Mar. 2013) para. 16.

2252. *African Commission on Human and Peoples' Rights v. Libya (Provisional Measures)*, African Court of Human and Peoples' Rights, App. No. 004/2011 (25 Mar. 2011) paras 17–18.

2253. *African Commission on Human and Peoples' Rights v. Republic of Kenya (Order of Provisional Measures)*, African Court of Human and Peoples' Rights, App. No. 006/2012 (15 Mar. 2013) para. 19.

2254. *African Commission on Human and Peoples' Rights v. Republic of Kenya (Order of Provisional Measures)*, African Court of Human and Peoples' Rights, App. No. 006/2012 (15 Mar. 2013) para. 24; *African Commission on Human and Peoples' Rights v. Libya (Order of Provisional Measures)*, African Court of Human and Peoples' Rights, App. No. 002/2013 (15 Mar. 2013) para. 19.

2255. Developments elsewhere have established that interim measures have binding effect, *see LaGrand Case* (*Germany v. United States of America*) I.C.J. Reports 2001, 466, paras 99–103; *Application of the Convention on the Prevention and Punishment of the Crime of Genocide* (*Bosnia and Herzegovina v. Serbia and Montenegro)* I.C.J. Reports 2007, 1, paras 452, 468; *Constitutional Court v. Peru (Provisional Measures)*, Ser. E, No. 3 (2000); *Mamatkulov and Abdurasulovic v. Turkey*, European Court of Human Rights, App. Nos 46827/99, 46951/99, Judgment of 6 Feb. 2003).

the verb 'order' rather than the previous verb 'prescribe' in old Rule 51(1).[2256] Further favouring the sense of a legal duty is the Human Rights Court's capacity under Rule 59(4) to 'make all such recommendations as it deems appropriate' in instances of non-compliance by States.[2257] In instances of non-compliance the Human Rights Court has ordered the Respondent to stay all acts adopted subsequent to the Ruling and adopted further measures.[2258] The Human Rights Court could do worse than adopt the Commission's approach declaring that a contracting party that has failed to abide by its indication of interim measures is in breach of the principle of *pacta sunt servanda* enshrined in Article 1 of the African Charter.[2259]

359. While the Protocol does not address the possibility of a non-appearing State party Rule 63(1) allows the Human Rights Court to proceed with the case and enter a decision in default at the request of the other party or on its own motion. However, the Human Rights Court must first satisfy itself that due notice was given to the defaulting party.[2260] A decision in default may be set aside by the Court if the defaulting party shows good cause.[2261]

360. The Applicant can discontinue a case by informing the Human Rights Court to that effect.[2262] The Respondent's consent to discontinue the case is not required. The Human Rights Court itself is empowered to strike out cases from its list at any stage of the proceedings if it believes that it is no longer justified to continue with the Application.[2263] A case may be restored to the Court's list at the Applicant's request in exceptional circumstances.[2264]

2256. Rules of Court 59(1), 684. *See also Mugesera v. Rwanda*, African Court of Human and Peoples' Rights, App. No. 012/2017, Judgment (27 Nov. 2020) para. 8.
2257. The Human Rights Court brought Libya's non-compliance with an Order to the attention of the AU Assembly, *African Commission on Human and Peoples' Rights v. Libya*, African Court of Human and Peoples' Rights, App. No. 002/2013 (3 Jun. 2016) para. 18.
2258. *Soro v. Côte d'Ivoire*, Provisional Measures, African Court of Human and Peoples' Rights, App. No. 012/2020 (15 Sep. 2020) para. 33.
2259. *See supra* paras 219–220.
2260. These are cumulative conditions, *Mugesera v. Rwanda*, African Court of Human and Peoples' Rights, App. No. 012/2017, Judgment (27 Nov. 2020) para. 14. *See also* Rule of Court 54(7) regarding hearings. *See African Commission on Human and Peoples' Rights v. Libya*, African Court of Human and Peoples' Rights, App. No. 002/2013 (3 Jun. 2016) paras 38–43. In his Separate Opinion, Judge Ouguergouz stated that the Court should have been guided by the jurisprudence of the ICJ and Inter-American Court of Human Rights in this area. He proceeded to express the view that the Court had failed to carry out a proper examination of the facts and law which had seemingly resulted in the Court pronouncing itself 'automatically' in favour of the Applicant, *ibid.*, *African Commission on Human and Peoples' Rights v. Libya*, African Court of Human and Peoples' Rights, App. No. 002/2013 (3 Jun. 2016), Separate Opinion of Judge Ouguergouz, paras 3–4, 27–28.
2261. Rule of Court 63(2).
2262. Rule of Court 65(1)(a).
2263. Rule of Court 65(1)(c).
2264. Rule of Court 65(3).

361. The procedure in contentious cases consists primarily of written proceedings, but oral proceedings only if considered necessary.[2265] Cases are heard in open court[2266] although it may decide, *propio motu* or at the request of the parties, that they be held in camera in the interests of public morality, safety or public order, or the best interests of a child.[2267] A safeguard exists in that the Human Rights Court must provide a reasoned explanation for its decision.[2268] At any stage of the pleadings the Human Rights Court may order the joinder of interrelated cases and pleadings if considered appropriate.[2269] The use of the term 'pleadings' rather than 'proceedings' suggests the Human Rights Court enjoys a narrower discretion in this field. Following the conclusion of the hearings the Human Rights Court deliberates in private[2270] and then delivers its judgment in open Court, or in exceptional circumstances, virtually.[2271] Judgments must be taken by majority, and shall be final and not subject to appeal.[2272] Moreover, judgments must be reasoned,[2273] and separate and dissenting opinions may be attached.[2274] The Rules make provision for the publication of the Human Rights Court's judgments, advisory opinions, orders, etc.[2275] Corrections may be made to clerical errors or omissions in its decisions.[2276] It is interesting to note that Article 28(1) of the Protocol and Rule of Court 69(1) require the Human Rights Court to render its judgment within ninety days of having completed its deliberations. This does not seem an unreasonable expectation in the context of the protection of human rights.

362. The decisions of the Human Rights Court are binding on the parties;[2277] thus, States parties to cases decided by the Human Rights Court 'undertake to

---

2265. Rule of Court 30(1). *See also* Rule of Court 52 on oral hearings. The Human Rights Court may put questions to the parties, Rule of Court 54(4).
2266. Protocol Art. 10(1); Rule of Court 52(2).
2267. Rule of Court 52(2), (3).
2268. Rule of Court 52(4). In *Mulindahabi v. Rwanda*, African Court of Human and Peoples' Rights, App. No. 004/2017 (26 Jun. 2020) para. 64., the Human Rights Court held that a reasoned decision is guaranteed by the African Charter Art. 7(1)(a).
2269. Rule of Court 62(1). This it did in *Tankanyika Law Society and The Legal and Human Rights Law Centre and Reverend Christopher Mtikila v. Tanzania*, African Court of Human and Peoples' Rights, App. No. 009 & 011/2011 (22 Sep. 2011), where the subject matter and the defendants were the same in both cases.
2270. Rule of Court 67.
2271. Protocol, Art. 28(5); Rule of Court 74. According to the Human Rights Court, 'publicity of a judgment is assured as long as it is rendered in a premises or open area; provided the public is notified of the place and ... can have free access to the same', *Mohamed Abubakri v. Tanzania*, African Court of Human and Peoples' Rights, App. No. 007/2013 (3 Jun. 2016), para. 225. However, this conclusion was criticized by the dissenting judges who argued that judgments in judges' chambers could not amount to 'open court'.
2272. Protocol, Art. 28(2); Rule of Court 69(2).
2273. Protocol, Art. 28(6); Rule of Court 71(1)(h).
2274. Protocol, Art. 28(7); Rule of Court 70.
2275. Rules of Court 21(2)(i) and 76. Also available at the Court's website, http://www.african-court.org.
2276. Rule of Court 79 . The Human Rights Court has issued corrected judgments, for example, *Ingabire Victoire Umuhoza v. Rwanda*, Ruling on Jurisdiction, African Court of Human and Peoples' Rights, App. No. 003/2014 (5 Sep. 2016) Corrigendum.
2277. Rule of Court 72(2).

comply with the judgment … and to guarantee its execution'.[2278] International practice suggests that the Human Rights Court's jurisprudence will have a persuasive effect on other States. In cases of non-compliance the Human Rights Court has no power to enforce its decisions although, in accordance with Rule of Court 81(3), it can issue an order to ensure compliance with its decisions. In addition, it can draw the Assembly's attention to any cases in which a State has not complied with a decision under Article 31 of the Protocol.[2279] Under Article 29(2) of the Protocol the EX (previously Council of Ministers) is entrusted with the task of monitoring the execution of judgments on the Assembly's behalf. In principle, there appears to be no legal obstacle to the Assembly imposing sanctions on a recalcitrant State pursuant to Article 23 of the Constitutive Act for breach of its obligations under the Protocol. Moreover, a creative interpretation of Article 27(1) could allow the Human Rights Court to award punitive damages in cases where the applicant establishes that a State has flouted a judgment of the Human Rights Court and has failed to make reparation to a victim.

363. Although the Human Rights Court's judgments are final,[2280] the Human Rights Court can review its decisions in the light of new facts or evidence which can have a decisive influence.[2281] According to Rule of Court 78(1), the new facts or evidence must not have been known with due diligence at the time the decision was delivered. A limitation period of six months of the discovery of new facts and evidence is imposed. In addition, the Human Rights Court has the power to interpret its decisions.[2282] Under Rule of Court 77(1) the Human Rights Court is competent to interpret a decision on application by any party. Significantly, the Court's power in this regard is narrow, limited 'for the purpose of *executing a decision* ' (emphasis added).[2283] The rationale seems to be in order 'to prevent a new dispute being submitted to the Human Rights Court in the guise of a request to interpret an earlier judgment'.[2284] A deadline of twelve months from the date of judgment is set unless the interests of justice dictate otherwise.[2285]

364. The Protocol bestows a broad advisory jurisdiction upon the Human Rights Court. Article 4(1) thus confers upon the Human Rights Court competence to give advisory opinions on any legal matter relating to the African Charter or other relevant human rights instrument[2286] at the request of a Member State of the AU, the

2278. Protocol Art. 30. *See also* Rules of Court 72(2), 80, 81(1).
2279. *See also* Rule of Court 81(4).
2280. Protocol Art. 28(2); Rule of Court 72(1).
2281. Protocol Art. 28(3); Rule of Court 78(1). An application for revision does not stay the execution of a decision unless the Human Rights Court decides otherwise, Rule of Court 78(5).
2282. Protocol Art. 28(4); Rule of Court 77.
2283. An application for interpretation does not stay the execution of a judgment unless the Human Rights Court decides otherwise, Rule of Court 77(4).
2284. S. Rosenne, *The World Court: What It is and How It Works* (5th edn, Dordrecht: Martinus Nijhoff, 1995), 151. Rosenne was writing about the ICJ but his comment seems equally valid with regard to the Human Rights Court.
2285. Rule of Court 77(1).
2286. *See also* Rule of Court 82(1)-(2). However, the Human Rights Court decided it could not consider the Rome Statute of the International Criminal Court (17 Jul. 1998), 2187 U.N.T.S. 91, 37 I.L.M.

AU, any AU organ,[2287] or any African organization recognized by the AU.[2288] In another application of the *lis pendens* principle the request must not relate to an application pending before the Commission.[2289] The fact that all Member States of the AU are able to request an opinion, whether or not they are parties to the Protocol, is noteworthy. The recognition of a broad range of applicants and wide-ranging subject matter could give rise to problems similar to those discussed above in relation to its contentious jurisdiction. However, such a wide jurisdiction has the potential of strengthening the commitment to human rights and giving rise to a rich jurisprudence.

365. It is important to note that the power of the Human Rights Court to render advisory opinions is discretionary, as evidenced by the inclusion of the word 'may' in Article 4(1).[2290] It remains to be seen in what circumstances, other than that specifically relating to an issue being examined by the Commission, the Human Rights Court may choose to decline to exercise its advisory jurisdiction.

---

999 (1998) (Rome Statute), as it raised issues of Public International Law and not human rights law, *Request for Advisory Opinion by the Coalition for* the *International Criminal Court, the Legal Defence & Assistance Project (LEDAP), the Civil Resource Development & Documentation Center (CIRDDOC) and the Women Advocates Documentation Center (WARDC)*, African Court of Human and Peoples' Rights, Request No. 001/2014 (5 Jun. 2015) para. 13i.

2287. *See Request by the Pan African Parliament (PAP) on the Application of the Principle of Regional Rotation in the Election of the Bureau of the PAP*, African Court of Human and Peoples' Rights, Request No. 001/2021 (16 Jul. 2021).

2288. The Human Rights Court has held that the Committee on the Rights of the Child is an AU organ with *locus standi*, *Request for Advisory Opinion by the African Committee of Experts on the Rights and Welfare of the Child on the Standing of the African Committee of Experts on the Rights and Welfare of the Child before the African Court of Human and Peoples' Rights*, African Court of Human and Peoples' Rights, Request No. 002/2013 (5 Dec. 2014), paras 56–57. The term 'organization' used in Art. 4(1) refers both to NGOs and Intergovernmental Organizations, *Request for Advisory Opinion by Socio-Economic Rights and Accountability Project (SERAP)*, African Court of Human and Peoples' Rights, Request No. 001/2013 (26 May 2017) para. 46. An 'organization' must be recognized by the AU itself, either through the granting of Observer Status or the signing of an MOU between the AU and the NGO, *ibid*., para. 53. The Human Rights Court has concluded in a number of cases that it is unable to give the Advisory Opinion requested of it because the organization had not been recognized by the AU, *see, e.g.*, *Request for Advisory Opinion by l'Association Africaine de Défense des Droits de l' Homme*, African Court of Human and Peoples' Rights, Request No. 002/2016 (28 Sep. 2017). Additionally, 'an organization may be considered as "African" if it is registered in an African country and has branches at the sub-regional, regional or continental levels, and if it carries out activities beyond the country where it is registered', *Request for Advisory Opinion by l'Association Africaine de Défense des Droits de l'Homme*, African Court of Human and Peoples' Rights, Request No. 002/2016 (28 Sep. 2017) para. 27. The potential for duplication again arises since, as has been observed, the Commission has the power of interpretation under the African Charter Art. 45(3), which has been described by an eminent author as amounting to authorization 'to issue what are in effect advisory opinions', A.H. Robertson & J.G. Merrills, *Human Rights in the World*(3rd edn, Manchester: Manchester University Press, 1992), 221. It is likely that the Court will assume primary competence, Nmehielle, 273.

2289. *See also* Rule of Court 82(1). *See Request for Advisory Opinion by Pan-African Lawyers' Union and Southern African Litigation Center*, African Court of Human and Peoples' Rights, Request No. 002/2012 (15 Mar. 2013).

2290. *Request for Advisory Opinion by the African Committee of Experts on the Rights and Welfare of the Child on the Standing of the African Committee of Experts on the Rights and Welfare of the*

366. In matters of procedure, it is important to note that Rule of Court 87 assimilates the advisory procedure to contentious procedure. However, the Human Rights Court has decided that it need not consider its territorial and temporal jurisdiction but only the requirements for personal and material jurisdiction.[2291] Preliminary objections to advisory proceedings are therefore permitted.[2292]

367. The rules make it clear that advisory proceedings consist of written[2293] and, if necessary, oral stages.[2294] Of particular interest is the fact that any 'entity' is allowed to enter written submissions on any of the issues raised in the request for an opinion.[2295] Such entities are those such as Member States, the Commission and AU organs. African organizations, NGOs and individuals may qualify as 'interested entities'.[2296] Other procedures are identical, *mutatis mutandis*, to those in contentious cases.[2297]

368. Article 4(2) and Rule 86(1) require the Human Rights Court to give reasons for its advisory opinions and enable the judges to deliver separate or dissenting opinions. This appears to be standard international judicial practice. Opinions must be read in open court unless circumstances dictate otherwise.[2298] This situation hardly seems consonant with basic notions of justice which demands openness, particularly in contemporary times when an expectation of transparency has arisen. It is difficult to conceive of circumstances where a 'secret opinion' may be justified. Regrettably, the rules are silent as to whether a 'secret opinion' could be made public at some future stage or whether it would remain 'secret' in perpetuity, or which body would be entitled ultimately to take a decision on this issue.

369. It is a trite observation that advisory opinions are not legally binding but it would be surprising if the Human Rights Court's opinions were not to acquire an authoritative status.

370. The Human Rights Court is given the power under Article 9 to attempt amicable settlements in accordance with the African Charter.[2299] Both Article 9 of the Protocol and the Rules of the Court envisage a proactive role, which is discretionary, for the Human Rights Court in reaching amicable, or friendly, settlements.[2300]

Child before the African Court of Human and Peoples' Rights, African Court of Human and Peoples' Rights, Request No. 002/2013 (5 Dec. 2014), para. 40.

2291. *Request for Advisory Opinion by the Pan African Lawyers Union (PALU)*, African Court of Human and Peoples' Rights, Request No. 001/2018 (4 Dec. 2020) para. 19.

2292. *See, e.g.*, *Request for Advisory Opinion by Socio-Economic Rights and Accountability Project (SERAP)*, African Court of Human and Peoples' Rights, Request No. 001/2013 (26 May 2017) paras 24–32.

2293. Rule of Court 84.

2294. Rule of Court 85.

2295. Rule of Court 83(2).

2296. *See* Rules of Court 83(2)(d), 84(2).

2297. Rule of Court 87.

2298. Rule of Court 86(2).

2299. *See also* Rule of Court 64(1).

2300. Rules of Court 64(1) and 29(2)(a).

It may therefore contact the parties and take suitable measures to facilitate an amicable settlement based on respect for human and peoples' rights.[2301] The parties may on their own initiative call upon the Human Rights Court to help settle their dispute.[2302] The agreement to settle in this instance must be mutual. A settlement may be reached at any time before the Human Rights Court renders judgment. The Human Rights Court will then deliver a judgment limited to a brief statement of the facts and the solution adopted.[2303] Notwithstanding such an agreement, the Human Rights Court may decide to proceed with the case.[2304] The rationale for doing so are in the interest of justice or to preserve public interest or order.[2305]

371. Under Article 10(2) and Rule of Court 31, any party to a case can be represented by a legal representative of their choice. Free legal representation may be provided in the interests of justice.[2306] Given the abject poverty in parts of Africa, this circumstance appears significant, but proper funding is important.[2307] As a general rule states, each party will bear its own costs unless the Human Rights Court decides otherwise.[2308]

372. According to Article 7 the Court shall apply the provisions of the African Charter and other human rights instruments ratified by the States concerned. The Human Rights Court can thus draw inspiration from the wealth of general and particular international law, including the ICCPR, the ECHR and the ACHR.[2309] No express mention is made of the norms of general international law but the Human Rights Court has had occasion to consider their relevance.[2310] Article 11(1) states that the Human Rights Court consists of eleven judges. This is only a fraction of the actual membership of the AU and should ensure that the bench does not become unwieldy. Cases are heard by the full Court; Article 23 of the Protocol provides that the Human Rights Court must consist of at least seven judges to be quorate.[2311] Neither the Protocol nor the Rules make provision for the creation of chambers. The judges must be nationals of AU Member States; it is not specified that a judge must be a national of a State that has ratified the Protocol.[2312] However, only States

2301. *See also* Rule of Court 64(1).
2302. Rule of Court 64(2).
2303. Rule of Court 64(4).
2304. Rule of Court 64(5).
2305. Rule of Court 64(5).
2306. *See also* Rule of Court 31(2).
2307. Rule of Court 31(3) provides that the Human Rights Court shall maintain a Legal Aid scheme. *See supra* note 466.
2308. Rule of Court 32(2). *See Michelot Yogogombaye v. Senegal*, African Court of Human and Peoples' Rights, App. No. 001/2008 (15 Dec. 2009) paras 41–45.
2309. *See, e.g., Wilfred Onyango Nganyi & 9 Others v. Tanzania*, African Court of Human and Peoples' Rights, App. No. 006/2013 (18 Mar. 2016), paras 169–179.
2310. *See, e.g., Ingabire Victoire Umuhoza v. Rwanda*, Ruling on Jurisdiction, African Court of Human and Peoples' Rights, App. No. 003/2014 (5 Sep. 2016) Corrigendum, on the withdrawal provisions of the Vienna Convention on the Law of Treaties.
2311. *See also* Rule of Court 25(1).
2312. Compare African Charter Art. 34, which stipulates that members of the Commission 'must have the nationality of one of the States Parties to the present Charter'.

Parties to the Protocol may nominate candidates,[2313] and in a welcome innovation, consideration must be given to 'adequate gender representation'.[2314] How this is to be achieved is unclear. Rule of Court 10(2) requires, *inter alia*, that the principle of gender parity be observed in the composition of the Bureau, that is, the President and Vice President of the Court.[2315] No two judges can be nationals of the same State.[2316] As is standard practice in international tribunals, judges may be drawn from a varied background.

373. Judges are elected by secret ballot by the AU Assembly,[2317] which requires a two-thirds majority, a not inconsiderable hurdle. Again, adequate gender representation must be observed,[2318] which implies that the candidatures of certain women must survive the nomination process. Article 14(2) requires that Africa's main regions and its principal legal traditions (civil, Roman-Dutch, common, and Islamic law, but is customary law included?) are represented on the Human Rights Court.[2319] It is curious that no similar direction is required at the nomination stage.

374. The judges' term of office is six years with the possibility of one further renewable period.[2320] All judges, except for the President,[2321] shall be part-time.[2322] A judge may be suspended or removed from office when the other members of the Human Rights Court are unanimously of the view that s/he no longer fulfils the requirements of office.[2323] The judge in question must be informed in writing by the President of the Court. The impugned judge will be able to defend himself/herself at a specially convened private session of the Human Rights Court, and a decision will be reached by the rest of the Court at a further special private session.[2324] The Human Rights Court's decision can be overturned by the AU Assembly.[2325]

375. The judges are elected in an individual capacity; that is, they must not follow instructions from any State or other agency. They must therefore desist from any activity that is incompatible with their independence or impartiality or the

2313. Protocol Art. 12(1), which stipulates that each State may propose up to three candidates, at least two of whom must be nationals of that State.
2314. Protocol Art. 12(2). *See also* Protocol Art. 14(3).
2315. Rule of Court 1(c).
2316. Protocol Art. 11(2).
2317. *Ibid.* Art. 14(1). *See* http://www.aict-ctia.org/courts_conti/achpr/achpr_bios.html.
2318. Protocol Art. 14(3).
2319. *See also* Rule of Court 10(2).
2320. Protocol Art. 15(1) and Rule of Court 2(3). At the end of two years following the first election, the terms of office shall expire after two years and the terms of four more judges shall expire at the end of four years.
2321. Protocol Art. 21(2). The President serves a term of office of two years and may be re-elected once, *ibid.*, Art. 20(1), Rule of Court 13(1).
2322. Protocol Art. 15(4). However, the Assembly may alter this arrangement; such circumstance might arise if the Human Rights Court develops a busy docket.
2323. *Ibid.*, Art. 19(1).
2324. Rule of Court 8.
2325. Protocol Art. 19(2).

demands of their office.[2326] Exactly what activities come within the scope of a prohibited activity was left to the Rules of Court to determine. Rule 5(2) specifically lists political, diplomatic or administrative positions or function as government legal advisers at the national level but the use of the adverb 'in particular' indicates that other occupations are not excluded.[2327] This requirement should also be read in conjunction with Article 17(1) of the Protocol which guarantees the independence of the judges. A general obligation exists to ensure that judges consider all cases impartially, free from inducements, pressure, influence, threats or other interference.[2328] Additionally, the judges enjoy all immunities extended to diplomatic agents under international law during their term of office.[2329] Article 17(2) seeks to avoid conflicts of interest by requiring a judge who has previously been involved in a case to recuse himself/herself. However, the rules of Court go further. Thus a judge who has a personal interest in the case, who has expressed public pronouncements, through the media or academic writings perhaps, or '*for any other reason*' (emphasis added), that may undermine or lead his/her impartiality and independence to be questioned is disqualified from the case.[2330] The President of the Court has no power to exclude a judge from a case. No provision is made for replacing a judge in such circumstances with an interim or substitute judge. In fact, the Protocol makes no provision whatsoever for the appointment of ad hoc judges. In order to avoid any semblance of partiality, Article 22 of the Protocol does not allow a judge who is a national of a State that is a party to a case to hear it.[2331] Additionally, a judge is also prohibited from hearing a case concerning the State that nominated him/her.[2332]

376. If the Human Rights Court concludes that human rights have been violated, Article 27(1) of the Protocol requires that it 'shall make appropriate orders to remedy the violation, including the payment of fair compensation or reparation'. Rule of Court 40(4) requires the Applicant to submit a request for reparation in the application commencing proceedings and allows him/her to submit a request for the amount of the reparation. The Human Rights Court will rule on the request for reparation either in the judgment or in a separate decision.[2333]

2326. Protocol Art. 18; Rule of Court 5(1).
2327. *See further* Rule of Court 5(3).
2328. Rules of Court 5(1), 9(4)(c), (d). *See also* Protocol Art. 16 and Rule of Court 3(1) on the oath of office.
2329. Protocol Art. 17(3). Vienna Convention on Diplomatic Relations (24 Apr. 1961) 500 U.N.T.S. 95; General Convention on the Privileges and Immunities of the OAU (25 Oct. 1965) 1000 U.N.T.S. 393.
2330. Rule of Court 9(4)(b)–(d).
2331. *See also* Rule of Court 9(2). In consequence Judge El Hadj Guissé, a national of Senegal, recused himself from hearing the case of *Michelot Yogogombaye v. Senegal*, African Court of Human and Peoples' Rights, App. No. 001/2008 (15 Dec. 2009). *See also, e.g., Association Juriste d'Afrique pour la Bonne Gouvernance v. Ivory Coast*, African Court of Human and Peoples' Rights, App. No. 006/2011 (16 Jun. 2011).
2332. Rule of Court 9(3).
2333. Rule of Court 69(3). *See, e.g., Zongo and Others v. Burkina Faso*, Judgment on Reparations, African Court of Human and Peoples' Rights, App. No. 013/2011 (5 Jun. 2015).

377. What constitutes 'fair compensation' or 'reparation' is undefined but the Human Rights Court has held that it can take the form of restitution, compensation and satisfaction.[2334] Awards of a pecuniary nature are clearly envisaged because by definition 'fair compensation' must include awards of a pecuniary nature, and this interpretation has been upheld by the Court which in the case of *Zongo and Others v. Burkina Faso* awarded monetary sums.[2335] The concept of 'reparation' extends to ordering consequential measures requiring States to take certain positive steps.[2336] In relation to the quantification of reparation, the Human Rights Court has held that the applicable principle is that of 'full reparation, commensurate with the prejudice suffered.'[2337]

378. In the case of *Zongo and Others v. Burkina Faso*, the Human Rights Court considered the issue of reparations at length.[2338] The first point of interest is that the Court will only consider awarding reparations where an application to that effect has been submitted and arguments made.[2339] The Court recalled that it is a basic principle of international law that a State must make reparation for a breach of its obligations,[2340] reflected in Article 27(1).[2341] But this was limited to 'identified wrongful acts'.[2342] The Court recognized two categories of damage, material and moral.[2343] In relation to moral prejudice, the Court first considered whether the Applicants, Zongo's beneficiaries, were 'victims' entitled to reparations. The Court opined that international human rights law did not restrict the notion of victim to direct heirs but extends to close relatives.[2344] In relation to proof of causal link between the wrongful act and the moral prejudice, the Court was of the view that such a link may result automatically from a violation of a human right without any need to prove otherwise.[2345]

2334. *Zongo and Others v. Burkina Faso*, Judgment on Reparations, African Court of Human and Peoples' Rights, App. No. 013/2011 (5 Jun. 2015), para. 29.
2335. *Ibid.*, para. 111(ii). *See also, e.g., Noudehouenou v. Benin*, African Court of Human and Peoples' Rights, App. No. 028/2020 (1 Dec. 2022) para. 203xiii.
2336. *See Zongo and Others v. Burkina Faso*, Judgment on Reparations, African Court of Human and Peoples' Rights, App. No. 013/2011 (5 Jun. 2015), para. 111(x), where the Court ordered the Respondent to reopen the investigation into the murder of the victim. On the Commission's practice *see supra* para. 330.
2337. *Zongo and Others v. Burkina Faso*, Judgment on Reparations, African Court of Human and Peoples' Rights, App. No. 013/2011 (5 Jun. 2015), para. 60.
2338. *Zongo and Others v. Burkina Faso*, Judgment on Reparations, African Court of Human and Peoples' Rights, App. No. 013/2011 (5 Jun. 2015).
2339. *Ibid.*, para. 2.
2340. *Case concerning the Factory at Chorzow (Germany v. Poland)*, Indemnity, Merits, P.C.I.J., Series A, No. 17 (1928).
2341. *Zongo and Others v. Burkina Faso*, Judgment on Reparations, African Court of Human and Peoples' Rights, App. No. 013/2011 (5 Jun. 2015), paras 20–22.
2342. *Ibid.*, para. 25.
2343. *Ibid.*, para. 27. The Court adopted the IACHR's definition of moral damage in *Cantoral Benevides v. Peru*, Reparations, Series C, No. 88 (2001).
2344. *Zongo and Others v. Burkina Faso*, Judgment on Reparations, African Court of Human and Peoples' Rights, App. No. 013/2011 (5 Jun. 2015), paras 46–49.
2345. *Ibid.*, para. 55.

379. The future of the Human Rights Court is currently subject to a degree of uncertainty, however. In July 2004 the AU decided that the Human Rights Court should be merged with the Court of Justice.[2346] While valid arguments may exist on practical grounds for reducing the number of AU organs, including a desire for rationalization,[2347] and the potential problem of overlapping jurisdiction between the two courts,[2348] the decision was not favourably received. Thus Amnesty International criticized it on the ground that it undermines the effective functioning of the Human Rights Court.[2349] Academics were also critical, drawing attention to the different roles played by the courts, particularly the fact that the Court of Justice has no explicit human rights mandate and its judges do not have to have expertise in human rights, and the different rules on *locus standi*.[2350] The Commission also expressed serious concern, fearing the 'negative impact' that the decision could have on the effectiveness of the Human Rights Court and drew attention to the different mandates and litigants of the two courts.[2351] These criticisms notwithstanding, in 2008 the Assembly adopted the Protocol on the ACJHR (2008 Protocol) establishing the ACJHR.[2352] Nevertheless, pending the merger the AU decided to allow the Human Rights Court to become operational.[2353] The 2008 Protocol contains transitional arrangements regarding the Human Rights Court. First, according to Article 4, the term of office of the judges of the Human Rights Court shall end when the judges of the ACJHR have been elected but shall remain in office until the latter have been sworn-in. Second, pursuant to Article 5, any cases pending before the Human Rights Court which have not been concluded before the 2008 Protocol enters into force, will be transferred to the Human Rights Section and will continue to be considered pursuant to the rules of the 1998 Protocol. Third, according to Article 7, once the 2008 Protocol has entered into force, the 1998 Protocol will remain in operation for a period of one year to allow for the assets and liabilities of the Human Rights Court to be transferred to the ACJHR. It is not inconceivable that the Human Rights Court may have a long life pending the entry into force of the 2008 Protocol.

2346. *Decision on the Merger of the African Court of Human and Peoples' Rights and the Court of Justice of the African Union*, AU Doc. Assembly/AU/Dec. 83 (V). *See* Protocol of the Court of Justice of the African Union, AU Doc. Assembly/AU/Dec. 25 (II).
2347. N.J. Udombana, 'An African Human Rights Court and an African Union Court: A Needful Duality or a Needless Duplication?', *Brooklyn J.I.L.* 28 (2003): 811.
2348. The Human Rights Court has the capacity to pronounce on the Constitutive Act on the basis that the promotion and protection of human rights are stated as core principles and objectives, under the Protocol, Art. 3(1), whereas the Court of Justice would seem to have had jurisdiction over the African Charter under the Protocol of the Court of Justice Art. 18(1)(b).
2349. *African Union: Assembly's decision should not undermine the African Court*, http://web.amnesty.org/library/print/ENGIOR300202004.
2350. F. Viljoen & E. Baimu, 'Courts for Africa: Considering the Co-Existence of the African Court on Human and Peoples' Rights and the African Court of Justice', *N.Q.H.R.* 22 (2004): 241; K.D. Magliveras & G.J. Naldi, 'The African Court of Justice', *Z.a.ö.R.V.* 66 (2006): 187, 212–213.
2351. Resolution on the Establishment of an Effective African Court on Human and Peoples' Rights, ACHPR/Res.76 (XXXVII) 05 (2005) http://www1.umn.edu/humanrts/africa/resolutions/rec81.html.
2352. *See supra* para. 119.
2353. AU Doc. Assembly/AU/Dec. 83 (V), para. 3.

§5. The Human Rights Section of the African Court of Justice and Human Rights

380. The AU sidestepped the potential difficulties thrown up by the proposed merger by creating two sections, one of which is the Human Rights Section with jurisdiction over alleged violations of human rights.[2354] Nonetheless, it appears true to say that one of the effects of the merger is that the distinctive identity of the Human Rights Court is diminished. According to the Preamble of the 2008 Protocol, the Human Rights Section's task is to secure the objectives of the African Charter, and to supplement and strengthen the mission of the Commission as well as of the African Committee of Experts on the Rights and Welfare of the Child.[2355] While this could simply be considered a statement of the intent to boost the existing protective system, it could also be seen as a reference to the fact that these two bodies have an enhanced role to play since, as is explained later, they have direct access to the Human Rights Section. Indeed, Article 27(2) of the Statute refers to the complementarity that the ACJHR maintains with the African Commission and the Committee of Experts.[2356]

381. Under Article 28(c) of the Statute the Human Rights Section[2357] has jurisdiction relating to the interpretation and application of the African Charter, the African Charter on the Rights of the Child, the Protocol on the Rights of Women in Africa, or of any other legal instrument pertaining to human rights. The inclusion of the latter clause is especially noteworthy because of its sweeping nature. The Human Rights Section appears to have been conferred jurisdiction to pronounce on multilateral instruments such as the International Covenants on Human Rights 1966 and the Convention on the Rights of the Child 1989, and on the constituent treaties of RECs with human rights commitments, for example, ECOWAS[2358] and the SADC.[2359] Given that the Constitutive Act contains general provisions on human rights there appears to be no valid reason why the Human Rights Section should not assume the authority to examine it, either under this provision or paragraph (a) thereof.[2360] The Human Rights Section is expressly granted jurisdiction over OAU/AU treaties, such as the Convention on Refugees, under Article 28(b) of the Statute.

2354. Statute of the African Court of Justice and Human Rights Art. 17(2) (Statute).
2355. *See infra* paras 385–390.
2356. *See also* Rule 114 of the Commission.
2357. Article 28 of the Statute setting out the ACJHR's contentious jurisdiction does not address the separate Sections but their discrete competences should be borne in mind.
2358. *See* Revised ECOWAS Treaty 1993 Art. 4(g), 35 I.L.M. 663 (1996). Thus, in *Hadijatou Mani Koraou v. Niger*, ECOWAS Community Court of Justice, Judgment No. ECW/CCJ/JUD/06/08 (27 Oct. 2008) paras 41–42, http://www.unhcr.org/refworld/docid/496b41fa2.html (accessed 16 Jan. 2013), the ECCJ invoked this particular treaty provision to state that it was charged with protecting human rights.
2359. Amended SADC Treaty 2001 Art. 4(c). In *Mike Campbell (Pvt) Ltd. et al. v. The Republic of Zimbabwe*, SADC (T) Case No. 2/2007, http://www.saflii.org/sa/cases/SADCT/2008/2.pdf (accessed 16 Jan. 2013), the SADC Tribunal held similarly that the SADC Treaty Art. 4(c) conferred upon it the competence to rule on human rights issues.
2360. The Human Rights Court has assumed the jurisdiction to consider the human rights provisions of the Constitutive Act, *Mohamed Abubakri v. Tanzania*, African Court of Human and Peoples' Rights, App. No. 007/2013 (3 Jun. 2016), para. 51.

It is interesting to note that in this particular instance the jurisdiction of the Human Rights Section extends to judging the *validity* of the treaties.

382. The following parties possess standing according to Article 30 of the Statute to submit cases to the Human Rights Section alleging human rights violations: (a) States Parties to the Protocol; (b) the African Commission on Human and Peoples' Rights; (c) the Committee of Experts on the Rights of the Child; (d) African IGOs; (e) African national human rights institutions; and (f) individuals and NGOs accredited to the AU or to its organs. Although not explicitly set out in the Statute it is likely that interstate cases are permissible. Whether States will be allowed to appeal adverse opinions issued by the Commission and by the Committee of Experts on the Rights of the Child is by no means certain but the language of the Statute suggests that it is likely to be so. That African IGOs, such as ECOWAS, and national human rights institutions have been listed as applicants is especially interesting. National human rights institutions could play a significant role if sufficiently independent. The fact that, in principle, the standing of duly accredited individuals and NGOs has been recognized is encouraging, although the requirement of accreditation may have a restrictive effect.[2361] Whether standing is afforded to associations and legal persons as is the case under the European system remains to be seen.[2362] An added difficulty is that the standing of NGOs and individuals is subject to the condition set out in Article 8(3) of the 2008 Protocol, the substantive section of which states that, '[a]ny Member State may ... make a declaration accepting the competence of the Court to receive cases under Article 30(f) [of the Statute] *involving a State which has not made such a declaration*' (emphasis added). That this provision lacks clarity is a matter of regret. If the intention is to make the jurisdiction of the Human Rights Section in this instance contingent upon States making a separate optional declaration,[2363] it would have made more sense to repeat verbatim Article 34(6) of the 1998 Protocol which is a model of simplicity. If, as is apparently the case, a separate declaration is required, then the situation is highly unfortunate because States with a poor human rights record are unlikely to accept the jurisdiction of the Human Rights Section in this regard. Whereas the Statute could be said to provide for what may amount to public interest litigation, it is regrettable that this will only prove possible in extremely restrictive circumstances.[2364] Applicants who are unable to proceed because of a contracting party's refusal to accept this head of jurisdiction will need to rely on other parties, the Commission or national human rights institutions for example, to champion their complaints before

---

2361. S. Sceats, *Africa's New Human Rights Court: Whistling in the Wind?*, Chatham House Briefing Paper IL BP 09/01. In *Association Juriste d'Afrique pour la Bonne Gouvernance v. Ivory Coast,* African Court of Human and Peoples' Rights, App. No. 006/2011 (16 Jun. 2011), the Human Rights Court dismissed the case as the applicant NGO did not have observer status with the Commission as required by the 1998 Protocol Art. 5(3). In July 2005, the Executive Council updated the criteria for accreditation which apply to NGOs only, Executive Council, *Criteria for Granting Observer Status and for a System of Accreditation within the AU* (EX.CL/Dec. 195 (VII)).

2362. Harris, O'Boyle, Warbrick, 788–796.

2363. Sceats, 9–10; *Interights*, http://www.interights.org/africansingleprotocoladopted/index.html (accessed 15 Jan. 2013).

2364. According to *Interights*, this limitation 'renders access to justice illusory for human rights victims', *ibid.*

the Human Rights Section. However, another avenue may emerge for an applicant found not to have standing, *forum prorogatum*.[2365] Under the Statute, a complainant is not required to be the victim of the alleged violation. It is commendable that the African system has opted for an expansive approach which can be justified on grounds such as poverty and lack of legal assistance.[2366] It should be observed that the Statute is silent on the issue of hurdles of admissibility. It must be assumed that detailed conditions governing admissibility will be laid down in the Rules of the Court.

§6. The African Charter on the Rights and Welfare of the Child

383. The rights of the child are not adequately addressed by the African Charter.[2367] In later years, however, the issue of children's rights came to the fore with the adoption of the UN Convention on the Rights of the Child (CRC) in 1989.[2368] Although the CRC attracted the support of many African States[2369] there was a consensus that the African child was exposed to particular dangers[2370] which demanded additional measures of protection in an African perspective.[2371] The result was the African Charter on the Rights and Welfare of the Child 1990 (ACRWC).[2372]

384. The ACRWC, the first regional instrument of its sort, complements the CRC.[2373] It guarantees a number of civil, political, economic, social, and cultural

2365. *Michelot Yogogombaye v. Senegal*, African Court of Human and Peoples' Rights, App. No. 001/2008 (15 Dec. 2009), Separate Opinion of Judge Ouguergouz, paras 31–39.

2366. F. Viljoen, 'Admissibility under the African Charter', in *The African Charter on Human and Peoples' Rights: The System in Practice, 1986–2000*, Evans & Murray (eds) (Cambridge: Cambridge University Press, 2002), 61, 75.

2367. *See* African Charter Art. 18(3).

2368. UN Convention on the Rights of the Child (20 Nov. 1989) 1577 U.N.T.S. 3, 28 I.L.M. 1448 (1989).

2369. The SADR is the only AU Member State not to have ratified the CRC. However, it has been argued that Africa has a whole had little input into the drafting of the CRC, O. Ekundayo, 'Does the African Charter on the Rights and Welfare of the Child (ACRWC) only Underlines and Repeats the Convention on the Rights of the Child (CRC)'s Provisions?: Examining the Similarities and the Differences between the ACRWC and the CRC', *International Journal of Humanities and Social Science* 5 (2015): 143, 147. *See also* J. Adu-Gyamfi & F. Keating, 'Convergence and Divergence between the UN Convention on the Rights of the Children and the African Charter on the Rights and Welfare of the Child', *Sacha Journal of Human Rights* 3 (20013): 47, 50.

2370. K.C.J.M. Arts, 'The International Protection of Children's Rights in Africa: The 1990 OAU Charter on the Rights and Welfare of the Child', *R.A.D.I.C.* 5 (1993): 139, 141–143.

2371. Ekundayo, 147–148; A. Lloyd, 'A Theoretical Analysis of the Reality of Children's Rights in Africa: An Introduction to the African Charter on the Rights and Welfare of the Child', *A.H.R.L.J.* 2 (2002): 11, 14–15; B. Thompson, 'Africa's Charter on Children's Rights: A Normative Break with Cultural Traditionalism', *I.C.L.Q.* 41 (1992): 434.

2372. African Charter on the Rights and Welfare of the Child (1 Jul. 1990), 28 I.L.M. 1456 (1989). The ACRWC entered into force on 29 Nov. 1999. As of February 2023, it had been ratified by fifty States. *See further* Arts; Lloyd; Viljoen, International Human Rights Law in Africa, 260–266; A. Kaviani Johnson & J. Sloth-Nielsen, 'Child protection, safeguarding and the role of the African Charter on the Rights and Welfare of the Child: Looking back and looking ahead', *A.H.R.L.J.* 20 (2020): 643.

2373. Ekundayo, 148.

rights to which State Parties must recognize and give effect.[2374] These rights are largely comparable to those protected by the CRC, although it would seem that such protection may on paper be not as forceful as under the CRC.[2375] However, this should not be considered a fundamental weakness since the ACRWC contains a safeguard clause and yields in those situations where it may not equal national or international standards.[2376] It should also be noted that the AU Protocol on the Rights of Women 2003 (Maputo Protocol) supplements some of the substantive rights enshrined in the ACRWC. In keeping with the African concept of rights, the ACRWC imposes responsibilities on the child towards his/her family, the community and the State.[2377] At the same time the family is stated to be the 'natural unit

---

2374. According to the African Committee of Experts on the Rights and Welfare of the Child (ACERWC) the obligation under the ACRWC Art. 1(1) to adopt legislative and other measures to give effect to said Charter 'is subject neither to progressive realization, nor to available resources', *Michelo Hunsungule and Others (on behalf of Children in Northern Uganda) v. Uganda* Communication No. 1/2005 (2013) para. 37. It has further stated that 'the implementation and realization of children's rights in Africa is not a matter to be relegated for tomorrow, but an issue that is in need of proactive immediate attention and action', *Institute for Human Right and Development in Africa and Finders Group Initiative on Behalf of TFA (A Minor) v. Cameroon* Communication No. 006/Com/002/2015 (2018) para. 56. It has proceeded to state that 'effective implementation of laws with due diligence is part of States parties obligation under the Charter', *Michelo Hunsungule and Others (on behalf of Children in Northern Uganda) v. Uganda* Communication No. 1/2005 (2013) para. 38. This requires that 'due diligence should be shown in prevention of human rights violations, investigation of violations, prosecution of perpetrators, and ensuring punishment of perpetrators', *Minority rights group international and Sos-esclaves on behalf of Said Ould Salem and Yarg Ould Salem v. Mauritania* Communication No. 007/Com/003/2015 (2018) para. 52. With regard to the State obligation on adopting 'other measures', the ACERWC has stated that the focus should be on administrative and judicial measures, *Institute for Human Right and Development in Africa and Finders Group Initiative on Behalf of TFA (A Minor) v. Cameroon* Communication No. 006/Com/002/2015 (2018) para. 43. *See further* ACERWC, General Comment No. 5 on State Party Obligations Under the African Charter on the Rights and Welfare of the Child (Article 1) and Systems Strengthening for Child Protection (2018) s. III (General Comment No. 5).

2375. Arts 147–149, identifies the freedom of expression and of thought, conscience and religion, the right to privacy, the right of access to information, the right to benefit from social security, and rights for minorities as especially problematic since they are made subordinate to the rights of parents, legal guardians or the State. *See further* B. Mezmur, 'The African Children's Charter @ 30: A distinction without a difference?', *International Journal of Children's Rights* 28 (2020): 693, 695. Compare *contra* Lloyd, 14–15, who asserts that the level of protection is higher under the ACRWC. It has been pointed out that the ACRWC has unique features, ACPF, Africa's 30-Year Journey with the African Children's Charter: Taking Stock, Rekindling Commitment, 10–11 https://resourcecentre.savethechildren.net/pdf/thecharter30narrativereportenglish_acpf.pdf/. The general consensus seems to be that the two instruments are complementary, Adu-Gyamfi & Keating, 56. It should be noted that under the African Charter on Democracy Art. 31(1), State Parties commit themselves to promoting Youth in the governance process. It should be observed that as with the rights protected by the African Charter, the those guaranteed by the ACRWC are considered indivisible, *IHRDA and Open Society Justice Initiative (OSJI)(on behalf of children of Nubian descent in Kenya) v. Kenya* Communication No. 2/09 (2011) para. 58.

2376. African Charter on the Rights of the Child ACRWC Art. 1(2); Arts 154–155.

2377. ACRWC Art. 31. *See* General Comment on Article 31 of ACRWC: Responsibilities of the Child (2017). *See also* Arts 153–154; Ekundayo, 154–155. However, it has been emphasized that children's rights are 'not contingent upon them fulfilling their "duties"', since duties co-exist interdependently with rights, *Michelo Hunsungule and Others (on behalf of Children in Northern*

and basis of society'[2378] and the child is entitled to parental care and protection.[2379] The ACRWC contains progressive features that have attracted praise. Crucially a child is defined as a person below the age of 18 years.[2380] The best interests of the child, which 'applies across cultural, political and geographical settings, to members of all ethnic groups',[2381] is *the* primary consideration, which sets a high standard.[2382] It is also 'a substantive right, an interpretative principle, and a rule of procedure.'[2383] The right of non-discrimination, described as 'a cardinal principle' of the ACRWC,[2384] applies.[2385] This may extend to discrimination based on the birth

---

Uganda) v. Uganda Communication No. 1/2005 (2013) para. 59. *See further* ACERWC, General Comment on Article 31 of ACRWC: Responsibilities of the Child (2017).

2378. ACRWC Art. 18(1). Compare African Charter Art. 18(1); American Convention on Human Rights Art. 17(1) (22 Nov. 1969), 1144 U.N.T.S. 144 (ACHR).

2379. ACRWC Art. 19. *See further ibid.*, Art. 20 on parental responsibilities. Compare ACHR Art. 19.

2380. ACRWC Art. 2. Compare CRC Art. 1, which is somewhat ambiguous. *See* Lloyd, 20. According to Ekundayo, 148–149, the definition of a child in African tradition is determined by a variety of factors of which age is not definitive. Some are therefore critical of this condition, *see, e.g.*, A. Twum-Danso, 'A Cultural Bridge, Not an Imposition: Legitimizing Children's Rights in the Eyes of Local Communities', *Journal of the History of Childhood and Youth* 1 (2008): 391, 393.

2381. General Comment No. 5 para. 4.2. In the words of the Human Rights Court, the principle 'is a cross-cutting principle which applies to children, irrespective of status, in diverse circumstances', *Request for Advisory Opinion by the Pan African Lawyers Union (PALU) on the Compatibility of Vagrancy Laws with the African Charter on Human and Peoples' Rights*, African Court of Human and Peoples' Rights, Request No. 001/2018, Judgment (4 Dec. 2020), para. 122.

2382. ACRWC Art. 4(1). According to the CRC Art. 3(1), the best interests of the child is simply *a* primary consideration. *See* Ekundayo, 149–150; Lloyd, 17–19. According to Adu-Gyamfi & Keating, 51–52, 'the best interest principle is plagued with vagueness and implementation difficulties'. Section 28(2) of the Constitution of South Africa, e.g., provides that, 'A child's best interests are of paramount importance...' The ACERWC has stated that, 'There are no conditions attached to this principle which could dilute its scope, reach or standard of application', General Comment No. 5 para. 4.2. The ACERWC has stated that the best interests of the child means that there can be no justification for female genital mutilation (FGM) given its harmful consequences to the health and well-being of affected girls, Joint General Comment on Female Genital Mutilation (2023) para. 9. In *Request for Advisory Opinion by the African Committee of Experts on the Rights and Welfare of the Child on the Standing of the African Committee of Experts on the Rights and Welfare of the Child before the African Court of Human and Peoples' Rights* Request No. 002/2013 (5 Dec. 2014) para. 95, the Human Rights Court emphasized the paramount nature of the best interests of the child which should take priority over technical points that could obstruct accessibility of justice for children. *See also IHRDA and Open Society Justice Initiative (OSJI)(on behalf of children of Nubian descent in Kenya) v. Kenya* Communication No. 2/09 (2011) para. 42. In *The Centre for Human Rights (University of Pretoria) v. Senegal* Communication No. 001/2012 (2014) paras 37–39, ACERWC found Senegal to be in breach of the ACRWC Art. 4 for failing to take the necessary measures against those forcing children into begging. It should be noted further that parents or guardians must 'ensure that the best interests of the child are their basic concern at all times', ACRWC Art. 20(1)(a).

2383. *Legal and Human Rights Centre and Centre for Reproductive Rights (on behalf of Tanzanian girls) v. Tanzania* Communication No. 0012/Com/001/2019 (2022) para. 70.

2384. *Institute for Human Right and Development in Africa and Finders Group Initiative on Behalf of TFA (A Minor) v. Cameroon* Communication No. 006/Com/002/2015 (2018) para. 59. This extends to 'any form of gender based discrimination against girls', *ibid.* The ACERWC expressed the view that gender-based violence amounts to gender-based discrimination, *ibid.* para. 62. Furthermore, it has stated that FGM is a form of gender discrimination embedded in gender inequality, Joint General Comment on Female Genital Mutilation (2023) para. 10.

2385. ACRWC Arts 3, 26. *See* General Comment No. 5 para. 4.1; Ekundayo, 153–154. Art. 3 has been held to be a non-derogable, 'general non-discrimination clause which applies to all substantive

of a child out of wedlock.[2386] According to the ACERWC there is a violation of the principle of non-discrimination if a child is not able to rely on the protection of the ACRWC simply because it is of a certain sex.[2387] Children with disabilities are entitled to special measures of protection.[2388] The child has an inherent right to life and States Parties are under a positive obligation to do their utmost to ensure the survival, protection and development of the child.[2389] The participation and recruitment of children in armed conflicts, which has been a problem in a number of African countries such as Burundi, the practices, which include FGM,[2390] are to be

---

rights' in the ACRWC, *African Centre of Justice and Peace Studies (ACJPS) and People's Legal Aid Centre (PLACE) v. Sudan* Communication No. 005/Com/001/2015 (2018) para. 32; as well as an 'absolute right', *Legal and Human Rights Centre and Centre for Reproductive Rights (on behalf of Tanzanian girls) v. Tanzania* Communication No. 0012/Com/001/2019 (2022) para. 53. *See further Legal and Human Rights Centre and Centre for Reproductive Rights (on behalf of Tanzanian girls) v. Tanzania* Communication No. 0012/Com/001/2019 (2022) paras 50–59, on discrimination with regard to expulsion of pregnant and married girls from school, denial of re-entry, mandatory pregnancy testing of schoolgirls, and detention of pregnant girls on the grounds of sex, age, health status (pregnancy) and marital status; *IHRDA and Open Society Justice Initiative (OSJI)(on behalf of children of Nubian descent in Kenya) v. Kenya* Communication No. 2/09 (2011) relating to discrimination in acquisition of nationality and the rights to health and education. *See further* ACERWC, General Comment on Article 6 of the African Charter on the Rights and Welfare of the Child. In *Request for Advisory Opinion by the Pan African Lawyers Union (PALU) on the Compatibility of Vagrancy Laws with the African Charter on Human and Peoples' Rights*, African Court of Human and Peoples' Rights, Request No. 001/2018, Judgment (4 Dec. 2020), para. 120, the Human Rights Court held that the enforcement of vagrancy laws resulting in the arrests, detention and forcible relocation of children was incompatible with children's right to non-discrimination under ACRWC Art. 3.

2386. In *Association pour le Progrès et la Défense des Droits des Femmes Maliennes (APDF) and the Institute for Human Rights and Development in Africa (IHRDA) v. Mali*, Application No. 046/2016 (11 May 2018) paras 114–115, the Human Rights Court held that Mali's Family Code which enshrines religious and customary law in matters of inheritance regarding children born out of wedlock was in breach of ACRWC Arts 3 and 4. In *Bhe and Others v. The Magistrate, Khayelitsha and Others* 2005 (1) SA 580 (CC), the Constitutional Court of South Africa invoked, *inter alia*, ACRWC Art. 3, to find that differential treatment between children born within and without of marriage amounted to unfair discrimination on the basis of birth. *See* ACHR Art. 17(5).

2387. *Institute for Human Right and Development in Africa and Finders Group Initiative on Behalf of TFA (A Minor) v. Cameroon* Communication No. 006/Com/002/2015 (2018) para. 64.

2388. ACRWC Art. 13. Note Protocol to the African Charter on Human and Peoples' Rights on the Rights of Persons with Disabilities in Africa (29 Jan. 2018) Art. 28.

2389. ACRWC Art. 5(1)–(2). *See* General Comment No. 5 para. 4.3. In *The Centre for Human Rights (University of Pretoria) v. Senegal* Communication No. 001/2012 (2014) paras 40–45, ACERWC stressed the significance of these principles in reinforcing the other rights guaranteed under the ACRWC.

2390. Arts 151. This practice has been condemned by the UN Fourth World Conference on Women (Beijing Platform for Action) para. 283(d), 35 I.L.M. 401 (1996). *See also* UN General Assembly Res. (2012). It has been reported that female genital mutilation, a practice which includes female circumcision and varying degrees of excision, exists in at least twenty-six countries in Africa, Report of Ms Halima Embarek Warzazi, Special Rapporteur, on traditional practices affecting the health of women and the girl child 10, UN Doc. E/CN.4/Sub.2/2005/36. According to this report in West Africa this practice is usually performed at the age of puberty, whereas in East Africa it is carried out at the earlier age of 7 or 8, UN Doc. E/CN.4/Sub.2/2005/36, 11. It is encouraging to note that in recent years the practice has been, or is being, prohibited by law and made a criminal offence in a number of African countries, Report of Ms Radhika Coomaraswamy, Special Rapporteur, on violence against women, its causes and consequences para. 17, UN Doc. E/CN.4/2002/83; *see also* UN Doc. E/CN.4/Sub.2/2005/36, 13. Female genital mutilation is prohibited in

eliminated.[2391] According to the ACERWC, practices are harmful if they: constitute a denial of the dignity and/or integrity of the individual and a violation of their human rights; constitute discrimination limiting the capacity of girls to participate fully in society; practices that are prescribed and/or kept in place by social norms that perpetuate male dominance and inequality of women and children, on the basis of, *inter alia*, sex, gender and age; are imposed on women and children by family members, the community or society at large regardless of the victim's lack of or inability to consent.[2392] Children are to be protected from all forms of abuse, torture and ill-treatment.[2393] The purpose is 'the protection of both the dignity as well as

---

Kenya under the Prohibition of Female Genital Mutilation Act, 2011 (the constitutionality of this Act was upheld by the High Court of Kenya in *Tatu Kamau v. Attorney General & 2 others; Equality Now & 9 others (Interested Parties)* [2021] KEHC 450 (KLR)), in South Africa under Children's Act, 2005 s. 12(3), in Uganda under Prohibition of Female Genital Mutilation Act, 2010. *See further* ACPF, 36. Western countries are also determined to eradicate this practice, *see, e.g.*, the UK's Female Genital Mutilation Act 2003 which not only makes it illegal in the UK but additionally makes it an offence to take girls to another country for female genital mutilation.

2391. ACRWC Art. 21(1). *See* Joint General Comment on Female Genital Mutilation (2023) paras 34-63.

See also, e.g., South Africa's Children's Act, 2005 s. 12. Begging, specifically prohibited by Art. 29(b), is one such practice, *see The Centre for Human Rights (University of Pretoria) v. Senegal* Communication No. 001/2012 (2014) paras 69–73. Other harmful practices include child marriage, virginity testing and breast ironing, ACHPR and ACERWC, Joint General Comment on the Rights and Welfare of the Child on Ending Child Marriage (2017) para. 49 (General Comment on Ending Child Marriage). *See further* CEDAW and CRC, Joint general recommendation No. 31 of the Committee on the Elimination of Discrimination against Women/general comment No. 18 of the Committee on the Rights of the Child (2019) on harmful practices UN Doc. CEDAW/C/GC/31/Rev.1–CRC/C/GC/18/Rev.1 para. 9. Mandatory pregnancy testing of schoolgirls, expulsion of pregnant and married girls from school and detention of pregnant girls also constitute harmful practices, *Legal and Human Rights Centre and Centre for Reproductive Rights (on behalf of Tanzanian girls) v. Tanzania* Communication No. 0012/Com/001/2019 (2022) paras 64–66. *See also* ACRWC Art. 1(3) which states that any custom, tradition, cultural or religious practice inconsistent with the ACRWC shall to the extent of the inconsistency be discouraged. *See Association pour le Progrès et la Défense des Droits des Femmes Maliennes (APDF) and the Institute for Human Rights and Development in Africa (IHRDA) v. Mali*, Application No. 046/2016 (11 May 2018) paras 124–125, where the Human Rights Court held that the discriminatory practices in Mali's Family Code violated ACRWC Arts 1(3) and 21. *See further* General Comment No. 5 para. 7.1. *See also* UN General Assembly Res. 52/99. According to a UN report little has been done to address these issues although Ghana has criminalized the practice of *trokosi*, the giving of 'virgin girls to priests as appeasement for past crimes committed by family members', UN Doc. E/CN.4/Sub.2/2005/36, para. 49. The report identifies traditional birth practices, which jeopardizes both mother and child, as prevalent throughout Africa, *ibid.*, paras 75–76. *See* I.L.O. Maternity Protection Convention 2000 No. 183. The problem of forced marriage, for instance, is not addressed expressly by the ACRWC.

2392. *Legal and Human Rights Centre and Centre for Reproductive Rights (on behalf of Tanzanian girls) v. Tanzania* Communication No. 0012/Com/001/2019 (2022) para. 62.

2393. ACRWC Art. 16(1). *See The Centre for Human Rights (University of Pretoria) v. Senegal* Communication No. 001/2012 (2014) paras 62–68. Forced pregnancy tests on girls are caught by this provision, *Legal and Human Rights Centre and Centre for Reproductive Rights (on behalf of Tanzanian girls) v. Tanzania* Communication No. 0012/Com/001/2019 (2022) para. 33. In *Michelo Hunsungule and Others (on behalf of Children in Northern Uganda) v. Uganda* Communication No. 1/2005 (2013) para. 76, ACERWC held that acts of sexual violence in armed conflicts were not only in violation of international criminal law but the ACRWC.

physical and mental integrity of the children.'[2394] However, punishment in the home is allowed as long as 'domestic discipline is administered with humanity and in a manner consistent with the inherent dignity of the child.'[2395] The sexual exploitation and abuse of children is prohibited[2396] as is the sale, trafficking and abduction of children.[2397] Child, or early, marriages are expressly prohibited[2398] and the fact that eighteen years is specified as the minimum age at which marriage can be lawfully entered into is noteworthy.[2399] In *APDF and IHRDA v. Mali* the Human Rights Court found that Mali's Family Code did not comply with the minimum age of marriage of eighteen years under the ACRWC, in violation of Article 2, defining the child as under eighteen years, and Article 21, obligations to prohibit marriage of children under eighteen years and to eliminate practices harmful to children.[2400] The

---

2394. *Institute for Human Right and Development in Africa and Finders Group Initiative on Behalf of TFA (A Minor) v. Cameroon* Communication No. 006/Com/002/2015 (2018) para. 68.

2395. ACRWC Art. 20(1)(c). *See* Ekundayo, 152.

2396. ACRWC Art. 27. *See also ibid.*, Art. 16(1), CRC Art. 34, I.L.O. Convention No. 182 on the Worst Forms of Child Labour Art. 3(b), and the Optional Protocol to the Convention on the Rights of the Child on the sale of children, child prostitution and child pornography (25 May 2000) 2171 U.N.T.S. 227, 39 I.L.M. 1285 (2000). *See also* General Comment on Article 27 of the ACRWC: "Sexual Exploitation" (2021). And *Institute for Human Right and Development in Africa and Finders Group Initiative on Behalf of TFA (A Minor) v. Cameroon* Communication No. 006/Com/002/2015 (2018) paras 70–71.

2397. ACRWC Art. 29. *See also* Kampala Convention Art. 7(5)(f), CRC Art. 35, the Optional Protocol to the Convention on the Rights of the Child on the sale of children, child prostitution and child pornography, and the Protocol to Prevent, Suppress and Punish Trafficking in Persons, Especially Women and Children, supplementing the UN Convention against Transnational Organized Crime (15 Nov. 2000) 2237 U.N.T.S. 319. *See also, e.g.*, South Africa's Children's Act, 2005 s. 284(1). In *The Centre for Human Rights (University of Pretoria) v. Senegal* Communication No. 001/2012 (2014) paras 74–81, ACERWC found that the children engaged in forced begging were victims of such practices.

2398. ACRWC Art. 21(2). *See also* Maputo Protocol Art. 6(b). And *see* ACPF, 37. Child marriage is also incompatible with the best interests of the child required by ACRWC Art. 4(1), General Comment on Ending Child Marriage para. 8. *See also* The Addis Ababa Declaration on Ending Child Marriage in Africa adopted by the ACERWC in 2014 stressing the importance of eliminating child marriage. It is estimated that over forty million women and girls in Africa under the age of fifteen entered into marriage or some other union, UNICEF, A Profile of Child Marriage in Africa, http://www.unicef.org/wcaro/english/UNICEF-Child-Marriage-Brochure-low-Single(1).pdf. *See also* Centre for Human Rights, A Report on Child Marriage in Africa, https://www.chr.up.ac.za/images/publications/centrepublications/documents/child_marriage_report.pdf.

2399. Arts 149. In *Mudzuru & Anor v. Ministry of Justice, Legal & Parliamentary Affairs N.O. & Ors* [2016] ZWCC 12 the Constitutional Court of Zimbabwe, relying in part on the ACRWC, held that s. 78(1) of the Constitution of Zimbabwe should be interpreted to mean that a person who has not attained the age of eighteen has no legal capacity to marry. *See* similarly *Attorney-General v. Gyumi* [2019] 1 T.L.R. 114 [CA]. A number of African States have adopted legislation setting eighteen as the minimum age at which a person can marry, *see, e.g.*, Botswana, Marriage Act, 2001 s. 14; Kenya, Marriage Act, 2014 s. 4; Malawi, Marriage, Divorce and Family Relations Act, 2015 s. 14.

2400. *Association pour le Progrès et la Défense des Droits des Femmes Maliennes (APDF) and the Institute for Human Rights and Development in Africa (IHRDA) v. Mali* Application No. 046/2016 (11 May 2018). In *Mudzuru & Anor v. Ministry of Justice, Legal & Parliamentary Affairs N.O. & Ors* [2016] ZWCC 12 the Constitutional Court of Zimbabwe Court held that s. 78(1) of the Constitution of Zimbabwe had effectively abolished all types of child marriages without exception.

prohibition on child labour is rather equivocal, however.[2401] Requiring States Parties to take legislative and administrative measures only to combat this problem has been criticized as inadequate.[2402] Yet the action required of States Parties is more extensive than under the CRC.[2403] Special provision is made for children caught up in the criminal justice system,[2404] including separation from adults in places of detention or imprisonment, a prohibition on torture, inhuman or degrading treatment or punishment,[2405] legal guarantees such as the presumption of innocence, and an age of capacity.[2406] According to the Human Rights Court, children are therefore entitled to all fair trial guarantees applicable to adults plus other special guarantees tailored to their special situation.' In addition, the judicial system 'must accord children in conflict with the law a treatment that is consistent with their sense of dignity and worth. This includes … treating children in a manner that accords with their age and promotes their reintegration into society.'[2407] The imposition of the death penalty on children is outlawed.[2408] The ACRWC also makes provision for other

2401. ACRWC Art. 15. Compare CRC Art. 32. *See also* I.L.O. Convention No. 182 on the Worst Forms of Child Labour. *See* Ekundayo, 151–152. In *The Centre for Human Rights (University of Pretoria) v. Senegal* Communication No. 001/2012 (2014) paras 57–61, ACERWC found that forced begging amounted to a worst form of child labour. In this case ACERWC interpreted the ACRWC Art. 15 in conjunction with other international law such as I.L.O. Convention No. 182.
2402. Arts 149–150. By comparison, CRC Art. 32(2) additionally requires social and educational measures. In *The Centre for Human Rights (University of Pretoria) v. Senegal* Communication No. 001/2012 (2014) paras 59–61, ACERWC found that in failing to take appropriate enforcement measures against begging Senegal had violated the ACRWC Art. 15(2). I.L.O. Convention No. 182 on the Worst Forms of Child Labour Art. 7(1), envisages the imposition of penal sanctions if appropriate.
2403. Arts 150.
2404. Compare ACHR Art. 5(5). In *Request for Advisory Opinion by the Pan African Lawyers Union (PALU) on the Compatibility of Vagrancy Laws with the African Charter on Human and Peoples' Rights*, African Court of Human and Peoples' Rights, Request No. 001/2018, Judgment (4 Dec. 2020), para. 125, the Human Rights Court stated that the best interests of the child should be a primary consideration in the administration of juvenile justice. *See also Rex v. Malefetsane Mohlomi and Others* [2013] LSHC 27 (High Court of Lesotho).
2405. The imposition of judicial corporal punishment on juveniles has been condemned by the highest courts of various African States, including Namibia, *Ex Parte Attorney-General, Namibia: In re Corporal Punishment by Organs of State* 1991 (3) SA 76 (NmS), South Africa, *S v. Williams and Others* 1995 (CC), and Zimbabwe, *S v. Juvenile* 1990 (4) SA 151 (ZS). In *S v. C (a Juvenile)* 2015 ZWHCC 718, the High Court of Zimbabwe stated that corporal punishment was unconstitutional under the new Constitution of Zimbabwe adopted in 2013. This conclusion was strengthened by the fact that Zimbabwe's international obligations in protecting the rights of the children, including the ACRWC, prohibited corporal punishment.
2406. African Charter on the Rights of the Child ACRWC Art. 17.
2407. *Request for Advisory Opinion by the Pan African Lawyers Union (PALU) on the Compatibility of Vagrancy Laws with the African Charter on Human and Peoples' Rights*, African Court of Human and Peoples' Rights, Request No. 001/2018, Judgment (4 Dec. 2020), paras 126–127.
2408. *Ibid.*, Art. 5(3); *Groupe de Travail sur les Dossiers Judiciaires Stratégiques v. Democratic Republic of Congo*, Communication No. 259/2002 (2011), para. 71. Compare CRC Art. 37(a), ACHR Art. 4(5), and UN General Assembly Res. 59/261. It would appear that this prohibition may have acquired the status of customary international law at the very least, Report of the Secretary-General, Capital punishment and implementation of the safeguards guaranteeing protection of the rights of those facing the death penalty, UN Doc. E/2005/3, para. 76.

important rights, that to education,[2409] described as 'an inherent right of all children',[2410] and to health.[2411] Furthermore, children have the right to leisure, recreational and cultural activities.[2412] The child also has a right to a name and nationality.[2413] Although not mentioned in the ACRWC itself it has been held that States Parties must provide a remedy which includes a right to reparation.[2414]

385. The ACRWC sets up a monitoring and implementation mechanism, the African Committee of Experts on the Rights and Welfare of the Child,[2415] (ACERWC) composed of eleven independent members,[2416] which, while it must meet at least once a year, can be convened whenever necessary.[2417] Extraordinary Sessions may also be called.[2418] ACERWC's mandate is to promote and protect the rights and welfare of the child, especially to collect and document information, assess problems relating to children, organize meetings, encourage national, and

---

2409. ACRWC Art. 11. *See* Ekundayo, 150–151. It is interesting to note that the school curriculum should promote African morals, traditional values and culture, ACRWC Art. 11(2)(c). *See IHRDA and Open Society Justice Initiative (OSJI)(on behalf of children of Nubian descent in Kenya) v. Kenya* Communication No. 2/09 (2011) paras 63–65; *The Centre for Human Rights (University of Pretoria) v. Senegal* Communication No. /2012 (2014) para. 50; *Michelo Hunsungule and Others (on behalf of Children in Northern Uganda) v. Uganda* Communication No. 1/2005 (2013) paras 72–73; *Legal and Human Rights Centre and Centre for Reproductive Rights (on behalf of Tanzanian girls) v. Tanzania* Communication No. 0012/Com/001/2019 (2022) paras 40–49. *See further* African Charter on Democracy Art. 43(1). In parts of Africa, almost half of all girls are excluded from formal education, Report of Mr Muñoz Villalobos, Special Rapporteur, on the right to education para. 45, UN Doc. E/CN.4/2005/45.

2410. *Legal and Human Rights Centre and Centre for Reproductive Rights (on behalf of Tanzanian girls) v. Tanzania* Communication No. 0012/Com/001/2019 (2022) para. 40. The ACERWC proceeded to hold that a policy of expulsion of pregnant and married girls from schools constituted a violation of ACRWC Art. 11, rejecting the Respondent State's argument that the policy was in keeping with the preservation and strengthening of positive African morals and traditional values enshrined in ACRWC Art. 11(2)(c), *ibid.*, paras 42, 49.

2411. ACRWC Art. 14. *See IHRDA and Open Society Justice Initiative (OSJI)(on behalf of children of Nubian descent in Kenya) v. Kenya* Communication No. 2/09 (2011) paras 59–62, where it was held that the health needs of Nubian children had not been adequately recognized or provided for.

2412. ACRWC Art. 12.

2413. ACRWC Art. 6. Compare ACHR Arts 18, 20.

2414. *Michelo Hunsungule and Others (on behalf of Children in Northern Uganda) v. Uganda* Communication No. 1/2005 (2013) para. 51; *Institute for Human Right and Development in Africa and Finders Group Initiative on Behalf of TFA (A Minor) v. Cameroon* Communication No. 006/Com/002/2015 (2018) paras 81–82. ACRWC Art. 46, which allows ACERWC to draw inspiration from the international law of human rights, appears to provide an explicit legal basis for these decisions.

2415. ACRWC Art. 32. *See* Lloyd, 23–30. ACERWC has been held to be an AU organ with a quasi-judicial function, *Request for Advisory Opinion by the African Committee of Experts on the Rights and Welfare of the Child on the Standing of the African Committee of Experts on the Rights and Welfare of the Child before the African Court of Human and Peoples' Rights* Request No. 002/2013 (5 December 2014) paras 56–57, 87.

2416. ACRWC Art. 33; Revised Rule of Procedure 1(2). The Revised Rules of Procedure are available at https://www.acerwc.africa/sites/default/files/2022-09/Revised-Rules-of-Procedure-ACERWC.pdf (Rules).

2417. *Ibid.*, Art. 37(3); Rule 24(1). Rule 25(1) specifies two ordinary sessions annually.

2418. Rule 26.

local institutions concerned with child welfare and to advise governments, to formulate and draft rules aimed at protecting children, to cooperate with African, regional and international institutions and organizations concerned with the rights and welfare of children, to monitor the implementation and ensure protection of the rights enshrined in the ACRWC, and to perform any other tasks entrusted to it by the AU,[2419] and has been praised as broader and better defined than that of the UN Committee on the Rights of the Child.[2420] As part of its monitoring activities, a reporting procedure requires States to submit its initial report to ACERWC within two years of the ACRWC's entry into force for that State and every three years thereafter.[2421]

386. A potentially effective enforcement weapon possessed by ACERWC, which the UN Committee on the Rights of the Child lacks, is jurisdiction to entertain communications relating to the ACRWC from persons, groups or NGOs.[2422] This provision allows ACERWC to consider individual complaints in the manner of the African Commission. In 2014 ACERWC adopted Guidelines on Communications, akin to rules of procedure, setting out the governing procedure.[2423] Any individual, including children, or group of natural or legal persons; a State Party, any IGO or NGO recognized in an AU Member State, a State Party or the UN; any specialized AU or UN organ or agency, have *locus standi*.[2424] It can be seen that this is a very broad category, patently designed to afford children the best possible representation. Communications may be submitted on their own behalf or on behalf of third parties.[2425] However, an interesting development is the fact that a communication can be brought on a child's behalf without his or her consent on condition that the complainant can demonstrate that the case is in 'the supreme interest of the child.'[2426] Given that children are the focus of this system, it is not a surprise that ACERWC's jurisdiction is conditional on the child's age at the time of the alleged

2419. ACRWC Art. 42. ACERWC considers that its 'primary mandate' is to 'interpret and monitor the implementation' of the African Charter on the Rights of the Child, *Michelo Hunsungule and Others (on behalf of Children in Northern Uganda) v. Uganda* Communication No. 1/2005 (2013) para. 39. ACERWC's mandate is supplemented by its Revised Rules of Procedure. The ACRWC cites the OAU but such references must now be taken to indicate the AU.
2420. Arts 155–157; Lloyd, 24.
2421. ACRWC Art. 43(1)(b); Rule 68(3).
2422. ACRWC Art. 44(1). *See, e.g., IHRDA and Open Society Justice Initiative (OSJI)(on behalf of children of Nubian descent in Kenya) v. Kenya* Communication No. 2/09 (2011); *Taha Fadul et al. v. Sudan* Communication No: 0015/Com/003/2020, Decision on Admissibility No. 001/2022 (2021).
2423. Revised Guidelines for the Consideration of Communications Provided for in Art. 44 of the African Charter on the Rights and Welfare of the Child, https://www.acerwc.africa/sites/default/files/2022-06/Guidelines-for-Consideration-of-Communications-and-Monitoring-Implementation-of-Decisions-by-the-African-Committee-of-Experts-on-the-Rights-and-Welfare-of-the-Child-English.pdf.
2424. Revised Guideline s.I(1).
2425. *Ibid. See Michelo Hunsungule and Others (on behalf of Children in Northern Uganda) v. Uganda* Communication No. 1/2005 (2013) para. 16.
2426. Revised Guideline s.I(3).

violation, and ACERWC retains jurisdiction over a communication that is submitted but not concluded before the child's eighteenth birthday.[2427] The latter provision takes notice of the concept of 'continuing violations' which is well established in international human rights law.[2428] ACERWC has made an important clarification of this provision. It has held, as an 'exceptional measure' in the best interests of the child, that the fact that the victim was over the age of eighteen at the time of the submission of the complaint does not render it inadmissible.[2429] This interpretation seems correct; the crucial issue must be the age of the person at the time of the alleged violations. Communications must comply with Requirements of Form, to all intents and purposes conditions of admissibility.[2430] Accordingly, the communication must not be anonymous and must be written in one of the official languages.[2431] Radically, a complaint against a non-State Party need not prove fatal if ACERWC considers the case to be in the 'overall best interests of the child'.[2432] Should a respondent State fail to appear ACERWC can proceed to consider the case on admissibility or the merits based on the complainant's submissions.[2433] Six conditions of admissibility must be satisfied, largely identical to those listed in Article 56 of the African Charter.[2434] However, a communication must additionally not be 'manifestly groundless'.[2435] The Revised Guidelines have adopted the principle of 'constructive' exhaustion of local remedies[2436] while ACERWC has invoked the practice of the African Commission in its decisions.[2437] It will also, in accordance

2427. Revised Guideline s.I(1)(4).

2428. *Loizidou v. Turkey*, 23 E.H.R.R. 513GC (1996); *Blake v. Guatemala*, Ser. C, No. 27 (1996); *Zitha & Zitha v. Mozambique*, Communication No. 361/08 (2010) paras 85–94. The principle was applied by ACERWC in *African Centre of Justice and Peace Studies (ACJPS) and Peoples' Legal Aid Centre (PLACE) v. Sudan* Communication No. 005/Com/001/2015, Decision on Admissibility No. 003/1016 (2016) paras 35–37.

2429. *African Centre of Justice and Peace Studies (ACJPS) and Peoples' Legal Aid Centre (PLACE) v. Sudan* Communication No. 005/Com/001/2015, Decision on Admissibility No. 003/2016 (2016) para. 38.

2430. Revised Guideline s.II(2). *See, e.g., APDF et IHRDA v. Mali* Communication No: 0013/Com/001/2020 (2021); *Taha Fadul et al. v. Sudan* Communication No: 0015/Com/003/2020, Decision on Admissibility No. 001/2022 (2021).

2431. Revised Guideline s.II(2)(a), (b).

2432. Revised Guideline s.II(2)(c), (ii).

2433. Revised Guideline s.XI(1).

2434. The case of *Etoungou Nko'o on behalf of Mr. and Mrs. Elogo Menye and Rev. Daniel Ezo'o Ayo v. Cameroon* Communication No. 10/Com/003/2016 (2017) was declared inadmissible for failing to establish a *prima facie* violation of the ACRWC.

2435. Revised Guideline s.IX(1)(b). This condition appears to be identical to that of 'manifestly groundless' in the European Convention on Human Rights Art. 35(3) (4 Nov. 1950), C.E.T.S. No. 204 (as amended).

2436. Revised Guideline s.IX(1)(d). *See IHRDA and Open Society Justice Initiative (OSJI)(on behalf of children of Nubian descent in Kenya) v. Kenya* Communication No. 2/09 (2011) para. 23. For an example of a case declared inadmissible for non-exhaustion of local remedies *see Etoungou Nko'o on behalf of Mr. and Mrs. Elogo Menye and Rev. Daniel Ezo'o Ayo v. Cameroon* Communication No. 10/Com/003/2016 (2017).

2437. *Michelo Hunsungule and Others (on behalf of Children in Northern Uganda) v. Uganda* Communication No. 1/2005 (2013) paras 19–21. *See also African Centre of Justice and Peace Studies (ACJPS) and Peoples' Legal Aid Centre (PLACE) v. Sudan* Communication No. 005/Com/001/2015, Decision on Admissibility No. 003/1016 (2016) paras 22–33.

with Article 46 ACRWC, draw inspiration from the international law of human rights, including UN and other AU instruments.[2438]

387. The Revised Guidelines also make provision for a number of other procedural matters. Thus a party may raise a preliminary objection before ACERWC takes a decision on the merits,[2439] which it must rule upon before considering any other matters in the communication.[2440] Third parties may be allowed to intervene if ACERWC considers that they may provide it with relevant information.[2441] It is noteworthy that ACERWC can solicit such intervention.[2442] The third party is required to state its interest in the case and the object of its intervention.[2443] These requirements extend to *amicus curiae* who may petition to submit briefs.[2444] ACERWC may review its decisions *proprio motu* or at the request of a party.[2445] The grounds justifying review are: the emergence of a decisive fact or evidence which was not known to ACERWC or the party;[2446] that ACERWC erred egregiously in its interpretation and application of the ACRWC or other relevant instrument;[2447] any other compelling reason ACERWC deems appropriate in the interests of justice.[2448] An application for review must be made within six months of the new fact's discovery, unless it is in the best interests of the child.[2449]

388. The Revised Guidelines' provisions on provisional measures are of particular interest because of their innovative nature. In cases of urgency, serious or massive violations of the ACRWC and the likelihood of irreparable harm to children ACERWC is authorized to indicate, *proprio motu* or at the request of a litigant party, provisional measures to prevent grave or irreparable harm to victims.[2450] Unlike other similar jurisdictions, there is no mention of preserving the respective rights of the parties, this is purely about protecting the victims. In considering a request for provisional measures ACERWC can take account of a number of factors, namely, the gravity and urgency of the situation, the irreparable nature and imminence of the harm in question, whether the situation or harm has been brought to the attention of the authorities or the reasons why not, whether the beneficiaries of the provisional measures can be individually or collectively identified, and

2438. *Institute for Human Right and Development in Africa and Finders Group Initiative on Behalf of TFA (A Minor) v. Cameroon* Communication No. 006/Com/002/2015 (2018) para. 79.
2439. Revised Guideline s. XVI(1).
2440. Revised Guideline s. XVI(4).
2441. Revised Guideline s. XVII(1)(i).
2442. *Ibid.*
2443. Revised Guideline s. XVII(1)(i)(b)(c).
2444. Revised Guideline s. XVII(2).
2445. Revised Guideline s. XX(1).
2446. Revised Guideline s. XX(2)(a).
2447. Revised Guideline s. XX(2)(c).
2448. Revised Guideline s. XX(2)(d).
2449. Revised Guideline s. XX(2)(b).
2450. Revised Guideline s. VII(1)(i). *See, e.g., Taha Fadul et al. v. Sudan* Communication No: 0015/Com/003/2020, Decision on Admissibility No. 001/2022 (2021) paras 14–17. The Secretariat must notify ACERWC immediately should a communication reveal serious or massive violations or in cases of emergency so that it can consider provisional measures, Revised Guideline s. III(2).

whether the beneficiaries' consent has been obtained.[2451] In order to verify the facts ACERWC may conduct on-site investigations.[2452] Nonetheless, ACERWC's decision must be taken within twenty-one days at most.[2453] The Revised Guidelines are silent on whether provisional measures are considered binding but in case of non-compliance ACERWC is empowered to take all necessary steps it considers appropriate.[2454] In a different but associated context, in cases where there are reasonable grounds to believe that the life or personal integrity of a child or children is in danger, ACERWC can request the speediest reply from the State Party.[2455]

389. As is usual, the Revised Guidelines envisage amicable settlements. These may be arranged between the parties themselves at any time prior to a decision,[2456] or under ACERWC's auspices. In both instances, amicable settlements must be based on respect for human rights.[2457] However, in the former case, ACERWC may decide to proceed with the communication despite the settlement,[2458] presumably because ACERWC may be of the view that justice is not being served or that important issues of public interest are at stake. While ACERWC has a mission to promote amicable settlements it may terminate its facilitation of such on various grounds. These are: if the issues are not susceptible to amicable settlement; if any party does not consent to an amicable settlement; of if it chooses not to continue with an amicable settlement; if any party is unwilling to reach an amicable settlement based on respect for children's rights and welfare; if serious or massive violations of children's rights are at issue.[2459]

390. In addition, ACERWC has been conferred broad powers of investigation.[2460] It may therefore 'resort to any appropriate method of investigating any matter falling within the ambit of the ... Charter', including measures a State Party has taken to implement the ACRWC, and 'request from the States Parties any information relevant to the implementation of the Charter'. ACERWC also possesses the weapon of publicity.[2461] ACERWC hence has at its disposal considerable powers to hold States to account. If exercised properly, the Committee could become a formidable guardian of children's rights. The few cases ACERWC has decided certainly suggest a robust approach. It should not be overlooked that alleged violations of the ACRWC can be referred to the African Court on Human and Peoples' Rights.[2462]

2451. Revised Guideline s. VII(2).
2452. Revised Guideline s. VII(3)(i).
2453. Revised Guideline s. VII(2)(iv).
2454. Revised Guideline s. VII(4)(iv).
2455. Revised Guideline s. IX(2)(v).
2456. Revised Guideline s. XIII(1)(i). *See Project Expedite Justice et al. v. Sudan* Communication No. 0011/Com/001/2018 (2020).
2457. Revised Guideline s. XIII(1)(ii), (2)(i).
2458. Revised Guideline s. XIII(1)(iv).
2459. Revised Guideline s. XIII(2)(iv).
2460. African Charter on the Rights of the Child ACRWC Art. 45(1).
2461. *Ibid.*, Art. 45(2)–(4).
2462. Although ACERWC itself does not have standing to bring an action before the Human Rights Court, a fact confirmed in *Request for Advisory Opinion by the African Committee of Experts on*

391. The ACRWC must be viewed as a positive development. It is the first regional document of its type.[2463] ACERWC's mandate compares favourably with that of the UN Committee. In substantive terms it complements the CRC. However, the fear that for many African States the ACRWC may simply have been too radical and progressive to attract widespread support since it challenges established traditions and customary and religious laws does not appear to have been borne out.[2464] In fact, the ACRWC appears to be exerting a positive influence on legislative and judicial developments throughout Africa.[2465]

§7. The Protocol on the Rights of Women

392. On 11 July 2003 the AU, meeting in Maputo, Mozambique, adopted a Protocol to the African Charter on women's rights.[2466] Although the African Charter enshrines the principle of non-discrimination on the grounds of, *inter alia*, sex[2467] and additionally calls specifically for the elimination of every discrimination against women and the protection of women's rights,[2468] women nevertheless continued to face considerable disadvantages.[2469] A patriarchal gender order meant that women in many African countries are legally considered minors, often described as 'junior males', and routinely encountered discrimination in areas such as succession, marriage and divorce.[2470] One of the least recognized rights is the right to an equal share

the Rights and Welfare of the Child on the Standing of the African Committee of Experts on the Rights and Welfare of the Child before the African Court of Human and Peoples' Rights Request No. 002/2013 (5 Dec. 2014). However, the Court expressed the view that there was no apparent reason why ACERWC was denied this capacity which may have been a mere oversight, *ibid.*, para. 75. *See further* Mezmur, 701.

2463. Lloyd, 13.
2464. In particular, family law, Arts 158; Thompson, 438–442.
2465. ACPF, 16–19; Mezmur, 695–699.
2466. Protocol to the African Charter on Human and Peoples' Rights on the Rights of Women in Africa (11 Jul. 2003), https://www.au.int/en/treaties, Heyns & Killander, 65 (Maputo Protocol). The Protocol entered into force on 25 Nov. 2005. As of Sept. 2023, it had been ratified by forty-four States. *See* generally F. Banda, 'Blazing a Trail: The African Protocol on Women's Rights Comes into Force', *J.A.L.* 50 (2006): 72; F. Banda, 'Protocol to the African Charter on the Rights of Women in Africa', in *The African Charter on Human and Peoples' Rights: The System in Practice, 1986–2006*, Evans & Murray (eds) (Cambridge: Cambridge University Press, 2008),441–474; C. Ocran, 'The Protocol to the African Charter on Human and Peoples' Rights on the Rights of Women in Africa', *R.A.D.I.C.* 15 (2007): 147; Viljoen, International Human Rights Law in Africa, 266–277.
2467. Maputo Protocol Art. 2. *See Egyptian Initiative for Personal Rights and INTERIGHTS v. Egypt*, Communication No. 323/2006 (2011), para. 121. For national decisions *see Ephraim v. Pastory* [1990] L.R.C. (Const) 757 (Tanzania High Court) para. 10; *Dow v. Attorney-General* [1992] L.R.C. (Const) 623 (Botswana Court of Appeal).
2468. Maputo Protocol Art. 18(3).
2469. According to the Report of Mrs Halima Embarek Warzazi, Special Rapporteur, on the situation regarding the elimination of traditional practices affecting the health of women and the girl child para. 66, UN Doc. E/CN.4/2002/83, the African Charter is not considered to be gender neutral. It does not give sufficient emphasis to women's fundamental rights to liberty, equality and dignity, and reflects a paternalistic conception of women that reduces them to the status of minors.
2470. *See* Report of Ms Radhika Coomaraswamy, Special Rapporteur, on violence against women, its causes and consequences paras 65–69, UN Doc. E/CN.4/2002/83. In many African countries the husband, or other male relative, is considered the custodian of the wife's person and property,

of an inheritance. Such adverse treatment can be compounded in traditional societies by resort to customary or religious laws that confer upon women a hierarchically inferior status.[2471,2472] The Maputo Protocol is the most obvious manifestation of the OAU/AU's promotion of gender perspective and thereby seeks to promote gender equality.[2473] More specifically, it seeks to extend 'the substantive scope of the existing law', 'to improve quasi-legal and legal means of ensuring compliance', and 'to extend the use of non-legal forms of implementation'.[2474] But the Maputo Protocol may be considered ground-breaking in that it is the first regional instrument that seeks to deal with women's rights in a comprehensive manner.

393. Like the African Charter the Maputo Protocol asserts different categories of rights, first-, second-, and third-generation rights. Under it States Parties undertake to combat all forms of discrimination against women[2475] and to include the principle of sex equality in municipal law.[2476] Significantly provision is made for 'corrective and positive action'.[2477] States Parties therefore commit themselves to eliminate all practices based on ideas of the inferiority or superiority of either of the

---

Ankumah, 153–154. *See* the controversial judgment of the Supreme Court of Zimbabwe in *Magaya v. Magaya* [1999] 3 L.R.C. 35. However, in recent years many African countries have enacted or amended legislation to strengthen the rights of women, and the girl child, though traditional attitudes may still persist, *see* UN Doc. E/CN.4/2004/SR.37. In *Bhe and Others v. The Magistrate, Khayelitsha and Others* 2005 (1) SA 580 (CC) the Constitutional Court of South Africa held that the African customary rule of male primogeniture in relation to the inheritance of property discriminated against women. *See also Ephraim v. Pastory* [1990] L.R.C. (Const) 757 (Tanzania High Court) para. 42.

2471. *See Magaya v. Magaya* [1999] 3 L.R.C. 35. Note also the *cause célèbre* of Amina Lawal who in September 2003 was finally acquitted by an Islamic Court of Appeal in Nigeria on charges of adultery, UN Doc. E/CN.4/2004/66/Add.1, para. 131.

2472. In *Association pour le Progrès et la Défense des Droits des Femmes Maliennes (APDF) and the Institute for Human Rights and Development in Africa (IHRDA) v. Mali*, Application No. 046/2016 (11 May 2018) paras 114–115, the Human Rights Court held that Mali's Family Code which enshrines religious and customary law in matters of inheritance was in breach of the Maputo Protocol Art. 21(2).

2473. One of the guiding principles of the AU is the promotion of gender equality, Constitutive Act Art. 4(l). Note that the Protocol on Amendments to the Constitutive Act Art. 3, additionally seeks to 'ensure the effective participation of women in decision-making, particularly in the political, economic and socio-cultural areas' as one of the objectives of the AU. *See also* African Charter on Democracy Art. 3(6).

2474. Viljoen, International Human Rights Law in Africa, 268.

2475. Maputo Protocol Art. 2(1). *See also* African Charter on Democracy Art. 8(1). Compare UN Convention on the Elimination of Discrimination against Women Art. 4 (18 Dec. 1979) 1249 U.N.T.S. 13 (CEDAW).

2476. Maputo Protocol Art. 2(1)(a). *See also ibid.*, Art. 8 ensuring equal protection before the law. And further African Charter on Democracy Art. 8(2); CEDAW Arts 2, 4(1). Section 9 of the South African Constitution enshrines the right to equality; relying on this provision, among others, the South Gauteng High Court has held that all parents, irrespective of gender, are entitled to equal parental leave, *Van Wyk and Others v. Minister of Employment and Labour* [2023] ZAGPJHC 1213.

2477. Maputo Protocol Art. 2(1)(d). Compare CEDAW Art. 2(b). *See* Viljoen, International Human Rights Law in Africa, 272. It appears that the term 'positive action' is equivalent to positive differentiation, or affirmative action, Progress Report submitted by Mr Bossuyt, Special Rapporteur, on the concept and practice of affirmative action paras 6–8, UN Doc. E/CN.4/Sub.2/2001/15.

sexes or stereotyped roles.[2478] Other salient features of the Maputo Protocol which are particularly worthy of note include a prohibition on the execution of pregnant or nursing women,[2479] a prohibition on the exploitation and degradation of women,[2480] and the adoption of measures to tackle trafficking in women,[2481] so that forced prostitution should be covered, the elimination of practices harmful to women, including a prohibition on female genital mutilation,[2482] protection of women against all forms of violence,[2483] including sexual violence and rape which if perpetrated in times of armed conflict should be considered war crimes, genocide and/or crimes against humanity,[2484] the principle of marriage based on consent,[2485] a minimum age of 18 years for a valid marriage,[2486] thus proscribing early marriage, the encouragement of monogamy as the preferred form of marriage,[2487] the right to be regarded

2478. Maputo Protocol Art. 2(2). Compare CEDAW Art. 5(1). *See Association pour le Progrès et la Défense des Droits des Femmes Maliennes (APDF) and the Institute for Human Rights and Development in Africa (IHRDA) v. Mali*, Application No. 046/2016 (11 May 2018) para. 125.
2479. Maputo Protocol Art. 4(j). *See also* ACRWC Art. 30(e). And see American Convention on Human Rights Art. 4(5) (22 Nov. 1969), 1144 U.N.T.S. 144 (ACHR).
2480. Maputo Protocol Art. 3(3). *See also ibid.*, Art. 13(m).
2481. *Ibid.*, Art. 4(g). *See, e.g.*, CEDAW Art. 6; Protocol to Prevent, Suppress and Punish Trafficking in Persons, Especially Women and Children (15 Nov. 2000), UN General Assembly Res. 55/25, which reinforces the Convention for the Suppression of the Traffic in Persons and of the Exploitation of the Prostitution of Others (21 Mar. 1950) 96 U.N.T.S. 271.
2482. Maputo Protocol Art. 5(b). *See* Joint General Comment on Female Genital Mutilation (2023) paras 28-32. It has been stated *supra* para. 384, that many African States are legislating to prohibit and criminalize this practice.
2483. Maputo Protocol Arts 3(4), 4(2) and 5(d). *See Egyptian Initiative for Personal Rights and INTERIGHTS v. Egypt*, Communication No. 323/2006 (2011), paras 142–153. *See also* UN Convention on the Elimination of Discrimination against Women (18 Dec. 1979); Inter-American Convention on the Prevention, Punishment and Eradication of Violence Against Women (9 June 1994) (Convention of Belem do Para) I.L.M. 33 (1994): 1534; European Convention on preventing and combating violence against women and domestic violence Arts 3(a), 4 (11 May 2011), C.E.T.S. No. 210 (Istanbul Convention).
There appears to be a strong correlation between violence against women and HIV/AIDS, Report of Yakin Ertürk, Special Rapporteur, on violence against women, UN Doc. E/CN.4/2005/72.
2484. Maputo Protocol Art. 11(3). *See also* Kampala Convention Arts 7(5)(f),9(1)(d). Compare Rome Statute Arts 7(1)(g) and 8(2)(xxii) and (2)(e)(vi). *See Prosecutor v. Akayesu* 37 I.L.M. 1399 (1998) para. 31, where the ICTR found as established a campaign of systematic rapes and other forms of sexual violence perpetrated by extremist Hutu militias. *See further Prosecutor v. Furundzija* 38 I.L.M. 317 (1999) paras 165–186 (ICTY). In *Prosecutor v. Charles Ghankay Taylor*, SCSL-03-1-T, Trial Chamber II, Judgment of 26 Apr. 2012, the accused was found guilty of aiding and abetting and planning the crimes of rape, sexual slavery and other crimes of a sexual nature. These findings were upheld by the Appeals Chamber, *Prosecutor v. Charles Ghankay Taylor*, SCSL-03-1-A, Judgment of 26 Sep. 2013.
2485. Maputo Protocol Art. 6(a). *See Association pour le Progrès et la Défense des Droits des Femmes Maliennes (APDF) and the Institute for Human Rights and Development in Africa (IHRDA) v. Mali*, Application No. 046/2016 (11 May 2018) paras 89-95.
2486. *Ibid.*, Art. 6(b). *See also* African Charter on the Rights of the Child Art. 21(2). The practice of early marriage is prevalent in parts of Africa, UN Doc. E/CN.4/Sub.2/1991/6, 7. *See further supra* para. 393.
2487. Maputo Protocol Art. 6(c). Polygamy, associated both with customary practices and Islam, is prevalent in many African countries. Note *Bhewa v. Government of Mauritius* (1990) MR 79, where the Supreme Court of Mauritius upheld the exclusive status of monogamous marriages.

as equal partners in marriage,[2488] the right of a married woman to retain and use her maiden name,[2489] the right to own and administer property,[2490] the right to divorce, separation or annulment,[2491] reciprocal rights and responsibilities with respect to the children upon divorce or separation,[2492] equitable sharing of joint property of the marriage,[2493] a widow's right to her children[2494] and to remarry,[2495] a widow's right to live in the matrimonial home[2496] and to an equitable share in the inheritance of her husband's property,[2497] a woman's right to participate equally in the political process,[2498] rights to education and training,[2499] employment rights, including equal remuneration,[2500] and reproductive rights,[2501] including termination of pregnancy in certain circumstances, for example, in cases of rape or incest, or where the mother's health or life is endangered.[2502] Vulnerable groups, such as elderly women, women with disabilities, and women in distress, are entitled to special measures of protection.[2503] The Human Rights Court has therefore held that vagrancy laws commit multiple violations of the rights of poor and marginalized women, including women's right to dignity, non-discrimination and equality.[2504]

2488. Maputo Protocol Rights Art. 6.
2489. *Ibid.*, Art. 6(f). *See Müller and Engelhard v. Namibia*, Communication No. 919/2000, UN Doc A/57/40, Vol II, Annex IX, CC, where the UN HRC found that differentiation on the basis of sex relating to the right of persons to assume the surname of the spouse on marriage amounted to discrimination in violation of ICCPR Art. 26.
2490. Maputo Protocol Art. 6(j). *See further supra*, paras 265, 393. But *see Rabah v. Mauritania,* Communication No. 197/97, 17th Activity Report, 2003–2004.
2491. Maputo Protocol Art. 7(b).
2492. *Ibid.*, Art. 7(c). *See also* Charter on the Rights of the Child Arts 18(2) and 19(2).
2493. Maputo Protocol Art. 7(d).
2494. *Ibid.*, Art. 20(b). *See also* Charter on the Rights of the Child Art. 18(2).
2495. Maputo Protocol Art. 20(c).
2496. *Ibid.*, Art. 21(a).
2497. *Ibid.* Customary law often adversely affects the woman's rights to succession, *see further supra* paras 265, 393.
2498. Maputo Protocol Art. 9. *See also* Protocol on Amendments to the Constitutive Act Art. 3(i), and African Charter on Democracy Arts 2(11), 3(6) and 29.
2499. Maputo Protocol Art. 12. *See also* African Charter on Democracy Art. 43(2).
2500. Maputo Protocol Art. 13(b). Equal opportunities in education has traditionally been problematic in many African countries, *see* G.J. Naldi, *The Organization of African Unity* (London & New York: Mansell, 1989), 195, n. 223.
2501. Maputo Protocol Art. 14.
2502. *Ibid.*, Art. 14(2)(c).
2503. *Ibid.*, Arts 22, 23, 24. In *Request for Advisory Opinion by the Pan African Lawyers Union (PALU) on the Compatibility of Vagrancy Laws with the African Charter on Human and Peoples' Rights* African Court of Human and Peoples' Rights, Request No. 001/2018, Judgment (4 Dec. 2020), para. 137, the Human Rights Court stated that Maputo Protocol Art. 24 'requires States to create an environment where poor and marginalised women can fully enjoy all their human rights.' Note Protocol on the Rights of Persons with Disabilities in Africa Art. 27 which lists an extensive elaboration of the rights of women with disabilities, requiring State Parties to ensure that the barriers that hinder the participation of women with disabilities in society are eliminated.
2504. *Request for Advisory Opinion by the Pan African Lawyers Union (PALU) on the Compatibility of Vagrancy Laws with the African Charter on Human and Peoples' Rights*, African Court of Human and Peoples' Rights, Request No. 001/2018, Judgment (4 Dec. 2020), para. 138.

394. Although no provision is made for a dedicated enforcement or regulatory mechanism,[2505] the African Commission on Human and Peoples' Rights has a supervisory role in that States Parties must account for the measures taken to realize the rights recognized by the Protocol in their periodic reports.[2506] Significantly the Maputo Protocol can be interpreted and applied by the African Court on Human and Peoples' Rights.[2507] A feature is the requirement on States Parties to provide appropriate remedies to women whose rights have been violated.[2508] Another important element is the obligation upon States Parties to implement the protocol at national level.[2509]

395. The Maputo Protocol seeks to bridge the 'gender gap'. In terms of substantive rights, the protocol is comprehensive and progressive in many respects and generally seems to reflect current developments in international human rights law, enshrined in documents such as UN Convention on the Elimination of Discrimination Against Women (CEDAW) and the Beijing Platform for Action.[2510] But it could also be considered revolutionary because it challenges many entrenched traditional, cultural, societal and religious values, although some of the more radical proposals submitted in the draft did not survived unscathed. States Parties are required to implement appropriate national measures to further the rights of women. The Maputo Protocol requires extensive law reform in many African countries, and while progress has been made in this regard in a number of countries women are still very vulnerable in others. Furthermore, the political will to transform entrenched attitudes must be found. The plight of women living with HIV/AIDS also requires urgent practical action. However, the fact that it is now in force should provide an added incentive.

§8. The Protocol on the Rights of Older Persons

396. Until recent times the rights of older persons in international law were set out in a number of soft law documents. In 1991 the UN General Assembly had adopted a resolution, the UN Principles for Older Persons, setting out a number of basic principles to which States should adhere.[2511] In 2002 the Madrid Plan of Action on Ageing became the foremost standard-setter in the field, and, *inter alia*,

2505. Compare the Committee on the Elimination of Discrimination against Women established under CEDAW which has a supervisory capacity, receiving national reports. An Optional Protocol (10 Dec. 1999), 38 I.L.M. 763 (1999), enables the Committee to consider individual petitions and to investigate reports of systematic violations.
2506. Maputo Protocol Art. 26(1). *See further* Viljoen, International Human Rights Law in Africa, 275–276.
2507. Maputo Protocol Art. 27.
2508. *Ibid.*, Art. 25.
2509. *Ibid.*, Art. 26(1).
2510. According to Murray, Human Rights in Africa, 151, the Maputo Protocol goes further than CEDAW in terms of substance. *See also* Viljoen, International Human Rights Law in Africa, 271–272, who additionally argues that the Maputo Protocol brings crucial 'specificity' to a number of areas. *See* Viljoen, International Human Rights Law in Africa, 272–273.
2511. UN General Assembly Res. 46/91.

addressed ageing issues from a human rights perspective.[2512] However, it was under the auspices of the OAS that the first treaty on the rights of older persons was adopted, in 2015.[2513]

397. An ageing population poses its own set of challenges to Africa.[2514] Despite various initiatives older persons cannot be said to have been at the forefront of vulnerable groups that the African Charter on Human and Peoples' Rights sought to protect in any meaningful way.[2515] The African Charter makes provision for the rights of the aged in a generalized way, stating that they have the right to 'special measures of protection in keeping with their physical or moral needs.'[2516] A similar provision can be found in Article 22 of the Protocol on Women's Rights. In addition, it seems that the principle of non-discrimination contained in Article 2 of the African Charter extends to the aged as they come within the scope of 'other status'. As with other vulnerable groups such as women and children it was felt in time that the rights of the aged would be better protected through an instrument that specifically addressed their needs and concerns. Accordingly, in 2016 the AU adopted a Protocol on the Rights of Older Persons.[2517]

398. The Protocol sets out a framework of the obligations of States regarding the rights of older persons. It enables States Parties to recognize, promote and protect older persons 'rights. Older persons are defined as persons aged 60 years and above[2518] and extends to persons with disabilities.[2519] The Protocol is framed in terms of duties and responsibilities upon States Parties which are required to implement appropriate national measures to further older persons 'rights.[2520] States will be required to adopt affirmative measures and allocate resources, for example, in relation to social security. The Protocol requires programmes that raise awareness on ageing and prepare persons for the challenges of old age.[2521] States Parties are placed under a general duty to gather and analyse national data and develop a national mechanism with the task of integrating and implementing older persons' rights in national policies and legislation.[2522]

2512. Madrid International Plan of Action on Ageing, http://www.un.org/en/events/pastevents/pdfs/Madrid_plan.pdf.
2513. Inter-American Convention on Protecting the Human Rights of Older Persons (A-70) (15 Jun. 2015), 55 I.L.M. 989 (2016).
2514. *See* I. Doron, B. Spannier & O. Lazar, 'The Rights of Older Persons Within the African Union', *Elder Law Review* 10 (2016): 1.
2515. *Ibid.*
2516. African Charter Art. 18(4).
2517. Protocol to the African Charter on Human and Peoples' Rights on the Rights of Older Persons in Africa (31 Jan. 2016), https://www.au.int/en/treaties, Heyns & Killander, 75. The Protocol, not yet in force, requires fifteen ratifications to enter into force, Art. 26(1). By Sept. 2023 it had been ratified by twelve States.
2518. Protocol on Older Persons Art. 1.
2519. Protocol on Older Persons Art. 13. Note the Protocol on the Rights of Persons with Disabilities in Africa Art. 30.
2520. Protocol on Older Persons Art. 2(1).
2521. *Ibid.*, Art. 19.
2522. *Ibid.*, Art. 21.

399. The Protocol enshrines a number of rights which States Parties must either protect or provide. A general obligation upon States Parties is the necessity to prohibit discrimination against older persons and eliminate social and cultural stereotypes.[2523] However, no definition of age discrimination is provided which might have proved useful. Protection from gender discrimination against older women is a specific requirement, however.[2524] Discrimination against older persons relating to access to employment must be removed.[2525] However, the Protocol has nothing to say on guaranteeing the same rights and benefits for all workers for equal work, regardless of age. Another general obligation is that of equal protection before the law and access to justice.[2526] This extends to the provision of legal assistance to protect their rights.[2527]

400. More specifically, the Protocol seeks to guarantee the autonomy of older persons by ensuring their rights to make decisions regarding their well-being without undue interference from other persons or entities and to appoint a party of their choice to carry out their wishes and instructions.[2528] In the case of incapacity older persons are to be provided with assistance in order to make decisions in their best interests.[2529] States must ensure that persons who retire have adequate pensions and other social security and must additionally ensure some form of universal social protection is in place for those who may not have contributed to any social security scheme.[2530] In addition, States should ensure that older persons can access buildings and public transport.[2531]

401. With respect to care and support the Protocol acknowledges the role of family members through the provision of incentives for family carers.[2532] It also seeks the promotion and strengthening of traditional support systems to enhance the ability of families and communities to care for older persons.[2533] Residential care should also be an affordable option for older persons.[2534] However, there is no explicit mention of long-term care. But the needs of older persons in palliative care are not overlooked.[2535] The Protocol does not in fact provide for a right to health as such, that is guaranteed by the African Charter, but it does oblige States Parties to

2523. *Ibid.*, Art. 3.
2524. *Ibid.*, Art. 9(1) Protocol on Older Persons. *See also* Maputo Protocol Art. 2(1). The importance of gender equality has been stressed by the European Court of Human Rights, *see Carvalho Pinto de Sousa Morais v. Portugal*, European Court of Human Rights, Appl. No. 17484/15, Judgment of 25 Jul. 2017.
2525. Protocol on Older Persons Art. 6(1).
2526. *Ibid.*, Art. 4(1).
2527. *Ibid.*, Art. 4(2).
2528. *Ibid.*, Art. 5(1).
2529. *Ibid.*, Art. 5(2).
2530. *Ibid.*, Art. 7(1)–(2).
2531. *Ibid.*, Art. 18.
2532. *Ibid.*, Art. 10(1).
2533. *Ibid.*, Art. 10(2).
2534. *Ibid.*, Art. 11(1).
2535. *Ibid.*, Art. 11(3).

grant older persons access to health services.[2536] In order to foster a healthy environment older persons should have access to education, cultural programmes, leisure and sports.[2537] Older persons taking care of vulnerable children should be provided with financial, material and other support but this support is limited to those who are 'indigent'.[2538]

402. Older women are deemed in need of special protection. Protection from discrimination has been previously noted but it also extends to property and land rights, and inheritance rights.[2539] Older women should be protected from violence and sexual abuse,[2540] including harmful traditional practices.[2541] Protection from violence is not defined but it can take many different forms and it is submitted that the Protocol should have made it clear that older persons, of either sex since men can also be at risk, have a right to a life free of violence of any kind.[2542]

403. The plight of older persons in conflict and disaster situations is not overlooked and the Protocol seeks to ensure that they are a prioritized group in such situations.[2543]

404. Inspired by traditional cultural values and in keeping with the African Charter, the Protocol incorporates a short list of duties owed by older persons towards their 'families, communities, the wider society, the state and the international community'.[2544] These responsibilities include mentoring and passing on knowledge to the younger generations and playing a role in mediation and conflict resolution.

405. In terms of implementation, States Parties are under an express obligation to implement the Protocol and they must give account for the measures taken to realize the rights recognized therein in their periodic reports to the African Commission on Human and Peoples' Rights.[2545] Both the African Commission and the African Court on Human and Peoples' Rights have the mandate to interpret and settle disputes over the Protocol.[2546] There is no discrete committee.

406. The Protocol on the Rights of Older Persons is the second regional instrument on this subject and in the absence of any global treaty is especially welcome. However, in some respects it seems like a missed opportunity. It cannot be described as a comprehensive document; it is not as detailed as the Inter-American Convention on the Human Rights of Older Persons. This may be due to the fact that the

2536. *Ibid.*, Art. 15(1)–(2).
2537. *Ibid.*, Arts 16 and 17.
2538. *Ibid.*, Art 12.
2539. *Ibid.*, Art. 9(2)–(3). *See also* Maputo Protocol Art. 21(a).
2540. Protocol on Older Persons Art. 9(1).
2541. *Ibid.*, Art. 8. *See also* Maputo Protocol Art. 5(b).
2542. Compare Inter-American Convention on Protecting the Human Rights of Older Persons Art. 9.
2543. Protocol on Older Persons Art. 14.
2544. *Ibid.*, Art. 20.
2545. *Ibid.*, Art. 22(1).
2546. *Ibid.*, Art. 22(2)–(4).

Protocol is a framework treaty that allows considerable latitude to States Parties as to how they achieve and implement their obligations. Neither are the rights protected in the Protocol as extensive as those in the Inter-American Convention on the Human Rights of Older Persons. For instance, the Protocol does not explicitly stipulate protection of the right to life and dignity in old age, a right not to be subjected to inhuman or degrading treatment, a right to give free and informed consent in medical matters, a right to personal liberty, a right to privacy and intimacy or a right to housing. Since States Parties are under an obligation to incorporate the UN Principles for Older Persons into national law,[2547] some of these rights, such as dignity, may be indirectly applicable but there is no guarantee in so far as other rights which do not feature therein. A potential weakness is evident. However, a positive attribute is that the Protocol contains a safeguard clause and must not therefore derogate from relevant 'instruments', which seems to be a reference to international treaties, realizing rights for older persons.[2548]

§9. The Protocol on the Rights of Persons with Disabilities

The African Charter on Human and Peoples' Rights contains a sweeping statement on the rights of persons with disabilities, providing that they have the right to 'special measures of protection in keeping with their physical or moral needs.'[2549] Persons with disabilities, be it children, women, older persons, have not been overlooked either.[2550] Nevertheless, it was felt that the special needs and problems faced by persons with disabilities, especially women and children, could be better handled by a discrete treaty. In 2018 a Protocol on the Rights of Persons with Disabilities was accordingly adopted.[2551]

407. The objective of the Protocol on Persons with Disabilities is to promote, protect and ensure the full and equal enjoyment of human rights by all persons with

2547. *Ibid.*, Art. 2(1).
2548. *Ibid.*, Art. 24(1).
2549. African Charter Art. 18(4). The African Commission on Human and Peoples' Rights has held that the rights guaranteed by the African Charter are equally available to persons with disabilities, *Purohit and Moore v. The Gambia*, Communication No. 241/2001, 16th Activity Report 2002–2003, paras 57–59.
2550. The ACRWC provides in greater detail that children with disabilities are entitled to special measures of protection, ACRWC Art. 13. *See* to a similar effect Maputo Protocol Art. 23; African Youth Charter Art. 24; Protocol on Older Persons Art. 13.
2551. Protocol to the African Charter on Human and Peoples' Rights on the Rights of Persons with Disabilities in Africa (29 Jan. 2018), Heyns & Killander, 83 (Protocol on Persons with Disabilities). As of Sept. 2023 the Protocol on Persons with Disabilities had been ratified by ten States. It shares features in common with the UN Convention on the Rights of Persons with Disabilities (13 Dec. 2006) 2515 U.N.T.S. 3 (CRPD), and the Inter-American Convention on the Elimination of All Forms of Discrimination Against Persons With Disabilities (7 Jun. 1999) (A-65). *See* K. Appiagyei-Atua, 'A Comparative analysis of the United Nations Convention on the Rights of Persons with Disability and the African Draft Protocol on the Rights of Persons with Disabilities', *Law, Development and Democracy* (2017) 21: 153. Only four African States have not ratified the CRPD.

disabilities and to ensure respect for their human dignity.[2552] Indeed, respect for human dignity, the worth of every person, and individual autonomy, the freedom to make reasonable life choices, are core principles of the Protocol.[2553] The Protocol defines persons with disabilities to 'include those who have physical, mental, psycho-social, intellectual, neurological, developmental or other sensory impairments which in interaction with environmental, attitudinal or other barriers hinder their full and effective participation in society on an equal basis with others.'[2554] It recognizes rights and freedoms for persons with disabilities but provides for duties as well. In this regard, the Protocol recognizes that persons with disabilities have duties on an equal basis with other persons as set out in the African Charter. However, States Parties must ensure that persons with disabilities are rendered assistance and support, including reasonable accommodations, in order to perform such duties.[2555] States parties assume a number of responsibilities in order to implement the Protocol, including legislative, administrative and other appropriate national measures, including the adoption of affirmative measures[2556] and allocation of adequate resources.[2557] In addition, the Protocol advocates the creation of an AU Commission Advisory Council on Disability to facilitate implementation.[2558]

408. The Protocol on Persons with Disabilities operates on the basis of a number of general principles,[2559] including non-discrimination,[2560] full participation and inclusion in society,[2561] equality of opportunity,[2562] accessibility,[2563] and the best interests of the child.[2564] The rights enshrined in the Protocol include non-discrimination,[2565] the right to equality and equal recognition before the law,[2566] the right to life,[2567] the right to liberty and security of person,[2568] freedom from torture or cruel, inhuman or degrading treatment or punishment,[2569] which in this context includes the right not to be subjected without free, prior and informed consent to

2552. Protocol on Persons with Disabilities Art. 2. Compare CRPD Art. 1.
2553. Protocol on Persons with Disabilities Art. 3(a).
2554. *Ibid.*, Art. 1. This definition is broader than that of the CRPD 1(2).
2555. Protocol on Persons with Disabilities Art. 31.
2556. *Ibid.*, Art. 4.
2557. *Ibid.*, Art. 4(i). By way of contrast the CRPD refers to 'available resources', Art. 4(2).
2558. Protocol on Persons with Disabilities Art. 33(d).
2559. *Ibid.*, Art. 3. Compare CRPD Art. 3 which is virtually identical.
2560. Protocol on Persons with Disabilities Art.3(b). *See also ibid.*, Art. 27(d) seeking to ensure that women and children with disabilities are protected from discrimination based on disability.
2561. *Ibid.*, Art. 3(c).
2562. *Ibid.*, Art. 3(e).
2563. *Ibid.*, Art. 3(f).
2564. *Ibid.*, Art. 3(i).
2565. *Ibid.*, Art. 5. Interestingly, it is acknowledged that parents, children and spouses of people with disabilities can experience discrimination by association, *ibid.*, Art. 5(2)(c).
2566. *Ibid.*, Arts 6, 7.
2567. *Ibid.*, Art. 8.
2568. *Ibid.*, Art. 9.
2569. *Ibid.*, Art. 10. Although the Protocol declares that persons with disabilities must be protected from all forms of exploitation, violence and abuse, *ibid.*, Art. 10(2)(d), it is not as detailed as the comparable provision in the CRPD, Art. 16.

medical or scientific experimentation or to sterilization or other invasive procedure,[2570] the right to access justice,[2571] which includes ensuring legal assistance, including legal aid,[2572] the right to live in the community,[2573] accessibility,[2574] the right to participate in political and public life,[2575] the right to self-representation,[2576] and the right to freedom of expression and opinion,[2577] and the right to marry and a family,[2578] participate in sports, recreation and culture, among others. Special provision is made for the rights of children, women and older persons with disabilities,[2579] more detailed than the comparable provisions in the CRPD.[2580]

409. The Protocol on Persons with Disabilities contains a number of second-generation rights. Included are the right to education,[2581] the right to health, habilitation and rehabilitation,[2582] the right to work,[2583] the right to an adequate standard of living,[2584] and the right to participate in sports, recreation and culture.[2585]

As with other such treaties, the Protocol on Persons with Disabilities contains provisions that are best considered in an African context. Accordingly, persons with disabilities are to be protected from harmful practices and superstitions which are to be eliminated.[2586] This includes witchcraft,[2587] abandonment and, shamefully, ritual killings.[2588] On education, the Protocol provides that the education of persons with disabilities shall be directed to supporting positive African values.[2589] On habilitation and rehabilitation, the Protocol urges the design and production of assistive devices and equipment adapted to local conditions.[2590]

The Protocol on Persons with Disabilities stands in comparison with the CRPD. As is to be expected, there are differences of emphasis. To take one example, the emphasis in Article 14 of the Protocol is on 'living in the community', whereas the

---

2570. Protocol on Persons with Disabilities Art. 10(2)(b), (c). *See also ibid.*, Art. 27(k). The CRPD does not mention invasive procedures.
2571. Protocol on Persons with Disabilities Art. 13.
2572. *Ibid.*, Art. 13(2).
2573. *Ibid.*, Art. 14.
2574. *Ibid.*, Art. 15. Compare CRPD Art. 9 which is more detailed. *See also ibid.*, Art. 20 on personal mobility.
2575. Protocol on Persons with Disabilities Art. 21.
2576. *Ibid.*, Art. 22.
2577. *Ibid.*, Art. 23.
2578. *Ibid.*, Art. 26.
2579. *Ibid.*, Arts 27, 28, 30.
2580. CRPD Arts 6, 7.
2581. Protocol on Persons with Disabilities Art. 16.
2582. *Ibid.*, Arts 17, 18.
2583. *Ibid.*, Art. 19.
2584. *Ibid.*, Art. 20.
2585. *Ibid.*, Art. 25.
2586. *Ibid.*, Art. 11(1). *See also ibid.*, Art. 4(d).
2587. *Ibid.*, Arts 11(1), 30(2)(e).
2588. Ritual killings refer to killings motivated by cultural, religious or superstitious beliefs, mostly associated with albinism, that a body or body parts has medicinal value, supernatural powers or brings good luck, *ibid.*, Preamble.
2589. Protocol on Persons with Disabilities Art. 16(4)(d).
2590. *Ibid.*, Art. 18(d)(e).

Article 19 CRPD stresses 'Living independently and being included in the community'. In this provision, the Protocol further provides for persons who require intensive support to have access to caregivers and respite services.[2591] Then, the Protocol includes rights which the CRPD omits altogether or possibly includes by implication. For example, on access to justice, the Protocol requires States to ensure legal assistance, including legal aid to persons with disabilities, on which the CRPD is silent.[2592] Unlike the Protocol, the CRPD does not contain specific provisions on youth or older persons with disabilities.[2593] And the Protocol is more far-reaching on the rights of women and girls with disabilities. However, at the same time, the CRPD addresses certain issues in greater detail than the Protocol or that are omitted altogether. Examples include the articles on accessibility, habilitation and rehabilitation, the right to an adequate standard of living, and education. But the Protocol does contain a safeguard clause. This is important in light of the instances where the Protocol seems to offer a lower level of protection than the CRPD. It does not therefore derogate from 'the principles and values contained in other relevant instruments for the realisation of the rights of persons covered' by it.[2594]

§10. The Protocol on Social Protection and Social Security

410. The second-generation right to social security is recognized in international and regional human rights instruments such as the ICESCR,[2595] the ILO Convention on Social Security (Minimum Standards) (No. 102),[2596] the Protocol on Economic, Social, and Cultural Rights (Protocol of San Salvador),[2597] the European Social Charter,[2598] and the EU Charter of Fundamental Rights.[2599] But the African Charter on Human and Peoples' Rights is not one of the instruments guaranteeing a right to social security or protection as such, although the African Commission on Human and Peoples' Rights has expressed the view that the State may need to provide some form of social security in order to fulfil its human rights obligations.[2600] Nevertheless, this right can be found in subsequent protocols, such as the Protocol

2591. *Ibid.*, Art. 14(2)(b).
2592. *Ibid.*, Art. 13(4).
2593. *Ibid.*, Arts 29, 30.
2594. *Ibid.*, Art. 36(1).
2595. International Covenant on Economic Social and Cultural Rights Art. 9 (16 Dec. 1966), 999 U.N.T.S. 3. *See also* UDHR Arts 22, 25, UN General Assembly Res. 217A (III). The right to social security is also enshrined in other UN instruments, *see* ILO, *Building social protection systems: International standards and human rights instruments* (Geneva: ILO, 2021) 2. The ICESCR has exerted a strong influence on the African Charter, M. Ssenyonjo, 'The Influence of the International Covenant on Economic, Social and Cultural Rights in Africa', *N.I.L.R.* 64 (2017): 259.
2596. ILO Convention on Social Security (Minimum Standards) (No. 102) (28 Jun. 1952) C102.
2597. Additional Protocol to the American Convention on Human Rights in theArea of Economic, Social, and Cultural Rights Art. 9 (17 Nov. 1988) OAS Treaty Series No. 69.
2598. European Social Charter (Revised) Art. 12 (3 May 1996) ETS No. 163.
2599. Charter of Fundamental Rights of the European Union Art. 34 (12 Dec. 2007) O.J. 2010/C 83/02.
2600. *The Social and Economic Rights Action Center and the Center for Economic and Social Rights v. Nigeria*, Communication No. 155/96, 15th Activity Report 2001–2002, para. 47.

on Women's Rights,[2601] the Protocol on the Rights of Older Persons[2602] and the Protocol on the Rights of Persons with Disabilities.[2603] The latter developments appear to have been inspired in part by the Goals and Priorities of Agenda 2063 which envisages social security and social protection as a priority areas (Aspiration 1). In furtherance of this goal the AU adopted the Protocol to Social Protection and Social Security in 2022 (Protocol to Social Protection).[2604]

The Protocol to Social Protection sets out a framework of State obligations concerning the right to social security, framed in terms of duties and responsibilities upon States Parties which are required to implement appropriate national measures to further this right. Absent accepted definitions,[2605] it should initially be noted that while the terms social security or social protection are used interchangeably in many legal instruments or cover a wide category of measures such as social assistance, social insurance, or other measures designed to secure social protection such as access to health care, the Protocol to Social Protection draws a distinction between such measures and provides definitions thereof. 'Social Protection' is described as 'public and private, or to mixed public and private measures', including all forms of social security, 'aimed at supporting and ensuring a minimum standard of livelihood and access to essential social health services and care for all people'.[2606] 'Social Assistance', which includes universal payments, refers to a form of social security, funded from government revenue, providing assistance in cash or in kind to persons who lack the means to support themselves and their dependants.[2607] 'Social Insurance' is defined as 'a contributory form of social security designed to protect income earners and their dependants against a reduction or loss of income'.[2608] And 'Social Security', included in the social protection concept, 'comprises social assistance, social insurance and social allowances, and refers to public and private, or to mixed public and private measures, designed to protect individuals and families against income insecurity caused by contingencies such as unemployment, employment injury, maternity, sickness, poor health, disability, old age, maintenance of children and death of a family member'.[2609]

According to the UN Committee on Economic, Social and Cultural Rights (CESCR), the right to social security comprises four key elements, which are: Availability (a social security system must be available and in place to ensure that benefits are provided for relevant social risks and contingencies); adequacy (benefits

2601. Protocol to the African Charter on Human and Peoples' Rights on the Rights of Women in Africa Art. 13(f) (11 Jul. 2003) (Maputo Protocol).
2602. Protocol to the African Charter on Human and Peoples' Rights on the Rights of Older Persons in Africa Art. 7 (31 Jan. 2016), https://www.au.int/en/treaties.
2603. Protocol to the African Charter on Human and Peoples' Rights on the Rights of Persons with Disabilities in Africa, Art. 20(2)(b) (9 Jan. 2018), https://www.au.int/en/treaties, commits States Parties to ensure access by persons with disabilities to social protection programmes.
2604. Protocol to the African Charter on Human and Peoples' Rights on the Rights of Citizens to Social protection and Social Security (6 Feb. 2022), Heyns & Killander, 100. No ratifications.
2605. S. G. Zamani & A. A. Evin, 'The Right To Social Security Under International Law ', *Mediterranean Journal of Social Sciences* 7 (2016): 45, 48.
2606. Protocol to Social Protection Art. 1(1)(p).
2607. *Ibid.*, Art. 1(1)(n).
2608. *Ibid.*, Art. 1(1)(o).
2609. *Ibid.*, Art. 1(1)(q).

must be adequate in amount and duration so that everyone may realize his or her rights to family protection and assistance, an adequate standard of living and adequate access to health care); accessibility (including coverage, i.e. all persons should be covered by the social security system, especially the most disadvantaged and marginalized groups, without discrimination; eligibility' i.e. qualifying conditions for benefits must be reasonable, proportionate and transparent; affordability, i.e. the costs associated with making contributions must be affordable for all; non-discrimination and equality, including gender equality.[2610] According to the UN this means that 'social protection systems are established and defined by law, supported by a long-term strategy, and reinforced by an appropriate and adequately funded long-term institutional framework'.[2611] A question that arises is whether the Protocol to Social Protection meets these standards.

In accordance with the Protocol to Social Protection, States Parties undertake to guarantee the right to social protection and social security.[2612] They must make 'continual progress' regarding the realization of these rights and obligations, and 'the taking of immediate steps within the means of States Parties towards the full realisation' of these rights and obligations.[2613] Each State Party must develop an integrated and comprehensive social protection system, which includes ensuring meaningful coverage in terms of social insurance schemes, social assistance measures and social services; and protecting against special and collective risks, including political conflict, climate change and natural disasters.[2614] It is interesting to note that the latter extend beyond the recommendations of the CESCR. The Protocol provides for a right to social protection which must be 'available, accessible, adequate, affordable and transparent.'[2615] States Parties must therefore establish and maintain a system of social protection;[2616] provide a minimum package of essential social protection, at least covering basic needs;[2617] and ensure that every citizen who has insufficient means of subsistence to support themselves and their dependants is entitled to adequate social assistance and other services provided by the State.[2618] With regard to social insurance, States Parties must legislate to compel all employers to enrol all employees into social insurance schemes;[2619] establish health insurance schemes that cover all the population groups;[2620] and put in place measures that enable everyone to prepare for retirement.[2621] The Protocol makes provision for a number of other benefits.[2622] These include health care and sickness

2610. CESCR, 'General Comment No. 19: The right to social security (art. 9)' E/C.12/GC/19.
2611. Report of the Secretary-General, Question of the realization in all countries of economic, social and cultural rights A/HRC/49/28, para. 19.
2612. *Ibid.*, Art. 2.
2613. *Ibid.*, Art. 2(c).
2614. *Ibid.*, Art. 2(g).
2615. *Ibid.*, Art. 3(a).
2616. *Ibid.*, Art. 3(b)(ii).
2617. *Ibid.*, Art. 3(b)(iii).
2618. *Ibid.*, Art. 3(b)(iv).
2619. *Ibid.*, Art. 4(a).
2620. *Ibid.*, Art. 4(b).
2621. *Ibid.*, Art. 4(c). *See also* Protocol on Older Persons Art. 19(2).
2622. Compare ILO Convention concerning Minimum Standards of Social Security (No. 102) (28 Jun. 1952) 210 *U.N.T.S.* 131.

benefits,[2623] maternity benefits,[2624] social protection schemes aimed at children,[2625] occupational health, safety and employment injury benefits,[2626] and death and survivors benefits.[2627] Other measures are to be adopted in the longer term. It thus calls upon States Parties to put in place unemployment benefits,[2628] retirement and other old age benefits,[2629] social protection schemes for persons with disabilities,[2630] and social protection and after care services for ex-prisoners, drug users and substance abusers.[2631] It should be observed that the private sector also has responsibilities in this regard, and therefore States Parties must ensure that the private sector provides and implements social protection programmes.[2632]

The Protocol to Social Protection must apply to all citizens,[2633] which includes the family unit.[2634] Vulnerable groups are specifically highlighted. These include groups such as refugees and other displaced persons,[2635] women and girls,[2636] children, adolescents and youth,[2637] older persons,[2638] and persons with disabilities.[2639] But the Protocol also applies to non-citizens in certain circumstances, taking into account the international obligations of States Parties, and the situation of migrants generally and certain migrant groups specifically considered vulnerable groups.[2640] Accordingly, migrant workers should be provided with social protection benefits.[2641] Additionally, so should displaced persons, unaccompanied children, asylum seekers, refugees and stateless persons.[2642] It should also be observed that States Parties must abide by the principle of non-discrimination so that every individual is entitled to these measures of support without distinction of any kind, such as age, disability, race, ethnic group, colour, sex, language, religion, political or any

2623. Protocol to Social Protection Art. 14.
2624. *Ibid.*, Art. 13.
2625. *Ibid.*, Art. 11(b).
2626. *Ibid.*, Art. 15.
2627. *Ibid.*, Art. 16.
2628. *Ibid.*, Art. 6(b).
2629. *Ibid.*, Art. 10. *See also* Protocol on Older Persons Art. 7(1), (2).
2630. *Ibid.*, Art. 12(a).
2631. *Ibid.*, Art. 17(a).
2632. *Ibid.*, Art. 23(e).
2633. *Ibid.*, Art. 2(e), i.e. a national of a Member State, *ibid.*, Art. 1(f).
2634. *Ibid.*, Art. 9. Compare Protocol of San Salvador Art. 15; European Social Charter (Revised) Art. 16; EU Charter of Fundamental Rights Art. 33(1).
2635. Protocol to Social Protection Art. 7.
2636. Protocol to Social Protection Art. 8. Compare UN Convention on the Elimination of Discrimination against Women Art. 11(1)(e) (18 Dec. 1979) 1249 U.N.T.S. 13 (CEDAW).
2637. Protocol to Social Protection Art. 11. *See also* Convention on the Rights of the Child Art. 26 (20 Nov. 1989) 2515 U.N.T.S. 3.
2638. Protocol to Social Protection Art. 10. *See also* Protocol on the Rights of Older Persons Art. 7. Compare Protocol of San Salvador Art. 17; European Social Charter (Revised) Art. 23.
2639. Protocol to Social Protection Art. 12. Compare Protocol of San Salvador Art. 18; Convention on the Rights of Persons with Disabilities Art. 28(2) (13 Dec. 2006) 1577 U.N.T.S. 3.
2640. *Ibid.*, Art. 2(f).
2641. *Ibid.*, Art. 7(a). *See also* International Convention on the Protection of the Rights of All Migrant Workers and Members of their Families Art. 27 (18 Dec. 1990) 2220 U.N.T.S. 3.
2642. Protocol to Social Protection Art. 7(d), (e).

other opinion, national and social origin, fortune, birth or other status.[2643] The Protocol proceeds to apply the principle of non-discrimination to specific, often vulnerable groups. It accordingly provides for gender equality by committing States Parties to abolish all gender-based discriminatory laws, customs and practices in their respective social protection systems.[2644] Women should also be protected against discrimination and dismissal in relation to maternity.[2645] Non-discriminatory measures should also be applied to older workers.[2646]

The Protocol complements social protection and social assistance measures with practical action, including effective access to education, including skills development,[2647] employment services,[2648] nutrition,[2649] water, sanitation and hygiene,[2650] childcare[2651] and housing,[2652] among others. Exceptional in this regard is Article 22 on the environment and climate change which commits States Parties, *inter alia*, to support measures to mitigate the effects of climate change and environmental degradation through social protection schemes.

In keeping with the established practice of the AU, the Protocol to Social Protection includes a list of duties owed by individuals towards their 'families, communities, the wider society and the state.'[2653] These include participating in social protection schemes designed to protect them and their families against risks, and providing support and protection to family members as required by national law.

The Protocol to Social Protection includes a safeguard clause.[2654] It contains an interesting provision, to the effect that, 'In the event of a contradiction between two (2) or more provisions of this Protocol, the interpretation which favours the rights of citizens and protects their legitimate interests shall prevail.'[2655]

Regarding implementation, States Parties must specify the measures taken to realize the rights recognized in the Protocol to Social Protection in their periodic reports to the African Commission on Human and Peoples' Rights.[2656] In addition, States Parties must establish or designate national machinery, including independent

---

2643. *Ibid.*, Art. 2(d). States Parties should additionally abide by the principle of equal treatment in relation to social protection, *ibid.*, Art. 2(a)(ii).
2644. Protocol to Social Protection Art. 8(a). *See further ibid.*, Art. 13(b) regarding social protection measures protecting women against discrimination and dismissal in relation to maternity. *See also* Maputo Protocol Art. 2. Compare UN Convention on the Elimination of Discrimination against Women Art. 11 (18 Dec. 1979) 1249 U.N.T.S. 13 (CEDAW).
2645. Protocol to Social Protection Art. 13(b). Compare CEDAW Art. 11(2)(a); European Social Charter (Revised) Art. 16(2); EU Charter of Fundamental Rights Art. 33(2).
2646. Protocol to Social Protection Art. 10(e). *See also* Protocol on Older Persons in Africa Arts 3, 6.
2647. Protocol to Social Protection Art. 18.
2648. *Ibid.*, Art. 6.
2649. *Ibid.*, Art. 19.
2650. *Ibid.*, Art. 20.
2651. *Ibid.*, Art. 11.
2652. *Ibid.*, Art. 21.
2653. *Ibid.*, Art. 27.
2654. *Ibid.*, Art. 31(a).
2655. *Ibid.*, Art. 31(b).
2656. Protocol to Social Protection Art. 28(a).

national institutions, to monitor the implementation of these rights.[2657] Both the African Commission and the African Court on Human and Peoples' Rights have jurisdiction over the Protocol.[2658]

The Protocol to Social Protection makes provision for dispute settlement between persons and the State. States Parties must therefore ensure that claimants, both individual and collective, have the right to complain or appeal with regard to any violations of their rights.[2659] These complaint mechanisms must meet procedural guarantees guaranteeing a fair hearing.[2660] Significantly, legal aid must be available for those whose rights have been violated.[2661]

The Protocol to Social Protection makes provision for reservations and withdrawals.[2662] An interesting point about the latter provision is that, as is sometimes the case with treaties of this nature, notice of withdrawal may only be given after three years from the date of the Protocol's entry into force.[2663]

Unlike many international and regional human rights instruments which recognize the right to social security in broad and general terms, in comparison, the Protocol to Social Protection is a relatively comprehensive and detailed document. It is a composition of separate elements. On the one hand, it imposes specific obligations on States Parties, while on the other, it provides for the gradual realization of the right to social security and social assistance. This raises a flaw with the Protocol. Because it does not set out any firm time frames for the delivery of these schemes, understandably so in some sense because of resource implications, their pace of introduction may turn out to be extremely slow.[2664] But even where it lays down specific obligations, States Parties have a wide discretion as to how these obligations are implemented and delivered.[2665] Funding is, of course, a crucial issue, and resources must be allocated, the Protocol therefore calling for the adequate funding of social protection systems.[2666]

The Protocol to Social Protection contains, as may have already been observed, a number of distinctive features relating to the environment and climate change, for instance. It seeks to address unemployment and underemployment by committing

---

2657. *Ibid.*, Art. 28(a).

2658. *Ibid.*, Art. 29. The jurisdiction of these bodies is contingent on domestic remedies being exhausted, Protocol to Social Protection Art. 26(f).

2659. *Ibid.*, Art. 26(a), (b).

2660. *Ibid.*, Art. 26(c).

2661. *Ibid.*, Art. 26(h).

2662. *Ibid.*, Art 34 and 37 respectively.

2663. *Ibid.*, Art. 37(a). Compare ILO Convention No. 102 Art. 82(1); European Social Charter (Revised) Art. M(1).

2664. Note the decision in *European Roma Rights Centre v. Bulgaria*, European Committee of Social Rights, Collective Complaint No. 31/2005, decision of 25 May 2005, para. II.1.02, that States Parties must attempt to achieve the objectives of the European Social Charter within a reasonable time, with measurable progress and making the best possible use of available resources.

2665. Note *ibid.*, Art. 23 which, *inter alia*, requires States Parties to include provisions in their constitutions and other national laws to ensure that an adequate framework for social protection is provided for. Art. 28 obligates States Parties to ensure the implementation of the Protocol.

2666. Protocol to Social Protection Art. 24. According to UNCTAD, thirty-three African economies are classified as least developed countries (LDCs), UNCTAD, 'UN list of least developed countries' https://unctad.org/topic/least-developed-countries/list.

States Parties to adopt proactive employment policies.[2667] Given the scale and significance of the informal and rural economies in Africa,[2668] the Protocol requires States Parties to adopt appropriate and adequate social security measures for informal and rural workers, including a minimum package of social protection.[2669] Furthermore, a system of social protection for women working in the informal and rural sectors must be established.[2670] It also includes a provision on data management.[2671] But the overarching philosophy is that social protection should, *inter alia*, be human rights-based, participatory, transformative, and inclusive.[2672] It therefore calls for the 'effective and meaningful participation of all stakeholders through social dialogue and citizen participation in social protection policy formulation, programme design, [and] implementation'.[2673]

2667. Protocol to Social Protection Art. 6.

2668. According to a recent ILO paper, informal employment is the main source of employment in Africa, accounting for 85.8% of total employment, rising to 89.2% in Sub-Saharan Africa; 97.9% of the agricultural sector is informal, A. Kiaga and V. Leung, 'The Transition from the Informal to the Formal Economy in Africa', 11–12 *Global Employment Policy Review* (Background Paper No. 4, December 2020), https://www.ilo.org/wcmsp5/groups/public/---ed_emp/documents/publication/wcms_792078.pdf.

2669. Protocol to Social Protection Art. 5(a), (d).

2670. *Ibid.*, Art. 5(e). *See also* Maputo Protocol Art. 13(f).

2671. *Ibid.*, Art. 25.

2672. *Ibid.*, Art. 2(b). *See also ibid.*, Art. 23(b).

2673. *Ibid.*, Art. 23(i).

Chapter 3. Refugees

§1. The OAU Convention on Refugees

411. The plight of Africa's refugees remains an ongoing tragedy. Conflict, environmental degradation,[2674] climate change, impoverishment, crop failures and famine, political unrest, and abuses of human rights[2675] have all contributed to the displacement of millions of people.[2676] As the flow of refugees has shown little sign of decreasing in recent years[2677] and mass exoduses have occurred from places such as the Sahel, Sudan,[2678] Somalia,[2679] and the Great Lakes region of Central Africa,[2680] the reception of refugees has led to serious problems for host States which, lacking the necessary resources and infrastructure, have expressed concern about the security and environmental implications caused by large population movements. Although the financial and material resources of African States to cope with the refugee burden are limited,[2681] it is perhaps ironic that the African States have contributed significantly to the progressive development of international refugee law.

2674. *See* Progress Achieved Towards Meeting Objectives of the Earth Summit, UN General Assembly Res. A/RES/S-19/2.

2675. The UN has established links between human rights violations and population displacements, *see, e.g.*, Vienna Declaration and Programme of Action, adopted by the World Conference on Human Rights in June 1993, pt. I, para. 23(2), 32 I.L.M. 1661 (1993); Report of the UN Secretary-General on Human Rights and Mass Exoduses, UN Doc. E/CN.4/1996/42, 4–12, 25. *See also* UN Commission on Human Rights Res. 2003/52, Human rights and mass exoduses. The UN Secretary-General identified weak national systems of human rights protection as being a significant contributing factor in mass displacement and argued that national systems of human rights protection had to be established and/or strengthened, UN Doc. A/57/387. The OAU also acknowledged this nexus, *see* Grand Bay (Mauritius) Declaration and Plan of Action 1999, para. 9, C. Heyns & M. Killander (eds), *Compendium of Key Human Rights Documents of the African Union* (7th edn, Pretoria: Pretoria University Law Press, 2022), 114.

2676. Report of the UN Secretary-General on the causes of conflict and the promotion of durable peace and sustainable development in Africa, UN Doc. A/52/871-S/1998/318 (1998) paras 7–15; T. Maluwa, *International Law in Post-Colonial Africa* 171–176 (The Hague: Kluwer Law International 1999). At the end of 2015 there were over five million refugees in Africa, *UNHCR Global Trends 2015*, http://www.unhcr.org/globaltrends/ (accessed 26 Apr. 2017).

2677. In 2015 the top countries of origin of refugees in Africa included the Central African Republic, Democratic Republic of Congo, Somalia, South Sudan and Sudan, *UNHCR Global Trends 2015*, http://www.unhcr.org/globaltrends/ (accessed 26 Apr. 2017). Note UN Security Council Res. 2349 (2017).

2678. The civil war between north and south in Sudan that lasted from 1983–2005 is said to have caused the internal displacement of four million southerners, while the more recent conflict in Darfur has displaced over two million people, UN Doc. E/CN.4/2006/71/Add.6, paras 6, 9. According to UN Security Council Res. 1556 (2004) the conflict in Darfur had led to two hundred thousand refugees fleeing to neighbouring Chad. *See also Sudan Human Rights Organization and Sudan Centre for Housing Rights and Evictions v. Sudan* Communication Nos 279/03, 296/05, 28th Activity Report 2010. By the end of 2015 there were over seven hundred thousand refugees in South Sudan and over six hundred thousand refugees in Sudan, *UNHCR Global Trends 2015*, http://www.unhcr.org/globaltrends/ (accessed 26 Apr. 2017).

2679. At the end of 2015 there were over three million refugees in the East and Horn of Africa, *UNHCR Global Trends 2015*, http://www.unhcr.org/globaltrends/ (accessed 26 Apr. 2017).

2680. At the end of 2015 there were over one and a half million refugees in the Great Lakes region, *ibid.*

2681. In Res. 2003/52 the Commission on Human Rights stressed the responsibility of States and international organizations to cooperate with States with large numbers of refugees to ensure that assistance and protection needs are addressed.

412. In 1969 the OAU adopted the Convention on Refugees.[2682] The OAU believed a regional treaty was necessary because the existing law, enshrined in the UN Convention on Refugees 1951,[2683] which seeks to protect the individual refugee and is not deemed applicable to flight *en masse*, was deemed inadequate.[2684] Such a narrow definition failed to take account of the particular difficulties facing Africa, such as wars of national liberation and natural disasters, which had given rise to mass exoduses and displaced whole populations. However, the OAU Convention does not seek to exclude the operation of the UN Convention from Africa;[2685] it simply seeks to solve the refugee problem in an African context. It is innovative in a number of respects.

413. The first item of significance is the broadening of the concept of the refugee. The OAU Convention on Refugees incorporates the UN Convention definition in Article 1(1), but it extends the definition in paragraph 2 to include those in need of complementary international protection based either on humanitarian grounds or human rights law, namely, internationally, or externally, displaced persons and humanitarian or de facto refugees,[2686] stating that:

2682. Convention Governing the Specific Aspects of Refugee Problems in Africa (10 Sep. 1969), 1001 U.N.T.S. 45, 8 I.L.M. 1288 (1969). The Convention entered into force on 20 Jan. 1974 and by June 2019 had been ratified by forty-six Member States. *See* generally P. Weis, *The Convention of the Organization of African Unity Governing the Specific Aspects of Refugee Problems*, 3 Revue de Droits de l'Homme 449 (1970); R.M. D'Sa, 'The African Refugee Problem, Relevant International Conventions and Recent Activities of the Organization of African Unity', *N.I.L.R.* 31 (1984): 378; F. Hofman, 'Refugee Law in an African Context', *Z.a.ö.R.V.* 52 (1992): 318; E.O. Awuku, 'Refugee Movements in Africa and the OAU Convention on Refugees', *J.A.L.* 39 (1995): 79; B.T. Mukirya-Nyanduga, 'Refugee Protection under the 1969 OAU Convention Governing the Specific Aspects of Refugee Problems in Africa', *German Y.B.I.L.* 47 (2004): 85. According to the African Commission on Human and Peoples' Rights States Parties are under an obligation to secure the rights protected by the African Charter to all persons within their jurisdiction, nationals and non-nationals alike, *Rencontre Africaine pour la Defense des Droits de l'Homme v. Zambia*, Communication No. 71/92, 10th Activity Report 1996–1997, para. 22, which extends to protecting the human rights of refugees, *African Institute for Human Rights and Development (on behalf of Sierra Leonean refugees in Guinea v. Republic of Guinea*, Communication No. 249/2002, 20th Activity Report 2005–2006, para. 68.

2683. Convention Relating to the Status of Refugees (28 Jul. 1951), 189 U.N.T.S. 137.

2684. *See* Weis. UN Convention on Refugees Art. 1(a)(2), defines a refugee as, *inter alia*, a person having a 'well-founded fear of being persecuted for reasons of race, religion, nationality, membership of a particular social group or political opinion'.

2685. OAU Convention on Refugees Art. 8(2), states that it is the effective regional complement to the UN Convention on Refugees. The preamble additionally acknowledges that the UN Convention on Refugees constitutes the basic instrument relating to the status and treatment of refugees. *See also Doebbler v. Sudan*, Communication No. 235/2000, 27th Activity Report 2009, para. 125.

2686. Hofman, 323; *Hirsi Jamaa and Others v. Italy*, Concurring Opinion of Judge Pinto de Albuquerque, European Court of Human Rights, Appl. No. 27765/09, Judgment of 23 Feb. 2012, http://www.echr.coe.int (accessed 24 Feb. 2012). According to the African Commission on Human and Peoples' Rights (Commission), 'International protection is granted to refugees because they do not enjoy the protection of their own home countries', *Doebbler v. Sudan*, Communication No. 235/2000, 27th Activity Report 2009, para. 149.

> The term 'refugee' shall also apply to every person who, owing to external aggression, occupation, foreign domination or events seriously disturbing public order in either part or the whole of his country of origin or nationality, is compelled to leave his place of habitual residence in order to seek refuge in another place outside his country of origin or nationality.

Excluded from acquiring refugee status are persons guilty of acts contrary to the purposes and principles of the OAU/AU.[2687]

414. The OAU definition therefore intended to cover mass exoduses brought about by the struggle for liberation. Although population displacement as a result of famine or other natural disasters may not have been originally envisaged as coming within the protective scope of the definition, it has subsequently been accepted that such displaced persons would qualify as refugees for the purposes of the Convention.[2688] This broader and more liberal regime was motivated, as stated in the Preamble to the OAU Convention, by 'the need for an essentially humanitarian approach towards solving the problems of refugees', and was therefore a step that was welcomed. It has nevertheless been suggested that the concept of the 'refugee' should be extended in line with the non-discrimination clause of Article 2 of the African Charter,[2689] to cover every person who fears being persecuted for belonging to an ethnic group, or for reasons of colour, sex, social origin, fortune, birth or other status.[2690] The ethnic conflict in the Great Lakes region of Central Africa from 1994–1996 in particular makes a compelling case for the extension of this definition.

2687. OAU Convention on Refugees Art. 1(5). This provision would seem to be applicable to those militants implicated in the genocide in Rwanda.

2688. C. d'Orsi, 'Sub-Saharan Africa: Is a New Special Regional Refugee Law Regime Emerging?', *Z.a.ö.R.V.* 68 (2008), 1057, 1065–1069. This conclusion is supported by the African Charter on the Rights and Welfare of the Child Art. 23(4) (1 Jul. 1990), 28 I.L.M. 1456 (1989). And *see* Vienna Declaration and Programme of Action pt. I, para. 23(5). *See also Hirsi Jamaa v. Italy*, Concurring Opinion of Judge Pinto de Albuquerque, European Court of Human Rights, Appl. No. 27765/09, Judgment of 23 Feb. 2012, who states, 'Groups of refugees cannot be subject to a diminished status based on an "inherent" mass-influx exception to "genuine" refugee status. To provide reduced, subsidiary protection … for people who arrive as part of a mass influx would be unjustified discrimination.' A simpler definition that reflects such causes is those who have fled for reasons 'traceable to conflicts, or radical political, social or economic changes', quoted in E.-I.A. Daes, *Status of the Individual and Contemporary International Law: Promotion, Protection and Restoration of Human Rights at National, Regional and International Levels* (New York: United Nations, 1992), 34.

2689. African Charter on Human and Peoples' Rights (17 Jun. 1981), 1520 U.N.T.S. 217, 21 I.L.M. 58 (1982).

2690. D'Sa, 378. This is because the OAU Convention on Refugees Art. 4, is narrower in scope, stating that the provisions of the Convention are to be applied to all refugees without discrimination as to, *inter alia*, race, religion, or nationality. However, note should be taken of the African Charter on Democracy Art. 8(2) (30 Jan. 2007), https://www.au.int/en/treaties, Heyns & Killander, 125, whereby State Parties are required to guarantee, *inter alia*, the rights of refugees and displaced persons. Nevertheless, the Commission has made this connection, *see Rencontre Africaine pour la Defense des Droits de l'Homme v. Zambia*, Communication No. 71/92, 10th Activity Report, 1996–1997, paras 21–22; and *Union Interafricaine des Droits de l'Homme et al. v. Angola*, Communication No. 159/96, 11th Activity Report 1997–1998, paras 16–17, where the Commission

415. Article 2 of the OAU Convention on Refugees notably enshrines a right of asylum,[2691] which is reinforced by Article 12(3) of the African Charter.[2692] However, it must be stressed that there is no automatic right to asylum; the use of the term 'best endeavours' is recommendatory rather than mandatory.[2693] States retain an absolute discretion, and ultimately the granting of asylum remains their prerogative.[2694] Furthermore, the granting of asylum is declared to be a peaceful and humanitarian act which must not be regarded as an unfriendly gesture by other OAU/AU Member States. Provision is made for burden-sharing if a State finds difficulty in continuing to grant asylum to refugees. A State may thus appeal directly to other States or through the AU for appropriate measures to be taken in the spirit of African solidarity and international cooperation to lessen that burden.

416. The OAU Convention on Refugees further emphasizes its humanitarian credentials by affirming in Article 2(3) the principle of *non-refoulement*,[2695] seemingly having a wider scope than that contained in its corresponding provision of the

stated that, 'Mass expulsions of any category of persons, whether on the basis of nationality, religion ethnic, racial or other considerations "constitute a special violation of human rights".' Similarly, in *African Institute for Human Rights and Development (on behalf of Sierra Leonean refugees in Guinea v. Republic of Guinea*, Communication No. 249/2002, 20th Activity Report 2005–2006, para. 69, the Commission held that mass expulsion of refugees amounted to discriminatory action contrary to the OAU Convention on Refugees Art. 4. Cumulative discriminatory measures affecting women constitutes persecution, Cases C-608/22 and C-609/22 *Bundesamt für Fremdenwesen und Asyl and Others (Afghan women)*, Advocate General's Opinion (9 Nov. 2023). It is interesting to note that in 2013 the CJEU held in relation to three African asylum seekers that sexual orientation could be a valid basis for having a well-founded fear of persecution, Case C-199/12, C-200/12, C-201/12 *X, Y, Z v. Minister voor Immigratie en Asiel*, Judgment of 7 Nov. 2013, C:2013: 720.

2691. Hofman, 318. At the very least it goes beyond that provided for in the UN Convention on Refugees, A.M. Rifaat, *Refugees and the right of asylum: an African perspective*, 40 Revue Egyptienne de droit international 71, 106 (1984). It should be observed that the right of asylum is a conventional right and not a customary right, *Asylum Case (Colombia v. Peru)* I.C.J. Reports 1950, 266; G.S. Goodwin-Gill, *The Refugee in International Law* (Oxford: Clarendon Press, 1996), Ch. 5. For a discussion on how Africa has contributed to the evolution of the law of asylum, *see* G.J. Naldi & C. d'Orsi, 'The Multi-Faceted Aspects of Asylum Law Applicable to Africa: Analysis for Reflection', *Loyola of Los Angeles International& Comparative Law Review* 36 (2014), 115–152.

2692. It appears that this provision applies a more restrictive approach to the granting of asylum in that asylum seekers are required to have suffered actual persecution rather than having a well-founded fear of persecution. In *Organisation Mondiale Contre La Torture and the Association Internationale des Juristes Democrates and Others v. Rwanda* Communication Nos 27/89, 46/91, 49/91, 99/93, 10th Activity Report 1993–1994, para. 30, the Commission expressed the view that this provision included 'a general protection of all those who are subject to persecution, that they may seek refuge in another state'.

2693. Weis, 457; Hofman, 324; Awuku, 82–83.

2694. D'Sa, 387; Hofman, 324; R. Murray, *Human Rights in Africa: From the OAU to the African Union* (Cambridge: Cambridge University Press, 2004), 221.

2695. According to the UNHCR *non-refoulement* is, in addition to a binding treaty obligation, a rule of customary international law and a human right, quoted in *M.S.S. v. Belgium and Greece*, European Court of Human Rights, Appl. No. 30696/09, Judgment of 21 Jan. 2011, para. 56. *See also* Daes, 34; Goodwin-Gill, 167–168. According to the Commission *non-refoulement* is a principle

UN Convention on Refugees, Article 33(1).[2696] In essence, the *non-refoulement* obligation in the OAU Convention amounts to an obligation to admit and host humanitarian refugees. Unlike the UN Convention on Refugees, no express reference is made to exceptions in the interests of national security or public order, or incidents of international crime.[2697] It would therefore seem that a bona fide refugee cannot be expelled.[2698] It has additionally been suggested that the OAU Convention on Refugees guarantees the principle of *non-refoulement* without exception.[2699] However, it has been argued to the contrary that this is not in fact the case since this provision must be read in the context of the Convention as a whole.[2700] Hence, according to Article 1(4)–(5) of the OAU Convention on Refugees, a person may lose their refugee status on various grounds of incompatibility.[2701] Since according to Article 3(1) thereof a refugee is under a duty to abide by the laws of the country of asylum, including measures taken for the maintenance of public order, any breach thereof may result in the loss of refugee status and expulsion may ensue. Nevertheless, a safeguard is provided by Article 12(4) of the African Charter which protects against arbitrary expulsions, stating that an alien lawfully in the territory of a State may be expelled only in accordance with the due process of law.[2702] It is significant that the principle of *non-refoulement* must be observed even in cases of mass influx of displaced persons, and this obligation is complemented by Article 12(5) of the

---

'which has taken an increasingly fundamental character, as one of the cornerstones of international refugee law', *Doebbler v. Sudan*, Communication No. 235/2000, 27th Activity Report 2009, para. 150.

2696. *See* D'Sa, 387–389; Goodwin-Gill, 140; Hofman, 320–321; d'Orsi, 1059–1065. But only if the UN Convention on Refugees is interpreted restrictively. In practice there may be little difference, Goodwin-Gill, 170–171. However, it appears that there is a lack of uniformity in the interpretation and scope of the principle in state practice, *see* generally E.F. D'Angelo, 'Non-refoulement: The Search for a Consistent Interpretation of Article 33', *Vanderbilt Journal Transnational Law* 42 (2009): 279.

2697. Such individuals do not qualify for, or lose, the status of refugees or protected person, UN Convention on Refugees Arts 32, 33(2); *see* generally Goodwin-Gill, Ch. 4. In *African Institute for Human Rights and Development (on behalf of Sierra Leonean refugees in Guinea v. Republic of Guinea*, Communication No. 249/2002, 20th Activity Report 2005–2006, paras 69, 72, the Commission held that the State was entitled to prosecute persons that posed a threat to the State. *See further* Cases C-57/09 and C-101/09 *Federal Republic of Germany v. B & D* [2010] E.C.R. I-10979, para. 101.

2698. Indeed, expelling refugees and refuge seekers to high-risk countries can constitute *arbitrary* repatriation, *Hirsi Jamaa v. Italy*, European Court of Human Rights, Appl. No. 27765/09, Judgment of 23 Feb. 2012, paras 153–156.

2699. Goodwin-Gill, 140.

2700. D'Sa, 388; Murray, 189. Awuku, 82, is of the view that the OAU's exclusion clause is stricter than that of the UN Convention on Refugees.

2701. Which would appear to extend to terrorist acts, Cases C-57/09 and C-101/09 *Federal Republic of Germany v. B & D* [2010] E.C.R. I-10979, paras 81–84; Case C-573/14. *Commissaire générale aux réfugiés et aux apatrides v. Mostafa Lounani*, Judgment of 31 Jan. 2017, C:2017:71.

2702. *Organisation Mondiale Contre La Torture and the Association Internationale des Juristes Democrates and Others v. Rwanda*, Communication Nos 27/89, 46/91, 49/91, 99/93, 10th Activity Report 1993–1994, para. 30; *Union Interafricaine des Droits de l'Homme et al. v. Angola*, Communication No.159/96, 11th Activity Report 1997–1998, paras 19–20.

African Charter which prohibits the mass expulsion of aliens.[2703] However, events in the Great Lakes region of Central Africa highlighted the difficulties faced by African States in coping with the reception of large numbers of refugees. In apparent defiance of their treaty obligations, borders were closed, and more than one million Rwandan and Burundian refugees were forced to leave Zaïre and Tanzania and return to their country of origin where they faced an uncertain future. However, these events may be explicable against a background of violence and infiltration by armed gangs as opponents of the new regimes in Rwanda and Burundi, many with complicity in the massacres perpetrated in those countries, used the refugee camps for subversive activities.[2704]

417. Note should be taken of the fact that under Article 2(6) of the OAU Convention on Refugees States granting the right of asylum are, for reasons of security, under an obligation to settle refugees a reasonable distance from the frontier of their country of origin. This requirement may appear, prima facie, to be incompatible with Article 26 of the UN Convention on Refugees and Article 12(1) of the African Charter which states that every individual shall have the right of freedom of movement and residence within the borders of a State. Nevertheless, States are under an obligation to ensure effective protection of refugees within their borders,[2705] and the wisdom of this provision has been substantiated by events in the Great Lakes region of Central Africa during 1996 when refugees along the Rwanda/Zaïre border often fell victim to acts of atrocities committed by different parties, and refugee camps were used to increase tension along the border.

418. A further distinguishing feature of the OAU Convention on Refugees is the prohibition on refugees engaging in subversive activities contained in Article 3. This

2703. In *Doebbler v. Sudan*, Communication No. 235/2000, 27th Activity Report 2009, para. 146, the question of whether the principle of *non-refoulement* applied to 14,000 Ethiopian refugees residing in Sudan was central to the case. Mass expulsions have been described as 'a special threat to human rights', *Rencontre Africaine pour la Defense des Droits de l'Homme v. Zambia*, Communication No. 71/92, 10th Activity Report, 1996–1997, para. 20. *See also African Institute for Human Rights and Development (on behalf of Sierra Leonean refugees in Guinea v. Republic of Guinea*, Communication No. 249/2002, 20th Activity Report 2005–2006, para. 69.

2704. UN Doc. E/CN/4/1997/61. Whilst the Commission will take note of the legitimate national security concerns of States their freedom of action is not unlimited however. In *Organisation Mondiale Contre La Torture and the Association Internationale des Juristes Democrates and Others v. Rwanda*, Communication Nos 27/89, 46/91, 49/91, 99/93, 10th Activity Report 1993–1994, the Commission found that the expulsion of Burundi nationals from Rwanda because they were considered to be a security risk amounted to a violation of, *inter alia*, the African Charter Art. 12(5). *See also African Institute for Human Rights and Development (on behalf of Sierra Leonean refugees in Guinea v. Republic of Guinea*, Communication No. 249/2002, 20th Activity Report 2005–2006. In *Democratic Republic of Congo v. Burundi, Rwanda and Uganda*, Communication No. 227/99, 20th Activity Report 2005–2006, para. 76, the Commission rejected as 'impermissible' Uganda's argument that it had launched operations in the DRC's territory in order to safeguard its national security interests since armed rebel groups hostile to Burundi, Rwanda and Uganda had sanctuary in the DRC. *See also Case concerning Armed Activities on the Territory of the Congo* (*Democratic Republic of Congo v. Uganda*) I.C.J. Reports 2005, 168.

2705. *See* Res. 2003/52 of the UN Commission on Human Rights.

principle is in keeping with Article 4(o) of the Constitutive Act,[2706] Article 23(2) of the African Charter and the OAU Declaration on the Problem of Subversion.[2707] Accordingly, a refugee is under a duty to abide by the laws of the country in which s/he finds herself/himself and to refrain from any subversive activities against any OAU/AU Member State. By restricting the prohibition towards OAU/AU Member States only, the national liberation struggle was left unhindered. A problem of definition may nevertheless arise. If the host State adopts a restrictive approach, legitimate political dissent or agitation in support of human rights could be suppressed, at variance with the freedom of expression enshrined in Article 9(2) of the African Charter.[2708] However, restrictions may be understandable to prevent unrest, acts of terror and incitement to violence.[2709] A person who does not abide by such a prohibition could lose his/her refugee status in accordance with Article 1(4)–(5) of the OAU Convention on Refugees and face expulsion. State parties are under a similar obligation to prohibit refugees residing in their territories from attacking, or engaging in any subversive activities, against any OAU/AU Member State.[2710] The political upheaval in the Great Lakes Region of Central Africa in recent years has highlighted the difficulties that these provisions seek to address. Mass population movements mingled genuine asylum seekers with armed gangs and individuals who had committed serious crimes, including crimes against humanity.[2711] Unrest was fomented in refugee camps which were used as bases from which to launch attacks against neighbouring territories. As a result, some refugee camps were stormed, and refugees were killed and dispersed.[2712] In order to protect bona fide refugees in these dangerous circumstances, the UNHCR reached an agreement with the governments of the region on security measures to ensure the civilian nature of the refugee

2706. And the OAU Charter Art. III(5) (25 May 1963), 479 U.N.T.S. 39, 2 I.L.M. 766 (1963), before it. *See further* Protocol on Amendments to the Constitutive Act, Art. 4(r) (9 Jul. 2002), https://www.au.int/en/treaties, Heyns & Killander, 12.

2707. In G.J. Naldi, *Documents of the Organization of African Unity* (London & New York: Mansell, 1992), 57.

2708. The term 'subversive activities' has been criticized for vagueness and the possibility that it could be invoked to curb legitimate activities, Weis, 457; Awuku, 83.

2709. In Res. 1161 the UN Security Council acknowledged the threat posed to the stability of the Great Lakes Region of Central Africa posed by malicious propaganda. *See also* Report of the UN Secretary-General on the causes of conflict and the promotion of durable peace and sustainable development in Africa, UN Doc. A/52/871-S/1998/318 (1998) para. 53.

2710. Under the Arusha Accords, the Governments of Burundi, Tanzania, Uganda and Zaïre agreed to the non-use of territories as bases for destabilizing Rwanda, UN Doc. E/CN.4/1995/50/Add. 2, para. 42.

2711. Report of the UN Secretary-General on the causes of conflict and the promotion of durable peace and sustainable development in Africa, UN Doc. A/52/871-S/1998/318 (1998) para. 53.

2712. UN Doc. E/CN.4/1995/50/Add.4. Similar problems arose in West Africa; in *African Institute for Human Rights and Development (on behalf of Sierra Leonean refugees in Guinea v. Republic of Guinea*, Communication No. 249/2002, 20th Activity Report 2005–2006, para. 71, the Commission acknowledged that Guinea held legitimate concerns about 'threats to its national security posed by the attacks from Sierra Leone and Liberia with a flow of rebels and arms across the borders.'

camps.[2713] Accordingly, the UNCHR put forward what it described as a 'ladder of options' identifying proportionate measures to perceived threats.[2714]

419. Article 5 of the OAU Convention on Refugees contains another distinctive right in making provision for voluntary repatriation.[2715] It is clear that repatriation must be voluntary, and, in light of the principle of *non-refoulement*, it declares that no refugee shall be repatriated against his/her will.[2716] If a refugee does wish to be repatriated, the country of origin and the country of asylum are obliged to collaborate to ensure the refugee's safe return. Neither should returning refugees be victimized for having left. In addition, refugees who freely decide to return to their homeland on their own initiative or as the result of assurances must have their return facilitated by the country of origin, the country of asylum, voluntary agencies, NGOs, and international organizations. While voluntary repatriation may offer one of the best solutions to the refugee crisis,[2717] it is apparent that unless the root causes that created the displacement in the first place are not remedied, the prospects of voluntary repatriation will prove negligible. Consequently, the return of relative stability and security to parts of Africa such as Liberia and Sierra Leone has led to the large-scale repatriation of refugees.[2718] Moreover, voluntary repatriation can only be made more effective if human rights are protected, the rule of law is respected, property restitution is addressed, and the safety of returnees can be assured.[2719]

420. It needs to be recalled that according to international human rights norms, a person cannot be arbitrarily deprived of the right to return to his/her country. The OAU Convention on Refugees does not address this issue, but under general international law, a national cannot be denied entry to his or her country of origin.[2720] Furthermore, according to Article 12(2) of the African Charter, an individual has the right to leave any country and to return to his or her country subject to the law of public order and security.[2721]

2713. UN Doc. E/CN.4/1997/61.

2714. The 'ladder of options' includes the following measures: (a) enhancing existing national law enforcement mechanisms; (b) international support for national security forces; (c) deployment of international fact-finding missions and observers; (d) deployment of international/regional police forces; (e) deployment of international/regional military forces under Ch. VI or Ch. VII UN Charter, UN Doc. E/CN.4/2005/80, para. 41.

2715. *See* d'Orsi, 1069–1076.

2716. *See* d'Orsi who highlights a number of cases of 'forced' repatriation, *ibid.*, 1077–1079.

2717. Awuku, 85. In Res. 2003/52 the UN Commission on Human Rights makes the point that return is not and should not be perceived as the only solution to forcible displacement but that resettlement and local integration are policies that should also be considered. *See further* Murray, 210–216. In 2015 one hundred and thirty thousand refugees in Africa returned, *UNHCR Global Trends 2015*, http://www.unhcr.org/globaltrends/ (accessed 26 Apr. 2017).

2718. UN Doc. E/CN.4/2005/80, para. 56. In *Doebbler v. Sudan*, Communication No. 235/2000, 27th Activity Report 2009, para. 161, the Commission found that thousands of Ethiopian refugees repatriated voluntarily following the end of the Ethiopian-Eritrean war.

2719. *See* the Kigali Declaration 2003 para. 14, Heyns & Killander, 154.

2720. Universal Declaration of Human Rights Art. 13(2), UN General Assembly Res. 217A (III); International Covenant on Civil and Political Rights Art. 12(2) (16 Dec. 1966), 999 U.N.T.S. 171, Protocol No. 4 to the European Convention on Human Rights Art. 3 (16 Sep. 1963), E.T.S. No. 46.

2721. *Alhassan Abubakar v. Ghana*, Communication No. 103/93, 10th Activity Report 1996–1997.

421. The importance of the OAU Convention on Refugees to international law lies in its progressive nature, setting a legal standard to which the international community should aspire.[2722] Particularly worthy of note are the extension of the definition of the concept of the refugee, the implementation of voluntary repatriation programmes and its provision of a right of asylum. Motivated in part by problems peculiar to Africa, these humanitarian developments were nonetheless welcome. These commitments have been subsequently endorsed by the OAU/AU and the UN in a number of special conferences convened to discuss the challenges posed by the refugee crises in Africa, which have also sought to address their root causes and offer practical proposals.[2723] Although these recommendations have no binding legal force, although they may have an impact as soft law, they nevertheless, in urging OAU/AU Member States to comply more effectively with their international obligations, constitute an important expression of the political will of OAU/AU Member States to reaffirm their legal and humanitarian obligations in accordance with the UN and OAU Conventions. However, in light of later developments, particularly the EU, it seems fair comment to suggest that the African response, once pioneering, now seems behind the times. For example, unlike the EU, there exists no uniform set of procedures for determination of refugee status and appeals.[2724] Yet the African Commission on Human and Peoples' Rights is having a positive influence on the development of the law in this area. The fact that the African Charter is deemed applicable to refugees is highly significant as it means, among other things, that refugees are entitled to basic rights and must be treated with dignity.[2725] However, in practical terms much remains to be done as African States generally lack the financial, logistical and material resources to deal with the challenges posed by refugee crises. But, as recent events in Europe have demonstrated, even Western States can struggle to cope with large numbers of refugees. It is clear that African States must acquire and develop early warning and early-action systems, as called for by resolution 2003/52 of the UN Commission on Human Rights, to react more promptly to evolving crises. Timely donor assistance, properly spent, is also important. But unless the root causes of mass displacement are effectively addressed, to

2722. The OAU Convention on Refugees has been described as creating 'an impressive normative framework', F. Viljoen, *International Human Rights Law in Africa* (Oxford: Oxford University Press, 2007), 258.

2723. Particular mention should be made of the Pan-African Conference on the Situation on Refugees in Africa held at Arusha, Tanzania, in May 1979, the Arusha Conference, which adopted a series of recommendations on 'The Situation of Refugees in Africa and Prospective Solutions to the Problem in the 1980s', *see* UN General Assembly Res. 34/61; the Addis Ababa Recommendations 1994; and the Conakry Comprehensive Action Plan 2000. *See further* Murray, 190–192.

2724. *Doebbler v. Sudan*, Communication No. 235/2000, 27th Activity Report 2009, para. 165. *See* EU Council Directive 2004/83 of 29 Apr. 2004 on minimum standards for the qualification and status of third country nationals or stateless persons as refugees or as persons who otherwise need international protection and the content of the protection granted, O.J. L 304/12, 30 Sep. 2004.

2725. *African Institute for Human Rights and Development (on behalf of Sierra Leonean refugees in Guinea v. Republic of Guinea*, Communication No. 249/2002, 20th Activity Report 2005–2006, paras 66–67.

be replaced by peace, security and stability, the international community is dealing with palliatives and the plight of refugees will continue to blight Africa.[2726]

422. The situation in Darfur is therefore of particular interest in this respect because it demonstrates the capacity of the international community to respond to threats to international peace and security in a collectively forceful manner when the political will exists. Since 2001, the conflict in the Darfur region of Sudan has engaged the international community. The Janjaweed militia especially had been carrying out attacks, and perpetrating atrocities, on civilian populations that led to forced displacement. The UN Security Council found that this conflict posed a threat to international peace and security.[2727] In demanding that the Sudanese Government put a stop to these attacks and disarm the militia the UN Security Council also called for measures to prevent or mitigate the humanitarian catastrophe.[2728] An international presence was initially established by the AU in 2004 as a monitoring mission in the form of the AMIS which was mandated, *inter alia*, to contribute to a secure environment for the delivery of humanitarian aid and the return of refugees and the internally displaced, or IDPs.[2729] A UN presence followed in the form of the UNMIS, established under Security Council resolution 1590(2005), which was additionally given the task of facilitating the voluntary return of IDPs and refugees by helping to establish the necessary security conditions. However, the numerous difficulties encountered by AMIS, which included suffering casualties from militia attacks and obstruction to humanitarian access, exposed its limitations, but this led to an extraordinary development, the creation of a hybrid AU/UN peacekeeping operation, AU/UN Hybrid Operation in Darfur (UNAMID).[2730] Furthermore, due to the destabilizing effect the Darfur conflict has been having on neighbouring countries, the UN has authorized, pursuant to Chapter VII of the UN Charter, the deployment of an EU operation in eastern Chad and northeastern CAR with a view, *inter alia*, to protecting refugees and IDPs.[2731]

2726. *See* Murray, 206–209. One important factor that is being addressed is ending impunity for human rights and humanitarian law violations. This has happened in relation to the conflict in Darfur, *see infra* para. 422 for fuller discussion. In 2004 the UN Secretary-General, pursuant to Security Council Res. 1564 (2004) acting under Ch. VII UN Charter, established an International Commission of Inquiry on Darfur with a view investigating alleged violations of human rights law and international humanitarian law in Darfur. The Commission found as established that the Government of Sudan and the Janjaweed were responsible for serious violations of human rights law and international humanitarian law amounting to crimes under international law and recommended that the Security Council refer the Darfur conflict to the ICC, UN Doc. S/2005/60. Under Res. 1593 (2005) the Security Council duly referred this matter to the ICC.

2727. Resolution 1556 (2004), adopted pursuant to Chapter VII UN Charter, which imposed sanctions on Sudan. *See also*, *e.g.*, Res. 1784 (2007).

2728. Resolutions 1556 (2004) and 1591 (2005), adopted pursuant to Ch. VII UN Charter. The African Commission on Human and Peoples' Rights has also expressed its concern at the situation in Darfur, *see*, *e.g.*, Resolution on the Situation of Human Rights in the Darfur Region in Sudan, 20th Activity Report, 2006.

2729. Communiqué of the Seventeenth Meeting of the Peace and Security Council of the AU, AU Doc. PSC/PR/Comm.(XVII), endorsed by UN Security Council Res. 1556 (2004).

2730. UN Security Council Res. 1769 (2007).

2731. UN Security Council Res. 1778 (2007). In January 2008 the Council of the EU adopted a Decision on the launching of operation EUFOR Tchad/RCA, Press Release 5625/08.

423. In 1964, the OAU set up as a permanent organ the Commission on Refugees with the task of considering all aspects of refugee problems in Africa and devising appropriate policies.[2732] With the advent of the AU, this body was transformed into the Sub-Committee on Refugees, Returnees and IDPs in Africa. Its expanded mandate includes assisting AU organs in formulating, developing and coordinating policy on issues affecting refugees, returnees and IDPs, promoting humanitarian law in Africa, examining the plight and needs of refugees, returnees and IDPs and providing policy recommendations, and collaborating with UN humanitarian agencies, RECs and NGOs.[2733]

§2. The AU Convention on Internally Displaced Persons

424. The OAU Convention on Refugees is not alone in having failed to address a problem of significant magnitude in Africa, of people who as a result of forced or involuntary movement find themselves in a refugee-like situation but do not legally qualify for refugee status because they remain within national frontiers, namely, IDPs. According to the UNHCR there were over eleven million IDPs in Africa at the end of 2015.[2734] The UN has stressed the importance of humanitarian aid and securing access to civilians.[2735] Although the OAU took some action to deal with the plight of IDPs[2736] it was only in 2009 that a Convention on IDPs in Africa (Kampala Convention) was adopted by the AU.[2737] The Kampala Convention may be considered ground-breaking due to the fact that currently it is the only existing specific universal or regional legal instrument providing for the comprehensive protection of IDPs.[2738] But the Kampala Convention is notable for a host of other reasons, including the comprehensive obligations owed by States and others, including humanitarian agencies and armed groups, towards IDPs, and human rights guarantees. Its basic premise may be said to that all persons have a right to be protected against arbitrary displacement.[2739]

2732. *See* G.J. Naldi, *The Organization of African Unity* (London & New York: Mansell, 1989), 97.
2733. *African Union Handbook 2014*, 98–99, https://www.au.int.
2734. *UNHCR Global Trends 2015*, http://www.unhcr.org/globaltrends/ (accessed 26 Apr. 2017).
2735. Vienna Declaration and Programme of Action pt. I, para. 23(4); Report of the High-Level Panel on Threats, Challenges and Change, A More Secure World: Our Shared Responsibility, UN Doc. A/59/565 (2004) paras 231–238.
2736. Murray, 222–225.
2737. Convention on the Protection and Assistance to Internally Displaced Persons in Africa (23 Oct. 2009), 49 I.L.M. 83 (2010). The Convention entered into force on 6 Dec. 2012 and by April 2022 had been ratified by Member States.
2738. However, the UN has drafted a 'soft law' document, Guiding Principles on Internal Displacement, setting out the humanitarian and human rights standards applicable to IDPs, which have been widely adopted, UN Doc. E/CN.4/1999/79. It has been described as 'an important international framework', UN General Assembly Resolution 60/1 (2005) on the 2005 World Summit Outcome, para. 132. *See further* F.M. Deng, 'The International Protection of the Internally Displaced', *International Journal of Refugee Law* 7 (1995): 7. The Kampala Convention closely mirrors the Guiding Principles on Internal Displacement.
2739. Kampala Convention Art. 4(4).

425. The Kampala Convention defines IDPs as, 'persons or groups of persons who have been forced or obliged to flee or to leave their homes or places of habitual residence, in particular as a result of or in order to avoid the effects of armed conflict, situations of generalized violence, violations of human rights or natural or human-made disasters, and who have not crossed an internationally recognized State border'.[2740] The broad scope of the definition adopted by the Kampala Convention is noteworthy; it expressly takes into consideration factors such as natural disasters that either were implicit in the OAU Convention on Refugees or became accepted due to subsequent practice. But especially significant is the fact that account is taken of human impact such as development projects, for example, the building of dams[2741] or the exploitation of natural resources.[2742] A definition of internal displacement is also provided, 'the involuntary or forced movement, evacuation or relocation of persons or groups of persons within internationally recognized state borders'.[2743] But the Kampala Convention protects against *arbitrary* displacement. Such displacement includes displacement caused by what may be termed 'ethnic cleansing',[2744] displacement caused by armed conflict,[2745] displacement caused by generalized violence or violations human rights,[2746] and displacement used as a collective punishment.[2747] Consequently, evacuations necessitated by imperative military reasons in accordance with international humanitarian law,[2748] or for health and safety reasons,[2749] for example, to protect a population at risk of drowning in floods, do not come within the scope of the definition.

426. The Kampala Convention imposes a series of general obligations upon States Parties,[2750] a number of which have special relevance to the lawlessness that has affected Somalia and Darfur. These include preventing arbitrary displacement,[2751] ensuring respect for human rights and international humanitarian law relating to IDPs,[2752] ensuring individual responsibility for acts of arbitrary displacement, including those of non-State actors,[2753] and meeting the basic needs of IDPs.[2754] More specifically, States Parties are required to ensure respect for human rights and international humanitarian law as a means of preventing situations giving

2740. *Ibid.*, Art. 1(k). It essentially repeats verbatim the description provided by the Guiding Principles on Internal Displacement, 5.
2741. Kampala Convention Art. 10.
2742. *Ibid.*, Art. 3(l)(i).
2743. *Ibid.*, Art. 1(l).
2744. *Ibid.*, Art. 4(4)(a).
2745. *Ibid.*, Art. 4(4)(b)–(c).
2746. *Ibid.*, Art. 4(4)(d).
2747. *Ibid.*, Art. 4(4)(g).
2748. *Ibid.*, Art. 4(4)(b).
2749. *Ibid.*, Art. 4(4)(f).
2750. *Ibid.*, Art. 3.
2751. *Ibid.*, Art. 3(l)(a)–(b).
2752. *Ibid.*, Art. 3(l)(c)–(e).
2753. *Ibid.*, Art. 3(l)(g)–(h). In addition, acts of arbitrary displacement that amount to genocide, war crimes or crimes against humanity shall be deemed offences punishable by law. *See also ibid.*, Arts 7(4), (5)(a). Such violations of international criminal law could therefore be prosecuted before the ICC.
2754. *Ibid.*, Art. 3(l)(k).

rise to arbitrary displacement,[2755] and to set up early warning systems.[2756] The Kampala Convention reiterates the basic principle of international law that the primary duty and responsibility, though not exclusive, for providing protection and humanitarian assistance to IDPs within their territory or jurisdiction rests with States.[2757] This extends to taking measures to protect and assist IDPs,[2758] including assessing the needs and vulnerabilities of IDPs,[2759] and taking the necessary steps to organize relief action.[2760] Where appropriate States Parties shall turn to international organizations and humanitarian agencies for assistance.[2761] They undertake to respect the mandates of the AU, UN, and humanitarian organizations to assist IDPs,[2762] and must therefore protect and refrain from attacking or harming humanitarian personnel and resources.[2763] However, in keeping with the traditional view that the legality of the delivery of humanitarian aid is contingent on the consent of the recipient State[2764] it is made clear that the sovereignty and territorial integrity of States remains unaffected.[2765]

427. More detailed obligations are set out in Article 9 of the Kampala Convention. These include preventing and refraining from violations of international humanitarian law, including genocide, war crimes or crimes against humanity,[2766] serious human rights violations, such as arbitrary killings, enforced disappearances and torture,[2767] all forms of sexual and gender-based violence,[2768] and starvation.[2769] States Parties must therefore ensure that IDPs live in satisfactory conditions so adequate humanitarian assistance, food, water, shelter, sanitation, medical care, must be provided.[2770] Those with special needs, children, mothers, the elderly,

2755. *Ibid.*, Art. 4(l).
2756. *Ibid.*, Art. 4(2).
2757. *Ibid.*, Art. 5(1). *See* Goodwin-Gill, 265.
2758. Kampala Convention Art. 5(4).
2759. *Ibid.*, Art. 5(5).
2760. *Ibid.*, Art. 5(7).
2761. *Ibid.*, Art. 5(6).
2762. *Ibid.*, Art. 5(3). *See also ibid.*, Art. 8(2) which reiterates the rights of States to request intervention from the AU in light of security problems caused by displacement.
2763. *Ibid.*, Art. 5(10). *See* UN Convention on Safety of United Nations and Associated Personnel (9 Dec. 1994) 2051 U.N.T.S. 363.
2764. *See* UN General Assembly Res. 46/182 (1991), Annex: Strengthening of the Coordination of Humanitarian Emergency Assistance of the United Nations, para. 3. However, at the same time it was acknowledged that victims of natural disasters are of concern to the international community. Moreover, UN practice has established that it can authorize enforcement action on humanitarian grounds, *see, e.g.*, UN Security Council Res. 794 (1992) on Somalia. *See also Military and Paramilitary Activities in and against Nicaragua (Nicaragua v. United States)* I.C.J. Reports 1986, paras 242–243.
2765. Kampala Convention Art. 5(12).
2766. *Ibid.*, Art 9(1)(b). It should be recalled that under Res. 1593 (2005) the UN Security Council referred the situation in Darfur to the ICC, resulting in the prosecution of the sitting President of Sudan, Omar Al Bashir, *The Prosecutor v. Omar Hassan Ahmad Al Bashir* ICC-02/05-01/09.
2767. Kampala Convention Art. 9(1)(c).
2768. *Ibid.*, Art. 9(1)(d).
2769. *Ibid.*, Art. 9(1)(e).
2770. *Ibid.*, Art. 9(2)(b).

must be provided for.[2771] States must do their utmost to trace and reunify separated families.[2772] The property of IDPs must be protected.[2773] The civilian nature of the camps must be maintained and protected against armed groups.[2774]

428. In light of events in Somalia and Darfur in particular where armed groups have attacked IDPs and disrupted the provision of humanitarian assistance, the Kampala Convention seeks to address the situation of IDPs in instances of armed conflict. It is made clear that there is nothing in the Kampala Convention that prevents a State from defending its sovereignty or re-establishing law and order by legitimate means,[2775] nor can the Kampala Convention be construed as affording legal status or recognition to armed groups.[2776] Members of armed groups are specifically prohibited from, *inter alia*, carrying out arbitrary displacement,[2777] from obstructing and impeding humanitarian assistance and resources to IDPs,[2778] attacking or harming humanitarian personnel,[2779] abduction and hostage taking, people trafficking and sexual slavery, as is forcible recruitment, including of children.[2780] Members of armed groups who violates the rights of IDPs will be held criminally liable under national and international law.[2781]

429. The Kampala Convention provides certain guarantees in relation to movement and settlement. IDPs have a right of freedom of movement, which is not absolute,[2782] and States must make provision for voluntary return, local integration or relocation.[2783] IDPs must be able to make a free and informed choice as to their resettlement.[2784] Significantly, States must create appropriate mechanisms to resolve property disputes and must, where possible, restore the lands of communities with 'special dependency and attachment to such lands'.[2785]

430. A particularly interesting feature of the Kampala Convention is the fact that it makes provision for effective remedies.[2786] States Parties must provide 'just and fair compensation and other forms of reparations' to IDPs for damage occurred as a result of dislocation where appropriate.[2787] In addition, a State incurs liability

2771. *Ibid.*, Art. 9(2)(c)–(d).
2772. *Ibid.*, Art. 9(2)(h).
2773. *Ibid.*, Art. 9(2)(i).
2774. *Ibid.*, Art. 9(2)(g). *See also ibid.*, Art. 7(5)(i).
2775. *Ibid.*, Art. 7(2).
2776. *Ibid.*, Art. 7(1).
2777. *Ibid.*, Art. 7(5)(a).
2778. *Ibid.*, Art. 7(5)(b), (g).
2779. *Ibid.*, Art. 7(5)(h).
2780. *Ibid.*, Art. 7(5)(e), (f).
2781. *Ibid.*, Art. 7(4).
2782. *Ibid.*, Art. 9(2)(f). *See also* African Charter Art. 12(1).
2783. Kampala Convention Art. 11(1).
2784. *Ibid.*, Art. 11(2).
2785. *Ibid.*, Art. 11(4)–(5). *See Centre for Minority Rights Development (Kenya) and Minority Rights Group International on behalf of Endorois Welfare Council v. Kenya*, Communication No. 276/2003 (2009).
2786. Kampala Convention Art.e 12(1).
2787. *Ibid.*, Art. 12(2).

when it fails to protect and assist IDPs in cases of natural disasters.[2788] The question arises as to what is meant by fair compensation, which by definition must include awards of a pecuniary nature as one option. Restitution in kind could be another possibility. But it could extend to ordering consequential measures requiring certain positive steps to be taken. However, the Kampala Convention may not be limited solely to material redress but appears to be open to the possibility of some form of amends for mental distress.

431. The AU has been the first organization of its type to tackle the significant predicament posed by IDPs. The Kampala Convention is a welcome development in that it seeks to establish a legal framework for resolving the causes of displacement and the problems arising in its wake. It sets out the rights of IDPs and the obligations of States towards them. In this respect, the fact that obligations are imposed on States towards humanitarian agencies and international organizations is important. Non-State actors, in the form of armed groups, are also under obligations towards IDPs, but how these are to be enforced is a matter of some doubt.[2789] The strengthening of the prohibition on arbitrary displacement is noteworthy. Its provisions on remedies are innovative but their effectiveness is to a degree dependent on the creation of appropriate mechanisms. Concern has been expressed that the human rights guarantees are imperfect but the fact that the African Charter is deemed applicable to IDPs makes this critique less plausible. All in all the Kampala Convention constitutes a creditable effort at dealing with the problem of IDPs.

2788. *Ibid.*, Art. 12(3).

2789. In general, a diligent State cannot be held responsible for the acts of rebels or insurrectionists, D.J. Harris, *Cases and Materials on International Law* (7th edn, London: Sweet & Maxwell, 2010), 430–431.

Chapter 4. Economic Cooperation

§1. The African Economic Community (AEC)

432. For many years after independence most African States largely experienced general economic decline. Economic growth tended to be uneven or unreliable. A combination of internal and external factors was responsible for this poor economic performance. The former include the pursuit of unsuccessful economic policies, lack of financial resources, deficiencies in institutional and physical infrastructures, insufficient managerial/administrative capacity, often leading to rampant corruption, kleptocracy, inadequate human resource development, and political instability. A business friendly environment often did not exist. External factors include adverse terms of trade, a decline in financial flows, overreliance on commodities, a decline in commodity prices and high debt and debt-servicing obligations.[2790] In a radical attempt to break the cycle of economic despair the African States came to the conclusion that a domestic solution, based on collective economic self-reliance, was not only necessary to reverse this trend and to ensure economic growth and prosperity but also feasible. The founding by the OAU of an AEC in 1991 represented one of the most ambitious developments in this field.[2791]

433. The AEC or Abuja, Treaty was adopted in June 1991 and entered into force in May 1994.[2792] Its objectives are: to promote economic, social, and cultural development and the integration of African economies in order to increase economic self-reliance and promote development; to harness and develop Africa's human and material resources; and to promote cooperation so as to raise the standard of living and enhance economic stability, foster peaceful relations among Member States and contribute to the progress, development and economic integration of Africa.[2793] These are to be achieved by, *inter alia*, the liberalization of trade through the abolition of customs duties on imports and exports and non-tariff barriers in order to establish a free trade area, the adoption of a common trade policy vis-à-vis third States, the harmonization of national policies in agriculture, industry, transport and communications, energy, trade, money and finance and science and technology, the

2790. *See* The Causes of Conflict and the Promotion of Durable Peace and Sustainable Development in Africa: Report of the Secretary-General, UN Doc. A/52/871-S/1998/318.

2791. Another significant initiative to promote economic and social development and to advance the economic integration of Africa was the Lagos Plan of Action for the Economic Development of Africa 1980, which sought to create favourable conditions to encourage economic growth in Africa. It also envisaged the creation of the AEC by the millennium. *See* R.M. D'Sa, 'The Lagos Plan of Action – Legal Mechanisms for Cooperation Between the Organization of African Unity and the United Nations Economic Commission for Africa', *J.A.L.* 27 (1983): 4.

2792. Treaty Establishing an African Economic Community (3 Jun. 1991), 30 I.L.M. 1241 (1991). As of January 2023, it has been ratified by fifty States. For analysis, *see* N.L. Lumu, *De la Nature de la Communauté Economique Africaine*, 8 R.A.D.I.C. 51 (1996); G.J. Naldi & K.D. Magliveras, 'The African Economic Community: Emancipation for African States or Yet Another Glorious Failure?', *North Carolina J. Int'l Law & Comm. Reg.* 24 (1999): 601; M. Ndulo, 'Harmonisation of Trade Laws in the African Economic Community', *I.C.L.Q.* 42 (1993): 101; B. Thompson, 'Economic Integration Efforts in Africa', *R.A.D.I.C.* 5 (1993): 743.

2793. AEC Treaty Art. 4(1).

establishment of a common external tariff, the removal of obstacles to the free movement of persons, goods, services and capital and the right of residence and establishment, and the establishment of a common market.[2794] Not unlike the EU, the AEC has the features of a supranational organization and foresees a role beyond the economic sphere, in the social and political worlds, leading eventually to political union, since achieved with the creation of the AU.[2795] The AEC Treaty is best described as a framework treaty setting down general policies with much of the detail to be provided in subsequent protocols.

434. The AEC Treaty seeks to regulate various areas of economic activity at both the regional and continental levels. The first important area concerns liberalization of trade and the creation of a customs union. Article 29 requires the progressive establishment of a customs union involving the elimination of customs duties, quota restrictions, other restrictions or prohibitions and administrative trade barriers, as well as all other non-tariff barriers, and the adoption of a common external customs tariff.[2796] The experience of the EU demonstrates that States are ingenious in developing barriers to the free movement of goods and it may therefore have been sensible to insert the phrase 'and measures of equivalent effect' where appropriate in the relevant provisions of the AEC Treaty.

435. Article 35 allows for derogation from the application of these provisions in a number of circumstances, none of which can be used as a means of arbitrary discrimination or a disguised restriction on trade. The grounds of derogation, which appear to be exhaustive, include national security, the control of arms and military equipment, protection of health and life of humans, animals and plants, public morality, protection of national treasures of artistic or archaeological value, protection of industrial, commercial and intellectual property, exports of strategic minerals and precious stones, the protection of infant industries, the control of hazardous and radioactive wastes and products and nuclear materials, the control of strategic products, balance of payment difficulties, and serious economic difficulties arising from imports from a Member State.[2797] It is submitted that the derogations should be subject to the principle of proportionality.

436. Another essential element of economic integration is the free movement of persons.[2798] Pursuant to Article 43 Member States undertake progressively to secure for their nationals the free movement of persons and the rights of residence and

2794. *Ibid.*, Art. 4(2).
2795. *See supra* Part II. Note that according to the Constitutive Act Art. 33(2) (26 May 2001), 2158 U.N.T.S. 3, its provisions take precedence over or supersede any inconsistent provisions of the AEC Treaty.
2796. The manner in which these objectives are to be achieved are specified in AEC Treaty Arts 30–34.
2797. This final exception is reinforced by AEC Treaty Art. 36 which prohibits the practice of 'dumping'.
2798. *See also ibid.*, Art. 71(2)(a). The free movement of persons is described as one of the 'fundamental freedoms' of EU Law, *see*, *e.g.*, Case 53/81 *Levin v. Staatssecretaris van Justicie* [1982] E.C.R. 1035. Thompson, 753–754, laments the lack of reference to 'Community citizenship' unlike the experience of ECOWAS, since she regards a common position on this issue as imperative for the accomplishment of the AEC's goals.

establishment within the AEC.[2799] By analogy with the EU experience,[2800] the issues that will need to be addressed include rights of entry and residence, the right to take up offers of employment, the right to look for employment,[2801] employment and associated rights, including equality in employment, unemployment and incapacity to work, the right to remain after employment, family rights, including schooling for dependants, the rights of non-AEC national dependants, entitlement to social security,[2802] public service employment, access to the professions, including the mutual recognition of qualifications, the rights of legal persons,[2803] and derogation on grounds of public policy, public security or public health, and the appropriate safeguards for persons whose rights of free movement may be restricted on such grounds.[2804]

437. Another crucial area is that of money and finance. Member States are to harmonize their monetary, financial and payment policies, including the insurance and banking sectors, with the eventual aim of establishing an African Monetary Union.[2805] Furthermore, the free movement of capital is to be achieved through the elimination of restrictions on the transfer of capital funds between Member States. The opening of bank accounts or the obtaining of loans from a financial institution in another Member State should therefore be facilitated. If the free movement of persons is to be properly secured then restrictions on the movement of capital belonging to persons resident in other Member States must be reduced. However, the very real risk exists that the liberalization of monetary controls, particularly exchange controls, could lead to the flight of money.

438. Other areas of cooperation addressed by the AEC Treaty include: agricultural development and food production;[2806] industrial development, science and technology, energy and natural resources, and the environment;[2807] transport and communications (post, telecommunications and broadcasting), including an integrated network;[2808] tourism;[2809] education, training and culture;[2810] and human resources, social affairs, health and population.[2811]

2799. The details as to how this freedom is to be guaranteed have been left to a later protocol. No express provision is made for the freedom to provide services, compare Treaty on the Functioning of the European Union (13 Dec. 2007), Art. 56 [2010] O.J. C 83 (30 Mar. 2010) 47, although the scope of the provision seems broad enough to encompass this freedom.
2800. A.M. Arnull, A.A. Dashwood, M.G. Ross & D.A. Wyatt, *European Union Law* (4th edn, London: Sweet & Maxwell, 2000), 380–494.
2801. *See also* AEC Treaty Art. 71(2)(b), (e).
2802. *See also ibid.*, Art. 72(2)(b).
2803. The application of this provision must be deemed to extend to legal persons, or the policy to be pursued would be substantially impeded.
2804. *See also* AEC Treaty Art. 72(2)(g).
2805. *Ibid.*, Art. 44.
2806. *Ibid.*, Arts 46–47.
2807. *Ibid.*, Arts 48–60.
2808. *Ibid.*, Arts 61–64.
2809. *Ibid.*, Art. 65.
2810. *Ibid.*, Arts 68–70.
2811. *Ibid.*, Arts 71–76.

439. The AEC's goals were to be effected gradually in six stages over a transitional period not exceeding forty years.[2812] While the AU seemed determined to accelerate the process of establishing the AEC[2813] progress was initially slow.[2814] It was only in 2012 that the AU adopted the First Plan of Action of the Minimum Integration Programme requesting that Member States speed up the integration process and initiate programmes to promote, *inter alia*, the free movement of persons, goods, services and capital.[2815] The AU also endorsed the Framework Road Map and Architecture for Fast Tracking the establishment of the CFTA and the Action Plan for Boosting Intra-African Trade.[2816] In its fiftieth anniversary Solemn Declaration in 2013 the AU reiterated its commitment to speed up the process of achieving the objectives of the AEC and implement promptly the CFTA.[2817] The vehicle for delivering these goals was Agenda 2063, considered more fully below.

§2. NEPAD

440. The transition to the AU presented African leaders with the opportunity to relaunch their campaign for economic development as progress on furthering the goals of the AEC Treaty stagnated. Economic cooperation is expressly listed as one of the purposes of the AU.[2818] The means chosen to this end was the New Partnership for Africa's Development (NEPAD) adopted in 2001.[2819] NEPAD is an AU 'strategic framework for pan-African socio-economic development' within the context of the AU.[2820] It seeks to eradicate poverty, promote sustainable growth and development, and integrate Africa into the global economy. One of the significant aspects of NEPAD is that it is based on an integrated approach, it accepts that a variety of factors, peace and security, democracy, good governance and human rights, are essential conditions for sustainable development.[2821] It seeks to enhance the

2812. *Ibid.*, Art. 6. *See* Thompson, 750–751; Y. Omorogbe, 'Economic Integration and African National Development', Proceedings African Social International & Comparative Law', 7 (1995): 279, 284–285.
2813. Constitutive Act, preamble.
2814. Assembly, *Decision on Economic Integration*, AU Doc. Assembly/AU/Dec. 178(X) (31 Jan.–2 Feb. 2008).
2815. Assembly, *Decision on African Integration*, AU Doc. Assembly/AU/Dec. 392(XVIII) (29–30 Jan. 2012).
2816. Assembly, *Decision on Boosting Intra-African Trade and Fast Tracking the Continental Free Trade Area*, AU Doc. Assembly/AU/Dec. 394(XVIII) (29–30 Jan. 2012).
2817. Assembly, *Solemn Declaration on the 50th Anniversary of the OAU/AU*, AU Doc. Assembly/AU/Decl. 3 (XXI) (26 May 2013) para. C.
2818. Constitutive Act Art. 2(b).
2819. The New Partnership for Africa's Development (NEPAD) Declaration 2001, C. Heyns & M. Killander (eds), *Compendium of Key Human Rights Documents of the African Union* (5th edn, Pretoria: Pretoria University Law Press, 2013), 486. *See* R. Murray, *Human Rights in Africa: From the OAU to the African Union* (Cambridge: Cambridge University Press, 2004), 38–42.
2820. In 2010 NEPAD was integrated into the AU structure, Assembly, *Decision on the Integration of the Transformation of the New Partnership for Africa's Development (NEPAD) into the Structures and Processes of the African Union including the Establishment of the NEPAD Planning and Co-ordinating Agency (NPCA)*, AU Doc. Assembly/AU/Dec. 283(XIV) (31 Jan.–2 Feb. 2010).
2821. NEPAD para. 71.

adoption of shared values and standards, policies, and good practice in these areas among its members. The RECs play an important role in its implementation.

441. But probably NEPAD's single most important practical feature is the peer review mechanism, the African Peer Review Mechanism (APRM), whereby a country's democratic and political governance, economic governance and management, corporate governance, and socioeconomic development record is subjected to periodic scrutiny in light of a number of benchmarks.[2822] Established in 2003, this self-monitoring and voluntary system allows for weaknesses to be identified and corrected.[2823] Member States' compliance with African and international standards in the areas of political and democratic governance, economic governance and good management, corporate governance, and socioeconomic development, is assessed. Crucially, any shortcomings identified by a review must be addressed by the State in question.

442. NEPAD's governing structure is based on three bodies: the AU Assembly, the NEPAD Heads of State and Government Orientation Committee (HGSOC), and the NEPAD Steering Committee. The AU Assembly is the body with ultimate responsibility; it oversees NEPAD and considers and adopts recommendations from the HGSOC Chair. The HGSOC sets policies and programmes of action. It is composed of twenty States, five permanent members (Algeria, Egypt, Nigeria, Senegal, South Africa) and fifteen others representing Africa's regions elected for a two-year period. The NEPAD Steering Committee develops the terms of reference for projects and programmes of action. It is made up of representatives nominated by the HGSOC from its members. A Sub-Committee, established in 2010, manages and supports activities promoting NEPAD. Mention must also be made of the NEPAD Planning and Co-ordinating Agency, an AU technical body. Its principal function is to facilitate and coordinate the implementation of the projects and programmes of action. To this end it cooperates actively with the UN.

443. Although NEPAD was welcomed by the UN[2824] it has nevertheless attracted some criticism, pointing to a lack of clear priorities[2825] or a lack of appreciation of the significance of human rights in realizing developmental goals.[2826] But these are surmountable problems. The one fundamental flaw that remains is that participation in the APRM is voluntary.

2822. Heyns & Killander, 497, 500; F. Viljoen, *International Human Rights Law in Africa* (Oxford: Oxford University Press, 2007), 211–216. Thirty-five AU Member States have joined the APRM.

2823. Although the APRM operated as an independent body, in 2014 it was integrated into the AU structure as an autonomous body, Assembly, *Decision on the Integration of the APRM into the African Union*, AU Doc. Assembly/AU/Dec. 527(XXIII) (26–27 Jun. 2014).

2824. World Summit Outcome, UN General Assembly Res. 60/1, UN Doc. A/Res/60/1, para. 68.

2825. Murray, 264.

2826. Viljoen, 216.

§3. AGENDA 2063

444. In 2015 the AU adopted Agenda 2063, a bold strategic people-driven plan for pan-African renewal of an 'integrated, prosperous and peaceful Africa' based on, *inter alia*, the structural transformation and integration of African economies through growth and sustainable socioeconomic development, peace, human rights and good governance, building upon the Lagos Plan of Action, the AEC Treaty and NEPAD.[2827] It reflects deeply held desires for unity and integration, peace and improved human security, progress and development, and a meaningful voice for Africa on the global stage. Its projects, or 'aspirations', are to be secured by a series of five ten-year plans over fifty years and the First Ten-Year Implementation Plan, a medium-term development plan involving Member States, RECs and the AU, has since been launched.[2828] It covers a number of areas, including sustainable economic growth, human capital development, employment creation, social protection, gender and youth development, infrastructure development, good governance, science and technology, peace and security, and culture, sports and arts. More specifically, it seeks to achieve these goals by, *inter alia*, encouraging private-public sector partnerships and greater involvement of the private sector, improving the public sector, preventing and combatting corruption, developing tax policies, increasing investment in agriculture, education, health and urban settlement, alleviating poverty and raising living standards, generating employment, providing basic social services, and sustainable natural resource management. Other goals include entrenching human rights, the rule of law and good governance, and bringing conflicts to an end. The achievement of many of these goals requires the establishment of financial institutions, such as the AIB, the Pan-African Stock Exchange and the African Central Bank, and of a regulatory framework. Among its foremost projects pertinent here are the CFTA and the African Passport and the free movement of persons. It is intended the CFTA will be launched in 2018, to be followed in later years by an African Customs Union, an African Common Market and African Monetary Union by 2023. The aim is to enhance free movement of persons by 2018.

445. The AEC Treaty, NEPAD and Agenda 2063 are ambitious projects that typify the global trends towards regional economic integration. But they additionally signify a concrete expression of the ultimate objective of economic integration.[2829] However, the future of these long-term projects face considerable hurdles. Political instability remains a major obstacle. The historical weakness and mismanagement of many African economies are obvious difficulties. In this regard, the African Charter on Democracy made a start in addressing these weaknesses by seeking

2827. Assembly, *Decision on the Report of the Commission on Development of the African Union Agenda 2063*, AU Doc. Assembly/AU/Dec. 565(XXIV) (30–31 Jan. 2015).

2828. African Union Commission, *Agenda 2063, The Africa We Want: First Ten-Year Implementation Plan* (2015).The Africa Progress Panel, a civil society organization, has stressed the need to secure universal access to energy across Africa, Africa Progress Panel, *Africa Progress Report 2013*, 14–19, http://www.africaprogresspanel.org (accessed 15 May 2013).

2829. *See, e.g.*, Assembly, *Decision on the Progress Report on the Transformation of the African Union Commission into the African Union Authority*, AU Doc. Assembly/AU/Dec. 454(XX) (27–28 Jan. 2013) para. 3.

to advance good and efficient economic governance. And Agenda 2063 recognizes these barriers to progress and acknowledges that they must be confronted and overcome. NEPAD is also important as it provides a structured framework that lays the foundations for development. More importantly, African States appear to take their NEPAD commitments seriously. But Agenda 2063 is especially significant. It brings together the aims and objectives set out in the earlier instruments and sets out new goals for both the immediate and longer terms. In light of the challenges facing Africa Agenda 2063 may be overambitious and some of its goals may not be attainable in the time frame without serious political commitment. Africa is, of course, exposed to global economic forces. Although much of Africa is resource-rich in terms of much sought-after commodities, oil and gas, minerals, etc., they are subject to the vagaries of the market. The last decade has witnessed economic growth and improvement in economic opportunities, and despite the economic downturn of recent years Africa's economic outlook remains optimistic.[2830] Wealth is being distributed more equitably, although the gap between the wealthy and the poor, the majority, is still enormous. If the African continent can sustain a peaceful and stable environment then economic development is likely to follow.

2830. *ECA Economic Report on Africa 2017* http://www.uneca.org/publications/economic-report-africa-2017 (accessed 10 May 2017). The Mo Ibrahim Foundation, a civil society organization, rated Mauritius as the clear leader in its Sustainable Economic Opportunity index for 2015, with South Africa, Morocco and Botswana some way behind, *2016 Ibrahim Index of African Governance: Sustainable Economic Opportunity*, http//:moibrahimfoundation.org/en (accessed 8 Mar. 2017). Mauritius, Rwanda and Botswana were the top three rated countries in its Business Environment index.

Chapter 5. Environment

446. Africa has been particularly susceptible to environmental degradation in recent times.[2831] That Africa suffers from drought and desertification,[2832] and the spoliation of natural resources, is common knowledge. Yet the OAU had been an early convert to conservation and the need to protect the environment. In 1968, the OAU had adopted the Convention on the Conservation of Nature and Natural Resources, according to which the parties undertake to conserve, utilize and develop soil, water, flora and fauna resources.[2833] Development is also a central element of this treaty.[2834] In 2003, this Convention was superseded by the Revised African Convention on the Conservation of Nature and Natural Resources.[2835] The objectives of the Revised Convention are, *inter alia*, to enhance environmental protection, and to foster the conservation and sustainable use of natural resources.[2836] Its guiding principles are the right to a sustainable environment and the right to development and the ensuing duty on States to ensure that both these needs are met in a sustainable, fair and equitable manner.[2837] Significantly, States agree as a fundamental obligation to take all necessary measures to achieve its objectives, especially through preventive measures and the application of the precautionary principle.[2838] Other important aspects of the Revised Convention are the inclusion of procedural rights,[2839] and an acknowledgement, albeit decidedly limited, of indigenous rights.[2840] Under Article 58(1) of the AEC Treaty, Member States commit themselves to promote a healthy environment. The Grand Bay Declaration affirmed the right to a healthy environment as a human right that was infringed by

---

2831. *See* UN General Assembly Res. A/RES/S-19/2 on Progress Achieved Towards Meeting Objectives of the Earth Summit, 36 I.L.M. 1639 (1997).
2832. Note the UN Convention to Combat Desertification (15 Sep. 1994), 1954 U.N.T.S. 3, 33 I.L.M. 1328 (1994), which, *inter alia*, establishes a regional programme for Africa to fight land degradation. Africa is vulnerable to climate change, Africa Progress Panel, *Africa Progress Report 2015*, 20–21, http://www.africaprogresspanel.org (accessed 29 Apr. 2017). Many African countries have therefore been supportive of the Paris Agreement (12 Dec. 2015) which seeks to impose reductions on greenhouse gas emissions.
2833. OAU Convention on the Conservation of Nature and Natural Resources (15 Sep. 1968), 1001 U.N.T.S. 3. The Convention was wide-ranging and innovative, F. Viljoen, *International Human Rights Law in Africa* (Oxford: Oxford University Press, 2007), 289. *See further* M. van der Linde, 'A Review of the African Convention on Nature and Natural Resources', *A.H.R.L.J.* 2 (2002): 33. It should be noted that South Sudan is the only African State not to have ratified the Convention on International Trade in Endangered Species of Wild Fauna and Flora and Fauna (3 Mar. 1973), 993 U.N.T.S. (CITES). Poaching remains a significant problem.
2834. OAU Convention on Nature and Natural Resources Art. 7.
2835. African Convention on the Conservation of Nature and Natural Resources (Revised) (11 Jul. 2003), https://www.au.int/en/treaties, C. Heyns & M. Killander (eds), *Compendium of Key Human Rights Documents of the African Union* (6th edn, Pretoria: Pretoria University Law Press, 2016), 98. The Convention entered into force on 23 July 2016. As of September 2023, it had been ratified by seventeen States. *See* Viljoen, 289–90.
2836. OAU Revised Convention on Nature and Natural Resources Art. 2(1)–(2).
2837. *Ibid.*, Art. 3. The nexus between the need to protect the environment in order to achieve sustainable development is reaffirmed by the African Charter on Democracy Art. 42.
2838. On the precautionary principle *see* para. 444 n. 2873 *infra*.
2839. OAU Revised Convention on Nature and Natural Resources Art. 16.
2840. *Ibid.*, Art. 17.

environmental degradation.[2841] But the most notable development is this regard had been the inclusion in the African Charter on Human and Peoples' Rights of the environment as a human, and justiciable, right.[2842] It will be recalled that the African Commission on Human and Peoples' Rights found that Article 24 of the African Charter placed an obligation on States to take reasonable steps, *inter alia*, to prevent polluting activities and ecological degradation, and to promote conservation.[2843] Of particular interest is the tough stance adopted by the Malabo Protocol according to which the illegal exploitation of natural resources is classified as a crime over which the ICL Section has jurisdiction.[2844] In this light it is therefore surprising, and regrettable, that the AU Constitutive Act is essentially silent on the issue of the environment.[2845]

447. But Africa has also been confronted with another menace, the practice of the illicit dumping of toxic and dangerous substances, sometimes described as 'toxic waste colonialism',[2846] with all the attendant risks that that implies for the well-being of local populations and the ecosystem, and which undeniably has adverse effects on the enjoyment of human rights.[2847] The OAU Council of Ministers therefore declared in 1988 that the dumping of nuclear and industrial wastes was 'a crime against Africa and the African people'.[2848] Growing hostility to these dangerous and

---

2841. Grand Bay (Mauritius) Declaration and Plan of Action 1999, paras 2, 8(n), Heyns & Killander, 149.

2842. *See* para. 284 *supra*.

2843. *The Social and Economic Rights Action Center and the Center for Economic and Social Rights v. Nigeria*, Communication No. 155/96, 15th Activity Report 2001–2002, para. 52.

2844. Statute on the Malabo Protocol Arts 28A(1)(13), and 28L*bis*. *See* M. V.S. Sirleaf, 'Prosecuting Dirty Dumping in Africa', in C.C. Jalloh, K. M. Clarke & V.O. Nmehielle, *The African Court of Justice and Human and Peoples' Rights in Context* (Cambridge: Cambridge University Press, 2019), 553, 573 *et seq*.

2845. But *see* Constitutive Act Art. 13(1)(f) which lists environmental protection as one of the policy areas of the Executive Council.

2846. *See* L. A. W. Pratt, 'Decreasing Dirty Dumping? A Reevaluation of Toxic Waste Colonialism and the Global Management of Transboundary Hazardous Waste', *William & Mary Environmental Law & Policy Review* 35 (2011): 581, 584, who defines this occurrence as 'where underdeveloped states are used as inexpensive alternatives for the export or disposal of hazardous waste pollution by developed states'.

2847. UN Commission on Human Rights, Adverse effects of the illicit movement and dumping of toxic and dangerous wastes on the enjoyment of human rights, Progress Report of the Special Rapporteur, UN Docs. E/CN.4/1998/10, E/CN.4/2001/55, para. 18. *See further* Sirleaf, 558–564; S. Atteh, 'Political Economy of Environmental Degradation: The Dumping of Toxic Waste in Africa', *International Studies* 30 (1993): 2, 19–26; D. Tladi, 'The quest to ban hazardous waste import into Africa: first Bamako and now Basel' (2000) 33 C.I.L.S.A.: 210, 211–12. The reasons why Africa became a dumping ground for hazardous wastes are various, *see* C.N. Eze, *The Bamako Convention on the Ban of the Import into Africa and the Control of the Transboundary Movement and Management of Hazardous Wastes within Africa: A Milestone in Environmental Protection?*, 15 R.A.D.I.C. 208, 209–210 (2007). According to Atteh, 26, the reasons include, *inter alia*, an acute shortage of disposal facilities in the developed countries, more stringent environmental laws, higher costs of waste disposal in exporting countries, and the willingness of developing countries to receive hazardous waste in exchange for payment. Another commentator states that the 'key driver is profit', Sirleaf, 557.

2848. Resolution 1153 (XLVIII) of 25 May 1988, Art. 1, 28 I.L.M. 567 (1989). The UN General Assembly also condemned the dumping of such wastes in Africa in Res. 43/75 T. Moreover, in the

often illegal practices resulted in international action regulating the movement and disposal of hazardous waste. This section focuses on the attempts of the OAU/AU to deal with the latter problem.[2849]

448. The response of the international community in seeking to police the dumping of toxic wastes was the adoption of the Basel Convention on Hazardous Wastes in 1989.[2850] The Basel Convention was a compromise between advocates of a complete ban on transboundary movements of wastes, mainly developing countries, which, often lacking the means to dispose properly of such wastes, argued that regulation was no guarantee against pollution, and those that wanted to establish a regulatory framework for the international transfer and treatment of wastes, ultimately opting for a partial ban on the transboundary movement of wastes.[2851] One commentator has described the Basel Convention as based on the key premise that hazardous waste can be exported from industrialized to developing countries subject to regulation and control.[2852] Additionally, it 'does not establish any regime of liability for harm caused by waste dumping.'[2853]As such the Basel Convention was a disappointment for the former which considered it inadequate as institutionalizing dangerous practices and hence prompted further action.

Vienna Declaration and Programme of Action 1993 pt. I, para. 11, 32 I.L.M. 1661 (1993), the international community recognized 'that the illicit dumping of toxic and dangerous substances and wastes potentially constitutes a serious threat to the human rights to life and health of everyone'. Accordingly, it called upon all States to adopt and implement rigorously existing treaties relating to the dumping of toxic and hazardous wastes and to cooperate in the prevention of illicit dumping.

2849. In the discussion of this section the author has relied considerably on the Progress Reports of the UN Special Rapporteur on Adverse effects of the illicit movement and dumping of toxic and dangerous wastes on the enjoyment of human rights.

2850. Basel Convention on the Control of Transboundary Movements of Hazardous Wastes and their Disposal (22 Mar. 1989), 1673 U.N.T.S. 57, 28 I.L.M. 657 (1989). The Basel Convention entered into force on 5 May 1992 and has been ratified by fifty-one African States as of July 2023. The Basel Convention has been amended twice; the Ban Amendment (22 Sep. 1995) prohibiting hazardous waste exports from Members of the Organization for Economic Co-operation and Development and the EU to developing countries which entered into force on 5 December 2019, and the Plastics Amendment (10 May 2019) to enhance the control of transboundary movements of plastic waste and clarify the Convention as it applies to such waste. For analysis of the Basel Convention, *see* P.W. Birnie & A.E. Boyle, *International Law and the Environment* (Oxford: Clarendon Press, 1992), 332–343; M. Bothé, 'International Regulation of Transboundary Movement of Hazardous Waste', *German Y.B.I.L.* 33 (1990): 422; K. Kummer, 'The International Regulation of Transboundary Traffic in Hazardous Wastes: The 1989 Basel Convention', *I.C.L.Q.* 41 (1992): 530. International efforts to control hazardous chemicals led to the adoption of the Stockholm Convention on Persistent Organic Pollutants (22 May 2001), 2256 U.N.T.S. 119, calling for the reduction and elimination in the release of these chemicals.

2851. According to Basel Convention Art. 4(1) any State has the right to ban the entry or disposal of foreign hazardous wastes and other wastes in its territory, and no State party may permit hazardous wastes to be exported to a party that has prohibited their import. *See further* Birnie & Boyle, 332–333; Tladi, 213–14.

2852. Viljoen, 290.

2853. R. V. Percival, 'Global Law and the Environment', *Washington Law Review* 86 (2011): 579, 622. However, in 1999 the Basel Protocol on Liability and Compensation for Damage Resulting from Transboundary Movements of Hazardous Waste and their Disposal (10 Dec. 1999) was adopted. Its objective is 'to provide for a comprehensive regime for liability as well as adequate and prompt

449. The Basel Convention requires that States Parties prevent the import of hazardous and other wastes where they had reason to believe that such wastes would not be managed in an environmentally sound manner.[2854] However, there was recognition that the transboundary movement of hazardous wastes to developing countries might be problematic since many of these States lacked the means to deal adequately with them. As a result, the decision was taken in 1995 to amend the Basel Convention, as from the end of 1997, in order to prohibit the export of hazardous wastes, even for recycling purposes, from Organization for Economic Cooperation and Development (OECD) member countries to non-member countries, thereby specifically addressing the criticisms of developing countries.[2855] This development came too late for the OAU, however, which, considering the Basel Convention flawed with respect to developing countries, in particular the failure to agree a total ban on the export of hazardous and other wastes to Africa, proceeded with its own initiative to combat the transboundary movement of hazardous wastes.

450. The Bamako Convention on Hazardous Wastes was adopted by the OAU in 1991[2856] as the regional complement to the Basel Convention which allows for the establishment of regional agreements of equal or added rigour.[2857] The basic characteristics of the regulatory system set in place by the Bamako Convention may be said to be 'prohibition and control'.[2858]

451. The Bamako Convention has adopted a broad definition of waste.[2859] Wastes are considered hazardous according to Article 2(1) when they are: (a) listed

---

compensation for damage resulting from the transboundary movement of hazardous wastes and other wastes, including incidents occurring because of illegal traffic in those wastes.'

2854. Basel Convention Art. 4(2)(g).

2855. Third Meeting of the Conference of the Parties to the Basel Convention, Decision 111/1, 18–22 Sep. 1995, UNEP/CHW.3/35. The so-called Basel Ban Amendment entered into force on 5 December 2019. However, States that have not ratified the amendment can continue to export hazardous substances. It seems developing countries believed recycling could provide a loophole for illegal imports, Tladi, 220.

2856. Bamako Convention on the Ban of the Import of Hazardous Wastes into Africa and on the Control of their Transboundary Movements within Africa (30 Jan. 1991), 2101 U.N.T.S. 177, 30 I.L.M. 773 (1991), entered into force on 22 Apr. 1998. As of February 2023, it had been ratified by – thirty States. For analysis, *see* Eze; Sirleaf, 568–570; Tladi& I. Cheyne, 'Africa and the International Trade in Hazardous Wastes', *R.A.D.I.C.* 6 (1994): 493; H.S. Kaminsky, 'Assessment of the Bamako Convention on the Ban of Import into Africa and the Control of Transboundary Movement and Management of Hazardous Wastes Within Africa', *The Georgetown International Environmental Law Review* 5 (1992): 77; F. Ouguergouz, 'The Bamako Convention on Hazardous Waste: A New Step in the Development of the African International Environmental Law', *A.Y.B.I.L.* 1 (1994): 19; K. Magliveras, 'A Comparative Examination of the African and South Pacific Radioactive Waste Management Regimes', *American Yearbook of International Law* 1 (2022): 370.

2857. *See* Basel Convention Art. 11(1). The view has been expressed that such a regional initiative is a more pragmatic way of protecting the interests of developing countries than a total international ban, Birnie & Boyle, 341–342.

2858. Ouguergouz, 200. Its features are described as being based upon prior informed consent, the prevention of illegal trade, a duty of reimport and environmentally sound treatment of waste, Birnie & Boyle, 334.

2859. Cheyne, 497–499; Eze, 217, 226; Tladi, 217–18.

in the Convention's annexes; (b) defined as hazardous by the domestic legislation of a State of export, import or transit; and (c) banned, cancelled or refused registration by a State, or voluntarily withdrawn from registration in the country of manufacture for human health or environmental reasons. Significantly radioactive wastes are included, by virtue of Article 2(2), in the scope of the Bamako Convention.[2860]

452. A distinction is drawn between waste generated outside of Africa and waste generated within Africa. With regard to the former, Parties to the Bamako Convention, 'aware of the risk of damage to human health and the environment caused by transboundary movements of hazardous wastes'[2861] and 'further recognizing the sovereignty of States to ban the importation into, and the transit through, their territory, of hazardous wastes and substances for human health and environmental reasons',[2862] hence introduce, first, a hazardous waste import ban; therefore, in accordance with Article 4(1), 'All Parties shall take appropriate legal, administrative and other measures within the area under their jurisdiction to prohibit the import of all hazardous wastes, for any reason, into Africa from non-Contracting Parties. Such import shall be deemed illegal and a criminal act.'[2863] And second, a ban on dumping of hazardous wastes at sea, internal waters and waterways; accordingly, under Article 4(2)(a), States parties shall 'adopt legal, administrative and other appropriate measures to control all carriers from non-Parties, and prohibit the dumping at sea of hazardous wastes'.[2864] The ban on hazardous wastes meets the basic demands of the African States and is reinforced by Article 59 of the AEC Treaty. And in its relations with the EU-African States have ensured that their concerns over the dumping of such wastes is taken into consideration.[2865]

453. The transboundary movement of wastes produced in Africa, or intra-African movement, is permitted but the Bamako Convention emphasizes the environmentally sound and efficient management of hazardous wastes, and thus prohibits exports to States where this cannot be guaranteed.[2866] It requires that each

2860. Whereas the Basel Convention excludes radioactive wastes, *see* Art. 4(3). The Basel Convention has been described as being essentially limited to household and hazardous wastes, Birnie & Boyle, 335. It has been suggested that the reason for the omission is because radioactive wastes are already subject to control by the International Atomic Energy Agency, Kummer, 543–544.
2861. Bamako Convention preambular para. 3.
2862. *Ibid.*, preambular para. 6.
2863. According to the Basel Convention Art. 4(3), 'illegal traffic in hazardous wastes or other wastes is criminal'. *See also* the European Convention on the Protection of the Environment Through Criminal Law (4 Nov. 1998), C.E.T.S. No. 172, 38 I.L.M. 259 (1999). As mentioned above, according to the Malabo Protocol Arts 28A(1)(12), and 28L, trafficking in hazardous wastes is a crime over which the ICL Section has jurisdiction.
2864. It should be observed that by virtue of Bamako Convention Art. 4(4)(c) general rights of navigation under international law through maritime zones subject to national jurisdiction remain unimpaired, *see further*, Birnie & Boyle, 336–337.
2865. Cotonou Agreement (23 Jun. 2000) O.J. L 317, 15 Dec. 2000, Declarations IX-X.
2866. Bamako Convention Art. 4(3)(i), (j), (k), (n), (o), (t); Tladi, 221.

Party, *inter alia*, 'impose strict, unlimited liability as well as joint and several liability on hazardous wastes generators',[2867] seemingly as a means of encouraging the appropriate disposal of hazardous wastes.[2868] The onus is on the generator because s/he is assumed to exercise effective responsibility.[2869]

454. The Bamako Convention additionally requires Parties to 'strive to adopt and implement the preventive, precautionary approach to pollution problems'.[2870] It should be noted that the Parties are also required to apply clean production methods,[2871] that is, production or industrial systems which avoid or eliminate the generation of hazardous wastes.[2872]

455. Article 6 establishes a system of prior informed consent and notification procedures for proposed transboundary movement of hazardous wastes.[2873] The

2867. Bamako Convention Art. 4(3)(b). *See further ibid.*, Art. 12 which calls for a protocol to establish the appropriate rules and procedures in the field of liabilities and compensation. Again, the Bamako Convention adopts a stricter regime than that of the Basel Convention since the latter, under Art. 12, merely requires Parties to cooperate 'with a view to adopting, as soon as practicable, a protocol setting out appropriate rules and procedures in the field of liability and compensation', *see* Birnie & Boyle, 340–341; Kummer, 554–555. Note that in 1993 the Council of Europe adopted a Convention on Civil Liability for Damage Resulting from Activities Dangerous to the Environment (21 Jun. 1993) E.T.S. No. 150, 32 I.L.M. 1228 (1993). *See* generally S.D. Murphy, 'Prospective Liability Regimes for the Transboundary Movement of Hazardous Wastes', *A.J.I.L.* 88 (1994): 24.

2868. C.R.H. Shearer, *Comparative analysis of the Basel and Bamako Conventions on hazardous waste*, 23 *Environmental Law* 141, 157–158 (1993).

2869. Kaminsky, 87.

2870. Bamako Convention Art. 4(3)(f). The Bamako Convention appears to have pioneered the inclusion of the precautionary principle in the operative section of the treaty, Kaminsky, 84. *See further*, Rio Declaration on Environment and Development (Principle 15). The ICJ seems to regard the precautionary principle as having persuasive authority as an emergent norm of international law, *Gabcíkovo-Nagymaros Project Case (Hungary v. Slovakia)* I.C.J. Reports 1997, 7, paras 112–113. And *see Pulp Mills on the River Uruguay (Argentina v. Uruguay)* I.C.J. Reports 2010, 14, para. 164. *See also* the Dissenting Opinions of Judges Weeramantry and Koroma in *Request for an Examination of the Situation in Accordance with paragraph 63 of the Court's Judgment in the 1974 Nuclear Tests Case* I.C.J. Reports 1995, 288, 342–344, and 368 respectively. However, it is instructive to note that the Bamako Convention specifies the 'precautionary approach' and a distinction has been drawn between the precautionary approach and the precautionary principle, the former seeming to possess the advantage of flexibility, *see* the Separate Opinions of Judges Laing and Treves in *Southern Bluefin Tuna Cases* (*New Zealand v. Japan*; *Australia v. Japan*) 38 I.L.M. 1624, 1641–1642, 1645 (1999), respectively. The 'precautionary approach' may now form part of customary law, *Responsibilities and Obligations of States Sponsoring Persons and Entities with respect to Activities in the Area, Advisory Opinion*, I.T.L.O.S. Reports 2011, 10, para. 135.

2871. Bamako Convention Art. 4(3)(f)–(g). *See also ibid.*, Art. 10. However, the attainability of such ambitious goals for many African States in the short term was questioned, Shearer, 176–177.

2872. Bamako Convention Art. 1(5).

2873. Kaminsky, 79–81; Shearer, 167–169. *See also* Bamako Convention Art. 4(3)(u). This is also the case with the Basel Convention, *see* Birnie & Boyle, 336–338; Kummer, 547–551. In addition, Bamako Convention Art. 13(1) provides that the Parties 'shall ensure that in the case of an accident occurring during the transboundary movement of hazardous wastes or their disposal which is likely to present risks to human health and the environment in other States those States are immediately informed'. Note the Rotterdam Convention on the Prior Informed Consent Procedure for Certain Hazardous Chemicals and Pesticides in International Trade (10 Sep. 1998), 2244 U.N.T.S. 337, 38 I.L.M. 1 (1999). By virtue of Bamako Convention Art. 7, Art. 6(2)–(4) applies

State of export may not allow the transboundary movement until it has received written consent by the State of import and written confirmation of the existence of a contract between the exporter and the disposer specifying environmentally sound management of the wastes in question.

456. A duty to reimport is imposed by Article 8. Where a legitimate transboundary movement of hazardous wastes cannot be completed in accordance with the terms of the contract, the State of export must ensure the reimport of the wastes by the exporter, if alternative arrangements cannot be made for their disposal in an environmentally sound manner within ninety days from the time the exporting State and the Secretariat have been informed by the importing State. The State of export and any State of transit must not oppose, hinder or prevent the return of the wastes to the State of export.[2874]

457. Article 9 addresses the issue of illegal waste. Hence, any transboundary movement of hazardous wastes:

> (a) if carried out without notification, pursuant to the provisions of this Convention, to all States concerned; or (b) if carried out without the consent, pursuant to the provisions of this Convention, of a State concerned; or (c) if consent is obtained from States concerned through falsification, misrepresentation or fraud; or (d) if it does not conform in a material way with the documents; or (e) if it results in deliberate disposal of hazardous wastes in contravention of this Convention and of general principles of international law is deemed to be illegal.[2875]

458. In addition to the imposition of liability under Article 4(3)(b), Article 9(2) requires States parties to legislate in order to provide for criminal sanctions, which must be sufficiently severe to punish and deter, to be imposed on illegal traffickers.[2876] If a movement is held to be illegal traffic as a result of conduct on the part of the exporter or generator the State of export must ensure that the waste is taken

---

mutatis mutandis to the movement of waste from a Party through a State which is not a Party. It now seems that customary international law requires comprehensive environmental impact assessments to be undertaken with a view to identifying potential threats to the environment and public health, *Gabcíkovo-Nagymaros Project Case* I.C.J. Reports 1997, 7, para. 112; *Pulp Mills on the River Uruguay*, I.C.J. Reports 2010, 14, para. 204; *Responsibilities and Obligations of States Sponsoring Persons and Entities with respect to Activities in the Area*, I.T.L.O.S. Reports 2011, paras 147–148. *See also* the Convention on Environmental Impact Assessment in a Transboundary Context (25 Feb. 1991) 1989 U.N.T.S. 310, 30 I.L.M. 800 (1991). The Libréville Declaration on Health and Environment in Africa, Libréville (29 Aug. 2008) calls for the setting up of systematic health and environmental risk assessments, para. 9.

2874. This provision is virtually identical to Art. 8 of the Basel Convention, *see* Kummer, 553–554, who asserts that illegal traffic is excluded from the scope of the provision. Moreover, she draws attention to the fact that no definition of non-completion of the contract is given.

2875. Compare Basel Convention Art. 9(1).

2876. *See also* Bamako Convention Art. 4(4)(a)–(b). Compare Basel Convention Art. 9(5), under which parties are required to 'introduce appropriate national/domestic legislation to prevent and punish illegal traffic'.

back by the exporter or generator or State of export within thirty days.[2877] The return of the wastes to the State of export shall not be opposed, hindered or otherwise prevented.[2878] Furthermore, if a movement is deemed to be illegal traffic as a result of conduct by the importer or disposer, the State of import must ensure that the wastes are returned to the exporter by the importer.[2879] It is not clear how such States are to be compelled to act in such manner but recourse could be had to the settlement of disputes procedure under the Convention.[2880]

459. The Bamako Convention's regulatory system would be ineffective in the absence of control and monitoring mechanisms. Particularly worthy of mention in this context is the Secretariat which is entrusted with a number of administrative functions.[2881] These include acting as a repository of information and assisting in the identification of cases of illegal traffic. The Secretariat also has the responsibility of verifying allegations made by a State Party that another State Party has violated its obligations under the Convention.[2882] For their part, States Parties must establish competent authorities.[2883]

460. It appears safe to conclude that the Bamako Convention is significantly stricter than the Basel Convention in many respects.[2884] Especially noteworthy are the wider scope of the Bamako Convention, the total ban on the importation of waste from outside Africa, and the adoption of the precautionary principle and the use of clean production methods. Given Africa's background as a dumping ground for toxic wastes and the lack of expertise on the part of African States it is understandable why the OAU should have favoured a restrictive approach.[2885] However, such inflexibility has been questioned. The inclusion of radioactive waste may prove problematic with commitments under other treaties.[2886] The total ban on imported waste may hamper the development of African industry.[2887] And the adoption of clean production methods may simply be beyond the capabilities of most African States at present.[2888] Nevertheless, the OAU set a standard for the international community to equal. Despite the acute nature of the problem and the profound feelings of the OAU/AU on the subject the Bamako Convention could prove too complex and too expensive for the majority of African States. The Libréville Declaration acknowledged in 2008 that it was not being implemented.

2877. Bamako Convention Art. 9(3).
2878. *Ibid.*
2879. *Ibid.*, Art. 9(4).
2880. *Ibid.*, Art. 20.
2881. *Ibid.*, Art. 16. *See* Eze, 221–222.
2882. Bamako Convention Art. 19.
2883. *Ibid.*, Art. 5.
2884. Eze, 225–229; Ouguergouz, 210–212.
2885. Cheyne, 499–503.
2886. Shearer, 175.
2887. *Ibid.*
2888. *Ibid.*, 176.

461. Nonetheless, much still remains to be done since there appears to be little sign of a reduction in the movement of hazardous wastes from industrialized countries to the Third World. Traffickers seem to be able to adapt to the changing international situation. One example is the dumping of toxic wastes in maritime space around Africa.[2889] However, the ban on hazardous wastes will not prove effective unless accompanied by practical measures for the detection of illicit operations. International cooperation, including the provision of financial and technical aid to Africa, seems vital.[2890] African States must be provided with the means of cleaning and remedying existing contamination. The technical capacities of developing countries to detect and prevent illicit traffic must therefore be strengthened. Particularly significant in this regard has been the First Continental Conference for Africa on the Environmentally Sound Management of Unwanted Stocks of Hazardous Wastes and their Prevention, convened by the secretariat of the Basel Convention in Rabat in January 2001. An action programme for Africa had been adopted, *inter alia*, to eliminate existing pesticides and the possibilities for international assistance and financing had been examined. The Libréville Declaration, which is not limited to the problem of hazardous waste, recognizes that strategies and policies must be put in place to develop, implement and monitor strategies and policies aimed at health and environmental security. Finally, national legislation to reduce and punish illegal transboundary movements of waste must be enacted and enforced.[2891]

2889. Assembly, *Decision on the Report of the Peace and Security Council on its Activities and the State of Peace and Security in Africa* (1–3 Jul. 2009) Thirteenth Ordinary Session, Assembly/AU/Dec. 252(XIII) para. 18.

2890. Some aid is being realized, UN Doc. E/CN.4/1999/SR.21, para. 63. Note the First Continental Conference for Africa on the Environmentally Sound management of Unwanted Stocks of Hazardous wastes and their Prevention, convened by the Secretariat of the Basel Convention in Rabat, 8–12 Jan. 2001.

2891. UN Commission on Human Rights, Adverse effects of the illicit movement and dumping of toxic and dangerous wastes on the enjoyment of human rights, Progress Report of the Special Rapporteur, UN Doc. E/CN.4/1998/10.

Chapter 6. Other Areas of Activity

§1. MERCENARISM

462. Mercenary activity has been a troubling element of post-colonial Africa. The involvement of mercenaries has been a feature of many of the armed conflicts that have affected Africa.[2892] Over many years mercenaries have threatened the sovereignty, independence, territorial integrity and security of many African States, undermining the right of self-determination, destabilizing governments and generally compromising peace and good order.[2893] More recently mercenaries have been departing from traditional mercenary activities, that is, fighting for financial gain in an armed conflict alien to their own nationality, and have diversified into new areas,[2894] implicated in the illegal exploitation and trafficking of natural resources such as diamonds and other precious stones in Angola and other conflict zones,[2895] and the provision of private security services, offering military and security services on the international market to governments and non-state actors.[2896] Non-State armed groups and private military and security companies (PMSCs) have become particularly active in the Sahel and the Central Africa region, plagued by terrorist

2892. *See* E. Kwakwa, 'The Current Status of Mercenaries in the Law of Armed Conflict', *Hastings International and Comparative Law Review* 14 (1990): 67, 75–78; M. Foaleng, 'African Mercenarism', in S. Gumedze, *Elimination of Mercenarism in Africa: A Need for a New Continental Approach* (Pretoria: ISS Monograph Series, 2008), 45, 52–57; L. Gómez del Prado, 'The Crime of Mercenarism A Challenge for the Judges of the New African Court', in C.C. Jalloh, K. M. Clarke & V.O. Nmehielle, *The African Court of Justice and Human and Peoples' Rights in Context* (Cambridge: Cambridge University Press, 2019), 449, 466–467.

2893. *See, e.g.*, UN General Assembly Res. 75/171 (2020). *See further* UN Commission on Human Rights, The use of mercenaries as a means of violating human rights and impeding the exercise of the right of peoples to self-determination, Report of the Special Rapporteur, UN Doc. E/CN.4/2000/20, 8–15. *See* F. Viljoen, *International Human Rights Law in Africa* (Oxford: Oxford University Press, 2007), 296, 298.

2894. *See* S. J. Ndlovu-Gatsheni & G. A. Dzinesa, '"One Man's Volunteer is Another Man's Mercenary?" Mapping the Extent of Mercenarism and its Impact on Human Security in Africa', in Gumedze, *Elimination of Mercenarism in Africa*, 75.

2895. UN Commission on Human Rights, The use of mercenaries as a means of violating human rights and impeding the exercise of the right of peoples to self-determination, Report of the Special Rapporteur 11–15, UN Doc. E/CN.4/2004/15.

2896. *Ibid.*, According to Ms Shameem, Special Rapporteur on the use of mercenaries as a means of violating human rights and impeding the right of peoples to self-determination, international private military companies have rendered the existing international legal framework 'totally ineffective', UN Doc. E/CN.4/2005/SR.12, para. 60. *See further* Report of the Working Group on the use of mercenaries as a means of violating human rights and impeding the exercise of the right of peoples to self-determination, UN Doc. A/HRC/51/25 examining, *inter alia*, violations of human rights and humanitarian law perpetrated by PMSCs. *And see* J.C. Zarate, 'The Emergence of a New Dog of War: Private International Security Companies, International Law, and the New World Disorder', *Stanford J.I.L.* 34 (1998): 75. Nonetheless, the UN General Assembly has condemned such mercenary-related activities, *see, e.g.*, UN General Assembly Res. 67/159 (2013). In Res. 75/171 (2020) para. 5 the UN General Assembly requested that States 'impose specific ban on such companies intervening in armed conflicts or actions to destabilize constitutional regimes'.

acts and violent extremism, undermining international peace efforts.[2897] Mercenaries belonging to the Wagner Group, a Russian PMSC, has been actively involved in a number of conflicts, particularly in the Central African Republic and Mali, attracting accusations of human rights abuses and violations of international humanitarian law.[2898] These new forms of mercenarism present their own threats to the peace and security of affected countries.

The menace posed by mercenarism led the OAU to adopt in 1977 the Convention for the Elimination of Mercenarism in Africa.[2899] A number of cumulative criteria have to be fulfilled in order to meet the definition of a mercenary, which may be summarized as a private individual who takes a direct part in an armed conflict affecting a country of which he is neither a national nor a resident for private gain.[2900] It proceeds to include in its definition of mercenarism individuals, groups or associations with the aim of opposing by armed violence a process of self-determination, and the stability or the territorial integrity of another State.[2901] These

2897. Report of the Secretary-General, Strengthening the partnership between the United Nations and the African Union on issues of peace and security in Africa, including on the work of the United Nations Office to the African Union, UN Doc. S/2021/763 (2021), paras 18–19; L. Brooke-Holland, 'UK military in the Sahel: Developments in 2022', Commons Library Research Briefing, 24 November 2022) https://researchbriefings.files.parliament.uk/documents/CBP-9634/CBP-9634.pdf; B. Petrini, 'Security in the Sahel and the end of *Operation Barkhane' IISS https://www.iiss.org/blogs/analysis/2022/09/security-in-the-sahel-and-the-end-of-operation-barkhane* (accessed 23 Dec. 2017).

2898. CAR: Russian Wagner Group harassing and intimidating civilians – UN experts, OHCHR Press Release (27 Oct. 2021), https://www.ohchr.org/en/press-releases/2021/11/car-russian-wagner-group-harassing-and-intimidating-civilians-un-experts; UN News, Mali: Independent rights experts call for probe into Wagner Group's alleged crimes (31 Jan. 2023), https://news.un.org/en/story/2023/01/1133007. According to the Montreux Document, a soft law document, PMSCs are obliged to comply with applicable international and national humanitarian law or human rights law, Montreux Document, paras 22, 26(a), https://www.icrc.org/en/publication/0996-montreux-document-private-military-and-security-companies. The U.S. Department of the Treasury's Office of Foreign Assets Control has designated the wagner group as a transnational criminal organization, U.S. Department of the Treasury, Treasury Sanctions Russian Proxy Wagner Group as a Transnational Criminal Organization, Press Release (26 Jan. 2023), https://home.treasury.gov/news/press-releases/jy1220.

2899. Convention for the Elimination of Mercenarism in Africa (3 Jul. 1977), 1490 U.N.T.S. 89. In force 22 Apr. 1985. As of July 2023, it had been ratified by thirty-two States. The commitment to fight mercenarism is reinforced by the Protocol to the OAU Convention on the Prevention and Combating of Terrorism Art. 3(1)(e) (8 Jul. 2004), https://www.au.int/en/treaties; C. Heyns & M. Killander (eds), *Compendium of Key Human Rights Documents of the African Union* (7th edn, Pretoria: Pretoria University Law Press, 2022), 134. In force 2 Jul. 2014. As of December 2022, it had been ratified by twenty-one States.

2900. OAU Convention on Mercenarism Art. 1(1). This definition corresponds in all material respects to those in the Additional Protocol I Relating to the Protection of Victims of International Armed Conflicts Art. 47(2) (8 June 1977), 1125 U.N.T.S. 3, and the International Convention against the Recruitment, Use, Financing and Training of Mercenaries Art. 1(1) (4 Dec. 1989), 2163 U.N.T.S. 75; I.L.M. 29 (1990): 89 (International Convention on Mercenaries). The International Convention on Mercenaries entered into force on 20 Oct. 2001 and has been ratified by ten African States. The definition of mercenarism is said to be 'largely unworkable in practice and open to abuse', H. P. Hestermeyer, 'Mercenaries', in R. Wolfrum (ed.), *Max Planck Encyclopedia of Public International Law, Vol. VII* (Oxford: Oxford University Law Press, 2012), 89, para. 13.

2901. OAU Convention on Mercenarism Art. 1(2). During the drafting of the International Convention on Mercenaries Western States would not accept opposition to the exercise of the right of peoples to self-determination as coming within the definition of mercenary activity, UN Commission on

definitions suffer from a number of limitations. First, meeting the criteria is extremely difficult, especially because of the requirement of motive, although it must be noted that this is a problem common to other international instruments.[2902] Second, in some crucial respects it is not as extensive as that provided in Article 1(2) of the International Convention on Mercenaries 1989. Thus, the International Convention on Mercenaries expands the definition of a mercenary to include those having the aim of overthrowing a government or undermining in any way the constitutional order of a State.[2903] Of course, such acts may come within the scope of undermining the 'stability' of a State. Both the International Convention on Mercenaries and the OAU Convention define a mercenary, *inter alia*, as a person who is recruited to fight in an armed conflict. The OAU Convention has been criticized for failing to address adequately the use of mercenaries in internal conflicts, dwelling 'almost exclusively [on] the question of extraterritorial deployment of mercenaries but...silent on internal deployment'.[2904] However, according to the ICRC, International humanitarian law recognizes only two types of armed conflicts, international and non-international armed conflicts.[2905] Hence, the use of the term 'armed conflicts' would appear to encompass both types of conflict. Furthermore, the use of the phrase 'armed violence' in Article 1(2) is of interest because it could be understood to extend the application of the concept of mercenarism to situations falling short of armed conflict.[2906] This apparent deficiency was acknowledged by the OAU which in its Declaration on Unconstitutional Changes of Government adopted in 2000 condemned the use of mercenaries to overthrow democratic governments.[2907] The reference to individuals, juridical persons, groups or associations

Human Rights, Report of the Meeting of Experts on the Traditional and New Forms of Mercenary Activities as a Means of Violating Human Rights and Impeding the Exercise of the Right of Peoples to Self-Determination para. 36, UN Doc. E/CN.4/2001/18. However, by way of compromise the International Convention on Mercenaries Art. 5(2) prohibits, *inter alia*, the use of mercenaries for the purpose of impeding the exercise of the right of self-determination. It appears that 'mercenarism' is a broader concept than that of 'mercenary' which includes the responsibilities of States and non-State actors involved in mercenary activities, para. 19.

2902. UN Commission on Human Rights, The use of mercenaries as a means of violating human rights and impeding the exercise of the right of peoples to self-determination, Report of the Special Rapporteur 22–24, UN Doc. E/CN.4/2000/20; UN Commission on Human Rights, Report of the Meeting of Experts on the Traditional and New Forms of Mercenary Activities as a Means of Violating Human Rights and Impeding the Exercise of the Right of Peoples to Self-Determination 6–7, UN Doc. E/CN.4/2001/18. *See further* Kwakwa, 69–74.

2903. International Convention on Mercenaries Art. 1(2)(a)(i)(ii).

2904. UN Commission on Human Rights, Report of the Meeting of Experts on the Traditional and New Forms of Mercenary Activities as a Means of Violating Human Rights and Impeding the Exercise of the Right of Peoples to Self-Determination para. 45, UN Doc. E/CN.4/2001/18. Additional Protocol I Art. 47(2) also applies only to international armed conflicts, Hestermeyer, para. 12.

2905. ICRC, 'How Is the Term "Armed Conflict" Defined in International Humanitarian Law?', https://www.icrc.org/en/doc/resources/documents/article/other/armed-conflict-article-170308.htm.

2906. Compare International Convention on Mercenaries Art. 1(2)(a) which includes in its definition of mercenary those who are specifically recruited to participate in concerted acts of violence.

2907. In C. Heyns & M. Killander (eds), *Compendium of Key Human Rights Documents of the African Union* (5th edn, Pretoria: Pretoria University Law Press, 2013), 159. *See also* African Charter on Democracy, Elections and Governance, Art. 23(2) (30 Jan. 2007), https://www.au.int/en/treaties, is also potentially significant because it is capable of extending the scope of the OAU Convention to contemporary forms of mercenary activities, such as PMSCs.[2908]

463. It seems that the AU associates mercenarism with terrorism. This conclusion arises from the fact that the Protocol to the OAU Convention on Terrorism makes reference to mercenarism.[2909] A further opportunity arose to expand the definition of mercenarism with the adoption of the Protocol on the Statute of the African Court of Justice and Human Rights (Malabo Protocol).[2910] The definition of mercenarism in Article 28H of the Malabo Protocol is broader in some respects than that under the OAU Convention and, in line with the AU's democratizing mandate, extends to those aiming to overthrow a government or undermine the constitutional order of a State, assisting a government to retain power, and assisting a group of persons to obtain power, i.e., a coup.[2911] The latter two elements are especially noteworthy. Because all these elements have to be satisfied in a cumulative manner, it may be 'an impossible task' to prove.[2912] The Malabo Protocol fails to take specific account of a current manifestation of mercenary activities in the form of PMSCs and it is not altogether clear if such companies could come within the scope of the definition.[2913]

Heyns & Killander, *Compendium of Key Human Rights Documents 2022*, 164 (African Charter on Democracy). In force 15 Feb. 2012. By February 2023 the African Charter on Democracy had been ratified by thirty-eight States.

2908. UN Commission on Human Rights, Report of the Meeting of Experts on the Traditional and New Forms of Mercenary Activities as a Means of Violating Human Rights and Impeding the Exercise of the Right of Peoples to Self-Determination para. 43, UN Doc. E/CN.4/2001/18. The adoption of an additional protocol to regulate the activities of private security services has been mooted, para. 46. It should be observed that the definition of the mercenary as given in the International Convention on Mercenaries has been criticized as flawed for failing to take adequate account of the current manifestations of mercenary activities, UN Commission on Human Rights, The use of mercenaries as a means of violating human rights and impeding the exercise of the right of peoples to self-determination, Report of the Special Rapporteur 14–21, UN Doc. E/CN.4/2001/19. The Special Rapporteur has proposed a new comprehensive legal definition, UN Commission on Human Rights, The use of mercenaries as a means of violating human rights and impeding the exercise of the right of peoples to self-determination, Report of the Special Rapporteur paras 37–47, UN Doc. E/CN.4/2004/15. Some of the proposals which are significant include those that mercenary activity must be considered a crime in and of itself and be internationally prosecutable, that States that sponsor mercenary activities should be held accountable, that the concept of the mercenary apply to both international and internal armed conflicts, and that the definition of a mercenary include PMSCs.

2909. Protocol to the OAU Convention on Terrorism Art. 3(1)(e).

2910. Protocol on Amendments to the Protocol on the Statute of the African Court of Justice and Human Rights (27 Jun. 2014), https://au.int/sites/default/files/treaties/36398-treaty-0045_-_protocol_on_amendments_to_the_protocol_on_the_statute_of_the_african_court_of_justice_and_human_rights_e-compressed.pdf, Heyns & Killander, *Compendium of Key Human Rights Documents 2022*, 62 (Malabo Protocol). Not yet in force.

2911. Although some elements defining the crime of mercenarism under the OAU Convention on Mercenarism have been omitted, Gómez del Prado, 468. *See ibid.*, 470 for criticism of Art. 28H.

2912. *Ibid.*, 462.

2913. Gómez del Prado, 470.

464. Under the terms of the OAU Convention, mercenarism, whether committed by individuals, 'natural or juridical', or sponsored by a State, is condemned as an international crime.[2914] Indeed, under the AU Non-Aggression and Common Defence Pact 2005 the sending by, or on behalf of a Member State or the provision of mercenaries, to carry out grave hostile acts against a Member State, can amount to aggression.[2915] Mercenarism is punishable by the severest penalties under domestic law, including capital punishment.[2916] Mercenaries are denied the status of combatants and are not entitled to prisoner-of-war status.[2917] State parties commit themselves to eradicate mercenarism; they therefore undertake, *inter alia*, to prohibit on their territory any activities promoting mercenarism or using mercenaries against any OAU/AU Member State or African people engaged in a liberation struggle; to prohibit the recruitment, training, financing, and equipping of mercenaries; to prevent their nationals or foreigners on their territory from engaging in mercenarism; and to prevent the entry and passage through their territory of mercenaries or their equipment.[2918] State parties are obliged to establish jurisdiction in order to prosecute or extradite offenders found on their territory (the principle *aut*

2914. OAU Convention on Mercenarism Art. 1(2), (3). Under Art. 2 thereof assuming command over or giving orders to mercenaries constitutes an aggravating circumstance. The OAU Convention on Mercenarism Preamble postulates that UN and OAU resolutions and State practice are indicative of the development of new rules of international lawmaking mercenarism an international crime. According to the International Convention on Mercenaries Arts 2 and 3 mercenarism and being a mercenary are offences for the purposes of the Convention. Mercenarism is not listed as a crime in the Rome Statute of the International Criminal Court, Gómez del Prado, 469. It is not clear whether mercenarism is prohibited by customary international law, J.P. Grant & J.C. Barker, *Parry & Grant Encyclopaedic Dictionary of International Law* (3rd edn, New York: Oxford University Press, 2009), 375, but *see Military and Paramilitary Activities In and Against Nicaragua (Nicaragua v. United States of America)* I.C.J. Reports 1986, 14, 103. Hestermeyer, para. 30, is of the view it does not. It is interesting to note that the UN General Assembly describes the International Convention on Mercenaries as a progressive development of international law, UN General Assembly Res. 44/34 (1989).

2915. African Union Non-Aggression and Common Defence Pact Art. 1(c)viii (31 Jan. 2005), https://www.au.int/en/treaties, Heyns & Killander, Compendium of Key Human Rights 2022, 150.

2916. OAU Convention on Mercenarism Art. 7. Art. 11 provides for due process.

2917. OAU Convention on Mercenarism Art. 3. *See also* Additional Protocol I Art. 47(1). For a critique of the latter *see* Kwakwa, 87–90. However, this is not to say that a mercenary was wholly unprotected by international humanitarian law, *see* UN Commission on Human Rights, Report of the Meeting of Experts on the Traditional and New Forms of Mercenary Activities as a Means of Violating Human Rights and Impeding the Exercise of the Right of Peoples to Self-Determination 5–6, UN Doc. E/CN.4/2001/18. Furthermore, according to the International Convention on Mercenaries Art. 16(b) the 'law of armed conflict and international humanitarian law, including the provisions relating to the status of combatant or of prisoner of war' shall apply. It should additionally be observed that mercenaries are entitled to judicial guarantees, *see* OAU Convention on Mercenarism Art. 11, Additional Protocol I Art. 75, and the International Convention on Mercenaries Arts 10(3)–11. According to the Montreux Document, para. 24, the 'status of the personnel of PMSCs is determined by international humanitarian law, on a case-by-case basis, in particular according to the nature and circumstances of the functions in which they are involved.'

2918. OAU Convention on Mercenarism Art. 6. *See also* AU Non-Aggression and Common Defence Pact Art. 5(c) under which States Parties shall prohibit the use of their territory for the stationing, withdrawal or incursions of mercenaries. Compare International Convention on Mercenaries Arts 5–6.

dedere aut judicare),[2919] and must also provide all necessary assistance to other States in matters of investigation.[2920] These obligations are reinforced by the undertaking under the AU Non-Aggression and Common Defence Pact State Parties to arrest and prosecute mercenaries.[2921] Interestingly, if a State is accused of an offence, by act or omission, any other Party to the OAU Convention may invoke it with the offending State and before competent OAU or International Organization tribunal or body, a reference it would seem to the International Court of Justice or the UN Security Council.[2922]

465. Given the difficulties that Africa faced with regard to mercenary activities, the OAU took the initiative to confront this problem through the adoption of a regional convention, anticipating action by the international community. Its approach to the problem may be said to be largely political rather than legal, which may be understandable against the background of the struggle against colonial domination, racist regimes and asserting political independence. However, this emphasis on external threats undermines the effectiveness of the OAU Convention and, unlike the International Convention on Mercenaries, seemingly narrows its scope to the extraterritorial, but not internal, deployment of mercenaries.[2923] It has therefore been suggested that the OAU Convention be amended so as extend its field of application to internal conflicts.[2924] However, it needs to be borne in mind that AU Member States have a right to request intervention from the AU to restore peace and security which could be invoked to deal with a threat from mercenaries.[2925] The AU could additionally take the initiative where a Member State faces an existential threat from mercenaries.[2926] Contemporary manifestations of mercenary-related activities pose a current threat to Africa and while the OAU Convention may be applicable to such activities again it has been suggested that dedicated legislation may be a preferable means of addressing the phenomenon.[2927]

2919. OAU Convention on Mercenarism Arts 8–9. Compare International Convention on Mercenaries Arts 10(1), 11–12. In 2004 Zimbabwe broke up an alleged conspiracy by mercenaries to carry out a coup d'état in Equatorial Guinea and extradited one of the alleged main conspirators to Equatorial Guinea para. 59, UN Doc. E/CN.4/2005/SR.12. In 2008, this person was given a sentence of over thirty years' imprisonment by a court in Equatorial Guinea. *See also Kaunda v. President of the Republic of South Africa* 2005 (4) SA 235 (CC). *See further* Viljoen, 298.

2920. OAU Convention on Mercenarism Art. 10. Compare International Convention on Mercenaries Art. 13(1).

2921. AU Non-Aggression and Common Defence Pact Art. 6(b).

2922. OAU Convention on Mercenarism Art. 5 (2).

2923. UN Commission on Human Rights, Report of the Meeting of Experts on the Traditional and New Forms of Mercenary Activities as a Means of Violating Human Rights and Impeding the Exercise of the Right of Peoples to Self-Determination, para. 45, UN Doc. E/CN.4/2001/18.

2924. *Ibid.*, para. 46.

2925. Constitutive Act of the African Union Art. 4(j) (26 May 2001), 2158 U.N.T.S. 3; Protocol Relating to the Establishment of the Peace and Security Council of the African Union Art. 4(k) (9 Jul. 2002), https://www.au.int/en/treaties, Heyns & Killander, Compendium of Key Human Rights 2022, 17 (PSC Protocol).

2926. PSC Protocol Art. 7(1)(o).

2927. UN Commission on Human Rights, Report of the Meeting of Experts on the Traditional and New Forms of Mercenary Activities as a Means of Violating Human Rights and Impeding the Exercise of the Right of Peoples to Self-Determination, *ibid.*

However, acting on such suggestions may be unnecessary as and when the Malabo Protocol is adopted as the ICL Section's jurisdiction *ratione materiae* extends to mercenarism[2928] which is classified as a crime thereunder.[2929]

§2. CORRUPTION

466. It is a sad fact that bribery and corruption are serious problems in parts of Africa,[2930] notwithstanding the fact that in Commonwealth Africa stringent criminal legislation has been adopted to curb these insidious practices.[2931] Their malign influence distorts socioeconomic development and undermines democracy, human rights and the rule of law.[2932] Corruption also puts at risk foreign aid and economic emancipation. The AU has therefore recognized the threat posed by corruption[2933]

2928. Malabo Protocol Art. 28H.

2929. *Ibid.*, Art. 28(1)A(7), reinforcing its designation as a crime under OAU Convention on Mercenarism Art. 1.

2930. It would not be an exaggeration to classify some regimes as kleptocracies. It is said that the reason why corruption is pervasive in Africa is because of 'a direct consequence of poorly developed and inappropriate institutional arrangements', J. M. Mbaku, *Corruption in Africa: Causes, Consequences and Cleanups* (Lanham: Lexington Books, 2010), 4. According to Transparency International, a civil society organization, sub-Saharan Africa is ranked as the most corrupt region in the world in 2022; Somalia is listed as the most corrupt country. Other African countries that are listed as highly corrupt are South Sudan, Libya, Equatorial Guinea, Burundi, Comoros and Chad, but many others are rated extremely poorly. Seychelles joins Botswana and Cabo Verde as the top cleanest African States. *See Corruptions Perceptions Index* 2022, https://www.transparency.org/en/cpi/2022. However, the Mo Ibrahim Foundation, another civil society organization, has noted increased improvement in reduced corruption in state institutions and the public sector in the period between 2015 and 2019, *2020 Ibrahim Index of African Governance*, https://mo.ibrahim.foundation/sites/default/files/2020-11/2020-index-report.pdf, pp. 54–55. It rated Rwanda, Mauritius and Tunisia the top three countries in its Anti-Corruption index for 2020, with Somalia, DR Congo and South Sudan the bottom three. However, in its 2022 Report it states that since 2017 progress in Anti-Corruption has stopped, *2022 IIAG: Key Findings*, 4 https://mo.ibrahim.foundation/sites/default/files/2023-01/2022-iiag-key-findings_en.pdf. In a high-profile scandal, South African President Jacob Zuma was forced to resign office in 2018 in light of mounting accusations of corruption, BBC, 'South Africa's Jacob Zuma resigns after pressure from party', 15 Feb. 2018, https://www.bbc.co.uk/news/world-africa-43066443.

2931. *See* S. Coldham, 'Legal Responses to State Corruption in Commonwealth Africa', J.A.L. 39 (1995): 115. The Constitutional Court of South Africa has held that the Constitution imposes an obligation on the State to establish and maintain an independent body to combat corruption and organized crime, *Glenister v. President of the Republic of South Africa & Others* 2011 (3) SA 347 (CC). In 2018 the Zondo Commission of Inquiry was established in South Africa to investigate allegations of corruption during the Zuma Administration. Zuma's refusal to appear before the Commission resulted in his being found in contempt of court and imprisoned, *Secretary of the Judicial Commission of Inquiry into Allegations of State Capture, Corruption and Fraud in the Public Sector including Organs of State v. Zuma and Others*, 2021 (5) SA 327 (CC).

2932. In the words of Transparency International, 'In SubSaharan Africa, armed conflict, violent transitions of power and increasing terrorist threats combined with poor enforcement of anti-corruption commitments rob citizens of their basic rights and services', *Corruptions Perceptions Index* 2021, p. 11.

2933. Grand Bay (Mauritius) Declaration and Plan of Action 1999 para. 8(g), Heyns & Killander, Compendium of Key Human Rights 2022, 187. NEPAD recognizes the imperative need to combat corruption, para. 83, Heyns & Killander, Compendium of Key Human Rights 2013, 486.

to Africa's attempts at reform and democratization, and the promotion of good governance has thus risen to the top of the political agenda.[2934] To that end the AU adopted in 2003 a Convention on Preventing and Combating Corruption.[2935]

467. The AU Convention provides a framework to address the menace of corruption; it seeks to assist State Parties to put in place or strengthen laws and mechanisms to deal with corruption and related offences and to foster transparency and accountability in public affairs, and thereby promote socioeconomic development.[2936] Because of the transnational dimension of the problem cross-border cooperation forms an essential element of the AU Convention. It encourages States Parties to harmonize national laws and policies.[2937] State Parties therefore condemn and reject corruption and related offences and commit themselves to, *inter alia*, human rights, transparency, the rule of law and good governance.[2938] The AU Convention proceeds on the basis of a series of preventive and punitive measures. Corruption is defined as 'the acts and practices including related offences' proscribed therein.[2939] However, 'proceeds of corruption' describe 'assets of any kind corporeal or incorporeal, movable or immovable, tangible or intangible and any document or legal instrument evidencing title to or interests in such assets acquired as a result of an act of corruption'.[2940] Whereas 'benefit' refers to 'gifts, favour, promise or advantage'.[2941] In terms of its scope, the AU Convention applies to the following acts of corruption: direct or indirect solicitation or acceptance by a public official[2942] (passive bribery), or the offering or granting, directly or indirectly, of any

2934. Grand Bay Declaration para. 3; Constitutive Act para. 3(g); NEPAD paras 7–15; African Charter on Democracy Arts 2(6), 12(1), 32 and 33. *See also* 50th Anniversary Solemn Declaration para. E (iii), Assembly, Twenty-First Ordinary Session, 26 May 2013. The Mo Ibrahim Foundation rated Mauritius, Cabo Verde and Botswana the top three countries in its Security & Rule of Law index for 2020, with Somalia, DR Congo and South Sudan the bottom three. South Africa, Mauritius and Cabo Verde were the top three countries in its Accountability index, with Somalia, Equatorial Guinea and Eritrea the bottom three, *2020 Ibrahim Index of African Governance*.

2935. Convention on Preventing and Combating Corruption (11 Jul. 2003), https://www.au.int/en/treaties, Heyns & Killander, Compendium of Key Human Rights 2022, 139. In force 5 Aug. 2006. By February 2023 it had been ratified by forty-eight States.

2936. AU Convention on Corruption Art. 2. *See also* Conference on Security, Stability, Development and Cooperation in Africa (2000) para. 12, Heyns & Killander, Compendium of Key Human Rights 2013, 163 (CSSDCA Solemn Declaration); African Charter on Values and Principles of Public Service and Administration Art. 3(8) (31 Jan. 2011), https://www.au.int/en/treaties. In force 23 Jul. 2016. By March 2022 it had been ratified by twenty States.

2937. AU Convention on Corruption Arts 2(3), 4(2)(f). The commitment to collaborate and cooperate in the fight against transnational crime is reinforced by the AU Non-Aggression and Common Defence Pact Art. 5(a).

2938. AU Convention on Corruption Art. 3. *See also* African Charter on Democracy Arts 3(9), 27(5) and 33(3).

2939. AU Convention on Corruption Art. 1(1). *See ibid.*, Art. 4(1).

2940. *Ibid.*, Art. 1(1).

2941. *Ibid.*, Art. 4(1)(a)–(b).

2942. That is, any official or employee of the State or its agencies who has been selected, appointed or elected to perform a function in the name of or in the service of the State at any level of hierarchy, Art. 1(1). Compare the much broader definition adopted by the UN Convention Against Corruption Art. 2 (31 Oct. 2003), 2349 U.N.T.S. 41 (UNCAC), which includes any person holding a legislative, executive, administrative or judicial State office. UNCAC entered into force on 14 Dec. 2005. As of 2021 UNCAC had been ratified by 189 States, fifty-three of them AU Member States.

item with monetary value, or other benefit for himself or herself or for another person or entity, in exchange for any act or omission in the performance of his or her public functions.[2943] Any act or omission in the performance of his or her public functions by a public official for the purpose of illicitly obtaining benefits for himself or herself or for a third party also comes within the definition of corruption.[2944] The diversion by a public official of public or private property, monies or securities for purposes unrelated to those for which they were intended also constitutes corruption.[2945] However, the AU Convention does not address bribery of a public official to induce the performance of an unlawful act. In addition, the AU Convention defines a public official as an 'official or employee of the State or its agencies' and its scope does not therefore extend to officials of international and regional organizations.[2946] The latter omission is surprising in view of the fact that the AU Convention seeks to deal with corruption in relation to international trade transactions and aid development.[2947] It is arguable that the AU Non-Aggression and Common Defence Pact could be applicable to corrupt practices given that one of its goals is to combat organized transnational crime,[2948] defined, *inter alia*, as having the purpose to obtain, directly or indirectly, financial and other material benefits.[2949]

468. The AU Convention extends its scope to cover persons working in the private sector.[2950] This includes persons who may be able to exert improper influence over the decision-making of a person performing functions in the public or private sectors.[2951] In addition, the tendering process must remain fair, and companies must be prevented from paying bribes to win tenders.[2952] It is worthy of note that the AU Convention applies to private-to-private corruption.[2953]

469. The AU Convention makes it plain that acts of corruption are also perpetrated when a direct or indirect offer or grant of a benefit is made to a public official[2954] or to persons who may be able to exert improper influence over the decision-making process (active bribery).[2955]

470. Illicit enrichment, defined as the 'significant increase in the assets of a public official or any other person which he or she cannot reasonably explain in relation to his or her income',[2956] also qualifies as corruption.[2957]

2943. AU Convention on Corruption Art. 4(1)(a), (b).
2944. *Ibid.*, Art. 4(1)(c). Nepotism might come within the scope of this definition.
2945. *Ibid.*, Art. 4(1)(d).
2946. *Ibid.*, Art. 1(1).
2947. *Ibid.*, Art. 19(2), (4).
2948. *Ibid.*, Art. 5(a).
2949. *Ibid.*, Art. 1(x).
2950. *Ibid.*, Art. 4(1)(e). *See further ibid.*, Art. 11.
2951. *Ibid.*, Art. 4(1)(f).
2952. *Ibid.*, Art. 11(2).
2953. *Ibid.*, Art. 11.
2954. *Ibid.*, Art. 4(1)(b).
2955. *Ibid.*, Art. 4(1)(f).
2956. *Ibid.*, Art. 1(1).
2957. *Ibid.*, Art. 4(1)(g). *See further ibid.*, Art. 8(2). Subject, however, to the caveat of domestic law.

471. Participation as a principal, agent, or accomplice in the commission, attempted commission or conspiracy to commit any of the above acts constitutes an act of corruption in itself.[2958]

472. It should be noted that the AU Convention does not preclude States Parties from applying the AU Convention among themselves with respect to other acts or practices of corruption not covered by the AU Convention.[2959]

473. In order to punish corrupt acts and practices a State Party must legislate to designate such as criminal offences.[2960] A State Party will be competent to prosecute in four circumstances: (1) where the offence is committed inside its territory; (2) where the offence is committed by a national or a resident individual; (3) where the alleged criminal is in its territory and it does not extradite such person; and where the offence, if committed abroad, has a prejudicial effect on the State Party.[2961] In light of the criminalization of certain practices the right to a fair trial is reaffirmed.[2962] It should be noted that under the Statute on the ACJHR corruption is listed as a crime[2963] over which the ICL Section has jurisdiction.[2964]

474. The AU Convention contains elaborate provisions on extradition. Said offences will be deemed extraditable offences.[2965] Where extradition is conditional on the existence of a treaty with the requesting State but such treaty does not exist, the AU Convention will serve as the relevant legal basis.[2966] However, extradition shall be carried out in accordance with domestic law or existing extradition treaties.[2967] Where a State Party refuses to extradite on the basis that it has jurisdiction over the offence, it must submit the case to the competent authorities for prosecution and report the outcome to the requesting State.[2968] At the request of the requesting State, the requested Party may take into custody a person whose extradition is sought or ensure that s/he is present at extradition proceedings, subject to domestic law, a relevant extradition treaty or a finding that the circumstances are urgent and so warrant.[2969] Furthermore, the requested State may seize and hand over to the requesting State objects which may be evidence of the offence or acquired as a result of the offence.[2970]

2958. *Ibid.*, Art. 4(1)(g).
2959. *Ibid.*, Art. 4(2).
2960. *Ibid.*, Art. 5(1). *See also* African Charter on Public Service and Administration Art. 12(1). Illicit enrichment should also be classified as an offence, AU Convention on Corruption Art. 8(1).
2961. AU Convention on Corruption Art. 13(1). Criminal jurisdiction exercised by a State Party in accordance with its domestic law is not precluded, *ibid.*, Art. 13(2).
2962. *Ibid.*, Art. 14.
2963. Statute on the ACJHR Art. 28I.
2964. *Ibid.*, Art. 28(1)A(8).
2965. AU Convention on Corruption Art. 15(2), (4).
2966. *Ibid.*, Art. 15(3).
2967. *Ibid.*, Art. 15(5).
2968. *Ibid.*, Art. 15(6).
2969. *Ibid.*, Art. 15(7).
2970. *Ibid.*, Art. 16(2).

475. State Parties are additionally required to adopt a series of other measures aimed at discouraging, preventing and eradicating corruption. These include establishing and strengthening anti-corruption agencies,[2971] which crucially should be independent, establishing and strengthening internal accounting and auditing procedures,[2972] protecting those who report or witness corruption,[2973] requiring public officials to declare their assets before they assume office,[2974] better training for public officials,[2975] the establishment of disciplinary mechanisms,[2976] restricting immunity for public officials,[2977] ensuring transparency in the management of tendering and hiring procedures in the public service,[2978] preventing the financing of political parties by the use of funds acquired through corruption,[2979] combating corruption in the private sector,[2980] establishing as a criminal offence the laundering of the proceeds of corruption,[2981] the confiscation and seizure of products of corruption, including asset recovery,[2982] the confiscation and seizure of bank documents,[2983] the waiver of banking secrecy,[2984] and allowing the media and civil society a role in holding governments to account.[2985] Interestingly, the private sector is also given a role in fighting corruption.[2986] It is therefore significant that access to information must be secured.[2987]

476. The AU Convention additionally contains provisions on mutual legal assistance. States Parties will therefore provide each other the greatest measure of assistance by dealing immediately with requests from appropriate authorities investigating corruption.[2988] Moreover, it seeks to foster international cooperation

2971. *Ibid.*, Art. 5(3). *See also ibid.*, Art. 20. *See further* African Charter on Public Service and Administration Art. 12(1); Declaration on Democracy, Political, Economic and Corporate Governance para. 14.
2972. AU Convention on Corruption Art. 5(4).
2973. *Ibid.*, Art. 5(5), (6).
2974. *Ibid.*, Art. 7(1). *See also* African Charter on Values and Principles of Public Service and Administration Art. 13.
2975. AU Convention on Corruption Art. 7(2). *See also* African Charter on Public Service and Administration Art. 12(2)–(4).
2976. AU Convention on Corruption Art. 7(3).
2977. *Ibid.*, Art. 7(5).
2978. *Ibid.*, Art. 7(4).
2979. *Ibid.*, Art. 10.
2980. *Ibid.*, Art. 11.
2981. *Ibid.*, Art. 6. The Malabo Protocol Art. 28A(1)(9) classifies money laundering as an international crime over which the ACJHR has jurisdiction. Money laundering is defined in Art. 28I *bis*. *See further* C. Rose, 'Money Laundering and the African Court of Justice and Human and Peoples' Rights', in Jalloh, Clarke & Nmehielle.
2982. *Ibid.*, Art. 16. Under the Malabo Protocol Art. 43A, the ACJHR is empowered to order the forfeiture and return of any property and assets acquired unlawfully.
2983. AU Convention on Corruption Art. 17(1).
2984. *Ibid.*, Art. 17(3), (4).
2985. *Ibid.*, Art. 12.
2986. *Ibid.*, Art. 11(2).
2987. *Ibid.*, Art. 9. It needs to be recalled that the African Charter Art. 9(1), guarantees the right to receive information.
2988. AU Convention on Corruption Art. 18(1).

to prevent corrupt practices.[2989] Noteworthy is the plea to developed countries to take measures to prevent corrupt public officials from enjoying stolen or illegally acquired gains.[2990]

477. Significantly the AU Convention envisages the creation of a transnational body within the AU, the Advisory Board on Corruption.[2991] Its functions include promoting and encouraging the adoption and application of anti-corruption measures in Africa,[2992] advising governments on how to deal with corruption,[2993] monitoring the behaviour of multinational corporations in Africa,[2994] developing and promoting the adoption of harmonized codes of conduct of public officials,[2995] and to liaise with the African Commission on Human and Peoples' Rights, civil society and IGOs and NGOs to facilitate the fight against corruption.[2996]

478. Later in 2003, the UN adopted the UN Convention Against Corruption (UNCAC).[2997] UNCAC's approach in preventing and combating corruption is comprehensive and thus more extensive than that of the AU Convention while sharing many features in common. UNCAC thus devotes detailed provisions to the issue of asset recovery.[2998] It deals with a number of issues unaddressed by the AU Convention. These include the criminal or civil liability of legal persons,[2999] and compensation for damage suffered by a victim of corruption.[3000] Other issues not explicitly addressed by the AU Convention include a statute of limitations,[3001] the suspension or removal of public officials,[3002] and the disqualification of persons found guilty of corruption from holding public office.[3003] It has been suggested that illegal financial flows should come within the scope of the AU Convention.[3004] Fair recruitment policies are required by the African Charter on Public Service and Administration.[3005] Only lax restrictions are imposed on former public officials taking up private sector employment so as to prevent conflicts of interest.[3006] But the positive features of the AU Convention should be stressed. These include private-to-private

2989. *Ibid.*, Art. 19.
2990. *Ibid.*, Art. 19(3).
2991. *Ibid.*, Art. 22(1).
2992. *Ibid.*, Art. 22(5)(a).
2993. *Ibid.*, Art. 22(5)(d).
2994. *Ibid.*, Art. 22(5)(e).
2995. *Ibid.*, Art. 22(5)(f).
2996. *Ibid.*, Art. 22(5)(g).
2997. *See supra* note. 2945.
2998. UNCAC Ch. V.
2999. *Ibid.*, Art. 26. But *see* AU Convention on Corruption Art. 19(1) which is of limited scope. Note that the Statute on the ACJHR Art. 46C, provides for corporate criminal liability.
3000. UNCAC Art. 35.
3001. *Ibid.*, Art. 29.
3002. *Ibid.*, Art. 30(6).
3003. *Ibid.*, Art. 30(7).
3004. Africa Progress Panel, *Africa Progress Report 2015*, 151, http://www.africaprogresspanel.org (accessed 29 Apr. 2017).
3005. AU Convention on Corruption Art. 19(2), (4). Compare UNCAC Art. 7.
3006. African Charter on Public Service and Administration Art. 11(5) requires only that they do not unduly profit from offices they previously occupied.

corruption, transparency in party political funding, the participation of civil society and the private sector in fighting corruption, and the strengthening of national control measures to ensure that foreign corporations in the territory of States Parties comply with national law.[3007] International, continental and regional cooperation is emphasized. Innovative in this respect is the undertaking to collaborate with countries of origin of multinationals to criminalize and punish secret commissions and other corrupt practices during international trade transactions.[3008]

The challenge of corruption is also addressed by the Malabo Protocol.[3009] It uniquely lists corruption as an international crime.[3010] The constitutive elements of the offence of corruption mirror closely those contained in Article 4 of the AU Convention on Corruption.

479. The AU is supportive of the efforts of other international and regional organizations in seeking to combat corruption.[3011] Given the complexities of the problem, it might have been useful for the AU Convention to have made some provision for technical assistance for States that felt it necessary. But UNCAC provides an opportunity to combat corruption more effectively on a global scale. Nevertheless, the AU's acknowledgement that corruption has had, has, and will have a negative and corrosive effect on the development and stability of Africa is an important initial step in dealing with this problem. In tandem with the African Charter on Public Service and Administration and national strategies, it is to be hoped that an enhanced culture of professionalism and ethical behaviour will be fostered and nourished. But corruption is a global problem that demands coordinated anti-corruption responses and policies. Bad corporate governance in other parts of the world, where there are failures to confront and prosecute irresponsible corporate behaviour that extends to bribing foreign officials, must also be addressed.[3012] Corporations and company directors must be made answerable for engaging in corrupt practices. Neither should politicians nor State entities evade responsibility. The inclusion of corporate and individual criminal liability for corruption under the

---

3007. AU Convention on Corruption Art. 5(2).
3008. *Ibid.*, Art. 19(1).
3009. *See* J. Hatchard, 'Combating Corruption Effectively? The Role of the African Court of Justice and Human Rights', in Jalloh, Clarke & Nmehielle.
3010. Malabo Protocol Art. 28I.
3011. *See, e.g.*, the UN Convention Against Transnational Organized Crime Art. 8 (2000), 2225 U.N.T.S. 209; the Inter-American Convention Against Corruption 1996, http//www.oas.org/juridico/English/treaties/b-58.html. The first African anti-corruption treaty was the SADC Protocol Against Corruption (14 Aug. 2001), http://www.sadc.int. This was followed shortly thereafter by the ECOWAS Protocol on the Fight Against Corruption (21 Dec. 2001), http://www.ecowas.int. Both latter treaties seek, *inter alia*, to criminalize a range of offences, harmonize national laws, and provide for international cooperation.
3012. Note the OECD Convention on Combating Bribery of Foreign Public Officials in International Business Transactions (1997), 2802 U.N.T.S. 225. The US Foreign Corrupt Practices Act 1997 is a stringent piece of legislation that imposes criminal penalties for engaging in foreign corruption. The United Kingdom's Bribery Act 2010 constitutes a modest development in this direction. The case of *SFO v. Rolls Royce plc* [2017] Lloyd's Rep. FC 249 revealed the Respondents to have engaged in bribery and corruption in various countries, including Nigeria.

Malabo Protocol is an indication that corruption will not be tolerated.[3013] The adoption of the AU Convention will send a powerful message that Africa is serious about dealing with the problem of corruption.

§3. Civil Society

480. Since the turn of the millennium in particular the concept of civil society has come to the fore in the body politic. Civil society refers to social or popular movements, socioeconomic organizations and associations independent of the state and can include churches and other religious groups, trade unions, the media, the private sector, public interest groups, academia, and NGOs, or CSOs.[3014] Civil society contributes to the enhancement of democracy; it promotes citizens' participation in public affairs and the decision-making process, and engages in public advocacy; it is a significant player in democratic accountability and responsiveness, helping to hold governments accountable and applying pressure on them to consider or reconsider particular policies. It can have an input at both national and international levels by developing proposals for legislation and policies. CSOs are thus considered as stakeholders in society. In the field of human rights, the development of civil society contributes to the creation of an environment conducive to human rights.[3015] The AU acknowledges the role of civil society, recognizing the participation of the people in its activities as one of its founding principles.[3016]

481. The process of reform and democratization in Africa led the OAU to accept the need to connect with the peoples of Africa and cooperate with African NGOs. The AEC Treaty recognizes this necessity at the socioeconomic level.[3017] However, particularly significant is the first OAU Ministerial Conference on Human Rights held in April 1999, resulting in the adoption of the Grand Bay Declaration and Plan of Action, where the OAU expressed a renewed sense of commitment to civil society.

3013. Malabo Protocol Art. 46B and 46C. It should be observed that corruption is also condemned under the African Charter on Democracy Art. 3(9).

3014. Compare the definition in the Glossary of the Panel of Eminent Persons on United Nations-Civil Society Relations, 'We the Peoples: Civil Society, the United Nations and Global Governance' (11 Jun. 2004) UN Doc. A/58/817.

3015. The Declaration on the Right and Responsibility of Individuals, Groups and Organs of Society to Promote and Protect Universally Recognized Human Rights and Fundamental Freedoms (Declaration on Human Rights Defenders), UN General Assembly Res. 53/144 (1998), acknowledges the role of individuals and groups. *See also* Vienna Declaration and Programme of Action pt. I, para. 38, 32 I.L.M. 1661 (1993). In relation to Africa *see* the Kigali Declaration paras 27–28, Heyns & Killander, Compendium of Key Human Rights 2016, 154; Resolution on the Protection of Human Rights Defenders in Africa, 17th Activity Report, 2003–2004, Annex IV.

3016. Constitutive Act Art. 4(c). *See also* the Cotonou Declaration on the strengthening and expanding the protection of all Human Rights Defenders in Africa, adopted by the International Symposium of Human Rights Defenders in Africa 2017, https://www.achpr.org/news/viewdetail?id=31.

3017. AEC Treaty Arts 90–91.

482. The Conference, recognizing that civil society contributes to the advancement of human rights,[3018] stressed the importance of promoting an African civil society, particularly NGOs, as a prerequisite for the healthy development of a State governed by the rule of law.[3019] The Conference therefore sought to safeguard the values that promote civil society. Recognizing the role of the media as a public watchdog, the Conference urged States to guarantee a free and independent press.[3020] Freedom of association was also emphasized.[3021] These conclusions were later reaffirmed by the Kigali Declaration.[3022] And in the CSSDCA Solemn Declaration, the role of civil society in the democratization of Africa is acknowledged.[3023]

483. In this context, the OAU held a conference in 2001 to establish a framework to enhance and consolidate cooperation between the OAU and African NGOs. It was accepted that CSOs required wider and more systematic access to the OAU. Furthermore, the preamble to the Constitutive Act recognizes 'the need to build a partnership between governments and all segments of civil society'. This is given expression to in the form of ECOSOCC under Article 22 of the Constitutive Act.[3024] In June 2002, a further conference was held with a view to establishing a mechanism to facilitate links between CSOs and the AU.[3025]

484. It is therefore encouraging to note that the role played by CSOs has been acknowledged by the AU. One of the objectives of the African Charter on Democracy, Elections and Governance 2007 is to foster citizen participation.[3026] State Parties are thus obliged to adopt a series of measures to promote and consolidate good governance, popular participation, accountability, transparency, the rule of law and

3018. Grand Bay Declaration para. 10.
3019. *Ibid.*, paras 17–19; preambular para. 13. *See also* Declaration on Democracy, Political, Economic and Corporate Governance para. 15.
3020. Grand Bay Declaration para. 21; preambular para. 8(m). Compare African Charter Art. 9. The African Commission on Human and Peoples' Rights has upheld the freedom of the press in *Constitutional Rights Projects and Civil Liberties Organization v. Nigeria* Communication No. 102/93, 12th Activity Report 1998–1999; *Media Rights Agenda and Constitutional Rights Project v. Nigeria* Communication Nos 105/93, 128/94, 130/94 and 152/96, 12th Activity Report 1998–1999. It has also adopted resolutions to that effect, *see* 8th Activity Report 1994–1995.
3021. Grand Bay Declaration para. 8(m). Compare African Charter Art. 10, and *see Civil Liberties Organization in respect of Nigerian Bar Association v. Nigeria* Communication No. 101/93, 8th Activity Report 1994–1995; *Media Rights Agenda and Constitutional Rights Project v. Nigeria* Communication Nos 105/93, 128/94, 130/94 and 152/96, 12th Activity Report 1998–1999; *Amnesty International v. Zambia* Communication No. 212/98 12th Activity Report 1998–1999.
3022. Kigali Declaration paras 27–28. *See also* the Cotonou Declaration on Human Rights Defenders in Africa.
3023. CCSSDCA Solemn Declaration para. 14 (c), Heyns & Killander, Compendium of Key Human Rights 2013, 163. *See also* Declaration on Democracy, Political, Economic and Corporate Governance para. 20.
3024. *See supra* paras 139–142; Viljoen, 226–29.
3025. In November 2003 the African Commission on Human and Peoples' Rights decided to establish a focal point for human rights defenders within the Commission's Secretariat in order to facilitate information on human rights defenders in Africa.
3026. African Charter on Democracy Art. 2(10).

so forth. For present purposes, what is salient is that State Parties must ensure effective participation of citizens in democratic processes and in the governance of public affairs.[3027] They must consolidate a culture of democracy and peace, which can be achieved by creating conducive conditions for CSOs to exist and operate.[3028] They must foster popular participation and partnership with CSOs.[3029] And they must ensure and promote partnership and dialogue between government, civil society and the private sector.[3030] Under the African Charter on Values and Principles of Public Service and Administration civil society is to participate in the planning and delivery of public services.[3031] The Libréville Declaration considers civil society as a partner in health and environmental issues.[3032] And it has previously been seen that civil society has a role to play in fighting corruption.[3033]

485. Civil society plays an immensely positive role in the promotion and implementation of human rights. One aspect of this role is the relationship of CSOs and NGOs with the African Commission on Human and Peoples' Rights, where they have assumed promotional and protective functions.[3034] The Commission has appointed a Special Rapporteur on Human Rights Defenders in Africa to cooperate with States, human rights defenders and NGOs with a view to raising awareness and developing strategies.[3035] But considerable obstacles confront civil society in Africa. Civil society requires an informed and active citizenship, problematic in much of Africa. If the ramifications of poverty are not the problem, then repressive regimes that do not tolerate opposition certainly are. Civil society cannot be expected to flourish in countries where restrictive regulations exist, where the media is cowed, where the activities of CSOs and NGOs, many of which face arbitrary difficulties in registering, where capricious funding restrictions are imposed, and its activists subjected to harassment, intimidation, legal proceedings and extrajudicial killings, and where the perpetrators of such violence can act with impunity.[3036] The Commission's Special Rapporteur has had cause on numerous occasions to raise

3027. *Ibid.*, Art. 3(7).
3028. *Ibid.*, Art. 12(3).
3029. *Ibid.*, Arts 27(2), 28.
3030. *Ibid.*, Art. 28.
3031. African Charter on Public Service and Administration Art. 5(4).
3032. Libréville Declaration on Health and Environment in Africa, Libréville para. 10 (29 Aug. 2008).
3033. *See supra* paras 475, 477.
3034. *See* N. Mbelle, 'The Role of Non-governmental Organisations and National Human Rights Institutions at the African Commission', in *The African Charter on Human and Peoples' Rights: The System in Practice, 1986–2006,* M. Evans & R. Murray (eds) (2nd edn, Cambridge: Cambridge University Press, 2008), Ch. 8.
3035. Resolution on the Protection of Human Rights Defenders in Africa. *See* R. Murray, *The Special Rapporteurs in the African System* in Evans & Murray, 344, 369–70. *See also* the Cotonou Declaration on Human Rights Defenders in Africa.
3036. Note that the UN Declaration on Human Rights Defenders obligates States not to subject human rights defenders to harassment or other adverse measures. *See also* the Cotonou Declaration on Human Rights Defenders in Africa. For examples of the violations being committed against human rights defenders in Africa and elsewhere, *see* UN Commission on Human Rights, Human Rights Defenders, Report of the Special Rapporteur, UN Doc. E/CN.4/2004/94.; Accord, *Civic Space Restrictions in Africa* (31 May 31, 2018), https://www.accord.org.za/conflict-trends/civic-space-restrictions-in-africa/.

concerns for the safety of human rights defenders and to report on their murders.[3037] The OAU/AU is to be congratulated for recognizing the need for strong partnerships with civil society. However, as is often the norm in Africa, the gap between public rhetoric and reality is immense.[3038]

§4. TERRORISM

486. Terrorism in its different manifestations has become a persistent and significant threat in recent years,[3039] described by the UN Security Council in Resolution 1377(2001) as 'one of the most serious threats to international peace and security in the twenty-first century' and as a 'threat to all states and to all humanity'. Africa has not escaped the blight of international terrorism,[3040] with countries in East Africa bearing the brunt of some horrific atrocities.[3041] Some countries, such as Algeria, Uganda and Nigeria, have faced long and brutal campaigns by domestic terrorists.[3042] Failed and weak States, such as Somalia, pose their own set of problems, as breeding grounds and havens for homegrown and international terrorist groups. Groups affiliated to Al-Qaeda of the Islamic Maghreb (AQIM) remain active in the Sahel region of Northwest Africa, as well as North Africa and Central and Southern Africa.[3043] The OAU/AU, acknowledging 'the scourge of terrorism as a source of serious human rights violation',[3044] therefore joined the war against terrorism. Hence, condemnation of acts of terrorism is one of the guiding principles of

3037. The Commission's Annual Activity Reports attest to this fact.
3038. According to its latest report, the Mo Ibrahim Foundation, a civil society organization, notes that the 'space for civil society has shrunk' across Africa, *Ibrahim Index of African Governance – Index Report* 49, https://mo.ibrahim.foundation/sites/default/files/2023-01/2022-index-report.pdf.
3039. Vienna Declaration and Programme of Action pt. I, para. 17.
3040. Report of the UN Secretary-General on strengthening the partnership between the United Nations and the African Union on issues of peace and security in Africa, UN Doc. S/2016/780, para. 5.
3041. Condemned by the UN Security Council in Res. 1189(1998) and 1450(2002). *See also* the condemnation of the terrorist bombing in Kampala by Al Shabab in 2010, Assembly, *Decision on the Report of the Peace and Security Council on its Activities and the State of Peace and Security in Africa,* AU Doc. Assembly/AU/Dec. 294 (XV) para. 7 (25–27 Jul. 2010).
3042. *See, e.g.*, UN Security Council Res. 2349(2017) condemning the activities of Boko Haram and ISIL in West Africa and the Sahel. In 2015 the AU mandated the Multinational Joint Task Force (MNJTF) to assist in restoring a safe and secure environment in the areas affected by Boko Haram and other terrorist groups. The Lord's Resistance Army (LRA) presented a persistent threat in Uganda which eventually led the AU to set up the Regional Cooperation Initiative for the Elimination of the Lord's Resistance Army (RCI-LRA) with the mandate to defeat the LRA.
3043. Sixteenth report of the Secretary-General on the threat posed by ISIL (Da'esh) to international peace and security and the range of United Nations efforts in support of Member States in countering the threat, UN Doc. S/2023/76, paras 17–26.
3044. Grand Bay Declaration para. 12; Kigali Declaration para. 9. *See also* Protocol to the OAU Convention on Terrorism Art. 1(a). In force 26 Feb. 2014. As of November 2022, it had been ratified by twenty-one States. *See* B. Saul, 'The Crime of Terrorism within the Jurisdiction of the African Court of Justice and Human and Peoples' Rights', in C.C. Jalloh, K. M. Clarke & V.O. Nmehielle, *The African Court of Justice and Human and Peoples' Rights in Context* (Cambridge: Cambridge University Press, 2019), 409, 417. According to the CSSDCA Declaration, para. 11(e), terrorism, 'in all its manifestations, is inimical to stability'.

the AU.[3045] Although the international community has not yet succeeded in agreeing to a comprehensive treaty dealing with terrorism,[3046] *inter alia*, because developing States had traditionally been reluctant to have wars of national liberation categorized as terrorism,[3047] the OAU was able to reach a consensus and at a conference held in Algiers in 1999 adopted a Convention on Terrorism.[3048]

487. The OAU Convention defines a 'terrorist act' as 'any act which is a violation of the criminal laws of a State Party and which may endanger the life, physical integrity or freedom of, or cause serious injury or death to, any person, any number or group of persons or causes or may cause damage to public or private property, natural resources, environmental or cultural heritage'.[3049] Moreover, any act calculated or intended to 'intimidate, put in fear, force, coerce or induce any government, body, institution, the general public or any segment thereof, to do or abstain from doing any act, or to adopt or abandon a particular standpoint, or to act according to certain principles', or to 'disrupt any public service, the delivery of any essential service to the public or create a public emergency', or to 'create general insurrection in a State' also comes within the definition.[3050] Aiding and abetting the commission of any of these acts also amount to terrorism.[3051] This definition is noteworthy for its breadth which goes significantly further than any existing international definition.[3052] While the inclusion of acts that damage the environment, for

---

3045. Constitutive Act Art. 4(o). *See also* PSC Protocol Art. 3(d), 50th Anniversary Solemn Declaration para. E(ii), Assembly, Twenty-First Ordinary Session, 26 May 2013.

3046. Although conventions dealing with specific aspects of terrorism, such as hijacking and financing, have been adopted, *see* A. Cassese, *International Law* (2nd edn, Oxford: Oxford University Press, 2005), 465–468.

3047. A. Cassese, *International Criminal Law* (2nd edn, Oxford: Oxford University Press, 2008), 162, n. 1. However, the UN Security Council's position is that any acts of terrorism are unjustifiable, *see, e.g.*, Res. 2178 (2014) preambular para. 1. The AU now shares this stance, *see, e.g.*, Assembly, *Decision on the Establishment of an African Union Special Fund on Prevention and Combating Terrorism and Violent Extremism in Africa*, AU Doc. Assembly/AU/Dec. 614(XXVII) (17–1 Jul. 2016), para. 3.

3048. Convention on the Prevention and Combating of Terrorism (14 Jul. 1999),2219 U.N.T.S. 179. In force 26 Dec. 2002. As of July 2023, it had been ratified by forty-three States. *See* generally Saul, 412–416; H. Boukrif, 'Quelques commentaires et observations sur la Convention de l'Organisation de l'Unité africaine sur la Prévention et la Lutte Contre le Terrorism', R.A.D.I.C. 11 (1999): 753.

3049. OAU Convention on Terrorism Art. 1(3)(a). The Malabo Protocol mirrors the definition in the OAU Convention on Terrorism is all essential respects; Art. 28G(A) thereof extends to the laws of the AU and RECs, and international law. *See* generally Saul, 419 *et seq.* Note that the Constitutive Act condemns political assassination Art. 4(o). *See also* OAU Charter Art. III(5).

3050. OAU Convention on Terrorism Art. 1(3)(a)(i)–(iii). *See also* Malabo Protocol Art. 28G(A)(1)-(3). The inclusion of the disruption of public services within the definition is problematic as it has the capacity of criminalizing the general public and of undermining freedom of industrial action, such as strikes.

3051. OAU Convention on Terrorism Art. 1(3)(b).

3052. Viljoen, 300. A comprehensive definition has thus far eluded the international community. Many treaties are subject specific, dealing with air safety, maritime navigation, or the suppression of the means by which terrorism can be supported. One specific example is the International Convention for the Suppression of Terrorist Bombings (25 Nov. 1997), 2149 U.N.T.S. 256. More recent treaties, such as the International Convention for the Suppression of the Financing of Terrorism (9 Dec. 1999), 2179 U.N.T.S. 197, and the European Convention on the Prevention of Terrorism (16

instance, is to be welcomed, concern must be expressed at the potential for abuse of such vague and broadly defined crimes by authoritarian-minded governments. Thus politically motivated strikes or even workers who strike in a labour dispute could find themselves charged with terrorist offences. It is important to note that wars of national liberation are excluded from the definition of terrorism.[3053] This should come as no surprise, given the African stance on the issue. With this notable exception, terrorist acts cannot be justified on political, philosophical, ideological, racial, ethnic, religious or other grounds.[3054] One of the consequences of this is that political or other motivation cannot provide a defence for terrorist acts for the purpose of extradition.

488. The OAU Convention also addresses the question of State-sponsored terrorism. This particular issue has assumed greater significance in recent years as a consequence of '9/11' and the threat posed by jihadist groups such as Al-Qaeda. The international community has defined the events of '9/11' as an armed attack setting off the right of self-defence under Article 51 of the UN Charter.[3055] The USA was of the view that the attack involved the state responsibility of the Afghan Taliban regime and force was used both to remove it from power and to eradicate the terrorists which it was believed the Taliban were harbouring.[3056] The well-known fact that certain African States have been accused of supporting terrorism thus gives this debate an added relevance.[3057] States must therefore refrain from, *inter alia*, organizing, supporting, financing, inciting or committing terrorist acts or providing havens for terrorists.[3058] States are further required to adopt measures, *inter alia*, to prevent their territories from being used for the preparation of terrorist acts,[3059] to

---

May 2005), C.E.T.S. 195, as well as UN Security Council Res. 1566(2004), determine what conduct should be depicted as 'terrorist' by linking it to pre-existing treaties on terrorism. Nevertheless, UN Security Council Res. 1566(2004) has established three cumulative elements: (i) acts, including against civilians, committed with the intention of causing death or serious bodily injury, or the taking of hostages; (ii) irrespective of whether motivated by considerations of a political, philosophical, ideological, racial, ethnic, religious or other similar nature, also committed for the purpose of provoking a state of terror in the general public or in a group of persons or particular persons, intimidating a population, or compelling a Government or an international organization to do or to abstain from doing any act; and (iii) such acts constituting offences within the scope of and as defined in the international instruments relating to terrorism. *See* generally, Report of the UN Special Rapporteur on the promotion and protection of human rights and fundamental freedoms while countering terrorism, UN Doc. E/CN.4/2006/98. Cassese argues that an agreed definition has emerged in customary law comprising three elements: (i) acts normally criminalized under municipal law; (ii) intended to provoke a state of terror in the population or to coerce a State or an international organization to take some action; (iii) are politically or ideologically motivated, Cassese, *International Criminal Law*, 165.

3053. OAU Convention on Terrorism Art. 3(1).

3054. *Ibid.*, Art. 3(2). *See further* UN Security Council Res. 1269(1999) and 1566(2004) which state that acts of terrorism are unjustifiable regardless of motivation.

3055. *See* UN Security Council Res. 1368(2001) and 1373(2001).

3056. *See* Cassese, *International Law*, 473–475.

3057. *Ibid.*, 468, 470.

3058. OAU Convention on Terrorism Art. 4(1). It should be observed that the AU condemns subversive activities, *see* of the Constitutive Act Art. 4(o). *See also* OAU Charter Art. III(5).

3059. OAU Convention on Terrorism Art. 4(2)(a).

deal with arms smuggling,[3060] to prevent the infiltration of their territory by terrorists,[3061] to promote the exchange of information[3062] and to prevent the establishment of terrorist support networks.[3063] In addition, under the Protocol to the OAU Convention on Terrorism States must prevent the entry into, and the training of terrorist groups on their territories.[3064] These proscriptions are reinforced by the AU Non-Aggression and Common Defence Pact, under which the encouragement, support, harbouring or provision of any assistance for the commission of terrorist acts constitutes aggression.[3065] States Parties must also prohibit the use of their territory for the stationing, withdrawal or incursions of terrorists.[3066] In light of the nihilistic threat posed by jihadist groups, States undertake under the Protocol to the OAU Convention on Terrorism States to ensure that terrorists do not acquire weapons of mass destruction.[3067] Many similar measures are advocated by UN Security Council Resolutions.[3068]

489. The OAU Convention adopts the *aut dedere aut judicare* principle. States are hence bound to arrest and prosecute or extradite perpetrators of terrorist acts.[3069] Terrorist acts as defined in the OAU Convention must become an extraditable offence within all extradition treaties.[3070] Jurisdiction is established on various grounds, principally where the act is committed in the territory of the State[3071] or on board a ship or aircraft registered there.[3072] However, jurisdiction is additionally provided for on the basis of the nationality, or active personality, principle,[3073] the passive personality principle[3074] and the protective principle.[3075] In view of the fact that there are compelling arguments for considering terrorist acts as international crimes or crimes against humanity,[3076] it seems regrettable that the drafters of the treaty did not have the foresight to make provision for universal jurisdiction. However, this omission loses significance as the Protocol on the Malabo Protocol classifies terrorism as a crime thereunder.[3077] The Protocol to the OAU Convention on

3060. *Ibid.*, Art. 4(2)(b).
3061. *Ibid.*, Art. 4(2)(c).
3062. *Ibid.*, Art. 4(2)(e). *See further ibid.*, Art. 5.
3063. *Ibid.*, Art. 4(2)(f).
3064. Protocol to the OAU Convention on Terrorism Art. 3(1)(b).
3065. AU Non-Aggression and Common Defence Pact Art. 1(e)(xi).
3066. *Ibid.*, Art. 5(c).
3067. Protocol to the OAU Convention on Terrorism Art. 3(f). *See further* UN Convention for the Supression of Acts of Nuclear Terrorism (13 Apr. 2003), 44 I.L.M. 815 (2005).
3068. *See, e.g.*, UN Security Council Res. 1904(2009).
3069. OAU Convention on Terrorism Art. 4(2)(h). *See also ibid.*, Arts 6(4), 7(2) and 8. *See further* AU Non-Aggression and Common Defence Pact Art. 6(b).
3070. OAU Convention on Terrorism Art. 9.
3071. *Ibid.*, Art. 6(1)(a).
3072. *Ibid.*, Art. 6(1)(b). *See further ibid.*, Art. 6(2)(d).
3073. *Ibid.*, Art. 6(1)(c). *See further ibid.*, Art. 6(2)(c).
3074. *Ibid.*, Art. 6(2)(a).
3075. *Ibid.*, Art. 6(2)(b), (e).
3076. Cassese, *International Criminal Law*, 175–77.
3077. Malabo Protocol Art. 28A(1)(6).

Terrorism provides an important safety net in that it constitutes an adequate legal basis for extradition for States Parties that do not have extradition arrangements.[3078]

490. Provision is made for mutual legal assistance.[3079] This extends to extraterritorial investigations (commission rogatoire). The parties therefore undertake to assist in, *inter alia*, the examination of witnesses and evidence,[3080] the collection of documents[3081] and serving of judicial documents,[3082] and the execution of searches and seizures.[3083] A commission rogatoire may be refused where each State Party has to execute a commission rogatoire relating to the same terrorist acts,[3084] if the request may affect efforts to expose crimes, impede investigations or the indictment of the accused in the requesting country,[3085] and the execution of a request would affect the sovereignty, security or public order of the requested State.[3086] However, a request for a commission rogatoire may not be refused on the grounds of the principle of confidentiality of bank operations or financial institutions.[3087] It is worth observing that the OAU Convention's provisions on mutual legal assistance do not match the detail of the UN Model Treaty on Mutual Legal Assistance.[3088]

491. The Protocol to the OAU Convention on Terrorism provides an important component in the fight against terrorism, that of the confiscation, freezing, and seizure of funds and assets 'for the purpose of committing a terrorist act'.[3089] It is submitted that the AU should have extended the scope of this provision, in line with UN Security Council Resolution 1373(2001), to cover entities and undertakings owned or controlled by terrorist groups and/or their supporters. Neither do the AU treaties follow the international practice of maintaining a Consolidated List of suspect individuals, groups, entities and undertakings subject to such measures.[3090] Holding hostages to ransom has been a favoured method employed by AQIM to boost its finances. This iniquitous practice has been condemned by the AU[3091] and the UN Security Council.[3092] While neither the OAU Convention nor the Protocol provide for the imposition of sanctions on State sponsors of terrorism it is clear that

3078. Protocol to the OAU Convention on Terrorism Art. 8(1).
3079. OAU Convention on Terrorism Art. 17. *See further* AU Non-Aggression and Common Defence Pact Art. 6(a). The OAU Convention on Terrorism allows States Parties to enter into further arrangements providing for greater specificity, *see* Art. 18.
3080. OAU Convention on Terrorism Art. 14(1)(a).
3081. *Ibid.*, Art. 14(1)(d).
3082. *Ibid.*, Art. 14(1)(g).
3083. *Ibid.*, Art. 14(1)(f).
3084. *Ibid.*, Art. 15(a).
3085. *Ibid.*, Art. 15(b).
3086. *Ibid.*, Art. 15(c).
3087. *Ibid.*, Art. 16.
3088. 30 I.L.M. 1419 (1991).
3089. Protocol to the OAU Convention on Terrorism Art. 3(c). *See further* International Convention for the Supression of the Financing of Terrorism Art. 8; UN Security Council Res. 1904 (2009) para. 1(a).
3090. *See* UN Security Council Res. 1267 (1999), 1333 (2000) and 1904 (2009).
3091. Assembly, *Decision to Combat the Payment of Ransom to Terrorist Groups,* AU Doc. Assembly/AU/Dec. 256 (XIII) para. 7 (3 Jul. 2009).
3092. *See* UN Security Council Res. 2085(2012) para. 5.

the AU could impose sanctions under Article 23 of the Constitutive Act.[3093] But the main purpose of the Protocol is to secure the effective implementation of the OAU Convention[3094] and to this end the PSC is given the primary role of harmonizing and coordinating continent-wide efforts in the fight against terrorism.[3095]

492. One final observation on these treaties remains to be made. It is an article of faith of liberal democratic societies that the war against terrorism should not undermine its values[3096] and should therefore be fought in conformity with the principles of international humanitarian law and international human rights.[3097] The OAU Convention enshrines this fundamental position,[3098] reinforced by the Protocol to the OAU Convention on Terrorism, which expressly outlaws torture, inhuman and degrading treatment of terrorist suspects.[3099]

The assessment of the OAU Convention on Terrorism is mixed. The definition of terrorist offences in the OAU Convention is, in general, more expansive than those in other regional treaties, which have therefore attracted criticism for being 'vague and over-broad' and 'ill-defined'.[3100] Notwithstanding this normative framework, the AU has continued to take steps to bolster its counter-terrorism efforts. In 2011 the AU adopted the African Model Law on Counter Terrorism to help States harmonize domestic legislation on terrorism.[3101] The Model Law's definition of terrorism is said to follow international standards more closely and to be 'more tightly circumscribed'.[3102] It is important to note that excluded from the definition of terrorism are acts which are the result of advocacy, protest, dissent or industrial action, liberation struggles and acts covered by international humanitarian law.[3103] In 2014 the PSC adopted the so-called Nairobi Communiqué setting out a series of objectives for the AU.[3104] One was an African arrest warrant for persons charged with or convicted of terrorist acts.[3105] Another was the creation of a Counter Terrorism

3093. It needs to be recalled that the UN Security Council has imposed sanctions on State sponsors of terrorism, *see* Cassese, *International Law*, 468.
3094. Protocol to the OAU Convention on Terrorism Art. 2(2).
3095. *Ibid.*, Art. 4. Regional mechanisms also have a role, *ibid.*, Art. 6.
3096. Concern has therefore been expressed about the anti-terrorism legislation of various African States, Viljoen, 302. The Cotonou Declaration on the strengthening and expanding the protection of all Human Rights Defenders in Africa draws attention to the fact that anti-terrorism legislation is often used against human rights defenders.
3097. *Gunme et al. v. Cameroon,* Communication No. 266/2003, 26th Activity Report 2008–2009, paras 113–114.
3098. OAU Convention on Terrorism Art. 22(1). *See also* UN Security Council Res. 1456 (2003) and Res. 2178 (2014).
3099. Protocol to the OAU Convention on Terrorism Art. 3(1)(k).
3100. Saul, 415–416.
3101. African Model Anti-Terrorism Law, https://archives.au.int/bitstream/handle/123456789/8313/african-model-law-E.pdf?sequence=1&isAllowed=y; Assembly, *Decision on the Report of the Peace and Security Council on its Activities and the State of Peace and Security in Africa*, AU Doc. Assembly/AU/Dec. 369(XVII) (30 Jun.–1 Jul. 2011), para. 30.
3102. Saul, 418.
3103. Model Law clause 5xl(a)-(c).
3104. AU Doc. PSC/AHG/Comm.(CDLV).
3105. *Ibid.*, para. 21(i).

Fund.[3106] And another, pursuant to the Non-Aggression and Common Defence Pact, was a call for the creation of specialized joint counter-terrorism units at the sub-regional level within the structure of the ASF.[3107]

§5. DEMOCRATIZATION

493. A global trend that became established in the late twentieth century has been that of democratization and constitutionalism.[3108] Included within these broad tenets are the principles of the rule of law, good governance, participatory, pluralistic and representative democracy and constitutional government.[3109] The causal link between repressive and bad governance, lack of security, underdevelopment and human rights abuses has long been accepted by the UN[3110] which thus maintains that participatory democracy fosters the full realization of peace, development and human rights.[3111] Africa has shared in this phenomenon of democratization.[3112] Of course, it must not be overlooked that mature, stable democracies exist in Africa, Botswana, Cabo Verde and Mauritius to name a few. There are newer democracies, with vibrant democratic cultures, such as South Africa.[3113] In 2011 popular revolutions known as the 'Arab Spring' swept through much of North Africa but their outcomes have been disappointing, resulting either in chaos, as in Libya, or

---

3106. *Ibid.*, para. 21(vii).
3107. *Ibid.*, para. 21(iii).
3108. Vienna Declaration and Programme of Action pt I, para. 8; UN Millennium Declaration Part V, UN General Assembly Res. 55/2, UN Doc. A/Res/55/2; World Summit Outcome paras 135–137, UN General Assembly Res. 60/1, UN Doc. A/Res/60/1. *See also* Constitutive Act of the African Union Art. 3(g) (26 May 2001), 2158 U.N.T.S. 3. It is increasingly argued that a legal entitlement to democratic rule exists, *see* T. Franck, 'The Emerging Right to Democratic Governance', *A.J.I.L.* 86 (1992): 46. However, in recent years democracy is being undermined throughout the world, *see* B. Herre, *The world has recently become less democratic* (6 Sep. 2022), https://ourworldindata.org/less-democratic; Z. Csaky, *Nations in Transit 2021: The Antidemocratic Turn* (Freedom House), https://freedomhouse.org/sites/default/files/2021-04/NIT_2021_final_042321.pdf.
3109. Described as the essence of a liberal democracy, J. Donnelly, *International Human Rights*(2nd edn, Boulder: Westview Press, 1997), 154–57. *See* World Summit Outcome, paras 119–120, 134.
3110. *See* in particular the Vienna Declaration and Programme of Action pt. I. In the World Summit Outcome, the UN General Assembly declared, *inter alia*, 'We recognize that development, peace and security and human rights are interlinked and mutually reinforcing', A/RES/60/1 para. 9. This fact was also accepted by the OAU, *see* Grand Bay Declaration para. 8; CSSDCA Declaration.
3111. Vienna Declaration and Programme of Action pt. I, para. 8; UN Millennium Declaration pt. I, para. 6.
3112. Vienna Declaration and Programme of Action pt. I, para. 9. *See* generally, J. Hatchard, M. Ndulo & P. Slinn, *Comparative Constitutionalism and Good Governance in the Commonwealth: An Eastern and Southern African Perspective* (Cambridge: Cambridge University Press, 2004), Ch. 3. Under the terms of the Harare Declaration 1991, http://www.thecommonwealth.org, members of the Commonwealth, which includes many African States, committed themselves to an agenda of democratization and human rights. This commitment was strengthened under the Commonwealth Charter 2012, http://www.thecommonwealth.org/files/252053/FileName/Charterof the Commonwealth.pdf. This agenda was accepted by the OAU rather late in the day, *see* CSSDCA Declaration.
3113. According to the *2022 Ibrahim Index of African Governance – Index Report*, https://assets.iiag.online/2022/2022-Index-Report.pdf, based on the category, Participation, Rights & Inclusion, the top five ranking countries were Seychelles, Cabo Verde, Mauritius, South Africa and Ghana.

the restoration of illiberal rule, as in Egypt and Tunisia. But too many regimes are of an autocratic and repressive nature, lacking popular support or a genuine democratic mandate.[3114] A fundamental principle of liberal democracy is that governments should be based on the consent of, and be representative of, the people who must be free to exercise their democratic rights. In order to acquire legitimacy genuine democratization must occur. A willingness to embrace and abide by the values of democracy must exist and a culture of constitutionalism, pluralism and participatory party politics must be nurtured; governments must be elected by and accountable to the people, transparent, free and fair elections on the basis of universal adult suffrage must be held at regular intervals and their results must be respected; democratic institutions must be established and supported; a free media must be allowed; civil society must be allowed to operate; corruption must be eliminated.[3115] Politicians must learn to respect the rule of law and act within the limitations imposed by the law; the executive must not interfere with judicial independence since an independent judiciary is vital to the existence of a State governed by the rule of law, restraining abuses of State power.[3116] A civil society organization, the Mo Ibrahim Foundation, has, however, issued a note of caution given worrying trends. It states that, 'Since the democratic expansion in Africa of the early 1990's, we have seen significant progress in the establishment of multiparty democracy and the entrenchment of democratic values … However … [t]he inclusiveness of democracies across Africa is in retreat and at the same time, improvements in good governance have stalled.'[3117]

494. Democratization is a core value of the AU. Explicit references to democratic ideals are made in the Constitutive Act and the fiftieth Anniversary Solemn Declaration reaffirms this commitment. They build upon the right to democratic government enshrined in Article 13(1) of the African Charter.[3118] Democratization is a key policy that will help secure progress in development, peace and social progress. Yet democratization can only be made effective if meaningful reforms are undertaken. Significantly, through the PSC the AU has assumed the capacity to take positive steps to promote and advance democratic values.[3119]

3114. *See* Hatchard, Ndulo & Slinn, 99–108. The five bottom ranking countries according to the *2022 Ibrahim Index of African Governance* were Equatorial Guinea, South Sudan, Eritrea, Somalia, and Egypt.
3115. UNHCR 'General Comment 25' in 'Note by the Secretariat, Compilation of General Comments and General Recommendations adopted by Human Rights Treaty Bodies' (2008) in HRI/GEN/1/Rev.9, vol. I. In 2016 the UN Secretary-General highlighted the fact that recent election-related disputes in countries such as Burundi were undermining democracy, Report of the UN Secretary-General on strengthening the partnership between the United Nations and the African Union on issues of peace and security in Africa, UN Doc. S/2016/780, para. 7.
3116. *See* UN Basic Principles on the Independence of the Judiciary, *Human Rights: A Compilation of International Instruments* vol. I (First Part) 409 (New York & Geneva: United Nations 2002); Kigali Declaration para. 5. *See* generally Hatchard, Ndulo & Slinn, Ch. 8.
3117. *2022 Ibrahim Index of African Governance – Index Report* 53.
3118. *See supra* paras 261–262.
3119. *See supra* paras 197–198. M. Wiebusch, *The Role of Regional Organizations in the Protection of Constitutionalism* (Stockholm: International IDEA Discussion Paper 17, 2016), 19–25.

495. The AU's acceptance of these ideals is openly expressed in the Constitutive Act's preamble where the AU undertakes, *inter alia*, to 'consolidate democratic institutions and culture, and to ensure good governance and the rule of law'. These principles are enshrined in the operative sections of the Constitutive Act, and supplemented by the PSC Protocol. One of the AU's objectives is the promotion of democratic principles and institutions, popular participation and good governance.[3120] Included among the AU's fundamental principles is respect for democratic values, the rule of law, and good governance.[3121] Attention has already been drawn to the existence of a 'democracy clause' in the Constitutive Act.[3122] But these core values form an essential part of NEPAD.[3123] In its Declaration on Democracy, Political, Economic and Corporate Governance the AU further reaffirmed its commitment to democracy and good political governance.[3124] Clearly the AU has the authority to assist transitional societies among its Member States in strengthening and consolidating democracy and constitutionalism.

496. Whereas the AU's commitment to democratic values is expressed in the Constitutive Act in general terms the African Charter on Democracy provides a detailed and wide-ranging set of values in common and undertakings by States Parties.[3125] Its aims, as set out in Article 2 thereof, include adherence to the principles of democracy, constitutionalism and the rule of law, the promotion of free and fair elections, the promotion and protection of an independent judiciary, securing good governance, and the rejection of unconstitutional seizures of power.[3126] Governing principles are listed in Article 3, including human rights and democratic principles; promotion of representative government; the separation of powers; gender equality; and condemnation and rejection of unconstitutional changes of government. Under Article 4(1) States Parties undertake to promote democracy, the rule of law and human rights, whereas under Article 5 they must ensure constitutional rule and constitutional transfers of power. States Parties commit themselves to promote and ensure these values.[3127] However, salient features that are particularly worthy of note include the following.

3120. Constitutive Act Art. 3(g). *See also* PSC Protocol Art. 3(f). An important development in this regard, reinforcing the AU's commitments to these values, is the adoption in 2007 of the African Charter on Democracy, Elections and Governance (30 Jan. 2007), https://www.au.int/en/treaties, Heyns & Killander, Compendium of Key Human Rights Documents 2022, 164 (African Charter on Democracy). In force 15 Feb. 2012. The African Charter on Democracy has been ratified by thirty-eight States as of February 2023.

3121. Constitutive Act Art. 4(g). *See also* PSC Protocol Art. 4(c), and African Charter on Democracy Arts 3 and 4(1).

3122. *See supra* para. 198.

3123. The New Partnership for Africa's Development (NEPAD) Declaration 2001, Heyns & Killander, Compendium of Key Human Rights 2013, 486.

3124. Heyns & Killander, Compendium of Key Human Rights 2013, 492.

3125. *See* S.-A. Elvy, 'Towards a New Democratic Africa: The African Charter on Democracy, Elections and Governance', *Emory International Law Review* 27 (2013): 41.

3126. *See also* Malabo Protocol Art. 28E(1)(e) which condemns 'any amendment or revision of the constitution or legal instruments, which is an infringement on the principles of democratic change of government'.

3127. African Charter on Democracy Arts 3–6.

497. First, developing a culture of democracy and peace.[3128] In addition, State Parties will promote a culture of respect, compromise, consensus and tolerance.[3129] To this end public, and inclusive, institutions that promote and support democracy and constitutional order must be established.[3130] Second, a commitment to participatory political systems, including the holding of democratic elections.[3131] To this end, the AU Commission may send electoral observer missions.[3132] Third, building upon the commitment in the Constitutive Act, unconstitutional changes of government will attract sanctions from the AU.[3133] In this regard, State Parties must ensure civilian control over the military and security forces.[3134] Fourth, State Parties commit themselves to a series of measures designed to advance political, economic and social governance.[3135]

498. Other, more specific, commitments to constitutionalism that attract comment include that of the supremacy of the constitution.[3136] The Westminster model of parliamentary sovereignty, which has not served Africa well, is therefore rejected.[3137] Another important pledge is that to the separation of powers.[3138] There is a commitment to local government, in that power should be decentralized to democratically elected local authorities.[3139] The extent of the devolution of such powers, and to which levels of local government, be it federal, district, county, etc. is a matter for the States themselves to determine. And significantly, State Parties undertake to ensure constitutional transfer of power.[3140] In this regard, it may be

---

3128. *Ibid.*, Arts 11–13, 38(1). *See Suy Bi Gohore Emile and Others v. Côte d'Ivoire*, African Court of Human and Peoples' Rights, App. No. 044/2019 (15 Jul. 2020) para. 170.
3129. *Ibid.*, Art. 39.
3130. *Ibid.*, Arts 15, 38(1).
3131. *Ibid.*, Arts 3(4), 3(11), 4(2), 17, 38(1). *See* Hatchard, Ndulo & Slinn, 108–114, 120–122. The regular conduct of transparent, free and fair elections has been held by the Human Rights Court as one of the fundamental principles of democracy. However, elections may be postponed in light of emergencies, such as the Covid pandemic. Such postponement must be for legitimate reasons, proportionate, in accordance with a general law, must be a last resort and cannot be a pretext to undermine democratic change, *Request for Advisory Opinion by the Pan African Lawyers Union (PALU) on the Right to Participate in the Government of One's Country in the Context of an Election Held during a Public Health Emergency or a Pandemic, such as the COVID-19 Crisis*, Advisory Opinion, African Court of Human and Peoples' Rights, App. No. 001/2020 (16 Jul. 2021) paras 51–54, 98–103. *See further Actions pour la Protection des Droit de l'Homme (APDH) v. Côte d'Ivoire*, African Court of Human and Peoples' Rights, App. No. 001/2014 (18 Nov. 2016). In this case the Human Rights Court stated that national electoral bodies must be independent and impartial, and perceived as such, and that their composition must be balanced to reassure the public about its ability to organize transparent, free and fair elections, *ibid.*, paras 118, 123, 125. *See also XYZ v. Benin*, Provisional Measures, African Court of Human and Peoples' Rights, App. No. 010/2020 (3 Apr. 2020) paras 123–125.
3132. African Charter on Democracy Art. 19(1). *See* generally Hatchard, Ndulo & Slinn, 114, 120.
3133. African Charter on Democracy Arts 3(10), 23–26. *See also ibid.*, Art. 14(2)–(3).
3134. *Ibid.*, Art. 14(1).
3135. *Ibid.*, Arts 27–43.
3136. *Ibid.*, Art. 10(1). *See, e.g.*, Constitution of Namibia Art. 1(6), Constitution of Zimbabwe s. 3.
3137. However, Hatchard, Ndulo & Slinn, 15–19, argue that criticisms of the imposition of inappropriate Westminster-style constitutions have been exaggerated.
3138. African Charter on Democracy Art. 3(5).
3139. *Ibid.*, Art. 34. *See* generally, Hatchard, Ndulo & Slinn, Ch. 9.
3140. African Charter on Democracy Art. 5.

helpful if limits on continuous terms of office of executive Presidents were adopted by State Parties, and more importantly, adhered to.[3141] These commitments have been renewed in Agenda 2063, which stresses that respect for democratic values and practices, human rights, the rule of law and good governance, and the creation of capable institutions, is essential for sustainable socioeconomic development.[3142]

499. Another phenomenon that has given rise to constitutional and democratic crises in a number of countries concerns questionable attempts at extending or abolishing limits on presidential terms, amounting in effect to the perpetuation of personal rule.[3143] Where such changes occur by legal means, such as by amending the constitution, it may be difficult, *prima facie,* to substantiate assertions of unconstitutional changes of government, however politically undesirable they may be.[3144] But they are hardly in keeping with the spirit of the law. An Africa-wide Summit on Constitutionalism and Democratic Consolidation, held in Gaborone in July 2022, organized by the NGO National Democratic Institute, the Government of Botswana and other partners,[3145] adopted the Gaborone Declaration on Constitutionalism which, *inter alia*, commends the peaceful transfer of executive power through credible elections and deplores the disregard of constitutional term limits which thereby deny opportunities for participation in the peaceful and orderly alternation of power and renewal of political leadership.[3146] An Advisory Opinion of the Inter-American Court of Human Rights (IACtHR) in 2021 on this issue is of immediate interest, however.[3147] The IACtHR observed that no universal or regional human rights treaty, including the African Charter, mention presidential re-election without term limits; however, while these treaties, including the African Charter, provided for a right to stand in elections[3148] it concluded that presidential re-election without term limits 'does not constitute an autonomous right protected...by the corpus iuris of

---

3141. *See* Hatchard, Ndulo & Slinn, 63–66. Violence has often broken out as a result of unconstitutional attempts at extending term limits, as in Burkina Faso in 2014 and Burundi in 2015.

3142. Assembly, *Decision on the Report of the Commission on Development of the African Union Agenda 2063*, AU Doc. Assembly/AU/Dec. 565(XXIV) (30–31 Jan. 2015).

3143. *See* generally, L. T. Chigowe, 'One Step Forward, Two Steps Backwards: The Threat of "Third Termism" on Democracy, Rule of Law and Governance in Africa', *Speculum Juris* 34 (2020): 12; M. Wiebusch & C. Murray, 'Presidential Term Limits and the African Union', *J.A.L.* 63 (2019): 131.

3144. Chigowe, 17-18. However, African Charter on Democracy Art. 10(2) requires that the process of constitutional amendment or revision rests on national consensus. *See XYZ v. Benin*, African Court of Human and Peoples' Rights, App. No. 010/2020 (27 Nov. 2020), paras 102–104; *Ajavon v. Benin*, African Court of Human and Peoples' Rights, App. No. 062/2019 (4 Dec. 2020) paras 340–342; *Noudehouenou v. Benin*, African Court of Human and Peoples' Rights, App. No. 003/2020, Judgment (4 Dec. 2020) paras 63–67.

3145. https://www.ndi.org/our-stories/current-and-former-african-presidents-support-term-limits-and-constitutionalism-summit.

3146. Gaborone Declaration in Support of Constitutionalism and Democratic Consolidation, https://www.ndi.org/sites/default/files/FINAL%20Gaborone%20Declaration.pdf.

3147. *Presidential Reelection Without Term Limits in the Context Of the Inter-American Human Rights System*, Inter-American Court of Human Rights, Advisory Opinion OC-28/21, Series A No. 28 (2021).

3148. *Ibid.*, para. 95, citing *Tankanyika Law Society and The Legal and Human Rights Law Centre and Reverend Christopher Mtikila v. Tanzania*, African Court of Human and Peoples' Rights, App. No. 009 & 011/2011 (22 Sep. 2011). *See further* Art. 13(1) African Charter.

international human rights law.'[3149] It considered that such a prohibition 'seeks to guarantee representative democracy' by preventing a person from holding on to power, and, in this way, to ensure political pluralism and rotation of power, while protecting the system of checks and balances that guarantee the separation of powers.'[3150] It noted that 'in view of how much power is concentrated in the presidency in a presidential system, restricting the possibility of reelection without term limits is a suitable means of ensuring that a person does not hold onto power, and thus that the fundamental principles of a representat*ive* democracy are not affected.'[3151] The IACtHR went on to warn of the gradual erosion of democratic safeguards that can lead to an authoritarian regime, even if popularly elected.[3152] It thus concluded that enabling indefinite presidential re-election is contrary to the principles of a representative democracy and, therefore, to the obligations established under the American system.[3153] The AU has put in place a comprehensive framework to bolster constitutionalism, good governance and participatory democracy which extends to practical measures through AU organs such as the PSC. Significantly, this includes the ability to impose sanctions on unconstitutional regimes.[3154] The AU accepts that progress in these fields is unlikely to be sustained unless socioeconomic conditions also improve since impoverishment can lead to apathy or instability and create conditions that undermine the legitimacy of governing regimes, including democratic ones. Recent events which have witnessed the unwelcome return of military coups, such as those in Mali,[3155] Burkina Faso,[3156] Niger,[3157]

3149. *Presidential Reelection Without Term Limits*, para. 102.
3150. *Ibid.*, para. 119.
3151. *Ibid.*, para. 120.
3152. *Ibid.*, para. 145.
3153. *Ibid.*, para. 146.
3154. *See supra* paras 84–90.
3155. Mali has been politically unstable since 2012 when a rebellion by a Tuareg rebel group broke out in northern Mali. In March 2012 disaffected soldiers overthrew the then President and an interim President installed. In 2013, the UN Multidimensional Integrated Stabilization Mission in Mali, MINUSMA, was established by UN Security Council Res. 2100 (2013) to support political developments in the country and carry out a number of security-related operations. It has a difficult relationship with the transitional authorities. In June 2015, the Malian Government and an alliance of rebel groups signed an agreement, known as the Algiers accords, to restore peace in the country but which was never implemented satisfactorily. In August 2020, President Ibrahim Boubacar Keïta was overthrown ousted by a military coup, replaced by a military officer who was himself ousted by another coup in May 2021, BBC News, 'Mali's coup leader Assimi Goïta seizes power again' (25 May 2021), https://www.bbc.co.uk/news/world-africa-57239805. See *further* UN Security Council Res. 2640 (2022).
3156. In 2014 Burkina Faso was thrown into political crisis following the President's attempt to amend the Constitution to allow him to stand for another term. In 2015 a section of the military carried out a coup d'état but pressure from the UN, AU and ECOWAS forced the putschists to hand over power, and a successful transition to civilian rule occurred, Report of the UN Secretary-General on strengthening the partnership between the United Nations and the African Union on issues of peace and security in Africa, UN Doc. S/2016/780, para. 22. In 2022 Burkina Faso experienced two military coups, BBC News, 'Burkina Faso military says it has seized power' (24 Jan. 2022), https://www.bbc.co.uk/news/world-africa-60118993.
3157. There was a failed coup attempt in March 2021, BBC News, 'Niger "coup" thwarted days before inauguration' (31 Mar. 2021), https://www.bbc.co.uk/news/world-africa-56589168.

Guinea,[3158] and Sudan,[3159] demonstrate that the AU's work in this field is a challenging one with much remaining to be done. The AU has not always been consistent in its approach to such difficult events[3160] but in collaboration with ECOWAS, it has reacted to such events by suspending membership of these countries.[3161] The AU's s mission to bolster democracy throughout Africa remains a work in progress.

§6. INTERNATIONAL CRIMINAL LAW

500. In June 2014 the AU adopted a Protocol on Amendments to the Protocol on the Statute of the ACJHR[3162] (Malabo Protocol) adding an International Criminal Law Section[3163] (ICL Section) to the ACJHR competent to hear all cases relating to international crimes listed in the amended Statute.[3164] This historic and controversial development appears to have been occasioned, in part, by a number of concerns that emerged in Africa regarding international criminal justice and the AU's consequent disenchantment with the ICC.[3165] In particular, these concerns

3158. In September 2021, President Alpha Condé, who had been elected in 2010, was overthrown by a coup, BBC News, 'Guinea coup leader to form new government in weeks' (6 Sep. 2021), https://www.bbc.co.uk/news/world-africa-58461436.

3159. In April 2019, President Bashir was overthrown in a military coup. That August a power-sharing deal, the Constitutional Document, was reached between military and civilian factions on the establishment of a new civilian-led transitional government. This led to the creation of the UN Integrated Transition Assistance Mission in Sudan, UNITAMS, pursuant to UN Security Council Res. 2524 (2020) to, *inter alia*, assist the political transition, progress towards democratic governance, and sustainable peace. On 3 October 2020, Sudan's Transitional Government and representatives of several rebel groups signed the Juba Agreement for Peace in Sudan, a complex constitution-building document, https://constitutionnet.org/sites/default/files/2021-03/Juba%20Agreement%20for%20Peace%20in%20Sudan%20-%20Official%20ENGLISH.PDF. Such progress was derailed in 2021 when the civilian government was ousted in another military coup. In December 2022, the Trilateral Mechanism, UNITAMS, AU, and IGAD, sponsored the signing of a Political Framework Agreement between the military and civilian groups in Sudan with a view towards reaching a political agreement on restorating the transitional period and the formation of a democratic government, https://igad.int/trilateral-mechanism-statement-on-the-signing-of-a-political-framework-agreement/.

3160. Wiebusch, 26.

3161. For example, Sudan was duly suspended from the AU, PSC/PR/COMM.(DCCCXLIV), Mali, PSC Communiqué PSC/PR/COMM.(1001(2021)), Burkina Faso, PSC Communiqué PSC/PR/COMM.1/1062(2022), and Guinea, PSC Communiqué PSC/PR/COMM.(1030(2021)).

3162. Protocol on Amendments to the Protocol on the Statute of the African Court of Justice and Human Rights (27 Jun. 2014) https://au.int/en/treaties, Heyns & Killander, Compendium of Key Human Rights 2016, 62. No ratifications to date. For comment, *see* G.J. Naldi & K.D. Magliveras, 'The International Criminal Law Section of the African Court of Justice and Human Rights: An Appraisal', *A.Y.B.I.L.* 21 (2015): 297; C.C. Jalloh, K. M. Clarke & V.O. Nmehielle, *The African Court of Justice and Human and Peoples' Rights in Context* (Cambridge: Cambridge University Press, 2019).

3163. Malabo Protocol Art. 16.

3164. Malabo Protocol Art. 17(3).

3165. K.D. Magliveras & G.J. Naldi, 'The International Criminal Court's Involvement with Africa: An Evaluation of a Fractious Relationship', *Nordic J.I.L.* 82 (2013): 417; G. Werle, L. Fernandez & M. Vormbaum (eds), *Africa and the International Criminal Court* (The Hague: T.M.C. Asser Press, 2014). The AU first raised the possibility of the ACJHR being empowered to try international crimes in 2009, Assembly, Assembly/AU/Dec. 213(XII).

touch upon the perceived abuse of the principle of universal jurisdiction by European States,[3166] and the ICC's pursuit of senior African officials, notably Sudanese President Al Bashir and Kenyan President Uhuru Kenyatta, and the perception that the ICC does not take account of the immunity of incumbent heads of state, contrary to established rules of international law;[3167] and the surrounding controversy on the reach of the Statute of the ICC[3168] (Rome Statute) to non-States Parties and whether the latter are obliged to give effect to ICC arrest warrants.[3169] In addition, because much of the ICC's work has focused on situations in Africa the opinion has formed that the ICC was culpable of selective justice by unjustly targeting Africa. The AU regards the arrest warrants against African Heads of State as undermining international law and as an affront to the 'dignity, sovereignty and integrity of the continent'.[3170] As a consequence, the AU has raised the threat of mass withdrawals by African States from the Rome Statute.[3171] But it has also been argued that the Malabo Protocol would permit the prosecution of certain actions, such as money laundering, trafficking in hazardous wastes and unconstitutional changes of government, which lie outside the jurisdiction of the ICC.[3172] Of course, the AU is perfectly within its rights in pursuing this course of action, there is nothing in international law that prevents it doing so.[3173] The question is about the political wisdom of so doing, whether the adoption of the Malabo Protocol could seriously undermine the mandate of the ICC and threaten the integrity of this developing branch of international law.

Assembly, *Decision on the Implementation of the Assembly Decision on the Abuse of the Principle of Universal Jurisdiction*, AU Doc. Assembly/AU/Dec. 213(XXII) (1–3 Feb. 2009), but the suggestion that Africa try international crimes goes much further back, A. Abass, 'Prosecuting International Crimes in Africa: Rationale, Prospects and Challenges', *E.J.I.L.* 24 (2013): 933, 936–937.

3166. Assembly, *Decision on the Report of the Commission on the Abuse of the Principle of Universal Jurisdiction*, AU Doc. Assembly/AU/ Dec. 199(XI) (30 Jun.–1 Jul. 2008). *See further* L. Arimatsu, *Universal Jurisdiction for International Crimes: Africa's Hope for Justice?* (London: Royal Institute of International Affairs, 2010).
3167. C.C. Jalloh, 'Reflections on the Indictment of Sitting Heads of State and Government and Its Consequences for Peace and Stability and Reconciliation in Africa', *African Journal Legal Studies* 7 (2014): 43. *See Arrest Warrant of 11 April 2000 (DR Congo v. Belgium)* I.C.J. Reports 2002, 3.
3168. Statute of the International Criminal Court (17 Jul. 1998), 2187 U.N.T.S. 3.
3169. *Prosecutor v. Omar Hassan Ahmad Al Bashir* (Decision Pursuant to Art. 87(7) of the Rome Statute on the Failure of the Republic of Malawi to Comply with the Cooperation Requests Issued by the Court with respect to the Arrest and Surrender Omar Hassan Ahmad Al Bashir) [2011] ICC-02/05-01/09, 51 I.L.M.397 (2012). *See* K. Magliveras & G. Naldi, 'The ICC Addresses Non-Cooperation by State Parties in Arresting President Al-Bashir: The Malawi Decision', *African Journal Legal Studies* 6 (2013): 1.
3170. Assembly, *Decision on the Report of the Commission on the Meeting of African States Parties to the ICC Statute of the International Criminal Court (ICC)*, AU Doc. Assembly/AU/Dec. 245 (XIII) (1–3 Jul. 2009).
3171. *See, e.g.*, Assembly, *Decision on the International Criminal Court*, AU Doc. Assembly/AU/Dec. 616 (XXVII) (17–18 Jul. 2016). In 2016 both Burundi and The Gambia gave notice of their withdrawal from the Rome Statute although the latter's was rescinded by the new government in 2017. More serious was South Africa's notice of withdrawal which in 2017 was held to be unconstitutional and invalid without prior parliamentary approval, *Democratic Alliance v. Minister of International Relations and Cooperation and Others* (Case No. 83145/2016, 22 Feb. 2017).
3172. Abass, 939–941.
3173. *Ibid.*, 941–943.

501. The rest of this section is given over to a discussion of the jurisdiction of the ICL Section. The temporal jurisdiction of the ICL Section extends only to crimes committed after the entry into force of the Malabo Protocol and the annexed Statute.[3174] AU Member States automatically accept the ICL Section's jurisdiction upon ratification of the Malabo Protocol and Statute.[3175] However, non-contracting parties may accept its jurisdiction in certain circumstances on an ad hoc basis by means of an express declaration.[3176] The ICL Section can thereby exercise jurisdiction over crimes committed in the territory of a non-State party.[3177] The bases of jurisdiction are wider than those envisaged in Article 12 of the Rome Statute and extend to crimes committed in the territory of a State, the State of which the accused is a national, the nationality of the victim (passive personality principle) and extraterritorial application, i.e., punishing acts committed abroad by non-nationals prejudicial to a contracting party's vital interests (protective principle).[3178] The latter assertions of jurisdiction are controversial. The passive personality principle has generally enjoyed little support but, since in recent years it has been incorporated into counter-terrorism conventions and finds expression in the African human rights system, it has its defenders. Alternatively, it could be considered an expression of the principle of diplomatic protection which can be found in some human rights treaties. The protective principle has again been applied in relation to terrorism and other serious offences against state security such as espionage, counterfeiting and smuggling.[3179]

502. Equally, the ICL Section's jurisdiction *ratione materiae* is considerably broader than that of the ICC. The Malabo Protocol takes an expansive stance; it does not restrict itself solely to the 'most serious crimes', it does not make distinctions based on the gravity of the offences. In contrast, it allows for flexibility by including a number of transnational crimes which are reflected in different legal sources, including the definition of international crimes in the Draft Code of Crimes against the Peace and Security of Mankind of 1996,[3180] as well as some proposals on a wide range of serious crimes considered by the Conference which drafted the Rome Statute.[3181] In addition to the core crimes of genocide, crimes against humanity and war crimes, it includes the crime of unconstitutional changes of government, mercenarism, piracy, terrorism, corruption, money laundering, drug trafficking, people trafficking, trafficking in hazardous wastes, and the illicit exploitation of natural

3174. Malabo Protocol Art. 46E(1).
3175. *Ibid.*, Art. 46E*bis* (1).
3176. *Ibid.*, Art. 46E*bis* (3).
3177. *Ibid.*, Art. 46E*bis* (2)(a).
3178. *Ibid.*, Art. 46E*bis* (2) (c)–(d).
3179. A. Aust, *Handbook of International Law* (Cambridge: Cambridge University Press, 2005), 45.
3180. International Law Commission, 'Draft Code of Crimes against the Peace and Security of Mankind', *Yearbook of the International Law Commission* vol. II(2) (1996).
3181. J. Dugard, 'Obstacles in the Way of an International Criminal Court', *Cambridge Law Journal* 56 (1997): 329; N. Boister, 'The Exclusion of Treaty Crimes from the Jurisdiction of the Proposed International Criminal Court: Law, Pragmatism, Politics', *Journal Armed Conflict Law* 3 (1998): 27, 27–28.

resources.[3182] Many of these practices may be considered as prohibited by customary and/or treaty law, even if regionally. However, several of the 'crimes' listed in the Malabo Protocol 'are not as yet fixed in the international criminal law firmament'[3183] since they include offences at an embryonic state of development, whereas others, e.g., coups d'état and mercenarism, reflect African concerns and priorities. Nevertheless, the question does arise as to whether some of these, again coups d'état and mercenarism, however reprehensible, meet the definition of 'most serious crimes of concern to the international community as a whole' as understood by Article 5(1) of the Rome Statute, or indeed, whether they constitute international crimes at all according to universal international law.[3184] Of course, the drafters of the Malabo Protocol are free to classify these practices as international crimes if they so wish. Moreover, the AU has notably succeeded in adopting a definition of the crime of aggression, something that eluded the ICC for many years.[3185] Finally, the list of crimes set out in the Malabo Protocol is not exhaustive as the Assembly can add further crimes in line with the development of international law.[3186] It is also important to note that the crimes are not be subject to any statute of limitations.[3187]

503. Jurisdiction *ratione personae* also merits attention. The question of head of state immunity has been a key concern of the AU in light of the controversy generated by the ICC indictments of Presidents Al Bashir and Kenyatta, and Colonel Gaddafi.[3188] Fundamental disagreement on this issue was one of the driving forces behind the AU's decision in drafting the Malabo Protocol. Notwithstanding jurisprudence that a rule of customary international law removing immunity from heads of states before international tribunals with respect to international crimes has crystallized,[3189] the AU's consistent position is that heads of state continue to enjoy immunity in accordance with traditional rules of international law unless waived

3182. Malabo Protocol Art. 28A. *See* G. Werle & M. Vormbaum (eds), *The African Criminal Court: A Commentary on the Malabo Protocol* (The Hague: T.M.C. Asser Press, 2017), Part II; N. Boister, 'Transnational Crimes Jurisdiction of the Criminal Chamber of the African Court of Justice and Human and Peoples' Rights', in Jalloh, Clarke & Nmehielle, 336.

3183. M. du Plessis, *Implications of the AU Decisions Giving the African Court Jurisdiction over International Crimes* (Institute for Security Studies Paper No. 235, 2012), 7–8.

3184. Cassese, *International Criminal Law* 12–13.

3185. Malabo Protocol Art. 28M. A text defining the crime of aggression was adopted at the ICC Review Conference by Resolution RC/Res.6 with a view to entry into force by 2017, 'First ICC Review Conference: Resolutions and Declarations', 49 I.L.M. 1328, 1334–1335 (2010). On 14 December 2017, States Parties to the Rome Statute adopted Resolution ICC-ASP/16/Res.5 by consensus enabling the ICC to prosecute the crime of aggression.

3186. Malabo Protocol Art. 28A(2).

3187. *Ibid.*, Art. 28A(3).

3188. *The Prosecutor v. Omar Hassan Ahmad Al Bashir* ICC-02/05-01/09; *The Prosecutor v. Uhuru Muigai Kenyatta*, ICC-01/09-02/11; *The Prosecutor v. Muammar Mohammed Abu Minyar Gaddafi, Saif Al-Islam Gaddafi and Abdullah Al-Senussi*, ICC-01/11-01/11. On the AU's reaction to these prosecutions *see, e.g.*, Assembly, *Decision on the Progress Report of the Commission on the Implementation of Decision Assembly/Au/Dec.270(XIV)*, AU Doc. Assembly/AU/Dec. 296(XV) (25–27 Jul. 2010), Assembly, *Decision on the Implementation of the Assembly Decisions on the International Criminal Court*, AU Doc. Assembly/AU/Dec. 366(XVII) (30 Jun.–1 Jul. 2011).

3189. *Prosecutor v. Omar Hassan Ahmad Al Bashir* (Decision Pursuant to Art. 87(7) of the Rome Statute on the Failure of the Republic of Malawi to Comply with the Cooperation Requests Issued by

explicitly.[3190] The Malabo Protocol therefore makes provision for absolute immunity for serving AU heads of state or government, and senior officials during their term of office.[3191] However, this does not mean that impunity for the perpetrators of human rights abuses is condoned.[3192] The Malabo Protocol makes provision for the attribution of individual criminal responsibility and establishes that the accused's previous position no longer provides a defence to absolve him/her from responsibility.[3193] This provision is in line with the traditional position that former officials may have to face criminal proceedings before transnational criminal courts.[3194]

504. Another significant innovation is that jurisdiction is extended over legal persons, including corporations.[3195] The inclusion of corporate legal liability may be understandable in the era of globalization and especially in light of the sometimes callous and irresponsible behaviour shown by transnational corporations (TNCs) especially in countries of the South.[3196] Given that international criminal law imposes obligations upon individuals, logic would dictate that, particularly since the Malabo Protocol includes corruption and illicit trade in hazardous wastes as core crimes, duties are extended to legal persons such as TNCs. That treaties may impose duties on TNCs is no longer to be considered exceptional and certainly an increasing trend exists to impose human rights standards on TNCs[3197] but a challenging difficulty remains: according to traditional international law corporations

---

the Court with respect to the Arrest and Surrender Omar Hassan Ahmad Al Bashir)[2011] ICC-02/05-01/09, 51 I.L.M. 397,405–407 (2012); Special Court of Sierra Leone, *Prosecutor v. Charles Ghankay Taylor*, Decision on Immunity from Jurisdiction, SCSL-2003-01-1 (3014–3039) (31 May 2004) paras 51–53. The ICC's conclusion was described by the AU as fundamentally flawed and contrary to international law, AU Commission, 'On the Decisions of Pre-Trial Chamber I of the International Criminal Court (ICC) Pursuant to Art. 87(7) of the ICC Statute', Press Release No. 002/2012 (9 Jan. 2012).

3190. Assembly, 'Decision on the Report of the Second Meeting of States Parties to the ICC Statute of the International Criminal Court (ICC)', Assembly/AU/Dec. 270(XIV) (31 Jan.–2 Feb. 2010) para. 8.

3191. Malabo Protocol Art. 46A*bis*. *See* D. Tladi, 'The Immunity Provision in the AU Amendment Protocol: Separating the (Doctrinal) Wheat from the (Normative) Chaff', *Journal International Criminal Justice* 13 (2015): 3.

3192. Constitutive Act Art. 4(o) rejects impunity.

3193. Malabo Protocol Art. 46B(1)–(2).

3194. *Arrest Warrant of 11 April 2000 (D.R. Congo v. Belgium)* I.C.J. Reports 2002, 3, paras 58–61.

3195. Malabo Protocol Art. 46C(1). *See* J. Kyriakakis, 'Article 46C: Corporate Criminal Liability at the African Criminal Court', in Jalloh, Clarke & Nmehielle, 793.

3196. *See The Social and Economic Rights Action Center and the Center for Economic and Social Rights v. Nigeria* Communication No. 155/96 (2001).

3197. The UN Norms on the Responsibilities of Transnational Corporations and Other Business Enterprises with Regard to Human Rights, adopted in August 2003 by the UN Sub-Commission on the Promotion and Protection of Human Rights Resolution 2003/16, UN Doc. E/CN.4/Sub.2/2003/12/Rev.2 (2003), provides a set of standard-setting principles for socially responsible corporate behaviour. In 2014 the UN Human Rights Council set up an intergovernmental working group on a legally binding instrument on transnational corporations with respect to human rights, UN Doc. A/HRC/26/L.22/Rev. 1. A revised draft text was published in 2022, UN Doc. A/HRC/49/65/Add.1.

are mere objects of international law or at best have limited international personality.[3198] However, in principle there exists no legal impediment to States agreeing to make corporations criminally liable under international law.[3199] There does appear to be an increasing trend towards criminal liability for corporations in international law which the Malabo Protocol reflects. But the end result could be to deter TNCs from conducting business in Africa at a time when the Continent is in need of foreign investments and seeks to improve its global image as an enterprise-friendly place.

505. The Malabo Protocol contains a complementarity clause.[3200] Accordingly, the jurisdiction of the ICL Section is complementary to national criminal jurisdictions whereby national courts are as a rule given precedence where the State is willing and able to investigate and prosecute the case.[3201] This principle has been understood as applying solely to national authorities[3202] but intriguingly the Malabo Protocol additionally mentions the courts of the Regional Economic Communities (RECs). This is problematic in that, at present, no REC court has jurisdiction over international crimes as such.[3203] Regrettably the Malabo Protocol is exceptionally vague on the relationship between the ICL Section and the courts of the RECs but references to 'other Court' and 'another Court' in Article 46I would suggest that the ICL Section would relinquish jurisdiction to the courts of the RECs.

506. Despite the fact that over thirty African States have ratified the Rome Statute, the Malabo Protocol does not contain a savings clause, in fact there is no mention of the ICC at all, so that the relationship between the two bodies is not addressed explicitly except to the effect that States that ratify the Malabo Protocol accept the jurisdiction of the Court.[3204] International law, set out in Article 30(3) of the Vienna Convention on the Law of Treaties regarding incompatibility between successive treaties on the same subject matter, indicates that the Malabo Protocol, when it enters into force, would prevail over the Rome Statute for those contracting parties that have ratified the latter if *incompatibility* were deemed to arise. There may be an incentive for some States in accepting the Malabo Protocol, even if on

3198. P. Malanczuk (ed.), *Akehurst's Modern Introduction to International Law* (7th rev. edn, London: Routledge, 1997), 100–103; Special Tribunal for Lebanon, *New TV S.A.L. v. Karma Mohamed Thasin al Khayat*, STL-14-05/I/CJ/ (31 January 2014) paras 18, 25; *Akhbar Beirut S.A.L. v. Ibrahim Mohamed al Amin*, STL-14-06/I/CJ/ (31 Jan. 2014) paras 18, 25.

3199. *New TV S.A.L. v. Karma Mohamed Thasin al Khayat*, STL-14-05/I/CJ/ (31 Jan. 2014) para. 26; *Akhbar Beirut S.A.L. v. Ibrahim Mohamed al Amin*, STL-14-06/I/CJ/ (31 Jan. 2014) para. 26.

3200. Malabo Protocol Art. 46H(1). *See* M. M. deGuzman, 'Complementarity at the African Court', in Jalloh, Clarke & Nmehielle, 645.

3201. *Ibid.*, Art. 46H(2); Cassese, *International Criminal Law*, 342–343. Thus, the ICL Section could assume jurisdiction where the national proceedings constitute a sham, Malabo Protocol Art. 46H(3)–(4), 46I(2). It has, however, been pointed out the word 'genuinely' which features in the corresponding provision of the Rome Statute has been omitted from the Malabo Protocol, deGuzman, 648–649.

3202. Cassese, *International Criminal Law*, 343.

3203. deGuzman, 647. However, the ECOWAS Court of Justice does have jurisdiction over human rights violations in Member States, Supplementary Protocol A/SP.1/01/05 Relating to the Community Court of Justice (19 Jan. 2005) Art. 3(4).

3204. Malabo Protocol Art. 46E*bis* (1).

an ad hoc basis, in that its list of crimes is more expansive than that in the Rome Statute. Of course, those unhappiest with the ICC but still keen on expressing support for international criminal justice may denounce the Rome Statute and transfer their allegiance to the African alternative.[3205] Such a development would have disturbing implications for the role and standing of the ICC should a significant number of African States withdraw. However, certain African countries, e.g., Botswana, are staunch ICC supporters. In fact, the deep divisions caused by this issue were on display at an extraordinary session of the Assembly that took place in October 2013 on the AU's relationship with the ICC where a call for mass withdrawal from the Rome Statute failed to be carried.[3206] The ICL Section is designed, *inter alia*, as an attractive option for those African regimes that would never contemplate accepting the Rome Statute, although whether some of the worst perpetrators of human rights abuses would choose even this course of action is open to doubt. But it should not be overlooked that the ICC has ruled that jurisdiction has also been conferred to it under the UN Security Council's Chapter VII powers in accordance with Article 13(b) of the Rome Statute.[3207] Therefore, if an African State's obligations under the Malabo Protocol and a suitable ICC decision proved incompatible, the latter would prevail consistent with Article 103 of the UN Charter.

§7. Cyber Security

507. The challenges posed by the digital age, access to information, the ease in communications, e-commerce, fraud and crime, computer security, data protection, among others, require responses which to be truly effective must be dealt with at a transnational level. This is because, to take one example, cybercrime is borderless, the perpetrators and victims of cybercrimes often located in different national jurisdictions. Europe took the lead in seeking to address these problems, adopting the Convention on Cybercrime in 2001 (Budapest Convention).[3208] The focus of the

---

3205. Burundi withdrew from the Rome Statute with effect from 27 October 2017, Press Release ICC-CPI-20161014-PR1244. In October 2016, South Africa deposited its instrument of withdrawal from the Rome Statute, Press Release ICC-CPI-20161021-PR1248. However, this move was revoked after a court ruling that it was unconstitutional, *Democratic Alliance v. Minister of International Relations and Cooperation and others* 2017 (3) SA 212 (GP). *See* UN Doc. C.N.121.2017.TREATIES-XVIII.10. In November 2016 The Gambia notified its decision to withdraw from the Rome Statute which was reversed by the new President in February 2017, Press Release ICC-ASP-20170217-PR1274. *See further* M. Ssenyonjo, 'State Withdrawal Notifications from the Rome Statute of the International Criminal Court: South Africa, Burundi and The Gambia', *Criminal Law Forum* 29 (2018): 63.

3206. Assembly, *Decision on Africa's Relationship with the International Criminal Court (ICC)*, AU Doc. Ext/Assembly/AU/Dec. 1 (12 Oct. 2013).

3207. *See, inter alia, The Prosecutor v. Omar Hassan Ahmad Al Bashir,* Decision Pursuant to Art. 87(7) of the Rome Statute on the Failure of the Republic of Malawi to Comply with the Cooperation Requests Issued by the Court with respect to the Arrest and Surrender Omar Hassan Ahmad Al Bashir, ICC-02/05-01/09. *See* E. De Wet, 'Concurrent Jurisdiction of the International Criminal Court and the African Criminal Chamber in the Case of Concurrent Referrals', in Jalloh, Clarke & Nmehielle, 180.

3208. European Convention on Cybercrime (23 Nov. 2001), E.T.S. No. 185. It is interesting to note that a number of African States are parties to the Budapest Convention, including Ghana, Mauritius,

Budapest Convention is on harmonizing national criminal law with regard to computer offences, providing national criminal law powers for the investigation and prosecution of cybercrime and enhancing international cooperation.[3209] In 2014 the AU followed suit with the adoption of the Convention on Cyber Security, or Malabo Convention.[3210] Unlike the Budapest Convention, the AU Convention on Cyber Security assumes a broader perspective bringing within its scope not only cybercrime but also electronic transactions or e-commerce, personal data protection and cybersecurity and cybercrime.[3211] It therefore borrows considerably from the, now repealed, EU Data Protection Directive. The AU Convention on Cyber Security establishes a standard legal and security framework for all these activities. However, the wisdom of this wide-ranging approach has attracted scepticism as overly ambitious and unrealistic.[3212] On the other hand, in relation to cybercrime and national criminal law powers, the AU Convention is not as far-reaching as the Budapest Convention, nor does it provide a framework for international cooperation.[3213] But it is important to note that the AU Convention is more in the nature of a traité cadre, leaving States with considerable discretion in establishing the detailed framework.[3214] The question has also been posed as to whether Africa has the practical and technical capacity to address many of these issues.[3215] Article 1 of the AU Convention on Cyber Security contains a list of definitions. However, it has been observed that some crucial definitions, such as 'service provider' and 'traffic data', have been omitted.[3216] But it is also true to say that the list of definitions in the AU Convention is more comprehensive than that of the Budapest Convention.

Senegal and South Africa. However, the EU had already taken the initiative, adopting EU Council Directive 95/46 of 24 Oct. 1995 on the protection of individuals with regard to the processing of personal data and on the free movement of such data, O.J. L 281/31, 24 Oct. 1995 (Data Protection Directive). The Data Protection Directive was superseded in 2018 by EU Council Regulation 2016/679 of 27 Apr. 2016 on the protection of natural persons with regard to the processing of personal data and on the free movement of such data, O.J. L 119/1, 27 Apr. 2016 (GDPR), an expanded and more coherent, protective framework with enhanced enforcement.

3209. *See* generally A.M. Weber, 'The Council of Europe's Convention on Cybercrime', *Berkeley Technology Law Journal* 18 (2003): 425; M.A. Vatis, *The Council of Europe Convention on Cybercrime*, Proceedings of a Workshop on Deterring Cyberattacks: Informing Strategies and Developing Options for US Policy http://www.nap.edu/catalog/12997.html. *See also* Second Additional Protocol to the Convention on Cybercrime on enhanced cooperation and disclosure of electronic evidence (12 May 2022), C.E.T.S. No. 224. It seeks, *inter alia*, to enhance cooperation on cybercrime and the ability of criminal justice authorities to collect evidence in electronic form of a criminal offence for the purpose of specific criminal investigations or proceedings.

3210. Convention on Cyber Security and Personal Data Protection (27 Jun. 2014) https://au.int/en/treaties. In force June 2023.

3211. G. Greenleaf & M. Georges, 'The African Union's Data Privacy Convention: A Major Step Toward Global Consistency?', *Privacy Laws & Business International Report* 131 (2014): 18; E. Tamarkin, *The AU's Cybercrime Response: A Positive Start, but Substantial Challenges Ahead* (ISS Policy Brief 73, Pretoria: Institute for Security Studies, 2015).

3212. Tamarkin, 4.

3213. Glacy+, *Comparative analysis of the Malabo Convention of the African Union and the Budapest Convention on cybercrime* 3–4 http://www.coe.int/cybercrime.

3214. Several passages in the Preamble support this interpretation.

3215. *Ibid.* 4–5.

3216. Glacy+, 5.

508. The AU Convention on Cyber Security seeks to ensure security of electronic transactions.[3217] E-commerce is to be exercised freely in the States Parties, the one exception being gambling.[3218] There may be sound public interest reasons for such a prohibition but it may have been preferable to have adopted an approach similar to that of EU Law where cross-border gambling is usually permissible subject to proportionate and non-discriminatory restrictions.[3219]

509. The AU Convention on Cyber Security establishes a legal and regulatory framework on personal data protection and cyber security. With regard to the former, the objective is to strengthen protection of data and punish any violation of privacy but 'without prejudice to the principle of free flow of personal data.'[3220] The AU Convention on Cyber Security extends to the collection, processing,[3221] transmission, storage or use of personal data, and the automated or non-automated processing of data, by the public and private sectors.[3222] Data processing relating to

---

3217. AU Convention on Cyber Security Art. 7.

3218. *Ibid.*, Art. 2(1)(a).

3219. *See, e.g.*, Case C-275/92 *HM Customs & Excise v. Schindler* [1994] E.C.R. I-1039; Case C-243/01 *Criminal proceedings against Piergiorgio Gambelli and others* [2003] E.C.R. I-13031.

3220. AU Convention on Cyber Security Art. 8. Personal data is defined as 'any information relating to an identified or identifiable natural person by which this person can be identified, directly or indirectly … by reference to an identification number or to one or more factors specific to his/her physical, physiological, mental, economic, cultural or social identity', *ibid.*, Art. 1. Compare GDPR Art. 4(1). Personal data can therefore include names, nationality, gender, ethnicity, religion, telephone numbers, fingerprints, images caught on camera. *See, e.g.*, Case C-101/01 *Criminal proceedings against Bodil Lindquist* [2003] E.C.R. I-12971, para. 24; Cases C-141/12 and C-372/12 *Minister voor Immigratie v. M.*, Judgment of 17 Jul. 2014, C:2014:2081, paras 34, 38–41; Case C-291/12 *Schwarz v. Bochum*, Judgment of 17 Oct. 2013, C:2013:670, para. 27; Case C-212/13 *Rynes v. Úřad pro Ochranu Údajů*, Judgment of 11 December 2014, C:2014:2428, para. 22.

3221. Processing is defined as 'any operation … which is performed upon personal data, whether or not by automatic means such as the collection, recording, organization, storage, adaptation, alteration, retrieval, backup, copy, consultation, use, disclosure by transmission, dissemination or otherwise making available, alignment or combination and locking, encryption, erasure or destruction of personal data', AU Convention on Cyber Security Art. 1. Compare GDPR Art. 4(2). Processing can include loading personal data on an internet page, communication of name and address, taking and storing fingerprints, video surveillance involving the recording and storage personal data. *See, e.g.*, Case C-101/01 *Lindquist* para. 25; Case C-461/10 *Bonnier Audio et al. v. Perfect Communication Sweden*, Judgment of 19 Apr. 2012, C:2012:219, para. 52; Case C-291/12 *Schwarz v. Bochum*, Judgment of 17 Oct. 2013, C:2013:670, paras 28–29; Case C-212/13 *Rynes v. Úřad pro Ochranu Údajů*, Judgment of 11 Dec. 2014, C:2014:2428, para. 24; Case C-205/21 *V.S. v. Ministerstvo na vatreshnite raboti, Glavna direktsia za borba s organiziranata prestapnost*, Judgment of 26 Jan. 2023, C:2023:49.

3222. AU Convention on Cyber Security Art. 9(1)(a)–(b). It is interesting to note that the CJEU has held that it is settled EU Law, in the light of Council Directive 2002/58/EC of 12 Jul. 2002 concerning the processing of personal data and the protection of privacy in the electronic communications sector, O.J. 2002 L 201/37, 12 Jul. 2002, as amended by Council Directive 2009/136/EC of 25 Nov. 2009, O.J. 2009 L 337/11, 25 Nov. 2009, precludes a general and indiscriminate retention of traffic and location data, Cases C-293/12 and C-594/12 *Digital Rights Ireland Ltd v. Minister for Communications, Marine and Natural Resources and Others*, Judgment of 8 Apr. 2014, C:2014:238; Cases C-203/15 and C-698/15 *Tele2 Sverige AB v. Post-och telestyrelsen*, Judgment of 21 Dec. 2016, C:2016:70; Case C-140/20 *G.D. v. The Commissioner of the Garda Síochána and Others*, Judgment of 5 Apr. 2022, C:2022:258.

public or State security, defence, research, or criminal prosecution is included subject to exceptions.[3223] However, data processing by an individual for his/her personal or household activities is excepted unless for 'systematic communication to third parties or for dissemination'.[3224] Also excepted is personal data processing for journalistic and research purposes and artistic and literary expression.[3225]

510. The processing of personal data is subject to a number of conditions.[3226] The central basic principles include that of consent (subject to certain exceptions);[3227] lawfulness and fairness; accuracy; transparency; and confidentiality and security.[3228] The collection and processing of sensitive data revealing racial and ethnic origin, parental filiation, political opinion, religious and philosophical beliefs, trade union membership, sex life and health is prohibited.[3229] This prohibition is not absolute and does not therefore apply in a variety of circumstances, including where written consent has been given, in the course of legal proceedings, or in the public interest for historical, statistical or scientific purposes.[3230]

511. The data subject[3231] is conferred a number of rights which are a right to information,[3232] a right of access,[3233] a right to object,[3234] and a right of rectification or erasure.[3235]

3223. AU Convention on Cyber Security Art. 9(1)(d). Compare GDPR Arts. 2(2)(d), 23(1). The CJEU has held that national measures providing for the retention of traffic and location data is justified if limited to what is strictly necessary, such as with the objective of fighting serious crime, Cases C-293/12 and C-594/12 *Digital Rights Ireland v. Minister for Communications, Marine and Natural Resources*, Judgment of 8 Apr. 2014, C:2014:238; Cases C-203/15 and C-698/15 *Tele2 Sverige AB v. Post-och telestyrelsen*, Judgment of 21 Dec. 2016, C:2016:70; Case C-205/21 *V.S. v. Ministerstvo na vatreshnite raboti, Glavna direktsia za borba s organiziranata prestapnost*, Judgment of 26 Jan. 2023, C:2023:49; or threats to national security, Cases C-511/18, C-512/18 and C-520/18 *La Quadrature du Net and Others v. Premier ministre and Others*, Judgment of 6 Oct. 2020, C:2020:791; Cases C-793/19 and C-794/19 *Bundesrepublik Deutschland v. SpaceNet AG and Telekom Deutschland GmbH*, Judgment of 20 Sep. 2022, C:2022:702.

3224. AU Convention on Cyber Security Art. 9(2)(a). Compare GDPR Art. 2(2)(c). *See* Case C-101/01 *Lindquist* paras 45–47.

3225. AU Convention on Cyber Security Art. 14(3). Compare GDPR Art. 85. In Case C-73/07 *Finnish Data Protection Ombudsman v. Satakunnan Markkinaporssi Oy and Satamedia Oy* [2007] E.C.R. I-7075, para. 61 the ECJ stated that activities may be categorized as journalistic if their sole object is the disclosure to the public of information or opinions irrespective of the medium used to transmit them.

3226. AU Convention on Cyber Security Art. 13.

3227. GDPR Art. 4(11) requires the consent to be unambiguous. *See also* Art. 7. However, circumventing consent may be justified, *inter alia*, in the legitimate interests pursued by the controller, *ibid.*, Art. 6(1)(f), a provision absent from the AU Convention on Cyber Security. A balance of interests is required, Case C-131/12 *Google Spain SL v. AEPD & Mario Costeja Gonzalez*, Judgment of 13 May 2014, C:2014:317, paras 70–75.

3228. *See* Case C-291/12 *Schwarz v. Bochum*, Judgment of 17 Oct. 2013, C:2013:670.

3229. AU Convention on Cyber Security Art. 14(1). Compare GDPR Art. 9(1). *See* Case C-101/01 *Lindquist* paras 50–51, where the CJEU stated that personal data regarding health must be given a broad interpretation so as to include mental and physical health.

3230. AU Convention on Cyber Security Art. 14(2). Compare GDPR Art. 8(2).

3231. According to AU Convention on Cyber Security Art. 1 the data subject refers to any 'natural person that is the subject of personal data processing'.

3232. AU Convention on Cyber Security Art. 16. Compare GDPR Arts 13–14.

512. The AU Convention on Cyber Security imposes a number of obligations on data controllers.[3236] These include confidentiality, security and storage responsibilities.[3237]

513. The AU Convention on Cyber Security requires States Parties to set up independent national personal data protection authorities (NPA) tasked with protecting personal data.[3238] In ensuring that information technologies do not threaten public freedoms and privacy NPAs have a broad mandate. These include responding to requests for an opinion regarding personal data processing; informing persons and data controllers of their rights and obligations; adjudging claims and complaints regarding the processing of personal data; informing the judicial authorities of offences that have come to their attention; imposing sanctions on data controllers; and authorizing transborder transfer of personal data.[3239] In addition, NPAs can warn and order data controllers to stop breaches of the AU Convention.[3240] Moreover, should a data controller fail to comply, the NPAs can withdraw their authorizations and impose monetary penalties.[3241] All decisions and sanctions by NPAs are subject to appeal.[3242] Unlike the GDPR the AU Convention does not compel States to provide a judicial remedy to persons whose rights may have been violated.[3243]

514. In relation to cybercrime, the AU Convention on Cyber Security requires States Parties to adopt legislative or regulatory measures providing for substantive

---

3233. AU Convention on Cyber Security Art. 17. Compare GDPR Art. 15. *See* Cases C-141/12 and C-372/12 *Minister voor Immigratie v. M.*, Judgment of 17 Jul. 2014, C:2014:2081, paras 44–46, 59–60. The CJEU has held that access must be without constraint, without excessive delay and without excessive expense, Case C-486/12 *X*, Judgment of 12 Dec. 2013, C:2013:836. Access may be subject to reasonable time limits, Case C-553/07 *College van Burgemeester en Wethouders van Rotterdam v. Rijkeboer* [2009] E.C.R. I-3889, paras 55–57.
3234. AU Convention on Cyber Security Art. 18. Compare GDPR Art. 15(1)(e).
3235. AU Convention on Cyber Security Art. 19. Compare GDPR Arts 16–17. *See* Case C-131/12 *Google Spain SL v. AEPD & Mario Costeja Gonzalez*, Judgment of 13 May 2014, C:2014:317, para. 98.
3236. Data controller refers to any natural or legal person, public or private, who collects and processes personal data, AU Convention on Cyber Security Art. 1. Compare GDPRArt. 4(7). *See* Case C-131/12 *Google Spain SL v. AEPD & Mario Costeja Gonzalez*, Judgment of 13 May 2014, C:2014:317, paras 33–41.
3237. AU Convention on Cyber Security Arts 20–23. Compare GDPR Arts 25–26. *See* Case C-342/12 *Worten-Equipamentos para o Lar v. Authority for Working Conditions*, Judgment of 30 May 2013, C: 2013: 355, paras 24–25.
3238. AU Convention on Cyber Security Art 11(1). State oversight of NPAs would be incompatible with the principle of independence, Case C-518/07 *Commission v. Germany* [2010] E.C.R. I-1885. *See also* Case C-614/10 *Commission v. Austria*, Judgment of 6 Oct. 2012, C:2012:631; Case C-288/12 *Commission v. Hungary*, Judgment of 8 Apr. 2014, C:2014:237.
3239. AU Convention on Cyber Security Art. 12(2).
3240. *Ibid.*, Art. 12(3).
3241. *Ibid.*, Art. 12(4).
3242. *Ibid.*, Art. 12(6).
3243. GDPR Arts 77–79. However, States Parties are free to do so, AU Convention on Cyber Security Art. 14(4).

law criminalizing cybercrime and procedural law powers necessary for the investigation and prosecution of these crimes.[3244] Cybercrime offences should be punishable by 'effective, proportionate and dissuasive criminal penalties' or other 'appropriate penalties', which may also be imposed on legal persons.[3245] National regulatory authorities must be put in place with the specific task of taking a leading role in all aspects of cyber security.[3246] Appropriate institutions to combat cybercrime should also be established.[3247] None of these measures should endanger the rights of individuals under national and international law.[3248]

515. The AU Convention on Cyber Security seeks to enhance international cooperation to combat cybercrime through the harmonization of the legislative or regulatory measures and respect for the principle of double criminal liability.[3249] States are encouraged to sign agreements on mutual legal assistance[3250] as well as information-sharing.[3251] The issue of how to settle competing claims to jurisdiction over an alleged offence between States, a likely eventuality, is thus addressed by implication.[3252]

516. States Parties are required to criminalize the following acts:[3253] attacks on computer systems (such as unauthorized access or entering or deleting data fraudulently);[3254] computerized data breaches (such as fraudulently intercepting data);[3255] content related offences (such as child pornography, racist or xenophobic propaganda, threats or insults based on race, national or ethnic origin or religion, genocide denial);[3256] and property offences (such as theft, fraud, money laundering or blackmail).[3257] No express provision is made for offences related to copyright infringement.[3258]

3244. AU Convention on Cyber Security Art. 25(1). *See also ibid.*, Art. 31(3). However, these powers do not appear to be as extensive as those under the Budapest Convention and incline to be somewhat imprecise and contain few safeguards, Glacy+, 4–5.
3245. AU Convention on Cyber Security Art. 31(1).*See also ibid.*, Art. 31(2). Art. 30(2) requires States Parties to enact laws providing for the criminal liability of legal persons.
3246. *Ibid.*, Art. 25(2).
3247. *Ibid.*, Art. 27(2).
3248. *Ibid.*, Art. 25(3).
3249. *Ibid.*, Art. 28(1).
3250. *Ibid.*, Art. 28(2).
3251. *Ibid.*, Art. 28(2)–(4).
3252. Compare Budapest Convention Art. 22(5).
3253. The point has been made that the AU Convention on Cyber Security omits a number of crucial *mens rea* elements, Glacy+, 4.
3254. AU Convention on Cyber Security Art. 29(1).
3255. *Ibid.*, Art. 29(2).
3256. *Ibid.*, Art. 29(3)(1). Compare the Additional Protocol concerning the Criminalization of Acts of a Racist and Xenophobic Nature through Computed Systems (28 Jan. 2003) E.T.S. 189.
3257. AU Convention on Cyber Security Art. 30(1). Although intellectual property is not specifically mentioned it is submitted that it comes within the scope of the term property, *Anheuser-Busch Inc. v. Portugal*, European Court of Human Rights [GC], 45 E.H.R.R. 830 (2007).
3258. Compare Budapest Convention Art. 10.

517. While the expectation is that States Parties will prosecute offenders the AU Convention on Cyber Security makes no explicit mention of the extradition of offenders although such a prospect may be envisaged in agreements on mutual legal assistance.

518. The AU Convention on Cyber Security has attracted criticism on human rights grounds.[3259] It is claimed that the criminalization of content related offences relating to hate speech, racist or xenophobic propaganda, or genocide denial, for instance, conflicts with the freedom of expression.[3260] However, it needs to be recalled that international human rights law does not consider the freedom of expression an absolute right but envisages limitations as lawful in certain circumstances[3261] or to prevent abuse.[3262]

519. In theory, these restrictions in the AU Convention do not appear sinister but seem compatible with international standards. More problematic, however, are the exceptions to the prohibitions on personal data processing on grounds of public interest or the exercise of official authority. These concepts are not defined in the AU Convention and could therefore be abused by national authorities. Another worrying provision is that whereby a court is permitted to authorize the search and seizure of computerized date when it is deemed 'useful in establishing the truth'.[3263] There is a certain Orwellian ring to this phrase. And while the AU Convention declares that all legal measures should be compatible with human rights law this guarantee is weakened by the fact that the African Charter on Human and Peoples' Rights does contain a right to privacy or private life.[3264] However, a safeguard clause provides that the AU Convention must not be interpreted in a manner inconsistent with international law.[3265]

3259. Tamarkin, 4–5.

3260. It is clear that the freedom of expression applies to cyberspace, *Animal Defenders International v. United Kingdom*, European Court of Human Rights [GC], 57 E.H.R.R. 21 (2013); *Delfi AS v. Estonia*, European Court of Human Rights [GC], App. No. 64569/09, Judgment of 18 Jun. 2015.

3261. European Convention on Human Rights Art. 10(2) (4 Nov. 1950), C.E.T.S. No. 194, as amended (ECHR); International Covenant on Civil and Political Rights Art. 19(3) (16 Dec. 1966), 999 U.N.T.S. 171 (ICCPR). Such as the protection of intellectual property and copyright, *Neij and Sunde Kolmisoppi v. Sweden,* European Court of Human Rights, App. No. 40397/12, Judgment of 19 Feb. 2013.

3262. ECHR Art. 17; ICCPR Art. 20(2); American Convention on Human Rights Art. 13(5) (22 Nov. 1969), 1144 U.N.T.S. 144; Protocol concerning the Criminalization of Acts of a Racist and Xenophobic Nature. *See Faurisson v. France*, Communication No. 550/1993 (1996). The Grand Chamber has assumed the stance that ECHR Art. 17 applies only on an exceptional basis and in extreme cases, *Paksas v. Lithuania*, European Court of Human Rights [GC], App. No. 34932/04, Judgment of 6 Jan. 2011; *Perinçek v. Switzerland*, European Court of Human Rights [GC], App. No. 27510/08, Judgment of 15 Oct. 2015.

3263. AU Convention on Cyber Security Art. 31(3)(a),(b).

3264. The centrality of a right to private life in accordance with ECHR Art. 8 has been stressed by the ECJ/CJEU, Cases C-465/00 and C-138/01 *Rechsnungshof v. Osterreichisher Rundfunk* [2003] E.C.R. I-4989, paras 70–71. *See also* Cases C-293/12 and C-594/12 *Digital Rights Ireland v. Minister for Communications, Marine and Natural Resources*, Judgment of 8 Apr. 2014, C:2014:238.

3265. AU Convention on Cyber Security Art. 33.

Part IV. The Relationship Between the African Union and Other International Organizations

520. A formal cooperative relationship between the OAU and the UN was first established in 1990 but a similar agreement between the UN and the AU was adopted only in November 2006.[3266] This framework agreement provided for cooperation between the two organizations across a wide range of areas, including economic and social development and peace and security. However, in light of changed circumstances and progress in Africa's political and economic governance, and cause for optimism in its prospects, the UN recognized that an updated partnership agreement was required.[3267] Accordingly, the New United Nations and African Union Partnership on Africa's Integration and Development Agenda (PAIDA) is designed to provide UN support for the AU as it proceeds with implementing Agenda 2063. In 2017, UN Secretary-General and Chairperson of the AU Commission signed the Joint UN-AU Framework for Enhanced Partnership in Peace and Security, building on peace and security cooperation in Africa between the two organizations.[3268]

521. Cooperation between the EU and African States dates back to the early days of the European Economic Community (EEC) (Yaoundé Convention 1963) but it was only at the Cairo Summit in 2000 that Africa-EU cooperation was placed on a formal footing. At the Lisbon Summit in December 2007 the Africa-EU Partnership was launched which adopted the Joint Africa-EU Strategy (JAES).[3269] The JAES seeks to move beyond donor-recipient cooperation, focusing rather on issues of joint political concern. It thus concentrates on a number of policy areas, including peace and security, democratic governance and human rights, trade and infrastructure, and millennium development goals, and is implemented through action

3266. *Enhancing UN-AU Cooperation: Framework for the ten-year capacity-building programme for the African Union*, UN Doc. A/61/630.

3267. Regional Coordination Mechanism for Africa, *Framework for a renewed United Nations and African Union Partnership on Africa's Integration and Development Agenda 2017–2027*. PAIDA was approved by the AU in 2015, Assembly, *Decision on the Framework for a Renewed UN/AU Partnership on Africa's Integration and Development Agenda [PAIDA] 2017–2027*, AU Doc. Assembly/AU/Dec. 587(XXV) (14–15 Jun. 2015).

3268. *Joint United Nations-African Union Framework for Enhanced Partnership in Peace and Security* (17 Apr. 2017), https://unoau.unmissions.org/sites/default/files/signed_joint_framework.pdf.

3269. *The Africa-EU Partnership: 2 unions, 1 vision*, http://www.africa-eu-partnership.org.

plans. The action plan (2014–2017) adopted at the 4th EU-Africa Summit in Brussels in 2014 focused on five priority areas of cooperation.[3270] These were: peace and security; democracy, good governance and human rights; human development; sustainable development, growth and continental integration; and global and emerging issues. Peace and security as essential prerequisites for development and prosperity was stressed. The declaration, A Joint Vision for 2030, adopted at the 6th EU-Africa Summit held in 2022 pursues key strategic objectives based on a commitment to multilateralism within the rules-based international order, with the UN at its core; reaffirmed increased cooperation on migration and mobility; increased cooperation for peace and security; and sustainable economic development, including an EU investment package.[3271]

3270. *4th EU-Africa Summit 2014 – Roadmap 2014-2017*, http://www.consilium.europa.eu/eudocs/cms_Data/docs/pressdata/en/ec/142094.pdf.
3271. 6th European Union – African Union Summit: A Joint Vision for 2030 https://international-partnerships.ec.europa.eu/policies/africa-eu-partnership_en#complementarity-with-other-cooperation-frameworks.

Chapter 1. Cooperation on Economic Affairs

§1. The African Union and the United Nations

522. The focus of economic cooperation between the AU and the UN centres on the UN Economic Commission for Africa (ECA), one of the regional economic commissions established by the UN Economic and Social Council (ECOSOC) under Article 68 of the UN Charter.[3272] Based in Addis Ababa, membership of the ECA comprises the UN Member States of the region and thus includes Morocco but excludes the SADR. The EX is the AU's coordinating body.[3273] The ECA's mandate in broad terms is to support the economic and social development of its Members and Africa in general, promote regional integration and support international efforts at development. More specifically, it concentrates on such areas as macroeconomic and structural policy, social development, gender issues, technological development, regional integration and trade, resource management, and good governance. The ECA's sessions are held annually.

523. In the 1980s Africa was faced with a series of serious socioeconomic crises which led the UN to adopt a programme of action designed to bolster Africa's economic recovery, the UN PAAERD.[3274] UN PAAERD aimed to assist Africa to achieve self-reliant and self-sustained economic development through a new era of cooperation. The sectors identified for special measures included trade and finance, economic management, food and agriculture, and human resource development. An immediate objective was to boost productivity, especially in the food and agricultural sectors. However, the achievements of UN PAAERD were deemed unsatisfactory and it was replaced by the UN New Agenda for the Development of Africa in the 1990s (UN-NADAF).[3275] UN-NADAF similarly aimed at strengthening African economies, with particular emphasis on integration and infrastructure programmes and projects. Regrettably, UN-NADAF was also deemed a disappointment and it was therefore decided that comprehensive support for NEPAD might bear greater success.[3276]

524. In response to an initiative from the AU, in 2006 the UN General Assembly approved the devising and implementation of a ten-year capacity-building plan for the AU.[3277] This plan came to fruition in the 2006 Declaration, 'Enhancing UN-AU Cooperation: Framework for the ten-year capacity-building programme for

---

3272. ECOSOC Res. 671A (XXV). ECOSOC is the UN's principal body in the field of economic and social cooperation, UN Charter Art. 62. The ECA has its own website, http://www.uneca.org.
3273. Constitutive Act of the African Union Art. 13 (26 May 2001), 2158 U.N.T.S. 3; Rule 5 of the Rules of Procedure of the Executive Council, 13 R.A.D.I.C. (2005) 55.
3274. UN General Assembly Res. S-13/2 (1986). *See* G.J. Naldi, *The Organization of African Unity* (London & New York: Mansell, 1989), 170–174.
3275. UN Doc. A/46/151 (annex).
3276. UN General Assembly Res. 57/7 (2002).
3277. UN General Assembly Res. 60/1 (2005).

the African Union.'[3278] This renewed partnership provided for enhanced cooperation between the two organizations across a range of areas, including economic and social development, human rights, conflict prevention, and peace and security.

525. This arrangement has since been superseded by PAIDA, a strategic partnership intended to provide UN collaboration and support for the AU in its endeavours to enhance economic and social conditions, particularly institutional and resource support. PAIDA is designed to be responsive to Africa's expressed aspirations, needs and priorities and is based on a number of principles, including AU ownership and leadership, accountability, consultation and coordination, observance of commitments made, and proactive engagement. The priority areas are: economic transformation; development, infrastructure and trade; regional integration; women's rights; agriculture; private sector development; health and nutrition; education and training; natural resource management; climate change; democracy and governance; human rights and the rule of law; and peace and security.

526. In 2021 the AfCFTA Secretariat and the UN Development Programme (UNDP) signed a strategic partnership to promote trade as an incentive for Africa's socioeconomic recovery from the COVID-19 pandemic, and as a stimulator of sustainable development. This new cooperation aims to address inequalities, increase growth and create jobs, especially for women and youth.

§2. The African Union and the European Union

527. The relationship between the AU and the EU is an important one. The EU is Africa's largest trading partner and makes substantial contributions to the AU's programme budget. The EU invests significant sums in Africa, on economic and human development, human rights, good governance and migration, energy and infrastructure projects, humanitarian assistance, and agri-food.[3279] This partnership is deepening. Early cooperation between the EEC and African States focused on providing financial support to French-speaking Africa to develop its infrastructure. This provided the basis for a series of agreements between the EC/EU and the African, Caribbean and Pacific (ACP) States (Lomé I-IV, Cotonou Agreement) which governed relations with sub-Saharan Africa.[3280] The Cotonou Agreement, adopted in 2000 but replaced in 2023, was characterized by non-reciprocal free trade arrangements for ACP States and aid packages designed to reduce and eradicate poverty, consistent with the objectives of sustainable development and the measured integration of the ACP countries into the world economy. The Cotonou Agreement was broader in scope than the previous arrangements and had three principal elements, or pillars: development cooperation; economic and trade cooperation; and

3278. UN Doc. A/61/630.
3279. European Commission, The EU-Africa Partnership, MEMO/15/4808 (22 Apr. 2015).
3280. *See* P. Sands & P. Klein, *Bowett's Law of International Institutions* (6th edn, London: Sweet & Maxwell, 2009), 147–148.

a political dimension.[3281] Trade between the EU and the ACPs was promoted chiefly through Economic Partnership Agreements (EPA). It is important to note, however, that these agreements were not concluded with the AU but with ACP States, including those of African RECs.[3282] Formal relations between the AU and the EU were established only in 2000 when the first Africa-EU Partnership Summit was held. Strengthening the partnership between the two continents led to the adoption of the JAES in 2007. Trade, economic development, growth and integration all form essential elements of the JAES.[3283] In 2023 the provisional application of a new agreement governing the legal framework for the next twenty years between the EU and the ACP to succeed the Cotonou Agreement was approved by the Council of the EU.[3284] The Partnership Agreement between the EU and ACP is based on six priority areas: democracy and human rights; sustainable economic growth and development; climate change; human and social development; peace and security; and migration and mobility.[3285] The Agreement includes three regional protocols, including one for Africa, the Africa Regional Protocol. In addition to the priority areas just mentioned, regional priority areas stressed in the EU-Africa Protocol include the environment and natural resources, the rule of law, justice and governance, and gender equality. It also gives an enhanced role to dialogue and cooperation with the AU.

3281. Cotonou Agreement (23 Jun. 2000) O.J. L 317, 15 Dec. 2000, revised 25 Jun. 2005, O.J. L 287, 28 Oct. 2005, revised 22 Jun. 2010, O.J. L 287, 4 Nov. 2010. *See* generally K. Arts, 'ACP-EC Relations in a New Era: The Cotonou Agreement', *Common Market Law Review* 40 (2003): 95.

3282. *See, e.g.*, Economic Partnership Agreement between the European Union and its Member States, of the one part, and the SADC EPA States, of the other part, O.J. L 250, 16 Sep. 2016. *See* generally European Parliament, Trade regimes applicable to developing countries, https://www.europarl.europa.eu/factsheets/en/sheet/162/trade-regimes-applicable-to-developing-countries.

3283. *Supra* para. 521.

3284. Council of the EU Press release, Post-Cotonou: Council gives greenlight to the new Partnership Agreement with the African, Caribbean and Pacific States (20 Jul. 2023).

3285. Partnership Agreement between the European Union and its Member States, of the one part, and the Members of the Organisation of African, Caribbean and Pacific States, of the other part, Council of the European Union, Consilium, ST_8372/1/23 REV 1 (19 Jul. 2023) (Partnership Agreement).

Chapter 2. Cooperation on Matters of Peace and Security

§1. The African Union and the United Nations

528. The UN Security Council has primary responsibility for the maintenance of international peace and security in accordance with Article 24(1) of the UN Charter. However, under Chapter VIII of the UN Charter the UN may have recourse to regional arrangements or agencies relating to international peace and security, including enforcement action. The AU, as the OAU before it, comes within the scope of such a regional arrangement or agency.[3286] In fact, the UN has had a long cooperative association with Africa and the OAU.[3287] As has been stated, in 2006 the two organizations adopted the 'Framework for the ten-year capacity-building programme for the African Union' which envisaged greater UN support in areas such as conflict prevention and peace and security.[3288] This partnership is succeeded by PAIDA which in April 2017 resulted in a framework agreement to strengthen the relationship on peace and security issues.[3289] The Framework for Partnership seeks to improve consultations between the UN and the AU on prevention and conflict management and resolution, post-conflict reconstruction and peace-building in Africa, particularly at operational levels, providing for regular meetings and consultations. One area is mediation. The UN supports the mediation capacity of the AU Commission, including support for the Panel of the Wise. More specifically, it has supported the African Initiative for Peace and Reconciliation in the CAR which directed by the AU with the support of ECCAS and the International Conference of the Great Lakes Region, resulted in a comprehensive peace agreement. Electoral support is another area, with the UN providing technical electoral assistance to many African States. And Peace Support Operations (PSOs) is another. The UN provides technical support for the African Standby Force Maputo as well as current AU-mandated peace support operations. In 2010 the United Nations Office to the African Union (UNOAU), designed to further the partnership in the area of peace and security, was duly established and acts as a liaison with UN agencies and the AU.[3290] The PSC is the AU organ that liaises with the UN on peace and security matters.[3291]

3286. *Repertoire of the Practice of the Security Council* 16th Supplement (2008–2009), http://www.un.org/en/sc/repertoire (accessed 26 Jul. 2013). *See* UN Security Council Res. 2320(2016).
3287. B. Boutros-Ghali, *Confronting New Challenges* (New York: United Nations, 1995), 340–341.
3288. UN Doc. A/61/630.
3289. Joint UN-AU Framework for Enhanced Partnership in Peace and Security, https://unoau.unmissions.org/sites/default/files/jount_un-au_framework_for_an_enhanced_partnership_in_peace_and_security.pdf.
3290. UN General Assembly Res. 64/288 (2010).
3291. Protocol Relating to the Establishment of the Peace and Security Council of the African Union Art. 17 (9 Jul. 2002), http://www.au.int, C. Heyns & M. Killander (eds), *Compendium of Key Human Rights Documents of the African Union* (5th edn, Pretoria: Pretoria University Law Press, 2013), 17.

529. One aspect of this relationship has concerned peacekeeping, the UN has deployed more peacekeeping missions in Africa than any other region;[3292] its involvement in the Congo, conducted by United Nations Operation in the Congo (ONUC), is one of its best known episodes;[3293] its involvement in Somalia is one of its most notorious;[3294] and its role in Rwanda is considered one of its most shameful.[3295] At present, there are six peacekeeping operations in Africa: the Central African Republic (CAR), the Democratic Republic of the Congo (DRC), Mali, Western Sahara, South Sudan and Sudan, one mission in Darfur, with the AU, and one in the disputed Abyei region. The UN's efforts to hold a referendum in Western Sahara, assisted by the MINURSO, have still not borne fruit.[3296] The situation in the DRC is still volatile.[3297] The same can be said for the CAR[3298] and South Sudan.[3299] The situations in the wider Sahel region and the Lake Chad Basin continue to deteriorate, with intercommunal conflict and atrocities attributed to terrorist, militia and armed groups. However, there have been positive outcomes. The UN played a major role in Namibia's struggle for independence; the UN Transitional Group (UNTAG) oversaw the South African departure and successfully organized and monitored the

3292. *Report of the UN Secretary-General on the causes of conflict and the promotion of durable peace and sustainable development in Africa* para. 29, UN Doc. A/52/871-S/1998/318 (1998).

3293. A. Parsons, *From Cold War to Hot Peace: UN Interventions 1947–1995* (London: Penguin, 1995), 77–93; M. Virally, *Les Nations Unies et l'affaire du Congo*, Annuaire Français de Droit International 557 (1960).

3294. Parsons, 198–207; C. Gray, *International Law and the Use of Force* (3rd edn, Oxford: Oxford University Press, 2008), 286–289.

3295. G. Robertson, *Crimes Against Humanity: The Struggle for Global Justice* (London: Penguin, 1999), 76–79.

However, Gray, 292–294, highlights the hesitant attitude of UN Member States, whereas Parsons, 213–214, points out that the UN force, UNAMIR, had neither the mandate nor the personnel or matérial to play an active part in suppressing the genocidal violence.

3296. *See, e.g.*, UN Security Council Res. 2051(2017). MINURSO was first deployed in Western Sahara in 1991.

3297. Gray, 316–319. *See* UN Security Council Res. 2293(2016). In an extraordinary development in 2013 the UN Security Council authorized the creation of an 'Intervention Brigade' as part of the UN force UN Organization Stabilization Mission in the DRC (MONUSCO) 'with the responsibility of neutralizing armed groups', UN Security Council Res. 2098(2013) para. 9.

3298. *See, e.g.*, UN Security Council Res. 2339(2017). Assembly, *Decision on the Report of the Peace and Security Council on its Activities and the State of Peace and Security in Africa*, AU Doc. Assembly/AU/Dec. 583(XXV) (14–15 Jun. 2015), para. 7.

3299. UN Security Council Res. 1996(2011). This resolution created another peacekeeping mission, the United Nations Mission in South Sudan (UNMISS), *inter alia,* to support peace consolidation, protect civilians, and provide security. In 2014 UNMISS was given a renewed mandate geared towards the protection of civilians, the safeguarding human rights and securing humanitarian assistance, UN Security Council Res. 2155(2014). Since independence South Sudan has been wracked by internecine warfare despite mediation by different parties including the AU and IGAD. A peace agreement between the South Sudanese leaders was signed in August 2015 but not implemented and serious fighting broke out again in July 2016. *See* UN Security Council Res. 2327(2016), where the Security Council, acting pursuant to Ch. VII, demanded, *inter alia*, the cessation of fighting throughout South Sudan and the implementation of agreed ceasefires. The Security Council had determined that the situation in South Sudan constituted a threat to international peace and security, UN Security Council Res. 2326(2016).

independence election.[3300] The UN facilitated the transition to peace in Mozambique's civil war.[3301] In Sierra Leone, the UN force UN Mission in Sierra Leone (UNAMSIL), with the assistance of British troops, eventually succeeded in bringing peace and stable government to a country wracked by violence since 1991.[3302] Nevertheless, the UN's failures in Africa and elsewhere led to increased calls for increased use of regional and sub-regional organizations under Chapter VIII of the UN Charter.[3303]

530. Increased cooperation with African organizations formed an important part of this agenda.[3304] A cooperative relationship had already been established between the UN and the OAU[3305] and between the UN and ECOWAS.[3306] But the advent of the AU signalled a transformation in this relationship. One of the crucial differences between the OAU and the AU is that the latter has an enhanced capacity for conflict management, mediation and peacemaking.[3307] The UN has expressed its support for the AU but it is accepted that it requires sustained capacity-building.[3308] The Ten-Year Capacity-Building Programme for the AU, adopted in 2006, was an important

3300. Parsons, Ch. 7.
3301. *Ibid.*, Ch. 10.
3302. Gray, 312–315. It should be observed that from 1997–1999 an ECOWAS force, EGOMOG, was present in Sierra Leone and ultimately resorted to the use of force to reinstate the legitimate government, *ibid.*, 411–417. In *Prosecutor v. Charles Ghankay Taylor* (Judgment) SCSL-03-1-T, T Ch. II (26 Apr. 2012) the former President of Liberia was found guilty by the SCSL of aiding and abetting and planning a number of crimes committed during the invasion of and retreat from Sierra Leone's capital, Freetown.
3303. *Report of the UN Secretary-General on the causes of conflict and the promotion of durable peace and sustainable development in Africa* paras 41–45; 'A More Secure World: Our Shared Responsibility', Report of the High-Level Panel on Threats, Challenges and Change paras 270–273, UN Doc. A/59/565 (2004).
3304. *Report of the UN Secretary-General on the causes of conflict and the promotion of durable peace and sustainable development in Africa ibid.*; UN General Assembly Res. 57/48(2003) on Cooperation between the United Nations and the African Union; UN General Assembly Res. 61/296(2007) on Cooperation between the United Nations and the African Union.
3305. Gray, 375–376.
3306. ECOWAS has played a major role in conflicts in West Africa. The civil war that erupted in Liberia in 1989 destabilized neighbouring States, particularly Sierra Leone, which led ECOWAS to take the pioneering step for an African sub-regional organization to send a peacekeeping force to Liberia, EGOMOG, *see* Parsons, 215–219. EGOMOG also established a presence in Sierra Leone and was instrumental in subduing rebel forces and restoring peace and security. The ECOWAS action in both countries generated legal controversy, focused on whether ECOWAS had prior UN authorization to use force, and whether EGOMOG was engaged in peacekeeping or peace-enforcement action, Gray, 400–407, 411–417. Subsequent missions by ECOWAS in Liberia and Côte d'Ivoire in 2003 were expressly authorized by the UN Security Council, Gray, 419–421. In 2017 ECOWAS intervened to resolve the constitutional crisis in The Gambia, *see* UN Security Council, Res. 2337 (2017). *See further* Report of the UN Secretary-General on strengthening the partnership between the United Nations and the African Union on issues of peace and security in Africa, UN Doc. S/2016/780, pt. VIII.
3307. *See* Protocol Relating to the Establishment of the Peace and Security Council of the African Union (9 Jul. 2002), http://www.au.int, Heyns & Killander, 17.
3308. *See, e.g.*, 2005 World Summit Outcome para. 93, UN General Assembly Res. 60/1 (2005); 'A More Secure World: Our Shared Responsibility' para. 272(c). *See further* Gray, 376–378.

initiative.[3309] UNOAU is engaged in developing the institutional capacity of the AU, assists in operationalizing AU decisions and coordinating the use of funds. UN support finds expression in several ways, for example, capacity-building for mediation in the development of an AU mediation strategy and in making operational the AU Panel of the Wise. It extends to electoral assistance to AU Member States, including providing election observers, bolstering security, enhancing the rule of law, integrating human rights into the conduct of operations and facilitating the participation of NGOs. The UN continues to provide support to recent peacemaking efforts in political crises in Burkina Faso, the Comoros, Libya and Madagascar, among others.[3310] But, as has been mentioned, peacekeeping missions have become a high-profile aspect of their collaborative efforts. The AU plays a key role in this respect because host-state consent is sometimes contingent on AU participation since certain African States harbour reservations about the UN's motives.[3311] These operations share certain features in that they have a UN mandate; they are created by a UN Security Council Resolution under Chapter VII of the UN Charter, deployed for a limited period of time before handing over to a UN force, and/or they are established by the AU, through the PSC, but approved by, and answerable to, the UN Security Council.[3312] Significantly, the AU has undertaken a number of high-profile operations.

531. One such operation concerns Somalia. AMISOM is a peacekeeping mission authorized by the UN.[3313] AMISOM was initially set up by the PSC in January 2007[3314] and was approved by the UN Security Council on 21 February 2007.[3315] Its mandate was to support transitional governmental structures, implement a national security plan, train the Somali security forces, and assist in creating a secure environment for the delivery of humanitarian aid.[3316] It also supported the Somali government against militants. In 2022, AMISOM was replaced by the African Union Transition Mission in Somalia (ATMIS) with the mandate to fight terrorist groups, provide security, develop the capacity of the Somali security forces, conduct a phased handover of security responsibilities to Somalia, and support peace and reconciliation efforts.[3317] In 2022, a new President was elected dedicated

---

3309. UN Doc. A/61/630. The UN organs continued to call for greater involvement with the AU on peace and security, *see* UN Security Council Res. 2033(2012), UN Security Council Res. 2167(2014) and UN General Assembly Res. 67/302 (2012).
3310. Report of the UN Secretary-General on strengthening the partnership between the United Nations and the African Union on issues of peace and security in Africa, UN Doc. S/2016/780, pt. IV. Joint SADC–AU–UN mediation facilitated the holding of elections in Madagascar in 2018.
3311. Gray, 301.
3312. *See, e.g.*, UN Security Council Res. 2085 (2012) para. 10, UN Security Council Res. 2127 (2013) paras 28, 32.
3313. *See* Gray, 378–380.
3314. AU Doc. PSC/PR/Comm (LXIX).
3315. UN Security Council Res. 1744 (2007).
3316. UN Security Council Res. 1772 (2007).
3317. AU Doc. PSC/PR/COMM.1068(2022) REV.1, endorsed by UN Security Council Res. 2628(2022).

to finalizing the constitution and intensifying dialogue and reconciliation but yet continuing the fight against al-Shabaab.[3318]

532. A fascinating facet of the situation in Somalia has been the extraordinary decision of the UN Security Council to combat piracy in Somali territorial waters which since the mid-2000s has posed a not insignificant threat to international shipping and security. Acting under Chapter VII of the UN Charter, the UN Security Council adopted Resolution 1816 (2008) authorizing States, with the permission of the Somali authorities, to take such steps within Somali territorial waters to deal with piratical acts consistent with that permitted by international law on the high seas.[3319]

533. The UN Security Council categorized the conflict in the Darfur region of Sudan as a threat to international peace and security.[3320] It also called for measures to prevent or mitigate a humanitarian catastrophe.[3321] The AMIS was initially established by the AU in 2004 as a monitoring mission,[3322] but its mandate was soon expanded, *inter alia*, to improve the security situation in Sudan, to monitor the Darfur Peace Agreement, to contribute to a secure environment for the delivery of humanitarian aid and the return of refugees and IDPs.[3323] In 2005, the UN Security Council established the UN Mission in Sudan (UNMIS), *inter alia*, to support AMIS.[3324] However, the numerous difficulties encountered by AMIS, which included militia attacks and obstruction to humanitarian access, exposed its limitations, but this led to a remarkable development, the merger of AMIS into a hybrid AU/UN peacekeeping operation, UNAMID.[3325] The AU's participation was crucial since it is clear that the Sudanese government would never have consented to a purely UN operation. UN and AU mediation led to the signing of a Roadmap Agreement between the Sudanese Government and opposition groups in 2016.[3326] With UNAMID's mediation, the Juba Peace Agreement was signed in 2020 between the Sudanese government and rebel groups.[3327] UNAMID was deemed to have accomplished its mandate and was terminated in December 2020. In June 2020, the UN Security Council established the United Nations Integrated Transition Assistance

3318. Report of the UN Secretary-General on strengthening the partnership between the United Nations and the African Union on issues of peace and security in Africa, UN Doc. S/2022/643, para. 18.
3319. *See also* UN Security Council Res. 1846 and 1851 (2008). UN Security Council Res. 2125(2013) renewed the authorization for another year. *See* generally O. Elagab, 'Somali Piracy and International Law: Some Aspects'. *Australia and New Zealand Maritime Law Journal* 24 (2010): 59.
3320. UN Security Council Res. 1556(2004). *See also*, *e.g.*, UN Security Council Res. 1784(2007).
3321. UN Security Council Res. 1556(2004) and 1591(2005).
3322. AU Doc. PSC/PR/Comm.(X).
3323. AU Doc. PSC/PR/Comm.(XVII), endorsed by UN Security Council Res. 1556(2004). *See further* Gray, 380–381.
3324. UN Security Council Res. 1590(2005).
3325. UN Security Council Res. 1769(2007). *See further* Gray, 381–382.
3326. Report of the UN Secretary-General on strengthening the partnership between the United Nations and the African Union on issues of peace and security in Africa, UN Doc. S/2016/780, para. 30.
3327. UN Security Council Press Statement on the Juba Peace Agreement (Sudan), SC/14323 (9 Oct. 2020).

Mission in Sudan (UNITAMS) with peace-building mandate, to support the country's democratic transition.[3328] A coup in October 2021 ushered in another political crisis giving rise to general unrest.[3329]

534. Another UN force operates in the Abyei region, disputed between Sudan and South Sudan, which had given rise to conflict and population displacement. The United Nations Interim Security Force for Abyei (UNISFA) was established with the mandate of monitoring the border and facilitating the delivery of humanitarian aid, and is authorized to use force in protecting civilians and humanitarian workers.[3330]

535. The toppling of Mali's democratic government in a military coup in March 2012 intensified a prolonged period of instability and violence, leading to terrorist and extremist groups taking control of the north of Mali. French military intervention succeeded in restoring a measure of security. Both the AU and ECOWAS became involved in mediation efforts to restore constitutional order and national unity. The UN Security Council found that the situation in Mali posed a threat to international peace and security,[3331] and approved the deployment of an African-led force, the African International Support Mission in Mali (AFISMA).[3332] AFISMA had robust rules of engagement; it was authorized to take 'all necessary measures', that is, use force, *inter alia*, to rebuild the Malian security forces, to support the Malian authorities in recovering territory under terrorist and extremist control, to support the Malian authorities in maintaining security and consolidating State authority, to support the Malian authorities in protecting civilians, and assist in creating a secure environment for the delivery of humanitarian aid.[3333] In 2013, the UN Security Council established the UN Multidimensional Integrated Stabilization Mission in Mali (MINUSMA) to take over from AFISMA from 1 July 2013.[3334] MINUSMA's mandate included support for the political process, protecting civilians, support for humanitarian assistance, support for cultural protection, and support for international justice.[3335] It was also authorized to take 'all necessary measures'.[3336] While a peace agreement was signed in June 2015,[3337] political instability returned to Mali with military coups in 2020 and 2021; moreover, increased

3328. UN Security Council Res. 2524(2020).
3329. Report of the UN Secretary-General on strengthening the partnership between the United Nations and the African Union on issues of peace and security in Africa, UN Doc. S/2022/643, para. 19. In 2023 intensive fighting broke out, ACLED, Sudan: Conflict Intensifies Following the Breakdown of Jeddah Talks, https://acleddata.com/2023/06/23/sudan-situation-update-june-2023-conflict-intensifies-following-the-breakdown-of-jeddah-talks/.
3330. UN Security Council Res. 1990(2011).
3331. UN Security Council Res. 2085(2012).
3332. AU Doc. PSC/AHG/Comm/2(CCCLIII).
3333. UN Security Council Res. 2085(2012), para. 9.
3334. UN Security Council Res. 2100(2013).
3335. *Ibid.*, para. 16.
3336. *Ibid.*, para. 17.
3337. *See* Assembly, *Decision on the Report of the Peace and Security Council on its Activities and the State of Peace and Security in Africa*, AU Doc. Assembly/AU/Dec. 583(XXV) (14–15 Jun. 2015), para. 7.

resentment by the country's authorities and people towards MINUSMA led to the UN terminating its mandate in June 2023.[3338]

536. The CAR provides another example. The security situation in the CAR has been on the UN Security Council's agenda since the 1990s.[3339] In order to help bring stability to the CAR, the UN set up the UN Integrated Peace-building Office in the Central African Republic (BINUCA) with an initial mandate to help consolidate peace, foster national reconciliation, strengthen democratic institutions, and strengthen the promotion and protection of human rights.[3340] In 2013, the security situation in the CAR deteriorated to a degree where there was a complete breakdown in law and order, leading the UN Security Council to designate the state of affairs as a threat to international peace and security.[3341] The UN Security Council additionally approved the deployment of an African-led force, the African International Support Mission in the Central African Republic (MISCA) which was to cooperate with the UN field office. MISCA's mandate was to help protect civilians, stabilize the country and restore state authority, and create conditions conducive to the provision of humanitarian assistance. It was authorized to take 'all necessary measures'.[3342] However, with a deteriorating security situation, the UN Security Council took the decision to subsume BINUCA into the UN Multidimensional Stabilizing Mission in the Central African Republic (MINUSCA), a peacekeeping operation, to which MISCA would transfer its authority[3343] and redeploy as part of that peacekeeping operation.[3344] MINUSCA's mandate includes protecting civilians, supporting the political process and extending state authority, facilitating the delivery of humanitarian assistance, promoting and protecting human rights, and supporting justice and the rule of law.[3345] Cooperative efforts with the AU, EU and ECCAS enabled a peace agreement in 2019.[3346] However, although the situation remains tense,[3347] the International Conference on the Great Lakes Region adopted a joint road map for peace in the Central African Republic in September 2021.[3348]

537. In 2015, a UN High-level Independent Panel on Peace Operations called for strengthening the UN-AU partnership.[3349] It stressed the importance of early

---

3338. UN Security Council Res. 2690(2023).
3339. *See* Gray, 303–304, 331–332.
3340. BINUCA's mandate was extended by UN Security Council Res. 2088(2013) and 2121(2013).
3341. UN Security Council Res. 2127(2013).
3342. *Ibid.*, para. 28.
3343. UN Security Council Res. 2149(2014) para. 21.
3344. *Ibid.*, para. 26.
3345. *Ibid.*, para. 30. In 2021 the UN Security Council decided to increase the size of MINUSCA to enable it better to perform its tasks, UN Security Council Res.2566(2021).
3346. Political Agreement for Peace and Reconciliation in the Central African Republic of 6 February 2019, Letter dated 14 February 2019 from the Secretary-General addressed to the President of the Security Council, Annex, UN Doc. S/2019/145.
3347. Security Council Report, Central African Republic: Briefing and Consultations, https://www.securitycouncilreport.org/whatsinblue/2022/06/central-african-republic-briefing-and-consultations-9.php.
3348. Report of the UN Secretary-General on strengthening the partnership between the United Nations and the African Union on issues of peace and security in Africa, UN Doc. S/2022/643, para. 18.
3349. UN Doc. A/70/95-S/2015/446.

engagement, continued consultation, joint planning and an integrated approach towards conflicts. The importance of sound politics in preventing, managing and resolving conflicts was also accentuated. Predictable financing for AU peace support operations was another important consideration. Support was forthcoming from the UN, and in May 2016, a joint UN-AU meeting was held on peace-building in Africa which endorsed many of the Panel's recommendations.[3350]

§2. The African Union and the European Union

538. Since the eve of the millennium, a cooperative relationship has been established between the UN and the EU on issues relating to peace and security and conflict management, including Africa.[3351] JAES highlighted the importance of peace and security to both parties. The key objectives on peace and security are to ensure a safe and secure environment, and to further political stability and effective governance. More specifically, to promote political dialogue on peace, justice and reconciliation; to strengthen the operationalization of APSA by training African forces; to address the root causes of conflict; and to consolidate human rights, among others. The EU provides funding and deploys civilian, military and election observation missions as part of its Common Security and Defence Policy (CSDP).[3352] The first concrete expression of this cooperative military relationship was Operation Artemis in the DRC following a request from the UN pursuant to UN Security Council Resolution 1484(2003) adopted under Chapter VII of the UN Charter. Operation Artemis, a rapid reaction force, was deployed for a few months in a supporting role to the UN force UN Observer Mission in the Democratic Republic of Congo (MONUC)[3353] to stabilize and strengthen the security and humanitarian conditions in the northern city of Bunia.[3354]

539. Another significant military operation undertaken by the EU was that of EUFOR Tchad/RCA in 2008 in Chad and CAR.[3355] Acting in accordance with Chapter VII of the UN Charter, EUFOR's role was to support the UN force MINURCAT in establishing a secure environment,[3356] but the problems encountered by MINURCAT meant that EUFOR became a 'first-entry force' paving the

3350. Report of the UN Secretary-General on strengthening the partnership between the United Nations and the African Union on issues of peace and security in Africa, UN Doc. S/2016/780, para. 40.
3351. Gray, 340–341; A. Novosseloff, *United Nations – European Union Cooperation in the Field of Peacekeeping: Challenges and Prospects* 6 (GGI Analysis Paper No. 4/2012), 8–12.
3352. Military and civilian missions and operations –European External Action Service https://www.eeas.europa.eu/eeas/missions-and-operations_en#9620.
3353. *See* Gray, 316–319.
3354. Novosseloff, 12.
3355. EU Council Decision on the launching of operation EUFOR Tchad/RCA, Press Release 5625/08. *See* Gray, *ibid.*, Novosseloff, 14–15.
3356. UN Security Council Res. 1778 (2007).

way for MINURCAT's eventual deployment.[3357] The deteriorating security situation in the CAR in 2013–2014 led the UN Security Council to authorize the deployment of an EU military force there with a mandate to use force.[3358] In April 2014, EUFOR RCA was launched to assist MISCA in achieving a safe and secure environment in the capital, Bangui.[3359]

540. In collaboration with AMISOM, the EU contributes significantly, especially in terms of financial support, to bringing peace and security to Somalia and strengthening its institutions and authorities. In April 2010 it launched a military Training Mission in Somalia (EUTM Somalia) to build up and professionalize its armed forces.[3360] In order to counter piracy off the coast of Somalia in December 2008, the EU launched the EU Naval Force (EU NAVFOR) Somalia – Operation Atalanta in accordance with relevant UN Security Council Resolutions.[3361] Operation Atalanta's mandate includes deterring, preventing and repressing acts of piracy and armed robbery at sea off the Somali coast, the protection of ships delivering aid to displaced persons in Somalia, the protection of AMISOM shipping, and protecting vulnerable shipping off the Somali coast on a case-by-case basis. In 2012, the area of operation was extended to include Somali coastal territory and internal waters.[3362] Operation Atalanta's mandate is ongoing.[3363]

541. Another important deployment is that of the EU's Regional Advisory and Coordination Cell for the Sahel (RACC).[3364] Created in 2019, its mandate is to facilitate peace and stability in a region experiencing terrorism and political instability.

542. EUTM Mozambique should also be mentioned. EUTM Mozambique was launched in October 2021 as part of the EU's response to the Government of Mozambique's request of assistance dealing with outbreaks of violence by non-state armed groups in Cabo Delgado.[3365] EUTM Mozambique provides humanitarian aid, peace-building, security and development.

3357. Novosseloff, 14.
3358. UN Security Council Res. 2134 (2014) paras 43–44.
3359. EU Council Press Release 7672/14. *See further* European Union Advisory Mission in Central African Republic (EUAM RCA), https://www.eeas.europa.eu/euam-rca_en, Established in 2019 to provide strategic advice; European Union Training Mission in Central African Republic (EUTM RCA), https://www.eeas.europa.eu/eutm-rca_en.
3360. *See* https://www.eutm-somalia.eu/.
3361. *Supra.* para. 540.
3362. Council Decision 2012/174/CFSP, O.J. L 89/69, 27 Mar. 2012.
3363. European Union Naval Force Operation ATALANTA – EUNAVFOR ATALANTA, https://eunavfor.eu/.
3364. EU RACC Sahel, https://www.eeas.europa.eu/eu-racc-sahel_en.
3365. EUTM Mozambique, https://www.eeas.europa.eu/eutm-mozambique_en. *See also* Report of the UN Secretary-General on strengthening the partnership between the United Nations and the African Union on issues of peace and security in Africa, UN Doc. S/2022/643, para. 16.

543. The triple relationship involving the AU took longer to develop, however.[3366] The Peace and Security partnership element of the JAES is based on three specific objectives: enhancing the political dialogue on peace and security; operationalizing APSA; and ensuring predictable funding for African-led peace support operations. A cooperative relationship has now been established, focusing on capacity-building in areas such as logistics, training and material.[3367] This it did with AMIS.[3368] A mission was dispatched to Mali to provide military training and advice to the Malian armed forces,[3369] the EU Training Mission in Mali (EUTM Mali).[3370] A number of other civilian missions in Africa have been undertaken.[3371]

544. Funding of operations is also an important element of the EU's projection of soft-power.[3372] The key EU financial instrument to support the Peace and Security partnership is the African Peace Facility (APF). The APF was established at the request of the AU.[3373] It is a multidisciplinary force made up of military, police and civilian components for deployment in crisis situations.[3374] Capacity-Building forms a large part of its work, but funding and technical support are provided for APSA and PSOs such as AMISOM, the MNJTF against Boko Haram and the RCI-LRA.

3366. Novosseloff, 23.
3367. *See* UN Security Council Res. 2167 (2014).
3368. *Ibid.*, 20.
3369. UN Security Council Res. 2085 (2012) para. 8.
3370. *See* http://www.eutmmali.eu.
3371. Military and civilian missions and operations – European External Action Service https://eeas.europa.eu/headquarters.
3372. The EU has provided funding for AFISMA in Mali, UN Security Council Res. 2085 (2012) para. 20, AMISOM in Somalia and MISCA in the CAR, UN Security Council Res. 2127 (2013) para. 42; *The Africa-EU Partnership: 2 unions, 1 vision*, 7–9. *See* generally Gray, 377–378.
3373. Assembly, *Decision on the Establishment by the European Union of a Peace Support Operation Facility for the African Union*, AU Doc. Assembly/AU/Dec. 21(II) (10–12 Jul. 2003).
3374. *The Africa-EU Partnership: 2 unions, 1 vision*, 9.

Part V. Appraisal

545. In 2013, the AU commemorated the fiftieth anniversary of the founding of the OAU amid much fanfare.[3375] The AU had cause for celebration as progress had been achieved across a number of areas such as peace and security, social and economic development, poverty reduction, human rights, the rule of law and good governance but, as it itself acknowledged, such advances were often fragile and much still remained to be done as some problems seem intractable.[3376] These challenges continue to be destabilizing and in turn have given rise in recent years to, *inter alia*, high levels of population movements, including forced migration. Nevertheless, in Agenda 2063, the AU has renewed its commitment to an African Renaissance.

546. For the last ten years, the AU has been geared to deal comprehensively with Africa's development challenges by concentrating on the political and economic integration of the continent. Respect for human rights and the rule of law, democratic principles and good governance constitute the values sustaining the AU and which at the same time are requested by such international partners/donors as the EU.[3377] Africa's commitment to these values is reinforced by NEPAD and Agenda 2063, according to which African countries have pledged to uphold, *inter alia*, human rights and good economic and political governance.

547. Institutionally, the AU has made good progress in enhancing the promotion of human rights. The AU recognizes the importance of democratic institutions. The promotion and protection of human rights, the consolidation of democratic institutions and cultures, and good governance and the rule of law form a core element of the AU. Significantly, the AU has indicated the high regard it has for these values by giving itself the power to deal with violations of these ideals. It can therefore impose sanctions on any Member State that fails to comply with the policies and

3375. 50th Anniversary Solemn Declaration para. E (iii), Assembly, Twenty-First Ordinary Session, 26 May 2013.

3376. *Ibid.*

3377. The EU has played a particularly important role in promoting democracy and human rights. Since 1992, a 'human rights clause' has formed part of cooperation agreements between the EU and third countries, emphasizing respect for democracy and human rights as 'essential elements' of the agreements. In 2003, the Cotonou Agreement (as revised) between the EU and African, Caribbean and Pacific (ACP) States entered into force. Art. 9 thereof is the 'human rights clause'. In the post-Cotonou Agreement (Partnership Agreement between the EU and its Member States and the Organisation of African, Caribbean and Pacific States (OACPS)) which, as mentioned above, was approved on 20 July 2023 by the EU Foreign Affairs Council, the principal provision on human rights is also Art. 9.

decisions of the AU, although so far it has not made use of this power. That this power has not been exercised is a matter of some concern. It could be attributed to Member States not wishing to antagonize other Member States by regarding them recalcitrant and saving the Organization from conflict and antiparathesis. On the other hand, the sanctions mechanism with which an IGO is equipped should be applied whenever the circumstances allow it. Such mechanisms exist to secure balance within the IGO and return to normalcy. Additionally, the AU Constitutive Act contains a 'democracy clause', whereby regimes that take power through unconstitutional means are not allowed to participate in its activities until the country has returned to democratic normalcy. In this work, attention has been drawn to a number of instances, the Comoros, Madagascar, Mali and the Gambia, where the AU, sometimes in collaboration with the UN, ECOWAS and other RECs, has taken action to restore constitutional order. And in several cases successfully so.

548. A number of important human rights instruments, including the Protocol to the African Charter on Human and Peoples' Rights establishing an African Court on Human and Peoples' Rights, and more recently, the Protocol on the Rights of Older Persons, the Protocol on the Rights of Persons with Disabilities in Africa, and the Protocol to the African Charter on Human and Peoples' Rights on the Rights of Citizens to Social Protection and Social Security not only have reinforced the regional protective system but also have arguably made it more advanced compared to other regional systems. The AU has succeeded in demonstrating its concern about human rights in a manner that the OAU never did. In its relatively short life, the African Court on Human and Peoples' Rights has shown evidence of the ability to hand down important decisions, a very welcome development. However, the AU's seeming indecision over its judicial organs, namely the non-operationalization of the African Court of Justice and the Member States' unwillingness to approve the Statute of the African Court of Justice and Human Rights, has left a question mark that should be dealt with expediency. Moreover, the AU's deteriorating relationship with the ICC has raised the spectre of the OAU's dark days of closing ranks with despots. But one of the fascinating aspects of this dispute has been the ructions within the Organization itself as a significant number of States have been open in their support for the ICC. The wisdom of having a Criminal Law Section attached to the African Court of Justice and Human Rights must be questioned. However, treaties alone cannot prevent human rights violations. At the end of the day, despite the fact that electoral democracy has made some progress in recent times, the fundamental obstacle towards guaranteeing human rights in Africa, in addition to economic underdevelopment, remains the unwillingness of too many regimes to build a State based on pluralist, inclusive democracy and the rule of law. Recent initiatives by the AU and NEPAD, in tandem with international partners, may facilitate efforts at securing concrete measures towards democratization and good governance.

549. It is also important that the implementation of existing human rights standards be strengthened. The African Commission on Human and People's Rights, mandated under the African Charter with promoting and ensuring their protection, attracted criticism as an institutionally weak guardian of rights.[3378] However, such pessimism no longer paints an accurate portrait. An analysis of its work and decisions in recent years demonstrates that the Commission has become more robust.[3379] The AU and initiatives such as the 'Silencing of the Guns' also strengthen Africa's commitment to conflict resolution. The capacity to adopt conflict prevention measures, such as the deployment of observers or missions of enquiry, has been enhanced and, arguably, Member States are not opposing them as in previous occasions. At the same time, with the assistance of the international community, the AU has set up its own peacekeeping forces and missions. However, they seem to be afflicted by the same drawbacks as UN peacekeeping, a lack of human, material and financial resources, a lack of political resolve as well as allegations of gross violations of the rules of engagement by peacekkeping forces. And security and instability remain persistent problems in most parts of the continent. As regards North Africa, the Arab Spring became the Arab Winter, the civil war in Libya is still being waged with the AU unable to handle it at least as a mediator, Tunisia, previously a model of democracy for the continent, now beyond the brink of totalitarialism, and Sudan engulfed in a deadly civil war. Ultimately, the root causes of interstate and intra-state conflict must be addressed, and so must their outcomes, including illegal and clandestine migration as well as the international crime of trafficking in human beings.

550. Poverty and underdevelopment have at one and the same time been both the cause and effect of many of Africa's ills. Despite many efforts, invariably financed by international partners, poverty reduction and eradication strategies do not yet appear to work. Addressing the root causes of conflict, strengthening democracy and human rights should encourage sustainable economic and human development. The implementation of the goals of Agenda 2063 and, first and foremost, the Agreement Establishing the African Continental Free Trade Area provide evidence of the commitment of African States to confront and solve their economic and associated social problems through indigenous solutions, what is referred to as 'African solutions to African problems'. However, the challenges are considerable. Globalization has always been a mixed blessing, and a large number of countries have actually lost out. While some African economies have shown impressive economic growth, too many remain either weak or mismanaged, or both. Furthermore, there is an inequitable distribution of wealth in the continent. Corruption is rampant, and one could talk of a prevailing ethos of corruption that degrades societies and undermines the future of the entire continent. The need for transparency is of course the answer, but the whole situation is being complicated by other factors, such as illiteracy and lack of schooling.

3378. Robertson, 58–59; H.J. Steiner & P. Alston, *International Human Rights in Context* (Oxford: Oxford University Press, 2000), 920.

3379. *See, e.g.*, *The Social and Economic Rights Action Center and the Center for Economic and Social Rights v. Nigeria*, Communication No. 155/96, *15th Activity Report 2001–2002*; *Gunme et al. v. Cameroon,* Communication No. 266/2003, 26th Activity Report 2008–2009; *Sudan Human Rights Organization and Sudan Centre for Housing Rights and Evictions v. Sudan* Communication Nos 279/03, 296/05, 28th Activity Report, 2010.

551. Twenty-one years after the commencement of its operation, not all AU organs envisaged in the Constitutive Act have been established and/or are functioning. Reference to the African Court of Justice has been made in the preceding paragraphs. None of the three financial institutions is in operation. The Pan-African Parliament has injected a welcome measure of democracy to the AU, even if limited, but it still does not enjoy any powers of substance. Member States should not tamper with PAP's potential. Even though one is not suggesting that overnight PAP should evolve to an organ akin to the European Parliament, Member States can ill-afford to overlook the advantages that an independent parliamentarian institution can lead to. And, when the Continental Free Trade Area finally becomes a reality, PAP should become the organ which, together with the Assembly of Heads of State and Government, will ensure that Member States apply its rules and regulations with diligence. The Peace and Security Council has already made its mark and, given the prevailing in the continent situation, it has managed to act as a trustworthy stakeholder in the continent. But the fact that the PSC is still not a proper AU organ no doubt limits its ability to fulfil its very important mandate to its full extent and undermines its authority as the organ that deals with the scourge of unconstitutional overthrow of governments and interstate conflicts. The need for the AU Constitutive Act to be urgently revised has been noted in other parts of this monograph. Here, it can only be emphasized that without a revised constitutive instrument the AU may be unable to face and address future problems and challenges. Indeed, if there is only one reason why the EU has been the very successful regional organization that it has become, it is the ability to reinvent itself by means of continuous amendments and revisions of its statutory instruments. But there has been another reason, which is of direct relevance to the AU. From early on, the EU has pressed the idea that it is creating its own legal system, an EU law, which requires absolute observance by Member States. The benefits of having uniform legislation and the same legal procedures in all EU Member States are obvious. As has been suggested above, an AU legal system has been developing and has the potential to radically change the continent. However, this requires a stable environment where Member States are not in constant antiparathesis and also an advanced constitutive instrument that will assist the process to have an AU law. The Constitutive Act is not capable to serve this purpose: it was no doubt a good instrument to secure the OAU's transformation into the AU. But now a different kind of transformation is required.

552. Naturally, the successful completion of a complex and multifaceted project such as the AU requires time, resources and unlimited quantities of willingness and continued cooperation among the membership. The evolutionary process of the EU, on which parts of the AU are said to be based, is a very good example. Therefore, it could be argued with some persuasion that the transformation still has a long way to go. However, the AU's sense of urgency is encouraging and significant progress has been made in the short period of twenty years. Many important treaties have been adopted, while the machinery for the implementation of the AU project is finally being put in place. Arguably, the AU is at a crucial crossroads and, unless it demonstrates a willingness to confront and deal resolutely with the continent's vested interests, the AU could have the fate of the unlamented OAU. But the much-suffered African people deserve a better and brighter future.

Part VI. Addresses and Networks

The African Union: Organs and Other Related Bodies

African Union (AU)
African Union Headquarters
P.O. Box 3243
Roosevelt Street
(Old Airport Area)
W21K19
Addis Ababa
Ethiopia
Tel: +251 11 551 77 00
Fax: +251 11 551 78 44
website: http://www.au.int

Economic, Social and Cultural Council
ECOSOCC Secretariat
8658 Kudu Road
Kabulonga, Lusaka
Zambia
Tel.: (260) 211429405
E-Mail: ecosocc@africa-union.org
Website: https://ecosocc.au.int/en

Pan-African Parliament
19 Richards Drive
Gallagher Estate
Midrand
Johannesburg

Republic of South Africa
Tel: +27 11 545 5000
Fax: +27 11 545 5136
E-mail: info@panafricanparliament.org
Website https://pap.au.int/en

AUDA-NEPAD Agency (formerly, New Partnership for Africa's Development (NEPAD))
230 15th Road
Midrand
Republic of South Africa
Tel.: +27 11 256 3600
E-mail: info@nepad.org
Website: https://www.nepad.org/

African Peer Review Mechanism (APRM)
Private Bag X09
Halfway House
Midrand
Johannesburg
Republic of South Africa
Tel.: +27 11 256 3400
E-mail: info@aprm-au.org
Website: http://aprm-au.org/

African Commission on Human and Peoples' Rights
31 Bijilo Annex Layout
Kombo North District
Western Region
P.O. Box 673
Banjul
The Gambia
Tel: +220 441 05 05/441 05 06
Fax: +220 441 05 04
E-mail: au-banjul@africa-union.org
Website: https://achpr.au.int/

African Committee of Experts on the Rights and Welfare of the Child
ACERWC Headquarters

Nala House, Balfour Road
Maseru, Kingdom of Lesotho
E-mail: acerwc-secretariat@africa-union.org
Website: http://www.acerwc.africa

Website: http://www.acerwc.africa

African Court on Human and Peoples' Rights
Dodoma Road
Mwalimu Julius Nyerere Conservation Centre
P.O. Box 6274
Arusha
United Republic of Tanzania
Tel: +255 272970430 ; +255 272970431 ; +255 272970432

E-mail: registrar@african-court.org
Website: http://www.african-court.org

African Union Commission on International Law
Office of Legal Councel
African Union Commission
P.O. Box 3243
Roosevelt Street (Old Airport Area)
W21K19 Addis Ababa
Ethiopia

African Union Advisory Board against Corruption
Arusha International Conference Centre (AICC)
Serengeti Wings, 3rd Floor,
East Africa Road, Sekei
P.O. Box 6071
Arusha

Tanzania
Tel: + 255 27 20 500 30
Fax: +255 27 205 0031
E-mail: info@auanticorruption.org
Website: https://anticorruption.au.int/en

African Centre for the Study and Research on Terrorism
B.P 141 Bureau de Poste
El-Mohammadia, Algiers
Algeria
Tel: (+123 21) 520 083
Fax: (+213 21) 520 378
E-mail: admin@caert.org.dz
Website: http://www.caert.org.dz

African Union Foundation
1258 Lever Road
Headway Hill
Midrand, 1685
Republic of South Africa
Tel.: Telephone: +27 11 313 5105
Website: https://www.africaunionfoundation.org/

Pan African University (PAU)
Pan African University Rectorate
Bastos
Yaoundé
Cameroon
E-mail: paurectorate@africa-union.org
Website: https://pau-au.africa

AFRICAN UNION PERMANENT REPRESENTATIONAL OFFICES:

AU Permanent Observer to the United Nations
3 Dag Hammarskjöld Plaza
305 East 47th Street, 5th Floor
New York, NY10017
United States of America
Tel: (+1 212) 319 5491
Fax: (+1 212) 319 6509

E-mail: au-newyork@africa-union.org
Website: https://www.africanunion-un.org/

AU Permanent Representative to the United Nations (Geneva Office) and to the World Trade Organization

127, Rue des Pâquis 36
CH-1211 Genève 22
Switzerland
Tel: (+41 22) 716 0640
Fax: (+41 22) 731 6818
E-Mail: au-geneva@africa-union.org
mission-observer.au@africanunion.ch

AU Permanent Representative to the United States

1919 Pennsylvania Ave, Suite 7001
Washington, DC 20006
United States of America
Tel: +1 202 293 8006
Fax: +1 202 293 8007
E-mail: au-washington@africa-union.org

Permanent Mission to the European Union (EU) and to the African, Caribbean and Pacific (ACP) Group of States (Brussels Office)

Avenue Gustave Demey 72–74
1160 Audergem
Belgium
Tel: +32 2 346 9747 or 346 9748
Fax: +32 2 346 9128
E-mail: au-brussels@africa-union.org
africanunion@skynet.be

Permanent Delegation to the League of Arab States – Cairo Office

Abd Allah Al Kateb
From Viny Square
Dokki, Cairo
Egypt
Tel: +20 2 3762 6154

Fax: +20 2 3762 6153
E-mail: au-cairo@africa-union.org

Permanent Mission to China (Beijing Office)
111/112, Unit 1 Tayuan Diplomatic Office Building
14 Liangmahe South Road
Beijing, China 100600

AFRICAN UNION SPECIALIZED AGENCIES, OTHER INSTITUTIONS AND REGIONAL ECONOMIC COMMUNITIES

African Civil Aviation Commission

Léopold Sédar Senghor International
Airport Road
B.P. 8898
Dakar-Yoff
Sénégal
Tel: +221 33 859 88 00
Fax: +221 33 820 70 18
E-Mail: secretariat@afcac.org
Website: http://www.afcac.org/en/

African Development Bank Group
01 BP 1387 Abidjan 01
Côte d'Ivoire
Tel: +225 2720263900
E-mail: afdb@afdb.org
Website: http://www.afdb.org

African Energy Commission (AFREC)
02 Rue Chenoua
BP 791 Hydra
16035 Algiers
Algeria
Tel: +213 (0) 2345 9198
Fax: +213 (0) 2345 9200
E-mail: afrec@africa-union.org
Website: https://au-afrec.org

African Telecommunications Union
P.O. Box 35282
00200 Nairobi
Kenya
Tel: +254 722 203132
E-mail: sg@atuuat.africa
Website: https://atuuat.africa/

Pan African Postal Union
Plot III, Block Z
Golf Course, Sekei
P.O. Box 6026
Arusha 23000
United Republic of Tanzania
Tel: +255 272543263
Fax: +255 272543265
E-mail: sg@papu.co.tz
Website: https://www.upap-papu.africa/

Pan African Youth Union
Rue Amir Abdelkader 5
10080 Agdal Riyad
Rabat
Morocco
Tel: +212-675-951-514
E-mail: info@panafricanyouthunion.org
Website: https://panafricanyouthunion.org/en/

African Rehabilitation Institute (ARI)
ARI Headquarters
Cnr Jason Moyo Ave and First St
P.O. Box 4056 Harare
Zimbabwe
Tel: (+263 4) 759 211
Fax: (+263 4) 759 218
E-mail: ari@ecoweb.co.zw

Economic Community of Western African States (ECOWAS)
101, Yakubu Gowon Crescent
Asokoro District
P.M.B. 401
Abuja
Nigeria
Tel: +234 9 3147 6479
Fax: (+234 9) 3143 005/3147 646
E-mail: info@ecowas.int
Website: http://www.ecowas.int

Common Market of Eastern and Southern Africa (COMESA)
COMESA Centre
Ben Bella Road
P.O. Box 30051
Lusaka
Zambia
Tel: +260 211 229725/32
Fax: +260 211 225107
E-Mail: info@comesa.int
Website: http://www.comesa.int

Southern Africa Development Community (SADC)
SADC House
Plot No. 54385
Central Business District
Private Bag 0095
Gaborone
Botswana
Tel: ++267 395 1863
Fax: +267 397 2848; +267 318 1070
E-mail: registry@sadc.int
Website: http://www.sadc.int

Intergovernmental Authority on Development (IGAD)
IGAD Secretariat
Avenue Georges Clemenceau
P.O. Box 2653 Djibouti
Republic of Djibouti
Tel: +253 354050
Fax: +253 356994
E-mail: igad@igad.org
Website: http://www.igad.org

Economic Community of Central African States (ECCAS)
Secrétariat Général de la CEEAC
BP 2112
Libreville
Gabon
Tel: +241-444731
Fax: +241-44732
E-mail: secretariat@ceeac-eccas.org
Website: http://www.ceeac-eccas.org

East African Community (EAC)
3 EAC Close
East African Community Headquarters
P.O. Box 1096
Arusha
Tanzania
Tel: +255 27 2162100
Fax: +255 27 2162190
E-mail: eac@eachq.org
Website: http://www.eac.int

Community of Sahel-Saharan States (CEN-SAD)
Secretariat General
P.O. Box 4041
Place D'Algeria
Tripoli

Libya
Tel: (+218 21) 361 4832
Fax: (+218 21) 333 216
E-mail: censadsg@yahoo.com
info@cen-sad.org
Website: http://www.censad.org

Arab Magreb Union (AMU)
AMU Secretariat
73, Rue Tensift Agdal
Rabat
Morocco
Tel: +212 537 6813 71-4
Fax: +212 537 681 377
Website: http://www.maghrebarabe.org/en/
E-mail: sg.uma@maghrebarabe.org

Appendix 1. The Constitutive Act of the African Union (2000)

We, Heads of State and Government of the Member States of the Organization of African Unity

Inspired by the noble ideals which guided the founding fathers of our Continental Organization and generations of Pan-Africanists in their determination to promote unity, solidarity, cohesion and cooperation among the peoples of Africa and African States;

Considering the principles and objectives stated in the Charter of the Organization of African Unity and the Treaty establishing the African Economic Community;

Recalling the heroic struggles waged by our peoples and our countries for political independence, human dignity and economic emancipation;

Considering that since its inception, the Organization of African Unity has played a determining and invaluable role in the liberation of the continent, the affirmation of a common identity and the process of attainment of the unity of our continent and has provided a unique framework for our collective action in Africa and in our relations with the rest of the world;

Determined to take up the multifaceted challenges that confront our continent and peoples in the light of the social, economic and political changes taking place in the world;

Convinced of the need to accelerate the process of implementing the Treaty establishing the African Economic Community in order to promote the socioeconomic development of Africa and to face more effectively the challenges posed by globalization;

Guided by our common vision of a united and strong Africa and by the need to build a partnership between governments and all segments of civil society, in particular women, youth and the private sector in order to strengthen solidarity and cohesion among our peoples;

Conscious of the fact that the scourge of conflicts in Africa constitutes a major impediment to the socio-economic development of the continent and of the need to promote peace, security and stability as a prerequisite for the implementation of our development and integration agenda;

Determined to promote and protect human and peoples' rights, consolidate democratic institutions and culture, and to ensure good governance and the rule of law;

Further determined to take all necessary measures to strengthen our common institutions and provide them with the necessary powers and resources to enable them discharge their respective mandates effectively;

Recalling the Declaration which we adopted at the Fourth Extraordinary Session of our Assembly in Sirte, the Great Socialist People's Libyan Arab Jamahiriya, on 9.9. 99, in which we decided to establish an African Union, in conformity with the ultimate objectives of the Charter of our Continental Organization and the Treaty establishing the African Economic Community;

Have agreed as follows:

Article 1. Definitions

In this Constitutive Act:

> 'Act' means the present Constitutive Act; 'AEC' means the African Economic Community; 'Assembly' means the Assembly of Heads of State and Government of the Union; 'Charter' means the Charter of the OAU;
> 'Committee' means a Specialized Technical Committee of the Union;
> 'Council' means the Economic, Social and Cultural Council of the Union;
> 'Court' means the Court of Justice of the Union;
> 'Executive Council' means the Executive Council of Ministers of the Union;
> 'Member State' means a Member State of the Union;
> 'OAU' means the Organization of African Unity;
> 'Parliament' means the Pan-African Parliament of the Union;
> 'Union' means the African Union established by the present Constitutive Act.

Article 2. Establishment

The African Union is hereby established in accordance with the provisions of this Act.

Article 3. Objectives

a. The objectives of the Union shall be to:
b. Achieve greater unity and solidarity between the African counties and the peoples of Africa;
c. Defend the sovereignty, territorial integrity and independence of its Member States;
d. Accelerate the political and socio-economic integration of the continent;
e. Promote and defend African common positions on issues of interest to the continent and its peoples;
f. Encourage international cooperation, taking due account of the Charter of the United Nations and the Universal Declaration of Human Rights;
g. Promote peace, security, and stability on the continent;
h. Promote democratic principles and institutions, popular participation and good governance;

i. Promote and protect human and peoples' rights in accordance with the African Charter on Human and Peoples' Rights and other relevant human rights instruments;
j. Establish the necessary conditions which enable the continent to play its rightful role in the global economy and in international negotiations;
k. Promote sustainable development at the economic, social and cultural levels as well as the integration of African economies;
l. Promote cooperation in all fields of human activity to raise the living standards of African peoples;
m. Coordinate and harmonize policies between existing and future Regional Economic Communities for the gradual attainment of the objectives of the Union;
n. Advance the development of the continent by promoting research in all fields, in particular in science and technology;
o. Work with relevant international partners in the eradication of preventable diseases and the promotion of good health on the continent.

Article 4. Principles

The Union shall function in accordance with the following principles:

a. Sovereign equality and interdependence among Member States of the Union;
b. Respect of borders existing on achievement of independence;
c. Participation of the African peoples in the activities of the Union;
d. Establishment of a common defence policy for the African continent;
e. Peaceful resolution of conflicts among Member States of the Union through such appropriate means as may be decided upon by the Assembly;
f. Prohibition of the use of force or threat to use force among Member States of the Union;
g. Non-interference by any Member State in the internal affairs of another;
h. The right of the Union to intervene in a Member State pursuant to a decision of the Assembly in respect of grave circumstances, namely war crimes, genocide and crimes against humanity;
i. Peaceful co-existence of Member States and their right to live in peace and security;
j. The right of Member States to request intervention from the Union in order to restore peace and security;
k. Promotion of self-reliance within the framework of the Union;
l. Promotion of gender equality;
m. Respect for democratic principles, human rights, the rule of law and good governance;
n. Promotion of social justice to ensure balanced economic development;
o. Respect for the sanctity of human life, condemnation and rejection of impunity and political assassination, acts of terrorism and subversive activities;
p. Condemnation and rejection of unconstitutional changes of governments.

Appendix 1, The Constitutive Act of the African Union (2000)

Article 5. Organs of the Union

1. The organs of the Union shall be:
   a. The Assembly of the Union;
   b. The Executive Council;
   c. The Pan-African Parliament;
   d. The Court of Justice;
   e. The Commission;
   f. The Permanent Representatives Committee;
   g. The Specialized Technical Committees;
   h. The Economic, Social and Cultural Council;
   i. The Financial Institutions;
2. Other organs that the Assembly may decide to establish.

Article 6. The Assembly

1. The Assembly shall be composed of Heads of States and Government or their duly accredited representatives.
2. The Assembly shall be the supreme organ of the Union.
3. The Assembly shall meet at least once a year in ordinary session. At the request of any MemberState and on approval by a two-thirds majority of the Member States, the Assembly shall meet in extraordinary session.
4. The Office of the Chairman of the Assembly shall be held for a period of one year by a Head of State or Government elected after consultations among the Member States.

Article 7. Decisions of the Assembly

1. The Assembly shall take its decisions by consensus or, failing which, by a two-thirds majority of the Member States of the Union. However, procedural matters, including the question of whether a matter is one of procedure or not, shall be decided by a simple majority.
2. Two-thirds of the total membership of the Union shall form a quorum at any meeting of the Assembly.

Article 8. Rules of Procedure of the Assembly

The Assembly shall adopt its own Rules of Procedure.

Article 9. Powers and Functions of the Assembly

1. The functions of the Assembly shall be to:
   a. Determine the common policies of the Union;

b. Receive, consider and take decisions on reports and recommendations from the other organs of the Union;
c. Consider requests for Membership of the Union;
d. Establish any organ of the Union;
e. Monitor the implementation of policies and decisions of the Union as well as ensure compliance by all Member States;
f. Adopt the budget of the Union;
g. Give directives to the Executive Council on the management of conflicts, war and other emergency situations and the restoration of peace;
h. Appoint and terminate the appointment of the judges of the Court of Justice;
i. Appoint the Chairman of the Commission and his or her deputy or deputies and Commissioners of the Commission and determine their functions and terms of office.

2. The Assembly may delegate any of its powers and functions to any organ of the Union.

Article 10. The Executive Council

1. The Executive Council shall be composed of the Ministers of Foreign Affairs or such other Ministers or Authorities as are designated by the Governments of Member States.
2. Council shall meet at least twice a year in ordinary session. It shall also meet in an extraordinary session at the request of any MemberState and upon approval by two-thirds of all Member States.

Article 11. Decisions of the Executive Council

1. The Executive Council shall take its decisions by consensus or, failing which, by a two-thirds majority of the Member States. However, procedural matters, including the question of whether a matter is one of procedure or not, shall be decided by a simple majority.
2. Two-thirds of the total membership of the Union shall form a quorum at any meeting of the Executive Council.

Article 12. Rules of Procedure of the Executive Council

The Executive Council shall adopt its own Rules of Procedure.

Article 13. Functions of the Executive Council

1. The Executive Council shall co-ordinate and take decisions on policies in areas of common interest to the Member States, including the following:
   a. Foreign trade;

   b. Energy, industry and mineral resources;
   c. Food, agricultural and animal resources, livestock production and forestry;
   d. Water resources and irrigation;
   e. Environmental protection, humanitarian action and disaster response and relief;
   f. Transport and communications;
   g. Insurance;
   h. Education, culture, health and human resources development;
   i. Science and technology;
   j. Nationality, residency and immigration matters;
   k. Social security, including the formulation of mother and child care policies, as well as policies relating to the disabled and the handicapped;
   l. Establishment of a system of African awards, medals and prizes.
2. The Executive Council shall be responsible to the Assembly. It shall consider issues referred to it and monitor the implementation of policies formulated by the Assembly.
3. The Executive Council may delegate any of its powers and functions mentioned in paragraph 1 of this Article to the Specialized Technical Committees established under Article 14 of this Act.

Article 14. The Specialized Technical Committees: Establishment and Composition

1. There is hereby established the following Specialized Technical Committees, which shall be responsible to the Executive Council:
   a. The Committee on Rural Economy and Agricultural Matters;
   b. The Committee on Monetary and Financial Affairs;
   c. The Committee on Trade, Customs and Immigration Matters;
   d. The Committee on Industry, Science and Technology, Energy, Natural Resources and Environment;
   e. The Committee on Transport, Communications and Tourism;
   f. The Committee on Health, Labour and Social Affairs; and
   g. The Committee on Education, Culture and Human Resources.
2. The Assembly shall, whenever it deems appropriate, restructure the existing Committees or establish other Committees.
3. The Specialized Technical Committees shall be composed of Ministers or senior officials responsible for sectors falling within their respective areas of competence.

Article 15. Functions of the Specialized Technical Committees

Each Committee shall within its field of competence:

a. Prepare projects and programmes of the Union and submit in to the Executive Council;

b. Ensure the supervision, follow-up and the evaluation of the implementation of decisions taken by the organs of the Union;
c. Ensure the coordination and harmonization of projects and programmes of the Union;
d. Submit to the Executive Council either on its own initiative or at the request of the Executive Council, reports and recommendations on the implementation of the provision of this Act; and
e. Carry out any other functions assigned to it for the purpose of ensuring the implementation of the provisions of this Act.

Article 16. Meetings

1. Subject to any directives given by the Executive Council, each Committee shall meet as often as necessary and shall prepare its rules of procedure and submit them to the Executive Council for approval.

Article 17. The Pan-African Parliament

1. In order to ensure the full participation of African peoples in the development and economic integration of the continent, a Pan-African Parliament shall be established.
2. The composition, powers, functions and organization of the Pan-African Parliament shall be defined in a protocol relating thereto.

Article 18. The Court of Justice

1. A Court of Justice of the Union shall be established; 2. The statute, composition and functions of the Court of Justice shall be defined in a protocol relating thereto.

Article 19. The Financial Institutions

The Union shall have the following financial institutions, whose rules and regulations shall be defined in protocols relating thereto:

a. The African Central Bank;
b. The African Monetary Fund;
c. The African Investment Bank.

Appendix 1, The Constitutive Act of the African Union (2000)

Article 20. The Commission

1. There shall be established a Commission of the Union, which shall be the Secretariat of the Union.
2. The Commission shall be composed of the Chairman, his or her deputy or deputies and the Commissioners. They shall be assisted by the necessary staff for the smooth functioning of the Commission.
3. The structure, functions and regulations of the Commission shall be determined by the Assembly.

Article 21. The Permanent Representatives Committee

1. There shall be established a Permanent Representatives Committee. It shall be composed of Permanent Representatives to the Union and other Plenipotentiaries of Member States.
2. The Permanent Representatives Committee shall be charged with the responsibility of preparing the work of the Executive Council and acting on the Executive Council's instructions. It may set up such sub-committees or working groups as it may deem necessary.

Article 22. The Economic, Social and Cultural Council

1. The Economic, Social and Cultural Council shall be an advisory organ composed of different social and professional groups of the Member States of the Union.
2. The functions, powers, composition and organization of the Economic, Social and Cultural Council shall be determined by the Assembly.

Article 23. Imposition of Sanctions

1. The Assembly shall determine the appropriate sanctions to be imposed on any Member State that defaults in the payment of its contributions to the budget of the Union in the following manner: denial of the right to speak at meetings, to vote, to present candidates for any position or post within the Union or to benefit from any activity or commitments therefrom.
2. Furthermore, any MemberState that fails to comply with the decisions and policies of the Union may be subjected to other sanctions, such as the denial of transport and communications links with other MemberStates, and other measures of a political and economic nature to be determined by the Assembly.

Article 24. The Headquarters of the Union

1. The Headquarters of the Union shall be in Addis Ababa in the Federal Democratic Republic of Ethiopia.
2. There may be established such other offices of the Union as the Assembly may, on the recommendation of the Executive Council, determine.

Article 25. Working Languages

The working languages of the Union and all its institutions shall be, if possible, African languages, Arabic, English, French and Portuguese.

Article 26. Interpretation

The Court shall be seized with matters of interpretation arising from the application or implementation of this Act. Pending its establishment, such matters shall be submitted to the Assembly of the Union, which shall decide by a two-thirds majority.

Article 27. Signature, Ratification and Accession

1. This Act shall be open to signature, ratification and accession by the Member States of the OAU in accordance with their respective constitutional procedures.
2. The instruments of ratification shall be deposited with the Secretary-General of the OAU.
3. Any Member State of the OAU acceding to this Act after its entry into force shall deposit the instrument of accession with the Chairman of the Commission.

Article 28. Entry into Force

This Act shall enter into force thirty (30) days after the deposit of the instruments of ratification by two-thirds of the Member States of the OAU.

Article 29. Admission to Membership

1. Any African State may, at any time after the entry into force of this Act, notify the Chairman of the Commission of its intention to accede to this Act and to be admitted as a member of the Union.
2. The Chairman of the Commission shall, upon receipt of such notification, transmit copies thereof to all Member States. Admission shall be decided by a simple majority of the Member States. The decision of each Member State shall be transmitted to the Chairman of the Commission who shall, upon receipt of the required number of votes, communicate the decision to the State concerned.

Article 30. Suspension

Governments which shall come to power through unconstitutional means shall not be allowed to participate in the activities of the Union.

Article 31. Cessation of Membership

1. Any State which desires to renounce its membership shall forward a written notification to the Chairman of the Commission, who shall inform Member States thereof. At the end of one year from the date of such notification, if not withdrawn, the Act shall cease to apply with respect to the renouncing State, which shall thereby cease to belong to the Union.
2. During the period of one year referred to in paragraph 1 of this Article, any Member State wishing to withdraw from the Union shall comply with the provisions of this Act and shall be bound to discharge its obligations under this Act up to the date of its withdrawal.

Article 32. Amendment and Revision

1. Any Member State may submit proposals for the amendment or revision of this Act.
2. Proposals for amendment or revision shall be submitted to the Chairman of the Commission who shall transmit same to Member States within thirty (30) days of receipt thereof.
3. The Assembly, upon the advice of the Executive Council, shall examine these proposals within a period of one year following notification of Member States, in accordance with the provisions of paragraph 2 of this Article.
4. Amendments or revisions shall be adopted by the Assembly by consensus or, failing which, by a two-thirds majority and submitted for ratification by all Member States in accordance with their respective constitutional procedures. They shall enter into force thirty (30) days after the deposit of the instruments of ratification with the Chairman of the Commission by a two-thirds majority of the Member States.

Article 33. Transitional Arrangements and Final Provisions

1. This Act shall replace the Charter of the Organization of African Unity. However, the Charter shall remain operative for a transitional period of one year or such further period as may be determined by the Assembly, following the entry into force of the Act, for the purpose of enabling the OAU/AEC to undertake the necessary measures regarding the devolution of its assets and liabilities to the Union and all matters relating thereto.
2. The provisions of this Act shall take precedence over and supersede any inconsistent or contrary provisions of the Treaty establishing the African Economic Community.

3. Upon the entry into force of this Act, all necessary measures shall be undertaken to implement its provisions and to ensure the establishment of the organs provided for under the Act in accordance with any directives or decisions which may be adopted in this regard by the Parties thereto within the transitional period stipulated above.
4. Pending the establishment of the Commission, the OAU General Secretariat shall be the interim Secretariat of the Union.
5. This Act, drawn up in four (4) original texts in the Arabic, English, French and Portuguese languages, all four (4) being equally authentic, shall be deposited with the Secretary-General of the OAU and, after its entry into force, with the Chairman of the Commission who shall transmit a certified true copy of the Act to the Government of each signatory State. The Secretary-General of the OAU and the Chairman of the Commission shall notify all signatory States of the dates of the deposit of the instruments of ratification or accession and shall upon entry into force of this Act register the same with the Secretariat of the United Nations.

In witness whereof, we have adopted this Act.

Appendix 1, The Constitutive Act of the African Union (2000)

Appendix 2. The Member States of the African Union (as of November 2023)

People's Democratic Republic of Algeria
Republic of Angola
Republic of Benin
Republic of Botswana
Burkina Faso (formerly, Republic of Upper Volta)
Republic of Burundi
Republic of Cameroon
Republic of Cape Verde/Republic of Cabo Verde
Central African Republic
Republic of Chad
Islamic Federal Republic of the Comoros
Republic of the Congo
Republic of Côte d'Ivoire
Democratic Republic of Congo
Republic of Djibouti
Arab Republic of Egypt
State of Eritrea
Kingdom of Eswatini (formerly, Kingdom of Swaziland)
Federal Democratic Republic of Ethiopia
Republic of Equatorial Guinea
Gabonese Republic
Republic of The Gambia
Republic of Ghana
Republic of Guinea

Appendix 2, The Member States of the African Union

Republic of Guinea-Bissau
Republic of Kenya
Kingdom of Lesotho
Republic of Liberia
State of Libya (formerly, Great Socialist People's Libyan Arab Jamahiriya)
Republic of Madagascar
Republic of Malawi
Republic of Mali
Islamic Republic of Mauritania
Republic of Mauritius
Kingdom of Morocco
Republic of Mozambique
Republic of Namibia
Republic of Niger
Federal Republic of Nigeria
Republic of Rwanda
Sahrawi Arab Democratic Republic
Republic of São Tomé and Príncipe
Republic of Senegal
Republic of Seychelles
Republic of Sierra Leone
Republic of Somalia
Republic of South Africa
Republic of South Sudan
Republic of The Sudan

United Republic of Tanzania
Togolese Republic
Republic of Tunisia
Republic of Uganda
Republic of Zambia
Republic of Zimbabwe

Appendix 3. Solemn Declaration on the 50th Anniversary of the OAU/AU (2013)

AU Doc. Assembly/AU/Decl. 3 (XXI)

We, Heads of State and Government of the African Union assembled to celebrate the Golden Jubilee of the OAU/AU established in the city of Addis Ababa, Ethiopia on 25 May 1963,

Evoking the uniqueness of the history of Africa as the cradle of humanity and a centre of civilization, and dehumanized by slavery, deportation, dispossession, apartheid and colonialism as well as our struggles against these evils, which shaped our common destiny and enhanced our solidarity with peoples of African descent;

Recalling with pride, the historical role and efforts of the Founders of the Pan-African Movement and the nationalist movements, whose visions, wisdom, solidarity and commitment continue to inspire us;

Reaffirming our commitment to the ideals of Pan-Africanism and Africa's aspiration for greater unity, and paying tribute to the Founders of the Organization of African Unity (OAU) as well as the African peoples on the continent and in the Diaspora for their glorious and successful struggles against all forms of oppression, colonialism and apartheid;

Mindful that the OAU/AU have been relentlessly championing for the complete decolonization of the African continent and that one of the fundamental objectives is unconditional respect for the sovereignty and territorial integrity of each of its Member States;

Stressing our commitment to build a united and integrated Africa;

Guided by the vision of our Union and affirming our determination to '*build an integrated, prosperous and peaceful Africa, driven and managed by its own citizens and representing a dynamic force in the international arena*';

Determined to take full responsibility for the realisation of this vision;

Guided by the principles enshrined in the Constitutive Act of our Union and our Shared Values, in particular our commitment to ensure gender equality and a people centred approach in all our endeavours as well as respect for sovereignty and territorial integrity of our countries.

ACKNOWLEDGE THAT:

I. ***The Organisation of African Unity (OAU)*** overcame internal and external challenges, persevered in the quest for continental unity and solidarity; contributed actively to the liberation of Africa from colonialism and apartheid; provided a political and diplomatic platform to generations of leaders on continental and international matters; and elaborated frameworks for Africa's development and integration agenda through programmes such as NEPAD and APRM.

II. ***The African Union (AU)*** carried forward our struggle for self-determination and drive for development and integration; formulated a clear vision for our Union; agreed that the ultimate goal of the Union is the construction of a united and integrated Africa; instituted the principle of non-indifference by authorizing the right of the Union to intervene in Member States in conformity with the Constitutive Act; and laid the groundwork for the entrenchment of the rule of law, democracy, respect for human rights, solidarity, promotion of gender equality and the empowerment of Women and Youth in Africa.

III. The implementation of the integration agenda; the involvement of people, including our Diaspora in the affairs of the Union; the quest for peace and security and preventing wars and genocide such as the 1994 Rwandan genocide; the alignment between our institutional framework and the vision of the Union; the fight against poverty; inequality and underdevelopment; and, assuring Africa's rightful place in the world, remain challenges.

WE HEREBY DECLARE:

A. On the African Identity and Renaissance

i) Our strong commitment to accelerate the African Renaissance by ensuring the integration of the principles of Pan Africanism in all our policies and initiatives;

ii) Our unflinching belief in our common destiny, our Shared Values and the affirmation of the African identity; the celebration of unity in diversity and the institution of the African citizenship;

iii) Our commitment to strengthen AU programmes and Member States institutions aimed at reviving our cultural identity, heritage, history and Shared values, as well as undertake, henceforth, to fly the AU flag and sing the AU anthem along with our national flags and anthems;

iv) Promote and harmonize the teaching of African history, values and Pan Africanism in all our schools and educational institutions as part of advancing our African identity and Renaissance;

v) Promote people to people engagements including Youth and civil society exchanges in order to strengthen Pan Africanism.

B. The struggle against colonialism and the right to self-determination of people still under colonial rule

i) The completion of the decolonization process in Africa; to protect the right to self-determination of African peoples still under colonial rule; solidarity with people of African descend and in the Diaspora in their struggles against racial discrimination; and resist all forms of influences contrary to the interests of the continent;
ii) The reaffirmation of our call to end expeditiously the unlawful occupation of the Chagos Archipelago, the Comorian Island of Mayotte and also reaffirm the right to self-determination of the people of Western Sahara, with a view to enable these countries and peoples, to effectively exercise sovereignty over their respective territories.

C. On the integration agenda

Our commitment to Africa's political, social and economic integration agenda, and in this regard, speed up the process of attaining the objectives of the African Economic Community and take steps towards the construction of a united and integrated Africa. Consolidating existing commitments and instruments, we undertake, in particular, to:

i) Speedily implement the Continental Free Trade Area; ensure free movement of goods, with focus on integrating local and regional markets as well as facilitate African citizenship to allow free movement of people through the gradual removal of visa requirements;
ii) Accelerate action on the ultimate establishment of a united and integrated Africa, through the implementation of our common continental governance, democracy and human rights frameworks. Move with speed towards the integration and merger of the Regional Economic Communities as the building blocks of the Union.

D. On the agenda for social and economic development

Our commitment to place the African people, in particular women, children and the youth, as well as persons with disabilities, at the centre of our endeavours and to eradicate poverty. In this regard, we undertake to:

i) Develop our human capital as our most important resource, through education and training, especially in science, technology and innovation, and ensure that Africa takes its place and contributes to humanity, including in the field of space sciences and explorations;
ii) Eradicate disease, especially HIV/AIDS, Malaria and Tuberculosis, ensure that no African woman dies while giving life, address maternal, infant and child mortality as well as provide universal health care services to our citizens;

iii) Accelerate Africa's infrastructural development, to link African peoples, countries and economies; and help to drive social, cultural and economic development. In this regard, we commit to meet our strategic targets in transport, ICT, energy and other social infrastructure by committing national, regional and continental resources to this end;
iv) Create an enabling environment for the effective development of the African private sector through meaningful public-private sector dialogue at all levels, in order to foster socially responsive business, good corporate governance and inclusive economic growth;
v) Take ownership of, use and develop, our natural endowments and resources, through value addition, as the basis for industrialization; promote intra-Africa trade and tourism, in order to foster economic integration, development, employment and inclusive growth to the benefit of the African people;
vi) Also take ownership, preserve, protect and use our oceanic spaces and resources, improve our maritime and transport industries to the benefit of the continent and its peoples, including by contributing to food security;
vii) Preserve our arable land for current and future generations, develop our rural economies, our agricultural production and agro-processing to eradicate hunger and malnutrition, as well as achieve food security and self-sufficiency;
viii) Expand and develop urban infrastructure and develop planned approaches to rapid urbanization and the emergence of new cities;
ix) Make our development agenda responsive to the needs of our peoples, anchored on the preservation of our environment for current and future generations, including in the fight against desertification and mitigation of the effects of climate change, especially with regards to island states and landlocked countries.

E. On peace and security

Our determination to achieve the goal of a conflict-free Africa, to make peace a reality for all our people and to rid the continent of wars, civil conflicts, human rights violations, humanitarian disasters and violent conflicts, and to prevent genocide. We pledge not to bequeath the burden of conflicts to the next generation of Africans and undertake to end all wars in Africa by 2020. In this regard, we undertake to:

i) Address the root causes of conflicts including economic and social disparities; put an end to impunity by strengthening national and continental judicial institutions, and ensure accountability in line with our collective responsibility to the principle of non-indifference;
ii) Eradicate recurrent and address emerging sources of conflict including piracy, trafficking in narcotics and humans, all forms of extremism, armed rebellions, terrorism, transnational organized crime and new crimes such as cybercrime.
iii) Push forward the agenda of conflict prevention, peace-making, peace support, national reconciliation and post-conflict reconstruction and development through the African Peace and Security Architecture; as well as, ensure enforcement of and compliance with peace agreements and build Africa's peacekeeping and enforcement capacities through the African Standby Force;

iv) Maintain a nuclear-free Africa and call for global nuclear disarmament, non-proliferation and peaceful uses of nuclear energy;
v) Ensure the effective implementation of agreements on landmines and the non-proliferation of small arms and light weapons;
vi) Address the plight of internally displaced persons and refugees and eliminate the root causes of this phenomenon by fully implementing continental and universal frameworks.

F. On democratic governance

Our determination to anchor our societies, governments and institutions on respect for the rule of law, human rights and dignity, popular participation, the management of diversity, as well as inclusion and democracy. In this regard, we undertake to:

i) Strengthen democratic governance including through decentralized systems, the rule of law and the capacities of our institutions to meet the aspirations of our people;
ii) Reiterate our rejection of unconstitutional change of government, including through any attempts to seize power by force but recognize the right of our people to peacefully express their will against oppressive systems;
iii) Promote integrity, fight corruption in the management of public affairs and promote leadership that is committed to the interests of the people;
iv) Foster the participation of our people through democratic elections and ensure accountability and transparency.

G. On Determining Africa's Destiny

Our determination to take responsibility for our destiny. We pledge to foster self-reliance and self-sufficiency. In this regard, we undertake to:

i) Take ownership of African issues and provide African solutions to African problems;
ii) Mobilize our domestic resources, on a predictable and sustainable basis to strengthen institutions and advance our continental agenda;
iii) Take all necessary measures, using our rich natural endowments and human resources, to transform Africa and make it a leading continent in the area of innovation and creativity;

H. Africa's place in the world

Our endeavour for Africa to take its rightful place in the political, security, economic, and social systems of global governance towards the realization of its Renaissance and establishing Africa as a leading continent. We undertake to:

i) Continue the global struggle against all forms of racism and discrimination, xenophobia and related intolerances;

ii) Act in solidarity with oppressed countries and peoples;
iii) Advance international cooperation that promotes and defends Africa's interests, is mutually beneficial and aligned to our Pan Africanist vision;
iv) Continue to speak with one voice and act collectively to promote our common interests and positions in the international arena;
v) Reiterate our commitment to Africa's active role in the globalization process and international forums including in Financial and Economic Institutions;
vi) Advocate for our common position for reform of the United Nations (UN) and other global institutions with particular reference to the UN Security Council, in order to correct the historical injustice with Africa as the only region without a permanent seat.

We pledge to articulate the above ideals and goals in our national development plans and in the development of the Continental Agenda 2063, through a people-driven process for the realization of our vision for an integrated, people-centred, prosperous Africa at peace with itself.

As Heads of State and Government, mindful of our responsibility and commitment, we pledge to act together with our Peoples and the African Diaspora to realize our vision of Pan Africanism and African Renaissance.

Adopted by the 21st Ordinary Session of the Assembly of Heads of State and Government of the African Union, at Addis Ababa, on 26 May 2013.

Selected Bibliography

Includes Both Works Which Were Cited in the Monograph and Works Which Were Not Cited. Readers may also consult the previous editions of the monograph for older works.

§1. Books, Book Chapters, Monographs & Yearbooks

Adebajo, A. & H. Scanlon (eds). *A Dialogue of the Deaf: Essays on Africa and the United Nations.* Johannesburg: Jacana, 2006.

Addney M. & Jegede A. (eds), *Human Rights and the Environment under African Union Law*. London: Palgrave Macmillan, 2020.

Adeleke, F. *International Investment Law and Policy in Africa: Exploring a Human Rights Based Approach to Investment Regulation and Dispute Settlement*. London: Routledge, 2018.

African Union Panel of the Wise. *Election-Related Disputes and Political Violence: Strengthening the Role of the African Union in Preventing, Managing, and Resolving Conflict.* The African Union Series, New York: International Peace Institute, July 2010.

Akokpari, J., A. Ndinga-Muvumba & T. Murithi (eds). *The African Union and Its Institutions.* Johannesburg: Jacana, 2008.

Amate, C.O.C. *Inside the OAU: Pan-Africanism in Practice.* London: Macmillan. 1986.

Amao O., *African Union Law: The Emergence of a Sui Generis Legal Order*, London: Routledge, 2019.

Amao O., M. Olivier & K. Magliveras (eds), *The Emergent African Union Law–Conceptualization, Delimitation, and Application.* Oxford: Oxford University Press, 2021.

Ankumah, A.H. *The African Commission on Human and Peoples' Rights.* The Hague: Martinus Nijhoff, 1996.

Bach, D. 'Regionalism in Africa: Concepts and Context'. In *Routledge Handbook of African Security*, edited by J.J. Hentz. London: Routledge, 2014, 181.

Bach, D. *Regionalism in Africa: Genealogies, Institutions and Trans-State Networks*. London: Routledge, 2015.

Banda, F. *African Migration, Human Rights, and Literature*. Oxford: Hart Publishing, 2020.

Boulden, J. (ed.). *Dealing with Conflict in Africa: The United Nations and Regional Organizations.* New York: Palgrave Macmillan, 2003.

Selected Bibliography

Brown, W. & S. Harman (eds), *African Agency in International Politics*. Abingdon: Routledge, 2013

Cheeseman, N. *Democracy in Africa: Successes, Failures, and the Struggle for Political Reform*. Cambridge: Cambridge University Press, 2015

El-Ayouty, Y. & I.W. Zartman (eds). *The OAU after Twenty Years*. New York: Praeger Press, 1984.

El-Ayouty, Y. (ed.). *The Organization of African Unity after Thirty Years*. Westport: Praeger, 1994.

Elias T. O. *Africa and the Development of International Law*. 2nd ed. Leiden: Martinus Nijhoff, 1988.

Engels, U. *Yearbook on the African Union*. Vol. 1, Vol. 2 & Vol. 3 Leiden: Brill 2021–2023.

Engo, P.B. 'Peaceful Co-existence and Friendly Relations among States: The African Contribution to the Progressive Development of Principles of International Law'. In *Africa and International Organization*, edited by Y. El-Ayouty & H. Brooks. The Hague: Martinus Nijhoff, 1974, 31.

Evans, M. & R. Murray (eds). *The African Charter on Human and Peoples' Rights: The System in Practice, 1986–2006*. 2nd edn. Cambridge: Cambridge University Press, 2008.

Falola, T. *The African Diaspora: Slavery, Modernity, and Globalization*. Rochester, NY: University of Rochester Press, 2013.

Hagmann, T. & F. Reyntjens (eds), *Aid and Authoritarianism in Africa: Development Without Democracy*. London: Zed Books, 2016.

Hatchard, J., M. Ndulo & P. Slinn. *Comparative Constitutionalism and Good Governance in the Commonwealth: An Eastern and Southern African Perspective*. Cambridge: Cambridge University Press 2004.

Heyns, C. & M. Killander (eds). *Compendium of Key Human Rights Documents of the African Union*. 7th edn. Pretoria: Pretoria University Law Press, 2022.

Huliaras, A. & S. Kalantzakos, 'Opportunities to Cooperation on New Global Challenges'. In T. Haastrup, L. Mah & N. Duggan (eds), *The Routledge Handbook of EU-Africa Relations*. London: Routledge, 2020, 295.

Huliaras, A. & S. Kalantzakos, 'Rethinking the Collapse of the First East African Community (1977): Lessons for the EU'. In J.-M. Trouille, H. Trouille & P. Uwimbabazi (eds), *The East-African Community: Intraregional Integration and Relations with the EU*. London: Routledge, 2021, 15.

Kabati, C. 'NATO Military Operations in Libya in Relation to International Humanitarian Law'. In *AU–NATO Collaboration: Implications and Prospects*, edited by B.A. Smith-Windsor. Rome: NATO Defense College, 2013, 135.

Kufuor, K. O. *African Unification: Law, Problems and Prospects*. Durham NC: Carolina Academic Press, 2016.

Le Floch, G., *La Cour africaine des droits de l'homme*. Paris: Pedone 2023.

Magliveras, K, 'The Multiple Sanctioning Regimes in the African Union: Analysis and Synthesis'. In F. Amao, M. Olivier & K. Magliveras (eds), *The Emergent African Union Law: Conceptualization, Delimitation, and Application*. Oxford: Oxford University Press, 2021, 359.

Magliveras, K. 'The Implications of African Union Law: Conceptual Analysis with Emphasis on the Institutional Consequences'. In F. Amao, M. Olivier & K.

Magliveras (eds), *The Emergent African Union Law: Conceptualization, Delimitation, and Application*. Oxford: Oxford University Press, 2021, 30.

Makinda, S.M., F. Wafula Okumu & D. Mickler, *The African Union: Addressing the Challenges of Peace, Security and Governance*. 2nd edn.London: Routledge, 2015.

Maluwa, T. *International Law in Post-Colonial Africa.* The Hague: Kluwer Law International, 1999.

Maluwa, T. 'African state practice and the formation of some peremptory norms of general international naw' in D. Tladi (ed.), *Peremptory norms of general international law (jus cogens)*, Leiden/Boston: Brill, 2021, 259.

Manga Fombad, C., Z. Kebonang & H. Melber. *African Union, NEPAD and the APRM Democratisation Efforts Explored*, Current African Issues No. 32. Uppsala: Nordiska Afrikainstitutet, 2006.

Martin, G. *Africa in World Politics – A Pan-African Perspective.* Trenton, New Jersey: Africa World Press, 2002.

Mazzeo, D. (ed.). *African Regional Organizations.* Cambridge: Cambridge University Press, 1984.

Mills, K. *International Responses to Mass Atrocities in Africa: Responsibility to Protect, Prosecute, and Palliate*. Philadelphia, PA: University of Pennsylvania Press, 2015.

Murray, R. & M. Evans. *Documents of the African Commission on Human and Peoples' Rights*. Oxford: Hart Publishing, 2001 & Vol. II. Oxford: Hart Publishing, 2008.

Naldi, G.J. *Documents of the Organization of African Unity*. London: Mansell, 1992.

Naldi, G.J. *The Organization of African Unity: An Analysis of Its Role*. London: Mansell, 1999.

Naldi, G.J. 'The Contribution of AU Human Rights Agreements to an Emergent AU Law'. In F. Amao, M. Olivier & K. Magliveras (eds), *The Emergent African Union Law: Conceptualization, Delimitation, and Application*. Oxford: Oxford University Press, 2021, 319.

Oche, O. (ed.). *African Legal Theory and Contemporary Problems*. New York: Springer, 2014.

Okumu, W. & Atta-Asamoah, A. (eds). *The African Union at 20: African perspectives on progress, challenges and prospects*. Institute of Security Studies, 2023.

Olivier, M. 'Conceptualizing AU Law within the Constitutional Framework of the AU'. In F. Amao, M. Olivier & K. Magliveras (eds), The Emergent African Union Law: Conceptualization, Delimitation, and Application. Oxford: Oxford University Press, 2021, 11.

Olufemi, A. *African Union Law: The Emergence of a Sui Generis Legal Order*. London: Routledge, 2018.

Okoye, F.C. *International Law and the New African States.* London: Sweet & Maxwell, 1972.

Resnick, D. & N. van de Walle (eds). *Democratic Trajectories in Africa: Unravelling the Impact of Foreign Aid*. Oxford: Oxford University Press, 2013.

Rudahindwa, J. R. *Regional Developmentalism through Law: Establishing an African Economic Community*. London: Routledge, 2018.

Schmidt, E. *Foreign intervention in Africa: From the Cold War to the War on Terror*. Cambridge: Cambridge University Press, 2013.

Stapel, S. *Regional Organizations and Democracy, Human Rights, and the Rule of Law: The African Union, Organization of American States, and the Diffusion of Institutions*. Palgrave Macmillan, 2022.

Tieku, T. K. *Governing Africa: 3D Analysis of the African Union's Performance*. New York, NY: Rowman & Littlefield, 2017.

Taylor, I. *Africa Rising? BRICS – Diversifying Dependency*. Oxford: James Currey, 2014.

Udombana N. *The African Union in International Law*. Ibadan: John Archers, 2020.

Umozurike, U.O. *The African Charter on Human and Peoples' Rights*. The Hague: Martinus Nijhoff, 1997.

Viljoen, F. *International Human Rights in Africa*. 2nd edn. Oxford: Oxford University Press, 2012.

§2. Journal Articles

Abrahamsen, A. 'Africa and International Relations: Assembling Africa, Studying the World'. *African Affairs* (London) 116 (462) (2017): 125.

Ajulo, S.B. 'Temporal Scope of ECOWAS and AEC Treaties: A Case for African Economic Integration'. *RADIC* 8 (1996): 111.

Amoah, P. 'The African Charter on Human and Peoples' Rights – An Effective Weapon for Human Rights?'. *RADIC* 4 (1992): 226.

Anand, R.P. 'Role of the New Asian-African Countries in the Present International Legal Order'. *AJIL* 56 (1962): 383.

Arts, K.C.J.M. 'The International Protection of Children's Rights in Africa: The 1990 OAU Charter on the Rights and Welfare of the Child'. *RADIC* 5 (1993): 139.

Akinkugbe, O.D. ' Dispute Settlement under the African Continental Free Trade Area Agreement: A Preliminary Assessment'. *RADIC* 28(Supplement) 2020: 138.

Ayeni, V.O. 'Implementation of the Decisions and Judgments of African Regional Human Rights Tribunals: Reflections on the Barriers to State Compliance and the Lessons Learnt'. *RADIC* (30) 2022: 560.

Bedjaoui, M. 'Le règlement pacifique des différends africains'. *Annuaire français de droit international* 18 (1972): 85.

Bekker, G. 'Recent Developments in the African Human Rights System 2011/12'. *International Human Rights Law Review* 1 (2012): 158.

Bello, E. 'The African Charter on Human and Peoples' Rights'. *Hague Recueil* 194 (1985/1986): 13.

Birkett, D.J. 'Victims' Justice? Reparations and Asset Forfeiture at the Extraordinary African Chambers'. *Journal of African Law* 63 (2019): 151.

Bu, Q. 'Chinese Multinational Companies in Africa: The Human Rights Discourse'. *African Journal of Legal Studies* 8 (2015): 33.

Cervenka, Z. 'The Settlement of Disputes among Members of the Organization of African Unity'. *Verfassung und Recht in Uerbersee* 7 (1974): 117.

Cheyne, I. 'Africa and the International Trade in Hazardous Wastes'. *RADIC* 6 (1994): 493.

Cowling, M. 'The African Union – An Evaluation'. *South African Yearbook of International Law* 27 (2002): 193.

Chidede, T. 'The right to regulate in Africa's international investment law regime'. *Oregon Review of International Law* 20 (2019) 437.

d'Orsi, C. 'Sub-Saharan Africa: Is a New Special Regional Refugee Law Regime Emerging?'. ZaöRV 68 (2008): 1057.

D'Sa, R.M. 'The African Charter on Human and Peoples' Rights: Problems and Prospects for Regional Action'. *Australian Yearbook of International Law* 10 (1981/83): 101.

D'Sa, R.M. 'The African Refugee Problem, Relevant International Conventions and Recent Activities of the Organization of African Unity'. *Netherlands International Law Review* 31 (1984): 378.

D'Sa, R.M. 'The Lagos Plan of Action – Legal Mechanisms for Cooperation Between the Organisation of African Unity and the United Nations Economic Commission for Africa'. *JAL* 27 (1983): 4.

Dersso, S.A. 'The Status and Legitimacy of Popular Uprisings in the AU Norms on Democracy and Constitutional Governance'. *Journal of African Law (Supplement 'The African Charter on Democracy, Elections and Governance at 10')* 63 (2019): 107.

Djoyou Kamga S.A. & C. Manga Fombad 'A Critical Review of the Jurisprudence of the African Commission on the Right to Development' *JAL* 57 (2013): 196.

Elias, T.O. 'The Commission of Mediation, Conciliation and Arbitration of the Organisation of African Unity'. *BYBIL* 40 (1964): 336.

Elvy, S.-A. 'Towards a New Democratic Africa: the African Charter on Democracy, Elections and Governance'. *Emory International Law Review* 27 (2013): 41.

Fombad, C. M. 'Fostering a Constructive Intra-African Legal Dialogue in Post-Colonial Africa'. *Journal of African Law* 66 (2022): 1.

Gittleman, R. 'The African Charter on Human and Peoples' Rights: A Legal Analysis'. *Virginia Journal of International Law* 22 (1982): 667.

Hastings, J.V. & Phillips S.G. 'Maritime Piracy Business Networks and Institutions in Africa'. *African Affairs* (London) 114 (457)(2015): 555.

Hofman, F. 'Refugee Law in an African Context'. ZaöRV 52 (1992): 318.

Huliaras, A. 'Qadhafi's Comeback: Libya and Sub-Saharan Africa in the 1990s'. *African Affairs*(London) 100 (2001): 5.

Isanga, J.M. 'The Constitutive Act of the African Union, African Courts and the Protection of Human Rights: New Dispensation?'. *Santa Clara Journal of International Law* 11 (2013): 267.

Jalloh, C.C., 'Reflections on the Indictment of Sitting Heads of State and Government and Its Consequences for Peace and Stability and Reconciliation in Africa'. *African Journal of Legal Studies* (7) 2014: 43.

Jonas, O. 'Neutering the SADC Tribunal by Blocking Individuals' Access to the Tribunal'. *International Human Rights Law Review* 2 (2013): 294.

Jordaan, E. 'The African Group on the United Nations Human Rights Council: Shifting Geopolitics and the Liberal International Order'. *African Affairs* (London) 115(460)(2016): 490.

Kaminsky, H.S. 'Assessment of the Bamako Convention on the Ban of Import into Africa and the Control of Transboundary Movement and Management of Hazardous Wastes Within Africa'. *The Georgetown International Environmental Law Review* 5 (1992): 77.

Kato, L.L. 'Recognition in International Law: Some Thoughts on Traditional Theory, Attitudes and Practice by African States'. *Indian Journal of International Law* 10 (1970): 299.

Krisch, N. 'The Establishment of an African Court on Human and Peoples' Rights'. ZaöRV 58 (1998): 713.

Kunig, P. 'The Protection of Human Rights by International Law in Africa'. *German Yearbook of International Law* 25 (1982): 138.

Kuwali, D. 'From Durable Solutions to Holistic Solutions: Prevention of Displacement in Africa'. *African Journal of Legal Studies* (6) 2013: 265.

Lloyd, A. 'A Theoretical Analysis of the Reality of Children's Rights in Africa: An Introduction to the African Charter on the Rights and Welfare of the Child'. *African Human Rights Law Journal* 2 (2002): 11.

Lumu, N.L. 'De la Nature de la Communauté Economique Africaine'. *RADIC* 8 (1996): 51.

Lubbe, W.D & Spijkers O. 'Taking Stock of United Nations and African Union Constitutionalism'. *RADIC* 29 (2021): 64.

Magliveras, K.D. & G.J. Naldi. 'The African Court of Justice'. *ZaöRV* 66 (2006): 187.

Magliveras, K.D. & G.J. Naldi. 'The African Union: A New Dawn for Africa?'. *ICLQ* 51 (2002): 415.

Magliveras, K.D. & G.J. Naldi. 'The ICC Addresses Non-Cooperation by State Parties in Arresting President Al-Bashir: The *Malawi* Decision'. *African Journal of Legal Studies* 6 (2013): 1.

Magliveras, K.D. & G.J. Naldi. 'The International Criminal Court's Involvement with Africa: Evaluation of a Fractious Relationship'. *Nordic Journal of International Law* 83 (2013): 417.

Magliveras, K.D. & G.J. Naldi. 'The Pan-African Parliament of the African Union: An Overview'. *African Human Rights Law Journal* 3 (2003): 222.

Magliveras, K.D. 'Fighting Impunity Unsuccessfully in Africa: A Critique of the African Union's Handling of the Hissène Habré Affair'. *RADIC* 22, no. 3 (2014): 420.

Majinge, C.R. 'The Future of Peacekeeping in Africa and the Normative Role of the African Union'. *Goettingen Journal of International Law* 2 (2010): 463.

Maluwa, T. 'The Peaceful Settlement of Disputes among African States, 1963–1983: Some Conceptual Issues and Practical Trends'. *ICLQ* 38 (1986): 299.

Martorana, C.S. 'The New African Union: Will It Promote Enforcement of the Decisions of the African Court of Human & Peoples' Rights?'. *George Washington International Law Review* 40 (2008): 583.

Mupangavanhu, Y. 'African Union Rising to the Need for Continental IP Protection? The Establishment of the Pan-African Intellectual Property Organization'. *JAL* 59 (2015) 1.

Murray, R. 'Serious or Massive Violations under the African Charter on Human and Peoples' Rights: A Comparison with the Inter-American and European Mechanisms'. *Netherlands Quarterly on Human Rights* 17 (1999): 109.

Mushkat, M. 'The African Approach to Some Basic Problems of Modern International Law'. *Indian Journal of International Law* 7 (1967): 335.

Naldi, G.J. & K.D. Magliveras. 'Reinforcing the African System of Human Rights: The Protocol on the Establishment of a Regional Court on Human and Peoples' Rights'. *Netherlands Quarterly on Human Rights* 16 (1998): 431.

Naldi, G.J. & K.D. Magliveras. 'The African Court of Justice and Human Rights: A Judicial Curate's Egg'. *International Organizations Law Review* 9 (2012): 387.

Naldi, G.J. & K.D. Magliveras. 'The African Economic Community: Emancipation for African States or Yet Another Glorious Failure?'. *North Carolina Journal of International Law and Commercial Regulation* 24 (1999): 601.

Naldi, G.J. & K.D. Magliveras. 'The Ever Difficult Symbiosis of Africa with the International Criminal Court'. *Revue Hellénique de Droit International* 66 (2013): 59.

Naldi, G.J. & K.D. Magliveras. 'The Proposed African Court of Human and Peoples' Rights: Evaluation and Comparison'. *RADIC* 8 (1996): 944.

Naldi, G.J. 'Interim Measures of Protection in the African System for the Protection of Human and Peoples' Rights'. *African Human Rights Law Journal* 2 (2002): 1.

Naldi, G.J. 'Limitation of Rights under the African Charter on Human and Peoples' Rights: The Contribution of the African Commission on Human and Peoples' Rights'. *South African Journal of Human Rights* 17 (2001): 109.

Niyungeko, G. 'The African Charter on Democracy, Elections and Governance as a Human Rights Instrument'. *Journal of African Law (Supplement 'The African Charter on Democracy, Elections and Governance at 10')* 63 (2019): 63.

Nwankwo, C. M. & Ajibo, C. C. 'Liberalizing Regional Trade Regimes Through AfCFTA: Challenges and Opportunities'. *Journal of African Law* 64 (2020): 297.

Ndulo, M. 'Harmonization of Trade Laws in the African Economic Community'. *ICLQ* 42 (1993): 101.

O'Shea, E. 'Responsibility to Protect (R2P) in Libya: Ghosts of the Past Haunting the Future'. *International Human Rights Law Review* 1 (2012): 173.

Obinna Okere, B. 'The Protection of Human Rights in Africa and the African Charter on Human and Peoples' Rights: A Comparative Analysis with the European and American Systems'. *Human Rights Quarterly* 6 (1984): 141.

Ocran, C. 'The Protocol to the African Charter on Human and Peoples' Rights on the Rights of Women in Africa'. *RADIC* 15 (2007): 147.

Odinkalu, C.A. 'The Individual Complaints Procedures of the African Commission on Human and Peoples' Rights: A Preliminary Assessment'. *Transnational Law & Contemporary Problems* 8 (1998): 359.

Okongwe, O. 'The OAU Charter and the Principle of Domestic Jurisdiction in Inter-African Affairs'. *Indian Journal of International Law* 13 (1973): 589.

Olivier, M.E. 'The Role of African Union Law in Integrating Africa'. *South African Journal of International Affairs* 22 (2015) 513.

Olugbuo, B.C. 'The African Union, the United Nations Security Council and the Politicisation of International Justice in Africa' *African Journal of Legal Studies* 7 (2014): 351.

Omorogbe, Y. 'A Club of Incumbents? The African Union and Coups d'Etat'. *Vanderbilt Journal of Transitional Law* 44 (2011): 123.

Onwubiko, J.N. 'The Biafran Self-Determination Question: Challenges and Prospects'. *RADIC* 31 (2023): 104.

Repousis, O.G. 'Multilateral investment treaties in Africa and the antagonistic narratives of bilateralism and regionalism'. *Texas International Law Journal* 52 (2017): 313.

Oppong, R.F. 'The African Union, The African Economic Community and Africa's Regional Economic Communities: Untangling a Complex Web'. *RADIC* 18 (2010): 92.

Ouguergouz, F. 'The Bamako Convention on Hazardous Waste: A New Step in the Development of the African International Environmental Law'. *African Yearbook of International Law* 1 (1994): 195.

Sarkin, J. 'The Role of the United Nations, the African Union and Africa's Sub-Regional Organizations in Dealing with Africa's Human Rights Problems: Connecting Humanitarian Intervention and the Responsibility to Protect'. *JAL* 53 (2009) 1.

Shearer, C.R.H. 'Comparative Analysis of the Basel and Bamako Conventions on Hazardous Waste'. *Environmental Law* 23 (1993): 141.

Ssenyonjo, M. 'Direct Access to the African Court on Human and Peoples' Rights by Individuals and Non- Governmental Organisations: An Overview of the Emerging Jurisprudence of the African Court 2008–2012'. *International Human Rights Law Review* 2 (2013): 294.

Thiam, D. 'L'Afrique demande un droit international nouveau'. *Verfassung und Recht in Uebersee* 1 (1968): 1.

Thompson, B. 'Africa's Charter on Children's Rights: A Normative Break with Cultural Traditionalism'. *ICLQ* 41 (1992): 434.

Thompson, B. 'Economic Integration Efforts in Africa'. *RADIC* 5 (1993): 743.

Tladi, D. 'The Quest to Ban Hazardous Waste Import into Africa: First Bamako and Now Basel'. *CILSA* 33 (2000): 210.

Udombana, N.J. 'Toward the African Court on Human and Peoples' Rights: Better Late than Never'. *Yale Human Rights and Development Law Journal* 3 (2000): 45.

Viljoen, F. & L. Louw. 'State Compliance with the Recommendations of the African Commission on Human and People's Rights 1994–2004'. *American Journal of International Law* 101 (2007): 1.

Williams, P.D. & A. Boutellis. 'Partnership Peacekeeping: Challenges and Opportunities in the United Nations-African Union Relationship'. *African Affairs* 113 (2014): 254.

Index

The numbers here refer to paragraph numbers.

Index

Index

www.ingramcontent.com/pod-product-compliance
Lightning Source LLC
LaVergne TN
LVHW021002300926
849160LV00007B/228
* 9 7 8 9 4 0 3 5 4 9 8 7 3 *